LEGAL PHILOSOPHY

MULTIPLE PERSPECTIVES

Larry May
Washington University

Nancy E. Snow
Marquette University

Angela Bolte
Washington University

Mayfield Publishing Company
Mountain View, California
London • Toronto

Copyright © 2000 by Mayfield Publishing Company

All rights reserved. No portion of this book may be reproduced in any form or by any means without written permission of the publisher.

Library of Congress Cataloging-in-Publication Data

Legal philosophy: multiple perspectives/[edited by] Larry May, Nancy E. Snow, Angela Bolte.
p. cm
Includes bibliographical references.
ISBN 0-7674-1009-2
1. Law—Philosophy. I. May, Larry. II. Snow, Nancy E. III. Bolte, Angela.

K235. L435 1999
340´.1 21—dc21 99-045908

Manufactured in the United States of America

10 9 8 7 6 5 4 3 2 1

Mayfield Publishing Company
1280 Villa Street
Mountain View, CA 94041

Sponsoring editor, Kenneth King; *production editor,* Julianna Scott Fein; *manuscript editor,* Molly Roth; *design manager,* Glenda King; *text designer,* Linda Robertson; *cover designer,* Jean Mailander; *manufacturing manager,* Randy Hurst. The text was set in 9.5/12 Plantin Light by Publication Services and printed on acid-free 45# Custom LG by Banta Book Group.

Acknowledgments and copyrights are at the back of the book on pages 806–808, which constitute an extension of the copyright page.

PREFACE

This textbook introduces students to the major areas of Anglo-American law and to the philosophical attempts to grapple with the theoretical underpinnings of each of these areas of law. In this discussion, students will be exposed to a very wide range of perspectives. Legal theorists are split between those who take an explicitly moral approach to the law and those who take an economic approach. Many of the essays in our collection take sides in this important dispute. We include seminal essays from the history of philosophy that have shaped the contemporary debates, including works from Thomas Hobbes, John Locke, John Austin, Jeremy Bentham, Immanuel Kant, and John Stuart Mill. We also include many contemporary classics by such authors as H. L. A. Hart, Ronald Dworkin, Robert Nozick, Richard Posner, Richard Epstein, Martha Minow, A. M. Honoré, and John Finnis.

In addition, our textbook puts much emphasis on the relatively new voices in legal philosophy debates: feminists, critical theorists, postmodernists, critical race theorists, and American Indians in our own society. We shall also explore viewpoints from the rest of the world where Anglo-American law has not been fully embraced: for example, Chinese conceptions of property law; Japanese conceptions of intellectual property; South African approaches to contract law and to affirmative action in employment law; French and Canadian approaches to "bad samaritanism"; and Indian, Irish, and Chinese approaches to fundamental constitutional rights.

By bringing these disparate voices into dialogue with each other, we try to show how they articulate the philosophical foundations of various areas of law. We work from the presumption that the Anglo-American system of justice is the most developed and sophisticated in the world, literally the envy of most other nations. But we also proceed from the belief that philosophy of law has too long been dominated by certain Western theorists who take it for granted that, for instance, property or crime must be conceived within a framework of advanced capitalist economics. Students need to know that there are other perspectives in these legal debates. This book aims to challenge students to think critically about law in the United States and in other societies and to seek a sense of law and justice that will motivate students to expect their legal institutions to confront injustice in all of its manifestations.

THE STRUCTURE OF THE BOOK

This book begins by considering the principles of legal reasoning, especially how a consideration of the facts of particular cases can evolve into a settled body of abstract rules. Throughout the book, we then introduce students to law cases, interspersed with theoretical essays by philosophers and lawyers. As discussed in law, real patterns of fact are quite different from hypothetical cases in several respects. First, a consideration of legal cases forces philosophers to think about concrete situations where a decision has to be made about what is to be done. Having an abstract conception of justice is not enough; one must also be able to see how such a conception can be applied to adjudicate a dispute between two equally well defended parties. And second, a consideration of real-life legal fact patterns makes us aware of how a change in just one fact may make a huge difference in deciding which rules apply and what types of remedy are appropriate.

Consider the case of a man who issues a curse against another man. Our view of the matter will change greatly if we are in an urban section of the United States where curses are routinely made, versus a rural section of Africa where curses are taken quite literally as part of a general practice of witchcraft. It will matter, of course, whether it is illegal for one person to curse another, but it will also matter whether the man cursed believes that curses are efficacious. Even in the urban setting, it will matter enormously what form the curse takes, for it may be either a slight insult or a grave affront to one's very being.

Unlike most of the standard texts in philosophy of law, we have organized our selections according to area of law so that students can see how the philosophical study of law relates to the normal set of courses taken in U.S. law schools. Sections of our text correspond to the standard first-year courses in torts, contracts, property, constitutional law, and criminal law. We also provide sections on the more advanced topics of jurisprudence, family law, employment law, and legal ethics, as well as a section on legal reasoning and punishments and remedies. Before each set of selections, we introduce students to the main concepts in these areas of law as well as set the stage for the detailed treatment of the various philosophical approaches to the core ideas in the essays that follow.

Our textbook offers a heavy dose of non-Western material, including a collection of essays that approach traditional topics in legal philosophy from the perspective of minority members within mainstream U.S. culture. All of this helps us focus the student's attention on the interplay of voices and outlooks that constitute today's multicultural society. Throughout, we have tried to offer essays that bring philosophical ideas alive by confronting them with the real-life predicaments of people struggling to interact with one another in an increasingly pluralistic age.

Finally, we have included a larger-than-normal number of essays from the law journals as well as essays by many prominent legal theorists teaching in U.S. law schools. This has two advantages over most other textbooks. First, it introduces undergraduates to the way that philosophy of law or jurisprudence is approached by lawyers as well as by philosophers. Second, for law students, it connects the philosophical study of law with some of the main figures in law that the students would already have encountered in their other courses.

In our view, philosophy of law has produced the richest literature of all of the subfields of ethics and political philosophy. Philosophy of law is a rigorous field of inquiry in its own right, as one can see especially clearly when work by lawyers is brought together with work by philosophers in a single volume then juxtaposed with the best work by contemporary critics of mainstream approaches. We hope that our book will inspire generations of students to bridge the gap between theory and practice and to look beyond the system of law in their own country, in considering the exciting writing in philosophy of law.

ACKNOWLEDGMENTS

We would like to thank those who reviewed the manuscript: Albert C. Cafagna, Michigan State University; J. Steven Kramer, University of Colorado at Boulder; Sidney Gendin, Eastern Michigan University; Heidi Malm, Loyola University of Chicago; Joan McGregor, Arizona State University; Ronald Moore, University of Washington; David Schmidtz, University of Arizona; Julie C. Van Camp, California State University at Long Beach; and Burleigh Wilkins, University of California at Santa Barbara.

CONTENTS

Preface iii

Introduction 1

Part 1 LEGAL REASONING 5

1. Frederick Schauer, "Formalism" 11
2. *Lochner v. New York* 20
3. Jerome Frank, from *Law and the Modern Mind* 25
4. Edward H. Levi, from *An Introduction to Legal Reasoning* 31
5. Ronald M. Dworkin, from *Law's Empire* 41
6. Cass R. Sunstein, "Incompletely Theorized Agreements" 53

Part 2 JURISPRUDENCE 65

7. John Austin, from *The Province of Jurisprudence Determined* 72
8. H. L. A. Hart, from *The Concept of Law* 79
9. Ronald M. Dworkin, "The Model of Rules I" 91
10. *Riggs v. Palmer* 98
11. John Finnis, "Natural Law and Legal Reasoning" 103
12. Richard A. Posner, "The Economic Approach to Law" 112
13. Roberto Mangabeira Unger, from *The Critical Legal Studies Movement* 117
14. Kimberlé Crenshaw, Neil Gotanda, Gary Peller, and Kendall Thomas, from *Critical Race Theory: The Key Writings That Formed the Movement* 126
15. Patricia Smith, "Feminist Legal Critics: The Reluctant Radicals" 132

Part 3 TORTS 143

16. H. L. A. Hart and A. M. Honoré, "Causation and Responsibility" 147
17. Joel Feinberg, "Sua Culpa" 154
18. George P. Fletcher, "Fairness and Utility in Tort Theory" 160
19. Jules L. Coleman, "Tort Liability and the Limits of Corrective Justice" 166

20. RICHARD A. EPSTEIN, "A Theory of Strict Liability" 173
21. MITCHELL MCINNES, "The Question of a Duty to Rescue in Canadian Tort Law: An Answer from France" 182
22. ROBERT B. LEFLAR, "Personal Injury Compensation Systems in Japan: Values Advanced and Values Undermined" 189
23. *Tarasoff v. Regents of University of California* 195

Part 4 CRIMINAL LAW 201

24. J. S. MILL, from *On Liberty and Utilitarianism* 209
25. PATRICK DEVLIN, from *The Enforcement of Morals* 216
26. *Bowers v. Hardwick* 221
27. EGBEKE AJA, "Crime and Punishment: An Indigenous African Experience" 228
28. ANTHONY KENNY, "The Mind and the Deed" 235
29. R. J. GERBER, "Is the Insanity Test Insane?" 243
30. JAMES WEINSTEIN, "First Amendment Challenges to Hate Crime Legislation: Where's the Speech?" 251
31. LOIS PINEAU, "Date Rape: A Feminist Analysis" 261

Part 5 PROPERTY 275

32. JOHN LOCKE, "Of Property" 281
33. ROBERT NOZICK, from *Anarchy, State, and Utopia* 287
34. A. M. HONORÉ, "Property, Title, and Redistribution" 291
35. JONAS ALSÉN, "An Introduction to Chinese Property Law" 297
36. RICHARD EPSTEIN, from *Takings: Private Property and the Power of Eminent Domain* 303
37. DAN ROSEN and CHIKAKO USUI, "The Social Structure of Japanese Intellectual Property Law" 313
38. A. JOHN SIMMONS, "Historical Rights and Fair Shares" 317
39. NELL JESSUP NEWTON, "Compensation, Reparations, and Restitution: Indian Property Claims in the United States" 321
40. CHERYL I. HARRIS, "Whiteness as Property" 328
41. *International News Service v. Associated Press* 342

Part 6 CONTRACTS 351

42. THOMAS HOBBES, from *Leviathan* 355
43. P. S. ATIYAH, "The Practice of Promising" 359
44. CHARLES FRIED, "Contract As Promise" 368
45. MICHAEL D. BAYLES, "Legally Enforceable Commitments" 380
46. ALAN WERTHEIMER, "Unconscionability and Contracts" 388

47. *Henningsen v. Bloomfield Motors, Inc.* 399
48. *Williams v. Walker-Thomas Furniture Company* 402
49. LYNN BERAT, "South African Contract Law: The Need for a Concept of Unconscionability" 405
50. MICHELE MOODY-ADAMS, "On Surrogacy: Morality, Markets, and Motherhood" 414

Part 7 CONSTITUTIONAL LAW 425

51. RONALD DWORKIN, "Constitutional Cases" 429
52. STEPHEN R. MUNZER and JAMES W. NICKEL, "Does the Constitution Mean What It Always Meant?" 440
53. R. P. PEERENBOOM, "What's Wrong with Chinese Rights? Toward a Theory of Rights with Chinese Characteristics" 451
54. JEREMY COOPER, "Poverty and Constitutional Justice: The Indian Experience" 468
55. ROBERT BORK, "The Right of Privacy: The Construction of a Constitutional Time Bomb" 481
56. JUDITH DECEW, "Constitutional Privacy, Judicial Interpretation, and *Bowers v. Hardwick*" 484
57. RORY O'CONNELL, "Natural Law: Alive and Kicking? A Look at the Constitutional Morality of Sexual Privacy in Ireland" 493
58. CHARLES R. LAWRENCE III, "If He Hollers Let Him Go: Regulating Racist Speech on Campus" 508
59. RONALD DWORKIN, "Do We Have a Right to Pornography?" 519
60. RAE LANGTON, "Whose Right? Ronald Dworkin, Women, and Pornographers" 527
61. *Plessy v. Ferguson* 533
62. *Brown v. Board of Education of Topeka, Kansas I* 539

Part 8 FAMILY LAW 543

63. MARTHA MINOW and MARY LYNDON SHANLEY, "Relational Rights and Responsibilities: Revisioning the Family in Liberal Political Theory and Law" 549
64. WILLIAM N. ESKRIDGE, JR., "Beyond Lesbian and Gay 'Families We Choose'" 562
65. RICHARD A. POSNER, from *Economic Analysis of Law* 572
66. JACQUELINE KRIKORIAN, "A Different Form of Apartheid? The Legal Status of Married Women in South Africa" 585
67. ANSHU NANGIA, "The Tragedy of Bride Burning in India: How Should the Law Address It?" 593
68. DEBORAH L. FORMAN, "Unwed Fathers and Adoption: A Theoretical Analysis in Context" 603

69. Mary L. Shanley, "Fathers' Rights, Mothers' Wrongs: Reflections on Unwed Fathers' Rights and Sex Equality" 613

70. *Stanley v. Illinois* 626

Part 9 EMPLOYMENT LAW 637

71. Albert G. Mosley, "Affirmative Action: Pro" 644

72. Nicholas Capaldi, "Affirmative Action: Con" 650

73. Wiseman Nkuhlu, "Affirmative Action for South Africa in Transition: From Theory to Practice" 657

74. "Extracts from a Working Document Entitled 'A Bill of Rights for a New South Africa' As Compiled by the Constitutional Committee of the ANC" 663

75. *California Constitution* 665

76. Larry May, "Sexual Harassment and Solidarity" 665

77. Jane Harris Aiken, "Sexual Character Evidence in Civil Actions: Refining the Propensity Rule" 676

78. *Faragher v. City of Boca Raton* 688

Part 10 REMEDIES, SENTENCING, AND PUNISHMENT 697

79. Immanuel Kant, "On the Right to Punish and to Grant Clemency" 704

80. Jeremy Bentham, from *An Introduction to the Principles of Morals and Legislation* 707

81. Dan M. Kahan, "What Do Alternative Sanctions Mean?" 715

82. Christine M. Wiseman, "Representing the Condemned: A Critique of Capital Punishment" 722

• 83. Martha C. Nussbaum, "Equity and Mercy" 734

84. *Payne v. Tennessee* 745

Part 11 LEGAL ETHICS 755

85. Charles Fried, "The Lawyer As Friend: The Moral Foundations of the Lawyer–Client Relation" 759

86. David Luban, "Why Have an Adversary System?" 769

87. Kenneth Kipnis, "Conflict of Interest and Conflict of Obligation" 774

88. Larry May, "Conflict of Interest" 785

89. *Wheat v. United States* 789

90. Monroe H. Freedman, "Professional Responsibility of the Criminal Defense Lawyer: The Three Hardest Questions" 793

91. Martha Minow, "Breaking the Law: Lawyers and Clients in Struggles for Social Change" 801

Credits 806

INTRODUCTION

THE RELATIONSHIP BETWEEN LAW AND PHILOSOPHY

Where there is law, there is injustice.
—TOLSTOY, *WAR AND PEACE*

This quotation from Tolstoy is interestingly ambiguous. On one level, we are told that law's primary goal or aim is to confront injustice and to attempt to remedy that injustice. In most societies, law functions as the chief institution entrusted with providing individual or collective remedies for those who have been harmed by the intentional or unintentional acts of others. On another level of meaning, we are told that where there are laws there will be injustice. This second meaning relates to the well-known fact that the law works through the application of general rules, but that general rules do not easily fit specific patterns of fact. The rules always overlap or underdetermine the facts. This means that the application of law to facts causes injustice to be done to someone. Law is based on an attempt to remedy injustice, but, by its very nature, law will create injustice as well. In both respects, we can see that law and justice are intertwined. Just as the idea of justice has intrigued philosophers for thousands of years, so has the idea of law. For several thousand years, the philosophical study of law has centered on the relationship between the concepts of justice and law.

In most contemporary law courses, the first few days are spent on the philosophical foundations of that legal subject. Property courses begin with discussions of how property rights are created in the state of nature, where there are no such rights. Contracts courses begin with discussions of the nature of promises and what it is about a promise that creates an obligation in the world where there was none before. Torts and criminal law begin with discussions of why harm is considered such a bad thing in a society, as well as what would be appropriate responses to acts that cause harm. Courses in constitutional law and legal ethics often begin with discussions of what is most foundational to any system of rules that calls itself law. As these and other courses progress, much additional discussion arises concerning "policy" considerations—namely, moral, social, political, and economic theorizing about the proper role of the law in regulating our lives.

The study of philosophy intersects with the study of law in many different ways. The very idea, or concept, of law has been studied by philosophers since the time of the ancient Greeks. Each branch of the law has at least one core question that has also been rigorously explored by philosophers. What differentiates a contract from a promise? Is the government ever justified in redistributing property? Should tort law hold people liable for failing to help one another? Should constitutions be interpreted narrowly or liberally? Do we punish criminals in order to attain retribution or deterrence? Should lawyers bend or twist the truth so as to serve their clients' interests vigorously?

THE LAW'S GOAL: STABILITY IN SOCIAL RELATIONSHIPS

The various fields of law all aim at one goal: providing mechanisms that allow individuals to order their lives and plan for the future. For example, contracts provide a mechanism by which obligations and rights can be created by mutual agreement. When you and I agree that you will clean my basement this weekend and that I will pay you fifty dollars to do so, the world for both of us has changed by our own free acts. You are no longer free to do whatever you want this weekend, and I am no longer free to do whatever I want with my money. You have an obligation to clean my basement, and I have an obligation to pay you fifty dollars. I have a right to have my basement cleaned by you, and you have a right to be paid fifty dollars by me. None of these rights and obligations existed until we exchanged promises. Such obligations are created, and recognized as enforceable at law, because we have made a contract. And the law will enforce such agreements unless the terms of the contract shock the conscience of society or otherwise violate common principles of fair dealing.

Property likewise provides a mechanism for regulating our lives concerning the acquisition and transfer of land and durable goods. Property law has created a stable base on which societies can achieve a certain kind of economic stability. If on my deathbed I transfer the deed for my acre of homestead to my favorite grandchild, the law will generally recognize and enforce the peaceful transfer of title to this piece of property. Such transfers create rights and obligations for my grandchild that she did not have before. Squabbles among my grandchildren over who should inherit the land are laid to rest, and all of these individuals can plan for the future with relative security. But if a squatter has been occupying and productively using my land for several decades, or if the state claims that it has a need for the land, these claims may be recognized over the claim of my grandchild. A debate has raged over the centuries about whether to call the squatter, or even the state, a thief. In England, squatters are often granted greater rights than deed holders are. In the United States, squatters normally lose to deed holders, although if one satisfies the conditions of "adverse possession," one will win over the rightful deed holders. States can seize lands by "eminent domain," regardless of the wishes of the title holders. But the state must pay the title holder a reasonable price for the seized land to compensate the title holder for the disruption of the landowner's expectations.

Most societies have established complex sets of rules regulating contracts and property transfers. These rules allow individuals to regulate their own lives with minimal interference from the state. Indeed, the courts operate mainly as a backdrop to the private relationships created in these areas of law. Law plays an important role nonetheless, because lawyers are largely responsible for drafting the enforceable legal documents that give voice to the intentions of the people who wish to contract with each other or transfer property. These rules vary in interesting ways stemming from the values of the members of the society.

In criminal law and torts, the larger objective is to secure a stable society, but this is accomplished in different ways than in contract and property law. Rather than helping people figure out how best to get what they want, the law intervenes to penalize or punish those who have acted in harmful and socially disruptive ways. The opportunity for individuals to be harmed by strangers or by neighbors and loved ones creates a different kind of insecurity on which the law focuses in criminal law and torts. If you are lying on a stretcher in an operating room, unconscious and at the mercy of the medical team, we want some assurance that a doctor will not neglect to take good care of you or, at very least, that you are not intentionally harmed or taken advantage of. The law functions to provide a basis for securing these goals, although many have wondered what standards of due care to set. When Princess Diana's limousine overturned on a highway in France, the reporters who stopped to take pictures but did not try to help were arrested by French police. If the same incident had occurred in the United States, no laws would have been broken by the reporters, because there is no legal duty to rescue here. What counts as harm worthy of legal sanction varies according to what the members of a society think they owe other citizens.

In family law and employment law, we find fascinating applications of some of the more abstract legal considerations. Consider the burgeoning area of sexual harassment suits in employment law or the attempts to regulate domestic violence through the family law courts. In both areas, notions of what counts as coercion and even what makes an act violent have been called into question as courts have tried to decide whether the law should be used for what was once thought of as purely private matters. Here we see the intersection of the issues just discussed. The law focuses on stability in private affairs and on protecting victims of harm. In earlier times, the fact that sexual harassment or domestic violence occurred in the home or between intimates was enough reason to think of it as a private matter that individuals should be free to regulate themselves. Today, these matters are thought to be public, because people now recognize that harm can be just as severe in the so-called private sphere as it is on the streets. As such, employment and family law have been reshaped to focus more on the potential for harm and the need to protect victims of that harm.

Finally, in constitutional law and legal ethics, we see attempts to regulate and stabilize societies concerning the behavior of high-placed political leaders. We have recently seen the functioning of constitutional law in the United States in providing a mechanism for determining whether a duly elected president, Bill Clinton, should be removed from office. Here, the Constitution serves to provide for the peaceful transition of power, or at least to provide checks on the possible abuse of power by the most powerful member of a society. Similarly, in legal ethics, we have seen the application of various legal mechanisms regarding whether members of the government can be held accountable for conflicts of interest when they let their judgments become influenced by personal or political gain. Here, the search for stability through law reaches to the highest levels of government. We see graphically how the law can adjudicate between parties often thought to be above the law because of their status as maker or enforcer of that law.

As you can see, the topics in this book reflect the intimate link between philosophy and law, a link recognized since the time of ancient Greece. In fact, Aristotle spent considerable time studying constitutions while writing about political philosophy. Constitutional law has been the richest area of intersection between law and philosophy, because the idea of founding or grounding is crucial for this area of law as well as for philosophy. In our text, we strive to display a wider overlap between law and philosophy, where each of the main areas of law is shown to raise significant philosophical issues. Just as Tolstoy is correct to say that where there is law there is also injustice, so we would say where there is injustice there have been philosophers. Whenever there have been discussions about justice or injustice, injury and responsibility, desert and punishment, there has also been a dialogue between philosophers and lawyers. The continuation of that dialogue is what this book is all about.

PART 1

LEGAL REASONING

Legal reasoning is at the heart of law. It is what lawyers do when they argue court cases. Even more importantly, it is what judges do when they decide cases. Most philosophical theories of legal reasoning—that is, philosophical explanations and justifications of legal reasoning, including those presented here—focus on what judges do or should be doing when they decide court cases. In the first reading selection offered here, "Formalism," Frederick Schauer defends a much maligned theory of legal reasoning, namely, formalism. Schauer's insight is that decision making according to rule lies at the heart of formalism. Because there is much to be said in favor of decision making according to rule, there is much, also, to commend formalism.

According to a familiar way of construing formalism, what judges do or should be doing when they decide cases is to apply mechanically rules of law to the facts of particular cases. After subsuming the facts of a case under the applicable legal rule, all that is left is for the judge to produce a verdict. Thus, legal reasoning is or should be analogous to logical deduction. What is wrong with this way of deciding cases?

According to Schauer, the main flaw of formalism is that it conceals the fact that, in deciding cases, judges make choices. Judges make three kinds of choices that formalism masks: choices within norms, choices between norms, and choices to create norms. Choices within norms can occur either when legal language is pervasively indeterminate or when penumbras of uncertainty exist around a clear and settled core of meaning. An illustration of how formalism masks choices that occur when legal language is pervasively indeterminate is given by Justice Peckham's reasoning in *Lochner v. New York* (1905), parts of which are included here. Justice Peckham simply took it to be analytic, or true by definition, that the meaning of the term *individual liberty* includes the idea that individuals are free to make labor contracts without government intervention. If so, then the norm that individuals are free to make labor contracts without government intervention has merely to be applied to the facts of *Lochner* for a correct verdict to be reached. Schauer's point, however, is that the meaning of *individual liberty* is broad, indeterminate, and subject to interpretation. The indeterminacy of *individual liberty* can support several interpretations. Justice Peckham's choice to interpret the term as he did was not the mechanical application of a clear and determinate legal rule, as a formalist would contend, but rather a conscious social and economic choice that was concealed by a formalist construing of legal reasoning.

Similar choices within norms are made in areas of uncertainty that surround clear cores of settled meaning. For example, in most cases, the meaning of the term *vehicle* in the rule "no vehicles in the park" is clear and settled. But do skateboards, rollerblades, or toy trucks count as vehicles? To decide whether they do requires a judge to interpret the meaning of the term *vehicle* as it appears in the context of the rule. One cannot mechanically or literally apply the rule in uncertain cases. Formalist descriptions of legal reasoning in such cases obscure two facts: that judges must make choices about how to interpret the meanings of rules and that the choices they make extend and thereby change the meanings of the rules in question.

Formalism can mask a different kind of choice—choices between norms, or the choice of whether to apply a clear norm. To illustrate this, Schauer discusses an obscure Vermont case, *Hunter v. Norman.*[1] Hunter, an incumbent state senator seeking reelection in Vermont, filed his nominating petition in the Windsor County Clerk's office three minutes past the deadline set by Vermont state statute. Jane Norman, the Windsor County Clerk, enforced the statute by refusing to accept Hunter's petition; as such, Hunter's name would not appear on the primary election ballot. Hunter claimed that he was late in filing because he relied on advice given to him by the county clerk's office. He filed an action against Norman, citing on his behalf *Ryshpan v. Cashman,*[2] in which the Vermont State Supreme Court held that when reliance on erroneous advice from the state puts citizens in inescapable time conflicts with statutory requirements, the statutory time schedule must yield. According to Schauer, the judge in *Hunter* had the choice of enforcing the statute, which clearly applied, or taking the escape provided by *Ryshpan*. In his view, when the statute and *Ryshpan* coexist, neither determines the outcome of *Hunter.* The choice of which is to prevail, the statute or *Ryshpan,* depends on factors external to both.

What would happen if *Ryshpan* did not exist? Would the judge have been forced to apply the Vermont statute in *Hunter?* Schauer thinks not. In the U.S. legal system, judges have ways to avoid the mechanical application of statutes. They can, for example, argue that mechanically applying the statute in a particular case would contravene the legislature's intent in passing the statute, or would fall foul of the statute's purpose. In other words, judges have the option of creating norms. Again, formalist reasoning conceals such judicial choices.

Schauer asks us to consider a legal system in which several conditions obtain. First, the meanings of legal rules are clear and settled. Second, the rules clearly apply in particular cases. Third, no escape routes exist. Fourth, no ways of creating escape routes exist. This kind of system, Schauer thinks, suggests a benign formalism—that is, a formalism that does not conceal judicial choices. This kind of system would display decision making according to rule. What can be said on its behalf?

For one thing, one could predict the decisions made in such a system. But decision making according to rule is predictable, Schauer argues, because of limited decisional jurisdiction. *Decisional jurisdiction* is the idea that the choices of decision makers can be more or less restricted in scope. When one restricts decision makers' scope of choice, one increases the predictability of their decisions by limiting the scope of factors that can influence such decisions. A system with limited decisional jurisdiction is inherently more stable and conservative than one in which decision makers have greater latitude of choice. A drawback of such a system is that it could tend toward rigidity and result in some absurd decisions. But formalism, Schauer claims, is not fundamentally about rigidity and absurdity. It is about power and its allocation. That formalism sometimes results in rigid and possibly absurd decisions might be offset by the fact that it requires modesty on the part of decision makers. Formalism is less than optimal when it prevents wise judges from making good decisions, but it is beneficial when it prevents corrupt or foolish judges from abusing power.

Toward the end of his essay, Schauer presents the outlines of a theory of presumptive formalism. According to this theory, there exist strong presumptions in favor of lower-level decisions made according to the literal meanings of the most locally applicable legal rules. But these presumptions are rebuttable under certain conditions. Schauer recognizes that such a system has risks and costs, but he believes that it would combine the virtues of decision making according to rule with the flexibility provided by escape routes.

The next selection, excerpts from *Lochner v. New York* (1905), gives an example of the kind of legal formalism Schauer finds objectionable. In that case, Lochner, the plaintiff, appealed a ruling by the New York Court of Appeals upholding his conviction by a lower court. The lower court convicted Lochner of a misdemeanor for violating New York's labor law by permitting and requiring an employee to work in his bakery for more than sixty hours in one week. Writing for a majority of the Supreme Court (5 to 4), Justice

[1]No. S197-86-WrC (Vt. July 28, 1986).
[2]132 Vt. 628, 326 A. 2d (1974).

Rufus Peckham overruled the Court of Appeals' decision and struck down the labor law in question as a violation of the U.S. Constitution. Central to Justice Peckham's disposition of the case is the bare assertion that the right to make business contracts is part of the liberty of the individual, which is protected by the Fourteenth Amendment. This assertion is bolstered by the subsidiary contentions that the freedom to make labor contracts extends to both parties, the employer and the employee, and that, in this case, there is no legitimate reason, such as public health concerns, for the state to restrict the hours of employment on which the parties agreed. Based on this reasoning, Justice Peckham concludes that New York's labor law is an unnecessary and unjustified intrusion of the police power of the state into the liberty of the individual as guaranteed by the Fourteenth Amendment, and strikes it down as unconstitutional.

As mentioned earlier, Justice Peckham took it to be true by definition that the meaning of the term *liberty* in the Fourteenth Amendment includes the right of employer and employee to make labor contracts without government intrusion. However, one might argue, following Justice Holmes, that Justice Peckham chose an interpretation of the term *liberty* that supports his own favorite economic theory, laissez-faire, and used it in this case to combat the emergence of the modern welfare state by attacking protective labor laws. The vice of formalism is that it can conceal an economic and social choice by representing it as a mechanical, value-neutral application of a clear and determinate rule of law. In their dissenting opinions, both Justice John Marshall Harlan and Justice Oliver Wendell Holmes criticize Peckham's decision on this ground. As Justice Harlan puts it, "Still less can I say that the statute is, beyond question, a plain, palpable invasion of rights secured by the fundamental law" (see p. 24). Justice Holmes is even more blunt: "General propositions do not decide concrete cases. The decision will depend on a judgment or intuition more subtle than any articulate major premise" (p. 25). So much, in Holmes's view, for legal formalism.

The next selection, excerpts from *Law and the Modern Mind,* by Jerome Frank, is an example of the legal realism movement, which gained currency in the 1920s and 1930s. Legal realists denied what legal formalists asserted to be true—that law is a system of certain, predictable rules and that judges do not invent new law but rather discover or derive it by applying preexisting legal principles to the facts of particular cases. According to legal realists, judges do indeed make new laws, sometimes on the basis of extralegal considerations such as political, moral, social, economic, or psychological factors. Legal realists readily admit that a variety of factors influence judges as they make the law; they further assert that the formalists' insistence on rule following obscures the true nature of judicial decision making.

Toward the beginning of the excerpt presented here, Frank attacks a well-known shibboleth of formalism, namely, that people need certainty and predictability in order to act in society without fear of breaking the law and incurring punishment. If judges were allowed to invent new laws, formalists avow, this certainty and predictability would be compromised, with dire practical effects. Against this claim, Frank makes two key points. The first is that the certainty and predictability of law is apparently not as crucial as formalism maintains, because legislatures routinely make new laws without incurring criticism from formalists. If legislatures can make new laws without undermining certainty and predictability, why think that judges cannot do the same? Second, ordinary folk do not know the law well enough to rely significantly on it in their practical affairs; if they took the time to learn the law well enough to become familiar with all possible legal consequences, they would never get married, make contracts, buy property, and so on. In short, he denies the formalists' claim that legal certainty and predictability are of paramount importance for people in their ordinary affairs.

What do legal realists make of the belief that judges derive new laws by mechanically applying legal rules to the facts of particular cases? According to Frank, this belief is a myth, "a false affirmation made without complete knowledge of its falsity" (p. 28). When judges believe that this is how particular cases are decided, they engage in self-deception. Then, what really happens when judges decide cases?

Judges believe that they rely on precedents and subsume the facts of particular cases under general legal rules to reach decisions. The reliance on precedents, Frank argues, is illusory, for precedents can be manipulated to apply to the facts of almost any case. Moreover, precedents do not give an accurate record of how the judge actually reached a verdict in any given case; judges use them as mere window dressing to justify decisions reached for other reasons.

The real reasons why a judge decides a case one way rather than another, says Frank, have to do with his or her personality, beliefs, and emotional experience of the case. If we could relive the judge's emotional experience of a case, which Frank believes is impossible, then and only then would we have the basis for an accurate precedent.

Willing to grant some truth to Frank's portrayal of how judges actually decide cases, one might contend that their illusory reliance on precedents does no real harm to the judicial system. Frank maintains that reliance on precedents causes judges to give too much weight to the force of past decisions and to be overly concerned with the consequences of present decisions for future litigation. This, he believes, produces unjust decisions in present cases. A contemporary example of the phenomenon that Frank criticizes is found in Justice Lewis Powell's reasoning in a death penalty case, *McCleskey v. Kemp.*[3] Warren McCleskey argued that his death sentence was invalidated by racial bias in the Georgia capital sentencing system. One of Powell's reasons for finding against McCleskey was his fear that doing so would open a floodgate of litigation based on all kinds of bias claims in all areas of the law. In his dissent, Justice Brennan mocks Powell's reasoning as a fear of "too much justice." Frank would, no doubt, agree with Brennan.

How judges create and use precedents is a central focus of the next selection, which is taken from Edward H. Levi's seminal book, *An Introduction to Legal Reasoning.* For Levi, the basic pattern of legal reasoning is reasoning by example, or reasoning from case to case. It proceeds in three basic steps: Similarity is seen between two cases, the rule of law inherent in the first case is articulated, and the rule is applied to the second case. Finding similarities or differences between cases, a function of judges, is central to this conception of legal reasoning. Law is a system of rules one discovers in the process of finding similarity and difference. Rather than unchanging, rules are dynamic, changing in meaning with each new application to a case. Reasoning by example explains how new ideas from the community enter the law, as well as how litigants participate in law making, for new ideas enter the law through arguments made by individual litigants in particular cases. Not only is reasoning by example the basic pattern of legal reasoning in case law, but it also applies with minor adjustments to the reasoning involved in statutory and constitutional interpretation.

Some argue that reasoning by example puts too much emphasis on the comparison of cases and too little on the development of legal concepts. Levi responds by identifying three stages in the evolution of legal concepts. In the first stage, judges struggle to formulate a legal concept through the comparison of a number of cases. In this initial stage, the concept is incompletely and confusedly articulated; equivocations of meaning can occur. In the second stage, the meaning of the concept becomes determinate. Classifications are made in which some cases fall within the meaning of the concept, and some fall outside of it. The third stage marks the breakdown of the concept. Cases arise that suggest that the concept is flawed or is no longer a useful classificatory tool. Reasoning by example lies at the heart of this process, which Levi illustrates in the rest of the selection presented here, with a sustained analysis of the rise and fall of the "inherently dangerous" rule.

The next reading, taken from Ronald M. Dworkin's book *Law's Empire,* presents a conception of judicial reasoning that differs markedly from those of formalists and of legal realists such as Frank and Levi. Dworkin's view, which has been called "law as integrity," is a normative theory of what judges should do when they decide hard cases. *Hard cases* are those in which settled legal rules do not clearly dictate an outcome. In deciding such cases, law as integrity requires judges to take a particular interpretive stance, namely, that which makes the best sense of their community's legal traditions and practices. According to this view, law making is a constructive process. One justifies new legal rules and principles by their coherence or "fit" with larger legal and political traditions.

Dworkin makes this abstract conception more concrete through the analogy of a chain novel. Each of several authors is responsible for a different chapter, and each must construct a chapter that fits with and makes the best interpretive sense of the previous chapters. Each author is constrained to some extent by the content and structure of previous chapters, yet each must make a creative contribution that advances the scope and purpose of the work as a whole. Writing a chapter in a chain novel is thus an exercise in interpretive construction. Similarly, making a deci-

---

[3]481 U. S. 279 (1987).

sion in a hard case is a unique creative activity. Instead of being constrained by previous chapters, however, judges must look to the entire body of law of their political community, then ask themselves which of a number of possible decisions provides the best interpretation of the entire network of law considered as a coherent whole.

As an interpretive theory, law as integrity can be applied to common-law cases as well as to statutory and constitutional interpretation. In our selection, Dworkin illustrates his view by applying it to a common-law case of emotional damages, *McLoughlin.* McLoughlin, whose husband and family were injured in an automobile accident in England in 1973, suffered nervous shock and subsequently tried to sue the driver, whose negligence had caused the accident, as well as other persons, for compensation for her emotional injuries. Dworkin considers no fewer than six interpretations of precedent cases that might control the decision in *McLoughlin,* thereby highlighting the level of nuance and complexity that his view of judicial decision making exacts.

As you will see in Part 2, law as integrity has become the prevailing paradigm in jurisprudence in the tradition of political liberalism. It has received attention from legal and political scholars who adopt the perspective of liberalism, as well as from some who reject that school of thought. In the next reading, "Incompletely Theorized Agreements," Cass R. Sunstein develops an alternative to law as integrity from within the liberal tradition. Contrary to Dworkin, Sunstein argues that particular legal conclusions are and should be reached on the basis of incompletely theorized agreements. To explain what this means, Sunstein argues that one can identify several levels of abstraction in legal reasoning. At the most concrete or specific level are the particular conclusions of law—that is, the individual decisions that judges make. At the next level are low-level principles, such as the clear-and-present-danger rule. Mid-level principles and generalizations, such as freedom of speech, are even more abstract. At the highest level of abstraction are general ethical theories, such as Kantianism and utilitarianism, or commitments to quite abstract values, such as equality or personal autonomy. Sunstein focuses on incompletely theorized agreements on particular outcomes that are accompanied by agreement on the low-level principles that account for them. His view is that even when judges and other participants in the legal and political system disagree on higher-level principles and theories, they can agree on particular conclusions and lower-level principles.

Sunstein advances this view as not only descriptively accurate but also normatively desirable. What can one say on behalf of incompletely theorized agreements? First, they reduce the political costs of enduring disagreements. If judges avoid large-scale theories, then losers in particular cases lose only the given cases. As such, they have not seen their deeper commitments rejected. This feature is especially advantageous in a pluralistic society of diverse and sometimes competing values, in which all citizens, regardless of the values they endorse, have claims to be treated fairly by legal and political institutions.

Second, incompletely theorized agreements help when we seek moral evolution over time. Not being tied to a completely articulated theory of constitutional equality, for example, helps us accommodate new facts and values.

Third, incompletely theorized agreements are reasonable to expect from people of limited time and resources. In other words, ordinary judges do not have the time and resources to develop full-scale theories to justify particular decisions.

Fourth, incompletely theorized agreements function well in a system in which precedents should or must be taken as fixed. Sunstein points out that, given the large number of participants in the legal system, as well as the variety of values implicated there, it would be unrealistic to expect law to speak with one voice—that is, to achieve widespread coherence. However, we can hope for pockets of consistency in restricted areas of law. Such limited consistency is often achieved through precedents. Incompletely theorized agreements can help us maintain consistency where possible without forcing broader agreement in areas not reached by precedent.

Finally, incompletely theorized agreements help preserve the ideal of the rule of law. Democratic societies are committed to rule by law, as opposed to rule by individuals. In discouraging the use of high-level theories to decide cases, incompletely theorized agreements prevent exercises of discretion in which individual judges might be tempted to impose their personal beliefs and values on others. This need to discipline judicial judgment is rooted in a theory of democratic institutions. There is no taboo, as Sunstein notes, on invoking high-level theories of value in legislatures, which are staffed by elected representatives, and presumably, reflect the will of the people. Though courts have used high-level theories at particular moments in history, democratic societies favor judicial modesty and qualified deference by courts to legislatures.

Before concluding the selection offered here, Sunstein considers an objection. Shouldn't judges aspire to a form of what Henry Sidgwick called "conceptual ascent"? That is, in an effort to gain deeper insight into the law itself, shouldn't they seek to understand the more abstract theories that presumably justify incompletely theorized agreements on particular cases? According to this view, abstract theories function as searchlights that broaden and deepen our understanding of lower- and mid-level principles and particular decisions. In the light of these theories, we could find that specific decisions based on incompletely theorized agreements are wrong, and we could discover more appropriate directions to develop the law.

Against this view, Sunstein makes two points. First, the actual situation of judges argues against grandiose theorizing. The decision-making scope of judges is limited by two things: that they are required to adjudicate particular cases, often of restricted scope, and that the institutional role of the courts is circumscribed. The bounded scope of judicial decision making, in Sunstein's view, argues in favor of theoretical modesty. Second, he challenges the rosy picture of theory that the objection assumes. Theories, in his view, have no special magic. As he puts it, "the abstract deserves no priority over the particular; neither should be treated as foundational" (p. 62).

The following selections offer an introduction to the complexities of scholarly work on legal reasoning. For further information, we urge you to consult the list of selected readings on legal reasoning, as well as the section on jurisprudence in this volume.

SELECTED READINGS

Alexander, Larry. "Constrained by Precedent." *Southern California Law Review* 63 (1989): 1–64.

Bork, Robert H. *The Tempting of America: The Political Seduction of the Law.* New York: Free Press, 1990.

Brooks, Peter, and Paul Gewirtz, eds. *Law's Stories: Narrative and Rhetoric in the Law.* New Haven, CT: Yale University Press, 1996.

Eskridge, William N., Jr. *Dynamic Statutory Interpretation.* Cambridge, MA: Harvard University Press, 1994.

Frank, Jerome. *Law and the Modern Mind.* New York: Tudor, 1930.

Holmes, Oliver Wendell, Jr. *The Common Law.* New York: Dover, 1991.

Kennedy, Duncan. *A Critique of Adjudication: (fin de siecle).* Cambridge, MA: Harvard University Press, 1998.

Nussbaum, Martha C. *Poetic Justice: The Literary Imagination and Public Life.* Boston: Beacon Press, 1995.

Minow, Martha, and Elizabeth Spelman. "In Context." *Southern California Law Review* 63 (1990): 1597–1652.

Posner, Richard A. *Law and Literature: A Misunderstood Relation.* Cambridge, MA: Harvard University Press, 1988.

Pound, Roscoe. *An Introduction to the Philosophy of Law.* New Haven, CT: Yale University Press, 1954.

Raz, Joseph. *The Authority of Law: Essays on Law and Morality.* Oxford, England: Clarendon Press, 1979.

Schauer, Frederick. *Playing By the Rules: A Philosophical Examination of Rule-based Decision-Making in Law and in Life.* Oxford, England: Clarendon Press, 1991.

Tushnet, Mark. "Following the Rules Laid Down: A Critique of Interpretivism and Neutral Principles." *Harvard Law Review* 96 (1983): 781–827.

Wechsler, Herbert. *Principles, Politics, and Fundamental Law: Selected Essays.* Cambridge, MA: Harvard University Press, 1961.

1

FREDERICK SCHAUER

Formalism

With accelerating frequency, legal decisions and theories are condemned as "formalist" or "formalistic." But what *is* formalism, and what is so bad about it? Even a cursory look at the literature reveals scant agreement on what it is for decisions in law, or perspectives on law, to be formalistic, except that whatever formalism is, it is not good. Few judges or scholars would describe themselves as formalists, for a congratulatory use of the word "formal" seems almost a linguistic error. Indeed, the pejorative connotations of the word "formalism," in concert with the lack of agreement on the word's descriptive content, make it tempting to conclude that "formalist" is the adjective used to describe any judicial decision, style of legal thinking, or legal theory with which the user of the term disagrees.

Yet this temptation should be resisted. There *does* seem to be descriptive content in the notion of formalism, even if there are widely divergent uses of the term. At the heart of the word "formalism," in many of its numerous uses, lies the concept of decisionmaking according to *rule*. Formalism is the way in which rules achieve their "ruleness" precisely by doing what is supposed to be the failing of formalism: screening off from a decisionmaker factors that a sensitive decisionmaker would otherwise take into account. Moreover, it appears that this screening off takes place largely through the force of the language in which rules are written. Thus the tasks performed by rules are tasks for which the primary tool is the specific linguistic formulation of a rule. As a result, insofar as formalism is frequently condemned as excessive reliance on the language of a rule, it is the very idea of decisionmaking by rule that is being condemned, either as a description of how decisionmaking can take place or as a prescription for how decisionmaking should take place.

Once we disentangle and examine the various strands of formalism and recognize the way in which formalism, rules, and language are conceptually intertwined, it turns out that there is something, indeed much, to be said for decision according to rule—and therefore for formalism. I do not argue that formalism is always good or that legal systems ought often or even ever be formalistic. Nevertheless, I do want to urge a rethinking of the contemporary aversion to formalism. For even if what can be said for formalism is not in the end persuasive, the issues should be before us for inspection, rather than blocked by a discourse of epithets.

FORMALISM AS THE DENIAL OF CHOICE

A. Choice within Norms

Few decisions are charged with formalism as often as *Lochner v. New York*. But what makes Justice Peckham's majority opinion in *Lochner* formalistic? Surely it is not just that the Court protected an unrestricted privilege of labor contracting against the first stirrings of the welfare state. For the Court to make such a political decision under the rubric of broad constitutional clauses like "liberty" is a far cry from what seems to be meant when decisions are criticized as being formal. To the extent that the charge of formalism suggests narrowness, *Lochner* is hardly a candidate. We criticize *Lochner* not for being narrow, but for being excessively broad.

Although *Lochner* is criticized for the length of its reach, a closer look reveals that it is not the result that is condemned as formalistic but rather the justification for that result. The formalism in *Lochner* inheres in its *denial* of the political, moral, social, and economic choices involved in the decision, and indeed in its denial that there was any choice at all. Justice Peckham simply announced that "[t]he general right to make a contract in relation to his business is part of the liberty of the individual protected by the Fourteenth Amendment"[1] and that "[t]he right to purchase or to sell labor is part of the liberty protected by this amendment."[2] To these pronouncements he added the confident statement that "[o]f course the liberty of contract relating to labor includes both parties to it."[3]

Justice Peckham's language suggests that he is explaining a precise statutory scheme rather than

[1] 198 U.S. 45 (1905) at 53.
[2] *Id.*
[3] *Id.* at 56.

expounding on one word in the Constitution. It is precisely for this reason that his opinion draws criticism. We condemn *Lochner* as formalistic not because it involves a choice, but because it attempts to describe this choice as compulsion. What strikes us clearly as a political or social or moral or economic choice is described in *Lochner* as definitionally incorporated within the *meaning* of a broad term. Thus, choice is masked by the language of linguistic inexorability.

When I say that pelicans are birds, the truth of the statement follows inexorably from the meaning of the term "bird." If someone disagrees, or points at a living, breathing, flying pelican and says "That is not a bird," she simply does not know what the word "bird" means. We criticize *Lochner* as formalistic because it treats the word "liberty" (or the words "life, liberty, or property, without due process of law") as being like the word "bird" and the privilege of contracting as being like a pelican, i.e., subsumed in the broader category. According to the reasoning in *Lochner,* if you don't know that contracting for labor without governmental control is an example of liberty, then you just don't know what the word "liberty" means.

Lochner is condemned as formalistic precisely because the analogy between pelicans (as birds) and unrestricted contracting (as liberty) fails. One can understand much about the concept of liberty and about the word "liberty" and yet still deny that they include the privilege of unconstrained labor contracting. Thus, a decisionmaker who knows or should know that such a choice is open, but treats the choice as no more available than the choice to treat a pelican as other than a bird, is charged with formalism for treating as definitionally inexorable that which involves nondefinitional, substantive choices.

Lochner is merely one example in which a false assertion of inexorability is decried as formalistic. Much contemporary criticism of Blackstone, Langdell, and others of their persuasion attacks their jurisprudence on similar grounds. They stand accused of presenting contestable applications of general terms as definitionally incorporated within the meaning of the general term. It is important, however, to understand the relationship between the linguistic and the ontological questions for those of Blackstone's vision. Blackstone's view that certain abstract terms definitionally incorporate a wide range of specific results is tied intimately to his perception of a hard and suprahuman reality behind these general terms. If the word "property," for example, actually describes some underlying and noncontingent reality, then it follows easily that certain specific embodiments are necessarily part of that reality, just as pelicans are part of the underlying reality that is the universe of birds. These instantiations might still follow even if the general term is not a natural kind whose existence and demarcation is beyond the control of human actors. There is nothing natural or noncontingent about the term "basketball," but it is nevertheless an error in this culture at this time to apply that word to a group of people hitting small hard balls with one of a collection of fourteen different sticks. Still, linguistic clarity and rigidity are both facilitated insofar as the words track the natural kinds of the world. To the extent that Blackstone and others believed that categories like liberty, property, and contract were natural kinds rather than human artifacts, they were less likely to perceive the choices we would now not think to deny. When one believes that a general term reflects a deep reality beyond the power of human actors, the view that certain particulars are *necessarily* part of that reality follows with special ease.

Thus, one view of the vice of formalism takes that vice to be one of deception, either of oneself or of others. To disguise a choice in the language of definitional inexorability obscures that choice and thus obstructs questions of how it was made and whether it could have been made differently. Use of the word "formalism" in this sense hinges on the existence of a term (or phrase, sentence, or paragraph) whose contested application generates the choice. Some terms, like "liberty" and "equality," are *pervasively indeterminate*. It is not that such terms have no content whatsoever; it is that *every* application, every concretization, every instantiation requires the addition of supplementary premises to apply the general term to specific cases. Therefore, any application of that term that denies the choice made among various eligible supplementary premises is formalistic in this sense.

More commonly, however, the indeterminacy to be filled by a decisionmaker's choice is not pervasive throughout the range of applications of a term. Instead, the indeterminacy is encountered only at the edges of a term's meaning. As H. L. A. Hart tells us, legal terms possess a core of settled meaning and a penumbra of debatable meaning. For Hart, formalism derives from the denial of choice in the penumbra of meaning, where applying the term in question is optional. Thus, Hart conceives of formalism as the unwillingness to acknowledge in cases of doubtful application, such as the question of whether a bicycle is a vehicle for purposes of the prohibition on vehicles in the park, that choices must be made that go far beyond merely ascertaining the meaning of a word.

Hart's conception of formalism is closely aligned with that undergirding those who criticize both Blackstone and *Lochner*. Hart's formalist takes the penumbra to be as clear as the core, while the *Lochner* formalist takes the general term to be as determinate as the specific. Both deny the extent of actual indeterminacy, and thus neither admits that the application of the norm involves a choice not determined by the words of the norm alone.

B. Choice among Norms

Implicit in Hart's conception of formalism is the view that in the core, unlike in the penumbra, legal answers are often tolerably determinate. Even if this is true, and I will examine this claim presently, the possibility remains that a decisionmaker has a choice of whether or not to follow a seemingly applicable norm even in its core of meaning. The question in this case is not whether a bus is a vehicle, or even whether the core of the rule excludes buses from the park, but whether the rule excluding vehicles must be applied in this case. At times a decisionmaker may have a choice whether to apply the clear and specifically applicable norm. In such cases we can imagine a decisionmaker having and making a choice but denying that a choice was in any way part of the process. Thus, a variant on the variety of formalism just discussed sees formalism as involving not denial of the existence of choices within norms, but denial that there are frequently choices about whether to apply even the clear norms.

As an example of this type of formalism, consider the unreported and widely unknown case of *Hunter v. Norman*.[4] Hunter, an incumbent state senator in Vermont seeking re-election, filed his nominating petition in the Windsor County Clerk's office on July 21, 1986 at 5:03 p.m. In doing so he missed by three minutes the petition deadline set by title 17, section 2356, of the Laws of Vermont.[5] The statute provides, in its entirety, that "Primary petitions shall be filed not later than 5:00 p.m. on the third Monday of July preceding the primary election prescribed by section 2351 of this title, and not later than 5:00 p.m. of the forty-second day prior to the day of a special primary election."[6] The Windsor County Clerk, Jane Norman, duly enforced the statute by refusing to accept Hunter's petition, observing that "I have no intention of breaking the law, not for Jesus Christ himself."[7] Hunter's name, consequently, was to be withheld from appearing on the September Democratic primary election ballot.

Hunter, not surprisingly, took his disappointment to the courthouse and filed an action in equity against Norman for extraordinary relief.[8] He asked that the court order her to accept his petition and to ensure that his name would appear on the primary ballot. At the hearing, Hunter alleged that he had called the clerk's office earlier on the date in question and been told that he was required to deliver the petition in person because of the necessity of signing forms consenting to his nomination. In fact, these consent forms were not due until a later date. Hunter claimed that had he not been led to appear in person by receiving this erroneous advice, the petition would have been filed earlier in the day. He argued that in light of the erroneous information given to Hunter by the Clerk's office, the clerk (and the state) were estopped from relying on the statutory deadline. In support of this proposition, Hunter offered *Ryshpan v. Cashman*,[9] in which the Vermont Supreme Court, on similar facts, held that because "reliance on erroneous actions on behalf of the State has put . . . its citizens in inescapable conflict with the literal terms of one of the time requirements instituted by that same sovereignty. . . [t]he statutory time schedule must . . . as a matter of equity . . . yield."[10]

---

[4]No. S197-86-WrC (Vt. July 28, 1986). The following account of the case is drawn from Judge Cheever's brief opinion, the pleadings, news accounts in *Rutland Herald* of July 22, 23, 24, and 26, 1986, and a conversation with Marilyn Signe Skoglund, Assistant Attorney General in the Office of the Attorney General, State of Vermont.

[5]VT. STAT. ANN. tit. 17, § 2356 (1982).

[6]*Id.*

[7]*Rutland Herald*, July 23, 1986, at 5, col. 4.

[8]The petition is unclear as to whether Hunter was seeking the extraordinary legal remedy of mandamus or a mandatory injunction in equity.

[9]132 Vt. 628, 326 A.2d 169 (1974).

[10]*Id.* at 630–31, 326 A.2d at 171.

Ultimately, Hunter prevailed, and it appears that *Ryshpan v. Cashman* saved the day—or at least saved Hunter's day. *Ryshpan* therefore seems to have operated as an escape route from the rigors of the statute. Suppose, however, that everything in Hunter's case had been the same, including the existence of *Ryshpan,* but that the judge had ruled against Hunter solely on the basis of the statutory language. Had this hardly unrealistic alternative occurred, it would seem but a small step from the brand of formalism discussed above to a formalist characterization of this hypothetical decision. As long as *Ryshpan* exists, the judge has a choice whether to follow the letter of the statute or instead to employ the escape route. To make this choice and merely cite the statute as indicating the absence of choice would therefore deny the reality of the choice that was made. The crux of the matter is that this choice was present as long as *Ryshpan* existed, whether the judge followed that case or not. The charge of formalism in such a case would be but a variation of formalism as the concealment of choice: Instead of a choice within a norm, as with either pervasively indeterminate language or language containing penumbras of uncertainty surrounding a core of settled meaning, here the choice is between two different norms.

This variation on *Ryshpan* reveals the reasons we condemn the masking of choice. When the statute and *Ryshpan* coexist, neither determines which will prevail. Thus, the choice of the escape route represented by *Ryshpan* over the result indicated by the statute, or vice versa, necessarily would be made on the basis of factors external to both. These factors might include the moral, political, or physical attractiveness of the parties; the particular facts of the case; the judge's own views about deadlines; the judge's own views about statutes; the judge's own views about the Vermont Supreme Court; the judge's own views about clerks of courts; and so on. Yet were any of these factors to cause a particular judge to decide that the statute should prevail, mere citation of the statute as inexorably dictating the result would conceal from the litigants and from society the actual determinative factors. Insofar as we expect the reasons for a decision to be open for inspection (and that, after all, is usually the reason judges write opinions), failure to acknowledge that a choice was made can be criticized because knowing how the choice was made helps to make legitimate the products of the system.

C. Is There Always a Choice?

Ryshpan v. Cashman is a trifle obscure, but it is hardly unique. Consider the number of *Ryshpan* equivalents that allow decisionmakers to avoid the specific mandates of a particular rule. A decisionmaker may determine that the literal language of a rule does not serve that rule's original intent, as the Supreme Court has interpreted the Civil Rights Act of 1964, the contracts clause of the Constitution, and the Eleventh Amendment. Or a decisionmaker may apply the "mischief rule" or its variants to determine that a literal application of the rule would not serve the rule's *purpose.* Or a decisionmaker may apply a more general rule that denies relief to a claimant entitled to relief under the most locally applicable rule; for example, she might apply the equitable principle of unclean hands or laches, the legal principle of *in pari delicto,* or the civil law principle of abuse of right. Any reader of this article could easily add to this list.

Yet, what if none of these established routes were available in a particular case—would a judge then be forced to apply the specifically applicable rule? To answer this question, let us examine another variation on *Hunter v. Norman.* Suppose that *Ryshpan v. Cashman* did *not* exist, but that everything else about the facts and the applicable law in *Hunter* remained the same. What choices, if any, would be open to the judge? The judge could, of course, simply hold that the statute applied and rule against Hunter. But must he? Could the judge instead "create" *Ryshpan* by concluding that Hunter should win because he was misled by the clerk's office?

This option of creating *Ryshpan* does not seem inconsistent with the way the American legal system operates. Despite the lack of any specific statute or case authorizing such a result, allowing Hunter to win because he was misled would raise no eyebrows in American legal circles. No one would call for an investigation of the judge's competence, as someone might had the judge ruled for Hunter because Hunter was a Capricorn and Norman a Sagittarius. If the creation of such an escape route would be consistent with American judicial traditions, then the judge can be seen to have had a choice between deciding for Hunter and deciding for Norman even without *Ryshpan.* Thus a judge who ruled against Hunter on the basis of the statute would be denying the extent to which there was still a choice to create *Ryshpan* and thereby rule for Hunter.

Of course, a judge who decided to "create" *Ryshpan* would probably not simply assert that Hunter should win because he relied on erroneous information from a state official. Rather, the judge would justify this conclusion by reference to general principles that lurk in various corners of the legal system. For example, the judge might say that, as a general principle, parties are estopped from relying on laws whose contents they have misstated to the disadvantage of another; a decision against the clerk would be merely a specific instance of the application of that general principle. Or, the judge might cite other particular principles, such as the principle of reliance in securities law, and analogize this case to those. Under either analysis the judge would attempt to ground the new principle in some already existing principle.

On the basis of these variations, we can distinguish three possible models of escape route availability. Under one model, the existing escape routes in the system represent an incomplete list of principles to ameliorate the rigidity of rules, and the judge may add to this list where amelioration is indicated but no applicable ameliorative principle exists. In such instances, the judge might discuss justice or fairness or some other general value and explain why this value supports the creation of a principle like that in *Ryshpan v. Cashman*. The implicit ideal of this system is the availability of an ameliorative principle whenever the circumstances demand it. Thus the judge who creates a new ameliorative principle on an appropriate occasion furthers the goals of this system.

Alternatively, we could develop a model of a system in which there is already a more or less complete stock of ameliorative principles. In such a system, a judge would *always* have some escape route available if all the circumstances indicated that the applicable norm was not the best result to be reached in that case. If *Ryshpan* itself did not exist, the judge would be able to pick other extant ameliorative principles that would get Hunter's name on the ballot.

Both the first model, which resembles Dworkin's account of the law, and the second, which borrows from Llewellyn's, acknowledge the persuasiveness of judicial choice in their recognition of the judge's opportunity (or perhaps even obligation) to avoid the arguably unjust consequences of mechanical application of the most directly applicable legal rule. If either of these models is an accurate rendition of some legal system, then a decisionmaker within such a system who simply applies the most directly applicable legal rule without further thought or explanation either denies herself a choice that the system permitted or required, or denies to others an explanation of why she chose not to use the escape routes permitted by the system. This failure to explain the choice to apply the most locally applicable rule is simply a variation on the more egregious forms of formalism as denial of choice.

These two models—one allowing the creation of rule-avoiding norms, and the other presenting a complete list of such norms for use—must be contrasted with a third model. Under this third model, the stock of extant rule-avoiding norms is not temporarily incomplete but completable, as in the first model, nor is it complete, as in the second. Instead, it is both incomplete and closed. A decisionmaker will therefore be confronted with situations in which the immediately applicable rule generates a result the decisionmaker wishes to avoid but for which the system neither contains an escape route nor permits one to be created. Under this model, a judge who followed the rule—rather than the course she otherwise would have taken on the basis of *all* relevant factors—would not have acted formalistically in the sense now under discussion. Where there was no choice, a decisionmaker following the mandates of the most directly applicable norm could not be accused of having a choice but denying its existence.

If we can imagine a model in which a rule-avoiding norm is both nonexistent and precluded in some instances, then we can also imagine a model in which no rule-avoiding norms exist at all. In such a system, a decisionmaker would be expected simply to decide according to the rule when there was a rule dealing specifically with the situation. Because there was no choice to be made, the decisionmaker could not be charged with masking a choice.

This third model presents the conceptual possibility of a different type of formalism than that which has been the focus of this section. In this third model, the charge of "formalism" would possess a different significance than in the other two models, for the decisionmaker accused of being formalistic might not be denying a choice made in the decisionmaking process, but might never have had a choice at all. To investigate the possibility of this type of formalism we must determine whether a system can truly foreclose choices from the decisionmaker. . . .

SHOULD CHOICE BE RESTRICTED?

Let me recapitulate. One conception takes the vice of formalism to consist of a decisionmaker's denial, couched in the language of obedience to clear rules, of having made any choice at all. Yet rules, if followed, may not leave a decisionmaker free choice. Rules *can* limit decisional choice, and decisionmakers *can* abide by those limitations. Those limitations come in most cases from the literal language of a rule's formulation, for to take a rule as anything other than the rule's formulation, or at least the meaning of the rule's formulation, is ultimately to deny the idea of a rule.

Thus, formalism merges into ruleness, and both are inextricably intertwined with literalism, i.e., the willingness to make decisions according to the literal meaning of words or phrases or sentences or paragraphs on a printed page, even if the consequences of that decision seem either to frustrate the purpose behind those words or to diverge significantly from what the decisionmaker thinks—the rule aside—should be done. But does demonstrating that formalism is ruleness rescue formalism? Restated, what is so good about decision according to rules?

The simple answer to this question, and perhaps also the correct one, is "nothing." Little about decision constrained by the rigidity of rules seems intrinsically valuable. Once we understand that rules get in the way, that they gain their ruleness by cutting off access to factors that might lead to the best resolution in a particular case, we see that rules function as impediments to optimally sensitive decisionmaking. Rules doom decisionmaking to mediocrity by mandating the inaccessibility of excellence.

Nor is there anything essentially *just* about a system of rules. We have scarce reason to believe that rule-based adjudication is more likely to be just than are systems in which rules do not block a decisionmaker, especially a just decisionmaker, from considering every reason that would assist her in reaching the best decision. Insofar as factors screened from consideration by a rule might in a particular case turn out to be those necessary to reach a just result, rules stand in the way of justice in those cases and thus impede optimal justice in the long term. We equate Solomon's wisdom with justice not because Solomon followed the rules in solving the dispute over the baby but because Solomon came up with exactly the right solution for that case. We frequently laud not history's rule followers, but those whose abilities at particularized decisionmaking transcend the inherent limitations of rules.

Still, that rules may be in one sense unjust, or even that they may be inappropriate in much of what we call a legal system, does not mean there is nothing to be said for rules. One of the things that can be said for rules is the value variously expressed as predictability or certainty. But if we pursue the predictability theme, we see that what most arguments for ruleness share is a focus on disabling certain classes of decisionmakers from making certain kinds of decisions. Predictability follows from the decision to treat all instances falling within some accessible category in the same way. It is a function of the way in which rules decide ahead of time how *all* cases within a class will be determined.

Predictability is fostered to the extent that four different requirements are satisfied. The first of the factors contributing to predictability is the capacity on the part of those relying on a rule to identify certain particulars as instances of a given category (for example, that pelicans are birds). When there is a more or less uniform and uncontroversial ability to say that some item is a member of some category, little in the way of potentially variable judgment clouds the prediction of whether the rule will apply to this particular item. This relates to the second factor: that the decisionmakers in the system will perceive those particulars as being members of the same category perceived by the addressees and will be seen as so perceiving by those affected. That is, people perceive pelicans as birds; decisionmakers perceive pelicans as birds; and people know that decisionmakers will perceive pelicans as birds. Third, the rule must speak in terms of an accessible category. Predictability requires that a rule cover a category whose denotation is substantially noncontroversial among the class of addressees of the rule and common to the addressees of the rule and those who apply it. Finally, the rule must treat all members of a category in the same way. Only if the consequences specified in the apodosis of the rule are as accessible and noncontroversial as the coverage specified in the protasis can a rule produce significant predictability of application. Thus, predictability comes from the knowledge that if this is a bird a certain result will follow, and from the confidence that what I now perceive to be a bird will be considered a bird by the ultimate decisionmaker.

This predictability comes only at a price. Situations may arise in which putting this particular into that category seems just too crude—something about this particular makes us desire to treat it specially. *This* vehicle is merely a statue, emits no fumes, makes no noise, and endangers no lives; it ought to be treated differently from those vehicles whose characteristics mesh with the purpose behind the rule. Serving the goal of predictability, however, requires that we ignore this difference, because to acknowledge this difference is also to create the power—the *jurisdiction*—to determine whether this vehicle or that vehicle serves the purpose of the "no vehicles in the park" rule. It is the jurisdiction to determine that only some vehicles fit the purpose of the rule that undermines the confidence that *all* vehicles will be prohibited. No longer is it the case that anything that is a *vehicle,* a moderately accessible category, is excluded. Instead, the category is now that of *vehicles whose prohibition will serve the purpose of the "no vehicle in the park" rule,* a potentially far more controversial category.

Thus, the key to understanding the relationship of ruleness to predictability is the idea of decisional jurisdiction. The issue is not whether the statue serves the purpose of the "no vehicles in the park" rule. It is whether giving some decisionmaker jurisdiction to determine what the rule's purpose is (as well as jurisdiction to determine whether some item fits that purpose) injects a possibility of variance substantially greater than that involved in giving a decisionmaker jurisdiction solely to determine whether some particular is or is not a vehicle. Note also that the jurisdictional question has a double aspect. When we grant jurisdiction we are first concerned with the range of equally correct decisions that might be made in the exercise of that jurisdiction. If there is no authoritative statement of the purpose behind the "no vehicles in the park" rule, granting jurisdiction to determine that purpose would allow a decisionmaker to decide whether the purpose is to preserve quiet, to prevent air pollution, or to prevent accidents, and each of these determinations would be equally correct. In addition to increasing the range of correct decisions, however, certain grants of jurisdiction increase the likelihood of erroneous determinations. Compare "No vehicles in the park" with "The park is closed to vehicles whose greatest horizontal perimeter dimension, when added to their greatest vertical perimeter dimension, exceeds the lesser of (a) sixty-eight feet, six inches and (b) the greatest horizontal perimeter dimension, added to the greatest vertical perimeter dimension, of the average of the largest passenger automobile manufactured in the United States by the three largest automobile manufacturers in the preceding year." The second adds no inherent variability, but it certainly compounds the possibility of decisionmaker error. Creating the jurisdiction to determine whether the purposes of a rule are served undermines predictability by allowing the determination of any of several possible purposes; in addition, the creation of that jurisdiction engenders the possibility that those who exercise it might just get it wrong.

Grants of decisional jurisdiction not only increase permissible variance and the possibility of "computational" error, they also involve decisionmakers in determinations that a system may prefer to have made by someone else. We may believe that courts are less competent to make certain decisions than other bodies; for example, we may feel that certain kinds of fact-finding are better done by legislatures. There may also be moral or political reasons to restrict the judge's discretion, for decisionmaking implicates profound questions of just who in a given domain may legitimately make certain decisions. It is, for example, a plausible position that the public rather than the University of Michigan philosophy department should make the moral determinations involved in governing the United States, even if the University of Michigan philosophy department would make better choices.

Although decreasing the possibility of variance and error by the decisionmaker contributes to the ability of addressees of rules to predict the consequences of application of those rules, limited variance can serve other values as well. If decisionmakers are denied jurisdiction to determine whether a particular instance actually justifies its inclusion in a larger generalization or are denied jurisdiction to determine the best result on the basis of all germane factors, the part of the system inhabited by those decisionmakers becomes more stable. Treating a large group of different particulars in the same way—the inevitable byproduct of the generalization of rules—dampens the range of variance in result by suppressing consideration of a wide range of potentially relevant differences. Thus, stability, not as a necessary condition for predictability but as a value in its own right, is fostered by truncating the decisionmaking authority.

Because rule-bound decisionmaking is inherently stabilizing, it is inherently conservative, in the nonpolitical sense of the word. By limiting the ability of decisionmakers to consider every factor relevant to an event, rules make it more difficult to adapt to a changing future. Rules force the future into the categories of the past. Note the important asymmetry here, the way in which rules operate not to enable but only to disable. A decisionmaker can never exceed the optimal result based on all relevant factors. Thus, a rule-bound decisionmaker, precluded from taking into account certain features of the present case, can never do better but can do worse than a decisionmaker seeking the optimal result for a case through a rule-free decision.

Yet this conservatism, suboptimization, and inflexibility in the face of a changing future need not be universally condemned. Rules stabilize by inflating the importance of the classifications of yesterday. We achieve stability, valuable in its place, by relinquishing some part of our ability to improve on yesterday. Again the issue is jurisdiction, for those who have jurisdiction to improve on yesterday also have jurisdiction to make things worse. To stabilize, to operate in an inherently conservative mode, is to give up some of the possibility of improvement in exchange for guarding against some of the possibility of disaster. Whether, when, and where the game is worth the candle, however cannot be determined acontextually.

In sum, it is clearly true that rules get in the way, but this need not always be considered a bad thing. It may be a liability to get in the way of wise decisionmakers who sensitively consider all of the relevant factors as they accurately pursue the good. However, it may be an asset to restrict misguided, incompetent, wicked, power-hungry, or simply mistaken decisionmakers whose own sense of the good might diverge from that of the system they serve. The problem, of course, is the difficulty in determining which characterization will fit decisionmakers; we must therefore decide the extent to which we are willing to disable good decisionmakers in order simultaneously to disable bad ones.

With these considerations in mind, let us approach formalism in a new light. Consider some of the famous marchers in formalism's parade of horribles, examples such as *R. v. Ojibway,* Fuller's statue of the truck in the park, and the poor Bolognese surgeon who, having opened the vein of a patient in the course of performing an emergency operation outdoors, was prosecuted for violating the law prohibiting "drawing blood in the streets." Each of these examples reminds us that cases may arise in which application of the literal meaning of words produces an absurd result. But now we can recast the question, for we must consider not only whether the result was absurd in these cases but also whether a particular decisionmaker should be empowered to determine absurdity. Even in cases as extreme as these, formalism is only superficially about rigidity and absurdity. More fundamentally, it is about power and its allocation.

Formalism is about power, but is also about its converse—modesty. To be formalistic as a decisionmaker is to say that something is not my concern, no matter how compelling it may seem. When this attitude is applied to the budget crisis or to eviction of the starving, it seems objectionable. But when the same attitude of formalism requires judges to ignore the moral squalor of the Nazis or the Ku Klux Klan in First Amendment cases, or the guilt of the defendant in Fourth Amendment cases, or the wealth of the plaintiff who seeks to recover for medical expenses occasioned by the defendant's negligence, it is no longer clear that refusal to take all factors into account is condemnable.

Modesty, of course, has its darker side. To be modest is at times good, but avoiding authority is also avoiding responsibility. In some circumstances we want our decisionmakers to take charge and accept the consequences of their actions. But it is by no means clear that just because it is good for some people to take charge some of the time, that taking charge, even accompanied by acceptance of responsibility, is a universal good. "I'm in charge here" has a long but not always distinguished history. Part of what formalism is about is its inculcation of the view that sometimes it is appropriate for decisionmakers to recognize their lack of jurisdiction and to defer even when they are convinced that their own judgment is best. The opposite of modesty is arrogance, not just responsibility. True, modesty itself carries responsibility, because an actor behaving modestly is participating and thus assisting in the legitimacy of the grant of authority to someone else. But this is a responsibility of a different and limited kind. That one accepts partial responsibility for the decisions of others does not entail the obligation to substitute one's judgment for that of others.

The distinctive feature of rules, therefore, lies in their ability to be formal, to exclude from consideration in the particular case factors whose exclusion was determined without reference to the particular case at hand. This formalism of rules is not only conceptually sound and psychologically possible, but it also, as I have tried to show, is on occasion normatively desirable. Insofar as formalism disables some decisionmakers from considering some factors that may appear important to them, it allocates power to some decisionmakers and away from others. Formalism therefore achieves its value when it is thought desirable to narrow the decisional opportunities and the decisional range of a certain class of decisionmakers.

I stress that all of this is compatible with agnosticism about how rulebound decisionmaking applies to legal systems in general, to particular legal systems, or to particular parts of legal systems. It is far from a necessary truth that legal systems must be exclusively or even largely operated as rule-governed institutions. Judgments about when to employ formalism are contextual and not inexorable, political and not logical, psychological and economic rather than conceptual. It would blunt my point about the simultaneously plausible and contingent nature of decision according to rule to offer in this acontextual setting my recommendations about what if any parts of the American or any other legal system should operate in such a fashion. My goal is only to rescue formalism from conceptual banishment. But having been readmitted to the community of respectable ideas, formalism, or decisionmaking according to rule in any strong sense, still has the burden of showing that it is appropriately used in a particular decisional domain. . . .

An alternative hypothesis posits some ground between no review and unfettered intrusiveness. There might be cases in which the presumption in favor of the result below would cause the decision to stand. Under this hypothesis, we can have rebuttable presumptions—cases in which the presumption might be overcome in particularly exigent circumstances but nevertheless controls in many or even most cases. . . .

If such instructions sometimes create presumptions, and if those presumptions sometimes work, then what does this say about the possibility of what we might call a *presumptive formalism?* In order to construct such a model, we would want to equate the literal mandate of the most locally applicable written rule with the judgment of the court below. The court below can be taken to have determined, for example, that in one case operable and operating automobiles are excluded from the park, in another case golf carts are excluded from the park, and in a third case immobile statues of trucks are excluded from the park. We can then equate the reviewing court with a determination of the correct result from the perspective of the reasons behind the rule rather than the literal language of the rule itself. We might conclude that in the first case even a de novo application of the reasons would generate the same result as generated by the formalistic reading, and therefore the formal mandate would prevail uncontroversially. In the second, a de novo application of reasons would generate a different result than that generated by the rule, but the result generated by the rule remains "in the ballpark" and therefore is upheld despite its divergence from the result that would be reached by direct application of the reasons. In the third, however, a de novo application of the reasons indicates that the result generated by the rule is so far out of bounds, so absurd, so preposterous that it is analogous to an abuse of discretion and would therefore be reversed—the rule would not be applied in this case.

Under such a theory of presumptive formalism there would be a presumption in favor of the result generated by the literal and largely acontextual interpretation of the most locally applicable rule. Yet that result would be presumptive only, subject to defeasibility when less locally applicable norms, including the purpose behind the particular norm, and including norms both within and without the decisional domain at issue, offered especially exigent reasons for avoiding the result generated by the presumptively applicable norm.

Such a system would bring the advantages of predictability, stability, and constraint of decisionmakers commonly associated with decision according to rule, but would temper the occasional unpleasant consequences of such a system with an escape route that allowed some results to be avoided when their consequences would be especially outrageous. Such a system would not be without cost. First of all, the escape route would necessarily decrease the amount of predictability, stability, and decisionmaker restraint. In short, it would diminish the amount of ruleness by placing more final authority in the decisionmaker than in the rule. Second, the presumptive force attached to the formalist reading of the applicable norms would still result in some odd or suboptimal results. In this sense, such a system would fail to honor all of the goals either of unrestrained particularism or unrestrained formalism. Finally, such a system would risk collapse into one in which the presumptions were for all practical purposes either absolute or nonexistent.

Even on the assumption that such a system might be desirable in some decisional domains, this does not mean that all or part of what we commonly call the legal system might be one of those domains. It might be that formalism, even only presumptively, is a good idea, but that the goals of the legal system, in light of the decisions we ask it to make, are such that it ought not to be designed along such a model. More likely, formalism ought to be seen as a tool to be used in some parts of the legal system and not in others. Determining which parts, if any, would be susceptible to such treatment is not my agenda here, for what I have attempted to offer is only an argument that formal systems are not necessarily to be condemned. That is not to say they are universally or even largely to be applauded, nor that they are to be pervasive or even frequent within that segment of society we call the legal system. To answer this last question we must ask what the legal system, in whole or in part, is supposed to do, for only when we answer that question can we determine what kinds of tools it needs to accomplish that task. . . .

2

Lochner v. New York

198 U.S. 45 (1905)

ERROR TO THE COUNTY COURT OF ONEIDA COUNTY, STATE OF NEW YORK

No. 292. Argued February 23, 24, 1905 —Decided April 17, 1905.

The general right to make a contract in relation to his business is part of the liberty protected by the Fourteenth Amendment, and this includes the right to purchase and sell labor, except as controlled by the State in the legitimate exercise of its police power.

Liberty of contract relating to labor includes both parties to it; the one has as much right to purchase as the other to sell labor.

There is no reasonable ground, on the score of health, for interfering with the liberty of the person or the right of free contract, by determining the hours of labor, in the occupation of a baker. Nor can a law limiting such hours be justified as a health law to safeguard the public health, or the health of the individuals following that occupation.

Section 110 of the labor law of the State of New York, providing that no employees shall be required or permitted to work in bakeries more than sixty hours in a week, or ten hours a day, is not a legitimate exercise of the police power of the State, but an unreasonable, unnecessary and arbitrary interference with the right and liberty of the individual to contract, in relation to labor, and as such it is in conflict with, and void under, the Federal Constitution.

This is a writ of error to the County Court of Oneida County, in the State of New York (to which court the record had been remitted), to review the judgment of the Court of Appeals of that State, affirming the judgment of the Supreme Court, which itself affirmed the judgment of the County Court, convicting the defendant of a misdemeanor on an indictment under a statute of that State. . . .

The indictment averred that the defendant "wrongfully and unlawfully required and permitted an employé working for him in his biscuit, bread and cake bakery and confectionery establishment, at the city of Utica, in this county, to work more than sixty hours in one week," after having been theretofore convicted of a violation of the same act; and therefore, as averred, he committed the crime or misdemeanor, second offense. The plaintiff in error demurred to the indictment on several grounds, one of which was that the facts stated did not constitute a crime. The demurrer was overruled, and the plaintiff in error having refused to plead further, a plea of not guilty was entered by order of the court and the trial commenced, and he was convicted of misdemeanor, second offense, as indicted, and sentenced to pay a fine of $50 and to stand committed until paid, not to exceed fifty days in the Oneida County jail. A certificate of reasonable doubt was granted by the county judge of Oneida County, whereon an appeal was taken to the Appellate Division of the Supreme Court, Fourth Department, where the judgment of conviction was affirmed. 73 App. Div. N.Y. 120. A further appeal was then taken to the Court of Appeals, where the judgment of conviction was again affirmed. 177 N.Y. 145. . . .

Mr. Justice Peckham, after making the foregoing statement of the facts, delivered the opinion of the court.

The indictment, it will be seen, charges that the plaintiff in error violated the one hundred and tenth section of article 8, chapter 415, of the Laws of 1897, known as the labor law of the State of New York, in that he wrongfully and unlawfully required and permitted an employé working for him to work more than sixty hours in one week. There is nothing in any of the opinions delivered in this case, either in the Supreme Court or the Court of Appeals of the State, which construes the section, in using the word "required," as referring to any physical force being used to obtain the labor of an employé. It is assumed that the word means nothing more than the requirement arising from voluntary contract for such labor in excess of the number of hours specified in the statute. There is no pretense in any of the opinions that the statute was intended to meet a case of involuntary labor in any form. All the opinions assume that there is no real distinction, so far as this question is concerned, between the words "required" and "permitted." The mandate of the statute that "no employé shall be required or permitted to work," is the substantial equivalent of an enactment that "no employé shall contract or agree to work," more than ten hours per day, and as there is no provision for special emergencies the statute is mandatory in all cases. It is not an act merely fixing the number of hours which shall constitute a legal day's work, but an absolute prohibition upon the employer, permitting, under any circumstances, more than ten hours work to be done in his establishment. The employé may desire to earn the extra money, which would arise from his working more than the prescribed time, but this statute forbids the employer from permitting the employé to earn it.

The statute necessarily interferes with the right of contract between the employer and employés, concerning the number of hours in which the latter may labor in the bakery of the employer. The general right to make a contract in relation to his business is part of the liberty of the individual protected by the Fourteenth Amendment of the Federal Constitution. *Allgeyer v. Louisiana,* 165 U. S. 578. Under that provision no State can deprive any person of life, liberty or property without due process of law. The right to purchase or to sell labor is part of the liberty protected by this amendment, unless there are circumstances which exclude the right. There are, however, certain powers, existing in the sovereignty of each State in the Union, somewhat vaguely termed police powers, the exact description and limitation of which have not been attempted by the courts. Those powers, broadly stated and without, at present, any attempt at a more specific limitation, relate to the safety, health, morals and general welfare of the public. Both property and liberty are held on such reasonable conditions as may be imposed by the governing power of the State in the exercise of those powers, and with such conditions the Fourteenth Amendment was not designed to interfere. *Mugler v. Kansas,* 123 U. S. 623; *In re Kemmler,* 136 U. S. 436; *Crowley v. Christensen,* 137 U. S. 86; *In re Converse,* 137 U. S. 624.

The State, therefore, has power to prevent the individual from making certain kinds of contracts, and in regard to them the Federal Constitution offers no protection. If the contract be one which the State, in the legitimate exercise of its police power, has the right to prohibit, it is not prevented from prohibiting it by the Fourteenth Amendment. Contracts in violation of a statute, either of the Federal or state government, or a contract to let one's property for immoral purposes, or to do any other unlawful act, could obtain no protection from the Federal Constitution, as coming under the liberty of person or of free contract. Therefore, when the State, by its legislature, in the assumed exercise of its police powers, has passed an act which seriously limits the right to labor or the right of contract in regard to their means of livelihood between persons who are *sui juris* (both employer and employé), it becomes of great importance to determine which shall prevail—the right of the individual to labor for such time as he may choose, or the right of the State to prevent the individual from laboring or from entering into any contract to labor, beyond a certain time prescribed by the State.

This court has recognized the existence and upheld the exercise of the police powers of the States in many cases which might fairly be considered as border ones, and it has, in the course of its determination of questions regarding the asserted invalidity of such statutes, on the ground of their violation of the rights secured by the Federal Constitution, been guided by rules of a very liberal nature, the application of which has resulted, in numerous instances, in upholding the validity of state statutes thus assailed. Among the later cases where the state law has been upheld by this court is that of *Holden v. Hardy,* 169 U. S. 366. A provision in the act of the legislature of Utah was there under consideration, the act limiting the employment of workmen in all underground mines or workings, to eight hours per day, "except in cases of emergency, where life or property is in imminent danger." It also limited the hours of labor in smelting and other institutions for the reduction or refining of ores or metals to eight hours per day, except in like cases of emergency. The act was held to be a valid exercise of the police powers of the State. A review of many of the cases on the subject, decided by this and other courts, is given in the opinion. It was held that the kind of employment, mining, smelting, etc., and the character of the employés in such kinds of labor, were such as to make it reasonable and proper for the State to interfere to prevent the employés from being constrained by the rules laid down by the proprietors in regard to labor. The following citation from the observations of the Supreme Court of Utah in that case was made by the judge writing the opinion of this court, and approved: "The law in question is confined to the protection of that class of people engaged in labor in underground mines, and in smelters and other works wherein ores are reduced and refined. This law applies only to the classes subjected by their employment to the peculiar conditions and effects attending underground mining and work in smelters, and other works for the reduction and refining of ores. Therefore it is not necessary to discuss or decide whether the legislature can fix the hours of labor in other employments."

It will be observed that, even with regard to that class of labor, the Utah statute provided for cases of emergency wherein the provisions of the statute would not apply. The statute now before this court has no emergency clause in it, and, if the statute is valid, there are no circumstances and no emergencies under which the slightest violation of the provisions of the act would be innocent. There is nothing in *Holden v. Hardy* which covers the case now before us. Nor does *Atkin v. Kansas,* 191 U. S. 207, touch the case at bar. The *Atkin* case was decided upon the right of the State to control its municipal corporations and to prescribe the conditions upon which it will permit work of a public character to be done for a municipality. *Knoxville Iron Co. v. Harbison,* 183 U. S. 13, is equally far from an authority for this legislation. The employés in that case were held to be at a disadvantage with the employer in matters of wages, they being miners and coal workers, and the act simply provided for the cashing of coal orders when presented by the miner to the employer.

The latest case decided by this court, involving the police power, is that of *Jacobson v. Massachusetts,* decided at this term and reported in 197 U. S. 11. It related to compulsory vaccination, and the law was held valid as a proper exercise of the police powers with reference to the public health. It was stated in the opinion that it was a case "of an adult who, for aught that appears, was himself in perfect health and a fit subject for vaccination, and yet, while remaining in the community, refused to obey the statute and the regulation adopted in execution of its provisions for the protection of the public health and the public safety, confessedly endangered by the presence of a dangerous disease." That case is also far from covering the one now before the court.

Petit v. Minnesota, 177 U. S. 164, was upheld as a proper exercise of the police power relating to the observance of Sunday, and the case held that the legislature had the right to declare that, as matter of law, keeping barber shops open on Sunday was not a work of necessity or charity.

It must, of course, be conceded that there is a limit to the valid exercise of the police power by the State. There is no dispute concerning this general proposition. Otherwise the Fourteenth Amendment would have no efficacy and the legislatures of the States would have unbounded power, and it would be enough to say that any piece of legislation was enacted to conserve the morals, the health or the safety of the people; such legislation would be valid, no matter how absolutely without foundation the claim might be. The claim of the police power would be a mere pretext—become another and delusive name for the supreme sovereignty of the State to be exercised free from constitutional restraint. This is not contended for. In every case that comes before this court, therefore, where legislation of this character is concerned and where the protection of the Federal Constitution is sought, the question necessarily arises: Is this a fair, reasonable and appropriate exercise of the police power of the State, or is it an unreasonable, unnecessary and arbitrary interference with the right of the individual to his personal liberty or to enter into those contracts in relation to labor which may seem to him appropriate or necessary for the support of himself and his family? Of course the liberty of contract relating to labor includes both parties to it. The one has as much right to purchase as the other to sell labor.

This is not a question of substituting the judgment of the court for that of the legislature. If the act be within the power of the State it is valid, although the judgment of the court might be totally opposed to the enactment of such a law. But the question would still remain: Is it within the police power of the State? and that question must be answered by the court.

The question whether this act is valid as a labor law, pure and simple, may be dismissed in a few words. There is no reasonable ground for interfering with the liberty of person or the right of free contract, by determining the hours of labor, in the occupation of a baker. There is no contention that bakers as a class are not equal in intelligence and capacity to men in other trades or manual occupations, or that they are not able to assert their rights and care for themselves without the protecting arm of the State, interfering with their independence of judgment and of action. They are in no sense wards of the State. Viewed in the light of a purely labor law, with no reference whatever to the question of health, we think that a law like the one before us involves neither the safety, the morals nor the welfare of the public, and that the interest of the public is not in the slightest degree affected by such an act. The law must be upheld, if at all, as a law pertaining to the health of the individual engaged in the occupation of a baker. It does not affect any other portion of the public than those who are engaged in that occupation. Clean and wholesome bread does not depend upon whether the baker works but ten hours per day or only sixty hours a week. The limitation of the hours of labor does not come within the police power on that ground.

It is a question of which of two powers or rights shall prevail—the power of the State to legislate or the right of the individual to liberty of person and freedom of contract. The mere assertion that the subject relates though but in a remote degree to the public health does not necessarily render the enactment valid. The act must have a more direct relation, as a means to an end, and the end itself must be appropriate and legitimate, before an act can be held to be valid which interferes with the general right of an individual to be free in his person and in his power to contract in relation to his own labor. . . .

It is impossible for us to shut our eyes to the fact that many of the laws of this character, while passed under what is claimed to be the police power for the purpose of protecting the public health or welfare, are, in reality, passed from other motives. We are justified in saying so when, from the character of the law and the subject upon which it legislates, it is apparent that the public health or welfare bears but the most remote relation to the law. The purpose of a statute must be determined from the natural and legal effect of the language employed; and whether it is or is not repugnant to the Constitution of the United States must be determined from the natural effect of such statutes when put into operation, and not from their proclaimed purpose. *Minnesota v. Barber,* 136 U. S. 313; *Brimmer v. Rebman,* 138 U. S. 78. The court looks beyond the mere letter of the law in such cases. *Yick Wo v. Hopkins,* 118 U. S. 356.

It is manifest to us that the limitation of the hours of labor as provided for in this section of the statute under which the indictment was found, and the plaintiff in error convicted, has no such direct relation to and no such substantial effect upon the health of the employé, as to justify us in regarding the section as really a health law. It seems to us that the real object and purpose were simply to regulate the hours of labor between the master and his employés (all being men, *sui juris*), in a private business, not dangerous in any degree to morals or in any real and substantial degree, to the health of the employés. Under such circumstances the freedom of master and employé to contract with each other in relation to their employment, and in defining the same, cannot be prohibited or interfered with, without violating the Federal Constitution.

The judgment of the Court of Appeals of New York as well as that of the Supreme Court and of the County Court of Oneida County must be reversed and the case remanded to the County Court for further proceedings not inconsistent with this opinion.

Reversed.

MR. JUSTICE HARLAN, with whom MR. JUSTICE WHITE and MR. JUSTICE DAY concurred, dissenting.

While this court has not attempted to mark the precise boundaries of what is called the police power of the State, the existence of the power has been uniformly recognized, both by the Federal and state courts.

All the cases agree that this power extends at least to the protection of the lives, the health and the safety of the public against the injurious exercise by any citizen of his own rights. . . .

Granting then that there is a liberty of contract which cannot be violated even under the sanction of direct legislative enactment, but assuming, as according to settled law we may assume, that such liberty of contract is subject to such regulations as the State may reasonably prescribe for the common good and the well-being of society, what are the conditions under which the judiciary may declare such regulations to be in excess of legislative authority and void? Upon this point there is no room for dispute; for, the rule is universal that a legislative enactment, Federal or state, is never to be disregarded or held invalid unless it be, beyond question, plainly and palpably in excess of legislative power. In *Jacobson v. Massachusetts, supra,* we said that the power of the courts to review legislative action in respect of a matter affecting the general welfare exists *only* "when that which the legislature has done comes within the rule that if a statute purporting to have been enacted to protect the public health, the public morals or the public safety, has no real or substantial relation to those objects, or is, beyond all question, a plain, palpable invasion of rights secured by the fundamental law"—citing *Mugler v. Kansas,* 123 U. S. 623, 661; *Minnesota v. Barber,* 136 U. S. 313, 320; *Atkin v. Kansas,* 191 U. S. 207, 223. If there be doubt as to the validity of the statute, that doubt must therefore be resolved in favor of its validity, and the courts must keep their hands off, leaving the legislature to meet the responsibility for unwise legislation. If the end which the legislature seeks to accomplish be one to which its power extends, and if the means employed to that end, although not the wisest or best, are yet not plainly and palpably unauthorized by law, then the court cannot interfere. In other words, when the validity of a statute is questioned, the burden of proof, so to speak, is upon those who assert it to be unconstitutional. *McCulloch v. Maryland,* 4 Wheat. 316, 421.

Let these principles be applied to the present case. By the statute in question it is provided that, "No employé shall be required or permitted to work in a biscuit, bread or cake bakery or confectionery establishment more than sixty hours in any one week, or more than ten hours in any one day, unless for the purpose of making a shorter work day on the last day of the week; nor more hours in any one week than will make an average of ten hours per day for the number of days during such week in which such employé shall work."

It is plain that this statute was enacted in order to protect the physical well-being of those who work in bakery and confectionery establishments. It may be that the statute had its origin, in part, in the belief that employers and employés in such establishments were not upon an equal footing, and that the necessities of the latter often compelled them to submit to such exactions as unduly taxed their strength. Be this as it may, the statute must be taken as expressing the belief of the people of New York that, as a general rule, and in the case of the average man, labor in excess of sixty hours during a week in such establishments may endanger the health of those who thus labor. Whether or not this be wise legislation it is not the province of the court to inquire. Under our systems of government the courts are not concerned with the wisdom or policy of legislation. So that in determining the question of power to interfere with liberty of contract, the court may inquire whether the means devised by the State are germane to an end which may be lawfully accomplished and have a real or substantial relation to the protection of health, as involved in the daily work of the persons, male and female, engaged in bakery and confectionery establishments. But when this inquiry is entered upon I find it impossible, in view of common experience, to say that there is here no real or substantial relation between the means employed by the State and the end sought to be accomplished by its legislation, *Mugler v. Kansas, supra.* Nor can I say that the statute has no appropriate or direct connection with that protection to health which each State owes to her citizens, *Patterson v. Kentucky, supra*; or that it is not promotive of the health of the employés in question, *Holden v. Hardy, Lawton v. Steele, supra;* or that the regulation prescribed by the State is utterly unreasonable and extravagant or wholly arbitrary, *Gundling v. Chicago, supra.* Still less can I say that the statute is, beyond question, a plain, palpable invasion of rights secured by the fundamental law. *Jacobson v. Massachusetts, supra.* Therefore I submit that this court will transcend its functions if it assumes to annul the statute of New York. . . .

MR. JUSTICE HOLMES dissenting.

I regret sincerely that I am unable to agree with the judgment in this case, and that I think it my duty to express my dissent.

This case is decided upon an economic theory which a large part of the country does not entertain. If it were a question whether I agreed with that theory, I should desire to study it further and long before making up my mind. But I do not conceive that to be my duty, because I strongly believe that my agreement or disagreement has nothing to do with the right of a majority to embody their opinions in law. It is settled by various decisions of this court that state constitutions and state laws may regulate life in many ways which we as legislators might think as injudicious or if you like as tyrannical as this, and which equally with this interfere with the liberty to contract. Sunday laws and usury laws are ancient examples. A more modern one is the prohibition of lotteries. The liberty of the citizen to do as he likes so long as he does not interfere with the liberty of others to do the same, which has been a shibboleth for some well-known writers, is interfered with by school laws, by the Post Office, by every state or municipal institution which takes his money for purposes thought desirable, whether he likes it or not. The Fourteenth Amendment does not enact Mr. Herbert Spencer's Social Statics. The other day we sustained the Massachusetts vaccination law. *Jacobson v. Massachusetts,* 197 U. S. 11. United States and state statutes and decisions cutting down the liberty to contract by way of combination are familiar to this court. *Northern Securities Co. v. United States,* 193 U. S. 197. Two years ago we upheld the prohibition of sales of stock on margins or for future delivery in the constitution of California. *Otis v. Parker,* 187 U. S. 606. The decision sustaining an eight hour law for miners is still recent. *Holden v. Hardy,* 169 U. S. 366. Some of these laws embody convictions or prejudices which judges are likely to share. Some may not. But a constitution is not intended to embody a particular economic theory, whether of paternalism and the organic relation of the citizen to the State or of *laissez faire*. It is made for people of fundamentally differing views, and the accident of our finding certain opinions natural and familiar or novel and even shocking ought not to conclude our judgment upon the question whether statutes embodying them conflict with the Constitution of the United States.

General propositions do not decide concrete cases. The decision will depend on a judgment or intuition more subtle than any articulate major premise. But I think that the proposition just stated, if it is accepted, will carry us far toward the end. Every opinion tends to become a law. I think that the word liberty in the Fourteenth Amendment is perverted when it is held to prevent the natural outcome of a dominant opinion, unless it can be said that a rational and fair man necessarily would admit that the statute proposed would infringe fundamental principles as they have been understood by the traditions of our people and our law. It does not need research to show that no such sweeping condemnation can be passed upon the statute before us. A reasonable man might think it a proper measure on the score of health. Men whom I certainly could not pronounce unreasonable would uphold it as a first installment of a general regulation of the hours of work. Whether in the latter aspect it would be open to the charge of inequality I think it unnecessary to discuss.

3

JEROME FRANK

From *Law and the Modern Mind*

CHAPTER IV / JUDICIAL LAW-MAKING

Have judges the right and power to make law and change law? Much good ink has been spilled in arguing that question. A brief survey of the controversy will illuminate our thesis.

The conventional view may be summarized thus:

Law is a complete body of rules existing from time immemorial and unchangeable except to the limited extent that legislatures have changed the rules by enacted statutes. Legislatures are expressly empowered thus to change the law. But the judges are not to make or change the law but to apply it. The law, ready-made, pre-exists the judicial decisions.

Judges are simply "living oracles" of law. They are merely "the speaking law." Their function is purely passive. They are "but the mouth which pronounces the law." They no more make or invent new law than Columbus made or invented America. Judicial opinions are evidence of what the law is; the best evidence, but no more than that. When a former decision is overruled, we must not say that the rule announced in the earlier decision was once the law and has now been changed by the later decision. We must not view the earlier decision as laying down an erroneous rule. It was a false map of the law just as a pre-Columbian map of the world was false. Emphatically, we must not refer to the new decision as making new law. It only seems to do so. It is merely a bit of revised legal cartography.

If a judge actually attempted to contrive a new rule, he would be guilty of usurpation of power, for the legislature alone has the authority to change the law. The judges, writes Blackstone, are "not delegated to pronounce a new law, but to maintain and expound the old law"; even when a former decision is abandoned because "most evidently contrary to reason," the "subsequent judges do not pretend to make new law, but to vindicate the old one from misrepresentation." The prior judge's eyesight had been defective and he made "a mistake" in finding the law, which mistake is now being rectified by his successors.

Such is the conventional notion. There is a contrary minority view, which any dispassionate observer must accept as obviously the correct view:

> "No intelligent lawyer would in this day pretend that the decisions of the courts do not add to and alter the law," says Pollock, a distinguished English jurist. "Judge-made law is real law," writes Dicey, another famous legal commentator, "though made under the form of, and often described by judges no less than jurists, as the mere interpretation of law. . . . The amount of such judge-made law is in England far more extensive than a student realizes. Nine-tenths, at least, of the law of contract, and the whole, or nearly the whole, of the law of torts are not to be discovered in any volume of the statutes. . . . Whole branches, not of ancient but of very modern law, have been built up, developed or created by action of the courts."

Judges, then, do make and change the law. The minority view is patently correct; the opposing arguments will not bear analysis. What, then, explains the belief so tenaciously held that the judiciary does not ever change the law or that, when it does, it is acting improperly? Why is it that judges adhere to what Morris Cohen has happily called "the phonographic theory of the judicial function"? What explains the recent remark of an eminent member of the Bar: "The man who claims that under our system courts make law is asserting that the courts habitually act unconstitutionally"? Why do the courts customarily deny that they have any law-making power and describe new law which they create to deal with essentially contemporary events, as mere explanations or interpretations of law which already exists and has existed from time immemorial? Why this obstinate denial of the juristic realities?

We revert to our thesis: The essence of the basic legal myth or illusion is that law can be entirely predictable. Back of this illusion is the childish desire to have a fixed father-controlled universe, free of chance and error due to human fallibility.

In early stages of legal development this desire was more intense than now and there was what Sir Henry Maine has called "a superstitious disrelish of change" which went to the extent of making men oppose any modification of existing law even by statutory legislation. We have partially overcome the superstitious antipathy to legal change so far as the change results from the action of legislative bodies, and no little part of law is modified each year by statutes enacted by state legislatures and by Congress.

But such statutory legislation, while it may alter the law, does so, ordinarily, only prospectively. It is the usual practice—to some extent it is required by constitutional prohibitions—that changes embodied in statutes enacted by legislative bodies should not be retroactive but should apply only to future conduct. Which is to say that, generally speaking, a legal novelty brought about through statutory legislation can be known *before* men do any acts which may be affected by the innovation. Insofar, a man can conduct himself in reliance upon the existing law, knowing, at the time he acts, that any changes thereafter made by a legislative body will not modify the law upon which he relied.

Consequently, absolute certainty and predictability are apparently not endangered by alterations of law made or adopted by legislatures.

But if it is once recognized that a judge, in the course of deciding a case, can for the first time create the law applicable to that case, or can alter the rules which were supposed to exist before the case was decided, then it will also have to be recognized that the rights and obligations of the parties to that case may be decided retroactively. A change thus made by a judge, when passing upon a case, is a change in the law made with respect to past events,—events which occurred before the law came into existence. Legal predictability is plainly impossible, if, at the time I do an act, I do so with reference to law which, should a lawsuit thereafter arise with reference to my act, may be changed by the judge who tries the case. For then the result is that my case is decided according to law which was not in existence when I acted and which I, therefore, could not have known, predicted or relied on when I acted.

If, therefore, one has a powerful need to believe in the possibility of anything like exact legal predictability, he will find judicial law-making intolerable and seek to deny its existence.

Hence the myth that the judges have no power to change existing law or make new law: it is a direct outgrowth of a subjective need for believing in a stable, approximately unalterable legal world—in effect, a child's world.

This remark might be challenged on the ground that the desire to avoid legal retroactivity is not "subjective" but practical, because, it may be said, men cannot and will not engage in affairs without having in mind the pertinent law. Yet reflection reveals the fact that the supposed *practical* importance of avoiding legal retroactivity and uncertainty is much overrated, since most men act without regard to the legal consequences of their conduct, and, therefore, do not act in reliance upon any given pre-existing law:

> "Practically," says John Chipman Gray, "in its application to actual affairs, for most of the laity, the law, except for a few crude notions of the equity involved in some of its general principles, is all *ex post facto.* When a man marries, or enters into a partnership, or buys a piece of land, or engages in any other transactions, he has the vaguest possible idea of the law governing the situation, and with our complicated system of Jurisprudence, it is impossible it should be otherwise. If he delayed to make a contract or do an act until he understood exactly all the legal consequences it involved, the contract would never be made or the act done. *Now the law of which a man has no knowledge is the same to him as if it did not exist.*"

Which is to say that the factor of uncertainty in law has little bearing on practical affairs. Many men go on about their business with virtually no knowledge of, or attention paid to, the so-called legal rules, be those rules certain or uncertain. If the law but slightly affects what a man does, it is seldom that he can honestly maintain that he was disadvantaged by lack of legal stability. Although, then, judges have made law, vast quantities of law, and judge-made innovations, retroactively applied, are devised yearly; although frequently a man must act with no certainty as to what legal consequences the courts will later attach to his acts; although complete legal predictability and with it safety from slippery change are therefore by no means possible,—yet retroactivity and the resulting unavoidable uncertainty are not as great practical evils as they are often assumed to be. The no judge-made law doctrine, it seems, is not, fundamentally, a response to practical needs. It appears rather to be due to a hunger and a craving for a non-existent and unattainable legal finality—which, in turn, may be ascribed to a concealed but potent striving to recapture in the law the child's conception of the fatherly attributes.

But what of it? What harm in this myth? No harm, if the denial of judicial law-making were a mere pleasantry, in the category of what Austin and Morris Cohen refer to as polite or euphemistic fictions; that is, statements contrary to fact, but known by all to be such and comparable to the fibs of daily social intercourse.

But the denial of the fact of judge-made law is no mere fib. At times, indeed, it seems to resemble an outright benevolent lie, a professional falsehood designed actually to deceive the laity for their own good; Gray suggests that the misrepresentation derives in part from a belief of the legal profession that it is "important that judges should say, *and that the people should believe,* that the rules according to which the judges decide these cases had a previous existence." The lay public, that is, are to be duped.

Now this dupery is not harmless. It leads, sooner or later, to a distrust of the judges, a disrespect for their opinions. For now and again the public becomes aware that in some actual cases the judges have made or changed the law. Then follow accusations of dishonesty, of corruption, of usurpation of authority, of revolutionary violation of the judicial oath of office, and the like. And it is difficult to reply to such accusations when the judges themselves deny that they have power to make law and yet go on (unavoidably and unmistakably) making it.

Why, then, do the judges deceive the public? Because they are themselves deceived. The doctrine of no judge-made law is not, generally speaking, a *"lie"*—for a lie is an affirmation of a fact contrary to the truth, made with knowledge of its falsity and with the intention of deceiving others. Nor is it a "fiction"—a false affirmation made with knowledge of its falsity but with no intention of deceiving others.

It is rather a myth—a false affirmation made without complete knowledge of its falsity. We are confronting a kind of deception which involves self-deception. The self-deception, of course, varies in degree; many judges and lawyers are half-aware that the denial of the existence of judicial legislation is what Gray has called "a form of words to hide the truth." And yet most of the profession insists that the judiciary cannot properly change the law, and more or less believes that myth. When judges and lawyers announce that judges can never validly make law, they are not engaged in fooling the public; they have successfully fooled themselves. . . .

CHAPTER XIV / ILLUSORY PRECEDENTS: THE FUTURE: JUDICIAL SOMNAMBULISM

Lawyers and judges purport to make large use of precedents; that is, they purport to rely on the conduct of judges in past cases as a means of procuring analogies for action in new cases. But since what was actually decided in the earlier cases is seldom revealed, it is impossible, in a real sense, to rely on these precedents. What the courts in fact do is to manipulate the language of former decisions. They could approximate a system of real precedents only if the judges, in rendering those former decisions, had reported with fidelity the precise steps by which they arrived at their decisions. The paradox of the situation is that, granting there is value in a system of precedents, our present use of illusory precedents makes the employment of real precedents impossible.

The decision of a judge after trying a case is the product of a unique experience. "Of the many things which have been said of the mystery of the judicial process," writes Yntema, "the most salient is that *decision is reached after an emotive experience in which principles and logic play a secondary part.* The function of juristic logic and the principles which it employs seem to be like that of language, to describe the event which has already transpired. These considerations must reveal to us the impotence of general principles to control decision. Vague because of their generality, they mean nothing save what they suggest in the organized experience of one who thinks them, and, because of their vagueness, they only remotely compel the organization of that experience. The important problem . . . is not the formulation of the rule but the ascertainment of the cases to which, and the extent to which, it applies. And this, even if we are seeking uniformity in the administration of justice, will lead us again to the circumstances of the concrete case. . . . The reason why the general principle cannot control is because it does not inform. . . . It should be obvious that when we have observed a recurrent phenomenon in the decisions of the courts, we may appropriately express the classification in a rule. But the rule will be only a mnemonic device, a useful but hollow diagram of what has been. It will be intelligible only if we *relive again the experience of the classifier.*"

The rules a judge announces when publishing his decision are, therefore, intelligible only if one can relive the judge's unique experience while he was trying the case—which, of course, cannot be done. One cannot even approximate that experience as long as opinions take the form of abstract rules applied to facts formally described. Even if it were desirable that, despite its uniqueness, the judge's decision should be followed, as an analogy, by other judges while trying other cases, this is impossible when the manner in which the judge reached his judgment in the earlier case is most inaccurately reported, as it now is. You are not really applying his decision as a precedent in another case unless you can say, in effect, that, having relived his experience in the earlier case, you believe that he would have thought his decision applicable to the facts of the latter case. And as opinions are now written, it is impossible to guess what the judge did experience in trying a case. The facts of all but the simplest controversies are complicated and unlike those of any other controversy; in the absence of a highly detailed account by the judge of how he reacted to the evidence, no other person is capable of reproducing his actual reactions. The rules announced in his opinions are therefore often insufficient to tell the reader why the judge reached his decision.

Dickinson admits that the "personal bent of the judge" to some extent affects his decisions. But this "personal bent," he insists, is a factor only in the selection of new rules for unprovided cases. However, *in a profound sense the unique circumstances of almost any case make it an "unprovided case" where no well-established rule "authoritatively" compels a given result.* The uniqueness of the facts and of the judge's reaction thereto is often concealed because the judge so states the facts that they appear to call for the application of a settled rule. But that concealment does not mean that the judge's personal bent has been inoperative or that his emotive experience is simple and reproducible.

Oliphant has argued that the courts have been paying too much attention to the language of prior cases and that the proper use of the doctrine of following the precedents should lead the courts to pay more attention to what judges in earlier cases have *decided* as against what they have *said* in their opinions. It may be true that in a limited number of simple cases we can guess what the judge believed to be the facts, and therefore can guess what facts, in any real sense, he was passing on. But usually there are so many and such diverse factors in the evidence which combine in impelling the judge's mind to a decision, that what he decided is unknown—except in the sense that he gave judgment for A, or sent B to prison for ten years, or enjoined C from interfering with D.

At any rate, that will be true while the present method of reporting and deciding cases is adhered to. If and when we have judges trained to observe their own mental processes and such judges with great particularity set forth in their opinions all the factors which they believe led to their conclusions, a judge in passing on a case may perhaps find it possible, to some considerable extent, intelligently to use as a control or guide, the opinion of another judge announced while passing on another case. But as matters stand, reliance on precedents is illusory because judges can seldom tell precisely what has been theretofore decided.

Every lawyer of experience comes to know (more or less unconsciously) that in the great majority of cases, the precedents are none too good as bases of prediction. Somehow or other, there are plenty of precedents to go around. A recent writer, a believer in the use of precedents, has said proudly that "it is very seldom indeed that a judge cannot find guidance of some kind, direct or indirect, in the mass of our reported decisions—by this time a huge accumulation of facts as well as rules." In plain English, as S. S. Gregory or Judge Hutcheson would have put it, a court can usually find earlier decisions which can be made to appear to justify almost any conclusion.

What has just been said is not intended to mean that most courts arrive at their conclusions arbitrarily or apply a process of casuistical deception in writing their opinions. The process we have been describing involves no insincerity or duplicity. The average judge sincerely believes that he is using his intellect as "a cold logic engine" in applying rules and principles derived from the earlier cases to the objective facts of the case before him.

A satirist might indeed suggest that it is regrettable that the practice of precedent-mongering does not involve *conscious* deception, for it would be comparatively easy for judges entirely aware of what they were doing, to abandon such conscious deception and to report accurately how they arrived at their decisions. Unfortunately, most judges have no such awareness. Worse than that, they are not even aware that they are not aware. Judges Holmes, Cardozo, Hand, Hucheson, Lehman and a few others have attained the enlightened state of awareness of their unawareness. A handful of legal thinkers off the bench have likewise come to the point of noting the ignorance of all of us as to just how decisions, judicial or otherwise, are reached. Until many more lawyers and judges become willing to admit that ignorance which is the beginning of wisdom and from that beginning work forward painstakingly and consciously, we shall get little real enlightenment on the subject.

Perhaps one of the worst aspects of rule-fetichism and veneration for what judges have done in the past is that the judges, in writing their opinions, are constrained to think of themselves altogether too much as if they were addressing posterity. Swayed by the belief that their opinions will serve as precedents and will therefore bind the thought processes of judges in cases which may thereafter arise, they feel obliged to consider excessively not only what has previously been said by other judges but also the future effect of those generalizations which they themselves set forth as explanations of their own decisions. When publishing the rules which are supposed to be the core of their decisions, they thus feel obligated to look too far both backwards and forwards. Many a judge, when unable to find old word-patterns which will fit his conclusions, is overcautious about announcing a so-called new rule for fear that, although the new rule may lead to a just conclusion in the case before him, it may lead to undesirable results in the future—that is, in cases not then before the court. Once trapped by the belief that the announced rules are the paramount thing in the law, and that uniformity and certainty are of major importance and are to be procured by uniformity and certainty in the phrasing of rules, a judge is likely to be affected, in determining what is fair to the parties in the unique situation before him, by consideration of the possible, yet scarcely imaginable, bad effect of a just opinion in the instant case on possible unlike cases which may later be brought into court. He then refuses to do justice in the case on trial because he fears that "hard cases make bad laws." And thus arises what may aptly be called "injustice according to law."

Such injustice is particularly tragic because it is based on a hope doomed to futility, a hope of controlling the future. Of course, present problems will be clarified by reference to future ends; but ends, although they have a future bearing, must obtain their significance in present consequences, otherwise those ends lose their significance. For it is the nature of the future that it never arrives. If all decisions are to be determined with reference to a time to come, then the law is indeed chasing a will-o'-the-wisp. "Yesterday today was tomorrow." To give too much attention to the future is to ignore the problem which is demanding solution today. Any future, when it becomes the present, is sure to bring new complicating and individualized problems. "Future problems" can never be solved. There is much wisdom in Valéry's reference to the "anachronism of the future."

Indeed, alleged interest in the future may be a disguise for too much devotion to the past, and a means of avoiding the necessity for facing unpleasant risks in the present. If the decision of a particular case takes the form of the enunciation of a rule with emphasis on its future incidence, the tendency will be to connect the past by smooth continuities with the future, and the consequence will be an overlooking of the distinctive novelties of the present. There will be undue stress on past, habitual ways of doing things.

What is more significant is that this regard for the future serves also to conceal that factor in judging which is most disturbing to the rule-minded—the personality of the judge. Thus in a recent book the author finds an advantage in the technique of abstract logic which judges purport to employ in that it requires the judge to

> "raise their minds above the facts of the immediate case before them and subordinate their feelings and impressions to a process of intricate abstract reasoning. *One danger in the administration of justice is that the necessities of the future and the interest of parties not before the court may be sacrificed in favor of present litigants.* . . . Nothing is so effective to prevent this outcome as that judges should approach the decision of a controversy with minds directed to considerations having no connection with the immediate situation or interest in the parties. Judges are human instruments, with prejudices, passions, and weaknesses. As it is, they often decide a new point or a doubtful point, ignore a principle, narrow a rule, or explain a concept under the influence of these human limitations. But this influence is enormously diminished by the necessity of centering their attention on a mass of considerations which lie outside the color of the case at bar; and by the habit of coming at every question from the angle of a dry and abstract logic."

It might be more accurately said that the influence of this point of view promotes judicial self-delusion and produces that ineffectual suppression of the judge's personality which leads to the indirect, unobserved and harmful effects of his personality on judicial decisions.

Present problems should be worked out with reference to present events. We cannot rule the future. We can only imagine it in terms of the present. And the only way to do that is as thoroughly as possible to know the present.

We come to this: The desire to regulate the future is in part a desire for impossible uniformity, security and certainty, for oversimplification, for a world regulated and controlled as a child would have it regulated and controlled.

In the interest of preserving the appearance of such a world, much effort is devoted to "keeping the record straight"; that is, to making it appear that decisions and opinions have more of the logical and less of the psychological than is possible. This desire manifests itself in many curious comments and suggestions.

Thus a writer, not long since, suggested that there was growing an unfortunate tendency of courts to decide cases on their merits, that this was making the law chaotic, but that a return to certainty and predictability could be procured, in spite of this tendency, if the courts would cease writing opinions. The suggestion was made naïvely and without cognizance of the fact that it meant merely that the failure of the courts to adhere to mechanical applications of rules would be less obvious, if the courts merely recorded their judgments without opinions and thus made it more difficult to scrutinize the means by which they arrived at their judgments.

And, again, it has been urged that, in the interest of maintaining respect for the courts, dissenting opinions should never be rendered, the intent being that thereby the public will not be made aware that able judges, sitting side by side and passing on the same set of facts, can disagree about the law.

The point of all such proposals is that they tacitly concede the impossibility of obtaining legal conformity, but seek to cover up the more obvious manifestations of this lack. The healthier method would be not only to recognize the gross evidences of uncertainty but to make evident the actual but now concealed circumstances which make certainty an impossibility, to the end that by describing accurately the real nature of the judicial process we may learn to better it.

The judge, at his best, is an arbitrator, a "sound man" who strives to do justice to the parties by exercising a wise discretion with reference to the peculiar circumstances of the case. He does not merely "find" or invent some generalized rule which he "applies" to the facts presented to him. He does "equity" in the sense in which Aristotle—when thinking most clearly—described it. "It is equity," he wrote in his Rhetoric, "to pardon human failings, and to look to the law giver and not to the law; . . . to prefer arbitration to judgment, for the arbitrator sees what is equitable, but the judge only the law, and for this an arbitrator was first appointed, in order that equity might flourish."The bench and bar usually try to conceal the arbitral function of the judge. (Dicey represents the typical view. A judge, he says, "when deciding any case must act, *not as an arbitrator, but strictly as a judge; . . . it is a judge's business to determine not what may be fair as between A and X in a given case,* but what according to some principle of law, are the respective rights of A and X.") But although fear of legal uncertainty leads to this concealment, the arbitral function is the central fact in the administration of justice. The concealment has merely made the labor of the judges less effective. . . .

And so in respect to the law: If we relinquish the assumption that law can be made mathematically certain, if we honestly recognize the judicial process as involving unceasing adjustment and individualization, we may be able to reduce the uncertainty which characterizes much of our present judicial output to the extent that such uncertainty is undesirable. By abandoning an infantile hope of absolute legal certainty we may augment markedly the amount of actual legal certainty. . . .

4

EDWARD H. LEVI

From *An Introduction to Legal Reasoning*

I

This is an attempt to describe generally the process of legal reasoning in the field of case law and in the interpretation of statutes and of the Constitution. It is important that the mechanism of legal reasoning should not be concealed by its pretense. The pretense is that the law is a system of known rules applied by a judge; the pretense has long been under attack.[1] In an important sense legal rules are never clear, and, if a rule had to be clear before it could be imposed, society would be impossible. The mechanism accepts the differences of view and ambiguities of words. It provides for the participation of the community in resolving the ambiguity by providing a forum for the discussion of policy in the gap of ambiguity. On serious controversial questions, it makes it possible to take the first step in the direction of what otherwise would be forbidden ends. The mechanism is indispensable to peace in a community.

[1]The controlling book is Frank, Law and the Modern Mind (1936).

The basic pattern of legal reasoning is reasoning by example. It is reasoning from case to case. It is a three-step process described by the doctrine of precedent in which a proposition descriptive of the first case is made into a rule of law and then applied to a next similar situation. The steps are these: similarity is seen between cases; next the rule of law inherent in the first case is announced; then the rule of law is made applicable to the second case. This is a method of reasoning necessary for the law, but it has characteristics which under other circumstances might be considered imperfections.

These characteristics become evident if the legal process is approached as though it were a method of applying general rules of law to diverse facts—in short, as though the doctrine of precedent meant that general rules, once properly determined, remained unchanged, and then were applied, albeit imperfectly, in later cases. If this were the doctrine, it would be disturbing to find that the rules change from case to case and are remade with each case. Yet this change in the rules is the indispensable dynamic quality of law. It occurs because the scope of a rule of law, and therefore its meaning, depends upon a determination of what facts will be considered similar to those present when the rule was first announced. The finding of similarity or difference is the key step in the legal process.

The determination of similarity or difference is the function of each judge. Where case law is considered, and there is no statute, he is not bound by the statement of the rule of law made by the prior judge even in the controlling case. The statement is mere dictum, and this means that the judge in the present case may find irrelevant the existence or absence of facts which prior judges thought important. It is not what the prior judge intended that is of any importance; rather it is what the present judge, attempting to see the law as a fairly consistent whole, thinks should be the determining classification. In arriving at his result he will ignore what the past thought important; he will emphasize facts which prior judges would have thought made no difference. It is not alone that he could not see the law through the eyes of another, for he could at least try to do so. It is rather that the doctrine of dictum forces him to make his own decision.

Thus it cannot be said that the legal process is the application of known rules to diverse facts. Yet it is a system of rules; the rules are discovered in the process of determining similarity or difference. But if attention is directed toward the finding of similarity or difference, other peculiarities appear. The problem for the law is: When will it be just to treat different cases as though they were the same? A working legal system must therefore be willing to pick out key similarities and to reason from them to the justice of applying a common classification. The existence of some facts in common brings into play the general rule. If this is really reasoning, then by common standards, thought of in terms of closed systems, it is imperfect unless some overall rule has announced that this common and ascertainable similarity is to be decisive. But no such fixed prior rule exists. It could be suggested that reasoning is not involved at all; that is, that no new insight is arrived at through a comparison of cases. But reasoning appears to be involved; the conclusion is arrived at through a process and was not immediately apparent. It seems better to say there is reasoning, but it is imperfect.

Therefore it appears that the kind of reasoning involved in the legal process is one in which the classification changes as the classification is made. The rules change as the rules are applied. More important, the rules arise out of a process which, while comparing fact situations, creates the rules and then applies them. But this kind of reasoning is open to the charge that it is classifying things as equal when they are somewhat different, justifying the classification by rules made up as the reasoning or classification proceeds. In a sense all reasoning is of this type, but there is an additional requirement which compels the legal process to be this way. Not only do new situations arise, but in addition peoples' wants change. The categories used in the legal process must be left ambiguous in order to permit the infusion of new ideas. And this is true even where legislation or a constitution is involved. The words used by the legislature or the constitutional convention must come to have new meanings. Furthermore, agreement on any other basis would be impossible. In this manner the laws come to express the ideas of the community and even when written in general terms, in statute or constitution, are molded for the specific case.

But attention must be paid to the process. A controversy as to whether the law is certain, unchanging, and expressed in rules, or uncertain, changing, and only a technique for deciding specific cases misses the point. It is both. Nor is it helpful to dispose of the process as a wonderful mystery possibly reflecting a higher law, by which the law can remain the same and yet change. The law forum is the most explicit demonstration of the mechanism required for a moving classification system. The folklore of law may choose to ignore the imperfections in legal reasoning, but the law forum itself has taken care of them.

What does the law forum require? It requires the presentation of competing examples. The forum protects the parties and the community by making sure that the competing analogies are before the court. The rule which will be created arises out of a process in which if different things are to be treated as similar, at least the differences have been urged. In this sense the parties as well as the court participate in the law-making. In this sense, also, lawyers represent more than the litigants.

Reasoning by example in the law is a key to many things. It indicates in part the hold which the law process has over the litigants. They have participated in the law-making. They are bound by something they helped to make. Moreover, the examples or analogies urged by the parties bring into the law the common ideas of the society. The ideas have their day in court, and they will have their day again. This is what makes the hearing fair, rather than any idea that the judge is completely impartial, for of course he cannot be completely so. Moreover, the hearing in a sense compels at least vicarious participation by all the citizens, for the rule which is made, even though ambiguous, will be law as to them.

Reasoning by example shows the decisive role which the common ideas of the society and the distinctions made by experts can have in shaping the law. The movement of common or expert concepts into the law may be followed. The concept is suggested in arguing difference or similarity in a brief, but it wins no approval from the court. The idea achieves standing in the society. It is suggested again to a court. The court this time reinterprets the prior case and in doing so adopts the rejected idea. In subsequent cases, the idea is given further definition and is tied to other ideas which have been accepted by courts. It is now no longer the idea which was commonly held in the society. It becomes modified in subsequent cases. Ideas first rejected but which gradually have won acceptance now push what has become a legal category out of the system or convert it into something which may be its opposite. The process is one in which the ideas of the community and of the social sciences, whether correct or not, as they win acceptance in the community, control legal decisions. Erroneous ideas, of course, have played an enormous part in shaping the law. An idea, adopted by a court, is in a superior position to influence conduct and opinion in the community; judges, after all, are rulers. And the adoption of an idea by a court reflects the power structure in the community. But reasoning by example will operate to change the idea after it has been adopted.

Moreover, reasoning by example brings into focus important similarity and difference in the interpretation of case law, statutes, and the constitution of a nation. There is a striking similarity. It is only folklore which holds that a statute if clearly written can be completely unambiguous and applied as intended to a specific case. Fortunately or otherwise, ambiguity is inevitable in both statute and constitution as well as with case law. Hence reasoning by example operates with all three. But there are important differences. What a court says is dictum, but what a legislature says is a statute. The reference of the reasoning changes. Interpretation of intention when dealing with a statute is the way of describing the attempt to compare cases on the basis of the standard thought to be common at the time the legislation was passed. While this is the attempt, it may not initially accomplish any different result than if the standard of the judge had been explicitly used. Nevertheless, the remarks of the judge are directed toward describing a category set up by the legislature. These remarks are different from ordinary dicta. They set the course of the statute, and later reasoning in subsequent cases is tied to them. As a consequence, courts are less free in applying a statute than in dealing with case law. The current rationale for this is the notion that the legislature has acquiesced by legislative silence in the prior, even though erroneous, interpretation of the court. But the change in reasoning where legislation is concerned seems an inevitable consequence of the division of function between court and legislature, and, paradoxically, a recognition also of the impossibility of determining legislative intent. The impairment of a court's freedom in interpreting legislation is reflected in frequent appeals to the constitution as a necessary justification for overruling cases even though these cases are thought to have interpreted the legislation erroneously.

Under the United States experience, contrary to what has sometimes been believed when a written constitution of a nation is involved, the court has greater freedom than it has with the application of a statute or case law. In case law, when a judge determines what the controlling similarity between the present and prior case is, the case is decided. The judge does not feel free to ignore the results of a great number of cases which he cannot explain under a remade rule. And in interpreting legislation, when the prior interpretation, even though erroneous, is determined after a comparison of facts to cover the case, the case is decided. But this is not true with a constitution. The constitution sets up the conflicting ideals of the community in certain ambiguous categories. These categories bring along with them satellite concepts covering the areas of ambiguity. It is with a set of these satellite concepts that reasoning by example must work. But no satellite concept, no matter how well developed, can prevent the court from shifting its course, not only by realigning cases which impose certain restrictions, but by going beyond realignment back to the over-all ambiguous category written into the document. The constitution, in other words, permits the court to be inconsistent. The freedom is concealed either as a search for the intention of the framers or as a proper understanding of a living instrument, and sometimes as both. But this does not mean that reasoning by example has any less validity in this field.

II

It may be objected that this analysis of legal reasoning places too much emphasis on the comparison of cases and too little on the legal concepts which are created. It is true that similarity is seen in terms of a word, and inability to find a ready word to express similarity or difference may prevent change in the law. The words which have been found in the past are much spoken of, have acquired a dignity of their own, and to a considerable measure control results. As Judge Cardozo suggested in speaking of metaphors, the word starts out to free thought and ends by enslaving it. The movement of concepts into and out of the law makes the point. If the society has begun to see certain significant similarities or differences, the comparison emerges with a word. When the word is finally accepted, it becomes a legal concept. Its meaning continues to change. But the comparison is not only between the instances which have been included under it and the actual case at hand, but also in terms of hypothetical instances which the word by itself suggests. Thus the connotation of the word for a time has a limiting influence—so much so that the reasoning may even appear to be simply deductive.

But it is not simply deductive. In the long run a circular motion can be seen. The first stage is the creation of the legal concept which is built up as cases are compared. The period is one in which the court fumbles for a phrase. Several phrases may be tried out; the misuse or misunderstanding of words itself may have an effect. The concept sounds like another, and the jump to the second is made. The second stage is the period when the concept is more or less fixed, although reasoning by example continues to classify items inside and out of the concept. The third stage is the breakdown of the concept, as reasoning by example has moved so far ahead as to make it clear that the suggestive influence of the word is no longer desired.

The process is likely to make judges and lawyers uncomfortable. It runs contrary to the pretense of the system. It seems inevitable, therefore, that as matters of kind vanish into matters of degree and then entirely new meanings turn up, there will be the attempt to escape to some overall rule which can be said to have always operated and which will make the reasoning look deductive. The rule will be useless. It will have to operate on a level where it has no meaning. Even when lip service is paid to it, care will be taken to say that it may be too wide or too narrow but that nevertheless it is a good rule. The statement of the rule is roughly analogous to the appeal to the meaning of a statute or of a constitution, but it has less of a function to perform. It is window dressing. Yet it can be very misleading. Particularly when a concept has broken down and reasoning by example is about to build another, textbook writers, well aware of the unreal aspect of old rules, will announce new ones, equally ambiguous and meaningless, forgetting that the legal process does not work with the rule but on a much lower level.

The movement of legal concepts in case law has frequently been shown by pointing to the breakdown of the so-called "inherently dangerous" rule. It is easy to do this because the opinion in *MacPherson v. Buick Motor Co.*[2] is the work of a judge acutely conscious of the legal process and articulate about it. But *MacPherson v. Buick* was only a part of a cyclical

[2] 217 N.Y. 382, 111 N. E. 1050 (1916); see Parker, Attorneys at Law, Ch. 8 (1942).

movement in which differences and similarities first rejected are then adopted and later cast aside. The description of the movement can serve as an example of case law. Roughly the problem has become: the potential liability of a seller of an article which causes injury to a person who did not buy the article from the seller. In recent times the three phases in the movement of the concepts used in handling this problem can be traced.

The first of these begins in 1816 and carries us to 1851. It begins with a loaded gun and ends with an exploding lamp. The loaded gun brought liability to its owner in the case of *Dixon v. Bell.*[3] He had sent his thirteen- or fourteen-year-old servant girl to get the gun; in playing with the gun she had shot it off into the face of the plaintiff's son, who lost his right eye and two teeth. In holding that the plaintiff might recover, Lord Ellenborough attempted no classification of dangerous articles. He was content to describe the gun "as by this want of care . . . left in a state capable of doing mischief."[4] Thus the pattern begins with commodities mischievous through want of care.

The pattern becomes complicated in 1837 in the case of *Langridge v. Levy,*[5] where a plaintiff complained that the defendant had sold his father a defective gun for the use of himself and his sons. The gun had blown up in the plaintiff's hand. The court allowed recovery, apparently on the theory that the seller had falsely declared that the gun was safe when he knew it was defective and had sold the gun to the father knowing it was to be used by the plaintiff. It was therefore both a case of fraud and, in some sense, one of direct dealing between the seller and the plaintiff. The example used by the court was the case of a direct sale to the plaintiff, or where the instrument had been "placed in the hands of a third person for the purpose of being delivered to and then used by the plaintiff."[6] The direct dealing point is also emphasized by the statement of one of the judges during the argument to the effect that it would have helped the plaintiff's case if he had alleged that his father "was an unconscious agent in the transaction" because "the act of an unconscious agent is the act of the part who sets him in motion."[7]

[3]5 Maule & Selwyn 198 (1816).
[4]Ibid., at 199.
[5]2 Meeson & Welsby 519 (1837).
[6]Ibid., at 531.
[7]Alderson, B., ibid at 525.

In the argument of *Langridge v. Levy,* counsel for the defendant had pointed to a distinction between things "immediately dangerous or mischievous by the act of the defendant" and "such as may become so by some further act to be done to it."[8] They had urged what might be considered the pattern suggested by *Dixon v. Bell.* But the court rejected the use of any such distinction, although it remarked in passing that the gun was not "of itself dangerous, but . . . requires an act to be done, that is to be loaded, in order to make it so." It rejected not only the distinction but any category of dangerous articles, because it "should pause before we made a precedent by our decision which would be an authority for an action against the vendors, even of such instruments and articles as are dangerous in themselves, at the suit of *any person* whomsoever into whose hands they might happen to pass and who should be injured thereby."[9]

Nevertheless the category of dangerous articles and the distinction between things of a dangerous nature and those which become so if improperly constructed (which need not be the same as requiring a further act to be done to make it dangerous) were again urged before the court five years later in *Winterbottom v. Wright.*[10] The court refused to permit a coachman to recover against the defendant who had provided a defective coach under contract with the Postmaster General. The plaintiff had been driving the coach from Hartford to Holyhead when it broke down due to some latent defect; the plaintiff was thrown from his seat and lamed for life. He could not recover because to extend liability this far would lead to "absurd and outrageous consequences." The court refused to discuss whether the defective coach was a weapon of a dangerous nature, even though defendant's counsel seemed to be willing to acknowledge the existence of a special rule of liability for that category. And as for the application of *Langridge v. Levy,* in that case there was "distinct fraud" and the plaintiff "was really and substantially the party contracting." The court refused to find similarity under

[8]Ibid., at 528; note also the hypothetical case set forth by counsel for the plaintiff in *Langridge v. Levy* reported in 6 L.J. (N.S.) Ex. 137, 138 (1837). "A case might be put of a wrong medicine sent from a chemist, which is received by a person, and placed by him in a cupboard, and afterwards taken by a third person, who, in consequence receives an injury; can it be said that he has no remedy against the chemist?"
[9]Ibid., at 530.
[10]10 Meeson & Welsby 109 (1842).

the fraud concept in the fact that the defendant had sold a coach as safe when he did not know it to be in good condition, or under the direct dealing concept in *Langridge v. Levy* in that "there was nothing to show that the defendant was aware even of the existence of the particular son who was injured" whereas here the coach "was necessarily to be driven by a coachman."[11] The further argument that the plaintiff had no opportunity of seeing that the coach was sound and secure was insufficient to bring liability.

But in 1851, in *Longmeid v. Holliday,*[12] the concept of things dangerous in themselves, twice urged before the court and rejected, finally won out. Longmeid had bought a lamp for the use of himself and his wife from Holliday, the defendant storekeeper, who called the lamp "Holliday's Patent Lamp" and had it put together by other persons from parts which he had purchased. When Eliza Longmeid, the wife and plaintiff, tried to light the lamp, it exploded; the naphtha ran over her and scorched and burned her. She was not permitted to collect from the storekeeper. It had not been shown that the defendant knew the lamp was unfit and warranted it to be sound. And the lamp was not in its nature dangerous. In discussing those cases where a third person, not a party to a contract, might recover damages, the court said:

> And it may be the same when any one delivers to another without notice an instrument in its nature dangerous, or under particular circumstances, as a loaded gun which he himself loaded, and that other person to whom it is delivered is injured thereby, or if he places it in a situation easily accessible to a third person, who sustains damage from it. A very strong case to that effect is *Dixon v. Bell.* But it would be going much too far to say that so much care is required in the ordinary intercourse of life between one individual and another, that, if a machine not in its nature dangerous,—a carriage for instance,—but which might become so by a latent defect entirely unknown, although discoverable by the exercise of ordinary care, should be lent or given by one person, even by the person who manufactured it, to another, the former should be answerable to the latter for a subsequent damage accruing by the use of it.[13]

Thus the doctrine of the distinction between things in their nature dangerous and those which become so by an unknown latent defect is announced as a way of explaining the difference between a loaded gun (which under the rule, however, is explained as a particular circumstance) and a defective lamp. As applied in the case, the doctrine describes the classification of the lamp as dangerous only through a latent defect and results in no liability. But a court could have found as much direct dealing in the purchase of a lamp for the use of the purchaser and his wife as in the case of the purchase of a gun for the use of the purchaser and his sons. Under the rule as stated a carriage is not in its nature dangerous.

The second phase of the development of the doctrine of dangerous articles is the period during which the rule as announced in the *Longmeid* case is applied. The phase begins with mislabeled poison and ends with a defective automobile. During this time also there is the inevitable attempt to soar above the cases and to find some great overall rule which can classify the cases as though the pattern were really not a changing one.

It was the purchase of belladonna, erroneously marked as extract of dandelion, which, in *Thomas v. Winchester*[14] in 1852, produced the first application and restatement of the rule announced in the *Longmeid* case. The poison had been bought at the store of Dr. Foord, but it had been put into its jar and incorrectly labeled in the shop of the defendant Winchester—probably through the negligence of his employee. Mrs. Thomas, who used what she thought was the extract of dandelion, reacted by having "coldness of the surface and extremities, feebleness of circulation, spasms of the muscles, giddiness of the head, dilatation of the pupils of the eye and derangement of mind." She was allowed to recover against Winchester. The defendant's negligence had "put human life in imminent danger." No such imminent danger had existed in the *Winterbottom* case, the Court explained. This was more like the case of the loaded gun in *Dixon v. Bell.* The imminent danger category would not include a defective wagon but it did include the poison.

Looking back, one might say today that the category of things by their nature dangerous or imminently dangerous soon came to include a defective hair wash. At least in *George v. Skivington*[15] in 1869, a chemist who compounded a secret hair wash was

---

[11]Ibid., at 112.
[12]155 Eng. Rep. 752 (1851).
[13]Ibid., at 755. The opinion was by Parke, B.

[14]6 N.Y. 397 (1852).
[15]5 L.R. Ex. 1 (1869).

liable to the wife of the purchaser for injuries caused by the wash. But the court went about its business without explicit regard for the imminently dangerous category. It thought that the imperfect hair was like the imperfect gun in the *Langridge* case. It chose to ignore the emphasis in the *Langridge* case on the purported fact that the seller there knew the gun was defective and lied. It said, "substitute the word 'negligence' for fraud and the analogy between *Langridge v. Levy* and this case is complete." And as for the case of the defective lamp where there was no liability, that was different because negligence had not been found. In constructing a pattern for the cases, it appears that loaded guns, defective guns, poison, and now hair wash were in the imminently dangerous category. Defective wagons and lamps were outside.

The next year it became known that a defective balance wheel for a circular saw was not imminently dangerous. The New York court stated: "Poison is a dangerous subject. Gunpowder is the same. A torpedo is a dangerous instrument, as is a spring gun, a loaded rifle or the like. . . . Not so, however, an iron wheel, a few feet in diameter and a few inches in thickness although one part may be weaker than another. If the article is abused by too long use, or by applying too much weight or speed, an injury may occur, as it may from an ordinary carriage wheel, a wagon axle, or the common chair in which we sit."[16] While applying the imminently dangerous category to defeat liability, the New York court took occasion to give a somewhat new emphasis to *Thomas v. Winchester*. It found that "the decision in *Thomas v. Winchester* was based upon the idea that the negligent sale of poisons is both at common law and by statute an indictable offense." And certainly that could be argued. At any rate, three years later the New York court said its opinion in the balance-wheel case showed that *Thomas v. Winchester* would not result in liability in a case where a boiler blew up.[17] But the imminently dangerous category received a new member in 1882 when the builder of a ninety-foot scaffold to be used in painting the dome of the courthouse was held liable to the estate of an employee-painter who was killed when the ledger gave way.[18] Yet if a defective scaffold was in, the court followed tradition in announcing that a defective carriage would be out.

In England, a defective scaffold was also put in the category. The plaintiff in *Heaven v. Pender*[19] was a ship painter who was injured, while engaged in his work, due to the breaking of defective ropes which held his support outside the ship. He was allowed to recover against the dock owner who had supplied the support and ropes. But the majority of the judges decided the case on the rather narrow point that the necessary workmen were in effect invited by the dock owner to use the dock and appliances. That could have been the explanation also for the American scaffold case. The most noteworthy feature of *Heaven v. Pender,* however, was the flight of one of the judges, Lord Esher, at that time Brett, toward a rule above the legal categories which would classify the cases.

Brett thought recovery should be allowed because:

> Whenever one person supplies goods or machinery, or the like for the purpose of their being used by another person under such circumstances that everyone of ordinary sense would, if he thought, recognize at once that unless he used ordinary care and skill with regard to the condition of the thing supplied or the mode of supplying it, there will be danger of injury to the person or property of him for whose use the thing is supplied, and who is to use it, a duty arises to use ordinary care and skill as to the condition or manner of supplying such thing.[20]

This statement was concocted by Brett from two types of cases: first, the case where two drivers or two ships are approaching each other and due care is required toward each other, and second, where a man is invited into a shop or warehouse and the owner must use reasonable care "to keep his house or warehouse that it may not endanger the person or property of the person invited." Since these two different situations resulted in the same legal rule, or stated differently, since two general principles when applied resulted in the same legal rule, Brett thought there must be "some larger proposition which involves and covers both set of circumstances." This was because "the logic of inductive reasoning requires that where two propositions lead to exactly similar premises there must be a more remote and larger premise which embraces both of the major propositions." Brett's rule of ordinary care ran into some difficulty in looking

[16] Loop v. Litchfield, 42 N.Y. 351, 359 (1870).
[17] Losee v. Clute, 51 N.Y. 494 (1873).
[18] Devlin v. Smith, 89 N.Y. 470 (1882).
[19] 11 L.R. Q.B. 503 (1883).
[20] Ibid., at 510; see also rule as stated at 509.

back at the *Langridge* case and its insistence on both fraud and direct dealing. But Brett said of the *Langridge* case, "It is not, it cannot be accurately reported," and in any event the fact that recovery was allowed on the basis of fraud "in no way negatives the proposition that the action might have been supported on the ground of negligence without fraud."

The majority opinion in *Heaven v. Pender,* while proceeding on the invitee point, and while refusing to follow Brett in his flight, agrees that liability for negligence follows when the instrument is dangerous "as a gun" or when the instrument is in such a condition as to cause danger "not necessarily incident to the use of such an instrument" and no due warning is given. Approving this statement, the New York court in 1908 held that the question of a manufacturer's negligence could be left to a jury where the plaintiff lost an eye due to the explosion of a bottle of aerated water.[21] The next year a defective coffee urn or boiler which blew up and killed a man was permitted to join the aerated bottle in the danger concept.[22] The coffee-urn case provided the occasion for explaining two of the names given the dangerous category. Given an "inherently dangerous" article, the court explained, a manufacturer becomes liable for negligent construction which, when added to its inherent characteristics, makes it "imminently dangerous."

The categories by now were fairly well occupied. The dangerous concept had in it a loaded gun, possibly a defective gun, mislabeled poison, defective hair wash, scaffolds, a defective coffee urn, and a defective aerated bottle. The not-dangerous category, once referred to as only latently dangerous, had in it a defective carriage, a bursting lamp, a defective balance wheel for a circular saw, and a defective boiler. Perhaps it is not too surprising to find a defective soldering lamp in *Blacker v. Lake*[23] joining the not-dangerous class. But the English court, in the opinions of its two judges, experienced some difficulty. For the first judge there appears to have been no difficulty in classifying the soldering lamp as not dangerous. Yet the *Skivington* case caused trouble because it appeared to suggest that negligence could be substituted for fraud and perhaps liability would follow even though the article was not dangerous. But in that event the *Skivington* case should not be followed because it was in conflict with *Winterbottom v. Wright.* Accordingly, the soldering lamp not being dangerous, it was error to leave the question of negligence to the jury. The second judge suggested a more surprising realignment of the cases which threatened the whole danger category. He suggested that no recovery should be permitted even though the lamp fell into the class of things dangerous in themselves. The duty of the vendor in such a case, he pointed out, would be a duty to warn, but that duty is discharged if the nature of the article is obvious or known, as was true in this case. Indeed, the *Skivington* and *Thomas v. Winchester* cases were explainable on the very ground that the articles appeared harmless and their contents were unknown. One might almost say that recovery was permitted in those cases because the danger was only latent.

The period of the application of the doctrine of dangerous articles as set forth in the *Longmeid* case and adopted in *Thomas v. Winchester* may be thought to come to an end in 1915 with its application by a federal court—the Circuit Court of Appeals for the Second Circuit. This was the way the law looked to the court. "One who manufactures articles inherently dangerous, e.g. poisons, dynamite, gunpowder, torpedoes, bottles of water under gas pressure, is liable in tort to third parties which they injure, unless he has exercised reasonable care with reference to the articles manufactured. . . . On the other hand, one who manufactures articles dangerous only if defectively made, or installed, e.g., tables, chairs, pictures or mirrors hung on the walls, carriages, automobiles, and so on is not liable to third parties for injuries caused by them, except in cases of willful injury or fraud."[24] Accordingly, the court denied recovery in a suit by the purchaser of a car from a dealer against the manufacturer when the front right wheel broke and the car turned over.

MacPherson v. Buick[25] begins the third phase of the life of the dangerous instrument concept. The New York Court of Appeals in 1916 had before it almost a repetition of the automobile case passed upon by the federal court the previous year. The plaintiff was driving his car, carrying a friend to the hospital, when the car suddenly collapsed due to a

[21]Torgesen v. Schultz, 192 N.Y. 156, 84 N.E. 956 (1908).
[22]Statler v. Ray, 195 N.Y. 478, 88 N.E. 1063 (1909).
[23]106 L.T. 533 (1912).

[24]Cadillac v. Johnson, 221 Fed. 801, 803 (C.C.A. 2d, 1915).
[25]217 N.Y. 382, 111 N.E. 1050 (1916); see Bohlen, Liability of Manufacturers to Persons Other than Their Immediate Vendors, 45 L.Q. Rev. 343 (1929).

defective wheel. The plaintiff was seriously injured. The Buick Motor Company, the defendant, had sold the car to a retail dealer who in turn had sold it to the plaintiff. The defective wheel had been sold to the Buick company by the Imperial Wheel Company.

As was to be expected, counsel for the plaintiff urged that an automobile was "dangerous to a high degree."[26] It was, in fact, similar to a locomotive. It was much more like a locomotive than like a wagon. "The machine is a fair rival for the Empire Express," he said. "This is evidenced further by the fact that the person running an automobile must have a license of competency, equally with the locomotive engineer and by the legal restrictions imposed by law in the use of the automobile." It was "almost childish to say that an automobile at rest is not dangerous. Neither is a locomotive with the fire drawn" nor a battery of coffee boilers nor a 42-centimeter gun. The automobile, propelled by explosive gases, was "inherently dangerous." The trial judge had charged the jury that "an automobile is not an inherently dangerous vehicle" but had said that they might find it "imminently dangerous if defective."[27] As to the difference between the two phrases, counsel said there was no point "juggling over definitions. 'Inherently' means 'inseparably.' 'Imminently' means 'threateningly.'" He did not comment on the request of the defendant that the judge charge the jury that recovery depended on the car being "eminently dangerous."[28] Counsel did write, however, that he "was powerfully impressed with a remark of Lord Chief Justice Isaacs, on his recent visit to this country, to the effect that in England they were getting away from merely abstract forms and were seeking to administer justice in each individual case."[29]

The New York Court of Appeals allowed recovery. Judge Cardozo recognized that "the foundations of this branch of the law . . . were laid in *Thomas v. Winchester*." He said that some of the illustrations used in *Thomas v. Winchester* might be rejected today (having in mind no doubt the example of the defective carriage), but the principle of the case was the important thing. "There never has in this state been doubt or disavowal of the principle itself." Even while remarking that "precedents drawn from the days of travel by stagecoach do not fit the conditions of travel today," he was quick to add the explanation: "The principle that the danger must be imminent does not change, but the things subject to the principle do change." And in addition there were underlying principles. They were stated, more or less, Cardozo said, by Brett in *Heaven v. Pender*.

To be sure, Cardozo was not certain that this statement of underlying principles was an accurate exposition of the law of England. He thought "it may need some qualification even in our own state. Like most attempts at comprehensive definition, it may involve errors of inclusion and exclusion." He thought, however, that "its tests and standards, at least in their underlying principles, with whatever qualifications may be called for as they are applied to varying conditions, are the tests and standards of our law." He did not comment on the statement of Brett concerning *Thomas v. Winchester* that it "goes a very long way. I doubt whether it does not go too far."

As to the cases, Cardozo recognized that the early ones "suggest a narrow construction of the rule." He had reference to the boiler and balance-wheel cases. But the way to set them aside had already been shown. They could be distinguished because there the manufacturer had either pointed out the defect or had known that his test was not the final one. The distinction was based upon a point unsuccessfully advanced by losing counsel in *Winterbottom v. Wright*. Other cases showed that it was not necessary to be destructive in order to be dangerous. "A large coffee urn . . . may have within itself, if negligently made, the potency of danger, yet no one thinks of it as an implement whose normal function is destruction." And "what is true of the coffee urn is equally true of bottles of aerated water." *Devlin v. Smith* was important too. "A scaffold," Cardozo pointed out, "is not inherently a dangerous instrument." He admitted that the scaffold and the coffee-urn cases may "have extended the rule of *Thomas v. Winchester*," but "If so, this court is committed to the extension. The defendant argues that things inherently dangerous to life are poisons, explosives, deadly weapons, things whose normal function is to injure or destroy. But whatever the rule in *Thomas v. Winchester* may once have been, it has no longer that restricted meaning."

He showed a certain impatience for what he called "verbal niceties." He complained that "subtle distinc-

---

[26]Brief for the Plaintiff 16, 17, 18.

[27]217 N.Y. 382, 396, 111 N.E. 1050, 1055 (1916).

[28]Ibid., at 399, 1056.

[29]Brief for the Plaintiff 23.

tions are drawn by the defendant between things inherently dangerous and things imminently dangerous." As to this it was sufficient to say, "If danger was to be expected as reasonably certain, there was a duty of vigilance, and this whether you call the danger inherent or imminent." The rule was: "If the nature of a thing is such that it is reasonably certain to place life and limb in peril, when negligently made, it is then a thing of danger." But "there must be a knowledge of a danger not merely possible but probable." Thus what was only latently dangerous in *Thomas v. Winchester* now became imminently dangerous or inherently dangerous, or, if verbal niceties are to be disregarded, just plain or probably dangerous.

Elsewhere in commenting on the case, Cardozo seems to make somewhat less of the matter of principles. He wrote: "What, however, was the posture of affairs before the *Buick* case had been determined? Was there any law on the subject? A mass of judgments, more or less relevant, had been rendered by the same and other courts. A body of particulars existed in which an hypothesis might be reared. None the less, their implications were equivocal. . . . The things classified as dangerous have been steadily extended with a corresponding extension of the application of the remedy. . . . They have widened till they include a scaffold or an automobile or even pies and cakes when nails and other foreign substances have supplied ingredients not mentioned in the recipes of cook books." Cardozo described the legal process in connection with these cases as one in which "logic and utility still struggle for the mastery."[30] One can forgive Judge Cardozo for this language. It is traditional to think of logic as fighting with something. Sometimes it is thought of as fighting with history and experience.

In a reversal of itself, not so striking because the membership of the court was different, the same federal court hearing another appeal in the same case in which it had been decided that a defective automobile was not inherently dangerous now stated with new wisdom: "We cannot believe that the liability of a manufacturer of an automobile has any analogy to the liability of a manufacturer of 'tables, chairs, pictures, or mirrors hung on walls.' The analogy is rather that of a manufacturer of unwholesome food or of a poisonous drug."[31]

MacPherson v. Buick renamed and enlarged the danger category. It is usually thought to have brought the law into line with "social considerations."[32] But it did not remove the necessity for deciding cases. Later the New York courts were able to put into the category of things of danger or probably dangerous a defective bottle[33] and another coffee urn,[34] although one less terrifying than the coffee boiler of 1909. But for some reason or other, admission was denied to a defective automobile when the defect was a door handle which gave way, causing one of the doors to open with the result that the plaintiff was thrown through the door and under the car. The defective handle did not make the car a "thing of danger."[35] And if one is comparing cases and examples, it has to be admitted that a door handle is less closely connected with those things which make a car like a locomotive than is the wheel on which it runs.

Nevertheless, a new freedom follows from *MacPherson v. Buick*. Under it, as the Massachusetts court has said, the exception in favor of liability for negligence where the instrument is probably dangerous has swallowed up the purported rule that "a manufacturer or supplier is never liable for negligence to a remote vendee."[36] The exception now seems to have the same certainty the rule once had. The exception is now a general principle of liability which can be stated nicely in the Restatement, and text writers can criticize courts for not applying what is now an obvious rule of liability.[37]

A somewhat similar development has occurred in England. In *Donoghue v. Stevenson*[38] in 1932, the manufacturer of a bottle of ginger beer was held liable to the plaintiff who had purchased the bottle through a friend at a café. The bottle contained the decomposed remains of a snail. The opinions of the

---

[30]Cardozo, The Growth of the Law 40–41, 76–78 (1924).
[31]Johnson v. Cadillac, 261 Fed. 878, 886 (C.C.A. 2d, 1919).
[32]See Torts: Liability of Manufacturer to Consumer for Article Dangerous Because of Defective Construction, 9 Corn. L.Q. 494 (1924).
[33]Smith v. Peerless Glass Co., 259 N.Y. 292, 181 N.E. 576 (1932); cf. Bates v. Batey & Co., [1913] 3 K.B. 351.
[34]Hoenig v. Central Stamping Co., 273 N.Y. 485, 6 N.E. 2d 415 (1936).
[35]Cohen v. Brockway Motor Corp., 240 App. Div. 18, 268 N.Y. Supp. 545 (1934).
[36]Carter v. Yardley & Co., 319 Mass. 92, 64 N.E. 2d 693 (1946).
[37]See Harper, Law of Torts § 106 (133).
[38][1932] A.C. 562. Note the reference to trade names and patents at 583.

majority judges stressed the close and almost direct relationship between the manufacturer and the remote vendee. The control of the manufacturer of this type of article was thought to be "effective until the article reaches the consumer. . . . A manufacturer puts up an article of food in containers which he knows will be opened by the actual consumer. There can be no inspection by any purchaser and no reasonable preliminary inspection by the consumer." Lord Atkin, while stating that Brett's rule in *Heaven v. Pender* was too broad, found that the moral rule requiring the love of one's neighbour in law was translated into the injunction "you must not injure your neighbour." The question then was: "Who is my neighbour?" The practical rule evolved was of persons "closely and directly affected" and as to acts "which you can reasonably foresee would be likely to injure your neighbour." The emphasis on control and proximity revives the notion of the unconscious agent in *Langridge v. Levy,* as well as the inability to inspect, unsuccessfully urged in *Winterbottom v. Wright* and apparently implicit in the *Skivington* case.

As for other prior cases it was now said that the distinction between things dangerous and those dangerous in themselves was "an unnatural one" and anyway the fact that there might be a special duty for one category no longer meant that a duty might not exist for others. *Winterbottom* and *Longmeid* were no longer controlling because negligence had not been alleged and proved in those cases. And as for the *Blacker* case, Lord Atkin had read and re-read it but had difficulty "in formulating the precise grounds upon which the judgment was given." Thus prior cases were realigned out of the way despite the protest of dissenting judges who adhered to the view of the exception only for dangerous articles in the more traditional sense.

While the emphasis was on continuing control in the *Donoghue* case, and counsel urged that the *Donoghue* case applied only to articles intended for internal consumption, its rule was applied in *Grant v. Australian Knitting Mills*[39] in 1936 to underpants defective due to the presence of an irritating chemical. Here the emphasis could be more on the point that the defect was hidden. While the *Blacker* case was in a sense disregarded, the point made by one of its judges was in fact accepted. Reasoning in a manner not unlike *Skivington*, which substituted negligence for fraud, the court put secrecy in the place of control. Donoghue's case was now seen not to "depend on the bottle being stopped and sealed; the essential point in this regard was that the article should reach the consumer or user subject to the same defect as it had when it left the manufacturer." The court realized that in applying its test of directness, control, proximity and hidden defect, "many difficult problems will arise. . . . Many qualifying conditions and many complications of fact may in the future come before the Courts for decision." But "in their Lordships' opinion it is enough for them to decide this case on its actual facts."

With the breakdown of the inherently dangerous rule, the cycle from *Dixon v. Bell* was complete. But it would be a mistake to believe that the breakdown makes possible a general rule, such as the rule of negligence, which now can be applied. A rule so stated would be equivalent to the flight of Brett. Negligence itself must be given meaning by the examples to be included under it. Unlimited liability is not intended. As the comparison of cases proceeds, new categories will be stressed. Perhaps, for example, there will be a category for trade-marked, patented, advertised, or monopolized articles. The basis for such a category exists. The process of reasoning by example will decide. . . .

[39][1936] A.C. 85.

5

Ronald M. Dworkin

From *Law's Empire*

CHAPTER SEVEN / INTEGRITY IN LAW

A LARGE VIEW

In this chapter we construct the third conception of law I introduced [previously]. Law as integrity denies that statements of law are either the backward-looking factual reports of conventionalism or the forward-looking instrumental programs of legal pragmatism. It insists that legal claims are interpretive judgments and therefore combine backward- and forward-looking elements; they interpret contemporary legal practice seen as an unfolding political narrative. So law as integrity rejects as unhelpful the ancient question whether judges find or invent law; we understand legal reasoning, it suggests, only by seeing the sense in which they do both and neither.

Integrity and Interpretation

The adjudicative principle of integrity instructs judges to identify legal rights and duties, so far as possible, on the assumption that they were all created by a single author—the community personified—expressing a coherent conception of justice and fairness. We form our third conception of law, our third view of what rights and duties flow from past political decisions, by restating this instruction as a thesis about the grounds of law. According to law as integrity, propositions of law are true if they figure in or follow from the principles of justice, fairness, and procedural due process that provide the best constructive interpretation of the community's legal practice. Deciding whether the law grants Mrs. McLoughlin compensation for her injury, for example, means deciding whether legal practice is seen in a better light if we assume the community has accepted the principle that people in her position are entitled to compensation.

Law as integrity is therefore more relentlessly interpretive than either conventionalism or pragmatism. These latter theories offer themselves *as* interpretations. They are conceptions of law that claim to show our legal practices in the best light these can bear, and they recommend, in their postinterpretive conclusions, distinct styles or programs for adjudication. But the programs they recommend are not themselves programs *of* interpretation: they do not ask judges deciding hard cases to carry out any further, essentially interpretive study of legal doctrine. Conventionalism requires judges to study law reports and parliamentary records to discover what decisions have been made by institutions conventionally recognized to have legislative power. No doubt interpretive issues will arise in that process: for example, it may be necessary to interpret a text to decide what statutes our legal conventions construct from it. But once a judge has accepted conventionalism as his guide, he has no further occasion for interpreting the legal record as a whole in deciding particular cases. Pragmatism requires judges to think instrumentally about the best rules for the future. That exercise may require interpretation of something beyond legal material: a utilitarian pragmatist may need to worry about the best way to understand the idea of community welfare, for example. But once again, a judge who accepts pragmatism is then done with interpreting legal practice as a whole.

Law as integrity is different: it is both the product of and the inspiration for comprehensive interpretation of legal practice. The program it holds out to judges deciding hard cases is essentially, not just contingently, interpretive; law as integrity asks them to continue interpreting the same material that it claims to have successfully interpreted itself. It offers itself as continuous with—the initial part of—the more detailed interpretations it recommends. We must therefore now return to the general study of interpretation we began [previously]. We must continue the account given . . . of what interpretation is and when it is done well, but in more detail and directed more to the special interpretive challenge put to judges and others who must say what the law is.

Integrity and History

History matters in law as integrity: very much but only in a certain way. Integrity does not require consistency in principle over all historical stages of a community's law; it does not require that judges try to understand the law they enforce as continuous in principle with the abandoned law of a previous century or even a previous generation. It commands a horizontal rather than vertical consistency of principle across the range of the legal standards the community now enforces. It insists that the law—the rights and duties that flow from past collective decisions and for that reason license or require coercion—contains not only the narrow explicit content of these decisions but also, more broadly, the scheme of principles necessary to justify them. History matters because that scheme of principle must justify the standing as well as the content of these past decisions. Our justification for treating the Endangered Species Act as law, unless and until it is repealed, crucially includes the fact that Congress enacted it, and any justification we supply for treating that fact as crucial must itself accommodate the way we treat other events in our political past.

Law as integrity, then, begins in the present and pursues the past only so far as and in the way its contemporary focus dictates. It does not aim to recapture, even for present law, the ideals or practical purposes of the politicians who first created it. It aims rather to justify what they did (sometimes including, as we shall see, what they said) in an overall story worth telling now, a story with a complex claim: that present practice can be organized by and justified in principles sufficiently attractive to provide an honorable future. Law as integrity deplores the mechanism of the older "law is law" view as well as the cynicism of the newer "realism." It sees both views as rooted in the same false dichotomy of finding and inventing law. When a judge declares that a particular principle is instinct in law, he reports not a simple-minded claim about the motives of past statesmen, a claim a wise cynic can easily refute, but an interpretive proposal: that the principle both fits and justifies some complex part of legal practice, that it provides an attractive way to see, in the structure of that practice, the consistency of principle integrity requires. Law's optimism is in that way conceptual; claims of law are endemically constructive, just in virtue of the kind of claims they are. This optimism may be misplaced: legal practice may in the end yield to nothing but a deeply skeptical interpretation. But that is not inevitable just because a community's history is one of great change and conflict. An imaginative interpretation can be constructed on morally complicated, even ambiguous terrain.

THE CHAIN OF LAW

The Chain Novel

. . . [C]reative interpretation takes its formal structure from the idea of intention, not (at least not necessarily) because it aims to discover the purposes of any particular historical person or group but because it aims to impose purpose over the text or data or tradition being interpreted. Since all creative interpretation shares this feature, and therefore has a normative aspect or component, we profit from comparing law with other forms or occasions of interpretation. We can usefully compare the judge deciding what the law is on some issue not only with the citizens of courtesy deciding what that tradition requires, but with the literary critic teasing out the various dimensions of value in a complex play or poem.

Judges, however, are authors as well as critics. A judge deciding *McLoughlin* or *Brown* adds to the tradition he interprets; future judges confront a new tradition that includes what he has done. Of course literary criticism contributes to the traditions of art in which authors work; the character and importance of that contribution are themselves issues in critical theory. But the contribution of judges is more direct, and the distinction between author and interpreter more a matter of different aspects of the same process. We can find an even more fruitful comparison between literature and law, therefore, by constructing an artificial genre of literature that we might call the chain novel.

In this enterprise a group of novelists writes a novel *seriatim;* each novelist in the chain interprets the chapters he has been given in order to write a new chapter, which is then added to what the next novelist receives, and so on. Each has the job of writing his chapter so as to make the novel being constructed the best it can be, and the complexity of this task models the complexity of deciding a hard case under law as integrity. The imaginary literary enterprise is fantastic but not unrecognizable. Some novels have actually been written in this way, though mainly for a debunking purpose, and certain parlor games for rainy weekends in English country houses have something of the same structure. Television soap operas span decades with the same characters and some minimal continuity of personality and plot, though they are written by different teams of authors even in different weeks. In our example, however, the novelists are expected to take their responsibilities of continuity more seriously; they aim jointly to create, so far as they can, a single unified novel that is the best it can be.[1]

Each novelist aims to make a single novel of the material he has been given, what he adds to it, and (so far as he can control this) what his successors will want or be able to add. He must try to make this the best novel it can be construed as the work of a single author rather than, as is the fact, the product of many different hands. That calls for an overall judgment on his part, or a series of overall judgments as he writes and rewrites. He must take up some view about the novel in progress, some working theory about its characters, plot, genre, theme, and point, in order to decide what counts as continuing it and not as beginning anew. If he is a good critic, his view of these matters will be complicated and multifaceted, because the value of a decent novel cannot be captured from a single perspective. He will aim to find layers and currents of meaning rather than a single, exhaustive theme. We can, however, in our now familiar way give some structure to any interpretation he adopts, by distinguishing two dimensions on which it must be tested. The first is what we have been calling the dimension of fit. He cannot adopt any interpretation, however complex, if he believes that no single author who set out to write a novel with the various readings of character, plot, theme, and point that interpretation describes could have written substantially the text he has been given. That does not mean his interpretation must fit every bit of the text. It is not disqualified simply because he claims that some lines or tropes are accidental, or even that some events of plot are mistakes because they work against the literary ambitions the interpretation states. But the interpretation he takes up must nevertheless flow throughout the text; it must have general explanatory power, and it is flawed if it leaves unexplained some major structural aspect of the text, a subplot treated as having great dramatic importance or a dominant and repeated metaphor. If no interpretation can be found that is not flawed in that way, then the chain novelist will not be able fully to meet his assignment; he will have to settle for an interpretation that captures most of the text, conceding that it is not wholly successful. Perhaps even that partial success is unavailable; perhaps every interpretation he considers is inconsistent with the bulk of the material supplied to him. In that case he must abandon the enterprise, for the consequence of taking the interpretive attitude toward the text in question is then a piece of internal skepticism: that nothing can count as continuing the novel rather than beginning anew.

He may find, not that no single interpretation fits the bulk of the text, but that more than one does. The second dimension of interpretation then requires him to judge which of these eligible readings makes the work in progress best, all things considered. At this point his more substantive aesthetic judgments, about the importance or insight or realism or beauty of different ideas the novel might be taken to express, come into play. But the formal and structural considerations that dominate on the first dimension figure on the second as well, for even when neither of two interpretations is disqualified out of hand as explaining too little, one may show the text in a better light because it fits more of the text or provides a more interesting integration of style and content. So the distinction between the two dimensions is less crucial or profound than it might seem. It is a useful analytical device that helps us give structure to any interpreter's working theory or style. He will form a sense of when an interpretation fits so poorly that it is unnecessary to consider its substantive appeal, because he knows that this cannot outweigh its embarrassments of fit in deciding whether it makes the novel better, everything taken into account, than its rivals. This sense will define the first dimension for him. But he need not reduce his intuitive sense to any precise formula; he would rarely need to decide whether some interpretation barely survives or barely fails, because a bare survivor, no matter how ambitious or interesting it claimed the text to be, would almost certainly fail in the overall comparison with other interpretations whose fit was evident.

We can now appreciate the range of different kinds of judgments that are blended in this overall comparison. Judgments about textual coherence and integrity, reflecting different formal literary values, are interwoven with more substantive aesthetic judgments that themselves assume different literary aims. Yet these various kinds of judgments, of each general kind, remain distinct enough to check one another in an overall assessment, and it is that possibility of contest, particularly between textual and substantive judgments, that distinguishes a chain novelist's assignment from more independent creative writing. Nor can we draw any flat distinction between the stage at which a chain novelist interprets the text he has been given and the stage at which he adds his own chapter, guided by the interpretation he has settled on. When he begins to write he might discover in what he has written a different, perhaps radically different, interpretation. Or he might find it impossible to write in the tone or theme he first took up, and that will lead him to reconsider other interpretations he first rejected. In either case he returns to the text to reconsider the lines it makes eligible. . . .

LAW: THE QUESTION OF EMOTIONAL DAMAGES

Law as integrity asks a judge deciding a common-law case like *McLoughlin* to think of himself as an author in the chain of common law. He knows that other judges have decided cases that, although not exactly like his case, deal with related problems; he must think of their decisions as part of a long story he must interpret and then continue, according to his own judgment of how to make the developing story as good as it can be. (Of course the best story for him means best from the standpoint of political morality, not aesthetics.) We can make a rough distinction once again between two main dimensions of this interpretive judgment. The judge's decision—his postinterpretive conclusions—must be drawn from an interpretation that both fits and justifies what has gone before, so far as that is possible. But in law as in literature the interplay between fit and justification is complex. Just as interpretation within a chain novel is for each interpreter a delicate balance among different types of literary and artistic attitudes, so in law it is a delicate balance among political convictions of different sorts; in law as in literature these must be sufficiently related yet disjoint to allow an overall judgment that trades off an interpretation's success on one type of standard against its failure on another. I must try to exhibit that complex structure of legal interpretation, and I shall use for that purpose an imaginary judge of superhuman intellectual power and patience who accepts law as integrity.

Call him Hercules.[2] In this and the next several chapters we follow his career by noticing the types of judgments he must make and tensions he must resolve in deciding a variety of cases. But I offer this caution in advance. We must not suppose that his answers to the various questions he encounters *define* law as integrity as a general conception of law. They are the answers I now think best. But law as integrity consists in an approach, in questions rather than answers, and other lawyers and judges who accept it would give different answers from his to the questions it asks. You might think other answers would be better. (So might I, after further thought.) You might, for example, reject Hercules' views about how far people's legal rights depend on the reasons past judges offered for their decisions enforcing these rights, or you might not share his respect for what I shall call "local priority" in common-law decisions. If you reject these discrete views because you think them poor constructive interpretations of legal practice, however, you have not rejected law as integrity but rather have joined its enterprise.

Six Interpretations

Hercules must decide *McLoughlin*. Both sides in that case cited precedents; each argued that a decision in its favor would count as going on as before, as continuing the story begun by the judges who decided those precedent cases. Hercules must form his own view about that issue. Just as a chain novelist must find, if he can, some coherent view of character and theme such that a hypothetical single author with that view could have written at least the bulk of the novel so far, Hercules must find, if he can, some coherent theory about legal rights to compensation for emotional injury such that a single political official with that theory could have reached most of the results the precedents report.

He is a careful judge, a judge of method. He begins by setting out various candidates for the best interpretation of the precedent cases even before he reads them. Suppose he makes the following short list: (1) No one has a moral right to compensation except for physical injury. (2) People have a moral right to compensation for emotional injury suffered at the scene of an accident against anyone whose carelessness caused the accident but have no right to compensation for emotional injury suffered later. (3) People should recover compensation for emotional injury when a practice of requiring compensation in their circumstances would diminish the overall costs of accidents or otherwise make the community richer in the long run. (4) People have a moral right to compensation for any injury, emotional or physical, that is the direct consequence of careless conduct, no matter how unlikely or unforeseeable it is that that conduct would result in that injury. (5) People have a moral right to compensation for emotional or physical injury that is the consequence of careless conduct, but only if that injury was reasonably foreseeable by the person who acted carelessly. (6) People have a moral right to compensation for reasonably foreseeable injury but not in circumstances when recognizing such a right would impose massive and destructive financial burdens on people who have been careless out of proportion to their moral fault.

These are all relatively concrete statements about rights and, allowing for a complexity in (3) we explore just below, they contradict one another. No more than one can figure in a single interpretation of the emotional injury cases. (I postpone the more complex case in which Hercules constructs an interpretation from competitive rather than contradictory principles, that is, from principles that can live together in an overall moral or political theory though they sometimes pull in different directions.)[3] Even so, this is only a partial list of the contradictory interpretations someone might wish to consider; Hercules chooses it as his initial short list because he knows that the principles captured in these interpretations have actually been discussed in the legal literature. It will obviously make a great difference which of these principles he believes provides the best interpretation of the precedents and so the nerve of his postinterpretive judgment. If he settles on (1) or (2), he must decide for Mr. O'Brian; if on (4), for Mrs. McLoughlin. Each of the others requires further thought, but the line of reasoning each suggests is different. (3) invites an economic calculation. Would it reduce the cost of accidents to extend liability to emotional injury away from the scene? Or is there some reason to think that the most efficient line is drawn just between emotional injuries at and those away from the scene? (5) requires a judgment about foreseeability of injury, which seems to be very different, and (6) a judgment both about foreseeability and the cumulative risk of financial responsibility if certain injuries away from the scene are included.

Hercules begins testing each interpretation on his short list by asking whether a single political official could have given the verdicts of the precedent cases if that official were consciously and coherently enforcing the principles that form the interpretation. He will therefore dismiss interpretation (1) at once. No one who believed that people never have rights to compensation for emotional injury could have reached the results of those past decisions cited in *McLoughlin* that allowed compensation. Hercules will also dismiss interpretation (2), though for a different reason. Unlike (1), (2) fits the past decisions; someone who accepted (2) as a standard would have reached these decisions, because they all allowed recovery for emotional injury at the scene and none allowed recovery for injury away from it. But (2) fails as an interpretation of the required kind because it does not state a principle of justice at all. It draws a line that it leaves arbitrary and unconnected to any more general moral or political consideration.

What about (3)? It might fit the past decisions, but only in the following way. Hercules might discover through economic analysis that someone who accepted the economic theory expressed by (3) and who wished to reduce the community's accident costs would have made just those decisions. But it is far from obvious that (3) states any principle of justice or fairness. . . . (3) supposes that it is desirable to reduce accident costs overall. Why? Two explanations are possible. The first insists that people have a right to compensation whenever a rule awarding compensation would produce more wealth for the community overall than a rule denying it. This has the form, at least, of a principle because it describes a general right everyone is supposed to have. . . . The second, quite different, explanation suggests that it is sometimes or even always in the community's general interest to promote overall wealth in this way, but it does not suppose that anyone has any right that social wealth always be increased. It therefore sets out a policy that government might or might not decide to pursue in particular circumstances. It does not state a principle of justice, and so it cannot figure in an interpretation of the sort Hercules now seeks.[4]

Law as integrity asks judges to assume, so far as this is possible, that the law is structured by a coherent set of principles about justice and fairness and procedural due process, and it asks them to enforce these in the fresh cases that come before them, so that each person's situation is fair and just according to the same standards. That style of adjudication respects the ambition integrity assumes, the ambition to be a community of principle. But . . . integrity does not recommend what would be perverse, that we should all be governed by the same goals and strategies of policy on every occasion. It does not insist that a legislature that enacts one set of rules about compensation today, in order to make the community richer on the whole, is in any way committed to serve that same goal of policy tomorrow. For it might then have other goals to seek; not necessarily in place of wealth but beside it, and integrity does not frown on this diversity. Our account of interpretation, and our consequent elimination of interpretation (3) read as a naked appeal to policy, reflects a discrimination already latent in the ideal of integrity itself.

We reach the same conclusion in the context of *McLoughlin* through a different route, by further reflection on what we have learned about interpretation. An interpretation aims to show what is interpreted in the best light possible, and an interpretation of any part of our law must therefore attend not only to the substance of the decisions made by earlier officials but also to how—by which officials in which circumstances—these decisions were made. A legislature does not need reasons of principle to justify the rules it enacts about driving, including rules about compensation for accidents, even though these rules will create rights and duties for the future that will then be enforced by coercive threat. A legislature may justify its decision to create new rights for the future by showing how these will contribute, as a matter of sound policy, to the overall good of the community as a whole. There are limits to this kind of justification. . . . The general good may not be used to justify the death penalty for careless driving. But the legislature need not show that citizens already have a moral right to compensation for injury under particular circumstances in order to justify a statute awarding damages in those circumstances.

Law as integrity assumes, however, that judges are in a very different position from legislators. It does not fit the character of a community of principle that a judge should have authority to hold people liable in damages for acting in a way he concedes they had no legal duty not to act. So when judges construct rules of liability not recognized before, they are not free in the way I just said legislators are. Judges must make their common-law decisions on grounds of principle, not policy: they must deploy arguments why the parties actually had the "novel" legal rights and duties they enforce at the time the parties acted or at some other pertinent time in the past.[5] A legal pragmatist would reject that claim. But Hercules rejects pragmatism. He follows law as integrity and therefore wants an interpretation of what judges did in the earlier emotional damage cases that shows them acting in the way he approves, not in the way he thinks judges must decline to act. It does not follow that he must dismiss interpretation (3) read in the first way I described, as supposing that past judges acted to protect a general legal right to compensation when this would make the community richer. For if people actually have such a right, others have a corresponding duty, and judges do not act unjustly in ordering the police to enforce it. The argument disqualifies interpretation (3) only when this is read to deny any such general duty and to rest on grounds of policy alone.

Expanding the Range

Interpretations (4), (5), and (6) do, however, seem to pass these initial tests. The principles of each fit the past emotional injury decisions, at least on first glance, if only because none of these precedents presented facts that would discriminate among them. Hercules must now ask, as the next stage of his investigation, whether any one of the three must be ruled out because it is incompatible with the bulk of legal practice more generally. He must test each interpretation against other past judicial decisions, beyond those involving emotional injury, that might be thought to engage them. Suppose he discovers, for example, that past decisions provide compensation for physical injury caused by careless driving only if the injury was reasonably foreseeable. That would rule out interpretation (4) unless he can find some principled distinction between physical and emotional injury that explains why the conditions for compensation should be more restrictive for the former than the latter, which seems extremely unlikely.

Law as integrity, then, requires a judge to test his interpretation of any part of the great network of political structures and decisions of his community by asking whether it could form part of a coherent theory justifying the network as a whole. No actual judge could compose anything approaching a full interpretation of all of his community's law at once. That is why we are imagining a Herculean judge of superhuman talents and endless time. But an actual judge can imitate Hercules in a limited way. He can allow the scope of his interpretation to fan out from the cases immediately in point to cases in the same general area or department of law, and then still farther, so far as this seems promising. In practice even this limited process will be largely unconscious: an experienced judge will have a sufficient sense of the terrain surrounding his immediate problem to know instinctively which interpretation of a small set of cases would survive if the range it must fit were expanded. But sometimes the expansion will be deliberate and controversial. Lawyers celebrate dozens of decisions of that character, including several on which the modern law of negligence was built.[6] Scholarship offers other important examples.[7]

Suppose a modest expansion of Hercules' range of inquiry does show that plaintiffs are denied compensation if their physical injury was not reasonably foreseeable at the time the careless defendant acted, thus ruling out interpretation (4). But this does not eliminate either (5) or (6). He must expand his survey further. He must look also to cases involving economic rather than physical or emotional injury, where damages are potentially very great: for example, he must look to cases in which professional advisers like surveyors or accountants are sued for losses others suffer through their negligence. Interpretation (5) suggests that such liability might be unlimited in amount, no matter how ruinous in total, provided that the damage is foreseeable, and (6) suggests, on the contrary, that liability is limited just because of the frightening sums it might otherwise reach. If one interpretation is uniformly contradicted by cases of that sort and finds no support in any other area of doctrine

Hercules might later inspect, and the other is confirmed by the expansion, he will regard the former as ineligible, and the latter alone will have survived. But suppose he finds, when he expands his study in this way, a mixed pattern. Past decisions permit extended liability for members of some professions but not for those of others, and this mixed pattern holds for other areas of doctrine that Hercules, in the exercise of his imaginative skill, finds pertinent.

The contradiction he has discovered, though genuine, is not in itself so deep or pervasive as to justify a skeptical interpretation of legal practice as a whole, for the problem of unlimited damages, while important, is not so fundamental that contradiction within it destroys the integrity of the larger system. So Hercules turns to the second main dimension, but here, as in the chain-novel example, questions of fit surface again, because an interpretation is *pro tanto* more satisfactory if it shows less damage to integrity than its rival. He will therefore consider whether interpretation (5) fits the expanded legal record better than (6). But this cannot be a merely mechanical decision; he cannot simply count the number of past decisions that must be conceded to be "mistakes" on each interpretation. For these numbers may reflect only accidents like the number of cases that happen to have come to court and not been settled before verdict. He must take into account not only the numbers of decisions counting for each interpretation, but whether the decisions expressing one principle seem more important or fundamental or wide-ranging than the decisions expressing the other. Suppose interpretation (6) fits only those past judicial decisions involving charges of negligence against one particular profession—say, lawyers—and interpretation (5) justifies all other cases, involving all other professions, and also fits other kinds of economic damage cases as well. Interpretation (5) then fits the legal record better on the whole, even if the number of cases involving lawyers is for some reason numerically greater, unless the argument shifts again, as it well might, when the field of study expands even more.

Now suppose a different possibility: that though liability has in many and varied cases actually been limited to an amount less than interpretation (5) would allow, the opinions attached to these cases made no mention of the principle of interpretation (6), which has in fact never before been recognized in official judicial rhetoric. Does that show that interpretation (5) fits the legal record much better, or that interpretation (6) is ineligible after all? Judges in fact divide about this issue of fit. Some would not seriously consider interpretation (6) if no past judicial opinion or legislative statement had ever explicitly mentioned its principle. Others reject this constraint and accept that the best interpretation of some line of cases may lie in a principle that has never been recognized explicitly but that nevertheless offers a brilliant account of the actual decisions, showing them in a better light than ever before.[8] Hercules will confront this issue as a special question of political morality. The political history of the community is *pro tanto* a better history, he thinks, if it shows judges making plain to their public, through their opinions, the path that later judges guided by integrity will follow and if it shows judges making decisions that give voice as well as effect to convictions about morality that are widespread through the community. Judicial opinions formally announced in law reports, moreover, are themselves acts of the community personified that, particularly if recent, must be taken into the embrace of integrity.[9] These are among his reasons for somewhat preferring an interpretation that is not too novel, not too far divorced from what past judges and other officials said as well as did. But he must set these reasons against his more substantive political convictions about the relative moral value of the two interpretations, and if he believes that interpretation (6) is much superior from that perspective, he will think he makes the legal record better overall by selecting it even at the cost of the more procedural values. Fitting what judges did is more important than fitting what they said.

Now suppose an even more unpatterned record. Hercules finds that unlimited liability has been enforced against a number of professions but has not been enforced against a roughly equal number of others, that no principle can explain the distinction, that judicial rhetoric is as split as the actual decisions, and that this split extends into other kinds of actions for economic damage. He might expand his field of survey still further, and the picture might change if he does. But let us suppose he is satisfied that it will not. He will then decide that the question of fit can play no more useful role in his deliberations even on the second dimension. He must now emphasize the more plainly substantive aspects of that dimension: he must decide which interpretation shows the legal record to be the best it can be from the standpoint of substantive political morality. He will compose and compare two stories. The first supposes that the community personified has adopted and is enforcing the principle of foreseeability as its test of moral responsibility for damage caused by negligence, that the various decisions it has reached are intended to give effect to that principle, though it has often lapsed and reached decisions that foreseeability would condemn. The second supposes, instead, that the community has adopted and is enforcing the principle of foreseeability limited by some overall ceiling on liability, though it has often lapsed from that principle. Which story shows the community in a better light, all things considered, from the standpoint of political morality?

Hercules' answer will depend on his convictions about the two constituent virtues of political morality we have considered: justice and fairness.[10] It will depend, that is, not only on his beliefs about which of these principles is superior as a matter of abstract justice but also about which should be followed, as a matter of political fairness, in a community whose members have the moral convictions his fellow citizens have. In some cases the two kinds of judgment—the judgment of justice and that of fairness—will come together. If Hercules and the public at large share the view that people are entitled to be compensated fully whenever they are injured by others' carelessness, without regard to how harsh this requirement might turn out to be, then he will think that interpretation (5) is plainly the better of the two in play. But the two judgments will sometimes pull in different directions. He may think that interpretation (6) is better on grounds of abstract justice, but know that this is a radical view not shared by any substantial portion of the public and unknown in the political and moral rhetoric of the times. He might then decide that the story in which the state insists on the view he thinks right, but against the wishes of the people as a whole, is a poorer story, on balance. He would be preferring fairness to justice in these circumstances, and that preference would reflect a higher-order level of his own political convictions, namely his convictions about how a decent government committed to both fairness and justice should adjudicate between the two in this sort of case.

Judges will have different ideas of fairness, about the role each citizen's opinion should ideally play in the state's decision about which principles of justice to enforce through its central police power. They will have different higher-level opinions about the best resolution of conflicts between these two political ideals. No judge is likely to hold the simplistic theory that fairness is automatically to be preferred to justice or vice versa. Most judges will think that the balance between the opinions of the community and the demands of abstract justice must be struck differently in different kinds of cases. Perhaps in ordinary commercial or private law cases, like *McLoughlin,* an interpretation supported in popular morality will be deemed superior to one that is not, provided it is not thought very much inferior as a matter of abstract justice. But many judges will think the interpretive force of popular morality very much weaker in constitutional cases like *Brown,* because they will think the point of the Constitution is in part to protect individuals from what the majority thinks right.[11]

Local Priority

I must call special attention to a feature of Hercules' practice that has not yet clearly emerged. His judgments of fit expand out from the immediate case before him in a series of concentric circles. He asks which interpretations on his initial list fit past emotional injury cases, then which ones fit cases of accidental damage to the person more generally, then which fit damage to economic interests, and so on into areas each further and further from the original *McLoughlin* issue. This procedure gives a kind of local priority to what we might call "departments" of law. If Hercules finds that neither of two principles is flatly contradicted by the accidental damage cases of his jurisdiction, he expands his study into, say, contract cases to see which of these principles, if either, fits contract decisions better. But in Hercules' view, if one principle does *not* fit accident law at all—if it is contradicted by almost every decision in the area that might have confirmed it—this counts dramatically against it as an eligible interpretation of that body of law, even if it fits other areas of the law superbly. He will not treat this doctrine of local priority as absolute, however; he will be ready to override it, as we shall soon see, in some circumstances.

The compartmentalization of law into separate departments is a prominent feature of legal practice. Law schools divide courses and their libraries divide treatises to distinguish emotional from economic or physical injury, intentional from unintentional torts, tort from crime, contract from other parts of common law, private from public law, and constitutional law from other parts of public law. Legal and judicial arguments respect these traditional divisions. Judicial opinions normally begin by assigning the case in hand to some department of law, and the precedents and statutes considered are usually drawn exclusively from that department. Often the initial classification is both controversial and crucial.

Compartmentalization suits both conventionalism and pragmatism, though for different reasons. Departments of law are based on tradition, which seems to support conventionalism, and they provide a strategy a pragmatist can manipulate in telling his noble lies: he can explain that his new doctrine need not be consistent in principle with past decisions because the latter, properly understood, belong to a different department. Law as integrity has a more complex attitude toward departments of law. Its general spirit condemns them, because the adjudicative principle of integrity asks judges to make the law coherent as a whole, so far as they can, and this might be better done by ignoring academic boundaries and reforming some departments of law radically to make them more consistent in principle with others.[12] But law as integrity is interpretive, and compartmentalization is a feature of legal practice no competent interpretation can ignore.

Hercules responds to these competing impulses by seeking a constructive interpretation of compartmentalization. He tries to find an explanation of the practice of dividing law into departments that shows that practice in its best light. The boundaries between departments usually match popular opinion; many people think that intentional harm is more blameworthy than careless harm, that the state needs a very different kind of justification to declare someone guilty of a crime than it needs to require him to pay compensation for damage he has caused, that promises and other forms of explicit agreement or consent are a special kind of reason for state coercion, and so forth. Dividing departments of law to match that sort of opinion promotes predictability and guards against sudden official reinterpretations that uproot large areas of law, and it does this in a way that promotes a deeper aim of law as integrity. If legal compartments make sense to people at large, they encourage the protestant attitude integrity favors, because they allow ordinary people as well as hard-pressed judges to interpret law within practical boundaries that seem natural and intuitive.

Hercules accepts that account of the point of compartmentalization, and he shapes his doctrine of local priority accordingly. He allows the doctrine most force when the boundaries between traditional departments of law track widely held moral principles distinguishing types of fault or responsibility, and the substance of each department reflects those moral principles. The distinction between criminal and civil law meets that test. Suppose Hercules thinks, contrary to most people's opinion, that being made to pay compensation is just as bad as being made to pay a fine, and therefore that the distinction between criminal and civil law is unsound in principle. He will nevertheless defer to local priority. He will not claim that criminal and civil law should be treated as one department; he will not argue that a criminal defendant's guilt need only be established as probable rather than beyond a reasonable doubt because the probable standard fits the combined department as well as any other.

But Hercules will not be so ready to defer to local priority when his test is not met, when traditional boundaries between departments have become mechanical and arbitrary, either because popular morality has shifted or because the substance of the departments no longer reflects popular opinion.[13] Compartments of law do sometimes grow arbitrary and isolated from popular conviction in that way, particularly when the central rules of the departments were developed in different periods. Suppose the legal tradition of a community has for many decades separated nuisance law, which concerns the discomfort of interference that activities on one person's land cause to neighbors, from negligence law, which concerns the discomfort of interference that activities on one person's land cause to neighbors, from negligence law, which concerns the physical or economic or emotional injuries someone's carelessness inflicts on others. Suppose that the judges who decided the crucial nuisance cases disdained any economic test for nuisance; they said that an activity counts as a nuisance, and must therefore be stopped, when it is not a "natural" or traditional use of the land, so that someone who starts a factory on land traditionally used for farming is guilty of nuisance even though the factory is an economically more efficient use. But suppose that in recent years judges have begun to make economic cost crucial for negligence. They say that someone's failure to take precautions against injuring others is negligent, so that he is liable for the resulting injury if the precaution was "reasonable" in the circumstances, and that the economic cost of the precaution counts in deciding whether it was in fact reasonable.

The distinction between negligence and nuisance law no longer meets Hercules' test, if it ever did. It makes some sense to distinguish nuisance from negligence if we assume that nuisance is intentional while negligence is unintentional; then the distinction tracks the popular principle that it is worse to injure someone knowingly than unknowingly. But the developments in negligence law I just described are not consistent with that view of the distinction, because failing to guard against an accident is not necessarily unintentional in the required sense. So Hercules would be ready to ignore the traditional boundary between these two departments of law. If he thought that the "natural use" test was silly, and the economic cost test much more just, he would argue that the negligence and nuisance precedents should be seen as one body of law, and that the economic cost test is a superior interpretation of that unified body. His argument would probably be made easier by other legal events that already had occurred. The intellectual climate that produced the later negligence decisions would have begun to erode the assumption of the earlier nuisance cases, that novel enterprises that annoy people are necessarily legal wrongs. Perhaps the legislature would have adopted special statutes rearranging liability for some new forms of inconvenience, like airport noise, that the "natural" theory has decided or would decide in what seems the wrong way, for example. Or perhaps judges would have decided airport cases by straining the historical meaning of "natural" to reach decisions that seemed sensible given developing technology. Hercules would cite these changes as supporting his interpretive argument consolidating nuisance and negligence. If he persuades the profession to his view, nuisance and negligence will no longer be distinct departments of law but joint tenants of a new province which will shortly attract a new name attached to new law school courses and new treatises. This process is in fact under way in Anglo-American law, as is, though less securely, a new unification of private law that blurs even the long-established and once much firmer boundary between contract and tort.

A PROVISIONAL SUMMARY

[Now] . . . we will take stock, though this means some repetition, and then consider certain objections to the argument so far. Judges who accept the interpretive ideal of integrity decide hard cases by trying to find, in some coherent set of principles about people's rights and duties, the best constructive interpretation of the political structure and legal doctrine of their community. They try to make that complex structure and record the best these can be. It is analytically useful to distinguish different dimensions or aspects of any working theory. It will include convictions about both fit and justification. Convictions about fit will provide a rough threshold requirement that an interpretation of some part of the law must meet if it is to be eligible at all. Any plausible working theory would disqualify an interpretation of our own law that denied legislative competence or supremacy outright or that claimed a general principle of private law requiring the rich to share their wealth with the poor. That threshold will eliminate interpretations that some judges would otherwise prefer, so the brute facts of legal history will in this way limit the role any judge's personal convictions of justice can play in his decisions. Different judges will set this threshold differently. But anyone who accepts law as integrity must accept that the actual political history of his community will sometimes check his other political convictions in his overall interpretive judgment. If he does not—if his threshold of fit is wholly derivative from and adjustable to his convictions of justice, so that the latter automatically provide an eligible interpretation—then he cannot claim in good faith to be interpreting his legal practice at all. Like the chain novelist whose judgments of fit automatically adjusted to his substantive literary opinions, he is acting from bad faith or self-deception.

Hard cases arise, for any judge, when his threshold test does not discriminate between two or more interpretations of some statute or line of cases. Then he must choose between eligible interpretations by asking which shows the community's structure of institutions and decisions—its public standards as a whole—in a better light from the standpoint of political morality. His own moral and political convictions are now directly engaged. But the political judgment he must make is itself complex and will sometimes set one department of his political morality against another: his decision will reflect not only his opinions about justice and fairness but his higher-order convictions about how these ideals should be compromised when they compete. Questions of fit arise at this stage of interpretation as well, because even when an interpretation survives the threshold requirement, any infelicities of fit will count against it, in the ways we noticed, in the general balance of political virtues. Different judges will disagree about each of these issues and will accordingly take different views of what the law of their community, properly understood, really is.

Any judge will develop, in the course of his training and experience, a fairly individualized working conception of law on which he will rely, perhaps unthinkingly, in making these various judgments and decisions, and the judgments will then be, for him, a matter of feel or instinct rather than analysis. Even so, we as critics can impose structure on his working theory by teasing out its rules of thumb about fit—about the relative importance of consistency with past rhetoric and popular opinion, for example—and its more substantive opinions or leanings about justice and fairness. Most judges will be like other people in their community, and fairness and justice will therefore not often compete for them. But judges whose political opinions are more eccentric or radical will find that the two ideals conflict in particular cases, and they will have to decide which resolution of that conflict would show the community's record in the best light. Their working conceptions will accordingly include higher-order principles that have proved necessary to that further decision. A particular judge may think or assume, for example, that political decisions should mainly respect majority opinion, and yet believe that this requirement relaxes and even disappears when serious constitutional rights are in question.

We should now recall two general observations we made in constructing the chain-novel model, because they apply here as well. First, the different aspects or dimensions of a judge's working approach—the dimensions of fit and substance, and of different aspects of substance—are in the last analysis all responsive to his political judgment. His convictions about fit, as these appear either in his working threshold requirement or analytically later in competition with substance, are political not mechanical. They express his commitment to integrity: he believes that an interpretation that falls below his threshold of fit shows the record of the community in an irredeemably bad light, because proposing that interpretation suggests that the community has characteristically dishonored its own principles. When an interpretation meets the threshold, remaining defects of fit may be compensated, in his overall judgment, if the principles of that interpretation are particularly attractive, because then he sets off the community's infrequent lapses in respecting these principles against its virtue in generally observing them. The constraint fit imposes on substance, in any working theory, is therefore the constraint of one type of political conviction on another in the overall judgment which interpretation makes a political record the best it can be overall, everything taken into account. Second, the mode of this constraint is the mode we identified in the chain novel. It is not the constraint of external hard fact or of interpersonal consensus, but rather the structural constraint of different kinds of principle within a system of principle, and it is none the less genuine for that.

No mortal judge can or should try to articulate his instinctive working theory so far, or make that theory so concrete and detailed, that no further thought will be necessary case by case. He must treat any general principles or rules of thumb he has followed in the past as provisional and stand ready to abandon these in favor of more sophisticated and searching analysis when the occasion demands. These will be moments of special difficulty for any judge, calling for fresh political judgments that may be hard to make. It would be absurd to suppose that he will always have at hand the necessary background convictions of political morality for such occasions. Very hard cases will force him to develop his conception of law and his political morality together in a mutually supporting way. But it is nevertheless possible for any judge to confront fresh and challenging issues as a matter of principle, and this is what law as integrity demands of him. He must accept that in finally choosing one interpretation over another of a much contested line of precedents, perhaps after demanding thought and shifting conviction, he is developing his working conception of law in one rather than another direction. This must seem to him the right direction as a matter of political principle, not just appealing for the moment because it recommends an attractive decision in the immediate case. There is, in his counsel, much room for deception, including self-deception. But on most occasions it will be possible for judges to recognize when they have submitted an issue to the discipline it describes. And also to recognize when some other judge has not. . . .

NOTES

1. Perhaps this is an impossible assignment; perhaps the project is doomed to produce not just an impossibly bad novel but no novel at all, because the best theory of art requires a single creator or, if more than one, that each must have some control over the whole. (But what about legends and

jokes? What about the Old Testament, or, on some theories, the *Iliad?*) I need not push that question further, because I am interested only in the fact that the assignment makes sense, that each of the novelists in the chain can have some grasp of what he is asked to do, whatever misgivings he might have about the value or character of what will then be produced

2. Hercules played an important part in *Taking Rights Seriously* chap. 4.
3. See the discussion of critical legal studies later in this chapter.
4. The disagreement between Lords Edmund Davies and Scarman in *McLoughlin,* described in Chapter 1, was perhaps over just this claim. Edmund Davies's suggestions, about the arguments that might justify a distinction between compensable and noncompensable emotional injury, seem to appeal to arguments of policy Scarman refused to acknowledge as appropriate.
5. See *Taking Rights Seriously,* chap. 4.
6. See *Thomas v. Winchester,* 6 N.Y. 397, and *MacPherson v. Buick Motor Co.,* 217 N.Y. 382, 111 N.E. 1050.
7. C. Haar and D. Fessler, *The Wrong Side of the Tracks* (New York, 1986), is a recent example of integrity working on a large canvas.
8. See, for example, Benjamin Cardozo's decision in *Hynes v. New York Central R.R. Co.,* 231 N.Y. 229.
9. These various arguments why a successful interpretation must achieve some fit with past judicial opinions as well as with the decisions themselves are discussed in Chapter 9 in the context of past legislative statements.
10. I have in mind the distinction and the special sense of fairness described in Chapter 6.
11. But see the discussions of "passivism" as a theory of constitutional adjudication in Chapter 10.
12. See the discussion of different levels of integrity in Chapter 11.
13. The disagreement between Lords Diplock and Edmund Davies, on the one hand, and Lord Dilthorne on the other, in the notorious blasphemy case *R. v. Lemon* [1979] 1 All ER 898, illustrates the importance of not ignoring this connection between changes in popular morality and the boundaries of local priority. The former insisted that the law of blasphemy be interpreted to reflect developments in other parts of criminal law; the latter that blasphemy, for some unexplained reason, be counted an isolated domain of its own.

6

Cass R. Sunstein

Incompletely Theorized Agreements

Incompletely theorized agreements play a pervasive role in law and society. It is quite rare for a person or group completely to theorize any subject, that is, to accept both a general theory and a series of steps connecting that theory to concrete conclusions. Thus we often have in law an *incompletely theorized agreement on a general principle*—incompletely theorized in the sense that people who accept the principle need not agree on what it entails in particular cases.

This is the sense emphasized by Justice Oliver Wendell Holmes in his great aphorism, "General principles do not decide concrete cases."[1] Thus, for example, we know that murder is wrong, but disagree about whether abortion is wrong. We favor racial equality, but are divided on affirmative action. We believe in liberty, but disagree about increases in the minimum wage. Hence the pervasive legal and political phenomenon of an agreement on a general principle alongside disagreement about particular cases. The agreement is incompletely theorized in the sense that it is *incompletely specified.* Much of the key work must be done by others, often through casuistical judgments at the point of application.

Often constitution-making becomes possible through this form of incompletely theorized agreement. Many constitutions contain incompletely specified standards and avoid rules, at least when it comes to the description of basic rights. Consider the cases of Eastern Europe and South Africa, where constitutional provisions include many abstract provisions on whose concrete specification there has been sharp dispute. Abstract provisions protect "freedom of speech," "religious liberty," and "equality under the law," and citizens agree on those abstractions in the midst of sharp dispute about what these provisions really entail.

Much lawmaking becomes possible only because of this phenomenon. Consider the fact that the creation of large regulatory agencies has often been feasible only because of incompletely specified agreements. In dealing with air and water pollution, occupational safety and health, or regulation of broadcasting, legislators converge on general, incompletely specified requirements—that regulation be "reasonable," or that it provide "a margin of safety." If the legislature attempted to specify these requirements—to decide what counts as reasonable regulation—there would be a predictably high level of dispute and conflict, and perhaps the relevant laws could not be enacted at all.

Incompletely specified agreements thus have important social uses. Many of their advantages are practical. They allow people to develop frameworks for decision and judgment despite large-scale disagreements. At the same time, they help produce a degree of social solidarity and shared commitment. People who are able to agree on political abstractions—freedom of speech, freedom from unreasonable searches and seizures—can also agree that they are embarking on shared projects. These forms of agreement help constitute a democratic culture. It is for this reason that they are so important to constitution-making. Incompletely specified agreements also have the advantage of allowing people to show one another a high degree of mutual respect. By refusing to settle concrete cases that raise fundamental issues of conscience, they permit citizens to announce to one another that society shall not take sides on such issues until it is required to do so.

So much for incompletely specified provisions. Let us turn to a second phenomenon. Sometimes people agree on a mid-level principle but disagree about both general theory and particular cases. These sorts of agreements are also incompletely theorized, but in a different way. Judges may believe, for example, that government cannot discriminate on the basis of race, without having a large-scale theory of equality, and also without agreeing whether government may enact affirmative action programs or segregate prisons when racial tensions are severe. Judges may think that government may not regulate speech unless it can show a clear and present danger—but disagree about whether this principle is founded in utilitarian or Kantian considerations, and disagree too about whether the principle allows government to regulate a particular speech by members of the Ku Klux Klan.

My particular interest here is in a third kind of phenomenon, of special interest for law: incompletely theorized agreements on particular outcomes, accompanied by agreements on the narrow or low-level principles that account for them. These terms contain some ambiguities. There is no algorithm by which to distinguish between a high-level theory and one that operates at an intermediate or lower level. We might consider, as conspicuous examples of high-level theories, Kantianism and utilitarianism, and see legal illustrations in the many distinguished (academic) efforts to understand such areas as tort law, contract law, free speech, and the law of equality as undergirded by highly abstract theories of the right or the good.[2] By contrast, we might think of low-level principles as including most of the ordinary material of legal "doctrine"—the general class of principles and justifications that are not said to derive from any large theories of the right or the good, that have ambiguous relations to large theories, and that are compatible with more than one such theory.

By the term "particular outcome," I mean the judgment about who wins and who loses a case. By the term "low-level principles," I refer to something relative, not absolute; I mean to do the same thing by the terms "theories" and "abstractions" (which I use interchangeably). In this setting, the notions "low-level," "high," and "abstract" are best understood in comparative terms, like the terms "big," "old," and "unusual." The "clear and present danger" standard is a relative abstraction when compared with the claim that members of the Nazi Party may march in Skokie, Illinois. But the "clear and present danger" idea is relatively particular when compared with the claim that nations should adopt the constitutional abstraction "freedom of speech." The term "freedom of speech" is a relative abstraction when measured against the claim that campaign finance laws are acceptable, but the same term is less abstract than the grounds that justify free speech, as in, for example, the principle of personal autonomy.

What I am emphasizing here is that when people diverge on some (relatively) high-level proposition, they might be able to agree when they lower the level of abstraction. Incompletely theorized judgments on particular cases are the ordinary material of law. And in law, the point of agreement is often highly particularized—absolutely as well as relatively particularized—in the sense that it involves a specific outcome and a set of reasons that do not venture far from the case at hand. High-level theories are rarely reflected explicitly in law.

Perhaps the participants in law endorse no such theory, or perhaps they believe that they have none, or perhaps they cannot, on a multimember court, reach agreement on a theory. Perhaps they find theoretical disputes confusing or annoying. What is critical is that they agree on how a case must come out. The argument very much applies to rules, which are, much of the time, incompletely theorized; indeed, this is one of the major advantages of rules. People may agree that a 60-mile-per-hour speed limit makes sense, and that it applies to defendant Jones, without having much of a theory about criminal punishment. They may agree that to receive social security benefits, people must show that they earn less than a certain sum of money, without having anything like a theory about who deserves what. Thus a key social function of rules is to allow people to agree on the meaning, authority, and even the soundness of a government provision in the face of disagreements about much else.

Much the same can be said about rule-free decisions made under standards, factors, and analogical reasoning. Indeed, all of the lawyer's conventional tools allow incompletely theorized agreements on particular outcomes. Consider analogical thinking. People might think that A is like B and covered by the same low-level principle, without agreeing on a general theory to explain why the low-level principle is sound. They agree on the matter of similarity, without agreeing on a large-scale account of what makes the two things similar. In the law of discrimination, for example, many people think that sex discrimination is "like" race discrimination and should be treated similarly, even if they lack or cannot agree on a general theory of when discrimination is unacceptable. In the law of free speech, many people agree that a ban on speech by a Communist is "like" a ban on speech by a member of the Ku Klux Klan and should be treated similarly—even if they lack or cannot agree on a general theory about the foundations of the free speech principle.

INCOMPLETE THEORIZATION AND THE CONSTRUCTIVE USES OF SILENCE

What might be said on behalf of incompletely theorized agreements, or incompletely theorized judgments, about particular cases? Some people think of incomplete theorization as quite unfortunate—as embarrassing or reflective of some important problem or defect. Perhaps people have not yet thought deeply enough. When people theorize, by raising the level of abstraction, they do so to reveal bias, confusion, or inconsistency. Surely participants in a legal system should not abandon this effort.

There is a good deal of truth in these usual thoughts. Sometimes more in the way of abstraction does reveal prejudice or confusion. But this is not the whole story. On the contrary, incompletely theorized judgments are an important and valuable part of both private and public life. They help make law possible; they even help make life possible. Most of their virtues involve *the constructive uses of silence*, an exceedingly important social and legal phenomenon. Silence—on something that may prove false, obtuse, or excessively contentious—can help minimize conflict, allow the present to learn from the future, and save a great deal of time and expense. In law, as elsewhere, what is said is no more important than what is left unsaid. Certainly this is true for ordinary courts, which have limited expertise and democratic accountability, and whose limits lead them to be cautious.

My principal concern is the question of how judges on a multimember body should justify their opinions in public; the argument therefore has a great deal to do with the problem of collective choice. But some of the relevant points bear on other issues as well. They have implications for the question of how an individual judge not faced with the problem of producing a majority opinion—a judge on a trial court, for example—might write; they bear on the question of how a single judge, whether or not a member of a collective body, might think in private; and they relate to appropriate methods of both thought and justification wholly outside of adjudication and even outside of law.

Multimember Institutions

Begin with the special problem of public justification on a multimember body. The first and most obvious point is that incompletely theorized agreements are well-suited to a world—and especially a legal world—containing social dissensus on large-scale issues. By definition, such agreements have the large advantage of allowing a convergence on particular outcomes by people unable to reach an accord on general principles. This advantage is associated not only with the simple need to decide cases, but also with social stability, which could not exist if fundamental disagreements broke out in every case of public or private dispute.

Second, incompletely theorized agreements can promote two goals of a liberal democracy and a liberal legal system: to enable people to live together and to permit them to show each other a measure of reciprocity and mutual respect.[3] The use of low-level principles or rules generally allows judges on multimember bodies and hence citizens to find commonality and thus a common way of life without producing unnecessary antagonism. Both rules and low-level principles make it unnecessary to reach areas in which disagreement is fundamental.

Perhaps even more important, incompletely theorized agreements allow people to show each other a high degree of mutual respect, civility, or reciprocity. Frequently ordinary people disagree in some deep way on an issue—the Middle East, pornography, homosexual marriages—and sometimes they agree not to discuss that issue much, as a way of deferring to each other's strong convictions and showing a measure of reciprocity and respect (even if they do not at all respect the particular conviction that is at stake). If reciprocity and mutual respect are desirable, it follows that judges, perhaps even more than ordinary people, should not challenge a litigant's or another person's deepest and most defining commitments, at least if those commitments are reasonable and if there is no need for them to do so. Thus, for example, it would be better if judges intending to reaffirm *Roe v. Wade* could do so without challenging the judgment that the fetus is a human being.[4]

To be sure, some fundamental commitments might appropriately be challenged in the legal system or within other multimember bodies. Some commitments are ruled off-limits by the authoritative legal materials. Many provisions involving basic rights have this purpose. Of course it is not always disrespectful to disagree with someone in a fundamental way; on the contrary, such disagreements may sometimes reflect profound respect. When defining commitments are based on demonstrable errors of fact or logic, it is appropriate to contest them. So too when those commitments are rooted in a rejection of the basic dignity of all human beings, or when it is necessary to undertake the challenge to resolve a genuine problem. But many cases can be resolved in an incompletely theorized way, and that is all I am suggesting here.

Institutional arguments in law—especially those involving judicial restraint—are typically designed to bracket fundamental questions and to say that however those questions might be resolved in principle, courts should stand to one side. The allocation of certain roles has an important function of allowing outcomes to be reached without forcing courts to make decisions on fundamental issues. Those issues are resolved by reference to institutional competence, not on their merits.

In particular, the principle of stare decisis, which instructs courts to respect precedent, helps produce incompletely theorized agreements, and it helps to avoid constant struggle over basic principle. It serves this function precisely because it prevents people from having to build the world again, and together, every time a dispute arises. People can agree to follow precedent when they disagree on almost everything else. As a prominent example, consider the United States Supreme Court's refusal to overrule *Roe v. Wade,* where the justices emphasized the difficulties that would be produced by revisiting so large-scale a social controversy.[5] Members of the Court can accept the rule of precedent from diverse foundations and despite their many disagreements. Thus the justifications of the rule of precedent are diverse—involving predictability, efficiency, fairness, constraints on official discretion—and people who disagree on those justifications can agree on the practice, at least as a general rule.

Multimember Institutions and Individual Judges

Turn now to reasons that call for incompletely theorized agreements whether or not we are dealing with a multimember body. The first consideration here is that incompletely theorized agreements have the crucial function of reducing the political cost of enduring disagreements. If judges disavow large-scale theories, then losers in particular cases lose much less. They lose a decision, but not the world. They may win on another occasion. Their own theory has not been rejected or ruled inadmissible. When the authoritative rationale for the result is disconnected from abstract theories of the good or the right, the losers can submit to legal obligations, even if reluctantly, without being forced to renounce their largest ideals. I have said that some theories should be rejected or ruled inadmissible. But it is an advantage, from the standpoint of freedom and stability, for a legal system to be able to tell most losers—many of whom are operating from foundations that have something to offer or that cannot be ruled out a priori—that their own deepest convictions may play a role elsewhere in the law.

The second point is that incompletely theorized agreements are valuable when we seek moral evolution over time. Consider the area of constitutional equality, where considerable change has occurred in the past and will inevitably occur in the future. A completely theorized judgment would be unable to accommodate changes in facts or values. If the legal culture really did attain a theoretical end-state, it would become too rigid and calcified; we would know what we thought about everything. This would disserve posterity.

Incompletely theorized agreements are a key to debates over constitutional equality, with issues being raised about whether gender, sexual orientation, age, disability, and others are analogous to race; such agreements have the important advantage of allowing a large degree of openness to new facts and perspectives. At one point, we might think that homosexual relations are akin to incest; at another point, we might find the analogy bizarre. Of course a completely theorized judgment would have many virtues if it is correct. But at any particular moment in time, this is an unlikely prospect for human beings, not excluding judges.

A particular concern here is the effect of changing understandings of both facts and values. Consider ordinary life. At a certain time, you may well refuse to make decisions that seem foundational in character—for example, whether to get married within the next year, whether to have two, three, or four children, or whether to live in San Francisco or New York. Part of the reason for this refusal is knowledge that your understandings of both facts and values may well change. Indeed, your identity may itself change in important and relevant ways and for this reason a set of commitments in advance—something like a fully theorized conception of your life course—would make no sense.

Legal systems and nations are not so very different. If the Supreme Court is asked to offer a fully theorized conception of equality—in areas involving, for example, the rights of disabled people, children, and homosexuals—it may well respond that its job is to decide cases rather than to offer fully theorized accounts, partly because society should learn over time and partly because society's understandings of facts and values, in a sense its very identity, may well shift in unpredictable ways. This point bears on many legal issues. It helps support the case for incompletely theorized agreements.

The third point is practical. Incompletely theorized agreements may be the best approach that is available for people of limited time and capacities. Full theorization may be far too much to ask. A single judge faces this problem as much as a member of a multimember panel. Here too the rule of precedent is crucial; attention to precedent is liberating, not merely confining, since it frees busy people to deal with a restricted range of problems. Incompletely theorized agreements have the related advantage, for ordinary lawyers and judges, of humility and modesty. To engage in analogical reasoning, for example, one ordinarily need not take a stand on large, contested issues of social life, some of which can be resolved only on what will seem to many a sectarian basis. . . .

Fourth, incompletely theorized agreements are well adapted to a system that should or must take precedents as fixed points. This is a large advantage over more ambitious methods, since ambitious thinkers, in order to reach horizontal and vertical coherence, will probably be forced to disregard many decided cases. In light of the sheer number of decided cases and adjudicative officials, law cannot speak with one voice; full coherence in principle is unlikely in the extreme.

It is notable in this connection that for some judges and lawyers (lower court judges, for example), precedents truly are fixed (short of civil disobedience), whereas for others, including Supreme Court Justices, they are revisable, but only in extraordinary circumstances. If a judge or a lawyer were to attempt to reach full theorization, precedents would have at most the status of considered judgments about particular cases, and these might be revised when they run into conflict with something else that he believes and that is general or particular. This would cause many problems. Participants in a legal system aspiring to stability should not be so immodest as to reject judgments reached by others whenever those judgments could not be made part of reflective equilibrium for those particular participants. Thus the area of contract law is unlikely fully to cohere with the field of tort law or property; contract law is itself likely to contain multiple and sometimes inconsistent strands.

We can find many analogies in ordinary life. A parent's practices with his children may not fully cohere. Precedents with respect to bedtime, eating, homework, and much else are unlikely to be susceptible to systematization under a single principle. Of course, parents do not seek to be inconsistent. A child may feel justly aggrieved if a sibling is permitted to watch more hours of television for no apparent reason; but full coherence would be a lot to ask. The problem of reaching full consistency is all the more severe in law, where so many people have decided so many things, and where disagreements on large principles lurk in the background.

There is a more abstract point here. Human morality recognizes irreducibly diverse goods, which cannot be subsumed under a single "master" value.[6] The same is true for the moral values reflected in the law. Any simple, general, and monistic or single-valued theory of a large area of the law—free speech, contracts, property—is likely to be too crude to fit with our best understandings of the multiple values that are at stake in that area. It would be absurd to try to organize legal judgments through a single conception of value.

What can be said about law as a whole can be said about many particular areas of law. Monistic theories of free speech or property rights, for example, will fail to accommodate the range of values that speech and property implicate. Free speech promotes not simply democracy, but personal autonomy, economic progress, self-development, and other goals as well. Property rights are important not only for economic prosperity, but for democracy and autonomy too. We are unlikely to be able to appreciate the diverse values at stake, and to describe them with the specificity they deserve, unless we investigate the details of particular disputes.

This is not a decisive objection to general theories; a "top down" approach might reject monism and point to plural values.[7] Perhaps participants in democracy or law can describe a range of diverse values, each of them at a high level of abstraction; acknowledge that these values do not fall under a single master value; and use these values for assessing law. But even if correct, any such approach would run into difficulty because of an important practical fact: social disagreements about how best to describe or specify the relevant values. Moreover, any such approach is likely to owe its genesis and its proof—its point or points—to a range of particular cases on which it can build. Of course full theorization of an area of law would be acceptable, or even an occasion for great celebration, if it accounted for the plural values at issue. But this would be a most complex task, one that requires identification of a wide range of actual and likely cases. At least we can say that incompletely theorized judgments are well-suited to a moral universe that is diverse and pluralistic, not only in the sense that people disagree, but also in the sense that each of us is attuned to pluralism when we are thinking well about any area of law.

None of these points suggests that incompletely theorized agreements always deserve celebration. The virtues of such agreements are partial. Some incompletely theorized agreements are unjust. If an agreement is more fully theorized, it will provide greater notice to affected parties. Moreover, fuller theorization—in the form of wider and deeper inquiry into the grounds for judgment—may be valuable or even necessary to prevent inconsistency, bias, or self-interest. If judges on a panel have actually agreed on a general theory, and if they are really committed to it, they should say so. Judges and the general community will learn much more if they are able to discuss the true motivating grounds for outcomes. All these are valid considerations, and nothing I am saying here denies their importance.

JUDGES, THEORY, AND THE RULE OF LAW

There is a close association between the effort to attain incompletely theorized agreements and the rule of law ideal. Insofar as a legal system involves rule by law rather than rule by individual human beings, it tries to constrain judgments in advance. Some people think that the rule of law, properly understood, is a law of rules. . . . For the moment we can understand the rule of law more modestly. It is opposed to rule by individual human beings, who should not be permitted to govern as they wish through making law entirely of their choice in the context of actual disputes. Insofar as the rule of law prevents this from happening, it tries to prevent people in particular cases from invoking their own theories of the right or the good so as to make decisions according to their own most fundamental judgments.

Indeed, a prime purpose of the rule of law is to rule off-limits certain deep ideas of the right or the good, on the view that those ideas ought not to be invoked, most of the time, by judges and officials occupying particular social roles. Among the forbidden or presumptively forbidden ideas are, often, high-level views that are taken as too hubristic or sectarian precisely because they are so high-level. The presumption against high-level theories is an aspect of the ideal of the rule of law to the extent that it is an effort to limit the exercise of discretion at the point of application.

In this way we might make distinctions between the role of high theory within the courtroom and the role of high theory in the political branches of government. To be sure, incompletely theorized agreements play a role in democratic arenas; consider laws protecting endangered species or granting unions a right to organize. But in democratic arenas, there is no taboo, presumptive or otherwise, on invoking high-level theories of the good or the right.[8] On the contrary, such theories have played a key role in many social movements with defining effects on American constitutionalism, including the Civil War, the New Deal, the women's movement, and the environmental movement. Abstract, high-level ideas are an important part of democratic discussion, and sometimes they are ratified publicly and placed in a constitution.

By contrast, development of large-scale theories by ordinary courts is problematic and usually understood as such within the judiciary. The skepticism about large-scale theories is partly a result of the fact that such theories may require large-scale social reforms, and courts have enormous difficulties in implementing such reforms.[9] When courts invoke a large-scale theory as a reason for social change, they may well fail simply because they lack the tools to bring about change on their own. An important reason for judicial incapacity is that courts must decide on the legitimacy of rules that are aspects of complex systems. In invalidating or changing a single rule, courts may not do what they seek to do. They may produce unfortunate systemic effects, with unanticipated bad consequences that are not visible to them at the time of decision, and that may be impossible for them to correct thereafter.[10] Legislatures are in a much better position on this score. Consider, for example, an effort to reform landlord-tenant law. Judges may require landlords to provide decent housing for poor tenants, but the result may be to require landlords to raise rents, with detrimental effects on the poor. To say this is not to say that judge-initiated changes are always bad. But it is to say that the piecemeal quality of such changes is a reason for caution.

The claim that courts are ineffective in producing large-scale reform is a generalization, and it has the limits of all generalizations. The point does not count decisively against more ambitious judicial rulings when those rulings have a powerful legal and moral foundation. An ambitious ruling might announce an uncontestable high-level principle, and the announcement of the principle might be right even if courts lack implementing tools. What seems clear is that the difficulties of judge-led social reform provide a basis for judicial modesty. . . .

More fundamentally, it is in the absence of a democratic pedigree that the system of precedent, analogy, and incompletely theorized agreement has such an important place. The need to discipline judicial judgment arises from the courts' complex and modest place in any well-functioning constitutional system. To be sure, judges have, in some societies, a duty to interpret the Constitution, and sometimes that duty authorizes them to invoke relatively large-scale principles, seen as part and parcel of the Constitution as democratically ratified. Many people think that judicial activity is best characterized by reference to use of such principles.[11] Certainly there are occasions on which this practice is legitimate and even glorious.

To identify those occasions it would be necessary to develop a full theory of legal interpretation. For present purposes we can say something more modest. Most of judicial activity does not involve constitutional interpretation, and the ordinary work of common law decision and statutory interpretation calls for low-level principles on which agreements are possible. Indeed, constitutional argument itself is based largely on low-level principles, not on high theory, except on those rare occasions when more ambitious thinking becomes necessary to resolve a case or when the case for the ambitious theory is so insistent that a range of judges converge on it. And there are good reasons for the presumption in favor of low-level principles—having to do with the limited capacities of judges, the need to develop principles over time, the failure of monistic theories of the law, and the other considerations traced above. . . .

HERCULES AND THEORY

An Ambitious Alternative

Enthusiasm for incompletely theorized agreements meets with many adversaries. Let us take Ronald Dworkin as an especially prominent example. In his illuminating work on legal reasoning, Dworkin urges, at least as an ideal, a high degree of theoretical self-consciousness in adjudication. Dworkin argues that when lawyers disagree about what the law is with respect to some hard question—Can the government ban hate speech? Cross-burning?—they are disagreeing about "the best constructive interpretation of the community's legal practice."[12] Thus Dworkin claims that interpretation in law consists of different efforts to make a governing text "the best it can be." This is Dworkin's conception of law as integrity. Under that conception, judges try to fit their rulings to preexisting legal materials, but they also invoke principle, in the sense that they try to cast those materials in their best light. The goal of the judge is to analyze the case at hand under the two dimensions of "fit" and "justification."

Hercules, Dworkin's infinitely patient and resourceful judge, approaches the law in this way. It is important for our purposes that on Dworkin's view, judges are obliged to account for the existing legal materials, whether judge-made or statutory, by weaving them together into a coherent framework. Hence judges are not supposed to impose large-scale theories of their own making. Here we might appear to have the makings of an appreciation for incompletely theorized agreements, for reliance on precedent is a large part of those agreements.

But Dworkin does not defend incompletely theorized agreements. On the contrary, his account appears to require judges to develop high-level theories and does not (to say the least) favor theoretical modesty. In Dworkin's hands, the relevant theories are large and abstract; they sound just like political philosophy or moral theory. On his view, the law of tort reflects a theory of equality, and the law of free speech a theory of autonomy. These theories are derived from and brought to bear on particular problems. But this is not how real lawyers proceed. They try to avoid broad and abstract questions. Such questions are too hard, large, and open-ended for legal actors to handle. They prevent people who disagree on large principles from reaching consensus on particular outcomes. In this way, Hercules could not really participate in ordinary judicial deliberations; he would be seen as a usurper, even an oddball.

In thinking about equal protection issues, for example, lawyers (and ordinary people) do not generate large-scale theories about the meaning of equality in a democracy. Instead they ask what particular sorts of practices seem clearly to violate the Fourteenth Amendment or the principle of equality, and then whether a measure discriminating against (for example) the handicapped is relevantly similar or relevantly different. Of course the description of relevant similarities and differences will have evaluative dimensions, and of course these should be made explicit. As we will see, an analogy depends for its plausibility on a principle of some sort. But lawyers and judges try not to engage in abstract political theorizing. They avoid such theorizing because it takes too much time and may be unnecessary; because it may go wrong insofar as it operates without close reference to actual cases; because it often prevents people from getting along at all; and because general theorizing can seem or be disrespectful insofar as it forces people to contend, unnecessarily, over their deepest and most defining moral commitments. Consider in this connection the idea that courts should not resolve constitutional issues unless they must in order to decide a case—an idea that imposes a presumptive taboo on judicial judgments about society's most basic or defining commitments.[13]

Dworkin anticipates an objection of this kind. He notes that it might be paralyzing for judges to seek a general theory for each area of law, and he acknowledges that Hercules is more methodical than any real-world judge can be. But Hercules, in Dworkin's view, "shows us the hidden structure of" ordinary "judgments and so lays these open to study and criticism."[14] Of course Hercules aims at a "comprehensive theory" of each area of law, whereas ordinary judges, unable to consider all lines of inquiry, must aim at a theory that is "partial." But Hercules's "judgments of fit and political morality are made on the same material and have the same character as theirs."

It is these points that I am denying here. The decisions of ordinary judges are based on different material and have a different character. They are less deeply theorized, not only because of limits of time and capacity, but also because of the distinctive morality of judging in a pluralistic society. I will qualify this claim below. But for the moment, the point suggests that the ordinary judge is no Hercules with less time on his hands, but a different sort of figure altogether.

CONCEPTUAL ASCENT?

Borrowing from Henry Sidgwick's writings on ethical method,[15] an enthusiast for ambitious thinking might respond in the following way. There is often good reason for judges to raise the level of abstraction and ultimately to resort to large-scale theory. As a practical matter, concrete judgments about particular cases will prove inadequate for morality or law. Sometimes people do not have clear intuitions about how cases should come out; their intuitions are uncertain or shifting. Sometimes seemingly similar cases provoke different reactions, and it is necessary to raise the level of theoretical ambition to explain whether those different reactions are justified or to show that the seemingly similar cases are different after all. Sometimes people simply disagree. By looking at broader principles, we may be able to mediate the disagreement. In any case there is a problem of explaining our considered judgments about particular cases, in order to see whether they are not just a product of accident,[16] and at some point the law will want to offer that explanation.

For these reasons, a judge who does not theorize might end up being Herculean too. At least he had better have that aspiration in mind. When our modest judge joins an opinion that is incompletely theorized, he has to rely on a reason or a principle, justifying one outcome rather than another. The opinion must itself refer to a reason or principle; it cannot just announce a victor. Perhaps the low-level principle is wrong because it fails to fit with other cases or because it is not defensible as a matter of (legally relevant) political morality.

In short, the incompletely theorized agreement may be nothing to celebrate. It may be wrong or unreliable. The fact that people converge may be a kind of coincidence or an accident, and when they start thinking more deeply, they may be able to tell whether the judgment is really right. Thus if a judge is reasoning well, he should have before him a range of other cases, C through Z, in which the principle is tested against others and refined. At least if he is a distinguished judge, he will experience a kind of "conceptual ascent," in which the more or less isolated and small low-level principle is finally made part of a more general theory. Perhaps this would be a paralyzing task, and perhaps our judge need not often attempt it. But it is an appropriate model for understanding law and an appropriate aspiration for judges.

The conceptual ascent seems especially desirable in light of the fact that incompletely theorized agreements will allow large pockets of inconsistency. Some areas of the law may appear coherent and make internal sense, but they may run into each other if they are compared. We may have a coherent category of law involving sex equality (though this would be fortunate indeed), and a coherent category involving racial equality (same qualification), but these categories may have a very strange and unsatisfactory relation to the categories involving sexual orientation and the handicapped. Various subcategories of tort law may make sense, but they may not fit together at all. More ambitious forms of reasoning seem necessary in order to test the low-level principles. In this way we might conclude that judges should think of incompletely theorized agreements as an early step toward something both wider and deeper. Many academic understandings of law, including economic analysis, undertake the task of showing that wider and deeper conception.[17]

There is some truth in this response. Moral reasoners should try to achieve vertical and horizontal consistency, not just the local pockets of coherence offered by incompletely theorized agreements. In democratic processes it is appropriate and sometimes indispensable to challenge existing practice in abstract terms. But the response ignores some of the distinctive characteristics of the arena in which real-world judges must do their work. Some of these limits involve bounded rationality and thus what should happen in a world in which judges face various constraints; some of them involve limits of role and appropriate judicial morality in a world in which judges are mere actors in a complex system, and in which people legitimately disagree on first principles. In light of these limits, incompletely theorized agreements have the many virtues described above, including the facilitation of convergence, the reduction of costs of disagreement, and the demonstration of humility and mutual respect.

As I have noted, incompletely theorized agreements are especially well-adapted to a system that must take precedents as fixed points; lawyers could not try to reach full integrity without severely compromising the system of precedent. Usually local coherence is the most to which lawyers may aspire. Just as legislation cannot be understood as if it came from a single mind, so too precedents, compiled by many people responding to different problems in many different periods, will not reflect a single authorial voice.

There are many lurking questions. How do we know whether moral or political judgments are right? What is the relation between provisional or considered judgments about particulars and corresponding judgments about abstractions? Sometimes people write as if abstract theoretical judgments, or abstract theories, have a kind of reality and hardness that particular judgments lack, or as if abstract theories provide the answers to examination questions that particular judgments, frail as they are, may pass or fail. On this view, theories are searchlights that illuminate particular judgments and show them for what they really are. But we might think instead that there is no special magic in theories or abstractions, and that theories are simply the (humanly constructed) means by which people make sense of the judgments that constitute their ethical and political worlds. The abstract deserves no priority over the particular; neither should be treated as foundational. A (poor or crude) abstract theory may be a confused way of trying to make sense of our considered judgments about particular cases, which may be much better than the theory. In fact it is possible that moral judgments are best described not as an emanation of a broad theory, but instead as part of a process of reflection about prototypical cases or "precedents" from which moral thinkers—ordinary citizens and experts—work.[18]

LEGITIMACY

There is a final issue. Dworkin's conception of law as integrity contains a theory of what it means for law to be legitimate. Hercules, Dworkin's idealized judge, can produce vertical and horizontal consistency among judgments of principle in law. The same cannot be said of those who urge incompletely theorized agreements. A legal system pervaded by such agreements need not yield anything like full coherence. Perhaps this is a decisive defect. Perhaps it suffers from the standpoint of those who seek legitimacy in law.

Of course principled consistency should not be disparaged, and of course a regime of principled judgments has many advantages over imaginable alternatives. Of course problems of legitimacy may arise precisely because of the absence of such consistency. If you are treated differently from someone else—if you are treated worse or better—there should be a reason for the difference in treatment. In fact, however, the idea of integrity—insofar as it is focused on the judiciary—does not provide a convincing theory of legitimacy. Integrity, if a product of good judicial judgment, is neither necessary nor sufficient for legitimacy. Legitimacy stems not simply from principled consistency on the part of adjudicators, but from a justifiable exercise of authority, which requires a theory of just institutions. That theory should in turn be founded in democratic considerations, suitably constrained by an account of what interests should be immunized from democratic intrusion. Legitimacy is an outcome of well-functioning democratic processes, not of a system of distinction-making undertaken by judges. Even if done exceptionally well, distinction-making by principled judges is too court-centered as a source of legitimacy.

Those who stress incompletely theorized agreements insist that adjudication is part of a complex set of institutional arrangements, most prominently including democratic arenas. They attempt to design their theory of judicial judgment as an aspect of a far broader set of understandings about appropriate institutional arrangements and about forums in which the (suitably constrained) public can deliberate about its judgments. For reasons of both policy and principle, the development of large-scale theories of the right and the good is a democratic task, not a judicial one. These remarks should suggest the ingredients of an account of legitimacy of which incompletely theorized agreements would be a part. . . .

NOTES

1. Lochner v. New York, 198 U.S. 48, 69 (1908) (Holmes, J., dissenting).
2. See, e.g., Charles Fried, *Contract as Promise: A Theory of Contractual Obligation* (Cambridge: Harvard University Press, 1981); Ronald M. Dworkin, *Law's Empire* (Cambridge: Harvard University Press, 1986).
3. See John Rawls, *Political Liberalism* (New York: Columbia University Press, 1993), pp. 16–17, 50.
4. This is the goal of the equal protection argument. See Cass R. Sunstein, *The Partial Constitution* (Cambridge: Harvard University Press, 1993), ch. 9.
5. See Planned Parenthood v. Casey, 112 S. Ct. 2791 (1992). . . .
6. I borrow here from Joseph Raz, "The Relevance of Coherence," in *Ethics in the Public Domain: Essays in the Morality of Law and Politics* (Oxford: Oxford University Press, 1994), p. 261.
7. See Amartya K. Sen, *Commodities and Capabilities* (Amsterdam: North-Holland, 1985).
8. I am putting to one side the questions raised by "comprehensive views," see Rawls, supra note [3].
9. See Gerald N. Rosenberg, *The Hollow Hope: Can Courts Bring about Social Change?* (Chicago: University of Chicago Press, 1991).
10. Examples are offered in R. Shep Melnick, *Regulation and the Courts: The Case of the Clean Air Act* (Washington, D.C.: Brookings Institution, 1983), and Donald Horowitz, *The Courts and Social Policy* (Washington, D.C.: Brookings Institution, 1977). The point is described from the theoretical point of view in Lon Fuller, The Forms and Limits of Adjudication, 92 Harv. L. Rev. 353 (1978), and Joseph Raz, The Inner Logic of the Law, in *Ethics in the Public Domain*, supra note [6], at 224.
11. This is the vision of judicial review in Bruce A. Ackerman, *We the People, vol. 1: Foundations* (Cambridge: Harvard University Press, 1991). Note that it differs dramatically from the understanding in Ronald Dworkin, *Law's Empire*, in the sense that Ackerman insists that large-scale principles have sources in actual judgments of "we the people." There is, however, a commonality between Ackerman and Dworkin in the sense that both see the use of such principles as a large part of the Court's work. It is along that dimension that I am doubting both of their accounts. . . .
12. Dworkin, supra note 2, at 224.
13. See Alexander M. Bickel, *The Least Dangerous Branch: The Supreme Court at the Bar of Politics* (New Haven: Yale University Press, 1986).
14. Dworkin, supra note 2, at 265.
15. See Henry Sidgwick, *The Methods of Ethics*, 7th ed. (New York: Dover, 1966), pp. 96–104.
16. "[T]he resulting code seems an accidental aggregate of precepts, which stands in need of some rational synthesis." Sidgwick, supra note [15], at 102.
17. See Richard A. Posner, *Economic Analysis of Law*, 4th ed. (Boston: Little Brown, 1992); see also the discussion of the law of tort in Dworkin, supra note 2.
18. "One's ability to recognize instances of cruelty, patience, meanness, and courage, for example, far outstrips one's capacity for verbal definition of those notions." Paul M. Churchland, *The Engine of Reason, the Seat of the Soul* (Cambridge: MIT Press, 1995), p. 145; see also id. at 144, 293.

PART 2

JURISPRUDENCE

The fundamental question of jurisprudence is "What is the nature of law?" This question has fascinated thinkers since at least the time of the Greeks. In fact, Sophocles' famous play, *Antigone,* presents two opposing answers that became prominent in subsequent jurisprudence.[1] In the play, Antigone's brother, Polyneices, has been killed in battle against Thebes. Creon, the King of Thebes, has forbidden the burial of Polyneices' body. Creon claims the right to make this law in virtue of his position as king. Antigone, however, refuses to obey; she attempts to bury Polyneices. As her authority, she cites a law higher than the one set by Creon—a law whose force derives from a divinely ordained natural order. This opposition represents two distinct answers to the nature-of-law question. Creon's view exemplifies what has come to be known as the tradition of legal positivism. This is the view that law is set by "position"; that is, laws are made by the rulers of political communities and derive all of their authority from that origin. According to this view, there is no essential connection between law and morality; the force of law is separate and distinct from that of morals. The alternative, expressed by Antigone, has become known as the natural law tradition. Natural law theorists believe that the authority of positive law rests in part on its conformity with moral standards. An extreme version of this belief is expressed in Augustine's claim that "an unjust law is no law at all." According to this view, positive laws must conform to a higher moral law if they are to retain legitimacy.

Natural law has had a long and venerable tradition. The Roman philosopher Cicero and the Stoics held early versions of natural law theory, and philosophers and theologians such as Augustine and Thomas Aquinas championed Christian versions of the view through the Middle Ages.[2] Hugo Grotius and Samuel Pufendorf developed it in the early modern period; it was embraced in the eighteenth century by the renowned English jurist William Blackstone.[3] In the twentieth century, versions of natural law theory have been developed by many thinkers, including Lon L. Fuller and John Finnis.[4]

In contrast, legal positivism remained relatively undeveloped until it was taken up by the philosophers

---

[1]Sophocles, *Antigone,* ed. Brendan Kennelly (Newcastle upon Tyne, England: Bloodaxe Books, 1996).

[2]See Cicero, *The Republic, and The Laws,* trans. Niall Rudd (New York: Oxford University Press, 1998); on the Stoics, see Martha C. Nussbaum, *The Therapy of Desire: Theory and Practice in Hellenistic Ethics* (Princeton, NJ: Princeton University Press, 1994); Augustine, *On Free Choice of the Will,* trans. Thomas Williams (Indianapolis, IN: Hackett, 1983); and Thomas Aquinas, *On Law, Morality, and Politics,* ed. William R. Baumgarth and Richard J. Regan, S.J. (Indianapolis, IN: Hackett, 1988).

[3]See Hugo Grotius, *The Law of War and Peace,* trans. Louise R. Loomis (Roslyn, NY: W. J. Black, 1949); Samuel Pufendorf, *On the Duty of Man and Citizen According to Natural Law,* ed. James Tully (Cambridge, England: Cambridge University Press, 1991); and William Blackstone, *Commentaries on the Laws of England,* vols. 1–4 (Chicago, IL: University of Chicago Press, 1979).

[4]See Fuller, *The Morality of Law* (New Haven, CT: Yale University Press, 1969); and Finnis, *Natural Law and Natural Rights* (Oxford, England: Clarendon, 1980).

Thomas Hobbes and Jeremy Bentham.[5] The readings of Part 2 begin with an excerpt from the first major legal positivist, John Austin, whose seminal work, *The Province of Jurisprudence Determined,* a series of lectures given at the University of London in the late 1820s and early 1830s, began what has become known as the command theory of law. Austin's theory is interesting not only as an example of early positivism, but also as one of the first attempts in the field of analytical jurisprudence, which has formed the backbone of Anglo-American jurisprudence. Central to analytical jurisprudence is the idea that one can construct theories of law and of legal systems by analyzing and exploring the interrelations among basic legal concepts.

Austin carefully distinguishes positive laws, or laws "from man to man," from natural law, or the law of God to man. The former, not the latter, is the proper province of jurisprudence. According to Austin, we should understand positive law in terms of a command. Austin defines *command* as an expressed desire from one person to another that the other should act or refrain from acting in some way, where the desire is backed up with the threat of punishment. The liability of being punished distinguishes commands from other expressions of desire. The one to whom the command is expressed becomes bound or obliged, or comes under a duty to obey. A *law* is a command that generally obliges a person or persons to the acts or forbearances of a class. Laws proceed from superiors and bind or oblige inferiors. One's "superiority" here means might, or the power of inflicting pain or evil on another and thereby forcing the other, through fear of that evil, to conform his or her conduct to one's wishes.

Austin admits exceptions to his general thesis that law is a species of command. First, some laws that are not commands are nonetheless properly included within the scope of jurisprudence. Second, some laws are commands but seem not imperative. Austin's awkward struggles with these exceptions to his general thesis should alert us that the idea of "command" is not as central or pervasive to the analysis of law as Austin claims.

The command theory is forcefully and elegantly critiqued in the next reading selection, which is excerpted from H. L. A. Hart's book, *The Concept of Law.* Hart, like Austin a positivist, compares the command of Austin's sovereign with a gunman's threat. As with Austin's sovereign, a gunman can express a desire that another act or refrain from acting, and this desire can be backed with the threat of a sanction in case of noncompliance. But no one thinks that the gunman's threat creates an obligation for the victim to comply. In Hart's terms, the victim is obliged, but not obligated, to comply with the gunman's threat. So, too, in the case of Austin's sovereign: A subject might be obliged to obey the sovereign's command, but no obligation to obey has been created. At most, Austin's theory allows us to predict that certain forms of behavior will conform with the requirements of legal rules. It thereby provides us with an external perspective on legal rules, the perspective of an outside observer who, without participating in a social practice, can nonetheless detect regular patterns of behavior from which he or she can make predictions. To understand the nature of legal obligation, and of social obligation more generally, we have to consider what Hart calls the internal perspective on rules. The *internal perspective* is that of a member of a social group who accepts and uses a rule or set of rules as a guide to conduct. Legal rules are a subset of obligation-imposing social rules that members of a group accept as normative for certain kinds of conduct.

In a legal system, legal rules are divided into two broad groups: primary rules that regulate action and secondary rules that are about primary rules. One can imagine fairly primitive societies characterized by only primary rules. Such pre-legal societies, Hart thinks, would exhibit three defects: uncertainty about what the rules are, static or unchanging rules, and inefficiency in enforcing compliance with the rules. For each of these defects, we can find a remedy in the form of a secondary rule. The remedy for uncertainty is the rule of recognition—the fundamental and often unstated rule that serves as the ultimate and authoritative source of all other rules in the legal system. The rule of recognition identifies valid sources of law and often provides ways of ranking these sources and their respective laws in cases of conflict. The remedy for the static character of rules in a pre-legal society is rules of change, that is, secondary rules for the introduction, revision, or repeal of primary rules. The remedy for inefficiency is rules of adjudication, that is, rules that identify judges, courts, jurisdictions, and procedures for judging.

---

[5]See Hobbes, *Leviathan,* ed. C. B. MacPherson (Harmondsworth, England: Penguin, 1968); and Jeremy Bentham, *An Introduction to the Principles of Morals and Legislation,* ed. J. H. Burns and H. L. A. Hart (London: Methuen, 1982).

Hart's theory of law as a union of primary and secondary rules is subjected to rigorous criticism by Ronald M. Dworkin in "The Model of Rules I." Law, Dworkin argues, consists not only of rules, but also of standards. Standards are of two types: principles and policies. Principles articulate requirements of justice, fairness, or morality. They frequently express rights. Policies, in contrast, set out some desirable economic, social, or political goal to be achieved. Dworkin makes his case not only by analyzing the distinctive logical properties of rules and standards, but also by examining actual legal cases. Two cases, *Riggs v. Palmer,* decided in New York in 1889, and *Henningsen v. Bloomfield Motors, Inc.,*[6] decided in New Jersey in 1960, are especially instructive. In *Riggs,* which is included here, the question before the court was whether a grandson who had murdered his grandfather could inherit under the terms of the will. The grandson was named as heir, and the statute of wills for New York state was silent on the question of whether a convicted murderer could inherit. The court admitted that the rules would allow the grandson to inherit, but it ruled against his claim on grounds of principle. In the court's opinion, the moral principle that no one should profit from his or her own wrongdoing controlled the statute of wills in *Riggs,* and thereby prevented the murderer from inheriting. Similar but more complex reasoning appears in *Henningsen.* Henningsen had signed a warranty limiting an automobile manufacturer's liability to covering the cost of defective parts. He argued, however, that the manufacturer should be held liable for medical and other expenses of persons hurt in a crash. Invoking a complex chain of reasoning consisting of policies as well as principles, the court ruled in Henningsen's favor, contrary to the explicit terms of the warranty he had signed.

Dworkin's theory is a decisive rejection of positivism. In claiming that law consists of standards as well as rules, his view implies that law has essential moral content—a claim traditionally rejected by positivists. His view also has implications for the positivists' theory of judicial discretion, their analysis of legal obligation, and their theory of the rule of recognition. For example, if law is a system of primary and secondary rules, as Hart contends, then there is a point at which legal rules end. Positivist judges who must adjudicate cases at the margins of legal rules must therefore look beyond the rules to extralegal considerations to decide such cases. A Dworkinian judge, however, would be obligated to look to legal standards in addition to legal rules. In addition, positivists believe that legal obligations are created only by rules. But if standards are also a part of law, as Dworkin believes, then standards, too, can legally obligate. Finally, positivists believe that in many legal systems, an overall rule of recognition can identify all of a system's laws. But belief in such a rule becomes untenable if we acknowledge a complex body of common-law principles and policies as part of law, as Dworkin urges.

Dworkin has developed his theory much further in subsequent works.[7] As was stated in Part 1, Dworkin's theory has become the prevailing liberal paradigm in contemporary jurisprudence and has been dubbed "law as integrity." Many philosophers and lawyers have attacked law as integrity from within the tradition of political liberalism. A recent liberal critique, by Cass R. Sunstein, is included in Part 1. Other theorists, representing entire schools of jurisprudential thought, reject altogether the liberal paradigm, and comment on the nature of law from other, quite distinctive vantage points. Among the latter is John Finnis, a contemporary natural law theorist, whose ideas are presented in Part 2 in an excerpt from "Natural Law and Legal Reasoning." In his view, a theory of natural law is essentially a theory of human good as principles of practical reasoning. He identifies seven basic human goods that ought to be pursued and respected in rational choices and actions: human life; knowledge; excellence in work and in play; harmony between individuals and groups; harmony between one's feelings and one's judgments and choices; harmony between one's judgments and choices and one's behavior; and harmony between oneself and the larger reality, including harmony between oneself and the divine. These basic goods are the ultimate reasons for choices and actions that instantiate and express human nature. Though they give us reasons for acting, they also, and more fundamentally, given the constraints of the human condition (we cannot actively

[6]32 N.J. 358, 161 A. 2d 69 (1960).

[7]See especially Dworkin, *Law's Empire* (London: Fontana Paperbacks, 1986). An excerpt from this book is included in Part 1 of this volume, and a more thorough discussion of it is included in the introduction to that part.

pursue every opportunity to realize every human good), give us reasons against acting in ways that destroy the instantiation of any of the basic goods in human persons. Thus, they provide a system of moral absolutes—absolute prohibitions on certain kinds of action. As Finnis states, these moral absolutes "give legal reasoning its backbone" (see p. 109). The prohibitions they articulate—for example, injunctions against violence to persons and theft of property—are fundamental to various branches of law.

Another important feature of the basic goods is that they are incommensurable values; that is, there is no single overarching standard or metric against which rational comparisons of the basic goods can be made. This does not make the choice of an instantiation of one good over another irrational, however. The choice to instantiate one good in preference to another can be perfectly rational yet motivated by the subjective dispositions and preferences of the chooser. The incommensurability of the basic goods is reflected in many of the dilemmas posed by legal reasoning and has direct implications, Finnis argues, for the analysis of judicial decision making offered in Dworkin's recent work. Contrary to Dworkin and to many other theorists, Finnis believes that the incommensurability of the basic goods shows that there are definite limits to the power and scope of legal reasoning.

Issues of rational choice raised by the incommensurability of the basic goods lead Finnis to comment briefly on a school of jurisprudential thought known as the economic analysis of law. One of the main champions, but now a skeptic, of this movement is Richard A. Posner, a federal judge for the U.S. Court of Appeals for the Seventh Circuit. The movement is sweeping in its assertions, contending that practically all branches and activities of law can be explained in terms of the workings of a few basic economic assumptions and principles. The claims of the economic analysts are both descriptive and normative. Not only can law and legal activities be described in terms of economic analysis, but law should be conducted in conformity with economic assumptions and principles.

The central assumption of economic analysis, according to Posner, is that all people, except for children and the retarded, as well as those suffering from temporary mental impairments, are rational maximizers of their satisfactions. This putative fact grounds both the descriptive and normative claims of the economic analysis movement, for economic analysts take as fundamental the notion that wealth maximization is and should be the overriding goal of the legal system. The "wealth" in "wealth maximization," Posner points out, does not refer to money only. Rather, it refers to the sum of all tangible and intangible goods and services, weighted by two kinds of prices: the offer price (the price someone is willing to pay for a good or service) and the asking price (the price someone wants to receive for a good or service). Posner argues that the activities of legislatures and judges and the operations of familiar common-law rules can be understood as roughly conforming to the dictates of wealth maximization. In fact, some economic analysts endeavor to explain the entire body of the common law with a handful of economic principles, such as cost-benefit analysis, free rider prevention, decision making under uncertainty, risk aversion, and the promotion of mutually beneficial exchanges.

Whether this descriptive enterprise will succeed remains to be seen. Whether wealth maximization is normatively desirable as the overriding goal of our legal system is a deeper and more complex issue. Posner himself indicates a serious drawback of the wealth maximization ethic—its reliance on market activities, which in turn depend on luck. As he points out, the distribution of productivity among a population might depend on factors that are arbitrary from a moral point of view, such as one's genetic makeup, social upbringing, or place of birth. The "luck of the draw" might well influence a person's prospects for wealth maximization at any given time in any given society. But should it also affect one's legal rights and duties and the principles of law that regulate society? At the end of his selection, Posner tends to answer, "No."

Natural law theorists and economic analysts have launched critiques of the prevailing liberal paradigm of justice from the conservative end of the political spectrum. However, a range of trenchant criticisms has also come from the left. One such family of criticisms, informed significantly by Marxist social theory, is the Critical Legal Studies (CLS) movement. We include here a selection by one of its foremost proponents, Roberto Mangabeira Unger. Unger discusses the critical and constructive dimensions of the CLS movement, which takes critical aim at objectivism on the one hand and formalism on the other. According to Unger, *objectivism* is the belief that authoritative legal materials—statutes, case law, and legal ideas—compose an acceptable scheme of human association and that they display, albeit imperfectly, the main contours of an intelligible moral order. By *formalism,* Unger means a commitment to, and belief in the possibility of, methods of legal justification that contrast with open-ended or ideological disputes about the basic terms of social life and, in virtue of that contrast, claim adjudicative authority. Formalism views impersonal purposes, principles, and policies as indispensable tools for conflict resolution.

Objectivism and formalism are exemplified by the prevailing liberal paradigm in jurisprudence, as well as by the economic analysis of law. The CLS movement takes aim at Dworkin's idea that current forms of legal reasoning and individual legal decisions can be justified by reference to a larger scheme of political morality that is historically embedded in Western democratic tradition. CLS also rejects the economic analysts' idea that a descriptive and normative legal framework of wealth maximization can be derived from and justified by the basis of principles of economic theory and assumptions about the economic nature of people. The scope of CLS critiques is sweeping—aiming at nothing less than the complete overthrow of prevailing ideas about the nature, purposes, and character of law and legal reasoning.

Among other critical methods that Unger mentions, two are of interest for their constructive implications: the methods of internal development and of visionary insight. The method of internal development sees transformative power as implicit in conflicts between social ideals and their flawed actualizations in present society. The method is essentially one of mutual correction and development: A flawed embodiment is corrected in light of an abstract social ideal; the ideal is then revised with reference to the new embodiment. The outcome is an ongoing process of social transformation. The method of internal development starts with the materials available within a particular legal tradition then gradually transforms that tradition from within. By contrast, the method of visionary insight presents an ideal of an entirely reordered social world. According to Unger, such an ideal should be supported by a credible theory of transformation, armed with insight into human personality and guided by the goal of extending the possibilities for human connection. The two transformative methods share similarities as well as differences. Whereas the method of visionary insight starts with an ideal of a reordered world, the method of internal development ends with it. Perhaps more important than this difference, however, is a similarity. Both techniques seize on deviations in current practice and either imagine them transformed or actually transform them into new legal and social realities.

The need for new legal and social realities is the leitmotif of Critical Race Theory (CRT), the historical, ideological, and methodological offspring of the CLS movement. Motivated by the persistent and pervasive presence of racism in law and society, critical race theorists have adopted the radical ideology and methods of the CLS movement in efforts to expose and transform the presently racist legal and social practice. The authors of the selection given here, which is part of an introduction to a volume of seminal essays by critical race theorists, discuss several of the dominant concerns of the CRT movement. Foremost among them is a disenchantment with the traditional civil rights discourse that emerged from the Civil Rights movement of the 1960s and early 1970s. Though it helped lead to the CRT movement, this discourse is firmly entrenched in mainstream political liberalism. One legacy of this discourse, according to CRT theorists, is that racial justice is conceptualized in a way that excludes the possibility of radical and transformative critique. In short, racism is narrowly defined from "the perpetrator's perspective," as an intentional, but irrational, deviation by a conscious wrongdoer from an otherwise neutral, and therefore just, status quo. The legal conception of racism in terms of discrete, identifiable acts of prejudice insulates from radical critique the pervasive and systemic racism of social institutions and everyday practices.

Debates on affirmative action aptly illustrate this. According to CRT theorists, mainstream liberal and conservative thought simply assumes the justice of the current system of meritocracy, or "just deserts," in employment and academia. Racial discrimination is constructed as an aberration against an otherwise just background. However, CRT maintains that the justice of background social institutions themselves must be questioned. In particular, the idea that the mythology of "merit" represents a race-neutral moral category, so crucial in the affirmative action debate, must be exploded.

Two other familiar stances taken in affirmative action debates also warrant mention. One position frequently taken in mainstream liberal and conservative thought is that social policy should be guided by a moral norm of "color blindness." This position implies that any race-based deviation from this norm amounts to unjustifiable racial discrimination. The view thereby obliterates the distinction, crucial for effective affirmative action, between race consciousness and racism itself. Another liberal view of affirmative action is that race-conscious preference in employment and academia is a necessary evil in efforts to overcome the effects of past racial discrimination. Both views, according to CRT theorists, betray the poverty of the liberal imagination insofar as both accept the basic justice of the status quo and equate racism with race-motivated departures from it. What is needed is to push beyond traditional liberal and conservative construals of race and racism to new understandings of race-conscious identity and the social meanings of these new understandings. In forging such a campaign, CRT sees itself as heir to a tradition of radicalism in legal thought that begins with the legal realist movement of the 1920s and 1930s (see the introduction to Part 1 in this volume) and continues with the CLS movement begun in the 1970s.

In the last article on jurisprudence, "Feminist Legal Critics: The Reluctant Radicals," Patricia Smith traces the philosophical history of the feminist movement in jurisprudential thought, which, like CRT theory, criticizes the prevailing liberal paradigm. Smith observes that in the early days of feminist legal analysis, feminist critics worked within the parameters of political liberalism. The liberal tradition in the United States began with the assumption that only white, Christian, property-owning men were entitled to rights. Persons who differed from the white-male standard, such as Negro slaves, Native Americans, Chinese immigrants, and women, were initially viewed as subhuman, inferior, and not entitled to the full panoply of rights and privileges enjoyed by white-male property owners or to equal treatment by the law. Early feminist battles, and significant gains for women, were won by extending to women the same legal rights and privileges accorded to white men under the dominant liberal paradigm. However, as Smith makes clear in her discussion of the evolution of sex discrimination in equal protection law, the central problem with liberalism is its reliance on allegedly neutral, impartial standards and principles. These standards are meant to apply with equal justice to men and women alike. Yet the standards themselves are not neutral; they incorporate a male bias. The inability of courts to recognize the bias of legal standards retards the courts' efforts to render unbiased justice in particular cases. Worse, it prevents courts from addressing systematic injustices that result from inherently patriarchal social institutions and norms. Thus, as with CLS and CRT scholars, feminist legal critics have challenged the liberal tradition's reliance on objectivism and formalism and have pushed toward increasingly radical critiques of the liberal paradigm in their pursuit of justice for women.

Radical feminist critiques focus on aspects of the unequal power dynamics between men and women that are embodied in and propagated by contemporary law. As Smith notes, Catherine MacKinnon's groundbreaking work, for example, exposes many current legal norms and practices as the means by which men dominate and subordinate women in society. Deborah Rhode and Christine Littleton analyze the unequal power dynamics in law in terms of disadvantage instead of domination. Martha Minow examines court practices, especially Supreme Court practices, in terms of unexamined assumptions that yield what she calls "dilemmas of difference," that is, choices that reinforce disadvantage, no matter which option is taken. These differing analyses make the same essential points: that law reflects and perpetuates the social subordination of women to men, that it does this by perpetuating a network of patriarchal norms and institutions, and that both law and the patriarchal structures it upholds are legitimated by hitherto unexamined, and thus unchallenged, sexist prejudice.

At the end of her article, Smith suggests that even radical feminist critiques are not incompatible with liberal values. Patriarchy, she argues, is not an essential part of political liberalism. We need to hold fast to legitimate liberal ideals, such as universal human rights and equality before the law, while rejecting the patriarchal structures and norms that deny those values. While this will require deep and extensive legal and social reforms, it will not, in Smith's opinion, mandate such radical tactics as revolution and the overthrow of the government and the Constitution. Though not all feminists would agree, even radical feminists are, in Smith's view, reluctant radicals.

We include the following selections with the hope of giving you some insight into the complexity of law, as well as some idea of the power and vitality of scholarship, both past and present, in jurisprudence. For more information, you should consult not only the list of selected readings at the end of Part 2 but also Part 1, on legal reasoning.

SELECTED READINGS

Baumgarth, William R., and Richard J. Regan, eds. *Saint Thomas Aquinas: On Law, Morality, and Politics.* Indianapolis, IN: Hackett, 1988.

Dworkin, Ronald M. *Freedom's Law: The Moral Reading of the American Constitution.* Cambridge, MA: Harvard University Press, 1996.

———. *Law's Empire.* London: Fontana Paperbacks, 1986.

Finnis, John. *Natural Law and Natural Rights.* Oxford, England: Clarendon Press, 1980.

Fitzpatrick, Peter, and Alan Hunt, eds. *Critical Legal Studies.* Oxford, England: Basil Blackwell, 1987.

Fuller, Lon. *The Morality of Law,* rev. ed. New Haven, CT: Yale University Press, 1964.

Hart, H. L. A., and Tony Honore. *Causation in the Law.* Oxford, England: Oxford University Press, 1985.

Helman, Mark. *A Guide to Critical Legal Studies.* Cambridge, MA: Harvard University Press, 1987.

Posner, Richard A. *The Economics of Justice.* Cambridge, MA: Harvard University Press, 1983.

———. *Overcoming Law.* Cambridge, MA: Harvard University Press, 1995.

———. *The Problem of Jurisprudence.* Cambridge, MA: Harvard University Press, 1990.

Rhode, Deborah L. *Justice and Gender.* Cambridge, MA: Harvard University Press, 1989.

Smith, Patricia, ed. *Feminist Jurisprudence.* New York: Oxford University Press, 1993.

Tully, James, ed. *Samuel Pufendorf: On the Duty of Man and Citizen.* Cambridge, England: Cambridge University Press, 1996.

7

JOHN AUSTIN

From *The Province of Jurisprudence Determined*

LECTURE I

The matter of jurisprudence is positive law: law, simply and strictly so called: or law set by political superiors to political inferiors. But positive law (or law, simply and strictly so called) is often confounded with objects to which it is related by *resemblance,* and with objects to which it is related in the way of *analogy:* with objects which are *also* signified, *properly* and *improperly,* by the large and vague expression *law.* To obviate the difficulties springing from that confusion, I begin my projected Course with determining the province of jurisprudence, or with distinguishing the matter of jurisprudence from those various related objects: trying to define the subject of which I intend to treat, before I endeavor to analyse its numerous and complicated parts.

[A law, in the most general and comprehensive acceptation in which the term, in its literal meaning, is employed, may be said to be a rule laid down for the guidance of an intelligent being by an intelligent being having power over him. Under this definition are included, and without impropriety, several species. It is necessary to define accurately the line of demarcation which separates these species from one another, as much mistiness and intricacy has been infused into the science of jurisprudence by their being confounded or not clearly distinguished. In the comprehensive sense above indicated, or in the largest meaning which it has, without extension by metaphor or analogy,][1] the term *law* embraces the following objects:—Laws set by God to His human creatures, and laws set by men to men.

The whole or a portion of the laws set by God to men is frequently styled the law of nature, or natural law: being, in truth, the only natural law of which it is possible to speak without a metaphor, or without a blending of objects which ought to be distinguished broadly. But, rejecting the appellation Law of Nature as ambiguous and misleading, I name those laws or rules, as considered collectively or in a mass, the *Divine law,* or the *law of God.*

Laws set by men to men are of two leading or principal classes: classes which are often blended, although they differ extremely; and which, for that reason, should be severed precisely, and opposed distinctly and conspicuously.

Of the laws or rules set by men to men, some are established by *political* superiors, sovereign and subject: by persons exercising supreme and subordinate *government,* in independent nations, or independent political societies. The aggregate of the rules thus established, or some aggregate forming a portion of that aggregate, is the appropriate matter of jurisprudence, general or particular. To the aggregate of the rules thus established, or to some aggregate forming a portion of that aggregate, the term *law,* as used simply and strictly, is exclusively applied. But, as contradistinguished to *natural* law, or to the law of *nature* (meaning, by those expressions, the law of God), the aggregate of the rules, established by political superiors, is frequently styled *positive* law, or law existing *by position.* As contradistinguished to the rules which I style *positive morality,* and on which I shall touch immediately, the aggregate of the rules, established by political superiors, may also be marked commodiously with the name of *positive law.* For the sake, then, of getting a name brief and distinctive at once, and agreeably to frequent usage, I style that aggregate of rules, or any portion of that aggregate, *positive law:* though rules, which are *not* established by political superiors, are also *positive,* or exist *by position,* if they be rules or laws, in the proper signification of the term.

Though *some* of the laws or rules, which are set by men to men, are established by political superiors, *others* are *not* established by political superiors, or are *not* established by political superiors, in that capacity or character.

[Closely analogous to human laws of this second class, are a set of objects frequently but *improperly* termed *laws,* being rules set and enforced by *mere opinion,* that is, by the opinions or sentiments held or felt by an indeterminate body of men in regard to human conduct. Instances of such a use of the term *law* are the expressions—"The law of honour"; "The

[1] [Bracketed materials from the original]

law set by fashion"; and rules of this species constitute much of what is usually termed "International law."

The aggregate of human laws properly so called belonging to the second of the classes above mentioned, with the aggregate of objects *improperly* but by *close analogy* termed laws, I place together in a common class, and denote them by the term] *positive morality*. The name *morality* severs them from *positive law*, while the epithet *positive* disjoins them from the *law of God*. And to the end of obviating confusion, it is necessary or expedient that they *should* be disjoined from the latter by that distinguishing epithet. For the name *morality* (or *morals*), when standing unqualified or alone, denotes indifferently either of the following objects: namely, positive morality *as it is*, or without regard to its merits; and positive morality *as it would be*, if it conformed to the law of God, and were, therefore, deserving of *approbation*.

[Besides the various sorts of rules which are included in the literal acceptation of the term law, and those which are by a close and striking analogy, though improperly, termed laws, there are numerous applications of the term law, which] rest upon a slender analogy and are merely metaphorical or figurative. Such is the case when we talk of *laws* observed by the lower animals; of *laws* regulating the growth or decay of vegetables; of *laws* determining the movements of inanimate bodies or masses. For where *intelligence* is not, or where it is too bounded to take the name of *reason*, and, therefore, is too bounded to conceive the purpose of a law, there is not the *will* which law can work on, or which duty can incite or restrain. Yet through these misapplications of a *name*, flagrant as the metaphor is, has the field of jurisprudence and morals been deluged with muddy speculation.

[Having] suggested the *purpose* of my attempt to determine the province of jurisprudence: to distinguish positive law, the appropriate matter of jurisprudence, from the various objects to which it is related by resemblance, and to which it is related, nearly or remotely, by a strong or slender analogy: I shall [now] state the essentials of *a law* or *rule* (taken with the largest signification which can be given to the term *properly*).

Every *law* or *rule* (taken with the largest signification which can be given to the term *properly*) is a *command*. Or, rather, laws or rules, properly so called, are a *species* of commands.

Now, since the term *command* comprises the term *law*, the first is the simpler as well as the larger of the two. But, simple as it is, it admits of explanation. And, since it is the *key* to the sciences of jurisprudence and morals, its meaning should be analysed with precision. . . .

If you express or intimate a wish that I shall do or forbear from some act, and if you will visit me with an evil in case I comply not with your wish, the *expression* or *intimation* of your wish is a *command*. A command is distinguished from other significations of desire, not by the style in which the desire is signified, but by the power and the purpose of the party commanding to inflict an evil or pain in case the desire be disregarded. If you cannot or will not harm me, in case I comply not with your wish, the expression of your wish is not a command, although you utter your wish in imperative phrase. If you are able and willing to harm me in case I comply not with your wish, the expression of your wish amounts to a command, although you are prompted by a spirit of courtesy to utter it in the shape of a request. "*Preces erant, sed quibus contradici non posset.*" Such is the language of Tacitus, when speaking of a petition by the soldiery to a son and lieutenant of Vespasian.

A command, then, is a signification of desire. But a command is distinguished from other significations of desire by this peculiarity: that the party to whom it is directed is liable to evil from the other, in case he comply not with the desire.

Being liable to evil from you if I comply not with a wish which you signify, I am *bound* or *obliged* by your command, or I lie under a *duty* to obey it. If, in spite of that evil in prospect, I comply not with the wish which you signify, I am said to disobey your command, or to violate the duty which it imposes.

Command and duty are, therefore, correlative terms: the meaning denoted by each being implied or supposed by the other. Or (changing the expression) wherever a duty lies, a command has been signified; and whenever a command is signified, a duty is imposed.

Concisely expressed, the meaning of the correlative expressions is this. He who will inflict an evil in case his desire be disregarded, utters a command by expressing or intimating his desire: He who is liable to the evil in case he disregard the desire, is bound or obliged by the command.

The evil which will probably be incurred in case a command be disobeyed or (to use an equivalent expression) in case a duty be broken, is frequently called a *sanction,* or an *enforcement of obedience.* Or (varying the phrase) the command or the duty is said to be *sanctioned* or *enforced* by the chance of incurring the evil.

Considered as thus abstracted from the command and the duty which it enforces, the evil to be incurred by disobedience is frequently styled a *punishment.* But, as punishments, strictly so called, are only a *class* of sanctions, the term is too narrow to express the meaning adequately. . . .

It appears, then, from what has been premised, that the ideas or notions comprehended by the term *command* are the following. 1. A wish or desire conceived by a rational being, that another rational being shall do or forbear. 2. An evil to proceed from the former, and to be incurred by the latter, in case the latter comply not with the wish. 3. An expression or intimation of the wish by words or other signs.

It also appears from what has been premised, that *command, duty,* and *sanction* are inseparably connected terms: that each embraces the same ideas as the others, though each denotes those ideas in a peculiar order or series. . . .

Commands are of two species. Some are *laws* or *rules.* The others have not acquired an appropriate name, nor does language afford an expression which will mark them briefly and precisely. I must, therefore, note them as well as I can by the ambiguous and inexpressive name of "*occasional* or *particular* commands."

The term *laws* or *rules* being not unfrequently applied to occasional or particular commands, it is hardly possible to describe a line of separation which shall consist in every respect with established forms of speech. But the distinction between laws and particular commands may, I think, be stated in the following manner.

By every command, the party to whom it is directed is obliged to do or to forbear.

Now where it obliges *generally* to acts or forbearances of a *class,* a command is a law or rule. But where it obliges to a *specific* act or forbearance, or to acts or forbearances which it determines *specifically* or *individually,* a command is occasional or particular. In other words, a class or description of acts is determined by a law or rule, and acts of that class or description are enjoined or forbidden generally. But where a command is occasional or particular, the act or acts, which the command enjoins or forbids, are assigned or determined by their specific or individual natures as well as by the class or description to which they belong.

The statement which I have given in abstract expressions I will now endeavour to illustrate by apt examples.

If you command your servant to go on a given errand, or *not* to leave your house on a given evening, or to rise at such an hour on such a morning, or to rise at that hour during the next week or month, the command is occasional or particular. For the act or acts enjoined or forbidden are specially determined or assigned.

But if you command him *simply* to rise at that hour, or to rise at that hour *always,* or to rise at that hour *till further orders,* it may be said, with propriety, that you lay down a *rule* for the guidance of your servant's conduct. For no specific act is assigned by the command, but the command obliges him generally to acts of a determined class.

If a regiment be ordered to attack or defend a post, or to quell a riot, or to march from their present quarters, the command is occasional or particular. But an order to exercise daily till further orders shall be given would be called a *general* order, and *might* be called a *rule.*

If Parliament prohibited simply the exportation of corn, either for a given period or indefinitely, it would establish a law or rule: a *kind* or *sort* of acts being determined by the command, and acts of that kind or sort being *generally* forbidden. But an order issued by Parliament to meet an impending scarcity, and stopping the exportation of corn *then shipped and in port,* would not be a law or rule, though issued by the sovereign legislature. The order regarding exclusively a specified quantity of corn, the negative acts or forbearances, enjoined by the command, would be determined specifically or individually by the determinate nature of their subject.

As issued by a sovereign legislature, and as wearing the form of a law, the order which I have now imagined would probably be *called* a law. And hence the difficulty of drawing a distinct boundary between laws and occasional commands.

Again: An act which is not an offence, according to the existing law, moves the sovereign to displeasure: and, though the authors of the act are legally innocent or unoffending, the sovereign commands that they shall be punished. As enjoining a specific punishment in that specific case, and as not enjoining generally acts or forbearances of a class, the order uttered by the sovereign is not a law or rule.

Whether such an order would be *called* a law, seems to depend upon circumstances which are purely immaterial: immaterial, that is, with reference to the present purpose, though material with reference to others. If made by a sovereign assembly deliberately, and with the forms of legislation, it would probably be called a law. If uttered by an absolute monarch, without deliberation or ceremony, it would scarcely be confounded with acts of legislation, and would be styled an arbitrary command. Yet, on either of these suppositions, its nature would be the same. It would not be a law or rule, but an occasional or particular command of the sovereign One or Number.

To conclude with an example which best illustrates the distinction, and which shows the importance of the distinction most conspicuously, *judicial commands* are commonly occasional or particular, although the commands which they are calculated to enforce are commonly laws or rules.

For instance, the lawgiver commands that thieves shall be hanged. A specific theft and a specified thief being given, the judge commands that the thief shall be hanged, agreeably to the command of the lawgiver.

Now the lawgiver determines a class or description of acts; prohibits acts of the class generally and indefinitely; and commands, with the like generality, that punishment shall follow transgression. The command of the lawgiver is, therefore, a law or rule. But the command of the judge is occasional or particular. For he orders a specific punishment, as the consequence of a specific offence.

According to the line of separation which I have now attempted to describe, a law and a particular command are distinguished thus. —Acts or forbearances of a *class* are enjoined *generally* by the former. Acts *determined specifically,* are enjoined or forbidden by the latter. . . .

It appears, from what has been premised, that a law, properly so called, may be defined in the following manner.

A law is a command which obliges a person or persons.

But, as contradistinguished or opposed to an occasional or particular command, a law is a command which obliges a person or persons, and obliges *generally* to acts or forbearances of a *class.*

In language more popular but less distinct and precise, a law is a command which obliges a person or persons to a *course* of conduct.

Laws and other commands are said to proceed from *superiors,* and to bind or oblige *inferiors.* I will, therefore, analyze the meaning of those correlative expressions; and will try to strip them of a certain mystery, by which that simple meaning appears to be obscured.

Superiority is often synonymous with *precedence* or *excellence.* We talk of superiors in rank; of superiors in wealth; of superiors in virtue: comparing certain persons with certain other persons; and meaning that the former precede or excel the latter in rank, in wealth, or in virtue.

But, taken with the meaning wherein I here understand it, the term *superiority* signifies *might:* the power of affecting others with evil or pain, and of forcing them, through fear of that evil, to fashion their conduct to one's wishes.

For example, God is emphatically the *superior* of Man. For his power of affecting us with pain, and of forcing us to comply with his will, is unbounded and resistless.

To a limited extent, the sovereign One or Number is the superior of the subject or citizen: the master, of the slave or servant: the father, of the child.

In short, whoever can *oblige* another to comply with his wishes, is the *superior* of that other, so far as the ability reaches: The party who is obnoxious to the impending evil, being, to that same extent, the *inferior.*

The might or superiority of God, is simple or absolute. But in all or most cases of human superiority, the relation of superior and inferior, and the relation of inferior and superior, are reciprocal. Or (changing the expression) the party who is the superior as viewed from one aspect, is the inferior as viewed from another.

For example, To an indefinite, though limited extent, the monarch is the superior of the governed: his power being commonly sufficient to enforce compliance with his will. But the governed, collectively or in mass, are also the superior of the monarch: who is checked in the abuse of his might by his fear of exciting their anger; and of rousing to active resistance the might which slumbers in the multitude.

A member of a sovereign assembly is the superior of the judge: the judge being bound by the law which proceeds from that sovereign body. But, in his character of citizen or subject, he is the inferior of the judge: the judge being the minister of the law, and armed with the power of enforcing it.

It appears, then, that the term *superiority* (like the terms *duty* and *sanction*) is implied by the term command. For superiority is the power of enforcing compliance with a wish: and the expression or intimation of a wish, with the power and the purpose of enforcing it, are the constituent elements of a command. . . .

Like most of the leading terms in the science of jurisprudence and morals, the term *laws* is extremely ambiguous. Taken with the largest signification which can be given to the term properly, *laws* are a species of *commands*. But the term is improperly applied to various objects which have nothing of the imperative character: to objects which are *not* commands; and which, therefore, are *not* laws, properly so called. . . .

1. Acts on the part of legislatures to *explain* positive law, can scarcely be called laws, in the proper signification of the term. Working no change in the actual duties of the governed, but simply declaring what those duties are, they properly *are* acts of *interpretation* by legislative authority. Or, to borrow an expression from the writers on the Roman Law, they are acts of *authentic* interpretation.

But, this notwithstanding, they are frequently styled laws; *declaratory* laws, or declaratory statutes. They must, therefore, be noted as forming an exception to the proposition "that laws are a species of commands."

It often, indeed, happens (as I shall show in the proper place), that laws declaratory in name are imperative in effect: Legislative, like judicial interpretation, being frequently deceptive; and establishing new law, under guise of expounding the old.

2. Laws to repeal laws, and to release from existing duties, must also be excepted from the proposition "that laws are a species of commands." In so far as they release from duties imposed by existing laws, they are not commands, but revocations of commands. They authorize or permit the parties, to whom the repeal extends, to do or to forbear from acts which they were commanded to forbear from or to do. And, considered with regard to *this,* their immediate or direct purpose, they are often named *permissive laws,* or, more briefly and more properly, *permissions.*

Remotely and indirectly, indeed, permissive laws are often or always imperative. For the parties released from duties are restored to liberties or rights: and duties answering those rights are, therefore, created or revived. . . .

3. Imperfect laws, or laws of imperfect obligation, must also be excepted from the proposition "that laws are a species of commands."

An imperfect law (with the sense wherein the term is used by the Roman jurists) is a law which wants a sanction, and which, therefore, is not binding. A law declaring that certain acts are crimes, but annexing no punishment to the commission of acts of the class, is the simplest and most obvious example.

Though the author of an imperfect law signifies a desire, he manifests no purpose of enforcing compliance with the desire. But where there is not a purpose of enforcing compliance with the desire, the expression of a desire is not a command. Consequently, an imperfect law is not so properly a law, as counsel, or exhortation, addressed by a superior to inferiors.

Examples of imperfect laws are cited by the Roman jurists. But with us in England, laws professedly imperative are always (I believe) perfect or obligatory. Where the English legislature affects to command, the English tribunals not unreasonably presume the legislature exacts obedience. And, if no specific sanction be annexed to a given law, a sanction is supplied by the courts of justice, agreeably to a general maxim which obtains in cases of the kind.

The imperfect laws, of which I am now speaking, are laws which are imperfect, in the sense of *the Roman jurists:* that is to say, laws which speak the desires of political superiors, but which their authors (by oversight or design) have not provided with sanctions. Many of the writers on *morals,* and on the so called *law of nature,* have annexed a different meaning to the term *imperfect.* Speaking of imperfect obligations, they commonly mean duties which are *not legal:* duties imposed by commands of God, or duties imposed by positive morality, as contradistinguished to duties imposed by positive law. An imperfect obligation, in the sense of the Roman jurists, is exactly equivalent to no obligation at all. For the term *imperfect* denotes simply, that the law wants the sanction appropriate to laws of the kind. An imperfect obligation, in the other meaning of the expression, is a religious or a moral obligation. The term *imperfect* does not denote that the law imposing the duty wants the appropriate sanction. It denotes that the law imposing the duty is *not* a law established by a political superior: that it wants that *perfect,* or that surer or more cogent sanction, which is imparted by the sovereign or state.

I believe that I have now reviewed all the classes of objects, to which the term *laws* is improperly applied. The laws (improperly so called) which I have here lastly enumerated, are (I think) the only laws which are not commands, and which yet may be properly included within the province of jurisprudence. But though these, with the so called laws set by opinion and the objects metaphorically termed laws, are the only laws which *really* are not commands, there are certain laws (properly so called) which may *seem* not imperative. Accordingly, I will subjoin a few remarks upon laws of this dubious character.

1. There are laws, it may be said, which *merely* create *rights:* And, seeing that every command imposes a *duty,* laws of this nature are not imperative.

But, as I have intimated already, and shall show completely hereafter, there are no laws *merely* creating *rights.* There are laws, it is true, which *merely* create *duties:* duties not correlating with correlating rights, and which, therefore may be styled *absolute.* But every law, really conferring a right, imposes expressly or tacitly a *relative* duty, or a duty correlating with the right. If it specify the remedy to be given, in case the right shall be infringed, it imposes the relative duty expressly. If the remedy to be given be not specified, it refers tacitly to pre-existing law, and clothes the right which it purports to create with a remedy provided by that law. Every law, really conferring a right, is, therefore, imperative: as imperative, as if its only purpose were the creation of a duty, or as if the relative duty, which it inevitably imposes, were merely absolute. . . .

2. According to an opinion which I must notice *incidentally* here, though the subject to which it relates will be treated *directly* hereafter, *customary laws* must be excepted from the proposition "that laws are a species of commands."

By many of the admirers of customary laws (and, especially, of their German admirers), they are thought to oblige legally (independently of the sovereign or state), *because* the citizens or subjects have observed or kept them. Agreeably to this opinion, they are not the *creatures* of the sovereign or state, although the sovereign or state may abolish them at pleasure. Agreeably to this opinion, they are positive law (or law, strictly so called), inasmuch as they are enforced by the courts of justice: But, that notwithstanding, they exist *as positive law* by the spontaneous adoption of the governed, and not by position or establishment on the part of political superiors. Consequently, customary laws, considered as positive law, are not commands. And, consequently, customary laws, considered as positive law, are not laws or rules properly so called.

An opinion less mysterious, but somewhat allied to this, is not uncommonly held by the adverse party: by the party which is strongly opposed to customary law; and to all law made judicially, or in the way of judicial legislation. According to the latter opinion, all judge-made law, or all judge-made law established by *subject* judges, is purely the creature of the judges by whom it is established immediately. To impute it to the sovereign legislature, or to suppose that it speaks the will of the sovereign legislature, is one of the foolish or knavish *fictions* with which lawyers, in every age and nation, have perplexed and darkened the simplest and clearest truths.

I think it will appear, on a moment's reflection, that each of these opinions is groundless: that customary law is *imperative,* in the proper signification of the term; and that all judge-made law is the creature of the sovereign or state.

At its origin, a custom is a rule of conduct which the governed observe spontaneously, or not in pursuance of a law set by a political superior. The custom is transmuted into positive law, when it is adopted as such by the courts of justice, and when the judicial decisions fashioned upon it are enforced by the power of the state. But before it is adopted by the courts, and clothed with the legal sanction, it is merely a rule of positive morality: a rule generally observed by the citizens or subjects; but deriving the only force, which it can be said to possess, from the general disapprobation falling on those who transgress it.

Now when judges transmute a custom into a legal rule (or make a legal rule not suggested by a custom), the legal rule which they establish is established by the sovereign legislature. A subordinate or subject judge is merely a minister. The portion of the sovereign power which lies at his disposition is merely delegated. The rules which he makes derive their legal force from authority given by the state: an authority which the state may confer expressly, but which it commonly imparts in the way of acquiescence. For, since the state may reverse the rules which he makes, and yet permits him to enforce them by the power of the political community, its sovereign will "that his rules shall obtain as law" is clearly evinced by its conduct, though not by its express declaration.

The admirers of customary law love to trick out their idol with mysterious and imposing attributes. But to those who can see the difference between positive law and morality, there is nothing of mystery about it. Considered as rules of positive morality, customary laws arise from the consent of the governed, and not from the position or establishment of political superiors. But, considered as moral rules turned into positive laws, customary laws are established by the state: established by the state directly, when the customs are promulgated in its statutes; established by the state circuitously, when the customs are adopted by its tribunals.

The opinion of the party which abhors judge-made laws, springs from their inadequate conception of the nature of commands.

Like other significations of desire, a command is express or tacit. If the desire be signified by *words* (written or spoken), the command is express. If the desire be signified by conduct (or by any signs of desire which are *not* words), the command is tacit.

Now when customs are turned into legal rules by decisions of subject judges, the legal rules which emerge from the customs are *tacit* commands of the sovereign legislature. The state, which is able to abolish, permits its ministers to enforce them: and it, therefore, signifies its pleasure, by that its voluntary acquiescence, "that they shall serve as a law to the governed."

My present purpose is merely this: to prove that the positive law styled *customary* (and all positive law made judicially) is established by the state directly or circuitously, and, therefore, is *imperative*. I am far from disputing, that law made judicially (or in the way of improper legislation) and law made by statute (or in the properly legislative manner) are distinguished by weighty differences. I shall inquire, in future lectures, what those differences are; and why subject judges, who are properly ministers of the law, have commonly shared with the sovereign in the business of making it.

I assume, then, that the only laws which are not imperative, [and which belong to the subject matter of jurisprudence,] are the following—1. Declaratory laws, or laws explaining the import of existing positive law. 2. Laws abrogating or repealing existing positive law. 3. Imperfect laws, or laws of imperfect obligation (with the sense wherein the expression is used by the Roman jurists). . . .

LECTURE VI

The superiority which is styled sovereignty, and the independent political society which sovereignty implies, is distinguished from other superiority, and from other society, by the following marks or characters. —1. The *bulk* of the given society are in a *habit* of obedience or submission to a *determinate* and *common* superior: let that common superior be a certain individual person, or a certain body or aggregate of individual persons. 2. That certain individual, or that certain body of individuals, is *not* in a habit of obedience to a determinate human superior. Laws (improperly so called) which opinion sets or imposes, may permanently affect the conduct of that certain individual or body. To express or tacit commands of other determinate parties, that certain individual or body may yield occasional submission. But there is no determinate person, or determinate aggregate of persons, to whose commands, express or tacit, that certain individual or body renders habitual obedience.

Or the notions of sovereignty and independent political society may be expressed concisely thus. —If a *determinate* human superior, *not* in a habit of obedience to a like superior, receive *habitual* obedience from the *bulk* of a given society, that determinate superior is sovereign in that society, and the society (including the superior) is a society political and independent.

To that determinate superior, the other members of the society are *subject:* or on that determinate superior, the other members of the society are *dependent.* The position of its other members towards that determinate superior, is *a state of subjection,* or *a state of dependence.* The mutual relation which subsists between that superior and them, may be styled *the relation of sovereign and subject,* or *the relation of sovereignty and subjection.*

Hence it follows, that it is only through an ellipsis, or an abridged form of expression, that the *society* is styled *independent.* The party truly independent (independent, that is to say, of a determinate human superior), is not the society, but the sovereign portion of the society: that certain member of the society, or that certain body of its members, to whose commands, expressed or intimated, the generality or bulk of its members render habitual obedience. Upon that certain person, or certain body of persons, the other members of the society are *dependent:* or to that certain person, or certain body of persons, the other members of the society are *subject*. By "an independent political society," or "an independent and sovereign nation," we mean a political society consisting of a sovereign and subjects, as opposed to a political society which is merely subordinate: that is to say, which is merely a limb or member of another political society, and which therefore consists entirely of persons in a state of subjection.

In order that a given society may form a society political and independent, the two distinguishing marks which I have mentioned above must unite. The *generality* of the given society must be in the *habit* of obedience to a *determinate* and *common* superior: whilst that determinate person, or determinate body of persons must *not* be habitually obedient to a determinate person or body. It is the union of that positive, with this negative mark, which renders that certain superior sovereign or supreme, and which renders that given society (including that certain superior) a society political and independent. . . .

8

H. L. A. HART

From *The Concept of Law*

CHAPTER 5 / LAW AS THE UNION OF PRIMARY AND SECONDARY RULES

2. THE IDEA OF OBLIGATION

It will be recalled that the theory of law as coercive orders, notwithstanding its errors, started from the perfectly correct appreciation of the fact that where there is law, there human conduct is made in some sense non-optional or obligatory. In choosing this starting-point the theory was well inspired, and in building up a new account of law in terms of the interplay of primary and secondary rules we too shall start from the same idea. It is, however, here, at this crucial first step, that we have perhaps most to learn from the theory's errors.

Let us recall the gunman situation. A orders B to hand over his money and threatens to shoot him if he does not comply. According to the theory of coercive orders this situation illustrates the notion of obligation or duty in general. Legal obligation is to be found in this situation writ large; A must be the sovereign habitually obeyed and the orders must be general, prescribing courses of conduct not single actions. The plausibility of the claim that the gunman situation displays the meaning of obligation lies in the fact that it is certainly one in which we would say that B, if he obeyed, was "obliged" to hand over his money. It is, however, equally certain that we should misdescribe the situation if we said, on these facts, that B "had an obligation" or a "duty" to hand over the money. So from the start it is clear that we need something else for an understanding of the idea of obligation. There is a difference, yet to be explained, between the assertion that someone *was obliged* to do something and the assertion that he *had an obligation* to do it. The first is often a statement about the beliefs and motives with which an action is done: B was obliged to hand over his money may simply mean, as it does in the gunman case, that he believed that some harm or other unpleasant consequences would befall him if he did not hand it over and he handed it over to avoid those consequences. In such cases the prospect of what would happen to the agent if he disobeyed has rendered something he would otherwise have preferred to have done (keep the money) less eligible.

Two further elements slightly complicate the elucidation of the notion of being obliged to do something. It seems clear that we should not think of B as obliged to hand over the money if the threatened harm was, according to common judgments, trivial in comparison with the disadvantage or serious consequences, either for B or for others, of complying with the orders, as it would be, for example, if A merely threatened to pinch B. Nor perhaps should we say that B was obliged, if there were no reasonable grounds for thinking that A could or would probably implement his threat of relatively serious harm. Yet, though such references to common judgments of comparative harm and reasonable estimates of likelihood, are implicit in this notion, the statement that a person was obliged to obey someone is, in the main, a psychological one referring to the beliefs and motives with which an action was done. But the statement that someone *had an obligation* to do something is of a very different type and there are many signs of this difference. Thus not only is it the case that the facts about B's action and his beliefs and motives in the gunman case, though sufficient to warrant the statement that B was obliged to hand over his purse, are *not sufficient* to warrant the statement that he had an obligation to do this; it is also the case that facts of this sort, i.e., facts about beliefs and motives, are *not necessary* for the truth of a statement that a person had an obligation to do something. Thus the statement that a person had an obligation, e.g., to tell the truth or report for military service, remains true even if he believed (reasonably or unreasonably) that he would never be found out and had nothing to fear from disobedience. Moreover, whereas the statement that he had this obligation is quite independent of the question whether or not he in fact reported for service, the statement that someone was obliged to do something, normally carries the implication that he actually did it.

Some theorists, Austin among them, seeing perhaps the general irrelevance of the person's beliefs, fears, and motives to the question whether he had an obligation to do something, have defined this notion not in terms of these subjective facts, but in terms of the *chance* or *likelihood* that the person having the obligation will suffer a punishment or "evil" at the hands of others in the event of disobedience. This, in effect, treats statements of obligation not as psychological statements but as predictions or assessments of chances of incurring punishment or "evil." To many later theorists this has appeared as a revelation, bringing down to earth an elusive notion and restating it in the same clear, hard, empirical terms as are used in science. It has, indeed, been accepted sometimes as the only alternative to metaphysical conceptions of obligation or duty as invisible objects mysteriously existing "above" or "behind" the world of ordinary, observable facts. But there are many reasons for rejecting this interpretation of statements of obligation as predictions, and it is not, in fact, the only alternative to obscure metaphysics.

The fundamental objection is that the predictive interpretation obscures the fact that, where rules exist, deviations from them are not merely grounds for a prediction that hostile reactions will follow or that a court will apply sanctions to those who break them, but are also a reason or justification for such reaction and for applying the sanctions. . . .

There is, however, a second, simpler, objection to the predictive interpretation of obligation. If it were true that the statement that a person had an obligation meant that *he* was likely to suffer in the event of disobedience, it would be a contradiction to say that he had an obligation, e.g., to report for military service but that, owing to the fact that he had escaped from the jurisdiction, or had successfully bribed the police or the court, there was not the slightest chance of his being caught or made to suffer. In fact, there is no contradiction in saying this, and such statements are often made and understood.

It is, of course, true that in a normal legal system, where sanctions are exacted for a high proportion of offences, an offender usually runs a risk of punishment; so, usually the statement that a person has an obligation and the statement that he is likely to suffer for disobedience will both be true together. Indeed, the connection between these two statements is somewhat stronger than this: at least in a municipal system it may well be true that, unless *in general* sanctions were likely to be exacted from offenders, there would be little or no point in making particular statements about a person's obligations. In this sense, such statements may be said to presuppose belief in the continued normal operation of the system of sanctions much as the statement "he is out" in cricket presupposes, though it does not assert, that players, umpire, and scorer will probably take the usual steps. None the less, it is crucial for the understanding of the idea of obligation to see that in individual cases the statement that a person has an obligation under some rule and the prediction that he is likely to suffer for disobedience may diverge.

It is clear that obligation is not to be found in the gunman situation, though the simpler notion of being obliged to do something may well be defined in the elements present there. To understand the general idea of obligation as a necessary preliminary to understanding it in its legal form, we must turn to a different social situation which, unlike the gunman situation, includes the existence of social rules; for this situation contributes to the meaning of the statement that a person has an obligation in two ways. First, the existence of such rules, making certain types of behavior a standard, is the normal, though unstated, background or proper context for such a statement; and, secondly, the distinctive function of such statement is to apply such a general rule to a particular person by calling attention to the fact that his case falls under it. . . . There is involved in the existence of any social rules a combination of regular conduct with a distinctive attitude to that conduct as a standard. We have also seen the main ways in which these differ from mere social habits, and how the varied normative vocabulary ("ought," "must," "should") is used to draw attention to the standard and to deviations from it, and to formulate the demands, criticisms, or acknowledgements which may be based on it. Of this class of normative words the words "obligation" and "duty" form an important sub-class, carrying with them certain implications not usually present in the others. Hence, though a grasp of the elements generally differentiating social rules from mere habits is certainly indispensable for understanding the notion of obligation or duty, it is not sufficient by itself.

The statement that someone has or is under an obligation does indeed imply the existence of a rule; yet it is not always the case that where rules exist the standard of behaviour required by them is conceived of in terms of obligation. "He ought to have" and "He had an obligation to" are not always interchangeable expressions, even though they are alike in carrying an implicit reference to existing standards of conduct or are used in drawing conclusions in particular cases from a general rule. Rules of etiquette or correct speech are certainly rules: they are more than convergent habits or regularities of behaviour; they are taught and efforts are made to maintain them; they are used in criticizing our own and other people's behaviour in the characteristic normative vocabulary. "You ought to take your hat off," "It is wrong to say 'you was.'" But to use in connection with rules of this kind the words "obligation" or "duty" would be misleading and not merely stylistically odd. It would misdescribe a social situation; for though the line separating rules of obligation from others is at points a vague one, yet the main rationale of the distinction is fairly clear.

Rules are conceived and spoken of as imposing obligations when the general demand for conformity is insistent and the social pressure brought to bear upon those who deviate or threaten to deviate is great. Such rules may be wholly customary in origin: there may be no centrally organized system of punishments for breach of the rules; the social pressure may take only the form of a general diffused hostile or critical reaction which may stop short of physical sanctions. It may be limited to verbal manifestations of disapproval or of appeals to the individuals' respect for the rule violated; it may depend heavily on the operation of feelings of shame, remorse, and guilt. When the pressure is of this last-mentioned kind we may be inclined to classify the rules as part of the morality of the social group and the obligation under the rules as moral obligation. Conversely, when physical sanctions are prominent or usual among the forms of pressure, even though these are neither closely defined nor administered by officials but are left to the community at large, we shall be inclined to classify the rules as a primitive or rudimentary form of law. We may, of course, find both these types of serious social pressure behind what is, in an obvious sense, the same rule of conduct; sometimes this may occur with no indication that one of them is peculiarly appropriate as primary and the other secondary, and then the question whether we are confronted with a rule of morality or rudimentary law may not be susceptible of an answer. But for the moment the possibility of drawing the line between law and morals need not detain us. What is important is that the insistence on importance or *seriousness* of social pressure behind the rules is the primary factor determining whether they are thought of as giving rise to obligations.

Two other characteristics of obligation go naturally together with this primary one. The rules supported by this serious pressure are thought important because they are believed to be necessary to the maintenance of social life or some highly prized feature of it. Characteristically, rules so obviously essential as those which restrict the free use of violence are thought of in terms of obligation. So too rules which require honesty or truth or require the keeping of promises, or specify what is to be done by one who performs a distinctive role or function in the social group are thought of in terms of either "obligation" or perhaps more often "duty." Secondly, it is generally recognized that the conduct required by these rules may, while benefiting others, conflict with what the person who owes the duty may wish to do. Hence obligations and duties are thought of as characteristically involving sacrifice or renunciation, and the standing possibility of conflict between obligation or duty and interest is, in all societies, among the truisms of both the lawyer and the moralist.

The figure of a *bond* binding the person obligated, which is buried in the word "obligation," and the similar notion of a debt latent in the word "duty" are explicable in terms of these three factors, which distinguish rules of obligation or duty from other rules. In this figure, which haunts much legal thought, the social pressure appears as a chain binding those who have obligations so that they are not free to do what they want. The other end of the chain is sometimes held by the group or their official representatives, who insist on performance or exact the penalty: sometimes it is entrusted by the group to a private individual who may choose whether or not to insist on performance or its equivalent in value to him. The first situation typifies the duties or obligations of criminal law and the second those of civil law where we think of private individuals having rights correlative to the obligations.

Natural and perhaps illuminating though these figures or metaphors are, we must not allow them to trap us into a misleading conception of obligation as essentially consisting in some feeling of pressure or compulsion experienced by those who have obligations. The fact that rules of obligation are generally supported by serious social pressure does not entail that to have an obligation under the rules is to experience feelings of compulsion or pressure. Hence there is no contradiction in saying of some hardened swindler, and it may often be true, that he had an obligation to pay the rent but felt no pressure to pay when he made off without doing so. To *feel* obliged and to have an obligation are different though frequently concomitant things. To identify them would be one way of misinterpreting, in terms of psychological feelings, the important internal aspect of rules. . . .

Indeed, the internal aspect of rules is something to which we must . . . refer before we can dispose finally of the claims of the predictive theory. For an advocate of that theory may well ask why, if social pressure is so important a feature of rules of obligation, we are yet so concerned to stress the inadequacies of the predictive theory; for it gives this very feature a central place by defining obligation in terms of the likelihood that threatened punishment or hostile reaction will follow deviation from certain lines of conduct. The difference may seem slight between the analysis of a statement of obligation as a prediction, or assessment of the chances, of hostile reaction to deviation, and our own contention that though this statement presupposes a background in which deviations from rules are generally met by hostile reactions, yet its characteristic use is not to predict this but to say that a person's case falls under such a rule. In fact, however, this difference is not a slight one. Indeed, until its importance is grasped, we cannot properly understand the whole distinctive style of human thought, speech, and action which is involved in the existence of rules and which constitutes the normative structure of society.

The following contrast again in terms of the "internal" and "external" aspect of rules may serve to mark what gives this distinction its great importance for the understanding not only of law but of the structure of any society. When a social group has certain rules of conduct, this fact affords an opportunity for many closely related yet different kinds of assertion; for it is possible to be concerned with the rules, either merely as an observer who does not himself accept them, or as a member of the group which accepts and uses them as guides to conduct. We may call these respectively the "external" and the "internal points of view." Statements made from the external point of view may themselves be of different kinds. For the observer may, without accepting the rules himself, assert that the group accepts the rules, and thus may from outside refer to the way in which *they* are concerned with them from the internal point of view. But whatever the rules are, whether they are those of games, like chess or cricket, or moral or legal rules, we can if we choose occupy the position of an observer who does not even refer in this way to the internal point of view of the group. Such an observer is content merely to record the regularities of observable behaviour in which conformity with the rules partly consists and those further regularities, in the form of the hostile reaction, reproofs, or punishments, with which deviations from the rules are met. After a time the external observer may, on the basis of the regularities observed, correlate deviation with hostile reaction, and be able to predict with a fair measure of success, and to assess the chances that a deviation from the group's normal behaviour will meet with hostile reaction or punishment. Such knowledge may not only reveal much about the group, but might enable him to live among them without unpleasant consequences which would attend one who attempted to do so without such knowledge.

If, however, the observer really keeps austerely to this extreme external point of view and does not give any account of the manner in which members of the group who accept the rules view their own regular behaviour, his description of their life cannot be in terms of rules at all, and so not in the terms of the rule-dependent notions of obligation or duty. Instead, it will be in terms of observable regularities of conduct, predictions, probabilities, and signs. For such an observer, deviations by a member of the group from normal conduct will be a sign that hostile reaction is likely to follow, and nothing more. His view will be like the view of one who, having observed the working of a traffic signal in a busy street for some time, limits himself to saying that when the light turns red there is a high probability that the traffic will stop. He treats the light merely as a natural *sign that* people will behave in certain ways, as clouds are a *sign that* rain will come. In so doing he will miss out a whole dimension of the social life of those whom he is watching, since for them the red light is not merely a sign that others will stop: they look upon it as a *signal for* them to stop, and so a reason for stopping in conformity to rules which make stopping when the light is red a standard of behaviour and an obligation. To mention this is to bring into the account the way in which the group regards its own behaviour. It is to refer to the internal aspect of rules seen from their internal point of view.

The external point of view may very nearly reproduce the way in which the rules function in the lives of certain members of the group, namely those who reject its rules and are only concerned with them when and because they judge that unpleasant consequences are likely to follow violation. Their point of view will need for its expression, "I was obliged to do it," "I am likely to suffer for it if . . . ," "You will probably suffer for it if . . . ," "They will do that to you if . . . ." But they will not need forms of expression like "I had an obligation" or "You have an obligation" for these are required only by those who see their own and other persons' conduct from the internal point of view. What the external point of view, which limits itself to the observable regularities of behaviour, cannot reproduce is the way in which the rules function as rules in the lives of those who normally are the majority of society. These are the officials, lawyers, or private persons who use them, in one situation after another, as guides to the conduct of social life, as the basis for claims, demands, admissions, criticism, or punishment, viz., in all the familiar transactions of life according to rules. For them the violation of a rule is not merely a basis for the prediction that a hostile reaction will follow but a *reason* for hostility.

At any given moment the life of any society which lives by rules, legal or not, is likely to consist in a tension between those who, on the one hand, accept and voluntarily cooperate in maintaining the rules, and so see their own and other persons' behaviour in terms of the rules, and those who, on the other hand, reject the rules and attend to them only from the external point of view as a sign of possible punishment. One of the difficulties facing any legal theory anxious to do justice to the complexity of the facts is to remember the presence of both these points of view and not to define one of them out of existence. Perhaps all our criticisms of the predictive theory of obligation may be best summarized as the accusation that this is what it does to the internal aspect of obligatory rules.

3. THE ELEMENTS OF LAW

It is, of course, possible to imagine a society without a legislature, courts, or officials of any kind. Indeed, there are many studies of primitive communities which not only claim that this possibility is realized but depict in detail the life of a society where the only means of social control is that general attitude of the group towards its own standard modes of behaviour in terms of which we have characterized rules of obligation. A social structure of this kind is often referred to as one of "custom"; but we shall not use this term, because it often implies that the customary rules are very old and supported with less social pressure than other rules. To avoid these implications we shall refer to such a social structure as one of primary rules of obligation. If a society is to live by such primary rules alone, there are certain conditions which, granted a few of the most obvious truisms about human nature and the world we live in, must clearly be satisfied. The first of these conditions is that the rules must contain in some form restrictions on the free use of violence, theft, and deception to which human beings are tempted but which they must, in general, repress, if they are to coexist in close proximity to each other. Such rules are in fact always found in the primitive societies of which we have knowledge, together with a variety of others imposing on individuals various positive duties to perform services or make contributions to the common life. Secondly, though such a society may exhibit the tension, already described, between those who accept the rules and those who reject the rules except where fear of social pressure induces them to conform, it is plain that the latter cannot be more than a minority, if so loosely organized a society of persons, approximately equal in physical strength, is to endure: for otherwise those who reject the rules would have too little social pressure to fear. This too is confirmed by what we know of primitive communities where, though there are dissidents and malefactors, the majority live by the rules seen from the internal point of view.

More important for our present purpose is the following consideration. It is plain that only a small community closely knit by ties of kinship, common sentiment, and belief, and placed in a stable environment, could live successfully by such a regime of unofficial rules. In any other conditions such a simple form of social control must prove defective and will require supplementation in different ways. In the first place, the rules by which the group lives will not form a system, but will simply be a set of separate standards, without any identifying or common mark, except of course that they are the rules which a particular group of human beings accepts. They will in this respect resemble our own rules of etiquette. Hence if doubts arise as to what the rules are or as to the precise scope of some given rule, there will be no procedure for settling this doubt, either by reference to an authoritative text or to an official whose declarations on this point are authoritative. For, plainly, such a procedure and the acknowledgement of either authoritative text or persons involve the existence of rules of a type different from the rules of obligation or duty which *ex hypothesi* are all that the group has. This defect in the simple social structure of primary rules we may call its *uncertainty.*

A second defect is the *static* character of the rules. The only mode of change in the rules known to such a society will be the slow process of growth, whereby courses of conduct once thought optional become first habitual or usual, and then obligatory, and the converse process of decay, when deviations, once severely dealt with, are first tolerated and then pass unnoticed. There will be no means, in such a society, of deliberately adapting the rules to changing circumstances, either by eliminating old rules or introducing new ones: for, again, the possibility of doing this presupposes the existence of rules of a different type from the primary rules of obligation by which alone the society lives. In an extreme case the rules may be static in a more drastic sense. This, though never perhaps fully realized in any actual community, is worth considering because the remedy for it is something very characteristic of law. In this extreme case, not only would there be no way of deliberately changing the general rules, but the obligations which arise under the rules in particular cases could not be varied or modified by the deliberate choice of any individual. Each individual would simply have fixed obligations or duties to do or abstain from doing certain things. It might indeed very often be the case that others would benefit from the performance of these obligations; yet if there are only primary rules of obligation they would have no power to release those bound from performance or to transfer to others the benefits which would accrue from performance. For such operations of release or transfer create changes in the initial positions of individuals under the primary rules of obligation, and for these operations to be possible there must be rules of a sort different from the primary rules.

The third defect of this simple form of social life is the *inefficiency* of the diffuse social pressure by which the rules are maintained. Disputes as to whether an admitted rule has or has not been violated will always occur and will, in any but the smallest societies, continue interminably, if there is no agency specially empowered to ascertain finally, and authoritatively, the fact of violation. Lack of such final and authoritative determinations is to be distinguished from another weakness associated with it. This is the fact that punishments for violations of the rules, and other forms of social pressure involving physical effort or the use of force, are not administered by a special agency but are left to the individuals affected or to the group at large. It is obvious that the waste of time involved in the group's unorganized efforts to catch and punish offenders, and the smouldering vendettas which may result from self-help in the absence of an official monopoly of "sanctions," may be serious. The history of law does, however, strongly suggest that the lack of official agencies to determine authoritatively the fact of violation of the rules is a much more serious defect; for many societies have remedies for this defect long before the other.

The remedy for each of these three main defects in this simplest form of social structure consists in supplementing the *primary* rules of obligation with *secondary* rules which are rules of a different kind. The introduction of the remedy for each defect might, in itself, be considered a step from the pre-legal into the legal world; since each remedy brings with it many elements that permeate law: certainly all three remedies together are enough to convert the regime of primary rules into what is indisputably a legal system. We shall consider in turn each of these remedies and show why law may most illuminatingly be characterized as a union of primary rules of obligation with such secondary rules. Before we do this, however, the following general points should be noted. Though the remedies consist in the introduction of rules which are certainly different from each other, as well as from the primary rules of obligation which they supplement, they have important features in common and are connected in various ways. Thus they may all be said to be on a different level from the primary rules, for they are all *about* such rules; in the sense that while primary rules are concerned with the actions that individuals must or must not do, these secondary rules are all concerned with the primary rules themselves. They specify the ways in which the primary rules may be conclusively ascertained, introduced, eliminated, varied, and the fact of their violation conclusively determined.

The simplest form of remedy for the *uncertainty* of the regime of primary rules is the introduction of what we shall call a "rule of recognition." This will specify some feature or features possession of which by a suggested rule is taken as a conclusive affirmative indication that it is a rule of the group to be supported by the social pressure it exerts. The existence of such a rule of recognition may take any of a huge variety of forms, simple or complex. It may, as in the early law of many societies, be no more than that an authoritative list or text of the rules is to be found in a written document or carved on some public monument. No doubt as a matter of history this step from the pre-legal to the legal may be accomplished in distinguishable stages, of which the first is the mere reduction to writing of hitherto unwritten rules. This is not itself the crucial step, though it is a very important one: what is crucial is the acknowledgement of reference to the writing or inscription as *authoritative,* i.e., as the *proper* way of disposing of doubts as to the existence of the rule. Where there is such an acknowledgement there is a very simple form of secondary rule: a rule for conclusive identification of the primary rules of obligation.

In a developed legal system the rules of recognition are of course more complex; instead of identifying rules exclusively by reference to a text or list they do so by reference to some general characteristic possessed by the primary rules. This may be the fact of their having been enacted by a specific body, or their long customary practice, or their relation to judicial decisions. Moreover, where more than one of such general characteristics are treated as identifying criteria, provision may be made for their possible conflict by their arrangement in an order of superiority, as by the common subordination of custom or precedent to statute, the latter being a "superior source" of law. Such complexity may make the rules of recognition in a modern legal system seem very different from the simple acceptance of an authoritative text: yet even in this simplest form, such a rule brings with it many elements distinctive of law. By providing an authoritative mark it introduces, although in embryonic form, the idea of a legal system: for the rules are now not just a discrete unconnected set but are, in a simple way, unified. Further, in the simple operation of identifying a given rule as possessing the required feature of being an item on an authoritative list of rules we have the germ of the idea of legal validity.

The remedy for the *static* quality of the regime of primary rules consists in the introduction of what we shall call "rules of change." The simplest form of such a rule is that which empowers an individual or body of persons to introduce new primary rules for the conduct of the life of the group, or of some class within it, and to eliminate old rules. . . . It is in terms of such a rule, and not in terms of orders backed by threats, that the ideas of legislative enactment and repeal are to be understood. Such rules of change may be very simple or very complex: the powers conferred may be unrestricted or limited in various ways: and the rules may, besides specifying the persons who are to legislate, define in more or less rigid terms the procedure to be followed in legislation. Plainly, there will be a very close connection between the rules of change and the rules of recognition: for where the former exists the latter will necessarily incorporate a reference to legislation as an identifying feature of the rules, though it need not refer to all the details of procedure involved in legislation. Usually some official certificate or official copy will, under the rules of recognition, be taken as a sufficient proof of due enactment. Of course if there is a social structure so simple that the only "source of law" is legislation, the rule of recognition will simply specify enactment as the unique identifying mark or criterion of validity of the rules. . . .

We have already described in some detail the rules which confer on individuals power to vary their initial positions under the primary rules. Without such private power-conferring rules society would lack some of the chief amenities which law confers upon it. For the operations which these rules make possible are the making of wills, contracts, transfers of property, and many other voluntarily created structures of rights and duties which typify life under law, though of course an elementary form of power-conferring rule also underlies the moral institution of a promise. The kinship of these rules with the rules of change involved in the notion of legislation is clear, and as recent theory such as Kelsen's has shown, many of the features which puzzle us in the institutions of contract or property are clarified by thinking of the operations of making a contract or transferring property as the exercise of limited legislative powers by individuals.

The third supplement to the simple regime of primary rules, intended to remedy the *inefficiency* of its diffused social pressure, consists of secondary rules empowering individuals to make authoritative determinations of the question whether, on a particular occasion, a primary rule has been broken. The minimal form of adjudication consists in such determinations, and we shall call the secondary rules which confer the power to make them "rules of adjudication." Besides identifying the individuals who are to adjudicate, such rules will also define the procedure to be followed. Like the other secondary rules these are on a different level from the primary rules: though they may be reinforced by further rules imposing duties on judges to adjudicate, they do not impose duties but confer judicial powers and a special status on judicial declarations about the breach of obligations. Again these rules, like the other secondary rules, define a group of important legal concepts: in this case the concepts of judge or court, jurisdiction and judgment. Besides these resemblances to the other secondary rules, rules of adjudication have intimate connections with them. Indeed, a system which has rules of adjudication is necessarily also committed to a rule of recognition of an elementary and imperfect sort. This is so because, if courts are empowered to make authoritative determinations of the fact that a rule has been broken, these cannot avoid being taken as authoritative determinations of what the rules are. So the rule which confers jurisdiction will also be a rule of recognition, identifying the primary rules through the judgments of the courts and these judgments will become a "source" of law. It is true that this form of rule of recognition, inseparable from the minimum form of jurisdiction, will be very imperfect. Unlike an authoritative text or a statute book, judgments may not be couched in general terms and their use as authoritative guides to the rules depends on a somewhat shaky inference from particular decisions, and the reliability of this must fluctuate both with the skill of the interpreter and the consistency of the judges.

It need hardly be said that in few legal systems are judicial powers confined to authoritative determinations of the fact of violation of the primary rules. Most systems have, after some delay, seen the advantages of further centralization of social pressure; and have partially prohibited the use of physical punishments or violent self help by private individuals. Instead they have supplemented the primary rules of obligation by further secondary rules, specifying or at least limiting the penalties for violation, and have conferred upon judges, where they have ascertained the fact of violation, the exclusive power to direct the application of penalties by other officials. These secondary rules provide the centralized official "sanctions" of the system.

If we stand back and consider the structure which has resulted from the combination of primary rules of obligation with the secondary rules of recognition, change and adjudication, it is plain that we have here not only the heart of a legal system, but a most powerful tool for the analysis of much that has puzzled both the jurist and the political theorist.

Not only are the specifically legal concepts with which the lawyer is professionally concerned, such as those of obligation and rights, validity and source of law, legislation and jurisdiction, and sanction, best elucidated in terms of this combination of elements. The concepts (which bestride both law and political theory) of the state, of authority, and of an official require a similar analysis if the obscurity which still lingers about them is to be dissipated. The reason why an analysis in these terms of primary and secondary rules has this explanatory power is not far to seek. Most of the obscurities and distortions surrounding legal and political concepts arise from the fact that these essentially involve reference to what we have called the internal point of view: the view of those who do not merely record and predict behavior conforming to rules, but *use* the rules as standards for the appraisal of their own and others' behaviour. This requires more detailed attention in the analysis of legal and political concepts than it has usually received. Under the simple regime of primary rules the internal point of view is manifested in its simplest form, in the use of those rules as the basis of criticism, and as the justification of demands for conformity, social pressure, and punishment. Reference to this most elementary manifestation of the internal point of view is required for the analysis of the basic concepts of obligation and duty. With the addition to the system of secondary rules, the range of what is said and done from the internal point of view is much extended and diversified. With this extension comes a whole set of new concepts and they demand a reference to the internal point of view for their analysis. These include the notions of legislation, jurisdiction, validity, and, generally, of legal powers, private and public. There is a constant pull towards an analysis of these in the terms of ordinary or "scientific," fact-stating or predictive discourse. But this can only reproduce their external aspect: to do justice to their distinctive, internal aspect we need to see the different ways in which the law-making operations of the legislator, the adjudication of a court, the exercise of private or official powers, and other "acts-in-the-law" are related to secondary rules.

In the next chapter we shall show how the ideas of the validity of law and sources of law, and the truths latent among the errors of the doctrines of sovereignty may be rephrased and clarified in terms of rules of recognition. But we shall conclude this chapter with a warning: though the combination of primary and secondary rules merits, because it explains many aspects of law, the central place assigned to it, this cannot by itself illuminate every problem. The union of primary and secondary rules is at the centre of a legal system; but it is not the whole, and as we move away from the centre we shall have to accommodate, in ways indicated in later chapters, elements of a different character.

CHAPTER 6 / THE FOUNDATIONS OF A LEGAL SYSTEM

1. RULE OF RECOGNITION AND LEGAL VALIDITY

. . . The foundations of a legal system consist of the situation in which the majority of a social group habitually obey the orders backed by threats of the sovereign person or persons, who themselves habitually obey no one. This social situation is, for this theory, both a necessary and a sufficient condition of the existence of law. We have already exhibited in some detail the incapacity of this theory to account for some of the salient features of a modern municipal legal system: yet none the less, as its hold over the minds of many thinkers suggests, it does contain, though in a blurred and misleading form, certain truths about certain important aspects of law. These truths can, however, only be clearly presented, and their importance rightly assessed, in terms of the more complex social situation where a secondary rule of recognition is accepted and used for the identification of primary rules of obligation. It is this situation which deserves, if anything does, to be called the foundations of a legal system. In this chapter we shall discuss various elements of this situation which have received only partial or misleading expression in the theory of sovereignty and elsewhere.

Wherever such a rule of recognition is accepted, both private persons and officials are provided with authoritative criteria for identifying primary rules of obligation. The criteria so provided may, as we have seen, take any one or more of a variety of forms: these include reference to an authoritative text; to legislative enactment; to customary practice; to general declarations of specified persons, or to past judicial decisions in particular cases. In a very simple system like the world of Rex I . . . where only what he enacts is law and no legal limitations upon his legislative power are imposed by customary rule or constitutional document, the sole criterion for identifying the law will be a simple reference to the fact of enactment by Rex I. The existence of this simple form of rule of recognition will be manifest in the general practice, on the part of officials or private persons, of identifying the rules by this criterion. In a modern legal system where there are a variety of "sources" of law, the rule of recognition is correspondingly more complex: the criteria for identifying the law are multiple and commonly include a written constitution, enactment by a legislature, and judicial precedents. In most cases, provision is made for possible conflict by ranking these criteria in an order of relative subordination and primacy. It is in this way that in our system "common law" is subordinate to "statute."

It is important to distinguish this relative *subordination* of one criterion to another from *derivation*, since some spurious support for the view that all law is essentially or "really" (even if only "tacitly") the product of legislation, has been gained from confusion of these two ideas. In our own system, custom and precedent are subordinate to legislation since customary and common law rules may be deprived of their status as law by statute. Yet they owe their status of law, precarious as this may be, not to a "tacit" exercise of legislative power but to the acceptance of a rule of recognition which accords them this independent though subordinate place. Again, as in the simple case, the existence of such a complex rule of recognition with this hierarchical ordering of distinct criteria is manifested in the general practice of identifying the rules by such criteria.

In the day-to-day life of a legal system its rule of recognition is very seldom expressly formulated as a rule; though occasionally, courts in England may announce in general terms the relative place of one criterion of law in relation to another, as when they assert the supremacy of Acts of Parliament over other sources or suggested sources of law. For the most part the rule of recognition is not stated, but its existence is *shown* in the way in which particular rules are identified, either by courts or other officials or private persons or their advisers. There is, of course, a difference in the use made by courts of the criteria provided by the rule and the use of them by others: for when courts reach a particular conclusion on the footing that a particular rule has been correctly identified as law, what they say has a special authoritative status conferred on it by other rules. In this respect, as in many others, the rule of recognition of a legal system is like the scoring rule of a game. In the course of the game the general rule defining the activities which constitute scoring (runs, goals, &c.) is seldom formulated; instead it is *used* by officials and players in identifying the particular phases which count towards winning. Here too, the declarations of officials (umpire or scorer) have a special authoritative status attributed to them by other rules. Further, in both cases there is the possibility of a conflict between these authoritative applications of the rule and the general understanding of what the rule plainly requires according to its terms. This . . . is a complication which must be catered for in any account of what it is for a system of rules of this sort to exist.

The use of unstated rules of recognition, by courts and others, in identifying particular rules of the system is characteristic of the internal point of view. Those who use them in this way thereby manifest their own acceptance of them as guiding rules and with this attitude there goes a characteristic vocabulary different from the natural expressions of the external point of view. Perhaps the simplest of these is the expression, "It is the law that . . . ," which we may find on the lips not only of judges, but of ordinary men living under a legal system, when they identify a given rule of the system. This, like the expression "Out" or "Goal," is the language of one assessing a situation by reference to rules which he in common with others acknowledges as appropriate for this purpose. This attitude of shared acceptance of rules is to be contrasted with that of an observer who records *ab extra* the fact that a social group accepts such rules but does not himself accept them. The natural expression of this external point of view is not "It is the law that . . ." but "In England they recognize as law . . . whatever the Queen in Parliament enacts. . . ." The first of these forms of expression we shall call an *internal statement* because it manifests the internal point of view and is naturally used by one who, accepting the rule of recognition and without stating the fact that it is accepted, applies the rule in recognizing some particular rule of the system as valid. The second form of expression we shall call an *external statement* because it is the natural language of an external observer of the system who, without himself accepting its rule of recognition, states the fact that others accept it.

If this use of an accepted rule of recognition in making internal statements is understood and carefully distinguished from an external statement of fact that the rule is accepted, many obscurities concerning the notion of legal "validity" disappear. For the word "valid" is most frequently, though not always, used, in just such internal statements, applying to a particular rule of a legal system, an unstated but accepted rule of recognition. To say that a given rule is valid is to recognize it as passing all the tests provided by the rule of recognition and so as a rule of the system. We can indeed simply say that the statement that a particular rule is valid means that it satisfies all the criteria provided by the rule of recognition. This is incorrect only to the extent that it might obscure the internal character of such statements; for, like the cricketers' "Out," these statements of validity normally apply to a particular case a rule of recognition accepted by the speaker and others, rather than expressly state that the rule is satisfied.

Some of the puzzles connected with the idea of legal validity are said to concern the relation between the validity and the "efficacy" of law. If by "efficacy" is meant that the fact that a rule of law which requires certain behaviour is obeyed more often than not, it is plain that there is no necessary connection between the validity of any particular rule and *its* efficacy, unless the rule of recognition of the system includes among its criteria, as some do, the provision (sometimes referred to as a rule of obsolescence) that no rule is to count as a rule of the system if it has long ceased to be efficacious.

From the inefficacy of a particular rule, which may or may not count against its validity, we must distinguish a general disregard of the rules of the system. This may be so complete in character and so protracted that we should say, in the case of a new system, that it had never established itself as the legal system of a given group, or, in the case of a once-established system, that it had ceased to be the legal system of the group. In either case, the normal context or background for making any internal statement in terms of the rules of the system is absent. In such cases it would be generally *pointless* either to assess the rights and duties of particular persons by reference to the primary rules of a system or to assess the validity of any of its rules by reference to its rules of recognition. To insist on applying a system of rules which had either never actually been effective or had been discarded would, except in special circumstances mentioned below, be as futile as to assess the progress of a game by reference to a scoring rule which had never been accepted or had been discarded.

One who makes an internal statement concerning the validity of a particular rule of a system may be said to *presuppose* the truth of the external statement of fact that the system is generally efficacious. For the normal use of internal statements is in such a context of general efficacy. It would however be wrong to say that statements of validity "mean" that the system is generally efficacious. For though it is normally pointless or idle to talk of the validity of a rule of a system which has never established itself or has been discarded, none the less it is not meaningless nor is it always pointless. One vivid way of teaching Roman Law is to speak *as if* the system were efficacious still and to discuss the validity of particular rules and solve problems in their terms; and one way of nursing hopes for the restoration of an old social order destroyed by revolution, and rejecting the new, is to cling to the criteria of legal validity of the old regime. This is implicitly done by the White Russian who still claims property under some rule of descent which was a valid rule of Tsarist Russia.

A grasp of the normal contextual connection between the internal statement that a given rule of a system is valid and the external statement of fact that the system is generally efficacious, will help us see in its proper perspective the common theory that to assert the validity of a rule is to predict that it will be enforced by courts or some other official action taken. In many ways this theory is similar to the predictive analysis of obligation which we considered and rejected in the last chapter. In both cases alike the motive for advancing this predictive theory is the conviction that only thus can metaphysical interpretations be avoided: that either a statement that a rule is valid must ascribe some mysterious property which cannot be detected by empirical means or it must be a prediction of future behaviour of officials. In both cases also the plausibility of the theory is due to the same important fact: that the truth of the external statement of fact, which an observer might record, that the system is generally efficacious and likely to continue so, is normally presupposed by anyone who accepts the rules and makes an internal statement of obligation or validity. The two are certainly very closely associated. Finally, in both cases alike the mistake of the theory is the same: it consists in neglecting the special character of the internal statement and treating it as an external statement about official action.

This mistake becomes immediately apparent when we consider how the judge's own statement that a particular rule is valid functions in judicial decision; for, though here too, in making such a statement, the judge presupposes but does not state the general efficacy of the system, he plainly is not concerned to predict his own or others' official action. His statement that a rule is valid is an internal statement recognizing that the rule satisfies the tests for identifying what is to count as law in his court, and constitutes not a prophecy of but part of the *reason* for his decision. There is indeed a more plausible case for saying that a statement that a rule is valid is a prediction when such a statement is made by a private person; for in the case of conflict between unofficial statements of validity or invalidity and that of a court in deciding a case, there is often good sense in saying that the former must then be withdrawn. Yet even here, . . . to investigate the significance of such conflicts between official declarations and the plain requirements of the rules, it may be dogmatic to assume that it is withdrawn as a statement now shown to be *wrong,* because it has falsely *predicted* what a court would say. For there are more reasons for withdrawing statements than the fact that they are wrong, and also more ways of being wrong than this allows.

The rule of recognition providing the criteria by which the validity of other rules of the system is assessed is in an important sense, which we shall try to clarify, an *ultimate* rule: and where, as is usual, there are several criteria ranked in order of relative subordination and primacy one of them is *supreme.* These ideas of the ultimacy of the rule of recognition and the supremacy of one of its criteria merit some attention. It is important to disentangle them from the theory, which we have rejected, that somewhere in every legal system, even though it lurks behind legal forms, there must be a sovereign legislative power which is legally unlimited.

Of these two ideas, supreme criterion and ultimate rule, the first is the easiest to define. We may say that a criterion of legal validity or source of law is supreme if rules identified by reference to it are still recognized as rules of the system, even if they conflict with rules identified by reference to the other criteria, whereas rules identified by reference to the latter are not so recognized if they conflict with the rules identified by reference to the supreme criterion. A similar explanation in comparative terms can be given of the notions of "superior" and "subordinate" criteria which we have already used. It is plain that the notions of a superior and a supreme criterion merely refer to a *relative* place on a scale and do not import any notion of legally *unlimited* legislative power. Yet "supreme" and "unlimited" are easy to confuse—at least in legal theory. One reason for this is that in the simpler forms of legal system the ideas of ultimate rule of recognition, supreme criterion, and legally unlimited legislature seem to converge. For where there is a legislature subject to no constitutional limitations and competent by its enactment to deprive all other rules of law emanating from other sources of their status as law, it is part of the rule of recognition in such a system that enactment by that legislature is the supreme criterion of validity. This is, according to constitutional theory, the position in the United Kingdom. But even systems like that of the United States in which there is no such legally unlimited legislature may perfectly well contain an ultimate rule of recognition which provides a set of criteria of validity, one of which is supreme. This will be so, where the legislative competence of the ordinary legislature is limited by a constitution which contains no amending power, or places some clauses outside the scope of that power. Here there is no legally unlimited legislature, even in the widest interpretation of "legislature"; but the system of course contains an ultimate rule of recognition and, in the clauses of its constitution, a supreme criterion of validity.

The sense in which the rule of recognition is the *ultimate* rule of a system is best understood if we pursue a very familiar chain of legal reasoning. If the question is raised whether some suggested rule is legally valid, we must, in order to answer the question, use a criterion of validity provided by some other rule. Is this purported by-law of the Oxfordshire County Council valid? Yes: because it was made in exercise of the powers conferred, and in accordance with the procedure specified, by a statutory order made by the Minister of Health. At this first stage the statutory order provides the criteria in terms of which the validity of the by-law is assessed. There may be no practical need to go farther; but there is a standing possibility of doing so. We may query the validity of the statutory order and assess its validity in terms of the statute empowering the minister to make such orders. Finally, when the validity of the statute has been queried and assessed by reference to the rule that what the Queen in Parliament enacts is law, we are brought to a stop in inquiries concerning validity: for we have reached a rule which, like the intermediate statutory order and statute, provides criteria for the assessment of the validity of other rules; but it is also unlike them in that there is no rule providing criteria for the assessment of its own legal validity.

There are, indeed, many questions which we can raise about this ultimate rule. We can ask whether it is the practice of courts, legislatures, officials, or private citizens in England actually to use this rule as an ultimate rule of recognition. Or has our process of legal reasoning been an idle game with the criteria of validity of a system now discarded? We can ask whether it is a satisfactory form of legal system which has such a rule at its root. Does it produce more good than evil? Are there prudential reasons for supporting it? Is there a moral obligation to do so? These are plainly very important questions; but, equally plainly, when we ask them about the rule of recognition, we are no longer attempting to answer the same kind of question about it as those which we answered about other rules with its aid. When we move from saying that a particular enactment is valid, because it satisfies the rule that what the Queen in Parliament enacts is law, to saying that in England this last rule is used by courts, officials, and private persons as the ultimate rule of recognition, we have moved from an internal statement of law asserting the validity of a rule of the system to an external statement of fact which an observer of the system might make even if he did not accept it. So too when we move from the statement that a particular enactment is valid, to the statement that the rule of recognition of the system is an excellent one and the system based on it is one worthy of support, we have moved from a statement of legal validity to a statement of value. . . .

In the simple system of primary rules of obligation sketched in the last chapter, the assertion that a given rule existed could only be an external statement of fact such as an observer who did not accept the rules might make and verify by ascertaining whether or not, as a matter of fact, a given mode of behaviour was generally accepted as a standard and was accompanied by those features which, as we have seen, distinguish a social rule from mere convergent habits. It is in this way also that we should now interpret and verify the assertion that in England a rule—though not a legal one—exists that we must bare the head on entering a church. If such rules as these are found to exist in the actual practice of a social group, there is no separate question of their validity to be discussed, though of course their value or desirability is open to question. Once their existence has been established as a fact we should only confuse matters by affirming or denying that they were valid or by saying that "we assumed" but could not show their validity. Where, on the other hand, as in a mature legal system, we have a system of rules which includes a rule of recognition so that the status of a rule as a member of the system now depends on whether it satisfies certain criteria provided by the rule of recognition, this brings with it a new application of the word "exist." The statement that a rule exists may now no longer be what it was in the simple case of customary rules—an external statement of the *fact* that a certain mode of behaviour was generally accepted as a standard in practice. It may now be an internal statement applying an accepted but unstated rule of recognition and meaning (roughly) no more than "valid given the system's criteria of validity." In this respect, however, as in others a rule of recognition is unlike other rules of the system. The assertion that it exists can only be an external statement of fact. For whereas a subordinate rule of a system may be valid and in that sense "exist" even if it is generally disregarded, the rule of recognition exists only as a complex, but normally concordant, practice of the courts, officials, and private persons in identifying the law by reference to certain criteria. Its existence is a matter of fact. . . .

9

RONALD M. DWORKIN

The Model of Rules I

3. RULES, PRINCIPLES, AND POLICIES

I want to make a general attack on positivism, and I shall use H. L. A. Hart's version as a target, when a particular target is needed. My strategy will be organized around the fact that when lawyers reason or dispute about legal rights and obligations, particularly in those hard cases when our problems with these concepts seem most acute, they make use of standards that do not function as rules, but operate differently as principles, policies, and other sorts of standards. Positivism, I shall argue, is a model of and for a system of rules, and its central notion of a single fundamental test for law forces us to miss the important roles of these standards that are not rules.

I just spoke of "principles, policies, and other sorts of standards." Most often I shall use the term "principle" generically, to refer to the whole set of these standards other than rules; occasionally, however, I shall be more precise, and distinguish between principles and policies. Although nothing in the present argument will turn on the distinction, I should state how I draw it. I call a "policy" that kind of standard that sets out a goal to be reached, generally an improvement in some economic, political, or social feature of the community (though some goals are negative, in that they stipulate that some present feature is to be protected from adverse change). I call a "principle" a standard that is to be observed, not because it will advance or secure an economic, political, or social situation deemed desirable, but because it is a requirement of justice or fairness or some other dimension of morality. Thus the standard that automobile accidents are to be decreased is a policy, and the standard that no man may profit by his own wrong a principle. The distinction can be collapsed by construing a principle as stating a social goal (*i.e.,* the goal of a society in which no man profits by his own wrong), or by construing a policy as stating a principle (*i.e.,* the principle that the goal the policy embraces is a worthy one) or by adopting the utilitarian thesis that principles of justice are disguised statements of goals (securing the greatest happiness of the greatest number). In some contexts the distinction has uses which are lost if it is thus collapsed.[1]

My immediate purpose, however, is to distinguish principles in the generic sense from rules, and I shall start by collecting some examples of the former. The examples I offer are chosen haphazardly; almost any case in a law school casebook would provide examples that would serve as well. In 1889 a New York court, in the famous case of *Riggs v. Palmer*[2], had to decide whether an heir named in the will of his grandfather could inherit under that will, even though he had murdered his grandfather to do so. The court began its reasoning with this admission: "It is quite true that statutes regulating the making, proof and effect of wills, and the devolution of property, if literally construed, and if their force and effect can in no way and under no circumstances be controlled or modified, give this property to the murderer."[3] But the court continued to note that "all laws as well as all contracts may be controlled in their operation and effect by general, fundamental maxims of the common law. No one shall be permitted to profit by his own fraud, or to take advantage of his own wrong, or to found any claim upon his own iniquity, or to acquire property by his own crime."[4] The murderer did not receive his inheritance.

In 1960, a New Jersey court was faced, in *Henningsen v. Bloomfield Motors, Inc.*[5] with the important question of whether (or how much) an automobile manufacturer may limit his liability in case the automobile is defective. Henningsen had bought a car, and signed a contract which said that the manufacturer's liability for defects was limited to "making good" defective parts—"this warranty being expressly in lieu of all other warranties, obligations or liabilities." Henningsen argued that, at least in the circumstances of his case, the manufacturer ought not to be protected by this limitation, and ought to be liable for the medical and other expenses of persons injured in a crash. He was not able to point to any statute, or to any established rule of law, that prevented the manufacturer from standing on the contract. The court nevertheless agreed with Henningsen. At various points in the court's argument the following appeals to standards are made: (a) "[W]e must keep in mind the general principle that, in the absence of fraud, one who does not choose to read a contract before signing it cannot later relieve himself of its burdens."[6] (b) "In applying that principle, the basic tenet of freedom of competent parties to contract is a factor of importance."[7] (c) "Freedom of contract is not such an immutable doctrine as to admit of no qualification in the area in which we are concerned."[8] (d) "In a society such as ours, where the automobile is a common and necessary adjunct of daily life, and where its use is so fraught with danger to the driver, passengers and the public, the manufacturer is under a special obligation in connection with the construction, promotion and sale of his cars. Consequently, the courts must examine purchase agreements closely to see if consumer and public interests are treated fairly."[9] (e) "'[I]s there any principle which is more familiar or more firmly embedded in the history of Anglo-American law than the basic doctrine that the courts will not permit themselves to be used as instruments of inequity and injustice?'"[10] (f) "'More specifically the courts generally refuse to lend themselves to the enforcement of a "bargain" in which one party has unjustly taken advantage of the economic necessities of other. . . .'"[11]

The standards set out in these quotations are not the sort we think of as legal rules. They seem very different from propositions like "The maximum legal speed on the turnpike is sixty miles an hour" or "A will is invalid unless signed by three witnesses." They

[1]See . . . Dworkin, "Wasserstrom: The Judicial Decision," 75 *Ethics* 47 (1964), reprinted as "Does Law Have a Function?," 74 *Yale Law Journal* 640 (1965).
[2]115 N.Y. 506, 22 N.E. 188 (1889).
[3]*Id.* at 509, 22 N.E. at 189.
[4]*Id.* at 511, 22 N.E. at 190.
[5]32 N.J. 358, 161 A.2d 69 (1960).
[6]*Id.* at 386, 161 A.2d at 84.
[7]*Id.*
[8]*Id.* at 388, 161 A.2d at 86.
[9]*Id.* at 387, 161 A.2d at 85.
[10]*Id.* at 389, 161 A.2d at 86 (quoting Frankfurter, J., in *United States v. Bethlehem Steel,* 315 U.S. 289, 326 [1942]).
[11]*Id.*

are different because they are legal principles rather than legal rules.

The difference between legal principles and legal rules is a logical distinction. Both sets of standards point to particular decisions about legal obligation in particular circumstances, but they differ in the character of the direction they give. Rules are applicable in an all-or-nothing fashion. If the facts a rule stipulates are given, then either the rule is valid, in which case the answer it supplies must be accepted, or it is not, in which case it contributes nothing to the decision.

This all-or-nothing is seen most plainly if we look at the way rules operate, not in law, but in some enterprise they dominate—a game, for example. In baseball a rule provides that if the batter has had three strikes, he is out. An official cannot consistently acknowledge that this is an accurate statement of a baseball rule, and decide that a batter who has had three strikes is not out. Of course, a rule may have exceptions (the batter who has taken three strikes is not out if the catcher drops the third strike). However, an accurate statement of the rule would take this exception into account, and any that did not would be incomplete. If the list of exceptions is very large, it would be too clumsy to repeat them each time the rule is cited; there is, however, no reason in theory why they could not all be added on, and the more that are, the more accurate is the statement of the rule.

If we take baseball rules as a model, we find that rules of law, like the rule that a will is invalid unless signed by three witnesses, fit the model well. If the requirement of three witnesses is a valid legal rule, then it cannot be that a will has been signed by only two witnesses and is valid. The rule might have exceptions, but if it does then it is inaccurate and incomplete to state the rule so simply, without enumerating the exceptions. In theory, at least, the exceptions could all be listed, and the more of them that are, the more complete is the statement of the rule.

But this is not the way the sample principles in the quotations operate. Even those which look most like rules do not set out legal consequences that follow automatically when the conditions provided are met. We say that our law respects the principle that no man may profit from his own wrong, but we do not mean that the law never permits a man to profit from wrongs he commits. In fact, people often profit, perfectly legally, from their legal wrongs. The most notorious case is adverse possession—if I trespass on your land long enough, some day I will gain a right to cross your land whenever I please. There are many less dramatic examples. If a man leaves one job, breaking a contract, to take a much higher paying job, he may have to pay damages to his first employer, but he is usually entitled to keep his new salary. If a man jumps bail and crosses state lines to make a brilliant investment in another state, he may be sent back to jail, but he will keep his profits.

We do not treat these—and countless other counter-instances that can easily be imagined—as showing that the principle about profiting from one's wrongs is not a principle of our legal system, or that it is incomplete and needs qualifying exceptions. We do not treat counter-instances as exceptions (at least not exceptions in the way in which a catcher's dropping the third strike is an exception) because we could not hope to capture these counter-instances simply by a more extended statement of the principle. They are not, even in theory, subject to enumeration, because we would have to include not only these cases (like adverse possession) in which some institution has already provided that profit can be gained through a wrong, but also those numberless imaginary cases in which we know in advance that the principle would not hold. Listing some of these might sharpen our sense of the principle's weight (I shall mention that dimension in a moment), but it would not make for a more accurate or complete statement of the principle.

A principle like "No man may profit from his own wrong" does not even purport to set out conditions that make its application necessary. Rather, it states a reason that argues in one direction, but does not necessitate a particular decision. If a man has or is about to receive something, as a direct result of something illegal he did to get it, then that is a reason which the law will take into account in deciding whether he should keep it. There may be other principles or policies arguing in the other direction—a policy of securing title, for example, or a principle limiting punishment to what the legislature has stipulated. If so, our principle may not prevail, but that does not mean that it is not a principle of our legal system, because in the next case, when these contravening considerations are absent or less weighty, the principle may be decisive. All that is meant, when we say that a particular principle is a principle of our law, is that the principle is one which officials must take into account, if it is relevant, as a consideration inclining in one direction or another.

The logical distinction between rules and principles appears more clearly when we consider principles that do not even look like rules. Consider the proposition, set out under "(d)" in the excerpts from the *Henningsen* opinion, that "the manufacturer is under a special obligation in connection with the construction, promotion and sale of his cars." This does not even purport to define the specific duties such a special obligation entails, or to tell us what rights automobile consumers acquire as a result. It merely states—and this is an essential link in the *Henningsen* argument—that automobile manufacturers must be held to higher standards than other manufacturers, and are less entitled to rely on the competing principle of freedom of contract. It does not mean that they may never rely on that principle, or that courts may rewrite automobile purchase contracts at will; it means only that if a particular clause seems unfair or burdensome, courts have less reason to enforce the clause than if it were for the purchase of neckties. The "special obligation" counts in favor, but does not in itself necessitate, a decision refusing to enforce the terms of an automobile purchase contract.

This first difference between rules and principles entails another. Principles have a dimension that rules do not—the dimension of weight or importance. When principles intersect (the policy of protecting automobile consumers intersecting with principles of freedom of contract, for example), one who must resolve the conflict has to take into account the relative weight of each. This cannot be, of course, an exact measurement, and the judgment that a particular principle or policy is more important than another will often be a controversial one. Nevertheless, it is an integral part of the concept of a principle that it has this dimension, that it makes sense to ask how important or how weighty it is.

Rules do not have this dimension. We can speak of rules as being *functionally* important or unimportant (the baseball rule that three strikes are out is more important than the rule that runners may advance on a balk, because the game would be much more changed with the first rule altered than the second). In this sense, one legal rule may be more important than another because it has a greater or more important role in regulating behavior. But we cannot say that one rule is more important than another within the system of rules, so that when two rules conflict one supersedes the other by virtue of its greater weight.

If two rules conflict, one of them cannot be a valid rule. The decision as to which is valid, and which must be abandoned or recast, must be made by appealing to considerations beyond the rules themselves. A legal system might regulate such conflicts by other rules, which prefer the rule enacted by the higher authority, or the rule enacted later, or the more specific rule, or something of that sort. A legal system may also prefer the rule supported by the more important principles. (Our own legal system uses both of these techniques.)

It is not always clear from the form of a standard whether it is a rule or a principle. "A will is invalid unless signed by three witnesses" is not very different in form from "A man may not profit from his own wrong," but one who knows something of American law knows that he must take the first as stating a rule and the second as stating a principle. In many cases the distinction is difficult to make—it may not have been settled how the standard should operate, and this issue may itself be a focus of controversy. The first amendment to the United States Constitution contains the provision that Congress shall not abridge freedom of speech. Is this a rule, so that if a particular law does abridge freedom of speech, it follows that it is unconstitutional? Those who claim that the first amendment is "an absolute" say that it must be taken in this way, that is, as a rule. Or does it merely state a principle, so that when an abridgement of speech is discovered, it is unconstitutional unless the context presents some other policy or principle which in the circumstances is weighty enough to permit the abridgement? That is the position of those who argue for what is called the "clear and present danger" test or some other form of "balancing."

Sometimes a rule and a principle can play much the same role, and the difference between them is almost a matter of form alone. The first section of the Sherman Act states that every contract in restraint of trade shall be void. The Supreme Court had to make the decision whether this provision should be treated as a rule in its own terms (striking down every contract "which restrains trade," which almost any contract does) or as a principle, providing a reason for striking down a contract in the absence of effective contrary policies. The Court construed the provision as a rule, but treated that rule as containing the word "unreasonable," and as prohibiting only "unreasonable" restraints of trade.[12] This

[12] *Standard Oil v. United States,* 221 U.S. 1, 60 (1911); *United States v. American Tobacco Co.,* 221 U.S. 106, 180 (1911).

allowed the provision to function logically as a rule (whenever a court finds that the restraint is "unreasonable" it is bound to hold the contract invalid) and substantially as a principle (a court must take into account a variety of other principles and policies in determining whether a particular restraint in particular economic circumstances is "unreasonable").

Words like "reasonable," "negligent," "unjust," and "significant" often perform just this function. Each of these terms makes the application of the rule which contains it depend to some extent upon principles or policies lying beyond the rule, and in this way makes that rule itself more like a principle. But they do not quite turn the rule into a principle, because even the least confining of these terms restricts the *kind* of other principles and policies on which the rule depends. If we are bound by a rule that says that "unreasonable" contracts are void, or that grossly "unfair" contracts will not be enforced, much more judgment is required than if the quoted terms were omitted. But suppose a case in which some consideration of policy or principle suggests that a contract should be enforced even though its restraint is not reasonable, or even though it is grossly unfair. Enforcing these contracts would be forbidden by our rules, and thus permitted only if these rules were abandoned or modified. If we were dealing, however, not with a rule but with a policy against enforcing unreasonable contracts, or a principle that unfair contracts ought not to be enforced, the contracts could be enforced without alteration of the law.

4. PRINCIPLES AND THE CONCEPT OF LAW

Once we identify legal principles as separate sorts of standards, different from legal rules, we are suddenly aware of them all around us. Law teachers teach them, lawbooks cite them, legal historians celebrate them. But they seem most energetically at work, carrying most weight, in difficult lawsuits like *Riggs* and *Henningsen*. In cases like these, principles play an essential part in arguments supporting judgments about particular legal rights and obligations. After the case is decided, we may say that the case stands for a particular rule (e.g., the rule that one who murders is not eligible to take under the will of his victim). But the rule does not exist before the case is decided; the court cites principles as its justification for adopting and applying a new rule. In *Riggs*, the court cited the principle that no man may profit from his own wrong as a background standard against which to read the statute of wills and in this way justified a new interpretation of that statute. In *Henningsen*, the court cited a variety of intersecting principles and policies as authority for a new rule respecting manufacturers' liability for automobile defects.

An analysis of the concept of legal obligation must therefore account for the important role of principles in reaching particular decisions of law. . . .

. . . Would we also have to abandon or modify the first tenet, the proposition that law is distinguished by tests of the sort that can be set out in a master rule like Professor Hart's rule of recognition? If principles of the *Riggs* and *Henningsen* sort are to count as law, and we are nevertheless to preserve the notion of a master rule for law, then we must be able to deploy some test that all (and only) the principles that do count as law meet. Let us begin with the test Hart suggests for identifying valid *rules* of law, to see whether these can be made to work for principles as well.

Most rules of law, according to Hart, are valid because some competent institution enacted them. Some were created by a legislature, in the form of statutory enactments. Others were created by judges who formulated them to decide particular cases, and thus established them as precedents for the future. But this test of pedigree will not work for the *Riggs* and *Henningsen* principles. The origin of these as legal principles lies not in a particular decision of some legislature or court, but in a sense of appropriateness developed in the profession and the public over time. Their continued power depends upon this sense of appropriateness being sustained. If it no longer seemed unfair to allow people to profit by their wrongs, or fair to place special burdens upon oligopolies that manufacture potentially dangerous machines, these principles would no longer play much of a role in new cases, even if they had never been overruled or repealed. (Indeed, it hardly makes sense to speak of principles like these as being "overruled" or "repealed." When they decline they are eroded, not torpedoed.)

True, if we were challenged to back up our claim that some principle is a principle of law, we would mention any prior cases in which that principle was cited, or figured in the argument. We would also mention any statute that seemed to exemplify that principle (even better if the principle was cited in the preamble of the statute, or in the committee reports or other legislative documents that accompanied it). Unless we could find some such institutional support, we would probably fail to make out our case, and the more support we found, the more weight we could claim for the principle.

Yet we could not devise any formula for testing how much and what kind of institutional support is necessary to make a principle a legal principle, still less to fix its weight at a particular order of magnitude. We argue for a particular principle by grappling with a whole set of shifting, developing and interacting standards (themselves principles rather than rules) about institutional responsibility, statutory interpretation, the persuasive force of various sorts of precedent, the relation of all these to contemporary moral practices, and hosts of other such standards. We could not bolt all of these together into a single "rule," even a complex one, and if we could the result would bear little relation to Hart's picture of a rule of recognition, which is the picture of a fairly stable master rule specifying "some feature or features possession of which by a suggested rule is taken as a conclusive affirmative indication that it is a rule. . . ."[13]

Moreover, the techniques we apply in arguing for another principle do not stand (as Hart's rule of recognition is designed to) on an entirely different level from the principles they support. Hart's sharp distinction between acceptance and validity does not hold. If we are arguing for the principle that a man should not profit from his own wrong, we could cite the acts of courts and legislatures that exemplify it, but this speaks as much to the principle's acceptance as its validity. (It seems odd to speak of a principle as being valid at all, perhaps because validity is an all-or-nothing concept, appropriate for rules, but inconsistent with a principle's dimension of weight.) If we are asked (as we might well be) to defend the particular doctrine of precedent, or the particular technique of statutory interpretation, that we used in this argument, we should certainly cite the practice of others in using that doctrine or technique. But we should also cite other general principles that we believe support that practice, and this introduces a note of validity into the chord of acceptance. We might argue, for example, that the use we make of earlier cases and statutes is supported by a particular analysis of the point of the practice of legislation or the doctrine of precedent, or by the principles of democratic theory, or by a particular position on the proper division of authority between national and local institutions, or something else of that sort. Nor is this path of support a one-way street leading to some ultimate principle resting on acceptance alone. Our principles of legislation, precedent, democracy, or federalism might be challenged too; and if they were we should argue for them, not only in terms of practice, but in terms of each other and in terms of the implications of trends of judicial and legislative decisions, even though this last would involve appealing to those same doctrines of interpretation we justified through the principles we are now trying to support. At this level of abstraction, in other words, principles rather hang together than link together.

So even though principles draw support from the official acts of legal institutions, they do not have a simple or direct enough connection with these acts to frame that connection in terms of criteria specified by some ultimate master rule of recognition. Is there any other route by which principles might be brought under such a rule?

Hart does say that a master rule might designate as law not only rules enacted by particular legal institutions, but rules established by *custom* as well. He has in mind a problem that bothered other positivists, including Austin. Many of our most ancient legal rules were never explicitly created by a legislature or a court. When they made their first appearance in legal opinions and texts, they were treated as already being part of the law because they represented the customary practice of the community, or some specialized part of it, like the business community. (The examples ordinarily given are rules of mercantile practice, like the rules governing what rights arise under a standard form of commercial paper.)[14] Since Austin thought that all law was the command of a determinate sovereign, he held that these customary practices were not law until the courts (as agents of the sovereign) recognized them, and that the courts were indulging in a fiction in pretending otherwise. But that seemed arbitrary. If everyone thought

[13]H. L. A. Hart, *The Concept of Law* 92 (1961).

[14]See Note, "Custom and Trade Usage: Its Application to Commercial Dealings and the Common Law," 55 *Columbia Law Review* 1192 (1955), and materials cited therein at 1193 n.1. As that note makes plain, the actual practices of courts in recognizing trade customs follow the pattern of applying a set of general principles and policies rather than a test that could be captured as part of a rule of recognition.

custom might in itself be law, the fact that Austin's theory said otherwise was not persuasive.

Hart reversed Austin on this point. The master rule, he says, might stipulate that some custom counts as law even before the courts recognize it. But he does not face the difficulty this raises for his general theory because he does not attempt to set out the criteria a master rule might use for this purpose. It cannot use, as its only criterion, the provision that the community regard the practice as *morally* binding, for this would not distinguish legal customary rules from moral customary rules, and of course not all of the community's long-standing customary moral obligations are enforced at law. If, on the other hand, the test is whether the community regards the customary practice as *legally* binding, the whole point of the master rule is undercut, at least for this class of legal rules. The master rule, says Hart, marks the transformation from a primitive society to one with law, because it provides a test for determining social rules of law other than by measuring their acceptance. But if the master rule says merely that whatever other rules the community accepts as legally binding are legally binding, then it provides no such test at all, beyond the test we should use were there no master rule. The master rule becomes (for these cases) a non-rule of recognition; we might as well say that every primitive society has a secondary rule of recognition, namely the rule that whatever is accepted as binding is binding. Hart himself, in discussing international law, ridicules the idea that such a rule could be a rule of recognition, by describing the proposed rule as "an empty repetition of the mere fact that the society concerned . . . observes certain standards of conduct as obligatory rules."[15]

Hart's treatment of custom amounts, indeed, to a confession that there are at least some rules of law that are not binding because they are valid under standards laid down by a master rule but are binding—like the master rule—because they are accepted as binding by the community. This chips at the neat pyramidal architecture we admired in Hart's theory: we can no longer say that only the master rule is binding because of its acceptance, all other rules being valid under its terms.

This is perhaps only a chip, because the customary rules Hart has in mind are no longer a very significant part of the law. But it does suggest that Hart would be reluctant to widen the damage by bringing under the head of "custom" all those crucial principles and policies we have been discussing. If he were to call these part of the law and yet admit that the only test of their force lies in the degree to which they are accepted as law by the community or some part thereof, he would very sharply reduce that area of the law over which his master rule held any dominion. It is not just that all the principles and policies would escape its sway, though that would be bad enough. Once these principles and policies are accepted as law, and thus as standards judges must follow in determining legal obligations, it would follow that *rules* like those announced for the first time in *Riggs* and *Henningsen* owe their force at least in part to the authority of principles and policies, and so not entirely to the master rule of recognition.

So we cannot adapt Hart's version of positivism by modifying his rule of recognition to embrace principles. No tests of pedigree, relating principles to acts of legislation, can be formulated, nor can his concept of customary law, itself an exception to the first tenet of positivism, be made to serve without abandoning that tenet altogether. One more possibility must be considered, however. If no rule of recognition can provide a test for identifying principles, why not say that principles are ultimate, and *form* the rule of recognition of our law? The answer to the general question "What is valid law in an American jurisdiction?" would then require us to state all the principles (as well as ultimate constitutional rules) in force in that jurisdiction at the time, together with appropriate assignments of weight. A positivist might then regard the complete set of these standards as the rule of recognition of the jurisdiction. This solution has the attraction of paradox, but of course it is an unconditional surrender. If we simply

[15]H. L. A. Hart, *The Concept of Law* 230 (1961). A master rule might specify some particular feature of a custom that is independent of the community's attitude; it might provide, for example, that all customs of very great age, or all customs having to do with negotiable instruments count as law. I can think of no such features that in fact distinguish the customs that have been recognized as law in England or America, however. Some customs that are not legally enforceable are older than some that are, some practices relating to commercial paper are enforced and others not, and so forth. In any event, even if a distinguishing feature were found that identified all rules of law established by custom, it would remain unlikely that such a feature could be found for principles which vary widely in their subject matter and pedigree and some of which are of very recent origin.

designate our rule of recognition by the phrase "the complete set of principles in force," we achieve only the tautology that law is law. If, instead, we tried actually to list all the principles in force we would fail. They are controversial, their weight is all important, they are numberless, and they shift and change so fast that the start of our list would be obsolete before we reached the middle. Even if we succeeded, we would not have a key for law because there would be nothing left for our key to unlock.

I conclude that if we treat principles as law we must reject the positivists' first tenet, that the law of a community is distinguished from other social standards by some test in the form of a master rule. We have already decided that we must then abandon the second tenet—the doctrine of judicial discretion—or clarify it into triviality. What of the third tenet, the positivists' theory of legal obligation?

This theory holds that a legal obligation exists when (and only when) an established rule of law imposes such an obligation. It follows from this that in a hard case—when no such established rule can be found—there is no legal obligation until the judge creates a new rule for the future. The judge may apply that new rule to the parties in the case, but this is *ex post facto* legislation, not the enforcement of an existing obligation.

The positivists' doctrine of discretion (in the strong sense) required this view of legal obligation, because if a judge has discretion there can be no legal right or obligation—no entitlement—that he must enforce. Once we abandon that doctrine, however, and treat principles as law, we raise the possibility that a legal obligation might be imposed by a constellation of principles as well as by an established rule. We might want to say that a legal obligation exists whenever the case supporting such an obligation, in terms of binding legal principles of different sorts, is stronger than the case against it.

Of course, many questions would have to be answered before we could accept that view of legal obligation. If there is no rule of recognition, no test for law in that sense, how do we decide which principles are to count, and how much, in making such a case? How do we decide whether one case is better than another? If legal obligation rests on an undemonstrable judgment of that sort, how can it provide a justification for a judicial decision that one party had a legal obligation? Does this view of obligation square with the way lawyers, judges and laymen speak, and is it consistent with our attitudes about moral obligation? Does this analysis help us to deal with the classical jurisprudential puzzles about the nature of law?

These questions must be faced, but even the questions promise more than positivism provides. Positivism, on its own thesis, stops short of just those puzzling, hard cases that send us to look for theories of law. When we read these cases, the positivist remits us to a doctrine of discretion that leads nowhere and tells nothing. His picture of law as a system of rules has exercised a tenacious hold on our imagination, perhaps through its very simplicity. If we shake ourselves loose from this model of rules, we may be able to build a model truer to the complexity and sophistication of our own practices.

10

Riggs v. Palmer

22 N.E. 188 (1889)

OPINION BY: EARL

Opinion: Earl, J. On the 13th day of August 1880, Francis B. Palmer made his last will and testament, in which he gave small legacies to his two daughters, Mrs. Riggs and Mrs. Preston, the plaintiffs in this action, and the remainder of his estate to his grandson, the defendant, Elmer E. Palmer, subject to the support of Susan Palmer, his mother, with a gift over to the two daughters, subject to the support of Mrs. Palmer, in case Elmer should survive him and die under age, unmarried and without any issue. The testator at the date of his will owned a farm and considerable personal property. He was a widower, and thereafter, in March 1882, he was married to Mrs. Bresee, with whom before his marriage he entered into an ante-nuptial contract in which it was agreed that, in lieu of dower and all other claims upon his estate in case she survived him, she should have her support upon his farm during her life, and such support was expressly charged upon the farm. At the date of the will, and, subsequently , to the death of the testator, Elmer lived with him as a member of his family, and at his death was sixteen years old. He knew of the provisions made in his favor in the will, and, that he might prevent his grandfather from revoking such provisions, which he had manifested some intention to do, and to obtain the speedy enjoyment and immediate possession of his property, he willfully murdered him by poisoning him. He now claims the property, and the sole question for our determination is, can he have it? The defendants say that the testator is dead; that his will was made in due form and has been admitted to probate and that, therefore, it must have effect according to the letter of the law.

It is quite true that statutes regulating the making, proof and effect of wills, and the devolution of property, if literally construed, and if their force and effect can in no way and under no circumstances be controlled or modified, give this property to the murderer.

The purpose of those statutes was to enable testators to dispose of their estates to the objects of their bounty at death, and to carry into effect their final wishes legally expressed; and in considering and giving effect to them this purpose must be kept in view. It was the intention of the law-makers that the donees in a will should have the property given to them. But it never could have been their intention that a donee who murdered the testator to make the will operative should have any benefit under it. If such a case had been present to their minds, and it had been supposed necessary to make some provision of law to meet it, it cannot be doubted that they would have provided for it. It is a familiar canon of construction that a thing which is within the intention of the makers of a statute is as much within the statute as if it were within the letter; and a thing which is within the letter of the statute is not within the statute, unless it be within the intention of the makers. The writers of laws do not always express their intention perfectly, but either exceed it or fall short of it, so that judges are to collect it from probable or rational conjectures only, and this is called rational interpretation; and Rutherforth, in his Institutes (p. 407) says: "When we make use of rational interpretation, sometimes we restrain the meaning of the writer so as to take in less, and sometimes we extend or enlarge his meaning so as to take in more than his words express."

Such a construction ought to be put upon a statute as will best answer the intention which the makers had in view, for *qui haeret in litera, haeret in cortice*. In Bacon's Abridgment (Statutes I, 5); Pufendorf (book 5, chapter 12), Rutherforth (pp. 422, 427), and in Smith's Commentaries (814), many cases are mentioned where it was held that matters embraced in the general words of statutes, nevertheless, were not within the statutes, because it could not have been the intention of the law-makers that they should be included. They were taken out of the statutes by an equitable construction, and it is said in Bacon: "By an equitable construction, a case not within the letter of the statute is sometimes holden to be within the meaning, because it is within the mischief for which a remedy is provided. The reason for such construction is that the law-makers could not set down every case in express terms. In order to form a right judgment whether a case be within the equity of a statute, it is a good way to suppose the law-maker present, and that you have asked him this question, did you intend to comprehend this case? Then you must give yourself such answer as you imagine he, being an upright and reasonable man, would have given. If this be that he did mean to comprehend it, you may safely hold the case to be within the equity of the statute; for while you do no more than he would have done, you do not act contrary to the statute, but in conformity thereto." In some cases the letter of a legislative act is restrained by an equitable construction; in others it is enlarged; in others the construction is contrary to the letter. The equitable construction which restrains the letter of a statute is defined by Aristotle, as frequently quoted, in this manner: *Aequitas est correctio legis generaliter latoe qua parti deficit.* If the law-makers could, as to this case, be consulted, would they say that they intended by their general language that the property of a testator or of an ancestor should pass to one who had taken his life for the express purpose of getting his property? In 1 Blackstone's Commentaries (91) the learned author, speaking of the construction of statutes, says: "If there arise out of them any absurd consequences manifestly contradictory to common reason, they are, with regard to those collateral consequences, void. When some collateral matter arises out of the general words, and happens to be unreasonable, then the judges are in decency to conclude that the consequence was not foreseen by the parliament, and, therefore, they are at liberty to expound the statute by equity and only *quoad hoc* disregard it;" and he gives as an illustration, if an act of parliament gives a man power to try all causes that arise within his manor of Dale, yet, if a cause should arise in which he himself is party, the act is construed not to extend to that because it is unreasonable that any man should determine his own quarrel.

There was a statute in Bologna that whoever drew blood in the streets should be severely punished, and yet it was held not to apply to the case of a barber who opened a vein in the street. It is commanded in the Decalogue that no work shall be done upon the Sabbath, and yet, giving the command a rational interpretation founded upon its design, the Infallible Judge held that it did not prohibit works of necessity, charity or benevolence on that day.

What could be more unreasonable than to suppose that it was the legislative intention in the general laws passed for the orderly, peaceable and just devolution of property, that they should have operation in favor of one who murdered his ancestor that he might speedily come into the possession of his estate? Such an intention is inconceivable. We need not, therefore, be much troubled by the general language contained in the laws.

Besides, all laws as well as all contracts may be controlled in their operation and effect by general, fundamental maxims of the common law. No one shall be permitted to profit by his own fraud, or to take advantage of his own wrong, or to found any claim upon his own iniquity, or to acquire property by his own crime. These maxims are dictated by public policy, have their foundation in universal law administered in all civilized countries, and have nowhere been superseded by statutes. They were applied in the decision of the case of the *New York Mutual Life Insurance Company* v. *Armstrong* (117 U.S. 591). There it was held that the person who procured a policy upon the life of another, payable at his death, and then murdered the assured to make the policy payable, could not recover thereon. Mr. Justice Field, writing the opinion, said: "Independently of any proof of the motives of Hunter in obtaining the policy, and even assuming that they were just and proper, he forfeited all rights under it when, to secure its immediate payment, he murdered the assured. It would be a reproach to the jurisprudence of the country if one could recover insurance money payable on the death of a party whose life he had feloniously taken. As well might he recover insurance money upon a building that he had willfully fired."

These maxims, without any statute giving them force or operation, frequently control the effect and nullify the language of wills. A will procured by fraud and deception, like any other instrument, may be decreed void and set aside, and so a particular portion of a will may be excluded from probate or held inoperative if induced by the fraud or undue influence of the person in whose favor it is. (*Allen* v. *M'Pherson,* 1 H.L. Cas. 191; *Harrison's Appeal,* 48 Conn. 202.) So a will may contain provisions which are immoral, irreligious or against public policy, and they will be held void.

Here there was no certainty that this murderer would survive the testator, or that the testator would not change his will, and there was no certainty that he would get this property if nature was allowed to take its course. He, therefore, murdered the testator expressly to vest himself with an estate. Under such circumstances, what law, human or divine, will allow him to take the estate and enjoy the fruits of his crime? The will spoke and became operative at the death of the testator. He caused that death, and thus by his crime made it speak and have operation. Shall it speak and operate in his favor? If he had met the testator and taken his property by force, he would have had no title to it. Shall he acquire title by murdering him? If he had gone to the testator's house and by force compelled him, or by fraud or undue influence had induced him to will him his property, the law would not allow him to hold it. But can he give effect and operation to a will by murder, and yet take the property? To answer these questions in the affirmative, it seems to me, would be a reproach to the jurisprudence of our state, and an offense against public policy.

Under the civil law evolved from the general principles of natural law and justice by many generations of jurisconsults, philosophers and statesmen, one cannot take property by inheritance or will from an ancestor or benefactor whom he has murdered. . . . In the Civil Code of Lower Canada the provisions on the subject in the Code Napoleon have been substantially copied. But, so far as I can find, in no country where the common law prevails has it been deemed important to enact a law to provide for such a case. Our revisers and law-makers were familiar with the civil law, and they did not deem it important to incorporate into our statutes its provisions upon this subject. This is not a *casus omissus.* It was evidently supposed that the maxims of the common law were sufficient to regulate such a case and that a specific enactment for that purpose was not needed.

For the same reasons the defendant Palmer cannot take any of this property as heir. Just before the murder he was not an heir, and it was not certain that he ever would be. He might have died before his grandfather, or might have been disinherited by him. He made himself an heir by the murder, and he seeks to take property as the fruit of his crime. What has before been said as to him as legatee applies to him with equal force as an heir. He cannot vest himself with title by crime.

My view of this case does not inflict upon Elmer any greater or other punishment for his crime than the law specifies. It takes from him no property, but simply holds that he shall not acquire property by his crime, and thus be rewarded for its commission.

Our attention is called to *Owens* v. *Owens* (100 N.C. 240), as a case quite like this. There a wife had been convicted of being an accessory before the fact to the murder of her husband, and it was held that she was, nevertheless, entitled to dower. I am unwilling to assent to the doctrine of that case. The statutes provide dower for a wife who has the misfortune to survive her husband and thus lose his support and protection. It is clear beyond their purpose to make provision for a wife who by her own crime makes herself a widow and willfully and intentionally deprives herself of the support and protection of her husband. As she might have died before him, and thus never have been his widow, she cannot by her crime vest herself with an estate. The principle which lies at the bottom of the maxim, *volenti non fit injuria,* should be applied to such a case, and a widow should not, for the purpose of acquiring, as such, property rights, be permitted to allege a widowhood which she has wickedly and intentionally created.

The facts found entitled the plaintiffs to the relief they seek. The error of the referee was in his conclusion of law. Instead of granting a new trial, therefore, I think the proper judgment upon the facts found should be ordered here. The facts have been passed upon twice with the same result, first upon the trial of Palmer for murder, and then by the referee in this action. We are, therefore, of opinion that the ends of justice do not require that they should again come in question.

The judgment of the General Term and that entered upon the report of the referee should, therefore, be reversed and judgment should be entered as follows: That Elmer E. Palmer and the administrator be enjoined from using any of the personalty or real estate left by the testator for Elmer's benefit; that the devise and bequest in the will to Elmer be declared ineffective to pass the title to him; that by reason of the crime of murder committed upon the grandfather he is deprived of any interest in the estate left by him; that the plaintiffs are the true owners of the real and personal estate left by the testator, subject to the charge in favor of Elmer's mother and the widow of the testator, under the ante-nuptial agreement, and that the plaintiffs have costs in all the courts against Elmer.

DISSENT BY: GRAY

DISSENT: Gray, J. (dissenting) This appeal presents an extraordinary state of facts, and the case, in respect of them, I believe, is without precedent in this state.

The respondent, a lad of sixteen years of age, being aware of the provisions in his grandfather's will, which constituted him the residuary legatee of the testator's estate, caused his death by poison in 1882. For this crime he was tried and was convicted of murder in the second degree, and at the time of the commencement of this action he was serving out his sentence in the state reformatory. This action was brought by two of the children of the testator for the purpose of having those provisions of the will in the respondent's favor canceled and annulled.

The appellants' argument for a reversal of the judgment, which dismissed their complaint, is that the respondent unlawfully prevented a revocation of the existing will, or a new will from being made, by his crime, and that he terminated the enjoyment by the testator of his property and effected his own succession to it by the same crime. They say that to permit the respondent to take the property willed to him would be to permit him to take advantage of his own wrong.

To sustain their position the appellants' counsel has submitted an able and elaborate brief, and, if I believed that the decision of the question could be affected by considerations of an equitable nature, I should not hesitate to assent to views which commend themselves to the conscience. But the matter does not lie within the domain of conscience. We are bound by the rigid rules of law, which have been established by the legislature and within the limits of which the determination of this question is confined. The question we are dealing with is, whether a testamentary disposition can be altered, or a will revoked, after the testator's death, through an appeal to the courts, when the legislature has, by its enactments, prescribed exactly when and how wills may be made, altered and revoked, and apparently, as it seems to me, when they have been fully complied with, has left no room for the exercise of an equitable jurisdiction by courts over such matters. Modern jurisprudence, in recognizing the right of the individual, under more or less restrictions, to dispose of his property after his death, subjects it to legislative control, both as to extent and as to mode of exercise. Complete freedom of testamentary disposition of one's property has not been and is not the universal rule; as we see from the provisions of the Napoleonic Code, from those systems of jurisprudence in other countries which are modeled upon the Roman law, and from the statutes of many of our states. To the statutory restraints, which are imposed upon the disposition of one's property by will, are added strict and systematic statutory rules for the execution, alteration and revocation of the will; which must be, at least, substantially, if not exactly, followed to insure validity and performance. The reason for the establishment of such rules, we may naturally assume, consists in the purpose to create those safeguards about these grave and important acts, which experience has demonstrated to be the wisest and surest. That freedom, which is permitted to be exercised in the testamentary disposition of one's estate by the laws of the state, is subject to its being exercised in conformity with the regulations of the statutes. The capacity and the power of the individual to dispose of his property after death, and the mode by which that power can be exercised, are matters of which the legislature has assumed the entire control, and has undertaken to regulate with comprehensive particularity.

The appellants' argument is not helped by reference to those rules of the civil law, or to those laws of other governments, by which the heir or legatee is excluded from benefit under the testament, if he has been convicted of killing, or attempting to kill, the testator. In the absence of such legislation here, the courts are not empowered to institute such a system of remedial justice. The deprivation of the heir of his testamentary succession by the Roman law, when guilty of such a crime, plainly, was intended to be in the nature of a punishment imposed upon him. The succession, in such a case of guilt, escheated to the exchequer. . . .

I concede that rules of law, which annul testamentary provision made for the benefit of those who have become unworthy of them, may be based on principles of equity and of natural justice. It is quite reasonable to suppose that a testator would revoke or alter his will, where his mind has been so angered and changed as to make him unwilling to have his will executed as it stood. But these principles only suggest sufficient reasons for the enactment of laws to meet such cases.

The statutes of this state have prescribed various ways in which a will may be altered or revoked; but the very provision, defining the modes of alteration and revocation, implies a prohibition of alteration or revocation in any other way. The words of the section of the statute are: "No will in writing, except in the cases hereinafter mentioned, nor any part thereof, shall be revoked or altered otherwise," etc. Where, therefore, none of the cases mentioned are met by the facts, and the revocation is not in the way described in the section, the will of the testator is unalterable. I think that a valid will must continue as a will always, unless revoked in the manner provided by the statutes. Mere intention to revoke a will does not have the effect of revocation. The intention to revoke is necessary to constitute the effective revocation of a will; but it must be demonstrated by one of the acts contemplated by the statute. As Woodworth, J., said in *Dan* v. *Brown* (4 Cow. 490): "Revocation is an act of the mind, which must be demonstrated by some outward and visible sign of revocation." The same learned judge said in that case: "The rule is that if the testator lets the will stand until he dies, it is his will; if he does not suffer it to do so, it is not his will." (*Goodright* v. *Glasier,* 4 Burr. 2512, 2514; *Pemberton* v. *Pemberton,* 13 Ves. 290.)

The finding of fact of the referee, that, presumably, the testator would have altered his will, had he known of his grandson's murderous intent, cannot affect the question. We may concede it to the fullest extent; but still the cardinal objection is undisposed of, that the making and the revocation of a will are purely matters of statutory regulation, by which the court is bound in the determination of questions relating to these acts. Two cases in this state and in Kentucky, at an early day, seem to me to be much in point. *Gains* v. *Gains* (2 Marshall, 190), was decided by the Kentucky Court of Appeals in 1820. It was there urged that the testator intended to have destroyed his will, and that he was forcibly prevented from doing so by the defendant in error or devisee, and it was insisted that the will, though not expressly, was thereby virtually revoked. The court held, as the act concerning wills prescribed the manner in which a will might be revoked, that as none of the acts evidencing revocation were done, the intention could not be substituted for the act. In that case the will was snatched away and forcibly retained. In 1854, Surrogate Bradford, whose opinions are entitled to the highest consideration, decided the case of *Leaycraft* v. *Simmons* (3 Bradf.35). In that case the testator, a man of eighty-nine years of age, desired to make a codicil to his will, in order to enlarge the provisions for his daughter. His son having the custody of the instrument, and the one to be prejudiced by the change, refused to produce the will, at testator's request, for the purpose of alteration. The learned surrogate refers to the provisions of the civil law for such and other cases of unworthy conduct in the heir or legatee, and says, "our statute has undertaken to prescribe the mode in which wills can be revoked (citing the statutory provision). This is the law by which I am governed in passing upon questions touching the revocation of wills. The whole of this subject is now regulated by statute, and a mere intention to revoke, however well authenticated, or however defeated, is not sufficient." And he held that the will must be admitted to probate. I may refer also to a case in the Pennsylvania courts. In that state the statute prescribed the mode for repealing or altering a will, and in *Clingan* v. *Mitcheltree* (31 Pa. State Rep. 25) the Supreme Court of the state held, where a will was kept from destruction by the fraud and misrepresentation of the devisee, that to declare it canceled as against the fraudulent party would be to enlarge the statute.

I cannot find any support for the argument that the respondent's succession to the property should be avoided because of his criminal act, when the laws are silent. Public policy does not demand it, for the demands of public policy are satisfied by the proper execution of the laws and the punishment of the crime. There has been no convention between the testator and his legatee, nor is there any such contractual element in such a disposition of property by a testator, as to impose or imply conditions in the legatee. The appellants' argument practically amounts to this: That as the legatee has been guilty of a crime, by the commission of which he is placed in a position to sooner receive the benefits of the testamentary provision, his rights to the property should be forfeited and he should be divested of his estate. To allow their argument to prevail would involve the diversion by the court of the testator's estate into the hands of persons, whom, possibly enough, for all we know, the testator might not have chosen or desired as its recipients. Practically the court is asked to make another will for the testator. The laws do not warrant this judicial action, and mere presumption would not be strong enough to sustain it.

But more than this, to concede appellants' views would involve the imposition of an additional punishment or penalty upon the respondent. What power or warrant have the courts to add to the respondent's penalties by depriving him of property? The law has punished him for his crime, and we may not say that it was an insufficient punishment. In the trial and punishment of the respondent the law has vindicated itself for the outrage which he committed, and further judicial utterance upon the subject of punishment or deprivation of rights is barred. We may not, in the language of the court in *People* v. *Thornton* (25 Hun, 456), "enhance the pains, penalties and forfeitures provided by law for the punishment of crime."

The judgment should be affirmed, with costs.

11

JOHN FINNIS

Natural Law and Legal Reasoning

Moral reasoning, legal reasoning, and their interrelationships can scarcely be understood reflectively without attention to two different sources of ambiguity. The source is, in each case, well known: the distinction between reasons and feelings; and the distinction between doing (the shaping of one's own "existence" by one's choices) and making (the exercise of technique by activity on some form of "cultural" object or method). But the distinctions are commonly not well understood, and the traps they lay for the analysis of morality and adjudication are usually neglected.

I

We are animals, but intelligent. Our actions all have an emotional motivation, involve our feelings and imagination and other aspects of our bodiliness, and can all be observed (if only, in some cases, by introspection) as pieces of behaviour. But rationally motivated actions also have an intelligent motivation—seek to realize (protect, promote) an intelligible good.

So our purposes, the states of affairs we seek to bring about, typically have a double aspect: the goal which we imagine and which engages our feelings, and the intelligible benefit which appeals to our rationality by promising to instantiate, either immediately or instrumentally, some basic human good. While some of the purposes we employ intelligence to pursue may be motivated ultimately by nothing more than feeling, others are motivated ultimately by (an understanding of) a basic human good. The idiom in which "reason" refers to purposes—"the reason he did that," equivalent to "his purpose in doing that"—fails to mark this distinction. But none of common speech's related terms—"purpose," "goal," "intention"—is free from the same ambiguity. So I stipulate that when I speak of "reasons" in this chapter, I refer (except when discussing technical reasons) to reason(s) as giving ground for intelligent action motivated ultimately by a basic human good (more precisely, by the intelligible benefit promised by the instantiation of a basic good).[1]

An account of basic reasons for action should not be rationalistic. Human flourishing is not to be portrayed in terms only of exercising capacities to reason. As animals, we are organic substances part of whose well-being is *bodily life,* maintained in health, vigour, and safety, and transmitted to new human beings. To regard human life as a basic reason for action is to understand it as a good in which indefinitely many beings can participate in indefinitely many ways, going far beyond any goal or purpose which anyone could envisage and pursue, but making sense of indefinitely many purposes, and giving rational support to indefinitely many goals.[2]

This sense of "(basic) reason for action" holds for all the other basic human goods: *knowledge* of reality (including aesthetic appreciation of it); *excellence in work and play* whereby one transforms natural realities to express meanings and serve purposes; *harmony between individuals and groups* of persons (peace, neighbourliness, and friendship); *harmony between one's feelings and one's judgments and choices* (inner peace); *harmony between one's choices and judgements and one's behaviour* (peace of conscience and authenticity in the sense of consistency between one's self and its expression); and *harmony between oneself and the wider reaches of reality* including the reality constituted by the world's dependence on a *more-than-human source of meaning and value.*

Such a statement of the basic human goods entails an account of human nature.[3] But it does not presuppose such an account. It is not an attempt to deduce reasons for action from some preexisting theoretical conception of human nature. Such an attempt would vainly defy the logical truth (well respected by the ancients)[4] that "ought" cannot be deduced from "is"—a syllogism's conclusion cannot contain what is not in its premisses. Rather, a full account of human nature can only be given by one who understands the human goods practically, i.e. as reasons for choice and action, reasons which make full sense of supporting feelings and spontaneities.

An account of practical reasonableness can be called a theory of "natural law" because practical reasoning's very first principles are those basic reasons which identify the basic human goods as ultimate reasons for choice and action—reasons for actions which will instantiate and express human nature precisely because participating in those goods, i.e. instantiating (actualizing, realizing) those ultimate aspects of human flourishing.[5]

II

To the extent that legal reasoning derives from and participates in practical reasonableness, a sound theory of legal reasoning must differ from some theories now current. At the heart of "Critical Legal Studies," for example, is a denial that there are any objective human goods. Of the four reasons (all bad) which Roberto Unger offers for denying that there are objective human goods, the argument closest to his heart, I think, is that by affirming that there are such goods one "denies any significance to choice other than the passive acceptance or rejection of independent truths . . . [and] disregards the significance of choice as an expression of personality."[6]

But, in reality, it is the diversity of *rationally* appealing human goods which makes free choice both possible and frequently necessary. Like every other term concerning human activity, "choice" is afflicted, in common idiom, by ambiguities originating particularly[7] in the distinction between reason and feeling. In its strong, central sense, free choice is the adoption of one amongst two or more rationally appealing and incompatible, alternative options, such that nothing but the choosing itself settles which option is chosen and pursued.[8] Many aspects of individual and social life, and many individual and social obligations, are structured by choice between rationally appealing options whose rational appeal can be explained only in terms, ultimately, of basic human opportunities understood to be objectively good (though variously realizable). No sound sense can be made of "objectivity" and "truth," here or elsewhere, otherwise than in terms of rational judgement, open to all relevant questions.

But if the basic human goods, for all their objectivity and truth, open up so much to free choice, what can be the basis for identifying choices which, though rational, ought to be rejected because unreasonable, wrong, immoral?

Moral thought is simply rational thought at full stretch, integrating emotions and feelings but *undeflected* by them. Practical rationality's fundamental principle is: take as a premiss at least one of the basic reasons for action, and follow through to the point at which you somehow bring about the instantiation of that good in action. Do not act pointlessly. The fundamental principle of moral thought is simply the demand to be fully rational: in so far as it is in your power, allow nothing but the basic reasons for action to shape your practical thinking as you find, develop, and use your opportunities to pursue human flourishing through your chosen actions. Be entirely reasonable.[9] Aristotle's phrase *orthos logos,* and his later followers' *recta ratio,* right reason, should simply be understood as "unfettered reason," reason undeflected by emotions and feelings. And so undeflected reason, and the morally good will, are guided by the first moral principle: that one ought to choose (and otherwise will) those and only those possibilities whose willing is compatible with a will towards the fulfillment of all human persons in all the basic goods, towards the ideal of integral human fulfillment.

Take a simple, paradigmatic form of immorality. Emotion may make one wish to destroy or damage the good of life in someone one hates, or the good of knowledge; so one kills or injures, or deceives, that person just out of feelings of aversion. It is immoral, because hereabouts there is a general, so to speak methodological, moral principle intermediate between the most basic principles of practical reason (the basic goods or reasons for action, and the first moral principle) and particular moral norms against killing or lying. This intermediate moral principle, which some call a mode of responsibility,[10] will exclude meeting injury with injury, or responding to one's own weakness or setbacks with self-destructiveness.

Perhaps more immediately relevant to political and legal theory is the intermediate moral principle requiring that one act fairly: that one not limit one's concern for basic human goods simply by one's feelings of self-preference or preference for those who are near and dear. Fairness (and its paradigmatic formulation in the Golden Rule) does not exclude treating different persons differently; it requires only that the differential treatment be justified either by inevitable limits on one's action or by intelligible requirements of the basic goods themselves. I shall say more (VII below) about the legitimate role of feelings in making fair choices in which one prioritizes goods (or instantiations of basic goods) by one's feelings without prioritizing persons simply by feelings.

There are other intermediate moral principles. Very important to the structuring of legal thought is the principle which excludes acting against a basic reason by choosing to destroy or damage any basic good in any of its instantiations in any human person (VI below). A basic human good always is a reason for action and always gives a reason *not* to choose to destroy, damage, or impede some instantiation of that good; but since the instantiations of human good at stake in any morally significant choice are not commensurable by *reason* prior to choice, there can never be a sufficient reason not to take that reason-not-to as decisive for choice. Only emotional factors such as desire or aversion could motivate a choice rejecting it.

Of course, the basic reasons for action, as the phrase suggests, present one with many reasons for choice and action, many reasons to . . . And since one is finite, one's choice of any purpose, however far-reaching, will inevitably have as a side-effect some negative impact on (minimally, the non-realization of) other possible instantiations of this and other basic goods. In that sense, every choice is "against some basic reason." But only as a side-effect. In the choices which are excluded by the intermediate moral principle now in question, the damaging or destruction or impeding of an instantiation of a basic good—the harming of some basic aspect of someone's existence and well-being—is chosen, as a means, i.e. *as part* of the description of the option adopted by choice. Whereas the first intermediate principle excludes making such damage or destruction one's end, the present principle excludes making it one's means. The concepts of (the) end and means (defining an option) come together in the conception so fundamental to our law: intention.[11] . . .

IV

Legal reasoning and rationality has, I suggest, its distinctiveness and its peculiar elusiveness because, in the service of a third-order, existential, moral, and chosen purpose—of living together in a just order of fair and right relationships—there has been and is being constructed a fourth-order object, "the law" (as in "the law of England"). This is a vastly complex cultural object, comprising a vocabulary with many artfully assigned meanings, rules identifying permitted and excluded arguments and decision, and correspondingly very many technical routines or processes (such as pleading, trial, conveyancing, etc.) constituted and regulated according to those formulae, their assigned meanings, and the rules of argument and decision.

This cultural object, constructed or (as we say) posited by creative human choices, is an instrument, a technique adopted for a moral purpose, and adopted because there is no other available way of agreeing over significant spans of time about precisely how to pursue the moral project well. Political authority in all its manifestations, including legal institutions, is a technique for doing without unanimity in making social choices—where unanimity would almost always be unattainable or temporary—in order to secure practical (near-)unanimity about how to coordinate the actions (including forbearances) of members of the society.[12]

Legal reasoning, then, is (at least in large part) technical reasoning—not moral reasoning. Like all technical reasoning, it is concerned to achieve a particular purpose, a definite state of affairs attainable by efficient dispositions of means to end. The particular end here is the resolution of disputes (and other allegations of misconduct) by the provision of a directive sufficiently definite and specific to identify one party as right (in-the-right) and the other as wrong (not-in-the-right).

Hence the law's distinctive devices: defining terms, and specifying rules, with sufficient and necessarily artificial clarity and definiteness to establish the "bright lines" which make so many real-life legal questions *easy questions*. Legal definitions and rules are to provide the citizen, the legal adviser, and the judge with an algorithm for deciding as many questions as possible—in principle every question—yes (or no), this course of action would (or would not) be lawful; this arrangement is valid; this contract is at an end; these losses are compensable in damages and those are not; and so forth. As far as it can, the law is to provide sources of reasoning—statutes and statute-based rules, common law rules, and customs—capable of ranking (commensurating) alternative dispute-resolutions as right or wrong, and thus better and worse.

Lawyers' tools of trade—their ability to find and use the authoritative sources—are means in the service of a purpose sufficiently definite to constitute a technique, a mode of technical reasoning. The purpose, again, is the unequivocal resolution of every dispute (and other question for just decision) which can be in some way foreseen and provided for. Still, this quest for certainty, for a complete set of uniquely correct answers, is itself in the service of a wider good which, like all basic human goods, is not reducible to a definite goal but is rather an open-ended good which persons and their communities can participate in without ever capturing or exhausting the good of just harmony. This good is a moral good just in so far as it is itself promoted and respected as one aspect of the ideal of integral human fulfillment. As a moral good its implications are specified by all the moral principles which could bear upon it.

Thus there emerges the tension around which Ronald Dworkin's work on legal reasoning revolves.

V

Dworkin seeks to resolve the tension between law's and legal reasoning's character as a culturally specified technique of attaining predictable answers to problems of social co-ordination and its character as, in each of its decisive legislative, executive and judicial moments, a moral act participating in justice (or injustice). His attempted resolution fails, I think, to grasp the real nature and implications of that tension.

In judicial reasoning as portrayed by Dworkin, two criteria of judgement are in use; as we shall see, there is between these two criteria a kind of incommensurability analogous to the incommensurability between the human goods involved in morally significant, rationally motivated choices. One of these criteria or dimensions belongs to what I have called the third (moral) order or rationality, and the other to the fourth (technical) order. The first dimension Dworkin calls "fit": coherence with the existing legal "materials" created by past political decisions, i.e. with legislation and authoritative judicial decision (precedent). The second dimension he now calls "justification."[13] And he tries to show that a *uniquely* correct ("the right") answer is available in "most" hard cases.

One can deny this last thesis without committing oneself to any scepticism about the objectivity of human good(s) or of correct judgements about right and wrong. Nor need one's denial be predicated on the popular argument which Dworkin is rightly concerned to scorn and demolish—the argument that disagreement is endemic and ineradicable. (For disagreement is a mere fact about people, and is logically irrelevant to the merits of any practical or other interpretative claim.) Nor need a denial of Dworkin's one-right answer thesis rest on the fact that no one has the "superhuman" powers of Dworkin's imaginary judge.

Even an ideal human judge, with superhuman powers, could not sensibly search for a uniquely correct answer to a hard case (as lawyers in sophisticated legal systems use the term "hard case"). For in such a case, the search for the one right answer is practically incoherent and senseless, in much the same way as a search for the English novel which is "most romantic and shortest" (or "funniest and best," or "most English and most profound").

Assuming with Dworkin that there are two "dimensions" or criteria of judicial assessment, we can say that a case for judicial decision is hard (not merely novel) when not only is there more than one answer which is not in evident violation of an applicable rule, but also the answers which are in that sense available can be ranked in different orders along each of the relevant criteria of evaluation: for novels, their brevity and their Englishness (or humour, or profundity, or . . .); for judicial judgements their fit with previous legislation and precedent, and—let us grant (not concede) to Dworkin—their *inherent* moral soundness. In such a case there is found what theorists of "rational choice" (in sense 3) call "intransitivity," a phenomenon which such theories confessedly cannot really handle: solution A is better than solution B on the scale of legal fit, and B than C, but C is better than A on the scale of "moral soundness"; so there is no sufficient reason to declare A, or B, or C the overall "best judicial decision." If the rank order was the same on both dimensions, of course, the case was not a hard one at all, and the legal system already had what one always desires of it: a uniquely correct answer.

In his works before *Law's Empire,* Dworkin tried to overcome this incommensurability of the dimensions or criteria of assessment by proposing a kind of lexicographical (in Rawls's terminology "lexical") ordering. Candidates for the "best account" of the law of England in 1980 must fit then existing English legal materials adequately, and of those which satisfy this threshold criterion, that which ranks highest on the other criterion (moral soundness) is overall, absolutely, "the best," even though it fits less well than (an)other(s).[14] But this solution was empty, since he identified no criteria, however sketchy or "in principle," for specifying when fit is "adequate," i.e. for locating the threshold (of fit) beyond which the criterion of soundness would prevail. (It was like being told to search for the funniest novel among those that are "short enough.") Presumably, candidates for the one right answer to the question "When is fit adequate?" would themselves be ranked in terms both of fit and of soundness. An infinite regress, of the vicious sort which nullifies purported rational explanations, was well under way.

In *Law's Empire,* Dworkin abandons the simple picture of a lexical ordering between these two criteria. We are left with little more than a metaphor: "balance"—as in "the general balance of political virtues" embodied in competing interpretations or accounts of the law (of England (in 1990)). But in the absence of any metric which could commensurate the different criteria, the instruction to balance (or, earlier, to weigh) can legitimately mean no more than "Bear in mind, conscientiously, all the relevant factors, and *choose.*" Or, in the legal sphere, "Hear the arguments, sitting in the highest court, and then *vote.*"

In understanding practical rationality in all its forms, one should notice a feature of the experience of choice. *After* one has chosen, the factors favouring the chosen option will usually seem to outweigh, overbalance, those favouring the rejected alternative options. The option chosen—to do *x*, to adopt rule or interpretation *y*—will commonly seem (to the person who chose, if not to onlookers) to have a supremacy, a unique rightness. But this sense of the supremacy, the rightness of one (the chosen) option will not alter the truth that the choice was not rationally determined, i.e. was not guided by an identification of one option or answer as "the right one." (And this does not mean that it was irrational; it was between rationally appealing options.) Rather, the choice established the "right" answer—i.e. established it in, and by reference ultimately to, the dispositions and sentiments of the chooser.[15] When the choice in a hard case is made by (the majority in the) highest appeal court (a mere brute fact), the unique rightness of the answer is established not only by and for the attitude of those who have chosen it, but also for the legal system or community for which it has thus been authoritatively decided upon, and laid down as or in a *rule*.

VI

The incommensurability of Dworkin's two dimensions or criteria for judicial judgement has significant similarities to the incommensurability of the goods (and reasons) at stake in alternative options available for morally significant choice in any context. The moral and political rationality which underpins (though does not exhaust) legal rationality cannot be understood without an understanding of incommensurability.

Incommensurability, the absence of any *rationally* identified metric for measuring, or scale for "weighing," the goods and bads in issue, is much more pervasive and intense than one would imagine from the simple Dworkinian picture of legal reasoning along the two dimensions of legal fit and moral soundness. One meets incommensurability in humble contexts such as having to choose between going to a lecture, reading a good book, going to the cinema, and talking to friends. One meets it in relation to grand social choices, such as whether to reject or renounce a nuclear deterrent:[16] exploring such a choice will amply illustrate the impotence of all forms of aggregative reasoning towards morally significant choice—choice outside the purely technical or technological task of identifying the most cost-efficient means to a single limited goal.

The reasoning most characteristic of technical rationality is "cost-benefit analysis," comparing the costs of alternative options with the probable benefits. This can be carried through with full rationality only when (*a*) goals are well defined, (*b*) costs can be compared with some definite unit (e.g. money), (*c*) benefits can also be quantified in a way that renders them commensurable with one another, and (*d*) differences among means, other than their efficiency, measurable costs, and measurable benefits, are not counted as significant. None of these conditions is fulfilled in moral reasoning.

Indeed, morally significant choice would be unnecessary and, with one qualification, impossible if one option could be shown to be *the best* on a single scale which, as all aggregative reasoning does, ranks options in a single, transitive order. If there were a reason (for doing *x*) which some rational method of comparison (e.g. aggregation of goods and bads in a complete cost-benefit analysis) identified as rationally preferable, the alternative reason (against doing *x*), being thus identified as rationally inferior, would cease to be rationally appealing in that situation of choice. The reason thus identified as dominant, as unqualifiedly preferable, and the option favoured by that reason, would be rationally unopposed. There would remain *no choice* of the sort that moral theories seek to guide. For, the morally significant choices which moral theories seek to guide are between alternative options which have rational appeal.

To identify options as morally wrong does not entail identifying one option as (morally) uniquely right. Indeed, even when one option can be judged the only (morally) right option for a given person (a moral judgement which only that person's prior commitments and dispositions will make possible), this entails only that the alternative, immoral options are not fully reasonable. It in no way entails that these alternative options are irrational, i.e. lack rational appeal in terms of genuine, intelligible human goods which would be secured by the immoral options and sacrificed by the morally upright option. Thus rationally motivated, morally significant choice remains possible—indeed characteristic of the human situation—even in the perhaps relatively uncommon case of the moral "one right answer (option)."

But when technical reasonings identify one option as uniquely correct, i.e. as dominant, they do so by demonstrating that it offers *all that the other options offer and some more;* it is unqualifiedly better. The other options then lack *rational* appeal. Such deliberation ends not in choice—in the rich, central sense of that ambiguous term—but rather in insight, "decision" (not choice, but rationally compelled judgement), and action.

One of morality's principles, I have said (II above), excludes acting against a basic reason by choosing to destroy or damage any basic human good in any of its instantiations in any human person. For these instantiations are nothing other than aspects of human persons, present and future, and human persons cannot rationally be reduced to the commensurable factors captured by technical reasoning. These instantiations of human good constitute *reasons against* any option which involves choosing (intending) to destroy or damage any of them. The significance of the incommensurability of goods involved in such morally significant options is that no reason *for* such an option can be rationally preferable to such a reason against. And the same is true of the *reason against* an option which is constituted by that option's unfairness.

What, it may be asked, are the grounds for regulating one's choice according to the reason-*against* rather than by any reason-*for*? Once again they cannot be stated without reference to some features of our world, the fundamental context of all human choosing. Options which there are reasons *for* my choosing are infinite in number. Being finite, I simply cannot do everything, cannot choose every option for which there are reasons. But I can refrain from doing anything; I can respect every serious reason-against. So, an unconditional or absolute affirmative duty (duty *to* . . .) would impose an impossible burden and be irrational; but negative moral absolutes (duties *not* to . . .), if correctly stated with attention to the distinction between intention and side-effect, can all be adhered to in any and every circumstance.

Moreover, many human goods (e.g. the lives of others) are gifts, givens, which we can destroy or damage, but cannot create. Here, too, is a ground of the intelligible asymmetry between reasons-for and reasons-against. Nor does the priority, within their ambit, of reasons-against give morality as a whole a negative cast, or elevate "moral purity" to the rank of a supreme goal. The first limb of practical reason's first principle remains that human good is to be done and pursued. Its second limb is that evil is to be avoided. But a full respect for and adherence to the absolute duties to forbear from evil leaves open a wide field of (more numerous) individual and social positive responsibilities.

VII

The moral absolutes give legal reasoning its backbone: the exclusion of intentional killing, of intentional injury to the person and even the economic interests of the person, of deliberate deception for the sake of securing desired results, of enslavement which treats a human person as an object of a lower rank of being than the autonomous human subject. These moral absolutes, which *are* rationally determined and essentially determinate, constitute the most basic human rights, and the foundations of the criminal law and the law of intentional torts or delicts, not to mention all the rules, principles, and doctrines which penalize intentional deception, withdraw from it all direct legal support, and exclude it from the legal process.

The rationality of these moral and legal norms depends upon the incommensurability of the human goods and bads at stake in morally significant options for choice. This incommensurability has further implications of importance to legal reasoning.

The core of the moral norm of fairness is the Golden Rule: "Do to others as you would have them do to you; do not impose on others what you would not want to be obliged by them to accept." This has two aspects. First: practical rationality, outside the limited technical context of competitive games, includes a rational norm of impartiality. This norm excludes not all forms and corresponding feelings of preference for oneself and those who are near and dear, bur rather all those forms of preference which are motivated only by desires, aversions, or hostilities which do not correspond to intelligible aspects of the real *reasons* for action, the basic human goods realizable in the lives of other human beings as in the lives of oneself or those close to one's heart.

The Golden Rule's second aspect is this. Although fairness is thus a rational norm requiring one to transcend all rationally unintegrated feelings, its concrete application in personal life presupposes a commensuration of benefits and burdens which reason is impotent to commensurate. For, to apply the Golden Rule one must know what burdens one considers too great to accept. And this knowledge, constituting a pre-moral commensuration, cannot be by rational commensuration. Therefore, it can only be one's intuitive awareness, one's discernment, of one's own differentiated *feelings* towards various goods and bads as concretely remembered, experienced, or imagined. This, I repeat, is not a rational and objective commensuration of goods and bads; but once established in one's feelings and identified in one's self-awareness, it enables one to measure one's options by a rational and objective standard of inter-personal impartiality.

Analogously, in the life of a community, the preliminary commensuration of rationally incommensurable factors is accomplished not by rationally determined judgements, but by *decisions* (choices). Is it fair to impose on others the risks inherent in driving at more than 10 m.p.h.? Yes, in our community, since our community has by custom and law *decided* to treat those risks and harms as *not too great.* Have we a rational critique of a community which decided to limit road traffic to 10 m.p.h. and to accept all the economic and other costs of that decision? Or not to have the institution of trusts, or constructive trusts? No, we have no rational critique of such a community. But we do have a rational critique of someone who drives at 60 m.p.h. but who, when struck by another, complains and alleges that the mere fact that the other's speed exceeded 10 m.p.h. established that other's negligence. Or of someone willing to receive the benefits (e.g. the tax benefits) of trusts but not willing to accept the law's distinction between trust and contract in his bankruptcy.

And, in general, we have a rational critique of one who accepts the benefits of this and other communal decisions but rejects the burdens as they bear on him and those in whom he feels interested. In short, the decision to permit road traffic to proceed faster than 10 m.p.h., or to define trusts just as English law does, was rationally underdetermined. (That is not to say that it was or is wholly unguided by reason; the good of human bodily life and integrity is a genuine reason always practically relevant, and the rational demand for consistency with our individual and communal tolerance or intolerance of other—non-traffic—threats to that good provides some rational criteria for decision. And similarly with that trust, whose rationality defied many legislative attempts, for centuries, to suppress this peculiar double ownership.) Still, though rationally underdetermined, the decision to permit fast-moving traffic, once made, provides an often fully determinate rational standard for treating those accused of wrongful conduct or wrongfully inflicting injury. Likewise with trusts, in bankruptcy.

In the working of the legal process, much turns on the principle—a principle of fairness—that litigants (and others involved in the process) should be treated by judges (and others with power to decide) *impartially,* in the sense that they are as nearly as possible to be treated by each judge as they would be treated by every other judge. It is this above all, I believe, that drives the law towards the artificial, the *techne* rationality of laying down and following a set of positive norms identifiable as far as possible simply by their "sources" (i.e. by the fact of their enactment or other constitutive event) and applied so far as possible according to their publicly stipulated meaning, itself elucidated with as little as possible appeal to considerations which, because not controlled by facts about sources (constitutive events), are inherently likely to be appealed to differently by different judges. This drive to insulate legal from moral reasoning can never, however, be complete.

Incommensurability has further, related implications for legal reasoning. It rules out the proposed technique of legal reasoning known as Economic Analysis of Law. For it is central to that technique that every serious question of social order can be resolved by aggregating the overall net good promised by alternative options, in terms of a simple commensurating factor (or maximand), namely wealth measured in terms of the money which relevant social actors would be willing and able to pay to secure their preferred option. Equally central to Economic Analysis is the assumption, or thesis, that there is no difference of principle between buying the right to inflict injury intentionally and buying the right not to take precautions which would eliminate an equivalent number of injuries caused accidentally.[17] A root and branch critique of Economic Analysis of Law will focus on these two features of it.

Less fundamental critiques, such as Dworkin's (helpful and worth while though it is),[18] leave those features untouched. Indeed, Dworkin's own distinction between rights and collective goals (the latter being proposed by Dworkin as the legitimate province of legislatures) is a distinction which uncritically assumes that collective goals can rationally be identified and preferred to alternatives by aggregation of value, without regard to principles of distributive fairness and other aspects of justice—principles which themselves constitute rights, and which cannot be traded off, according to some rational methodology, against measurable quantities of value.[19]

VIII

In sum: much academic theory about legal reasoning greatly exaggerates the extent to which reason can settle what is greater good and lesser evil. At the same time, such theory minimizes the need for authoritative sources. Such sources, so far as they are clear, and respect the few absolute moral rights and duties, are to be respected as the only reasonable basis for judicial reasoning and decision, in relation to those countless issues which do not directly involve those absolute rights and duties. A natural law theory in the classical tradition makes no pretence that natural reason can identify the one right answer to those countless questions which arise for the judge who finds the sources unclear.

In a classical view, expressed by Aquinas with a clear debt to Aristotle,[20] there are many ways of going wrong and doing wrong; but in very many, perhaps most situations of personal and social life there are a number of incompatible *right* (i.e. not-wrong) options. Prior personal choice(s) or authoritative social decision-making can greatly reduce this variety of options for the person who has made that commitment or the community which accepts that authority. Still, those choices and decisions, while rational and reasonable, were in most cases not required by reason. They were not preceded by any rational judgment that *this* option is *the* right answer, or the best solution.

NOTES

1. For my use here of "purpose," "goal," "feeling," "benefit," motivated," and "basic human good," see Germain Grisez, Joseph Boyle, and John Finnis, "Practical Principles, Moral Truth, and Ultimate Ends," *American Journal of Jurisprudence,* 32 (1987), 99–151 at 99–110.
2. See John Finnis, Joseph Boyle, and Germain Grisez, *Nuclear Deterrence, Morality and Realism* (Oxford: Oxford University Press, 1987), 277–8; John Finnis, *Natural Law and Natural Rights* (Oxford: Clarendon Press, 1980), 84–5, 100.
3. See John Finnis, *Fundamentals of Ethics* (Oxford: Oxford University Press, 1983), 20–2; Finnis, "Natural Inclinations and Natural Rights . . . ," in L. Elders and K. Hedwig, eds., *Lex et Libertas* (*Studi Tomistici* 30, Libereria Editrice Vaticana, 1987), 43 at 43–9.
4. So Aristotle's principal treatise on human nature is his *Ethics,* which is an attempt to identify the human good, and is, according to its author, from beginning to end an effort of practical, as opposed to theoretical, understanding (see e.g. *Nicomachean Ethics,* 1.1 $1094^a26–^b12$ with Aquinas' commentary); Finnis, *Fundamentals of Ethics,* 24. Aristotle's *Ethics* is not derivative from some prior treatise on human nature, not even his *De Anima.*
5. In Aristotle, "natural" (as in "natural right" or "right by nature") also connotes objectivity or truth: see *Fundamentals of Ethics,* 24.
6. Roberto Mangabeira Unger, *Knowledge and Politics* (New York: Free Press, 1975), 77. On this, and the other arguments, see Finnis, "On 'The Critical Legal Studies Movement,'" in J. Eekelaar and J. Bell, eds., *Oxford Essays in Jurisprudence: Third Series* (Oxford: Oxford University Press, 1987), 144–65 at 163–5; or in *American Journal of Jurisprudence,* 30 (1985), 21–42 at 40–2.
7. But not exclusively; ambiguities arise here also from various phenomenal and cultural sources; so movements can be said to be "chosen" and "free" just in so far as they are not subject to physical constraints, or external constraint, or social constraints; and so on.
8. On free choice and its conditions, see e.g. Finnis, Boyle, and Grisez, *Nuclear Deterrence,* 256–60; Joseph Boyle, Germain Grisez, and Olaf Tollefsen, *Free Choice: A Self-Referential Argument* (Notre Dame, Ind.: Notre Dame University Press, 1976); Aquinas, *De Malo,* q. 6, a. un.
9. See Finnis, Boyle, and Grisez, *Nuclear Deterrence,* 119–25.
10. Thus *Nuclear Deterrence,* at 284–7. In *Natural Law,* 100–13, I call them "basic requirements of

practical reasonableness," and in *Fundamentals of Ethics,* 69–70, 74–6, I call them "intermediate moral principles."

11. On intention, see Finnis, "Intention and Side-Effects" in R. G. Frey and Christopher Morris, eds., *Liability and Responsibility: Essays in Law and Morals* (Cambridge: Cambridge University Press, 1991), 32–64; for the relation between the analysis of action here sketched and the mode of responsibility which excludes choosing to destroy, damage, or impede any instantiation of any basic human good, see *Nuclear Deterrence,* 286–90. . . .
12. See further Finnis, *Natural Law,* 231–7; Finnis, "The Authority of Law in the Predicament of Contemporary Social Theory," *Notre Dame Journal of Law, Ethics and Public Policy,* 1 (1984), 115–37; Finnis, "Law as Co-ordination," *Ratio Juris,* 2 (1989), 97–104.
13. See Ronald Dworkin, *Law's Empire* (Cambridge, Mass.: Harvard University Press, 1986), 255. . . .
14. See e.g. Dworkin, *Taking Rights Seriously,* 340–2.
15. See Grisez, "Against Consequentialism," *American Journal of Jurisprudence,* 23 (1978), 21–72 at 46–7.
16. See Finnis, Boyle, and Grisez, *Nuclear Deterrence, Morality and Realism,* 207–72. Joseph Raz, *The Morality of Freedom* (Oxford: Oxford University Press, 1986), 321–66, explores incommensurability with some similar conclusions.
17. See Finnis, "Allocating Risks and Suffering," *Cleveland State Law Rev.,* 38 (1990) 193–207 at 200–5.
18. Dworkin, *A Matter of Principle* (Cambridge, Mass.: Harvard University Press, 1985), pt. IV.
19. See Finnis, "A Bill of Rights for Britain? The Moral of Contemporary Jurisprudence," *Proc. Brit. Acad.* 71 (1985), 303–31 at 318–22.
20. See Aquinas, *Summa Theologiae,* Ia IIae, q. 95, a.2; Aristotle, *Nicomachean Ethics,* 5. 10. 1134^{b}19–1135^{a}6; Finnis, *Natural Law,* 281–90, 294–5.

12

RICHARD A. POSNER

The Economic Approach to Law

The most ambitious and probably the most influential effort in recent years to elaborate an overarching concept of justice that will both explain judicial decision making and place it on an objective basis is that of scholars working in the interdisciplinary field of "law and economics," as economic analysis of law is usually called.[1] I am first going to describe the most ambitious version of this ambitious effort and then use philosophy to chip away at it and see what if anything is left standing.

THE APPROACH

The basic assumption of economics that guides the version of economic analysis of law that I shall be presenting is that people are rational maximizers of their satisfactions—all people (with the exception of small children and the profoundly retarded) in *all* of their activities (except when under the influence of psychosis or similarly deranged through drug or alcohol abuse) that involve choice. Because this definition embraces the criminal deciding whether to commit another crime, the litigant deciding whether to settle or litigate a case, the legislator deciding whether to vote for or against a bill, the judge deciding how to cast his vote in a case, the party to a contract deciding whether to break it, the driver deciding how fast to drive, and the pedestrian deciding how boldly to cross the street, as well as the usual economic actors, such as businessmen and consumers, it is apparent that most activities either reg-

[1] The literature is vast; for diverse viewpoints, see *The Economic Approach to Law* (Paul Burrows and Cento G. Veljanovski eds. 1981); Robert Cooter and Thomas Ulen, *Law and Economics* (1988); Mark Kelman, *A Guide to Critical Legal Studies,* chs. 4–5 (1987); A. Mitchell Polinsky, *An Introduction to Law and Economics* (2d ed. 1989); Steven Shavell, *Economic Analysis of Accident Law* (1987); "Symposium: The Place of Economics in Legal Education," 33 *Journal of Legal Education* 183 (1983); and my book *Economic Analysis of Law* (3d ed. 1986).

ulated by or occurring within the legal system are grist for the economic analyst's mill. It should go without saying that nonmonetary as well as monetary satisfactions enter into the individual's calculus of maximizing (indeed, money for most people is a means rather than an end) and that decisions, to be rational, need not be well thought out at the conscious level—indeed, need not be conscious at all. Recall that "rational" denotes suiting means to ends, rather than mulling things over, and that much of our knowledge is tacit.

Since my interest is in legal doctrines and institutions, it will be best to begin at the legislative (including the constitutional) level. I assume that legislators are rational maximizers of their satisfactions just like everyone else. Thus nothing they do is motivated by the public interest as such. But they want to be elected and reelected, and they need money to wage an effective campaign. This money is more likely to be forthcoming from well-organized groups than from unorganized individuals. The rational individual knows that his contribution is unlikely to make a difference; for this reason and also because voters in most elections are voting for candidates rather than policies, which further weakens the link between casting one's vote and obtaining one's preferred policy, the rational individual will have little incentive to invest time and effort in deciding whom to vote for. Only an organized group of individuals (or firms or other organizations—but these are just conduits for individuals) will be able to overcome the informational and free-rider problems that plague collective action.[2] But such a group will not organize and act effectively unless its members have much to gain or much to lose from specific policies, as tobacco farmers, for example, have much to gain from federal subsidies for growing tobacco and much to lose from the withdrawal of those subsidies. The basic tactic of an interest group is to trade the votes of its members and its financial support to candidates in exchange for an implied promise of favorable legislation. Such legislation will normally take the form of a statute transferring wealth from unorganized taxpayers (for example, consumers) to the interest group. If the target were another interest group, the legislative transfer might be effectively opposed. The unorganized are unlikely to mount effective opposition, and it is their wealth, therefore, that typically is transferred to interest groups.

On this view, a statute is a deal. . . . But because of the costs of transactions within a multiheaded legislative body, and the costs of effective communication through time, legislation does not spring full-grown from the head of the legislature; it needs interpretation and application, and this is the role of the courts. They are agents of the legislature. But to impart credibility and durability to the deals the legislature strikes with interest groups, courts must be able to resist the wishes of current legislators who want to undo their predecessors' deals yet cannot do so through repeal because the costs of passing legislation (whether original or amended) are so high, and who might therefore look to the courts for a repealing "interpretation." The impediments to legislation actually facilitate rather than retard the striking of deals, by giving interest groups some assurance that a deal struck with the legislature will not promptly be undone by repeal. An independent judiciary is one of the impediments.

Judicial independence makes the judges imperfect agents of the legislature. This is tolerable not only for the reason just mentioned but also because an independent judiciary is necessary for the resolution of ordinary disputes in a way that will encourage trade, travel, freedom of action, and other highly valued activities or conditions and will minimize the expenditure of resources on influencing governmental action. Legislators might appear to have little to gain from these widely diffused rule-of-law virtues. But if the aggregate benefits from a particular social policy are very large and no interest group's ox is gored, legislators may find it in their own interest to support the policy. Voters understand in a rough way the benefits to them of national defense, crime control, dispute settlement, and the other elements of the night watchman state, and they will not vote for legislators who refuse to provide these basic public services. It is only when those services are in place, and when (usually later) effective means of taxation and redistribution develop, that the formation of narrow interest groups and the extraction by them of transfers from unorganized groups become feasible.

The judges thus have a dual role: to interpret the interest-group deals embodied in legislation and to

---

[2]A free rider is someone who derives a benefit without contributing to the cost of creating the benefit. For example, even if A and B both favor the enactment of a statute, X, each will prefer the other to invest what is necessary in getting X enacted, since the benefit of X to A or to B will be the same whether or not he contributes to the cost of obtaining it. . . . [N]ational defense [is] an example of an activity that would encounter severe free-rider problems if provided privately.

provide the basic public service of authoritative dispute resolution. They perform the latter function not only by deciding cases in accordance with preexisting norms, but also—especially in the Anglo-American legal system—by elaborating those norms. They fashioned the common law out of customary practices, out of ideas borrowed from statutes and from other legal systems (for example, Roman law), and out of their own conceptions of public policy. The law they created exhibits, according to the economic theory that I am expounding, a remarkable (although not total—remember the extension of the rule of capture to oil and gas) substantive consistency. It is as if the judges *wanted* to adopt the rules, procedures, and case outcomes that would maximize society's wealth.

I must pause to define "wealth maximization," a term often misunderstood. The "wealth" in "wealth maximization" refers to the sum of all tangible and intangible goods and services, weighted by prices of two sorts: offer prices (what people are willing to pay for goods they do not already own); and asking prices (what people demand to sell what they do own). If A would be willing to pay up to $100 for B's stamp collection, it is worth $100 to A. If B would be willing to sell the stamp collection for any price above $90, it is worth $90 to B. So if B sells the stamp collection to A (say for $100, but the analysis is qualitatively unaffected at any price between $90 and $100—and it is only in that range that a transaction will occur), the wealth of society will rise by $10. Before the transaction A had $100 in cash and B had a stamp collection worth $90 (a total of $190); after the transaction A has a stamp collection worth $100 and B has $100 in cash (a total of $200). The transaction will not raise measured wealth—gross national product, national income, or whatever—by $10; it will not raise it at all unless the transaction is recorded, and if it is recorded it is likely to raise measured wealth by the full $100 purchase price. But the real addition to social wealth consists of the $10 increment in *nonpecuniary* satisfaction that A derives from the purchase, compared with that of B. This shows that "wealth" in the economist's sense is not a simple monetary measure, and explains why it is a fallacy (the Earl of Lauderdale's fallacy) to think that wealth would be maximized by encouraging the charging of monopoly prices. The wealth of producers would increase but that of consumers would diminish—and actually by a greater amount, since monopoly pricing will induce some consumers to switch to goods that cost society more to produce but, being priced at a competitive rather than a monopoly price, appear to the consumer to be cheaper. The fallacy thus lies in equating business income to social wealth.[3]

Similarly, if I am given a choice between remaining in a job in which I work forty hours a week for $1,000 and switching to a job in which I would work thirty hours for $500, and I decide to make the switch, the extra ten hours of leisure must be worth at least $500 to me, yet GNP will fall when I reduce my hours of work. Suppose the extra hours of leisure are worth $600 to me, so that my full income rises from $1,000 to $1,100 when I reduce my hours. My former employer presumably is made worse off by my leaving (else why did he employ me?), but not more than $100 worse off; for if he were, he would offer to pay me a shade over $1,100 a week to stay—and I would stay. (The example abstracts from income tax.)

Wealth is *related* to money, in that a desire not backed by ability to pay has no standing—such a desire is neither an offer price nor an asking price. I may desperately desire a BMW, but if I am unwilling or unable to pay its purchase price, society's wealth would not be increased by transferring the BMW from its present owner to me. Abandon this essential constraint (an important distinction, also, between wealth maximization and utilitarianism—for I might derive greater utility from the BMW than its present owner or anyone else to whom he might sell the car), and the way is open to tolerating the crimes committed by the passionate and avaricious against the cold and the frugal.

The common law facilitates wealth-maximizing transactions in a variety of ways. It recognizes property rights, and these facilitate exchange. It also protects property rights, through tort and criminal law. (Although today criminal law is almost entirely statutory, the basic criminal protections—for example, those against murder, assault, rape, and theft—have, as one might expect, common law origins.) Through contract law it protects the process of exchange. And it establishes procedural rules for resolving disputes in these various fields as efficiently as possible.

The illustrations given thus far of wealth-maximizing transactions have been of transactions

---

[3]On these and other technical details of wealth maximization, see my article "Wealth Maximization Revisited," 2 *Notre Dame Journal of Law, Ethics, and Public Policy* 85 (1985).

that are voluntary in the strict sense of making everyone affected by them better off, or at least no worse off. Every transaction has been assumed to affect just two parties, each of whom has been made better off by it. Such a transaction is said to be Pareto superior, but Pareto superiority is not a necessary condition for a transaction to be wealth maximizing. Consider an accident that inflicts a cost of $100 with a probability of .01 and that would have cost $3 to avoid. The accident is wealth-maximizing "transaction" (recall Aristotle's distinction between voluntary and involuntary transactions) because the expected accident cost ($1) is less than the cost of avoidance. (I am assuming risk neutrality. Risk aversion would complicate the analysis but not change it fundamentally.) It is wealth maximizing even if the victim is not compensated. The result is consistent with Learned Hand's formula, which defines negligence as the failure to take cost-justified precautions. If the only precaution that would have averted the accident is not cost-justified, the failure to take it is not negligent and the injurer will not have to compensate the victim for the costs of the accident.

If it seems artificial to speak of the accident as the transaction, consider instead the potential transaction that consists of purchasing the safety measure that would have avoided the accident. Since a potential victim would not pay $3 to avoid an expected accident cost of $1, his offer price will be less than the potential injurer's asking price and the transaction will not be wealth maximizing. But if these figures were reversed—if an expected accident cost of $3 could be averted at a cost of $1—the transaction would be wealth maximizing, and a liability rule administered in accordance with the Hand formula would give potential injurers an incentive to take the measures that potential victims would pay them to take if voluntary transactions were feasible. The law would be overcoming transaction-cost obstacles to wealth-maximizing transactions—a frequent office of liability rules.

The wealth-maximizing properties of common law rules have been elucidated at considerable length in the literature of the economic analysis of law.[4] Such doctrines as conspiracy, general average (admiralty), contributory negligence, equitable servitudes, employment at will, the standard for granting preliminary injunctions, entrapment, the contract defense of impossibility, the collateral-benefits rule, the expectation measure of damages, assumption of risk, attempt, invasion of privacy, wrongful interference with contract rights, the availability of punitive damages in some cases but not others, privilege in the law of evidence, official immunity, and the doctrine of moral consideration have been found—at least by some contributors to this literature—to conform to the dictates of wealth maximization. . . . It has even been argued that the system of precedent itself has an economic equilibrium. Precedents are created as a by-product of litigation. The greater the number of recent precedents in an area, the lower the rate of litigation will be. In particular, cases involving disputes over legal as distinct from purely factual issues will be settled. The existence of abundant, highly informative (in part because recent) precedents will enable the parties to legal disputes to form more convergent estimates of the likely outcome of a trial . . . if both parties agree on the outcome of trial they will settle beforehand because a trial is more costly than a settlement. But with less litigation, fewer new precedents will be produced, and the existing precedents will obsolesce as changing circumstances render them less apt and informative. So the rate of litigation will rise, producing more precedents and thereby causing the rate of litigation again to fall.

This analysis does not explain what drives judges to decide common law cases in accordance with the dictates of wealth maximization. Prosperity, however, which wealth maximization measures more sensitively than purely monetary measures such as GNP, is a relatively uncontroversial policy, and most judges try to steer clear of controversy: their age, method of compensation, and relative weakness vis-à-vis the other branches of government make the avoidance of controversy attractive. It probably is no accident, therefore, that many common law doctrines assumed their modern form in the nineteenth century, when laissez-faire ideology, which resembles wealth maximization, had a strong hold on the Anglo-American judicial imagination; Shaw's opinion in the *Farwell* case . . . is a good example.

It may be objected that in assigning ideology as a cause of judicial behavior, the economist strays outside the boundaries of his discipline; but he need not rest on ideology. The economic analysis of legislation

[4]See *Economic Analysis of Law,* note 1 above, pt. 2 and ch. 21; William M. Landes and Richard A. Posner, *The Economic Structure of Tort Law* (1987).

implies that fields of law left to the judges to elaborate, such as the common law fields, must be the ones in which interest–group pressures are too weak to deflect the legislature from pursuing goals that are in the general interest. Prosperity is one of these goals, and one that judges are especially well equipped to promote. The rules of the common law that they promulgate attach prices to socially undesirable conduct, whether free riding or imposing social costs without corresponding benefits.[5] By doing this the rules create incentives to avoid such conduct, and these incentives foster prosperity. In contrast, judges can, despite appearances, do little to redistribute wealth. A rule that makes it easy for poor tenants to break leases with rich landlords, for example, will induce landlords to raise rents in order to offset the costs that such a rule imposes, and tenants will bear the brunt of these higher costs. Indeed, the principal redistribution accomplished by such a rule may be from the prudent, responsible tenant, who may derive little or no benefit from having additional legal rights to use against landlords—rights that enable a tenant to avoid or postpone eviction for nonpayment of rental—to the feckless tenant. That is a capricious redistribution. Legislatures, however, have by virtue of their taxing and spending powers powerful tools for redistributing wealth. So an efficient division of labor between the legislative and judicial branches has the legislative branch concentrate on catering to interest-group demands for wealth distribution and the judicial branch on meeting the broad-based social demand for efficient rules governing safety, property, and transactions. Although there are other possible goals of judicial action besides efficiency and redistribution, many of these (various conceptions of "fairness" and "justice") are labels for wealth maximization,[6] or for redistribution in favor of powerful interest groups; or else they are too controversial in a heterogeneous society, too ad hoc, or insufficiently developed to provide judges who desire a reputation for objectivity and disinterest with adequate grounds for their decisions.

Finally, even if judges have little commitment to efficiency, their inefficient decisions will, by definition, impose greater social costs than their efficient ones will. As a result, losers of cases decided mistakenly from an economic standpoint will have a greater incentive, on average, to press for correction through appeal, new litigation, or legislative action than losers of cases decided soundly from an economic standpoint—so there will be a steady pressure for efficient results. Moreover, cases litigated under inefficient rules tend to involve larger stakes than cases litigated under efficient rules (for the inefficient rules, by definition, generate social waste), and the larger the stakes in a dispute the likelier it is to be litigated rather than settled; so judges will have a chance to reconsider the inefficient rule.

Thus we should not be surprised to see the common law tending to become efficient, although since the incentives of judges to perform well along any dimension are weak (this is a by-product of judicial independence), we cannot expect the law ever to achieve perfect efficiency. Since wealth maximization is not only a guide in fact to common law judging but also a genuine social value and the only one judges are in a good position to promote, it provides not only the key to an accurate description of what the judges are up to but also the right benchmark for criticism and reform. If judges are failing to maximize wealth, the economic analyst of law will urge them to alter practice or doctrine accordingly. In addition, the analyst will urge—on any legislator sufficiently free of interest-group pressures to be able to legislate in the public interest—a program of enacting only legislation that conforms to the dictates of wealth maximization.

Besides generating both predictions and prescriptions, the economic approach enables the common law to be reconceived in simple, coherent terms and to be applied more objectively than traditional lawyers would think possible. From the premise that the common law does and should seek to maximize society's wealth, the economic analyst can deduce in logical—if you will, formalist—fashion (economic theory is formulated nowadays largely in mathematical terms) the set of legal doctrines that will express and perfect the inner nature of the common law, and can compare

---

[5]Such imposition is well illustrated by acquisitive crimes: the time and money spent by the thief in trying to commit thefts and the property owner in trying to prevent them have no social product, for they are expended merely in order to bring about, or to prevent, a redistribution of wealth. Overall wealth decreases, as in the case of monopoly, discussed earlier.

[6]For example, it is unclear whether Weinrib's Kantian theory of tort law . . . has different substantive implications from the economic theory; the differences may be in vocabulary only.

these doctrines with the actual doctrines of common law. After translating from the economic vocabulary back into the legal one, the analyst will find that most of the actual doctrines are tolerable approximations to the implications of economic theory and so are formalistically valid. Where there are discrepancies, the path to reform is clear—yet the judge who takes the path cannot be accused of making rather than finding law, for he is merely contributing to the program of realizing the essential nature of the common law.

The project of reducing the common law—with its many separate fields, its thousands of separate doctrines, its hundreds of thousands of reported decisions—to a handful of mathematical formulas may seem quixotic, but the economic analyst can give reasons for doubting this assessment. Much of the doctrinal luxuriance of common law is seen to be superficial once the essentially economic nature of the common law is understood. A few principles, such as cost-benefit analysis, the prevention of free riding, decision under uncertainty, risk aversion, and the promotion of mutually beneficial exchanges, can explain most doctrines and decisions. Tort cases can be translated into contract cases by recharacterizing the tort issue as finding the implied pre-accident contract that the parties would have chosen had transaction costs not been prohibitive, and contract cases can be translated into tort cases by asking what remedy if any would maximize the expected benefits of the contractual undertaking considered ex ante. The criminal's decision whether to commit a crime is no different in principle from the prosecutor's decision whether to prosecute; a plea bargain is a contract; crimes are in effect torts by insolvent defendants because if all criminals could pay the full social costs of their crimes, the task of deterring antisocial behavior could be left to tort law. Such examples suggest not only that the logic of the common law really is economics but also that the teaching of law could be simplified by exposing students to the clean and simple economic structure beneath the particolored garb of legal doctrine.

If all this seems reminiscent of Langdell, it differs fundamentally in being empirically verifiable. The ultimate test of a rule derived from economic theory is not the elegance or logicality of the derivation but the rule's effect on social wealth. The extension of the rule of capture to oil and gas was subjected to such a test, flunked, and was replaced (albeit through legislative rather than judicial action) by efficient rules. The other rules of the common law can and should be tested likewise. . . .

. . Wealth maximization is an ethic of productivity and social cooperation—to have a claim on society's goods and services you must be able to offer something that other people value—while utilitarianism is a hedonistic, unsocial ethic. . . And an ethic of productivity and cooperation is more congruent with the values of the dominant groups in our society than the pure utilitarian ethic would be. Unfortunately, wealth maximization is not a pure ethic of productivity and cooperation, not only because even lawful efforts at maximizing wealth often make some other people worse off, but more fundamentally because luck plays a big role in the returns to market activities. What is worse, it is always possible to argue that the distribution of productivity among a population is itself the luck of the genetic draw, or of upbringing, or of where one happens to have been born, and that these forms of luck have no ethical charge. There are counterarguments, of course, but they are not decisive. So, once again, the foundations of an overarching principle for resolving legal disputes are rotten, and one is driven back to the pragmatic ramparts. . . .

13

ROBERTO MANGABEIRA UNGER

From *The Critical Legal Studies Movement*

INTRODUCTION / THE TRADITION OF LEFTIST MOVEMENTS IN LEGAL THOUGHT AND PRACTICE

The critical legal studies movement has undermined the central ideas of modern legal thought and put another conception of law in their place. This conception implies a view of society and informs a practice of politics.

What I offer here is more a proposal than a description. But is a proposal that advances along one of the paths opened up by a movement of ideas that has defied in exemplary ways perplexing, widely felt constraints upon theoretical insight and transformative effort. . . .

The antecedents were unpromising. Critical legal studies arose from the leftist tradition in modern legal thought and practice. Two overriding concerns have marked this tradition.

The first concern has been the critique of formalism and objectivism. By formalism I do not mean what the term is usually taken to describe: belief in the availability of a deductive or quasi-deductive method capable of giving determinate solutions to particular problems of legal choice. Formalism in this context is a commitment to, and therefore also a belief in the possibility of, a method of legal justification that contrasts with open-ended disputes about the basic terms of social life, disputes that people call ideological, philosophical, or visionary. Such conflicts fall far short of the closely guarded canon of inference and argument that the formalist claims for legal analysis. This formalism holds impersonal purposes, policies, and principles to be indispensable components of legal reasoning. Formalism in the conventional sense—the search for a method of deduction from a gapless system of rules—is merely the anomalous, limiting case of this jurisprudence.

A second distinctive formalist thesis is that only through such a restrained, relatively apolitical method of analysis is legal doctrine possible. Legal doctrine or legal analysis is a conceptual practice that combines two characteristics: the willingness to work from the institutionally defined materials of a given collective tradition and the claim to speak authoritatively within this tradition, to elaborate it from within in a way that is meant, at least ultimately, to affect the application of state power. Doctrine can exist, according to the formalist view, because of a contrast between the more determinate rationality of legal analysis and the less determinate rationality of ideological contests.

This thesis can be restated as the belief that lawmaking, guided only by the looser and more inconclusive arguments suited to ideological disputes, differs fundamentally from law application. Lawmaking and law application diverge in both how they work and how their results may properly be justified. To be sure, law application may have an important creative element. But in the politics of lawmaking the appeal to principal and policy, when it exists at all, is supposed to be both more controversial in its foundations and more indeterminate in its implications than the corresponding features of legal analysis. Other modes of justification allegedly compensate for the diminished force and precision of the ideal element in lawmaking. Thus, legislative decisions may be validated as results of procedures that are themselves legitimate because they allow all interest groups to be represented and to compete for influence or, more ambitiously, because they enable the wills of citizens to count equally in choosing the laws that will govern them.

Objectivism is the belief that the authoritative legal materials—the system of statutes, cases, and accepted legal ideas—embody and sustain a defensible scheme of human association. They display, though always imperfectly, an intelligible moral order. Alternatively they show the results of practical constraints upon social life—constraints such as those of economic efficiency—that, taken together with constant human desires, have a normative force. The laws are not merely the outcome of contingent power struggles or of practical pressures lacking in rightful authority.

The modern lawyer may wish to keep his formalism while avoiding objectivist assumptions. He may feel happy to switch from talk about interest group politics in a legislative setting to invocations of impersonal purpose, policy, and principle in an adjudicative or professional one. He is plainly mistaken; formalism presupposes at least a qualified objectivism. For if the impersonal purposes, policies, and principles on which all but the most mechanical versions of the formalist thesis must rely do not come, as objectivism suggests, from a moral or practical order exhibited, however partially and ambiguously, by the legal materials themselves, where could they come from? They would have to be supplied by some normative theory extrinsic to the law. Even if such a theory could be convincingly established on its own ground, it would be miraculous if its implications coincided with any large portion of the received doctrinal understandings. At least it would be miraculous unless you had already assumed the truth of objectivism. But if the results of this alien theory failed to overlap with the greater part of received understandings of the law, you would need to reject broad areas of established law and legal doctrine as "mistaken." You would then have trouble maintaining the contrast of doctrine to ideology and political prophecy that represents an essential part of the formalist creed: you would have become a practitioner of the free-wheeling criticism of established arrangements and received ideas. No wonder theorists committed to formalism and the conventional view of doctrine have always fought to retain a remnant of the objectivist thesis. They have done so even at a heavy cost to their reputation among the orthodox, narrow-minded lawyers who otherwise provide their main constituency.

Another, more heroic way to dispense with objectivism would be to abrogate the exception to disillusioned, interest group views of politics that is implicit in objectivist ideas. This abrogation would require carrying over to the interpretation of rights the same shameless talk about interest groups that is thought permissible in a legislative setting. Thus, if a particular statute represented a victory of sheepherders over cattlemen, it would be applied, strategically, to advance the sheepherders' aims and to confirm the cattlemen's defeat. To the objection that the correlation of forces underlying a statute is too hard to measure, the answer may be that this measurement is no harder to come by than the identification and weighting of purposes, policies, and principles that lack secure footholds in legislative politics. This "solution," however, would escape objectivism only by discrediting the case for doctrine and formalism. Legal reasoning would turn into a mere extension of the strategic element in the discourse of legislative jostling. The security of rights, so important to the ideal of legality, would fall hostage to context-specific calculations of effect.

If the criticism of formalism and objectivism is the first characteristic theme of leftist movements in modern legal thought, the purely instrumental use of legal practice and legal doctrine to advance leftist aims is the second. The connection between skeptical criticism and strategic militancy seems both negative and sporadic. It is negative because it remains almost entirely limited to the claim that nothing in the nature of law or in the conceptual structure of legal thought—neither objectivist nor formalist assumptions—constitutes a true obstacle to the advancement of leftist aims. It is sporadic because short-run leftist goals might occasionally be served by the transmutation of political commitments into delusive conceptual necessities.

These themes of leftist legal thought and practice have now been reformulated while being drawn into a larger body of ideas. The results offer new insight into the struggle over power and right within and beyond the law, and they redefine the meaning of radicalism.

CHAPTER 1 / THE CRITICISM OF LEGAL THOUGHT

We have transformed the received critique of formalism and objectivism into two sets of more precise claims that turn out to have a surprising relation. The two groups of critical ideas state the true lesson of the law curriculum—what it has actually come to teach, rather than what the law professors say it teaches, about the nature of law and legal doctrine. The recitation of the lesson carries the criticism of formalist and objectivist ideas to an unprecedented extreme. This very extremism, however, makes it possible to draw from criticism elements of a constructive program.

THE CRITIQUE OF OBJECTIVISM

In refining the attack upon objectivism, we have reinterpreted contemporary law and legal doctrine as the ever more advanced dissolution of the project of the classical, nineteenth-century lawyers. Because both the original project and the signs of its progressive breakdown remain misunderstood, the dissolution has not yet been complete and decisive. The nineteenth-century jurists were engaged in a search for the built-in legal structure of democracy and the market. The nation, at the Lycurgan moment of its history, had opted for a particular type of society: a commitment to a democratic republic and to a market system as a necessary part of that republic. The people might have chosen some other type of social organization. But in choosing this one, in choosing it for example over an aristocratic and corporatist polity on the old-European model, they also chose the legally defined institutional structure that went along with it. This structure provided legal science with its topic and generated the purposes, policies, and principles to which legal argument might legitimately appeal. Two ideas played a central role in this enterprise. One was the distinction between the foundational politics, responsible for choosing the social type, and the ordinary politics, including the ordinary legislation, operating within the framework established at the foundational moment.

The other idea was that an inherent and distinct legal structure existed for each type of social organization.

Many may be tempted to dismiss out of hand as wholly implausible and undeserving of criticism this conception of a logic of social types, each type with its intrinsic institutional structure. It should be remembered, however, that in less explicit and coherent form the same idea continues to dominate the terms of modern ideological debate and to inform all but the most rigorous styles of microeconomics and social science. It appears, for example, in the conceit that we must choose between market and command economies or at most combine these two exhaustive and well-defined institutional options into a "mixed economy." The abstract idea of the market as a system in which a plurality of economic agents bargain on their own initiative and for their own account becomes more or less tacitly identified with the particular market institutions that triumphed in modern Western history. Moreover, the abandonment of the objectivist thesis would leave formalism, and the varieties of doctrine that formalism wants to defend, without a basis, a point to which my argument will soon return. The critique of objectivism that we have undertaken challenges the idea of types of social organization with a built-in legal structure, as well as the more subtle but still powerful successors of this idea in current conceptions of substantive law and doctrine. We have conducted this assault on more than one front.

Successive failures to find the universal legal language of democracy and the market suggests that no such language exists. An increasing part of doctrinal analysis and legal theory has been devoted to containing the subversive implications of this discovery.

The general theory of contract and property provided the core domain for the objectivist attempt to disclose the built-in legal content of the market, just as the theory of protected constitutional interests and of the legitimate ends of state action was designed to reveal the intrinsic legal structure of a democratic republic. But the execution kept belying the intention. As the property concept was generalized and decorporealized, it faded into the generic conception of right, which in turn proved to be systematically ambiguous (Hohfeld's insight) if not entirely indeterminate. Contract, the dynamic counterpart to property, could do no better. The generalization of contract theory revealed, alongside the dominant principles of freedom to choose the partner and the terms, the counterprinciples: that freedom to contract would not be allowed to undermine the communal aspects of social life and that grossly unfair bargains would not be enforced. Though the counterprinciples might be pressed to the corner, they could be neither driven out completely nor subjected to a system of metaprinciples that would settle, once and for all, their relation to the dominant principles. In the most contested areas of contract law, two different views of the sources of obligation still contend. One, which sees the counterprinciples as mere ad hoc qualifications to the dominant principles, identifies the fully articulated act of will and the unilateral imposition of a duty by the state as the two exhaustive sources of obligation. The other view, which treats the counterprinciples as possible generative norms of the entire body of law and doctrine, finds the standard source of obligations in the only partly deliberate ties of mutual dependence and redefines the two conventional sources as extreme, limiting cases. Which of these clashing conceptions provides the real theory of contract? Which describes the institutional structure inherent in the very nature of a market?

The development of constitutional law and constitutional theory throughout the late nineteenth and the twentieth centuries tells a similar story of the discovery of indeterminacy through generalization. This discovery was directly connected with its private law analogue. The doctrines of protected constitutional interests and of legitimate ends of state action were the chief devices for defining the intrinsic legal-institutional structure of the scheme of ordered liberty. They could not be made coherent in form and precise in implication without freezing into place, in a way that the real politics of the republic would never tolerate, a particular set of deals between the national government and organized groups. Legitimate ends and protected interests exploded into too many contradictory implications; like contract and property theory, they provided in the end no more than retrospective glosses on decisions that had to be reached on quite different grounds.

The critique of this more specific brand of objectivism can also develop through the interpretation of contemporary law and doctrine. The current content of public and private law fails to present a single, unequivocal version of democracy and the market. On the contrary, it contains in confused and undeveloped form the elements of different versions. These small-scale variations, manifest in the nuances of contemporary doctrine, suggest larger possible variations.

The convergent result of these two modes of attack upon objectivism—the legal-historical and the legal-doctrinal—is to discredit, once and for all, the conception of a system of social types with a built-in institutional structure. The very attempt to work this conception into technical legal detail ends up showing its falsehood. Thus, a cadre of seemingly harmless and even toadying jurists partly authored the insight required to launch the attack against objectivism—the discovery of the indeterminate content of abstract institutional categories such as democracy or the market—with its far-reaching subversive implications. Those who live in the temple may delight in the thought that the priests occasionally outdo the prophets.

THE CRITIQUE OF FORMALISM

We have approached the critique of formalism in an equally distinctive way. The starting point of our argument is the idea that every branch of doctrine must rely tacitly if not explicitly upon some picture of the forms of human association that are right and realistic in the areas of social life with which it deals. For example, a constitutional lawyer needs a theory of the democratic republic that describes the proper relation between state and society or the essential features of social organization and individual entitlement that government must protect come what may.

Without such a guiding vision, legal reasoning seems condemned to a game of easy analogies. It will always be possible to find, retrospectively, more or less convincing ways to make a set of distinctions, or failures to distinguish, look credible. A common experience testifies to this possibility; every thoughtful law student or lawyer has had the disquieting sense of being able to argue too well or too easily for too many conflicting solutions. Because everything can be defended, nothing can; the analogy-mongering must be brought to a halt. It must be possible to reject some of the received understandings and decisions as mistaken and to do so by appealing to a background normative theory of the branch of law in question or of the realm of social practice governed by that part of the law.

Suppose you could determine on limited grounds of institutional propriety how much a style of doctrinal practice may regularly reject as mistaken. With too little rejection, the lawyer fails to avoid the suspect quality of endless analogizing. With too much, he forfeits his claim to be doing doctrine as opposed to ideology, philosophy, or prophecy. For any given level of revisionary power, however, different portions of the received understandings in any extended field of law may be repudiated.

To determine which part of established opinion about the meaning and applicability of legal rules you should reject, you need a background prescriptive theory of the relevant area of social practice, a theory that does for the branch of law in question what a doctrine of the republic or of the political process does for constitutional argument. This is where the trouble starts. No matter what the content of this background theory, it is, if taken seriously and pursued to its ultimate conclusions, unlikely to prove compatible with a broad range of the received understandings. Yet just such a compatibility seems to be required by a doctrinal practice that defines itself by contrast to open-ended ideology. For it would be strange if the results of a coherent, richly developed normative theory were to coincide with a major portion of any extended branch of law. The many conflicts of interest and vision that lawmaking involves, fought out by countless minds and wills working at cross-purposes, would have to be the vehicle of an immanent moral rationality whose message could be articulated by a single cohesive theory. The dominant legal theories in fact undertake this daring and implausible sanctification of the actual, and the unreflective common sense of orthodox lawyers tacitly presupposes it. Most often, the sanctification takes the form of treating the legal order as a repository of intelligible purposes, policies, and principles, in abrupt contrast to the standard, disenchanted view of legislative politics.

This argument against formalism may be criticized on the ground that the claimed contrast between the game of analogy and the appeal to a background conception of right is untenable; from the outset analogy is guided by such a conception, so the criticism would suggest. But for analogy to be guided by such a conception would require the miracle of preestablished harmony between the content of the laws and the teachings of a coherent theory of right. Or, again, it may be objected that in law such background views benefit from a self-limiting principle, introduced by the constraints of institutional context. Such a principle, however, must rely either upon a more or less tacit professional consensus about the rightful limits of institutional roles or upon an explicit and justifiable theory of institutional roles. Even if a consensus of this sort could claim authority, it simply does not exist. The proper extent of revisionary power—the power to declare some portion of received legal opinion mistaken—remains among the most controversial legal topics, as the American debates about judicial "activism" and "self-restraint" show. An explicit theory of institutional roles can make sense and find support only within a substantive theory of politics and rights. We thus return to the initial implausibility of a widespread convergence of any such theory with the actual content of a major branch of law.

Having recognized this problem with doctrine, modern legal analysis tries to circumvent it in a number of ways. It may, for example, present an entire field of law as the expression of certain underlying theoretical approaches to the subject. According to one suggestion, these implicit models fit into a coherent scheme or, at least, point toward a synthesis. In this way it seems possible to reconcile the recognition that legal analysis requires an appeal to an underlying theory of right and social practice with the inability to show that the actual content of law and doctrine in any given area coincides, over an appreciable area of law, with a particular theory. But this recourse merely pushes the problem to another level. No extended body of law in fact coincides with such a metascheme, just as no broad range of historical experiences coincides with the implications of one of the evolutionary views that claim to provide a science of history. (That this counts as more than a faint resemblance is a point to which I shall return.) It is always possible to find in actual legal materials radically inconsistent clues about the range of application of each of the models and indeed about the identity of the models themselves.

Once the lawyer abandons these methods of compensation and containment, he returns to a cruder and more cynical device. He merely imposes upon his background conceptions—his theories of right and social practice—an endless series of ad hoc adjustments. The looseness of the theories and the resulting difficulty of distinguishing the ad hoc from the theoretically required make this escape all the easier. There emerges the characteristic figures of the modern jurist who wants—and needs—to combine the cachet of theoretical refinement, the modernist posture of seeing through everything, with the reliability of the technician whose results remain close to the mainstream of professional and social consensus. Determined not to miss out on anything, he has chosen to be an outsider and an insider at the same time. To the achievement of this objective he has determined to sacrifice the momentum of his ideas. We have denounced him wherever we have found him, and we have found him everywhere.

One more objection might be made to this attack upon formalism and upon the type of doctrinal practice that formalism justifies. According to this objection, the attack succeeds only against the systematic constructions of the most ambitious academic jurists, not against the specific, problem-oriented arguments of practical lawyers and judges. It is hard, though, to see how such arguments could be valid, how indeed they might differ from rhetorical posturing, unless they could count as tentative fragments of a possible cohesive view of an extended body of law.

The implication of our attack upon formalism is to undermine the attempt to rescue doctrine through these several strategems. It is to demonstrate that a doctrinal practice that puts its hope in the contrast of legal reasoning to ideology, philosophy, and political prophecy ends up as a collection of makeshift apologies.

THE CRITIQUES OF OBJECTIVISM AND FORMALISM RELATED: THEIR SIGNIFICANCE FOR CURRENT LEGAL THEORIES

Once the arguments against objectivism and formalism have been rendered in these specific ways, their relation to each other gains a new and surprising clarity. As long as the project of the nineteenth-century jurists retained its credibility, the problem of doctrine did not emerge. The miracle required and promised by objectivism could take place: the coincidence of the greater part of substantive law and doctrine with a coherent theory, capable of systematic articulation and relentless application. The only theory capable of performing the miracle would have been one that described the inner conceptual and institutional structure of the type of social and governmental organization to which the nation had committed itself at its foundational moment. Such a theory would not have needed to be imported from outside. It would not have been just somebody's favorite system. It would have translated into legal categories the abiding structure of ordinary political and economic activity. Once the objectivist project underlying the claim to reveal the inherent content of a type of social organization ceased to be believable, doctrine in its received form was condemned to the self-subversion that our critique of formalism has elucidated. But because the nature and defects of the project appeared only gradually, so did the permanent disequilibrium of doctrine.

This view of the flaws in objectivism and formalism and of the close link between the two sets of ideas and the two critiques explains our approach to the most influential and symptomatic legal theories in America today: the law and economics and the rights and principles schools. Each of these theories is advanced by a group that stands at the margin of high power, despairs of seeing its aims triumph through governmental politics, and appeals to some conceptual mechanism designed to show that the advancement of its program is a practical or moral necessity. The law and economics school has mainly addressed private law; the rights and principles school, public law. The law and economics school has invoked practical requirements (with normative implications) that supposedly underlie the legal system and its history; the rights and principles school, moral imperatives allegedly located within the legal order itself. The law and economics school has chiefly served the political right; the rights and principles school, the liberal center. But both theoretical tendencies can best be understood as efforts to recover the objectivist and formalist position. It is as restatements of objectivism and formalism that we have rejected them.

The chief instrument of the law and economics school is the equivocal use of the market concept. These analysts give free rein to the very mistake that the increasing formalization of microeconomics was largely meant to avoid: the identification of the abstract market ideas or the abstract circumstance of maximizing choice with a particular social and institutional complex. As a result, an analytic apparatus intended, when rigorous, to be entirely free of restrictive assumptions about the workings of society and entirely subsidiary to an empirical or normative theory that needs independent justification gets mistaken for a particular empirical and normative vision. More particularly, the abstract market idea is identified with a specific version of the market—the one that has prevailed in most of the modern history of most Western countries—with all its surrounding social assumptions, real or imagined. The formal analytic notion of allocational efficiency is equated with a particular theory of economic growth or, quite simply, with the introduction, the development, or the defense of this particular institutional and social order. Such are the sophistries by which the law and economics school pretends to discover both the real basis for the overall evolution of the legal order and the relevant standard by which to criticize occasional departure, of that order from its alleged vocation. From this source supposedly come the purposes and policies that do and should play the paramount role in legal reasoning.

The rights and principles school achieves similar results through very different means. It claims to discern in the leading ideas of the different branches of law, especially when illuminated by a scrupulous, benevolent, and well-prepared professional elite, the signs of an underlying moral order that can then serve as the basis for a system of more or less natural rights. This time, the objective order that guides the main line of legal evolution and serves to criticize the numerous though marginal aberrations is a harshly simplified version of moral ideas supposedly expressed in authoritative legal materials. No longer able to appeal to the idea of the built-in institutional structure of a type of social organization, this school alternates confusedly between two options, both of which it finds unacceptable as a basis for legal theory. One option is that moral consensus (if only it could actually be identified) carries weight just because it exists. The alternative view is that the dominant legal principles count as the manifestations of a transcendent moral order whose content can be identified quite apart from the history and substance of a particular body of law. The third, mediating position for which the school grasps—that consensus on the received principles somehow signals a moral order resting mysteriously upon more than consensus—requires several connected intellectual maneuvers. One is a drastic minimization of the extent to which the law already incorporates conflict over the desirable forms of human association. Another is the presentation of the dominant legal ideas as expressions of higher moral insight, an insight duly contained and corrected by a fidelity to the proprieties of established institutional roles, a fidelity that must itself be mandated by the moral order. Yet another is the deployment of a specific method to reveal the content and implications of this order: generalize from particular doctrines and intuitions, then hypostasize the generalizations into moral truth, and finally use the hypostasis to justify and correct the original material. The intended result of all this hocus-pocus is far clearer than the means used to achieve it. The result is to generate a system of principles and rights that overlaps to just the appropriate extent with the positive content of the laws. Such a system has the suitable degree of revisionary power, the degree necessary to prove that you are neither an all-out and therefore ineffective apologist nor an irresponsible revolutionary.

The law and economics and the rights and principles schools supply a watered-down version of the enterprise of nineteenth-century legal science. The endeavor of the classical nineteenth-century jurists in turn represented a diluted version of the more common, conservative social doctrines that preceded the emergence of modern social theory. These doctrines pretended to discover a canonical form of social life and personality that could never be fundamentally remade and reimagined even though it might undergo corruption or regeneration. At each succeeding stage of the history of these ideas, the initial conception of a natural form of society becomes weaker: the categories more abstract and indeterminate, the champions more acutely aware of the contentious character of their own claims. Self-consciousness poisons their protestations. Witnessing this latest turn in the history of modern legal thought, no one could be blamed for recalling hopefully Novalis's remark that "when we dream that we dream we are about to awake."

A large part of this history consists in the attempt to deflect the critique of formalism and objectivism by accepting some of its points while saving increasingly less of the original view. The single most striking example in twentieth-century American legal thought has been development of a theory of legal process, institutional roles, and purposive legal reasoning as a response to legal realism. The most creditable pretext for these endless moves of confession and avoidance has been the fear that, carried to the extreme, the critique of objectivism and formalism would leave nothing standing. The results might destroy the very possibility of legal doctrine, even of normative argument generally. Thus, ramshackle and plausible compromises have been easily mistaken for theoretical insight. For many of us, the turning point came when we decided, at the risk of confusion, paralysis, and marginality, to pursue the critical attack *à outrance*. When we took the negative ideas relentlessly to their final conclusions, we were rewarded by seeing these ideas turn into the starting points of a constructive program.

CHAPTER 2 / FROM CRITIQUE TO CONSTRUCTION

THE CONSTRUCTIVE OUTCOME OF THE CRITIQUE OF FORMALISM: DEVIATIONIST DOCTRINE

The defense of the received forms of doctrine has always rested on an implicit challenge: either accept the ruling style, with its aggressive contrast to controversy over the basic terms of social life, as the true dorm of doctrine, or find yourself reduced to the inconclusive contest of political visions. This dilemma is merely one of the many specific conceptual counterparts to the general choice: either resign yourself to some established version of social order, or face the war of all against all. The implication of our critique of formalism is to turn the dilemma of doctrine upside down. It is to say that, if any conceptual practice similar to what lawyers now call doctrine can be justified, the class of legitimate doctrinal activities must be sharply enlarged. The received style of doctrine must be redefined as an arbitrarily restricted subset of this larger class. We agree neither on whether we can in fact develop this expanded or deviationist doctrine nor on what exactly its methods and boundaries should be. But we know that only such an expansion could generate a conceptual practice that maintains the minimal characteristics of doctrine—the willingness to take the extant authoritative materials as starting points and the claim to normative authority—while avoiding the arbitrary juxtaposition of easy analogy and truncated theorizing that characterizes the most ambitious and coherent examples of legal analysis today.

It may fairly be asked why radicals should be interested in preserving doctrine at all. At stake in the defense of a suitably expanded doctrinal practice is the validity of normative and programmatic argument itself; at least this must be true when such argument takes the standard form of working from within a tradition rather than the exceptional one of appealing to transcendent insight. As long as necessitarian theories of historical change—the belief that the content and sequence of social systems reflect inescapable economic or psychological imperatives—remained persuasive, views of how society ought to be changed seemed misguided and superfluous. The disintegration of such theories, which has been the dominant feature of recent social thought, creates an opportunity for normative and programmatic ideas while depriving these ideas of an available criterion of political realism.

Expanded doctrine—the genre of legal writing that our movement has begun to develop—may be defined by several complementary or substantially equivalent criteria. On one description its central feature is the attempt to cross both an empirical and a normative frontier: the boundaries that separate doctrine from empirical social theory and from argument over the proper organization of society—that is, from ideological conflict. Enlarged doctrine crosses the normative boundary by deploying a method that differs in no essential way from the loose form of criticism, justification, and discovery that is possible within ideological controversy. Deviationist doctrine moves across the empirical boundary in two different ways. One way is familiar and straightforward: to explore the relations of cause and effect that lawyers dogmatically assume rather than explicitly investigate when they claim to interpret rules and precedents in the light of imputed purpose. The settled interpretation of a rule is often justified by a two-step operation: the interpreter first imputes to the rule a purpose, such as the promotion of family cohesion, then decides which reasonable understanding of the rule is best calculated to advance this end. Characteristically, however, he makes no serious effort to support or revise the causal assumptions taken for granted in the second stage of this procedure. The causal dogmatism of legal analysis is all the more remarkable given the star role that our ordinary understanding of history assigns to the unintended consequences of action and the paradoxical quality of causal connections. The other way the empirical element counts is more subtle and systematic: it opens up the petrified relations between abstract ideals or categories, such as freedom of contract or political equality, and the legally regulated social practices that are supposed to exemplify them. The method is to show, as a matter of truth about history and society, that these abstractions can receive—and almost invariably have received—alternative institutional embodiments, each of which gives a different cast to their guiding intentions.

On another description the crucial feature of deviationist doctrine is the willingness to recognize and develop the conflicts between principles and counterprinciples that can be found in any body of law. Critical doctrine does this by finding in these disharmonies the elements of broader contests among prescriptive conceptions of society.

Yet another description of expanded doctrine is presupposed by the previous two and makes explicit what they have in common. The revised style of doctrine commits itself to integrate into standard doctrinal argument the explicit controversy over the right and feasible structure of society, over what the relations among people should be like in the different areas of social activity. In the rich North Atlantic countries of today, the imaginative vision of the ways in which people can have a life in common appeals to a particular ideal of democracy for the state and citizenship, to a picture of private community in the domain of family and friendship, and to an amalgam of contract and impersonal technical hierarchy in the everyday realm of work and exchange. This social vision helps make the entire body of law look intelligible and even justifiable. Above all it serves to resolve what would otherwise be incorrigible indeterminacy in the law. Just as the ambiguities of rules and precedents require recourse to imputed purposes or underlying policies and principles, so the ambiguities of these policies and principles can be avoided only by an appeal to some background scheme of association of the sort just described. Yet the conflicting tendencies within law constantly suggest alternative schemes of human association. The focused disputes of legal doctrine repeatedly threaten to escalate into struggles over the basic imaginative structure of social existence.

The dominant styles of legal doctrine often included all three levels of analysis: the authoritative rules and precedents; the ideal purposes, policies, and principles; and the conceptions of possible and desirable human association to be enacted in different areas of social practice. Each such set of conceptions made a particular version of society stand in the place of the indefinite possibilities of human connection. To identify this set is to see how power-ridden and manipulable materials gain a semblance of authority, necessity, and determinacy and thus how formalism and objectivism seem plausible. It is to illuminate the mental world within which impersonal purposes, policies, and principles make sense and claim authority.

Most legal traditions of the past incorporated the final level of legal argument by relying upon a secular or sacred vision of the one right and necessary order of social life. Modern legal doctrine, however, works in a social context in which society has increasingly been forced open to transformative conflict. It exists in a cultural context in which, to an unprecedented extent, society is understood to be made and imagined rather than merely given. To incorporate the final level of legal analysis in this new setting would be to transform legal doctrine into one more arena for continuing the fight over the right and possible forms of social life. Modern jurists and their philosophers have generally wanted to avoid this result. They have avoided it at the cost of a series of violent and arbitrary intellectual restrictions whose ultimate effect is to turn legal doctrine into an endless array of argumentative tricks. Through its constructive attempts to devise a less confined genre of legal analysis, the critical legal studies movement has insisted upon avoiding this avoidance.

The rationality for which this expanded version of legal doctrine can hope is nothing other than the modest and potential but nevertheless significant rationality of the normal modes of moral and political controversy. You start from the conflicts between the available ideals of social life in your own social world or legal tradition and their flawed actualizations in present society. You imagine the actualizations transformed, or you transform them in fact, if only by extending an ideal to some area of social life from which it had previously been excluded. Then you revise the ideal conceptions in the light of their new practical embodiments. Call this process internal development. To engage in it self-reflectively you need make only two crucial assumptions: that no one scheme of association has conclusive authority and that the mutual correction of abstract ideals and their institutional realizations represents the last best hope of the standard forms of normative controversy. The weakness of such a method is its dependence upon the starting points provided by a particular tradition; its strength, the richness of reference to a concrete collective history of ideas and institutions. Legal doctrine, rightly understood and practiced, is the conduct of internal argument through legal materials.

The distinctive character of internal development becomes clear when this method is compared to the other major recourse of normative thought: the visionary insight into a reordered social world. Such insight presents an entirely new plan of collective life, a plan supported by a credible theory of transformation, informed by an image of personality, and guided by the effort to extend opportunities of human connection. Whereas internal argument starts by exploring conflicts between ruling ideals and established arrangements, or among those ideals themselves, and then pushes by gradual steps toward ever more drastic ways of reimagining society, visionary insight begins with the picture of a reordered human world. But the political prophet can be understood and he can persuade only because the principles of the world he invokes may be discerned already at work in the anomalies of personal encounter and social practice. No clearcut contrast exists between the normal and the visionary modes of argument, only a continuum of escalation. The strongest proof of their similarity is that both resort to the same preferred device: they try to seize upon deviations in current experience and to imagine them transformed, or to transform them in fact, into organizing conceptions and practices. A resemblance in character underlies this similarity of method. Short of claiming access to authoritative revelation or privileged intuition, every normative argument must in some wider sense be internal. If not internal to the interplay between ideals and institutions within a particular tradition, it must be internal to an analogous interplay on the scale of world history. . . .

14

KIMBERLÉ CRENSHAW, NEIL GOTANDA, GARY PELLER, AND KENDALL THOMAS

From *Critical Race Theory: The Key Writings That Formed the Movement*

INTRODUCTION

This volume offers a representative, though by no means exhaustive, compilation of the growing body of legal scholarship known as Critical Race Theory (CRT). As we conceive it, Critical Race Theory embraces a movement of left scholars, most of them scholars of color, situated in law schools, whose work challenges the ways in which race and racial power are constructed and represented in American legal culture and, more generally, in American society as a whole. In assembling and editing these essays, we have tried both to provide a sense of the intellectual genesis of this project and to map the main methodological directions that Critical Race Theory has taken since its inception. Toward these ends, the essays in the first few parts are arranged roughly in the chronological order of their publication. The remaining parts, however, are devoted to the most important methodological strands of Critical Race Theory today. We have chosen to present the substance of the original essays rather than small portions of a greater number of works, in the interest of providing the reader with texts that retain as much of their complexity, context, and nuance as possible.

As these writings demonstrate, there is no canonical set of doctrines or methodologies to which we all subscribe. Although Critical Race scholarship differs in object, argument, accent, and emphasis, it is nevertheless unified by two common interests. The first is to understand how a regime of white supremacy and its subordination of people of color have been created and maintained in America, and, in particular, to examine the relationship between that social structure and professed ideals such as "the rule of law" and "equal protection." The second is a desire not merely to understand the vexed bond between law and racial power but to *change* it. The essays gathered here thus share an ethical commitment to human liberation—even if we reject conventional notions of what such a conception means, and though we often disagree, even among ourselves, over its specific direction.

This ethical aspiration finds its most obvious concrete expression in the pursuit of engaged, even adversarial, scholarship. The writings in this collaboration may be read as contributions to what Edward Said has called "antithetical knowledge," the development of counteraccounts of social reality by subversive and subaltern elements of the reigning order. Critical Race Theory—like the Critical Legal Studies movement with which we are often allied—rejects the prevailing orthodoxy that scholarships should be or could be "neutral" and "objective." We believe that legal scholarship about race in America can never be written from a distance of detachment or with an attitude of objectivity. To the extent that racial power is exercised legally and ideologically, legal scholarship about race is an important site for the construction of that power, and thus is always a factor, if "only" ideologically, in the economy of racial power itself. To use a phrase from the existentialist tradition, there is "no exit"—no scholarly perch outside the social dynamics of racial power from which merely to observe and analyze. Scholarship—the formal production, identification, and organization of what will be called "knowledge"—is inevitably political. Each of the texts in this volume seeks in its own way not simply to explicate but also to intervene in the ideological contestation of race in America, and to create new, oppositionist accounts of race.

The aspect of our work which most markedly distinguishes it from conventional liberal and conservative legal scholarship about race and inequality is a deep dissatisfaction with traditional civil rights discourse. As several of the authors in this collection demonstrate, the reigning contemporary American ideologies about race were built in the sixties and seventies around an implicit social compact. This compact held that racial power and racial justice would be understood in very particular ways. Racial justice was embraced in the American mainstream in terms that excluded radical or fundamental challenges to status quo institutional practices in American society by treating the exercise of racial power as rare and aberrational rather than as systemic and ingrained. The construction of "racism" from what Alan Freeman terms the "perpetrator perspective" restrictively conceived racism as an intentional, albeit irrational, deviation by a conscious wrongdoer from otherwise neutral, rational, and just ways of distributing jobs, power, prestige, and wealth. The adoption of this perspective allowed a broad cultural mainstream both explicitly to acknowledge the fact of racism and, simultaneously, to insist on its irregular occurrence and limited significance. As Freeman concludes, liberal race reforms thus served to legitimize the basic myths of American meritocracy.

In Gary Peller's depiction, this mainstream civil rights discourse on "race relations" was constructed in this way partly as a defense against the more radical ideologies of racial liberation presented by the Black Nationalist and Black Consciousness movements of the sixties and early seventies, and their less visible but intellectually subversive scholarly presentations by people such as James Turner, now a teacher in black studies at Cornell. In the construction of "racism" as the irrational and backward bias of believing that someone's race is important, the American cultural mainstream neatly linked the black left to the white racist right: according to this quickly coalesced consensus, because race-consciousness characterized both white supremacists and black nationalists, it followed that both were racists. The resulting "center" of cultural common sense thus rested on the exclusion of virtually the entire domain of progressive thinking about race within colored communities. With its explicit embrace of race-consciousness, Critical Race Theory aims to reexamine the terms by which race and racism have been negotiated in American consciousness, and to recover and revitalize the radical tradition of race-consciousness among African-Americans and other peoples of color—a tradition that was discarded when integration, assimilation and the ideal of color-blindness became the official norms of racial enlightenment.

The image of a "traditional civil rights discourse" refers to the constellation of ideas about racial power and social transformation that were constructed partly by, and partly as a defense against, the mass mobilization of social energy and popular imagination in the civil rights movement of the late fifties and sixties. To those who participated in the civil rights movements firsthand—say, as part of the street and body politics engaged in by Reverend Martin Luther King, Jr.'s cadres in town after town across the South—the fact that they were part of a deeply subversive movement of mass resistance and social transformation was obvious. Our opposition to traditional civil rights discourse is neither a criticism of the civil rights movement nor an attempt to diminish its significance. On the contrary, as Anthony Cook's radical reading of King's theology and social theory makes explicit, we draw much of our inspiration and sense of direction from that courageous, brilliantly conceived, spiritually inspired, and ultimately transformative mass action.

Of course, colored people made important social gains through civil rights reform, as did American society generally: in fact, but for the civil rights movement's victories against racial exclusion, this volume and the Critical Race Theory movement generally could not have been taught at mainstream law schools. The law's incorporation of what several authors here call "formal equality" (the prohibition against explicit racial exclusion, like "whites only" signs) marks a decidedly progressive moment in U.S. political and social history. However, the fact that civil rights advocates met with some success in the nation's courts and legislatures ought not obscure the central role the American legal order played in the deradicalization of racial liberation movements. Along with the suppression of explicit white racism (the widely celebrated aim of civil rights reform), the dominant legal conception of racism as a discrete and identifiable act of "prejudice based on skin color" placed virtually the entire range of everyday social practices in America—social practices developed and maintained throughout the period of formal American apartheid—beyond the scope of critical examination or legal remediation.

The affirmative action debate . . . provides a vivid example of what we mean. From its inception, mainstream legal thinking in the U.S. has been characterized by a curiously constricted understanding of race and power. Within this cramped conception of racial domination, the evil of racism exists when—and only when—one can point to specific, discrete acts of racial discrimination, which is in turn narrowly defined as decision-making based on the irrational and irrelevant attribute of race. Given this essentially negative, indeed, dismissive view of racial identity and its social meanings, it was not surprising that mainstream legal thought came to embrace the ideal of "color-blindness" as the dominant moral compass of social enlightenment about race. Mainstream legal argument regarding "race relations" typically defended its position by appropriating Dr. King's injunction that a person should be judged "by the content of his character rather than the color of his skin" and wedding it to the regnant ideologies of equal opportunity and American meritocracy. Faced with this state of affairs, liberal proponents of affirmative action in legal and policy arenas—who had just successfully won the formal adoption of basic antidiscrimination norms—soon found themselves in a completely defensive ideological posture. Affirmative action requires the use of race as a socially significant category of perception and representation, but the deepest elements of mainstream civil rights ideology had come to identify such race-consciousness as racism itself. Indeed, the problem here was not simply political and strategic: the predominant legal representation of racism as the mere recognition of race matched the "personal" views of many liberals themselves, creating for them a contradiction in their hearts as well as their words.

Liberal antidiscrimination proponents proposed various ways to reconcile this contradiction: they characterized affirmative action as a merely "exceptional" remedy for past injustice, a temporary tool to be used only until equal opportunity is achieved or a default mechanism for reaching discrimination that could not be proved directly. Separate but related liberal defenses of affirmative action hold that its beneficiaries have suffered from "deprived" backgrounds that require limited special consideration in the otherwise fully rational and unbiased competition for social goods, or that affirmative action promotes social "diversity," a value which in the liberal vision is independent of, perhaps even at odds with, equality of opportunity or meritocracy.

The poverty of the liberal imagination is belied by the very fact that liberal theories of affirmative action are framed in such defensive terms, and so clearly shaped by the felt need to justify this perceived departure from purportedly objective findings of "merit" (or the lack thereof). These apologetic strategies testify to the deeper ways civil rights reformism has helped to legitimize the very social practices—in employment offices and admissions departments—that were originally targeted for reform. By constructing "discrimination" as a deviation from otherwise legitimate selection processes, liberal race rhetoric affirms the underlying ideology of just deserts, even as it reluctantly tolerates limited exceptions to meritocratic mythology. Despite their disagreements about affirmative action, liberals and conservatives who embrace dominant civil rights discourse treat the category of merit itself as neutral and impersonal, outside of social power and unconnected to systems of racial privilege. Rather than engaging in a broad-scale inquiry into why jobs, wealth, education, and power are distributed as they are, mainstream civil rights discourse suggests that once the irrational biases of race-consciousness are eradicated, everyone will be treated fairly, as equal competitors in a regime of equal opportunity.

What we find most amazing about this ideological structure in retrospect is how very little actual social change was imagined to be required by "the civil rights revolution." One might have expected a huge controversy over the dramatic social transformation necessary to eradicate the regime of American apartheid. By and large, however, the very same whites who administered explicit policies of segregation and racial domination kept their jobs as decision makers in employment offices of companies, admissions offices of schools, lending offices of banks, and so on. In institution after institution, progressive reformers found themselves struggling over the implementation of integrationist policy with the former administrators of segregation who soon regrouped as an old guard "concerned" over the deterioration of "standards."

The continuity of institutional authority between the segregationist and civil rights regimes is only part of the story. Even more dramatic, the same criteria for defining "qualifications" and "merit" used during the period of explicit racial exclusion continued to be used, so long as they were not directly "racial." Racism was identified only with the outright formal exclusion of people of color; it was simply assumed that the whole rest of the culture, and the de facto segregation of schools, work places, and neighborhoods, would remain the same. The sheer taken-for-grantedness of this way of thinking would pose a formidable and practically insurmountable obstacle. Having rejected race-consciousness in toto, there was no conceptual basis from which to identify the cultural and ethnic character of mainstream American institutions; they were thus deemed to be racially and culturally neutral. As a consequence, the deeply transformative potential of the civil rights movement's interrogation of racial power was successfully aborted as a piece of mainstream American ideology.

Within the predominantly white law school culture where most of the authors represented in this volume spend professional time, the law's "embrace" of civil rights in the Warren Court era is proclaimed as the very hallmark of justice under the rule of law. In our view, the "legislation" of civil rights movement and its "integration" into the mainstream commonsense assumptions in the late sixties and early seventies were premised on a tragically narrow and conservative picture of the goals of racial justice and the domains of racial power. In the balance of this introduction, we describe as matters both of institutional politics and intellectual inquiry how we have come to these kinds of conclusions.

In his essay on the Angelo Herndon case, Kendall Thomas describes and pursues a central project of Critical Race scholarship: the use of critical historical method to show that the contemporary structure of civil rights rhetoric is not the natural or inevitable meaning of racial justice but, instead, a collection of strategies and discourses born of and deployed in particular political, cultural, and institutional conflicts and negotiations. Our goal here is similar. We hope to situate the strategies and discourses of Critical Race

Theory within the broader intellectual and social currents from which we write, as well as within the specific work place and institutional positions where we are located and from which we struggle.

The emergence of Critical Race Theory in the eighties, we believe, marks an important point in the history of racial politics in the legal academy and, we hope, in the broader conversation about race and racism in the nation as a whole. As we experienced it, mostly as law students or beginning law professors, the boundaries of "acceptable" race discourse had become suddenly narrowed, in the years from the late sixties to the late seventies and early eighties, both in legal institutions and in American culture more generally. In the law schools we attended, there were definite liberal and conservative camps of scholars and students. While the debate in which these camps engaged was clearly important—for example, how the law should define and identify illegal racial power—the reigning discourse seemed, at least to us, ideologically impoverished and technocratic.

In constitutional law, for example, it was well settled that government-sanctioned racial discrimination was prohibited, and that legally enforced segregation constituted such discrimination. That victory was secured in *Brown v. Board of Education* and its progeny. In the language of the Fourteenth Amendment, race is a "suspect classification" which demands judicial strict scrutiny. "Race relations" thus represent an exception to the general deference that mainstream constitutional theory accords democratically elected institutions. Racial classifications violate the equal protection clause unless they both serve a compelling governmental interest and further, are no broader than necessary to achieve that goal. Within the conceptual boundaries of these legal doctrines, mainstream scholars debated whether discrimination should be defined only as intentional government action . . . or whether the tort-like "de facto" test should be used when government actions had predictable, racially skewed results . . . or whether the racial categories implicit in affirmative action policy should be legally equivalent to those used to burden people of color and therefore also be subject to strict scrutiny . . . and then whether remedying past social discrimination was a sufficiently compelling and determinate goal to survive strict scrutiny . . . and so on.

In all these debates we identified, of course, with the liberals against the intent requirement established in *Washington v. Davis*, the affirmative action limitations of *Bakke* (and later *Croson*), the curtailment of the "state action" doctrine resulting in the limitation of sites where constitutional antidiscrimination norms would apply, and so on. Yet the whole discourse seemed to assume away the fundamental problem of racial subordination whose examination was at the center of the work so many of us had spent our college years pursuing in Afro-American studies departments, community mobilizations, student activism, and the like.

The fact that affirmative action was seen as such a "dilemma" or a "necessary evil" was one symptom of the ultimately conservative character of even "liberal" mainstream race discourse. More generally, though, liberals and conservatives seemed to see the issues of race and law from within the same structure of analysis—namely, a policy that legal rationality could identify and eradicate the biases of race-consciousness in social decision-making. Liberals and conservatives as a general matter differed over the degree to which racial bias was a fact of American life: liberals argued that bias was widespread where conservatives insisted it was not; liberals supported a disparate effects test for identifying discrimination, where conservatives advocated a more restricted intent requirement; liberals wanted an expanded state action requirement, whereas conservatives wanted a narrow one. The respective visions of the two factions differed only in scope: they defined and constructed "racism" the same way, as the opposite of color-blindness.

In any event, however compelling the liberal vision of achieving racial justice through legal reform overseen by a sympathetic judiciary may have been in the sixties and early seventies, the breakdown of the national consensus for the use of law as an instrument for racial redistribution rendered the vision far less capable of appearing even merely pragmatic. By the late seventies, traditional civil rights lawyers found themselves fighting, and losing, rearguard attacks on the limited victories they had only just achieved in the prior decade, particularly with respect to affirmative action and legal requirements for the kinds of evidence required to prove illicit discrimination. An increasingly conservative judiciary made it clear that the age of ever expanding progressive law reform was over.

At the same time that these events were unfolding, a predominantly white left emerged on the law school scene in the late seventies, a development which played a central role in the genesis of Critical Race Theory. Organized by a collection of neo-Marxist intellectuals, former New Left activists, ex-counter-culturalists, and other varieties of oppositionists in law schools, the Conference on Critical Legal Studies established itself as a network of openly leftist law teachers, students, and practitioners committed to exposing and challenging the ways American law served to legitimize an oppressive social order. Like the later experience of Critical Race writers vis-à-vis race scholarship, "crits" found themselves frustrated with the presuppositions of the conventional scholarly legal discourse: they opposed not only conservative legal work but also the dominant liberal varieties. Crits contended that liberal and conservative legal scholarship operated in the narrow ideological channel within which law was understood as qualitatively different from politics. The faith of liberal lawyers in the gradual reform of American law though the victory of the superior rationality of progressive ideas depended on a belief in the central ideological myth of the law/politics distinction, namely, that legal institutions employ a rational, apolitical, and neutral discourse with which to mediate the exercise of social power. This, in essence, is the role of law as understood by liberal political theory. Yet politics was embedded in the very doctrinal categories with which law organized and represented social reality. Thus the deeply political character of law was obscured in one way by the obsession of mainstream legal scholarship with technical discussions about standing, jurisdiction and procedure; and the political character of judicial decision-making was—or could be—determined by preexisting legal rules, standards, and policies, all of which were applied according to professional craft standards encapsulated in the idea of "reasoned elaboration." Law was, in the conventional wisdom, distinguished from politics because politics was open-ended, subjective, discretionary, and ideological, whereas law was determinate, objective, bounded, and neutral.

This conception of law as rational, apolitical, and technical operated as an institutional regulative principle, defining what was legitimate and illegitimate to pursue in legal scholarship, and symbolically defining the professional, businesslike culture of day-to-day life in mainstream law schools. This generally characterized the entire post-war period in legal education, with virtually no organized dissent. Its intellectual and ideological premises had not been seriously challenged since the Legal Realist movement of the twenties and thirties—a body of scholarship that mainstream scholars ritually honored for the critique of the "formalism" of turn-of-the-century legal discourse but marginalized as having "gone too far" in its critique of the very possibility of a rule of law. Writing during the so-called liberty of contract period (characterized by the Supreme Court's invalidation of labor reform legislation on the grounds that it violated the "liberty" of workers and owners to contract with each other over terms of employment) the legal realists set out to show that the purportedly neutral and objective legal interpretation of the period was really based on politics, on what Oliver Wendell Holmes called the "hidden and often inarticulate judgments of social policy."

The crits unearthed much of the Legal Realist work that mainstream legal scholars had ignored for decades, and they found the intellectual and theoretical basis for launching a full-scale critique of the role of law in helping to rationalize an unjust social order. While the Realist critique of American law's pretensions to neutrality and rationality was geared toward the right-wing libertarianism of an "Old Order" of jurists, crits redirected it at the depoliticized and technocratic assumptions of legal education and scholarship in the seventies. Moreover, in the sixties tradition from which many of them had come, they extended the intellectual and ideological conflict they engendered to the law school culture to which it was linked.

By the late seventies, Critical Legal Studies existed in a swirl of formative energy, cultural insurgency, and organizing momentum: It had established itself as a politically, philosophically, and methodologically eclectic but intellectually sophisticated and ideologically left movement in legal academia, and its conferences had begun to attract hundreds of progressive law teachers, students, and lawyers; even mainstream law reviews were featuring critical work that reinterpreted whole doctrinal areas of law from an explicitly ideological motivation. Moreover, in viewing law schools as work-places, and thus as organizing sites for political resistance, "CLSers" actively recruited students and left-leaning law teachers from around the country to engage in the construction of left legal scholarship and law school transformation. CLS quickly became the organizing hub for a huge burst of left legal scholarly production and for various oppositional political challenges in law school institutional life. Several left scholars of color identified with the movement, and most important for the eventual genesis of Critical Race Theory a few years later, CLS succeeded in at least one aspect of its frontal assault on the depoliticized character of legal education. By the late seventies, explicitly right-wing legal scholarship had developed its own critique of the conventional assumptions, just as the national mood turned to the right with the election of Ronald Reagan. The law school as an institution was, by then, an obvious site for ideological contestation as the apolitical pretensions of the "nonideological" center began to disintegrate.

Critical Race Theory emerged in the interstices of this political and institutional dynamic. Critical Race Theory thus represents an attempt to inhabit and expand the space between two very different intellectual and ideological formations. Critical Race Theory sought to stage a simultaneous encounter with the exhausted vision of reformist civil rights scholarship, on the one hand, and the emergent critique of left legal scholarship on the other. Critical Race Theory's engagement with the discourse of civil rights reform stemmed directly from our lived experience as students and teachers in the nation's law schools. We both saw and suffered the concrete consequences that followed from liberal legal thinkers' failure to address the constrictive role that racial ideology plays in the composition and culture of American institutions, including the American law school. Our engagement with progressive left legal academics stemmed from our sense that their focus on legal ideology, legal scholarship and politics of the American law school provided a language and a practice for viewing the institutions in which we studied and worked both as sites and targets for our developing critique of law, racism, and social power.

In identifying the liberal civil rights tradition and the Critical Legal Studies movement as key factors in the emergence of Critical Race Theory, we do not mean to offer an oversimplified genealogy in which Critical Race Theory appears as a simple hybrid of the two. We view liberal civil rights scholarship and the work of the critical legal theorists not so much as rudimentary components of Critical Race Theory, but as elements in the conditions of its possibility. In short, we intend to evoke a particular atmosphere in which progressive scholars of color struggled to piece together an intellectual identity and a political practice that would take the form both of a left intervention into race discourse and a race intervention into left discourse. . . .

15

PATRICIA SMITH

Feminist Legal Critics: The Reluctant Radicals

Feminist legal criticism began not as a radical critique, but as a liberal argument for the universal application of traditional legal categories.[1] The early campaigns for universal suffrage are the first obvious examples. The arguments for women's suffrage were radical only in the limited sense that they tended to restrict traditional patriarchal power and to equalize the political power of women in a very limited way. Women's suffrage was in that sense socially radical, but this fact was hardly recognized at the time. That is, giving women the vote was not widely expected to change the social, legal, or political situation of women in any radical way at all.

And conceptually, the arguments for women's suffrage were not radical in any sense; they were liberal. It was not necessary for them to be radical. This was because of an interesting contradiction between universal liberal rhetoric and patriarchal social structures that depended for its resolution on ultimately unsustainable factual assumptions about the differences between the basic nature of men and women. These assumptions were explicitly built into law in the form of overt prohibitions against the participation of women in various aspects of public life.

In the case of voting, for example, the prohibition against women voting was most generally based on the view that women were incapable of understanding political issues. Incompetence (along with danger, including moral danger) has been the most common argument throughout all of history against women doing almost everything. The incompetence argument has struck contemporary feminists as ironic in the face of apparently powerful counterexamples, such as Cleopatra and Queen Elizabeth, to name only two powerful female leaders who seemed to understand not only political issues but political strategy quite as well as any man. But human beings have never allowed powerful but inconvenient counterexamples to stand in the way of powerful and convenient theories, and we still do not. We call them exceptions, and early political thinkers called them exceptions too. Queens didn't count. But eventually, as women gradually became more generally educated, the exceptions overpowered the rule of incompetence as to voting, and the prohibition was overcome. This development was based on a liberal rather than a radical view. The liberal view is that all human beings are presumptively entitled to equal treatment, or equality before the law. Eighteenth-century political rhetoric speaks this way about human rights, often referred to as the "rights of man." Now, the fact is that a significant portion of the human population was excluded from these "human" rights. Apparently you had to prove you were human. Native Americans, Chinese immigrants, and African-American slaves had no more rights than women; and the justification was that these groups of individuals were different (What they were different from was left unspecified, but the assumption was that they were different from the norm, which was taken as given, and which in this country had the characteristics of white, male, heterosexual Christians of European heritage.) The presumption of equality was overridden when it came to the rights of others or did not apply to them because of "intrinsic" differences of race and sex.

Thus, the great liberal debate of the nineteenth and twentieth centuries has been over who gets included in the ranks of personhood, citizenship, and humanity. Over time the circle was expanded to include more and more groups that had previously been considered unfit for rights: non-property owners, working men, different nationalities, different races, and finally even women. In all of these cases the decision to include these groups was based on the conclusion that differences that were previously thought significant were not significant after all. For purposes of law it was decided that differences between the excluded groups and the included group were largely irrelevant. What never changed was the norm—the standard of evaluation or the standard of comparison. That standard was based on the status quo founded in the assumptions of those in power. The standard was never questioned because it was assumed to be necessary, neutral and universal—simply a description of the world. Thus, the great liberal debate was over which classes of people are factually or materially (as opposed to morally) equal (that is, psychologically, dispositionally, and intellectually equal to the norm), then and only then were you entitled to formal equality or equality before the law.

That was the forum entered by liberal feminists, and it is in fact the forum of greatest advance in the cause of women's rights. One thing that shows is that much of the liberal ideal is correct—most differences between groups of people should be considered irrelevant to law. But in recent decades women have discovered that the liberal program has certain serious limitations, and that discovery has led many feminists to a more radical evaluation of law and to the greatest intellectual contribution that feminists have made to legal analysis, namely the critique of traditional discriminatory norms. Nowadays, feminists are asking why, as a matter of justice, those in power are entitled to formulate standards that favor themselves by which to measure all others. As a matter of power this is easily understood. As a matter of justice it is quite puzzling. The answer to the puzzle is that the norms formulated by those in power are not characterized as favoring themselves, but as neutral descriptions of necessary features of the world. So the current challenge for feminist scholars is to show how norms traditionally considered neutral are actually biased. The feminist critique of equal protection law provides the clearest illustration of both the liberal approach and its limits, while some recent work of feminist legal critics in this area and others demonstrates the new and radicalized challenge feminism now presents to previously unexamined discriminatory legal norms. In the next two sections I consider each of these to illustrate the development of feminist legal analysis as a certain form of radical legal critique.

THE EVOLUTION OF SEX DISCRIMINATION IN EQUAL PROTECTION LAW

The 1950s and 1960s marked the first serious consideration among the American people of the possibility that a legal system overall might be biased against an entire class of people, and in particular an entire race of people. (Of course, the Marxists had been making the class argument for years, but it had very little impact in the United States.) With the struggle for civil rights for American blacks came the realization that law itself was at least sometimes used systematically to disadvantage an entire group with no apparent justification, because by the 1960s it had become embarrassing to argue that blacks are not human beings, or not human "in the relevant sense."

It is interesting that it took more than a decade for any serious analogies to be drawn between the legal treatment of blacks and the legal treatment of women, but at least by the 1970s effective arguments were being made that sexism was in some sense analogous to racism. In 1971 the Supreme Court struck down for the first time a sex-based classification as a violation of the equal protection clause of the Fourteenth Amendment.[2] The arguments made in this case and others of the time were analogous to the liberal arguments being made against race discrimination. For example, in 1973 ACLU counsel Ruth Bader Ginsberg argued in *Frontiero v. Richardson* that sex-based classifications, like racially based classifications, should be recognized as constitutionally suspect on three grounds. First, historically women have been subjugated and restricted as a class. Second, women ought to be judged on their individual merits rather than on the basis of stereotypes that are often inaccurate, and even if accurate in general may be inaccurate as applied to a particular individual. (In other words, if an individual woman meets the standard norm she ought not to be eliminated by a blanket prohibition against women as a class.) Third, sex is an immutable characteristic that often bears no relation to the ability to perform or contribute.[3]

Thus, the typical argument for the advancement of women's rights in the early 1970s was the liberal argument that challenged the dominant power to make good on its universal claims for impartiality and justice by opposing historical oppression, recognizing the value of individuality, and avoiding the individual unfairness of frequently inaccurate stereotypes. This argument worked well initially, at least in blatant cases of overt discrimination, and well it should since it employs the dominant ideology of the classical liberal tradition, which is central to western legal thought. However, it did not take long for problems to crop up.

Since the basis of sex discrimination claims was the traditional idea of similarly situated persons being differentially treated on irrelevant grounds, the Court saw no basis for deciding cases in which persons were not similarly situated. Thus, when *Roe v. Wade* was decided shortly after *Frontiero,* the woman's right to choose abortion was based on the right to privacy, with no mention of a foundation in equal protection law based on sex.[4] Similarly, when mandatory unpaid maternity leaves for schoolteachers were challenged in *Cleveland Board of Education v. LaFleur,* the Court avoided the sex discrimination claim by striking down the policy on other grounds.[5] Having thus hemmed itself into an analysis of sex discrimination based only on the differential treatment of similarly situated persons, when the Court was faced squarely and unavoidably with the sex discrimination claims of pregnant women in *Geduldig v. Aiello* in 1974, it reached the stunning conclusion that discrimination based on pregnancy does not involve a sex-based classification.[6] *Geduldig* does not represent one of the Court's shining hours. It generated an enormous wave of critical commentary. The extension of the reasoning in *Geduldig* to a Title VII case prompted a swift amendment (the Pregnancy Disability Act) by Congress, repudiating the Court's reasoning. And the Court itself in more recent decisions has backed away from this holding, though it has not changed its general rationale for sex discrimination under the equal protection clause.[7]

The problems caused by the general rationale that bases a discrimination claim solely on the differential treatment of similarly situated persons show that it cannot deal with questions of fair treatment where differences are real. There is something so obviously wrong with the idea that where differences are real equal protection of the law cannot apply, that a raft of critical commentary has been generated which has led to a more radical feminist critique of law. What feminists have realized is that equal protection law itself, while claiming to be neutral, in fact assumes a male standard of what is normal. For example, the average working woman will be pregnant twice during her working career. Pregnancy is abnormal only for a working man. Thus, the standard of normality that discounts pregnancy for working persons is male. The question, of course, is why should that be the standard?

Christine Littleton has summarized the feminist critique of current equality analysis in the following three points that demonstrate its male bias. First, it defines as beyond its scope precisely those issues that women find crucial to their concrete experience as women (such as pregnancy). Second, it construes difference (which is created by the relationship of women to particular, contingent social structures, such as home and work responsibilities) as natural (that is, unchangeable and inherent) and as located solely in the woman herself (women are naturally domestic). Third, it assumes (without evidence) the gender neutrality of social institutions, as well as the notion that practices must distinguish themselves from "business as usual" in order to be seen as unequal.[8]

More briefly put, equality analysis is biased against women in three respects: (1) it is inapplicable once it encounters a "real" difference from men; (2) it locates the difference in women, rather than in relationships; and (3) it fails to question the assumption that social institutions are gender neutral, and that women and men are therefore similarly related to those institutions.

This analysis made many feminists acutely aware of the arbitrariness of norms and of the fact that the inability of the courts to deal with sex discrimination in many cases is directly related to the inability to evaluate biased norms. And some feminists reasoned that if the liberal presumption of neutral legal processes retards the ability to evaluate norms as biased, then the liberal approach is sharply limited in its ability to correct systematic injustice, such as that which grows out of systematic patriarchal norms.

THE DEVELOPMENT OF FEMINIST LEGAL CRITIQUE AS RADICAL REFORM

Feminists have recognized that a significant part of law is the legitimation of the dominant ideology and that a significant part of the dominant ideology of most societies is patriarchal. This is the focus of some recent feminist legal critique. It is the embodiment of the observation that norms are often systematically biased in ways that reinforce the subordination of women to men by assuming a male standard of what is normal, or a male perspective of what is real, and then entrenching these assumptions by characterizing them as neutral. A number of feminists have developed this position in a variety of ways.

Perhaps the best known are the views of Catherine MacKinnon. In a recent book, MacKinnon sets out a radical feminist thesis of law and jurisprudence.[9] She is concerned with the transformation of belief into reality. Law, she points out, is a crucial factor in that transformation. Virtually all societies, she notes, are organized in social hierarchies that subordinate women to men on the basis of sex, as well as subordinating certain people to others on the basis of race and class. These facts of social organization which institutionalize social power are embodied in the organization of states as law. That is, through law, social domination is made both legitimate and invisible. It becomes reality—just the way things are. Liberal legalism or positivist jurisprudence buries the embodiment of patriarchal dominance even further by insisting that the proper domain of jurisprudence is descriptive, not evaluative or normative. As she puts it:

> Liberal legalism [i.e., legal positivism] is thus a medium for making male dominance both invisible and legitimate by adopting the male point of view in law at the same time as it enforces that view on society. . . . Through legal mediation, male dominance is made to seem a feature of life, not a one-sided construct imposed by force for the advantage of a dominant group. To the degree it succeeds ontologically, male dominance does not look epistemological: control over being produces control over consciousness. . . . Dominance reified becomes difference. Coercion legitimated becomes consent. . . . In the liberal state, the rule of law—neutral, abstract, elevated, pervasive—both institutionalizes the power of men over women and institutionalizes power in its male form.[10]

There are many variations on this theme. Quite a number of feminists have suggested that legal standards often uncritically reinforce social disadvantages imposed on women. For example, Deborah Rhode[11] and Christine Littleton[12] have both suggested moderate versions of the radical thesis that recognize the need to address structural problems of patriarchy that entrench inequality, but argue for addressing them in terms of disadvantage rather than domination. Both are examples of feminist theories that call for accepting diversity in all its forms, using law to ensure that diversity is not penalized. Both require the equal acceptance of cultural differences and concentrate on eliminating the unequal consequences of sex differences, whatever their origin or nature. One of the attractive features of this approach is that it makes no particular assumptions about the intrinsic psychological nature of men or women. It does not presume that we can know what the intrinsic differences or similarities might be, or what the sexes would be like if social conditioning were different. It holds only that no cultural position should be penalized—it should not be a disadvantage to be one sex or race or nationality rather than another. The idea, as Littleton puts it, is to embrace diversity and make difference costless.

In another interesting proposal from a rather different direction, Nadine Taub and Wendy Williams[13] have suggested one way in which the courts could formulate in legal doctrine the ideal that difference should not be penalized. Taub and Williams advocate the expansion of what the Court has called the *Griggs* doctrine of discriminatory impact.[14] Very generally speaking, the *Griggs* doctrine says that if a norm or practice has a disproportionate impact on a suspect class (such as a race or sex) then that norm or practice is subject to reevaluation. Unfortunately, the Court has chosen to restrict rather than expand the *Griggs* doctrine, but suggestions like that of Taub and Williams show that equal protection could be made an effective device for the protection of disadvantaged classes if the dominant class saw fit to develop it in that direction.

Whether these critiques are formulated in terms of disproportionate impact, the domination of women or their disadvantage, all represent a shift from liberal claims for inclusion in traditional norms to a radical critique of those norms as fundamentally biased. Martha Minow[15] has generalized this position to a critique of the inability of courts (and particularly the Supreme Court's inability) to deal with the problem of differences in a pluralistic society. Unexamined assumptions create what Minow calls dilemmas of difference for the courts. Minow points out that the Supreme Court is often faced with the apparent dilemma of reinforcing disadvantage no matter which choice it makes. If it recognizes a disadvantage so as to correct it, it may reinforce stereotypes that perpetuate it. On the other hand, if the Court ignores the difference so as to counter the stereotypes associated with it, then there is no way to address the disadvantage attached to the difference.[16] This is a serious problem for all classes that are systematically disadvantaged, since the "neutral" (that is, disinterested and detached) application of biased standards simply reproduces systematic disadvantage, thus calling into question the very meaning of neutrality. Minow suggests that courts could defuse these dilemmas by recognizing the unexamined assumptions that generate them.

First, she points out, we commonly assume that differences are intrinsic rather than relational or comparative. Women are considered intrinsically different rather than different as compared to men. Jews are intrinsically different rather than different as compared to Christians, and so forth. As Minow points out, men are as different from women as women are from men; Christians are as different from Jews as Jews are from Christians. The question is why the norm should be male and Christian? Second, we typically adopt an unstated norm as a point of reference in evaluating others. This norm is not neutral or inevitable, but it seems so when left unstated and unexamined. It is taken as given rather than recognized as chosen. It is assumed universal rather than recognized as particular. Third, we treat the perspective of the person doing the judging as objective, even though in fact no one can see fully from someone else's point of view or without a point of view. Fourth, we assume that the perspective of those being judged is either irrelevant or already covered by the supposedly objective and universal perspective of the judge. Fifth, it is assumed that the status quo—the existing social and economic arrangement—is natural, neutral, inevitable, uncoerced, and good. So departures from the status quo risk non-neutrality and interference with individual freedom. Minow believes that making these assumptions explicit will require judges to examine the foundations of their own perspectives, which are often not recognized as perspectives at all. Once recognized as perspectives, the views must be defended as compared to other perspectives rather than being erroneously assumed as universal.[17]

The above examples illustrate that many feminists today recognize that a significant part of law is the legitimation of the status quo (which is to say, the dominant power or ideology) and that a significant part of the dominant ideology of our society (and most others) is patriarchal. Thus, standard traditional norms must be examined and defended in terms of the interests of all people rather than assumed as inevitable and neutral.

However, a fact that many feminists do not mention but most presume is that patriarchy is not the only or the entire dominant ideology of this society. Our society is also individualist, committed to justice and freedom, committed to the ideals of impartiality, the rule of law and equality before the law. These are not patriarchal ideals as such.[18] They are universal, humanistic ideals. In fact, they are not particularly compatible with patriarchy; and this contradiction between what is often called liberal ideology (but what might be called humanist ideology) and patriarchy can still be exploited in the cause of justice for women. That is, the contradiction between patriarchy and humanistic liberal ideals that are both embodied in Anglo-American law enables even radical feminists to advocate reform rather than revolution. Thus, even radical feminists are radical only in the sense of advocating far-reaching reforms. They need not advocate the overthrow of government, or even the amendment of the Constitution. On the other hand, a commitment to the elimination of patriarchy is a commitment to revolutionize fundamental social and legal institutions.

The view of Taub and Williams illustrates this clearly. On the one hand, the proposal they make is very moderate—a simple and reasonable extension of a doctrine already formulated by the Court and regularly used in one form in Title VII cases. In another respect the proposal is a radical one because the effect of it would be to counteract the disadvantages imposed on certain classes of people by social organization itself. Yet, the rationale is perfectly compatible with humanistic liberal ideals verbally expressed in the Anglo-American legal tradition for two hundred years.

Similarly, Minow's suggestions would have a radical impact on the process of judging itself, yet on the other hand, all she is really arguing is that those in power should be accountable to the point of examining their own assumptions. This is so reasonable a requirement that one wonders how anyone committed to rational thinking could argue against it. Certainly, liberals would not.

Even MacKinnon, one of the most radical of feminists, utilizes the distinction between humanistic liberal rhetoric and patriarchal practices. In her recent analysis of equality, MacKinnon argues that the law of equality provides a peculiar opportunity for challenging the inequality of law on behalf of women, since law does not usually guarantee rights to something that does not exist. Equality in law is understood formally, and so it is presumed that by and large women already have it. Many, if not most, formal legal barriers for women have been dismantled. Women can now own property, execute contracts, attend universities, and engage in businesses and professions without formal prohibition. But, as many feminists have observed, this formal equality does not eliminate informal discrimination, nor does it provide equal opportunity in fact. MacKinnon argues that it is up to feminists to make equality law meaningful for women by defining it in terms of the concrete experience of women's lives, and challenging the male forms of power that are affirmatively embodied as rights in law. MacKinnon recognizes that equality is not about character traits or even human nature. It is not about "sameness and difference," as it is so often construed, but about domination and subordination. Equality and inequality are about the distribution of power. To confront that distribution of power directly, recognizing it for what it is, and to remove the mask of legitimacy raised by its legalization is the critical task of feminist jurisprudence, according to MacKinnon.[19]

These positions recognize implicitly or explicitly that there are serious contradictions between the universal values that we profess and the patriarchal institutions that structure our lives. This is a consistent factor in feminist legal analysis that connects recent work with early liberal feminist views. But early liberal feminist criticism was effective only while it was directed at explicitly patriarchal legal doctrines. These patriarchal legal doctrines made the contradiction explicit and clear.[20]

However, feminists today recognize that the form of the contradiction has changed. It is no longer an explicit contradiction between two clearly articulated legal rules. At least much of the time the contradiction is now between two (or more) rather vaguely understood legal norms that are the embodiment of traditional social standards. Thus, traditional standards cannot simply be taken as given. Rebutting false claims of factual difference between men and women is not enough. The contradictions between universal values and patriarchal practices cannot be effectively utilized for freedom and justice for women until the bias of certain norms is recognized.

These problems are far from over, and a major aggravating factor in their solution is the common claim that they have already been solved.[21] I believe that the remaining problems can be usefully characterized in the form of two remaining hurdles.

The first hurdle is simply a development of the original liberal battle: how to keep the discrimination that used to come in overtly through the front door from sneaking covertly through the back door. Old stereotypes die hard, and despite our best efforts to combat unfounded and untestable assumptions about differences between men and women, these assumptions seem able to reinstitute themselves like chameleons in new forms.

The second hurdle is how to get those who occupy positions of power to see that the norms they use are, after all, just the norms they choose, and that many traditional norms in fact benefit men at the expense of women and/or reinforce traditional social arrangements that restrict the freedom of women. Negotiating this hurdle requires a more radical approach to challenging basic norms. Such an approach is not incompatible with classical liberal ideals of justice and equality, but does set up serious tensions with traditional presumptions of neutral legal processes.

The case of *EEOC v. Sears*[22] provides a good example of the issues involved in the first hurdle. This case involved a Title VII class action lawsuit charging Sears Roebuck and Co. with employment discrimination against women in hiring and promotion. The charge was based on statistical evidence that women were greatly underrepresented in higher-paying commission sales positions although the pool of applicants was more or less equal, and lower-paying jobs were predominantly filled by women. This approach relied on a typical focus of Title VII class action suits which utilizes statistics that indicate a disproportionate impact from facially neutral practices as presumptive evidence of discrimination. In other words, if a disproportionate impact is shown, Title VII presumes that discrimination is the reason for it. This, then, shifts the burden of proof to the defendant to provide nondiscriminatory reasons for the differences shown by the statistics.

To meet this burden of proof, Sears argued successfully that women were not underrepresented in the high-paying commission sales jobs because of discrimination, but because women as a class really are not interested in such jobs.[23] Ironically, Sears used the language of certain feminist scholars to support its claim that women dislike competition and value good relationships more than money. According to this view, women tend to sacrifice monetary advancement for less stressful working conditions and more limited hours that enable them to meet their responsibilities at home. So disparities in high-paying jobs are not due to discrimination but to women's own choices. This argument was accepted by the court, even in the face of contradicting testimony from women who had actually applied to Sears for commission sales positions.[24]

Joan Williams[25] has done a good job of pointing out that this reasoning simply re-enshrines old stereotypes of women as passive, domestic, and self-sacrificing. These old stereotypes are powerful and entrenched. It is always easier to fall back into them than it is to get rid of them. What is particularly distressing about the *Sears* case is that it inserts sexist stereotypes into precisely the legislation that was enacted to counteract them. Even if the stereotypes are true as generalizations, Title VII was designed to protect those women who do not fit that generalization, specifically those women who applied for the commission sales positions at Sears. Sears simply discounted these women and so did the court. That is, Sears assumed that those women who applied for commission sales and supervisory positions did not really want those jobs. They were padding their applications to increase their chances of getting hired, it was claimed.[26] Since most women applied for low-level clerking positions, Sears reasoned, that must be what all women prefer. That outrageously invalid argument is the argument that the court accepted as the basis of its interpretation of Title VII. This will disadvantage all future claimants. Furthermore, if actual testimony cannot rebut the Sears argument that women are not interested in competitive work, how could any plaintiff overcome that argument on the part of any employer? One wonders how any woman can ever win a Title VII claim based on disproportionate impact again. Cases like *Sears* show how easy it is to go backward, even with regard to the old liberal argument that we are all human and are entitled to equal treatment based on our individual merits. We have far to go before men and women will be presumed equal, and discriminatory assumptions about the "intrinsic" differences in male and female disposition and intellect are overcome.

There are no easy examples of the issues connected with the second hurdle, because in the evaluation of traditional norms what seems normal is what everyone is used to, and that is the status quo. The challenge always carries the burden of persuasion, always seems at least initially less plausible than the norm, and that is true whether or not the norm is just.[27] Feminists have found that norms are most difficult to challenge where the differences (physical or social) between men and women are real, and where the interests of men and women are perceived to be at odds. In such cases it is the status quo itself that disadvantages women, and it cannot be corrected unless the norm is changed. This involves new evaluations at very fundamental levels.

Consider, for example, the formulation of harm or injury. What constitutes an injury is central to legal action. It has long been a truism that justice and law require interpersonal respect, at least to the extent that we may not intentionally harm, defraud, or interfere with the freedom of other individuals. We are not entitled to cause injury. Virtually all moral and legal theories agree that this is the core of interpersonal responsibility. One person's freedom ends with the freedom and bodily integrity of another. Any individual's rights are limited by the basic rights of all other persons. Thus, coercion, intimidation, fraudulent deception, and bodily injury are prohibited by justice and law without question. That is the settled core of our moral tradition, but it does not specify what counts as harm or injury, or what qualifies as coercion, intimidation, or deception at a level that can be prohibited.

Somehow injury does not apply the same way to women, at least with respect to men who are related to them or even who know them. If assault is prohibited, why are husbands so often not prosecuted for beating their wives? If exploitation is wrong, why are employers so often not prosecuted for pressuring their employees into sexual relations? If rape is illegal, why are men so often not prosecuted if they are acquainted with the women they coerce into sex? If bodily integrity is a fundamental right, how could decisions regarding pregnancy rest ultimately with anyone other than the women whose body is involved? All of these are areas that involve real differences between men and women, and they are areas in which the interests of men and women can now be interpreted as possibly conflicting.

As Minow has pointed out, contrary to assumptions of universality, all law is formulated from a perspective. So we can hardly be surprised if it turns out to be the perspective of those who formulated it, which is to say, the perspective of powerful men—the traditional patriarchs. It is difficult to assume the perspective of someone else. It takes a level of self-awareness that is truly rare. Nor is it more common for people in power to recognize the limits of their own views and the value of understanding and accommodating the views of others.

Until almost the twentieth century, women were not considered to have interests or views of their own. Women were not independent or free. In fact, they were not separate individuals legally. A woman could not have an interest that conflicted with the interests of her husband or father. Thus, she could not be harmed or injured by her husband or father (unless he killed her). The man to whom she was related was responsible for her and in charge of her.

So it is hardly surprising that wife beating was construed as discipline, which is not a harm. It is not surprising that rape, unlike any other crime, was defined from the perspective of the perpetrator rather than the victim. Nor is it surprising that until recently sexual harassment simply did not exist, and procreation (both in terms of contraception and abortion) was controlled by government rather than by women. Women did not have separate interests; their interests were defined by men, from the perspective of men, in terms of the interests of men, because that is who formulated the law. This was not a commitment of liberalism. It is not even compatible with liberalism. It was an assumption of patriarchy that was left unexamined because it was the norm (a) that women had no interests separate from their husbands or fathers, and (b) that the law should not intrude into family matters. The challenge for feminists is then how to change such norms and others like them, which have been taken as given—as normal—for hundreds or even thousands of years.

The very fact that such issues are now being addressed, that such topics are being publicly discussed, is the first sign of social progress. Yet we have far to go before women are recognized as entitled to bodily integrity that cannot be coercively usurped by men who know them and by legislators who presume to define their interests. The great divide between the protection of women from strangers and the nonprotection of women from men who know them reflects old and deeply embedded notions of male supremacy, domination, and the ownership of women. Until recently these views were supported by overt acceptance of male authority and supremacy. Today, many people say that these old presumptions of patriarchy no longer hold. Today we say that women are entitled to determine their own physical integrity by their own voluntary choices.

Yet these abstract ideals have serious concrete limits. Powerful forces have mobilized to oppose reproductive freedom for women on the assumption that women are not entitled to make such choices. The physical integrity of women does not include the right to control their reproductive capacities. Pregnancy is not a harm; it is a blessing. Thus, the norm is still that women are essentially mothers, first and foremost. The choice not to be a mother (i.e., to be in actual control of one's reproductive capacities), while formally acknowledged in law, is still highly controversial and is flatly rejected by many. The long-standing commitment to individual autonomy is a fundamental norm of our society that has never been and still is not applied equally to men and women. That is because (a) men and women are different, so deciding what an equal commitment to autonomy means is not a simple matter; (b) autonomy was never considered important for women in the past; and (c) those who decided legal, moral, and religious policy about motherhood and procreation were not the same people who were subject to the disadvantages of such policies. So the fight over who should be in control of women's bodies is still far from settled.

And old patterns of social interaction based on norms that subordinate women are perpetuated, largely by denial and by blaming the victim. If a woman is raped or beaten not by a stranger but in the course of normal life, then she must have brought it on herself. If she is harassed by her employer she must have led him on. And anyway, date rape has to be rare. Wife battering is surely uncommon. Sexual harassment must be largely imaginary. We do not want to hear about these problems.

Statistical surveys clearly indicate that women are harmed much more often by men who know them than by any other cause. For example, 4 million women are battered in their homes in the United States each year. Women are harassed, beaten, raped, and killed by men who know them far more often than by strangers. Yet these offenses, with the exception of killing, are still largely unprosecuted. Why? Because we the people excuse the abuse of women as a form of control or an outlet for frustration ("If you can't beat your wife who can you beat?"). This behavior is a hangover from an earlier and more overtly sexist day, and we don't want to know about it. So we pretend that it is a rarity committed by a few outlaws like ordinary crimes. But it is not.[28]

The pervasiveness of these abusive practices attests to the worst features of the continuing sexism of our society. Old norms die hard. Physical coercion and violence remain an option for male domination in personal relations as a last resort. The more women struggle for freedom and equality, the more some men will respond with violence. The more women compete, the more they will be harassed by those who feel threatened or offended by the changing status quo.

And the failure to prosecute attests to the continuing sexism of our law.[29] This will not change significantly until traditional norms are changed that condone it. Until police and prosecutors, judges and juries recognize such injuries as serious harms and stop making excuses for them, women will not be protected. But police and prosecutors, judges and juries by and large reflect the attitudes of the general public.

So long as overpowering your date is not the same as raping a stranger, and beating your wife is not as serious as assaulting someone on the street, and pressuring your secretary into sex is just the way life is, and pregnancy is characterized by Supreme Court justices as an inconvenience, the physical integrity of women will not be determined by their own voluntary choices. Thus, many women today are still dominated by physical force and restrictive legislation, denied the most basic protections of justice by a society and a legal system that pretends that some physical coercion is not real harm, and in any case that women can avoid it by "proper behavior," by understanding their limits. Such a view is not compatible with the liberal commitment to freedom and equal treatment, as liberal feminists have argued for many years. It can only be made compatible by assuming the normative commitments of patriarchy as a fact of life. And that is not actually hard to do (in fact it is actually harder not to do) since patriarchal assumptions have set the standard of normal social relations, religious ideals, moral expectations, and legal standards for thousands of years. Patriarchy is the norm—or more accurately, it is an enormously complex network of norms. It is challenging those norms and that network that constitutes the radical agenda of modern feminists. It is an agenda that does not conflict with liberal values; it does not require overthrow of the government, or even amending the Constitution, but it does require the eventual transformation of our most fundamental institutions, including extensive legal reform.

NOTES

1. "Radical" and "liberal" are terms of multiple definition and use. I consider a radical critique to be one that calls for revolutionary or fundamental change of some sort, but not necessarily military overthrow, or political upheaval, or even immediate social change. That is, on my view, a radical critique can call for incremental or evolutionary change, so long as the ultimate goal is monumental or profound. "Liberal" is harder to define because it standardly encompasses a broad swath of views ranging from communitarian to libertarian. But usually liberals are thought to fall somewhere between those two poles. I believe that all liberals are committed to freedom, justice, and the significance of individuals, although they may interpret these values in very different ways. Thus, on my view, it is possible for a radical critique to rest on liberal values. The two positions are not categorically antagonistic. However, whether a particular radical critique is compatible with a particular liberal view depends on the particulars of both. I will use the term "liberal" to stand for a commitment to freedom, justice in the form of equal treatment, and the significance of individuals.
2. *Reed v. Reed,* 404 U.S. 71 (1971).
3. 411 U.S. 677 (1973).
4. 410 U.S. 113 (1973).
5. 414 U.S. 632 (1974).
6. 417 U.S. 484 (1974).
7. See *Newport News Ship, and Dry Dock v. E.E.O.C.,* 103 S. Ct. 2622 (1983). The general rationale is that individuals cannot be treated differently on the basis of sex unless there is some clearly specifiable difference that justifies different treatment. Thus, so long as the sexes are similar they must be treated the same.
8. C. Littleton, "Reconstructing Equality," *Calif. L. Rev.* 75 (1987): 1279.
9. C. MacKinnon, *Toward a Feminist Theory of the State* (Cambridge: Harvard University Press, 1989).
10. Ibid., 237–38.
11. D. Rhode, *Justice and Gender* (Cambridge: Harvard University Press, 1989).
12. Littleton, "Reconstructing Equality."
13. N. Taub and W. Williams, "Will Equality Require More . . . ?" *Rutgers L. Rev./Civ. Rts. Dev.* 37 (1985): 825.
14. See *Griggs v. Duke Power,* 401 U.S. 424 (1971).
15. M. Minow, "Foreword: Justice Engendered," *Harvard L. Rev* 101 (1987): 10.
16. The common formulation of the early debate over women's rights illustrates the problem. It was asked whether women, being different, should argue for equal rights or for special rights. Equal rights (i.e., identical rights) seemed to disadvantage women sometimes (e.g., as to pregnancy benefits), and so some argued that special rights were needed to accommodate women's special needs and circumstances. Others argued that only equal (i.e., identical) rights should be claimed because any special needs or differences acknowledged by women are always used to limit women in the long run, and special rights will be viewed as special favors that accommodate women's deficiencies. The problem is that if that is the way the issue is formulated, then women lose either way because the (unstated) norm is male. After all, who is it that women are different from? Whose rights (if equality is the standard) should women's rights be equal to? And if women's rights should sometimes be different from men's, why is it women's rights that are characterized as special? Why not formulate rights in terms of women's needs and characterize men's rights as special? One way makes as much sense as the other. The question is, who is the norm?
17. Minow, "Justice Engendered."
18. Some feminists consider all these principles to be patriarchal, but most feminists either do not specify their position on this point or hold a more contextually based view rather like that expressed here.
19. MacKinnon, *Toward a Feminist Theory.*
20. In *Reed v. Reed,* for example, it was held that a woman could not be barred from being the executrix of an estate on the basis of her sex, since there was no demonstrable difference between men and women in regard to administering an estate. The (patriarchal) state law that excluded all women as a class from that activity was clearly contradicted by our supposedly universal commitment to freedom and equal treatment and by our constitutional commitment to equal protection of the law.
21. See, e.g., D. Rhode, "The 'No Problem' Problem: Feminist Challenges and Cultural Change," *Yale L. J.* 100 (1991): 1731.

22. 628 F. Supp. 1264 (N.D. Ill. 1986).
23. It is worth noting that in *Castro v. Beecher,* 334 F. Supp. 930, 936 (D. Mass. 1976), an almost identical argument, that the underrepresentation of blacks in law enforcement was simply due to their lack of interest, was rejected by the court as racist. And in *Glover v. Johnson,* 478 F. Supp. 1075, 1086–88 (E.D. Mich. 1979), the argument that women did not need vocational training since women preferred unskilled jobs anyway was also rejected as prejudice. Thus, in the past courts have rejected justifications of disparities based on supposed lack of interest.
24. The court also ignored expert testimony from a historian who argued that history shows that women accept more competitive jobs whenever they become available. See J. Williams, "Deconstructing Gender," *Mich. L. Rev.* 87 (1989): 797.
25. Ibid.
26. The Sears managers, the statistical analyst, and the guidebook for hiring all systematically discounted applications of women for traditionally male positions (such as commission sales). The statistical analyst explained on the witness stand exactly how she went about discounting all applications of women for "male" jobs. Yet the court accepted this approach as appropriately reflecting the (supposed) interests of women, despite conflicting testimony by women that they had in fact wanted commission sales positions. This demonstrates the power of stereotypes, once accepted. See ibid., 813–20.
27. For example, in *Plessy v. Ferguson,* 163 U.S. 537, the case that established the legitimacy of racial segregation under the equal protection clause, the Court said (among other things): "The object of the amendment was undoubtedly to enforce the absolute equality of the two races before the law, but, in the nature of things, it could not have been intended to abolish distinctions based upon color, or to enforce social, as distinguished from political, equality, or a commingling of the two races upon terms unsatisfactory to either." Segregation was the norm. A mere constitutional amendment requiring racial equality could not rebut the presumption of the legitimacy of the status quo, hence the Court's interpretation of "equal protection" allowed the norm to stand. It appears clearly unjust to us today, but at the time it seemed perfectly reasonable, which attests to the strength of the status quo. How many reasonable and defensible sexist judgments of the 1980s and 1990s will seem similarly outrageous fifty years from now? We haven't the distance to tell.
28. During the Vietnam War 59,000 soldiers were killed, causing a storm of public outrage. During the same period 54,000 women were killed by their male partners, without so much as a whisper of public protest. We can say we didn't know. (That's what the Germans said about the Jews.) But why didn't we know? It was public record. We didn't want to know. And we still don't. Women's voices are louder now, but we still mostly ignored the recent Senate report (Senate Report no. 197, 102nd Cong., 1st Sess. (1991)) noting that both rape and domestic violence have sharply increased in the past decade. Four million women are severely battered every year, the leading cause of injury for U.S. women (much greater than assault by strangers). From 2000 to 4000 women are now murdered by their male partners yearly. In 1990 more women were beaten by their male partners than were married. Nor can the increase of rape and battery be fully explained by better reporting, because the government systematically underestimates the numbers of such victims. See Senate Report no. 197.
29. Again using domestic violence as my example, women cannot escape this harm without legal intervention. Three-fourths of all reported domestic violence assaults occur after a woman has left her partner, and the majority of murdered battered women are killed after they leave. Between 1983 and 1987 battered women shelters reported over a 100 percent increase in women seeking refuge, and 1 million per year were turned away for lack of space. Yet funding in the past five years has been decreased. Half of all homeless women in the United States in the past decade were refugees of domestic violence. But legal response has been slow. Only fifteen states have laws that prosecute batterers and protect victims. See *gen.* K. Culliton, "Domestic Violence Legislation in Chile and the U.S." (unpublished manuscript).

PART 3

TORTS

Although difficult to define, broadly speaking a *tort* is a "civil wrong."[1] In part, some of the difficulty in defining torts concerns the fact that tort law is connected to many, if not all, other areas of the law. Many attempts have been made to define the domain of tort law. Some, such as Sir John Salmond, have argued that there is no law of tort, only unconnected torts that, when combined, form tort law as we know it. Others have argued that there are general principles at work that are broader than any single identified category of tort, even though formulating those general principles is difficult or seems impossible. Still others claim that a single principle, rather than many principles, operates in tort law: "Any harm done to another is wrong, and calls for redress, unless 'justification' for it can be shown."[2]

The function of tort law is easier to define. Tort law is designed to help compensate individuals for the losses they have incurred as a result of the activities of another. This definition is quite broad, but it is aided by what people commonly hold as the guiding principle of tort law, namely, that "liability must be based on conduct which is socially unreasonable."[3] The notion of unreasonableness is specified in this manner to avoid being too individualized, because, without general standards, *all* activity might be considered unreasonable. The "reasonable person" standard often implements this principle in tort law.

[1]W. Paige Keeton, ed., *Prosser and Keeton on Torts*, 5th ed. (St. Paul, MN: West,1984), 2.
[2]Ibid., 4.
[3]Ibid., 6.

Perhaps because of its vagueness, tort law has been an especially rich area for philosophers, as evidenced by the variety of philosophical views presented here. Issues such as causation, responsibility, retribution, and reasonableness, to name only a few, echo and re-echo through these selections. For example, in "Causation and Responsibility," H. L. A. Hart and A. M. Honoré focus on the role of causation in determining legal as compared with moral responsibility. They focus on three cases that illustrate the potential difficulties in tracing the consequences from what seem initially to be simple causes. In case one, the investigation of a forest fire reveals that person A flung a lighted cigarette into the bracken at the forest's edge, the bracken caught fire, and a breeze sprang up, fanning the flames toward the forest. Though saying that A caused the forest fire seems easy, Hart and Honoré point out that to do so means that we have not taken the breeze to be a cause in the same way that we have taken A's flinging of the lighted cigarette to be a cause. In case two, A flings the lighted cigarette into the bracken. Just as the flames are about to die out, person B deliberately pours gasoline on the dying embers. The fire then spreads and burns down the forest. Here, Hart and Honoré state that, unlike case one, A is not the cause of the forest fire—B is. Because B has exploited the circumstances, B is the cause of the forest fire no matter what we think of either A's or B's actions. In case three, A hits B and B falls to the ground, stunned. At the very moment B falls, a tree also falls to the ground and kills B. According to Hart and Honoré, while A is surely the cause of any bruises

B might have sustained in hitting the ground, A is not the cause of B's death. While the fall of the tree resembles the breeze in case one, in that it is independent of and subsequent to A's actions, the falling tree holds a much different place in the causal chain than the breeze does. In a sense, the falling tree causes B's death.

In the selection "Sua Culpa," Joel Feinberg explores the more specific notion of "his fault" and defends the procedure of levying liability on the basis of fault. When a harm has occurred, blame often needs to be fixed through a careful examination of the actions of those who potentially are at fault. This allows determination of who is in possession of the fault or, in other words, which fault is "his fault." Feinberg fixes blame in this fashion by using the "triconditional analysis." This analysis allows us to conclude that a harm is "his fault" if (1) the person was at fault in acting, (2) the faulty act caused the harm, and (3) the aspect that made the act faulty was also one of the aspects that caused the harm. According to Feinberg, this manner of fixing blame is necessary so that the innocent do not have to bear the costs of injustice; instead, the faulty injurer must bear these costs so as to protect the innocence of the injured party. Feinberg claims that liability should be fixed in this way, which he calls the "weak retributive principle," rather than under a more conventional retributive account designed to punish any person at fault. He argues that the latter, which he calls a "strong retributive principle," does not take into account the fact that we are all faulty at one time or another.

In "Fairness and Utility in Tort Theory," George P. Fletcher argues that there are two opposed paradigms for resolving tort disputes: reciprocity and reasonableness. The paradigm of reciprocity compares the risk-creating activity of both parties and the possibility of an excuse. If there is not an equal creation of risk and a basis for excuse, then the risk-creator is liable. The paradigm of reasonableness tests solely for the existence of an unreasonable risk. If the risk is unreasonable, the defendant is liable. A simple cost-benefit analysis determines the notion of reasonableness. Fletcher finds that though the paradigm of reasonableness has a certain allure, given its appeal in the modern U.S. legal system, the paradigm of reciprocity is overall a better tort theory. According to Fletcher, the latter paradigm offers a greater overall level of protection for individuals than that provided by the former.

Jules L. Coleman, in "Tort Liability and the Limits of Corrective Justice," disagrees with Feinberg's weak retributive principle for imposing fault. Finding this principle too limited, Coleman proposes allocating costs on the basis of fault according to a method that rests on the principle of corrective justice. Under this principle, liability is not imposed to protect the innocence of the victims; rather, justice lies in the duties that the injurer owes to the victim. This means that an individual may owe a duty to a victim because that victim has suffered a loss, even if she is not at fault for creating that loss. For example, Coleman holds that someone may be an optimal risk-reducer and thus may be found to owe a duty to the victim although she is not directly responsible for creating the loss the victim suffered. Yet, the duty owed to the victim is not the same in every case. Coleman states that the duties owed to a particular victim depend on the surrounding social and legal practices. For example, with a no-fault plan by which we compensate victims from a pool that all pay into, no additional duty is owed to the victim, except perhaps an apology.

Richard A. Epstein begins the next selection, "A Theory of Strict Liability," by pointing out the oppositional relationship between common-law notions of common sense and fairness within tort law and the more recent economic theory of torts. While some prefer this theory because it reduces the need for an examination of the fairness question, some fairness questions that cannot be answered in economic terms remain. Epstein points out that this argument contains a presupposition regarding the theory of fairness itself—namely, that one can explain it in such a way that leaves room for economic theory. Given this supposition, Epstein attempts to raise these fairness questions within traditional legal theory so as to determine whether the argument for economic theory holds. To accomplish this task, Epstein focuses on the conflict between negligence theories and theories of strict liability.

In "The Question of a Duty to Rescue in Canadian Tort Law: An Answer from France," Mitchell McInnes argues that Canadian tort law can be expanded to include a general duty to rescue. This is due in part to the possibility of expanding the many currently existing exceptions to the general lack of a duty to rescue in Canadian tort law. For example, the Canadian courts have found that a duty to rescue can arise in relationships of economic benefit, relationships of control or benefit, creations of danger, gratuitous undertakings, and statutory duties. Though some theories attempt to explain these exceptions, Mclnnes believes that these exceptions are simply a product of policy decisions. Further, though some policy arguments reject the duty to rescue, McInnes finds overall stronger policy arguments in favor of the duty to rescue. Thus, he claims the lack of a duty to rescue in Canadian law is an "anachronism" that ought to be changed.

Taken from a symposium on Japanese law, the next selection, by Robert Leflar, compares Japanese and American tort law. Although Leflar finds retribution and public participation to be goals of both systems, he questions the extent to which these goals are realized in Japan. When Leflar examines the goals of compensation and deterrence, using the examples of medical malpractice and products liability, he finds so few suits filed in Japan that the potential is high for neither of these goals being achieved. In the case of medical malpractice, Leflar speculates that harm to the doctors' reputations rather than pocketbooks could potentially serve as a deterrent. Finally, Leflar focuses on two additional values of the Japanese tort system: transaction cost and fairness. These goals are achieved quite readily in the case of many product liability cases because of standardized damage guidelines that outline monetary damages no matter what the status of the parties. These guidelines make many lawsuits unnecessary, because each side knows exactly how much a claim is worth, unlike in the United States. Overall, Leflar claims that any evaluation of the Japanese tort system must depend on the particular goals under examination. Regarding fairness or cost containment, the Japanese system is quite effective, but regarding deterrence, the Japanese system will likely seem inferior when compared with the U.S. tort system.

Finally, we provide the *Tarasoff v. Regents of University of California* lawsuit as an example of tort law. Here, Prosenjit Poddar, while under the care of the psychologist Dr. Lawrence Moore, killed Tatiana Tarasoff. Poddar had informed Dr. Moore of his intention to kill Tarasoff. Dr. Moore had Poddar detained by campus police, but Poddar was released when he seemed rational. Moreover, Dr. Moore never informed Tarasoff of Poddar's intention. In this appeal, Dr. Moore's employer is found liable for Dr. Moore's failure to warn Tarasoff of the immediate danger posed by his patient. The court's justification for this ruling is based on a notion of a professional's duty to exercise reasonable care. Because he failed in this duty, Dr. Moore is found by the court to be negligent.

We hope that, after reading these selections, you come to a greater appreciation of tort law and the vast philosophical concerns it generates. For more information, please consult the list of selected readings that follows.

SELECTED READINGS

Ashworth, Andrew, and Eva Steiner. "Criminal Omission and Public Duties: The French Experience." *Legal Studies* 10 (1990): 153–64.

Besser, Anne Cucchiara, and Kalman J. Kaplan. "The Good Samaritan: Jewish and American Legal Perspectives." *The Journal of Law and Religion* 10 (1994): 193–219.

Calabresi, Guido. *The Cost of Accidents.* New Haven, CT: Yale University Press, 1971.

Coleman, Jules. "Moral Theories of Tort: Their Scope and Limits." *Law and Philosophy* 1, 2 (1982, 1983): 5–36.

Cottrell, Jill. "The Function of the Law of Torts in Africa." *Journal of African Law* 31 (1987): 161–84.

Cullen, W. Douglas. "The Liability of the Good Samaritan." *Juridical Review* (1995): 20–27.

Denton, Frank E. "The Case Against a Duty to Rescue." *Canadian Journal of Law and Jurisprudence* 4 (1991): 101–32.

Eliash, Ben Zion. "To Leave or Not to Leave: The Good Samaritan in Jewish Law." *Saint Louis University Law Journal* 38 (1994): 619–28.

Feinberg, Joel. *Doing and Deserving.* Princeton, NJ: Princeton University Press, 1970.

Geis, Gilbert. "Sanctioning the Selfish: The Operation of Portugal's New 'Bad Samaritan' Statute." *International Review of Victimology* 1 (1991): 297–313.

Husak, Douglas. "Omissions, Causation, and Liability." *Philosophical Quarterly* 30 (1980): 318–26.

Jones, Michael. "Remoteness and Rescuers." *Modern Law Review* 45 (1982): 342–45.

Mawby, R. I. "Bystander Responses to the Victims of Crime: Is the Good Samaritan Alive and Well?" *Victimology* 10 (1985): 461–75.

Mclnnes, Mitchell. "The Economic Analysis of Rescue Laws." *Manitoba Law Journal* 21 (1992): 237–73.

———. "Restitution and the Rescue of Life." *Alberta Law Review* 32 (1994): 37–70.

McPherson v. Buick Motor Co., 217 N.Y. 382, 111 N.E. 1050 (1916).

Owen, David, ed. *Philosophical Foundations of Tort Law.* Oxford, England: Clarendon Press, 1995.

Palsgraf v. The Long Island Railroad Co., 248 N.Y. 339 (1928).

Posner, Richard. "A Theory of Negligence." *Journal of Legal Studies* 1 (1972): 29–96.

———. *Economic Analysis of the Law.* 4th ed. Boston: Little, Brown, 1992.

Thomson, Judith Jarvis. "The Decline of Cause." *Georgetown Law Journal* 137 (1987): 137–50.

United States v. Carroll Towing Co., 159 F. 2d 169 (2d Cir. 1947).

Zion, James W. "Harmony among the People: Torts and Indian Courts." *Montana Law Review* 45 (1984): 265–79.

16

H. L. A. HART
A. M. HONORÉ

Causation and Responsibility

I. RESPONSIBILITY IN LAW AND MORALS

. . . In the moral judgments of ordinary life, we have occasion to blame people because they have caused harm to others, and also, if less frequently, to insist that morally they are bound to compensate those to whom they have caused harm. These are the moral analogues of more precise legal conceptions; for, in all legal systems, liability to be punished or to make compensation frequently depends on whether actions (or omissions) have caused harm. Moral blame is not of course confined to such cases of causing harm. We blame a man who cheats or lies or breaks promises, even if no one has suffered in the particular case: this has its legal counterpart in the punishment of abortive attempts to commit crimes, and of offences constituted by the unlawful possession of certain kinds of weapons, drugs, or materials, for example, for counterfeiting currency. When the occurrence of harm is an essential part of the ground for blame the connection of the person blamed with the harm may take any of the forms of causal connection we have examined. His action may have initiated a series of physical events dependent on each other and culminating in injury to persons or property, as in wounding and killing. These simple forms are paradigms for the lawyer's talk of harm "directly" caused. But we blame people also for harm which arises from or is the consequence of their neglect of common precautions; we do this even if harm would not have come about without the intervention of another human being deliberately exploiting the opportunities provided by neglect. The main legal analogue here is liability for "negligence." The wish of many lawyers to talk in this branch of the law of harm being "within the risk of" rather than "caused by" the negligent conduct manifests appreciation of the fact that a different form of relationship is involved in saying that harm is the consequence, on the one hand, of an explosion and, on the other, of a failure to lock the door by which a thief has entered. Again, we blame people for the harm which we say is the consequence of their influence over others, either exerted by non-rational means or in one of the ways we have designated "interpersonal transactions." To such grounds for responsibility there correspond many important legal conceptions: the instigation of crimes ("commanding" or "procuring") constitutes an important ground of criminal responsibility and the concepts of enticement and of inducement (by threats or misrepresentation) are an element in many civil wrongs as well as in criminal offences.

The law, however, especially in matters of compensation, goes far beyond these casual grounds for responsibility in such doctrines as the vicarious responsibility of a master for his servant's civil wrongs and that of the responsibility of an occupier of property for injuries suffered by passers-by from defects of which the occupier had no knowledge and which he had no opportunity to repair. There is a recognition, perhaps diminishing, of this non-causal ground of responsibility outside the law; responsibility is sometimes admitted by one person or group of persons, even if no precaution has been neglected by them, for harm done by persons related to them in a special way, either by family ties or as members of the same social or political association. Responsibility may be simply "placed" by moral opinion on one person for what others do. The simplest case of such vicarious moral responsibility is that of a parent for damage done by a child; its more complex (and more debatable) form is the moral responsibility of one generation of a nation to make compensation for their predecessors' wrong, such as the Germans admitted in payment of compensation to Israel.

At this point it is necessary to issue a caveat about the meaning of the expression "responsible" if only to avoid prejudicing a question about the character of *legal* determinations of causal connection . . . Usually in discussion of the law and occasionally in morals, to say that someone is responsible for some harm means that in accordance with legal rules of moral principles it is at least permissible, if not mandatory, to blame or punish or exact compensation from him. In this use[1] the expression "responsible for" does not refer to a factual connection between the person held responsible and the harm but simply to his liability under the rules to be blamed, punished, or made to pay. The expressions "answerable for" or "liable for" are practically synonymous with "responsible for" in *this* use, in which there is no implication that the person held responsible actually *did* or *caused* the harm. In this sense a master is (in English law) responsible for the damage done by his servants acting within the scope of their authority and a parent (in French and German law) for that done by his children; it is in this sense that a guarantor or surety is responsible for the debts or the good behaviour of other persons and an insurer for losses sustained by the insured. Very often, however, especially in discussion of morals, to say that someone is responsible for some harm is to assert *(inter alia)* that he *did* the harm or *caused* it, though such a statement is perhaps rarely confined to this for it usually also carries with it the implication that it is at least permissible to blame or punish him. This double use of the expression no doubt arises from the important fact that doing or causing harm constitutes not only the most usual but the primary type of ground for holding persons responsible in the first sense. We still speak of inanimate or natural causes such as storms, floods, germs, or the failure of electricity supply as "responsible for" disasters; this mode of expression, now taken only to mean that they caused the disasters, no doubt originated in the belief that all that happens is the work of spirits when it is not that of men. Its survival in the modern world is perhaps some testimony to the primacy of causal connection as an element in responsibility and to the intimate connection between the two notions.

We shall consider later an apparent paradox which interprets in a different way the relationship between cause and responsibility. Much modern thought on causation in the law rests on the contention that the statement that someone has caused harm either means no more than that the harm would not have happened without ("but for") his action or where (as in normal legal usage and in all ordinary speech), it apparently means more than this, it is a disguised way of asserting the "normative" judgment that he is responsible in the first sense, i.e. that it is proper or just to blame or punish him or make him pay. On this view to say that a person caused harm is not really, though ostensibly it is, to give a *ground* or *reason* for holding him responsible in the first sense; for we are only in a position to say that he has caused harm when we have decided that he is responsible. Pending consideration of the theories of legal causation which exploit this point of view we shall use the expression "responsible for" only in the first of the two ways explained, i.e. without any implication as to the type of factual connection between the person held responsible and the harm; and we shall provisionally, though without prejudicing the issue, treat statements that a person caused harm as one sort of non-tautologous ground or reason for saying that he is responsible in this sense.

. . . Yet, in order to understand the extent to which the causal notions of ordinary thought are used in the law, we must bear in mind the many factors which must differentiate moral from legal responsibility in spite of their partial correspondence. The law is not only bound to follow the moral patterns of attribution of responsibility but, even when it does, it must take into account, in a way which the private moral judgment need not and does not, the general social consequences which are attached to its judgments of responsibility; for they are of a gravity quite different from those attached to moral censure. . . . Always to follow the private moral judgment here would be far too expensive for the law: not only in the crude sense that it would entail a vast machinery of courts and officials, but in the more important sense that it would inhibit or discourage too many other valuable activities of society. To limit the *types* of harm which the law will recognize is not enough; even if the types of harm are limited it would still be too much for any society to punish or exact compensation from individuals whenever their connection with harm of such types would justify moral censure. Conversely, social needs may require that compensation should be paid and even (though less obviously) that punishment be inflicted where no such connection between the person held responsible and the harm exists. . . .

[1]Cf. *OED sub tit.* Responsible: Answerable, accountable (*to* another *for* something); liable to be called to account: "being responsible to the King for what might happen to us," 1662; Hart, "Varieties of Responsibility" (1967) 83 *LQR* 346, reprinted with additions as "Responsibility and Retribution" in Hart, *Punishment and Responsibility* (Oxford, 1968), chap. IX.

II. TRACING CONSEQUENCES

"To consequences no limit can be set": "Every event which would not have happened if an earlier event had not happened is the consequence of that earlier event." These two propositions are not equivalent in meaning and are not equally or in the same way at variance with ordinary thought. They have, however, both been urged sometimes in the same breath by the legal theorist[2] and the philosopher: they are indeed sometimes said by lawyers to be "the philosophical doctrine" of causation. It is perhaps not difficult even for the layman to accept the first proposition as a truth about certain physical events; an explosion may cause a flash of light which will be propagated as far as the outer nebulae; its effects or consequences continue indefinitely. It is, however, a different matter to accept the view that whenever a man is murdered with a gun his death was the consequence of (still less an "effect" of or "caused by") the manufacture of the bullet. The first tells a perhaps unfamiliar tale about unfamiliar events; the second introduces an unfamiliar, though, of course, a possible way of speaking about familiar events. It is not that this unrestricted use of "consequence" is unintelligible or never found; it is indeed used to refer to bizarre or fortuitous connections or coincidences: but the point is that the various causal notions employed for the purposes of explanation, attribution of responsibility, or the assessment of contributions to the course of history carry with them implicit limits which are similar in these different employments.

It is, then, the second proposition, defining consequence in terms of "necessary condition," with which theorists are really concerned. This proposition is the corollary of the view that, if we look into the past of any given event, there is an infinite number of events, each of which is a necessary condition of the given event and so, as much as any other, is its cause. This is the "cone"[3] of causation, so called because, since any event has a number of simultaneous conditions, the series fans out as we go back in time. . . .

Legal theorists have developed this account of cause and consequence to show what is "factual," "objective," or "scientific" in these notions: this they call "cause in fact" and it is usually stressed as a preliminary to the doctrine that any more restricted application of these terms in the law represents nothing in the facts or in the meaning of causation, but expresses fluctuating legal policy or sentiments of what is just or convenient. Moral philosophers have insisted in somewhat similar terms that the consequences of human action are "infinite." . . . The point is that though we could, we do not think in this way in tracing connections between human actions and events. Instead, whenever we are concerned with such connections, whether for the purpose of explaining a puzzling occurrence, assessing responsibility, or giving an intelligible historical narrative, we employ a set of concepts restricting in various ways what counts as a consequence. These restrictions colour *all* our thinking in causal terms; when we find them in the law we are not finding something invented by or peculiar to the law, though of course it is for the law to say when and how far it will use them and, where they are vague, to supplement them. . . .

. . . [W]e shall consider the detail of three simple cases.

(i) A forest fire breaks out, and later investigation shows that shortly before the outbreak *A* had flung away a lighted cigarette into the bracken at the edge of the forest, the bracken caught fire, a light breeze got up, and fanned the flames in the direction of the forest. If, on discovering these facts, we hesitate before saying that *A*'s action caused the forest fire this would be to consider the alternative hypothesis that in spite of appearances the fire only succeeded *A*'s action in point of time, that the bracken flickered out harmlessly and the forest fire was caused by something else. To dispose of this it may be necessary to examine in further detail the process of events between the ignition of the bracken and the outbreak of fire in the forest and to show that these exemplified certain types of continuous change. If this is shown, there is no longer any room for doubt: *A*'s action *was* the cause of the fire, whether he intended it or not. This seems and is the simplest of cases. Yet it is important to notice that even in applying our general knowledge to a case as simple as this, indeed in regarding it as simple, we make an implicit use of a distinction between types of factor which constitute a limit in tracing consequences and those which we regard as mere circumstances "through" which we trace them. For the breeze which sprang up after *A* dropped the cigarette, and without which the fire would not have spread to the forest, was

[2]Lawson, *Negligence in the Civil Law*, p. 53.
[3]Glanville Williams, *Joint Torts and Contributory Negligence*, p. 239.

not only subsequent to his action but entirely independent of it: it was, however, a common recurrent feature of the environment, and, as such, it is thought of not as an "intervening" force but as merely part of the circumstances in which the cause "operates." The decision so to regard it is implicitly taken when we combine our knowledge of the successive stages of the process and assert the connection.

It is easy here to be misled by the natural metaphor of a causal "chain," which may lead us to think that the causal process consists of a series of single events each of which is dependent upon (would not have occurred without) its predecessor in the "chain" and so is dependent upon the initiating action or event. In truth in any causal process we have at each phase not single events but complex sets of conditions, and among these conditions are some which are not only subsequent to, but independent of the initiating action or event. Some of these independent conditions, such as the evening breeze in the example chosen, we classify as mere conditions in or on which the cause operates; others we speak of as "interventions" or "causes." To decide how such independent elements shall be classified is also to decide how we shall combine our knowledge of the different general connections which the successive stages exemplify, and it is important to see that nothing *in* this knowledge itself can resolve this point. We may have to go to science for the relevant general knowledge before we can assert with proper confidence that *A*'s action did cause the fire, but science, though it tells us that an air current was required, is silent on the difference between a current in the form of an evening breeze and one produced by someone who deliberately fanned the flames as they were flickering out in the bracken. Yet an air current in this deliberately induced form is not a "condition" or "mere circumstance" through which we can trace the consequence; its presence would force us to revise the assertion that *A* caused the fire. Conversely if science helped us to identify as a necessary factor in producing the fire some condition or element of which we had previously been totally ignorant, e.g. the persistence of oxygen, this would leave our original judgment undisturbed if this factor were a common or pervasive feature of the environment or of the thing in question. There is thus indeed an important sense in which it is true that the distinction between cause and conditions is not a "scientific" one. It is not determined by laws or generalizations concerning connections between events.

When we have assembled all our knowledge of the factors involved in the fire, the residual question which we then confront (the attributive question) may be typified as follows: Here is *A*'s action, here is the fire; can the fire be attributed to *A*'s action as its consequence given that there is also this third factor (the breeze or *B*'s intervention) without which the fire would not have happened? It is plain that, both in raising questions of this kind and in answering them, ordinary thought is powerfully influenced by the analogy between the straightforward cases of causal attribution (where the elements required for the production of harm in addition to the initiating action are all "normal" conditions) and even simpler cases of responsibility which we do not ordinarily describe in causal language at all but by the simple transitive verbs of action. These are the cases of the direct manipulation of objects involving changes in them or their position: cases where we say "He pushed it," "He broke it," "He bent it." The cases which we do confidently describe in causal language ("The fire was caused by his carelessness," "He caused a fire") are cases where no other human action or abnormal occurrence is required for the production of the effect, but only normal conditions. Such cases appear as mere long-range or less direct versions or extensions of the most obvious and fundamental case of all for the attribution of responsibility: the case where we can simply say "He did it." Conversely in attaching importance to thus causing harm as a distinct ground of responsibility and in taking certain kinds of factor (whether human interventions or abnormal occurrences), without which the initiating action would not have led to harm, to preclude the description of the case in simple causal terms, common sense is affected by the fact that here, because of the manner in which the harm eventuates, the outcome cannot be represented as a mere extension of the initiating action; the analogy with the fundamental case for responsibility ("He did it") has broken down. . . .

(ii) *A* throws a lighted cigarette into the bracken which catches fire. Just as the flames are about to flicker out, *B*, who is not acting in concert with *A*, deliberately pours petrol on them. The fire spreads and burns down the forest. *A*'s action, whether or not he intended the forest fire, was not the cause of the fire: *B*'s was.

The voluntary intervention of a second human agent, as in this case, is a paradigm among those factors which preclude the assimilation in causal judgments of the first agent's connection with the eventual harm to the case of simple direct manipulation. Such an intervention displaces the prior action's title to be called the cause and, in the persistent metaphors found in the law, it "reduces" the earlier action and its immediate effects to the level of "mere circumstances" or "part of the history." *B* in this case was not an "instrument" through which *A* worked or a victim of the circumstances *A* has created. He has, on the contrary, freely exploited the circumstances and brought about the fire without the co-operation of any further agent or any chance coincidence. Compared with this the claim of *A*'s action to be ranked the cause of the fire fails. That this and not the moral appraisal of the two actions is the point of comparison seems clear. If *A* and *B* both intended to set the forest on fire, and this destruction is accepted as something wrong or wicked, their moral wickedness, judged by the criterion of intention, is the same. Yet the causal judgment differentiates between them. If their moral guilt is judged by the outcome, this judgment though it would differentiate between them cannot be the source of the causal judgment; for it presupposes it. The difference just is that *B* has caused the harm and *A* has not. Again, if we appraise these actions as good or bad from different points of view, this leaves the causal judgments unchanged. *A* may be a soldier of one side anxious to burn down the enemy's hide-out: *B* may be an enemy soldier who has decided that his side is too iniquitous to defend. Whatever is the moral judgment passed on these actions by different speakers it would remain true that *A* had not caused the fire and *B* had.

There are, as we have said, situations in which a voluntary action would not be thought of as an intervention precluding causal connection in this way. These are the cases discussed further below where an opportunity commonly exploited for harmful actions is negligently provided, or one person intentionally provides another with the means, the opportunity, or a certain type of reason for wrongdoing. Except in such cases a voluntary intervention is a limit past which consequences are not traced. By contrast, actions which in any of a variety of different ways are less than fully voluntary are assimilated to the means by which or the circumstances in which the earlier action brings about the consequences. Such actions are not the outcome of an informed choice made without pressure from others, and the different ways in which human action may fall short in this respect range from defective muscular control, through lack of consciousness or knowledge, to the vaguer notions of duress and predicaments, created by the first agent for the second, in which there is no "fair" choice.

In considering examples of such actions and their bearing on causal judgments there are three dangers to avoid. It would be folly to think that in tracing connections through such actions instead of regarding them, like voluntary interventions, as a limit, ordinary thought has clearly separated out their non-voluntary aspect from others by which they are often accompanied. Thus even in the crude case where *A* lets off a gun (intentionally or not) and startles *B*, so that he makes an involuntary movement of his arm which breaks a glass, the commonness of such a reaction as much as its compulsive character may influence the judgment that *A*'s action was the cause of the damage.

Secondly we must not impute to ordinary thought all the fine discriminations that could be made and in fact are to be found in a legal system, or an equal willingness to supply answers to complex questions in causal terms. Where there is no precise system of punishment, compensation or reward to administer, ordinary men will not often have faced such questions as whether the injuries suffered by a motorist who collides with another in swerving to avoid a child are consequences attributable to the neglect of the child's parents in allowing it to wander on to the road. Such questions courts have to answer and in such cases common judgments provide only a general, though still an important indication of what are the relevant factors.

Thirdly, though very frequently non-voluntary actions are assimilated to mere conditions or means by which the first agent brings about the consequences, the assimilation is never quite complete. This is manifested by the general avoidance of many causal locutions which are appropriate when the consequences are traced (as in the first case) through purely physical events. Thus even in the case in which the second agent's role is hardly an "action" at all, e.g. where *A* hits *B*, who staggers against a glass window and breaks it, we should say that *A*'s blow made *B* stagger and break the glass, rather than that *A's* blow caused the glass to break, though in any explanatory or attributive context the case would be *summarized* by saying that *A*'s action was the cause of the *damage*.

In the last two cases where *B*'s movements are involuntary in the sense that they are not part of any action which he chose or intended to do, their connection with *A*'s action would be described by saying that *A*'s blow *made B* stagger or *caused* him to stagger or that the noise of *A*'s shot *made* him jump or *caused* him to jump. This would be true, whether *A* intended or expected *B* to react in this way or not, and the naturalness of treating *A*'s action as the cause of the ultimate damage is due to the causal character of this part of the process involving *B*'s action. The same is, however, true where *B*'s actions are not involuntary movements but *A* is considered to have made or caused *B* to do them by less crude means. This is the case if, for example, *A* uses threats or exploits his authority over *B* to make *B* do something, e.g. knock down a door. At least where *A*'s threats are of serious harm, or *B*'s act was unquestionably within *A*'s authority to order, he too has made or forced or (in formal quasi-legal parlance) "caused" *B* to act.

Outside the area of such cases, where *B*'s will would be said either not to be involved at all, or to be overborne by *A*, are cases where *A*'s act creates a predicament for *B narrowing* the area of choice so that he has either to inflict some harm on himself or others, or sacrifice some important interest or duty. Such cases resemble coercion in that *A* narrows the area of *B*'s choice but differ from it in that this predicament need not be intentionally created. *A* sets a house on fire (intentionally or unintentionally): *B* to save himself has to jump from a height involving certain injury, or to save a child rushes in and is seriously burned. Here, of course, *B*'s movements are not involuntary; the "necessity" of his action is here of a different order. His action is the outcome of a choice between two evils forced on him by *A*'s action. In such cases, when *B*'s injuries are thought of as the consequence of the fire, the implicit judgment is made that his action was the lesser of two evils and in this sense a "reasonable" one which he was obliged to make to avoid the greater evil. This is often paradoxically, though understandably, described by saying that here the agent "had no choice" but to do what he did. Such judgments involve a comparison of the importance of the respective interests sacrificed and preserved, and the final assertion that *A*'s action was the cause of the injuries rests on evaluations about which men may differ.

Finally, the ground for treating some harm which would not have occurred without *B*'s action as the consequence of *A*'s action may be that *B* acted in ignorance of or under a mistake as to some feature of the situation created by *A*. Poisoning offers perhaps the simplest example of the bearing on causal judgments of actions which are less than voluntary in this Aristotelian sense. If *A* intending *B*'s death deliberately poisons *B*'s food and *B*, knowing this, deliberately takes the poison and dies, *A* has not, unless he coerced *B* into eating the poisoned food, caused *B*'s death: if, however, *B* does not know the food to be poisoned, eats it, and dies, *A* has caused his death, even if he put the poison in unwittingly. Of course only the roughest judgments are passed in causal terms in such cases outside law courts, where fine degrees of "appreciation" or "reckless shutting of the eyes" may have to be discriminated from "full knowledge." Yet, rough as these are, they indicate clearly enough the controlling principles.

Though in the foregoing cases *A*'s initiating action might often be described as "the cause" of the ultimate harm, this linguistic fact is of subordinate importance to the fact that, for whatever purpose, explanatory, descriptive, or evaluative, consequences of an action are traced, discriminations are made (except in the cases discussed later) between free voluntary interventions and less than voluntary reactions to the first action or the circumstances created by it.

(iii) The analogy with single simple actions which guides the tracing of consequences may be broken by certain kinds of conjunctions of physical events. *A* hits *B* who falls to the ground stunned and bruised by the blow; at that moment a tree crashes to the ground and kills *B*. *A* has certainly caused *B*'s bruises but not his death: for though the fall of the tree was, like the evening breeze in our earlier example, independent of and subsequent to the initiating action, it would be differentiated from the breeze in any description in causal terms of the connection of *B*'s death with *A*'s action. It is to be noticed that this is not a matter which turns on the intention with which *A* struck *B*. Even if *A* hit *B* inadvertently or accidentally his blow would still be the cause of *B*'s bruises: he would have caused them, though unintentionally. Conversely even if *A* had intended his blow to kill, this would have been an attempt to kill but still not the cause of *B*'s death, unless *A* knew that the tree was about to fall just at that moment. On this legal and ordinary judgments would be found to agree; and most legal systems would distinguish for the purposes of punishment[4] an

[4]For the bearing of the principles of punishment on such problems see Chap. XIV.

attempt with a fatal upshot, issuing by such chance or anomalous events, from "causing death"—the terms in which the offences of murder and manslaughter are usually defined.

Similarly the causal description of the case does not turn on the moral appraisal of *A*'s action or the wish to punish it. *A* may be a robber and a murderer and *B* a saint guarding the place *A* hoped to plunder. Or *B* may be a murderer and *A* a hero who has forced his way into *B*'s retreat. In both cases the causal judgment is the same. *A* had caused the minor injuries but not *B*'s death, though he tried to kill him. *A* may indeed be praised or blamed but not for causing *B*'s death. However intimate the connection between responsibility and causation, it does not determine causal judgments in this simple way. Nor does the causal judgment turn on a refusal to attribute grave consequences to actions which normally have less serious results. Had *A*'s blow killed *B* outright and the tree, falling on his body, merely smashed his watch we should still treat the coincidental character of the fall of the tree as determining the form of causal statement. We should then recognize *A*'s blow as the cause of *B*'s death but not the breaking of the watch.

The connection between *A*'s action and *B*'s death in the first case would naturally be described in the language of *coincidence*. "It was a coincidence: it just happened that, at the very moment when *A* knocked *B* down, a tree crashed at the very place where he fell and killed him." The common legal metaphor would describe the fall of the tree as an "extraneous" cause. This, however, is dangerously misleading, as an analysis of the notion of coincidence will show. It suggests merely an event which is subsequent to and independent of some other contingency, and of course the fall of the tree has both these features in relation to *A*'s blow. Yet in these respects the fall of the tree does not differ from the evening breeze in the earlier case where we found no difficulty in tracing causal connection.[5] The full elucidation of the notion of a coincidence is a complex matter for, though it is very important as a limit in tracing consequences, causal questions are not the only ones to which the notion is relevant. The following are its most general characteristics. We speak of a coincidence whenever the conjunction of two or more events in certain spatial or temporal relations (1) is very unlikely by ordinary standards and (2) is for some reason significant or important, provided (3) that they occur without human contrivance and (4) are independent of each other. It is therefore a coincidence if two persons known to each other in London meet without design in Paris on their way to separate independently chosen destinations; or if two persons living in different places independently decide to write a book on the same subject. The first is a coincidence of time and place ("It just happened that we were at the same place at the same time"), and the second a coincidence of time only ("It just happened that they both decided to write on the subject at the same time"). . . .

One further criterion in addition to these four must be satisfied if a conjunction of events is to rank as a coincidence and as a limit when the consequences of the action are traced. This further criterion again shows the strength of the influence which the analogy with the case of the simple manipulation of things exerts over thought in causal terms. An abnormal *condition* existing at the time of a human intervention is distinguished both by ordinary thought and, with a striking consistency, by most legal systems from an abnormal event or conjunction of events subsequent to that intervention; the former, unlike the latter, are not ranked as coincidences or "extraneous" causes when the consequences of the intervention come to be traced. Thus *A* innocently gives *B* a tap over the head of a normally quite harmless character, but because *B* is then suffering from some rare disease the tap has, as we say, "fatal results." In this case *A* has caused *B*'s death though unintentionally. The scope of the principle which thus distinguishes contemporaneous abnormal conditions from subsequent events is unclear; but at least where a human being initiates some physical change in a thing, animal, or person, abnormal physical states of the object affected, existing at the time, are ranked as part of the circumstances in which the cause "operates." In the familiar controlling imagery these are part of "the stage already set" before the "intervention." . . .

[5]Above, [pp. 149–50 ff.]

17

JOEL FEINBERG

Sua Culpa

I

. . . It may seem that most of those who quibble and quarrel about "his fault" are either children or lawyers; and even lawyers, therefore, can seem childish when they are preoccupied with the question. But investigators, editorialists, and executives must assign blame for failures and thereby judge the faults of their fellows. (Indeed, their inquiries and debates are most childish when they do *not* carefully consider fault and instead go scapegoat-hunting.) My assumption in what follows is that the faults that concern nonlawyers, both children and adults, are faults in the same sense of the word as those that concern the lawyer, that the concept of "his fault" is imported into the law from the world of everyday affairs. On the other hand, "proximate cause" (to pick just one of a thousand examples) is a technical term of law invented by lawyers to do a special legal job and subject to continual refashioning in the interests of greater efficiency in the performance of its assigned legal task. To explain this term to a layman is precisely to explain what *lawyers* do with it; if it should ever happen that a child, or a sportswriter, or an historian should use the expression, that fact would be of no relevance to its proper analysis. But to explain the concept of "his fault," we must give an account that explains what both lawyers and laymen do with it and how it is possible for each to understand and to communicate with the other by means of it.

An equivalent way of saying that some result is a man's fault is to say that he is to *blame* for it. Precisely the same thing can also be said in the language of *responsibility*. Of course, to be responsible for something (after the fact) may also mean that one did it, or caused it, or now stands answerable, or accountable, or liable to unfavorable responses from others for it. One can be responsible for a result in all those senses without being to blame for it. One can be held liable for a result either because it is one's fault or for some quite different kind of reason; and one can be to blame for an occurrence and yet escape all liability for it. Still, when one is to blame for a harm, one can properly be said to be "responsible for it *really*"; that is, there is a sense of "responsible for" that simply means "chargeable to one as one's fault." One of the commonest uses of the expression "*morally* responsible for" is for being responsible for something in this sense. (Another is for chargeability to a fault of a distinctively moral kind. Still another is for being *liable* to responses of a distinctively moral kind.)

II

The word "fault" occurs in three distinct idioms. We can say of a man that *he has a fault,* or that he is (or was) *at fault,* or that he is "to blame" for a given harm, which is to say that the harm is (or was) *his fault*. In this essay I shall be directly concerned only with the last of these idioms. . . .

III

We come now to the main business at hand: the analysis of the concept of "his fault." It should be clear at the outset that, in order for a given harm to be someone's fault, he must have been somehow "at fault" in what he did or omitted to do, and also that there must have been some sort of causal connection between his action or omission and the harm. It is equally obvious that neither of these conditions by itself can be sufficient. Thus a motorist may be at fault in driving with an expired license or in exceeding the speed limit by five miles per hour, but unless his faulty act is a cause of the collision that ensues, the accident can hardly be his fault. Fault without causally determining action, then, is not sufficient. Similarly, causation without fault is not sufficient for the caused harm to be the causer's fault. It is no logical contradiction to say that a person's action caused the harm yet the harm was not his fault.

The Triconditional Analysis

It is natural at this point to conclude that a harm is "his fault" if and only if (1) he was at fault in acting (or omitting) and (2) his faulty act (or omission) caused the harm. This analysis, however, is incomplete, being still vulnerable to counterexamples of faulty actions causing harm that is nevertheless not the actor's fault. Suppose that *A* is unlicensed to drive an automobile but drives anyway, thereby "being at fault." The appearance of him driving in an (otherwise) faultless manner causes an edgy horse to panic and throw his rider. His faultily undertaken act caused a harm that cannot be imputed to him because the respect in which his act was faulty was causally irrelevant to the production of the harm. (When we come to give a causal explanation of the harm, we will not mention the fact that the driver had no license in his pocket. *That* is not what scared the horse.) This example suggests that a further condition is required to complete the analysis: (3) the aspect of the act that was faulty was also one of the aspects in virtue of which the act was a cause of the harm. . . .

We can refer to this account as "the triconditional analysis" and to its three conditions as (in order) "the fault condition," "the causal condition" (that the act was a cause of the harm), and "the causal relevance condition" (that the faulty aspect of the act was its causal link to the harm). I shall conclude that the triconditional analysis goes a long way toward providing a correct account of the commonsense notion of "his fault" and that its three conditions are indeed necessary to such an account even if, in the end, they must be formulated much more carefully and even supplemented by other conditions in an inevitably more complicated analysis. The remainder of this section discusses difficulties for the analysis as it stands which, I think, it can survive (at least after some tinkering, modifying, and disclaiming). One of these difficulties stems from a heterogeneous group of examples of persons who, on our analysis, would be blamed for harms that are clearly not their fault. I try to sidestep these counterexamples by affixing a restriction to the fault condition and making corresponding adjustments in the formulation of the relevance condition. The other difficulties directly concern the causal condition and the relevance condition. Both of these can involve us quickly in some fundamental philosophical problems.

Restrictions on the Fault Condition

There are some exceptional cases (but readily accessible to the philosophical imagination) in which a person who is clearly not to blame for a given harm nevertheless is the sole person who satisfies the conditions of the tripartite analysis. These cases, therefore, constitute counterexamples to that analysis if it is taken to state not only necessary but sufficient conditions for blame. Nicholas Sturgeon has suggested an especially ingenious case:

> *A* has made a large bet that no infractions of the law will occur at a certain place in a certain period of time; but *B*, at that place and time, opens a pack of cigarettes and fails to destroy the federal tax seal thereby breaking the law. *A*, seeing *B*'s omission, is so frustrated that he suffers a fatal heart attack on the spot. (To simplify matters, we may suppose that no one has any reason to suppose *A* is endangering his health by gambling in this way.)[1]

Clearly, *A*'s death is not *B*'s fault. Yet (1) *B* was at fault in acting contrary to law; (2) his faulty act frustrated *A*, causing the heart attack; and (3) the aspects of *B*'s act (omission) that were faulty (the illegality of his omission to destroy the tax stamps) were also among the aspects of it in virtue of which there was a causal connection between it and the harm. . . .

. . . We can attempt to avoid counterexamples of the sort Sturgeon . . . suggested by tampering with the first condition (the fault condition). We can say now (of course, only tentatively and not without misgiving) that, for the purpose of this analysis, the way of being at fault required by the fault condition is to be understood as the harm-threatening way, not the nonbenefiting, offense-threatening, harmless faith-breaking, or law-violating ways. The fault condition then can be reformulated as follows (in words suggested by Sturgeon): a given harm is *A*'s fault only if (1) *A* was at fault in acting or omitting to act and "the faultiness of his act or omission consisted, at least in part, in the creation of either a certainty or an unreasonable risk of harm. . . ."[2] Now the faulty smoker in Sturgeon's example . . . [is] no longer "at fault" in the requisite way, and the revised analysis no longer pins the blame for coincidental harms on [him]. To open a cigarette package in an overly fastidious fashion is not to endanger unduly the health of others. . . .

. . . We can now say that the (harm-threatening) "faulty aspect" of an act is a cause of subsequent harm

[1]The example is from a very helpful letter sent to me by Professor Sturgeon after I read an earlier version of this paper at Cornell in May 1969.
[2]*Ibid.*

when the risk or certainty of harm in virtue of which the act was at fault was a risk or certainty of "just the sort of harm that was in fact caused,"[3] and not harm of some other sort. The resultant harm, in other words, must be within the scope of the risk (or certainty) in virtue of which the act is properly characterized as faulty. This is more than a mere explication of the original way of putting the third condition. It is a definite modification designed to rule out cases of *coincidence* where the faulty aspect of an act, even when it is of the harm-threatening sort, may be causally linked to a subsequent harm via such adventitious conditions as standing wagers. . . . Under the revised formulation, the very same considerations involved in the explanation of *why* the act is faulty are also involved, essentially and sufficiently, in the explanation of *how* the harm was caused. . . .

Fault and Cause: Dependent and Independent Determinations

Can we tell whether an act caused a given harm independently of knowing whether the actor was at fault in acting? The answer seems to be that we can determine the causal question independently of the fault question in some cases but not in others. Part of our problem is to explain this variation. Consider first some examples. . . . [T]he motorist in our earlier example, by driving (whether with or without fault is immaterial to this point) along a rarely traveled stretch of country road, caused a nervous horse to bolt. That is, it was his activity as he conducted it then and there, with its attendant noise and dust, that caused the horse to bolt; and we can know this independently of any determination of fault.

Examples provided by J. L. Mackie . . . however, seem to cut the other way. Mackie[4] describes an episode in which a motorcyclist exceeded a speed limit and was chased by a policeman, also on a motorcycle, at speeds up to seventy miles per hour. An absentminded pedestrian stepped off a bus into the policeman's path and was killed instantly. The newspapers for the next few days were full of debates over the question of whose conduct was the "real cause" of the death, debates that seemed to center on the question of whose conduct was the least *reasonable* intrusion into the normal course of events. To express an opinion at all on the causal question seemed to be to take a stand, plain and simple, about the *propriety* of pursuits by police in heavily populated areas. . . .

To clarify the relations between cause and fault, it will be necessary to digress briefly and remind ourselves of certain features of causal judgments as they are made in ordinary life. That one condition is causally necessary or, in a given context, sufficient for the occurrence of a given event is normally a question simply for empirical investigation and the application of a scientific theory. Normally, however, there will be a plurality of distinguishable causal conditions (often called "causal factors") for any given event, and the aim of a causal inquiry will be to single out one[5] of these to be denominated "the cause" of the event in question.[6] A judgment that cites one of the numerous eligible causal conditions for an event as "the cause" I call a *causal citation*. The eligibility of an event or state as a causal factor is determined empirically via the application of inductive criteria.[7] On the other hand, the citation of one of the eligible candidates as "the cause" is normally made, as we shall see, via the application of what Dray calls "pragmatic criteria." In Dray's convenient phrase, the inductive inquiry establishes the "importance of a condition to the event," whereas the causal citation indicates its "importance to the inquirer."

The point of a causal citation is to single out one of the certified causal candidates that is especially

[3]*Ibid.*

[4]"Responsibility and Language," *Australasian Journal of Philosophy,* 33 (1955), 145.

[5]In unusual cases, two or three.

[6]The distinction in common sense between a "causal factor" and "the cause" corresponds roughly—very roughly—to the technical legal distinction between "cause in fact" and "proximate cause."

[7]A causal factor is an earlier necessary condition in at least the weaker sense of "necessary condition," *viz.,* a member of a set of jointly sufficient conditions whose presence was necessary to the sufficiency of the set; but it need not be necessary in the stronger sense, *viz.,* a necessary element in every set of conditions that would be jointly sufficient, as oxygen is necessary to every instance of combustion. Not all prior necessary conditions, of course, are genuine causal factors. Analytic connections ("But for his having been born, the accident would not have happened") are ruled out, and so are "incidental connections" (earlier speeding bringing one to a given point just at the moment a tree falls on the road). Unlike necessary conditions connected in a merely incidental way to results, causal factors are "necessary elements in a set of conditions generally connected through intermediate stages with it." See H. L. A. Hart and A. M. Honoré, *Causation in the Law* (Oxford: Clarendon Press, 1959), 114. See also [Robert] Keeton [*Legal Cause in the Law of Torts* (Columbus: Ohio State University Press, 1963)], 62.

interesting to us, given our various practical purposes and cognitive concerns. These purposes and concerns provide a convenient way of classifying the "contexts of inquiry" in which causal citations are made. The primary division is between explanatory and nonexplanatory contexts. The occasion for an explanatory citation is one in which there is intellectual puzzlement of a quite specific kind. A surprising or unusual event has occurred which is a deviation from what is understood to be the normal course of things. . . .

Very often one of the causal conditions for a given upshot is a faulty human action. . . .

. . . [C]ausal citations can be divided into those made from explanatory and those made from nonexplanatory standpoints, and the latter group into those made from the "engineering" and those made from the "blaming" standpoints. Explanatory citations single out abnormal interferences with the normal course of events or hitherto unknown missing links in a person's understanding. They are designed simply to remove puzzlement by citing the causal factor that can shed the most light. Hence we can refer to the criterion of selection in explanatory contexts (for short) as *the lantern criterion.* Causal citations made from the "engineering standpoint" are made with a view to facilitating control over future events by citing the most efficiently and economically manipulable causal factor. The criterion for selection in engineering contexts can thus be called (for short) *the handle criterion.* The point of causal citations in purely blaming contexts is simply to pin the label of blame on the appropriate causal factor for further notice and practical use. These judgments cite a causal factor that is a human act or omission "stained" (as an ancient figure of speech would have it) with fault. The criterion in blaming contexts can be called (for short) *the stain criterion.* When we look for "the cause," then, we may be looking for the causal factor that has either a lantern, a handle, or a stain on it.

Purely blaming citations can be interpreted in two different ways. On the first model, to say that a person's act was the cause of the harm is precisely equivalent to saying that he is to blame for the harm, that is, that the harm is his fault. The causal inquiry undertaken from the purely blaming perspective, according to this view, is one and the same as the inquiry into the question of who was to blame or of whose fault it was. On this model, then, causal citation is not a condition for the fixing of blame; it is, rather, precisely the same thing. . . .

On the second model of interpretation, which is also sometimes *a propos,* the truth of the causal citation "His act was the cause of the harm" is only one of the *conditions* for the judgment that "The harm was his fault." Here we separate cause and fault before bringing them together again in a "his fault" judgment, insisting that the harm was his fault *only if* his action caused it. The causal inquiry, so conceived, is undertaken for the sake of the blame inquiry, but its results are established independently. . . .

The Causal Relevance Condition: Is It Always Necessary?

Does the analysis of commonsense "his fault" judgments really require a causal relevance condition? Many people, I suspect, are prepared to make "his fault" judgments in particular cases even when they know that a causal relevance condition has not been satisfied; and many puzzling cases are such as to make even most of us hesitate about the matter. . . .

. . . [O]thers might prefer to reject the causal relevance condition out of hand as too restrictive and urge instead that the blame always be placed on the person *most at fault,* whether the fault is causally relevant or not, providing his faulty action was a genuine causal factor. . . . It does not commend itself to the intuitive understanding in a quiet reflective hour, however, and seems to me to have no other merit than that of letting the indignation and vindictiveness occasioned by harm have a respectable outlet in our moral judgments. . . . Rather, if we are vindictively inclined, we can say that to impose liability on a person to enforced compensation or other harsh treatment for some harm does not always require that the harm be his fault. This would be the moral equivalent of a departure from what is called "the fault principle" in the law of torts. It is an attempt to do justice to our spontaneous feelings, without confusing our concepts, and has the merits at least of openness and honesty.

Disinterested parties might reject causal relevance as a condition for being to blame in a skeptical way, offering as an alternative to it a radical contextual relativism. . . . This skeptical theory, however, strikes me as a combined insight and *non sequitur.* The insight is that we are not *forced* to pinpoint blame unless some practical question like liability hinges on it and that it is often the better part of wisdom to decline to do so when one can. But it does not follow from the fact that "his fault" judgments can sometimes be avoided that it is logically open to us to make them in any way we wish when we do make them. I hold, therefore, to the conclusion that, in fixing the blame for harm, we are restricted by our very concepts to the person(s) whose faulty act was a causal factor in the production of the harm in virtue of its causally relevant faulty aspect.

There often is room for discretion in the making of "his fault" judgments, but it comes at a different place and is subject to strict limitations. The person whose fault the harm is said to be *must* satisfy the conditions of the triconditional analysis (and perhaps others as well); but when more than one person is so qualified, the judgment-maker may sometimes choose between them on "pragmatic grounds," letting some of them off the hook. When this discretion is proper, the three conditions of our analysis must be honored as necessary, but they are no longer taken to be sufficient. . . . [I]f it is given that we must, for some practical purpose, single out a wrongdoer more narrowly, then we have discretion to choose among those (but only those) who satisfy the necessary conditions of the tripartite analysis.[8]

Fault and Tort Liability

Suppose we accept the revised triconditional analysis of "his fault" but jettison the causal relevance condition as a requisite for tort *liability*. . . . The prime consequence of dropping the causal relevance condition is to downgrade the role of causation as a ground for liability and to increase the importance of simply being at fault. If causal relevance is not required, it would seem that being at fault is the one centrally important necessary condition for liability, and indeed so important as to render the causal condition itself a mere dispensable formality. To upgrade the fault condition to that extent is most likely to seem reasonable when the fault is disproportionately greater than the harm it occasions. . . .

It is another matter, however, when the harm is disproportionately greater than the fault, when a mere slap causes an unsuspected hemophiliac to bleed to death, or a clumsy slip on the sidewalk leads one to bump an "old soldier with an egg shell skull," causing his death. Hart and Honoré suggest that even here commonsense considerations can help justify abandonment, in some cases at least, of the causal relevance condition by mitigating its apparent harshness:

> The apparent unfairness of holding a defendant liable for a loss much greater than he could foresee to some extent disappears when we consider that a defendant is often negligent without suffering punishment or having to pay compensation. I may drive at an excessive speed a hundred times before the one occasion on which my speeding causes harm. The justice of holding me liable, should the harm on that occasion turn out to be extraordinarily grave, must be judged in the light of the hundred other occasions on which, without deserving such luck, I have incurred no liability.[9]

. . . If justice truly requires (as the Hart-Honoré argument suggests) that blame and liability be properly apportioned to *all* a person's faults as accumulated in the long run, causal linkage to harm aside, why not go all the way in this direction and drop the "causal factor" condition altogether in the interest of Aristotelian "due proportion" and fairness? To say that we are all negligent is to say that on other occasions, at least, we have all created unreasonable risk of harms, sometimes great harms, of one kind or another, to other persons. Even in circumstances where excessive harm actually results, we may have created other risks of a different kind to other individuals, risks which luckily failed to eventuate in harm. . . .

The system just described could be called a system of "liability without *contributory* fault," since it bypasses a causation requirement. It is a system of liability based on fault simply, whether or not the fault contributes to harm. It thus differs sharply from the traditional system of liability based in part upon what is called *the fault principle,* which requires that accidental losses be borne

---

[8]If it is given that a particular "his fault" judgment on a particular occasion must single out one or a small number to be assigned the blame, then the concept of "his fault" can perhaps be understood to limit discretion by providing two additional necessary conditions to the triconditional analysis: (4) there is no other person to whom conditions (1)–(3) apply who was substantially more at fault than the present assignee(s); and (5) there is no other person to whom conditions (1)–(3) apply whose act was a more striking deviation from routine, or of a kind patently more manipulable, or otherwise a more "direct" or "substantial" cause. . . .

[9]Hart and Honoré, *op.cit.,* 243.

by the party whose fault the accident was. This is liability based on "his fault" ascriptions, rather than "at fault" imputations. In contrast, the principle underlying a system of liability based on fault without causation might well be called the *retributive theory of torts*. . . .

One way to understand the retributive theory of torts is to relate it to, or derive it from, a general moral theory that bears the name of retributivism. In treating of this more general theory, it is very important to distinguish a strong from a weak version, for failure to do so has muddled discussions of retribution in criminal law and would very likely do the same in discussions of principles of tort liability. According to the strong version of the general retributive principle, *all* evil or, more generally still, all *fault* deserves its comeuppance; it is an end in itself, quite apart from other consequences, that all wrongdoers (or faulty doers) be made to suffer some penalty, handicap, or forfeiture as a requital for their wrongdoing. Similarly, it is an end in itself, morally fitting and proper irrespective of other consequences, that the meritorious be rewarded with the means to happiness. . . .

The weaker version of general retributivism, on the other hand, is essentially a comparative principle, applying to situations in which it is given that someone or other must do without, make a sacrifice, or forfeit his interest. The principle simply asserts the moral priority, *ceteris paribus,* of the innocent party. Put most pithily, it is the principle that *fault forfeits first,* if forfeit there must be. If someone must suffer, it is better, *ceteris paribus,* that it be the faulty than the meritorious. This weaker version of retributivism, which permeates the law, especially the criminal law, has strong support in common sense. It commonly governs the distribution of that special kind of benefit called "the benefit of the doubt," so that, where there is doubt, for example, about the deterrent efficacy of a particular mode of punishment for a certain class of crimes, the benefit of that doubt is given to potential victims instead of convicted criminals.

I find the weaker version of retributivism much more plausible intuitively than the stronger, though even it is limited—for example, by the values of intimacy and friendship. . . .

Now let us return to our tort principles. What is called the "fault principle" (or, better, the "his fault" principle) does not derive from, and indeed is not even compatible with, the strong version of general retributivism. As we have seen, the causal component of "his fault" ascriptions introduces a fortuitous element, repugnant to pure retributivism. People who are very much at fault may luckily avoid causing proportionate harm, and unlucky persons may cause harm in excess of their minor faults. In the former case, little or no harm may be a person's fault even though he is greatly at fault; hence his liability, based on "his fault," will not be the burden he deserves, and the moral universe will be out of joint. In the latter case, unhappily coexistent circumstances may step up the normal magnitude of harm resulting from a minor fault, and again the defendant's liability will not do proper justice to his actual fault.

The tort principle that is called for by strong retributivism is that which I have called "the retributive theory of torts." Being at fault gets its proper comeuppance from this principle, whether or not it leads directly to harm; and the element of luck—except for luck in escaping detection—is largely eliminated. Hence fault suffers its due penalty, and if that is an end in itself, as strong retributivism maintains, then the retributive theory of torts is well recommended indeed. But the lack of intuitive persuasiveness of the general theory, I think, diminishes the plausibility of its offshoot in torts. Weak retributivism, which is generally more plausible, in my opinion, than its strong counterpart, does not uniquely favor either the retributive theory of torts or the "his fault" principle. Except in straightforwardly comparative contexts where the necessity of forfeiture is given, it takes no stand whatever about principles of tort liability. . . .

One final point remains to be made. If we hold that we are all more or less equally sinners in respect to a certain area of conduct or a certain type of fault—if, for example we are all as likely, more or less, to be erring defendants as wronged plaintiffs in driving accident suits—then the principle of strong retributivism itself would call for the jettisoning of the "his fault" principle in that area of activity. If fault is distributed equally, the "his fault" principle, in distributing liability *unequally* among a group, will cause a lack of correspondence between fault and penalty. On the assumption of equal distribution of fault, the use of the "his fault" principle would lead to *less* correspondence, less exact proportioning of penalty to fault, even than various principles of social insurance that have the effect of spreading the losses as widely as possible among a whole community of persons presumed to be equally faulty. But then these schemes of nonfault liability are supported by strong reasons of their own, principles both of justice and economy,[10] and hardly need this bit of surprising added support from the principle of strong retributivism.

18

GEORGE P. FLETCHER

Fairness and Utility in Tort Theory

I. TWO PARADIGMS OF LIABILITY

. . . [T]ort theorists tend to regard the existing doctrinal framework of fault and strict liability as sufficiently rich to express competing views about fairly shifting losses. This conceptual framework accounts for a number of traditional beliefs about tort law history. One of these beliefs is that the ascendancy of fault in the late nineteenth century reflected the infusion of moral sensibility into the law of torts. That new moral sensibility is expressed sometimes as the principle that wrongdoers ought to pay for their wrongs. Another traditional view is that strict tort liability is the analogue of strict criminal liability, and that if the latter is suspect, so is the former. The underlying assumption of both these tenets is that negligence and strict liability are antithetical rationales of liability. This assumed antithesis is readily invoked to explain the ebbs and flows of tort liability. Strict liability is said to have prevailed in early tort history, fault supposedly held sway in the late nineteenth century, with strict liability now gaining ground.

[10]E.g., the *benefit principle* (of commutative justice) that accidental losses should be borne according to the degree to which people benefit from an enterprise or form of activity; the *deep pocket principle* (of distributive justice) that the burden of accidental losses should be borne by those most able to pay in direct proportion to that ability; the *spread-it-out principle* that the cost of accidental losses should be spread as widely as possible "both interpersonally and intertemporally"; the *safety* or *loss-diminution principle* that the method of distributing losses that leads to the smallest net amount of loss to be distributed is the best one.

These beliefs about tort history are ubiquitously held, but to varying degrees they are all false or at best superficial. There has no doubt been a deep ideological struggle in the tort law of the last century and a half. But, as I shall argue, it is not the struggle between negligence and fault on the one hand, and strict liability on the other. Rather, the confrontation is between two radically different paradigms for analyzing tort liability—paradigms which represent a complex of views about (1) the appropriate standard of liability, (2) the appropriate style of legal reasoning, and (3) the relationship between the resolution of individual disputes and the community's welfare.

These paradigms of liability cut across traditional doctrinal lines, creating a deep ideological cleavage between two ways of resolving tort disputes. . . .

Of the two paradigms, I shall call the first the paradigm of reciprocity. According to this view, the two central issues of tort law—whether the victim is entitled to recover and whether the defendant ought to pay—are distinct issues, each resolvable without looking beyond the case at hand. Whether the victim is so entitled depends exclusively on the nature of the victim's activity when he was injured and on the risk created by the defendant. The social costs and utility of the risk are irrelevant, as is the impact of the judgment on socially desirable forms of behavior. Further, according to this paradigm, if the victim is entitled to recover by virtue of the risk to which he was exposed, there is an additional question of fairness in holding the risk creator liable for the loss. This distinct issue of fairness is expressed by asking whether the defendant's creating the relevant risk was excused on the ground, say, that the defendant could not have known of the risk latent in his conduct. To find that an act is excused is in effect to say that there is no rational, fair basis for distinguishing between the party causing harm and other people. Whether we can rationally single out the defendant as the loss-bearer depends on our expectations of when people ought to be able to avoid risks. As will become clear in the course of this discussion, these expectations should not always depend upon the social utility of taking risks; rather they should often depend on non-instrumentalist criteria for judging when men ought to be able to avoid excessive risks of harm. For example, the standard of uncommon "ultra-hazardous activities," introduced by the first *Restatement* is apparently a non-instrumentalist standard: one looks only to the risk and not to its social utility to determine whether it is ultrahazardous. Yet it is never made clear by the *Restatement* why extra-hazardous risks warrant "strict liability" while ordinarily hazardous risks do not.

As part of the explication of the first paradigm of liability, I shall propose a specific standard of risk that makes sense of the *Restatement*'s emphasis on uncommon, extra-hazardous risks, but which shows that the *Restatement*'s theory is part of a larger rationale of liability that cuts across negligence, intentional torts, and numerous pockets of strict liability. The general principle expressed in all of these situations governed by diverse doctrinal standards is that a victim has a right to recover for injuries caused by a risk greater in degree and different in order from those created by the victim and imposed on the defendant—in short, for injuries resulting from nonreciprocal risks. Cases of liability are those in which the defendant generates a disproportionate, excessive risk of harm, relative to the victim's risk-creating activity. For example, a pilot or an airplane owner subjects those beneath the path of flight to nonreciprocal risks of harm. Conversely, cases of nonliability are those of reciprocal risks, namely those in which the victim and the defendant subject each other to roughly the same degree of risk. For example, two airplanes flying in the same vicinity subject each other to reciprocal risks of a mid-air collision. Of course, there are significant problems in determining when risks are nonreciprocal, and we shall turn to these difficulties later. For now, it is sufficient to note that the paradigm of reciprocity represents (1) a bifurcation of the questions of who is entitled to compensation and who ought to pay, (2) a commitment to resolving both of those issues by looking only to the activity of the victim and the risk-creator, and (3) a specific criterion for determining who is entitled to recover for loss, namely all those injured by nonreciprocal risks.

The conflicting paradigm of liability—which I shall call the paradigm of reasonableness—represents a rejection of noninstrumentalist values and a commitment to the community's welfare as the criterion for determining both who is entitled to receive and who ought to pay compensation. Questions that are distinct under the paradigm of reciprocity—namely, is the risk nonreciprocal and was it unexcused—are collapsed in this paradigm into a single test: was the risk unreasonable? The reasonableness of the risk thus determines both whether the victim is entitled to compensation and whether the defendant ought to be held liable. Reasonableness is determined by a straightforward balancing of costs and benefits. If the risk yields a net social utility (benefit), the victim is not entitled to recover from the risk-creator; if the risk yields a net social disutility (cost), the victim is entitled to recover.[1] The premises of this paradigm are that reasonableness provides a test of activities that ought to be encouraged and that tort judgments are an appropriate medium for encouraging them. . . .

II. THE PARADIGM OF RECIPROCITY

A. The Victim's Right to Recover

Our first task is to demonstrate the pervasive reliance of the common law on the paradigm of reciprocity. The area that most consistently reveals this paradigm is the one that now most lacks doctrinal unity—namely, the disparate pockets of strict liability. . . .

I shall attempt to show that the paradigm of reciprocity accounts for the typical cases of strict liability—crashing airplanes,[2] damage done by wild animals,[3] and the more common cases of blasting, fumigating and crop dusting.[4] To do this, I shall consider in detail two leading, but seemingly diverse instances of liability for reasonable risk-taking—*Rylands v. Fletcher*[5] and *Vincent v. Lake Erie Transportation Co.*[6] The point of focusing on these two cases is to generate a foundation for inducing the claim that unexcused nonreciprocity of risk is the unifying feature of a broad spectrum of cases imposing liability under rubrics of both negligence and strict liability.

In *Rylands v. Fletcher* the plaintiff, a coal mine operator, had suffered the flooding of his mine by water that the defendant had pumped into a newly-erected reservoir on his own land. The water broke through to an

---

[1]This is a simpler statement of the balancing test known as the "Learned Hand formula," defined in United States v. Carroll Towing Co., 159 F. 2d 169 (2d Cir. 1947). . . .

[2]*See* . . . PROSSER 514–16.

[3]*E.g.,* Collins v. Otto, 149 Colo. 489, 369 P.2d 564 (1962) (coyote bite); Filburn v. People's Palace & Aquarium Co., 25 Q.B.D. 258 (1890) (escaped circus elephant). *See generally* PROSSER 496–503.

[4]*Eg.,* Exner v. Sherman Power Constr. Co., 54 F.2d 510 (2d Cir. 1931) (storing explosives); Western Geophysical Co. of America v. Mason, 240 Ark. 767, 402 S.W.2d 657 (1966) (blasting); Luthringer v. Moore, 31 Cal. 2d 489, 190 P.2d 1 (1948) (fumigating); Young v. Darter, 363 P.2d 829 (Okla. 1961) (crop dusting).

[5]159 Eng. Rep. 737 (Ex. 1865), *rev'd,* L.R.1 Ex. 265 (1866), *aff'd,* L.R. 3 H.L. 330 (1868).

[6]109 Minn. 456, 124 N.W. 221 (1910).

abandoned mine shaft under the defendant's land and thus found its way to the plaintiff's adjoining mine. The engineers and contractors were negligent in not providing stronger supports for the reservoir; yet because they were independent contractors, the defendant was not liable for their negligence. Though the defendant's erecting and maintaining the reservoir was legally permissible, the Exchequer Chamber found for the plaintiff,[7] and the House of Lords affirmed.[8] Blackburn's opinion in the Exchequer Chamber focused on the defendant's bringing on to his land, for his own purposes, "something which, though harmless whilst it remain there, will naturally do mischief if it escape."[9] Lord Cairns, writing in the House of Lords, reasoned that the defendant's activity rendered his use of the land "non-natural"; accordingly, "that which the Defendants were doing they were doing at their own peril."[10]

Neither Blackburn's nor Cairns' account provides an adequate rationale for liability. It may be that a body of water will "naturally do mischief if it escapes," but so may many other things, like water in a pipe, oil in a furnace tank, and fire in a fireplace. It is unlikely that Blackburn would favor liability for the harmful consequences of these risky practices. Cairns' rationale of non-natural use, for all its metaphysical pretensions, may be closer to the policy issue at stake in the dispute. The fact was that the defendant sought to use his land for a purpose at odds with the use of land then prevailing in the community. He thereby subjected the neighboring miners to a risk to which they were not accustomed and which they would not regard as a tolerable risk entailed by their way of life. Creating a risk different from the prevailing risks in the community might be what Lord Cairns had in mind in speaking of a non-natural use of the land. A better term might have been "abnormal" or "inappropriate" use. Indeed these are the adjectives used in the proposed revision of the *Restatement* to provide a more faithful rendition of the case law tradition of strict liability.[11]

A seemingly unrelated example of the same case law tradition is *Vincent v. Lake Erie Transportation Co.,* a 1910 decision of the Minnesota Supreme Court.[12] The dispute arose from a ship captain's keeping his vessel lashed to the plaintiff's dock during a two-day storm when it would have been unreasonable, indeed foolhardy, for him to set out to sea. The storm battered the ship against the dock, causing damages assessed at five hundred dollars. The court affirmed a judgment for the plaintiff even though a prior case had recognized a ship captain's right to take shelter from a storm by mooring his vessel to another's dock, even without consent.[13] The court's opinion conceded that keeping the ship at dockside was justified and reasonable, yet it characterized the defendant's damaging the dock as "prudently and advisedly [availing]" himself of the plaintiff's property. Because the incident impressed the court as an implicit transfer of wealth, the defendant was bound to rectify the transfer by compensating the dock owner for his loss.[14]

The rationales of *Rylands* and *Vincent* are obviously not interchangeable. Building a reservoir is not availing oneself of a neighbor's property. And mooring a ship to a wharf is not an abnormal or "non-natural" use of either the ship or the wharf. Yet by stripping the two cases of their rhetoric and by focusing on the risks each defendant took, one can bring the two cases within the same general principle. The critical feature of both cases is that the defendant created a risk of harm to the plaintiff that was of an order different from the risks that the plaintiff imposed on the defendant. . . .

Expressing the standard of strict liability as unexcused, nonreciprocal risk-taking provides an account not only of the *Rylands* and *Vincent* decisions, but of strict liability in general. It is apparent, for example, that the uncommon, ultra-hazardous activities pinpointed by the *Restatement* are readily subsumed under the rationale of nonreciprocal risk-taking. If uncommon activities are those with few participants, they are likely to be activities generating nonreciprocal risks. Similarly, dangerous activities like blasting, fumigating, and crop dusting stand out as distinct, nonreciprocal risks in the community. They represent threats of harm that exceed the level of risk to which all members of the community contribute in roughly equal shares.

[7]L.R. 1 Ex. 265 (1866).
[8]L.R. 3 H.L. 330 (1868).
[9]L.R. 1 Ex. at 279.
[10]L.R. 3 H.L. at 339.
[11]Restatement (Second) of Torts §520 (Tent. Draft No 10, 1964).
[12]109 Minn. 456, 124 N.W. 221 (1910).

[13]*See* Ploof v. Putnam, 81 Vt. 471, 71 A. 188 (1908) (defendant dock owner, whose servant unmoored the plaintiff's ship during a storm, held liable for the ensuing damage to the ship and passengers).
[14]109 Minn. at 460, 124 N.W. at 222.

The rationale of nonreciprocal risk-taking accounts as well for pockets of strict liability outside the coverage of the *Restatement*'s sections on extra-hazardous activities. For example, an individual is strictly liable for damage done by a wild animal in his charge, but not for damage committed by his domesticated pet.[15] Most people have pets, children, or friends whose presence creates some risk to neighbors and their property. These are risks that offset each other; they are, as a class, reciprocal risks. Yet bringing an unruly horse into the city goes beyond the accepted and shared level of risks in having pets, children, and friends in one's household. If the defendant creates a risk that exceeds those to which he is reciprocally subject, it seems fair to hold him liable for the results of his aberrant indulgence. . . .

Negligently and intentionally caused harms also lend themselves to analysis as nonreciprocal risks. As a general matter, principles of negligence liability apply in the context of activities, like motoring and sporting ventures, in which the participants all normally create and expose themselves to the same order of risk. These are all pockets of reciprocal risk-taking. . . . To establish liability for harm resulting from these activities, one must show that the harm derives from a specific risk negligently engendered in the course of the activity. Yet a negligent risk, an "unreasonable" risk, is but one that unduly exceeds the bounds of reciprocity. . . .

To complete our account of the paradigm of reciprocity, we should turn to one of its primary expressions: intentional torts, particularly the torts of battery and assault. . . . An intentional assault or battery represents a rapid acceleration of risk, directed at a specific victim. These features readily distinguish the intentional blow from the background of risk. Perceiving intentional blows as a form of nonreciprocal risk helps us understand why the defendant's malice or animosity toward the victim eventually became unnecessary to ground intentional torts.[16] The nonreciprocity of risk, and the deprivation of security it represents, render irrelevant the attitudes of the risk-creator.

All of these manifestations of the paradigm of reciprocity—strict liability, negligence and intentional battery—express the same principle of fairness: all individuals in society have the right to roughly the same degree of security from risk. By analogy to John Rawls' first principle of justice,[17] the principle might read: we all have the right to the maximum amount of security compatible with a like security for everyone else. This means that we are subject to harm, without compensation, from background risks, but that no one may suffer harm from additional risks without recourse for damages against the risk-creator. . . .

B. Excusing Nonreciprocal Risks

If the victim's injury results from a nonreciprocal risk of harm, the paradigm of reciprocity tells us that the victim is entitled to compensation. Should not the defendant then be under a duty to pay? Not always. For the paradigm also holds that nonreciprocal risk-creation may sometimes be excused, and we must inquire further, into the fairness of requiring the defendant to render compensation. We must determine whether there may be factors in a particular situation which would excuse this defendant from paying compensation.

Though the King's Bench favored liability in its 1616 decision of *Weaver v. Ward*,[18] it digressed to list some hypothetical examples where directly causing harm would be excused and therefore exempt from liability. . . .

The hypotheticals of *Weaver v. Ward* correspond to the Aristotelian excusing categories of compulsion and unavoidable ignorance.[19] Each of these has spawned a line of cases denying liability in cases of inordinate risk-creation. The excuse of compulsion has found expression in the emergency doctrine, which excuses excessive risks created in cases in which the defendant is caught in an unexpected, personally dangerous situation. In *Cordas v. Peerless Transportation Co.*, for example, it was thought excusable for a cab driver to jump from his moving cab in order to escape from a threatening gunman on the running board. In view of the crowd of pedestrians

[15]*See, e.g.,* Fowler v. Helck, 278 Ky. 361, 128 S.W. 2d 564 (1939); Warrick v. Farley, 95 Neb. 565, 145 N.W. 1020 (1914).

[16]*See* Vosburg v. Putney, 80 Wis. 523, 50 N.W. 403 (1891). Animosity would obviously be relevant to the issue of punitive damages, *see* PROSSER 9–10, the formal rationales for which are retribution and deterrence, not compensation.

[17]Rawls, *Justice as Fairness,* 67 PHILOSOPHICAL REV. 164, 165 (1958) ("[E]each person participating in a practice, or affected by it, has an equal right to the most extensive liberty compatible with a like liberty for all."). . . .

[18]80 Eng. Rep 284 (K.B. 1616).

[19]THE NICOMACHEAN ETHICS OF ARISTOTLE, [Ross transl. World Classics ed. 1954] Book III, ch. 1, at 48 ("Those things, then, are thought involuntary, which take place under compulsion or owing to ignorance.")

nearby, the driver clearly took a risk that generated a net danger to human life. It was thus an unreasonable, excessive, and unjustified risk. Yet the overwhelmingly coercive circumstances meant that he, personally, was excused from fleeing the moving cab. An example of unavoidable ignorance excusing risk-creation is *Smith v. Lampe,* in which the defendant honked his horn in an effort to warn a tug that seemed to be heading toward shore in a dense fog. As it happened, the honking coincided with a signal that the tug captain expected would assist him in making port. Accordingly the captain steered his tug toward the honking rather than away from it. That the defendant did not know of the prearranged signal excused his contributing to the tug's going aground. Under the facts of the case, the honking surely created an unreasonable risk of harm. If instantaneous injunctions were possible, one would no doubt wish to enjoin the honking as an excessive, illegal risk. Yet the defendant's ignorance of that risk was also excusable. Under the circumstances he could not fairly have been expected to inform himself of all possible interpretations of honking in a dense fog. . . .

. . . [W]e can formulate two significant claims about the role of excuses in cases decided under the paradigm of reciprocity. First, excusing the risk-creator does not, in principle, undercut the victim's right to recover. In most cases it is operationally irrelevant to posit a right to recovery when the victim cannot in fact recover from the excused risk-creator. . . .

Secondly, an even more significant claim is that these excuses—compulsion and unavoidable ignorance—are available in all cases in which the right to recovery springs from being subjected to a nonreciprocal risk of harm. We have already pointed out the applicability of these excuses in negligence cases like *Cordas* and *Smith v. Lampe.* What is surprising is to find them applicable in cases of strict liability as well; strict liability is usually thought of as an area where courts are insensitive to questions of fairness to defendants. . . . In *Madsen v. East Jordan Irrigation Co.,*[20] for example, the defendant's blasting operations frightened the mother mink on the plaintiff's farm, causing them to kill 230 of their offspring. The Utah Supreme Court affirmed a demurrer to the complaint. In the court's judgment, the reaction of the mother mink "was not within the realm of matters to be anticipated."[21] This is precisely the factual judgment that would warrant saying that the company's ignorance of this possible result was excused, yet the rubric of proximate cause provided a doctrinally acceptable heading for dismissing the complaint.

It is hard to find a case of strict liability raising the issue of compulsion as an excuse. Yet if a pilot could flee a dangerous situation only by taking off in his plane, as the cab driver in *Cordas* escaped danger by leaping from his moving cab, would there be rational grounds for distinguishing damage caused by the airplane crash from damage caused by *Cordas'* cab? One would think not. Both are cases of nonreciprocal risk-taking and both are cases in which unusual circumstances render it unfair to expect the defendant to avoid the risk he creates. . . .

III. THE PARADIGM OF REASONABLENESS

. . . In the course of the nineteenth century, . . . the concepts underlying the paradigm of reciprocity gradually assumed new contours. A new paradigm emerged, which challenged all traditional ideas of tort theory. . . .

The core of this revolutionary change was a shift in the meaning of the word "fault." At its origins in the common law of torts, the concept of fault served to unify the medley of excuses available to defendants who would otherwise be liable in trespass for directly causing harm. As the new paradigm emerged, fault came to be an inquiry about the context and the reasonableness of the defendant's risk-creating conduct. . . .

The difference between justifying and excusing conditions is most readily seen in the case of intentional conduct, particularly intentional crimes. Typical cases of justified intentional conduct are self-defense and the use of force to effect an arrest. These justificatory claims assess the reasonableness of using force under the circumstances. The questions asked in seeking to justify an intentional battery as self-defense

[20] 101 Utah 552, 125 P.2d 794 (1942).

[21] *Id.* at 555, 125 P.2d at 795.

relate to the social costs and the social benefits of using force and to the wrongfulness of the initial aggressor's conduct in attacking the defendant. The resolution of this cost-benefit analysis speaks to the legal permissibility and sometimes to the commendability of the *act* of using force under the circumstances. Excuses, in contrast, focus not on the costs and benefits of the *act,* but on the degree of the *actor's* choice in engaging in it. Insanity and duress are raised as excuses even to concededly wrongful acts. To resolve a claim of insanity, we are led to inquire about the *actor's* personality, his capacities under stress and the pressures under which he was acting. Finding that the *actor* is excused by reason of insanity is not to say that the *act* was right or even permissible, but merely that the actor's freedom of choice was so impaired that he cannot be held accountable for his wrongful deed. . . .

That the fault requirement shifted its orientation from excusing to justifying risks had the following consequences: (1) fault became a judgement about the risk, rather than about the responsibility of the individual who created the risk; (2) fault was no longer a question of fairness to the individual, but an inquiry about the relative costs and benefits of particular risks; (3) fault became a condition for recognizing the right of the victim to recover. These three postures of the fault requirement diverged radically from the paradigm of reciprocity. Together, they provided the foundation for the paradigm of reasonableness, a way of thinking that was to become a powerful ideological force in tort thinking of the late nineteenth and twentieth centuries.

The reasonable man became a central, almost indispensable figure in the paradigm of reasonableness. By asking what a reasonable man would do under the circumstances, judges could assay the issues both of justifying and excusing risks. Reasonable men, presumably, seek to maximize utility; therefore to ask what a reasonable man would do is to inquire into the justifiability of the risk. . . .

No single appellate decision ushered in the paradigm of reasonableness. It derived from a variety of sources. If there was a pivotal case, however, it was *Brown v. Kendall,* decided by the Massachusetts Supreme Judicial Court in 1850. . . .

. . . Chief Justice Shaw's opinion created possibilities for an entirely new and powerful use of the fault standard, and the judges and writers of the late nineteenth and early twentieth centuries responded sympathetically.

Shaw's revision of tort doctrine made its impact in cases in which the issue was not one of excusing inadvertent risk-creation, but one of justifying risks of harm that were voluntarily and knowingly generated. Consider the following case of risk-creation: . . . the defendant police officer shoots at a fleeing felon, knowing that he thereby risks hitting a bystander. . . . All of these victims could receive compensation for their injuries under the paradigm of reciprocity, as incorporated in the doctrine of trespassory liability; the defendant or his employees directly and without excuse caused the harm in each case. Yet as *Brown v. Kendall* was received into the tort law, the threshold of liability became whether, under all the circumstances, the defendant acted with ordinary, prudent care. But more importantly, the test of ordinary care transcended its origins as a standard for determining the acceptability of ignorance as an excuse, and became a rationale for determining when individuals could knowingly and voluntarily create risks without responsibility for the harm they might cause. The test for justifying risks became a straightforward utilitarian comparison of the benefits and costs of the defendant's risk-creating activity. The assumption emerged that reasonable men do what is justified by a utilitarian calculus, that justified activity is lawful, and that lawful activities should be exempt from tort liability.

In the case mentioned above, the arguments are readily at hand for maximizing utility by optimizing accidents: . . . capturing fleeing felons is sufficiently important to warrant a few risks to onlookers. . . . More generally, if promoting the general welfare is the criterion of rights and duties of compensation, then a few individuals must suffer. One might fairly wonder, however, why . . . law enforcement . . . should prosper at the expense of innocent victims.

IV. UTILITY AND THE INTERESTS OF THE INDIVIDUAL

The accepted reading of tort history is that the rise of the fault standard in the nineteenth century manifested a newly found sensitivity to the morality of legal rules. James Barr Ames captured orthodox sentiments with his conclusion that "[t]he ethical standard of reasonable conduct has replaced the unmoral standard of acting at one's peril."[22]. . .

But the issue in the nineteenth century was not the choice between strict liability on the one hand and liability based on fault on the other. Nor was it a simplistic choice between an "unmoral" standard and an ethical one. Rather, the question of the time was the shape that the fault standard would take. Should the absence of fault function as an excuse within a paradigm of reciprocity? Or should it function as a standard for exempting from liability risks that maximize utility? That was the moral and policy question that underlay the nineteenth century revolution in tort thinking. The question posed by the conflict of paradigms was whether traditional notions of individual autonomy would survive increasing concern for the public welfare. If the courts of the time had clearly perceived and stated the issue, they would have been shaken by its proportions. . . .

V. THE INTERPLAY OF SUBSTANCE AND STYLE

The conflict between the paradigm of reasonableness and the paradigm of reciprocity is, in the end, a struggle between two strategies for justifying the distribution of burdens in a legal system. . . .

On the whole, however, the paradigm of reasonableness still holds sway over the thinking of American courts. The reasonable man is too popular a figure to be abandoned. The use of litigation to pursue social goals is well entrenched. Yet the appeal to the paradigm might well be more one of style than substance. . . .

The paradigm of reciprocity, on the other hand, for all its substantive and moral appeal, puts questions that are hardly likely to engage the contemporary legal mind: When is a risk so excessive that it counts as a nonreciprocal risk? When are two risks of the same category and thus reciprocally offsetting? . . .

. . . Yet why should the rhetoric of reasonableness and foreseeability appeal to lawyers as a more scientific or precise way of thinking? The answer might lie in the scientific image associated with passing through several stages of argument before reaching a conclusion. The paradigm of reasonableness requires several stages of analysis: defining the risk, assessing its consequences, balancing costs and benefits. The paradigm of reciprocity requires a single conclusion, based on perceptions of similarities, of excessiveness, and of directness. If an argument requires several steps, it basks in the respectability of precision and rationality. Yet associating rationality with multistaged argumentation may be but a spectacular lawyerly fallacy. . . .

[22]Ames, Law and Morals [22 Harv. L. Rev. 97, 99 (1908)].

19

JULES L. COLEMAN

Tort Liability and the Limits of Corrective Justice

This essay tries to make sense of and defend both of the following claims: . . . (1) Many of the important rights and duties sustained in tort law are justifiable departures from tort law's corrective justice core; and (2) the extent to which corrective justice (as a moral principle) creates reasons for acting in a community depends on the nature and scope of nonmoral, including legal, practices. So it is a mistake to think of law only in terms of the extent to which it implements or is otherwise influenced by morality. The scope of morality can itself be determined in part by legal practice; or so I will argue.

FOUR KINDS OF CASES

With regard to the claim that many of the duties sustained in tort law do not implement corrective justice, it will be helpful to distinguish among four different kinds of cases.

1. The victim has suffered a loss owing to the fault of the injurer or as a result of a right of his being invaded. The victim's loss is imposed on the injurer whose fault or conduct is responsible for it.
2. The victim has suffered a loss owing to the fault of the injurer or as a result of a right of his being invaded. The victim's loss is imposed on

someone other than his injurer, someone who is not responsible for the occurrence.

3. The victim has suffered a loss that is no one's fault and which does not involve a right of his being invaded. (For example, he loses out to another in a competitive business context.) The victim's loss is imposed on the party whose conduct is causally responsible for the loss, but who is otherwise faultless.
4. The victim has suffered a loss that is no one's fault and which does not involve a right of his being invaded. But instead of the loss being imposed on the party whose conduct is causally responsible for the loss (as in case 3), it is imposed on someone else altogether.

Whereas tort law provides us with examples of all four kinds of cases, only cases of the first sort implicate corrective justice. If I am right that corrective justice represents the core of tort law, then these other cases must be departures from corrective justice. The question is whether, and under what conditions, these departures are justifiable or defensible.

Suppose a manufacturer provides an ineffective (or inefficient) warning. It is inefficient because it fails fully or adequately to warn and, therefore, to deter. Someone uses the product and injures himself as a result. In order for his loss to be wrongful under corrective justice, the warning would have had to be ineffective; the victim would have had to have read it; had the warning been adequate it would have deterred him from using the product; he would have had to use the product believing that it was safe for him and so on. An optimal warning would have deterred him from using the product had he read it. The warning on the product would not have. In fact, the victim never read the warning. The warning is not optimal, but it does not in fact contribute to the victim's loss. Though there is no denying that the manufacturer is at fault, the victim's loss is not the manufacturer's fault. The victim has suffered a loss, but not one for which he has a claim in corrective justice to repair. One might even say that the loss is his own fault.

Nevertheless, a court might well impose liability on the product manufacturer for the purpose of encouraging more efficient warnings. Though he has no right to it, compensation provides the victim with an incentive to litigate. By litigating, he acts as a private regulator. The manufacturer has a defective warning that needs to be improved. If part of the goal of the law is to encourage product manufacturers to provide optimal warnings, why should a court wait until a victim comes along who has a valid claim to repair in justice? The goal of encouraging efficient warnings does not discriminate between those victims who have suffered wrongful losses and those who have not.

Presumably few would object if the state fined the manufacturer an amount equal to the damage that results from a defective warning. Suppose the money from that fine were to go toward funding the relevant public regulatory scheme. In private litigation, the victim is acting as a private prosecutor. The liability judgment works like a fine. Instead of funding the public regulatory scheme, it funds a private regulatory scheme. On what grounds could one object to holding the manufacturer liable to the "victim"? He is being paid to "prosecute."

The plausibility or desirability of the private prosecutor approach does not depend on the legitimacy of the underlying claim. Whether or not the victim has a right in corrective justice to repair, imposing his loss on the manufacturer can be defended on the grounds that it creates an attractive system of incentives to litigate and to invest in safety.

Here, then, is a case in which the plaintiff recovers against a defendant, though they are not brought together by considerations of corrective justice. The defendant has acted wrongfully, but his wrongdoing is not responsible for the plaintiff's loss. The plaintiff has no right to repair in justice; the defendant has no duty either.

This sort of case differs, therefore, from others in which the plaintiff has a right to repair in justice, but liability for his loss is imposed on someone other than the wrongdoer or injurer. Let's now consider such cases.

LIABILITY AND THE CHEAPEST COST-AVOIDER

In the case I am imagining, the victim has a claim in justice to repair, but the defendant does not have a duty in justice to him. The interesting feature of this case is that someone other than the defendant owes a duty of repair to the victim. Thus, there are the victim who has the sort of claim that would be valid under the principle of corrective justice, as well as an agent who has the duty to the victim because he is responsible for having created the loss, and some third party who the court is prepared to hold liable to the victim because he is the cheapest cost-avoider, though he is in no way responsible for the harm. (For example, suppose you wrongfully injure me causing me substantial damage, but instead of me suing you, I sue your Dean who is not responsible for my loss or your conduct, but who, I believe, might be a good person to sue for a variety of reasons. Perhaps he has "deeper" pockets, or he is the cheapest cost-avoider, that is, he can optimally reduce (in the future) the probability of harm at the lowest cost.)

Were the court to impose liability on the cheapest cost-avoider, it would be enforcing a claim valid in corrective justice, but it would not otherwise be implementing corrective justice (it would not be imposing the loss on someone who has the duty to repair it). The question here is whether in imposing the victim's loss on the third party tort law violates corrective justice.

One reason for thinking that imposing the victim's loss on someone other than the individual who has the moral duty to repair it is wrong in that the third party does not volunteer to have the loss imposed upon him; another is that the third party is innocent of wrongdoing. Suppose Donald Trump volunteers to pay all my debts of repair. If he pays them off, all claims against me are extinguished thereby; no injustice is done. The example suggests that someone other than the injurer can shoulder the victim's loss without violating corrective justice. In that example, however, Trump volunteers to bear my costs, and it is for that reason, one might say, that no violation of corrective justice occurs. Had my costs been imposed on him without his consent, our moral assessment of the situation would have been very different. This suggests that corrective justice is violated when the costs of accidents are imposed on someone who does not agree so to bind herself.

Involuntariness is not an adequate criterion of wrongfulness, however. . . .

Neither the cheapest cost-avoider nor the wrongdoer agrees to bear the victim's costs. Though neither agrees to shoulder the relevant costs, there is an obvious difference between them; the cheapest cost-avoider is, ex hypothesi, innocent of mischief, the wrongdoer is not. This suggests that the reason that it is permissible to impose the victim's loss upon the wrongdoer, but not on the cheapest cost-avoider (if he is not the wrongdoer), is that the latter is innocent of wrongdoing, whereas the former is not. The reason that imposing the victim's loss on the cheapest cost-avoider violates corrective justice, then, is that corrective justice prohibits imposing losses on innocent persons. Thus, imposing the loss on the wrongdoer is compatible with corrective justice (even required by it perhaps), but imposing the same loss on the cheapest cost-avoider violates justice.

In fact, imposing liability on someone innocent of wrongdoing need not constitute a corrective injustice. Innocent individuals can sometimes have a duty in corrective justice to repair. Far from being an offense to justice, imposing liability on them may be required by it. An individual who justifiably infringes the right of another may have a duty in justice to repair, a duty grounded in the fact that his conduct constitutes a wrong to the person injured. . . .

By showing that it is not always permissible to impose a loss on an innocent and unwilling party, we have not shown that the state would always be justified in doing so. . . . For all we have shown, the state may have authority to impose liability on someone only if they have a duty in corrective justice to repair. It's just that innocence and voluntariness are not essential to determining whether a person has such a duty.

On the other hand, we could view these examples as illustrating a different point, namely that the state must have a good reason for imposing liability. If it does not, then it acts beyond the scope of its authority, and in doing so, it may impose its own corrective injustices. . . .

The manufacturing example shows that creating a system of effective incentives to reduce the incidence of accidents could count as a good reason for imposing liability. In that case imposing the victim's loss on the cheapest cost-avoider would not violate corrective justice.

If the state is free to impose liability on the wrongdoer (under the auspices of corrective justice) or on the cheapest cost-avoider (under the auspices of efficiency consistent with corrective justice), then, provided the costs of searching out the best risk reducer are low enough, why would the state ever choose to implement corrective justice?[1] If the state chooses to implement corrective justice, then it will miss an opportunity to create a scheme of accident-cost-minimizing incentives, and for no good reason. As long as the victim who has a claim in corrective justice is compensated, why should the state foolishly impose the loss on the person with the moral duty in corrective justice to make repair if imposing it on the cheapest cost-avoider promises to accomplish some good and does not itself violate corrective justice? And, remember, imposing the loss on the cheapest cost-avoider does not violate corrective justice because the state has a good reason for imposing the loss on him, and therefore does him (the cheapest cost-avoider) no wrong.

If this is a sound argument, then it is problematic that a state would ever concern itself with making sure that the victim's loss is imposed on the party who has the duty in corrective justice to repair it. As long as the victim is compensated and some good is accomplished by imposing the loss on someone who can do something about such losses, why bother? But the argument may not be sound. Imposing the loss on an innocent cheapest cost-avoider may in fact violate corrective justice. What might the argument that it does look like?

... Perhaps the real problem with imposing the victim's loss on the cheapest cost-avoider is that it is unjust to do so *when there is someone else who has the duty in corrective justice to make repair.* It may be permissible to impose a loss on the cheapest cost-avoider, even if that person is free of mischief and unwilling to bear the costs voluntarily—provided there is no individual who has a duty in justice to bear those costs. If there is such a person, as there is in our example, then imposing the loss on the cheapest cost-avoider is wrongful for exactly that reason. . . .

... This conclusion follows only if corrective justice demands an absolute priority with respect to all other goals the state may legitimately pursue within a tort system. This conclusion cannot be sustained, however.

We might distinguish between two different ways in which imposing liability on someone unconnected or otherwise not responsible for an accident's occurrence might be viewed as imposing a wrongful loss. In one case there are no good reasons whatsoever for imposing the loss on her. She did not cause the harm; she was not negligent or otherwise at fault in any way; nor is she in a good position to reduce or spread risk. In this sense, the loss is imposed on her for no good reason connected to any plausible account of the point or purpose of accident law; it is imposed entirely without justification, and is wrongful in that sense. . . .

Suppose, instead, that there exist good reasons of the sort recognized as legitimate within the relevant political morality for imposing the loss on her. Perhaps, she is the optimal risk-reducer. In the sense of wrongful just characterized, imposing liability would not be wrongful. However, we can imagine another sense of the term or criterion for its application that makes it wrongful to impose liability (even if there are good reasons of the sort the state is authorized to implement for doing so), that is, whenever liability could have been imposed on someone else who has the duty in corrective justice to make repair. Because there are good reasons for imposing the loss in some way other than that dictated by corrective justice, the only ground for holding that doing so is wrongful is that any such liability judgment forgoes the opportunity to do corrective justice. And that in turn can be wrongful only if doing corrective justice has some kind of absolute priority over other legitimate goals the state may pursue through its tort system.

I accept the first and reject the second way in which imposing losses on third parties can constitute a corrective injustice. The state must allocate costs for a reason that is within its authority to implement, and it must do so in a way that falls within the constraints of the relevant principles of justice and political morality. If it has no good reason of the relevant sort for imposing liability, it violates corrective justice, and, very likely, other principles of justice as well. On the other hand, if it acts on the basis of good reasons within the scope of its authority, it does not violate corrective justice, even though it does not implement it. Imposing the loss on an innocent third party may not be a good idea on other grounds, but it is not wrongful just because in doing so the state misses a chance to impose the loss on that person who has the duty in corrective justice. On the other hand, imposing the loss on a third party who is not a good risk-reducer or -spreader may create a wrongful loss, whether or not there is someone who has the duty in corrective justice to make repair, simply because there exists no justification for imposing the loss on him. The fact that someone has a duty to make repair in corrective justice has little, if anything, to do with the wrongfulness of imposing liability without a good reason for doing so.

In this account, corrective justice does not invariably or absolutely cancel or override reasons for acting that the state may be otherwise authorized to implement. It has no absolute priority with respect to the state's other legitimate goals. . . .

LIMITING CORRECTIVE JUSTICE

. . . Implementing corrective justice requires a set of substantive liability rules, for example, a rule of liability for negligence. In addition to substantive liability rules, implementing corrective justice requires administrative rules establishing burdens of proof and evidence. . . .

Two cases famous in torts case books help to illustrate the relationship between administrative rules and the principles they are designed to implement. Consider first *Ybarra v. Spangard.*[2] In *Ybarra,* the plaintiff undergoes surgery, and, while under general anesthetic, is apparently mistreated. The plaintiff can establish neither negligence or responsibility. He can prove that he suffered an injury. The court holds that the most plausible explanation of his injury suggests negligence on someone's part. The court applies the doctrine of res ipsa loquitur in order to shift the burden of proof to the defendants to show that no negligence transpired. In effect, the court holds that under the circumstances, each of the named parties within the operating room should have the burden of showing that he or she was not the responsible party. A defendant who cannot show that he or she was not responsible will remain subject to liability. And this will be true even if that defendant is not someone who has the duty in corrective justice to repair; even if, moreover, that person is not in a good position to reduce or spread the relevant risk.

Nevertheless, it is easy to see how such a rule for shifting the burden of proof could be thought of as constituting a plausible way of implementing corrective justice. In *Ybarra,* the best way for a defendant to free herself of the burden of liability is to identify the party who is responsible for the plaintiff's misfortune. Presumably, at least some of the defendants know who that person is. Being excused from liability provides each defendant with the incentive to reveal that information. If the information is revealed, then that person who is in fact responsible for the loss will be solely liable for it, and corrective justice will have been served.[3]

Summers v. Tice[4] can be given a similar rationale. In that case, two hunters negligently fire in the direction of a third. The plaintiff is hit by one bullet, but there is no way he can determine whose bullet is responsible for his injury. If, in order to recover, he had to identify the responsible party, he would be out of luck. Instead, the court allows the burden to be shifted to the defendants, both of whom acted negligently. Either could free himself of liability by showing that his bullet was not the effective one. In that case the other party whose bullet is responsible for the damage would be solely liable and corrective justice done. As it happens, the defendants are in no better position to identify the responsible bullet than is the plaintiff. Neither can free himself of liability. Both are liable to the plaintiff, when in fact only one has the duty in corrective justice to repair. Still, it is a mistake to infer that *Summers* marks a departure from corrective justice simply because someone other than the person who has the relevant duty must bear some of the costs. Rather, the outcome in *Summers* is a predictable consequence of applying evidentiary rules designed to implement corrective justice under conditions of uncertainty.

It is tempting to extend the rationale of *Summers* to modern tort cases like *Sindell*[5] and *Hymowitz.*[6] If *Summers* can be understood as an effort to extend the ambit of corrective justice, then *Sindell* and *Hymowitz* might be subject to a similar analysis. In each case plaintiffs had been injured as the result of diethylstilbestrol (DES) administered to their mothers during pregnancy as a miscarriage preventive, and the defendants were the manufacturers and marketers of the drug. During the period the defendants marketed DES, they knew or should have known that it causes cancerous or precancerous vaginal and cervical growths in the daughters of the mothers who took it, but they failed to test for efficacy and safety or to warn of its potential danger. Because of the passage of time between ingestion of the drug by the mother and harm to the daughter, and the large number of manufacturers using the same drug formula, the plaintiffs in DES cases usually are not able to identify which defendant manufactured the drug ingested by their respective mothers.

Although the court in *Sindell* found inapplicable theories of "alternate liability," "concert of action" liability, and industry-wide ("enterprise") liability, it adopted a "market share" theory in order to find for the plaintiffs. Under the court's market share formula, the plaintiff joins as defendant the manufacturers of a substantial share of the particular market of DES from which her mother might have taken. Damages are apportioned to each defendant's share of that particular market, and each defendant may cross-claim against other manufacturers or demonstrate that it, in fact, could not have produced the particular drug ingested by the plaintiff's mother. . . .

Following the line of reasoning in *Ybarra* and *Summers,* one could argue that the burden can be shifted legitimately to each of the many defendants to show that he is not responsible for anyone's wrongdoing. Indeed, that is part of the holding in *Sindell.* In other words, if a particular defendant can show that none of the drugs he manufactures is responsible for any of the harms suffered by members of the plaintiff class, he can free himself of liability. Because there is no practical way of determining which harms are the responsibility of those manufacturers who are not able to free themselves of liability, the court adopts the principle that each should be liable for that percentage of the total damages that corresponds to its share of the market. This is the principle of market share liability. If market share is a reasonable proxy for causal responsibility, then one can view *Sindell* as an extension of *Summers* and *Ybarra,* which in turn can be understood as efforts to pursue the overarching goal of corrective justice when facing substantial epistemic obstacles.

The problem with this, the standard interpretation of *Sindell,* is revealed by the ruling in *Hymowitz.* In *Hymowitz,* one of the defendants in fact establishes that his product is not causally responsible for any of the harms suffered by members of the plaintiff class. Under the *Sindell* formula, any defendant who can establish his freedom from causal responsibility is able to free himself of liability. The *Hymowitz* court, however, rejects this option, and allows the defendant liability reflecting his share of the national market.

One response to *Hymowitz* is to treat it as a mistake that does not conform to the administration of corrective justice story we have been weaving. Another alternative is to contend that *Hymowitz* in fact fits within the corrective justice account of tort law. This is Richard Wright's view.[7] According to Wright, *Hymowitz* establishes that the relevant *harm* for which people can be justly held liable in torts (in cases of this sort) is the *wrongful imposition of risk.* The defendant in *Hymowitz* cannot show that he did not impose unjustifiable risks. Indeed, he did. All he can show is that the risks he imposed did not mature into full blown harms of the relevant sort. . . .

The problem with Wright's argument is that it is unmotivated and ad hoc. It is not helpful to say that *Hymowitz* introduces another category of harms particularly appropriate to cases of a certain sort (market share cases). Either the imposition of unjustifiable risk is the relevant harm in all cases, both those in which the risk matures and those in which it does not, or it is not. One cannot claim that in the uncomplicated torts case, the relevant harm is the injury the victim suffers whereas in other cases in which this conception of the harm is problematic—those like *Hymowitz*—the relevant harm is the risk imposed. This is simply an ad hoc solution to a difficult problem. . . .

The standard interpretation rejects *Hymowitz* as a mistake, an unjustifiable departure from tort law's preoccupation with implementing corrective justice under the conditions of uncertainty bound to obtain. To his credit, Wright rejects this interpretation. His mistake is in thinking that *Hymowitz* can be defended as a form of corrective justice in which the relevant harm is the wrongful imposition of risk. The best interpretation of *Hymowitz,* however, does not view it as a mistake or as an attempt to implement corrective justice for a distinct category of harms. To understand *Hymowitz* and *Sindell,* we have to consider the principle of corrective justice once again.

Suppose that we all lived in New Zealand or that our community, wherever it was, decided to implement a no-fault plan like New Zealand's. Let's now set aside all questions about whether doing so would be a smart or otherwise desirable thing to do. The question we need to address is in what way does this no-fault plan affect or otherwise relate to the principle of corrective justice? . . .

. . . The New Zealand plan neither affronts corrective justice, nor is its existence irrelevant to corrective justice . . . [because] whether or not corrective justice in fact imposes moral duties on particular individuals is *conditional* upon the existence of other institutions for making good victims' claims to repair. The capacity within a particular community of corrective justice to impose the relevant *moral* duties depends on the existence of certain *legal* or *political* institutions or social practices. . . .

The view I am suggesting is that whether or not corrective justice itself imposes moral duties on individuals in a community will depend on other practices that are in effect. The reason is this. Corrective justice links agents with losses. It provides individuals with agent-relative reasons for acting. These reasons for acting can be superseded by other practices that create reasons for acting, both agent-neutral and agent-relative. Such practices can sometimes sever the relationship between agents and losses. The victim's wrongful loss may give her a right to recover. That right is part of the normative basis for imposing a duty to repair. The nature and scope of the duty depend on the practices in place. The content of the duty and the reasons for acting to which it gives rise do not follow logically from the nature of the right to repair, but from the normative practices in place within the community, practices that, in conjunction with the victim's right, give rise to specific obligations.

My view is not that other social and legal practices sever all of the relationships between wrongdoer and victim. After all, the wrongdoer may be responsible for the victim's loss. The question is to which duties does this relationship give rise. And my argument is that the nature and scope of the duties depend on the prevailing practices. Moreover, even if no-fault practices exist for handling accident costs, the injurer, and no one else, may have the duty to apologize, or the like.

The question before the state is not whether to forgo corrective justice; instead, it is, what ought to be done about losses including those that result from wrongful conduct. If there is a comprehensive plan put into effect for dealing with those losses by imposing them on everyone or on all those individuals who are at fault, whether or not their fault results in harm to others, then corrective justice itself imposes no duties within that community.[8] Thus, although corrective justice is private justice—justice between the parties—whether or not it imposes obligations between the parties depends on other social, political and legal practices. This, I take it, is a controversial, but I think inescapable truth about corrective justice. It may be true of other moral principles as well.

If corrective justice is conditional in this sense, then the state may choose to allocate accident costs in any number of ways. . . .

With this discussion in mind, let's return to the troubling cases of *Sindell* and *Hymowitz*. . . .

The problem comes from trying to reconcile *Sindell* with *Hymowitz*. According to *Sindell*, although at fault, a defendant who could establish that his fault was not responsible for anyone's damage would free himself of liability. In *Hymowitz*, the absence of responsibility is inadequate to free the defendant of liability. *Hymowitz* is, in fact, the correct interpretation of the basic principles set forth in *Sindell*. *Sindell* is not an extension of corrective justice. Instead, it involves a localized at-fault plan. . . .

. . . One can have either a corrective justice scheme or an at-fault pool but not both at the same time. For that reason, *Sindell* does not fully comprehend the underlying principles of liability that it creates. It is caught between two paradigms: corrective justice and at-fault liability. Perhaps, the *Sindell* court fails to see that the two cannot be reconciled; perhaps the court believes that imposing liability on the basis of fault or market share is at the heart of corrective justice, and that because it is, any defendant who can in fact show that he did not cause any harm should be able to free himself of liability. Whatever the reason, *Sindell* is torn between two conflicting approaches to allocating the relevant costs: one that imposes the duty in corrective justice; the other that imposes losses according to a localized at-fault scheme. Therefore, rather than being an unjustifiable departure from the logic of *Sindell*, *Hymowitz* represents the correct understanding of *Sindell*'s underlying logic.

NOTES

1. For the sake of this argument we are assuming that the wrongdoer is not the cheapest cost-avoider, although there is no reason to think that the two will always be different individuals. We are concerned with that case in which they are different, however, because we want to know whether imposing the loss on the cheapest cost-avoider violates corrective justice, and it could only if the two were different individuals.
2. Ybarra v. Spangard, 25 Cal. 2d 486, 154 P.2d 687 (1944).
3. It is a further question whether such a burden shifting rule will actually prove effective. The point here is simply to illustrate how various rules can

still be interpreted as part of a general plan to implement an ideal, say, of corrective justice, even if the results the rules generate in particular cases do not fully correspond to the results corrective justice would require.

4. Summers v. Tice, 33 Cal. 2d. 80, 199 P.2d 1 (1948).
5. Sindell v. Abbott Laboratories, 26 Cal. 3d 588, 607 P.2d 924, 163 Cal. Rptr. 132 (1980).
6. Hymowitz v. Eli Lilly and Co., 73 N.Y. 2d 487, 539 N.E. 2d 941 (1989), cert. denied sub nom. Rexall Drug Co. v. Tigue, 110 S. Ct. 350 (1989).
7. Richard W. Wright, "Responsibility, risk, probability, naked statistics, and proof: Pruning the bramble bush by clarifying the concepts" 73 *Iowa L. Rev.* 1001 (1988).
8. There are some conditions that must be satisfied before this is valid. First, the victims must be fully compensated under the alternative plan, or they must be as fully compensated under the alternative as they would be under a scheme that implements corrective justice. Second, the alternative must accomplish some additional goals not secured by a corrective justice plan. Third, the alternative must conform to the relevant demands of justice and morality.

   In my earlier work, I claimed that the duties in corrective justice could be discharged by parties other than those who are responsible for creating wrongful losses. Thus, my claim was that no-fault plans were ways of discharging duties in corrective justice (provided other conditions like those mentioned above were met). I still accept the claim that it is possible for someone other than the wrongdoer to discharge the wrongdoer's obligations, otherwise insurance would be unthinkable, but I reject the idea that no-fault plans are ways of meeting the demands of corrective justice. Instead, certain practices simply mean that no duties in corrective justice arise in a particular community. Thus, it is not as if New Zealand has an unusual approach to meeting the demands of corrective justice with respect to accident-related losses. Rather, in New Zealand, there is no practice of corrective justice with respect to such losses. After all, in corrective justice, the faulty injurer has a duty to repair, and under the plans we are talking about, there simply is no agent-relative duty of any sort. The victim's right grounds a duty, but the duty it grounds depends on the practice. The practice of corrective justice imposes that duty on the faulty injurer. Other practices or social conventions might well impose different duties.

   Whereas I used to say that other practices can *discharge* the wrongdoer's duty, I now say that such practices either *extinguish* duties in corrective justice that would otherwise arise or that duties in corrective justice simply do not arise. The difference between the latter two approaches is important. In one view, corrective justice is like a default rule. If no other practices of the appropriate sort exist, then corrective justice does, and it imposes duties of a certain agent-relative kind. In the other, if there is no practice of corrective justice, there are no duties of corrective justice, whatever other practices may exist. I have settled on a view about which of these alternatives is correct, but everything I have said so far is compatible with both interpretations.

20

RICHARD A. EPSTEIN

A Theory of Strict Liability

INTRODUCTION

Torts is at once one of the simplest and one of the most complex areas of the law. It is simple because it concerns itself with fact patterns that can be understood and appreciated without the benefit of formal legal instruction. . . .

But the simplicity of torts based upon its use of ordinary language is deceptive. . . . While an intuitive appreciation of the persistent features of ordinary language may help decide easy cases, more is required for the solution of those difficult cases where the use of ordinary language pulls in different directions at the same time. There is need for a systematic inquiry which refines, but which does not abandon, the shared impressions of everyday life. The task is to develop a normative theory of torts that takes into account common sense notions of individual responsibility. . . .

This common sense approach to torts as a branch of common law stands in sharp opposition to much of the recent scholarship on the subject because it does not regard economic theory as the primary means to establish the rules of legal responsibility. A knowledge of the economic consequences of alternative legal arrangements can be of great importance, but even among those who analyze tort in economic terms there is acknowledgment of certain questions of "justice" or "fairness" rooted in common sense beliefs that cannot be explicated in terms of economic theory.[1] . . . But once it is admitted that there are questions of fairness as between the parties that are not answerable in economic terms, the exact role of economic argument in the solution of legal questions becomes impossible to determine. It may well be that an acceptable theory of fairness can be reconciled with the dictates of economic theory in a manner that leaves ample room for the use of economic thought. But that judgment presupposes that some theory of fairness has been spelled out, which, once completed, may leave no room for economic considerations of any sort.

In order to raise these fairness questions in the context of traditional legal doctrine, I shall focus on the conflict that has persisted in the common law between theories of negligence and theories of strict liability. . . .

I. A CRITIQUE OF NEGLIGENCE

The development of the common law of tort has been marked by the opposition between two major theories. The first holds that a plaintiff should be entitled, prima facie, to recover from a defendant who has caused him harm only if the defendant intended to harm the plaintiff or failed to take reasonable steps to avoid inflicting the harm. The alternative theory, that of strict liability, holds the defendant prima facie liable for the harm caused whether or not either of the two further conditions relating to negligence and intent is satisfied. . . .

But the law of negligence never did conform in full to the requisites of the "moral" system of personal responsibility invoked in its behalf. In particular, the standard of the reasonable man, developed in order to insure injured plaintiffs a fair measure of protection against their fellow citizens, could require a given person to make recompense even where no amount of effort could have enabled *him* to act in accordance with the standard of conduct imposed by the law. . . .

Even if these exceptions to the general rule of negligence affect only a few of the cases to be decided, they do indicate a theoretical weakness that helps to explain efforts to find alternative justifications for the law of negligence couched in economic rather than moral terms. Thus, it was suggested that a defendant should be regarded as negligent if he did not take the precautions an economically prudent man would take in his own affairs, and, conversely, that where the defendant *did* conduct himself in an economically prudent manner, he could successfully defend himself in an action brought by another person whom he injured.

Although positions of this sort had been suggested from the beginning of this century, they received their most famous exposition in the opinion of Learned Hand in *United States v. Carroll Towing Co.*[2] The narrow point for decision in *Carroll Towing* was whether the owner of a barge owed to others a duty to keep a barge or attendant on board while his barge was moored inside a harbor. . . . Hand expresses his conclusion in mathematical terms in order to demonstrate its applicability to the entire law of tort:

> if the probability be called P; the injury, L; and the burden, B; liability depends upon whether B is less than L multiplied by P: i.e., whether B [is less than] PL.[3]

. . . Hand proceeds to examine the conduct, not of the owner, but of the bargee and in the traditional manner so often used to decide the "reasonableness" of the defendant's conduct in negligence cases. The evidence showed that the bargee had been off the ship for a period in excess of twenty-one hours before the accident took place. Moreover, all he had to offer to

---

[1]See Guido Calabresi & A. Douglas Melamed, Property Rules, Liability Rules, and Inalienability: One View of the Cathedral, 85 Harv. L. Rev. 1089, 1102–05 (1972). But see Richard A. Posner, A Theory of Negligence, 1 J. Leg. Studies 29 (1972).

[2]159 F. 2d 169 (2d Cir. 1947)

[3] [*Id.* at 173.]

explain his absence was some "fabricated" tale.[4] There was "no excuse for his absence," and it followed:

> In such circumstances we hold—and it is all that we do hold—that it was a fair requirement that the Conners Company should have a bargee aboard (unless he had some excuse for his absence), during the working hours of daylight.[5]

The use of the concept of "excuse" in Hand's formulation of the particular grounds for decision suggests that some of the elements material to determining "blameworthiness" in the moral sense are applicable with full force even after the statement of the general economic formula. But it is unclear what counts for Hand as an appropriate excuse within the framework of the law of tort. . . .

But even if the notion of "excuse" is put to one side, Hand's formula is still not free from difficulty. It is difficult to decide how to apply the formula when there is a need for but a single precaution which one party is no better suited to take than the other. If, for example, there were two boats in a harbor, and need for but a single bargee, what result is appropriate if the two boats collide when both are unmanned? Is there negligence, or contributory negligence, or both? The formula is silent on the question of which ship should be manned. Yet that is the very question which must be answered, since in economic terms no bargee provides too little accident protection while two bargees provide too much. . . .

. . . In any system of common law liability, a court must allocate, explicitly or implicitly, a loss that has already occurred between the parties—usually two—before it. It could turn out that neither of the parties acted in a manner that was unreasonable or improper from either an economic or a moral point of view, but a decision that the conduct of both parties was "proper" under the circumstances does not necessarily decide the legal case; there could well be other reasons why one party should be preferred to another.

The point is illustrated by the famous case of *Vincent v. Lake Erie Transport Co.*[6] During a violent storm, defendant ordered his men to continue to make the ship fast to the dock during the course of the storm in order to protect it from the elements. The wind and waves repeatedly drove it into the dock, damaging it to the extent of $500. Although there had been a prior contract between the plaintiff and defendant, the case was treated by the court as though the parties to the suit were strangers, since the terms of the contract did not cover the incident in question. Moreover, it was accepted without question that the conduct of the defendant was reasonable in that there was no possible course of action open to the captain of the ship that would have enabled him to reduce the aggregate damage suffered by the ship and the dock. On these facts the court concluded that the defendant had to pay the plaintiff for the $500 damage.

The result in *Vincent* seems inconsistent with either of the customary explanations, moral or economic, of negligence in the law of tort. There is no argument that the conduct of the defendant was "blameworthy" in any sense. . . . Similarly, if the economic conception of negligence is adopted, the same result must be reached once it is admitted that the conduct of the defendant served to minimize the total amount of damage suffered; the expected benefits of further precautions were outweighed by their costs.

Had the Lake Erie Transportation Company owned both the dock and the ship, there could have been no lawsuit as a result of the incident. . . . The action in tort in effect enables the injured party to require the defendant to treat the loss he has inflicted on another as though it were his own. If the Transportation Company must bear all the costs in those cases in which it damages its own property, then it should bear those costs when it damages the property of another. The necessity may justify the decision to cause the damage, but it cannot justify a refusal to make compensation for the damage so caused. . . .

II. AN ANALYSIS OF CAUSATION

Implicit in the development of the prior arguments is the assumption that the term causation has a content which permits its use in a principled manner to help solve particular cases. In order to make good on these arguments that concept must be explicated and shown to be a suitable basis for the assignment of responsibility. Those two ends can be achieved only if much of the

[4] *Id.* at 173–74

[5] *Id.* at 174.

[6] 109 Minn. 456, 124 N.W. 221 (1910).

standard rhetoric on causation in negligence cases is first put to one side.

Under the orthodox view of negligence, the question of causation is resolved by a two-step process. The first part of the inquiry concerns the "cause in fact" of the plaintiff's injury. The usual test to determine whether or not the plaintiff's injury was in fact caused by the negligence of the defendant is to ask whether, "but for the negligence of the defendant, the plaintiff would not have been injured." But this complex proposition is not in any sense the semantic equivalent of the assertion that the defendant caused the injury to the plaintiff. The former expression is in counterfactual form and requires an examination of what *would have* been the case if things had been otherwise. The second expression simply asks in direct indicative form what in fact *did* happen. The change in mood suggests the difference between the two concepts.

The "but for" test does not provide a satisfactory account of the concept of causation if the words "in fact" are taken seriously. *A* carelessly sets his alarm one hour early. When he wakes up the next morning he has ample time before work and decides to take an early morning drive in the country. While on the road he is spotted by *B,* an old college roommate, who becomes so excited that he runs off the road and hurts *C*. But for the negligence of *A, C* would never have been injured, because *B* doubtless would have continued along his uneventful way. Nonetheless, it is common ground that *A,* even if negligent, is in no way responsible for the injury to *C,* caused by *B*.

Its affinity for absurd hypotheticals should suggest that the "but for" test should be abandoned as even a tentative account of the concept of causation. But there has been no such abandonment. . . . [T]here is no merit, philosophic or otherwise, to an account of any concept which cannot handle the simplest of cases, and only a mistaken view of philosophic inquiry demands an acceptance of an account of causation that conflicts so utterly with ordinary usage.

Once the "philosophical" account of causation was accepted, it could not be applied in legal contexts without modification because of the unacceptable results that it required. The concept of "cause in law" or "proximate" cause became necessary to confine the concept within acceptable limits. . . . [T]he question of proximate cause has been said to reduce itself to the question whether the conduct of the defendant is a "substantial factor" contributing to the loss of the plaintiff, or whether the harm suffered was "reasonably foreseeable." But these formulations of the test of proximate cause do not give much guidance for the solution of particular cases. One might think that this would be treated as a defect in an account of a concept like causation, but in large measure it has been thought to be its strength. Once it is decided that there is no hard content to the term causation, the courts are free to decide particular lawsuits in accordance with the principles of "social policy" under the guise of the proximate-cause doctrine.

. . . But the term [proximate cause] cannot be banished from the lexicon on the ground that it is "metaphysical." The concept is dominant in the law because it is dominant in the language that people, including lawyers, use to describe conduct and to determine responsibility.[7] . . .

. . . [T]he concept of causation, as it applies to cases of physical injury, can be analyzed in a matter that both renders it internally coherent and relevant to the ultimate question who shall bear the loss.

There will be no attempt to give a single semantic equivalent to the concept of causation. Instead, the paper will consider in succession each of four distinct paradigm cases covered by the proposition "*A* caused *B* harm." . . . Briefly put, they are based upon notions of force, fright, compulsion and dangerous conditions.

Force

We begin with the simplest instance of causation: the application of force to a person or thing. In a physical sense, the consequences of the application of force may be quite varied. In some cases the object acted upon will move; it others it will be transformed; in still others it will be damaged. It is this last case that will be of exclusive concern here, because it is accepted without question that the minimum condition of tort liability is damage to the person or property of the plaintiff.

The identification of causation with force does not of itself complete the first instance of the proposition "*A* caused harm to *B*." It is still necessary to show that the force in question was applied by human and not

---

[7]H. L. A. Hart & A. M. Honoré, [Causation in the Law (1959)], at 59–62.

natural agencies, and thus to tie the concept of force to that of human volition. The term "volition" is a primitive in the language whose function is to mark off the class of human acts from the class of events; to distinguish between "I raised my arm," and "my arm went up." But even if the term cannot be defined, its function can be made clear by some simple examples. In the old case of *Smith v. Stone,*[8] the defendant was carried on to the plaintiff's land by a band of armed men. The court held that the plaintiff could not recover in trespass, because it was "the trespasse of the party that carried the defendant upon the land, and not the trespasse of the defendant." True, the physical requirement of entrance was satisfied in the case, but the defendant's movement was in no sense an "action" because, if anything, it was contrary to his will. . . .

The combination of force and volition is expressed in the simple transitive sentence, *A* hit *B*. It is true that this proposition as stated is consistent with the assertion that *A* did not harm *B*. But in many contexts the implication of harm follows fairly from the assertion, as anyone hit by a car will admit. Where the issue is in doubt, the verb can be changed, even as the form of the proposition remains constant, to bring the element of harm more sharply into relief. Thus instead of "*A* hit *B*," another proposition of the requisite form could be "*A* pummeled *B*," or "*A* beat *B*." But since the specifics of the harm go only to the measure of damages and not to the issue of liability, the proposition "*A* hit *B*" will serve as the model of the class of propositions to be considered.

The grammatical structure of the proposition "*A* hit *B*" is crucial to analysis of the problem of causation because it describes a situation both where the parties are *linked* to each other and where their respective roles are still *differentiated*. . . . But it may well be necessary as a matter of fact to assess the role of those forces that are *instruments* of the defendant. Take a simple case where *A* drives his car into *B*. It could be argued that *A*'s act extended no further than the depression of the gas pedal or, perhaps, *A*'s movement of his leg muscles. But the constant and inveterate use of the English language militates against the restriction of an act to the physical movements of *A*'s body. "*A* drove his car into *B*" is a true description of the event; we might explain its significance away, but we can never deny it in good faith. Reference to those subsequent mechanical complications does not falsify that description. . . .

Finally, the proposition of the form "*A* hit *B*" does not depend upon the two-part theory of causation developed by the law of negligence. No question of "but for" is ever raised, much less answered. . . .

Once this simple causal paradigm is accepted, its relationship to the question of responsibility for the harm so caused must be clarified. Briefly put, the argument is that proof of the proposition *A* hit *B* should be sufficient to establish a prima facie case of liability.[9] . . . The doctrine of strict liability holds that proof that the defendant caused harm creates that presumption because proof of the nonreciprocal source of the harm is sufficient to upset the balance where one person must win and the other must lose. There is no room to consider, as part of the prima facie case, allegations that the defendant intended to harm the plaintiff, or could have avoided the harm he caused by the use of reasonable care. The choice is plaintiff or defendant, and the analysis of causation is the tool which, prima facie, fastens responsibility upon the defendant. . . .

Fright and Shock

The structure of the prima facie case for assault—the historical companion to trespass to the person—parallels the paradigm for the prima facie case of the tort of trespass, and illustrates the means by which the concept of causation can be extended in a principled manner. The case in assault is *A* frightened *B*. That paradigm indicates, as in trespass, that *A* and *B* do not have symmetrical roles. There is the same close connection between the conduct of the defendant and the harm of the plaintiff. There is, however, a difference between the cases of assault and those of trespass. In trespass actions the plaintiff's conduct is not in issue in the prima facie case. But the *reactions* of the plaintiff must be taken into account before the prima facie case of assault can be completed. Still, the roles of the parties are not identical. The reactions of the plaintiff do not rise to the level of acts because they are in no sense volitional.

---

[8]Style 65, 82 Eng. Rep. 533 (1647).

[9]The argument depends upon "a deep sense of common law morality that one who hurts another should compensate him." Leon Green. Foreseeability in Negligence Law 61 *Colum. L. Rev.* 1412 (1961).

Nonetheless, the paradigm does raise some troublesome issues. Suppose, for example, the defendant frightened the plaintiff when he raised his hand to mop the sweat off his face at a time when the plaintiff was standing about fifty yards away. Do facts such as these disclose a prima facie case of assault? Our first response to the allegation does not address the issue of substantive law at all. Rather, it says that the harm suffered by the plaintiff is so trivial that it is inappropriate to use, at public expense, the legal machinery to resolve the case. . . .

But the case can be made more difficult by assuming that the plaintiff has suffered serious injuries as a result of his fright. If anyone could be frightened by that kind of conduct, however, most likely he could not have survived long enough in life's hustle and bustle to be injured by the defendant. . . .

But even after these odd cases are put to one side, the paradigm of assault does raise problems of proof that are not present in trespass cases since the allegation "*A* frightened *B*," unlike the allegation "*A* hit *B*," can be proved in the given case only after the responses of *B* are taken into account. . . .

. . . The crucial question is that of causation and if a defendant frightens or shocks a plaintiff, the recovery should, prima facie, be allowed. . . .

Compulsion

The concept of causation is not limited to cases of the form "*A* hit *B*" or "*A* frightened *B*." There are other relationships that exhibit more complex grammatical forms to which it also applies. Indeed, the proposition "*A* hit *B*" represents only a special case of a more complex relationship, capable of indefinite extension, which for three persons takes the form "*A* compelled *B* to hit *C*.". . .

. . . In the analysis of this more complex proposition and its relationship to the question of responsibility, there is the same interaction between nonreciprocity and causation as in the simple cases already analyzed. In order to unpack these relationships, consider the case from the standpoint of the injured party, *C*. If the proposition "*A* compelled *B* to hit *C*" is true, then it follows that "*B* hit *C*." The last proposition can be analyzed in accordance with the notions of causation based upon force and volition that have already been developed. Given that paradigm, it follows that *C* has a prima facie case against *B*. *B* cannot escape liability by showing that he did not hit *C*, for a demonstration that he acted under compulsion is not the same as a demonstration that he did not act at all. . . . Nor, if the observations about the defense of "necessity" made earlier are sound, can *B* plead as a defense that he was compelled by *A* to hit *C*. Even if this conduct were reasonable, it does not follow that *B* need not pay. . . . *B* will have an action over against *A* after he has paid *C*, on the theory that *A* compelled him (to his loss) to hit *C*.

The analysis is not yet complete, because *C* is not limited to an action against *B*. He can bring in the alternative an action against *A*. That action, however, could not rely on trespassory theories of causation. *A* did not hit *C*; *B* did. But the roles of *A* and *C* are still both linked, and differentiated, because *A* compelled *B* to hit *C*; *C* did not compel *B* to hit *A*. . . .

The changes in causal theory have their effect on questions of proof. Proof of compulsion upon *B* is crucial if *C*'s action against *A* is to succeed. . . .

In particular, two points must be observed. First, the question whether *B* was negligent under the circumstances is, at best, evidence on the question of compulsion. . . . Second, it is not strictly material whether *B* intended to harm *C*, because he could have been compelled to act as he did whether or not that harm was intended. . . .

One further problem remains. Suppose *C* is able to bring actions against both *A* and *B*. He will not be entitled to a double recovery for the single harm, so it will be necessary to decide whether *A* or *B* will be saddled with the ultimate loss. Here again the causal paradigm permits us to link and differentiate the roles of the parties to the suit. *A* compelled *B* to hit *C*; *B* did not compel *A* to hit *C*. Hence it follows that, prima facie, *B* should prevail over *A*. . . .

Causation and Dangerous Conditions

The forms of causation thus far developed are the easiest to comprehend and accept. But an analysis of causation is seriously incomplete if made only in terms of force, fright, and compulsion. Both ordinary thought and legal theory also use a causal paradigm which covers cases involving the creation of dangerous conditions that result in harm to either person or property. . . .

. . . [T]here are significant differences between this paradigm and those that have come before. First, it makes use of the expression, "result in." While it could be objected that this term defines causation in terms of itself, that is not the case. The term "result in" is intended to cover only those cases of causation—force, fright and compulsion—already developed in previous sections of this paper. . . .

Second, this paradigm applies only to dangerous conditions. It is possible to divide the most common instances of dangerous conditions into three classes.[10] The first includes things that are "inherently" dangerous, of which stored explosives are the most common example. They are inherently dangerous because they retain their *potential* energy in full, even if they are stored or handled with the highest possible care. . . .

The second kind of dangerous condition is created when a person places a thing—not dangerous in itself—in a dangerous position. Instances of this form of dangerous condition are of two sorts. The first class presupposes the recognition of rights of way: highways, footpaths, and the like. . . .

Other situations in this class involve any unstable position where the application of a small force will permit the release of some greater force. . . .

The third kind of dangerous situation concerns products or other things dangerous because defective. . . .

It can . . . be shown that this account of causation is consistent with the rules of strict liability. It is true that the term "dangerous" often carries with it suggestions of both the degree of risk and the probability of harm, but in the restricted sense the term is used here—with the emphasis upon the "potential" to cause harm in the narrow sense of that term—more than a verbal mutation is at stake. The law of negligence, as expressed in the formula of Learned Hand, requires balancing the risk and probable extent of harm against the burden of the costs needed either to eliminate or reduce it. No cost-benefit analysis is required, however, when the theories of dangerous conditions are used to establish the causal connection between the defendant's conduct and the plaintiff's harm. It could well be that the defendant acts in a reasonable manner when he creates a dangerous condition that results in harm to the plaintiff. It may not be worthwhile for him to see that all of his manufactured products are free from defects; but nonetheless he will be held liable if any of them should prove defective and cause harm. . . .

III. THE PROBLEM OF THE GOOD SAMARITAN

. . . The theories of strict liability explain and justify, as the rules of reasonableness cannot, the common law's refusal to extend liability in tort to cases where the defendant has not harmed the plaintiff by his affirmative action.[11] The problem arises in its starkest form in the case of the good Samaritan. *A* finds himself in a perilous situation which was not created by *B*, as when *A* is overwhelmed by cramps while swimming alone in a surging sea. *B*, moreover, is in a position where he could, without any danger of injury to himself, come to *A*'s assistance with some simple and well-nigh costless steps, such as throwing a rope to the plaintiff. The traditional common law position has been that there is no cause of action against *B* solely because *B*, in effect, permitted *A* to drown.

It is important to note the manner in which such cases should be decided under a negligence system. . . .

[If] one considers the low costs of prevention to *B* of rescuing *A*, and the serious, if not deadly, harm that *A* will suffer if *B* chooses not to rescue him, there is no reason why the *Carroll Towing* formula or the general rules of negligence should not require, under pain of liability, the defendant to come to the aid of the plaintiff. Nonetheless, the good Samaritan problem receives special treatment even under the modern law of torts. . . . No matter how the facts are manipulated, it is not possible to argue that *B* caused *A* harm in any of the senses of causation which were developed in the earlier portions of this article when he failed to render assistance to *A* in his time of need. In typical negligence cases, all the talk of avoidance and reasonable care may shift attention from the causation requirement, which the general "but for" test distorts beyond recognition. But its importance is revealed by its absence in the good Samaritan cases where the presence of all those elements immaterial to tortious liability cannot, even in

[10]The classification that follows was developed in John Charlesworth, Liability for Dangerous Things (1992).

[11]I put aside here all those cases in which there are special relationships between the plaintiff and the defendants: parent and child, invitor and invitee, and the like.

combination, persuade judges who accept the negligence theory to apply it in the decisive case.

The principles of strict liability do more than explain the reasons behind the general common law refusal to require men to be good Samaritans. They also explain why it is that in some cases there are strong arguments to support apparent exceptions to the common law position. . . .

. . . *Montgomery v. National C. & T.,* is described by Gregory as follows:

> Consider this situation: Two of defendant's trucks, due to no fault of the drivers, became stalled on a narrow road, completely blocking the highway. Also, without fault, the men were unable to get the trucks started again. This was at the foot of a short hill, which obscured the view of approaching drivers. Moreover, the hill was somewhat icy. Plaintiff came driving along at a normal speed. By the time he saw the stalled trucks, he was unable to stop and crashed into them. Had one of defendant's truck drivers climbed the hill and posted a warning, this accident would not have happened.[12]

. . . [T]he South Carolina court found that the defendant could be held liable on account of the actionable negligence of its employees in the course of their employment, because on the facts of the case the employees had both the opportunity and the means to place warnings in some form at the top of the hill which would have enabled the plaintiff to avoid the crash in question. The court insisted that this duty rested upon the defendant's employees even though two propositions are settled: first, that no passerby would have been charged with that duty, even if he had the time and means to have taken those steps; and second, that the defendant's employees would have been under no duty to place those warnings if the road had been blocked, say, by a falling tree.[13] In effect, the position of the court is that simply because the defendant's employees blocked the road, they were under a duty to take those precautions reasonably calculated to prevent possible injury to other users of the highway. . . .

. . . The defendant is liable because harm resulted when the plaintiff's car ran into its truck after his employees blocked the road. It is immaterial that the defendant's employees had an opportunity to place warnings at the top of the hill, because the theory of dangerous conditions, too, is a theory of strict liability. Once it is shown that the plaintiff's conduct (he hit the defendant's truck) only serves to complete the prima facie case, the liability follows, because the facts do not even suggest the basis for an affirmative defense.[14]

Theories of strict liability, therefore, support the result . . . in a simple and direct fashion. But it is not clear that these results are correct under a system of negligence which accepts as one of its premises that a man is under no duty to confer aid upon a stranger. . . .

. . . Defendant's drivers would have been under no duty to warn oncoming vehicles of the possible danger if the road had been blocked by a falling tree. Once it is accepted that an allegation that the defendant blocked the highway does not create a prima facie case, then . . . it seems improper to take refuge in a halfway house which says that the conduct of the defendant is nonetheless sufficient to obligate him to take reasonable steps for the benefit of the plaintiff. . . . [T]he act of the defendant must be treated like an Act of God. . . .

These variations on the good Samaritan rule illustrate the evasive responses that courts are prepared to make in order to restrict a rule that they accept but do not like. . . .

There is a further class of exceptions to the good Samaritan rule, motivated by the same judicial distaste for the doctrine, which also cannot be rationalized by an appeal to the theories of strict liability. Consider the case where the defendant gratuitously takes steps to aid the plaintiff only to discontinue his efforts before the plaintiff is moved to a position of comparative safety. For example, *A* sees *B* lying unconscious on the public street. Immediately, he runs to the phone, dials an emergency room, and then hangs up the receiver. Or, in the alternative, he picks *B* up and places him in his automobile, only to return him to his original position on the sidewalk when he thinks, for whatever reason, better of the involvement.

---

[12]Charles O. Gregory, The Good Samaritan and the Bad, in The Good Samaritan and the Law, 22, 27 (James Ratcliff ed. 1966).

[13]Charles O. Gregory, *supra* note [12], at 27.

[14]If the owner of the truck brought an action against the driver, claiming as its prima facie case, "you struck my truck," that action would fail because the defendant could plead as its affirmative defense, "you (plaintiff) blocked my right of way." Observe that there is no appeal here to a notion of contributory negligence, even though the defense puts plaintiff's conduct into issue.

It has often been argued that the good Samaritan doctrine in these situations is of no application on the ground that once the defendant undertakes to assist the plaintiff in distress, he can no longer claim that his conduct amounted to a "simple nonfeasance," no longer maintain that the two were still strangers in the eyes of the law. . . .

This position must be rejected. The act requirement in the law of tort is but a combination of the volition and the causation requirements already discussed. The law of tort cannot be invoked simply because the defendant has done something; it must be shown that the act in question has caused harm to the plaintiff. Where the defendant has dialed the phone only to put the receiver back on the hook, he has acted, but those acts have not caused harm. The theories of force, fright, compulsion and dangerous condition are inapplicable, either alone or in combination, to the facts as described. . . .

Properly conceived, these situations should be discussed together with other forms of gratuitous undertakings and the obligations they generate. The common law has never found a home for such obligations. They should not be part of the law of tort because they do not satisfy the causation requirement; and the unfortunate doctrine of consideration prevents their easy inclusion in the law of contracts. . . .

The same issue involved in the good Samaritan problem frequently arises when it is the *defendant* who claims in effect that the plaintiff was under an affirmative duty to take steps for his, the defendant's, benefit. The point is most clearly raised in connection with the maxim that a tortfeasor takes his victim as he finds him. The maxim applies where the defendant has tortiously harmed the plaintiff, and the issue is whether the latter is entitled to recover for those injuries which would not have occurred had the plaintiff had, in all material respects, a "normal" constitution.

The situation is illustrated by the facts of *Vosburg v. Putney*.[15] The plaintiff was suffering from the after effects of a prior injury to his leg. The defendant kicked the leg at its sore point and caused a serious inflammation. Little or no harm would have been done to an individual with a sound leg. Once it is accepted that the plaintiff has a prima facie case against the defendant, whether on a theory of strict liability, negligence, or "wrongful" intent, the question arises whether the plaintiff should be able to recover for that portion of the damages that would not have been suffered by a plaintiff with a healthy constitution. If he takes no precaution to protect his knee, it should be possible for the defendant to argue that the plaintiff's negligence bars his recovery if the *Carroll Towing* formula is used to determine the reasonableness of the plaintiff's conduct. . . .

If this line of reasoning is accepted, the defendant in cases like *Vosburg v. Putney* could argue that the plaintiff was in breach of his duties to the defendant when he failed, say, to wear a shinguard which at low cost would protect him from accidental harm. . . . But the law does not take this position. It holds instead that the plaintiff is under no duty to package and bandage himself (though the costs are low) in order to reduce the damages to be paid by those who might harm him. Where the plaintiff is in a weakened condition, he has not caused the harm in any of the senses developed in part II, even if he had the opportunity to prevent them from occurring. As in the case of the good Samaritan, one man is not under a common law duty to take steps to aid a stranger. . . .

. . . Strong arguments can be advanced to show that the common law position on the good Samaritan problem is in the end consistent with both moral and economic principles.

The history of Western ethics has been marked by the development of two lines of belief. One line of moral thought emphasizes the importance of freedom of the will. It is the intention (or motive) that determines the worth of the act; and no act can be moral unless it is performed free from external compulsion.[16] Hence the expansion of the scope of positive law could only reduce the moral worth of human action. . . .

On the other hand there are those theories that concern themselves not with the freedom of the will, but with the external effects of individual behavior. There is no room for error, because each act which does not further the stated goals (usually, of the maximization of welfare) is in terms of these theories a bad act. Thus a system of laws must either require the individual to

---

[15] 80 Wis. 523, 50 N.W. 403 (1891). . . .

[16] See, *e.g.*, James Street Fulton, The Free Person and Legal Authority, in Responsibility in Law and in Morals 1–11 (Arthur L. Harding ed. 1960).

act, regardless of motive, in the socially desired manner, or create incentives for him to so behave. . . .

. . . [M]ost systems of conventional morality try to distinguish between those circumstances in which a person should be compelled to act for the benefit of his fellow man, and those cases where he should be allowed to do so only if prompted by the appropriate motives. To put the point in other terms, the distinction is taken between that conduct which is required and that which, so to speak, is beyond the call of duty. If that distinction is accepted as part of a common morality, then the argument in favor of the good Samaritan rule is that it, better than any possible alternatives, serves to mark off the first class of activities from the second. . . .

The defense of the good Samaritan rule in economic terms takes the same qualified form. . . .

. . . [T]he incentive effects created by the absence of a good Samaritan rule must be examined in the context of other rules of substantive law. Thus it is critical to ask about the incentives which are created by rules which permit a rescuer to bring an action against the person he saved on quasi-contractual theories. It is also important to ask what modifications of behavior could be expected if the scope of this kind of action were expanded, and important, too, to know about the possible effects of systems of public honors and awards for good Samaritans. None of these arguments is designed to show that the common law approach can be justified on economic grounds, but they do show how perilous it is to attempt to justify legal rules by the incentives that they create. . . .

But it is a mistake to dwell too long upon questions of cost, for they should not be decisive in the analysis of the individual cases. Instead it is better to see the law of torts in terms of what might be called its political function. The arguments made here suggest that the first task of the law of torts is to define the boundaries of individual liberty. To this question and the rules of strict liability based upon the twin notions of causation and volition provide a better answer than the alternative theories based upon the notion of negligence, whether explicated in moral or economic terms. In effect, the principles of strict liability say that the liberty of one person ends when he causes harm to another. Until that point he is free to act as he chooses, and need not take into account the welfare of others.

But the law of tort does not end with the recognition of individual liberty. Once a man causes harm to another, he has brought himself within the boundaries of the law of tort. It does not follow, however, that he will be held liable in each and every case in which it can be showed that he caused harm, for it may still be possible for him to escape liability, not by an insistence upon his freedom of action, but upon a specific showing that his conduct was either excused or justified. Thus far in this paper we have only made occasional and unsystematic references to the problems raised by both pleas of excuses and justification. Their systematic explication remains crucial to the further development of the law of tort. That, task, however, is large enough to deserve special attention of its own.

21

MITCHELL McINNES

The Question of a Duty to Rescue in Canadian Tort Law: An Answer from France

Dal. L.J. (1990)

I. INTRODUCTION

A man witnesses a canoeist drowning a short distance from the shore.[1] For over forty minutes the tenants of an apartment complex listen to the tortured screams of a woman being murdered in the streets below.[2] A handful of railway employees watch a boy bleed to death for want of medical attention after he was struck by a passing car.[3] The owner of a pleasure craft learns that one of his passengers has fallen overboard into an icy lake.[4] An innocent party to a motor vehicle accident finds that the driver at fault was injured as a result of the mishap.[5] In each of these

[1] *Osterlind* v. *Hill* (1928), 263 Mass. 73, 160 N.E. 301.
[2] These were the facts surrounding the murder of Kitty Genovese in New York City, March 26, 1964. . . .
[3] *Union Pacific R.R.* v. *Cappier* (1903), 66 Kan. 649, 72 P. 281.
[4] *Horsley* v. *McLaren* [1972] S.C.R. 441, 22 D.L.R. (3d) 545; *affg.* [1970] 2 O.R. 487, 11 D.L.R. (3d) 277; *revg.* [1969] 2 O.R. 137, 4 D.L.R. (3d) 557.
[5] *See e.g.* Alberta Motor Vehicle Administration Act, R.S.A. 1980, c. M-22, s.76 (1).

examples the first mentioned party (or parties) could have safely rendered assistance to the helpless victim. The aim of the present discussion is to show that there ought to be a *legal* obligation to do so in Canadian tort law. . . .

II. HISTORY OF DUTY TO ACT AT COMMON LAW AND IN FRENCH LAW

. . .

1. History of Duty to Act in French Law

Before 1941 the law in France was much the same as it was in the common law world—generally speaking, legal sanctions would not follow upon a refusal to rescue someone. . . . While an increasing number of European countries had come to impose a positive obligation to render aid,[6] remarkable and unfortunate circumstances provided French legislators with a unique impetus.

In 1941 a German officer serving in France was murdered while witnesses stood idly by, refusing to intervene. By way of reprisal the Nazis executed 50 hostages. The Vichy government, coerced by the Germans, hoped to obviate the future need for such drastic measures by providing a means of redress through the more humane channels of the French courts.[7] The result was the enactment of a statute which required intervention for the prevention of crimes and for the assistance of persons in peril.[8] . . . A free French government, declaring the law void, sought not to repudiate the existence of the duty, but rather to retain it in an expanded form. The year 1945 saw the implementation of articles 61–63 of the Penal Code,[9] of which article 63§2 is, for the present purposes, the most pertinent. It provides that:

> Whoever abstains voluntarily from giving such aid to a person that he would have been able to give him without risk to himself or third persons by his personal action or by calling help . . .

shall be liable.

The statute is primarily penal in nature, the criminal punishment for a breach being a term of imprisonment of between three months and five years, or a fine of between 36,000 and 1,500,000 francs, or both. Of more relevance for the present purposes, of course, is the fact that a breach can also give rise to civil liability. . . .

III. ARTICLE 63§2 OF THE FRENCH PENAL CODE AND A PROPOSED DUTY

Professor Tunc has distilled from the statute and related case law four conditions which must be met before liability can be incurred.[10] First, the person must be in danger. . . . Second, the statute is breached only where something *could* have been done, though that "something" is not exhausted by possibilities of personal intervention. . . . Third, one is required to act only in the absence of risk to himself or third parties. . . . Finally, the refusal to rescue must be voluntary. It will not be so where one is unaware of the need for assistance. . . .

The French statute provides a sensible, comprehensive model for the duty which should be imposed in Canada. First of all, the policy underlying a duty to rescue would not be well served if an obligation existed only where the victim's *life* was in danger. . . . Further, while there will be instances where the gravity of the situation will be readily apparent, it would seem to invite problems to restrict the imposition of a duty to such cases. . . . The French statute should also be followed insofar as it does not require the rescue of property which is at risk. Whereas the imposition of a duty is justified where a person is facing danger, it may not be where a *thing* is facing danger. . . .

On whom should a duty be imposed? Again, the French legislation gives an appropriate response, congruent with the policy of a duty. Some have suggested that only those actually witness to the peril should be obliged to act. It is not at all clear, however, why a duty should be so dependant on chance. . . . Of course, the

---

[6]Portugal (1867), Switzerland (1808), Netherlands (1881), Italy (1889), Norway (1902), Russia (1903), Turkey (1926), Denmark (1930), Poland (1932), Germany (1871, 1935). Rudzinski's seminal survey, "The Duty to Rescue: A Comparative Analysis" in *The Good Samaritan and the Law,* [J. Ratcliffe ed., 1966] should be consulted for a detailed discussion.

[7]Magnol [1946] Semaine Juridique I. 531.

[8]Tunc, Commentaire [1946] Dalloz Legislation 33, 38.

[9][1947] Dalloz Legislation 130. The most significant difference between the two versions is that the later one does not require proof that serious bodily harm or death actually resulted from the failure to give succour.

[10]Tunc, "The Volunteer and the Good Samaritan" in *The Good Samaritan and the Law supra* n. [6] at 47.

line must be drawn at some point—but it is a point which French courts have been able to locate. Thus, a duty should be imposed on one who is either present at the scene or who is "reliably informed." The "reasonable man" standard should be used in deciding whether a person so informed assessed the circumstances and the need for help properly. . . .

Depending on the nature of the situational demands, the requirement under French law is to personally intervene, or obtain help, or both. This is sensible. The spirit of the duty would not be observed if one could walk away simply because personal involvement was impossible if others, who could help, were summonable. Whatever action is called for, however, the rescuer should not be expected to satisfy too high a standard of care. . . .

IV. CURRENT LAW: GENERAL ABSENCE OF DUTY AND EXCEPTIONS

Common law courts have long felt uncomfortable with the law's general denial of a duty to assist one in peril. . . . Inevitably, time began to see the crystallization of conscience into law as the number of "exceptional" situations in which a duty would be imposed grew even larger. Today liability for a failure to act will lie in widely disparate circumstances, many of which would not have been actionable under the traditional common law position. . . .

1. Exceptions to the General Rule

(i) *Relationships of Economic Benefit*

The Supreme Court of Canada has on a number of occasions recognized that a duty *may* arise where a relationship of economic benefit exists. In *Jordan House Ltd.* v. *Menow,*[11] Mr. Justice Laskin (as he then was) agreed with the lower court's decision to impose liability upon a hotel which had served beer to a patron who was past the point of visible intoxication and later ejected him out into the night. The action was brought by the parton after he was struck by a vehicle as he weaved his way down a much-traveled highway on foot. It was held that while motorists might be expected to succumb to Good Samaritan impulses and take steps to ensure that the plaintiff safely reached his destination, they were under no legal duty to do so. The hotel, on the other hand, was under such a duty. The basis for the difference seems primarily to have been that the hotel stood in an invitor-invitee relationship with its patron, although, significantly, it was stressed that "a great deal turned on the knowledge of the [hotel] of the patron and his conditions. . . ."[12] Not every tavern-owner would be obliged to "act as a watch dog for all patrons who enter his place of business and drink to excess."[13] The litigants in the *Jordan House* case were particularly well acquainted, and the plaintiff's propensity to over-consumption and subsequent reckless behaviour was well known to the defendant. Indeed, the defendant had earlier ordered its employees not to serve the plaintiff unless he was accompanied by a responsible person.[14] . . .

(ii) *Relationships of Control or Supervision*

Individuals often stand in a relationship of control or supervision in which one is dominant over the other. In some instances the price consequent on that power is the obligation to protect the subordinate party from harm. . . . [I]n an employer-employee relationship where the former may dictate working conditions, a duty exists.[15] An obligation has also been recognized as between school and pupil,[16] innkeeper and guest,[17] ship master and passenger,[18] jail and prisoner,[19] and hospital and patient.[20]

Frequently a relationship of control or supervision may give rise to a duty which is owed not to the party under control, but rather to a third party. Thus,

[11][1974] S.C.R. 239, 38 D.L.R. (3d) 105; *affg.* [1971] 1 O.R. 129, 14 D.L.R. (3d) 345; *affg.* [1970] 1 O.R. 54, 7 D.L.R. (3d) 494.

[12]*Id.* at 113. Mr. Justice Ritchie, concurring on the result based his decision on narrower grounds. For him the duty imposed was simply to not serve the plaintiff alcohol when he was drunk.

[13]*Id.* at 113.

[14]*Id.* at 107.

[15]Fleming, *Law of Torts* (1983) 142; *Remedies in Tort* [(1987)] at 16.1-102.

[16]*Williams* v. *Eady* (1893), 10 T.L.R. 41; *Moddejonge* v. *Huron Couty Bd. of Educ.,* [1972] 2 O.R. 437 (HC.J.); *Portelance* v. *Bd. of Trustees R.C. Sep. Sch. of Grantham,* [1962] 2 O.R. 365, 32 D.L.R. (2d) 337 (C.A.).

[17]Fleming, *Law of Torts, supra* n. [15] at 142; *Remedies in Tort, supra* n. [15] at 16.1-102.

[18]*Horsley* v. *McLaren supra* n. [4].

[19]*Timm* v. *R.* [1965] 1 Ex. C.R. 174; *Ellis* v. *Home Office* [1953] 2 All E.R. 149; *Howley* v. *R.,* [1973] F.C. 184.

[20]*Lawson* v. *Wellesley* (1975), 9 O.R. (2d) 677; *affd. on other grounds,* [1978] 1 S.C.R. 893.

a parent owes a duty to ensure that a child does not cause injuries to third parties,[21] and prisons and psychiatric institutions are obliged to protect the public from escaped prisoners[22] and patients.[23]. . . Finally, an affirmative obligation may also be imposed on one who has control over a dangerous object.[24]

(iii) *Creation of Danger*

Related to the idea that a duty will be imposed on one who has control over an instrument of danger is the idea that a duty will be imposed on one who non-negligently creates a danger. In *Oke* v. *Weide Transport and Carra*[25] the defendant non-negligently collided with a sign post, leaving it bent and protruding from the pavement at right angles. The deceased was later "speared" by the post when it penetrated the floor boards of his car and deflected up into his chest. The majority of the Manitoba Court of Appeal dismissed the plaintiff's action on the grounds of foreseeability, reserving judgment on the question of whether or not the defendant was under a duty to the deceased to do anything about the post. In a celebrated dissent Freedman, J.A. argued that the defendant should be held liable. . . . The essence of Mr. Justice Freedman's opinion is supported elsewhere, affirmative obligations being imposed in various circumstances where a defendant's actions created a situation of peril.[26]

(iv) *Gratuitous Undertakings*

. . .

Generally, a mere promise, unsupported by consideration, will not ground an action in either tort or contract. There is, however, an underdeveloped body of law which suggests that where the undertaking is coupled with reliance, a tortious duty may be imposed. In effect, a party, through past conduct, may create a self-imposed obligation to act. Such was the case in *Mercer* v. *South Eastern and Chatham Railway Co.*[27] The defendant there had voluntarily commenced a routine of locking a gate which opened onto its railway tracks whenever a train passed by. The object of the practice was to prevent that which in fact occurred. The plaintiff, aware of and relying on the defendant's custom, was run down by a locomotive after passing through the unlocked gate. Regrettably, through carelessness the defendant had deviated from its usual procedure. Liability followed. . . .

The second issue to be addressed in regards to gratuitous undertakings concerns the standard of care which will be imposed on one who commences to effect a rescue in the absence of a duty to do so. On the one hand, the famous American case of *Zelenko* v. *Gimbel Bros.*[28] stands for the proposition that one who gratuitously undertakes a rescue must not fail to do what "an ordinary man would do in performing the task." A different approach was adopted in *East Suffolk Catchment Board* v. *Kent*[29] where it was held that a public body would not be liable for failing to expediently continue on with a rescue operation unless by doing so it inflicted injury on the plaintiff. The Ontario Court of Appeal subsequently expanded that principle to cover private individuals who gratuitously intervene. . . .

(v) *Statutory Duties*

. . (While much of the legislation imposing positive obligations is only peripherally related to the issue of a duty to rescue . . . , "hit-and-run" statutes bear directly on the matter. Illustrative is the Alberta Motor Vehicle Administration Act:[30]

---

[21]*Hatfield* v. *Pearson* (1956), 6 D.L.R. (2d) 593; *Starr* v. *Crone*, [1950] 4 D.L.R. 433.

[22]*Home Office* v. *Dorset Yacht Co.*, [1970] A.C. 1004, [1970] 2 W.L.R. 1140, [1970] 2 All E.R. 294; *affg.* [1969] 2 Q.B. 412, [1969] 2 All E.R. 564.

[23]*Holgate* v. *Lancashire Mental Hosp. Bd.*, [1937] 4 All E.R. 19. In the United States the duty is even broader. *See Tarasoff* v. *Regents of Univ. of Calif.* (1976), 131 Cal. Rptr. 14. . . .

[24]*See eg. Stermer* v. *Lawson* (1977), 79 D.L.R. (3d) 366; *affd.* (1979), 11 C.C.L.T. (B.C.C.A.) lending a motorcycle to a young, unlicensed driver; Rudolph, "The Duty to Act: A Proposed Rule" [(1965)] at 503; *Ayers* v. *Hicks* (1942), 40 N.E. 2d. 334.

[25](1963), 41 D.L.R. (2d) 53.

[26]*Jordan House* v. *Menow, supra* n. [11]; *Depeu* v. *Flatau* (1907), 100 Minn. 299, 11 N.W. 1 . . . *Ontario Hospital Services Commission* v. *Borsoski* (1973), 54 D.L.R. (3d) 339, 7 O.R. (2d) 83 . . . *Haynes* v. *Harwood,* [1935] 1 K.B. 146, [1934] All E.R. Rep. 103. . . .

[27][1922] K.B. 549.

[28](1935), 287 N.Y.S. 134; *affd. without reasons* (1935), 287 N.Y.S. 136.

[29][1941] A.C. 74, [1940] 4 All E.R. 527. The case has been much criticized, and subsequent decisions have put its status into doubt. *City of Kamloops* v. *Nielsen,* [1984] 2 S.C.R. 2, 29 C.C.L.T. 97, [1984] 2 W.W.R.1, (*per* Wilson J.); *Anns* v. *Merton London Borough Council,* [1978] A.C. 728, [1977] 2 W.L.R. 1024, [1977] 2 All E.R. 492.

[30]*Supra* n. [5]. *See also* Canadian Criminal Code R.S.C. 1985, c. C-46, s.252(1); Highway Traffic Act R.S.O. 1980, c. 198, s.174(1)(6); Motor Vehicle Act R.S.B.C. 1979, c. 288, s. 62(1).

> 76(1) When an accident occurs on a highway, the driver or other person in charge of the vehicle that was directly or indirectly involved in the accident . . .
>
> (b) shall render all reasonable assistance. . . .

Failure to do so may result in a fine of $500 or imprisonment for a term not exceeding six months.[31] Significantly, the statute is also said to ground a civil action if breached.[32] The provision is interesting for its scope of applicability. . . . More to the point, one must render aid regardless of fault,[33] and even though one's involvement in the accident may only be "indirect". . . .

The policy of section 76(1) of the Alberta Motor Vehicle Administration Act, and of similar legislation, is clear. Parliament and provincial legislatures have indicated a new direction for the law by getting involved in the business of encouraging, nay, requiring Good Samaritanism. . .

2. Summary of the Exceptions

A number of commentators have sought to distil from the various exceptions a common basis upon which affirmative obligations are imposed and can be rationalized. Most popular is the "benefit theory" which holds that a duty will be placed upon one who has "voluntarily brought himself into a certain relationship with others from which he obtains or expects a benefit."[34] . . . It is suggested, however, that unless stretched to an untenable extent, the existence of a benefit (actual or potential) moving to obligor provides at best only a partial explanation. . . .

. . . However, the mere fact that one derives an economic benefit does not inevitably lead to the conclusion that a duty will be incurred, nor does the incurrence of a duty necessarily depend on the presence of a benefit. Mr. Justice Laskin (as he then was), while holding that a duty did exist on the facts before the court in *Jordan House Ltd.* v. *Menow,* went on to say that not every tavern owner would be under a similar duty to all his customers. "A great deal turns on the knowledge of the operator (or his employees) of the patron and his condition. . . ."[35]

The benefit analysis is most unacceptable in regards to parent-child relationships. There is something very distasteful about a legal system which would purportedly downplay altruistic behaviour within the family unit, and seek rather to explain the duty owed by a mother or father as the price to be paid for some benefit actually or potentially moving to the parent. . . .

Gratuitous undertakings by definition can not be explained by the benefit principle, a fact which even the most forceful advocates of the theory concede.[36] . . .

Other theories as to why or when tort law will impose a duty to act are similarly unsatisfying. Professor Weinrib, starting from the proposition that "[the] common law position on nonfeasance generally relies on contract law, and hence on the market, to regulate the provision of aid to others for independently existing dangers,"[37] goes on to argue that an affirmative obligation will be imposed in tort where there is an absence of any social value in the liberty to contract. The evidence offered in defence of this thesis, while somewhat supportive, is sparse and ultimately unpersuasive. Weinrib begins by offering an explanation for the decision of the Supreme Court of Canada in *O'Rourke* v. *Schacht*[38] in which a police officer was held to be under a duty to warn drivers of dangerous conditions on a highway. . . . Similarly, duties owed by family members to one another are explained on the basis that "family relations [are] never appropriate for market regulation."[39] Finally it is noted that contracts which have been made between rescuers and rescuees have been declared unenforceable as unconscionable or made under duress.[40]

The theory is fatally flawed. First of all, it is rather limited in scope. Weinrib does not, for example, even attempt to explain the basis of the duty found in cases like *Jordan House Ltd.* v. *Menow.* . . .

---

31 R.S.A. 1980, c. M-22, s. 101(1).

32 Linden, *Canadian Tort Law* (4th ed. 1988) 283.

33 There exists, independently of the statute, a duty to render aid where the driver was tortiously responsible for the injury of the other. *Racine* v. *CNR,* [1923] 2 D.L.R. 572, [1923] 1 W.W.R. 1439, 19 Alta. L.R. 529 (C.A.).

34 McNeice & Thornton, "Affirmative Duties in Tort," [(1949), 58 *Yale L.J.*] at 1282–1283; Bohlen, "The Moral Duty to Aid Others As a Basis of Tort Liability" [(1908), 56 *U.Pa.L.Rev.* 217 and 316] at 220.

35 . . . 38 D.L.R. (3d) 113.

36 McNeice & Thornton, "Affirmative Duties in Tort," *supra* n. [34] at 1286–1287.

37 Weinrib, "The Case for a Duty to Rescue" (1980), 90 *Yale L.J.* 247 at 269.

38 [1976] 1 S.C.R. 53 D.L.R. (3d) 96; *affg.* [1973] 1 O.R. 221, 30 D.L.R. (3d) 641.

39 [*Supra* n. 37] at 271.

40 *Id.* at 271. . . .

On a more fundamental level it appears that whether or not a duty will be imposed is a policy decision. Neither the benefit theory nor Weinrib's theory are capable of adequately explaining all of the affirmative obligations which exist in tort law, though both may represent factors which, along with others, are at play in the policy field. . . .

V. POLICY BASIS OF TORT DEVELOPMENT

A duty to rescue could be either judicially or statutorily created. Although both approaches have features which recommend them, it is the former which is preferred here. . . .

A general duty to rescue, if it is to be recognized judicially, rather than statutorily, will find its home in the tort of negligence. That it could fit within the test set forth by Lord Atkin's famous dictum in *Donoghue* v. *Stevenson* seems clear.[41]

> The rule that you are to love your neighbour becomes in law that you are not to injure your neighbour, and the lawyer's question is, Who is my neighbour? receives a restricted reply. You must take reasonable care to avoid acts or *omissions* which you can reasonably foresee would be likely to injure your neighbour. Who, then, in law is my neighbour? The answer seems to be—persons who are so closely and directly affected by my act that I ought reasonably to have them in contemplation as being so affected when I am directing my mind to the acts or *omissions* which are called in question. (emphasis added) . . .

VI. POLICY CONSIDERATIONS

1. Policy Arguments Against a Duty to Rescue

Reflecting the values and attitudes of the times, the development of the early common law was premised upon a philosophy of "rugged individualism."[42] . . . Quite naturally it was considered inappropriate for the government or the courts to intervene in regards to omissions—their function was more narrowly aimed at preventing *positive* harm from being done.[43] . . .

. . . Such harsh judgements are today unlikely. Condemnation is unlikely to follow upon a cry for help if the situation was truly one of imminent danger. Indeed, silence in such circumstances might be regarded as obstinate and irresponsible. From all that has been said, it seems clear that modern Canadian society is not based on a philosophy of rugged individualism.[44] The view that a duty to rescue is unnecessary and undesirable, so typical of the earlier era, should similarly seem anachronistic. . . .

Implicit throughout the discussion so far has been the assumption that a general duty to rescue would be consistent with commonly held notions of morality. . . .

The best indicator that a duty to rescue would be consistent with morality or conscience, however, is seen in the possible responses to a call for help. Basically, two are possible. First of all, the bystander may become involved and personally provide relief or summon one who is better equipped to do the job. Morality would surely underlie the altruistic response. Alternatively, the bystander may pass by. . . . If, as in most cases, the bystander later tried to justify his inaction, the role of morality is again evident. "I'm not a doctor—I couldn't have helped." "Someone else will stop for the poor guy." "It's none of my business." Such responses are unfortunately familiar to all but the most saintly among us. What is clear is that if not for the pangs of guilt, if not for the need to placate one's bothersome conscience, if not for the knowledge that the morally correct choice was not made, such rationalizations would be pointless and would not occur.

Epstein has argued that in a society in which the government can force one to gratuitously confer a benefit upon another, "it becomes impossible to tell where liberty ends and obligation begins."[45] . . . True,

---

[41][1932] A.C. 562, 580. Similar statements appeared in earlier decisions, but it is Lord Atkin's which has withstood the test of time, *Heaven* v. *Pender* (1883), 11 Q.B.D. 503 as limited by *LaLievre* v. *Gould*, [1893] 1 Q.B. 491; *Buckley* v. *Mott* (1920), 50 D.L.R. 508 (N.S.).

[42]Hope, "Officiousness" 1929), 15 *Cornell L.Q.* 25, 29.

[43]Hale, "Prima Facie Torts, Combination and Non-feasance" (1946), 46 *Col. L. Rev.* 196, 214.

[44]*Crocker* v. *Sundance Northwest Resorts Ltd.* [1988] 1 S.C.R., 1186, 51 D.L.R. (4th); 321, 44 C.C.L.L. 225, *revg.* (1985), 20 D.L.R. (4th) 552, 33 C.C.L.T. 73, *which revd.* (1983), 150 D.L.R. (3d) 178, 25 C.C.L.T. 201.

[45]Epstein, "A Theory of Strict Liability" (1973), 2 *J. Legal Stud.* 151 at 199.

if Canadian society is to retain its basic nature, liberty must at some point prevail over the call for personal sacrifice. However, practically speaking, the duty advocated would seldomly be invoked, and when it was, it would only require action which would not expose the rescuer to danger. The extent to which freedom would be threatened would not be great. . . .

In defence of the traditional common law view it has been said that the law should not require one to jeopardize his pocket-book or safety in an attempt to save a person in peril.[46] This argument is no longer supportable because recent developments have seen tort law soften its attitude towards rescuers, and also because it assumes the imposition of a duty in *all* cases. First, while the early common law did invoke the concepts of *volenti*[47] and causation[48] to deny the claims of rescuers who are injured as a result of their efforts, jurists of the 20th century have increasingly come to praise and encourage Good Samaritans.[49] Consequently, compensation is available to the reasonable[50] rescuer from one who negligently created the perilous situation . . . or from a third party responsible for supervening negligence. . . .

Secondly, while it is inevitable that mishaps would occur under the proposed duty, a bystander need not court disaster in order to fulfil his obligations. To reiterate, the model advocated, based on the French experience, would only require that which could be done safely. . . .

[46]McNeice & Thornton, "Affirmative Duties in Tort" [(1949), 58 *Yale L.J.*] at 1288; Linden, "Tort Liability for Criminal Nonfeasance" [(1966), 44 *Can. Bar Rev.* 25] at 30.

[47]*See e.g. Kimball* v. *Butler Bros.* [(1910), 15 O.W.R. 221 (C.A.)].

[48]*See e.g. Anderson v. Northern Ry. Co.* [(1875), 25 U.C.C.P. 301 (C.A.)].

[49]*See e.g. Attorney General for Ontario* v. *Crompton* (1976), 1 C.C.L.T. 81. A detailed analysis of the position in civil law countries can be found in Dawson, "Rewards for the Rescue of Human Life?" in *The Good Samaritan and the Law, supra* n. [6] at 62.

[50]The "foolhardy" and the "rash" will not be compensated. *Baker* v. *Hopkins,* [1958] 3 All E.R. 147 (Q.B.D.); *affd.* [1959] 1 W.L.R. 966, [1959] 3 All E.R. 225 (C.A.); *Haigh* v. *Grand Trunk Pacific Ry. Co.* (1914), 7 W.W.R. (N.S.) 806. Recent developments suggest that the courts may also be willing to employ the doctrine of contributory negligence to deny compensation in part. *See e.g. Sayers* v. *Harlow Urban District Council,* [1958] 2 All E.R. 342 (C.A.); *Holomis* v. *Dubuc* (1974), 56 D.L.R. (3d) 351.

2. Policy Arguments in Favour of a Duty to Rescue

Most of what has been said up to this point has simply rebutted arguments made against the imposition of a duty to rescue. That, of course, only takes the issue half of the way home. It is necessary to show not only that bad things would not come from a duty, but also that good things would.

From a practical viewpoint, the best possible result which could come from the imposition of a duty would be an increase in the number of rescues which are undertaken. . . .

Assuming that people would be aware of a duty to rescue if it existed, the question then becomes whether they would more often aid those in peril. Posner's suggestion that the existence of an obligation would paradoxically lead to fewer rescuers is, in the absence of empirical support, difficult to accept.[51] First, his prediction that (for example) a strong swimmer would avoid the beach because there might be a call for help is dubious to say the least. Given that the sacrifice required would be minimal and non-life threatening, it seems unlikely that such a person would shun the water and the pleasure that it brings her, as well as the possibility of glory and personal pride which would follow upon a rescue. Secondly, Posner's prediction that altruists, who would otherwise become involved, would refuse on the grounds that a legal duty would be coercive and would deprive them of the power of choice, is untenable. It is certainly a cynical view, but beyond that it seems to fly in the face of common sense. How likely is it that a person, otherwise predisposed to benevolent behaviour, would be so offended by legal recognition of his own values that he would consciously commit a tort and incur liability and public condemnation? . . . [I]t does seem far more probable that, if anything, a duty would lead to more, not fewer, rescues. . . .

The imposition of a duty to rescue would also be a positive development in that it would serve the various goals of tort law. It would likely lessen the incidence of socially undesirable behaviour as it would provide an incentive (the avoidance of liability) to those who are capable of action and who are aware of the moral call for help, but who are simply callous or recalcitrant. That is, it would act as a deterring factor. . . .

[51]Posner, *Economic Theory of Law,* [(1986) at §6.9].

VII. CONCLUSIONS

. . . From all that has been said, however, it appears abundantly clear that the view embodied in the law's general denial of a duty to undertake a rescue is an anachronism. Accordingly, the law should be altered so as to reflect the settled convictions of Canadians today.

Admittedly, affecting such a change would not be easy. Developments might continue to be slow and uncertain as judges and legislators cautiously invoke various devices as means of justifying their progressive steps. . . .

The policy considerations which must be accounted for in answering this question are many. On the basis of the experience in France over the past four decades it has been shown that the administrative and philosophical fears of those who oppose a duty are largely unfounded. So, too, it has been shown that the existence of an obligation to assist those in peril would have many positive effects. Prosser has said that "changing social conditions lead constantly to the recognition of new duties."[52] One can hope.

[52]*Handbook on the Law of Torts* (1964) 334.

22

ROBERT B. LEFLAR

Personal Injury Compensation Systems in Japan: Values Advanced and Values Undermined

. . . This paper explores the relative emphasis placed by the Japanese tort system on the various posited goals of personal injury law. The paper begins by stressing the importance to Japan of the retributive and public participation functions of tort law. It proceeds to focus on the extent to which Japanese law fulfills the goals of compensation and deterrence in the fields of medical malpractice and certain areas of products liability. The paper concludes that although transaction costs are relatively low in Japan, and the tort system operates fairly at least among those litigants who engage it, the goals of systematic compensation for injury and appropriate deterrence of injury-causing activity are incompletely met.

"HETERODOX" FUNCTIONS OF TORT LAW: RETRIBUTION AND PUBLIC PARTICIPATION

In my view, retribution (or, put another way, vengeance) is a legitimate function of the tort system as well as the criminal law system, both in Japan and in the United States. . . .

I doubt that any Japanese will ever forget the images of plaintiffs' groups demonstrating outside the headquarters of the various companies responsible for mercury pollution,[1] arsenic contamination of powdered milk,[2] and other toxic tragedies.[3] The bereaved, carrying black-edged portraits of the deceased, demanded formal apologies from the presidents of the companies involved. The extraction of a formal apology is, in some sense, a form of vengeance. The act inflicts humiliation. It is a process familiar to any observer of Japanese tort litigation.

The American public, too, views the tort system as a means of inflicting peaceful retribution upon wrongdoers. The fact that punitive damages are a firmly established feature of American tort law[4] leaves the point beyond dispute, even without considering the literature on jurors' motivations in straight compensatory

[1]Judgment of March 20, 1973, Kumamoto District Court, 696 HANREI JIHŌ 15 (translated in JULIAN GRESSER, KŌICHIRŌ FUJIKURA & AKIO MORISHIMA, ENVIRONMENTAL LAW IN JAPAN 106 (1981)); Judgment of June 14, 1977, Tokyo High Court, 853 HANREI JIHŌ 3; Judgment of the Supreme Court, First Petty Bench, Dec. 17, 1980, 984 HANREI JIHŌ 37.

[2]Judgment of the Supreme Court, Feb. 27, 1969, 547 HANREI JIHŌ 92; Judgment of Nov. 28, 1973, Tokushima District Court, 721 HANREI JIHŌ 7. *See generally* WAGAKUNI NO SEIZŌBUTSU SEKININ HŌ [JAPANESE PRODUCT LIABILITY LAW] (AKIO TAKEUCHI, ED.) 38–39 (1990).

[3]*See, e.g.,* Akio Morishima & Malcolm Smith, *Accident Compensation Schemes in Japan: A Window on the Operation of Law in a Society,* 20 U. BRITISH COLUMBIA L. REV. 491, 492–93 (1986); Michael Reich, *Public and Private Responses to a Chemical Disaster in Japan: The Case of Kanemi Yushō,* 15 LAW IN JAPAN 102 (1982).

[4]*See, e.g.,* Pacific Mutual Life Ins. Co. v. Haslip, 111 S.Ct. 1032, 1041–43 (1991); *id.* at 1047–48 (Scalia, J., concurring).

damage actions. I suppose that even the economists, champions of logical calculation that they are, could conceivably recognize this psychological reality by inserting a "vengeance factor" into their utility analyses. I have never detected any tendency among the practitioners of that noble science, however, to allow a retributive component to creep into their equations.

Our Japanese colleagues have also stressed the importance to their tort system of its public participation function. That function takes on added significance because political channels are less responsive to the public in Japan than in the United States.

In a system where hierarchy is the social norm, where administrative control by an elite class is a given, and where meaningful public input into the policymaking process is usually limited to a few select academics such as Professor Morishima who serve on advisory committees and (to some extent) to the mass media, ordinary citizens are essentially shut out.

The phenomenon described by Professor Matsumoto whereby public-interest lawsuits are brought that make no financial sense, in which the costs of litigation could not possibly be recouped through the likely damage award, constitutes an important means for citizens to be heard. There are simply few other avenues for participation in the policymaking process.

Retribution and public participation are considered legitimate goals of the Japanese tort system. The extent to which these goals are actually realized, however, is problematic. The pollution cases are examples of successful fulfillment of some of those goals. The subsequent judicial retreat from the activist stance of the pollution cases is of considerable significance: as Professor Tanaka pointed out, defeat in political litigation entails the real political risk that the government can use the judicial outcome as justification for not responding to social needs.

COMPENSATION AND DETERRENCE FUNCTIONS OF JAPANESE TORT LAW: MEDICAL MALPRACTICE

What of the other functions of the civil law system that Western scholars are more accustomed to debating, such as compensation and deterrence?

Consider first medical malpractice. As Professors Morishima and Tejima pointed out, on the whole medical malpractice law in Japan is rather similar to that in the United States, at least as a matter of judicial rhetoric and doctrine.[5] Some case law suggests that the standard of care applied to doctors may be even stricter in Japan.[6]

In my view, subtle doctrinal formulations explain very little for comparative purposes. Allow me to draw your attention instead to some figures.

Professor Tejima mentioned the steady increase of medical malpractice cases in Japan. In 1987 the number of cases filed in court rose to 335, an increase of not quite 40 percent from ten years earlier.[7] In addition, to assess the total number of medical claims for comparative purposes, one should add perhaps half of the 250 claims made to the extrajudicial arbitration system sponsored by the Japan Medical Association (JMA).[8] One should also count some portion—two-thirds would be a generous approximation—of the 220 claims per year that Professor Tejima mentioned from the drug side effect compensation act,[9] many of which, if brought in the United States, would probably involve a malpractice claim. That gives us a rough estimate of slightly more than 600 malpractice-related claims per year in Japan.

---

[5] *See, e.g.*, Ikufumi Niimi and Itsuko Matsuura, *Iryō Jiko to Minji Sekinin* [*Medical Injury and Civil Liability*], in ICHIRŌ KATŌ & AKIO MORISHIMA (EDS.), IRYŌ TO JINKEN [MEDICAL CARE AND HUMAN RIGHTS] 366–404 (1984).

[6] In a 1961 case, the Supreme Court stated that the "highest duty of care [saizen no chūi gimu]" necessary for avoiding danger is required of physicians, as professionals charged with managing human life and health. Judgment of Feb. 16, 1961, Supreme Court, 15(2) *Saikōsai Minji Hanreishū* 244. Later cases have tended to phrase the standard of care in a less exacting way, for example, as that generally prevailing in the practice of clinical medicine at the time of the incident in question. *See, e.g.*, Judgment of March 30, 1982, Supreme Court, 1039 HANREI JIHŌ 66.

[7] SUPREME COURT OF JAPAN, IRYŌ KAGO KANKEI MINJI SOSHŌ JIKEN SHITSUMU SHIRYŌ [MATERIALS ON CIVIL ACTIONS RELATING TO MEDICAL MALPRACTICE] 9 (1989) (TABLE 3).

[8] Ichirō Katō, Tatsuo Kuroyanagi et al., *Fuhō Kōi Seido no Higaisha Kyūsai* [*Compensation of the Injured under the Tort Law System*], 926 JURISUTO 17, 23 (1989), *citing* KŌICHI HABA, IRYŌ JIKO NO BAISHŌ IGAKU-TEKI KENKYŪ [MEDICAL RESEARCH ON COMPENSATION FOR MEDICAL ACCIDENTS] (2463 cases submitted from 1974 to 1983, averaging 246 per year).

[9] Iyakuhin Fukusayō Higai Kyū sai Kenkyū Shinkō Kikin Hō [Drug Side-Effect Injury Relief and Research Promotion Fund Law], Law No. 55 of 1979.

Professor Tejima indicated there were 2,645 claims filed with the fund during the 12 years from 1980–1991, an average of 220 claims per year. . . . Most of these claims would fall primarily in the products liability field if brought in the United States, but malpractice claims against the prescribing physician would also be brought in many cases.

Comparisons among the per capita medical malpractice case filing rate in Japan and the rates in the United States, Canada and the United Kingdom are instructive. In the United States there are perhaps thirty claims per 100,000 people per year.[10] Rates in the United Kingdom are said to vary between six and twenty claims per 100,000 people per year, somewhat less than the Canadian rate.[11]

In Japan, a nation of 120 million people, there appear to be roughly 0.5 claims per 100,000 people per year. So the increase in medical malpractice litigation in Japan has brought the rate up close to two percent of the United States per capita claim rate. Perhaps if it continues to skyrocket, it may soon hit one-tenth of the British rate.

The best illustration of the differences among societies on this score is to compare medical malpractice insurance premiums. In the United States, premiums are differentiated according to geography and medical specialization. In 1986, premiums ranged from roughly $1,900 per year in Arkansas for general practitioners doing only minor surgery,[12] to $115,000 per year for neurological surgeons in the Miami area.[13]

In Japan, by contrast, medical malpractice insurance premiums are standardized; there is no differentiation either by geography or by specialty. In 1988, a physician typically paid a total of about ¥60,000 per year,[14] which was less than US $500. Hospitals, which are defined as having 20 or more beds, typically paid ¥8,310 (US $60) per bed per year for malpractice insurance.[15]

As the Harvard Medical Practice Study has demonstrated, the vast majority of Americans injured by medical error receive no compensation for their injuries.[16] There is no good reason to believe that the extent of actual medical error is significantly greater or significantly less in Japan than in the United States, although statistics to support that assertion are difficult to obtain.

There are fewer surgeries in Japan for equivalent conditions,[17] by and large, so there is probably less unnecessary surgery. On the other hand, there are more unnecessary drug prescriptions in Japan than the United States, largely because Japanese private physicians and hospitals both derive a great deal of their income from the prescription and overprescription of drugs.

Moreover, until very recently Japan has not required that patients be informed of the fact that they were participating in drug trials. In 1990, at last the Ministry of Health and Welfare instituted such a requirement.[18] That is to say, the rule is on the books now; the extent to which it is being followed is unclear. For present purposes, the point is that what would be considered widespread violations of patients' rights in the United States have long gone unnoticed (and unlitigated) in Japan.

To summarize, only a small proportion of patients injured by medical malpractice is ever compensated in the United States. But that proportion is likely far smaller in Japan.

Some downplay the significance of this problem. After all, Japan has universal health care insurance.

---

[10]*See, e.g.,* Patricia Danzon, *The "Crisis" in Medical Malpractice: A Comparison of Trends in the United States, Canada, the United Kingdom and Australia,* [18 LAW, MEDICINE, AND HEALTH CARE 48, 50 (1990)]. *See also* Patricia Danzon, *The Frequency and Severity of Medical Malpractice Claims: New Evidence,* [49, LAW AND CONTEMP. PROBS. 57 (1986)].

[11]C. HAM, R. DINGWALL, P. FENN & D. HARRIS, MEDICAL NEGLIGENCE: COMPENSATION AND ACCOUNTABILITY (1988), cited in Patricia Danzon, *The "Crisis" in Medical Malpractice: A Comparison of Trends in the United States, Canada, the United Kingdom and Australia, supra* note [10] at 48, 50 n.23 (1990).

[12]GENERAL ACCOUNTING OFFICE, MEDICAL MALPRACTICE: SIX STATE CASE STUDIES SHOW CLAIMS AND INSURANCE COSTS STILL RISE DESPITE REFORMS 16 (1986) (Table 2.2).

[13]David Nye, Donald Gifford, Bernard Webb & Marvin Dewar, *The Causes of the Medical Malpractice Crisis: An Analysis of Claims Data and Insurance Company Finances,* 76 GEO. L.J. 1495, 1502 (1988) (Table 2).

[14]. . . YASUDA FIRE & MARINE INS. CO., ISHI BAISHŌ SEKININ HOKEN NO GO-ANNAI [GUIDE TO PHYSICIANS' LIABILITY INSURANCE] 6 (1988). . . .

[15]YASUDA FIRE & MARINE INS. CO., ISHI BAISHŌ SEKININ HOKEN NO GO-ANNAI [GUIDE TO PHYSICIANS' LIABILITY INSURANCE] 6 (1988).

[16]A. Russell Localio et al., *Relation Between Malpractice Claims and Adverse Events Due to Negligence,* 325 NEW ENGLAND J. MED. 245 (1991). *See also* Troyen A. Brennan et al., *Incidence of Adverse Events and Negligence in Hospitalized Patients,* 324 NEW ENGLAND J. MED. 370 (1991); Lucian L. Leape et al. *The Nature of Adverse Events in Hospitalized Patients,* 324 NEW ENGLAND J. MED. 377 (1991).

[17]The overall number of surgical operations per 1,000 population was 22.0 in Japan in 1984, and 91.0 in the United States in 1986. Naoki Ikegami, *Japanese Health Care: Low Cost through Regulated Fees,* 10(3) HEALTH AFFAIRS 87, 99 (1991). . . .

[18]MINISTRY OF HEALTH & WELFARE, PHARMACEUTICAL AFFAIRS BUREAU NOTIFICATION No. 874 (October 2, 1989), *reprinted in English in* DRUG REGISTRATION REQUIREMENTS IN JAPAN 203–212 (YAKUJI NIPPŌ, 4TH ED. 1991). These "Good Clinical Practice" (GCP) rules became effective on October 1, 1990.

People who are injured by medical malpractice have their iatrogenic injuries competently treated at reasonable cost. That response ignores the fact that people who die from malpractice do not have their injuries competently treated. Moreover, to rely on the social welfare net as virtually the sole means of redressing medical malpractice injuries is to ignore the issues of compensating wage loss and pain and suffering.

Perhaps the picture in Japan is not quite so bleak as I have painted it. An anecdotal, but perhaps representative, example of the kind of compensation that never gets into the official statistics is the story I heard from a colleague of the physician whose misdiagnosis inconvenienced a certain patient but caused no lasting damage. The physician in question went to the patient's house, made a sincere apology and presented as a token of that sincerity an envelope containing ¥50,000 (then about US $400).

That act is unthinkable in the United States. Imagine the liability consequences! But it is probably not atypical in Japan. There exists outside our purview an informal compensation system that also may have the effect of satisfying, to some extent, the retributional values of the tort system. Nevertheless, it is unlikely that this informal system compensates more than a small minority of patients harmed by malpractice.

If tort law is not satisfactorily serving even a compensatory function in the area of medical malpractice, then one might conclude *a fortiori* that it could not possibly have any deterrent effect. Certainly there is no significant financial deterrent imposed by the level of medical malpractice insurance premiums prevalent in Japan.

This line of reasoning is not necessarily persuasive, though. As Professor Tejima suggested, perhaps physicians in Japan place an extraordinarily high reputational value on not being sued. The mere publication of a report of a malpractice action can have grave implications for a community physician's standing in the competition for patients. In Japanese medical education, too, a common professorial admonition is that if the student persists in whatever diagnostic or treatment error is under discussion, the student will likely wind up in court.

We are all familiar with the phenomenon of overvaluing a tiny risk of catastrophic harm. In that respect, perhaps Japanese physicians are to malpractice risks what American consumers were to Alar-treated apples.

Moreover, reputational losses are not covered by liability insurance benefits. They fall directly on the physician. So to some extent, there is a sentinel effect derived simply from the existence of a medical malpractice system, whether the system is functioning or not. A perception of danger, whatever the reality, can be a powerful motivator.

Central to medical quality control, however, is accountability. I will follow up on one of Professor Tejima's points (perhaps at the risk of slight exaggeration) by stating boldly that formal accountability is entirely lacking in Japanese medical practice.

There is, for example, no system of specialization exams. The physician declares himself (or, rarely, herself) a specialist in a particular area, starts practicing in that area and simply continues. There are no requirements for continuing medical education.

Systematic risk evaluation programs and outcome-based clinical studies of treatment effectiveness are quite rare in Japan. Risk management systems and risk management specialists, now common in American hospitals, are virtually unknown in the Japanese setting.

Utilization review is virtually impossible; usable data are not even kept in any systematic fashion. Insurance claim records are jealously guarded. A study along the lines of the Harvard Medical Practice Study would be scarcely imaginable in Japan.

Peer review in an American sense is entirely foreign to Japan. The hierarchical structure of Japanese medicine requires that one not subject the members of one's own group to outside evaluation or criticism. Such problems are dealt with internally. Certainly it is conceivable that a physician of questionable competence might be shuffled out of neurosurgery into general practice. But there is no institutional equivalent, for example, of American hospitals' review committees that sometimes exercise the power of suspension or revocation of hospital privileges. In fact, more than one-third of Japanese physicians practice on their own, owning their own hospitals and clinics, without admitting privileges to large hospitals. These physicians practice entirely outside any accountability structure.

Not least important, the Japan Medical Association disciplinary system shares with its American counterparts the quality of laxity in searching out quality control problems. The list of difficulties could go on. These facts simply illustrate that however intractable the problem of preventing medical injury by law-related means may be in the United States, it is a far more intractable problem in Japan.

COMPENSATION AND DETERRENCE FUNCTIONS: PRODUCTS LIABILITY

A noteworthy difference between American and Japanese products liability litigation is the almost total absence in Japan of two categories of cases that occupy a large proportion of American courts' civil dockets: asbestos cases, and design and manufacturing defect cases against automobile manufacturers.

Asbestos claimants, in Japan as in the United States, may seek redress either through civil litigation or through the workers' compensation system. Regarding civil litigation, Japanese courts have seen only a handful of lawsuits, consolidating approximately 40 plaintiffs' claims.

Available statistics on workers' compensation claims arising from asbestos exposure are fragmentary. Statistics for the 20-year period 1960–1979 for Osaka Prefecture, where much of the Japanese asbestos-producing and -processing industry has been concentrated, show a total of 116 asbestosis cases authorized for workers' compensation due to permanent disability.[19] As for lung cancer and mesothelioma, from 1981 through 1987 the Labor Ministry recognized a nationwide total of 56 cases caused by asbestos exposure.[20] Although in both data sets the numbers rise gradually over time, one can nevertheless draw the firm conclusion that in comparison with the United States experience, the absolute number of asbestos-related cases and the total amount of compensation are extremely small.

Perhaps the disparity between the volume of asbestos cases in the United States and Japan could be explained by differences between the two countries in asbestos consumption over time. If Japan was using far smaller quantities of asbestos in earlier years, then taking account of the latency periods for asbestos-related diseases, the consequent disparity in the extent of human asbestos exposure could explain the differences in subsequent claim frequencies.

To compare Japan's asbestos consumption with that of the United States, one may use Japanese asbestos import figures as a proxy for consumption figures, because Japan produces very little asbestos domestically. In the United States, asbestos consumption peaked from about 1950 to the early 1970s and then declined precipitously. In Japan asbestos imports peaked shortly after 1970 and then leveled off. In 1989 Japanese asbestos imports were almost triple United States usage. In the past few years imports have started to decline.

It may therefore be the case that much of the difference in claims experience between the two countries is due to the latency factor, and that the cases simply have not started pouring in yet in Japan. But with the very high male smoking rates in Japan and the synergistic effect between tobacco consumption and asbestos consumption in disease causation,[21] it is likely that the number of Japanese asbestos victims will dramatically increase over time, together with the amount of asbestos litigation.

Regarding automobile defects, there is virtually no litigation in Japan against automobile manufacturers.[22] Absence of defects is not the explanation; even the Japanese automakers have not yet attained a state of perfection. The National Highway Traffic Safety Administration has reported numerous recent recalls and defects in Japanese cars sold in the United States.

Professor Matsumoto's presentation provided a revealing explanation. The traffic accident compensation system covers injuries that might have been caused by automobile defects. A vehicle owner, to escape liability for damages that he or she has caused, must prove not only lack of fault on the owner's part but also absence of defect in the vehicle. So the vehicle owner is legally responsible for injuries to others that are caused by an automobile defect, jointly with the automobile manufacturer.

---

[19]K. Morinaga et al., *Mortality and Survival of Workers Receiving Compensation for Asbestos in Osaka, Japan,* 2 PROCEEDINGS OF VITH INTERNATIONAL PNEUMOCONIOSIS CONFERENCE 1983 768 (ILO 1984).

[20]Personal communication from Mr. Isao Koga, Labor Ministry, Labor Standards Bureau, Compensation Division, May 29, 1989.

[21]*See, e.g.,* Occupational Exposure to Asbestos, Tremolite, Anthophyllite, and Actinolite, 51 Fed. Reg. 22,612, 22,625 (1986) (Hammond and Selikoff studies).

[22]*See, e.g.,* Gary T. Schwartz, *Product Liability and Medical Malpractice in Comparative Context,* in THE LIABILITY MAZE: THE IMPACT OF LIABILITY LAW ON SAFETY AND INNOVATION 51 (Peter W. Huber & Robert E. Litan eds. 1991).

The injured party can recover the standardized damage amount from the vehicle owner's insurance company. All drivers carry compulsory insurance, and about 60 percent also carry optional insurance.[23] Therefore, seldom does the injured party have a strong incentive to take on the enormous burden of litigating a defect case against Toyota or Nissan.

TRANSACTION COST REDUCTION AND FAIRNESS

Other values that the Japanese civil code system treasures are transaction cost reduction and fairness, in the sense of equivalent treatment of similarly situated injured parties.

Concerning transaction costs, Professor Priest suggested that in the United States high litigation rates derive in part from the existence of the jury system. Outcomes are unpredictable, so plaintiffs' and defendants' attorneys' estimates of likely outcomes tend to vary widely. As a result, settlements are often difficult to reach.

Actually, there are two components to that unpredictability. One is the probability of winning, a form of unpredictability that may or may not relate to the presence of lay jurors as fact finders. The other factor is the amount of damage, a form of unpredictability that probably is connected to the jury system.

In Japan, one of those sources of unpredictability is largely removed because of the standardized damage guidelines based on the traffic accident schedule that Professor Morishima has described. Where liability of the defendant is probable, attorneys for each side know precisely how much the case is worth. Litigation is unnecessary.

Insurance companies have theoretical incentives to litigate nevertheless. One such incentive is to delay payment of benefits in order to obtain the use of the money not yet paid. Also, as Professors Ramseyer and Nakazato have pointed out, defendants have somewhat cheaper litigation costs than plaintiffs.[24] Plaintiffs have to buy legal services at what Professor Matsumoto has characterized as cartelized attorney's fee schedule rates. Insurance companies and manufacturers, by contrast, can obtain cut-rate legal services from the large corps of non-attorney legal specialists trained in law at the undergraduate level and employed by the company. This cost imbalance may also give defendants an incentive to litigate, or at least to threaten to litigate. Whether these theoretical incentives actually affect defendants' and insurers' behavior, increasing their tendency to litigate and to delay, is a question resolvable only by empirical evidence.

Concerning the goal of fairness, the standardized damage guidelines characteristic of much of Japanese tort litigation promote fairness among similarly situated litigants. However, as Professor Morishima pointed out, there is significant variation from one compensation scheme to the next.

The arguments here are familiar from the workers' compensation arena. Standardized damages are appealing in curtailing the crap-shoot aspect of litigation. But such systems are also characterized by undercutting of the deterrence goal. Liability is easily calculable by a manufacturer. It becomes just another cost of doing business. In systems such as Japan's, in which there is a paucity of litigation and insurers do not adopt responsive premium rating policies, the deterrent function of tort law is undermined, and the larger part of the cost of injuries is externalized to the injured public.

EVALUATING THE JAPANESE TORT SYSTEM AS A WHOLE

Finally, I would like to address Ramseyer's and Nakazato's interesting and provocative article, "The Rational Litigant: Settlement Amounts and Verdict Rates in Japan," published three years ago in the Journal of Legal Studies. They looked at the traffic accident system as "typical" of Japanese litigation and concluded: "Litigation is scarce in Japan not because the system is bankrupt. It is scarce because the system works."[25]

I agree with Professor Tanaka that their generalization from the traffic accident system is too sweep-

---

[23]Takao Tanase, *The Management of Disputes: Automobile Accident Compensation in Japan*, 24 LAW & SOCIETY REV. 651, 670 (1990).

[24]J. Mark Ramseyer & Minoru Nakazato, *The Rational Litigant: Settlement Amounts and Verdict Rates in Japan,* 18 J. LEGAL STUDIES 263, 274–76 (1989).

[25]*Id.* at [24].

ing. Traffic accidents are the exception in Japanese litigation rather than the rule. Unlike medical malpractice, and unlike drug litigation, fact issues in traffic accident cases can be readily resolved. Police reports are presumptively complete and accurate. Insurance records exist. One can identify the injured and fix liability with relative ease.

Moreover, insurance companies do not have the same incentives to litigate as obstinately over traffic accidents in Japan as they do in American jurisdictions without no-fault systems. As Professor Tanase has pointed out in a persuasive article, with reference to compulsory insurance (which is the basis for more than three-fourths of total payouts), the insurance companies are all in a risk pool that shares profits and losses evenly, giving the closely regulated industry a quasi-administrative function.

So when Professor Ramseyer says "the system works," the question becomes, with reference to what goals does it work?

If one of the goals is to keep administrative costs down, the Japanese system certainly is successful. If one goal is to achieve equity in damage recoveries among the injured, Japan is relatively successful in that respect as well, at least to the extent that the injured engage the system. If a goal is to keep the development of safety standards in administrative hands and out of the reach of the courts and plaintiffs' attorneys, the system generally works very well indeed. In times past, the courts have served as a channel for public participation; that role appears to have diminished in significance.

But if the goals of systematic compensation and injury prevention are considered important, then with the possible exception of traffic accident compensation, one has to look outside the Japanese legal system for their fulfillment.

23

Tarasoff v. Regents of University of California

17 Cal. 3d 425, 551 P.2d 334,
131 Cal. Rptr. 14 (1976)

Tobriner, J. On October 27, 1969, Prosenjit Poddar killed Tatiana Tarasoff. Plaintiffs, Tatiana's parents, allege that two months earlier Poddar confided his intention to kill Tatiana to Dr. Lawrence Moore, a psychologist employed by the Cowell Memorial Hospital at the University of California at Berkeley. They allege that on Moore's request, the campus police briefly detained Poddar, but released him when he appeared rational. They further claim that Dr. Harvey Powelson, Moore's superior, then directed that no further action be taken to detain Poddar. No one warned plaintiffs of Tatiana's peril.

Concluding that these facts set forth causes of action against neither therapists and policemen involved, nor against the Regents of the University of California as their employer, the superior court sustained defendants' demurrers to plaintiffs' second amended complaints without leave to amend. This appeal ensued.

[Plaintiffs' second amended complaints set forth four causes of action: (1) a claim that defendants negligently failed to detain a dangerous patient; (2) a claim that defendants negligently failed to warn Tatiana's parents; (3) a claim for punitive damages on the ground that defendants acted "maliciously and oppressively"; and (4) a claim that defendants breached their duty to their patient and the public. The court concludes that plaintiffs' first and fourth causes of action are barred by governmental immunity, and that plaintiffs' third cause of action is barred by a rule precluding exemplary damages in a wrongful death action. Therefore, the court addresses the question of whether plaintiffs' second cause of action can be amended to state a basis for recovery.]

The second cause of action can be amended to allege that Tatiana's death proximately resulted from defendants' negligent failure to warn Tatiana or others likely to apprise her of her danger. Plaintiffs contend that as amended, such allegations of negligence and proximate causation, with resulting damages, establish a cause of action. Defendants, however, contend that in the circumstances of the present case they owed no duty of care to Tatiana or her parents and that, in the absence of such duty, they were free to act in careless disregard of Tatiana's life and safety.

In analyzing this issue, we bear in mind that legal duties are not discoverable facts of nature, but merely conclusory expressions that, in cases of a particular type, liability should be imposed for damage done. As stated in Dillon v. Legg (1968) 68 Cal. 2d 728, 734, 69 Cal. Rptr. 72, 76, 441 P.2d 912, 916: "The assertion that liability must . . . be denied because defendant bears no 'duty' to plaintiff 'begs the essential question—whether the plaintiff's interests are entitled to legal protection against the defendant's conduct. . . . [Duty] is not sacrosanct in itself, but only an expression of the sum total of those considerations of policy which lead the law to say that the particular plaintiff is entitled to protection.' (Prosser, Law of Torts [3d ed. 1964] at pp. 332–333.)"

In the landmark case of Rowland v. Christian (1968) 69 Cal. 2d 108, 70 Cal. Rptr. 97, 443 P.2d 561, Justice Peters recognized that liability should be imposed "for an injury occasioned to another by his want of ordinary care or skill" as expressed in section 1714 of the Civil Code. Thus, Justice Peters, quoting from Heaven v. Pender (1883) 11 Q.B.D. 503, 509 stated: "'whenever one person is by circumstances placed in such a position with regard to another . . . that if he did not use ordinary care and skill in his own conduct . . . he would cause danger of injury to the person or property of the other, a duty arises to use ordinary care and skill to avoid such danger.'"

We depart from "this fundamental principle" only upon the "balancing of a number of considerations"; major ones "are the foreseeability of harm to the plaintiff, the degree of certainty that the plaintiff suffered injury, the closeness of the connection between the defendant's conduct and the injury suffered, the moral blame attached to the defendant's conduct, the policy of preventing future harm, the extent of the burden to the defendant and consequences to the community of imposing a duty to exercise care with resulting liability for breach, and the availability, cost and prevalence of insurance for the risk involved."

The most important of these considerations in establishing duty is foreseeability. As a general principle, a "defendant owes a duty of care to all persons who are foreseeably endangered by his conduct, with respect to all risks which make the conduct unreasonably dangerous." As we shall explain, however, when the avoidance of foreseeable harm requires a defendant to control the conduct of another person, or to warn of such conduct, the common law has traditionally imposed liability only if the defendant bears some special relationship to the dangerous person or to the potential victim. Since the relationship between a therapist and his patient satisfies this requirement, we need not here decide whether foreseeability alone is sufficient to create a duty to exercise reasonable care to protect a potential victim of another's conduct.

Although, as we have stated above, under the common law, as a general rule, one person owed no duty to control the conduct of another, nor to warn those endangered by such conduct, the courts have carved out an exception to this rule in cases in which the defendant stands in some special relationship to either the person whose conduct needs to be controlled or in a relationship to the foreseeable victim of that conduct. Applying this exception to the present case, we note that a relationship of defendant therapists to either Tatiana or Poddar will suffice to establish a duty of care; as explained in section 315 of the Restatement Second of Torts, a duty of care may arise from either "(a) a special relation . . . between the actor and the third person which imposes a duty upon the actor to control the third person's conduct, or (b) a special relation . . . between the actor and the other which gives to the other a right of protection."

Although plaintiffs' pleadings assert no special relation between Tatiana and defendant therapists, they establish as between Poddar and defendant therapists the special relation that arises between a patient and his doctor or psychotherapist. Such a relationship may support affirmative duties for the benefit of third persons. Thus, for example, a hospital must exercise reasonable care to control the behavior of a patient which may endanger other persons. A doctor must also warn a patient if the patient's condition or medication renders certain conduct, such as driving a car, dangerous to others.

Although the California decisions that recognize this duty have involved cases in which the defendant stood in a special relationship *both* to the victim and to the person whose conduct created the danger, we do not think that the duty should logically be constricted to such situations. Decisions of other jurisdictions hold that the single relationship of a doctor to his patient is sufficient to support the duty to exercise reasonable care to protect others against dangers emanating from the patient's illness. The courts hold that a doctor is liable to persons infected by his patient if he negligently fails to diagnose a contagious disease or, having diagnosed the illness, fails to warn members of the patient's family. . . .

Defendants contend, however, that imposition of a duty to exercise reasonable care to protect third persons is unworkable because therapists cannot accurately predict whether or not a patient will resort to violence. In support of this argument amicus representing the American Psychiatric Association and other professional societies cites numerous articles which indicate that therapists, in the present state of the art, are unable reliably to predict violent acts; their forecasts, amicus claims, tend consistently to overpredict violence, and indeed are more often wrong than right. Since predictions of violence are often erroneous, amicus concludes, the courts should not render rulings that predicate the liability of therapists upon the validity of such predictions.

The role of the psychiatrist, who is indeed a practitioner of medicine, and that of the psychologist who performs an allied function, are like that of the physician who must conform to the standards of the profession and who must often make diagnoses and predictions based upon such evaluations. Thus the judgment of the therapist in diagnosing emotional disorders and in predicting whether a patient presents a serious danger of violence is comparable to the judgment which doctors and professionals must regularly render under accepted rules of responsibility.

We recognize the difficulty that a therapist encounters in attempting to forecast whether a patient presents a serious danger of violence. Obviously we do not require that the therapist, in making that determination, render a perfect performance; the therapist need only exercise "that reasonable degree of skill, knowledge, and care ordinarily possessed and exercised by members of [that professional specialty] under similar circumstances." Within the broad range of reasonable practice and treatment in which professional opinion and judgment may differ, the therapist is free to exercise his or her own best judgment without liability; proof, aided by hindsight, that he or she judged wrongly is insufficient to establish negligence.

In the instant case, however, the pleadings do not raise any question as to failure of defendant therapists to predict that Poddar presented a serious danger of violence. On the contrary, the present complaints allege that defendant therapists did in fact predict that Poddar would kill, but were negligent in failing to warn.

Amicus contends, however, that even when a therapist does in fact predict that a patient poses a serious danger of violence to others, the therapist should be absolved of any responsibility for failing to act to protect the potential victim. In our view, however, once a therapist does in fact determine, or under applicable professional standards reasonably should have determined, that a patient poses a serious danger of violence to others, he bears a duty to exercise reasonable care to protect the foreseeable victim of that danger. While the discharge of this duty of due care will necessarily vary with the facts of each case, in each instance the adequacy of the therapist's conduct must be measured against the traditional negligence standard of the rendition of reasonable care under the circumstances. . . .

Contrary to the assertion of amicus, this conclusion is not inconsistent with our recent decision in People v. Burnick, supra, 14 Cal. 3d 306, 121 Cal. Rptr. 488, 535 P.2d 352. Taking note of the uncertain character of therapeutic prediction, we held in *Burnick* that a person cannot be committed as a mentally disordered sex offender unless found to be such by proof beyond a reasonable doubt. The issue in the present context, however, is not whether the patient should be incarcerated, but whether the therapist should take any steps at all to protect the threatened victim; some of the alternatives open to the therapist, such as warning the victim, will not result in the drastic consequences of depriving the patient of his liberty. Weighing the uncertain and conjectural character of the alleged damage done the patient by such a warning against the peril to the victim's life, we conclude that professional inaccuracy in predicting violence cannot negate the therapist's duty to protect the threatened victim.

The risk that unnecessary warnings may be given is a reasonable price to pay for the lives of possible victims that may be saved. We would hesitate to hold that the therapist who is aware that his patient expects to attempt to assassinate the President of the United States would not be obligated to warn the authorities because the therapist cannot predict with accuracy that his patient will commit the crime.

Defendants further argue that free and open communication is essential to psychotherapy; that "Unless a patient . . . is assured that . . . information [revealed by him] can and will be held in utmost confidence, he will be reluctant to make the full disclosure upon which diagnosis and treatment . . . depends." (Sen. Com. on Judiciary, comment on Evid. Code, §1014.) The giving of a warning, defendants contend, constitutes a breach of trust which entails the revelation of confidential communications. . . .

We realize that the open and confidential character of psychotherapeutic dialogue encourages patients to express threats of violence, few of which are ever executed. Certainly a therapist should not be encouraged routinely to reveal such threats; such disclosures could seriously disrupt the patient's relationship with his therapist and with the persons threatened. To the contrary, the therapist's obligations to his patient require that he not disclose a confidence unless such disclosure is necessary to avert danger to others, and even then that he do so discreetly, and in a fashion that would preserve the privacy of his patient to the fullest extent compatible with the prevention of the threatened danger.

The revelation of a communication under the above circumstances is not a breach of trust or a violation of professional ethics; as stated in the Principles of Medical Ethics of the American Medical Association (1957), section 9: "A physician may not reveal the confidence entrusted to him in the course of medical attendance . . . *unless he is required to do so by law or unless it becomes necessary in order to protect the welfare of the individual or of the community.*" (Emphasis added.) We conclude that the public policy favoring protection of the confidential character of patient-psychotherapist communications must yield to the extent to which disclosure is essential to avert danger to others. The protective privilege ends where the public peril begins.

Our current crowded and computerized society compels the interdependence of its members. In this risk-infested society we can hardly tolerate the further exposure to danger that would result from a concealed knowledge of the therapist that his patient was lethal. If the exercise of reasonable care to protect the threatened victim requires the therapist to warn the endangered party or those who can reasonably be expected to notify him, we see no sufficient societal interest that would protect and justify concealment. The containment of such risks lies in the public interest. For the foregoing reasons, we find that plaintiffs' complaints can be amended to state a cause of action against defendants Moore, Powelson, Gold, and Yandell and against the Regents as their employer, for breach of a duty to exercise reasonable care to protect Tatiana.

[The majority concludes that the police defendants did not have a special relationship to either Tatiana or Poddar to impose upon them a duty to warn. The court also concludes that the defendant therapists are not protected by governmental immunity in connection with their failure to warn Tatiana's parents because their decisions were not "basic policy decisions" within the meaning of earlier precedent.]

For the reasons stated, we conclude that plaintiffs can amend their complaints to state a cause of action against defendant therapists by asserting that the therapists in fact determined that Poddar presented a serious danger of violence to Tatiana, or pursuant to the standards of their profession should have so determined, but nevertheless failed to exercise reasonable care to protect her from that danger. To the extent, however, that plaintiffs base their claim that defendant therapists breached that duty because they failed to procure Poddar's confinement, the therapists find immunity in Government Code section 856. Further, as to the police defendants we conclude that plaintiffs have failed to show that the trial court erred in sustaining their demurrer without leave to amend.

The judgment of the superior court in favor of defendants Atkinson, Beall, Brownrigg, Hallernan, and Teel is affirmed. The judgment of the superior court in favor of defendants Gold, Moore, Powelson, Yandell, and the Regents of the University of California is reversed, and the cause remanded for further proceedings consistent with the views expressed herein.

WRIGHT, C.J., and SULLIVAN and RICHARDSON, JJ., concur.

MOSK, J. (concurring and dissenting).

I concur in the result in this instance only because the complaints allege that defendant therapists did in fact predict that Poddar would kill and were therefore negligent in failing to warn of that danger. Thus the issue here is very narrow: we are not concerned with whether the therapists, pursuant to the standards of their profession, "should have" predicted potential violence; they allegedly did so in actuality. Under these limited circumstances I agree that a cause of action can be stated.

Whether plaintiffs can ultimately prevail is problematical at best. As the complaints admit, the therapist *did* notify the police that Poddar was planning to kill a girl identifiable as Tatiana. While I doubt that more should be required, this issue may be raised in defense and its determination is a question of fact.

I cannot concur, however, in the majority's rule that a therapist may be held liable for failing to predict his patient's tendency to violence if other practitioners, pursuant to the "standards of the profession," would have done so. The question is, what standards? Defendants and a responsible amicus curiae, supported by an impressive body of literature demonstrate that psychiatric predictions of violence are inherently unreliable. . . .

I would restructure the rule designed by the majority to eliminate all reference to conformity to standards of the profession in predicting violence. If a psychiatrist does in fact predict violence, then a duty to warn arises. The majority's expansion of that rule will take us from the world of reality into the wonderland of clairvoyance.

CLARK, J. (dissenting).

Until today's majority opinion, both legal and medical authorities have agreed that confidentiality is essential to effectively treat the mentally ill, and that imposing a duty on doctors to disclose patient threats to potential victims would greatly impair treatment. . . . Moreover, . . . imposing the majority's new duty is certain to result in a net increase in violence.

Overwhelming policy considerations weigh against imposing a duty on psychotherapists to warn a potential victim against harm. While offering virtually no benefit to society, such a duty will frustrate psychiatric treatment, invade fundamental patient rights and increase violence.

The importance of psychiatric treatment and its need for confidentiality have been recognized by this court. . . .

Assurance of confidentiality is important for three reasons.

DETERRENCE FROM TREATMENT

First, without substantial assurance of confidentiality, those requiring treatment will be deterred from seeking assistance. It remains an unfortunate fact in our society that people seeking psychiatric guidance tend to become stigmatized. Apprehension of such stigma—apparently increased by the propensity of people considering treatment to see themselves in the worst possible light—creates a well-recognized reluctance to seek aid. This reluctance is alleviated by the psychiatrist's assurance of confidentiality.

FULL DISCLOSURE

Second, the guarantee of confidentiality is essential in eliciting the full disclosure necessary for effective treatment. The psychiatric patient approaches treatment with conscious and unconscious inhibitions against revealing his innermost thoughts. "Every person, however well-motivated, has to overcome resistances to therapeutic exploration. These resistances seek support from every possible source and the possibility of disclosure would easily be employed in the service of resistance." (Goldstein & Katz, supra, 36 Conn. Bar J. 175, 179; see also, 118 Am. J. Psych. 734, 735.) Until a patient can trust his psychiatrist not to violate their confidential relationship, "the unconscious psychological control mechanism of repression will prevent the recall of past experiences." (Butler, Psychotherapy and Griswold: Is Confidentiality a Privilege or a Right? (1971) 3 Conn. L. Rev. 599, 604.)

SUCCESSFUL TREATMENT

Third, even if the patient fully discloses his thoughts, assurance that the confidential relationship will not be breached is necessary to maintain his trust in his psychiatrist—the very means by which treatment is effected. "[T]he essence of much psychotherapy is the contribution of trust in the external world and ultimately in the self, modeled upon the trusting relationship established during therapy." (Dawidoff, The Malpractice of Psychiatrists, 1966 Duke L.J. 696, 704). Patients will be helped only if they can form a trusting relationship with the psychiatrist. All authorities appear to agree that if the trust relationship cannot be developed because of collusive communication between the psychiatrist and others, treatment will be frustrated.

Given the importance of confidentiality to the practice of psychiatry, it becomes clear the duty to warn imposed by the majority will cripple the use and effectiveness of psychiatry. Many people, potentially violent—yet susceptible to treatment—will be deterred from seeking it; those seeking it will be inhibited from making revelations necessary to effective treatment; and, forcing the psychiatrist to violate the patient's trust will destroy the interpersonal relationship by which treatment is effected.

VIOLENCE AND CIVIL COMMITMENT

By imposing a duty to warn, the majority contributes to the danger to society of violence by the mentally ill and greatly increases the risk of civil commitment—the total deprivation of liberty—and those who should not be confined. The impairment of treatment and risk of improper commitment resulting from the new duty to warn will not be limited to a few patients but will extend to a large number of the mentally ill. Although under existing psychiatric procedures only a relatively few receiving treatment will ever present a risk of violence, the number making threats is huge, and it is the latter group—not just the former—whose treatment will be impaired and whose risk of commitment will be increased. . . .

Neither alternative open to the psychiatrist seeking to protect himself is in the public interest. The warning itself is an impairment of the psychiatrist's ability to treat, depriving many patients of adequate treatment. It is to be expected that after disclosing their threats, a significant number of patients, who would not become violent if treated according to existing practices, will engage in violent conduct as a result of unsuccessful treatment. In short, the majority's duty to warn will not only impair treatment of many who would never become violent but worse, will result in a net increase in violence.

The second alternative open to the psychiatrist is to commit his patient rather than to warn. Even in the absence of threat of civil liability, the doubts of psychiatrists as to the seriousness of patient threats have led psychiatrists to overcommit to mental institutions. This overcommitment has been authoritatively documented in both legal and psychiatric studies. . . .

Given the incentive to commit created by the majority's duty, this already serious situation will be worsened, contrary to Chief Justice Wright's admonition "that liberty is no less precious because forfeited in a civil proceeding than when taken as a consequence of a criminal conviction." (In re W. (1971) 5 Cal. 3d 296, 307, 96 Cal Rptr. 1, 9, 486 P.2d 1201, 1209.) . . .

[T]he majority impedes medical treatment, resulting in increased violence from—and deprivation of liberty to—the mentally ill.

We should accept . . . medical judgment, relying upon effective treatment rather than on indiscriminate warning.

The judgment should be affirmed.

McComb, J., concurs.

PART 4

CRIMINAL LAW

Criminal law is rich in philosophical interest. Any serious study of criminal law should begin with some basics. First, what is a crime? Broadly speaking, a *crime* is any act or omission that violates a criminal law. Though this definition has the virtue of relativizing what counts as a crime to specific criminal codes, aside from that, it is not very illuminating. However, some traditional distinctions and typologies shed more light on what constitutes crime. For example, the eminent English jurist William Blackstone distinguished between crimes that are *mala in se*—that is, evil in themselves or crimes against nature, such as murder—and those that are *mala prohibita*—that is, acts or omissions that are not intrinsically evil but count as crimes only because they have been prohibited by criminal law, such as certain regulatory offenses.[1] Another useful typology is suggested by Lawrence M. Friedman, who identifies property crimes, crimes against persons, morals offenses such as gambling and certain forms of sexual activity (often called "victimless crimes" because they usually involve the consent of participants), offenses against public order, and regulatory crimes.[2] Another familiar distinction is between felonies, which are relatively more serious crimes such as aggravated assault, and misdemeanors, which are deemed less serious crimes, such as simple assault.

Many, though not all, crimes can be analyzed into two components: an *actus reus,* or guilty act, and a *mens rea,* or guilty mind. The *actus reus* is the act or omission that has been prohibited by law, and the *mens rea* is the culpable mental state, identified by law, that the offender was in at the time of acting. For a person to be charged with a crime, a guilty act must have been committed, but the specific crime with which an alleged offender is charged often depends on both the accused's mental state at the time of acting and the circumstances in which the act was committed. Consider, for example, homicide. In general, "A person is guilty of criminal homicide if he purposely, knowingly, recklessly, or negligently causes the death of another human being."[3] The words *purposely, knowingly, recklessly,* and *negligently* refer to the accused's mental state at the time of acting and influence the degree of seriousness of the crime as well as the specific crime—such as murder or voluntary or involuntary manslaughter—with which the accused is charged. The circumstances in which the guilty act is committed can also affect both the seriousness of the crime with which an accused is charged and the severity of the sentence if the accused is convicted. Aggravating circumstances increase the severity of a crime and/or penalty, whereas mitigating circumstances can have the opposite effect. For example, the crime of simple rape becomes aggravated rape, a more serious crime, when a weapon is present. In some states, such as Georgia, a convicted murderer becomes eligible for the death penalty if the victim was a police officer killed in the line of duty. Sometimes the circumstances of the act provide a legal excuse or justification for the act; that is, they fur-

[1]See Blackstone, *Commentaries on the Laws of England,* vol. 4 (Chicago, IL: University of Chicago Press, 1979), 7–8.

[2]See Friedman, *Crime and Punishment in American History* (New York: Basic Books, 1993), 7.

[3]Henry Campbell Black, *Black's Law Dictionary,* 5th ed. (St. Paul, MN: West, 1979), 661.

nish a reason for acting that shows that the act is not one that the law prohibits. Killing in self-defense, intentional killing from necessity in the line of duty, and sometimes accidental killing are cases in point.

Three more aspects of criminal law merit mention. First, a few crimes import the idea of strict liability into criminal law. *Strict liability* is the doctrine that someone is liable for a prohibited act regardless of his or her mental state at the time of acting. Statutory rape, or sexual intercourse with a minor, provides a good example. No jurisdictions allow as a defense to this crime the accused's belief that the minor was over the legally specified age of consent, and it was not until recently that some jurisdictions and the Model Penal Code allowed as a defense the accused's reasonable belief under some circumstances.[4]

A second fascinating and controversial aspect of the criminal law is the *doctrine of diminished capacity,* which refers to a defendant's lack of capacity to achieve the mental state required for a particular crime. Also known as partial insanity, the doctrine allows the trier of fact to regard the defendant's impaired mental state as mitigating the punishment or the degree of the offense even though the defendant does not qualify as insane under the insanity test. Many courts have adopted the doctrine of diminished capacity and applied it to cases involving defendants who are mentally retarded or of extremely low intelligence (see *Black's Law Dictionary,* p. 412). Interesting contemporary twists on the doctrine of diminished capacity include "victimization syndromes." Victimization syndromes encompass Vietnam War veteran syndrome, battered women's syndrome, and hostage syndrome. All of these are types of posttraumatic stress disorder, which has recently been recognized as an official disorder by the American Psychiatric Association. As with other uses of the diminished capacity doctrine, "syndrome" defenses have been used to negate the specific intent element of a crime, thereby resulting in a reduced charge, such as from murder to manslaughter.[5]

Yet a third aspect of the criminal law is the insanity defense. Whereas the doctrine of diminished capacity is a partial defense, the insanity defense is a complete defense. The doctrine of diminished capacity relegates to the defendant some degree of responsibility for the commission of a crime. By contrast, the term *insanity* is used in law "to denote that degree of mental illness which negates the individual's legal responsibility or capacity" (*Black's Law Dictionary,* p. 714). As we shall discuss later in this introduction, several tests of insanity have been used in criminal law since the insanity defense came into British law in 1843.

Armed with these introductory remarks about crime and criminal law, we can now turn to a more detailed discussion of the essays presented in this section. Among the most fundamental philosophical questions we can ask is, "What is the function or purpose of the criminal law?" What is it for? The essays by John Stuart Mill and Patrick Devlin, with which the section on criminal law begins, offer contrasting answers to these questions. Their answers have important implications both for what constitutes a crime, and for the proper reach that the law should have into the private lives of individuals. Mill's piece, an excerpt from his famous work, *On Liberty and Utilitarianism,* sets forth the "harm principle," according to which the government may intervene in the private affairs of individuals only for the sake of preventing harm to nonconsenting third parties. The state may not intervene for the good of the individual, nor may it intrude in the private activities of consenting rational adults. Mill makes clear that the harm principle applies only to mature adults of undiminished rational capacities. Children, adults of diminished rational capacities, and, to Mill's discredit, primitive peoples living in quasi-barbaric states, are not protected by the harm principle. Because of their lack of rational capacity, these people need and, in Mill's view, are rightly subject to regulation by others, including the state.

Motivating these limits on the power of government to intervene in the affairs of rational adults is a commitment to the autonomy of the individual. Mill firmly believes in the right of people to make their own choices, set their own goals, and frame their own life plans. He advocates a list of liberties that comprises some of the most basic freedoms of the liberal political tradition: the rights to freedom of thought and conscience, of speech and opinion, of expression and publication; the right to cultivate one's prefer-

---

[4]See Sanford H. Kadish, Stephen J. Schulhofer, and Monrad G. Paulsen, *Criminal Law and Its Processes: Cases and Materials,* 4th ed. (Boston: Little, Brown, 1983), 285–86; the Model Penal Code is a model code of criminal law suggested by the National Conference of Commissioners of Uniform State Laws for adoption by state legislatures. On the Model Penal Code, see *Black's Law Dictionary,* 5th ed., p. 905.

[5]See Donald Alexander Downs, *More Than Victims: Battered Women, the Syndrome Society, and the Law* (Chicago: University of Chicago Press, 1996), 4.

ences and tastes and to frame one's life plan as one chooses; and the freedom to unite. All of these liberties are constrained by the proviso that engaging in them may not cause harm to others.

Mill offers an optimistic vision of the value of personal autonomy, of the possibilities of human flourishing, and of the limited role of government. However, one can raise many questions about, for example, his harm principle. What constitutes harm? Are psychological as well as physical harms regulated by the harm principle? Should the criminal law intervene to regulate offensive behavior, such as the production, dissemination, and consumption of hard-core pornography, that only some members of society believe can cause harm to a certain group, such as women?

Patrick Devlin takes quite a different perspective on the function of the criminal law as well as on the limits of the law's right to intervene in the private affairs of consenting adults. In this excerpt from *The Enforcement of Morals,* he argues that the function of the criminal law is to enforce society's morals. This view has been called *legal moralism.* As his primary defense of this position, he offers an argument from analogy. Just as political structures, such as forms of government, are essential for the continuation of society, so, too, are ongoing moral institutions, practices, and beliefs. Moral institutions, such as monogamous marriage, and moral beliefs, such as the Christian belief in the sanctity of the family (father and mother, united in holy wedlock, and their children), are the bonds that hold society together. Just as treason threatens the government and may be prohibited by the criminal law for the sake of preserving society, so, too, whatever threatens the moral institutions and beliefs that hold society together may also be criminally prohibited. Following this argument Devlin claims that homosexuality ought to be criminalized. Far from being a victimless "morals crime," the "victim", of homosexual behavior, even when practiced in private between consenting adults, is the institution of heterosexual marriage, which is weakened by homosexual practices. By threatening marriage, homosexuality threatens society's morals and thus should be criminally prohibited. Since we are all, Devlin thinks, weak and vulnerable in matters of sexual morality, there are no theoretical limits to the law's right to enforce morality, only practical ones. We must look to legislatures to determine the practical limits of the law's reach into private affairs; legislatures, in turn, must look to the opinions of the average reasonable man to ascertain the limits of society's tolerance for a particular practice. If a practice would elicit from the average reasonable "man on the street" genuine feelings of disgust, coupled with a deliberate judgment that it is injurious to society, then, Devlin thinks, the practice lies beyond the limits of what society can tolerate, and legislation should criminalize it.

Devlin's view is weak on several points. First, one can question the aptness of his argument from analogy. Treason is a direct threat to government, but how is homosexual activity a direct threat to heterosexual marriage? Traitors act with the intent to undermine a government, but it is doubtful that gays and lesbians engage in homosexual activity with the intent of undermining heterosexual marriage. Though the use of the criminal sanction is appropriate in the former case, it seems grossly unwarranted in the latter. Second, Devlin assumes that society is homogenous in its moral beliefs and practices, as well as united in the common practice of Christianity. In many contemporary Western societies, this is no longer true. In a multicultural society comprising many divergent moral and religious traditions, Devlin's view that the criminal law should enforce morality is problematic. If one religious or moral tradition is enforced with criminal sanctions, practitioners of other religious or moral perspectives can rightly complain of unequal treatment. Third, in pluralistic societies characterized by moral diversity, the average reasonable man, whose view truly represents all or most members of society, might not be found. Instead, we might find the average reasonable woman, or the average reasonable Muslim, or Hispanic, or African American. Whose view should the legislature consult? The view that represents the most potential votes in the next election? Finally, prostitution and adultery can threaten heterosexual marriage, but Devlin evidently believes that they do not constitute as great a threat as homosexuality does. Surely, he owes some explanation why.

The issues with which Mill and Devlin grapple came before the United States Supreme Court in the landmark case of *Bowers v. Hardwick* (1986). In 1982, Hardwick was charged with violating the Georgia statute criminalizing consensual sodomy (defined by the statute as oral or anal sex) by engaging in oral sex with another adult male in the bedroom of Hardwick's home. Hardwick challenged the constitutionality of the Georgia statute on five grounds. A narrow majority of the Court (5–4) rejected Hardwick's claims. Justice Byron White wrote the majority opinion.

Hardwick's first argument is that homosexuals have a constitutional right of privacy to engage in consensual sexual activity. The Georgia statute violates this privacy right. Hardwick premises his claim on a line of Supreme Court precedents. In *Griswold v. Connecticut,*[6] the Supreme Court articulated a right to privacy out of the penumbra of several constitutional amendments to protect the right of married couples to use contraceptives without government intrusion. In subsequent cases, the privacy right was upheld and extended to other private sexual and reproductive choices. Most famously, *Roe v. Wade*[7] drew on the right to privacy to grant women the right to have an abortion during the first two trimesters of pregnancy. Justice White, however, refused to extend this line of precedent to the right to engage in consensual sodomy.

In his second argument, Hardwick claims that a fundamental liberty to engage in consensual sodomy is "implicit in the concept of ordered liberty" that has been protected by the Supreme Court (see pp. 222, 223) and that this freedom is among those that are "deeply rooted in this Nation's history and traditions" (pp. 222, 224). White rejects these claims, as well as Hardwick's third argument that the due process clauses of the Fifth and Fourteenth Amendments should be extended to cover the right to engage in consensual sodomy. Hardwick's fourth and fifth arguments, that homosexual conduct that occurs in the privacy of the home merits constitutional protection under the precedent of *Stanley v. Georgia,*[8] and that the Georgia statute lacks a rational basis, also receive short shrift by Justice White.

The moralizing tone of the Supreme Court's decision is best captured in Chief Justice Burger's concurring opinion. Quoting Blackstone, he calls sodomy "the infamous crime against nature," "an offense of deeper malignity than rape," "a heinous act," and "a crime not fit to be named"(p. 224). Against such Devlinesque comments, Justice Blackmun's dissenting remarks reflect Mill. The case, he contends, is not about a fundamental right to engage in homosexual sodomy, but about "the right to be let alone" (p. 224). In Blackmun's words, "This case involves no real interference with the rights of others, for the mere knowledge that other individuals do not adhere to one's value system cannot be a legally cognizable interest . . . let alone an interest that can justify invading the houses, hearts, and minds of citizens who choose to live their lives differently" (p. 228).

The fourth selection in Part 4, "Crime and Punishment: An Indigenous African Experience," by Egbeke Aja, provides an interesting non-Western perspective on legal moralism, on what constitutes a crime, and on the appropriate limits of the law's reach into individual lives. Aja offers an example of a society with a universally accepted moral code and in which the criminal law was used to enforce morality. He examines the traditional, precolonial morality of the Igbo, an ethnic group in Nigeria with a population of about ten million. Traditional Igbo morality stresses the primacy of the world order over the individual. Personal morality does not exist in traditional Igbo thinking. Moral action consists in acts intended to maintain harmony among the various forces of nature: animal, vegetable, and mineral. There is, moreover, an ontological dimension to Igbo morality: To do wrong is not merely to be in individual disharmony with these natural forces, but to disrupt the natural order itself. Unimportant in themselves, an individual's actions matter only insofar as they affect the larger socionatural scheme. Traditional Igbo morality consists of prohibitions, taboos, and the Omenala, a set of customs that comprises the collective values of the Igbo tradition. The identification of the self with the community is the essential requirement of the Omenala.

In precolonial Igbo society, communities were isolated from outside influences, self-supporting, and largely self-contained. Any deliberate or unconscious harm to the fabric of society constituted a crime. Aja gives examples of the three main types of crime—capital, minor crimes, and abomination—and their respective punishments. Because they bear on the conception of responsibility central to the Igbo notion of crime, two features of these crimes are especially noteworthy. First, guilt for a crime was not limited to an individual perpetrator. The guilt or pollution associated with a crime affected a person's entire household, contaminating anything that was related to him or her—people, animals, or property. Second, the Igbo idea of the guilty mind, or *mens rea,* as an element of a criminal offense evidently differed from the idea in Western criminal law. This is seen in the Igbo idea that newly

[6]381 U.S. 479 (1965).
[7]410 U.S. 113 (1973).
[8]394 U.S. 557 (1969).

born infants, and even fetuses, were held responsible for certain crimes. For example, a breach baby was to be thrown into the evil forest after birth. The baby was judged to have had the intention to take the life of the mother. We include Aja's article here because it provides a perspective on crime and punishment that challenges traditional Western ways of thinking. Indeed, as a final comment, Aja notes how Western influences have changed contemporary Igbo culture, bringing with them a weakening of traditional social bonds and new forms of crime, without introducing corresponding modes of punishment. Interestingly, Aja attributes the inability of contemporary Igbo society to cope with crime to the Western legal system's emphasis on evidence.

Anthony Kenny's article, "The Mind and the Deed," defends the traditional Western common-law conception of criminal responsibility. Recall that, according to the traditional view, two elements compose a criminal offense: an *actus reus,* or guilty act, and *mens rea,* or guilty mind. A range of culpable mental states exists in criminal law: negligence, which is voluntary unawareness in performing an act; recklessness, which is the belief that one is performing or is probably performing an act; intent, which is performing the act as an end in itself or as a means to some other end; and specific intention, which is performing an act with an intent specified by law. Each of these mental states implies a progressively higher degree of criminal liability.

Kenny defends the traditional conception against several objections he believes are conceptually confused. For example, he rejects the suggestion, made in England in 1974 by the National Association for Mental Health, that crime is a form of social illness best dealt with by importing strict liability into the criminal law. According to this view, an offender would be held responsible for committing a criminal action, regardless of his or her mental state at the time of acting. Not only does the association misrepresent strict liability, Kenny claims, but following the suggestion would lead to a host of absurd consequences.

Another objection to the traditional conception is epistemological: How can we know for sure that someone had a particular mental state at the time of committing a criminal act? Here Kenny invokes the views of the philosopher Ludwig Wittgenstein to argue that (1) observing certain forms of physical behavior can allow us to infer a person's mental state and (2) assuming that someone is in a certain mental state can enable us to make sense of his or her physical actions. For example, if I see tears running down your face and hear you sobbing, I can infer that you are sorrowful or grief stricken. If I am puzzled by the fact that you suddenly drop to the floor and begin feeling the carpet with outstretched palms and fingers, I can make sense of this behavior by hypothesizing that you have lost a contact lens and want to find it. Despite the prevalence of such examples, determining *mens rea* in criminal cases is often no mean feat.

In an interesting twist on the usual problems, Kenny discusses a 1967 case from the High Court of Malawi, *Nyuzi and Kudemera v. Republic.* Alarmed at the high infant mortality rate, a village in Malawi suspected that witchcraft had caused the deaths. Accordingly, the villagers employed Nyuzi and an assistant to conduct an ordeal for the purpose of determining whether a group of suspects were witches. Several people died after ingesting a nonpoisonous substance administered by Nyuzi and the assistant. In Malawi at the time, witchcraft was a strict liability offense; consequently, Nyuzi and his assistant were convicted. However, Kenny raises the question of whether the two were also guilty of killing the deceased—that is, whether an *actus reus* has occurred. Questions of *mens rea* at least appear to be more tractable. Among the cluster of questions that *Nyuzi* raises is the reasonableness of the defendants' belief that they were intervening to prevent deaths. This query underscores the difficulty of using the average reasonable man standard in multicultural contexts. According to whose standards of reasonableness should the defendants' belief be judged—the average Englishman on the street or the average Malawian?

In "Is the Insanity Test Insane?" R. J. Gerber questions how the law has dealt with an ongoing challenge to the traditional conception of criminal responsibility—namely, criminal insanity. The first modern insanity test, the M'Naghten Rule, derives from an English court case in 1843. According to the test, an accused is not criminally responsible if a mental disease prevented him or her, at the time of acting, from knowing either the nature and quality of the act or that the act was wrong. Among other complaints, critics point out that the M'Naghten Rule is a purely cognitive test that does not address the possibility of volitional impairments. That is, M'Naghten does not address types of mental illness that keep people who know that the act that they are doing is wrong from being able to use that knowledge to control their actions. Moreover, the rule calls for total impairment.

The first alternative to M'Naghten, the irresistible impulse test, centers on the accused's ability to control his or her actions. This test, Gerber claims, suffers from two flaws. First, in focusing on the immediacy of "impulse," the test causes judges and jurors to overlook mental impairments that cause a gradual loss of control. Second, the test gives no criteria for distinguishing an impulse that could not be resisted from one that simply was not resisted. A third, broader test of insanity is the Durham rule, adopted in 1954 by the United States Court of Appeals for the District of Columbia Court. It exonerates an accused of criminal responsibility if his or her unlawful act was the product of mental disease or defect. Use of the Durham test dramatically increased reliance on psychiatric testimony. It was finally abandoned in 1972 in *U.S. v. Brawner*,[9] when the District of Columbia adopted the American Law Institute's proposal that an accused can be excused of criminal responsibility for unlawful conduct if, at the time of acting, he or she, as a result of mental disease or defect, lacked substantial capacity either to appreciate the criminality (wrongfulness) of the conduct or to conform the conduct to the requirements of law.

Controversy about the insanity test has not gone away. Gerber tries to disentangle some of the issues that fuel the fire. Foremost among these puzzles, he believes, is the mistaken notion that insanity is a *mens rea* issue. Insanity, he argues, is an excuse to an established crime. Insanity does not negate the crime or preclude the possibility that insane people can form culpable mental states such as premeditation or recklessness. Insanity indicates psychological dysfunctionality and, thus, reason for diminished criminal responsibility. Therefore, the fates of *mens rea* and the insanity defense are and should be kept separate.

The last two articles, by James Weinstein and by Lois Pineau, examine specific kinds of crimes that raise difficult issues for the criminal justice system: hate crimes and date rape. In Weinstein's article, "First Amendment Challenges to Hate Crime Legislation: Where's the Speech?" the issue is whether the state may enhance penalties for bias in the selection of crime victims without violating the First Amendment. Representative of such statutes, the Wisconsin hate crimes statute enhances the penalty for certain crimes if the victim was selected because of race, religion, color, disability, sexual orientation, national origin, or ancestry. Susan Gellman has recently argued that hate crimes statutes punish thought and are facially invalid under the First Amendment. Her argument can be posed as a simple question. If hate crimes statutes enhance the penalties for acts that are already crimes, what do they punish, if not the thought of the offender? Based on Gellman's arguments, the Wisconsin Supreme Court struck down the state's statute in *State v. Mitchell.* Weinstein argues that Gellman is wrong, and he mounts an extensive defense of hate crimes statutes.

He points out that a statute can be facially invalid under the First Amendment in two ways. First, there might be no conditions in which a statute can be applied without violating the amendment. Second, although conditions exist in which one can apply a statute to, say, speech *not* protected by the First Amendment, applying the statute in these circumstances has a chilling effect on speech that *is* protected. Weinstein argues that in neither sense are hate crimes statutes of the Wisconsin type facially invalid. In addition, he explores five justifications for enhancing penalties for hate crimes to negate the contention that hate crimes statutes exist only to punish bigoted thought.

Weinstein begins his arguments by claiming that, contra Gellman, courts routinely take the thoughts of offenders into account when sentencing. Courts look more kindly, for example, on mercy killers than on those who kill for profit, and sentencing practices reflect this fact. Weinstein offers support for this view from the record of a Supreme Court decision, *Dawson v. Delaware*, in which the court claimed, contrary to the actual facts of the case, that if an offender's membership in a racist organization had been implicated in the murder he committed, the court would be warranted in taking this fact into account in sentencing. If courts can do this, Weinstein maintains, legislatures should be able to as well.

If hate crimes statutes do not punish bigoted thought, what is their justification? Weinstein offers five possibilities. First, hate crimes statutes reflect the retributivist view that bias crimes are intrinsically more reprehensible than nonbias crimes. Second, Weinstein

---

[9] 471 F. 2d 969 (1972).

invokes a version of legal moralism to argue that society regards hate crimes as especially evil and thus deserving of enhanced punishment. His third, fourth, and fifth arguments identify three distinct kinds of harms that make racially motivated violence worse than other kinds of violence: (1) hate crimes are more damaging to the victim than are other kinds of violence, (2) hate crimes have a powerful terrorizing effect on members of the victim's community, and (3) hate crimes are especially pernicious and disruptive for society as a whole.

Weinstein's harm-based arguments raise further free speech issues. If the threat of further violence to the victim and members of the victim's community is part of the terroristic harm caused by hate crimes, can the expression of these threats be considered protected speech under the First Amendment? Weinstein responds by arguing that the threat of further violence that is communicated by battery is the same as a verbal threat. But a verbal threat of violence is considered "fighting words" and is not protected by the First Amendment. Consequently, the threat of further violence made by hate crimes should not be considered protected speech, either. What if the harm inflicted by a hate crime is psychological distress, not the threat of further violence? Weinstein replies that the First Amendment does not protect someone from being sued for wantonly and maliciously inflicting psychological distress on another person. Similarly, it should not protect someone from suffering an enhanced penalty under criminal law if psychological distress is part of the harm inflicted during an attack.

Two further free speech issues deserve mention. *R. A. V. v. City of St. Paul* is a Supreme Court decision striking down St. Paul's ordinance prohibiting the use of certain racist symbols and graffiti. The majority concluded that because the ban extended only to racist "fighting words," the ordinance had engaged in viewpoint discrimination in violation of the First Amendment. Does *R. A. V.* apply to Wisconsin-style statutes? Weinstein thinks not, for two reasons. First, the St. Paul ordinance proscribed expression, whereas hate crimes statutes prohibit violence that is neither purely verbal nor symbolic conduct. Second, the *R.A.V.* court made clear that it is unconstitutional for the government to regulate unprotected speech in order to prohibit viewpoints it finds offensive. The purpose of hate crimes statutes, however, is not to prohibit offensive speech but to prevent threats and emotional injury caused by bias-motivated violence.

Finally, are hate crimes statutes facially invalid in the second sense mentioned earlier? That is, do they have a chilling effect on protected speech? The primary problem is that racist speech uttered during or before an attack could be misused by prosecutors seeking an enhanced penalty under a hate crimes statute. Admitting that this is a possibility, Weinstein contends that it should be dealt with by prosecutorial discretion and evidentiary safeguards. The solution is not to strike down hate crimes statutes as unconstitutional.

Hate crimes are currently of great concern in U. S. society. Date rape is another such crime, discussed by Pineau in "Date Rape: A Feminist Analysis." Defining date rape as nonconsensual sex that does not involve physical injury, she points out that the lack of physical evidence of assault frequently results in date rape being mistaken for seduction. New laws that replace "rape" with "sexual assault" do nothing to resolve this problem.

The crime of rape hinges on the issue of consent. In some common-law jurisdictions, defendants can show that they lacked the *mens rea* necessary for conviction for rape by successfully arguing that their belief that the plaintiff consented was reasonable. Pineau asks, reasonable according to whose standards—the man's or the woman's? She develops criteria for the reasonableness of belief in consent based on a woman's perspective. These criteria are grounded in what she calls the "theory of communicative sexuality." This theory provides a normative framework for conducting and evaluating sexual encounters that differs markedly from the prevailing framework, which Pineau dubs the "aggressive-acquiescence" model of seduction.

The aggressive-acquiescence model incorporates a variety of interlocking myths about male and female sexuality, including the notion that aggression is a normal part of sexual encounters, and is given normative clout by its reliance on a contract model of interaction. According to the aggressive-acquiescence model, it is natural and normal for men to initiate and aggressively pursue sex with women, and it is equally natural and normal for women initially to resist these overtures. Here we find two myths: that male sexuality is necessarily (and rightly) insistent, and that a woman's "no" really means "yes." A further myth that supports the "no means yes" myth is that women are fundamentally dishonest about sex. Even though they pretend to resist men's sexual overtures, women secretly desire sex with men. Moreover, the model assumes that although women somehow provoke or invite sexual encounters with men, perhaps by dressing a certain way or by going to a bar, the correct role for women is to submit to men's sexual desires passively. Thus, through their provocative dress or behavior, women, and not men, are responsible for sexual encounters (the "she asked for it" myth), even though women's sexual autonomy is denied. Further, the aggressive-acquiescence framework gains normative shape and force by its reliance on a contract model of interaction. According to the contract model, by entering into a sexual encounter with a man, a woman thereby agrees to deliver whatever sexual services the man expects. She thus finds herself on a "slippery slope" that could lead to sexual intercourse, without the option of changing her mind and reneging should her own expectations of the encounter be disappointed.

The theory of communicative sexuality supplies a healthier way of viewing and conducting sexual encounters than does the aggressive-acquiescence view. Central to the communicative theory is the idea that it is reasonable for women (or anyone, for that matter) to agree to the kind of sex they would enjoy. Debunking the myths about sexuality on which the aggressive-acquiescence model relies, Pineau cites recent empirical studies showing that people are more likely to enjoy sex if it occurs in a relaxed, open atmosphere of trust and mutual respect in which each partner is willing to discover and comply with the other's desires. Sex is better if, to use a Kantian phrase, each partner adopts the other's sexual ends as her or his own. Crucial to this project is the role of communication in discovering each other's desires. Good conversations provide a model for the kind of responsive communication that should inform sexual encounters. As good conversationalists are intuitive, sympathetic, and charitable, Pineau argues, these characteristics should inform communication in sexual encounters. Communicative sexuality should also be responsive to what Pineau calls the "dialectics of desire." Each partner's desires should be informed by and responsive to the desires of the other. This ensures that, if one of the partners does not desire to continue the encounter, this fact will be respected by the other.

Adopting the theory of communicative sexuality has implications for rape trials. Because communicative sex is the kind of sex it is reasonable for a woman to enjoy and, thus, reasonable for her to consent to, the presence of communicative sexuality is *prima facie* evidence that a woman consents to a sexual encounter. Lacking evidence of communicative sexuality, however, the burden of proof is on the male defendant to show that it is reasonable for a woman to consent to sex that she would not enjoy. This approach would change the kind of evidence that is admissible and probative in rape trials and would, Pineau contends, bring the crime of date rape more firmly within the province of criminal law.

The following selections offer an introduction to philosophical work on criminal law, which is a rich area for philosophical scrutiny. The list of selected readings provides the interested reader with further avenues for exploration.

SELECTED READINGS

Burgess-Jackson, Keith, ed. *A Most Detestable Crime: New Philosophical Essays on Rape*. New York: Oxford University Press, 1999.

Downs, Donald Alexander. *More Than Victims: Battered Women, the Syndrome Society, and the Law.* Chicago: The University of Chicago Press, 1996.

Friedman, Lawrence M. *Crime and Punishment in American History.* New York: Basic Books, 1993.

Gross, Hyman. *A Theory of Criminal Justice*. New York: Oxford University Press, 1979.

Herek, Gregory M., and Kevin T. Berrill, eds. *Hate Crimes: Confronting Violence against Lesbians and Gay Men*. Newbury Park, CA: Sage, 1992.

Husak, Douglas N. *Philosophy of Criminal Law.* Totowa, NJ: Rowman and Littlefield, 1987.

Jacobs, James B., and Kimberly Potter. *Hate Crimes: Criminal Law and Identity Politics.* New York: Oxford University Press, 1998.

Kahan, Dan M., and Martha Nussbaum. "Two Conceptions of Emotion in Criminal Law." *Columbia Law Review* 96 (1996): 269–374.

Kennedy, Randall. *Race, Crime, and the Law.* New York: Pantheon Books, 1997.

Kleinig, John, ed. "Symposium: Penalty Enhancement for Hate Crimes." *Criminal Justice Ethics* 11 (1992).

Mackay, R. D. "Post-Hinckley Insanity in the U.S.A." *Criminal Law Review* (February 1988): 88–96.

Packer, Herbert L. *The Limits of the Criminal Sanction.* Stanford, CA: Stanford University Press, 1968.

Robinson, Daniel N. *Wild Beasts and Idle Humours: The Insanity Defense from Antiquity to the Present.* Cambridge, MA: Harvard University Press, 1996.

Schulhofer, Stephen J. *Unwanted Sex: The Culture of Intimidation and the Failure of Law.* Cambridge, MA: Harvard University Press, 1998.

Sistare, Christine. *Responsibility and Criminal Liability.* Boston: Kluwer Academic, 1989.

24

J. S. MILL

From *On Liberty and Utilitarianism*

CHAPTER I / INTRODUCTORY

. . . The object of this Essay is to assert one very simple principle, as entitled to govern absolutely the dealings of society with the individual in the way of compulsion and control, whether the means used be physical force in the form of legal penalties, or the moral coercion of public opinion. That principle is, that the sole end for which mankind are warranted, individually or collectively, in interfering with the liberty of action of any of their number, is self-protection. That the only purpose for which power can be rightfully exercised over any member of a civilized community, against his will, is to prevent harm to others. His own good, either physical or moral, is not a sufficient warrant. He cannot rightfully be compelled to do or forbear because it will be better for him to do so, because it will make him happier, because, in the opinions of others, to do so would be wise, or even right. These are good reasons for remonstrating with him, or reasoning with him, or persuading him, or entreating him, but not for compelling him, or visiting him with any evil in case he do otherwise. To justify that, the conduct from which it is desired to deter him must be calculated to produce evil to some one else. The only part of the conduct of any one, for which he is amenable to society, is that which concerns others. In the part which merely concerns himself, his independence is, of right, absolute. Over himself, over his own body and mind, the individual is sovereign.

It is, perhaps, hardly necessary to say that this doctrine is meant to apply only to human beings in the maturity of their faculties. We are not speaking of children, or of young persons below the age which the law may fix as that of manhood or womanhood. Those who are still in a state to require being taken care of by others, must be protected against their own actions as well as against external injury. For the same reason, we may leave out of consideration those backward states of society in which the race itself may be considered as in its nonage. The early difficulties in the way of spontaneous progress are so great, that there is seldom any choice of means for overcoming them; and a ruler full of the spirit of improvement is warranted in the use of any expedients that will attain an end, perhaps otherwise unattainable. Despotism is a legitimate mode of government in dealing with barbarians, provided the end be their improvement, and the means justified by actually effecting that end. Liberty, as a principle, has no application to any state of things anterior to the time when mankind have become capable of being improved by free and equal discussion. Until then, there is nothing for them but implicit obedience to an Akbar or a Charlemagne, if they are so fortunate as to find one. But as soon as mankind have attained the capacity of being guided to their own improvement by conviction or persuasion (a period long since reached in all nations with whom we need here concern ourselves), compulsion either in the direct form or in that of pains and penalties for non-compliance, is no longer admissible as a means to their own good, and justifiable only for the security of others.

It is proper to state that I forego any advantage which could be derived to my argument from the idea of abstract right, as a thing independent of utility. I regard utility as the ultimate appeal on all ethical questions; but it must be utility in the largest sense, grounded on the permanent interests of a man as a progressive being. Those interests, I contend, authorize the subjection of individual spontaneity to external control, only in respect to those actions of each, which concern the interest of other people. If any one does an act hurtful to others, there is a *prima facie* case for punishing him, by law, or, where legal penalties are not safely applicable, by general disapprobation. There are also many positive acts for the benefit of others, which he may rightfully be compelled to perform; such as to give evidence in a court of justice; to bear his fair share in the common defense, or in any other joint work necessary to the interest of the society of which he enjoys the protection; and to perform certain acts of individual beneficence, such as saving a fellow-creature's life, or interposing to protect the defenseless against ill-usage, things which whenever it is obviously a man's duty to do, he may rightfully be made responsible to society for not doing. A person may cause evil to others not only by his actions but by his inaction, and in either case he is justly accountable to them for the injury. The latter case, it is true, requires a much more cautious exercise of compulsion than the former. To make any one answerable for doing evil to others is the rule; to make him answerable for not preventing evil is, comparatively speaking, the exception. Yet there are many cases clear enough and grave enough to justify that exception. In all things which regard the external relations of the individual, he is *de jure* amenable to those whose interests are concerned, and, if need be, to society as their protector. There are often good reasons for not holding him to the responsibility; but these reasons must arise from the special expediencies of the case: either because it is a kind of case in which he is on the whole likely to act better, when left to his own discretion, than when controlled in any way in which society have it in their power to control him; or because the attempt to exercise control would produce other evils, greater than those which it would prevent. When such reasons as these preclude the enforcement of responsibility, the conscience of the agent himself should step into the vacant judgment seat, and protect those interests of others which have no external protection; judging himself all the more rigidly, because the case does not admit of his being made accountable to the judgment of his fellow-creatures.

But there is a sphere of action in which society, as distinguished from the individual, has, if any, only an indirect interest; comprehending all that portion of a person's life and conduct which affects only himself, or if it also affects others, only with their free, voluntary, and undeceived consent and participation. When I say only himself, I mean directly, and in the first instance; for whatever affects himself, may affect others through himself; and the objection which may be grounded on this contingency, will receive consideration in the sequel. This, then, is the appropriate region of human liberty. It comprises, first, the inward domain of consciousness; demanding liberty of conscience in the most comprehensive sense; liberty of thought and feeling; absolute freedom of opinion and sentiment on all subjects, practical or speculative, scientific, moral, or theological. The liberty of expressing and publishing opinions may seem to fall under a different principle, since it belongs to that part of the conduct of an individual which concerns other people; but, being almost of as much importance as the liberty of thought itself, and resting in great part on the same reasons, is practically inseparable from it. Secondly, the principle requires liberty of tastes and pursuits; of framing the plan of our life to suit our own character; of doing as we like, subject to such consequences as may follow: without impediment from our fellow-creatures, so long as what we do does not harm them, even though they should think our conduct foolish, perverse, or wrong. Thirdly, from this liberty of each individual, follows the liberty, within the same limits, of combination among individuals; freedom to unite, for any purpose not involving harm to others: the persons combining being supposed to be of full age, and not forced or deceived.

No society in which these liberties are not, on the whole, respected, is free, whatever may be its form of government; and none is completely free in which they do not exist absolute and unqualified. The only freedom which deserves the name, is that of pursuing our own good in our own way, so long as we do not attempt to deprive others of theirs, or impede their efforts to obtain it. Each is the proper guardian of his own health, whether bodily, or mental and spiritual. Mankind are greater gainers by suffering each other to live as seems good to themselves, than by compelling each to live as seems good to the rest. . . .

CHAPTER II / OF THE LIBERTY AND THOUGHT AND DISCUSSION

. . . We have now recognised the necessity to the mental well-being of mankind (on which all their other well-being depends) of freedom of opinion, and freedom of the expression *of* opinion, on four distinct grounds; which we will now briefly recapitulate.

First, if any opinion is compelled to silence, that opinion may, for aught we can certainly know, be true. To deny this is to assume our own infallibility.

Secondly, though the silenced opinion be an error, it may, and very commonly does, contain a portion of truth; and since the general or prevailing opinion on any subject is rarely or never the whole truth, it is only by the collision of adverse opinions that the remainder of the truth has any chance of being supplied.

Thirdly, even if the received opinion be not only true, but the whole truth; unless it is suffered to be, and actually is, vigorously and earnestly contested, it will, by most of those who receive it, be held in the manner of a prejudice, with little comprehension or feeling of its rational grounds. And not only this, but, fourthly, the meaning of the doctrine itself will be in danger of being lost, or enfeebled, and deprived of its vital effect on the character and conduct: the dogma becoming a mere formal profession, inefficacious for good, but cumbering the ground, and preventing the growth of any real and heartfelt conviction, from reason or personal experience. . . .

CHAPTER IV / OF THE LIMITS TO THE AUTHORITY OF SOCIETY OVER THE INDIVIDUAL

. . . What, then, is the rightful limit to the sovereignty of the individual over himself? Where does the authority of society begin? How much of human life should be assigned to individuality, and how much to society?

Each will receive its proper share, if each has that which more particularly concerns it. To individuality should belong the part of life in which it is chiefly the individual that is interested; to society, the part which chiefly interests society.

Though society is not founded on a contract, and though no good purpose is answered by inventing a contract in order to deduce social obligations from it, every one who receives the protection of society owes a return for the benefit, and the fact of living in society renders it indispensable that each should be bound to observe a certain line of conduct towards the rest. This conduct consists, first, in not injuring the interests of one another; or rather certain interests, which, either by express legal provision or by tacit understanding, ought to be considered as rights; and secondly, in each person's bearing his share (to be fixed on some equitable principle) of the labours and sacrifices incurred for defending the society or its members from injury and molestation. These conditions society is justified in enforcing, at all costs to those who endeavour to withhold fulfillment. Nor is this all that society may do. The acts of an individual may be hurtful to others, or wanting in due consideration for their welfare, without going to the length of violating any of their constituted rights. The offender may then be justly punished by opinion, though not by law. As soon as any part of a person's conduct affects prejudicially the interests of others, society has jurisdiction over it, and the question whether the general welfare will or will not be promoted by interfering with it, becomes open to discussion. But there is no room for entertaining any such question when a person's conduct affects the interests of no persons besides himself, or needs not affect them unless they like (all the persons concerned being of full age, and the ordinary amount of understanding). In all such cases, there should be perfect freedom, legal and social, to do the action and stand the consequences.

It would be a great misunderstanding of this doctrine to suppose that it is one of selfish indifference, which pretends that human beings have no business with each other's conduct in life, and that they should not concern themselves about the well-doing or well-being of one another, unless their own interest is involved. Instead of any diminution, there is need of a great increase of disinterested exertion to promote the good of others. But disinterested benevolence can find other instruments to persuade people to their good than whips and scourges, either of the literal or the metaphorical sort. I am the last person to undervalue the self-regarding virtues; they are only second in importance, if even second, to the social. It is equally the business of education to cultivate both. But even education works by conviction and persuasion as well as by compulsion, and it is by the former only that, when the period of education is passed, the self-regarding virtues should be inculcated. Human beings owe to each other help to distinguish the better from the worse, and encouragement to choose the former and avoid the latter. They should be forever stimulating each other to increased exercise of their higher faculties, and increased direction of their feelings and aims towards wise instead of foolish, elevating instead of degrading, objects and contemplations. But neither one person, nor any number of persons, is warranted in saying to another human creature of ripe years, that he shall not do with his life for his own benefit what he chooses to do with it. He is the person most interested in his own well-being: the interest which any other person, except in cases of strong personal attachment, can have in it, is trifling, compared with that which he himself has; the interest which society has in him individually (except as to his conduct to others) is fractional, and altogether indirect; while with respect to his own feelings and circumstances, the most ordinary man or woman has means of knowledge immeasurably surpassing those that can be possessed by any one else. The interference of society to overrule his judgment and purposes in what only regards himself must be grounded on general presumptions; which may be altogether wrong, and even if right, are as likely as not to be misapplied to individual cases, by persons no better acquainted with the circumstances of such cases than those are who look at them merely from without. In this department, therefore, of human affairs, Individuality has its proper field of action. In the conduct of human beings towards one another it is necessary that general rules should for the most part be observed, in order that people may know what they have to expect: but in each person's own concerns his individual spontaneity is entitled to free exercise. Considerations to aid his judgment, exhortations to strengthen his will, may be offered to him, even obtruded on him, by others: but he himself is the final judge. All errors which he is likely to commit against advice and warning are far outweighed by the evil of allowing others to constrain him to what they deem his good.

I do not mean that the feelings with which a person is regarded by others ought not to be in any way affected by his self-regarding qualities or deficiencies. This is neither possible nor desirable. If he is eminent in any of the qualities which conduce to his own good, he is, so far, a proper object of admiration. He is so much the nearer to the ideal perfection of human nature. If he is grossly deficient in those qualities, a sentiment the opposite of admiration will follow. There is a degree of folly, and a degree of what may be called (though the phrase is not unobjectionable) lowness or depravation of taste, which, though it cannot justify doing harm to the person who manifests it, renders him necessarily and properly a subject of distaste, or, in extreme cases, even of contempt: a person could not have the opposite qualities in due strength without entertaining these feelings. Though doing no wrong to any one, a person may so act as to compel us to judge him, and feel to him, as a fool, or as a being of an inferior order: and since this judgment and feeling are a fact which he would prefer to avoid, it is doing him a service to warn him of it beforehand, as of any other disagreeable consequence to which he exposes himself. It would be well, indeed, if this good office were much more freely rendered than the common notions of politeness at present permit, and if one person could honestly point out to another that he thinks him in fault, without being considered unmannerly or presuming. We have a right, also, in various ways, to act upon our unfavorable opinion of any one, not to the oppression of his individuality, but in the exercise of ours. We are not bound, for example, to seek his society; we have a right to avoid it (though not to parade the avoidance), for we have a right to choose the society most acceptable to us. We have a right, and it may be our duty, to caution others against him, if we think his example or conversation likely to have a pernicious effect on those with whom he associates. We may give others a preference over him in optional good offices, except those which tend to his improvement. In these various modes a person may suffer very severe penalties at the hands of others for faults which directly concern only himself; but he suffers these penalties only in so far as they are the natural and, as it were, the spontaneous consequences of the faults themselves, not because they are purposely inflicted on him for the sake of punishment. A person who shows rashness, obstinacy, self-conceit—who cannot live within moderate means—who cannot restrain himself from hurtful indulgences—who pursues animal pleasures at the expense of those of feeling and intellect—must expect to be lowered in the opinion of others, and to have a less share of their favourable sentiments; but of this he has no right to complain, unless he has merited their favour by special excellence in his social relations, and has thus established a title to their good offices, which is not affected by his demerits towards himself.

What I contend for is, that the inconveniences which are strictly inseparable from the unfavourable judgment of others, are the only ones to which a person should ever be subjected for that portion of his conduct and character which concerns his own good, but which does not affect the interest of others in their relations with him. Acts injurious to others require a totally different treatment. Encroachment on their rights; infliction on them of any loss or damage not justified by his own rights; falsehood or duplicity in dealing with them; unfair or ungenerous use of advantages over them; even selfish abstinence from defending them against injury—these are fit objects of moral reprobation, and, in grave cases, of moral retribution and punishment. And not only these acts, but the dispositions which lead to them, are properly immoral, and fit subjects of disapprobation which may rise to abhorrence. Cruelty of disposition; malice and ill-nature; that most anti-social and odious of all passions, envy; dissimulation and insincerity, irascibility on insufficient cause, and resentment disproportioned to the provocation; the love of domineering over others; the desire to engross more than one's share of advantages (the πλεονεξια of the Greeks); the pride which derives gratification from the abasement of others; the egotism which thinks self and its concerns more important than everything else, and decides all doubtful questions in its own favour;—these are moral vices, and constitute a bad and odious moral character: unlike the self-regarding faults previously mentioned, which are not properly immoralities, and to whatever pitch they may be carried, do not constitute wickedness. They may be proofs of any amount of folly, or want of personal dignity and self-respect; but they are only a subject of moral reprobation when they involve a breach of duty to others, for whose sake the individual is bound to have care for himself. What are called duties to ourselves are not socially obligatory, unless circumstances render them at the same time duties to others. The term duty to oneself, when it means anything more than prudence, means self-respect or self-development, and for none of these is any one accountable to his fellow-creatures, because for none of them is it for the good of mankind that he be held accountable to them.

The distinction between the loss of consideration which a person may rightly incur by defect of prudence or of personal dignity, and the reprobation which is due to him for an offence against the rights of others, is not a merely nominal distinction. It makes a vast difference both in our feelings and in our conduct towards him whether he displeases us in things in which we think we have a right to control him, or in things in which we know that we have not. If he displeases us, we may express our distaste, and we may stand aloof from a person as well as from a thing that displeases us; but we shall not therefore feel called on to make his life uncomfortable. We shall reflect that he already bears, or will bear, the whole penalty of his error; if he spoils his life by mismanagement, we shall not, for that reason, desire to spoil it still further: instead of wishing to punish him, we shall rather endeavour to alleviate his punishment, by showing him how he may avoid or cure the evils his conduct tends to bring upon him. He may be to us an object of pity, perhaps of dislike, but not of anger or resentment; we shall not treat him like an enemy of society: the worst we shall think ourselves justified in doing is leaving him to himself, if we do not interfere benevolently by showing interest or concern for him. It is far otherwise if he has infringed the rules necessary for the protection of his fellow-creatures, individually or collectively. The evil consequences of his acts do not then fall on himself, but on others; and society, as the protector of all its members, must retaliate on him; must inflict pain on him for the express purpose of punishment, and must take care that it be sufficiently severe. In the one case, he is an offender at our bar, and we are called on not only to sit in judgment on him, but, in one shape or another, to execute our own sentence: in the other case, it is not our part to inflict any suffering on him, except what may incidentally follow from our using the same liberty in the regulation of our own affairs, which we allow to him in his.

The distinction here pointed out between the part of a person's life which concerns only himself, and that which concerns others, many persons will refuse to admit. How (it may be asked) can any part of the conduct of a member of society be a matter of indifference to the other members? No person is an entirely isolated being; it is impossible for a person to do anything seriously or permanently hurtful to himself, without mischief reaching at least to his near connections, and often far beyond them. If he injures his property, he does harm to those who directly or indirectly derived support from it, and usually diminishes, by a greater or less amount, the general resources of the community. If he deteriorates his bodily or mental faculties, he not only brings evil upon all who depended on him for any portion of their happiness, but disqualifies himself for rendering the services which he owes to his fellow-creatures generally; perhaps becomes a burden on their affection or benevolence; and if such conduct were very frequent, hardly any offence that is committed would detract more from the general sum of good. Finally, if by his vices or follies a person does no direct harm to others, he is nevertheless (it may be said) injurious by his example; and ought to be compelled to control himself, for the sake of those whom the sight or knowledge of his conduct might corrupt or mislead.

And even (it will be added) if the consequences of misconduct could be confined to the vicious or thoughtless individual, ought society to abandon to their own guidance those who are manifestly unfit for it? If protection against themselves is confessedly due to children and persons under age, is not society equally bound to afford it to persons of mature years who are equally incapable of self-government? If gambling, or drunkenness, or incontinence, or idleness, or uncleanliness, are as injurious to happiness, and as great a hindrance to improvement, as many or most of the acts prohibited by law, why (it may be asked) should not law, so far as is consistent with practicability and social convenience, endeavour to repress these also? And as a supplement to the unavoidable imperfections of law, ought not opinion at least to organise a powerful police against these vices, and visit rigidly with social penalties those who are known to practise them? There is no question here (it may be said) about restricting individuality, or impeding the trial of new and original experiments in living. The only things it is sought to prevent are things which have been tried and condemned from the beginning of the world until now; things which experience has shown not to be useful or suitable to any person's individuality. There must be some length of time and amount of experience after which a moral or prudential truth may be regarded as established: and it is merely desired to prevent generation after generation from falling over the same precipice which has been fatal to their predecessors.

I fully admit that the mischief which a person does to himself may seriously affect, both through their sympathies and their interests, those nearly connected with him and, in a minor degree, society at large. When, by conduct of this sort, a person is led to violate a distinct and assignable obligation to any other person or persons, the case is taken out of the self-regarding class, and becomes amenable to moral disapprobation in the proper sense of the term. If, for example, a man, through intemperance or extravagance, becomes unable to pay his debts, or, having undertaken the moral responsibility of a family, becomes from the same cause incapable of supporting or educating them, he is deservedly reprobated, and might be justly punished; but it is for the breach of duty to his family or creditors, not for the extravagance. If the resources which ought to have been devoted to them had been diverted from them for the most prudent investment, the moral culpability would have been the same. George Barnwell murdered his uncle to get money for his mistress, but if he had done it to set himself up in business, he would equally have been hanged. Again, in the frequent case of a man who causes grief to his family by addiction to bad habits, he deserves reproach for his unkindness or ingratitude; but so he may for cultivating habits not in themselves vicious, if they are painful to those with whom he passes his life, or who from personal ties are dependent on him for their comfort. Whoever fails in the consideration generally due to the interests and feelings of others, not being compelled by some more imperative duty, or justified by allowable self-preference, is a subject of moral disapprobation for that failure, but not for the cause of it, nor for the errors, merely personal to himself, which may have remotely led to it. In like manner, when a person disables himself, by conduct purely self-regarding, from the performance of some definite duty incumbent on him to the public, he is guilty of a social offence. No person ought to be punished simply for being drunk; but a soldier or a policeman should be punished for being drunk on duty. Whenever, in short, there is a definite damage, or a definite risk of damage, either to an individual or to the public, the case is taken out of the province of liberty, and placed in that of morality or law.

But with regard to the merely contingent, or, as it may be called, constructive injury which a person causes to society, by conduct which neither violates any specific duty to the public, nor occasions perceptible hurt to any assignable individual except himself; the inconvenience is one which society can afford to bear, for the sake of the greater good of human freedom. If grown persons are to be punished for not taking proper care of themselves, I would rather it were for their own sake, than under pretence of preventing them from impairing their capacity of rendering to society benefits which society does not pretend it has a right to exact. But I cannot consent to argue the point as if society had no means of bringing its weaker members up to its ordinary standard of rational conduct, except waiting till they do something irrational, and then punishing them, legally or morally, for it. Society has had absolute power over them during all the early portion of their existence: it has had the whole period of childhood and nonage in which to try whether it could make them capable of rational conduct in life. The existing generation is master both of the training and the entire circumstances of the generation to come; it cannot indeed make them perfectly wise and good, because it is itself so lamentably deficient in goodness and wisdom; and its best efforts are not always, in individual cases, its most successful ones; but it is perfectly well able to make the rising generation, as a whole, as good as, and a little better than, itself. If society lets any considerable number of its members grow up mere children, incapable of being acted on by rational consideration of distant motives, society has itself to blame for the consequences. Armed not only with all the powers of education, but with the ascendancy which the authority of a received opinion always exercises over the minds who are least fitted to judge for themselves; and aided by the *natural* penalties which cannot be prevented from falling on those who incur the distaste or the contempt of those who know them; let not society pretend that it needs, besides all this, the power to issue commands and enforce obedience in the personal concerns of individuals, in which, on all principles of justice and policy, the decision ought to rest with those who are to abide the consequences. Nor is there anything which tends more to discredit and frustrate the better means of influencing conduct than a resort to the worse. If there be among those whom it is attempted to coerce into prudence or temperance any of the material of which vigorous and independent characters are made, they will infallibly rebel against the yoke. No such person will ever feel that others have a right to control him in his concerns, such as they have to prevent him from injuring them in theirs; and it easily comes to be considered a mark of spirit and courage to fly in the face of such usurped authority, and do with ostentation the exact opposite of what it enjoins; as in the fashion of grossness which succeeded, in the time of Charles II, to the fanatical moral intolerance of the Puritans. With respect to what is said of the necessity of protecting society from the bad example set to others by the vicious or the self-indulgent; it is true that bad example may have a pernicious effect, especially the example of doing wrong to others with impunity to the wrong-doer. But we are now speaking of conduct which, while it does no wrong to others, is supposed to do great harm to the agent himself: and I do not see how those who believe this can think otherwise than that the example, on the whole, must be more salutary than hurtful, since, if it displays the misconduct, it displays also the painful or degrading consequences which, if the conduct is justly censured, must be supposed to be in all or most cases attendant on it.

But the strongest of all the arguments against the interference of the public with purely personal conduct is that, when it does interfere, the odds are that it interferes wrongly, and in the wrong place. On questions of social morality, of duty to others, the opinion of the public, that is, of an overruling majority, though often wrong, is likely to be still oftener right; because on such questions they are only required to judge of their own interests; of the manner in which some mode of conduct, if allowed to be practised, would affect themselves. But the opinion of a similar majority, imposed as a law on the minority, on questions of self-regarding conduct, is quite as likely to be wrong as right; for in these cases public opinion means, at the best, some people's opinion of what is good or bad for other people; while very often it does not even mean that; the public, with the most perfect indifference, passing over the pleasure or convenience of those whose conduct they censure, and considering only their own preference. There are many who consider as an injury to themselves any conduct which they have a distaste for, and resent it as an outrage to their feelings; as a religious bigot, when charged with disregarding the religious feelings of others, has been known to retort that they disregard his feelings, by persisting in their abominable worship or creed. But there is no parity between the feeling of a person for his own opinion, and the feeling of another who is offended at his holding it; no more than between the desire of a thief to take a purse, and the desire of the right owner to keep it. And a person's taste is as much his own peculiar concern as his opinion or his purse. Is easy for any one to imagine an ideal public which leaves the freedom and choice of individuals in all uncertain matters undisturbed, and only requires them to abstain from modes of conduct which universal experience has condemned. But where has there been seen a public which set any such limit to its censorship? Or when does the public trouble itself about universal experience? In its interferences with personal conduct it is seldom thinking of anything but the enormity of acting or feeling differently from itself; and this standard of judgment, thinly disguised, is held up to mankind as the dictate of religion and philosophy, by nine-tenths of all moralists and speculative writers. These teach that things are right because they are right; because we feel them to be so. They tell us to search in our own minds and hearts for laws of conduct binding on ourselves and on all others. What can the poor public do but apply these instructions, and make their own personal feelings of good and evil, if they are tolerably unanimous in them, obligatory on all the world? . . .

25

PATRICK DEVLIN

From *The Enforcement of Morals*

. . . I think it is clear that the criminal law as we know it is based upon moral principle. In a number of crimes its function is simply to enforce a moral principle and nothing else. The law, both criminal and civil, claims to be able to speak about morality and immorality generally. Where does it get its authority to do this and how does it settle the moral principles which it enforces? Undoubtedly, as a matter of history, it derived both from Christian teaching. But I think that the strict logician is right when he says that the law can no longer rely on doctrines in which citizens are entitled to disbelieve. It is necessary therefore to look for some other source.

In jurisprudence, as I have said, everything is thrown open to discussion and, in the belief that they cover the whole field, I have framed three interrogatories addressed to myself to answer:

1. Has society the right to pass judgment at all on matters of morals? Ought there, in other words, to be a public morality, or are morals always a matter for private judgment?
2. If society has the right to pass judgment, has it also the right to use the weapon of the law to enforce it?
3. If so, ought it to use that weapon in all cases or only in some; and if only in some, on what principles should it distinguish?

I shall begin with the first interrogatory and consider what is meant by the right of society to pass a moral judgment, that is, a judgment about what is good and what is evil. The fact that a majority of people may disapprove of a practice does not of itself make it a matter for society as a whole. Nine men out of ten may disapprove of what the tenth man is doing and still say that it is not their business. There is a case for a collective judgment (as distinct from a large number of individual opinions which sensible people may even refrain from pronouncing at all if it is upon somebody else's private affairs) only if society is affected. Without a collective judgment there can be no case at all for intervention. Let me take as an illustration the Englishman's attitude to religion as it is now and as it has been in the past. His attitude now is that a man's religion is his private affair; he may think of another man's religion that it is right or wrong, true or untrue, but not that it is good or bad. In earlier times that was not so; a man was denied the right to practise what was thought of as heresy, and heresy was thought of as destructive of society.

The language used in the passages I have quoted from the Wolfenden Report suggests the view that there ought not to be a collective judgment about immorality *per se*. Is this what is meant by "private morality" and "individual freedom of choice and action"? Some people sincerely believe that homosexuality is neither immoral nor unnatural. Is the "freedom of choice and action" that is offered to the individual, freedom to decide for himself what is moral or immoral, society remaining neutral; or is it freedom to be immoral if he wants to be? The language of the Report may be open to question, but the conclusions at which the Committee arrive answer this question unambiguously. If society is not prepared to say that homosexuality is morally wrong, there would be no basis for a law protecting youth from "corruption" or punishing a man for living on the "immoral" earnings of a homosexual prostitute, as the Report recommends.[1] This attitude the Committee make even clearer when they come to deal with prostitution. In truth, the Report takes it for granted that there is in existence a public morality which condemns homosexuality and prostitution. What the Report seems to mean by private morality might perhaps be better described as private behavior in matters of morals.

This view—that there is such a thing as public morality—can also be justified by *a priori* argument. What makes a society of any sort is community of ideas, not only political ideas but also ideas about the way its members should behave and govern their lives; these latter ideas are its morals. Every society has a moral structure as well as a political one: or rather, since that might suggest two independent systems, I should

---

[1] Para. 76.

say that the structure of every society is made up both of politics and morals. Take, for example, the institution of marriage. Whether a man should be allowed to take more than one wife is something about which every society has to make up its mind one way or the other. In England we believe in the Christian idea of marriage and therefore adopt monogamy as a moral principle. Consequently the Christian institution of marriage has become the basis of family life and so part of the structure of our society. It is there not because it is Christian. It has got there because it is Christian, but it remains there because it is built into the house in which we live and could not be removed without bringing it down. The great majority of those who live in this country accept it because it is the Christian idea of marriage and for them the only true one. But a non-Christian is bound by it, not because it is part of Christianity but because, rightly or wrongly, it has been adopted by the society in which he lives. It would be useless for him to stage a debate designed to prove that polygamy was theologically more correct and socially preferable; if he wants to live in the house, he must accept it as built in the way in which it is.

We see this more clearly if we think of ideas or institutions that are purely political. Society cannot tolerate rebellion; it will not allow argument about the rightness of the cause. Historians a century later may say that the rebels were right and the Government was wrong and a percipient and conscientious subject of the State may think so at the time. But it is not a matter which can be left to individual judgment.

The institution of marriage is a good example for my purpose because it bridges the division, if there is one, between politics and morals. Marriage is part of the structure of our society and it is also the basis of a moral code which condemns fornication and adultery. The institution of marriage would be gravely threatened if individual judgments were permitted about the morality of adultery; on these points there must be a public morality. But public morality is not to be confined to those moral principles which support institutions such as marriage. People do not think of monogamy as something which has to be supported because our society has chosen to organize itself upon it; they think of it as something that is good in itself and offering a good way of life and that it is for that reason that our society has adopted it. I return to the statement that I have already made, that society means a community of ideas; without shared ideas on politics, morals, and ethics no society can exist. Each one of us has ideas about what is good and what is evil; they cannot be kept private from the society in which we live. If men and women try to create a society in which there is no fundamental agreement about good and evil they will fail; if, having based it on common agreement, the agreement goes, the society will disintegrate. For society is not something that is kept together physically; it is held by the invisible bonds of common thought. If the bonds were too far relaxed the members would drift apart. A common morality is part of the bondage. The bondage is part of the price of society; and mankind, which needs society, must pay its price. . . .

. . . You may think that I have taken far too long in contending that there is such a thing as public morality, a proposition which most people would readily accept, and may have left myself too little time to discuss the next question which to many minds may cause greater difficulty: to what extent should society use the law to enforce its moral judgments? But I believe that the answer to the first question determines the way in which the second should be approached and may indeed very nearly dictate the answer to the second question. If society has no right to make judgments on morals, the law must find some special justification for entering the field of morality: if homosexuality and prostitution are not in themselves wrong, then the onus is very clearly on the lawgiver who wants to frame a law against certain aspects of them to justify the exceptional treatment. But if society has the right to make a judgment and has it on the basis that a recognized morality is as necessary to society as, say, a recognized government, then society may use the law to preserve morality in the same way as it uses it to safeguard anything else that is essential to its existence. If therefore the first proposition is securely established with all its implications, society has a prima facie right to legislate against immorality as such.

The Wolfenden Report, notwithstanding that it seems to admit the right of society to condemn homosexuality and prostitution as immoral, requires special circumstances to be shown to justify the intervention of the law. I think that this is wrong in principle and that any attempt to approach my second interrogatory on these lines is bound to break down. I think that the attempt by the Committee does break down and that this is shown by the fact that it has to define or describe its special circumstances so widely that they can be supported only if it is accepted that the law *is* concerned with immorality as such.

The widest of the special circumstances are described as the provision of "sufficient safeguards against exploitation and corruption of others, particularly those who are specially vulnerable because they are young, weak in body or mind, inexperienced, or in a state of special physical, official or economic dependence."[2] The corruption of youth is a well-recognized ground for intervention by the State and for the purpose of any legislation the young can easily be defined. But if similar protection were to be extended to every other citizen, there would be no limit to the reach of the law. The "corruption and exploitation of others" is so wide that it could be used to cover any sort of immorality which involves, as most do, the cooperation of another person. Even if the phrase is taken as limited to the categories that are particularized as "specially vulnerable," it is so elastic as to be practically no restriction. This is not merely a matter of words. For if the words used are stretched almost beyond breaking-point, they still are not wide enough to cover the recommendations which the Committee make about prostitution.

Prostitution is not in itself illegal and the Committee do not think that it ought to be made so.[3] If prostitution is private immorality and not the law's business, what concern has the law with the ponce or the brothel-keeper or the householder who permits habitual prostitution? The Report recommends that the laws which make these activities criminal offences should be maintained or strengthened and brings them (so far as it goes into principle; with regard to brothels it says simply that the law rightly frowns on them) under the head of exploitation.[4] There may be cases of exploitation in this trade, as there are or used to be in many others, but in general a ponce exploits a prostitute no more than an impresario exploits an actress. The Report finds that "the great majority of prostitutes are women whose psychological makeup is such that they choose this life because they find in it a style of living which is to them easier, freer and more profitable than would be provided by any other occupation. . . . In the main the association between prostitute and ponce is voluntary and operates to mutual advantage."[5] The Committee would agree that this could not be called exploitation in the ordinary sense. They say: "It is in our view an over-simplification to think that those who live on the earnings of prostitution are exploiting the prostitute as such. What they are really exploiting is the whole complex of the relationship between prostitute and customer; they are, in effect, exploiting the human weaknesses which cause the customer to seek the prostitute and the prostitute to meet the demand."[6]

All sexual immorality involves the exploitation of human weaknesses. The prostitute exploits the lust of her customers and the customer the moral weakness of the prostitute. If the exploitation of human weaknesses is considered to create a special circumstance, there is virtually no field of morality which can be defined in such a way as to exclude the law.

I think, therefore, that it is not possible to set theoretical limits to the power of the State to legislate against immorality. It is not possible to settle in advance exceptions to the general rule or to define inflexibly areas of morality into which the law is in no circumstances to be allowed to enter. Society is entitled by means of its laws to protect itself from dangers, whether from within or without. Here again I think that the political parallel is legitimate. The law of treason is directed against aiding the king's enemies and against sedition from within. The justification for this is that established government is necessary for the existence of society and therefore its safety against violent overthrow must be secured. But an established morality is as necessary as good government to the welfare of society. Societies disintegrate from within more frequently than they are broken up by external pressures. There is disintegration when no common morality is observed and history shows that the loosening of moral bonds is often the first stage of disintegration, so that society is justified in taking the same steps to preserve its moral code as it does to preserve its government and other essential institutions. The suppression of vice is as much the law's business as the suppression of subversive activities; it is no more possible to define a sphere of private morality than it is to define one of

[2] Para. 13.
[3] Paras. 224, 285, and 318.
[4] Para. 223.
[5] Paras. 302 and 320.
[6] Para. 306.

private subversive activity. It is wrong to talk of private morality or of the law not being concerned with immorality as such or to try to set rigid bounds to the part which the law may play in the suppression of vice. There are no theoretical limits to the power of the State to legislate against treason and sedition, and likewise I think there can be no theoretical limits to legislation against immorality. You may argue that if a man's sins affect only himself it cannot be the concern of society. If he chooses to get drunk every night in the privacy of his own home, is anyone except himself the worse for it? But suppose a quarter or a half of the population got drunk every night, what sort of society would it be? You cannot set a theoretical limit to the number of people who can get drunk before society is entitled to legislate against drunkenness. The same may be said of gambling. The Royal Commission on Betting, Lotteries, and Gaming took as their test the character of the citizen as a member of society. They said: "Our concern with the ethical significance of gambling is confined to the effect which it may have on the character of the gambler as a member of society. If we were convinced that whatever the degree of gambling this effect must be harmful we should be inclined to think that it was the duty of the state to restrict gambling to the greatest extent practicable."[7]

In what circumstances the State should exercise its power is the third of the interrogatories I have framed. But before I get to it I must raise a point which might have been brought up in any one of the three. How are the moral judgments of society to be ascertained? By leaving it until now, I can ask it in the more limited form that is now sufficient for my purpose. How is the law-maker to ascertain the moral judgments of society? It is surely not enough that they should be reached by the opinion of the majority; it would be too much to require the individual assent of every citizen. English law has evolved and regularly uses a standard which does not depend on the counting of heads. It is that of the reasonable man. He is not to be confused with the rational man. He is not expected to reason about anything and his judgment may be largely a matter of feeling. It is the viewpoint of the man in the street—or to use an archaism familiar to all lawyers—the man in the Clapham omnibus. He might also be called the right-minded man. For my purpose I should like to call him the man in the jury box, for the moral judgment of society must be something about which any twelve men or women drawn at random might after discussion be expected to be unanimous. This was the standard the judges applied in the days before Parliament was as active as it is now and when they laid down rules of public policy. They did not think of themselves as making law but simply as stating principles which every right-minded person would accept as valid. It is what Pollock called "practical morality," which is based not on theological or philosophical foundations but "in the mass of continuous experience half-consciously or unconsciously accumulated and embodied in the morality of common sense." He called it also "a certain way of thinking on questions of morality which we expect to find in a reasonable civilized man or a reasonable Englishman, taken at random."

Immorality then, for the purpose of the law, is what every right-minded person is presumed to consider to be immoral. Any immorality is capable of affecting society injuriously and in effect to a greater or lesser extent it usually does; this is what gives the law its *locus standi*. It cannot be shut out. But—and this brings me to the third question—the individual has a *locus standi* too; he cannot be expected to surrender to the judgment of society the whole conduct of his life. It is the old and familiar question of striking a balance between the rights and interests of society and those of the individual. . . .

. . . [I]t is possible to make general statements of principle which it may be thought the legislature should bear in mind when it is considering the enactment of laws enforcing morals.

I believe that most people would agree upon the chief of these elastic principles. There must be toleration of the maximum individual freedom that is consistent with the integrity of society. It cannot be said that this is a principle that runs all through the criminal law. Much of the criminal law that is regulatory in character—the part of it that deals with *malum prohibitum* rather than *malum in se*—is based upon the opposite principle, that is, that the choice of the individual must give way to the convenience of the many. But in all matters of conscience the principle I have stated is generally held to prevail. It is not confined to thought and speech; it extends to action, as is shown by the recognition of the right to conscientious objection in

[7] (1951) Cmd. 8190, para. 159.

war-time; this example shows also that conscience will be respected even in times of national danger. The principle appears to me to be peculiarly appropriate to all questions of morals. Nothing should be punished by the law that does not lie beyond the limits of tolerance. It is not nearly enough to say that a majority dislike a practice; there must be a real feeling of reprobation. Those who are dissatisfied with the present law on homosexuality often say that the opponents of reform are swayed simply by disgust. If that were so it would be wrong, but I do not think one can ignore disgust if it is deeply felt and not manufactured. Its presence is a good indication that the bounds of toleration are being reached. Not everything is to be tolerated. No society can do without intolerance, indignation and disgust; they are the forces behind the moral law, and indeed it can be argued that if they or something like them are not present, the feelings of society cannot be weighty enough to deprive the individual of freedom of choice. I suppose that there is hardly anyone nowadays who would not be disgusted by the thought of deliberate cruelty to animals. No one proposes to relegate that or any other form of sadism to the realm of private morality or to allow it to be practised in public or private. It would be possible no doubt to point out that until a comparatively short while ago nobody thought very much of cruelty to animals and also that pity and kindliness and the unwillingness to inflict pain are virtues more generally esteemed now than they have ever been in the past. But matters of this sort are not determined by rational argument. Every moral judgment, unless it claims a divine source, is simply a feeling that no right-minded man could behave in any other way without admitting that he was doing wrong. It is the power of a common sense and not the power of reason that is behind the judgments of society. But before a society can put a practice beyond the limits of tolerance there must be a deliberate judgment that the practice is injurious to society. There is, for example, a general abhorrence of homosexuality. We should ask ourselves in the first instance whether, looking at it calmly and dispassionately, we regard it as a vice so abominable that its mere presence is an offence. If that is the genuine feeling of the society in which we live, I do not see how society can be denied the right to eradicate it. Our feeling may not be so intense as that. We may feel about it that, if confined, it is tolerable, but that if it spread it might be gravely injurious; it is in this way that most societies look upon fornication, seeing it as a natural weakness which must be kept within bounds but which cannot be rooted out. It becomes then a question of balance, the danger to society in one scale and the extent of the restriction in the other. On this sort of point the value of an investigation by such a body as the Wolfenden Committee and of its conclusions is manifest.

The limits of tolerance shift. This is supplementary to what I have been saying but of sufficient importance in itself to deserve statement as a separate principle which law-makers have to bear in mind. I suppose that moral standards do not shift; so far as they come from divine revelation they do not, and I am willing to assume that the moral judgments made by a society always remain good for that society. But the extent to which society will tolerate—I mean tolerate, not approve—departures from moral standards varies from generation to generation. It may be that overall tolerance is always increasing. The pressure of the human mind, always seeking greater freedom of thought, is outwards against the bonds of society forcing their gradual relaxation. It may be that history is a tale of contraction and expansion and that all developed societies are on their way to dissolution. I must not speak of things I do not know; and anyway as a practical matter no society is willing to make provision for its own decay. I return therefore to the simple and observable fact that in matters of morals the limits of tolerance shift. Laws, especially those which are based on morals, are less easily moved. It follows as another good working principle that in any new matter of morals the law should be slow to act. By the next generation the swell of indignation may have abated and the law be left without the strong backing which it needs. But it is then difficult to alter the law without giving the impression that moral judgment is being weakened. This is now one of the factors that is strongly militating against any alteration to the law on homosexuality.

A third elastic principle must be advanced more tentatively. It is that as far as possible privacy should be respected. This is not an idea that has ever been made explicit in the criminal law. Acts or words done or said in public or in private are all brought within its scope without distinction in principle. But there goes with this a strong reluctance on the part of judges and legislators to sanction invasions of privacy in the detection of crime. The police have no more right to trespass than the ordinary citizen has; there is no general right of search; to this extent an Englishman's home is still his castle. The Government is extremely careful in the exercise even of those powers which it claims to be undisputed. Telephone tapping and interference with the mails afford a good illustration of this. A Committee of three Privy Councillors who recently inquired into these activities found that the Home Secretary and his predecessors had already formulated strict rules governing the exercise of these powers and the Committee were able to recommend that they should be continued to be exercised substantially on the same terms. But they reported that the power was "regarded with general disfavour."

This indicates a general sentiment that the right to privacy is something to be put in the balance against the enforcement of the law. Ought the same sort of consideration to play any part in the formation of the law? Clearly only in a very limited number of cases. When the help of the law is invoked by an injured citizen, privacy must be irrelevant; the individual cannot ask that his right to privacy should be measured against injury criminally done to another. But when all who are involved in the deed are consenting parties and the injury is done to morals, the public interest in the moral order can be balanced against the claims of privacy. The restriction on police powers of investigation goes further than the affording of a parallel; it means that the detection of crime committed in private and when there is no complaint is bound to be rather haphazard and this is an additional reason for moderation. These considerations do not justify the exclusion of all private immorality from the scope of the law. I think that, as I have already suggested, the test of "private behaviour" should be substituted for "private morality" and the influence of the factor should be reduced from that of a definite limitation to that of a matter to be taken into account. Since the gravity of the crime is also a proper consideration, a distinction might well be made in the case of homosexuality between the lesser acts of indecency and the full offence, which on the principles of the Wolfenden Report it would be illogical to do. . . .

26

Bowers v. Hardwick

478 U.S. 186 (1986)

Justice White delivered the opinion of the Court.

In August 1982, respondent Hardwick (hereafter respondent) was charged with violating the Georgia statute criminalizing sodomy by committing that act with another adult male in the bedroom of respondent's home. After a preliminary hearing, the District Attorney decided not to present the matter to the grand jury unless further evidence developed.

Respondent then brought suit in the Federal District Court, challenging the constitutionality of the statute insofar as it criminalized consensual sodomy. He asserted that he was a practicing homosexual, that the Georgia sodomy statute, as administered by the defendants, placed him in imminent danger of arrest, and that the statute for several reasons violates the Federal Constitution. The District Court granted the defendants' motion to dismiss for failure to state a claim, relying on *Doe* v. *Commonwealth's Attorney for the City of Richmond,* 403 F. Supp. 1199 (ED Va. 1975), which this Court summarily affirmed, 425 U. S. 901 (1976).

A divided panel of the Court of Appeals for the Eleventh Circuit reversed. 760 F. 2d 1202 (1985). The court first held that, because *Doe* was distinguishable and in any event had been undermined by later decisions, our summary affirmance in that case did not require affirmance of the District Court. Relying on our decisions in *Griswold* v. *Connecticut,* 381 U. S. 479 (1965); *Eisenstadt* v. *Baird,* 405 U. S. 438 (1972); *Stanley* v. *Georgia,* 394 U. S. 557 (1969); and *Roe* v. *Wade,* 410 U. S. 113 (1973), the court went on to hold that the Georgia statute violated respondent's fundamental rights because his homosexual activity is a private and intimate association that is beyond the reach of state regulation by reason of the Ninth Amendment and the Due Process Clause of the Fourteenth Amendment. The case was remanded for trial, at which, to prevail, the State would have to prove that the statute is supported by a compelling interest and is the most narrowly drawn means of achieving that end.

Because other Courts of Appeals have arrived at judgments contrary to that of the Eleventh Circuit in this case, we granted the Attorney General's petition for certiorari questioning the holding that the sodomy statute violates the fundamental rights of homosexuals. We agree with petitioner that the Court of Appeals erred, and hence reverse its judgment.

This case does not require a judgment on whether laws against sodomy between consenting adults in general, or between homosexuals in particular, are wise or desirable. It raises no question about the right or propriety of state legislative decisions to repeal their laws that criminalize homosexual sodomy, or of state-court decisions invalidating those laws on state constitutional grounds. The issue presented is whether the Federal Constitution confers a fundamental right upon homosexuals to engage in sodomy and hence invalidates the laws of the many States that still make such conduct illegal and have done so for a very long time. The case also calls for some judgment about the limits of the Court's role in carrying out its constitutional mandate.

We first register our disagreement with the Court of Appeals and with respondent that the Court's prior cases have construed the Constitution to confer a right of privacy that extends to homosexual sodomy and for all intents and purposes have decided this case. The reach of this line of cases was sketched in *Carey* v. *Population Services International,* 431 U. S. 678, 685 (1977). *Pierce* v. *Society of Sisters,* 268 U. S. 510 (1925), and *Meyer* v. *Nebraska,* 262 U. S. 390 (1923), were described as dealing with child rearing and education; *Prince* v. *Massachusetts,* 321 U. S. 158 (1944), with family relationships; *Skinner* v. *Oklahoma ex rel. Williamson,* 316 U. S. 535 (1942), with procreation; *Loving* v. *Virginia,* 388 U. S. 1 (1967), with marriage; *Griswold* v. *Connecticut, supra,* and *Eisenstadt* v. *Baird, supra,* with contraception; and *Roe* v. *Wade,* 410 U. S. 113 (1973), with abortion. The latter three cases were interpreted as construing the Due Process Clause of the Fourteenth Amendment to confer a fundamental individual right to decide whether or not to beget or bear a child. *Carey* v. *Population Services International, supra,* at 688–689.

Accepting the decisions in these cases and the above description of them, we think it evident that none of the rights announced in those cases bears any resemblance to the claimed constitutional right of homosexuals to engage in acts of sodomy that is asserted in this case. No connection between family, marriage, or procreation on the one hand and homosexual activity on the other has been demonstrated, either by the Court of Appeals or by respondent. Moreover, any claim that these cases nevertheless stand for the proposition that any kind of private sexual conduct between consenting adults is constitutionally insulated from state proscription is insupportable. Indeed, the Court's opinion in *Carey* twice asserted that the privacy right, which the *Griswold* line of cases found to be one of the protections provided by the Due Process Clause, did not reach so far. 431 U. S., at 688, n. 5, 694, n. 17.

Precedent aside, however, respondent would have us announce, as the Court of Appeals did, a fundamental right to engage in homosexual sodomy. This we are quite unwilling to do. It is true that despite the language of the Due Process Clauses of the Fifth and Fourteenth Amendments, which appears to focus only on the processes by which life, liberty, or property is taken, the cases are legion in which those Clauses have been interpreted to have substantive content, subsuming rights that to a great extent are immune from federal or state regulation or proscription. Among such cases are those recognizing rights that have little or no textual support in the constitutional language. *Meyer, Prince,* and *Pierce* fall in this category, as do the privacy cases from *Griswold* to *Carey.*

Striving to assure itself and the public that announcing rights not readily identifiable in the Constitution's text involves much more than the imposition of the Justices' own choice of values on the States and the Federal Government, the Court has sought to identify the nature of the rights qualifying for heightened judicial protection. In *Palko* v. *Connecticut,* 302 U. S. 319, 325, 326 (1937), it was said that this category includes those fundamental liberties that are "implicit in the concept of ordered liberty," such that "neither liberty nor justice would exist if [they] were sacrificed." A different description of fundamental liberties appeared in *Moore* v. *East Cleveland,* 431 U. S. 494, 503 (1977) (opinion of POWELL, J.), where they are characterized as those liberties that are "deeply rooted in this Nation's history and tradition." *Id.,* at 503 (POWELL, J.). see also *Griswold* v. *Connecticut,* 381 U. S., at 506.

It is obvious to us that neither of these formulations would extend a fundamental right to homosexuals to engage in acts of consensual sodomy. Proscriptions against that conduct have ancient roots. . . . Sodomy was a criminal offense at common law and was forbidden by the laws of the original 13 States when they ratified the Bill of Rights. In 1868, when the Fourteenth Amendment was ratified, all but 5 of the 37 States in the Union had criminal sodomy laws. In fact, until 1961, all 50 States outlawed sodomy, and today, 24 States and the District of Columbia continue to provide criminal penalties for sodomy performed in private and between consenting adults. . . . Against this background, to claim that a right to engage in such conduct is "deeply rooted in this Nation's history and tradition: or "implicit in the concept of ordered liberty" is, at best, facetious.

Nor are we inclined to take a more expansive view of our authority to discover new fundamental rights imbedded in the Due Process Clause. The Court is most vulnerable and comes nearest to illegitimacy when it deals with judge-made constitutional law having little or no cognizable roots in the language or design of the Constitution. That this is so was painfully demonstrated by the face-off between the Executive and the Court in the 1930's, which resulted in the repudiation of much of the substantive gloss that the Court had placed on the Due Process Clauses of the Fifth and Fourteenth Amendments. There should be, therefore, great resistance to expand the substantive reach of those Clauses, particularly if it requires redefining the category of rights deemed to be fundamental. Otherwise, the Judiciary necessarily takes to itself further authority to govern the country without express constitutional authority. The claimed right pressed on us today falls far short of overcoming this resistance.

Respondent, however, asserts that the result should be different where the homosexual conduct occurs in the privacy of the home. He relies on *Stanley* v. *Georgia,* 394 U. S. 557 (1969), where the Court held that the First Amendment prevents conviction for possessing and reading obscene material in the privacy of one's home: "If the First Amendment means anything, it means that a State has no business telling a man, sitting alone in his house, what books he may read or what films he may watch." *Id.,* at 565.

Stanley did protect conduct that would not have been protected outside the home, and it partially prevented the enforcement of state obscenity laws; but the decision was firmly grounded in the First Amendment. The right pressed upon us here has no similar support in the text of the Constitution, and it does not qualify for recognition under the prevailing principles for construing the Fourteenth Amendment. Its limits are also difficult to discern. Plainly enough, otherwise illegal conduct is not always immunized whenever it occurs in the home. Victimless crimes, such as the possession and use of illegal drugs, do no escape the law where they are committed at home. *Stanley* itself recognized that its holding offered no protection for the possession in the home of drugs, firearms, or stolen goods. *Id.,* at 568, n. 11. And if respondent's submission is limited to the voluntary sexual conduct between consenting adults, it would be difficult, except by fiat, to limit the claimed right to homosexual conduct while leaving exposed to prosecution adultery, incest, and other sexual crimes even though they are committed in the home. We are unwilling to start down that road.

Even if the conduct at issue here is not a fundamental right, respondent asserts that there must be a rational basis for the law and that there is none in this case other that the presumed belief of a majority of the electorate in Georgia that homosexual sodomy is immoral and unacceptable. This is said to be an inadequate rationale to support the law. The law, however, is constantly based on notions of morality, and if all laws representing essentially moral choices are to be invalidated under the Due Process Clause, the courts will be very busy indeed. Even respondent makes no such claim, but insists that majority sentiments about the morality of homosexuality should be declared inadequate. We do not agree, and are unpersuaded that the sodomy laws of some 25 States should be invalidated on this basis.

Accordingly, the judgment of the Court of Appeals is

Reversed.

CHIEF JUSTICE BURGER, concurring.

I join the Court's opinion, but I write separately to underscore my view that in constitutional terms there is no such thing as a fundamental right to commit homosexual sodomy.

As the Court notes, *ante,* at 192, the proscriptions against sodomy have very "ancient roots." Decisions of individuals relating to homosexual conduct have been subject to state intervention throughout the history of Western civilization. Condemnation of those practices is firmly rooted in Judeo-Christian moral and ethical standards. Homosexual sodomy was a capital crime under Roman law. See Code Theod. 9.7.6; Code Just. 9.9.31. See also D. Bailey, Homosexuality and the Western Christian Tradition 70–81 (1975). During the English Reformation when powers of the ecclesiastical courts were transferred to the King's Courts, the first

English statute criminalizing sodomy was passed. 25 Hen. VIII, ch. 6. Blackstone described "the infamous *crime against nature*" as an offense of "deeper malignity" than rape, a heinous act "the very mention of which is a disgrace to human nature," and "a crime not fit to be named." 4 W. Blackstone, Commentaries *215. The common law of England, including its prohibition of sodomy, became the received law of Georgia and the other Colonies. In 1816 the Georgia Legislature passed the statute at issue here, and that statute has been continuously in force in one form or another since that time. To hold that the act of homosexual sodomy is somehow protected as a fundamental right would be to cast aside millennia of moral teaching.

This is essentially not a question of personal "preferences" but rather of the legislative authority of the State. I find nothing in the Constitution depriving a State of the power to enact the statute challenged here.

JUSTICE POWELL, concurring.

I join the opinion of the Court. I agree with the Court that there is no fundamental right—*i. e.,* no substantive right under the Due Process Clause—such as that claimed by respondent Hardwick, and found to exist by the Court of Appeals. This is not to suggest, however, that respondent may not be protected by the Eighth Amendment of the Constitution. The Georgia statute at issue in this case, Ga. Code Ann. § 16–6–2 (1984), authorizes a court to imprison a person for up to 20 years for a single private, consensual act of sodomy. In my view, a prison sentence for such conduct—certainly a sentence of long duration—would create a serious Eighth Amendment issue. Under the Georgia statute a single act of sodomy, even in the private setting of a home, is a felony comparable in terms of the possible sentence imposed to serious felonies such as aggravated battery, § 16–5–24, first-degree arson, § 16–7–60, and robbery, § 16–8–40.

In this case, however, respondent has not been tried, much less convicted and sentenced. Moreover, respondent has not raised the Eighth Amendment issue below. For these reasons this constitutional argument is not before us.

JUSTICE BLACKMUN, with whom JUSTICE BRENNAN, JUSTICE MARSHALL, and JUSTICE STEVENS join, dissenting.

This case is no more about "a fundamental right to engage in homosexual sodomy," as the Court purports to declare, *ante,* at 191, than *Stanley* v. *Georgia,* 394 U. S. 557 (1969), was about a fundamental right to watch obscene movies, or *Katz* v. *United States,* 389 U. S. 347 (1967), was about a fundamental right to place interstate bets from a telephone booth. Rather, this case is about "the most comprehensive of rights and the right most valued by civilized men," namely, "the right to be let alone." *Olmstead* v. *United States,* 277 U. S. 438, 478 (1928) (BRANDEIS, J., dissenting).

The statute at issue, Ga. Code Ann. § 16–6–2 (1984), denies individuals the right to decide for themselves whether to engage in particular forms of private, consensual sexual activity. The Court concludes that § 16–6–2 is valid essentially because "the laws of . . . many States . . . still make such conduct illegal and have done so for a very long time." *Ante,* at 190. But the fact that the moral judgments expressed by statutes like § 16–6–2 may be "'natural and familiar . . . ought not to conclude our judgment upon the question whether statutes embodying them conflict with the Constitution of the United States.'" *Roe* v. *Wade,* 410 U. S. 113, 117 (1973), quoting *Lochner v. New York,* 198 U.S. 45, 76 (1905) (HOLMES, J., dissenting). Like Justice Holmes, I believe that "[i]t is revolting to have no better reason for a rule of law than that so it was laid down in the time of Henry IV. It is still more revolting if the grounds upon which it was laid down have vanished long since, and the rule simply persists from blind imitation of the past." Holmes, The Path of the Law, 10 Harv. L. Rev. 457, 469 (1897). I believe we must analyze respondent Hardwick's claim in the light of the values that underlie the constitutional right to privacy. If that right means anything, it means that, before Georgia can prosecute its citizens for making choices about the most intimate aspects of their lives, it must do more than assert that the choice they have made is an "'abominable crime not fit to be named among Christians.'" *Herring* v. *State,* 119 Ga. 709, 721, 46 S. E. 876, 882 (1904).

I

In its haste to reverse the court of Appeals and hold that the Constitution does not "confe[r] a fundamental right upon homosexuals to engage in sodomy," *ante,* at 190, the Court relegates the actual statute being challenged to a footnote and ignores the procedural posture of the case before it. A fair reading of the statute and of the complaint clearly reveals that the majority has distorted the question this case presents.

First, the Court's almost obsessive focus on homosexual activity is particularly hard to justify in light of the broad language Georgia has used. Unlike the Court, the Georgia Legislature has not proceeded on the assumption that homosexuals are so different from other citizens that their lives may be controlled in a way that would not be tolerated if it limited the choices of those other citizens. Cf. *ante,* at 188, n. 2. Rather, Georgia has provided that "[a] person commits the offense of sodomy when he performs or submits to any sexual act involving the sex organs of one person and the mouth or anus of another." Ga. Code Ann. § 16–6–2(a) (1984). The sex or status of the persons who engage in the act is irrelevant as a matter of state law. In fact, to the extent I can discern a legislative purpose for Georgia's 1968 enactment of § 16–6–2, that purpose seems to have been to broaden the coverage of the law to reach heterosexual as well as homosexual activity. I therefore see no basis for the Court's decision to treat this case as an "as applied" challenge to § 16–6–2, see *ante,* at 188, n. 2, or for Georgia's attempt, both in its brief and at oral argument, to defend § 16–6–2 solely on the grounds that it prohibits homosexual activity. Michael Hardwick's standing may rest in significant part on Georgia's apparent willingness to enforce against homosexuals a law it seems not to have any desire to enforce against heterosexuals. See Tr. of Oral Arg. 4–5; cf. 760 F. 2d 1202, 1205–1206 (CA11 1985). But his claim that § 16-6-2 involves an unconstitutional intrusion into his privacy and his right of intimate association does not depend in any way on his sexual orientation. . . .

II

"Our cases long have recognized that the Constitution embodies a promise that a certain private sphere of individual liberty will be kept largely beyond the reach of government." *Thornburgh* v. *American College of Obstetricians & Gynecologists,* 476 U. S. 747, 772 (1986). In construing the right to privacy, the Court has proceeded along two somewhat distinct, albeit complementary, lines. First, it has recognized a privacy interest with reference to certain decisions that are properly for the individual to make. *E. g., Roe* v. *Wade,* 410 U. S. 113 (1973); *Pierce* v. *Society of Sisters,* 268 U. S. 510 (1925). Second, it has recognized a privacy interest with reference to certain *places* without regard for the particular activities in which the individuals who occupy them are engaged. *E. g., United States* v. *Karo,* 468 U. S. 705 (1984); *Payton* v. *New York,* 445 U.S. 573 (1980); *Rios* v. *United States,* 364 U. S. 253 (1960). The case before us implicates both the decisional and the spatial aspects of the right to privacy.

A

The Court concludes today that none of our prior cases dealing with various decisions that individuals are entitled to make free of governmental interference "bears any resemblance to the claimed constitutional right of homosexuals to engage in acts of sodomy that is asserted in this case." *Ante,* at 190–191. While it is true that these cases may be characterized by their connection to protection of the family, see *Roberts* v. *United States Jaycees,* 468 U.S. 609, 619 (1984), the Court's conclusion that they extend no further than this boundary ignores the warning in *Moore* v. *East Cleveland,* 431 U. S. 494, 501 (1977) (plurality opinion), against "clos[ing] our eyes to the basic reasons why certain rights associated with the family have been accorded shelter under the Fourteenth Amendment's Due Process Clause." We protect those rights not because they contribute, in some direct and material way, to the general public welfare, but because they form so central a part of an individual's life. "[The] concept of privacy embodies the 'moral fact that a person belongs to himself and not others nor to society as a whole.'" *Thornburgh* v. *American College of Obstetricians & Gynecologists,* 476 U. S., at 777, n. 5 (STEVENS, J., concurring), quoting Fried, Correspondence, 6 Phil. & Pub. Affairs 288–289 (1977). And so we protect the decision whether to marry precisely because marriage "is an association that promotes a way of life, not causes; a harmony in living, not political faiths; a bilateral loyalty, not commercial or social projects." *Griswold* v. *Connecticut,* 381 U. S., at 486. We protect the decision whether to have a child because parenthood alters so dramatically an individual's self-definition, not because of demographic considerations or the Bible's command to be fruitful and multiply. . . . And we protect the family because it contributes so powerfully to the happiness of individuals, not because of a preference for stereotypical households. . . . The Court recognized in *Roberts,* 468 U. S., at 619, that the "ability independently to define one's identity that is central to any concept of liberty" cannot truly be exercised in a vacuum; we all depend on the "emotional enrichment from close ties with others." *Ibid.*

Only the most willful blindness could obscure the fact that sexual intimacy is "a sensitive, key relationship of human existence, central to family life, community welfare, and the development of human personality," *Paris Adult Theatre I* v. *Slaton,* 413 U. S. 49, 63 (1973); see also *Carey* v. *Population Services* individuals define themselves in a significant way through their intimate sexual relationships with others suggests, in a nation as diverse as ours, that there may be many "right" ways of conducting those relationships, and that much of the richness of a relationship will come from the freedom an individual has to *choose* the form and nature of these intensely personal bonds. . . .

In a variety of circumstances we have recognized that a necessary corollary of giving individuals freedom to choose how to conduct their lives is acceptance of the fact that different individuals will make different choices. For example, in holding that the clearly important state interest in public education should give way to a competing claim by the Amish to the effect that extended formal schooling threatened their way of life, the Court declared: "There can be no assumption that today's majority is 'right' and the Amish and others like them are 'wrong.' A way of life that is odd or even erratic but interferes with no rights or interests of others is not to be condemned because it is different." *Wisconsin* v. *Yoder,* 406 U. S. 205, 223–224 (1972). The Court claims that its decision today merely refuses to recognize a fundamental right to engage in homosexual sodomy; what the Court really has refused to recognize is the fundamental interest all individuals have in controlling the nature of their intimate associations with others.

B

The behavior for which Hardwick faces prosecution occurred in his own home, a place to which the Fourth Amendment attaches special significance. The Court's treatment of this aspect of the case is symptomatic of its overall refusal to consider the broad principles that have informed our treatment of privacy in specific cases. Just as the right to privacy is more than the mere aggregation of a number of entitlements to engage in specific behavior, so too, protecting the physical integrity of the home is more than merely a means of protecting specific activities that often take place there. Even when our understanding of the contours of the right to privacy depends on "references to a 'place,'" *Katz* v. *United States,* 389 U. S., at 361 (HARLAN, J., concurring), "the essence of a Fourth Amendment violation is 'not the breaking of [a person's] doors, and the rummaging of his drawers,' but rather is 'the invasion of his indefeasible right of personal security, personal liberty and private property.'" *California* v. *Ciraolo,* 476 U. S. 207, 226 (1986) (POWELL, J., dissenting), quoting *Boyd* v. *United States,* 116 U. S. 616, 630 (1886).

The Court's interpretation of the pivotal case of *Stanley* v. *Georgia,* 394 U. S. 557 (1969), is entirely unconvincing. Stanley held that Georgia's undoubted power to punish the public distribution of constitutionally unprotected, obscene material did not permit the State to punish the private possession of such material. According to the majority here, *Stanley* relied entirely on the First Amendment, and thus, it is claimed, sheds no light on cases not involving printed materials. *Ante,* at 195. But that is not what *Stanley* said. Rather, the *Stanley* Court anchored its holding in the Fourth Amendment's special protection for the individual in his home:

> "'The makers of our Constitution undertook to secure conditions favorable to the pursuit of happiness. They recognized the significance of man's spiritual nature, of his feelings and of his intellect. They knew that only a part of the pain, pleasure and satisfactions of life are to be found in material things. They sought to protect Americans in their beliefs, their thoughts, their emotions and their sensations.'
>
> . . .
>
> "These are the rights that appellant is asserting in the case before us. He is asserting the right to read or observe what he pleases—the right to satisfy his intellectual and emotional needs in the privacy of his own home." 394 U. S., at 564–565, quoting *Olmstead* v. *United States,* 277 U. S., at 478 (BRANDEIS, J., dissenting).

The central place that *Stanley* gives Justice Brandeis' dissent in *Olmstead,* a case raising *no* First Amendment claim, shows that *Stanley* rested as much on the Court's understanding of the Fourth Amendment as it did on the First. Indeed, in *Paris Adult Theatre I* v. *Slaton,* 413 U. S. 49 (1973), the Court suggested that reliance on the Fourth Amendment not only supported the Court's outcome in *Stanley* but actually was *necessary* to it: "If obscene material unprotected by the First Amendment in itself carried with it a 'penumbra' of constitutionally protected privacy, this Court would not have found it necessary to decide *Stanley* on the narrow basis of the 'privacy of the home,' which was hardly more than a reaffirmation that 'a man's home is his castle.'" 413 U. S., at 66. "The right of the people to be secure in their . . . houses," expressly guaranteed by the Fourth Amendment, is perhaps the most "textual" of the various constitutional provisions that inform our understanding of the right to privacy, and thus I cannot agree with the Court's statement that "[t]he right pressed upon us here has no . . . support in the text of the Constitution," *ante,* at 195. Indeed, the right of an individual to conduct intimate relationships in the intimacy of his or her own home seems to me to be the heart of the Constitution's protection of privacy.

III

The Court's failure to comprehend the magnitude of the liberty interests at stake in this case leads it to slight the question whether petitioner, on behalf of the State, has justified Georgia's infringement on these interests. I believe that neither of the two general justifications for § 16–6–2 that petitioner has advanced warrants dismissing respondent's challenge for failure to state a claim.

First, petitioner asserts that the acts made criminal by the statute may have serious adverse consequences for "the general public health and welfare," such as spreading communicable diseases or fostering other criminal activity. Brief for Petitioner 37. Inasmuch as this case was dismissed by the District Court on the pleadings, it is not surprising that the record before us is barren of any evidence to support petitioner's claim. In light of the state of the record, I see no justification for the Court's attempt to equate the private, consensual sexual activity at issue here with the "possession in the home of drugs, firearms, or stolen goods," *ante,* at 195, to which *Stanley* refused to extend its protection. 394 U. S., at 568, n. 11. None of the behavior so mentioned in *Stanley* can be properly viewed as "[v]ictimless," *ante,* in 195: drugs and weapons are inherently dangerous, see, *e.g., McLaughlin* v. *United States,* 476 U. S. 16 (1986), and for property to be "stolen," someone must have been wrongfully deprived of it. Nothing in the record before the Court provides any justification for finding the activity forbidden by § 16–6–2 to be physically dangerous, either to the persons engaged in it or to others.

The core of petitioner's defense of § 16–6–2, however, is that respondent and others who engage in the conduct prohibited by § 16–6–2 interfere with Georgia's exercise of the "'right of the Nation and of the States to maintain a decent society,'" *Paris Adult Theatre I* v. *Slaton,* 413 U. S., at 59–60, quoting *Jacobellis* v. *Ohio,* 378 U. S. 184, 199 (1964) (Warren, C. J., dissenting). Essentially, petitioner argues, and the Court agrees, that the fact that the acts described in § 16–6–2 "for hundreds of years, if not thousands, have been uniformly condemned as immoral" is a sufficient reason to permit a State to ban them today. Brief for Petitioner 19; see *ante,* at 190, 192–194, 196.

I cannot agree that either the length of time a majority has held its convictions or the passions with which it defends them can withdraw legislation from this Court's scrutiny. . . As Justice Jackson wrote so eloquently for the Court in *West Virginia Board of Education* v. *Barnette,* 319 U. S. 624, 641–642 (1943), "we apply the limitations of the Constitution with no fear that freedom to be intellectually and spiritually diverse or even contrary will disintegrate the social organization. . . . [F]reedom to differ is not limited to things that do not matter much. That would be a mere shadow of freedom. The test of its substance is the right to differ as to things that touch the heart of the existing order." . . . It is precisely because the issue raised by this case touches the heart of what makes individuals what they are that we should be especially sensitive to the rights of those whose choices upset the majority.

The assertion that "traditional Judeo-Christian values proscribe" the conduct involved, Brief for Petitioner 20, cannot provide an adequate justification for § 16–6–2. That certain, but by no means all, religious groups condemn the behavior at issue gives the State no license to impose their judgments on the entire citizenry.

The legitimacy of secular legislation depends instead on whether the State can advance some justification for its law beyond its conformity to religious doctrine. . . .Thus, far from buttressing his case, petitioner's invocation of Leviticus, Romans, St. Thomas Aquinas, and sodomy's heretical status during the Middle Ages undermines his suggestion that § 16–6–2 represents a legitimate use of secular coercive power. A State can no more punish private behavior because of religious intolerance than it can punish such behavior because of racial animus. . . . No matter how uncomfortable a certain group may make the majority of this Court, we have held that "[m]ere public intolerance or animosity cannot constitutionally justify the deprivation of a person's physical liberty." *O'Connor* v. *Donaldson,* 422 U. S. 563, 575 (1975). . . .

Nor can § 16–6–2 be justified as a "morally neutral" exercise of Georgia's power to "protect the public environment," *Paris Adult Theatre I,* 413 U. S., at 68–69. Certainly, some private behavior can affect the fabric of society as a whole. Reasonable people may differ about whether particular sexual acts are moral or immoral, but "we have ample evidence for believing that people will not abandon morality, will not think any better of murder, cruelty and dishonesty, merely because some private sexual practice which they abominate is not punished by the law." H. L. A. Hart, Immorality and Treason, reprinted in The Law as Literature 220, 225 (L. Blom-Cooper ed. 1961). Petitioner and the Court fail to see the difference between laws that protect public sensibilities and those that enforce private morality. Statutes banning public sexual activity are entirely consistent with protecting the individual's liberty interest in decisions concerning sexual relations: the same recognition that those decisions are intensely private which justifies protecting them from governmental interferences can justify protecting individuals from unwilling exposure to the sexual activities of others. But the mere fact that intimate behavior may be punished when it takes place in public cannot dictate how States can regulate intimate behavior that occurs in intimate places." . . .

This case involves no real interference with the rights of others, for the mere knowledge that other individuals do not adhere to one's value system cannot be a legally cognizable interest, cf. *Diamond* v. *Charles,* 476 U. S. 54, 65–66 (1986), let alone an interest that can justify invading the houses, hearts, and minds of citizens who choose to live their lives differently. . . .

27

EGBEKE AJA

Crime and Punishment: An Indigenous African Experience

1. INTRODUCTION

This essay is an attempt to peep through rather a small keyhole into the phenomena of crime and punishment in an indigenous African society—the Igbo society—an ethnic group in Nigeria with an estimated population of about ten million. My concern is not merely a theoretical one. Behind the analyses and issues raised are proffered answers to the nagging questions of:

1. How can the Igbo harmonize borrowed values with the indigenous ones; and
2. What are the effective ways of dealing with the alarming increase in crime with its bewildering sophistication, without running foul of inherited law?

2. MORALITY IN THE INDIGENOUS IGBO SOCIETY

A people's happiness and even their survival depend on the degree of harmony between them and the other beings or forces that inhabit their world. Morality, for the Igbo consisted in all acts and usages intended to maintain harmony among the various forces: human, vegetable, and mineral. Humankind is at the vortex of these forces. Moral goodness, therefore, has an ontological dimension: To do wrong in the indigenous Igbo society means not merely to be individually in disharmony with the order in nature but to harm and disorganize this order itself. Igbo morality is objective morality, for "The objective ethics of the Africans is an ontological ethics, immanent and intrinsic. It is attached to the essence of things ontologically perceived."[1] There is an intrinsic order of things which is the essential condition for the integrity of being. Hence, in the indigenous Igbo society, and African society generally, there is no purely personal morality.

We might say that, what an individual does has no importance in itself, but only on account of the deleterious influence the action is likely to have on the group and on the forces of nature which ensure the group's survival: rain, health, fertility, etc. Herein lies the basis of Igbo morality. The *summum bonum* for an indigenous Igbo is the performance of those acts which will enhance the ontological well-being of the Igbo community. All ethical concepts hinge on this. Consequently, the indigenous Igbo morality is a metaphysical ethics because (1) it emphasizes the innate harmony between human beings and the universe; (2) it respects the mechanism of the interaction among beings; and most importantly, (3) it has as its centerpiece, the community or the group. It can be described as "ethical communalism."[2]

Little wonder that in the indigenous Igbo society the perfect person was the person with a good heart, that is, a person who has learned the art of living and promoting the essential harmonies in life. Human beings, for the traditional Igbo, reach their full stature only in the solidarity of their community.

I have argued that the underlying factor of all African (Igbo) indigenous moral conduct was ontological. The greatest happiness and good of the group was the end and aim of each individual member of the indigenous Igbo society. The morality was utilitarian. However, it was not egoistic utility. It was communal and to a large extent, altruistic in outlook.[3] The Yorubas, another major ethnic group in Nigeria, share the same view of the inter-relatedness of beings inhabiting the universe. For the Yorubas, "Gentle character it is which enables the rope of life to stay unbroken in one's hand."[4]

The indigenous Igbo morality, in essence, was a morality of conduct rather than that of being. It was a dynamic morality, for it defined what X did rather than what X was. A person was what she was because of what she did. Human beings, for the Igbo, were not by nature either good or bad except in terms of what they did or did not do. As a result, the traditional Igbo morality was characterized by the following features:

1. *Prohibitions*—which include general prescriptions such as: Do not take the life of another person; do not steal; do not commit incest; do not defraud strangers, etc. These, though moral in content, were religious in expression. They were all rooted in religious beliefs and observances connected with *Ala*, the earth divinity.

2. *Taboos*—these were either general or specific. General taboos were applicable to all persons and included such taboos observed at various moments demanded by tradition or divination irrespective of time and place. For example, during a designated period of the year a man was not allowed to beat up his wife. Another example is that one kind of snake, the green snake, was not to be killed or eaten by a member of the Igbo community.

Specific taboos were for special people. For example, the traditional medical practitioner was not allowed to eat *ojukwu*—the yellow palm fruits which render her or his medicine powerless. Some priests were not to eat any food cooked by a mother of twins, nor were they expected to be under the same roof with such a mother.

3. *Customs*—the *Omenala* constituted the customs. Like the taboos, and prohibitions, they were couched in religious practices. The values of the indigenous Igbo society were summed up by the *Omenala*, that is, that which happens or is approved of in the community. Customs ranged from serious subjects like moral sanctions used to maintain social control to matters of etiquette and polite behavior. For example, anybody who picked up a fallen fruit which was not hers/his was accounted as having stolen. A child dared not beat up her parents or even elders. A woman or a man was not to have a child before marriage. All these values made up the Igbo tradition—a pattern of thought and action expressed in religious or social customs. The values made for cultural continuity in communal attitudes and institutions. They formed the index of what was accepted in the traditional Igbo culture. The essential requirement of *Omenala*, or tradition, on the part of the individual was the identification of self with the totality of beings. This identification was manifested in the individual's compliance with the specific beliefs and customs prevalent in the community.

3. WHAT CONSTITUTED CRIME IN THE INDIGENOUS IGBO SOCIETY

In the pre-colonial Igbo society, influences—natural and artificial—were steady, uniform, harmonious, and consistent. The individual was a member, not only of her immediate family, but also of her extended family, of the village at large, and even of the Igbo race. This group-membership, though mythical, was accepted by the Igbo as real and as such had reality. Each member belonged to the group in a very practical sense. Hence, to be out adrift from one's kith and kin was a living death; thus, the sanctions of ostracism was like outlawry in feudal England.

However, the indigenous Igbo society had little or no contact with the outside world. Each community was self-supporting and self-contained. "This 'splendid' isolation was conducive to consistency in behavior patterns of the individual members of the group."[5] Within the group, few crimes were possible, and as a result less crimes were committed because "society prepares the crime, the criminal commits it." Though in modern societies crime may just be a revolt by the criminal against the ills and shortcomings of the society, in the indigenous Igbo society, it was a kink on the ontological well-being of the group, a negation or violation of what ought-to-be. In the traditional Igbo society, there were no white collar crimes, like forgery and fraud; no bank robberies, since the communities had no banks. Property was sparse, and stealing was rare and limited in scope. Morality was high, since the individual would not dare break the moral norms of the community. The Igbo were so closely knit by consanguinity that strife was scarcely present and violence was strenuously avoided. Yet, there were limited areas of individual and group offenses.

For the indigenous Igbo, moral goodness had an ontological dimension. It was utilitarian, for all acts and usages were geared toward the attainment of perfect harmony which ought to exist in and between the physical, social, and religious dimensions of life. This, in the main, constituted the ontological locus of the traditional Igbo conscience. In the traditional Igbo society, a plurality of co-ordinated forces occur. The order in which these forces occur and interact comes from God. It must be respected and religiously maintained.[6] But, just as one stone thrown into a pond breaks up the reflections you could previously see in the water, so any criminal act can disrupt the existential harmony in the traditional Igbo society. Such an act effectively breaks the ontological harmony of the community of forces.

Crime was, in the indigenous Igbo society, "a disruptive factor in the fabric of the universe, a kink in the normal web of relationships between beings or an obstruction in the lines of flow of the life-forces which keep the social order alive."[7] That is, any deliberate or unconscious harm to the fabric of the organized society itself constituted crime. The principles at stake were basic to the ordering of society, and a breach of those principles impinged on the well-being of the entire community. With this understanding, for the indigenous Igbo, the unborn child or the newly born child could be a criminal. A disturbance of the ontological order, whether by the individual or by the corporate group, was ultimately an offense by the corporate body—the Igbo society. Hence, for the traditional Igbo,

> The guilt of one person involves his entire household including his animals and property. The pollution of the individual is corporately the pollution of those related to him whether they are human beings, animals or material goods.[8]

Any breach in the unity of *Omenala*—customs and traditions—was recognized by the indigenous Igbo, and Africans generally, as a breach of peace likely to result in tragedy for the community. A breach, therefore, was treated as a community affair. For instance, if a person committed a crime, the Igbo of old did not wait for the police to come to start mulling over the matter under the pretense of conducting a high-powered investigation. Instead, the first person to catch a glimpse of the culprit instantaneously pounced on him or her and exerted the appropriate justice once and for all. This instantaneous action was based on the principle that delaying justice was breaking the tradition or *Omenala* whose fundamental *raison d'être* was ensuring peace and harmony in the community of beings.

4. KINDS OF CRIMES

In the indigenous Igbo society crimes could be categorized into three main kinds:

1. *Capital crimes.* These involve one taking the life of a member of one's community either by omission or commission. They also included other offenses that attracted capital punishment. For instance, if a baby presents a breach position during birth, such a baby after birth is thrown away into the evil forest. The baby is deemed to have had the intention of taking the life of its mother. This, for the Igbo, was a

heinous crime on the part of the baby. The traditional Igbo was and is still at pains in understanding the modern English criminal procedure adopted in our courts where a person known to be a murderer is pronounced not guilty and set free for want of evidence and some other technicalities. Up till now, these are beyond the comprehension of the traditional Igbo who is still of a piece with the philosophy of the group. For the traditional Igbo, only one law exists for murder: death by hanging.

In Igbo thought, the word is a force. As a force, it influences and is being influenced by other forces in the Igbo universe. Thoughts or words wishing that someone be harmed in some way, are seen as an ill-wind that blows no good either on the individual who expressed the word, or the entire Igbo society. The word must be directed toward the maintenance of the group's ontological solidarity and harmony—the highest good. For, "the whole tone of the philosophy of most African people is distinctly life affirming."[9] Hearsay, therefore, was enough evidence in determining the guilt of a suspect.

The traditional Igbo distinguished four kinds of murder or *Ochu*.

(1) *Accidental killing.* In modern legal language, this is referred to as manslaughter. In traditional Igbo society, the slayer was notified of the death of the victim of the act. The slayer was given an opportunity to flee the community. The criminal remained in exile—uprooted from his roots—for a specific period. After the period, he may return if he so desired. If he returned, he then paid compensation to the relatives of the deceased. This is known as *Igwa ochu.* In keeping with the people's life-affirming philosophy, the compensation to the relatives of the deceased often ended in the family of the criminal giving a young girl in marriage to a member of the family of the deceased. The children of such a marriage are reckoned by the deceased family to have adequately redressed the social and ontological imbalance caused by the loss of their relative at the hand of the manslayer.

(2) *Killing in a fight.* In the indigenous Igbo society, dangerous weapons were not allowed in a fight between relatives or people of the same town or ethnic group. However, machetes, spears, bows and arrows, and similar weapons, though dangerous weapons, were permitted in a fight between communities. But care was exercised in the use of these weapons. If it happened that a member of one community was killed in a fight by a member of another community, members of the offending community would flee their village to another. The Igbo refer to this as *Iso ochu.* While in flight, the property left behind will be confiscated by the relatives of the deceased. More often than not, the offending community was sacked, their huts burnt down, their walls pulled down, and their economic trees felled all in the bid to restore the loss of joy of life sustained by the bereaved. The community remained desolate for a specified period, say three years, after which the offending community would pay compensation, such as grant of land known as *Ala ochu,* or female members of the community would be given away into forced marriage into the deceased person's community or village.

(3) *Decapitation.* For the traditional Igbo, to kill a human being was an odious crime; to decapitate the deceased was an unpardonable crime. The traditional Igbo could not imagine the prospect of their relatives going to the spirit world headless. As a result, the cutting off of the head amounted to an ontological sacrilege and led to eternal enmity between the opposing communities.

To forestall this singular crime, in tribal wars, it was customary to conclude a treaty between the belligerents whereby it was agreed that in the event of a member being killed, the corpse must not be decapitated.

(4) *Willful murder.* It was an atrocity for you to willfully and deliberately kill a member of your community. The houses and property of your entire family were then destroyed. You, the slayer, would in addition be expected to hang yourself. Should you delay in taking the rope, your relatives would be prompted to hand to you a suitable rope showing you, symbolically, the way you were to go. But, if the murderer was a coward and ran away, he remained in exile until the bitter feelings toward him had died down. In some cases, the criminal was exiled for life; in others, it lasted only for seven years. However, should any of the deceased relatives see the murderer return to the community, they had a right to kill her or him at sight. But after the stipulated period of exile, negotiations are opened. If these succeed, the fugitive returned to the community, and before he was integrated into the community, he performed all the appropriate sacrifices and made all prescribed restitutions.

In some cases, the criminal could run into the sanctuary of some local juju shrine where no one can touch her or him in retaliation. This phenomenon is one of the origins of the *Osu* caste system in some parts of Igboland. The fugitive, having surrendered to a shrine, becomes sacred and immune to human attacks. But the whole family's property was destroyed or forbidden to be used by anyone in the community as a sign of reparation.

A person with the Western mind-set would criticize these measures as drastic and unjust. In contradistinction to the European conception of justice which measures liability in terms of material damage, the traditional Igbo conception measures liability in terms of the loss in the joy of life. That is what is evaluated. For the Igbo, the taking of the life of a member of one's community was an ontological sacrilege; it was just like breaking off one of the cogs in a wheel. The whole system will no longer work smoothly, for a gap has been created in the traditional cobweb relationship. Anything that affects a member of the traditional society, affects the whole group. Hence, no price was deemed too grave for reinstating the group's ontological equilibrium.

2. *Minor crimes.* These are called minor in that they do not directly involve the taking of someone's life. Instead, they are acts that disturb the ontological harmony of the individual and the whole group. But some of them could attract capital punishment. This category of crimes concerns violations of other people's right over property. They include stealing, witchcraft, adultery, and breaking of taboos.

Stealing. Notorious thieves, wicked traditional medical practitioners, those who engaged in the nefarious practice of witchcraft, those who betrayed and sold out community secrets, those who were unruly and also refused to submit to the protests of relatives or who acted in such a manner that they placed the family or the community in jeopardy, were treated as criminals. The indigenous Igbo society got rid of this class of criminals by putting them to death.

In respect of the thief, the article stolen was of importance in determining the gravity of the punishment. For instance, yam theft was and is still regarded as a serious crime against not just humanity but also *Ala,* the earth goddess. The Igbo regard yam as the chief of all crops in Igboland. As such, yam is not expected to be subjected to a mean act such as stealing. So, a yam thief was punished severely in traditional Igbo society. But if the criminal is proved not a habitual offender, in some Igbo communities, she or he was made to dance around the village naked. The criminal was taunted, beaten, stoned, and jeered at as she or he went round the town-squares. In the indigenous Igbo society, loss of face was counted a grave punishment. But a notorious yam thief was required to take her or his life. Or, the relatives would be advised to arrange with people of another community to rid the family of the nuisance. Under one pretext or another, the criminal was induced to pass a chosen pathway where hired executioners, lying in ambush, would get rid of her or him. After they finished with the criminal, a tuber of yam would be placed on the chest of the slain criminal. People who indulged in habitual stealing of other people's property suffered similar fate in traditional Igbo cultures.

Adultery was also judged an offense against humanity and the gods. Adultery with the wife of a Chief was adjudged more grievous than with the wife of an ordinary member of the society. For the Igbo, a Chief is the spiritual head of the people. He is the link between the dead and the living. Anything, therefore, that disturbs his well-being affects the entire society, even the spirit world. As a result, adultery with his wife attracted the death penalty. Though the adulterer was held responsible, the wife of the Chief might be forgiven. But the same offense committed with the wife of any other member of the society demanded sacrifice and propitiation on the part of the man and the woman adulterers.

Nowadays, though still practiced in many Igbo communities, such killings would amount to murder, but in the indigenous Igbo culture they were justifiable homicide. It was a crude justice but an effective deterrent to evil-doing. The action was to forestall the Igbo adage that *Otu mkpisi aka ruta manu, ozue umuaka dum.* When one finger is oiled, it spreads to the others. In consonance with the Biblical injunction that if one part of one's body would make you sin, you should cut it off. The Igbo society got rid of any member of the society who habitually violated the rights of others over property. A person who tampered with the people's main source of sustenance, yam, or source of joy, deserved no other punishment than severance from the kith and kin.

3. *Abomination* consists of crimes which may or may not have been committed through the actions of the criminal. They include child infanticide and the breaking of taboos and customs of the people. They

are acts or events which are contrary to what used to be—a deviation from the normal state of affairs.

In the indigenous Igbo society, any abnormality in child-bearing was regarded as an abomination and by deduction, a crime or *aru*. The practice was to kill such a baby immediately after birth. This practice, dictated by and deeply rooted in the people's customs, was a common phenomenon; examples of *aru* in Igbo culture included the following:

(1) *Twin delivery or ejima*. The unfortunate twins were usually placed in a water pot and deposited in a "bad bush" or otherwise destroyed.

(2) *Nwa oghom* (Accidental birth). A child born before an elder brother or sister has been weaned committed an abomination. The baby was deemed to have interfered with the progress and wellbeing of its predecessor. For the Igbo, the first to be born has a greater right to live than the later "intruder," an indication of the high premium the indigenous Igbo placed on seniority of birth, and the order in the ontological hierarchy of beings or forces.

(3) *A breach birth—Iji okpa puta*. This was considered an abomination, and, therefore, demanded the death of the baby who chose to come into the world by that way whether the mother survived or not.

(4) A baby born with teeth or a child cutting the upper teeth first. In either case the penalty was death for the child or baby. The baby born with teeth is referred to as *Nwa pu eze n'afo;* while the child who cuts upper teeth first is known as *Nwa ezc clu*.

Other minor crimes or abominations that could be committed by a baby or a child included failure to cry vigorously at birth, being born with six toes or six fingers. In the first case, the baby forfeited its life; whereas, as a general rule, in the second case, the baby was abandoned to die on its own.

The above crimes indicate fundamental beliefs among the indigenous Igbo. For the Igbo, a human fetus becomes a human being directly it is conceived and must be accorded that status. The idea of an age of reason is alien to traditional Igbo jurisprudence, which holds that a superior force or being is always the guardian of an inferior force or being. Maintenance of the intrinsic harmony in nature is paramount in the mind of the indigenous Igbo. Any act of omission or commission that threatened the corporate existence of the society never went unpunished. Anything that would anger the gods was counted an abomination; so to be safe from the wrath of the gods, the indigenous society did everything to guard its members against the group's declared abominations.

By certain acts of speech, one could commit an abomination. It was a crime or abomination for any man to beat up his wife at a particular period of the year. For instance, in Chinua Achebe's *Things Fall Apart,* Okonkwo beat up Ekwefi, his wife, during the holy week.[10] By that singular act, Okonkwo offended both the community, *Umuofia,* and the gods. That amounted to a disruption of the desired peace, quiet, and harmony in both the human and spirit world, of *Umuofia*. When such an offense was committed, an appropriate propitiation was made to appease both the living and the dead. Okonkwo, of *Things Fall Apart,* atoned for the beating of his wife during the holy week.

By killing and eating a revered animal or totem, an indigenous Igbo was deemed to have committed a crime. Specific sacrifice was demanded. In Igbo thought, the animal world is part and parcel of the human world. Killing a python, a totem in some Igbo communities, called for a compensation and a befitting burial rite for the slain python. Such were some of the crimes and punishment in the simple, harmonious, indigenous Igbo culture.

5. PROOF IN THE INDIGENOUS IGBO CULTURES

In Igbo jurisprudence, grave suspicion amounts to *prima facie* proof. Should a murderer not admit guilt, the onus to establish her or his innocence was on that person. Proof in such cases was usually by means of trial by ordeal or by the invocation and the intervention of the gods in juju-swearing. The gods were needed because for the Igbo, and the Africans in general, the departed and the gods are the guardians of morality. In ordeal or juju swearing, the gods decided on the issue of the guilt or the innocence of the accused. One popular form of ordeal was to wash a corpse and collect the bath-water. A relative of the deceased took a sip of the water to assure witnesses that no poison had been mixed with it, then the accused person took a mouthful of the water. A period, usually twelve months, was agreed upon. If the suspected murderer died within the period, then her or his guilt would have been confirmed by the gods. If the suspect did not die, then she or he danced around the village, proclaiming her or his innocence.

Relatives and friends of the suspect were advised to refrain from interacting with her or him till after the expiration of the agreed period. In some cases, the water used in washing the corpse was poured across the road along which the suspect lived.

By modern standards, these means of detecting and punishing criminals may seem crude. But in a society with deep and tender religious feelings, such as the indigenous Igbo, ordeals and juju-swearing are accepted methods of proof. Admittedly, a guilty criminal may die by sheer auto-suggestion or by qualms of conscience, but for the traditional Igbo, the juju or the gods would have done their job as guardians of indigenous Igbo morals.

6. CRIME IN CONTEMPORARY IGBO CULTURE

Colonialism had a tremendous influence on the Igbo in spite of their resilience to change. Western civilization, with its money economy and materialism, descended on the indigenous Igbo society which was hitherto homogenous, simple, and with few incidences of crime. From colonialism resulted a cultural synthesis which has produced a curious cultural hybrid. This, in turn, has produced conflict of norms, divergent aims, and disparate rules of conduct.

The erstwhile simple society has gradually been undermined and progressively eroded and is threatened to be over-thrown. Consequently, the contemporary Igbo society is rife with sophisticated crimes. The group ideology that characterized the traditional Igbo culture has been replaced with a new one which is individualist in concept and materialist in content. The emphasis has shifted to individual enterprise and to the acquisition of material wealth. As a result, the average Igbo has started to disregard the old traditional system of social welfare which is fast giving way to the advancing avalanche of self-satisfaction. With the new materialism, wealth has soon been identified with worth. Hence, the saying in Igbo: *Onye nkirika akwa bu onye nkirika okwu,* meaning that the poor cannot possibly make any meaningful contribution to public debate.

Worse still, the traditional distinction between a rich and a virtuous person is fast disappearing in the contemporary Igbo society. Little wonder that the desire now is for more personal wealth which is both the key to and the symbol of success. The desire and trend obviously have led to more conflicts of interests and ultimately to more crime. A high crime rate is expected generally in a social system in which great emphasis is placed on the success goal and the attainment of wealth, whereas little or no emphasis is placed upon the proper means of achieving those goals.

The new neighborhood-township created by Western ideas and civilization has failed to function as an effective check on crime, since it is lacking in those pressures for conformity dictated by similar customs, religions, etc. reminiscent of the primordial indigenous Igbo neighborhood. The confusion has been compounded by the increase in commerce and travel as well as by the impact of newspapers, radio, and television. The danger of criminal contact and criminal contamination have become greater, when control over behavior has become weaker and more ineffective.

Expectedly, the Igbo of today is caught up in intense cultural conflict he is called upon by existential conditions to dance the rhythm of new religions, new values, new world views, and new political and legal systems. The Igbo value system has thus become distorted. Consequently, the crime rate is on the increase. The society appears unable to check the ugly trend; nor is it able to administer commensurate punishments to criminals. The Western legal system, with its emphasis on evidence, is responsible for the inability of the society to cope with crime in contemporary Igbo societies. . . .

NOTES

1. Placide Temples, *Bantu Philosophy* (Paris: Pr'esence Africaine, 1959), p. 81.
2. Egbeka Aja, "The Ontological Foundations of African Communalism" Unpublished M.A. Philosophy Dissertation (University of Nigeria, Nsukka, 1986), p. 98.
3. Edmund Ilogu, *Igbo Life and Thought* (Onitsha: University Publishing Company, 1985), p. 29.
4. John S. Mbiti, *African Religions and Philosophy* (London: Heinemann, 1969), p. 212.
5. C. A. Oputa, "Crime and the Nigerian Society," T. O. Elias, et al., eds. *African Indigenous Laws* (Nsukka: Institute of African Studies, University of Nigeria, Nsukka, 1975), p. 8
6. Tempels, *Bantu Philosophy,* p. 80.
7. K. C. Anyanwu and E. A. Ruch, *African Philosophy* (Rome: Catholic Book Agency, 1980), p. 135.

8. Mbiti, *African Religions and Philosophy,* p. 206.
9. E. C. Parrinder, *West African Psychology* (London: Lutherworth Press, 1951), p. 223.
10. Chinua Achebe, *Things Fall Apart* (London: Heinemann, 1980), ch. 5.

28

ANTHONY KENNY

The Mind and the Deed

The topic of responsibility is an area in which the interests of the philosopher and of the lawyer overlap. One branch of philosophy is the philosophy of mind and action, and one of the concerns of the criminal lawyer is the mental element in crime. This area of overlap will be the subject of this book.

Philosophers of mind are concerned with the analysis of the relationship between mind and behavior. When we understand, respond to, and evaluate each other's actions we make constant use of mentalistic concepts. On the basis of what people do, and in order to explain what they do, we attribute to them certain desires and beliefs. We ascribe their actions to choices, and we invoke, to explain their conduct, various intentions, motives, and reasons. These mentalistic concepts, such as *desire, belief, intention, motive,* and *reason,* are the subject matter of the philosophy of mind. In human action we look for a mental element; in the philosophy of human action we study the relationship between the mental element and the overt behaviour.

Actions are sometimes the subject of moral and legal evaluation: some actions we regard as admirable and praiseworthy; others we condemn and punish as criminal. Those human actions which are crimes are of special interest and have long been a subject of special study. Crimes, like other actions, involve a mental element. For this mental element lawyers have a special name: *mens rea,* which is the Latin for "guilty mind." There was a maxim of the English common law: *actus non facit reum nisi mens sit rea:* an act does not make a man guilty unless his mind is guilty too. The "guilty mind" need not be any consciousness of wickedness nor any malevolent intent: in most cases it is simply a knowledge of what one is doing, where what one is doing is something illegal. But where *mens rea* is required, no act can be criminal unless accompanied by a certain mental state. The particular mental state indicated by *mens rea* differs, as we shall see, from crime to crime: the expression means, in general, the state of mind which must accompany an act which is on the face of it criminal if the agent is to be held responsible, and therefore liable for punishment, for the action.

This notion of responsibility will be the major topic of this book. The scope and method of the chapters will be philosophical in the narrow sense of the word current in Anglo-American academic circles: I shall be engaged in the analysis and clarification of certain concepts which are central to our understanding of human nature and activity. I shall not be advancing empirical hypotheses about human behaviour, nor reporting scientific discoveries about human mental processes. Nor shall I be offering an elementary course in aspects of criminal law. But I shall constantly draw upon actual legal cases to illustrate the conceptual points that I wish to make. This is not because I believe that the notions of belief, intention, choice, and the like are only at home in the formal context of criminal proceedings: on the contrary, as I have said, I believe that the use of them is indispensable at every step when we endeavour to understand and communicate with each other. But the reports of the courts and the decisions of judges provide a fund of material for philosophical study which is more concrete, vivid, and credible, while at the same time often more extraordinary and thought-provoking, than any product of philosophers' imaginations. Moreover, the needs of the courts to reach a decision, and the experience of legal systems over long periods of practical operation, have in some areas brought a precision into legal concepts which can contrast favourably with the achievement of philosophers. Finally, by concentrating on legal cases in which matters of life and death are considered and in which the lifetime fate of the accused may be in the balance, we remind ourselves that the philosophy of action, while it may operate at a very abstract level, is a subject of great practical importance whose aim is to dispel confusions that can have far-reaching social consequences.

For several reasons the notion of responsibility and the cluster of concepts that combine to provide its habitat have been looked on with disfavour in recent years. To many people the apparatus of responsibility as administered in the criminal courts seems antiquated and inhumane: many social reformers look forward to a day when the courts of the criminal law have gone the way of rotten boroughs and ordeal by combat. They look forward to a time when law courts are replaced by something more scientific and clinical: when the determination of responsibility and the handing down of penalties by judicial bodies is replaced by the diagnosis of social illness and the prescription of appropriate medicinal procedures by teams of social scientists.

In these lectures I shall argue that many attacks on the common-law notion of responsibility are based on misunderstandings of an essentially philosophical nature. Conceptual confusions, I shall argue, often distort the benevolent and liberal intentions of social reformers and ensnare them into making proposals whose effects are abhorrent.

To illustrate the type of objection made by social reformers to the notions of *mens rea* and responsibility I shall quote from the evidence laid by the National Association for Mental Health before the Butler Committee which inquired into the treatment of mentally abnormal offenders and which reported in 1974. Under the heading "The Determination of Criminal Responsibility" the Association submitted as follows:[1]

> Until very recently the concept of "mens rea" was the basis of all decisions regarding responsibility. This position was eroded by the introduction of the concept of diminished responsibility in the 1958 Homicide Act. We recognise and applaud the liberal intention behind the concept, but it is all the same a difficult one, particularly as in some cases of mental illness the diminution of responsibility may be periodic and not permanent. The position is further complicated by the fact that there are now a number of "absolute" offences, where a person may be found guilty although he had no knowledge that what he was doing was an offence and no intention of committing an offence. Examples of such offences range from parking offences to being in possession of dangerous drugs.
>
> The Association has considerable reservations about the present confused situation. The difficulty arises over the imprecise nature of psychiatric definition of mental disorder. This means that we constantly see the unedifying clash of psychiatric experts for the defense and the prosecution in an effort to determine the state of man's mind, when this is very often not susceptible of scientific proof. Indeed such proof would only be obtainable in the highly unlikely event of a psychiatrist observing and assessing the offender at the precise time of his offence.
>
> We accordingly suggest for the Committee's consideration that the accused's state of mind could more profitably be taken into account in the disposal of his case than in assessing his responsibility. The disposal of cases of this kind ought to follow a very careful statement of psychiatric opinion and a full review of the social history.
>
> Given adequate provision for taking into account a convicted person's state of mind in the decision about disposal, we suggest that the concept of *"mens rea"* and criminal responsibility could be dispensed with in favour of the concept of strict accountability for one's actions in criminal charges. We recognise, however, the radical change in sentencing procedure that would be required in this case.

The Association, therefore, wished the requirement of *mens rea* as an ingredient in crime to be replaced by a system of strict accountability for action plus a professional investigation into the accused's state of mind at the time of sentencing. In attacking *mens rea,* the Association does not seem to have had a single target in mind. It devotes itself in the paper to the consideration of when it is proper to consider an accused person's "state of mind." But by this expression it clearly meant several different things. Most commonly the expression is used in the paper to refer to the accused's state of mental health: Is he or she sane or insane, mentally normal or abnormal? This is naturally what the Association is most interested in and what it wants professionally investigated at the time of disposal. But in other places, by "state of mind" the Association means such things as whether the accused knew that what he was doing was an offence and whether he had any intention of committing an offence. To investigate a state of mind in this sense is very different from inquiring into a person's state of mental health. To decide whether someone is mentally ill may well call for difficult expert inquiry by a psychiatrist—an inquiry whose difficulties would not necessarily be resolved by "observing and assessing the offender at the precise time of his offence." To discover whether someone knew a particular place to be a No Parking zone does not call for similar professional expertise.

The Association seems to have believed that *"mens rea"* meant knowledge that one is committing an offence, or the intention to commit an offence. This is not correct. Certainly for many crimes one needs to know that one is doing the action which is, as a matter of fact, an offence; but one does not need to know *that* it is an offence. The common law, which imposed the requirement of *mens rea,* contained also the maxim that ignorance of law was no defence. The *mens rea* which is needed for most crimes is not knowledge that X, which one is doing, is a crime; but simply the knowledge that one is doing X.

The state of mind which constitutes *mens rea* in fact varies from crime to crime. Let us suppose that the law wishes to prohibit a certain action, and let us suppose further that it gives a description of the prohibited action in terms which contain no reference to the agent's state of mind: e.g., a description such as "being in charge of a motor vehicle" or "entering a prohibited place." There are many different provisos which the law can go on to make concerning what the mental state of the agent must be if his performance of the prohibited act is to constitute a crime.

1. Let us suppose the law makes no such proviso at all, so that the act will be punishable no matter whether the accused did know or could have known what he was doing. In that case no *mens rea* will be required for the crime and it will be an "absolute" offence, an offence of "strict liability."

2. If the law does not wish it to be punishable absolutely in this manner, let us next suppose that it wishes it to be punishable whether or not the agent actually knows that he is performing the action, provided only that he could and should have known that he was. In that case the crime will be a crime of negligence. Where there is negligence, there is voluntary unawareness of the nature of one's action. The question arises. Is negligence a form of *mens rea?* Some argue that unawareness is not a state of mind and so negligence is not *mens rea;* others argue that because negligence is voluntary and culpable unawareness, the requirement of *mens rea* is present in crimes of negligence. The terminological point is perhaps not of great importance: what is important is to distinguish crimes of negligence from crimes of strict liability.

3. If the law does not thus wish an act to be punishable when performed by an agent who is unaware that he is performing it, let us next suppose that it wishes it to be punishable whether or not the agent intends to perform it (in the sense of wanting to perform it as an end in itself or as a means to some other end), provided only that he believes or thinks it likely that he is performing it. In that case the crime will be one of recklessness: recklessness will be the *mens rea* required for the action to be punishable.

4. If the law does not wish an action to be punishable whenever performed by an agent with this degree of awareness, it may wish it to be punishable only when performed intentionally by an agent as an end in itself or as a means to some other end. In this case the *mens rea* required will be the act's being intentional.

5. Finally, the law may not wish any and every intentional performance of an action to be punishable, but only in cases where the action is done with a particular intention which the law goes on to specify. In this case the *mens rea* will be the specific intent mentioned in the definition of the crime; crimes of this kind are called crimes of specific intent, and are contrasted with the crimes in the previous category which are sometimes called crimes of basic intent.

"Mens rea," then, may mean anything from mere negligence to a specific intention such as the intention to assist the enemy in wartime. Later, we shall have occasion to give detailed examples of types of crime in each of these five categories, and indeed on the borderlines between them. For the moment it is enough to note that as we go from the beginning to the end of this scale, the requirement of *mens rea* becomes more strict: as we go further in the scale the prosecution has to establish more and more about the accused's state of mind in order to secure conviction. The issue of soundness or unsoundness of mind is a quite separate issue, which may apply differently to different categories of crime, as we shall see later. But the general background assumption to these gradations of *mens rea* is that the accused is of sound mind: even in the cases of strict liability this is so.

The nature of strict liability is misleadingly represented in the National Association for Mental Health's submission quoted above. It is in no way a special feature of crimes of strict liability that the accused can be convicted though he has no knowledge that he is committing an offence: this is so in the great majority of crimes. Nor is it peculiar to crimes of strict liability that one can be convicted even though one did not know that one was doing the act which is, as a matter of fact, an offence: this is the case with all offences of negligence. One can, for instance, be guilty of driving without due care and attention even though at the time one did not know that one's driving was careless. The peculiar feature of absolute offences is that one can be found guilty even though one did not know, and could not reasonably have known, that one was performing the prohibited action. Selling adulterated milk and driving a motor car uninsured have been held in English law to be offences of this kind. A supplier of milk may be guilty of the former offence if milk reaches his customer in an adulterated form even though he delivered it in sound condition to a reputable carrier. If the requirement to provide third-party insurance is interpreted strictly, then I can be found guilty of driving a car uninsured if my insurers go bankrupt as I drive along the motorway.

It is not clear whether the National Association of Mental Health wishes *mens rea* to be replaced in all offences with liability that is absolute in this strict sense. If so, the proposal is surely totally unacceptable. If it were accepted, many innocent people could find themselves convicted and then—if the psychiatrists decided that it was in their or the public interest—detained against their will for indefinite periods. Suppose that I absentmindedly walk out of a bookstore with a book I have not paid for, and that as soon as I leave the store I realize what I have done and instantly go back to pay. According to the Association's proposal I would be guilty of theft, having appropriated the property of another, and evidence that I had no dishonest intent would be neither here nor there. When I had been found guilty, there would then follow "a very careful statement of psychiatric opinion and a full review of the social history." If the psychiatrists discovered that I had a history of odd, though not criminal, behaviour, then in accordance with a proposal of the Association not reproduced above, I would be liable to be committed to a special secure hospital.

It has been often remarked that the undesirable consequences of any proposal to abolish the requirement of *mens rea* come out particularly clearly in the case of the law of perjury. In any situation in which witnesses contradict each other on oath, one of them is making a statement which is objectively false. As things are, of course, no perjury is involved in this utterance of falsehood as long as the witness honestly believes that he is speaking the truth. But if the consideration of the accused's state of mind were to be abolished in the criminal law, then such things as his beliefs and his intentions would become irrelevant. In every clash between two witnesses one at least would be guilty of perjury and could be handed over to the psychiatrists at the Queen's pleasure forthwith.

Consider again the law of treason. English wartime defence regulations made it an offence to do an act likely to assist the enemy with intent to assist the enemy. On the reformers' proposal, of course, the mentalistic proviso, "with intent to assist the enemy," would have to be omitted. This would no doubt have the advantage of securing rapid promotion for junior officers, as their seniors were tried for treason and removed to strict security hospitals for mistaken orders in the field. Few, indeed, at any level would be secure. During the German invasion of Greece in 1941, Churchill ordered several British North African divisions to Greece. This act, as was foreseeable, materially assisted the German war effort: it failed to prevent the conquest of Greece, and it enabled the Axis to make substantial gains in Libya and Egypt. If the question of intent were to be ruled immaterial, this order, and countless others like it, could count as treasonable.

Objections to the notion of responsibility, I have claimed, are often based on conceptual confusion. But the objections, and the confusions on which I claim they are based, are of several different kinds. The principal ones can be grouped into three classes: the epistemological, the metaphysical, and the ethical. The epistemological objection to the notion of *mens rea* stems from the idea that it is impossible, or at least impracticably difficult, to ascertain the state of mind of a man in a way sufficient to determine *mens rea*. The metaphysical one starts from a presumption that science has shown, or made it extremely likely, that determinism is true. If every act of every human being is determined in advance by inexorable laws of nature—so the objection runs—then it seems unfair to single out particular actions for judgment and reprobation. Moreover, it may well seem pointless to try to change or affect people's actions by punishments or the threat of punishments, if everything they will ever do is predictable in advance from laws and conditions that obtained before ever they were born. Finally, the ethical objection to the notion of responsibility envisages it as tied up with a theory of retributive punishment, a view of punishment as allotting to a criminal his strict deserts, rendering evil for evil, an eye for an eye and a tooth for a tooth, in a barbarously vindictive manner.

. . . In this chapter I will attack the epistemological root of the objection to responsibility, which is the philosophical error often called by professional philosophers "dualism."

Dualism is the idea that mental events and states belong to a private world which is inaccessible to public observation: the belief in two separate realms of mental and physical realities which interact, if at all, only in a highly mysterious manner that transcends the normal rules of causality and evidence. The most impressive modern presentation of dualism was the philosophy of Descartes in the seventeenth century. Most contemporary philosophers reject such Cartesian dualism but its influence is great even upon those who explicitly renounce it. In extreme reaction to Cartesian ideas there grew up in the present century a school of behaviourists, who denied the existence of the mental realm altogether, maintaining that when we attribute mental states or events to people we are really making roundabout statements about their actual or hypothetical bodily behaviour. Behaviourism was for long very influential among psychologists; and among the philosophers a subtle and not quite thoroughgoing form of behaviourism was espoused in our own times by Gilbert Ryle.

The most significant philosopher of mind in the twentieth century, however, was Ludwig Wittgenstein: and Wittgenstein thought that both dualists and behaviourists were victims of confusion. Wittgenstein's own position was a middle stance between dualism and behaviourism. Mental events and states, he believed, were neither reducible to their bodily expressions (as the behaviourists had argued) nor totally separable from them (as the dualists had concluded). According to Wittgenstein the connection between mental processes and their manifestations in behaviour is not a causal connection discoverable, like other causal connections, from the regular concomitance between the two types of events. To use Wittgenstein's technical term, the physical expression of a mental process is a *criterion* for that process: that is to say, it is part of the concept of a mental process of a particular kind (a sensation such as pain, for instance, or an emotion such as grief) that it should have a characteristic manifestation. To understand the very notion of a given mental state, one has to understand what kinds of behaviour count as evidence for its occurrence; and the relation between the behavioural evidence and the mental state is not an inductive one, not, that is to say, a connection established by the observation of the co-occurrence of two sets of independently identifiable events.

I do not intend here to expound or to defend Wittgenstein's philosophy of mind: I have tried to do so elsewhere.[2] I merely observe that in so far as the epistemological objection to the notion of responsibility rests upon philosophical presuppositions, those presuppositions have in recent times been the subject of decisive criticism within philosophy itself. If Wittgenstein is right, there is no epistemological reason to reject the mentalistic concepts which are used in the legal assessment of responsibility, and no reason to think that we are setting judges and juries an impossible task in requiring them to have regard to the state of mind of an accused at the time of the commission of a criminal act. When we infer from behaviour and testimony to mental states and activities, we are not making a shaky inductive inference to events in an inaccessible realm; the very concepts of mental states have as their function to enable us to interpret and understand the conduct of human beings. The mind itself can be defined as the capacity to acquire the abilities to behave in the complicated and symbolic ways which constitute the linguistic, social, moral, cultural, economic, scientific, and other characteristically human activities of men in society.[3]

The mentalistic concepts which are used in the law cannot be understood apart from their function in explaining and rendering intelligible the behaviour of human agents. But this must not be misunderstood. When we explain action in terms of desires and beliefs we are not putting forward any explanatory *theory* to account for action. It is true that desires and beliefs explain action; but the explanation is not of any causal hypothetical form. It is not as if the actions of human beings constitute a set of raw data—actions identifiable on their faces as the kinds of actions they are—for which we then seek an explanatory hypothesis. On the contrary, many human actions are not identifiable as actions of a particular kind unless they are already seen and interpreted as proceeding from a particular set of desires and beliefs. Brief reflection suffices to show this in the case of such human actions as buying and selling, promising and marrying, lying and story-telling. But it can be true also of the most basic, apparently purely physical, actions, such as killing and letting die. In legal contexts it may well be easier to identify the state of mind of the accused and of others involved than it is to decide what, in purely physical terms, they actually did.

I would like to illustrate this by a detailed consideration of an African trial: the case of *Nyuzi and Kudemera* v *Republic,* heard on appeal by the High Court of Malawi in February 1967.[4] The case demonstrates clearly that it may be easier to decide whether an accused's state of mind fulfills the requirements of *mens rea* than to decide whether his actions answer to the description of a particular *actus reus. . .*

I quote from the African Law Reports:

> The appellants were charged jointly in the Resident Magistrate's Court, Mwanza, with (a) agreeing to hold a trial by ordeal contrary to s.3(2) of the Witchcraft Ordinance (*cap.*31) and (b) directing, controlling and presiding at a trial by ordeal contrary to s.3(1) of the Ordinance.
>
> The evidence revealed that the inhabitants of a certain village called on the first appellant, who professed to be a witchdoctor, to find out why the children born in the village were dying soon after birth. The first appellant agreed to hold a trial by ordeal to discover whether there were any witches in the village who might be responsible for the deaths. Sixteen people submitted themselves voluntarily for a test by *muabvi,* the belief being that the *muabvi* would kill any witches who drank it but would not affect the innocent. The first appellant prepared the *muabvi* which was handed to the 16 participants by the second appellant. Four of the 16 died and several others became ill as a result of the trial. The *muabvi* was submitted to a government analyst, who reported that it was not poisonous, and the pathologist who examined the deceased found no cause of death and no trace of poison in the bodies. The first appellant was convicted on both counts; the second appellant was acquitted on the first count but convicted on the second.
>
> The first appellant appealed on the grounds that he was an experienced witchdoctor who, in holding the trial by ordeal, was performing a useful service at the villagers' own request, and that the deaths were caused by magic because the deceased were magicians. The second appellant appealed on the ground that he did not profess to be a witchdoctor and had merely acted as an assistant to the first appellant.

One of the issues before the Court was whether the second appellant—the acolyte—had been rightly convicted: his conviction was in fact varied on appeal, for reasons of no current interest. I will consider only questions which arise concerning the first appellant, Nyuzi; and I shall concentrate on three questions: Did he kill the deceased? If he did kill them, did he kill them intentionally? If he did kill them intentionally, did he murder them?

First, then, did the witchdoctor kill, or cause the deaths of the villagers who died? From several remarks in the course of his judgment it is clear that the High Court judge, Cram J., thought it correct to say that Nyuzi had killed his victims. But this must be something of a question, given what we are told in the course of the judgment:

> A government analyst examined bark and powder found in the possession of the appellant but reported that they were not poisonous; experiments on animals showed that *muabvi* was not fatal, at least to guinea pigs. The pathologist found no cause of death in the deceased, but she believed that the cause of death might be poison. She conceded, however, that she found no poison.

The judge referred to an interesting, but unsubstantiated, theory that *muabvi* while not in itself fatal to human beings becomes toxic when associated with adrenalin: so that a person frightened by the ordeal, whose glands were activated, would internally manufacture a poison. The defence case was, in a manner, parallel to this: that the deaths were the result not of Nyuzi's action but of the internal activity of the witches' magic.

Among the members of seminars and classes to whom I have described this case in England and the USA I have found that opinion is fairly evenly divided on the question, Did Nyuzi kill the deceased? Some feel strongly in favour of an affirmative answer, some feel strongly in favour of a negative answer, and some are undecided. By contrast, it is usually easy to secure unanimous agreement about the description of Nyuzi's state of mind: he intended to submit the villagers to a test which, if they were witches, would lead to their death. Here is a case, then, in which it is much easier to reach a decision about a relatively complicated form of *mens rea* than about a relatively simple type of *actus reus.*

Those of us who feel, as the judge did, that it is natural on the facts of the case to say that Nyuzi killed his victims must admit, as the judge did, that no one knows how he did it. The reason that we say, if we do, that he killed the deceased is that we know that he believed the application of the ordeal could cause the death of witches, and that he intended to apply the ordeal. The action can only be identified as a killing because we have previously identified the state of mind as a type of conditional intent to kill. It might be objected that we do not need to identify the witchdoctor's state of mind in order to regard his action as a killing: we need merely believe that he possesses mysterious powers which he exercised in this case. But this suggestion does not, in fact, escape the route through a judgment about the witchdoctor's mind: for the only reason we say—if we do—that he possesses special powers is that this kind of thing happens when he *wants* it to happen.

It was not, in fact, necessary in the case of *Nyuzi* to decide whether the accused had caused the death of the deceased, since the trial was not for murder but for violation of the law against witchcraft. The Malawi witchcraft ordinance reads, in part: "trial by the ordeal of *muabvi* . . . or by any ordeal which is likely directly or indirectly to result in the death of or bodily injury to any person shall be and is hereby prohibited." Directing a trial by ordeal, if death results, is punishable by life imprisonment; if not, by seven years' hard labor.

No doubt it is in part at least because *muabvi* is non-toxic that witchfinders who administer it are not charged with murder: there must arguably be ground for reasonable doubt as to whether the administration of it actually causes death. In earlier times, witchdoctors offering *muabvi* have been charged and convicted of murder. One such, Palamba, had his appeal against conviction allowed by the Court of Appeal for Eastern Africa in 1947: not, however, because he did not cause death, but because he had no intent to kill.[5] *Muabvi,* the court argued, was not believed in the appellant's culture to be poison: an additional element was needed to cause death: the guilt of sorcery in the person who died after taking it. But witchcraft, the court went on to say, did not exist; therefore the deceased was innocent of witchcraft. "On the basis that the deceased was innocent of witchcraft, where was malice aforethought in the appellant who, *ex hypothesi,* believed that the administration of *muabvi* to a person innocent of witchcraft would not cause death?"

The argument of the court in *Palamba* seems to have been that the accused's intent can be expressed thus: I intend to kill X if X is a witch. This is a conditional intention, not an absolute intention. But it is a conditional the antecedent of which is necessarily false, since there are no such things as witches. Therefore it is a tantamount to no intent at all.

There is no doubt that, if a witchfinder has an intent to kill, it is only a conditional intent; and conditional intention is a difficult topic. . . . But there seems to be no doubt that a conditional intent can be a sufficient *mens rea* in murder as in other crimes; and whether the antecedent of the conditional is necessarily false seems to be less to the point than whether the accused believes it to be necessarily false. The argument of the court in *Palamba* was brushed aside by the judge in *Nyuzi* with the words: "This hardly takes account of the intent to kill a guilty witch."

"The real defence," the judge continued, "even with intent to kill, is self-defence or defence of the person of others." The trial, to repeat, was not a murder trial: but if self-defence can provide a defence to murder, clearly it can provide one against the lesser offence prohibited by the witchcraft ordinance. It is well established in English and Malawi law that defence of the person of others against a felonious attack is as legitimate a defence in law as self-defence: but the difficulty of admitting the defence in the present case is that the belief in the existence of the threat which is to be warded off depends upon the belief in witchcraft, and the question arises: Is this belief a reasonable one?

> The deaths of the children complained of by the villagers were, no doubt, explicable in scientific terms, such as invasion of their bodies by a harmful organism, genetic defects, lack of care and attention or malnutrition. A person in ignorance of scientific knowledge, believing the deaths caused by sorcery, can regard the killing of the witch reputed responsible for the deaths as justified in defense of person. In this culture to destroy the witch may be considered non-culpable and even meritorious. In the light of knowledge of a modern scientific culture, he acts under a mistake of fact. Section 10 of the Penal Code (*cap.* 23) runs:
>
> "A person who does . . . an act under an honest and reasonable, but mistaken, belief in the existence of any state of things is not criminally responsible for the act . . . to any greater extent than if the real state of things had been such as he believed to exist. . . ."
>
> The kernel of the problem appears in the word "reasonable." To what or to whom can what is "reasonable" be related?

The issue of the reasonableness of belief in witchcraft has been raised in a number of African cases which were murder cases, in which the death of supposed witches had been brought about not by an ordeal but by perfectly normal means. In *Jackson* the accused believed that an elderly female relation had put a spell on him, and he killed her with a bow and arrow and a hoe in the belief that this was the only way of averting his own imminent death.[6] His defence of self-defence was allowed at the trial, on the grounds that there was "no difference in principle between a physical and a metaphysical attack." On appeal, however, by the Attorney-General, it was held that the proper verdict should have been one of murder: the Federal Supreme Court was of the opinion that under the English common law a belief in the efficacy of witchcraft was unreasonable because it would not be accepted by the man in the street in England. This decision was queried by a number of courts before it was finally overruled in 1967 by the Supreme Court of Appeal of Malawi. As the High Court judge put it in the case of *Lufazema* which led to the overruling of *Jackson*:[7]

> Granted that the use of force in defense of person or property is governed by the principles of the English common law, does that, however, necessitate going the further step of choosing the average man in an English street? . . . Surely one does no violence to the principle (that the test of reasonableness is the reaction of the man in the street) by insisting that when it is applied in Malawi, it must mean a Malawi street.

On the other hand, a court argued in a parallel case (*Ifereonwe*),[8] the mere prevalence of a belief does not make it reasonable.

> It would be a dangerous precedent to recognise that because of a superstition, which may lead to a terrible result as is disclosed by the facts of this case, is generally prevalent among a community, it is therefore reasonable.

The case with which we have been principally concerned, *Nyuzi,* was heard before *Jackson* had been overruled; but the judge did not hesitate to dissent from it, remarking that what seems reasonable according to today's science in Manchester might not be the appropriate criterion by which to judge a person whose pre-scientific beliefs had been inculcated in the bush on the banks of the Zambesi river. In the view of the pre-scientific culture in which he was steeped, the appellant was intervening to prevent felonious deaths by the evil powers of witchcraft. "The common law requires *mens rea* as an element of a criminal offence. If a person, however, does not know the factual basis for the criminality of his act, how can he know his act is wrong?"

The judge eventually upheld the conviction, though clearly with grave misgivings about the ethical propriety of his decision. The legislature, he said, had enacted an absolute statutory liability for acts of witchcraft: "inherent in the statute is the requirement that the actor realises what he is doing, but he need not have *mens rea.*" He concluded:

> What is required is some solution which will keep this potentially dangerous person under some sort of control until he can be safely released on society, but which will also meet the ethical objection raised when a person without moral guilt is used as an example to others. It must be conceded that this kind of control simply does not exist. The only power the court has to segregate or to restrain is by imprisonment. The court must be guided as to the extent of loss of liberty by the certain risk to the community should the appellant be released in the present state of his beliefs. In all these circumstances, although a sentence of seven years' imprisonment with hard labour may offend ethical principles, it does give a practical solution to the risk to the community. Were the appellant to receive and accept some scientific explanations or to renounce his beliefs, consideration might be given in another place to a release upon licence, but not otherwise. For these reasons the appeal against conviction and sentence is dismissed.

The case was clearly a very difficult one, and the judge's manifest efforts to be fair to all concerned and his embarrassment at the apparent impossibility of doing so cannot but evoke sympathy and admiration. None the less, there is something rather puzzling both about his own account of the effect of his decision and the reasons which he gives for reaching it. The effect of the decision was to rule out self-defence as a defence to the charge of holding a trial by ordeal, and this decision was clearly necessary if the entire prohibition on ordeals was not to be nullified, since if the defence applied once it would apply always. But this does not make the offence into an absolute one: the intent to perform the prohibited action must be there, and that is the form that *mens rea* takes in the majority of crimes. Moreover, in order to rule out self-defence there is no need to make the test of a reasonable belief the reactions of an English man in the street. As was observed by the court in *Lufazema:* "belief in the efficacy of witchcraft might have been held unreasonable for the average man in Malawi also." If legislation is imposed with the express purpose of stamping out a system of beliefs with evil social consequences—whether it be the belief in witchcraft or the belief in the superiority of one race over another—then the belief that it is introduced to eliminate cannot be regarded as reasonable. The reference is not to English culture or to expediency in contrast with justice, but with reference to what the Malawi legislature wished to obtain in Malawi. Assuming that the Malawi legislature was right in imposing the witchcraft statute, then a court would surely be right in holding that a belief in witchcraft was not a reasonable belief.

If there is something wrong with punishing an accused such as Nyuzi, it is surely not that he believed what he was doing to be morally right, nor that the majority of the members of his community would share his belief. The question which really imposes an objection to the enforcement of witchcraft statutes in cases such as *Nyuzi* is rather: Is it right to punish someone for an action undertaken in the light of beliefs which in his situation he could not help but have? This is a particular form of the very general question of whether it is justifiable to blame or punish a person for something he has done when he could not have done otherwise.

Whether in truth the members of communities such as Nyuzi's are in such a condition of unshakeable conviction of the truth of witchcraft is a matter of fact on which it would be impudent for one unacquainted with them to express an opinion. But the question of general principle is one of the most fundamental philosophical questions that arise concerning the criminal law, . . . The metaphysical objection to responsibility, as I have said, arises from the supposition of determinism. If determinism is true, and if people should not be held responsible in cases where they could not do otherwise than they have done, then it seems that no one should ever be held responsible for anything. Supposing, then, that determinism is true—and surely many intelligent and well-informed people believe that it is—how can we any longer uphold the notion of responsibility in our courts of law?

NOTES

1. The National Association for Mental Health, Evidence for Submission to the Committee on Mentally Abnormal Offenders unpublished paper, pp. 1–2.
2. In A. Kenny, *Wittgenstein,* Penguin, Harmondsworth, 1975.
3. This account of the mind is expounded in the first chapter of A. Kenny, *Will, Freedom and Power,* Blackwell, Oxford, 1975.
4. *Nyuzi and Kudemera* v *Republic,* (1966–8) African Law Reports, 249.
5. (1947), 14 E. A. C. A. 96.
6. (1923–60) A. L. R. Malawi 488.
7. High Court of Malawi, 1 May 1967.
8. West African Court of Appeal, unreported; considered in *Nyuzi and Kudemera, op. cit.,* p. 259.

29

R. J. GERBER

Is the Insanity Test Insane?

M'NAGHTEN AND HIS SICK MIND

The modern insanity defense derives from a bizarre English trial in 1843. Daniel M'Naghten, a wood turner in Glasgow, suffered the delusion that Sir Robert Peel, the British prime minister, as well as the Jesuits and the Pope, were all conspiring against him. He couldn't get at the Pope or the Jesuits, so he determined that Peel must die. M'Naghten went to London with his gun, and on January 20, 1843, in a garden next to the prime minister's house, he shot and killed Peel's secretary, Edward Drummond, believing him the prime minister.

His trial developed into a battle between medical knowledge and ancient legal authority. . . .

THE M'NAGHTEN TEST

At M'Naghten's trial in 1843, nine medical witnesses testified that M'Naghten was totally insane. Dr. Isaac

Ray's book on forensic psychiatry was quoted to the court to attack Lord Hale's more restricted test of criminal insanity and the English cases resting on it. The testimony was so convincing that Chief Justice Tindal nearly directed a verdict of insanity, surprisingly commenting to the jury: ". . . I cannot help remarking . . . that the whole of the medical evidence is on one side, and that there is no part of it which leaves any doubt in the mind." Instead he committed the case to the jurors who found the defendant not guilty on the ground of insanity. M'Naghten was committed to Broadmoor, a mental institution, where he later died.

After M'Naghten's trial, both Houses of Parliament and Queen Victoria debated whether M'Naghten's acquittal presaged a dangerously liberalized state of affairs. The fifteen common law judges were required to respond to five parliamentary questions. Their answers constitute the famous M'Naghten test of insanity. Lord Chief Justice Tindal's answer became the official statement of the test now used by the courts of thirty states and of Great Britain. Tindal wrote:

> Your Lordships are pleased to inquire of us, secondly: "What are the proper questions to be submitted to the jury, where a person alleged to be afflicted with insane delusion respecting one or more particular subjects or persons, is charged with the commission of a crime (murder, for example), and insanity is set up as a defence?" And, thirdly: "In what terms ought the question to be left to the jury as to the prisoner's state of mind at the time when the act was committed?" And as these two questions appear to us to be more conveniently answered together, we have to submit our opinion to be, that the jury ought to be told in all cases that every man is to be presumed to be sane, and to possess a sufficient degree of reason to be responsible for his crimes, until the contrary be proved to their satisfaction; and that, to establish a defence on the ground of insanity, it must be clearly proved, that, at the time of the committing of the act, the party accused was labouring under such a defect of reason, from disease of the mind, as not to know the nature and quality of the act he was doing, or if he did know it, that he did not know he was doing what was wrong. The mode of putting the latter part of the question to the jury on these occasions has generally been whether the accused at the time of doing the act knew the differences between right and wrong; which mode, though rarely, if ever, leading to any mistake with the jury, is not, as we conceive, so accurate when put generally, and in the abstract, as when put with reference to the party's knowledge of right and wrong in respect to the very act with which he is charged. If the question were to be put as to the knowledge of the accused, solely and exclusively with reference to the law of the land, it might tend to confound the jury, by inducing them to believe that an actual knowledge of the law of the land was essential in order to lead to a conviction; whereas the law is administered upon the principle that every one must be taken conclusively to know it, without proof that he does know it. If the accused was conscious that the act was one which he ought not to do, and if that act was at the same time contrary to the law of the land, he is punishable; and the usual course, therefore, has been to leave the question to the jury, whether the party accused had a sufficient degree of reason to know that he was doing an act that was wrong; and this course we think is correct, accompanied with such observations and explanations as the circumstances of each particular case may require.

The judge's response was only an advisory opinion, "a hotchpotch of the law as laid down from the time of Bracton." Yet it has influenced the law for nearly the entire English-speaking world since his day. As Professor Wingo and others have observed, M'Naghten may be seen as the culmination of a series of attempts to solidify British thinking on the troublesome insanity issue. M'Naghten's unequivocal recognition of the "right and wrong" standard as an established rule and the national attention it attracted at the time make it a case of special significance. With its sharp focus on the offender's ability to know right from wrong with respect to the particular act charged, M'Naghten clarified and brought order out of existing but confusing precedent and produced a distinct, workable rule from which the more modern tests for insanity have evolved. It is the formula used in the clear majority of the states, including Arizona, which applied it strictly in *Everett,* supra, to require cognitional defects and to disregard emotional and other noncognitive disorders. It is a formula filled with paradox, not the least of which is that its own moral and cognitional criteria should have convicted rather than acquitted its namesake.

ANALYSIS OF THE M'NAGHTEN TEST

Under the M'Naghten Rule, the accused is not criminally responsible if a mental disease at the time of the act prevented him from knowing (a) the nature and quality of the act or (b) that it was wrong. The basic postulate of the test is capacity to follow the right course once one is able to perceive it. Its emphasis is on the cognitive capacity to understand the moral nature of acts. The assumption is that when cognition is defective the personality as a whole is so impaired that the accused cannot "know" the wrongfulness of his actions.

The objects of knowledge differ in the two branches of the test. The first branch is satisfied by a description; the other requires an evaluation. The first question really is whether an accused had sufficient ability to appreciate the nature and quality of his action. This question probes the defendant's comprehension of the effects of his act and evokes a description from him of his deliberations. The requirement to describe the nature and quality of the act is the ordinary way of specifying what is meant by the psychiatrist's "reality principle," i.e., knowledge of actions and their everyday consequences. The second branch of the test assumes that an accused knew the nature and quality of his act and asks whether he had the capacity to appreciate that his act was wrong. This standard requires an evaluative statement, not a description of the context of the act.

Above all, two phrases of the M'Naghten test cause major trouble: "disease of the mind" and "know." Courts have not precisely defined "disease of the mind," but this phrase clearly is not equivalent to all the various medical classifications of mental diseases. It takes its meaning instead from the rest of the test and thus becomes limited by the word "know." Noncognitive mental disorders are therefore not "diseases of the mind." Few of the psychoses and severe forms of other mental disorders literally come within "disease of the mind." In effect, to qualify as a "disease of the mind," a malady must touch an accused's reflective powers so severely that he is deprived of knowledge of the nature and quality of his act, so that he did not know what he was doing was wrong.

The word "know" may become ambiguous for persons suffering from serious mental illness not directly cognitional. A sick person's knowledge is often divorced from all affect, somewhat like the knowledge that children have of propositions they can recite but cannot understand. The knowledge crucial for criminal responsibility ought to be an appreciation or awareness of legal and moral consequences, not an abstract philosophical assent to a proposition. This cognitional limitation, as Judge Cardozo pointed out, is faithful neither to the facts of mental illness nor to the demands of legal, ethical, or social policies. Mental illness usually does not destroy the minimal moral awareness required by the test; it may, however, destroy the capacity to use such knowledge to control behavior.

The M'Naghten test literally calls for total impairment; the accused must not know at all. Thus the traditional English hallmark of "total" insanity enshrined in the test continues to require a near impossibility. Few if any persons are "total" madmen; insanity is rather a matter of degree and context.

Finally, "know" is an ambiguous term. Many psychiatrists see at least two types of knowing. There is a fundamental difference between verbal or purely intellectual knowledge and the mysterious other kind of knowledge familiar to every clinical psychiatrist; it is the difference between knowing divorced from affect (emotional appreciation) and knowledge so fused with affect that it becomes a human reality. Since everyday understanding is not confined to abstract intellectual processes like geometry, the word "know" in the phrasing of the test needs a practical sense (affect) totally different from purely intellectual assent to a moral proposition.

To be sure, this emphasis on cognition reflects a rationalist era. At the time of M'Naghten, cognition was believed the highest function of the personality. Cartesian philosophers of the period aptly expressed the accepted notion that the mind ran human behavior like an angel driving a machine. Today this view has been rejected by most scholars of human behavior. Psychologists as diverse as Freud, Jung, Rogers, and Skinner believe that cognition is not the sole or even the principal controlling function of the psyche. Volition, impulse, the subconscious, or the environment may each at times overpower control and/or cognition.

Since psychiatrists normally utilize other criteria apart from a defect in cognition to determine responsibility, the M'Naghten language widens the chasm between legal and medical insanity. Psychiatrists are forced to make wholly personal judgments about the guilt of the defendant. One psychiatrist has expressed the extreme viewpoint that answers supplied by a psychiatrist to questions of rightness or wrongness of an act or knowing its nature constitute a "professional perjury" because of lack of reliability. Furthermore, the M'Naghten limitation on cognition deprives the jury of relevant psychiatric information concerning emotional disorder, and thus causes many defendants such as Everett who are emotionally but not cognitively ill to be found legally sane. . . .

There also lingers a murky, linguistic issue. . . . Insane persons clearly *do* know; they *do* intend their acts. A paradigm of many examples, M'Naghten himself manifestly intended a killing, carefully premeditated it, and knew it to be wrong and punishable—this is precisely what his lengthy deliberation and careful concealment of plans connote. A strictly honest reading of his test on its face would exonerate neither M'Naghten nor many, if any, similarly insane defendants. To this linguistic problem it is inadequate to reply that the cognitional and moral language of the test requires a "commendably broad" interpretation, that the test should mean "fully" or "really appreciate one's behavior"; this amounts to admitting that the test not only does not mean what it says but also that it will exculpate nearly all of us. Thus a dilemma: the exact language of the test would literally convict nearly all insane persons; its liberal interpretation ("really appreciate") would acquit nearly all sane persons, none of whom "really" or "fully" appreciates all the moral implications of behavior.

THE IRRESISTIBLE IMPULSE TEST

Other tests have sought to remedy *M'Naghten*'s defects. One of these, the infrequent "Irresistible Impulse" test, is well put by New Mexico's Supreme Court, which typically joins it to the *M'Naghten* test:

> Assuming defendant's knowledge of the nature and quality of his act and his knowledge that the act is wrong, if, by reason of disease of the mind, defendant has been deprived of or has lost the power of his will which would enable him to prevent himself from doing the act, he can not be found guilty.

The test represents the first wholesale amendment of *M'Naghten*. Text writers have misnamed this the "irresistible impulse" test; it is really a control test. Goldstein has found so many differing formulations of the test that "there is no monolith called the 'irresistible impulse' test." Their central idea, however, is loss of control, and their universal motivation is to remedy *M'Naghten*'s omission of noncognitive control data.

Weighty objections, however, cut against a narrowly formulated control test that connotes the idea of sudden, impulsive or irresistible loss of control. Just as an intellectual interpretation of the *M'Naghten* knowledge requirement ignores emotional factors, a "sudden impulse" interpretation of the control test may restrict evidence and jury deliberations solely to immediacy, thus keeping from the jury the durational nature of an accused's mental condition. The "impulse" connotation fails to account for cases where loss of volition takes place not suddenly but gradually, as in cases of melancholia and paranoia.

The "irresistible impulse" test, while giving consideration to the defendant's capacity to control his actions, is deficient insofar as it implies a "sudden and immediate gratification of an urge," where temporary postponement is generally possible. It gives no consideration to the defendant whose mental disease is characterized by brooding, introspection and reflection. The connotation ascribed to "control" means that an individual with sufficient powers temporarily to control or forestall his impulses is legally sane even though he ultimately surrendered completely to these impulses. If the capacity for temporary control existed, the jury reasons, the impulse was not actually irresistible. The resulting standard thus becomes an arbitrary juggling of definitions rather than an assessment of individual behavior. Only the most obvious forms of loss of control receive due consideration, whereas more subtle but just as compelling behavioral problems are virtually ignored. In effect, the irresistible impulse test, like all its variant control tests, gives no criteria for distinguishing an impulse which could not be resisted from one which merely *was not* resisted. . . .

In 1954, in Washington, D.C., the United States Court of Appeals for the District of Columbia Circuit reversed the conviction of a Monte Durham for housebreaking and petit larceny. The court held that Durham had presented enough evidence on the question of his insanity to raise an issue for decision under the District of Columbia's version of the *M'Naghten* test for criminal responsibility. In the course of an extensive opinion, however, the court rejected the *M'Naghten* rule in all its formulations and held that "a broader test" should be adopted for the District of Columbia: "[A]n accused is not criminally responsible if his unlawful act was the product of a mental disease or mental defect."

Before 1954 the District of Columbia employed the right-wrong rule of *M'Naghten* taken together with the irresistible impulse test. Two principal problems arose in attempting to apply this standard. First, the antiquated terminology of *M'Naghten* ceased to represent society's notion of who should be punished relative to the existing state of psychiatric knowledge. Second, expert witnesses felt obliged to go outside their expertise into the realm of law and social morality in testifying as to whether defendants knew right from wrong. The issue of responsibility was framed so narrowly that experts felt precluded from adequately describing the ramifications and manifestations of a defendant's illness relevant to an assessment of criminal responsibility.

If a single theme pervaded Judge Bazelon's opinion in *Durham* it was encouraging the fullest possible range of psychiatric testimony on the question of responsibility. Instead of attempting to restrict testimony before it was heard, *Durham* intended to encourage the psychiatrist, "[W]hatever the state of psychiatry," to present the court and jury with all the information that he could provide that would illuminate the question, "Why did this defendant do these things?" The jury's inquiry might include, but was not to be limited to, the traditional test. After all the evidence had been presented, the jury was to apply the ultimate standard:

> [A] accused is not criminally responsible if his unlawful act was the product of mental disease or mental defect. . . . The question will be simply whether the accused acted because of a mental disorder, and not whether he displayed particular symptoms which medical science has long recognized do not necessarily, or even typically, accompany even the most serious mental disorder.

The *Durham* opinion deliberately left undefined the key term in its test: "mental disease or defect." Early cases under *Durham* show little concern with the missing definition. Lawyers and judges turned to the psychiatrists, who responded that a psychosis was a mental disease (or a "mental disorder," or a "mental illness") and that anything else was not.

Widely hailed by both jurists and psychiatrists, *Durham* seemingly represented a scientific advance in criminal jurisprudence. Clearly, it represents the psychiatrization of the criminal law, an attempt to transform into legal terms the notion that there are two modes of existence—one sane, and the other insane. The *Durham* standard views mental functioning as essentially unitary but multifaced. No single mental faculty determines the existence or nonexistence of sanity, just as no single faculty is responsible for the control of human behavior. Impaired control may result from a wide variety of causes in the psyche, not all of which are cognitional.

Yet ambiguities lingered with *Durham*. While the approach permitted the psychiatrist to testify on the full range of rational, emotional, and volitional elements influencing an individual's psyche, this test drew a single line on one side of which a defendant was held criminally responsible for his actions and on the other side of which he was completely exculpated. The test does not account for the psychic reality of a continuous graduated scale of responsibility. This absolute distinction between the responsible and the nonresponsible is rejected by much of modern psychiatry, which views an individual as responsible only to the extent that he is free to control his action. Freedom is a floating variable, not a fixed state. If psychiatrists had to suggest a criterion for distinguishing free from unfree, "they would say a person's freedom is present in inverse proportion to his neuroticism; in other words, the more his acts are determined by a malevolent consciousness, the less free he is." The psyche manifests degrees of freedom and degrees of responsibility.

Defining "mental disease" became another acute problem. Early experience under *Durham* was that "mental disease" was synonymous with psychosis, with the apparent agreement of all the participants in the trial process. Psychiatrists believed that they were using a legal term with an understood legal meaning; lawyers believed they were using a medical term with a standard medical content. The problem burst into the open in 1957, when the staff of Saint Elizabeth's Hospital decided that nonpsychotic diagnosis—particularly, the diagnosis of "sociopathic personality disturbances"—would be explicitly recorded in reports of mental examinations, thus opening the insanity defense to a larger number of defendants. St. Elizabeth's psychiatrists at trial began to testify that personality disorders were, indeed, "mental disease." The number of acquittals by reason of insanity rose dramatically: in the four years following *Durham* (1954–1957), there had been 34 such acquittals; in the four years following the change in policy (1958–1961), there were 150, and in 1961 and 1962 the acquittal rate was running at 66 per year. . . . The increase seemingly came not at the cost of a decrease in the conviction rate but at the expense of adjudications for incompetence, followed by dismissal of the criminal charges.

Ultimately at least four intertwined problems arose with the vague "mental disease" concept in *Durham.* In the first place, *Durham* failed to define the parameters of mental disease clearly enough to determine whether sociopathy would count. Durham himself was diagnosed a sociopath and held sane. Shortly thereafter one Blocker, on trial for murdering his wife, pled insanity, was diagnosed a sociopath, and also found guilty. One month later, however, when the St. Elizabeth's staff broadened its forensic concept of mental disease to include sociopathy, Blocker appealed and was granted a new trial. This sudden reversal of psychiatric opinion on the legal process provoked judicial tempers. Judge Burger angrily stated:

> The terms [now] mean in any given case whatever the expert witnesses say they mean . . . No rule of law can possibly be sound or workable which is dependent upon the terms of another discipline whose members are in profound disagreement about what those terms mean. . . . We tacitly conceded the power of St. Elizabeth's Hospital staff to alter drastically the scope of a rule of a law by a "weekend" change in nomenclature which was without any scientific basis.

The innuendo was clear: St. Elizabeth's had changed its labels to bring a greater number of defendants under the protective umbrella.

This first problem brought a second: the domination of the courtroom by psychiatrists. Whereas Judge Bazelon merely wanted to open the door to liberal psychiatric testimony, he in fact opened the floodgates to medical conjecture frequently inscrutable and just as frequently overbearing for judges and jurors. Particularly onerous to the jury's role was the tendency by psychiatrists to make unfounded statements regarding the vexing issue of just which psychic conditions did or did not cause the criminal act, thus permitting psychiatrists to determine criminal responsibility.

Durham also sparked a philosophical debate which echoes the problems that have always beset the insanity defense. As Judge Bazelon looked at the product test, his perspective was that of a man versed in the knowledge of psychodynamics and inclined toward the theory of psychic determinism. Judge Burger, however, insisted on the traditional rationalist arguments from Aristotle through Bentham, to the effect that men choose freely. The Bazelon test was for Burger a denial of the concept of free will. Judge Bazelon's positions were gradually eroded in subsequent decisions where sociopathy was eliminated as a mental disease.

Finally, most psychiatrists responded to *Durham* by providing a conclusory diagnosis. In 1962 Judge Burger warned that *Durham* was supposed "to open the inquiry to the widest possible scope of medical testimony, but in case after case we have tended to narrow the inquiry rigidly to the magic words 'disease' and 'product.'" Judge Bazelon, too, was less and less enchanted with psychiatrists in the courtroom. In *Rollerson* v. *United States,* he added his own warning: "The frequent failure to adequately explain and support expert psychiatric opinion threatens the administration of the insanity defense in the District of Columbia." The stage was set for another definitional foray.

BRAWNER: A NEW TEST

In the 1972 case of *United States* v. *Brawner,* the District of Columbia formally abandoned *Durham,* opting for a variant of the American Law Institute's proposal. Chief Judge Bazelon, author of *Durham,* wrote a separate opinion emphasizing his agreement that *Durham* should be retired; he disagreed with almost everything else in the majority opinion.

In the *Brawner* case, the defendant's jaw had been broken in a fight. He returned half an hour later with a gun, fired five shots through a closed apartment door, and killed one of the occupants. Four expert witnesses agreed that Brawner was suffering from a psychiatric or neurological abnormality, variously described as "epileptic personality disorder," "personality disorder associated with epilepsy." The prosecution witnesses apparently regarded Brawner's actions as a normal response in the circumstances, a more or less legitimate response. He had been severely injured in a fight and was very vindictive. As one of the doctors testified, "I think I would, too, under the same circumstances, want to get even with somebody who broke my jaw."

Determined to abandon *Durham,* the *Brawner* court turned to the ALI's proposed rule of criminal responsibility:

> (1) A person is not responsible for criminal conduct if at the time of such conduct as a result of mental disease or defect he lacks substantial capacity either to appreciate the criminality [wrongfulness] of his conduct or to conform his conduct to the requirements of law.
> (2) As used in this Article, the terms "mental disease or defect" do not include an abnormality manifested only by repeated criminal or otherwise antisocial conduct.

The court observed that the adoption of the American Law Institute rule would alleviate the undue influence of expert testimony which had permeated *Durham.* Less stultified, less likely to create the mystique surrounding expert testimony, the ALI language of "result" and "substantial capacity" presumably would permit better communication among experts, judge, and jury. Feeling that the "product" language of *Durham* led to its downfall, the court endorsed the ALI proposal "as a result of" language, stressing that some causal relationship was a necessary element of any insanity defense. The "substantial capacity" requirement sought to correct the longstanding reference in earlier cases to the need for total impairment. The *Brawner* court also adopted the ALI proposal which provides "appreciates the wrongfulness of his conduct" rather than the version which focuses upon "criminality" of conduct so as to include emotional trauma. The court ruled that the *caveat* in paragraph (2) be available to a judge as a rule of application but not for inclusion in instructions to the jury. Evidence of past criminal and antisocial actions would be inadmissible as evidence of mental disease unless accompanied by expert testimony.

More importantly, the opinion dispensed with two alternative proposals for handling insanity. Abolition of the defense was rejected as only within legislative rather than judicial prerogative. The court also rejected Judge Bazelon's suggestion that the jury be instructed that a defendant lacks criminal responsibility "if mental disease impairs his capacity or controls to such an extent that he cannot justly be held responsible." Apparently the court felt that such a freewheeling rule would allow subjective notions of justice, sympathy, and prejudice to color jury determinations.

Critical reading of *Brawner in toto* reveals serious inconsistencies touching the insanity defense relative to *mens rea.* The court's jury instruction on insanity provides: "You are not to consider this defense unless you have first found that the government has proved beyond a reasonable doubt each essential element of the offense." This instruction obviously means that insanity becomes an issue only after a prior finding that the defendant (1) did the criminal act (2) with its defining mental element, viz., intentionally, knowingly, etc. The defense comes alive then only for defendants already inculpated in crime. As a separate issue from *mens rea,* the defense is not an evidentiary standard for weighing intent or free will at all but an escape valve for persons whose mental state, while criminal, is disturbed beyond the range of full responsibility.

Having established this commendable distinction between *mens rea* and the insanity defense, the court next erases that distinction completely in saying it refuses to abolish the insanity defense because its abolition would eliminate free will from the criminal law. The court could reach this conclusion only by confusing the proposal to abolish the insanity defense with the quite broader proposal to abolish *mens rea.* It further mistakenly assumes that the abolition of insanity would inaugurate strict liability crimes, i.e., criminality apart from criminal intent, when in fact that result follows only from the abolition of *mens rea.* These assumptions are inconsistent with the court's own suggested jury instruction. They contribute nothing toward clarifying the role of insanity relative to *mens rea.*

The issue in *Brawner* was neither *mens rea* nor the abolition of the insanity defense as such; the issue was the propriety of the *Durham* test. In rejecting *Durham,* the court wandered into pastures far afield and became lost in a dark forest of alien issues. While *Brawner's* abolition of *Durham* is a plus factor, the rest of the opinion serves only to increase the confusion on the larger issues of what *mens rea* and insanity are for and how they relate. The decision more than fulfills Judge Bazelon's comment: "While the generals are designing an inspiring new insignia for the standard, the battle is being lost in the trenches."

In hopes of clearing the air for a possible solution, *Brawner* generates the need to analyze the following propositions anew: (1) insanity is not a *mens rea* issue; (2) *mens rea* should not be abolished, and (3) the insanity defense needs to be restructured.

INSANITY IS NOT A *MENS REA* ISSUE

Ennui over the proliferation of tests has spawned the proposal to abolish the insanity defense completely. Some critics have gone considerably further to urge the abolition of the defense not merely for its own sake but as a first step toward abolishing *mens rea* from criminal law. Before the ultimate merits of either proposal can be considered, it is imperative to realize that insanity is not properly a *mens rea* question, but a unique issue distinct from criminal intent.

Mens rea means criminal intent. It refers to the mental element which, together with a physical act, constitutes a crime. These mental elements, as defined by the Model Penal Code and most revised state codes, basically can appear in any one of three forms: (1) "Intentionally," (2) "Knowingly," or (3) "Recklessly, i.e., with disregard of known risks." Intentionally means acting toward a conscious criminal goal. Knowingly refers to acting with the awareness that certain dangerous results are likely to occur. Any one of the three mental states constitutes *mens rea*.

Absence of criminal intent means that no crime has been committed, in effect, that a bodily movement occurred independently of the mind's acquiescence. The absence of *mens rea* thus establishes an innocence claim. This claim is not a defense but a denial that any crime occurred at all.

Insanity is a wholly separate matter. It is not an innocence claim denying a crime, but an excuse to an established crime. Insanity asserts that although a crime has occurred, some sort of irrationality colored the guilty criminal intent. It acts as a second wind, as a second string in the bow of an already guilty defendant. As *Brawner* confusedly perceived, insanity is not really a negation of intent or knowledge or disregard of risk but a psychic distortion coloring these guilty and quite compatible mental states. Like the similar excuses of infancy and necessity, insanity tacitly admits both the act and the guilty criminal intent but asserts the need for some exception from the punitive consequences of guilt.

The foregoing analysis supports two conclusions: the first is that the fates of *mens rea* and insanity are separate. Altering the defense does not entrain the abolition of *mens rea* or of the free will postulate upholding *mens rea*. Hence the disutility of the widespread bellowing that the insanity defense is necessary in order to retain the entire concept of free will at the heart of the criminal law system.

The second conclusion is more psychiatric and factual: as any defense lawyer knows, the vast majority if not all insane criminals do actually intend or know or recklessly risk their criminal acts. To take one example which stands for all, M'Naghten himself quite obviously intended the death of the prime minister. He knew what he was doing, wanted its result, and knew that it was frowned upon by his peers. The same can be said for every or nearly every insane defendant. It is simply not the case that the insane are incapable of intention, deliberation, moral understanding, etc.; rather, like "wild beasts" and children, their mental operations occur within an unusually restricted context of a certain few misinterpreted objects, the context of which prevents the usual inhibitions from arresting the criminal plan. One may say, of course, that the insane defendant didn't "fully" or "really" know what he was doing; but such an interpretation cannot cloud the fact that the insane's knowledge and intention nonetheless are notably at work in the planning of the criminal act, often to the point of being overbearing. In a word, insanity rarely if ever precludes a criminal *mens rea*.

If the insane do in fact intend and know their criminal acts, such evidence properly touches on a finding of *mens rea*, not of insanity. Hence, their fate on the guilt-innocence issue should be dependent upon the much-debated fate of *mens rea*, not on the role of insanity. . . .

30

JAMES WEINSTEIN

First Amendment Challenges to Hate Crime Legislation: Where's the Speech?

INTRODUCTION

In a recent article Susan Gellman argues that hate crime legislation, such as the model legislation drafted by the Anti-Defamation League of B'nai B'rith ("ADL") violates the First Amendment.[1] The ADL model statute, which has been enacted in several states, provides as follows:

> A. A person commits the crime of intimidation if, by reason of the actual or perceived race, color, religion, national origin or sexual orientation of another individual or group of individuals, he violates Section __ of the Penal Code [insert code provision for criminal trespass, criminal mischief, harassment, menacing, assault and/or any other appropriate statutorily proscribed criminal conduct].
> B. Intimidation is a __ misdemeanor/felony [the degree of criminal liability should be made contingent upon the severity of the injury incurred or the property lost or damaged].[2]

Relying heavily on Gellman's critique, the Supreme Court of Wisconsin, in *State* v. *Mitchell,* recently struck down a hate crime law similar to the ADL model.[3] The Wisconsin law enhanced the penalty for certain crimes, including battery, if the defendant "[i]ntentionally selects the person against whom the crime . . . is committed . . . because of the race, religion, color, disability, sexual orientation, national origin or ancestry of that person . . . ."[4] The court, in an opinion written by Chief Justice Nathan Heffernan, found that the law, on its face, violated the First Amendment right to free speech.[5]

In this paper I will challenge the argument that hate crime legislation such as the ADL model statute is facially inconsistent with the First Amendment. I want to emphasize at the outset, however, that my disagreement extends only to the charge that such statutes are invalid on their face—in other words, that regardless of the circumstances in which they are applied, a statute that enhances the punishment for racially motivated crimes violates the First Amendment. Like any criminal statute, hate crime legislation can be *applied* in an unconstitutional manner, and for two reasons such laws present particular risk of unconstitutional application. First, to the extent that hate crime legislation is applied to enhance the punishment for crimes committed through speech, such as harassment by repeated use of racist epithets, or through symbolic conduct, such as burning a cross on a black family's lawn, obvious First Amendment problems arise.[6] In addition, it is possible for hate crime legislation to be misused in order to punish a defendant not for racial motivation in committing a crime but for using racist language or expressing bigoted ideas. Such possible unconstitutional applications must be taken seriously, and at the end of this article I will suggest prophylactic measures to prevent misuse. But as I also will discuss, such potential misapplication does not warrant voiding the statute on its face.

The bulk of this paper, however, will be devoted to answering the charge that enhancing punishment for racially motivated crimes violates the First Amendment, regardless of the type of crime at issue and irrespective of the circumstances under which the crime was committed. Specifically, I will show that the argument that a statute enhancing the punishment for racially motivated crimes is at its core a violation of the First Amendment is wrong both as a matter of doctrine and as sound free speech policy. In addition, I will show that the argument employed by Gellman and the Wisconsin court to attack the constitutionality of hate crime legislation undermines the validity of all antidiscrimination laws.

IN SEARCH OF THE SPEECH

That prohibition of hate crimes, other than those committed through speech or expressive conduct, should even present a free speech *issue,* let alone a First Amendment violation, is far from obvious. Unlike the typical statute that raises a free speech issue—for instance, a law forbidding the "dissemination of any materials . . . which promotes and incites hatred against persons by reason of their race, national origin, or religion"[7]—neither the model ADL statute nor the law struck down by the Wisconsin court in *Mitchell,* on its face, prohibits expression. Nor, despite potential application to expressive conduct, such as burning a cross on another's property, does the model statute or the Wisconsin law single out expressive conduct for prohibition. Rather, both statutes apply to crimes such as racially motivated assault, battery, murder, and arson, which even the critics of hate crime legislation do not argue qualify as "expressive conduct" possessing "sufficient communicative elements to bring the First Amendment into play."[8] Such facial neutrality contrasts sharply with the statutes at issue in the recent cross burning and flag desecration cases, which applied *only* to expressive conduct and, moreover, outlawed the conduct in question precisely because of governmental hostility to the expressive element of the conduct.[9]

What, then, is the argument that a statute boosting the punishment for racially motivated crimes, as compared to the same crimes committed without racial animus, violates the First Amendment? As Ms. Gellman explained, and the Wisconsin Supreme Court repeated verbatim:

> Under the ADL model, a charge of ethnic intimidation must always be predicated on certain offenses proscribed elsewhere in a state's criminal code. As those offenses are already punishable, all that remains is an additional penalty for the actor's reasons for his or her actions. The model statute does not address effects, state of mind, or a change in the character of the offense, *but only the thoughts and ideas that propelled the actor to act.* The government could not, of course, punish these thoughts and ideas independently. That they are held by one who commits a crime because of his or her beliefs does not remove this constitutional shield.[10]

Thus, according to Gellman, hate crime legislation creates a "thought crime" in violation of the First Amendment.[11]

The basic flaw in Gellman's argument is the incorrect assertion that when the state increases punishment because the defendant has acted with a particular motive it must be punishing him merely for having certain "thoughts and ideas" and not for "effects, state of mind, or change in the character of the offense." It is of course possible to punish someone merely for holding certain thoughts and beliefs as would be the case, for instance, if a law enhanced the penalty for any bigot convicted of drunk driving. Enhancing the punishment because of the defendant's motive for committing the crime presents a very different situation, however. As Professor Douglas Husak has pointed out in a previous issue of this journal,[12] and as my colleague Professor Jeffrie Murphy discusses in this issue, it is common for the degree of punishment to depend upon the defendant's motive for committing the crime.

We would not think it unusual, for instance, if a judge gave a defendant who killed his rich uncle in order to inherit his fortune a more severe sentence than a nephew who killed his uncle in order to save him further suffering from a painfully debilitative disease. Whatever moral and legal problems may be presented by such disparate punishment, free speech concerns are not among them. Rather, we recognize immediately that the greedy nephew is being punished not for having certain thoughts but for *acting* on those thoughts in a way that makes his conduct more reprehensible, and perhaps even more dangerous, than that of the compassionately motivated nephew. Nor would any greater First Amendment problem be presented if an enhanced punishment for murders for monetary gain were set by statute rather than left up to judicial discretion. Gellman's broad claim that a statute that enhances punishment because of the defendant's motive thereby violates the First Amendment is thus simply wrong.

A recent United States Supreme Court decision, *Dawson* v. *Delaware,*[13] underscores the distinction between punishing a person merely for holding abstract beliefs and punishing him for acting on those beliefs in such a way as to make the act particularly morally reprehensible or especially dangerous. In *Dawson,* the defendant's membership in the Aryan Brotherhood, a racist prison organization, was introduced into evidence at the penalty phase of a murder trial, and the defendant was sentenced to death. The Court held that because this evidence had "no relevance to the issues being decided in the [sentencing] proceeding,"[14] and in particular "was not tied in any way to the murder of [the defendant's] victim," such evidence "proved nothing more than [the defendant's] abstract beliefs" in violation of the First Amendment.[15] The Court emphasized, however, that if membership in the Aryan Brotherhood had in any way been relevant to the issues in the sentencing proceeding, the introduction of such evidence would not have violated the First Amendment. In making this distinction, the Court referred to a previous case in which it had found that a black defendant's membership in the Black Liberation Army, and his desire to start "a racial war," made it "most proper" for the sentencing judge to take into account "the elements of racial hatred" in the murder of a white hitchhiker.[16] The Court concluded by stating that in "many cases associational evidence might serve a legitimate purpose in showing that a defendant represents a future danger to society" or might otherwise be relevant "in proving . . . aggravating circumstances."[17]

If "elements of racial hatred" may constitutionally be considered by a sentencing judge or jury to enhance a penalty from life imprisonment to death when "relevant in proving aggravating circumstances," it follows that racist animus can similarly be taken into account by a legislature in enhancing punishment for hate crimes *when relevant to any of the considerations that the state may legitimately look to in formulating the degree of punishment for a crime.*

There are at least five plausible justifications for enhancing the punishment for racially motivated violence that are relevant to legitimate considerations that the state commonly looks to in determining punishment, all of which are distinct from the punishment of mere abstract thoughts and beliefs. These justifications fall into two categories. The first category comprises the retributivist justification that racial violence is inherently more reprehensible because of the racial motivation, as well as the legal moralist justification that society regard racial violence as especially reprehensible. The second category entails the additional injury caused or likely to be caused by racial violence vis-à-vis the same violent act without racial motivation. This category includes the justification that racial violence causes injury to the victim above and beyond physical damage, that racial violence causes injury not only to the immediate victim but also to the victim's racial or ethnic group, and that racial violence has particularly pernicious ramifications for society as a whole.

I will discuss each of these justifications in turn. But before doing so, let me make clear that I am not suggesting that any of these justifications is grounds for prohibiting beliefs or their expression. Rather, my point is that the *existence* of justifications for enhancement that are relevant to usual penological considerations refutes the claim that the sole purpose of enhanced penalties for racially motivated violence is to punish the defendant for holding certain abstract beliefs that the state finds offensive. Thus, *Dawson*'s relevancy standard serves much the same purpose as the key step in the Supreme Court's test for determining the validity of statutes regulating expressive conduct.

When a statute regulating expressive conduct, such as draft card burning or flag desecration, is challenged on First Amendment grounds, the crucial inquiry is whether the state can point to a plausible justification for the regulation of that conduct.[18] The existence of such a justification tends to show that the state is regulating the conduct *despite* its expressive nature, not *because* of it. Conversely, the absence of a speech-neutral justification shows that the statute is aimed at the expressive part of the speech/conduct amalgam. However, this initial identification of a speech-neutral justification is not invoked as a basis for suppressing expression that the state thinks is harmful (for example, a message of opposition to the Vietnam war) but rather as a preliminary step in determining whether the statute is aimed at speech in the first place.

So too with the inquiry here. The following justifications for enhancing punishment for racially motivated violence are thus not offered as grounds for punishing bigoted beliefs or the expression of such beliefs. Indeed, in a previous article I argued at length that there are no constitutionally adequate grounds for prohibiting racist beliefs expressed as part of public discourse.[19] Rather, these justifications are offered to refute the claim that the only possible purpose of enhancement statutes is to punish a person for holding bigoted beliefs.

RETRIBUTIVISM AND LEGAL MORALISM

Let us return for a moment to the case of the two homicidal nephews. I take it that neither Gellman nor the Wisconsin court would maintain that punishing someone who kills for monetary gain more severely than someone who engages in mercy killing is an unconstitutional attempt to punish greedy people for their thoughts and beliefs. What dispels any notion that the disparate punishment is an attempt to punish mere abstract beliefs is the existence of the obvious retributivist justification that killing for monetary gain is more reprehensible than killing out of compassion for the victim. Similarly, beating someone because of animosity to the color of his skin is, at least according to my intuition, more morally reprehensible than hitting someone because of a dispute about a parking space. Precisely why we feel that some deeds are more reprehensible than others raises interesting and difficult philosophical and psychological questions.[20] But we do not need to answer these questions or, indeed, even to subscribe to a retributivist theory of punishment to recognize that intuitive notions about the relative evil of an act have long been recognized as legitimate ingredients in determining the degree of punishment.[21] If relative judgments about the evil of the crime may legitimately be made relevant to determining punishment, however, then *Dawson* permits the state to justify enhancing the punishment for hate crimes on the grounds that violence motivated by "elements of racial hatred" is particularly deplorable. Put less doctrinally, if the state enhances the punishment for racially motivated crimes because it finds such acts particularly reprehensible, then it is not the case that the only purpose for enhancing the punishment is to penalize the defendant for holding racist beliefs.

Even if my intuition is wrong and racially motivated violence cannot be shown to be objectively more reprehensible than non-racial violence, there is nonetheless a strong indication that society—whether reasonably or not—finds racial violence especially evil. Enforcement of the community's sense of morality without regard to the objective validity of the underlying moral judgments—dubbed "legal moralism" by H.L.A. Hart[22]—provides another justification for enhanced punishment for racial violence. Soldiers brutalizing civilians is always despicable, yet recently the world was especially morally outraged by such atrocities committed as part of a campaign of "ethnic cleansing." On several occasions the United States Supreme Court has recognized the constitutional legitimacy of the state's interest in enforcing the community's concept of morality, even when violation of these norms causes no palpable harm.[23] But if the state may generally enforce the community's sense of morality, then under *Dawson* it is constitutional for a state to express its moral outrage for racially motivated violence by enhancing the punishment for such crimes. Of course it is not a valid argument to object that the Court has never held that such legal moralism is grounds for curtailing the exercise of a fundamental right,[24] for the question on the table is whether hate crime legislation infringes a fundamental right protected by the First Amendment.

Both the retributivist and legal moralist justification, then, might well be sufficient under *Dawson* to rebut a First Amendment challenge to penalty enhancing laws. More generally, because hate crime statutes on their face are aimed primarily at subject matter that is neither pure speech nor expressive conduct, I think it likely that the Court would subject hate crime legislation to only minimal scrutiny, thus accepting retributivism and legal moralism as sufficient speech-neutral justifications for enhancing the penalties for racially motivated crimes. As a matter of free speech policy, however, I am uncomfortable with these justifications in this context. The First Amendment claim against hate crime laws is that, despite the nonexpressive nature of the proscribed conduct, these laws are aimed nonetheless at "thoughts and ideas." Invoking justifications that are so subjective and unverifiable that they can almost always be plausibly asserted does little, however, to rebut this charge. Retributivism is particularly subjective, turning as it does on each individual's moral intuition. As for legal moralism, shared perceptions of morality are too amorphous and much too majoritarian to adequately dispel the charge that the enhancement is really only a penalty for holding certain offensive beliefs. Particularly against a background of repeated unconstitutional attempts to punish hate *speech,*[25] more palpable justifications should be required to dispel the claim that hate crime legislation is merely an indirect attempt to punish racist ideas.

THE ADDED INJURY OF RACIAL VIOLENCE

Suppose that one night a gang of high school kids, upset by their football team's loss to its cross-town rival, roams through the neighborhood near the victorious high school throwing rocks through shop windows. Now suppose that on another evening a group of skinheads, as part of an anti-Semitic campaign, smashes the windows of shops owned by Jews. As I have already mentioned, many intuitively find such ethnically or religiously motivated hooliganism more reprehensible than vandalism motivated by the home team's loss. But perhaps it is possible to defend this intuition with some consequentialist considerations.

One reason that we may feel that violence motivated by race hatred is particularly reprehensible is that such violence can inflict damage above and beyond the physical injury caused by a garden-variety assault, both to the immediate victim and to other members of the group to which the victim belongs. The effect of Kristallnacht on German Jews was greater than the sum of the damage to buildings and assaults to individual victims. Unlike vandalism in response to the loss of a football game, hate crimes can have a powerful *in terrorem* effect, particularly for members of minority groups who historically have been, or currently are, victims of racist violence. Vandalism of a fishing boat takes on a particularly sinister significance for both the boat owner and the entire Vietnamese immigrant community when it is discovered that the boat was damaged not by an undirected act of juvenile delinquency but as part of a racist campaign by white fishermen to stop these immigrants from plying their trade. Similarly, if a man is severely injured during a barroom brawl, the fact that he was beaten not because he was a Dodger fan but because he was gay has an impact, both on him and on other gays, far beyond the physical injury. In both cases the violence, in addition to inflicting physical injury, constitutes a threat of more violence to minority group members. In this regard it is significant that the name of the crime created by the ADL model is "intimidation."

Even when racially motivated violence does not carry with it such a clear threat of repeated attacks, memories of pogroms or lynchings might nevertheless make racially or ethnically based attacks especially horrific for some members of the community. Even isolated racist violence can inflict psychic injury above and beyond the physical and psychological damage associated with most other types of assaults. Consider the analogy to rape, which in some important sense is a gender-based "hate crime." In explaining why rape is a crime "deserving of serious punishment," the Supreme Court noted that among other especially harmful consequences, rape can "inflict mental and psychological damage" on the immediate victim and, in addition, "undermine[ ] the community's sense of security."[26] In short, the extra punishment given to perpetrators of racially motivated crimes can be justified by the extra harm that those crimes may cause. Such a justification belies the charge that the ADL model statute "does not address effects . . . but only the thoughts and ideas that propelled the actor to act."

While sufficient to rebut the charge that hate crime legislation punishes merely bigoted "thoughts and ideas," the justification of extra punishment raises another free speech problem (one not considered by Gellman or the Wisconsin court). The problem arises because the two types of harm I just described—threats of further violence and infliction of psychic injury—both depend on the message that hate crimes deliver to the victim and the victim's community. Indeed, one of the many horrible things about the racially motivated lynchings commonplace in this country not too many decades ago was the terroristic message such violence intended to and did send black citizens. However, to the extent that hate crime laws increase the punishment because hate crimes are intended to and do deliver a message to their victims, such laws punish expression. The question then becomes whether penalizing such expression violates the First Amendment. Analysis shows that it does not.

Suppose a white man, baseball bat in hand, comes up to a black man playing tennis at a public playground in a predominantly white neighborhood and says, "We don't like your kind here. I'll give you exactly one minute to leave this park, or I'll bash your head in and will do the same to any other of your kind who comes into this park!" Assume further that the African-American, not wanting to see if the speaker will make good his threat, packs up and leaves. I take it that no one would seriously maintain that the speaker had a First Amendment right to make this threat. Whatever free speech interest the speaker might have in expressing himself in this way is surely outweighed by black people's interest in not having to choose between forfeiting their right to use the park and risking serious injury.[27]

Now suppose that instead of making a verbal threat the white man walks up to the black man and immediately hits him with the bat. Assume further that the message the white man intended to convey by this conduct was that any black who comes into the park will be violently attacked, and that both the immediate victim and the rest of the African-American community in this town understand this message. If the purely verbal threat is not expression protected by the First Amendment, then surely the same message accomplished through conduct is not protected expression. Indeed, the message sent by the conduct is even less worthy of First Amendment protection than the purely verbal threat because the expression conveyed by the conduct is a much more effective threat now that the "speaker" has demonstrated that he is prepared to back it up. As applied to such an instance of racial violence, the ADL model statute enhances the punishment for battery because, in addition to the physical injury associated with the usual battery, this attack also sends a terroristic message.

Lest there be any confusion on this point, let me make clear that the message triggering the enhanced punishment in this example case is *not* that blacks are inferior—expression that is protected by the First Amendment[28]—or even that blacks should be beaten if they come into the neighborhood, advocacy that is protected unless it creates an imminent risk of violence.[29] What is being punished is the message, delivered in the most emphatic way imaginable, that blacks *will* be brutalized if they come into the park.

Of course, not all cases of racist violence will convey an actual threat of further imminent harm. In some cases the harmful communicative impact of the violence will be "merely" to inflict psychological distress on the victim and the victim's community as a result of association with past violence against the victimized group. If such psychic injury is just an unfortunate by-product of the violence rather than the result of some particularized message intended by the perpetrator (which, as with sexual assault, will often be the case) then there is no free speech problem with punishing the defendant for this added injury. For the sake of argument, however, I will assume that the attacker intends for this violence to communicate fear and anxiety not only to his immediate victim but also to the group to which the victim belongs (or the attacker intends to communicate some other particularized message that has this effect).

As I have recently discussed in another article, preventing psychic injury is not sufficient grounds for prohibiting speech that can fairly be considered to be within the realm of public discourse.[30] When expression other than public discourse is at issue, however, government has considerable First Amendment leeway to prohibit expression in order to prevent psychic injury. Consider the example of the malicious prankster who falsely tells a woman that her five-year-old child has just been run over by a car. Allowing the mother to recover for the emotional damage caused by this expression would not violate the prankster's free speech rights precisely because the communication at issue is no part of the exchange of ideas on matters of public concern. Similarly, under any reasonable definition the term *racist violence* does not qualify as public discourse. Therefore, just as the First Amendment permits the prankster to be penalized for the emotional injury his verbal expression causes, the state can constitutionally take account of the psychic injury that racial violence inflicts and enhances the punishment accordingly.

Demonstrating that the message which racist violence sends is not protected speech does not, however, get us completely out of the First Amendment woods. In a recent free speech decision, *R.A.V. v. City of St. Paul,*[31] the United States Supreme Court held that St. Paul's ban on the use of certain racist symbols and graffiti was unconstitutional. The Minnesota Supreme Court had construed the statute as applying only to such expression as also constituted "fighting words," a category of speech that the United States Supreme Court had often said was without First Amendment protection.[32] Nonetheless, the Court held that by singling out only *racist* fighting words for proscription St. Paul had engaged in viewpoint discrimination in violation of the First Amendment.[33] In light of *R.A.V.,* it could be argued that, to the extent that hate crime laws enhance punishment because of threats and psychic injury arising from racially motivated violence but do not similarly enhance the penalty for threats and psychic injury arising from other types of violence, these laws are unconstitutionally viewpoint oriented.

The reach of *R.A.V.* has yet to be made clear, but for two reasons I do not read that decision as rejecting a justification for hate crime legislation based on the terroristic impact of racial violence. First, although *R.A.V.* dealt with the proscription of a subset of unprotected expression, the Court emphasized that it was nonetheless *expression* that St. Paul had proscribed.[34] Unlike "fighting words," which must be manifest either in purely verbal form such as epithets or by symbolic conduct such as the cross burning involved in *R.A.V.,* the racist violence under discussion here is neither purely verbal nor symbolic conduct. Thus I have considerable doubt that the Supreme Court would extend *R.A.V.*'s searching scrutiny to a statute that proscribes primarily nonexpressive conduct, even though a justification for the statute involves the communicative impact of that conduct. I would thus be greatly surprised if the particularly harsh sentences meted out for sexual assault as compared with other forms of violent assault were subject to tough First Amendment scrutiny, even if the harshness of the sentences were justified by reference to the terroristic impact that rape has on women.

Even if *R. A. V.* were held to be applicable to hate crime legislation, a justification based on the communicative impact of racial violence might nonetheless be upheld. The Court in *R. A. V.* made clear that not all selective prohibitions of unprotected speech are unconstitutional, but emphasized that the evil to be avoided was government regulating unprotected speech in order to suppress certain viewpoints or ideas it finds offensive.[35] Thus the Court found particular fault with St. Paul's explanation that it was proscribing the use of certain racist symbols and graffiti because such expressions send a message of "racial supremacy" and because this prohibition shows minority groups that such expressions of racism are not condoned by the majority.[36] The justification for enhancing the penalty for racial violence because of the terroristic message it sends is very different. The purpose is not to suppress racist ideas but to prevent threats and emotional injury. Unlike fighting words—all of which by definition "inflict injury or tend to incite an immediate breach of the peace"[37]—not all the predicate crimes covered by hate crime legislation constitute a threat of further violence or inflict psychic injury, at least not to the extent that racially motivated crimes do.

I do not think, therefore, that justifying enhanced penalties by reference to the *in terrorem* effects of racial violence is contrary to the rationale of *R. A. V.* Nonetheless, given the uncertainties created by that decision, hate crime legislation will be on safer ground if it is justified by an interest less bound up with the communicative impact of racial violence. One such justification for enhanced punishment is simply that racially motivated violence is often more disruptive than the same violent act without the racial motivation. What starts as an isolated, racially motivated attack on one student at the local high school can all too easily escalate into a major fracas that involves dozens of students, and poisons the atmosphere at school for months to come. Other types of schoolyard violence, such as a scuffle over a disputed call at first base or a jealous boyfriend hitting a rival for his girlfriend's affection, are not likely to have such widespread or prolonged ramifications. The sad truth is that racial tensions lie just beneath the surface of much daily interaction in this society—a tension that can become paralyzing when exacerbated by overt racial violence.

Government could constitutionally punish securities fraud more severely than other types of fraud on the theory that such conduct undermines public confidence of financial institutions. Similarly, it could single out for particularly harsh punishment violence that disrupts interstate transportation because such conduct has a particularly disruptive impact on trade. But if government can mete out especially harsh punishment to protect the economy, I am hard pressed to see what constitutional obstacle—particularly what free speech impediment—there is to government enhancing punishment in an attempt to prevent the disruptive consequences commonly associated with racial violence.

Much can be said in support of the proposition that harsher punishment for racial violence will not help matters, that a problem as complex and as deep-rooted as tense race relations cannot be solved by the heavy hand of the criminal law. Indeed, such laws might even be counterproductive. But doubts about the wisdom of such laws do not make them unconstitutional.

In summary, I have identified five legitimate interests that the state may have in enhancing the punishment for racially motivated crimes: (1) such crimes are especially morally reprehensible; (2) there is a societal consensus that such crimes are particularly deplorable; (3) racially motivated violence is often more damaging to the victim than the same violent act lacking racial motivation; (4) racial violence can often have an *in terrorem* effect on members of the victim's community; and (5) such violence has an especially pernicious effect on society as a whole. Each of these justifications belies the claim that hate crime legislation is nothing more than an unconstitutional attempt to punish a defendant for holding bigoted thoughts and beliefs. . . .

THE POTENTIAL CHILLING EFFECT OF HATE CRIME LEGISLATION

There are two distinct ways in which a statute can be facially invalid under the First Amendment. First, a statute may be unconstitutional at its core in that it is aimed at protected expression. Such a statute—a prohibition of flag desecration, for example—will be unconstitutional regardless of the circumstances in which it is applied. I have spent the greater part of this paper rebutting the charge that the model ADL statute and the similar statute involved in *Mitchell* are facially unconstitutional in this way. But even if a statute has a legitimate core and is thus capable of some application consistent with the First Amendment, it may nonetheless be struck down on its face as "overbroad," that is, if there is too great a risk that it will be applied to protected expression. The rationale of the overbreadth doctrine is that the very existence of a statute with a real potential for application to protected speech unconstitutionally "chills" the exercise of First Amendment rights. The Supreme Court has emphasized, however, that the overbreadth doctrine is "strong medicine" to be applied "sparingly and only as a last resort."[38] Particularly where proscription of conduct rather than pure speech is involved, "the overbreadth of a statute must not only be real, but substantial as well, judged in relation to the statute's plainly legitimate sweep."[39] Otherwise, the prevention of a speculative or even a real but relatively small chilling effect will disable a state from enforcing its statute against conduct that it has undoubted power to prohibit.

In addition to finding the Wisconsin statute unconstitutional at its core for punishing "offensive thought," the Wisconsin Court also invoked the overbreadth doctrine to hold the statute void on its face.[40] In several respects hate crime laws such as the ADL model statute and the Wisconsin statute do present some risk of unconstitutional application. Any such potential unconstitutional application does not, however, present anywhere near the real and substantial deterrence of speech needed to void a statute on its face.

As I discussed in the introduction, application of hate crime legislation to pure speech, such as verbal harassment, or to symbolic conduct, such as cross burning or graffiti, may well be unconstitutional in light of *R. A. V.* States that have enacted hate crime legislation would therefore do well to amend such laws to make clear that they do not apply to pure speech or symbolic conduct, and, in the absence of legislative action, courts should so construe hate crime legislation. But even without corrective amendments or narrowing constructions, hate crime legislation such as the ADL model is not so substantially overbroad as to be invalid on its face. The point of *R. A. V.* is not that burning a cross on someone else's lawn or scrawling a swastika on a synagogue is protected speech but that Minnesota's singling out such otherwise illegal symbolic speech for special prohibition violated the First Amendment's ban on viewpoint discrimination.[41] Accordingly, to the extent that a hate crime statute especially proscribes speech or expressive conduct that the state could admittedly proscribe under a broader statute, no *protected* speech is thereby deterred. Invalidation of an entire hate crime statute on the grounds that there might be some minimal amount of unconstitutionally underinclusive application is therefore inappropriate.

The way in which hate crime laws are most likely to be misused involves prosecutions in which the evidence of the racial motivation rests entirely on racial epithets uttered in the heat of the altercation constituting the predicate crime. Suppose that during a fight about a parking space, a white man calls a black man a "dirty nigger" as he punches the black man in the mouth. If this is all the evidence that the state has of racial motivation for the attack, there is a risk that the enhanced punishment would result not because the attack was in fact racially motivated but because the defendant used a racial epithet. One would hope that prosecutors would not misuse hate crime laws in this way but would reserve them for cases in which the racial motivation is clear, and in which the additional harms associated with racist violence discussed above are manifest. If such inappropriate prosecutions are brought, courts should summarily dismiss them for insufficient evidence of racial motivation or, if need be, as a violation of the First Amendment under *R.A.V.*'s prohibition against singling out racial fighting words.

Even if hate crime legislation were improperly invoked against people for using racial epithets while committing violent acts, the chilling effect on *protected* speech would be minimal, and thus facial invalidation would be unwarranted. To the extent that such laws deter people who use racist epithets from engaging in violence, all the better. Conversely, if hate crime laws deter people engaging in violence from using racial epithets during their attacks, once again there is no chilling of *protected* speech since the use of racial epithets in these circumstances would be proscribable under the "fighting words" doctrine.

On the other hand, a real potential for chilling protected speech can arise if the prosecution uses a defendant's expression of racist beliefs as evidence of his motivation for committing the predicate crime. Suppose that in a case in which a defendant has been charged with assaulting someone because he is Jewish, the prosecution introduces evidence that in conversation with friends the defendant often refers to Jews as "kikes" and on several occasions had expressed the opinion that Jews were "cheap" and "subversive." Unlike the utterance of face-to-face insults during an altercation, use of racial or ethnic epithets not directed to anyone is protected speech, as is the expression of derogatory sentiments about racial or ethnic groups. If such abstract expressions of bigotry are used as evidence of racial motivation in hate crime prosecutions, racists may be deterred from exercising their First Amendment right to express their beliefs for fear that if they ever get into a physical confrontation with a member of the group they hate this expression will be used to enhance punishment. This potential chilling effect must be taken seriously. But it can be largely avoided, and certainly mitigated, by sensible application of ordinary rules of evidence that balance the probative value of proffered evidence against its likely prejudicial effect,[42] or if necessary, a prophylactic First Amendment rule excluding evidence of racist beliefs not directly linked to the conduct with which the defendant is charged. Thus racial motivation would have to be shown by direct evidence, such as a statement by the defendant that such was the reason he attacked the victim, or a call to racist violence immediately preceding the crime, as in *Mitchell*.[43] In sum, hate crime laws should not have a substantial chilling effect on protected speech, but even if they do, the solution is evidentiary safeguards, not facial invalidation.

CONCLUSION

I carry no brief for the wisdom of hate crime legislation. If I were a member of a state legislature I doubt that I would vote in favor of such a law. Enhancing punishment for racially motivated crimes seems to me to be part of a larger American syndrome of adopting harsh punishment as an expedient response that deals only with the most superficial manifestations of complex, deep-seated problems. Moreover, hate crime laws promise to be difficult to administer, may well be counterproductive in that they might be used disproportionately against the very minority groups they were primarily designed to protect, and to some limited extent may even deter protected speech. But these potential problems do not begin to warrant invoking the First Amendment to void such laws on their face.

The "background noise" from recent attempts to prohibit hate speech perhaps justifies scrutinizing hate crime legislation somewhat more carefully than other laws prohibiting nonexpressive conduct. This scrutiny, however, should be no greater than that used to determine whether a prohibition of expressive conduct is aimed at the expressive element of the speech-conduct amalgam. If the state can point to a plausible interest other than an attempt to punish racist ideology, a facial attack on the statute should fail. Otherwise, the First Amendment runs the risk of becoming a vehicle by which judges can void legislation not because it presents any threat to the vigorous and uninhibited exchange of ideas but because of disagreement with the wisdom of the legislation, or even because of outright hostility to its goals.

NOTES

1. Gellman, *Sticks and Stones Can Put You in Jail, But Can Words Increase Your Sentence? Constitutional and Policy Dilemmas of Ethnic Intimidation Laws,* 39 UCLA L. REV. 333 (1991).
2. *Id.* at 344.
3. 169 Wis. 2d. 153, 485 N.W.2d. 807 (1992). The case involved an attack by a group of black youths led by Todd Mitchell on Gregory Riddick, a fourteen-year-old white boy. Just before the attack the group of black youths had been discussing a scene in the movie "Mississippi Burning" in which a white man beat a young black boy while he was praying. Mitchell, who was an older member of the group, asked the others, "Do you all feel hyped up to move on some white people?" A short time later when Riddick happened by, Mitchell said: "You all want to fuck somebody up? There goes a white boy; go get him." Mitchell then pointed in Riddick's direction, and the group ran toward him, knocked him to the ground and beat him severely. *Id.* at 809.
4. 485 N.W.2d. at 809 n.1.
5. Judges Abrahamson and Bablitch dissented.
6. *See* R.A.V. v. City of St. Paul, 112 S.Ct. 2538 (1992) (prosecution of a white juvenile for burning a cross on a black family's lawn). This case, and the United States Supreme Court's reasons for finding unconstitutional the statute under which the prosecution was brought, are discussed in more detail below at text accompanying notes 31 to 37.

7. One of the ordinances used in the attempt to bar members of the American Nazi Party from marching in Skokie, Illinois. *See* Collin v. Smith, 578 F.2d 1197, 1199 (1978).
8. . . . *See* Texas v. Johnson, 491 U.S. 397, 404 (1989) . . . ; *see also* Wisconsin v. Mitchell, 485 N.W.2d. at 814 n.15 (activity covered by hate crime legislation is not "expressive conduct" protected by the First Amendment).
9. *See* R.A.V. v. City of St. Paul, 112 S.Ct. 2538 (1992); United States v. Eichman, 496 U.S. 310 (1990); Texas v. Johnson, 491 U.S. 397 (1989).
10. Gellman, *supra* note 1, at 363 (emphasis added), quoted in Mitchell, 485 N.W.2d at 812.
11. Gellman, *supra* note 1, at 362. After this article was prepared, the Supreme Court of Ohio held a law similar to the ADL model to be unconstitutional. See State v. Wyant, 64 Ohio St. 3d 566 (1992). The Ohio Court's rationale for invalidating the law was the same as that adopted by the Wisconsin Court—namely, that by enhancing a penalty due to the motive of the defendant the statute creates a "thought crime" in violation of the First Amendment.
12. Husak, *Motive and Criminal Liability,* CRIM JUST. ETHICS (Winter/Spring 1989), at 3.
13. 112 S.Ct. 1093 (1992).
14. *Id.* at 1095.
15. *Id.* at 1098.
16. *Id.* at 1097–98 (relying on Barclay v. Florida, 463 U.S. 939 (1983)).
17. 112 S.Ct. at 1098.
18. *See* Texas v. Johnson, 491 U.S. at 406–07; United States v. O'Brien, 391 U.S. 367, 377 (1968).
19. *See* Weinstein, *A Constitutional Roadmap to the Regulation of Campus Hate Speech,* 38 WAYNE L. REV. 163, 164–90 (1991).
20. The heightened repugnance that some of us feel towards racially motivated violence may well relate to the fact that the victim has been injured for a characteristic over which he has no control and which is central to his identity.
21. *See, e.g.,* J. MURPHY, RETRIBUTION, JUSTICE AND THERAPY 223–49 (1979); Moore, *The Moral Worth of Retribution,* in RESPONSIBILITY, CHARACTER AND THE EMOTIONS 179–219 (F. Schoeman ed. 1987). Indeed, in some contexts a retributivist ceiling—the concept that a defendant should not be punished in excess of his blameworthiness—is constitutionally required. *See* Coker v. Georgia, 433 U.S. 584, 597–98 (1977) (in finding imposition of death penalty for rape of adult women to be "disproportionate punishment" in violation of the Eighth Amendment prohibition of cruel or unusual punishment, Court relies in part upon its judgment that rape is not comparable to murder "in terms of moral depravity").
22. H.L.A. HART, LAW, LIBERTY AND MORALITY 6 (1963). Hart coined this term to describe Lord Patrick Devlin's position in his THE ENFORCEMENT OF MORALS (1959) that moral norms can legitimately be enforced regardless of their objective validity to protect the glue that binds the community—a position with which Hart disagrees.
23. *See* Paris Adult Theater I v. Slaton, 413 U.S. 49, 61 (1973); Bowers v. Hardwick, 478 U.S. 186, 196 (1986); *see also* Barnes v. Glen Theater, 111 S.Ct. 2456, 2462 (1991) (opinion of Rehnquist CJ., joined by O'Connor and Kennedy, JJ.), *id.* at 2467–68 (opinion of Scalia, J.).
24. Thus in *Paris Adult Theater* the Court was dealing with obscenity, which it had long ago held to be outside the protection of the First Amendment. *See* Roth v. United States, 354 U.S. 476, 480 (1957). Similarly in *Bowers* the court held that there was no fundamental right to engage in homosexual sodomy. In *Barnes,* however, Chief Justice Rehnquist's plurality opinion did find the societal interest in maintaining morality sufficient grounds to outlaw nude dancing, which Rehnquist acknowledged qualified as expressive conduct "within the outer perimeters of the First Amendment, though . . . only marginally so" (111 S.Ct. at 2460).
25. *E.g.,* the attempt to keep the members of the American Nazi Party from marching in Skokie discussed in note 7, *supra.* More recently there has been a spate of codes restricting racist speech on campus, some of which have been declared unconstitutional. *See* UMW Post. Inc. v. Board of Regents of the Univ. Wis. System, 774 F. Supp 1163 (E.D. Wis. 1991); Doe v. University of Michigan, 721 F. Supp 852 (E.D. Mich. 1989); *see also* Levin v. Harleston, 966 F. 2d 85 (2d Cir. 1992) (finding unconstitutional sanctions imposed by City University of New York administrators on professor for expressing racist ideas in letter to the *New York Times* and in a scholarly journal). *See generally* Weinstein, *supra* note 20, at 239-43.

26. Coker v. Georgia, 433 U.S. 584, 598 (1977).
27. For more on the subject of the First Amendment implications of punishing threats, *see* K. GREENAWALT, SPEECH, CRIME, AND THE USES OF LANGUAGE 90–109 (1989).
28. *See* R.A.V. v. City of St. Paul, 112 S.Ct. 2538, 2548 (1992) ("messages based on virulent notions of racial supremacy" is speech protected by the First Amendment).
29. *See* Brandenburg v. Ohio, 395 U.S. 444, 447 (1969).
30. *See* Weinstein, *supra* note 20 at 176–80. *See generally* Hustler Magazine v. Falwell, 485 U.S. 46, 55 (1988) (First Amendment forbids recovery by public figure for international infliction of emotional distress caused by publication, unless public figure can also show that the publication contains a false statement of fact made with knowledge of its falsity or reckless disregard as to whether or not it was true.)
31. 112 S.Ct. 2538.
32. *Id.* at 2541–42.
33. *Id.* at 2547.
34. *Id.* at 2543.
35. *Id.* at 2545–47.
36. *Id.* at 2548.
37. Chaplinsky v. New Hampshire, 315 U.S. 568, 572 (1942).
38. Broaderick v. Oklahoma, 413 U.S. 601, 613 (1973).
39. *Id.* at 615.
40. *Mitchell,* 485 N.W.2d at 815–16 *accord* Gellman, *supra* note 1, at 358–62.
41. *See supra* notes 35–36, and accompanying text.
42. *E.g.,* FED. R. OF EVID. 404.
43. 485 N.W.2d at 809.

31

LOIS PINEAU

Date Rape: A Feminist Analysis

ABSTRACT: This paper shows how the mythology surrounding rape enters into a criterion of "reasonableness" which operates through the legal system to make women vulnerable to unscrupulous victimization. It explores the possibility for changes in legal procedures and presumptions that would better serve women's interests and leave them less vulnerable to sexual violence. This requires that we reformulate the criterion of consent in terms of what is reasonable from a woman's point of view.

The feminist recognition that dominant ideologies reinforce conceptual frameworks that serve patriarchal interests lies behind what must now be seen as a revolution in political analysis, one which for the first time approaches the problems that women face from a woman's point of view. One of those problems is the ongoing difficulty of dealing with a society that practices and condones violence against women. This is particularly the case with date rape.

Date rape is nonaggravated sexual assault, nonconsensual sex that does not involve physical injury, or the explicit threat of physical injury. But because it does not involve physical injury, and because physical injury is often the only criterion that is accepted as evidence that the *actus reas* is nonconsensual, what is really sexual assault is often mistaken for seduction. The replacement of the old rape laws with the new laws on sexual assault have done nothing to resolve this problem.

Rape, defined as nonconsensual sex, usually involving penetration by a man of a woman who is not his wife, has been replaced in some criminal codes with the charge of sexual assault.[1] This has the advantage of extending the range of possible victims of sexual assault, the manner in which people can be assaulted, and replacing a crime which is exclusive of consent, with one for which consent is a defense.[2] But while the consent of a woman is now consistent with the conviction of her assailant in cases of aggravated assault, nonaggravated sexual assault is still distinguished from normal sex solely by the fact that it is not consented to. Thus the question of whether someone has consented to a sexual encounter is still important, and the criteria for consent continue to be the central concern of discourse on sexual assault.[3]

However, if a man is to be convicted, it does not suffice to establish that the *actus reas* was nonconsensual. In order to be guilty of sexual assault a man must have the requisite *mens rea,* i.e., he must either have believed that his victim did not consent or that she was probably not consenting.[4] In many common law jurisdictions a man who sincerely believes that a woman consented to a sexual encounter is deemed to lack the required *mens rea,* even though the woman did not consent, and even though his belief is not reasonable.[5] Recently, strong dissenting voices have been raised against the sincerity condition, and the argument made that *mens rea* be defeated only if the defendant has a reasonable belief that the plaintiff consented.[6] The introduction of legislation which excludes "honest belief" (unreasonable sincere belief) as a defence, will certainly help to provide women with greater protection against violence. But while this will be an important step forward, the question of what constitutes a reasonable belief, the problem of evidence when rapists lie, and the problem of the entrenched attitudes of the predominantly male police, judges, lawyers, and jurists who handle sexual assault cases, remains.

The criteria for *mens rea,* for the reasonableness of belief, and for consent are closely related. For although a man's sincere belief in the consent of his victim may be sufficient to defeat *mens rea,* the court is less likely to believe his belief is sincere if his belief is unreasonable. If his belief is reasonable, they are more likely to believe in the sincerity of his belief. But evidence of the reasonableness of his belief is also evidence that consent really did take place. For the very things that make it reasonable for *him* to believe that the defendant consented are often the very things that incline the court to believe that she consented. What is often missing is the voice of the woman herself, an account of what it would be reasonable for *her* to agree to, that is to say, an account of what is reasonable from *her* standpoint.

Thus, what is presented as reasonable has repercussions for four separate but related concerns: (1) the question of whether a man's belief in a woman's consent was reasonable; (2) the problem of whether it is reasonable to attribute *mens rea* to him; (3) the question of what could count as reasonable from the woman's point of view; (4) the question of what is reasonable from the court's point of view. These repercussions are of the utmost practical concern. In a culture which contains an incidence of sexual assault verging on epidemic, a criterion of reasonableness which regards mere submission as consent fails to offer persons vulnerable to those assaults adequate protection.

The following statements by self-confessed date rapists reveal how our lack of a solution for dealing with date rape protects rapists by failing to provide their victims with legal recourse:

> All of my rapes have been involved in a dating situation where I've been out with a woman I know. . . . I wouldn't take no for an answer. I think it had something to do with my acceptance of rejection. I had low self-esteem and not much self-confidence and when I was rejected for something which I considered to be rightly mine, I became angry and I went ahead anyway. And this was the same in any situation, whether it was rape or it was something else.7

> When I did date, when I was younger, I would pick up a girl and if she didn't come across I would threaten her or slap her face then tell her she was going to fuck—that was it. But that's because I didn't want to waste time with any come-ons. It took too much time. I wasn't interested because I didn't like them as people anyway, and I just went with them just to get laid. Just to say that I laid them.[8]

There is, at this time, nothing to protect women from this kind of unscrupulous victimization. A woman on a casual date with a virtual stranger has almost no chance of bringing a complaint of sexual assault before the courts. One reason for this is the prevailing criterion for consent. According to this criterion, consent is implied unless some emphatic episodic sign of resistance occurred, and its occurrence can be established. But if no episodic act occurred, or if it did occur, and the defendant claims that it didn't, or if the defendant threatened the plaintiff but won't admit it in court, it is almost impossible to find any evidence that would support the plaintiff's word against the defendant. This difficulty is exacerbated by suspicion on the part of the courts, police, and legal educators that even where an act of resistance occurs, this act should not be interpreted as a withholding of consent, and this suspicion is especially upheld where the accused is a man who is known to the female plaintiff.

In Glanville Williams's classic textbook on criminal law we are warned that where a man is unknown to a woman, she does not consent if she expresses her rejection in the form of an episodic and vigorous act at the "vital moment." But if the man is known to the woman she must, according to Williams, make use of "all means available to her to repel the man."[9] Williams warns that women often welcome a "mastery advance" and present a token resistance. He quotes Byron's couplet,

> A little still she strove, and much repented
> And whispering "I will ne'er consent"—consented

by way of alerting law students to the difficulty of distinguishing real protest from pretense.[10] Thus, while in principle, a firm unambiguous stand, or a healthy show of temper ought to be sufficient, if established, to show nonconsent, in practice the forceful overriding of such a stance is apt to be taken as an indication that the resistance was not seriously intended, and that the seduction had succeeded. The consequence of this is that it is almost impossible to establish the defendant's guilt beyond a reasonable doubt.

Thus, on the one hand, we have a situation in which women are vulnerable to the most exploitive tactics at the hands of men who are known to them. On the other hand, almost nothing will count as evidence of their being assaulted, including their having taken an emphatic stance in withholding their consent. The new laws have done almost nothing to change this situation. Yet clearly, some solution must be sought. Moreover, the road to that solution presents itself clearly enough as a need for a reformulation of the criterion of consent. It is patent that a criterion that collapses whenever the crime itself succeeds will not suffice.

The purpose of this paper is to develop such a criterion, and I propose to do so by grounding this criterion in a conception of the "reasonable." Part of the strength of the present criterion for consent lies in the belief that it is reasonable for women to agree to the kind of sex involved in "date rape," or that it is reasonable for men to think that they have agreed. My argument is that it is not reasonable for women to consent to that kind of sex, and that there are furthermore, no grounds for thinking that it is reasonable. Since what we want to know is when a woman has consented, and since standards for consent are based on the presumed choices of reasonable agents, it is what is reasonable from a woman's point of view that must provide the principal delineation of a criterion of consent that is capable of representing a woman's willing behaviour. Developing this line of reasoning further, I will argue that the kind of sex to which it would be reasonable for women to consent suggests a criterion of consent that would bring the kind of sex involved in date rape well within the realm of sexual assault.

THE PROBLEM OF THE CRITERION

The reasoning that underlies the present criterion of consent is entangled in a number of mutually supportive mythologies which see sexual assault as masterful seduction, and silent submission as sexual enjoyment. Because the prevailing ideology has so much informed our conceptualization of sexual interaction, it is extraordinarily difficult for us to distinguish between assault and seduction, submission and enjoyment, or so we imagine. At the same time, this failure to distinguish has given rise to a network of rationalizations that support the conflation of assault with seduction, submission with enjoyment. I therefore want to begin my argument by providing an example which shows both why it is so difficult to make this distinction, and that it exists. Later, I will identify and attempt to unravel the lines of reasoning that reinforce this difficulty.

> The woman I have in mind agrees to see someone because she feels an initial attraction to him and believes that he feels that same way about her. She goes out with him in the hope that there will be mutual enjoyment and in the course of the day or evening an increase of mutual interest. Unfortunately, these hopes of *mutual* and *reciprocal* interest are not realized. We do not know how much interest she has in him by the end of their time together, but whatever her feelings she comes under pressure to have sex with him, and she does not want to have the kind of sex he wants. She may desire to hold hands and kiss, to engage in more intense caresses or in some form of foreplay, or she may not want to be touched. She may have reasons unrelated to desire for not wanting to engage in the

kind of sex he is demanding. She may have religious reservations, concerns about pregnancy or disease, a disinclination to be just another conquest. She may be engaged in a seduction program of her own which sees abstaining from sexual activity as a means of building an important emotional bond. She feels she is desirable to him, and she knows, and he knows that he will have sex with her if he can. And while she feels she doesn't owe him anything, and that it is her prerogative to refuse him, this feeling is partly a defensive reaction against a deeply held belief that if he is in need, she should provide. If she buys into the myth of insistent male sexuality she may feel he is suffering from sexual frustration and that she is largely to blame.

We do not know how much he desires her, but we do know that his desire for erotic satisfaction can hardly be separated from his desire for conquest. He feels no dating obligation, but has a strong commitment to scoring. He uses the myth of "so hard to control" male desire as a rhetorical tactic, telling her how frustrated she will leave him. He becomes overbearing. She resists, voicing her disinclination. He alternates between telling her how desirable she is and taking a hostile stance, charging her with misleading him, accusing her of wanting him, and being coy, in short of being deceitful, all the time engaging in rather aggressive body contact. It is late at night, she is tired and a bit queasy from too many drinks, and he is reaffirming her suspicion that perhaps she has misled him. She is having trouble disengaging his body from hers, and wishes he would just go away. She does not adopt a strident angry stance, partly because she thinks he is acting normally and does not deserve it partly because she feels she is partly to blame, and partly because there is always the danger that her anger will make him angry, possibly violent. It seems that the only thing to do, given his aggression, and her queasy fatigue, is to go along with him and get it over with, but this decision is so entangled with the events in process it is hard to know if it is not simply a recognition of what is actually happening. She finds the whole encounter a thoroughly disagreeable experience, but he does not take any notice, and wouldn't have changed course if he had. He congratulates himself on his sexual prowess and is confirmed in his opinion that aggressive tactics pay off. Later she feels that she has been raped, but paradoxically tells herself that she let herself be raped.

The paradoxical feelings of the woman in our example indicate her awareness that what she feels about the incident stands in contradiction to the prevailing cultural assessment of it. She knows that she did not want to have sex with her date. She is not so sure, however, about how much her own desires count, and she is uncertain that she has made her desires clear. Her uncertainty is reinforced by the cultural reading of this incident as an ordinary seduction.

As for us, we assume that the woman did not want to have sex, but just like her, we are unsure whether her mere reluctance, in the presence of high-pressure tactics, constitutes nonconsent. We suspect that submission to an overbearing and insensitive lout is no way to go about attaining sexual enjoyment, and we further suspect that he felt no compunction about providing it, so that on the face of it, from the outside looking in, it looks like a pretty unreasonable proposition for her.

Let us look at this reasoning more closely. Assume that she was not attracted to the kind of sex offered by the sort of person offering it. Then it would be *prima facie* unreasonable for her to agree to have sex, unreasonable, that is, unless she were offered some pay-off for her stoic endurance, money perhaps, or tickets to the opera. The reason is that in sexual matters, agreement is closely connected to attraction. Thus, where the presumption is that she was not attracted, we should at the same time presume that she did not consent. Hence, the burden of proof should be on her alleged assailant to show that she had good reasons for consenting to an unattractive proposition.

This is not, however, the way such situations are interpreted. In the unlikely event that the example I have described should come before the courts, there is little doubt that the law would interpret the woman's eventual acquiescence or "going along with" the sexual encounter as consent. But along with this interpretation would go the implicit understanding that she had consented because when all was said and done, when the "token" resistances to the "masterful advances" had been made she had wanted to after all. Once the courts have constructed this interpretation, they are then forced to conjure up some horror story of feminine revenge in order to explain why she should bring charges against her "seducer."

In the even more unlikely event that the courts agreed that the woman had not consented to the above encounter, there is little chance that her assailant would be convicted of sexual assault.[11] The belief that the man's aggressive tactics are a normal part of seduction means that *mens rea* cannot be

DISPELLING THE MYTHS

The "she asked for it" justification of sexual assault incorporates a conception of a contract that would be difficult to defend in any other context and the presumptions about human sexuality which function to reinforce sympathies rooted in the contractual notion of just deserts are not supported by empirical research.

The belief that a woman generates some sort of contractual obligation whenever her behaviour is interpreted as seductive is the most indefensible part of the mythology of rape. In law, contracts are not legitimate just because a promise has been made. In particular, the use of pressure tactics to extract agreement is frowned upon. Normally, an agreement is upheld only if the contractors were clear on what they were getting into, and had sufficient time to reflect on the wisdom of their doing so. Either there must be a clear tradition in which the expectations involved in the contract are fairly well known (marriage), or there must be an explicit written agreement concerning the exact terms of the contract and the expectations of the persons involved. But whatever the terms of a contract, there is no private right to enforce it. So that if I make a contract with you on which I renege, the only permissible recourse for you is through due legal process.

Now it is not clear whether sexual contracts can be made to begin with, or if so, what sort of sexual contracts would be legitimate. But assuming that they could be made, the terms of those contracts would not be enforceable. To allow public enforcement would be to grant the State the overt right to force people to have sex, and this would clearly be unacceptable. Granting that sexual contracts are legitimate, state enforcement of such contracts would have to be limited to ordering nonsexual compensation for breaches of contract. So it makes no difference whether a sexual contract is tacit or explicit. There are no grounds whatsoever that would justify enforcement of its terms.

Thus, even if we assume that a woman has initially agreed to an encounter, her agreement does not automatically make all subsequent sexual activity to which she submits legitimate. If during coitus a woman should experience pain, be suddenly overcome with guilt or fear of pregnancy, or simply lose her initial desire, those are good reasons for her to change her mind. Having changed her mind, neither her partner nor the state has any right to force her to continue. But then if she is forced to continue she is assaulted. Thus, establishing that consent occurred at a particular point during a sexual encounter should not conclusively establish the legitimacy of the encounter.[17] What is needed is a reading of whether she agreed throughout the encounter.

If the "she asked for it" contractual view of sexual interchange has any validity, it is because there is a point at which there is no stopping a sexual encounter, a point at which that encounter becomes the inexorable outcome of the unfolding of natural events. If a sexual encounter is like a slide on which I cannot stop halfway down, it will be relevant whether I enter the slide of my own free will, or am pushed.

But there is no evidence that the entire sexual act is like a slide. While there may be a few seconds in the "plateau" period just prior to orgasm in which people are "swept" away by sexual feelings to the point where we could justifiably understand their lack of heed for the comfort of their partner, the greater part of a sexual encounter comes well within the bounds of morally responsible control of our own actions. Indeed, the available evidence shows that most of the activity involved in sex has to do with building the requisite level of desire, a task that involves the proper use of foreplay, the possibility of which implies control over the form that foreplay will take. Modern sexual therapy assumes that such control is universally accessible, and so far there has been no reason to question that assumption. Sexologists are unanimous, moreover, in holding that mutual sexual enjoyment requires an atmosphere of comfort and communication, a minimum of pressure, and an ongoing check-up on one's partner's state. They maintain that different people have different predilections, and that what is pleasurable for one person is very often anathema to another. These findings show that the way to achieve sexual pleasure, at any time at all, let alone with a casual acquaintance, decidedly does not involve overriding the other person's express reservations and providing them with just any kind of sexual stimulus.[18] And while we do not want to allow science and technology a voice in which the voices of particular women are drowned, in this case science seems to concur with women's perception that aggressive incommunicative sex is not what they want. But if science and the voice of women concur, if aggressive seduction does not lead to good sex, if women do not like it or want it, then it is not rational to think that they would agree to it. Where such sex takes place, it is therefore rational to presume that the sex was not consensual.

The myth that women like to be raped, is closely connected, as we have seen, to doubt about their honesty in sexual matters, and this suspicion is exploited by defence lawyers when sexual assault cases make it to the courtroom. It is an unfortunate consequence of the presumption of innocence that rape victims who end up in court frequently find that it is they who are on trial. For if the defendant is innocent, then either he did not intend to do what he was accused of, or the plaintiff is mistaken about his identity, or she is lying. Often the last alternative is the only plausible defence, and as a result, the plaintiff's word seldom goes unquestioned. Women are frequently accused of having made a false accusation, either as a defensive mechanism for dealing with guilt and shame, or out of a desire for revenge.

Now there is no point in denying the possibility of false accusation, though there are probably better ways of seeking revenge on a man than accusing him of rape. However, we can now establish a logical connection between the evidence that a woman was subjected to high-pressure aggressive "seduction" tactics, and her claim that she did not consent to that encounter. Where the kind of encounter is not the sort to which it would be reasonable to consent, there is a logical presumption that a woman who claims that she did not consent is telling the truth. Where the kind of sex involved is not the sort of sex we would expect a woman to like, the burden of proof should not be on the woman to show that she did not consent, but on the defendant to show that contrary to every reasonable expectation she did consent. The defendant should be required to convince the court that the plaintiff persuaded him to have sex with her even though there are no visible reasons why she should.

In conclusion, there are no grounds for the "she asked for it" defence. Sexually provocative behaviour does not generate sexual contracts. Even where there are sexual agreements, they cannot be legitimately enforced either by the State, or by private right, or by natural prerogative. Secondly, all the evidence suggests that neither women nor men find sexual enjoyment in rape or in any form of non-communicative sexuality. Thirdly, male sexual desire is containable, and can be subjected to moral and rational control. Fourthly, since there is no reason why women should not be sexually provocative, they do not "deserve" any sex they do not want. This last is a welcome discovery. The taboo on sexual provocativeness in women is a taboo both on sensuality and on teasing. But sensuality is a source of delight, and teasing is playful and inspires wit. What a relief to learn that it is not sexual provocativeness, but its enemies, that constitutes a danger to the world.

COMMUNICATIVE SEXUALITY: REINTERPRETING THE KANTIAN IMPERATIVE

The present criterion of consent sets up sexual encounters as contractual events in which sexual aggression is presumed to be consented to unless there is some vigorous act of refusal. As long as we view sexual interaction on a contractual model, the only possibility for finding fault is to point to the presence of such an act. But it is clear that whether or not we can determine such a presence, there is something strongly disagreeable about the sexual aggression described above.

In thinking about sex we must keep in mind its sensual ends, and the facts show that aggressive high-pressure sex contradicts those ends. Consensual sex in dating situations is presumed to aim at mutual enjoyment. It may not always do this, and when it does, it might not always succeed. There is no logical incompatibility between wanting to continue a sexual encounter, and failing to derive sexual pleasure from it.[19]

But it seems to me that there is a presumption in favour of the connection between sex and sexual enjoyment, and that if a man wants to be sure that he is not forcing himself on a woman, he has an obligation either to ensure that the encounter really is mutually enjoyable, or to know the reasons why she would want to continue the encounter in spite of her lack of enjoyment. A closer investigation of the nature of this obligation will enable us to construct a more rational and a more plausible norm of sexual conduct.

Onara O'Neill has argued that in intimate situations we have an obligation to take the ends of others as our own, and to promote those ends in a non-manipulative and non-paternalistic manner.[20] Now it seems that in honest sexual encounters just this is required. Assuming that each person enters the encounter in order to seek sexual satisfaction, each person engaging in the encounter has an obligation to help the other seek his or her ends. To do otherwise is to risk acting in opposition to what the other desires, and hence to risk acting without the other's consent.

But the obligation to promote the sexual ends of one's partner implies the obligation to know what those ends are, and also the obligation to know how those ends are attained. Thus, the problem comes down to a problem of epistemic responsibility, the responsibility to know. The solution, in my view, lies in the practice of a communicative sexuality, one which combines the appropriate knowledge of the other with respect for the dialectics of desire.

So let us, for a moment, conceive of sexual interaction on a communicative rather than a contractual model. Let us look at it the way I think it should be looked at, as if it were a proper conversation rather than an offer from the Mafia.

Conversations, when they are proper conversations, as opposed to lectures, diatribes, or interrogations, illustrate the logical relation between communicative interaction and treating someone as an end in herself in O'Neill's sense. This logical relation can be illustrated by the difference in kind between a typical contract and a proper sort of conversation, a difference that derives primarily from the different relation each bears to the necessity for cooperation. The difference is this: typically, where contracts are concerned, cooperation is primarily required as a means to some further end set by the contract. In proper conversations, as I shall define them here, cooperation is sought as an end in itself.

It is not inimical to most contracts that the cooperation necessary for achieving its ends be reluctant, or even hostile. Although we can find fault with a contractor for failing to deliver goods or services, we do not normally criticize her for her attitude. And although there are situations where we employ people on the condition that they be congenial, even then we do not require that their congeniality be the real thing. When we are having a proper conversation, however, we do, typically, want the real thing. In conversation, the cooperation with the other is not just a means to an interesting conversation; it is one of the ends we seek, without which the conversation ceases to satisfy.

The communicative interaction involved in conversation is concerned with a good deal more than didactic content and argument. Good conversationalists are intuitive, sympathetic, and charitable. Intuition and charity aid the conversationalist in her effort to interpret the words of the other correctly and sympathy enables her to enter into the other's point of view. Her sensitivity alerts her to the tone of the exchange. Has her point been taken good-humoredly or resentfully? Aggressively delivered responses are taken as a sign that *ad hominems* are at work, and that the respondent's self-worth has been called into question. Good conversationalists will know to suspend further discussion until this sense of self-worth has been reestablished. Angry responses, resentful responses, bored responses, even over-enthusiastic responses require that the emotional ground be cleared before the discussion be continued. Often it is better to change the topic, or to come back to it on another day under different circumstances. Good conversationalists do not overwhelm their respondents with a barrage of their own opinions. While they may be persuasive, the forcefulness of their persuasion does not lie in their being overbearing, but rather in their capacity to see the other's point of view, to understand what it depends on, and so to address the essential point, but with tact and clarity.

Just as communicative conversationalists are concerned with more than didactic content, persons engaged in communicative sexuality will be concerned with more than achieving coitus. They will be sensitive to the responses of their partners. They will, like good conversationalists, be intuitive, sympathetic, and charitable. Intuition will help them to interpret their partner's responses; sympathy will enable them to share what their partner is feeling; charity will enable them to care. Communicative sexual partners will not overwhelm each other with the barrage of their own desires. They will treat negative, bored, or angry responses, as a sign that the erotic ground needs to be either cleared or abandoned. Their concern with fostering the desire of the other must involve an ongoing state of alertness in interpreting her responses.

Just as a conversationalist's prime concern is for the mutuality of the discussion, a person engaged in communicative sexuality will be most concerned with the mutuality of desire. As such, both will put into practice a regard for their respondent that is guaranteed no place in the contractual language of rights, duties, and consent. The dialectics of both activities reflect the dialectics of desire insofar as each person's interest in continuing is contingent upon the other person wishing to do so too, and each person's interest is as much fueled by the other's interest as it is by her own. Each respects the subjectivity of the other not just by avoiding treading on it, but by fostering and protecting the quality of that subjectivity. Indeed, the requirement to avoid treading on the subjectivity of the other entails the obligation to respect the dialectics of desire.[21] For in intimacy there is no passing by on the other side. To be intimate just is to open up in emotional and personal ways, to share personal knowledge, and to be receptive to the openness of the other. This openness and sharing normally takes place only in an atmosphere of confidence and trust. But once availed of this knowledge, and confidence, and trust, one has, as it were, responsibility thrust upon one, the responsibility not to betray the trust by misusing the knowledge. And only by respecting the dialectics of desire can we have any confidence that we have not misused our position of trust and knowledge.

CULTURAL PRESUMPTIONS

Now it may well be that we have no obligation to care for strangers, and I do not wish to claim that we do. Nonetheless, it seems that O'Neill's point about the special moral duties we have in certain intimate situations is supported by a conceptual relation between certain kinds of personal relationships and the expectation that it should be a communicative relation. Friendship is a case in point. It is a relation that is greatly underdetermined by what we usually include in our sets of rights and obligations. For the most part, rights and obligations disappear as terms by which friendship is guided. They are still there, to be called upon, in case the relationship breaks down, but insofar as the friendship is a friendship, it is concerned with fostering the quality of the interaction and not with standing on rights. Thus, because we are friends, we share our property, and property rights between us are not invoked. Because we are friends, privacy is not an issue. Because we are friends we may see to each other's needs as often as we see to our own. The same can be said for relations between lovers, parents and dependent children, and even between spouses, at least when interaction is functioning at an optimal level. When such relations break down to the point that people must stand on their rights, we can often say that the actors ought to make more of an effort, and in many instances fault them for their lack of charity, tolerance, or benevolence. Thus, although we have a right to end friendships, it may be a reflection on our lack of virtue that we do so, and while we cannot be criticized for violating other people's rights, we can be rightfully deprecated for lacking the virtue to sustain a friendship.

But is there a similar conceptual relation between the kind of activity that a date is, and the sort of moral practice which that it requires? My claim is that there is, and that this connection is easily established once we recognize the cultural presumption that dating is a gesture of friendship and regard. Traditionally, the decision to date indicates that two people have an initial attraction to each other, that they are disposed to like each other, and look forward to enjoying each other's company. Dating derives its implicit meaning from this tradition. It retains this meaning unless other aims are explicitly stated, and even then it may not be possible to alienate this meaning. It is a rare woman who will not spurn a man who states explicitly, right at the onset, that he wants to go out with her solely on the condition that he have sexual intercourse with her at the end of the evening, and that he has no interest in her company apart from gaining that end, and no concern for mutual satisfaction.

Explicit protest to the contrary aside, the conventions of dating confer on it its social meaning, and this social meaning implies a relationship which is more like friendship than the cutthroat competition of opposing teams. As such, it requires that we do more than stand on our rights with regard to each other. As long as we are operating under the auspices of a dating relationship, it requires that we behave in the mode of friendship and trust. But if a date is more like a friendship than a business contract, then clearly respect for the dialectics of desire is incompatible with the sort of sexual pressure that is inclined to end in date rape. And clearly, also, a conquest mentality which exploits a situation of trust and respect for purely selfish ends is morally pernicious. Failure to respect the dialectics of desire when operating under the auspices of friendship and trust is to act in flagrant disregard of the moral requirement to avoid manipulative, coercive, and exploitive behaviour. Respect for the dialectics of desire is *prima facie* inconsistent with the satisfaction of one person at the expense of the other. The proper end of friendship relations is mutual satisfaction. But the requirement of mutuality means that we must take a communicative approach to discovering the ends of the other, and this entails that we respect the dialectics of desire.

But now that we know what communicative sexuality is, and that it is morally required, and that it is the only feasible means to mutual sexual enjoyment, why not take this model as the norm of what is reasonable in sexual interaction. The evidence of sexologists strongly indicates that women whose partners are aggressively uncommunicative have little chance of experiencing sexual pleasure. But it is not reasonable for women to consent to what they have little chance of enjoying. Hence it is not reasonable for women to consent to aggressive noncommunicative sex. Nor can we reasonably suppose that women have consented to sexual encounters which we know and they know they do not find enjoyable. With the communicative model as the norm, the aggressive contractual model should strike us as a model of deviant sexuality, and sexual encounters patterned on that model should strike us as encounters to which *prima facie* no one would reasonably agree. But if acquiesence to an encounter counts as consent only if the acquiescence is reasonable, something to which a reasonable person, in full possession of knowledge relevant to the encounter, would agree, then acquiescence to aggressive noncommunicative sex is not reasonable. Hence, acquiescence under such conditions should not count as consent.

Thus, where communicative sexuality does not occur, we lack the main ground for believing that the sex involved was consensual. Moreover, where a man does not engage in communicative sexuality, he acts either out of reckless disregard, or out of willful ignorance. For he cannot know, except through the practice of communicative sexuality, whether his partner has any sexual reason for continuing the encounter. And where she does not, he runs the risk of imposing on her what she is not willing to have. All that is needed then, in order to provide women with legal protection from "date rape" is to make both reckless indifference and willful ignorance a sufficient condition of *mens rea* and to make communicative sexuality the accepted norm of sex to which a reasonable woman would agree.[22] Thus, the appeal to communicative sexuality as a norm for sexual encounters accomplishes two things. It brings the aggressive sex involved in "date rape" well within the realm of sexual assault, and it locates the guilt of date rapists in the failure to approach sexual relations on a communicative basis.

THE EPISTEMOLOGICAL IMPLICATIONS

Finding a proper criterion for consent is one problem, discovering what really happened, after the event, when the only eye witnesses give conflicting accounts is another. But while there is no foolproof way of getting the unadulterated truth, it can make a significant difference to the outcome of a prosecution, what sort of facts we are seeking. On the old model of aggressive seduction we sought evidence of resistance. But on the new model of communicative sexuality what we want is evidence of an ongoing positive and encouraging response on the part of the plaintiff. This new goal will require quite different tactics on the part of the cross-examiners, and quite different expectations on the part of juries and judges. Where communicative sexuality is taken as the norm, and aggressive sexual tactics as a presumption against consent, the outcome for the example that I described above would be quite different. It would be regarded as sexual assault rather than seduction.

Let us then consider a date rape trial in which a man is cross-examined. He is asked whether he was presuming mutual sexual enjoyment. Suppose he answers in the negative. Then he would have to account for why he persisted in the face of her voiced reluctance. He cannot give as an excuse that he thought she liked it, because he believes that she did not. If he thought that she had consented even though she didn't like it, then it seems to me that the burden of proof would lie with him to say why it was reasonable to think this. Clearly, her initial resistance, her presumed lack of enjoyment, and the pressure tactics involved in getting her to "go along" would not support a reasonable belief in consent, and his persisting in the face of her dissatisfaction would surely cast doubt on the sincerity of his belief in her consent.

But suppose he answers in the affirmative. Then the cross-examiner would not have to rely on the old criteria for non-consent. He would not have to show either that she had resisted him, or that she was in a fearful or intimidated state of mind. Instead he could use a communicative model of sexuality to discover how much respect there had been for the dialectics of desire. Did he ask her what she liked? If she was using contraceptives? If he should? What tone of voice did he use? How did she answer? Did she make any demands? Did she ask for penetration? How was that desire conveyed? Did he ever let up the pressure long enough to see if she was really that interested? Did he ask her which position she preferred? Assuming that the defendant does not perjure himself, he would lack satisfactory answers to these questions. But even where the defendant did lie, a skilled cross-examiner who was willing to go into detail could probably establish easily enough when the interaction had not been communicative. It is extraordinarily difficult to keep up a consistent story when you are not telling the truth.

On the new criterion, the cross-examination focuses on the communicative nature of the ongoing encounter, and the communicative nature of an encounter is much easier to establish than the occurrence of an episodic act of resistance. For one thing, it requires that a fairly long, yet consistent story be told, and this enables us to assess the plausibility of the competing claims in light of a wider collection of relevant data. Secondly, in making noncommunicative sex the primary indicator of coercive sex it provides us with a criterion for distinguishing consensual sadomasochism from brutality. For even if a couple agree to sadomasochistic sex, bondage and whippings and the rest of it, the court has a right to require that there be a system of signals whereby each partner can convey to the other whether she has had enough.[23] Thirdly, the use of a new criterion of communicative sexuality would enable us to introduce a new category of nonaggravated sexual assault which would not necessarily carry a heavy sentence but which would nonetheless provide an effective recourse against "date rape."[24]

CONCLUSION

In sum, using communicative sexuality as a model of normal sex has several advantages over the "aggressive-acquiescence" model of seduction. The new model ties the presumption that consensual sex takes place in the expectation of mutual desire much more closely to the facts about how that desire actually functions. Where communicative sex does not occur, this establishes a presumption that there was no consent. The importance of this presumption is that we are able, in criminal proceedings, to shift the burden of proof from the plaintiff, who on the contractual model must show that she resisted or was threatened, to the defendant who must then give some reason why she should consent after all. The communicative model of sexuality also enables us to give a different conceptual content to the concept of consent. It sees consent as something more like an ongoing cooperation than the one-shot agreement which we are inclined to see it as on the contractual model. Moreover, it does not matter, on the communicative model, whether a woman was sexually provocative, what her reputation is, what went on before the sex began. All that matters is the quality of communication with regard to the sex itself.

But most importantly, the communicative model of normal sexuality gives us a handle on a solution to the problem of date rape. If noncommunicative sexuality establishes a presumption of nonconsent, then where there are no overriding reasons for thinking that consent occurred, we have a criterion for a category of sexual assault that does not require evidence of physical violence or threat. If we are serious about date rape, then the next step is to take this criterion as objective grounds for establishing that a date rape has occurred. The proper legislation is the shortest route to establishing this criterion.

There remains, of course, the problem of education. If we are going to change the rules about what is socially acceptable in sexual relations, then it is only fair to let the public know. In a mass media society, this is not hard to do. A public information campaign will spread the news in no time at all. The real problem is the reluctance of the mass media to deal with questions of sexual relations and sexual intimacy. Its politicians are still curiously reluctant to stand up to an increasingly small sector of society that is unwilling to admit, despite all the evidence to the contrary, that anyone but well-meaning husbands and wives ever have sex. I would not be surprised if this sort of puritanical holdout were the very source of the problem of rape. Certainly, sexual ignorance must contribute significantly to the kind of social environment conducive to rape.

NOTES

1. Geis, G. and R. Geis. "Rape Reform: An Appreciative-Critical Review," *Bulletin of the American*

Academy of Psychiatry and the Law 6, 301–312. Also see, Michael Davis, "Setting Penalties: What Does Rape Deserve," *Law and Philosophy* 3, 61–110.

2. Under Common Law a person cannot consent to aggravated assault. Also, consent may be irrelevant if the victim was unfit to consent. See Michael Davis, "Setting Penalties: What Does Rape Deserve," 104–105.
3. Discussion Paper No. 2, *Rape and Allied Offenses: Substantive Aspects,* Law Reform Commission of Victoria, August (1986).
4. In a recent Australian case a man was convicted of being an accomplice to a rape because he was reckless in determining whether the woman raped by his friend was consenting. The judge ruled that his "reckless indifference" sufficed to establish *mens rea.* This ruling was possible, however, only because unreasonable belief is not a rape defence in Australia. *Australian Law Review* 71, 120.
5. This is true, at present, in jurisdictions which follow the precedent set by Morgan vs. Morgan. In this case, four men were acquitted of rape because they sincerely thought that their victim had consented, despite their admitting that she had protested vigorously. See Mark Thornton's "Rape and Mens Rea," *Canadian Journal of Philosophy,* Supp. Vol. VIII, 119-146.
6. *Ibid.*
7. *Why Men Rape,* Sylvia Levine and Joseph Loenig, eds., (Toronto: Macmillan, 1980), p. 83.
8. *Ibid.,* p. 77.
9. Williams, *Textbook of Criminal Law* (1983), p. 238.
10. *Ibid.*
11. See Jeanne C. Marsh, Allison Geist, and Nathan Caplan, *Rape and The Limits of Law Reform* (Boston: Auburn House, 1982), p. 32. According to Marsh's study on the impact of the Michigan reform of rape laws, convictions were increased for traditional conceptions of rape, i.e., aggravated assault. However date-rape, which has a much higher incidence than aggravated assault, has a very low rate of arrest and an even lower one of conviction.
12. See Marsh, p. 61, for a particular good example of this response. Also see John M. MacDonald, "Victim-Precipitated Rape," *Rape: Offenders and their Victims* (Illinois: Charles C. Thomas, 1971), pp. 78–89, for a good example of this response in academic thinking. Also see Menachem Amir, *Patterns in Forcible Rape* (University of Chicago Press, 1972), p. 259.
13. See Eugene Borgida and Nancy Brekke, "Psycholegal Research on Rape Trials," in *Rape and Sexual Assault,* Ann Wobert Burgess, ed., (New York: Garland Press, 1985), p. 314. Also see M. J. Lerner, "The Desire for Justice and Reactions to Victims," *Altruism and Helping Behaviour,* J. Macaulay and L. Berkowitz, eds. (New York: Academic Press, 1970).
14. As, for example, Lorenne Clark and Debra Lewis do in *Rape: The Price of Coercive Sexuality* (Toronto: The Women's Press, 1977), pp. 152–153.
15. See Sue Bessner, *The Laws of Rape* (New York: Praeger Publications, 1984), pp. 111–121, for a discussion of the legal forms in which this suspicion is expressed.
16. *Ibid.*
17. A speech-act like "OK, let's get it over with" is taken as consent, even though it is extracted under high pressure, the sex that ensues lacks mutuality, and there are no ulterior reasons for such an agreement. See Davis, p. 103. Also see Carolyn Shafer and Marilyn Frye, "Rape and Respect," *Readings in Recent Feminist Philosophy,* ed. by Marilyn Pearsell (California: Wadsworth, 1986), p. 189, for a characterization of the common notion of consent as a formal speech-act.
18. It is not just women who fail to find satisfaction in the "swept away" approach to sexual interaction. Studies of convicted rapists, and of conquest oriented men, indicate that men are frequently disappointed when they use this approach as well. In over half of aggravated sexual assaults penetration fails because the man loses his erection. Those who do succeed invariably report that the sex experienced was not enjoyable. This supports the prevailing view of sexologists that men depend on the positive response of their partners in order to fuel their own responsive mechanisms. See A. N. Groth, *Rape and Sexual Assault.* Also see *Why Men Rape,* edited by Sylvia Levine and Joseph Koenig (Toronto: Macmillan, 1982) or consult any recent manual on male sexuality.
19. Robin Morgan comes perilously close to suggesting that there is when she defines rape as any sexual encounter that is not initiated by a woman out of her own heartfelt desire. See *Going Too Far* (New York: Random House, 1968), p. 165.

20. O'Neill, "Between Consenting Adults," *Philosophy and Public Affairs* 14, 252-277.
21. The sort of relationship I have in mind exemplifies the "feminist" approach to ethics argued for by Nell Noddings, *Caring: A Feminine Approach to Ethics* (Berkeley: University of California Press, 1984). In particular, see her discussion of teaching as a "duality," p. 195.
22. As now seems to be the case in Australian Law. See note 4.
23. The SAMOIS justification of sadomasochism rests on the claim that sadomasochistic practice can be communicative in this way. See *Coming to Power,* Samois (Boston: Alyson Publications, 1981).
24. See sections 520e, Act No. 266, State of Michigan. Sexual assault in the fourth degree is punishable by imprisonment of not more than two years or a fine of not more than $500, or both.

PART 5

PROPERTY

Issues of property have long intrigued philosophers. Not only have they questioned how we form property, but they have also explored the implications of property for humanity. Some philosophers have argued that property instigated the move away from a more peaceful state of nature; others have argued for a less pessimistic view of property and a less idyllic view of the state of nature. Given that, for better or worse, property is a part of all of our lives, philosophers have also explored the role that the state should play in enforcing property rights. One key question is whether or not the state should ever play a role in the redistribution of property even if society overall would benefit from such a redistribution.

Such issues particularly matter in regard to property that may be unfairly held by its owner. For example, property rights have been quite important in government interactions with indigenous peoples. If the government unfairly took land, should it repay the original owners? If justice demands that it must, the question remains how this should be done. After all, if many current citizens' ancestors had not immigrated at the time of the taking, or even soon after the taking, must they be forced either to give up title to property they purchased or to provide tax dollars to repay this unfairness?

To begin to explore these questions, we need to examine John Locke's highly influential work "Of Property," a selection from his *Second Treatise of Government*. Here, Locke presents his theory on the origin of property. Originally, Locke argues that God gave the earth and the creatures on it to all of humankind. While these items were owned in common, each individual owned his or her own person and labor. Thus, according to Locke, when an individual takes an item from the state of nature and mixes her labor with it, she creates private property. Additionally, Locke argues that each individual is entitled to take as much as she wants from the commons, if she uses the items before they spoil. If an individual takes too much and some spoils, that selfish person has robbed the rest of humankind.

Locke argues that we may also apply this theory to the ownership of land. Each individual may enclose a plot of land for personal cultivation and, by doing so, the land becomes his private property. The only limit to the enclosure of land for personal use is that no one should take more land than she can use; to take more is robbery. Locke claims that the appropriation of land actually improves life for all of humankind because cultivated land produces crop yields that far outstrip those of uncultivated land. Moreover, it is the privatization of land that leads to the use of money. Although it is wrong to hoard a crop and allow it to spoil, anyone can give or barter the crop away. For example, part of a crop of apples, which are perishable, might be bartered for nuts, which last much longer, or for gold, which is not perishable at all. The apple grower can keep as much gold as she likes, because having a large amount of something is not wrong—rather, allowing spoilage is wrong. Finally, Locke argues money is what allows for the unequal possession of land that exists in a modern society. With the use of money, an individual can possess more land and produce more crops than he can use alone, because he can trade those crops for nonperishable money. Without money, having too much of a surplus would lead to the general harm of spoilage.

Robert Nozick offers an analysis of Locke's theory of property in a selection from his *Anarchy, State, and Utopia*. In exploring a variety of questions he believes Locke's theory leaves unanswered, Nozick focuses on what he finds to be the crucial question: Does appropriation of property by some worsen the plight of others? This question hinges on Locke's assertion that, in any appropriation of property, there should be "enough and as good left in common for others" (see p. 281). Nozick focuses on two possible ways one's appropriation might worsen others' circumstance. First, the lack of opportunity for appropriation might prevent an individual from improving her situation through appropriating property. Second, the appropriation might worsen an individual because he can no longer use property freely as he once did. Nozick argues that a stringent proviso will exclude both possibilities, while a weaker proviso will exclude only the second possibility.

While Nozick explores the position that Locke's proviso is a stringent one, he claims that its characterization as a weak proviso is more accurate because of the variety of benefits that flows from the appropriation of property. For example, appropriation provides alternative sources of employment and increases the total amount of social product because those who can best use them possess the means of production. Nozick also claims that all adequate theories of justice in appropriation need a proviso similar to this weaker model. Nevertheless, while Nozick claims the need for a proviso modeled after the weak version, he argues that there are legitimate ways of circumventing such a proviso. For example, a person who wishes to appropriate some item might compensate others whom such an appropriation would harm so that she does not worsen their situation. Additionally, Nozick argues that if we include such a proviso to regulate justice in acquisition, there must be a similar proviso to regulate justice in transfer. Nevertheless, Nozick claims this concern does not illustrate that whenever someone owns all of something others are left worse off. He argues that if someone appropriates a small amount of chemicals and invents a drug, he makes no one worse off, because there are still chemicals available for appropriation. Thus, according to Nozick, the Lockean proviso will allow the free operation of a market system.

In "Property, Title and Redistribution," A. M. Honoré focuses on Robert Nozick's argument that the state has no duty to redistribute benefits equally throughout society, as confined to property. Honoré claims that this view rests on the idea that a person is allowed to keep "exclusively and indefinitely" for her own use whatever she makes or produces. This, Honoré argues, can be true of a person in isolation, but no argument illustrates that this is true for a social being. In Honoré's opinion, Nozick's attempt to reproduce Western property law assumes and omits too much. For example, Nozick's theory rests on the assumption that we can determine just title to property in abstraction from the historical or social context. This means that a just acquisition 200 years ago remains the just root for a title held today. As such, we are forced to say, for example, either that the acquisition of slaves was always unjust or that the descendants of slaveholders are entitled to own the descendants of slaves today. If we argue the former, Honoré questions how we are to know that there are no similarly unjustified forms of acquisition and ownership today. In fact, Honoré claims that outside of a Utopia, Nozick's theory has no application.

Moreover, Honoré argues that Nozick is too quick to reject other systems of property law. Such systems actually exist and are morally defensible. Further, we can imagine a system in which private property is inherently distributive. For example, an inventor of an item "owns" that property in that his right to its use is greater than that of the others of his community, but the other members of the community each have a right to use it also. Such a system, Honoré argues, is not obviously unjust; in fact, it positively reinforces the interdependence of all members of the community. Nevertheless, Honoré recognizes such a system will likely not survive the division of labor obtained through specialization, but taxation of the inventor could replace the lost benefits of use. According to Honoré, the fact that similar arrangements exist in some non-Western societies illustrates there is nothing unnatural about distributive property arrangements. Thus, compulsory sharing should not be dismissed out of hand for societies where the division of labor complicates such sharing; instead, the state has a role to play in seeing that sharing takes place.

In "An Introduction to Chinese Property Law," Jonas Alsén explains the development of and distinctions within Chinese property law. Given that ownership rights are seldom absolute, Alsén argues that we should see ownership as a bundle of rights. In socialist systems like China, the degree of ownership is simply less than that in capitalist systems. In the 1950s, real property was state owned and managed by peoples' communes. In 1978 the Deng government realized this system was not leading to economic prosperity and shifted to the Household Contract System. Under this system and subsequent revisions, China allowed some degree of private ownership through the contracting out of farms and urban land. Under this system, land is transferred from the state for a given time, the length of which hinges on its proposed use, in return for a fee paid to the state. This move was justified by the claim that China was still in the first stage of socialism and so still needed a market economy in order to develop. This move has given land value that it lacked before, created a real estate market, and removed the burden of urban development from the state.

With this move, Chinese conceptions of ownership were forced to shift. Originally, Chinese conceptions of ownership were based on the Japanese civil code rather than on Roman law. These foundations were further changed in 1987 with the institution of the Civil Code. Property ownership is now divided into four constituent "powers and functions": possession, use, the right to benefit, and disposition. The justification for this breakdown is to allow for a building of new rights with new combinations of the old parts. Alsén points out that the protection of property rights nevertheless remains limited because the legal system is weak and there is no true rule of law.

Richard Epstein, in a selection from *Takings: Private Property and the Power of Eminent Domain,* defends the use of eminent domain as a government tool. In Epstein's opinion, eminent domain is key to the development of a state, because the need for such a power motivates the move from a voluntary protective association to a true state. Epstein defines the power of eminent domain as the state's right to force exchanges of property rights, but these exchanges must leave the individuals with rights that are more valuable than the ones that the government has taken. Additionally, there are two limitations to this right: these forced exchanges are only for the public use, and the exchanges require compensation.

Epstein defends his view of eminent domain by comparing it with three competing views: Robert Nozick's, John Rawls', and civic virtue. Under Nozick's version of libertarianism, the government cannot be allowed to exercise forced exchanges, but Epstein finds this view lacking. Without forced exchange, Epstein argues, society cannot achieve true social order, because there will be too many holdouts and free riders. Next, Epstein finds Rawls' contractarianism too uncertain. Additionally, while Rawls has designed his theory to achieve fair distributions, it does so at the expense of the total amount to be distributed. Epstein believes eminent domain avoids these problems. Finally, Epstein critiques the view that eminent domain ignores the role of civic virtue. Epstein argues that civic virtue is a by-product of sound institutional arrangements. As such, eminent domain works toward civic virtue by attempting to achieve such sound institutional arrangements. According to Epstein, eminent domain is a necessary part of just government because it connects private property and public law.

In "The Social Structure of Japanese Intellectual Property Law," Dan Rosen and Chikako Usui explore the basis for Japanese attitudes toward intellectual property laws. Rosen and Usui suggest that, given widespread use of Western intellectual property laws by Japanese businesses, many would think that the Japanese would argue for intellectual property laws. Yet, when the authors examine Japanese intellectual property laws, they find these laws weak and Japanese attitudes toward them ambivalent. Rosen and Usui argue that the reason for this lack of support within Japan is due to the larger social system; moreover, looking at the law as a small part of the larger culture is the best way to understand the law overall.

Rosen and Usui suggest that within the United States, copyright law functions as a sort of bribe, in that the government gives inventors exclusive access to the economic benefits of their work with the hope that this economic incentive will motivate the inventor to produce more. Further, free riders in the United States must show "strong reasons" why the holder of the copyright ought not benefit. In Japan, the law does not assume exclusive access by the inventor; instead, there is wide consideration to fair exploitation. This wide consideration allows both widespread personal and privileged uses that benefit society overall, such as allowing fixed fees from textbook manufacturers for copyrighted material. This difference in attitude, according to Rosen and Usui, stems from Chinese Confucianism. Following Confucianism, Japanese society recognizes the interdependence that exists among all its members. This attitude allows for intellectual property laws that are much less protective of individual rights than are similar laws within the United States.

A. John Simmons, in "Historical Rights and Fair Shares," offers two approaches to dealing with property claims of American Indians based on past property rights violations. First, the state can treat American Indians like any other group, with the fact of their original occupation excluded as irrelevant. Second, the state can take seriously American Indians' historical claims to land and see these claims as the basis of the persistent right to rectification. Simmons argues that the second method is the most acceptable of the two because it both preserves the particularity of the American-Indian claims and can be sensitive to changing circumstances because the content of these historical rights can be particularized (but not particular) fair shares. For example, American-Indian historical rights are to fair portions of the actual land that they used; yet, if the state or any of its citizens have destroyed or irreversibly altered those lands, then native tribes are due the closest approximations.

Given his argument for rectification in this context, Simmons looks at two potential problems. First is the death of the original wrongdoer, but Simmons claims this problem is no worse in American-Indian land claims than in any other case. Second is the death of the victim of wrongdoing. If the rights die with the original victim, then there are no unique American-Indian rights to rectification at issue, and the state should treat them as any other group. Given this problem, Simmons examines several justifications for assuming the original property holders have passed down these rights to rectification to their descendants, rather than assuming, absent the wrong, the original property holders would have lost or given away the property. First, counterfactual judgments regarding what would have happened without the wrong must be conservative. Second, children have rights against their parents to the receipt of property that they need for a decent life. This means that even if the land was lost or given away, the children would have a claim to the land. Finally, the land and resources were tribal, not individual; therefore, the rights to rectification were also tribal. This means that the death of individuals is irrelevant to the issue of persisting historical rights. Essentially, this view of property ties tribal identity to the land; thus, tribal ownership of their historical land is essential and inalienable. Simmons also claims that a Lockean view of property, when abstracted from Locke's particular views of American Indians, supports this conclusion. Because Locke's theory allows individuals to join their property or to produce property through collective labor, it supports Simmons' claim that native tribes possess historical rights to rectification of past property injustices.

In "Compensation, Reparations, and Restitution: Indian Property Claims in the United States," Nell Jessup Newton argues that uncompensated confiscations are wrongs that the state ought to restitute. Many governments attempt to avoid restitution by claiming they have not committed a taking or that the land was not really property. For example, when governments nationalized private property in communist Eastern Europe, the involved states claimed there was no right to own private property, so they did not actually take the land. Many now seeking restitution from these states look to the United States as a good model because they see that country as a "safe haven" for such rights. Yet the United States struggled with similar issues when it was a newly developing state, because of conflicts with American Indian tribes. Newton examines past treatment of these tribes in order to illustrate the following: (1) There is no single method of compensation; instead, the United States developed various models for compensating American Indians for land taken. (2) The invocation of property rights as sacred is overly simple, because the United States often violated the property rights of American Indians. (3) The United States itself confiscated property from native tribes, so any invocation of national property rights may hide other motives. With awareness of these factors, the U.S. government's various attempts at compensation provide multiple models for similar attempts elsewhere.

To illustrate the complexity of the issue, Newton explores the history of U.S. land policy regarding American Indians. Initially the United States government struck a variety of treaties with native tribes through bargaining, but some negotiators also used fraud and threats of force. In 1871, Congress ended the practice of treaties, making federal statutes the vehicles of dispossession. During this time, the government took approximately one billion acres with either token compensation or none. Additionally, United

States Supreme Court rulings legitimized these takings, thus allowing the citizens to view these takings as fair. The rulings in *Johnson v. McIntosh, Cherokee Nation v. Georgia,* and *Worcester v. Georgia* formed *The Marshall Trilogy* that set the boundaries of American-Indian property law. The principles that Chief Justice John Marshall articulated in these three cases declared the following: that there would be federal superiority over the individual states and foreign nations regarding American-Indian affairs, which the Court rooted in the Constitution's Commerce Clause, and that the American-Indian tribes were considered "domestic dependent nations." In the second half of the nineteenth century, Congress instituted a policy of forced privatization of tribal land. Under this policy, the government individualized all tribal land, each head of household received enough acreage to become self-sufficient, and the government sold the rest to settlers. This was done in an attempt to civilize and assimilate native tribes. Additionally, approximately two-thirds of the tribal land was lost, but because individual tribal members benefited by being given their own plots of land, there was no tribal compensation. Supreme Court rulings supported this policy by claiming that tribal land was no different from any other land in that the government could claim it for public use. Also, the Court ruled that any disputes between the tribes and the federal government were political questions and therefore immune from judicial review and subject to the presumption that the government acted in good faith.

Cheryl Harris, in "Whiteness As Property," argues that whites have intermingled conceptions of property and race for centuries. Harris argues that the basic intersection of race and property played a critical role in establishing white superiority over both African Americans and American Indians. In the case of the former, the white majority made them property. In the case of the latter, the white majority supported the government's occupation and possession of tribal lands. The Representation Clause of the Constitution readily illustrates this combining of humanness and property through its claim that one slave equaled only three-fifths of a person. Harris also argues that whiteness fits broad historical conceptions of property. Whiteness helped determine a person's legal status as slave or free and, thus, became a jealously guarded possession. Moreover, whiteness fits the functional criteria of property. First, although most property is thought to be alienable, some forms are not. Here, whiteness functions like a professional degree that one party cannot transfer to another. Second, whiteness fulfills the right to use and enjoyment, because of the privileges accorded whites simply because they are white. Third, whiteness conforms to the conception of reputation as property, given the long legal history of classifying incorrect characterizations of blackness as defamation. Finally, whiteness fulfills the absolute right to exclude that is generally attached to property. Harris points to the lengthy history of courts guarding definitions of whiteness—for example, the "one-drop test," which declared as black anyone who had at least one drop of so-called black blood. Additionally, when we explore the white working class, they more closely tie their self-conceptions to race than class. Working-class whites benefited from this through higher salaries than their African-American counterparts. The "passing" that often occurred, and still occurs, in the African-American community illustrates the value in whiteness. African Americans valued the ability to pass as white because it enabled access to higher wages.

Harris claims that while whiteness does not have all the value it once did, such as the ability to confer citizenship, it still has value. Given the attached political value of being white, Harris claims that today not all whites win, but none lose. Illustrating the current value of whiteness is a recent study in which researchers asked white college students how much they would seek if they changed them from white to black. Many felt that a lump sum of $50 million or $1 million per year would not be too much to ask. Harris concludes by arguing that the United States needs affirmative action programs in order to delegitimize the property interest in whiteness. These programs, in her opinion, will not subordinate whites by reestablishing a property interest in blackness; instead, affirmative action will simply guarantee that no one is subordinated.

Finally, *International News Service v. Associated Press* is provided as an example of property law. Here, both parties are competitors in gathering and selling the news to individual newspapers. The main value of this news is in its promptness or freshness. The International News Service admitted that it was pirating the Associated Press's news, by copying it from news billboards and early editions of subscribing newspapers, but claimed this was lawful because the news is not property. The Associated Press contradicted this claim, stating that the International News Service violated their property rights. Additionally, such practices constituted unfair competition in business, because the International News Service was benefiting at the expense of the Associated Press's time and money. The Supreme Court ruled in the Associated Press's favor, claiming that there are three main questions at stake. First, is there property in news? Second, if there is, does it survive publication? Finally, is this practice unfair competition in trade?

The Court ruled that the news is not property the way a literary novel is property, because it is not a creation; instead, it is simple reporting of events. However, because both parties pay to collect and distribute it and receive money for it like any other type of merchandise, the Court ruled that the news takes the form of "quasi-property." Given this characterization, the Court focused on the final question, expanding it as follows: Does someone who gathers news for sale at considerable pain and expense have an interest in its publication without interference? Given that the complainant's business hinges on providing fresh news, it has a serious interest in preventing others from pirating the news and providing it at the same time or earlier. The Court ruled that the defendant was essentially a free rider engaged in unfair business practices. Because the Associated Press fairly paid the necessary price for the news, it should have the benefit of that news just as any property owner who justly paid for her property should have the benefit of it.

Clearly, many social and moral as well as philosophical issues arise from considerations of property law. For those of you interested in further information, we have included a list of selected readings related to the selections presented here.

SELECTED READINGS

Alsén, Jonas. "An Introduction to Chinese Property Law." *Maryland Journal of International Law and Trade* 20 (1996): 1–60.

Becker, Lawrence. "The Moral Basis of Property Rights." *NOMOS XXII: Property,* 187–220. New York: New York University Press, 1980.

Dutson, Stuart. "The Internet, Conflict of Laws, International Litigation and Intellectual Property: The Implications of the International Scope of the Internet on Intellectual Property Infringements." *Journal of Business Law* (Nov. 1997), 495–513.

Ederington, Benjamin. "Property as a Natural Institution: The Separation of Property from Sovereignty in International Law." *American University International Law Review* 13 (1997): 263–331.

Gardner, Royal. "Taking the Principle of Just Compensation Abroad: Private Property Rights, National Sovereignty, and the Cost of Environmental Protection." *University of Cincinnati Law Review* 65 (1997): 539–93.

Howes, David. "Comparing Cultural Appropriation in the American Southwest: Lessons from the Hopi Experience Concerning Uses of Law." *Canadian Journal of Law and Society* 10 (1995): 129–54.

Macpherson, C. B. "A Political Theory of Property." In Macpherson, *Democratic Theory: Essays in Retrieval.* Oxford, England: Clarendon, 1983.

Matsushita, Mitsuo. "A Japanese Perspective on Intellectual Property Rights and the GATT." *Columbia Business Law Review* 70 (1992): 81–95.

Moga, Thomas. "Recent Intellectual Property Developments in Japan, Taiwan, and China." *University of Detroit Mercy Law Review* 70 (1993): 313–26.

Newton, Nell. "Compensation, Reparations, and Restitution: Indian Property Claims in the United States." *Georgia Law Review* 28 (1994): 453–67.

Radin, Margaret Jane. "Diagnosing the Takings Problem." *NOMOS XXXIII: Compensatory Justice,* 248–78. New York: New York University Press, 1991.

Springer, James. "American Indians and the Law of Real Property in Colonial New England." *American Journal of Legal History* 30 (1986): 25–58.

Sunstein, Cass. "Lochner's Legacy." *Columbia Law Review 87* (1987): 873–979.

32

JOHN LOCKE

Of Property

25. Whether we consider natural reason, which tells us that men, being once born, have a right to their preservation, and consequently to meat and drink and such other things as nature affords for their subsistence; or revelation, which gives us an account of those grants God made of the world to Adam, and to Noah and his sons; it is very clear that God, as King David says (Psalm CXV. 16), "has given the earth to the children of men," given it to mankind in common. But this being supposed, it seems to some a very great difficulty how any one should ever come to have a property in anything. I will not content myself to answer that if it be difficult to make out property upon a supposition that God gave the world to Adam and his posterity in common, it is impossible that any man but one universal monarch should have any property upon a supposition that God gave the world to Adam and his heirs in succession, exclusive of all the rest of his posterity. But I shall endeavor to show how men might come to have a property in several parts of that which God gave to mankind in common, and that without any express compact of all the commoners.

26. God, who has given the world to men in common, has also given them reason to make use of it to the best advantage of life and convenience. The earth and all that is therein is given to men for the support and comfort of their being. And though all the fruits it naturally produces and beasts it feeds belong to mankind in common, as they are produced by the spontaneous hand of nature; and nobody has originally a private dominion exclusive of the rest of mankind in any of them, as they are thus in their natural state; yet, being given for the use of men, there must of necessity be a means to appropriate them some way or other before they can be of any use or at all beneficial to any particular man. The fruit or venison which nourishes the wild Indian, who knows no enclosure and is still a tenant in common, must be his, and so his, i.e., a part of him, that another can no longer have any right to it before it can do him any good for the support of his life.

27. Though the earth and all inferior creatures be common to all men, yet every man has a property in his own person; this nobody has any right to but himself. The labor of his body and the work of his hands, we may say, are properly his. Whatsoever then he removes out of the state that nature has provided and left it in, he has mixed his labor with, and joined to it something that is his own, and thereby makes it his property. It being by him removed from the common state nature has placed it in, it has by this labor something annexed to it that excludes the common right of other men. For this labor being the unquestionable property of the laborer, no man but he can have a right to what that is once joined to, at least where there is enough and as good left in common for others.

28. He that is nourished by the acorns he picked up under an oak, or the apples he gathered from the trees in the wood, has certainly appropriated them to himself. Nobody can deny but the nourishment is his. I ask, then, When did they begin to be his? When he digested or when he ate or when he boiled or when he brought them home? Or when he picked them up? And it is plain, if the first gathering made them not his, nothing else could. That labor put a distinction between them and common; that added something to them more than nature, the common mother of all, had done; and so they became his private right. And will anyone say he had no right to those acorns or apples he thus appropriated because he had not the consent of all mankind to make them his? Was it a robbery thus to assume to himself what belonged to all in common? If such a consent as that was necessary, man had starved, notwithstanding the plenty God had given him. We see in commons, which remain so by compact, that it is the taking any part of what is common and removing it out of the state nature leaves it in which begins the property, without which the common is of no use. And the taking of this or that part does not depend on the express consent of all the commoners. Thus the grass my horse has bit, the turfs my servant has cut, and the ore I have digged in any place where I have a right to them in common with others, become my property without the assignation or consent of anybody. The labor that was mine, removing them out of that common state they were in, has fixed my property in them.

29. By making an explicit consent of every commoner necessary to any one's appropriating to himself any part of what is given in common, children or servants could not cut the meat which their father or master had provided for them in common without assigning to every one his peculiar part. Though the water running in the fountain be every one's, yet who can doubt but that in the pitcher is his only who drew it out? His labor has taken it out of the hands of nature where it was common and belonged equally to all her children, and has thereby appropriated it to himself.

30. Thus this law of reason makes the deer that Indian's who has killed it; it is allowed to be his goods who has bestowed his labor upon it, though before it was the common right of every one. And amongst those who are counted the civilized part of mankind, who have made and multiplied positive laws to determine property, this original law of nature, for the beginning of property in what was before common, still takes place; and by virtue thereof what fish any one catches in the ocean, that great and still remaining common of mankind, or what ambergris any one takes up here, is, by the labor that removes it out of that common state nature left it in, made his property who takes that pains about it. And even amongst us, the hare that anyone is hunting is thought his who pursues her during the chase; for, being a beast that is still looked upon as common and no man's private possession, whoever has employed so much labor about any of that kind as to find and pursue her has thereby removed her from the state of nature wherein she was common, and has begun a property.

31. It will perhaps be objected to this that "if gathering the acorns, or other fruits of the earth, etc., makes a right to them, then any one man may engross as much as he will." To which I answer: not so. The same law of nature that does by this means give us property does also bound that property, too. "God has given us all things richly" (1 Tim. vi. 17), is the voice of reason confirmed by inspiration. But how far has he given it us? To enjoy. As much as any one can make use of to any advantage of life before it spoils, so much he may by his labor fix a property in; whatever is beyond this is more than his share and belongs to others. Nothing was made by God for man to spoil or destroy. And thus considering the plenty of natural provisions there was a long time in the world, and the few spenders, and to how small a part of that provision the industry of one man could extend itself and engross it to the prejudice of others, especially keeping within the bounds set by reason of what might serve for his use, there could be then little room for quarrels or contentions about property so established.

32. But the chief matter of property being now not the fruits of the earth and the beasts that subsist on it, but the earth itself, as that which takes in and carries with it all the rest, I think it is plain that property in that, too, is acquired as the former. As much land as a man tills, plants, improves, cultivates, and can use the products of, so much is his property. He by his labor does, as it were, enclose it from the common. Nor will it invalidate his right to say everybody else has an equal title to it, and therefore he cannot appropriate, he cannot enclose, without the consent of all his fellow commoners—all mankind. God, when he gave the world in common to all mankind, commanded man also to labor, and the penury of his condition required it of him. God and his reason commanded him to subdue the earth, i.e., improve it for the benefit of life, and therein lay out something upon it that was his own, his labor. He that in obedience to this command of God subdued, tilled, and sowed any part of it, thereby annexed to it something that was his property, which another had no title to, nor could without injury take from him.

33. Nor was this appropriation of any parcel of land by improving it any prejudice to any other man, since there was still enough and as good left, and more than the yet unprovided could use. So that, in effect, there was never the less left for others because of his enclosure for himself; for he that leaves as much as another can make use of does as good as take nothing at all. Nobody could think himself injured by the drinking of another man, though he took a good draught, who had a whole river of the same water left him to quench his thirst; and the case of land and water, where there is enough for both, is perfectly the same.

34. God gave the world to men in common; but since he gave it them for their benefit and the greatest conveniences of life they were capable to draw from it, it cannot be supposed he meant it should always remain common and uncultivated. He gave it to the use of the industrious and rational—and labor was to be his title to it—not to the fancy or covetousness of the quarrelsome and contentious. He that had

as good left for his improvement as was already taken up needed not complain, ought not to meddle with what was already improved by another's labor; if he did, it is plain he desired the benefit of another's pains which he had no right to, and not the ground which God had given him in common with others to labor on, and whereof there was as good left as that already possessed, and more than he knew what to do with, or his industry could reach to.

35. It is true, in land that is common in England or any other country where there are plenty of people under government who have money and commerce, no one can enclose or appropriate any part without the consent of all his fellow commoners; because this is left common by compact, i.e., by the law of the land, which is not to be violated. And though it be common in respect of some men, it is not so to all mankind, but is the joint property of this country or this parish. Besides, the remainder after such enclosure would not be as good to the rest of the commoners as the whole was when they could all make use of the whole; whereas in the beginning and first peopling of the great common of the world it was quite otherwise. The law man was under was rather for appropriating. God commanded, and his wants forced, him to labor. That was his property which could not be taken from him wherever he had fixed it. And hence subduing or cultivating the earth and having dominion, we see, are joined together. The one gave title to the other. So that God, by commanding to subdue, gave authority so far to appropriate; and the condition of human life which requires labor and material to work on necessarily introduces private possessions.

36. The measure of property nature has well set by the extent of men's labor and the conveniences of life. No man's labor could subdue or appropriate all, nor could his enjoyment consume more than a small part, so that it was impossible for any man, this way, to entrench upon the right of another, or acquire to himself a property to the prejudice of his neighbor, who would still have room for as good and as large a possession—after the other had taken out his—as before it was appropriated. This measure did confine every man's possession to a very moderate proportion, and such as he might appropriate to himself without injury to anybody, in the first ages of the world, when men were more in danger to be lost by wandering from their company in the then vast wilderness of the earth than to be straitened for want of room to plant in. And the same measure may be allowed still without prejudice to anybody, as full as the world seems; for supposing a man or family in the state they were at first peopling of the world by the children of Adam or Noah, let him plant in some inland, vacant places of America; we shall find that the possessions he could make himself, upon the measures we have given, would not be very large, nor, even to this day, prejudice the rest of mankind, or give them reason to complain or think themselves injured by this man's encroachment, though the race of men have now spread themselves to all the corners of the world and do infinitely exceed the small number which was at the beginning. Nay, the extent of ground is of so little value without labor that I have heard it affirmed that in Spain itself a man may be permitted to plough, sow, and reap, without being disturbed, upon land he has no other title to but only his making use of it. But, on the contrary, the inhabitants think themselves beholden to him who by his industry on neglected and consequently waste land has increased the stock of corn which they wanted. But be this as it will, which I lay no stress on, this I dare boldly affirm—that the same rule of property, viz., that every man should have as much as he could make use of, would hold still in the world without straitening anybody, since there is land enough in the world to suffice double the inhabitants, had not the invention of money and the tacit agreement of men to put a value on it introduced—by consent—larger possessions and a right to them; which, how it has done, I shall by-and-by show more at large.

37. This is certain, that in the beginning, before the desire of having more than man needed had altered the intrinsic value of things which depends only on their usefulness to the life of man, or had agreed that a little piece of yellow metal which would keep without wasting or decay should be worth a great piece of flesh or a whole heap of corn, though men had a right to appropriate, by their labor, each one to himself as much of the things of nature as he could use, yet this could not be much, nor to the prejudice of others, where the same plenty was still left to those who would use the same industry. To which let me add that he who appropriates land to himself by his labor does not lessen but increase the common stock of mankind; for the provisions serving to the support of human life produced by one acre of

enclosed and cultivated land are—to speak much within compass—ten times more than those which are yielded by an acre of land of an equal richness lying waste in common. And therefore he that encloses land, and has a greater plenty of the conveniences of life from ten acres than he could have from a hundred left to nature, may truly be said to give ninety acres to mankind; for his labor now supplies him with provisions out of ten acres which were by the product of a hundred lying in common. I have here rated the improved land very low in making its product but as ten to one, when it is much nearer a hundred to one; for I ask whether in the wild woods and uncultivated waste of America, left to nature, without any improvement, tillage, or husbandry, a thousand acres yield the needy and wretched inhabitants as many conveniences of life as ten acres of equally fertile land do in Devonshire, where they are well cultivated.

Before the appropriation of land, he who gathered as much of the wild fruit, killed, caught, or tamed as many of the beasts as he could; he that so employed his pains about any of the spontaneous products of nature as any way to alter them from the state which nature put them in, by placing any of his labor on them, did thereby acquire a propriety in them; but, if they perished in his possession without their due use, if the fruits rotted or the venison putrified before he could spend it, he offended against the common law of nature and was liable to be punished; he invaded his neighbor's share, for he had no right further than his use called for any of them and they might serve to afford him conveniences of life.

38. The same measures governed the possession of land, too: whatsoever he tilled and reaped, laid up and made use of before it spoiled, that was his peculiar right; whatsoever he enclosed and could feed and make use of, the cattle and product was also his. But if either the grass of his enclosure rotted on the ground, or the fruit of his planting perished without gathering and laying up, this part of the earth, notwithstanding his enclosure, was still to be looked on as waste and might be the possession of any other. Thus, at the beginning, Cain might take as much ground as he could till and make it his own land, and yet leave enough to Abel's sheep to feed on; a few acres would serve for both their possessions. But as families increased and industry enlarged their stocks, their possessions enlarged with the need of them; but yet it was commonly without any fixed property in the ground they made use of till they incorporated, settled themselves together, and built cities; and then, by consent, they came in time to set out the bounds of their distinct territories, and agree on limits between them and their neighbors, and by laws within themselves settled the properties of those of the same society; for we see that in that part of the world which was first inhabited, and therefore like to be best peopled, even as low down as Abraham's time they wandered with their flocks and their herds, which was their substance, freely up and down; and this Abraham did in a country where he was a stranger. Whence it is plain that at least a great part of the land lay in common, that the inhabitants valued it not, nor claimed property in any more than they made use of. But when there was not room enough in the same place for their herds to feed together, they, by consent, as Abraham and Lot did (Gen. xiii. 5), separated and enlarged their pasture where it best liked them. And for the same reason Esau went from his father and his brother and planted in Mount Seir (Gen. xxxvi. 6).

39. And thus, without supposing any private dominion and property in Adam over all the world exclusive of all other men, which can in no way be proven, nor any one's property be made out from it; but supposing the world given, as it was, to the children of men in common, we see how labor could make men distinct titles to several parcels of it for their private uses, wherein there could be no doubt of right, no room for quarrel.

40. Nor is it so strange, as perhaps before consideration it may appear, that the property of labor should be able to overbalance the community of land; for it is labor indeed that put the difference of value on everything; and let anyone consider what the difference is between an acre of land planted with tobacco or sugar, sown with wheat or barley, and an acre of the same land lying in common without any husbandry upon it, and he will find that the improvement of labor makes the far greater part of the value. I think it will be but a very modest computation to say that, of the products of the earth useful to the life of man, nine-tenths are the effects of labor; nay, if we will rightly estimate things as they come to our use and cast up the several expenses about them, what in them is purely owing to nature, and what to labor, we shall find that in most of them ninety-nine hundredths are wholly to be put on the account of labor.

41. There cannot be a clearer demonstration of anything than several nations of the Americans are of

this, who are rich in land and poor in all the comforts of life; whom nature having furnished as liberally as any other people with the materials of plenty, i.e., a fruitful soil, apt to produce in abundance what might serve for food, raiment, and delight, yet for want of improving it by labor have not one-hundredth part of the conveniences we enjoy. And a king of a large and fruitful territory there feeds, lodges, and is clad worse than a day-laborer in England.

42. To make this a little clear, let us but trace some of the ordinary provisions of life through their several progresses before they come to our use and see how much of their value they receive from human industry. Bread, wine, and cloth are things of daily use and great plenty; yet, notwithstanding, acorns, water, and leaves, or skins must be our bread, drink, and clothing, did not labor furnish us with these more useful commodities; for whatever bread is more worth than acorns, wine than water, and cloth or silk than leaves, skins, or moss, that is wholly owing to labor and industry: the one of these being the food and raiment which unassisted nature furnishes us with; the other, provisions which our industry and pains prepare for us, which how much they exceed the other in value when anyone has computed, he will then see how much labor makes the far greatest part of the value of things we enjoy in this world. And the ground which produces the materials is scarce to be reckoned in as any, or at most but a very small, part of it; so little that even amongst us land that is left wholly to nature, that has no improvement or pasturage, tillage, or planting, is called, as indeed it is, "waste"; and we shall find the benefit of it amount to little more than nothing.

This shows how much numbers of men are to be preferred to largeness of dominions; and that the increase of lands and the right employing of them is the great art of government; and that prince who shall be so wise and godlike as by established laws of liberty to secure protection and encouragement to the honest industry of mankind, against the oppression of power and narrowness of party, will quickly be too hard for his neighbors; but this by the bye.

To return to the argument in hand.

43. An acre of land that bears here twenty bushels of wheat, and another in America which with the same husbandry would do the like, are, without doubt, of the same natural intrinsic value; but yet the benefit mankind receives from the one in a year is worth £5, and from the other possibly not worth a penny if all the profit an Indian received from it were to be valued and sold here; at least, I may truly say, not one-thousandth. It is labor, then, which puts the greatest part of the value upon land, without which it would scarcely be worth anything; it is to that we owe the greatest part of all its useful products; for all that the straw, bran, bread of that acre of wheat is more worth than the product of an acre of as good land which lies waste is all the effect of labor. For it is not barely the ploughman's pains, the reaper's and thresher's toil, and the baker's sweat [that] is to be counted into the bread we eat; the labor of those who broke the oxen, who digged and wrought the iron and stones, who felled and framed the timber employed about the plough, mill, oven, or any other utensils, which are a vast number requisite to this corn, from its being seed to be sown to its being made bread, must all be charged on the account of labor, and received as an effect of that; nature and the earth furnished only the almost worthless materials as in themselves. It would be a strange "catalogue of things that industry provided and made use of, about every loaf of bread" before it came to our use, if we could trace them: iron, wood, leather, bark, timber, stone, bricks, coals, lime, cloth, dyeing drugs, pitch, tar, masts, ropes, and all the materials made use of in the ship that brought any of the commodities used by any of the workmen to any part of the work; all which it would be almost impossible, at least too long, to reckon up.

44. From all which it is evident that, though the things of nature are given in common, yet man, by being master of himself and proprietor of his own person and the actions or labor of it, had still in himself the great foundation of property; and that which made up the greater part of what he applied to the support or comfort of his being, when invention and arts had improved the conveniences of life, was perfectly his own and did not belong in common to others.

45. Thus labor, in the beginning, gave a right of property wherever anyone was pleased to employ it upon what was common, which remained a long while the far greater part and is yet more than mankind makes use of. Men, at first, for the most part contented themselves with what unassisted nature offered to their necessities; and though afterwards, in some parts of the world—where the increase of people and stock, with the use of money, had made land scarce and so of some value—the several communities settled the bounds of their distinct territories and, by laws within themselves, regulated the properties of

the private men of their society, and so, by compact and agreement, settled the property which labor and industry began. And the leagues that have been made between several states and kingdoms either expressly or tacitly disowning all claim and right to the land in the others' possession have, by common consent, given up their pretenses to their natural common right which originally they had to those countries, and so have, by positive agreement, settled a property amongst themselves in distinct parts and parcels of the earth; yet there are still great tracts of ground to be found which—the inhabitants thereof not having joined with the rest of mankind in the consent of the use of their common money—lie waste, and are more than the people who dwell on it do or can make use of, and so still lie in common; though this can scarce happen amongst that part of mankind that have consented to the use of money.

46. The greatest part of things really useful to the life of man, and such as the necessity of subsisting made the first commoners of the world look after, as it does the Americans now, are generally things of short duration, such as, if they are not consumed by use, will decay and perish of themselves; gold, silver, and diamonds are things that fancy or agreement has put the value on, more than real use and the necessary support of life. Now of those good things which nature has provided in common, every one had a right, as has been said, to as much as he could use, and property in all that he could effect with his labor; all that his industry could extend to, to alter from the state nature had put it in, was his. He that gathered a hundred bushels of acorns or apples had thereby a property in them; they were his goods as soon as gathered. He was only to look that he used them before they spoiled, else he took more than his share and robbed others. And indeed it was a foolish thing, as well as dishonest, to hoard up more than he could make use of. If he gave away a part to anybody else so that it perished not uselessly in his possession, these he also made use of. And if he also bartered away plums that would have rotted in a week for nuts that would last good for his eating a whole year, he did no injury; he wasted not the common stock, destroyed no part of the portion of the goods that belonged to others, so long as nothing perished uselessly in his hands. Again, if he would give his nuts for a piece of metal, pleased with its color, or exchange his sheep for shells, or wool for a sparkling pebble or a diamond, and keep those by him all his life, he invaded not the right of others; he might heap as much of these durable things as he pleased; the exceeding of the bounds of his just property not lying in the largeness of his possession, but the perishing of anything uselessly in it.

47. And thus came in the use of money—some lasting thing that men might keep without spoiling, and that by mutual consent men would take in exchange for the truly useful but perishable supports of life.

48. And as different degrees of industry were apt to give men possessions in different proportions, so this invention of money gave them the opportunity to continue and enlarge them; for supposing an island, separate from all possible commerce with the rest of the world, wherein there were but a hundred families, but there were sheep, horses, and cows, with other useful animals, wholesome fruits, and land enough for corn for a hundred thousand times as many, but nothing in the island, either because of its commonness or perishableness, fit to supply the place of money; what reason could anyone have there to enlarge his possessions beyond the use of his family and a plentiful supply to its consumption, either in what their own industry produced or they could barter for like perishable, useful commodities with others? Where there is not something both lasting and scarce, and so valuable to be hoarded up, there men will not be apt to enlarge their possessions of land were it ever so rich, ever so free for them to take. For, I ask, what would a man value ten thousand or a hundred thousand acres of excellent land, ready cultivated and well stocked, too, with cattle, in the middle of the inland parts of America where he had no hopes of commerce with other parts of the world to draw money to him by the sale of the product? It would not be worth the enclosing, and we should see him give up again to the wild common of nature whatever was more than would supply the conveniences of life to be had there for him and his family.

49. Thus in the beginning all the world was America, and more so than that is now; for no such thing as money was anywhere known. Find out something that has the use and value of money amongst his neighbors, you shall see the same man will begin presently to enlarge his possessions.

50. But since gold and silver, being little useful to the life of man in proportion to food, raiment, and carriage, has its value only from the consent of men, whereof labor yet makes, in great part, the measure, it

is plain that men have agreed to a disproportionate and unequal possession of the earth, they having, by a tacit and voluntary consent, found out a way how a man may fairly possess more land than he himself can use the product of, by receiving in exchange for the overplus gold and silver which may be hoarded up without injury to any one, these metals not spoiling or decaying in the hands of the possessor. This partage of things in an inequality of private possessions men have made practicable out of the bounds of society and without compact, only by putting a value on gold and silver, and tacitly agreeing in the use of money; for, in governments, the laws regulate the right of property, and the possession of land is determined by positive constitutions.

51. And thus, I think, it is very easy to conceive how labor could at first begin a title of property in the common things of nature, and how the spending it upon our uses bounded it. So that there could then be no reason of quarreling about title, nor any doubt about the largeness of possession it gave. Right and convenience went together; for as a man had a right to all he could employ his labor upon, so he had no temptation to labor for more than he could make use of. This left no room for controversy about the title, nor for encroachment on the right of others; what portion a man carved to himself was easily seen, and it was useless, as well as dishonest, to carve himself too much or take more than he needed.

33

ROBERT NOZICK

From *Anarchy, State, and Utopia*

LOCKE'S THEORY OF ACQUISITION

Before we turn to consider other theories of justice in detail, we must introduce an additional bit of complexity into the structure of the entitlement theory. This is best approached by considering Locke's attempt to specify a principle of justice in acquisition. Locke views property rights in an unowned object as originating through someone's mixing his labor with it. This gives rise to many questions. What are the boundaries of what labor is mixed with? If a private astronaut clears a place on Mars, has he mixed his labor with (so that he comes to own) the whole planet, the whole uninhabited universe, or just a particular plot? Which plot does an act bring under ownership? The minimal (possibly disconnected) area such that an act decreases entropy in that area, and not elsewhere? Can virgin land (for the purposes of ecological investigation by high-flying airplane) come under ownership by a Lockean process? Building a fence around a territory presumably would make one the owner of only the fence (and the land immediately underneath it).

Why does mixing one's labor with something make one the owner of it? Perhaps because one owns one's labor, and so one comes to own a previously unowned thing that becomes permeated with what one owns. Ownership seeps over into the rest. But why isn't mixing what I own with what I don't own a way of losing what I own rather than a way of gaining what I don't? If I own a can of tomato juice and spill it in the sea so that its molecules (made radioactive, so I can check this) mingle evenly throughout the sea, do I thereby come to own the sea, or have I foolishly dissipated my tomato juice? Perhaps the idea, instead, is that laboring on something improves it and makes it more valuable; and anyone is entitled to own a thing whose value he has created. (Reinforcing this, perhaps, is the view that laboring is unpleasant. If some people made things effortlessly, as the cartoon characters in *The Yellow Submarine* trail flowers in their wake, would they have lesser claim to their own products whose making didn't *cost* them anything?) Ignore the fact that laboring on something may make it less valuable (spraying pink enamel paint on a piece of driftwood that you have found). Why should one's entitlement extend to the whole object rather than just to the *added value* one's labor has produced? (Such reference to value might also serve to delimit the extent of ownership; for example, substitute "increases the value of" for "decreases entropy in" in the above entropy criterion.) No workable or coherent value-added property scheme has yet been devised, and any such scheme presumably would fall to objections (similar to those) that fell the theory of Henry George.

It will be implausible to view improving an object as giving full ownership to it, if the stock of unowned objects that might be improved is limited. For an object's coming under one person's ownership changes the situation of all others. Whereas previously they were at liberty (in Hohfeld's sense) to use the object, they now no longer are. This change in the situation of others (by removing their liberty to act on a previously unowned object) need not worsen their situation. If I appropriate a grain of sand from Coney Island, no one else may now do as they will with *that* grain of sand. But there are plenty of other grains of sand left for them to do the same with. Or if not grains of sand, then other things. Alternatively, the things I do with the grain of sand I appropriate might improve the position of others, counterbalancing their loss of the liberty to use that grain. The crucial point is whether appropriation of an unowned object worsens the situation of others.

Locke's proviso that there be "enough and as good left in common for others" (sect. 27) is meant to ensure that the situation of others is not worsened. (If this proviso is met is there any motivation for his further condition of nonwaste?) It is often said that this proviso once held but now no longer does. But there appears to be an argument for the conclusion that if the proviso no longer holds, then it cannot ever have held so as to yield permanent and inheritable property rights. Consider the first person *Z* for whom there is not enough and as good left to appropriate. The last person *Y* to appropriate left *Z* without his previous liberty to act on an object, and so worsened *Z*'s situation. So *Y*'s appropriation is not allowed under Locke's proviso. Therefore the next to last person *X* to appropriate left *Y* in a worse position, for *X*'s act ended permissible appropriation. Therefore *X*'s appropriation wasn't permissible. But then the appropriator two from last, *W*, ended permissible appropriation and so, since it worsened *X*'s position, *W*'s appropriation wasn't permissible. And so on back to the first person *A* to appropriate a permanent property right.

This argument, however, proceeds too quickly. Someone may be made worse off by another's appropriation in two ways: first, by losing the opportunity to improve his situation by a particular appropriation or any one; and second, by no longer being able to use freely (without appropriation) what he previously could. A *stringent* requirement that another not be made worse off by an appropriation would exclude the first way if nothing else counterbalances the diminution in opportunity, as well as the second. A *weaker* requirement would exclude the second way, though not the first. With the weaker requirement, we cannot zip back so quickly from *Z* to *A*, as in the above argument; for though person *Z* can no longer *appropriate*, there may remain some for him to *use* as before. In this case *Y*'s appropriation would not violate the weaker Lockean condition. (With less remaining that people are at liberty to use, users might face more inconvenience, crowding, and so on; in that way the situation of others might be worsened, unless appropriation stopped far short of such a point.) It is arguable that no one legitimately can complain if the weaker provision is satisfied. However, since this is less clear than in the case of the more stringent proviso, Locke may have intended this stringent proviso by "enough and as good" remaining, and perhaps he meant the non-waste condition to delay the end point from which the argument zips back.

Is the situation of persons who are unable to appropriate (there being no more accessible and useful unowned objects) worsened by a system allowing appropriation and permanent property? Here enter the various familiar social considerations favoring private property: it increases the social product by putting means of production in the hands of those who can use them most efficiently (profitably); experimentation is encouraged, because with separate persons controlling resources, there is no one person or small group whom someone with a new idea must convince to try it out; private property enables people to decide on the pattern and types of risks they wish to bear, leading to specialized types of risk bearing; private property protects future persons by leading some to hold back resources from current consumption for future markets; it provides alternate sources of employment for unpopular persons who don't have to convince any one person or small group to hire them, and so on. These considerations enter a Lockean theory to support the claim that appropriation of private property satisfies the intent behind the "enough and as good left over" proviso, *not* as a utilitarian justification of property. They enter to rebut the claim that because the proviso is violated no natural right to private property can arise by a Lockean process. The difficulty in working such an argument to show that the proviso is satisfied is in fixing the appropriate base line for comparison. Lockean appropriation makes people no worse off than they would be *how?* This question of fixing the baseline needs more detailed investigation than we are able to give it here. It would be desirable to have an estimate of the general economic importance of original appropriation in order to see how much leeway there is for differing theories of appropriation and of the location of the baseline. Perhaps this importance can be measured by the percentage of all income that is based upon untransformed raw materials and given resources (rather than upon human actions), mainly rental income representing the unimproved value of land, and the price of raw material *in situ,* and by the percentage of current wealth which represents such income in the past.[1]

We should note that it is not only persons favoring *private* property who need a theory of how property rights legitimately originate. Those believing in collective property, for example those believing that a group of persons living in an area jointly own the territory, or its mineral resources, also must provide a theory of how such property rights arise; they must show why the persons living there have rights to determine what is done with the land and resources there that persons living elsewhere don't have (with regard to the same land and resources).

THE PROVISO

Whether or not Locke's particular theory of appropriation can be spelled out so as to handle various difficulties, I assume that any adequate theory of justice in acquisition will contain a proviso similar to the weaker of the ones we have attributed to Locke. A process normally giving rise to a permanent bequeathable property right in a previously unowned thing will not do so if the position of others no longer at liberty to use the thing is thereby worsened. It is important to specify *this* particular mode of worsening the situation of others, for the proviso does not encompass other modes. It does not include the worsening due to more limited opportunities to appropriate (the first way above, corresponding to the more stringent condition), and it does not include how I "worsen" a seller's position if I appropriate materials to make some of what he is selling, and then enter into competition with him. Someone whose appropriation otherwise would violate the proviso still may appropriate provided he compensates the others so that their situation is not thereby worsened; unless he does compensate these others, his appropriation will violate the proviso of the principle of justice in acquisition and will be an illegitimate one.[2] A theory of appropriation incorporating this Lockean proviso will handle correctly the cases (objections to the theory lacking the proviso) where someone appropriates the total supply of something necessary for life.[3]

A theory which includes this proviso in its principle of justice in acquisition must also contain a more complex principle of justice in transfer. Some reflection of the proviso about appropriation constrains later actions. If my appropriating all of a certain substance violates the Lockean proviso, then so does my appropriating some and purchasing all the rest from others who obtained it without otherwise violating the Lock-

---

[1]I have not seen a precise estimate. David Friedman, *The Machinery of Freedom* (N.Y.: Harper & Row, 1973), pp. xiv, xv, discusses this issue and suggests 5 percent of U.S. national income as an upper limit for the first two factors mentioned. However he does not attempt to estimate the percentage of current wealth which is based upon such income in the past. (The vague notion of "based upon" merely indicates a topic needing investigation.)

[2]Fourier held that since the process of civilization had deprived the members of society of certain liberties (to gather, pasture, engage in the chase), a socially guaranteed minimum provision for the persons was justified as compensation for the loss (Alexander Gray, *The Socialist Tradition* (New York: Harper & Row, 1968), p. 188). But this puts the point too strongly. This compensation would be due those persons, if any, for whom the process of civilization was a *net loss,* for whom the benefits of civilization did not counterbalance being deprived of these particular liberties.

[3]For example, Rashdall's case of someone who comes upon the only water in the desert several miles ahead of others who also will come to it and appropriates it all. Hastings Rashdall, "The Philosophical Theory of Property," in *Property, its Duties and Rights* (London: MacMillan, 1915).

We should note Ayn Rand's theory of property rights ("Man's Rights" in *The Virtue of Selfishness* (New York: New American Library, 1964), p. 94), wherein these follow from the right to life, since people need physical things to live. But a right to life is not a right to whatever one needs to live; other people may have rights over these other things. . . . At most, a right to life would be a right to have or strive for whatever one needs to live, provided that having it does not violate anyone else's rights. With regard to material things, the question is whether having it does violate any right of others. (Would appropriation of all unowned things do so? Would appropriating the water hole in Rashdall's example?) Since special considerations (such as the Lockean proviso) may enter with regard to material property, one *first* needs a theory of property rights before one can apply any supposed right to life (as amended above). Therefore the right to life cannot provide the foundation for a theory of property rights.

ean proviso. If the proviso excludes someone's appropriating all the drinkable water in the world, it also excludes his purchasing it all. (More weakly, and messily, it may exclude his charging certain prices for some of his supply.) This proviso (almost?) never will come into effect; the more someone acquires of a scarce substance which others want, the higher the price of the rest will go, and the more difficult it will become for him to acquire it all. But still, we can imagine, at least, that something like this occurs: someone makes simultaneous secret bids to the separate owners of a substance, each of whom sells assuming he can easily purchase more from the other owners; or some natural catastrophe destroys all of the supply of something except that in one person's possession. The total supply could not be permissibly appropriated by one person at the beginning. His later acquisition of it all does not show that the original appropriation violated the proviso (even by a reverse argument similar to the one above that tried to zip back from *Z* to *A*). Rather, it is the combination of the original appropriation *plus* all the later transfers and actions that violates the Lockean proviso.

Each owner's title to his holding includes the historical shadow of the Lockean proviso on appropriation. This excludes his transferring it into an agglomeration that does violate the Lockean proviso and excludes his using it in a way, in coordination with others or independently of them, so as to violate the proviso by making the situation of others worse than their baseline situation. Once it is known that someone's ownership runs afoul of the Lockean proviso, there are stringent limits on what he may do with (what it is difficult any longer unreservedly to call) "his property." Thus a person may not appropriate the only water hole in a desert and charge what he will. Nor may he charge what he will if he possesses one, and unfortunately it happens that all the water holes in the desert dry up, except for his. This unfortunate circumstance, admittedly no fault of his, brings into operation the Lockean proviso and limits his property rights.[4] Similarly, an owner's property right in the only island in an area does not allow him to order a castaway from a shipwreck off his island as a trespasser, for this would violate the Lockean proviso.

Notice that the theory does not say that owners do have these rights, but that the rights are overridden to avoid some catastrophe. (Overridden rights do not disappear; they leave a trace of a sort absent in the cases under discussion.) There is no such external (and *ad hoc?*) overriding. Considerations internal to the theory of property itself, to its theory of acquisition and appropriation, provide the means for handling such cases. The results, however, may be coextensive with some condition about catastrophe, since the baseline for comparison is so low as compared to the productiveness of a society with private appropriation that the question of the Lockean proviso being violated arises only in the case of catastrophe (or a desert-island situation).

The fact that someone owns the total supply of something necessary for others to stay alive does *not* entail that his (or anyone's) appropriation of anything left some people (immediately or later) in a situation worse than the baseline one. A medical researcher who synthesizes a new substance that effectively treats a certain disease and who refuses to sell except on his terms does not worsen the situation of others by depriving them of whatever he has appropriated. The others easily can possess the same materials he appropriated; the researcher's appropriation or purchase of chemicals didn't make those chemicals scarce in a way so as to violate the Lockean proviso. Nor would someone else's purchasing the total supply of the synthesized substance from the medical researcher. The fact that the medical researcher uses easily available chemicals to synthesize the drug no more violates the Lockean proviso than does the fact that the only surgeon able to perform a particular operation eats easily obtainable food in order to stay alive and to have the energy to work. This shows that the Lockean proviso is not an "end-state principle"; it focuses on a particular way that appropriative actions affect others, and not on the structure of the situation that results.

Intermediate between someone who takes all of the public supply and someone who makes the total supply out of easily obtainable substances is someone who appropriates the total supply of something in a way that does not deprive the others of it. For example, someone finds a new substance in an out-of-the-

[4]The situation would be different if his waterhole didn't dry up, due to special precautions he took to prevent this. Compare our discussion of the case in the text with Hayek, *The Constitution of Liberty,* p. 136; and also with Ronald Hamowy, "Hayek's Concept of Freedom; A Critique," *New Individualist Review,* April 1961, pp. 28–31.

way place. He discovers that it effectively treats a certain disease and appropriates the total supply. He does not worsen the situation of others; if he did not stumble upon the substance no one else would have, and the others would remain without it. However, as time passes, the likelihood increases that others would have come across the substance; upon this fact might be based a limit to his property right in the substance so that others are not below their baseline position; for example, its bequest might be limited. The theme of someone worsening another's situation by depriving him of something he otherwise would possess may also illuminate the example of patents. An inventor's patent does not deprive others of an object which would not exist if not for the inventor. Yet patents would have this effect on others who independently invent the object. Therefore, these independent inventors, upon whom the burden of proving independent discovery may rest, should not be excluded from utilizing their own invention as they wish (including selling it to others). Furthermore, a known inventor drastically lessens the chances of actual independent invention. For persons who know of an invention usually will not try to reinvent it, and the notion of independent discovery here would be murky at best. Yet we may assume that in the absence of the original invention, sometime later someone else would have come up with it. This suggests placing a time limit on patents, as a rough rule of thumb to approximate how long it would have taken, in the absence of knowledge of the invention, for independent discovery.

I believe that the free operation of a market system will not actually run afoul of the Lockean proviso. (Recall that crucial to our story in Part I of how a protective agency becomes dominant and a *de facto* monopoly is the fact that it wields force in situations of conflict, and is not merely in competition, with other agencies. A similar tale cannot be told about other businesses.) If this is correct, the proviso will not play a very important role in the activities of protective agencies and will not provide a significant opportunity for future state action. Indeed, were it not for the effects of previous *illegitimate* state action, people would not think the possibility of the proviso's being violated as of more interest than any other logical possibility. (Here I make an empirical historical claim; as does someone who disagrees with this.) This completes our indication of the complication in the entitlement theory introduced by the Lockean proviso.

34

A. M. HONORÉ

Property, Title and Redistribution

This discussion paper is concerned with the relationship between the institution of private property and the notion of economic equality. Is it inconsistent, or morally obtuse to recognize the value of the institution and at the same time to argue that each member of a society is entitled to an equal or approximately equal standard of living? I shall be particularly concerned with the argument of *R. Nozick*, in *Anarchy, State and Utopia*[1] to the effect that under a system of "just entitlements" such as he specifies there is no room to admit that the state has the right or duty to redistribute benefits so as to secure an equal or more equal spread, because "the particular rights over things fill the space of rights, leaving no room for general rights to be in a certain material condition."[2] Though *Nozick's* "just entitlements"[3] are not confined to titles to property I shall so confine myself. Rights of a more personal character could in theory be the subjects of redistribution and indeed *Nozick* discusses the case for transplanting organs from A to B in order to correct physical maldistribution of parts of the body.[4] Fascinating as such speculations may be, the physical and technical difficulties involved in such a programme would be stupendous and the moral objections to the invasion of people's bodies for whatever purpose are much stronger than they are when what is proposed is to tax or, in some cases, to expropriate. Nor can one concede the argument that the redistribution of part of what A has earned to B

[1]Oxford 1974.
[2]Nozick p. 238.
[3]Nozick pp. 150–182.
[4]Nozick p. 206.

goes beyond the invasion of property rights and amounts to a system of forced labour[5] by which A is compelled to work part of his day for B, so that redistribution of property is really an invasion of the status and freedom of the person taxed or expropriated. This is no more compelling than the Marxist argument that a wage-earner whose surplus product is appropriated by the employer is a sort of wage slave. The objection to this is not that the income-earner freely works under a system in which he knows that part of what he produces will be appropriated by his employer or transferred to other people by means of taxes. He may have no choice, if he is to earn a living, but to accept a system which he dislikes. The argument is open to attack rather because it rests on the morally questionable view that a person is entitled to keep exclusively and indefinitely for himself whatever he makes or produces. This would be true of a man working in complete isolation; no serious argument has been advanced to show that it is true of a social being.

Nozick's argument depends on accepting this questionable view. Against those who favour a principle of social justice by which things are to be distributed according to need, desert, the principle of equal claims or the like, he argues that the just allocation is the historically justifiable one. This can be ascertained, in relation to any given item of property, by asking whether the holder acquired it by a just title or derived his title justly from another who so held it, either originally or by derivation from such a just acquirer. Consequently just distribution depends on just acquisition and transfer, and redistribution is confined to those instances in which the original acquisition or the subsequent transmission of the property was unjust.

All therefore turns on what count as just principles of acquisition and transfer of title. According to *Nozick*—

1. a person who acquires a holding in accordance with the principle of justice in acquisition is entitled to that holding
2. a person who acquires a holding in accordance with the principle of justice in transfer from some one else entitled to the holding is entitled to the holding
3. no one is entitled to a holding except by (repeated) applications of 1 and 2

The complete principle of distributive justice would say simply that a distribution is just if everyone is entitled to the holdings they possess under the distribution.

What is presupposed by this set of rules for tracing title is apparently only that the principles of acquisition and transfer should be morally respectable. For acquisition something like *Locke's* theory of property is understood.[6] Transfers in a free society will be consensual. But that is only the appearance. What *Nozick* additionally presupposes, without seeking to justify, is that the interest acquired and transmitted is the ownership of property as conceived in western society on the model of Roman law.[7] He is assuming, first, that the acquirer obtains an exclusive right to the thing acquired, that he is entitled, having cleared the land, made the tool etc. to deny access and use to everyone else. Secondly he is supposing that the right acquired is of indefinite duration. The man who has made the clearing can remain there for his lifetime. He is not obliged to move on after so many years, and leave the fruits of his labour to another, nor does he lose his right by leaving. Thirdly the right is supposed to be transmissible inter vivos and on death, so that it can be sold, given, inherited, mortgaged and the like again without limit of time. Under such a system of property law, of course, the initial acquisition is decisive. Once A has cleared the land his neighbours, friends, associates and, if it comes to that, his family are obliged to look on while he enjoys and transmits his "entitlement" to whomsoever he chooses, irrespective of the fact that in a wider context they, along with him, form part of a single group[8] which is dedicated, among other objects, to the preservation of all. This system of property law, whatever its economic merits, is not self-evidently just. If the interest acquired (western type ownership) is greater than can be morally justified, then however just the methods by which A

[5]Nozick pp. 169 f, arguing that redistributive arrangements give B a sort of Property right in A. This mistake stems from the Lockean argument that we own ourselves and *hence* what we make etc. If human beings are free they cannot own themselves; their relationship to themselves and their bodies is more like one of "sovereignty" which cannot be alienated or foregone, though it can be restricted by (lawful) contract or treaty.

[6]Nozick pp. 174 ff.

[7]For an analysis see Honoré, "Ownership," in: Guest, *Oxford Essays in Jurisprudence* (London 1961).

[8]For an analysis see Honoré ARSP 61 (1975) 161.

acquires the thing in question and transfers it to X, the distribution of property under which the thing is allocated to X is not thereby saved from criticism. Indeed, quite the contrary. If the interest awarded to owners under the system is greater than can reasonably be justified on moral, as opposed to economic grounds, any distribution of property will be inherently unjust. Hence the intervention of the state will be needed if justice is to be done.

There is no doubt that the *Nozick* rules about just acquisition, transfer and distribution reproduce in outline western systems of property law based on the liberal conception of ownership. According to these notions, ownership is a permanent, exclusive and transmissible interest in property. But this type of property system is neither the only conceivable system, nor the easiest to justify from a moral point of view, nor does it predominate in those societies which are closest to a "state of nature."

In so far as the *Nozick* principles are meant to reproduce western property law they are incomplete in that they omit provision for lapse of title and for compulsory acquisition. Lapse of title is not perhaps of great moral importance, but it is worth noting that legal rules about limitation of actions and prescription embody the idea that an owner who neglects his property may be deprived of it. The acquirer (squatter or the like) obtains it by a sort of private expropriation. More important is expropriation by the state or public authority. It is not at all clear why the parts of western property law favourable to the private owner should be reproduced in the system of entitlements to the exclusion of those which favour the claims of the community. The latter, after all, balance the former. The individualistic bias of property law is corrected by the admission of state claims to tax and expropriate.

Aside from the omission of rules about lapse and compulsory acquisition one may note that *Nozick's* principles rest on the assumption that whether a justification exists for acquiring or transferring property can be decided in abstraction from the historical and social context. A just acquisition in 1066 or 1620 remains a just root of title in 1975. If this were really so one would have to say either that the acquisition of slaves is seen in retrospect always to have been unjust and that the state would have been justified in intervening in a slave-owning society to correct the injustice, or that the descendants of slave-owners are entitled to own the descendants of freed slaves. So with colonies, *mutatis mutandis*. Are we to say that as a result of the post-war movement to free colonies we now see that the acquisition of colonies, apparently valid at the time in international law and morality, was always wrong and that the international society would have been justified, had it been so minded, in intervening even in the nineteenth century to free the existing colonies and prevent further acquisitions? If so, how can we be sure that there are not equally unjustified forms of property ownership in present-day society which in fact justify state intervention in a redistributive sense? And how can we be sure in any future society that these objectionable forms of acquisition are not present? In which case, outside Utopia, the thesis advanced by *Nozick* has no application. But if the acquisition of slaves and colonies was initially just, surely some provision should be made in his system for the redistribution of entitlements when the moral basis on which they originally rested has become eviscerated. These instances would count morally as cases of lapse of title owing to changing views of right and wrong. Legally they would furnish examples of just expropriation. There would have to be a further exception in *Nozick's* system to cater for changing conditions of fact. Suppose, apart from any question of the justification for colonies, that in the nineteenth century Metropolitania occupied a deserted tract which it proceeded to colonize, building roads and irrigating the land. As a result a numerous indigenous population crowded in from the neighbouring areas. These people now claim to be free and to decide their own destinies. Whether or not colonization is in general thought a permissible form of "entitlement" the changed situation must surely change one's moral evaluation of Metropolitania's title to the formerly deserted tract. So with the Mayflowerite who bagged a large stretch of unoccupied land in 1620. If the situation is now that irrespective of title the tracts in question are occupied by people who have nowhere else to live surely the moral basis of the title of the Mayflowerite's successors must at least be open to debate. Once there was more than enough to go round, now there is not. And is the case very different if the thousands without property instead of occupying the colonies or tracts in question crowd the periphery and make claims on the unused resources inside: All this is intended to make the simple point that it is obtuse to suppose that the justification for acquiring or transmitting property could be settled once and for all at the date of acquisition or transfer. Legally it may be so, subject to the rules of lapse and expropriation. This is because of the need to frame rules of law in such a way as to ensure certainty of title. They are meant however to be applied in a context in which social and moral criticism may be directed against their operation and in which their defects may be corrected by legislation or similar means. Apart from positive law, can it seriously be maintained that the rules about what constitutes a just acquisition or transfer both express unchanging verities and, in their application to the facts of a given acquisition or transfer, are exempt from reassessment in the light of changed circumstances?

Systems of property law which diverge from the orthodox western type based on liberal conceptions of ownership are conceivable, morally defensible and have actually obtained in certain societies. To begin with the conceivable, let us take an imaginary case. Suppose that, in a "state of nature" a group of people live near a river and subsist on fish, which they catch by hand, and berries. There is great difficulty in catching fish by hand. Berries are however fairly plentiful. There are bits of metal lying around and I discover how to make one of them into a fishhook. With this invention I quadruple my catch of fish. My neighbours cannot discover the knack and I decline to tell them. They press me to lend them the fishhook or to give them the lessons in acquiring the technique. I have however acquired western notions of property law and Lockean ideas about entitlement, I point out that I have a just title to the fishhook, since according to *Nozick's* version of *Locke* they are no worse off as a result of my invention. I am therefore entitled to the exclusive, permanent and transmissible use of the fishhook. My neighbours may try their hands at finding out how to make one, of course, but if they fail they may look forward to eating berries and from time to time a bit of fish while I and those persons whom I choose to invite to a meal propose to enjoy ourselves with daily delicacies. If they object that this is unfair I shall point out (though the relevance is not obvious) that they are not actually starving. Nor am I monopolizing materials. There are other pieces of metal lying around. They are no worse off than they were before or than they would have been without my find (in fact they *are* worse off, relatively to me). As to the parrot cry that they protect me and my family from marauders, wild animals and the like, so that I ought to share my good fortune with them, I reply that they have not grasped what is implied by a system of just entitlements. Are they saying that I am not entitled to the fishhook?

One of my brighter neighbours might well answer me as follows. "I do not deny that you have a right to the fishhook. As you say you made it and you invented the system of using it to catch fish. But it does not follow that, as you assert, your right to it is exclusive, permanent and transmissible. Your views seem to be coloured by reading books about sophisticated societies. In those societies men are dedicated to increasing production, come what may, and in order to achieve that they accept institutions which to us seem very unfair. We are simple people used to sharing our fortunes and misfortunes. We recognize that you have a right to the fishhook but not that the right has the unlimited content which you assign to it. You ought to allow each of us to use it in turn. Naturally as the maker and inventor you are entitled to a greater share in the use than the rest of us individually, and if you like to call that share 'ownership' we shall not object. But please stop looking up the definition of 'ownership' in foreign books. These notions will only disrupt our way of life."

The point my neighbour is making is that a system of private property can be inherently distributive. In the system envisaged there is an "owner" in the sense of a person whose right to the use of the thing is greater than that of others, who has a residual claim if others do not want to use the thing, and in whom powers of management will be vested. He will be responsible for lending the fishhook out, it will be returned to him each evening, he will keep it in repair. But these powers of use, management and reversion fall short of western conception of ownership. In such a system the redistributive power of the state will be unnecessary unless the members of the group fail to keep the rules. For the rules themselves ensure an even distribution of property, subject to the recognition of desert and choice—a recognition which is not allowed to subvert the principle of sharing.

Is the projected system of property law obviously unjust? How does it compare with western notions of ownership? From the point of view of justice, though perhaps not of economic efficiency, it seems to compare rather favourably. It is designed to give effect to the interdependence of the members of the group and to recognize overtly that they cannot survive in isolation. It rejects the notion that I do no harm to a member of my group if as a result of my effort I am better off, and he is no worse off than he would otherwise be. That notion, which is common to the outlook of *Nozick* and *Rawls,* however much they otherwise differ, rests on the assumption that a person who is *comparatively* worse off is not worse off. But he is, and the precise wrong he suffers is that of being treated as an unequal by the more fortunate member or members of the group.

The fruits of an invention which raises production have therefore, in the projected system, to be shared, either by a system of compulsory loan or, in a weaker version, by a system of surplus sharing, under which what an owner "has in excess of his needs or is not using must be made available to other members of his group."[9]

The sort of system envisaged is unlikely to survive the division of labour, viz. specialisation. The members of the group other than the inventor are likely to feel that he can fish better than they and that they would do well to get him to fish for them. But then they must pay him. At first perhaps the payment is a fraction of the catch. Later the inventor is bemused by the idea that he is entitled to the whole product of his invention. So he argues that his neighbours owe him the whole of his catch and, if they want any of it, must pay in some other way, as by repairing his hut. As he has possession on his side his views may prevail. We slide insensibly, therefore, from a participatory to an exclusive system of property law, and it is difficult to keep alive, in a society of economic specialisation, the notion that each participates in a common enterprise. The remedy for this is not, or is only to a minor extent, a return to rotatory labour. It is rather that the community as a whole, the state, must act as the surrogate of the participatory principles. The inventor of the fishhook will have to be taxed. In that way the economic advantages of specialisation can be combined with a just, or juster distribution of the benefits derived from it. The tax will be used to give the other members of the group benefits corresponding to their former rights to use the fishhook.

There is no point in attempting to work out in detail what a participatory system of property law would be like. The idea is easy to grasp. If such a system is morally sound, then it follows that in a western-type system the intervention of the state, so far from being, as *Nozick* thinks, ruled out except in peripheral instances, (initially unjust acquisitions, subsequently unjust transfers) is essential in order to achieve justice in distribution.[10] Whether one says that this is because in a western-type system all the holdings are unjust (because they are holdings of an unjust sort of property interest) or that they were initially just but that their permanent retention cannot be justified, is debatable: the former seems more appealing. In any event either *Nozick's* conclusion is empty because the premises are never fulfilled, or if the premises are fulfilled, they do not lead to the conclusion to which they seem to lead.

If it is accepted that the sort of property system described is conceivable and morally defensible, that is sufficient to rebut the argument which denies a redistributive function to the state. It is not irrelevant, however, to draw attention to the fact that among the variety of property arrangements found in simple societies there are some which approximate to the distributive arrangement outlined. Among other things this will serve to rebut any argument that I am relying on a gimmicky obligatory principle of transfer.[11] A convenient outline of the variety of such property systems is to be found in *M. J. Herskowitz'* work.[12] They are of course multifold: apart from arrangements which resemble the western institution of ownership there are to be found types of group (e.g. family or clan) ownership, public ownership, rotating individual use (e.g. of fishing grounds) and also the sort of arrangement here envisaged, namely what may be called private ownership subject to compulsory loan or sharing. Thus among the Bushmen[13] "all kinds of food are private property" and "one who takes without the permission of the owner is liable to punishment for theft" but "one who shoots a buck or

---

[9]Herskowitz, below n. 12, p. 372

[10]Nozick, pp. 174 ff. However one interprets Locke's requirement that the acquirer must leave enough and as good in common for others (Second Treatise sec. 27) the intention behind is not satisfied unless entitlements are adjusted from time to time according to what *then* remains for others.

[11]Nozick p. 157.

[12]M. J. Herskowitz, *Economic Anthropology* (New York 1952), part IV. Property.

[13]Herskowitz pp. 321–322, citing L. Schapera, *The Khosian Peoples of South Africa, Bushmen and Hottentots* (London 1930) p. 148.

discovers a terrain where vegetable food is to be gathered is nevertheless expected to share with those who have nothing," so that "all available food, though from the point of view of customary law privately owned, is actually distributed among the members of a given group." The dividing is done by the owner and the skin, sinews etc. belong to him to deal with as he pleases. Among the Indians of the Pacific North-West[14] a man is said to have "owned" an economically important tract and this "ownership" was expressed by his "giving permission," to his fellows to exploit the locality each season but "no instance was ever heard of an 'owner' refusing to give the necessary permission. Such a thing is inconceivable." The individual "ownership" is a sort of stewardship or ownership in trust carrying with it management and the right to use but not excluding the right of others to a similar use. Among certain tribes of Hottentots[15] a person who dug a waterhole or opened a spring made this his property and all who wished to use it had to have his permission, but he was under an obligation to see that no stranger or stranger's stock was denied access to it. Among the Tswana[16] where the chief allocates (and in that sense "owns") the land he will allot cattle-posts to individuals, but not exclusively. The allocee, whose position is closest to that of the private owner, "must share with a number of other people the pastures of the place where his cattle-post is situated, although no one else may bring his cattle there without permission." Yet occupation does give a certain prior right. "If a man builds a hut and so indicates that it is not merely for temporary use, he established a form of lien over the place, and can return to it at any time."

There are also examples of what I have termed surplus sharing, which give effect to the principle that what a person has in excess of his needs, or is not using must be made available to other members of the group. Among the Eskimos the principle that "personal possession is conditioned by actual use of the property" comes into play. A fox-trap lying idle may be taken by anyone who will use it. In Greenland a man already owning a tent or large boat does not inherit another, since it is assumed that one person can never use more than one possession of this type. "Though what a person uses is generally acknowledged to be his alone any excess must be at the disposal of those who need it and can make good use of it."[17]

These examples show that there is nothing unnatural about distributive property arrangements in a simple society. The mechanism, or one of the possible mechanisms by which such arrangements are secured, is that of what it seems preferable to call private ownership subject to a trust or a duty to permit sharing. The "ownership" is not of course ownership of the classical western type, but neither is it "primitive communism." Its essential feature is that the titles to acquisition are much the same as in modern societies—finding, invention, occupation, making and the like—and the types of transfer—sale, gift, inheritance—are not necessarily dissimilar, but the type of interest acquired and transmitted is different. The principle of sharing is written into the delineation of interests of property.

There is no special reason to think that our moral consciousness is superior to that of simple societies. So if compulsory sharing commends itself to some of them it should not be dismissed out of hand for societies in which the division of labour has made those simple arrangements out of date: but in these, given the weakened social cohesion which the division of labour introduces, the central authority (the state) is needed to see that sharing takes place.

---

[14]Herskowitz pp. 332–333, citing P. Drucker "Rank, Wealth and Kinship in Northwest Coast Society," *Amer. Anth.* 41 (1939) p. 59.

[15]Herskowitz pp. 343–344, citing Schapera, above n. 13, at pp. 286–291.

[16]Herskowitz p. 344, citing L. Schapera and A. J. H. Goodwin "Work and Wealth" in *The Bantu-Speaking Tribes of South Africa* (ed. L. Schapera) pp. 156–157.

[17]Herskowitz pp. 373–374 citing K. Birket-Smith, *The Eskimos* (London 1936) pp. 148–151.

35

JONAS ALSÉN

An Introduction to Chinese Property Law

PROPERTY LAW

Property Theory

Introduction

> *There is nothing which so generally strikes the imagination, and engages the affections of mankind, as the right of property; or that sole and despotic dominion which one man claims and exercises over external things of the world, in total exclusion of the right of any other individual in the universe.*
>
> —William Blackstone, Commentaries*2.

All societies impose at least some limitations on what may be owned privately and on what may be the proper use or disposition of private property. Even a man who always claims exclusive rights, can rarely exercise those rights in total exclusion of any other. Ownership rights are seldom absolute. Many things, such as dwellings, cannot be used or transferred without having any restrictions at all placed on them. Instead of absolute rights, ownership should be seen as a bundle of rights held by the property owner. Therefore, the question of control over property becomes one of degree of ownership. Acceptable degrees of ownership are in turn enforced through a legal system.

In a socialist society, the level of permissible private ownership is lower than that in a capitalist society. In communist theory, the control of property has long been viewed as the key to success of the socialist revolution. To create a socialist society and give this order an economic power base, Marx meant that all means of production had to be controlled by the state. Private ownership of these means had to be abolished. This would deprive the exploiting capitalists of their powerbase and bring the working class to power. Public ownership is viewed as vital to assure that the means of production will be used for the good of many instead of the enrichment of a few.

In line with Marxist theory, the industries in the urban areas as well as the arable land in China were all confiscated during the 1950s. The state created huge state enterprises that became small societies in their own right, caring for food allowances, health care, housing, schools and the retired workers. In the countryside, the government created collectives of the villages and then, in turn, integrated the collectives into huge people's communes comprised of approximately some 5000 households each. These mammoth units (*danwei*) made sense from a communist ideological standpoint, but they often did not make economical sense.

Realizing that a centrally-planned, state-run economy was not leading to economic prosperity, the Deng government changed course and began to allow a degree of private ownership in 1978. The commune system was abolished and the land was contracted out to the farmers. The state encouraged small scale, light industry operated by collectives in the rural areas. In the cities, small private enterprises in manufacturing and services were encouraged. As the economy grew, large privately-run companies appeared. These firms employed many people and the owners did not themselves engage in labor. Such people looked very much like capitalists. As China was on its way to being transformed into a capitalistic society, it became harder theoretically to justify communist rule and the power monopoly exercised by the CCP. This problem was solved by arguing that China was still in the "primary stage of socialism" (*shehuizhuyi chuji jieduan*).[1] According to this theory, the Chinese society had bypassed an essential stage of economic order by going directly from a feudal peasant society to a socialist society. To reach the goal of a real communistic society where the state eventually would wither away, a stage of market economy had to be experienced. This primary stage is expected to last one hundred years from the 1950s. Public ownership plays the dominant role even during this phase of

[1] Allison W. Conner, *To Get Rich is Precarious: Regulation of Private Enterprise in the P.R.C.*, 5 J. of Chinese L. 1, 14 n.66 (1991). The "primary stage" theory was first launched by the then CCP general secretary Zhao Ziyang in a speech to the CCP Thirteenth National Congress in October 1987. *Id.*

development, but private ownership is also permissible. It is acknowledged that the private sector of the economy involves wage labor and this will lead to unequal income, but this is tolerated since the private sector provides employment and helps meet people's needs. Moreover, Chinese theorists argue that private enterprise in China is meant to be different from private enterprise elsewhere (i.e., capitalist societies) because it developed long after China's socialist transformation. The public sector clearly occupies the dominant position in the economy and the owners of private enterprise are expected to use most of their profits in expanding production instead of using it for personal consumption.[2]

The "primary stage" theory provides an ideological justification, however weak, for the permittance of private ownership of property and the development of private business in the Chinese socialist society. Legal protection for private business was given in a 1988 constitutional amendment article 11 not long after the launch of this theory.[3]

Concept of Property

The Chinese word for property is *caichan,* which includes both tangible and intangible property.[4] The latter includes intellectual property rights such as patents, trademarks, copyrights and any other scientific or intellectual achievements.[5]

Tangible property is by Chinese jurisprudence divided into specific property (*tedingwu*) and class property (*zhongleiwu*).[6] The former refers to identifiable items such as a painting or a building, and the latter refers to property that has common characteristics and can be measured and determined by quantities or types, such as rice. When a piece of class property is separated from its class, it becomes identifiable and is then considered specific property. There are mainly three areas where this distinction has legal effect. First, if a contract is made to use specific property, the same piece of property must be returned, but if class property such as rice is used, it is sufficient to return the same kind of product of identical quantity and quality. Second, if specific property is destroyed prior to delivery, the seller is relieved of his duty to perform, but in the case of class property, the seller is not relieved of the same obligation since the delivery can be replaced by a new shipment. Third, specific property is transferred when the contract is entered into, whereas class property is transferred when the goods are actually delivered. This last distinction has lost its relevance after the promulgation of the *General Principles of Civil Law*[7] (colloquially known as the Civil Code) in 1987. The new law provides a uniform rule in article 72 that governs transfer of both types of property. Under this article, property is transferred when the goods are delivered unless the parties have stipulated otherwise.[8]

As with most other legal systems, Chinese jurisprudence differentiates between movable and immovable property. The latter, which cannot be removed, is real property. To transfer real property, or land-use rights, a registration procedure has to be followed. A registration of movable property is only required when vehicles, ships, airplanes and securities are involved.[9]

Another distinction made in Chinese jurisprudence is between severable and unseverable property. The former refers to property that can be divided without changing the intended utility or harming the expected use of the thing, like a shipment of grain. Unseverable properties are things that cannot be divided without changing the intended utility or harming the use, like a horse. This distinction is not only of theoretical value. Severable property may be divided among different owners, but unseverable property may only be given to one owner and the rest will have to accept monetary compensation. When co-owned unseverable property is subject to debt, the owners are jointly liable for the debt, which would not be the case if the property could be divided.[10]

Other classifications include the distinction between the main property (e.g. lock) and subordinated property (e.g. key) and between the original

---

[2]*Id.* at 14.

[3]*See* section 7.4 *infra.*

[4]*See* MINFA DA CIDIAN 97–98, 343.

[5]*Id.*

[6]MINFA XUE [STUDIES IN CIVIL LAW] 90, 94 (Zhang Li & Wang Zuotang eds., 1994).

[7]*See* CIVIL CODE [General Principles of the Civil Code, 6th Nat'l People's Cong., 4th Sess. (effective 1987)].

[8]The parties may regulate their own relation in a contract, but not third party rights. The CIVIL CODE is silent on when a buyer of property gains protection from the seller's creditors.

[9]Secured Interests Law of the P.R.C., arts. 41–43, 8th Nat'l People's Cong., 14 Sess. (1995). Nationwide real estate mortgage and chattel registration systems are provided for in this law.

[10]STUDIES IN CIVIL LAW, supra note [6].

property (e.g. tree) and accrued property (e.g. fruit). Unless law or contract provides otherwise, the rule is that subordinated or accrued property is transferred when the main or original property is transferred.[11]

The classifications above have been stated in Chinese jurisprudence. Other classifications of property can be found in statutory law, which divides property into (1) state property, (2) collective property and (3) individual or private entity property.[12] This classification was inherited from Soviet legal thinking and is increasingly criticized by Chinese legal scholars for its impracticality.

Property is protected by articles in the Constitution and the Civil Code.[13] However, the wording is different depending on whether the property is state, collective or individually owned. State property is "sacred and inviolable"[14] whereas collective property and "lawful property"[15] of citizens are simply protected by law. Apparently, state property is given a higher legal status than collective and individual property. It follows that if a dispute involves individual property, the first question is whether the ownership itself is lawful. For state property, there seems to be a presumption of lawfulness. This distinction may have significant implications when the property interests of the state, collectives and individuals are in conflict. Even so, the practical difference between these provisions is not so great, as the basic principle of the Civil Code is that all civil law subjects, including state institutions and citizens, enjoy equal status in civil activities.[16]

Ownership

The definition of ownership (suoyouquan) is found in article 71 of the Civil Code: "Ownership means an owner's right in accordance with law to possess, use, benefit from and dispose of his own property."

This division of property rights is different from the typical western civil codes rooted in Roman law. Roman law distinguished between ownership (*dominium*) and property rights without ownership, such as possession, easements, and usufruct. The Roman system formed the basis for the formal classifications of property rights in 1804 for the French *Code Civil* and, more completely, in 1896 for the German civil code (the BGB). Even before the BGB was promulgated in 1900, the Japanese had put a more or less virtual carbon copy of it into effect in 1898. The Japanese Civil Code, in turn, influenced the Republic of China (ROC). The ROC's Civil Code, published between 1929 and 1931, acquired its terminology for the classification of property rights from its Japanese and German counterparts. Like the BGB and the Japanese Civil Code, book 3 of the ROC's Civil Code is titled "Rights in Things" (*wuquan*)[17] and deals with ownership, possession, easements, liens, and mortgages as well as related matters such as joint ownership and registration of rights.[18]

The ROC's Civil Code was abolished on mainland China along with all other ROC laws by the communists in 1949, because the bourgeois laws were regarded as having no place in the new socialist republic. Drafting of a PRC Civil Code began in the 1950s but was never completed. In spite of the civil code never having been put into effect, it was influential as laterdate Chinese legal textbooks were often based on its thinking.[19] The acute need for a statutory property rights system became evident after the economic reforms began in 1978. To satisfy this need, the government promulgated the Civil Code on January 1, 1987.[20]

As stated in article 71 of the Civil Code, the Chinese concept of property ownership is divided into

---

[11] *Id.*

[12] P.R.C. CONST., arts. 5, 7–10.

[13] Property rights are also dealt with in the Criminal Code. The Criminal Code states in its general provisions (art.2) that it protects citizens' ownership rights to their lawful property. Art. 31 of the Criminal Code states that those whose criminal acts cause economic loss to persons will be required, according to the circumstances, to make compensation for said loss in addition to criminal punishment. Criminal Law of the P.R.C. [CRIMINAL CODE], arts. 2, 31, 5th Nat'l People's Cong., 2d Sess. (1980).

[14] P.R.C. CONST., art. 12 and Civil Code, art. 73.

[15] P.R.C. CONST., art. 13 and Civil Code, arts. 74–75.

[16] CIVIL CODE, arts. 3, 5.

[17] The German term is Sachenrecht and the Japanese term is *Bukken*.

[18] Edward J. Epstein, The Theoretical System of Property Rights in China's General Principles of Civil Law: Theoretical Controversy in the Drafting Process and Beyond, 52 LAW AND CONTEMPORARY PROBLEMS 176, 183 (1989).

[19] *Id.* at 181.

[20] *See* CIVIL CODE. Chinese legal scholars do not like to call the General Principles of Civil Law a civil code, because they want to reserve that name for a more comprehensive CIVIL CODE in the future. However, since the law is a civil code, albeit short and incomplete, most Western legal scholars call it the "Civil Code." Interview with Wang Weiguo, Professor of Law, Chinese University of Politics and Law, Beijing, P.R.C. (July 8, 1995).

four constituent "powers and functions" (*quanneng*): Possession (*zhanyou*), use (*shiyong*), the right to benefit (*shouyiquan*)[21] and disposition (*chufen*).[22] These four powers and functions of ownership can be distilled from ownership individually or in combination. The reason for breaking down ownership into four constituent parts is that legal theorists can build new rights with novel combinations of the old parts. This might be described as a process of borrowing bourgeois theoretical tools to produce new "socialist" legal concepts.[23] Although property rights in the Civil Code might be classified differently, a closer look at the ownership system reveals that even Chinese civil law has its roots in the Roman legal tradition.

Textbook authors argue that in addition to ownership rights themselves, five other property rights can be found in Chapter 5, section 1 of the Civil Code. These are:

1. The right of state-owned or collective units to "use and benefit from" land owned by the state [art. 80(1)] or things on the land owned by the state [art. 81(1)];
2. The right, acquired by contract, of citizens or collectives to operate publicly owned land [art. 80(2)] and things on the land [art. 81(3)];
3. The right of the state or collective units or citizens to exploit natural resources [art. 81(2)];
4. The right of an enterprise owned by the whole people (i.e., state-owned enterprise) to operate property given to it by the state [art. 82]; and
5. Limitation of property rights necessary for the conduct of "neighborhood relationships" [art. 83].[24]

These rights can be classified as "rights in things" in the sense of the German BGB and the later denounced ROC Civil Code. The first right above can be described as a usufruct (*yongyiquan*); the second right is another kind of usufruct, called a contract usufruct. The third right, the right to exploit resources (*caikuang quan*) is more problematic when viewed from a strictly Western view of usufruct. In Roman law, a usufruct could not be consumed. This was solved by allowing the usufructary to be the owner of the fungible goods with a duty to restore the equivalent amount to the original owner. This solution is, however, not acceptable to Chinese Civil Law, since natural resources belong to the state[25] and the land on which the resources stand is non-transferrable. Chinese law solves this problem by allowing exploitation of natural resources for a fee. Since it is not the fruits of the land that are taken, but parts of the actual land itself, it seems as if the state is effectively transferring ownership. The fourth right, the right to operate, is also a form of usufruct. Neighborhood rights, the fifth civil right listed above, are property rights only in the sense that they limit the exercise of property rights by the owner or occupier of the immovable property.[26]

REAL PROPERTY ("IMMOVABLES")

Overview

Nothing is so closely connected with the word property as land, especially so in China with its large peasant population. Promise of land reform was an important reason why the communists succeeded in rallying the peasants to their side during the civil war. Under the ensuing land reform, land was initially redistributed to the peasants with ownership rights. However, after the collectivization in 1955, individual land ownership was abolished and formal ownership of land was transferred from the peasants to the collectives organized at the village level. Urban land was nationalized.

Still today, all land in China is either owned by the State or the Collectives. Generally speaking, all urban land belongs to the state and most rural land belongs to the collectives. The foundation for land ownership is laid out in the 1982 Constitution.

Article 9 of the Constitution states that all mineral resources, waters, forests, mountains, grasslands, unreclaimed land, beaches and other natural resources are

[21]"The right to benefit" was added to legal textbooks in the 1980s. Possession or use do not seem to be prerequisites to enjoying the right to benefit. This allows for the enjoyment of unearned income, which was not permitted according to earlier textbooks and CCP theory. In the 1950s, the right to benefit was regarded as a disguise for the exploiting classes' extraction of blood and sweat from the workers and consequently denounced. Current textbooks give such examples of right to benefit as interest from savings and eggs from a chicken. Epstein, supra note [18] at 285 n.26.

[22]*Id.* at 185

[23]*Id.*

[24]*Id.* at 188.

[25]P.R.C. CONST., art. 9

[26]Epstein, *supra* note [18] at 191.

owned by the state with the exception of forests, mountains, grasslands, unreclaimed land and beaches that are owned by collectives in accordance with the law.[27]

Article 10 originally stated that:[28]

> Land in the cities is owned by the state.
> Land in the rural and suburban areas is owned by collectives except for those portions which belong to the state in accordance with the law; house sites and private plots of cropland and hilly land are also owned by collectives.
> The state may in the public interest take over land for its use in accordance with the law.
> No organization or individual may appropriate, buy, sell, or lease land or otherwise engage in the transfer of land by unlawful means.
> All organizations and individuals who use land must make rational use of the land.

After the collectivization, the collectives formally owned their land. In practice, however, the state assumed tight control over transfer rights including the sale, rent or exchange of land. Use rights were vested in the collective, but crop choice and sale prices were all decided by the state.[29] This changed with the household contract system introduced by Deng Xiaoping in 1978. The collectives still could not sell the land but were now given the right to contract out land use rights to individual farmers who paid for their rent by selling a part of their crop to the state. The household system was a tremendous success and agricultural production increased rapidly.

A large part of the real property is managed by the SOEs, which have been allocated use rights to the land for an indefinite term without any significant compensation. Usually, the SOEs pay only a small annual fee. The land rights are limited. The SOEs cannot transfer their allocated land to a third party. However, since the early 1980s the SOEs have been allowed to use their land as in-kind contribution to a JV (provided the government approved). This right was still severely restricted and did not grant the JV the power to buy, sell or mortgage the property. In light of the current Chinese real estate boom, it seems hard to believe that land was regarded as almost worthless until the late 1980s and the acquisition of land was only a bureaucratic arrangement.

As China opened up to foreign investment, it became more and more evident that untransferrable land ownership rights were not very practical. In the new Special Economic Zones (SEZ), a system that allowed the rental of state land was attempted. However, neither the Chinese nor the foreign investors were pleased with the system which required the foreign investors to pay an annual rent. The fee was specified by law, without regard to changing conditions of the real estate market.[30] Nor could the JVs mortgage the land as a mean of getting funds. Chinese-foreign JVs were not the only losing parties in this system. The city governments did not get much money from these short-term land use leases.[31] Denying others land ownership, the state itself had to bear the burden of developing land in the cities. As the State lacked funds for this development, prime real estate parcels in big cities like Beijing could idle for decades and infrastructure construction went slow.

However, to allow private land ownership was ideologically hard for the CCP to accept, since privatization would create new landlords, the old class enemy. The solution was to allow purchase of land usage rights which were valid for a limited duration of time. The first land transfers took place in 1987 in the SEZ of Shenzhen.[32] At that time, this practice lacked support in the Constitution, but shortly afterwards, on April 12, 1988, the fourth paragraph of article 10 of the Constitution was amended to read:

> No organization or individual may appropriate, buy, sell or unlawfully transfer land in other ways. *The right to the use of land may be assigned in accordance with the provisions of the law.* (Emphasis added.)

[27]Chinese law makes a difference between resources and land itself. Therefore article 9 of the Constitution regulates resources and article 10 the land itself.

[28]The fourth paragraph of article 10 was amended in 1988. This is discussed later in this section.

[29]Mark Seldon & Aiguo Lu, *The Reform of Land Ownership and the Political Economy of Contemporary China, in* THE POLITICAL ECONOMY OF CHINESE DEVELOPMENT 187, 187 (Mark Seldon & Aiguo Lu, eds., 1993).

[30]The fees are dealt with in the Implementing Regulations to the Equity Joint Venture Law . . . arts. 47–53.

[31]According to the official Chinese statistics, the land-use fees and other related charges that the government of the Shenzhen SEZ collected from 1980 to 1987 were only 38 million Yuan. This was not even sufficient to pay for the interest on the 600 million Yuan investment by the Chinese Government in land development and infrastructure during the same time. *See* Henry Z. Zheng, *The Special Economic Zones and Coastal Cities, in* DOING BUSINESS IN CHINA, 43 (W. Strong & A. Wilcox eds., 1993).

[32]CHINA BUSINESS LAW GUIDE ϶ 85–620 (Sally A. Harpole ed., 1991).

The same year, article 2 of the Land Administration Law was amended to allow state-owned and collective-owned land to be alienated for value.[33] Detailed national regulations had yet to be issued but the legal foundation for using property as a commodity had been created. In 1990, a few years after the SEZs promulgated their land-use rights regulations, a national regulation on granting land use rights was passed.[34]

The local and national land grant regulations gave land value and created a real estate market. This new market, combined with double digit economic growth, soon created a booming real estate industry. The SEZs and the major cities soon looked like big construction sites. The development sometimes went out of control. Zoning laws were disregarded and in some places, like Shanghai, office construction increased past any reasonable demand forecast.[35] Another result of the real estate boom was increasing corruption. Since the land-use grants involve large sums of money and are administered by poorly paid civil servants, the potential for corruption is large.[36] In the suburban and rural areas, large areas of precious agricultural land were taken for housing construction as the cities grew.[37]

Urban Land

Land-Use Rights

The national regulations concerning land use rights are the 1986 Land Administration Law (LAL),[38] the 1991 implementation rules to the LAL,[39] the 1990 Grant Regulations,[40] the 1992 Allocated Land Measures,[41] and the 1994 Urban Real Estate Management Law (UML).[42] While also providing new provisions, the UML to a large extent repeats what already had been stated in previous legislation.

The regulations draw a distinction between urban and collective land. All urban land belongs to the state and the surrounding suburban land normally belongs to different collectives.[43] Only state-owned land can be transferred to a third party.[44] Therefore, land belonging to the collectives has to be nationalized before it can be granted.[45]

Another distinction is drawn between "Granted" and "Allocated" land. Granted land has a time limit on usage and can be transferred for value. Allocated land is given without consideration and normally has no time limit, but cannot be transferred.[46]

Granted Land-Use Rights

The definition of a grant of land is found in article 8¶ of the 1990 Grant Regulations: "The term 'grant of the right to use land' refers to the act by which the State, in its capacity as land owner, grants the right to use land for a certain number of years to a land user and the land user pays to the State a fee for the grant of the right to use land."

The maximum time limits of the land-use right are determined by the purpose of the use.[47]. . .

CONCLUSION

Since the beginning of reform in 1978, Chinese society has undergone tremendous changes. In the mid-1970s, there was no real need for an advanced property law in China since all companies and all land were owned or *de facto* controlled by the state. However, in the last fifteen years, China has made rapid economic advancements and property ownership has been diversified. Average incomes have tripled, private enterprise is allowed and new venture capital can be raised through stock markets. The

[33]Law of the P.R.C. on Land Management (also known as the Land Administration Law), 6th Nat'l People's Cong., 16th Sess. (1986) (amended 1986) [hereinafter LAL].

[34]Provisional Regulations of the People's Republic of China Concerning the Grant and Assignment of the Right to Use State Land in Urban Areas, (1990) [hereinafter 1990 Grant Regulations].

[35]*Survey: China* THE ECONOMIST (INT'L EDITION), March 18, 1995.

[36]*See* Finder [Susan Finder, "Inside the People's Courts: China's Litigation System and the Resolution of Commercial Disputes," *China Law and Practice,* Feb. 1996] at 20.

[37]*Growing Pains,* THE ECONOMIST (INT'L EDITION), March 18, 1995 at 24.

[38]*See* LAL, *supra* note [33].

[39]Rules for implementation of the Law of the P.R.C. on Land Management, promulgated Jan. 4, 1991 by the State Council.

[40]*See* 1990 Grant Regulations, *supra* note [34].

[41]Provisional Measures on Administration of Allocated Land Use Rights (1992) [hereinafter Allocated Land Measures].

[42]Urban Real Estate Management Law of the P.R.C., 8th Nat'l People's Cong., 8th Sess. (effective 1995) [hereinafter UML].

[43]LAL, art. 6.

[44]*See for example* P.R.C. CONST. art. 10, ¶ 4, and LAL art.2, ¶ 2.

[45]UML, *supra* note [42], art. 8. That only state land may be transferred is implied in the 1990 Grant Regulations but UML makes it explicit.

[46]1990 Grant Regulations, *supra* note [34], arts. 8, 42–44.

[47]*Id.* art. 12.

farmers have a land-use right to the land they cultivate and urban land can be transferred for value.

With the demands of an advanced market economy, it may only be a few years before China has established modern economic legislation, including an advanced property law bearing great resemblance to Western law. The momentum for legal reform is strong in the PRC today, and many important laws are being passed every year. Compared to other emerging markets, the legal reform in China has been quick.

However, protection of property rights is another matter altogether. The legal system is still weak in China and there exists no true rule of law. As long as the CCP holds absolute power, the courts will never be strong, independent organs. Regional protectionism makes it difficult to enforce a claim from another part of the country. In the metropolitan areas of Beijing, Shanghai and Guangzhou (Canton), the enforcement of property rights will work better than in the interior regions. Even in these cities, the function of property law will not be comparable to Western standards in the foreseeable future. Protection of property rights will slowly be strengthened, but the PRC still has a long way to go before the actual possession without title is a *de facto* weaker right than having the title to the property but no possession.

36

RICHARD EPSTEIN

From *Takings: Private Property and the Power of Eminent Domain*

PHILOSOPHICAL IMPLICATIONS

A SUMMING UP

The explication of the eminent domain clause in the previous nineteen chapters has covered cases that range from outright acquisition of land to the manifold modes of regulation and taxation so characteristic of the modern state. My central concern in this concluding chapter is not with the legal status of the takings clause, but with the larger questions of normative political theory: what are the intrinsic merits of the eminent domain provision when it is stripped of its present constitutional authority? If we were now in a position to organize a government from scratch, would its constitution include an eminent domain clause as interpreted here? My thesis is that the eminent domain approach, as applied both to personal liberty and private property, offers a principled account of both the function of the state and the limitations upon its powers.

Representative government begins with the premise that the state's rights against its citizens are no greater than the sum of the rights of the individuals whom it benefits in any given transaction. The state qua state has no independent set of entitlements, any more than a corporation has rights qua corporation against any of its shareholders.[1] All questions of public right are complex amalgams of questions of individual entitlements, so the principles of property, contract, and tort law can be used to explain the proper extent of government power. These rules determine the proper relationships among private individuals, which are preserved when the state intervenes as an agent on one side of the transaction. These entitlement principles obey very simple rules of summation and hence apply with undiminished vigor to large-number situations involving modifications of liability rules, regulation, and taxation. A system of private rights provides an exhaustive and internally consistent normative baseline of entitlements against which all the complex schemes of governance can be tested. As there are no gaps in rights when ownership is first established, no gaps

[1]It is precisely on this view that limited liability has been often attacked as an anomaly. Within the framework of a liberty-based analysis, there is no particular difficulty with the position of contract claimants, for the agreement to reach only corporate assets in satisfaction of a claim is no more problematic than a nonrecourse mortgage which limits the mortgagee's rights of collection only to the subject property. Tort claims are a very different matter. Here the legitimation of the corporate form is best understood as a set of complex forced exchanges. As a quid pro quo for limited liability, a corporation can be properly compelled to have liability insurance to meet its anticipated risks. And more generally, without limited liability no one could venture into any pooled investment, given the general rules of agency that hold all investors responsible for the actions of their employees. Limited liability thus channels suits for and against responsible parties, reducing transaction costs. Given its general nature and the positive welfare effects, it is very easy to conclude that limited liability meets the standards for implicit in-kind compensation.

emerge when private ownership is transformed by state intervention, whatever its form.

The state, however, cannot simply arise (even conceptually) out of a series of voluntary transactions from an original distribution of rights. Free riders, holdouts, and radical uncertainty thwart any omnibus agreement before its inception. The question then arises, what minimum of additional power must be added for the state to become more than a voluntary protective association and to acquire the exclusive use of force within its territory? The eminent domain analysis provides the answer: the only additional power needed is the state's right to force exchanges of property rights that leave individuals with rights more valuable than those they have been deprived of. The specter of the unlimited Hobbesian sovereign is averted by two critical limitations upon the nature of the exchanges that the state can force. First, the eminent domain logic allows forced exchanges only for the public use, which excludes naked transfers from one person to another. Second, it requires compensation, so everyone receives something of greater value in exchange for the *rights* surrendered.

In the final analysis the two conditions blend into one, because the power to coerce is limited to cases in which positive-sum games may go forward with a pro rata division of the surplus they generate. It is always easy to construct examples whereby some individuals with distinctive personal tastes will be worse off in fact, because they will lose the power to rape, kill, pillage, and plunder. Yet the baseline for forced exchanges is individual entitlements to personal autonomy, not individual preferences regardless of their content. Aggrieved parties cannot complain if they lose under the state something they were not entitled to against other individuals as a matter of right. No requirement of unanimous consent prevents the move to a system of governance.[2] The single pervert cannot block the state. Once organized, the state has the power to govern because within its own territory it has the monopoly of force sufficient to protect all persons against aggression in all its forms. Finally, by a system of unbiased judges (long recognized as part of the tradition of natural justice) the state insures that all disputes can be resolved. The gains of final adjudication are the substantial gains of social order, while the errors tend to be randomly distributed, so all persons share pro rata in the surplus created.[3]

This eminent domain framework does not depend upon a hidden assumption that before the formation of a government all individuals, real or hypothetical, reside in a "state of nature." Quite the contrary, political theory is quite unintelligible if it assumes that prior to the establishment of a government, individuals have no common language, no conception of right and wrong, no common culture or tradition, and no means of socialization outside the state. The question of the state is narrower than is sometimes supposed. The state is not the source of individual rights or of social community. It presupposes that these exist and are worth protecting and that individuals reciprocally benefit from their interactions with one another. A unique sovereign emerges solely in response to the demands to preserve order. The state becomes a moral imperative precisely because there is something of value that is worth protecting from the unbridled use of force by those who forsake tradition, family, and friends. A set of forced exchanges from existing rights does not create the original rights so exchanged; like the constitutional vision of private property, forced exchanges presuppose them. A forced exchange does not create culture and sense of community, it protects them by removing the need for compelling or allowing everyone to act as a policeman in his own cause. The state arises because the rates of error and abuse in pure self-help regimes become intolerable. The strength of a natural law theory is in its insistence that individual rights (and their correlative obligations) exist independent of agreement and prior to the formation of the state.

---

[2]The insistence upon subjective preferences is developed in Frank I. Michelman, "Ethics, Economics and the Law of Property," in *Ethics, Economics, and the Law* 3 (J. Roland Pennock and John W. Chapman eds.) (NOMOS Monograph No. 24, 1982), but is forcefully criticized by Harold Demsetz, "Professor Michelman's Unnecessary and Futile Search for the Philosopher's Touchstone," id. at 41.

[3]In principle one could argue that judges do not need absolute immunity, but that they should be liable when they act beyond their jurisdiction or with malice. Yet the dangers of that are great, because any disappointed litigant could seize on some exception. For this reason absolute immunity has remained inviolate even under statutes, such as Section 1983 of the Civil Rights Act, which on their face seem to subject judges to suit for decisions that wrongly award the property of A to B. See Pierson v. Ray, 386 U.S. 547 (1967). For my views on the relationship between official immunity to private suit and other forms of control of judicial abuse, see Richard A. Epstein, "Private-Law Models for Official Immunity," 1978 *Law and Contemp. Probs.* 53.

RIVAL THEORIES

To get some sense of the power of the eminent domain approach, it is instructive to compare this view with two rival theories that have been very influential in recent times, theories with which it has both important similarities and important differences. These theories are the ones associated with the work of Robert Nozick in *Anarchy, State, and Utopia* and that of John Rawls in *A Theory of Justice*. After reviewing them, I shall consider whether the theory of eminent domain is consistent with a vision of civic virtue in public life or is nullified by past acts that violate the theory itself.

Nozick

Nozick's theory incorporates the first part of the eminent domain approach in its respect for the principles of individual rights. Nozick relies heavily upon "historical" principles of justice to account for the institution of private property and the inequalities in wealth it engenders. At one time those principles were widely accepted in both common and constitutional discourse.[4] Nozick's rules of acquisition have close affinity to the first-possession rules of property. His principles of rectification cover the terrain of the law of tort, and those of transfer cover the law of contract.[5] One great attraction of his normative theory is its powerful congruence with basic social institutions and human practices which provides a convenient data base on which to examine its implications. Another strong point is that by striking a responsive chord, the theory requires no great cost to be legitimated, because people do not need to be persuaded to abandon their customary moral views, as they would to embrace a highly abstract theory (like Rawls's) that cuts against the grain and commits them to outcomes they cannot understand by procedures they sorely distrust.

But there are difficulties with Nozick's theory. The first concerns its origin and the status of individual rights. Nozick follows closely in the Lockean and common law tradition, for his historical theory of justice begins with the proposition that ownership is acquired by taking possession of an unowned thing. Nonetheless, the proposition that possession is the root of title is not a necessary truth.[6] The linkage between possession and title can be denied without self-contradiction. Arguably, all things in an initial position are subject to some form of collective ownership. Some nondeductive procedure must be available to let us choose between competing visions of the correct original position. Nozick's view depends upon an intuitive appreciation of the need for autonomy and self-determination. In one sense his position looks like a bare assertion: private property and personal liberty are important because they are important or because they are inherent in human nature. Such efforts at self-justification are always uneasy, but they are not for that reason wrong. One way to look at Nozick's simple theory is to ask what the world would look like if the popular conception of autonomy was abandoned. On what grounds could one categorically condemn murder, rape, mayhem, theft, and pillage? Our instincts of revulsion are so powerful that one is loathe to adopt a theory of individual rights that rests solely upon the shifting sands of utilitarian calculation. Slavery by conquest is regarded as a categorical evil.[7] Do we want even to consider the argument that slavery is justified if the agency costs of control and supervision are small in comparison with the resource gains from subjecting an incompetent slave to the will of a competent master? Or is the incompetence of one person only an argument for guardianship by another? Is it really an open question whether the parent-child relationship is one of guardianship or ownership? Simple faith may not serve as the ideal foundation of an ethical theory, but it may be much better than the next best alternative.

Nozick writes in an antiutilitarian vein that places his historical theory in sharp opposition to a consequentialist one. Yet in one sense the intuitive base for

---

[4]See Coppage v. Kansas, 236 U.S. 1 (1915).

[5]See Robert Nozick, *Anarchy, State, and Utopia* ch. 7 (1974).

[6]For a deeper exploration of the theme, see Richard A Epstein, "Possession as the Root of Title," 13 *Ga. L. Rev.* 1221 (1979).

[7]The question of slavery by contract is far more difficult, but two points do stand out. First, the illustrations of it in practice are so infrequent that one can doubt whether it ever comes about except by force or fraud. Even indentured servant contracts were of limited duration and imposed special duties upon the master. Second, and less often noticed, slaves also bargain away the rights of their offspring and thus are in breach of their natural obligations. Third, slavery has a corrosive effect on individual participation in public governance. None of these points is decisive, and each has counterexamples, but their combined weight supports the view that everyone is better off, ex ante, if slavery is banned altogether, as the theory of forced exchanges and implicit in-kind compensation allows.

much libertarian doctrine might be strengthened by a direct appeal to considerations of utility. Utilitarianism does not purport to rest upon mere assertion or past practice but seeks to show how these rules can be harmonized in the service of an end that is itself justified. If everyone is better off in World One than they are in World Two, who would want to interpose an argument about rights that, if respected, consigned everyone to the inferior world? A utilitarian argument is always filled with gigantic pitfalls because it makes all small decisions turn upon some vast social construct. Still, we shall not be too quick to attack a theory for mistakes in its application, especially if these can be corrected without abandoning the major premise.

Indeed, a sensible utilitarian theory does provide powerful support for Nozick's substantive commitment to individual liberty and private property. The simplicity of Nozick's system is surely commendable, for it cuts down the number of negative-sum games by setting boundary lines that other persons cannot cross without the owner's consent. The theory also tends to foster many separate sources of power, whether in personal talents or external things. It thereby tends to create competitive structures and to prevent the concentration of wealth and power in a few hands. Thus the first-possession rule itself makes it highly unlikely that any one person will reduce all things to ownership, especially when others enjoy the same privilege of original acquisition. Unifying the possession, use, and disposition of a determinate thing in the hands of individuals makes it far easier to organize subsequent transactions to correct original errors of allocation. Similarly, leaving things with their initial possessor creates a system of ownership that does not begin with state entanglements and that removes the dead-weight costs of shifting property from its present possessor to its rightful owner under the new system.[8] A utilitarian theory, especially of the indirect sort, thus looks quite consistent with the simple rules of thumb to which common practice conforms and to which libertarians gave great respect.[9]

Utilitarian theory is often criticized because it is said to ignore differences between persons and to make rights turn on consequences, not origins. But quite the opposite is true. A good utilitarian should be driven to respect differences among persons, if only to avoid the common pool problems that the principle of autonomy is able in large measure to overcome. Similarly, future happiness depends upon a system of stable and well-defined rights. These can be had only if entitlements are made to turn upon individual past actions which, once their consequences are understood, can offer the signposts for intelligent planning. The contrast between ontological and consequentialist theories in ethics is much overdrawn.

The defense of liberty and property can be made in either libertarian or utilitarian terms, yet it does not follow that distributional issues are ignored. Even before the advent of the welfare state, many social institutions developed to share and pool risk. Certainly the family has this function, and the same role can be ascribed to the large clans of primitive society. Friendly societies and fraternal organizations have had a similar role, and voluntary support for charitable activities has worked to preserve the social fabric against all sorts of external shocks. There is a certain amount of luck as to who is born smart and who is not, who has a congenital defect and who has great talent. No libertarian could consistently oppose voluntary aid to the poor and needy, or the complex private arrangements used to secure it. This obligation can be recognized as an "imperfect" one that is not simply a matter of ordinary consumption, even if the dangers of state coercion in principle make transfer payments an improper function of the state.

The original position taken first by Locke and adopted by Nozick has enormous appeal. Everyone does own himself, and no one owns any external things, and there are natural status obligations of support within the family. Nonetheless, Nozick's libertarian theory fails in its central mission because it cannot justify the existence of the state. Its chief weakness is that it views all entitlements as absolute, so all forced exchanges are ruled out of bounds, regardless of their terms. Yet without forced exchanges, social order cannot be achieved, given the holdout and free-rider problems. Nozick presents a wonderful discussion of the invisible-hand mechanisms that lead to the creation of multiple collective protection associations.[10] But no

---

[8]Donald Wittman, "Liability for Harm or Restitution for Benefit?" 13 *J. Legal Stud.* 57 (1984).

[9]See John Gray, "Indirect Utility and Fundamental Rights," 1 Soc. Phil. and Pol. 73 (1984).

[10]Nozick, supra note 5, at 12–25.

invisible-hand mechanism explains the emergence of an exclusive sovereign within any given territory. The need for forced exchanges makes this last leap from many associations to a single state, and the eminent domain argument supplies this step. Individual entitlements are respected always as claims for compensation and frequently, but not uniformly, as absolutes.

There are still limits on what the eminent domain theory can do. It cannot explain which protective association should become the exclusive one; for example, the place of honor might be awarded to the association with the most members. (Even here the specification of the territory can be decisive in choosing between rival claims.) The critical point is that any association which assumes power is hemmed in by a nondiscrimination provision: it owes the same obligations toward outsiders that it owes to its own members. Exploitation is made more difficult, if not precluded, when those who are bound without their consent must on average be left better off in their entitlement than before. The libertarian theory augmented by a willingness to tolerate some forced exchanges is vastly richer than a libertarian theory that wholly shuns them.

Rawls

The theory of governance implicit in the eminent domain clause also has strong elements of similarity to, and distinction from, the contractarian theory of justice most prominently associated with John Rawls. Rawls has two central principles: liberty and the difference principle.[11] According to the first, the proper purpose of social organization is to expand the liberties of all individuals to act, without interfering with others' liberties. By the second principle, any adjustment in the position of the original liberties must work to the advantage of the most disadvantaged in society. These substantive principles are justified by an appeal to the idea of reflective equilibrium, which itself depends upon a set of procedures to determine the proper substantive rules. Rawls's recurrent question is, what practices would all members in society adopt if they made their fundamental choices about the social structure behind a veil of ignorance? So located, their only knowledge is of human nature in general and of the laws of physical and social interaction, such as that most individuals are risk averse and are motivated by an uneasy mix of self-interest, family affections, and a sense of obligation. They are systematically denied knowledge of their own personal preferences and social niche.

Rawls's contractarian theory permits a richness of discussion that cannot be generated by simple libertarian premises, but it is open to powerful and familiar criticisms of a different sort, which I need not recount at length. First, it is quite impossible to understand Rawls's use of contract as it relates to abstractions.[12] Contract within the private law is an effort to vindicate the unique tastes of discrete persons who are far more concerned with their particular places and preferences than with the general social good. The Hobbesian cry, "The value of all things contracted for, is measured by the Appetite of the Contractors; and therefore the just value, is that which they be contented to give,"[13] is as succinct a statement and justification of freedom of contract as one can hope to give. Voluntary exchanges presuppose that in general every person has reliable information as to what he values and how much he values it or, at least, that he has better information about those things than those who would limit his choices. Trades are a positive-sum game because each person attaches greater value to what he receives than to what he surrenders. To argue for contracts by disinterested, indeed disembodied, persons is simply to strain a metaphor beyond its breaking point. By removing all traces of psychological struggle and individual self-interest, the theory departs radically from any plausible view of the private agreements based upon personal knowledge that lie at its analogical root. The metaphor of contract is best dropped altogether from Rawls's conception, because a single composite individual could do everything that is required of a contracting group. Indeed it is only the residual allure of the contract idea of consensus that drives Rawls to consider the preferences of hypothetical groups. By the terms of his theory, the choice of the single mean (or median?) person should suffice as well.

A second line of criticism is that Rawls's method of inquiry suffers from radical, indeed fatal, uncertainty. What results does the procedure generate, and how do these tie in with any common intuitions of individual rights and duties that are supposed to be generated? Rawls admitted that he could not be certain whether

[11]John Rawls, *A Theory of Justice* (1971).

[12]See Ronald Dworkin, "The Original Position," 40 *U. Chi. L. Rev* 500 (1973).

[13]Thomas Hobbes, *Leviathan,* ch. 15 (1651).

his view of the system tolerated the private ownership of productive property,[14] a startling indeterminacy in itself and a troublesome admission for anyone committed either to human freedom or to the power of normative discourse. Will the most ordinary of transactions—getting married to the spouse of one's own choice, having children, buying a home—be permissible under his theory? Nozick rightly points out that the theory offers no clear and powerful linkages between the micro level and the macro level.[15]

By degrees, the difference principle becomes the spider's web that traps the individual. Every individual's action will influence the utility others derive from their own holdings, whatever they may be. The irony should become apparent. The original objection to utilitarian thought was that it failed to respect the differences between persons. Yet that same objection can be leveled against Rawls's position, as the philosophical doctrine of internal relations is thus pressed into service to make the independence of human action, and with it individual liberty, a logical impossibility. If those left worse off are viewed as being harmed, then every human action contains a built-in justification for government intervention, even under the restrictive Millian principle that governments may intervene only to prevent harm to others. The libertarian position on rights does not suffer from this embarrassment. It contains a strong threshold condition—against the taking of private property, against the use of force or fraud—which must be crossed before one can regard the loss in welfare sustained by others as an actionable wrong. The proposition that all decisions must be collective because every action creates external harm can be rejected on principled grounds.[16]

The eminent domain approach to the question of political obligation meets these two central objections to Rawls's theory. The eminent domain theory does not have to deal with the entitlements of lifeless abstractions. Instead of relying upon a set of complex procedures to generate the needed substantive rights, it starts with a substantive account of individual rights, beginning with first possession and covering every aspect of the use and disposition of property. The radical uncertainty of Rawlsian procedures is thereby averted.

The eminent domain approach also eliminates the need to resort to hypothetical persons with incomplete personal knowledge. All persons are treated as their own masters, who are entitled to the full benefits of their natural talents and abilities. When a person takes possession of that which was previously unowned, he does not do so both as an agent for himself *and* as trustee for all other persons with claims upon him. He does so only for himself. In contrast, the Rawlsian approach regards the distribution of original talents (and hence the gains derived from their application) as morally arbitrary, the product of luck, and thus worthy of no protection. The opposition to Locke's view that each person owns his own labor cannot be more vivid.

Rawls's position has none of the operational simplicity of Locke's, but instead gives each person a lien upon the product of every other person, so that the personal destinies of all persons, present and future, are forever intertwined. His position forces upon every individual obligations that run contrary to biological instincts of egoism, whereby some special genetic linkage, such as parent to child, helps explain why one person takes into account another's gain or loss. The strong opposition between obligations within the family and within society at large is largely suppressed in Rawls's picture of human obligation. It is as if every person enjoyed the fruits of his own labor by leave of some central authority, so taxation becomes no longer a charge on individual wealth for supplying public goods but an efficient means for the state to reclaim the product of human talents that it already owns as trustee for the public at large. This conception strikes at the very heart of personal self-definition and individual self-expression. It presupposes the kind of detachment from, and impartiality toward, self that no human being emerging from his evolutionary past of remorseless self-interest can hope to achieve.[17] Each person becomes so enmeshed in the affairs of others

---

[14]Rawls, supra note [11], at 270–274.

[15]Nozick, supra note 5, at 204–213.

[16]For development, see Richard A. Epstein, "Intentional Harms," 4 *J. Legal Stud.* 391, 421–422 (1975), which deals with the question of *damnum absque iniuria*—harm without legal injury—which was the common law technique of restricting compensable harms so that all purposive human conduct does not become actionable.

[17]See, generally, Jack Hirschleifer, "Economics from a Biological Viewpoint," 20 *J. Law & Econ.* 1 (1977). For my views, see Richard A. Epstein, "A Taste for Privacy? Evolution and the Emergence of a Naturalistic Ethic," 9 *J. Legal Stud.* 665 (1980). "One central contribution of sociobiology to economics lies in demonstrating that tastes themselves are governed by discernible principles, and that self-interest, far from being merely an economic premise, is in the guise of inclusive fitness a biological conclusion." Id. at 679.

that even heroic efforts will never get them out. The theory is advanced in the cause of freedom, but the totalitarian abuse that it risks should be evident, for what happens if the wrong people gain control of the central machinery of social control?

The problems are also economic. The Rawlsian view is that personal talents are arbitrarily distributed in nature. That observation is used to justify social efforts to correct for the original imbalance, thereby expanding the occasions for social intervention. At common law the class of individual wrongs only reaches harms inflicted by one person against another. Acts of God and of the injured person himself are outside the domain of legal rectification, either by courts or by legislatures. But once the distribution of native talents becomes a matter of social concern, then coercion is necessary to neutralize natural differences attributable to the luck of the draw. In principle, social intervention will now be routinely justified to correct for acts of God, that is, for all harms caused by natural events, running the gamut from birth defects to injury by lightning, and even some forms of self-inflicted harm, at least if not deliberately caused. On either view, the scope of legitimate government actions is expanded enormously, without any clear indication of their form or content. It is quite impossible to say that rectification of acts of God requires the return to some status quo ante, because there is no benchmark to return to. Before the levels of overall compensation are set, there must be some assurance that the resources are there to allow the transfers to take place, for it is no longer enough to say that where the defendant wrongdoer is insolvent the matter comes to an end. There need not be any wrongdoer in the sense that the private law uses that term; all assets are held in social solution, even if in possession of those who claim to be their natural owners.

This collectivization of risk in turn leads to the very types of managerial problems that well-functioning markets seek to avoid. If an individual does not own himself, then there is a classic agency-cost question, because he must bear all the costs of his own labor while retaining only some portion of the gain. When everyone perceives the conflict between production and yield, the problems become additive. If individual misfortune is socialized, then some common pool must be formed to determine what fraction of each risk each person must bear. This pooling is designed to remove arbitrary individual differences that are distasteful to risk-averse parties. But the diversification of this risk comes at a very high cost. Transactional freedom is reduced because no one has clear title to anything that he wishes to purchase or sell, so property rights remain ill defined over time. The system downplays the natural, if imperfect, form of risk pooling provided by family and religious units.

The system also tends to cut against the formation of voluntary insurance markets. In the effort to control the problems of adverse selection (that is, only a small number of self-selected people being part of the insurance pool) the system increases the risks of moral hazard—the tendency of individuals to take steps to reduce their share of the total burden while keeping their full share of the benefits. The lesson derived from the development of natural resources is that pooling should be undertaken only when that solution is dictated by the nature of the resource. Where individual property rights can be well defined, pooling should be avoided—hence the difference between land and oil. The Rawlsian instinct runs the opposite way. Every thing is thrown into a common pool, even though the natural limits of the human body make it an ideal candidate for individual ownership, which the classical liberal theories provide.

The dangers of totalitarian excess become greater because of the built-in justifications for extensive social control. The creation of collective enterprises where none existed before does not eliminate self-interest; it only finds new and destructive avenues of expression. Individuals blessed with natural talents will seek to conceal them to escape the taxation or external controls that are the concrete expressions of the social lien. Their conduct offers an ironclad justification for other persons to monitor their "personal" affairs, which can never be wholly personal because they always involve the use and deployment of collective goods, to wit, unearned individual talents. The Rawlsian system is designed to yield fairer distributions, but if it takes people as they are, then the price is paid in the enormous shrinkage of the pie, which goes along with the implicit truncation of any sense of individual responsibility and self-worth, the indispensable glue of any social order. Why opt for a system of cross-ownership of persons? The Lockean creed of individual ownership of individual labor is a far simpler and more profound starting point. When meshed with a system of forced exchanges, it gives a far more consistent and well-ordered vision of both government and society.

All of this is not to say that the eminent domain approach does not incorporate elements of Rawlsian theory. Determining implicit in-kind compensation often turns on whether parties lie behind a veil of ignorance. With Rawls the veil is a construct, but under the eminent domain clause it is a simple fact of life, and the doubts about hypothetical constructs disappear. Concrete individuals are free to seek their own self-interest with whatever vigor they possess. But there are certain general rules (as with tort liability), which in the future are as apt to help as to hurt them, in the same proportions that they help or hurt others in society. Acting out of self-interest, the individual will maximize the wealth of the whole because that is the best way to maximize his own slice of the pie.

Second, the difference principle bears a close kinship to the disproportionate impact test, sometimes called the equal protection dimension of the eminent domain clause. Within Rawls's system the difference principle is a way of judging the soundness of institutional arrangements by improving the position of the worst off in society. Yet the difference principle works far better when it is moored to a system of Lockean entitlements, where it sorts out permissible from impermissible forced exchanges. The object of the rule is to move everyone to a more valuable set of fixed rights. Where the increase in wealth is accompanied by a radical shift in shares, compensation is required to ensure that all participate evenly in the social gains, so that wealth orderings are left unaffected by collective action. In contrast, Rawls's difference principle tends to compress the distribution of wealth and other benefits, compromising the position of the well-off for the benefit of the less fortunate. The redistributive element in the difference principle is plain. Yet one can invoke (as Rawls indeed does) ideas of insurance and risk aversion to suggest that, ex ante, all will accept that arrangement because when everyone is behind the veil of ignorance the gains of extreme success are smaller than the losses of great privation. But the benefits of the bedrock foundation of personal autonomy and private property remain secure, as it is far easier to work transformations with an existing baseline than without one. Risk aversion still remains relevant because it requires a downward evaluation of compensation packages that contain contingent benefits and more favorable attitude to government actions that substitute fixed payouts for uncertain ones. Nonetheless, risk aversion is still only one element in the package, not the package itself.

Civic Virtue

A final critique of the eminent domain theory comes from a very different quarter. It is often said that a theory that stresses the importance of private property and the fragility of government institutions ignores the role of civic virtue—devotion to public service, protection of the weak, advancement of the arts, participation in public life—which is central to understanding the highest aspirations of political life.[18] To be sure, there is something wrong with a view of the world that treats the renunciation of force and fraud as the noblest of human endeavors. Music, art, literature, science, and humanitarian endeavors speak eloquently against such a view. But civic virtue in public affairs is akin to happiness in private affairs. To make it the direct end of human conduct is to guarantee that it will not be obtained. Discreet indirection becomes the order of the day. As personal happiness is the by-product of a rich and productive life, so civic virtue is the by-product of sound institutional arrangements. The eminent domain approach works toward civic virtue, not by trumpeting its evident goodness, but by creating a sound institutional environment where it can flourish.

Consider the point that virtue and poverty do not go well together. Persons who are pressed to the edge of subsistence cannot render aid to others. Hunger breeds fear; fear breeds aggression; aggression, conflict; and conflict, civil disorder and decay. Civic virtue, then, depends upon sufficient personal liberty, security, and wealth to keep most people far from the thin edge. What set of institutions will tend to guarantee these political conditions? The first is the facilitation of voluntary transactions, which are generally positive-sum games, because people deal only with their own property. The second is control of legislatures, which have a propensity for negative-sum games because they allow people to deal in the property of others. To speak of the protection of markets is not to speak of

---

[18]See, e.g., Frank I. Michelman, "Politics and Values or What's Really Wrong with Rationality Review?" 13 *Creighton L. Rev.* 487 (1979). Frank I. Michelman, "Property as a Constitutional Right," 38 *Washington & Lee Law Rev.* 1097 (1981); Carol Rose, "*Mahon* Reconstructed: Or Why the Takings Issue Is Still a Muddle" 57 *So. Cal. L. Rev.* 561 (1984).

unlicensed liberty to act as one pleases. At the very least, the ordinary law of contract rules out all forms of force, duress, misrepresentation, and sharp practice. Contract law forbids many things, and its commands are not easy to comply with, judging from the frequency of their violation. Nor is it necessary to license every voluntary transaction: the antitrust laws find their most powerful voice in preventing voluntary transactions with negative social yields, such as monopoly. Similarly, to speak of the dangers of legislation is not to condemn all legislative practices, for there are public goods that private markets cannot provide, such as police, highways, and regulation of common pool resources.

Civic virtue will be under constant siege if factions have free rein in the public arena. Those who possess civic virtue must constantly fend off initiatives, such as endless farm subsidies or import protection, that should be ruled out of bounds at the start. When the virtuous people fail, they are bound to feel cynical: why shouldn't I get mine too? Degenerative noncooperative games emerge in which everyone is a net loser. It is a subdued version of the war of all against all, transformed into a more genteel, but still destructive, game in a different arena. In such a world everyone can plausibly claim that he should get his because everyone else has, or will, get his too. How can civic virtue survive persistent temptation? The bad will drive out the good in a Gresham's law of political life.

The only way to foster virtue is to reduce the opportunities for illicit gains from legislative intrigue. Civic virtue can emerge in private charitable behavior. It can emerge in responsible participation in the provision of public goods—deciding how much should be spent on defense, highways, and courts or when war should be declared or peace negotiated—matters which cannot, by any stretch of the imagination, be regulated by the eminent domain clause. Civic virtue does not prosper in a world in which courts refuse to protect either personal autonomy or property rights. The eminent domain clause thus improves the soil from which civic virtue can grow. It controls abuse by demanding that losers in the legislative process retain rights that leave them as well off as they were before.

Past Injustices

Thus far the theory has talked about the principle of eminent domain against rival conceptions of political order. But it may be said that the theory is incomplete because it does not account for prior injustices in the distribution of rights. These prior errors undermine all present entitlements, even if sound normative theory protects private property while allowing forced exchanges. Much of the current stores of wealth were acquired by improper means, and these imperfections necessarily infect the system as it now stands. To insist that the game now be played straight (which assumes, rightly, that we know how to play it straight) is to entrench for all time the present imperfections. Since the preconditions of the normative theory are not met, the theory must be rejected no matter what strength it has on the blank slate, the state of nature.

This argument stands in opposition to the parallel problem . . . on welfare rights, where the question was whether the power of embedded expectations was so great that one could not undo, especially by constitutional means, the social legislation of the New Deal and beyond, no matter how infirm its constitutional foundations. Nonetheless, there is a curious reversal, as the present argument places the claims of original justice above those of subsequent reliance on the current order. Yet the question has no conclusive answer.

One way to approach the argument, is to consider its principled analogy within the framework of the private law: the problem of *ius tertii*.[19] In the simplest case A owns property, which is then taken by B. C then takes the property from B. The question is whether the infirmity in B's title is sufficient to defeat his action to recover possession of the thing from C. The common law answer is no. Note what happens if the rule is otherwise. If B cannot recover from C, there is no way to prevent C taking the thing from B in the first place. Yet C secures no title hence he cannot prevent D from taking the thing from him. Denying B's action has the unhappy consequence that once the possession of property deviates from the proper chain of title, it must forever remain beyond the pale of private ownership. The common pool problem that the law tries to avoid is now created with a vengeance. The consequences for economic development and social peace are easy to envision, given that it is impossible to make productive use of an ever-increasing fraction of resources.

---

[19]See, e.g., F. Pollock and R. Wright, *Possession in the Common Law* 91–93 (1888); The Winkfield [1902] p. 42.

The doctrine of *relative title,* then, is the common law response to the problem. B by his wrong has title superior to all the world save A and those persons who claim through A. Let C, a stranger, take B's property, and B may recover it or its proceeds. Yet both of these actions may be trumped by A, either by a suit against B or a direct action against the party in possession. Nor does the story end here. B may die and leave his cause of action to D. C may die and leave his property to E. To the extent of assets descended, D has a course of action against E, as the relative title extends across persons and across generations.

Still, A or his successors cannot always have the right of action. With property titles as with contract claims, some statute of limitations is needed to wipe ancient titles off the books. As the classical article on adverse possession notes,[20] barring old valid claims is the price worth paying to protect valid titles against ceaseless attack. The social gains from forcing quick resolution of disputes are so enormous that everyone is better off with the limitation than without it. The abrogation of property rights by these statutes is fully and easily justified by the theories of implicit in-kind compensation already discussed. The private law can specify the consequences of wrongful conduct, chiefly by drawing a radical distinction between the claims of the original owner and those of the rest of the world: flawed possession counts for naught against the owner but is dispositive against the world. Once the flawed title is cleared by a statute of limitations, the normal process of mutually beneficial transactions can improve everyone's lot, notwithstanding the initial deviation from the ideal position.

As befits the subject, this theory can be carried into the public domain. Statutes of limitation may cut off (by our principle of summation) all claims for compensation demanded by one group for the property that was taken from another group. The fact that property was taken from the Indians, for example, affords no principled reason why the property should be redistributed from the present owners to the non-Indian poor. But the question is usually not so simple, for it must be asked whether each individual claimant is in the position of A, the original owner, or of C, the stranger to the title. The factual question may often prove intractable, as some of the claimants will be descendants of original owners, and others will be strangers, and still others a bit of both. Sorting out the claims introduces both administrative and error costs that come quickly to dominate the analysis. The doctrines of adverse possession and *ius tertii* depend upon being able to trace benefits and burdens across generations. There have been, in fact, so many false steps between the original error and the current position that it is quite impossible to go back and do things right, just as it is impossible to undo a system of Social Security after it has been in effect for fifty years. Any such efforts could well generate more errors than they eliminate. Can everyone claim to be the victim and not the perpetrator of improper government action? Efforts to sort out individual claims are wholly unpersuasive. Categorical efforts, those to assist blacks because of slavery and Indians because of dispossession, are likewise met with very powerful obstacles. Should other claimants be admitted to the list, given the vast amount of unjust regulation that falls short of total confiscation? Is it worth reducing total wealth, including that held by innocent parties, in an effort to run a compensation scheme that is sure to go awry if it is ever implemented?

Consider the practical obstacles to trying the large claims on their merits. It is not easy to figure out where the injured parties would have been if they had not been harmed in the first place. Is life in America for the descendants of slaves worse than life in Africa? Would migration have taken place on other and better terms? Would the Indian tribes subdued by the United States have been slaughtered by rivals, as happened in many tribal wars? If a cause of action can be established, what is the remedy? Is it possible to restore the property taken when it cannot be identified and when it has been improved by good-faith purchasers who reasonably believed that their claims were incontestable? Do we limit recoveries to damages? From whom and in what amount? Should some setoff be given for payments under government welfare programs, which were perhaps designed to offset these past injustices? How much have blacks, disadvantaged by slavery, received by block grants or welfare

---

[20] Henry Ballantine, "Title by Adverse Possession," 32 *Harv. L. Rev.* 135 (1918). "The statute [of limitations in adverse possession cases] has not for its object to reward the diligent trespasser for his wrong nor yet to penalize the negligent and dormant owner for sleeping upon his rights; the great purpose is automatically to quiet all titles which are openly and consistently asserted, to provide proof of meritorious titles, and correct errors in conveyancing." In other words, good titles can be protected against false claims of prior ownership only if bad claims are so protected as well.

payments or private charitable actions? What about the efforts of the federal government on behalf of, or against, Indians? No one could ever get the information to answer these questions if they were litigated under the set of applicable private law rules, aggregated over all individuals.

Not only is the baseline of rights insecure, but the source of the compensation is likewise problematic. One can say that the burdens of compensation all fall on the state, but this only conceals the persistent problem that the state must tax (and hence take) from individuals who have no direct responsibility for past wrongs. Many Americans reached this country after the abolition of slavery, in the great migrations from Eastern Europe between 1880 and 1920, for example. Many who were here earlier fought and gave their lives to abolish slavery. The costs of undoing the past are greater than the cost of trying to reshape the future. It may be possible to take limited steps at feasible cost to rectify the greatest abuse. Doing this would be more easily justified in a country that has been plagued with recent caste discrimination or apartheid than in our own. My own judgment is that any effort to use massive social transfers to right past wrongs will create far more tensions than it is worth, so treating all errors as a giant wash is the best of a bad lot. In contrast to my stand on welfare rights, I would give zero weight to the reliance claims of those who want to maintain a system of caste or segregation. But it is best to recognize the limits of any principle of rectification and to set about building from the base we have instead of trying to reconstruct its foundations anew.

We have thus come a complete circle. It is possible, both as a matter of constitutional law and political theory, to articulate common conceptions of right and wrong to resolve disputes that individuals have with each other and with the state. These principles do not rest upon any single value but seek to merge the three dominant strands of thought—libertarian, utilitarian, and even redistributive—into a coherent theory of individual rights and political obligations. The difficulties that remain are factual, given the complexity of our history and the legal institutions we have organized. As constructed, this argument about the eminent domain clause provides a decisive linkage between private property and public law. The received judicial wisdom about the linkage recognizes all the important parts of the picture but combines them in ways that are indefensible to anyone who is seriously concerned with either private property or limited government. The extensive discussion of the decided cases is designed to show how to reconstruct the link between individual rights and political institutions in order to demonstrate the intellectual and cultural unity of private and public law.

37

DAN ROSEN
CHIKAKO USUI

The Social Structure of Japanese Intellectual Property Law

I. INTRODUCTION

In a documentary entitled "The Japanese Version,"[1] the film-makers introduce us to a bar in Tokyo. The bar is dedicated to American cowboy culture. Western memorabilia hang on the walls; country and western music plays on the loudspeakers; and classic films play on video monitors. One customer in the bar, a dentist, regularly dresses like a character out of a Hoot Gibson movie. When asked why American Westerns are so popular in Japan, he answers without hesitation. The cowboy represents traditional Japanese society, the dentist says. Whenever there's trouble, the cowboys all gather together into a group and take care of each other's interests, just like people in Japan.

Of course, in America, the cowboy is the quintessential individualist, roaming the prairies alone and living by his own rules. Like the Lone Ranger, he rides into town, confronts evil, and then rides off into the sunset.

If both Japanese and Americans see an image as well-defined as the American cowboy so differently, it should come as no surprise that they also see intellectual property very differently.[2] To say that Japan is

[1]THE JAPANESE VERSION (The Center for New American Media 1990).

[2]*See generally* Samson Helfgott, *Cultural Differences Between the U.S. and Japanese Patent Systems,* 72 J. PAT. [& TRADEMARK] OFF. SOC'Y 231–38 (1990).

a group-oriented culture and America is an individualistic one is a cliché, but there is enough truth in the stereotypes to retain them despite the exceptions that can be found. With intellectual property, as with American Westerns, what you see depends on who you are.

In general, the intellectual property world is divided along two axes: (1) importing versus exporting nations, and (2) private enterprise versus nonmarket economies. On both of these scales, one would expect Japan to be a strong proponent of patent, trademark, and copyright laws. In the U.S., six of the top ten companies receiving patents are Japanese.[3] In Germany, as well, Japanese companies constitute the most prominent foreign applicants for patents, having applied for 2,910 in 1992, compared with 1,139 applications from American companies.[4] Japanese companies benefit greatly from trademark laws that prevent others from calling their cars "Honda Accord" or tape players "Sony Walkman." And although Japanese artistic works do not command worldwide audiences (because of the lack of knowledge of the Japanese language, not because of quality), Japanese corporations now export music and movies through their acquisition of American companies such as Columbia (Sony) and MCA (Matsushita), as well as the European EMI (Toshiba).

So, by all conventional measures, Japan should be a bastion of protection for intellectual property. And yet, compared with many Western countries and particularly the United States, the Japanese version of intellectual property law is porous and the attitude is often ambivalent. The roots of this lie in social attitudes towards the role of individuals within a society, interlocking relationships, the speed of progress, and interaction with outside entities. The argument put forward here is not that culture causes legal form, but rather that the law can best be understood as part of a much larger social system. This article will follow the threads of Japanese sociological thought and how they wind their way through patent, trade secret, trademark, and copyright.

[3] *IBM Won Most U.S. Patents in '93,* UPI, Jan. 10, 1994. . . .

[4] In Germany, however, domestic companies are at the top of the list. The most active applicants, in order, in 1992 were Siemens AG, Boscho (Robert) Gmbh, Bayer AG, BASF AG, IBM (U.S.), Hoechest AG, and Canon (Japan). *Japan Tops German Patent List,* JAPAN TIMES, Apr. 21, 1993, at 10.

II. TRADITIONAL JAPANESE THOUGHT AND THE ROLE OF INTELLECTUAL PROPERTY

In the United States, the copyright clause to the Constitution reveals the purpose of intellectual property law: "To promote the Progress of Science and the useful Arts, by securing for limited Times to Authors and Inventors the exclusive Right to their respective Writings and Discoveries."[5] Copyright is a social bribe, or at least a payoff. We promise to give the artists or inventors the sole ability to make money from their work[6] to encourage them to continue producing.[7] In a system predicated on private gain, such an incentive seems not only appropriate, but also necessary. Without it, the fear is that talented people would select other ways to use their skills—ways in which they could maximize their own economic rewards.

In contrast, Japan's copyright law reveals a balancing of interests between individual inventors and society. Rather than securing exclusive rights, the law's purpose "is to prescribe the rights of authors."[8] Unlike American patent and copyright law, which assumes exclusive rights from the outset, Japanese copyright law speaks of "promot[ing] the protection of the rights of authors, etc., giving consideration to a fair exploitation of these cultural products, and thereby . . . contributing to the development of culture."[9]

In America, the most scarred battlefield of copyright law is the fair use doctrine. Section 107 of the Copyright Act attempts to consider the interests of the public within the context of the author's exclusive

[5] U.S. CONST. art. I, § 8, cl.8.

[6] *See* Alfred C. Yen, *Restoring the National Law: Copyright as Labor and Possession,* 51 OHIO ST. L.J. 517 (1990).

[7] The other competing viewpoint, especially associated with France, provides intellectual property rights not as an incentive but rather as a recognition of the creator's dignity. *See* Dan Rosen, *Artists' Moral Rights: A European Evolution,* 2 CARDOZO ARTS & ENT. L.J. 155 (1983). Despite the theoretical aversion to the moral rights concept, it has made its way into American law, adjacent to copyright. *See, e.g.,* Russ VerSteeg, *Moral Rights for the Visual Artist: Contract Theory and Analysis,* 67 WASH. L. REV. 827 (1992); Edward J. Damich, *The Visual Artists Rights Act of 1990: Toward a Federal System of Moral Rights Protection for the Visual Arts,* 39 CATH. U. L. REV. 945 (1990). *See generally* Carl H. Settlemeyer III, *Between Thought and Possession: Artists' "Moral Rights" and Public Access to Creative Works,* 81 GEO. L.J. 2291 (1993).

[8] Chosaku-ken Hō [Copyright Law], Law No. 48 of 1970, art. 1 (Japan).

[9] *Id.*

rights, but it does so in a hesitant and, at best, Delphic manner. A variety of factors are to be considered, none of which is talismanic.[10] Wars over photocopying,[11] home videorecording,[12] and getting a scoop on the memoirs of an ex-President have been waged over the interpretation of these factors.[13] The law assumes that the private right of the copyright holder prevails unless the would-be copier can show a strong reason to be allowed a "free ride." In most fair use disputes, neither the plaintiff nor the defendant can be sanguine about the outcome.[14]

Japan takes a very different approach: simple and direct—one that prescribes the rights of authors and defines a fair exploitation. A copyrighted work "may be reproduced by a user for the purpose of his personal use, family use, or other use similar thereto within a limited area. . . ."[15] Japan does not make the interest of the public an exception to copyright; it includes the public interest in the allocation of rights. Article 33 further clarifies this "public welfare" idea. Article 33 provides publishers of government-approved school textbooks an absolute right to copy copyrighted material "for the use of children or pupils in their education in primary schools, junior and senior high schools or other similar schools."[16] The Commissioner of the Agency for Cultural Affairs then fixes an appropriate amount of payment for the use. In American copyright parlance, this is known as a compulsory license.[17] What is crucial here is that the ability to use the material is never in doubt because the public purpose is compelling.[18]

This illustrates a more general point that Japanese copyright law, like Japanese society, considers the interaction of individuals and the society simultaneously and values the correlative responsibilities at least as highly as the individual rights. American copyright law, like American society, begins with the premise that the whole prospers by giving as much protection to the individual as possible.[19]

The origins of this theme may be found in Chinese Confucianism which even today exerts a strong (if perhaps silent) influence on Japanese society. Confucianism posits a good society by mutual consideration of the needs of others. I take care of your needs; you take care of mine.[20] American thought is dominated by looking out for oneself. "Look out for number one." "Every man for himself." "It's a dog eat dog world." These are not idle proverbs.

Several writers, most notably Robert Whiting, have noted how this cultural difference affects the playing of America's national pastime in Japan. American players are accustomed to doing their best, and, by doing so, helping the entire team. The Japanese train

---

[10] *Notwithstanding the provision of sections 106 and 106A, the fair use of a copyrighted work . . . for purposes such as criticism, comment, news reporting, teaching (including multiple copies for classroom use), scholarship, or research is not an infringement of copyright. In determining whether the use made of a work in any particular case is a fair use the factors to be considered shall include—*

1. *the purpose and character of the use, including whether such use is of a commercial nature or is for nonprofit educational purposes;*
2. *the nature of the copyrighted work;*
3. *the amount and substantiality of the portion used in relation to the copyrighted work as a whole; and*
4. *the effect of the use upon the potential market for or value of the copyrighted work.*

17 U.S.C. § 107 (1988 & Supp. IV 1992).

[11] Williams & Wilkins Co. v. United States, 487 F.2d 1345 (Ct. Cl. 1973), *aff'd by an equally divided court,* 420 U.S. 376 (1975).

[12] Sony Corp. of Am. v. Universal City Studios, Inc., 464 U.S. 417 (1984).

[13] Harper & Row, Publishers, Inc. v. Nation Enters., 471 U.S. 539 (1985).

[14] *See, e.g.,* L. Ray Patterson, *Understanding Fair Use,* 55 LAW & CONTEMP. PROBS. 249 (1992); Jay Dratler, Jr., *Distilling the Witches' Brew of Fair Use in Copyright Law,* 43 MIAMI L. REV. 233 (1988).

[15] Chosaku-ken Hō, *supra* note 9, art. 30.

[16] *Id.* art. 33.

[17] Examples of compulsory license in American copyright law have included cable television retransmission of broadcast signals (17 U.S.C. § 111) (1988 & Supp. IV 1992), retransmission of satellite signals to home receiving dishes (17 U.S.C. § 119) (1988 & Supp. IV 1992), jukeboxes (17 U.S.C. §§ 116, 116A) (1988 & Supp. IV 1992) and the use of copyrighted nondramatic works by public broadcasting (17 U.S.C. 118) (1988 & Supp. IV 1992).

[18] American practice, in contrast, is the product of a compromise agreement reached among publishers', authors', educators', and trade organizations. It sets numerical limits on the amount of material that can be copied for classroom use, e.g., "an excerpt from any prose work of not more than 1,000 words or 10% of the work, whichever is less, but in any event a minimum of 500 words." *Agreement on Guidelines for Classroom Copying in Not-for-Profit Educational Institutions* II (ii) (b), *in* COPYRIGHT FOR THE NINETIES 645, 646 (Alan Latman et al. eds., 1989).

[19] Recent cases to the contrary seem to result from an inability to control the technology, rather than from any redefinition of the rights of copyright holders. *See generally* Dan Rosen, *A Common Law for the Ages of Intellectual Property,* 38 U. MIAMI L. REV. 769 (1984).

[20] Confucianism, however, frequently has been misused to justify rigid stratification and inflexible government. Some would argue that the Tokugawa shogunate in Japan adopted this approach implicitly. In seventeenth century China, it was used explicitly to strengthen the government's control. *See* JONATHAN D. SPENCE, THE SEARCH FOR MODERN CHINA 58–60 (1990).

their players to work incrementally for the progress of the team, each person sacrificing his personal goals (such as more home runs) to the immediate team objectives (bunt).[21] . . .

Takeo Doi's book, *The Anatomy of Dependence,*[22] is so often cited for this proposition that perhaps no more elaboration is necessary. Unfortunately, the translation of the title of his work obscures Doi's point that the Japanese are trained from birth to rely on others rather than to operate independently. The Japanese word in question is *amaeru*. It is not simply dependence, but rather interdependence—an elaborate interlocking system in which people look to one another (often as a kind of surrogate family) to have their needs fulfilled while they, in turn, fulfill the needs of others.

What bedevils many Western nations is that Japan's economy operates this way as well. It is an oversimplification to say that American antitrust law discourages the conglomeration of corporate power while Japanese law encourages it,[23] but not much of one.[24] Banks all offer the same services at the same cost, despite ongoing deregulation.[25] A taxi company in Kyoto recently incurred the wrath of all of its competitors by lowering prices by ten percent at a time when the others wanted a rate increase. The government gave permission to offer the discount as an experiment. The government also regulates the prices of airline flights in Japan. Prices are higher than in the U.S., and business has been bad in recent years, but the quality of service is high.[26]

Shigenori Matsui has described succinctly the difference between the American and the Japanese views of uniformity and unbridled competition. "Whereas in the United States the governmental regulation tends to be deemed justified only where the market failure or malfunction exists, it tends to be deemed justified in Japan even when no market failure or malfunction exists. . . . The role of the Government as a promoter and protector of the economy has long been accepted in Japan."[27]

Until quite recently, most Japanese corporations followed the lead of the Ministry of International Trade and Industry ("MITI"), in setting their goals. MITI set these goals by instigating interaction between corporate players, rather than by passing down Stalinistic decrees.[28] John Haley has called this process of Japanese administration "consensual administrative management."[29] The government would decide generally the most beneficial direction for industry, and then "Japan Inc.," as it was called sometimes, would head in that direction together; not like the legs of the same animal, but rather like the parade of different animals all headed toward Noah's ark. Everyone would be able to get on board, but each in its own way. Those who wanted more space, or who wished to steer the boat a different way, however, would be cast overboard quickly.

Frank Upham's retelling of the tale of Sato Taiji illustrates the point. Sato, a born iconoclast, decided it would be a good idea to import gas and sell it cheaply. Good for business and good for consumers. MITI, however, saw his plan differently. In its eyes, Sato's success would undermine the carefully main-

---

[21]ROBERT WHITING, YOU GOTTA HAVE WA (1989); ROBERT WHITING, THE CHRYSANTHEMUM AND THE BAT (1977).

[22]TAKEO DOI, THE ANATOMY OF DEPENDENCE (John Bester trans., 1971).

[23]*See generally* MITSUO MATSUSHITA, INTRODUCTION TO JAPANESE ANTIMONOPOLY LAW (1990); Alex Y. Seita & Jiro Tamura, *The Historical Background of Japan's Antimonopoly Law,* 1994 U. ILL. L. REV. 115 (1994).

[24]*See generally* J. D. Richards, Comment, *Japan Fair Trade Commission Guidelines Concerning Distribution Systems and Business Practices: An Illustration of Why Antitrust Law is a Weak Solution to U.S. Trade Problems With Japan,* 2 WIS. L. REV. 921 (1993).

[25]For example, the Japanese subsidiary of Citibank, from the United States, is the only bank in Japan that has 24-hour automatic teller machines (ATMs).

[26]Maintaining quality and guarding against the ill effects of unrestrained price competition are the main reasons given for government control of "excessive competition." *See generally* DANIEL OKIMOTO, BETWEEN MITI AND THE MARKET: JAPANESE INDUSTRIAL POLICY FOR HIGH TECHNOLOGY (1989). It should be noted that the airline business in the deregulated U.S. market has been bad too, with many carriers going out of business and others struggling. *See generally* AIRLINE DEREGULATION: THE EARLY EXPERIENCE (John R. Meyer & Clinton V. Oster, Jr. eds., 1981); ANTHONY E. BROWN, THE POLITICS OF AIRLINE DEREGULATION (1987); STEVEN MORRISON & CLIFFORD WINSTON, THE ECONOMIC EFFECTS OF AIRLINE DEREGULATION (1986).

[27]Shigenori Matsui, *Lochner v. New York in Japan: Protecting Economic Liberties in a Country Governed by Bureaucrats, in* LAW AND TECHNOLOGY IN THE PACIFIC COMMUNITY 199, 299 (Philip S. C. Lewis ed. 1994). Professor Matsui, however, believes that "it is more likely that the term 'excessive competition' is used as a pretext for protectionist regulation for the industry." *See also* J. Mark Ramseyer, *The Cost of the Consensual Myth: Antitrust Enforcement and Institutional Barriers to Litigation in Japan,* 94 YALE L.J. 604 (1985).

[28]Western writers, especially, have many different interpretations of MITI's role. *See, e.g.,* CHALMERS JOHNSON, MITI AND THE JAPANESE MIRACLE (1982); DAVID FRIEDMAN, THE MISUNDERSTOOD MIRACLE: INDUSTRIAL DEVELOPMENT AND POLITICAL CHANGE IN JAPAN (1988).

[29]JOHN O. HALEY, AUTHORITY WITHOUT POWER: LAW AND THE JAPANESE PARADOX 144 (1991).

tained balance of oil company profitability, employment, and stability of supply. And so, MITI, through "administrative guidance" (*gyō-sei shidō*)[30] and its network of influence throughout the economy made sure that he would be stopped.[31]

In recent years, increased trading with countries that do not share this worldview has caused some breakdown in this system. . . .

38

A. JOHN SIMMONS

Historical Rights and Fair Shares

V

. . . There are, I think, two broadly liberal approaches to dealing with the claims and problems of groups like the Native American peoples, only one of which is historical in the sense discussed here. Some theorists treat Native Americans simply as one of a number of disadvantaged groups in our society, all of whom need to be made better off until they enjoy the social and economic rights and goods that justice demands be provided to all. Native Americans may require some special rights, based on the special vulnerability of their cultural context; but their tribes' historical standings as the original occupants of the Americas are irrelevant to their current moral claims.[1] The alternative liberal approach to this end-state view is to take seriously the historical claims of Native Americans to land and resources as the basis of persistent rights to rectification, beyond anything to which they are entitled simply as equal citizens (or persons).[2] The virtue of the historical approach, as I see it, is that it preserves the particularity of Native American claims. Their rights are not, I think, just rights to some fair share of American resources; they are rights to a particular (or a particularized) fair share. Treating Native American rights as exclusively end-state rights means denying that the actual arguments made by Native American tribes for historical rights to particular lands and resources have any moral force at all, or any appeal beyond ungrounded emotionalism. But I do not think most of us regard Native American demands for control over portions of their historical homelands simply as unmotivated, sentimental nonsense.

It is tempting to embrace the nonhistorical, end-state view if we think that passing time and changing circumstances simply wipe out such historical rights. But I have suggested some ways in which historical rights can be sensitive to changing circumstances without simply dissolving in the face of change. I've argued that we can have genuinely historical rights whose content is nonetheless imprecise. This imprecision of content, however, does not reduce such rights to general, nonhistorical (i.e., end-state) rights to any fair share. Rather, such rights can be to particularized, though not particular, fair shares of land or resources.

These arguments enable us to defend a conception of Native American rights to rectification that preserves at least some of the particularity of the claims actually advanced in lawsuits and published

---

[30]*See id.* at 160–66 (1991).

[31]MITI's network of influence throughout the economy may extend as far as China—one of Sato's shipments never made it on the ship. Frank K. Upham, *The Man Who Would Import: A Cautionary Tale About Bucking the System in Japan,* 17 J. Japanese Stud. 323 (1991) (reviewing Sato Taiji, Ore Wa Tsūsansho ni Barasareta! [I Was Butchered by MITI!] (1986)).

In May of 1994, Nagoya-based Kanare Beikoku—a rice retailer—opened a discount gas station in Akomaki, Aichi prefecture, without a government license. It was said to be the first gas station in Japan to sell gas for less than ¥100 per liter. MITI refused the company's registration papers twice because it was unsatisfied with the documentation of the source of the gasoline. Eventually, in late June, MITI relented and the station received authorized status. *See Cheap Gas Fuels Debate Over Regulations,* Daily Yomiuri, June 14, 1994, at 9; *Gas Station Gets License,* Japan Times, July 1, 1994, at 14.

[1]This is roughly the approach taken by Will Kymlicka in *Liberalism, Community, and Culture* (Oxford: Oxford University Press, 1989). See especially the long footnote on pp. 158–61 in which Kymlicka expresses scepticism about the moral importance of "the fact of original occupancy." Lyons also concludes that "it is highly doubtful that [Native Americans] have any special claims based upon their distant ancestors' original occupation of the land" ("The New Indian Claims . . .": 268). Waldron seems sympathetic to this approach as well ("Superseding Historic Injustice": 26–28).

[2]A good recent example of this approach can be found in James Tully, "Rediscovering America: the *Two Treatises* and Aboriginal Rights," in *An Approach to Political Philosophy: Locke in Contexts* (Cambridge: Cambridge University Press, 1993).

arguments by (or on behalf of) Native American tribes. There is, I think, a range of acceptable rectificatory outcomes in these cases. Native American historical rights are to particularized shares; but the relevant entitlements were seldom made precise by any freely chosen (or otherwise responsibly accomplished) just downsizing of holdings. This means the historical rights of Native Americans are in certain ways imprecise (in addition to being exceptionally difficult to trace). But their rights are to (currently) fair portions of the actual lands they lived, hunted, and worked on, not to generic fair shares of American land. And these particularized rights are to portions of what were once their central holdings—for instance, to portions of lands they held sacred, lands on which they resided, or lands in which they invested labor through agriculture or other improvements (like ecological management). Where lands or resources within the acceptable range of particularized shares have been destroyed or irreversibly altered (by commercial development, say), the best rectification will be accomplished by returning land or goods that most closely approximate those to which Native Americans have particularized rights, or lands or goods that best facilitate duplicating the condition they would have enjoyed in the absence of the original injustice. Our counterfactual judgments in these cases should be conservative, assuming an absence of rashness and of extraordinary developments. And additional compensation for losses incurred during the changing of circumstances that required downsizing must also be considered.

It will certainly turn out that some past property injustices are simply unrectifiable. And it will certainly turn out as well that our judgments about just rectification will be fuzzy at best, complicated as they are both by evidentiary problems and by the imprecision of historical rights to shares (and of the concept of a fair share generally). The calculations required to determine even a reasonably specific range of acceptable rectificatory outcomes will be, to say the least, extraordinarily complex. But the principles noted here can at least provide some very broad guidelines for the proper way to particularize the reparations made to Native American peoples. We will always face, of course, the problems of conflicting claims by current generations of (largely) innocent third parties, those "newcomers" to the Americas whose expectations are firmly based on an assumed continuation of current distributions of land and resources. Those of us in this group are not, of course, quite like the completely innocent person who unwittingly builds his life around holdings that just turn out to have been stolen by an earlier possessor. For we all know the history of theft, broken agreements, and brutal subjugation on which our holdings in land and natural resources historically rest. But the claims of current generations of Americans must still be taken seriously. They can only be taken seriously in the right measure, however, if we first understand at least some of the force of the historical rights of Native Americans with which these claims are alleged to conflict.

Now it may seem that in these suggestions I have blithely ignored the two largest obstacles to understanding or accepting historical rights: the changes in cast that accompany long passages of time, and the dramatically different conceptions of property in fact favored by most Native American tribes. I will close this discussion with a few brief remarks on these two problems. Taking changes of cast first, there are obviously two central, relevant possibilities of this sort: those involving the death of the victim of wrongdoing and those involving the death of the wrongdoer. Both sorts of cases are complicated. When the wrongdoer dies, he may leave behind nothing that could adequately compensate his victim for the wrong, in which case rectification will simply be impossible. Where land is at issue, of course, this will generally not be the case (though we will still need to deal with the conflicting claims on the land of the children or dependents of the wrongdoer or of innocent third party holders of stolen land). But set all of this aside for now; the impossibility of full rectification in certain kinds of cases is not, I think, any more of a problem here than is the impossibility of retributive justice in cases where offenders die before they can be punished. The more troubling questions, I believe, clearly concern those cases in which the victim of wrongdoing dies. If the victim's rights die with him, of course, then Native American rights cannot possibly have persisted through the centuries in the ways my previous remarks suggested.

And why should we suppose that rights of rectification have simply been passed down family lines, from the original victims of injustice all the way to their current descendants? After all, those original victims might, in the absence of the injustice, have later sold their holdings or lost them in a poker game or given them to a needy friend, so that the relevant rights never would have passed to their children anyway. Why should inheritance of rights to rectification simply be assumed in this way,[3] particularly when we know that inherited property is the source of many apparent social injustices?[4] To this I think there are three appropriate responses. First, our counterfactual judgments about how things would have gone on in the absence of the wrong should be conservative.... Second, I think children have rights against their parents to the receipt of property (including in this "property" parental rights to the return of stolen property) that is needed by those children for a decent life; and in the case of the children of hunter-gatherers, this will invariably mean rights to use of the land and natural resources. Even if the parents did freely give away or sell the land their children needed for a decent life, then, the children would still have claims against the recipients of that land to the portions they needed.[5] Their parents were not entitled to dispose of the land without regard for the needs of their offspring. Finally, and perhaps most obviously relevant, we have the fact that the land and resources at issue were taken by Native Americans to be tribal property, not individual property.[6] If the property was thus held jointly, so were the relevant rights to rectification of injustice; and then, of course, the death of individual Native Americans was irrelevant to the question of persisting historical rights, as was the question of inheritance of rights (since the tribe as a whole never died, in at least many actual historical cases).

Now this last response may seem to solve the problem of the changing cast of characters only at the price of introducing new difficulties into our attempts to make sense of historical rights. First, there is no doubt that most Native American tribes understood the nature of their property in land and resources quite differently than, say, Locke and Nozick understand property rights. Tribes regarded themselves as inseparably connected to certain territories, so that their identities depended on continued and in some cases exclusive use of the land. Tribal ownership (or, better, stewardship) of the land was typically viewed as essential and inalienable, with ownership not so much derived from productive use as demanding productive uses that harmonized with the land.[7] And this amounts, of course, to a view of property in land which is more national than simply joint or collective. On such a conception of property in land, mandatory downsizing to make room for newcomers makes no clear sense. Newcomers may be permitted to use (nonsacred) tribal lands, but they cannot come to have any kind of property in the land that excludes tribal use.

From a Lockean historical perspective, this Native American conception of property rights will probably be viewed as in certain ways simply mistaken. Persons have rights of fair access to land and natural resources, and even a nation is not entitled to insist on control over a territory of inflexible size.[8] We must make room for everyone.[9] Native American beliefs that they need not yield to newcomers exclusive control over portions of their territories would then be viewed as a kind of nonculpable moral ignorance, an ignorance that perhaps excuses their acts of resistance to settlement of their territories, but that in no way limits the rights of fair access (and self-defense) of newcomers. The alternative (i.e., non-Lockean) historical perspectives are

---

[3]Waldron, "Superseding Historic Injustice": 15.

[4]Lyons, "The New Indian Claims . . .": 258.

[5]I discuss this view in *The Lockean Theory of Rights*, pp. 204–12.

[6]Waldron, "Superseding Historic Injustice": 15; Lyons, "The New Indian Claims . . .": 257.

[7]Tully, "Rediscovering America," pp. 138, 153–54. This view of property thus had more in common with pre-Lockean (than with Lockean) European conceptions of property, according to which land was sometimes taken to define the family that possessed it and consequently to be inalienable for that family.

[8]Locke himself regarded national territories as set by understandings or contracts (treaties) between nations, in which members of each society give up rights of fair access to land within the agreed-upon boundaries of other societies (*Second Treatise*, §45). But it is unclear why such agreements should be taken to bind or protect (a) new residents of these societies (prior to their consenting to membership); (b) individuals in the state of nature (such as Locke imagined Native Americans to be); or (c) nations that lack this understanding or were not otherwise party to any tacit or express agreements concerning national territory. Locke could, of course, have tried recognizing the Native American nations as genuine political societies, and then placed them with the nations in group (c), thus justifying appropriation of their territories by European settlers. But this would have entailed that those same Native Americans were free to appropriate European territory. It was thus safer from Locke's perspective (which included his desire to defend European settlement of the Americans) to place Native Americans in class (b), as Locke in fact did.

[9]This implication for national property is one of the least discussed features of historical rights theories. A Lockean alternative is to view the right of fair access as a right of access not to land and natural resources, but to the means for living a decent life. This right of fair access might, then, in developed societies entail, not rights to land for newcomers, but rights to wealth or to nonalienating opportunities for paid employment. See *The Lockean Theory of Rights*, pp. 293–94.

either conventionalist, relativizing property claims within a territory to those acknowledged by the dominant conventions in that territory,[10] or use-oriented, denying that exclusive private property in land or natural resources is possible.

But it may seem that the problems for a Lockean historical theory run still deeper. We might think, for example, that Lockeans simply can't handle joint or collective property claims at all, that all Lockean property is individual. This view, I think, is clearly confused. Joint property is certainly possible on a Lockean view.[11] Any individual property that individuals freely join together is then the (private) joint property of that collective. And further, if property acquisition turns on labor or on the incorporation of objects into purposive activities, joint property will be produced wherever objects are incorporated into collective projects. Thus, Native American tribes can certainly be supposed even on a Lockean view to have joint property in bodies of land or in natural resources. They can thus have historical rights to land or resources that can persist through time; they can have rights to the rectification of property injustices (i.e., injustices consisting in violations of those historical rights); and they can have rights that may be affected (in the ways we have discussed) by changing circumstances.

This conclusion needs two final points of clarification. First, even joint or collective property is subject to the individualistic limit set by the idea of a fair share. Collectives may hold no more property than the sum of the fair shares of their individual members.[12] And mandatory downsizing will be determined in terms of the proportionate downsizing of individual shares. Second, our Lockean conclusions about Native American tribal property cannot be derived by strict adherence to the letter of Locke's own arguments. Locke himself took Native Americans to have property only in their artifacts and in the products of their hunting and gathering. They had no property in land, for they did not use the land itself in any efficient way, as did the European settlers who enclosed and cultivated portions of the earth. Thus, for Locke there was no question of required reparations for encroachments on tribal lands, for those lands constituted vacant waste still awaiting original appropriation.[13]

If, though, we take seriously the idea that property can be acquired by incorporation into our purposive activities, then the collective tribal activities of hunting, fishing, migratory residence, nonsedentary agriculture, and the like, could certainly have grounded tribal property rights in land and resources. But while Locke may have been wrong on that point, he was certainly right about the inefficiency of aboriginal land use, at least in this one sense—there is not enough land in the world to support us all at the population density levels characteristic of original Native American tribal life. Even if hunting and gathering remain legitimate sources of property in land, the fair shares of land available for exclusive use by hunter-gatherers must be far smaller than those originally occupied by aboriginal Americans. Thus, mandatory downsizing enters our theory even if we reject Locke's assump-

---

[10]The Lockean view "naturalizes" property rights, I think, precisely to avoid such conventionalism. For if property rests simply on social convention, our property cannot be secure, given the possibility of simple alterations in social convention. The Lockean has to argue that while agreements between persons or within groups may change property relations between those involved, such agreements cannot change the rights of those not party to the agreements—such as white settlers, who could insist, on natural moral grounds, on their rights of fair access to land and resources.

[11]Indeed, national territory is for Locke in one sense all joint, for though it is composed of private land holdings, this private land is "united" to the commonwealth (*Second Treatise,* §120). And the commons within each nation's boundaries is the pure joint property of all the nation's members (ibid., §35). On the acquisition of collective property in Pufendorf and Locke, see my "Original Acquisition Theories," section III.

[12]The truth of this claim rests on (at least) three assumptions. First, of course, I assume that collectives are the kinds of things that can possess rights. Second, I assume no insuperable difficulties are introduced by the changing composition of the collectives. Third, I assume that members of a collective may hold in trust the rights to fair shares of other members who have been wrongfully killed or who have died after being unjustly deprived of their shares. Thus, we cannot reduce the fair share of a tribe by killing off its members or by stealing their land and waiting for them to die off. Tribes are entitled to hold shares in trust for future members under such circumstances (for some reasonable time period, at least), just as family members are entitled to do in cases of joint familial property. Morris has objected to the second of these assumptions by suggesting that since the collective will have "radically different" histories in the possible worlds containing and not containing the injustice, the actual and the possible collectives cannot be identical ("Existential Limits": 181). But here, unlike the case of individuals conceived after the injustice, the identity of the group across possible worlds can be supported by continuity with the previous (i.e., pre-injustice) history of the group in all similar worlds. Even more obviously, the "counterpart relation" (that can be used instead of identity in such cases) can be supported by that same previous history.

[13]Tully, "Rediscovering America," pp. 148, 162.

tions about which activities constituted productive (hence, appropriative) uses of the land.

We are left, then, with a characteristically liberal idea, one that we can now see is embraced by both purely historical and purely end-state theories of property rights and social justice (and so, we can surmise, one that will be embraced by any hybrid theory as well). Justice cares about insuring to all persons (access to) their fair share of goods and resources; it cares far less about the manner in which persons use these goods to advance their life plans and particular projects, or in the perceived virtues of those plans or projects themselves.

39

NELL JESSUP NEWTON

Compensation, Reparations, and Restitution: Indian Property Claims in the United States

Calls for restitution in Eastern Europe present legal scholars in the United States with an opportunity to reexamine the legal and moral justifications for laws of property distribution in general and laws permitting confiscation and mandating restitution in particular. Western legal and constitutional theory accepts that government may take property from its citizens for public purposes upon payment of compensation that is more than merely symbolic. Uncompensated confiscations are deemed wrongs that ought to be remedied by restitution[1] *in natura* or in the form of money damages, even when these confiscations were declared to be legal under the law of the discredited regime.[2]

Even assuming *arguendo* that the emerging consensus of states favors the principle of compensation, nonetheless, many regimes have confiscated property without compensation. Some states have enacted positive laws legitimating their own seizures by such devices as declaring the state's actions not to be "takings" or the land taken not to be "property." During the Communist regimes in Eastern Europe, for example, much private property was nationalized. This uncompensated nationalization was theoretically a redistribution to the people of the property seized; since no one had a right to own private property, the property taken was not compensable because it was not property. In the alternative, seizure was justified as a legitimate remedy against the former owners for their crimes against the state.

As the process of democratic reform began to sweep Eastern Europe in 1989, many citizens called for restitution of property nationalized during the Communist regimes, especially small landholders whose land had been nationalized during Communist rule.[3] The new democratic governments in Eastern Europe are seriously considering making restitution of property, justifying their demands on moral as well as practical grounds. Rights-based arguments regarding the sanctity of property and the obligation to give something back when one has been unjustly enriched, as well as pragmatic consequentialist arguments, seem to concur in creating this favorable climate for restitution. A restitution policy designed to right the wrongs of the past can help the new regime build credibility and legitimacy as a justice-administering state and can attract foreign capital by ensuring foreign investors that their property rights will be respected. Because a broad restitution plan can also be an efficient mechanism in the privatization movement by placing property in private hands, the intuitive appeal of restitution is enormous.

All the decisions regarding restitution require rethinking of first principles, including whether to attempt any restitution. Jon Elster has argued eloquently the position that restitution should be eschewed.[4] He asserts that so many lost so much, including physical and psychological suffering and lost opportunities as well as land, that, therefore, the most moral and efficient position would be to eschew backward-looking remedies like restitution in favor of distributing property to all citizens. According to Elster,

---

[1]Frank Bönker & Claus Offe, The Morality of Restitution: Considerations on Some Normative Questions Raised by the Transition to a Private Economy 13 (May, 1993) (unpublished manuscript, on file with author).

[2]*Id.* at 13 n.9.

[3]For a background on the history of the Hungarian Smallholders Party and its impact on the restitution process in Hungary, see Ellen Comisso, Legacies of the Past or New Institutions? The Struggle over Restitution in Hungary 7 (1993) (unpublished manuscript, on file with author).

[4]*See* Jon Elster, *On Doing What One Can,* 1 E. EUR. CONST. REV. 15 (1992).

such a distribution, perhaps through a voucher system, would be morally superior in both deontological and consequentialist terms, because it would benefit a much wider group than those who had owned land. It would be efficient because it would avoid litigation to establish the identity of those in desert of restitution. It would also expedite the return to a market economy.[5]

For political and moral reasons, most Eastern European nations have decided to make individual restitution for illegitimate takings either by compensation or by actual restoration of land. Consequently, the debates have focused more narrowly on many questions: which injustices deserve restitution, what kind of property should be restored, what is the relevant cut-off date for restitution, who deserves restitution, for what seizures, whether restitution should be *in natura* or money damages, and finally, whether restitution can be accomplished without creating new demands for compensation.

In all the debates about restitution, the assumption is made that the stability of both the United States political and economic systems is promoted by a strong market system and the reinforcing sanctity of private property in its legal regime. The security of property rights in the United States extends to large and small landholdings whether or not landholders plan to sell the property or otherwise put it to productive use. In other words, this stable property regime, which includes the promise that confiscation must be compensated, encourages both investment-backed expectations and the expectations of those whose land lies idle because it protects all owners of property. Consequently, many of those calling for restitution in Eastern Europe invoke this vision of property in the United States legal regime as both a reproach and an aspiration.

In other words, the United States property system is valorized as a safe haven for property rights and a model for new emerging market economies. Yet the United States also has had to struggle with the problem of a new democratic successor state confronting different concepts of property tied to pre-existing sovereign entities. I am referring, of course, to the handling of Indian property rights in the courts of the United States. An examination of the treatment of the property of American Indian tribes serves three useful purposes.

First, on the most pragmatic level, the United States has developed various models for compensating Indian tribes for land taken, including restitution plans. As part of these models, the government has dealt with many of the same questions bedeviling policymakers in Eastern Europe: who should be eligible, the owner at the time of confiscation alone, or his or her heirs? What is the appropriate cutoff date for restitution? What methods of restitution should be used, whether *in natura* or in money damages?

Second, an examination of United States Indian land policy reveals that the invocation of the sanctity of private property rights as the basis of the market economy is overly simplified. The United States is not a successor state grappling with the question of the extent to which it owes a duty to those harmed by its predecessor. In contrast, it is the very government that confiscated land from Indian tribes by methods both naked and subtle despite the high sounding words of the Fifth Amendment Takings Clause. Thus, countries invoking the United States as a model should be aware that invocations of national property rights may themselves hide other motives.

In short, the successes and failures of the various plans tried in the United States may serve as models for proposals in the East.

In other words, attention paid to the marginalization of Indian property rights in American law may refocus the debate more clearly. It will reveal much about political decisions masked by calls for restitution based on principles of natural justice. The same focus also may alert policymakers to the pitfalls of various restitution systems.

This paper will first present a short history of the land policy in the United States, focusing on the formal mechanisms used to wrest most Indian land from American tribes. As with the Communist regimes in Eastern Europe, American law developed to justify these takings as perfectly legal and presumptively moral. The federal courts have spun a web of rules to enforce treaties of cession whether coerced or consensual, to declare aboriginal Indian property as not property within the meaning of the Fifth Amendment to the United States Constitution, and to declare physical invasions of Indian land that result in the transfer of land from the tribe to the United States as not necessarily "takings." Outrageous self-serving justifications

[5] *See* David Franklin, The Pull of the Past: Restitution and Rehabilitation in Post-Revolutionary Czechoslovakia, Report to the Center for the Study of Constitutionalism in Central and Eastern Europe 4–6 (Aug. 1, 1991) (unpublished manuscript, on file with author) (giving history and major justifications for voucher plan).

for seizing Indian land and destroying tribalism have alternated with frank acknowledgment of the wrongs done to Native Americans and the moral duty to make amends. After describing these legal developments, some of which have taken place in the years since the 1940s, the paper will discuss the various methods advocated to make restitution for some of these actions in the form of special claims tribunals and other methods to provide compensation/reparations, and *in natura* restitution. The paper ends by drawing a few preliminary conclusions about the similarities and differences in the treatment of the Indian tribal experience with the treatment of groups to be benefitted by some of the restitution plans currently being debated.

A cautionary note is in order. This paper focuses solely on land claims. Although compensation or reparation proposals in Eastern Europe often include compensation for personal harms, American law has not provided any mechanism to compensate Indian tribes for loss of political freedom, the destruction of culture, and other intangible harms.[6]

I. THE DISPOSSESSION OF INDIAN PROPERTY

Contrary to what Francis Jennings has called the "cant of conquest,"[7] words rather than the sword accomplished the dispossession of the United States' original Indian inhabitants from their aboriginal land. Although land transfers did result from armed conflicts with Indian tribes, much more land was acquired through treaties negotiated with Indian tribes.[8] In the early nineteenth century, Alexis de Tocqueville noted ironically that, although American law regarding treatment of Indians was inspired "by the most chaste affection for the legal formalities,"[9] in practice a combination of the rapacity of the settlers, the formal niceties of American treaty law, and the willingness of the government to back up the settlers resulted in "the Americans cheaply acquir[ing] whole provinces which the richest sovereigns of Europe could not afford to buy."[10]

In other words, although some treaties executed in the eighteenth and early nineteenth century were the products of arms-length bargaining,[11] many were procured by fraud or simply by the threat of force so great that tribes had no choice but to cede more land, further blurring the line between consent and coercion in American Indian policy.[12] Of over two billion

---

[6]*See, e.g.,* Fort Sill Apache Tribe v. United States, 477 F.2d 1360 (Ct. Cl. 1973) (holding claim for false imprisonment for 27 years was not justiciable); *see also* Nell Jessup Newton, *Indian Claims in the Courts of the Conqueror,* 41 A.U. L. REV. 753, 776-84 (1992) (discussing *Fort Sill Apache Tribe* case and another unsuccessful claim based on breach of trust).

[7]FRANCIS JENNINGS, THE INVASION OF AMERICA: INDIANS, COLONIALISM AND THE CANT OF CONQUEST (1975) (recounting history of Colonial land dealings with Indian tribes).

[8]Felix Cohen, a twentieth century jurisprudence and Indian law scholar, asserted that far more land was purchased from tribes in a regular fashion than ever seized by the United States government. Felix S. Cohen, *Original Indian Title,* 32 MINN. L. REV. 28, 35 (1947). To accept Cohen's conclusion requires a minimizing of any coercion in the treaty process that elevates the form of contract over its circumstances and substance. In addition, Cohen's discussion omitted the land seizures by most of the thirteen original states, which claimed a right to deal with Indians superior to that of the newly created federal government. *See* Robert W. Clinton & Margaret Tobey Hotopp, *Judicial Enforcement of the Federal Restraints on Alienation of Indian Land: The Origins of the Eastern Land Claims,* 31 Me. L. Rev. 17 (1979) (describing process leading up to Nonintercourse Act claims of modern era).

[9]ALEXIS DE TOCQUEVILLE, DEMOCRACY IN AMERICA 339 (J.P. Mayer ed. & George Lawrence trans. 1969).

[10]*Id.* at 325.

[11]*See* FRANCIS PAUL PRUCHA, AMERICAN INDIAN POLICY IN THE FORMATIVE YEARS 142–44 (1962) (arguing that many treaties of period 1790–1834 were fairly negotiated and enforced).

[12]Although the treaty terms were translated from the English language, even well-meaning translators had trouble accurately rendering feudal concepts of fee simple title to peoples who believed in the common ownership of land. Sloppy and dishonest translations obfuscated the true nature of the transactions. Consequently, tribes often assumed they were granting usage rights in treaties ceding land in perpetuity. Since the translations were oral, for the most part (the Cherokees and some of the so-called Five Civilized Tribes had developed a written language), disputes were judged against the plain meaning of the document. In addition, government negotiators often engaged in the process Indian people call chief-naming: selecting friendly natives to put their marks on documents as tribal chiefs or headmen capable of acting in the interest of their members. *See* JENNINGS, *supra* note [7] at 105–45 (providing examples of such chicanery during Colonial era). *See generally* PRUCHA, *supra* note [11] (recounting treaty policies in years 1790–1834). For accounts of the various methods used to obtain treaties with the Cherokees requiring them to move from Georgia, see Joseph C. Burke, *The Cherokee Cases: A Study in Law, Politics and Morality,* 21 STAN. L. REV. 500 (1969); William F. Swindler, *Politics as Law: The Cherokee Cases,* 3 AM. INDIAN L. REV. 7 (1975). Although chiefs of the Sioux Nation signed a treaty ceding the Black Hills, they did so because a "sell or starve" rider Congress had attached to an appropriation act was having its intended effect. Nevertheless, the agreement violated a previous treaty promise that the government would not take any land from the tribe without the agreement of three-fourths of the male members of the tribe. Congress then cured this defect by enacting a law abrogating the earlier treaty. For the background, see II FRANCIS PAUL PRUCHA, THE GREAT FATHER 631–33 (1984).

acres of Indian land acquired by the United States, approximately one billion acres were compensated at an average rate of 7¢ per acre.[13] Like contracts of adhesion, many of these treaties share the qualities of statutory law.

In recognition of the one-sided nature of the treaty process, the courts of the United States have adopted maxims of treaty construction to mitigate the impact of the treaties on tribal property and sovereignty rights.[14] Not always honored, these maxims nevertheless state an ideal that shapes results in some cases as well as rhetoric.

In 1871, Congress formally ended the practice of making treaties with Indian tribes.[15] Although the new policy was principally propelled by the House of Representatives' demand to be included in Indian policy-setting, the United States Supreme Court interpreted the action as an unreviewable political decision to domesticate Indian affairs under the plenary power of Congress.[16]

Federal statutes took the place of treaties as the vehicles of dispossession of Indian tribal land. According to Russel Barsh, nearly one-fourth of the contiguous forty-eight states were acquired during one decade: 1865–1875.[17] Approximately one billion acres were taken outright with either no compensation or only token compensation.[18] Another ninety million acres of land that had been unilaterally privatized was lost to tribal ownership during the allotment era, reducing the Indian land mass by two-thirds.[19] Although not technically a taking under American law, for reasons to be detailed later, the 1971 congressional law that confiscated some 335 million acres of Alaska in return for $900 million and shares of stock in corporations formed to own 44 million acres of Alaskan land, represents an uncompensated transfer of tribal ownership of land to newly created corporations and, I would argue, an undercompensated taking of property at less than fair market value.[20]

The greed for land and the cultural and racial superiority of the white settlers and their supporters created the popular will to confiscate Indian land. Unfortunately the United States Supreme Court gave its imprimatur to these takings. Judicial decisions legitimizing takings in turn permitted the citizenry to accept the results as fair. In other words, the words that have been the most effective in "conquering" the Indians are the words of the great legal decisions setting the premises of American Indian Law as it relates to land rights: *The Marshall Trilogy,* decided between 1823 and 1832;[21] the *Plenary Power Cases* of the late nineteenth and early twentieth century;[22] and the more recent cases establishing the legitimacy of rules of formal inequality relating to Indian land: *Tee-Hit-Ton Indians v. United States*[23] in 1955, which would legitimize the confiscation of Alaska in 1971, and *United States v. Sioux Nation of Indians*[24] in 1980.

A. The Marshall Trilogy

Beginning in 1823, Chief Justice John Marshall wrote a series of opinions for the United States Supreme Court stating essential principles primarily designed to ensure federal superiority over the states and national superiority over other foreign nations with regard to Indian policy. Simply put, these principles asserted the primacy of federal control over Indian affairs, rooted in the Consti-

[13]Russel Lawrence Barsh, *Indian Land Claims Policy in the United States,* 58 N.D. L. REV. 7 (1982).

[14]*See, e.g.,* United States v. Winans, 198 U.S. 371, 380–81 (1905) (construing as "justice and reason demand in all cases where power is exerted by the strong over those to whom they owe care and protection"); *accord, e.g.,* Choctaw Nation v. Oklahoma, 397 U.S. 620, 631 (1970).

[15]Act of Mar. 3, 1871, ch. 120, 16 Stat. 544, 566 (codified as amended at 25 U.S.C. § 71 (Supp. 1993).

[16]*See* United States v. Kagama, 118 U.S. 375 (1886) (holding that Act of Mar. 3, 1885 gave United States courts jurisdiction over Indians belonging to Indian tribes).

[17]Barsh, *supra* note [13], at 8 n.3.

[18]Approximately 325,000 acres in the Great Basin were taken without compensation. Barsh, *supra* note [13], at 7. The entire State of California was taken by statute after the Senate failed to ratify treaties entered into by all the California Indian tribes who would have retained substantial land. *See* Indians of California v. United States, 102 Ct. Cl. 837 (1944) (awarding California Indians $5,024,842); Ralph L. Beals, *The Anthropologist as Expert Witness, in* IRREDEEMABLE AMERICA: THE INDIANS' ESTATE AND LAND CLAIMS 139 (Imre Sutton ed. 1985) (describing California land claim case).

[19]S. LYMAN TYLER, A HISTORY OF INDIAN POLICY 124 (1973).

[20]Although compensation was paid for Alaska's 335 million acres, the settlement suffers from two flaws: it was not, despite its name, an agreement with the Alaskan natives. Second, the natives did not receive anything close to fair market value for the land taken.

[21]Johnson v. McIntosh, 21 U.S. (8 Wheat.) 543 (1823); Cherokee Nation v. Georgia, 30 U.S. (5 Pet.) 1 (1831); Worcester v. Georgia, 31 U.S. (6 Pet.) 515 (1832).

[22]Stephens v. Cherokee Nation, 174 U.S. 445 (1899); Lone Wolf v. Hitchcock, 187 U.S. 553 (1903).

[23]348 U.S. 272 (1955).

[24]448 U.S. 371 (1980).

tution's Commerce Clause and the provisions explicitly and implicitly entrusting the foreign relations power to the national government. Rejecting an argument that Indian tribes had no status under the Constitution, Chief Justice Marshall declared that tribes were neither states of the Union nor foreign nations.[25] Nevertheless, they remained sovereign states with authority over events within their borders.[26] He referred to them as "domestic dependent nations"[27] and quoted with approval from Vattel's treatise in drawing the analogy to "[t]ributary and feudatory states . . .[which] do not thereby cease to be sovereign and independent states."[28] This recognition of the self-governing status of Indian tribes remains unique in the world's treatment of aboriginal peoples. Despite later Supreme Court cases that have weakened the protection accorded by United States law to Indian tribal sovereignty,[29] tribes retain considerable power over their own members[30] as well as those living and working on reservations or doing business with Indian people.[31]

The Marshall Trilogy also created a land policy that provided a rationale both for accepting what had been done before as well as securing Indian tribes' land rights in the future. In *Johnson v. McIntosh*,[32] the first of the *Trilogy* cases, Chief Justice Marshall constructed a legal framework for incorporating Indian property rights within the United States legal regime. Rejecting the argument that tribes could claim no natural rights to their land, he also rejected the notion that tribes' rights were superior to those of the United States, declaring:

> [The Indians] were admitted to be the rightful occupants of the soil, with a legal as well as just claim to retain possession of it, and to use it according to their own discretion; but their rights to complete sovereignty, as independent nations, were necessarily diminished, and their power to dispose of the soil, at their own will, to whomsoever they pleased, was denied by the original fundamental principle, that discovery gave exclusive title to those who made it.[33]

This "doctrine of discovery," announced in *Johnson* and later developed in *Worcester v. Georgia*[34] provided that, as between the European nations claiming hegemony in the Americas, the nation that claimed to have discovered a country had the prior claim to deal with that country's native inhabitants, including the first right to acquire land from the natives "by purchase or by conquest."[35] Until such land was acquired, even grants of land "were considered as blank paper so far as the rights of the natives were concerned."[36] A phrase first appearing in a concurring opinion in one

[25]Cherokee Nation v. Georgia, 30 U.S. (5 Pet.) 1, 17 (1831).
[26]*Id.*
[27]*Id.*
[28]Worcester v. Georgia, 31 U.S. (6 Pet.) 515, 561 (1832).
[29]*See, e.g.,* Oliphant v. Suquamish Indian Tribe, 435 U.S. 191 (1978) (holding Indian tribes have no criminal jurisdiction over non-Indians for crimes committed on Indian reservations). The Court noted, however: "Indian tribes do retain elements of 'quasisovereign' authority after ceding their lands to the United States and announcing their dependence on the Federal Government." *Id.* at 208. For criticisms of this case as dishonest and ahistorical, see Robert A. Williams, Jr., *The Algebra of Federal Indian Law: The Hard Trail of Decolonizing and Americanizing the White Man's Indian Jurisprudence,* 1986 WIS. L. REV. 219: Milner S. Ball, *Constitution, Court, Indian Tribes,* 1987 AM. B. FOUND. RES. J. 1.
[30]*See, e.g.,* United States v. Wheeler, 435 U.S. 313, 322 (1978) ("It is undisputed that Indian tribes have power to enforce their criminal laws against tribe members."); Santa Clara Pueblo v. Martinez, 436 U.S. 49, 72 n.32 (1978) ("A tribe's right to define its own membership for tribal purposes has long been recognized as central to its existence as an independent political community."); Runs After v. United States, 766 F.2d 347 (8th Cir. 1985) (dismissing for lack of federal court jurisdiction tribal members' complaint challenging tribal political process).
[31]*See, e.g.,* Brendale v. Confederated Tribes & Bands of the Yakima Indian Nation, 492 U.S. 408, 444 (1989) (upholding tribal authority to zone land owned by non-Indians in the closed area of the reservation); National Farmers Union Ins. Cos. v. Crow Tribe of Indians 471 U.S. 845 (1985) (requiring federal courts to abstain from challenges to tribal court jurisdiction in civil cases over non-Indians in cases arising on reservation until tribal court has had opportunity to determine its own jurisdiction); New Mexico v. Mescalero Apache Tribe, 462 U.S. 324 (1983) (upholding tribal wildlife regulations applied to nonmembers of tribal land); Merrion v. Jicarilla Apache Tribe, 455 U.S. 130 (1982) (upholding tribal authority to tax oil companies extracting gas on reservations).
[32]21 U.S. (8 Wheat.) 543 (1823).
[33]*Id.* at 574.
[34]31 U.S. (6 Pet.) 515 (1832).
[35]*Johnson,* 21 U.S. (8 Wheat.) at 587. Although a broad reading of the concept of conquest could make this distinction merely a nice one, Chief Justice Marshall clarified this point in *Worcester v. Georgia,* in which he stated his understanding of international law that acquisition of land by conquest was limited to the aftermath of just wars, in which the Indian tribe had been the aggressor. *Worcester,* 31 U.S. (6 Pet.) at 543–44. In describing England's policy toward acquiring lands from Indian tribes, which was then adopted by the United States, Chief Justice Marshall noted that the English charters authorized "offensive as well as defensive war, but only 'on just cause.'" *Id.* at 545. Summing up the whole history, he asserted: "The power of war is given only for defence, not for conquest." *Id.* at 546.
[36]*Worcester,* 31 U.S. (6 Pet.) at 546.

of the *Trilogy* cases stated that Indian title was "as sacred as the fee-simple, absolute title of the whites."[37]

These statements regarding the sacredness of Indian tribal property rights were honored more in the breach, however, as were the early treaty promises that remaining tribal land would be protected from settlers. Nevertheless, periodic efforts to make compensation and even restitution were made. Early treaties, whether or not consensual, did provide for compensation for land taken; the removal treaties also promised in lieu lands to the tribes willing to leave the East Coast for Indian territory.[38] In the abstract, this removal policy was designed to provide the tribes with in lieu lands alleged to be far better than the lands they had been asked to relinquish. Promises were made that no further land cessions would be needed, and some in lieu land was granted in fee simple absolute (seven million acres to the Cherokee Nation alone). Finally, the United States agreed that the land would never be made part of a state without tribal approval.[39]

The experience of the Cherokee Nation illustrates the dissonance between promise and reality in these removal treaties. Winning a victory against the State of Georgia's attempt to confiscate all of its land did not protect the tribe when the federal government, led by a President, Andrew Jackson, hostile to the Court's decisions in the Cherokee cases,[40] moved the tribe to Indian Territory. The government enforced treaties executed with a rump faction of the tribe and the Army forcibly marched the tribe from Georgia to Indian country.[41] One-fifth of the tribe died on this "Trail of Tears," a defining moment for the Cherokee people.[42]

These promises were broken for the many tribes that had moved to the Indian Territory when Congress adopted a policy of forced privatization of Indian land in the second half of the nineteenth century. Reasoning that communal ownership of land only exacerbated tribal Indians' uncivilized lifestyles and prevented the land from being fully exploited, Congress adopted the policy of allotment and assimilation. Under this policy, all tribal land would be individualized, with each head of household receiving enough acreage to become self-sufficient.[43] So-called "surplus" land—land not needed for these purposes—would then be sold to the next wave of settlers, who would in turn serve as role models for their Indian neighbors. Ownership of private property alone would turn Indians into farmers and ranchers; Christianization and civilization were sure to follow. It is important to note that some of the most progressive reformers of the day, Eastern whites known as the "Friends of the Indians," argued passionately that allotment and assimilation were the only mechanisms that would save Indians from white settlers and from their own cultural backwardness.[44] In the perverse logic of a time in which it was thought necessary "that all the Indian there is in the race should be dead . . . [k]ill the Indian in him, and save the man,"[45] destroying tribal land was regarded as the only way to save any land for Indians. According to Father Prucha, "Division of the Great Sioux Reserve was the most blatant example of reduction of a large reservation as a humanitarian measure in order to force the Indians into an economic and social pattern acceptable to the whites.[46]

During this destructive period, which continued into the twentieth century, tribes lost ninety million acres[47]—two-thirds of their land mass, including most

---

[37]Cherokee Nation v. Georgia, 30 U.S. (5 Pet.) 1, 48 (1831) (Baldwin, J., concurring). *See also, e.g.,* Mitchel v. United States, 34 U.S. (9 Pet.) 711, 746 (1835) (stating that Indian title is as sacred as fee-simple absolute); Beecher v. Wetherby, 95 U.S. 517, 526 (1877) (same).

[38]For background on the removal policy, see PRUCHA, *supra* note [12], at 183–213 (1984).

[39]*Id.* at 234.

[40]*See* Joseph L. Burke, *The Cherokee Cases: A Study in Law, Politics and Morality,* STAN. L. REV. 500 (1969). It was concerning *Worcester v. Georgia* that Jackson reportedly said: "John Marshall has made his decision, let him enforce it." *Id.* at 524–25. Most historians regard the story as apocryphal, however. *Id.*

[41]*See generally* JOHN EHLE, TRAIL OF TEARS: THE RISE & FALL OF THE CHEROKEE NATION (1988) (providing detailed history of removal of the Cherokee Nation).

[42]A doctor accompanying the Cherokee people on their march reported the death rate. *See* GRANT FOREMAN, THE FIVE CIVILIZED TRIBES 281–82 (1934).

[43]For an excellent history and analysis of the allotment era, see FREDERICK E. HOXIE, A FINAL PROMISE: THE CAMPAIGN TO ASSIMILATE THE INDIANS, 1880–1920 (1984).

[44]*See generally* AMERICANIZING THE AMERICAN INDIAN (Francis Paul Prucha ed. 1973) (providing collection of writings of the "Friends of the Indians").

[45]Richard H. Pratt, *The Advantages of Mingling Indians with Whites, in* AMERICANIZING THE AMERICAN INDIAN, *supra* note [44], at 260–61. Captain Pratt was the founder and superintendent of the Carlisle Indian School, a boarding school for Indian children. *Id.* at 260.

[46]II PRUCHA, *supra* note [12], at 631–32.

[47]This is a conservative estimate because the figures are given as the reduction in "Indian" land holdings from 138 million to 48 million acres. In other words, the 48 million acre figure includes tribal land as well as land allotted to individual Indians

of the present State of Oklahoma, which was created out of the Indian country.[48] Since individual members of the group were to benefit, no thought was given to compensating the tribal entity for this massive loss of land. Attempts by tribes to block allotment on various grounds, including the invocation of the fee simple status of Cherokee land and promises that no new states would be created, were blocked by the Supreme Court in 1902 on the ground that Indian land must be treated the same as all other land in the United States, and thus was subject to the sovereign's right to take land for public use.[49] In another decision less than two months later and with no apparent sense of irony, the Court also noted that Indian land was different from all other land because Indian tribes were under the guardianship of the United States.[50] As a consequence, the Court strongly implied that compensation need not be paid as long as the government acted as a guardian.[51] There was no need to reach the merits of the tribe's complaint, however, because the Court labeled disputes regarding land between the federal government and Indian tribes as political questions, immune from judicial review and subject to a presumption that the government would always act in good faith toward Indian tribes.[52]

This separate treatment of Indian land continued when Congress created the Court of Claims in 1855 for those with claims for money damages, including compensation for property seized by the government.[53] Shortly thereafter, an amendment excepted any claims based on treaties with Indian tribes and foreign nations from the new court's jurisdiction.[54] With all parties assuming that the exception for Indian treaties included any claims brought by Indian tribes, tribes with land claims could turn only to Congress for relief. During this period, which lasted until after World War II, tribes with the resources for lobbying obtained what were called "special jurisdictional acts" permitting claims to be brought in the Court of Claims seeking compensation for a variety of wrongs, including seizures of land.[55] The Court of Claims interpreted these special acts so narrowly that few tribes prevailed.[56] In addition, the special statutes often permitted the court to offset against the damages awarded any gratuities the federal government had given the tribe. Since gratuities included everything given—whether it was requested or not—and the cost of administering federal programs, the final net judgment was considerably reduced.[57]. . .

---

that escaped the many mechanisms by which this individualized land was acquired by non-Indians. These mechanisms are described in ROBERT N. CLINTON, NELL JESSUP NEWTON & MONROE PRICE, AMERICAN INDIAN LAW: CASES AND MATERIALS 147–52, 787–89 (3d ed. 1991). Although a government's breaking up of a closely held private business corporation into shares of stock distributed to all the workers in the corporation would surely be a compensable confiscation of private property under United States constitutional law, specifically the Fifth Amendment Takings Clause, tribes as entities were never compensated for the loss of property individualized during allotment. *See* U.S. CONST. amend. V ("nor shall private property be taken for public use, without just compensation").

[48] *See* RENNARD STRICKLAND, THE INDIANS IN OKLAHOMA 31–54 (1980) (describing Oklahoma statehood process).

[49] Cherokee Nation v. Hitchcock, 187 U.S. 294 (1902); *see also* Stephens v. Cherokee Nation, 174 U.S. 445 (1899).

[50] Lone Wolf v. Hitchcock, 187 U.S. 553, 565, 567 (1903).

[51] *See id.* at 568.

[52] *Id.* at 565.

[53] *See* Act of Feb. 24, 1885, ch. 122, 10 Stat. 612, 612 (creating Court of Claims).

[54] Act of Mar. 3, 1863, ch. 92, § 9, 12 Stat. 765, 767 (excluding claims dependent on treaty stipulations entered into with Indians).

[55] *See* PETRA T. SHATTUCK & JILL NORGREN, PARTIAL JUSTICE: FEDERAL INDIAN LAW IN A LIBERAL CONSTITUTIONAL SYSTEM 143 (1991) (noting problems created by this system).

[56] II PRUCHA, *supra* note [12], at 1018 (reporting that only 29 out of nearly 200 claims were not dismissed on technicalities).

[57] For example, the Indians of California were awarded $17,053,941 before offsets reduced the award to $5,024,842. Indians of California v. United States, 102 Ct. Cl. 837 (1944).

40

CHERYL I. HARRIS

Whiteness as Property

she walked into forbidden worlds
impaled on the weapon of her own pale skin
she was a sentinel
at impromptu planning sessions
of her own destruction. . . .

—CHERYL I. HARRIS, "POEM FOR ALMA"

[P]etitioner was a citizen of the United States and a resident of the state of Louisiana of mixed descent, in the proportion of seven eighths Caucasian and one eighth African blood; that the mixture of colored blood was not discernible in him, and that he was entitled to every recognition, right, privilege and immunity secured to the citizens of the United States of the white race by its Constitution and laws . . . and thereupon entered a passenger train and took possession of a vacant seat in a coach where passengers of the white race were accommodated.

—PLESSY V. FERGUSON[1]

I. INTRODUCTION

In the thirties, some years after my mother's family became part of the great river of black migration that flowed north, my Mississippi-born grandmother was confronted with the harsh matter of economic survival for herself and her two daughters. Having separated from my grandfather, who himself was trapped on the fringes of economic marginality, she took one long hard look at her choices and presented herself for employment at a major retail store in Chicago's central business district. This decision would have been unremarkable for a white woman in similar circumstances, but for my grandmother it was an act of both great daring and self-denial—for in so doing she was presenting herself as a white woman. In the parlance of racist America, she was "passing."

Her fair skin, straight hair, and aquiline features had not spared her from the life of sharecropping into which she had been born in anywhere/nowhere, Mississippi—the outskirts of Yazoo City. In the burgeoning landscape of urban America, though, anonymity was possible for a black person with "white" features. She was transgressing boundaries, crossing borders, spinning on margins, traveling between dualities of Manichean space, rigidly bifurcated into light/dark, good/bad, white/black. No longer immediately identifiable as "Lula's daughter," she could thus enter the white world, albeit on a false passport, not merely passing but trespassing.

Every day my grandmother rose from her bed in her house in a black enclave on the south side of Chicago, sent her children off to a black school, boarded a bus full of black passengers, and rode to work. No one at her job ever asked if she was black; the question was unthinkable. By virtue of the employment practices of the "fine establishment" in which she worked, she could not have been. Catering to the upper middle class, understated tastes required that blacks not be allowed.

She quietly went about her clerical tasks, not once revealing her true identity. She listened to the women with whom she worked discuss their worries—their children's illnesses, their husband's disappointments, their boyfriends' infidelities—all of the mundane yet critical things that made up their lives. She came to know them but they did not know her, for my grandmother occupied a completely different place. That place—where white supremacy and economic domination meet—was unknown turf to her white coworkers. They remained oblivious to the worlds within worlds that existed just beyond the edge of their awareness and yet were present in their very midst.

Each evening, my grandmother, tired and worn, retraced her steps home, laid aside her mask, and reentered herself. Day in and day out, she made herself invisible, then visible again, for a price too inconsequential to do more than barely sustain her family and at a cost too precious to conceive. She left the job some years later, finding the strain too much to bear.

From time to time, as I later sat with her, she would recollect that period, and the cloud of some painful memory would pass across her face. Her voice would remain subdued, as if to contain the still-remembered tension. On rare occasions, she would wince, recalling some particularly racist comment made in her presence because of her presumed shared group affiliation. Whatever retort might have been called for had been suppressed long before it reached her lips, for the price of her family's well-being was her silence. Accepting the risk of self-annihilation was the only way to survive.

Although she never would have stated it this way, the clear and ringing denunciations of racism she delivered from her chair when advanced arthritis had rendered her unable to work were informed by those experiences. The fact that self-denial had been a logical choice and had made her complicit in her own oppression at times fed the fire in her eyes when she confronted some daily outrage inflicted on black people. Later, these painful memories forged her total identification with the civil rights movement. Learning about the world at her knee as I did, these experiences also came to inform my outlook and my understanding of the world.

My grandmother's story is far from unique. Indeed, there are many who crossed the color line never to return. Passing is well known among black people in the United States; it is a feature of race subordination in all societies structured on white supremacy. Notwithstanding the purported benefits of black heritage in an era of affirmative action, passing is not an obsolete phenomenon that has slipped into history.

The persistence of passing is related to the historical and continuing pattern of white racial domination and economic exploitation, which has invested passing with a certain economic logic. It was a given for my grandmother that being white automatically ensured higher economic returns in the short term and greater economic, political, and social security in the long run. Becoming white meant gaining access to a whole set of public and private privileges that materially and permanently guaranteed basic subsistence needs and, therefore, survival. Becoming white increased the possibility of controlling critical aspects of one's life rather than being the object of others' domination.

My grandmother's story illustrates the valorization of whiteness as treasured property in a society structured on racial caste. In ways so embedded that it is rarely apparent, the set of assumptions, privileges, and benefits that accompany the status of being white have become a valuable asset—-one that whites sought to protect and those who passed sought to attain, by fraud if necessary. Whites have come to expect and rely on these benefits, and over time these expectations have been affirmed, legitimated, and protected by the law. Even though the law is neither uniform nor explicit in all instances, in protecting settled expectations based on white privilege, American law has recognized a property interest in whiteness that, although unacknowledged, now forms the background against which legal disputes are framed, argued, and adjudicated.

This article investigates the relationships between concepts of race and property, and it reflects on how rights in property are contingent on, intertwined with, and conflated with race. Through this entangled relationship between race and property, historical forms of domination have evolved to reproduce subordination in the present. [. . .]

II. THE CONSTRUCTION OF RACE AND THE EMERGENCE OF WHITENESS AS PROPERTY

The racialization of identity and the racial subordination of blacks and Native Americans provided the ideological basis for slavery and conquest. Although the systems of oppression of blacks and Native Americans differed in form—the former involving the seizure and appropriation of labor, the latter entailing the seizure and appropriation of land—undergirding both was a racialized conception of property implemented by force and ratified by law.

The origins of property rights in the United States are rooted in racial domination. Even in the early years of the country, it was not the concept of race alone that operated to oppress blacks and Indians; rather, it was the interaction between conceptions of race and property which played a critical role in establishing and maintaining racial and economic subordination.

The hyperexploitation of black labor was accomplished by treating black people themselves as objects of property. Race and property were thus conflated by establishing a form of property contingent on race: only blacks were subjugated as slaves and treated as property. Similarly, the conquest, removal, and extermination of Native American life and culture were ratified by conferring and acknowledging the property rights of whites in Native American land. Only white possession and occupation of land was validated and therefore privileged as a basis for property rights. These distinct forms of exploitation each contributed in varying ways to the construction of whiteness as property.

A. Forms of Racialized Property: Relationships Between Slavery, Race, and Property

1. *The Convergence of Racial and Legal Status*

Although the early colonists were cognizant of race, racial lines were neither consistently nor sharply delineated among or within all social groups. Captured Africans sold in the Americas were distinguished from the population of indentured or bond servants—"unfree" white labor—but it was not an irrebuttable presumption that all Africans were "slaves," or that slavery was the only appropriate status for them. The distinction between African and white indentured labor grew, however, as decreasing terms of service were introduced for white bond servants. Simultaneously, the demand for labor intensified, resulting in a greater reliance on African labor and a rapid increase in the number of Africans imported to the colonies.

The construction of white identity and the ideology of racial hierarchy were intimately tied to the evolution and expansion of the system of chattel slavery. The further entrenchment of plantation slavery was in part an answer to a social crisis produced by the eroding capacity of the landed class to control the white labor population. The dominant paradigm of social relations, however, was that while not all Africans were slaves, virtually all slaves were not white. It was their racial Otherness that came to justify the subordinated status of blacks. The result was a classification system that "key[ed] official rules of descent to national origin" so that "[m]embership in the new social category of 'Negro' became itself sufficient justification for enslaveability."[2] Although the cause of the increasing gap between the status of African and white labor is contested by historians, it is clear that "[t]he economic and political interests defending Black slavery were far more powerful than those defending indentured servitude."[3]

By the 1660s, the especially degraded status of blacks as chattel slaves was recognized by law. Between 1680 and 1682, the first slave codes appeared, enshrining the extreme deprivations of liberty already existing in social practice. Many laws parceled out differential treatment based on racial categories: blacks were not permitted to travel without permits, to own property, to assemble publicly, or to own weapons—nor were they to be educated. Racial identity was further merged with stratified social and legal status: "black" racial identity marked who was subject to enslavement, whereas "white" racial identity marked who was "free" or, at minimum, not a slave. The ideological and rhetorical move from "slave" and "free" to "black" and "white" as polar constructs marked an important step in the social construction of race.

2. *Implications for Property*

The social relations that produced racial identity as a justification for slavery also had implications for the conceptualization of property. This result was predictable, as the institution of slavery, lying at the very core of economic relations, was bound up with the idea of property. Through slavery, race and economic domination were fused.[4]

Slavery produced a peculiar, mixed category of property and humanity—a hybrid with inherent instabilities that were reflected in its treatment and ratification by the law. The dual and contradictory character of slaves as property and persons was exemplified in the Representation Clause of the Constitution. Representation in the House of Representatives was apportioned on the basis of population computed by counting all persons and "three-fifths of all other persons"—slaves. Gouveneur Morris's remarks before the Constitutional Convention posed the essential question: "Upon what principle is it that slaves shall be computed in the representation? Are they men? Then make them Citizens & let them vote? Are they property? Why then is no other property included?"[5]

The cruel tension between property and humanity was also reflected in the law's legitimation of the use of blackwomen's bodies as a means of increasing property.[6] In 1662, the Virginia colonial assembly provided that "[c]hildren got by an Englishman upon a Negro woman shall be bond or free according to the condition of the mother. . . ."[7] In reversing the usual common law presumption that the status of the child was determined by the father, the rule facilitated the reproduction of one's own labor force. Because the children of black women assumed the status of their mother, slaves were bred through blackwomen's bodies. The economic significance of this form of exploitation of female slaves should not be underestimated. Despite Thomas Jefferson's belief that slavery should be abolished, like other slaveholders, he viewed slaves as economic assets, noting that their value could be realized more efficiently from breeding than from labor. A letter he wrote in 1805 stated, "I consider the labor of a breeding woman as no object, and that a child raised every 2 years is of more profit that the crop of the best laboring man."[8]

Even though there was some unease in slave law, reflective of the mixed status of slaves as humans and property, the critical nature of social relations under slavery was the commodification of human beings. Productive relations in early American society included varying forms of sale of labor capacity, many of which were highly oppressive; but slavery was distinguished from other forms of labor servitude by its permanency and the total commodification attendant to the status of the slave. Slavery as a legal institution treated slaves as property that could be transferred, assigned, inherited, or posted as collateral.[9] For example, in *Johnson v. Butler,*[10] the plaintiff sued the defendant for failing to pay a debt of $496 on a specified date; because the covenant had called for payment of the debt in "money or negroes," the plaintiff contended that the defendant's tender of one negro only, although valued by the parties at an amount equivalent to the debt, could not discharge the debt. The court agreed with the plaintiff. This use of Africans as a stand-in for actual currency highlights the degree to which slavery "propertized" human life.

Because the "presumption of freedom [arose] from color [white]" and the "black color of the race [raised] the presumption of slavery," whiteness became a shield from slavery, a highly volatile and unstable form of property. In the form adopted in the United States, slavery made human beings market-alienable and in so doing, subjected human life and personhood—that which is most valuable—to the ultimate devaluation. Because whites could not be enslaved or held as slaves, the racial line between white and black was extremely critical; it became a line of protection and demarcation from the potential threat of commodification, and it determined the allocation of the benefits and burdens of this form of property. White identity and whiteness were sources of privilege and protection; their absence meant being the object of property.

Slavery as a system of property facilitated the merger of white identity and property. Because the system of slavery was contingent on and conflated with racial identity, it became crucial to be "white," to be identified as white, to have the property of being white. Whiteness was the characteristic, the attribute, the property of free human beings. . . .

B. Critical Characteristics of Property and Whiteness

1. *Whiteness As a Traditional Form of Property*

Whiteness fits the broad historical concept of property described by classical theorists. In James Madison's view, for example, property "embraces every thing to which a man may attach a value and have a right," referring to all of a person's legal rights. Property as conceived in the founding era included not only external objects and people's relationships to them, but also all of those human rights, liberties, powers, and immunities that are important for human well-being, including freedom of expression, freedom of conscience, freedom from bodily harm, and free and equal opportunities to use personal faculties.

Whiteness defined the legal status of a person as slave or free. White identity conferred tangible and economically valuable benefits, and it was jealously guarded as a valued possession, allowed only to those who met a strict standard of proof. Whiteness—the right to white identity as embraced by the law—is property if by "property" one means all of a person's legal rights.

Other traditional theories of property emphasize that the "natural" character of property is derivative of custom, contrary to the notion that property is the product of a delegation of sovereign power. This "bottom-up" theory holds that the law of property merely codifies existing customs and social relations. Under that view, government-created rights such as social welfare payments cannot constitute legitimate property interests because they are positivistic in nature. Other theorists have challenged this conception, and argued that even the most basic of "customary" property rights—the rule of first possession, for example—is dependent on its acceptance or rejection in particular instances by the government. Citing custom as a source of property law begs the central question: Whose custom?

Rather than remaining within the bipolar confines of custom or command, it is crucial to recognize the dynamic and multifaceted relationship among custom, command, and law, as well as the extent to which positionality determines how each may be experienced and understood. Indian custom was obliterated by force and replaced with the regimes of common law which embodied the customs of the conquerors. The assumption of American law as it related to Native Americans was that conquest did give rise to sovereignty. Indians experienced the property laws of the colonizers and the emergent American nation as acts of violence perpetuated by the exercise of power and ratified through the rule of law. At the same time, these laws were perceived as custom and "common sense" by the colonizers. The founders, for instance, so thoroughly embraced Lockean labor theory as the basis for a right of acquisition because it affirmed the right of the New World settlers to settle on and acquire the frontier. It confirmed and ratified their experience.

The law's interpretation of those encounters between whites and Native Americans not only inflicted vastly different results on them but also established a pattern—a custom—of valorizing whiteness. As the forms of racialized property were perfected, the value and protection extended to whiteness increased. Regardless of which theory of property one adopts, the concept of whiteness—established by centuries of custom (illegitimate custom, but custom nonetheless) and codified by law—may be understood as a property interest.

2. *Property and Expectations*

"Property is nothing but the basis of expectation," according to Jeremy Bentham, "consist[ing] in an established expectation, in the persuasion of being able to draw such and such advantage from the thing possessed."[11] The relationship between expectations and property remains highly significant, as the law "has recognized and protected even the expectation of rights as actual legal property."[12] This theory does not suggest that all values or all expectations give rise to property, but those expectations in tangible or intangible things which are valued and protected by the law are property.

In fact, the difficulty lies not in identifying expectations as a part of property but, rather, in distinguishing which expectations are reasonable and therefore merit the protection of the law as property. Although the existence of certain property rights may seem self-evident, and the protection of certain expectations may seem essential for social stability, property is a legal construct by which selected private interests are protected and upheld. In creating property "rights," the law draws boundaries and enforces or reorders existing regimes of power. The inequalities that are produced and reproduced are not givens or inevitabilities; rather, they are conscious selections regarding the structuring of social relations. In this sense, it is contended that property rights and interests are not "natural" but "creation[s] of law." In a society structured on racial subordination, white privilege became an expectation and, to apply Margaret Radin's concept, whiteness became the quintessential property for personhood. The law constructed "whiteness" as an objective fact, although in reality it is an ideological proposition imposed through subordination. This move is the central feature of "reification": "Its basis is that a relation between people takes on the character of a thing and thus acquires a 'phantom objectivity,' an autonomy that seems so strictly rational and all-embracing as to conceal every trace of its fundamental nature: the relation between people."[13] Whiteness was an "object" over which continued control was—and is—expected. . . .

Because the law recognized and protected expectations grounded in white privilege (albeit not explicitly in all instances), these expectations became tantamount to property that could not permissibly be intruded upon without consent. As the law explicitly ratified those expectations in continued privilege or extended ongoing protection to those illegitimate expectations by failing to expose or to disturb them radically, the dominant and subordinate positions within the racial hierarchy were reified in law. When the law recognizes, either implicitly or explicitly, the settled expectations of whites built on the privileges and benefits produced by white supremacy, it acknowledges and reinforces a property interest in whiteness that reproduces black subordination.

3. *The Property Functions of Whiteness*

In addition to the theoretical descriptions of property, whiteness also meets the functional criteria of property. Specifically, the law has accorded "holders" of whiteness the same privileges and benefits accorded holders of other types of property. The liberal view of property is that it includes the exclusive rights of possession, use, and disposition. Its attributes are the right to transfer or alienability, the right to use and enjoyment, and the right to exclude others. Even when examined against this limited view, whiteness conforms to the general contours of property. It may be a "bad" form of property, but it is property nonetheless.

a. Rights of Disposition Property rights are traditionally described as fully alienable. Because fundamental personal rights are commonly understood to be inalienable, it is problematic to view them as property interests. However, as Margaret Radin notes, "inalienability" is not a transparent term; it has multiple meanings that refer to interests that are nonsalable, nontransferable, or non-market-alienable. The common core of inalienability is the negation of the possibility of separation of an entitlement, right, or attribute from its holder.

Classical theories of property identified alienability as a requisite aspect of property; thus, that which is inalienable cannot be property. As the major exponent of this view, John Stuart Mill argued that public offices, monopoly privileges, and human beings—all of which were or should have been inalienable—should not be considered property at all. Under this account, if inalienability inheres in the concept of property, then whiteness, incapable of being transferred or alienated either inside or outside the market, would fail to meet a criterion of property.

As Radin notes, however, even under the classical view, alienability of certain property was limited. Mill also advocated certain restraints on alienation in connection with property rights in land and, probably, other natural resources. In fact, the law has recognized various kinds of inalienable property. For example, entitlements of the regulatory and welfare states, such as transfer payments and government licenses, are inalienable; yet they have been conceptualized and treated as property by law. Although this "new property" has been criticized as being improper—that is, not appropriately cast as property—the principal objection has been based on its alleged lack of productive capacity, not on its inalienability.

The law has also acknowledged forms of inalienable property derived from nongovernmental sources. In the context of divorce, courts have held that professional degrees or licenses held by one party and financed by the labor of the other is marital property whose value is subject to allocation by the court. A medical or law degree is not alienable either in the market or by voluntary transfer. Nevertheless, it is included as property when dissolving a legal relationship.

Indeed, Radin argues that as a deterrent to the dehumanization of universal commodification, market-inalienability may be justified to protect property important to the person and to safeguard human flourishing. She suggests that noncommodification or market-inalienability of personal property or those things essential to human flourishing is necessary to guard against the objectification of human beings. To avoid that danger, "we must cease thinking that market alienability is inherent in the concept of property." Following this logic, then, the inalienability of whiteness should not preclude the consideration of whiteness as property. Paradoxically, its inalienability may be more indicative of its perceived enhanced value rather than of its disqualification as property.

b. Right to Use and Enjoyment Possession of property includes the rights of use and enjoyment. If these rights are essential aspects of property, it is because "the problem of property in political philosophy dissolves into . . . questions of the will and the way in which we use the things of this world."[14] As whiteness is simultaneously an aspect of identity and a property interest, it is something that can both be experienced and deployed as a resource. Whiteness can move from being a passive characteristic as an aspect of identity to an active entity that—like other types of property—is used to fulfill the will and to exercise power. The state's official recognition both of a racial identity that subordinated blacks and of privileged rights in property based on race, elevated whiteness from a passive attribute to an object of law and a resource deployable at the social, political, and institutional level to maintain control. Thus, a white person "used and enjoyed" whiteness whenever she took advantage of the privileges accorded white people simply by virtue of their whiteness—when she exercised any number of rights reserved for the holders of whiteness. Whiteness as the embodiment of white privilege transcended mere belief or preference; it became usable property, the subject of the law's regard and protection. In this respect, whiteness, as an active property, has been used and enjoyed.

c. . . . The conception of reputation as property found its origins in early concepts of property which encompassed things (such as land and personalty), income (such as revenues from leases, mortgages, and patent monopolies), and one's life, liberty, and labor. . . . The idea of self-ownership, then, was particularly fertile ground for the idea that reputation, as an aspect of identity earned through effort, was similarly property. Moreover, the loss of reputation was capable of being valued in the market.

The direct manifestation of the law's legitimation of whiteness as reputation is revealed in the well-established doctrine that to call a white person "black" is to defame her.[15] Although many of the cases were decided in an era when the social and legal stratification of whites and blacks was more absolute, as late as 1957 the principle was reaffirmed, notwithstanding significant changes in the legal and political status of blacks. As one court noted, "there is still to be considered the social distinction existing between the races," and the allegation was likely to cause injury.[16] A black person, however, could not sue for defamation if she was called "white." Because the law expressed and reinforced the social hierarchy as it existed, it was presumed that no harm could flow from such a reversal.

Private identity based on racial hierarchy was legitimated as public identity in law, even after the end of slavery and the formal end of legal race segregation. Whiteness as interpersonal hierarchy was recognized externally as race reputation. Thus, whiteness as public reputation and personal property was affirmed.

d. The Absolute Right to Exclude Many theorists have traditionally conceptualized property as including the exclusive rights of use, disposition, and possession, with possession embracing the absolute right to exclude. The right to exclude was the central principle, too, of whiteness as identity, for whiteness in large part has been characterized not by an inherent unifying characteristic but by the exclusion of others deemed to be "not white." The possessors of whiteness were granted the legal right to exclude others from the privileges inhering in whiteness; whiteness became an exclusive club whose membership was closely and grudgingly guarded. The courts played an active role in enforcing this right to exclude—determining who was or was not white enough to enjoy the privileges accompanying whiteness. In that sense, the courts protected whiteness as they did any other form of property.

Moreover, as it emerged, the concept of whiteness was premised on white supremacy rather than on mere difference. "White" was defined and constructed in ways that increased its value by reinforcing its exclusivity. Indeed, just as whiteness as property embraced the right to exclude, whiteness as a theoretical construct evolved for the very purpose of racial exclusion. Thus, the concept of whiteness is built on exclusion and racial subjugation. This fact was particularly evident during the period of the most rigid racial exclusion, for whiteness signified racial privilege and took the form of status property.

At the individual level, recognizing oneself as "white" necessarily assumes premises based on white supremacy: it assumes that black ancestry in any degree, extending to generations far removed, automatically disqualifies claims to white identity, thereby privileging "white" as unadulterated, exclusive, and rare. Inherent in the concept of "being white" was the right to own or hold whiteness to the exclusion and subordination of blacks. Because "[i]dentity is . . . continuously being constituted through social interactions,"[17] the assigned political, economic, and social inferiority of blacks necessarily shaped white identity. In the commonly held popular view, the presence of black "blood"—including the infamous "one-drop"—consigned a person to being "black" and evoked the "metaphor . . . of purity and contamination" in which black blood is a contaminant and white racial identity is pure. Recognizing or identifying oneself as white is thus a claim of racial purity, an assertion that one is free of any taint of black blood. The law has played a critical role in legitimating this claim.

C. White Legal Identity: The Law's Acceptance and Legitimation of Whiteness as Property

The law assumed the crucial task of racial classification, and accepted and embraced the then-current theories of race as biological fact. This core precept of race as a physically defined reality allowed the law to fulfill an essential function—to "parcel out social standing according to race" and to facilitate systematic discrimination by articulating "seemingly precise definitions of racial group membership." This allocation of race and rights continued a century after the abolition of slavery.

The law relied on bounded, objective, and scientific definitions of race—what Neil Gotanda has called "historical-race"[18]—to construct whiteness as not merely race, but race plus privilege. By making race determinant and the product of rationality and science, dominant and subordinate positions within the racial hierarchy were disguised as the product of natural law and biology rather than as naked preferences. Whiteness as racialized privilege was then legitimated by science and was embraced in legal doctrine as "objective fact."

Case law that attempted to define race frequently struggled over the precise fractional amount of black "blood"—traceable black ancestry—that would defeat a claim to whiteness. Although the courts applied varying fractional formulas in different jurisdictions to define "black" or, in the terms of the day, "negro" or "colored," the law uniformly accepted the rule of hypodescent[19]—racial identity was governed by blood, and white was preferred.

This legal assumption of race as blood-borne was predicated on the pseudo-sciences of eugenics and craniology, which saw their major development during the eighteenth and nineteenth centuries. The legal definition of race was the "objective" test propounded by racist theorists of the day, who described race to be immutable, scientific, biologically determined—an unsullied fact of the blood rather than a volatile and violently imposed regime of racial hierarchy.

In adjudicating who was "white," courts sometimes noted that, by physical characteristics, the individual whose racial identity was at issue appeared to be white and, in fact, had been regarded as white in the community. Yet if an individual's blood was tainted, she could not claim to be "white" as the law understood, regardless of the fact that phenotypically she may have been completely indistinguishable from a white person, may have lived as a white person, and may have descended from a family that lived as whites. Although socially accepted as white, she could not legally be white. Blood as "objective fact" predominated over appearance and social acceptance, which were socially fluid and subjective measures.

In fact, though, "blood" was no more objective than that which the law dismissed as subjective and unreliable. The acceptance of the fiction that the racial ancestry could be determined with the degree of precision called for by the relevant standards or definitions rested on false assumptions that racial categories of prior ancestors had been accurately reported, that those reporting in the past shared the definitions currently in use, and that racial purity actually existed in the United States.[20] Ignoring these considerations, the law established rules that extended equal treatment to those of the "same blood," albeit of different complexions, because it was acknowledged that, "[t]here are white men as dark as mulattoes, and there are pure-blooded albino Africans as white as the whitest Saxons."[21]

The standards were designed to accomplish what mere observation could not: "That even Blacks who did not look Black were kept in their place."[22] Although the line of demarcation between black and white varied from rules that classified as black a person containing "any drop of Black blood" to more liberal rules that defined persons with a preponderance of white blood to be white,[23] the courts universally accepted the notion that white status was something of value that could be accorded only to those persons whose proofs established their whiteness as defined by the law.[24] Because legal recognition of a person as white carried material benefits, "false" or inadequately supported claims were denied like any other unsubstantiated claim to a property interest. Only those who could lay "legitimate" claims to whiteness could be legally recognized as white, because allowing physical attributes, social acceptance, or self-identification to determine whiteness would diminish its value and destroy the underlying presumption of exclusivity. In effect, the courts erected legal "no trespassing" signs.

In the realm of social relations, racial recognition in the United States is thus an act of race subordination. In the realm of legal relations, judicial definition of racial identity based on white supremacy reproduced that race subordination at the institutional level. In transforming white to whiteness, the law masked the ideological content of racial definition and the exercise of power required to maintain it: "It convert[ed an] abstract concept into [an] entity."[25]

1. *Whiteness As Racialized Privilege*

The material benefits of racial exclusion and subjugation functioned, in the labor context, to stifle class tensions among whites. White workers perceived that they had more in common with the bourgeoisie than with fellow workers who were black. Thus, W. E. B. Du Bois's classic historical study of race and class, *Black Reconstruction,*[26] noted that, for the evolving white working class, race identification became crucial to the ways that it thought of itself and conceived its interests. There were, he suggested, obvious material benefits, at least in the short term, to the decision of white workers to define themselves by their whiteness: their wages far exceeded those of blacks and were high even in comparison with world standards. Moreover, even when the white working class did not collect increased pay as part of white privilege, there were real advantages not paid in direct income: whiteness still yielded what Du Bois termed a "public and psychological wage" vital to white workers.[27] Thus, Du Bois noted that whites

> were given public deference . . . because they were white. They were admitted freely with all classes of white people, to public functions, to public parks. . . . The police were drawn from their ranks, and the courts, dependent on their votes, treated them with . . . leniency. . . . Their vote selected public officials, and while this had small effect upon the economic situation, it had great effect on their personal treatment. . . . White schoolhouses were the best in the community, and conspicuously placed, and they cost anywhere from twice to ten times as much per capita as the colored schools.[28]

The central feature of the convergence of "white" and "worker" lay in the fact that racial status and privilege could ameliorate and assist in "evad[ing] rather than confront[ing class] exploitation."[29] Although not accorded the privileges of the ruling class, in both the North and South, white workers could accept their lower class position in the hierarchy "by fashioning identities as 'not slaves' and as 'not Blacks.'"[30] Whiteness produced—and was reproduced by—the social advantage that accompanied it.

Whiteness was also central to national identity and to the republican project. The amalgamation of various European strains into an American identity was facilitated by an oppositional definition of black as Other. As Andrew Hacker suggests, fundamentally, the question was not so much "who is white" but, rather, "who may be considered white," for the historical pattern was that various immigrant groups of different ethnic origins were accepted into a white identity shaped around Anglo-American norms. Current members then "ponder[ed] whether they want[ed] or need[ed] new members as well as the proper pace of new admissions into this exclusive club."[31] Through minstrel shows in which white actors masquerading in blackface played out racist stereotypes, the popular culture put the black at "'solo spot centerstage, providing a relational model in contrast to which masses of Americans could establish a positive and superior sense of identity,' . . . [one] . . . established by an infinitely manipulable negation comparing whites with a construct of a socially defenseless group."[32]

It is important to note the effect of this hypervaluation of whiteness. Owning white identity as property affirmed the self-identity and liberty of whites and, conversely, denied the self-identity and liberty of blacks. The attempts to lay claim to whiteness through "passing" painfully illustrate the effects of the law's recognition of whiteness. The embrace of a lie, undertaken by my grandmother and the thousands like her, could occur only when oppression makes self-denial and the obliteration of identity rational and, in significant measure, beneficial. The economic coercion of white supremacy on self-definition nullifies any suggestion that passing is a logical exercise of liberty or self-identity. The decision to pass as white was not a choice, if by that word one means voluntariness or lack of compulsion. The fact of race subordination was coercive, and it circumscribed the liberty to define oneself. Self-determination of identity was not a right for all people but a privilege accorded on the basis of race. The effect of protecting whiteness at law was to devalue those who were not white by coercing them to deny their identity in order to survive.

2. *Whiteness, Rights, and National Identity*

The concept of whiteness was carefully protected because so much was contingent upon it. Whiteness conferred on its owners aspects of citizenship which were all the more valued because they were denied to others. Indeed, the very fact of citizenship itself was linked to white racial identity. The Naturalization Act of 1790 restricted citizenship to persons who resided in the United States for two years, who could establish their good character in court, and who were "white." Moreover, the trajectory of expanding democratic rights for whites was accompanied by the contraction of the rights of blacks in an ever-deepening cycle of oppression. The franchise, for example, was broadened to extend voting rights to unpropertied white men at the same time that black voters were specifically disenfranchised, arguably shifting the property required for voting from land to whiteness. This racialized version of republicanism—this

Herrenvolk republicanism—constrained any vision of democracy from addressing the class hierarchies adverse to many who considered themselves white.

The inherent contradiction between the bondage of blacks and republican rhetoric that championed the freedom of "all" men was resolved by positing that blacks were different. The laws did not mandate that blacks be accorded equality under the law because nature—not man, not power, not violence—had determined their degraded status. Rights were for those who had the capacity to exercise them, a capacity denoted by racial identity. This conception of rights was contingent on race, on whether one could claim whiteness—a form of property. This articulation of rights that were contingent on property ownership was a familiar paradigm, as similar requirements had been imposed on the franchise in the early part of the Republic. For the first two hundred years of the country's existence, the system of racialized privilege in the public and private spheres carried through this linkage of rights and inequality, of rights and property. Whiteness as property was the critical core of a system that affirmed the hierarchical relations between white and black. . . .

III. THE PERSISTENCE OF WHITENESS AS PROPERTY

A. The Persistence of Whiteness As Valued Social Identity

Even as the capacity of whiteness to deliver is arguably diminished by the elimination of rigid racial stratifications, whiteness continues to be perceived as materially significant. Because real power and wealth never have been accessible to more than a narrowly defined ruling elite, for many whites the benefits of whiteness as property, in the absence of legislated privilege, may have been reduced to a claim of relative privilege only in comparison to people of color. Nevertheless, whiteness retains its value as a "consolation prize": it does not mean that all whites will win, but simply that they will not lose, if losing is defined as being on the bottom of the social and economic hierarchy—the position to which blacks have been consigned.

Andrew Hacker, in his 1992 book *Two Nations,*[33] recounts the results of a recent exercise that probed the value of whiteness according to the perceptions of whites. The study asked a group of white students how much money they would seek if they were changed from white to black. "Most seemed to feel that it would not be out of place to ask for $50 million, or $1 million for each coming black year." Whether this figure represents an accurate amortization of the societal cost of being black in the United States, it is clear that whiteness is still perceived to be valuable. The wages of whiteness are available to all whites, regardless of class position—even to those whites who are without power, money, or influence. Whiteness, the characteristic that distinguishes them from blacks, serves as compensation even to those who lack material wealth. It is the relative political advantages extended to whites, rather than actual economic gains, that are crucial to white workers. Thus, as Kimberlé Crenshaw points out, whites have an actual stake in racism.[34] Because blacks are held to be inferior, although no longer on the basis of science as antecedent determinant but, rather, by virtue of their position at the bottom, it allows whites—all whites—to "include themselves in the dominant circle. [Although most whites] hold no real power—[all can claim] their privileged racial identity."[35]

White workers often identify themselves primarily as white rather than as workers because it is through their whiteness that they are afforded access to a host of public, private, and psychological benefits. It is through the concept of whiteness that class-consciousness among white workers is subordinated and attention is diverted from class oppression.

Although dominant societal norms have embraced the ideas of fairness and nondiscrimination, removal of privilege and antisubordination principles are actively rejected or at best ambiguously received, because expectations of white privilege are bound up with what is considered essential for self-realization. Among whites, the idea persists that their whiteness is meaningful. Whiteness is an aspect of racial identity surely, but it is much more; it remains a concept based on relations of power, a social construct predicated on white dominance and black subordination.

B. Subordination through Denial of Group Identity

Whiteness as property is also constituted through the reification of expectations in the continued right of white-dominated institutions to control the legal meaning of group identity. This reification manifests itself in the law's dialectical misuse of the concept of group identity as it pertains to racially subordinated peoples. The law has recognized and codified racial group identity as an instrument of exclusion and exploitation; however, it has refused to recognize group identity when asserted by racially oppressed groups as a basis for affirming or claiming rights. The law's approach to group identity reproduces subordination, in the past through "race-ing" a group—that is, by assigning a racial identity that equated with inferior status and, in the present, by erasing racial group identity.

In part, the law's denial of the existence of racial groups is not only predicated on the rejection of the ongoing presence of the past, but it is also grounded on a basic tenet of liberalism—that constitutional protections inhere in individuals, not in groups. As informed by the Lockean notion of the social contract, the autonomous, free will of the individual is central; indeed, it is the individual who, in concert with other individuals, elects to enter into political society and to form a state of limited powers. This philosophical view of society is closely aligned with the antidiscrimination principle—the idea being that equality mandates only the equal treatment of individuals under the law. Within this framework, the idea of the social group has no place.

Although the law's determination of any "fact," including that of group identity, is not infinitely flexible, its studied ignorance of the issue of racial group identity ensures wrong results by assuming a pseudo-objective posture that does not permit it to hear the complex dialogue concerning identity questions, particularly as they pertain to historically dominated groups.

Instead, the law holds to the basic premise that definition from above can be fair to those below, that beneficiaries of racially conferred privilege have the right to establish norms for those who have historically been oppressed pursuant to those norms, and that race is not historically contingent. Although the substance of race definitions has changed, what persists is the expectation of white-controlled institutions in the continued right to determine meaning—the reified privilege of power—that reconstitutes the property interest in whiteness in contemporary form. . . .

IV. DELEGITIMATING THE PROPERTY INTEREST IN WHITENESS THROUGH AFFIRMATIVE ACTION

Within the worlds of de jure and de facto segregation, whiteness has value, whiteness is valued, and whiteness is expected to be valued in law. The legal affirmation of whiteness and white privilege allowed expectations that originated in injustice to be naturalized and legitimated. The relative economic, political, and social advantages dispensed to whites under systematic white supremacy in the United States were reinforced through patterns of oppression of blacks and Native Americans. Materially, these advantages became institutionalized privileges; ideologically, they became part of the settled expectations of whites—a product of the unalterable original bargain. The law masks as natural what is chosen; it obscures the consequences of social selection as inevitable. The result is that the distortions in social relations are immunized from truly effective intervention, because the existing inequities are obscured and rendered nearly invisible. The existing state of affairs is considered neutral and fair, however unequal and unjust it is in substance. Although the existing state of inequitable distribution is the product of institutionalized white supremacy and economic exploitation, it is seen by whites as part of the natural order of things, something that cannot legitimately be disturbed. Through legal doctrine, expectation of continued privilege based on white domination was reified; whiteness as property was reaffirmed.

The property interest in whiteness has proven to be resilient and adaptive to new conditions. Over time it has changed in form but it has retained its essential exclusionary character and continued to distort outcomes of legal disputes by favoring and protecting settled expectations of white privilege. The law expresses the dominant conception of constructs such as "rights," "equality," "property," "neutrality," and "power": rights mean shields from interference; equality means formal equality; property means the settled expectations that are to be protected; neutrality means the existing distribution, which is natural; and power is the mechanism for guarding all of this. . . .

Affirmative action begins the essential work of rethinking rights, power, equality, race, and property from the perspective of those whose access to each of these has been limited by their oppression.[. . .] From this perspective, affirmative action is required on moral and legal grounds to delegitimate the property interest in whiteness—to dismantle the actual and expected privilege that has attended "white" skin since the founding of the country. Like "passing," affirmative action undermines the property interest in whiteness. Unlike passing, which seeks the shelter of an assumed whiteness as a means of extending protection at the margins of racial boundaries, affirmative action denies the privileges of whiteness and seeks to remove the legal protections of the existing hierarchy spawned by race oppression. What passing attempts to circumvent, affirmative action moves to challenge.

Rereading affirmative action to delegitimate the property interest in whiteness suggests that if, historically, the law has legitimated and protected the settled whites' expectations in white privilege, delegitimation should be accomplished not merely by implementing equal treatment but also by equalizing treatment among the groups that have been illegitimately privileged or unfairly subordinated by racial stratification. Obviously, the meaning of equalizing treatment would vary, because the extent of privilege and subordination is not constant with reference to all societal goods. In some instances, the advantage of race privilege to poorer whites may be materially insignificant when compared to their class disadvantage against more privileged whites. But exposing the critical core of whiteness as property—the unconstrained right to exclude—directs attention toward questions of redistribution and property that are crucial under both race and class analysis. The conceptions of rights, race, property, and affirmative action as currently understood are unsatisfactory and insufficient to facilitate the self-realization of oppressed people. . . .

A. Affirmative Action: A New Form of Status Property?

If whiteness as property is the reification, in law, of expectations of white privilege, then according privilege to blacks through systems of affirmative action might be challenged as performing the same ideological function, but on the other side of the racial line. As evidence of a property interest in blackness, some might point out that, recently, some whites have sought to characterize themselves as belonging to a racial minority. Equating affirmative action with whiteness as property, however, is false and can only be maintained if history is ignored or inverted while the premises inherent in the existing racial hierarchy are retained. Whiteness as property is derived from the deep historical roots of systematic white supremacy which have given rise to definitions of group identity predicated on the racial subordination of the Other, and have reified expectations of continued white privilege. This reification differs in crucial ways from the premises, intent, and objectives of affirmative action.

Fundamentally, affirmative action does not reestablish a property interest in blackness, because black identity is not the functional opposite of whiteness. Even today, whiteness is still intertwined with the degradation of blacks and is still valued because "the artifact of 'whiteness'. . . sets a floor on how far [whites] can fall." Acknowledging black identity does not involve the systematic subordination of whites, nor does it even set up a danger of doing so. Affirmative action is based on principles of antisubordination, not principles of black superiority.

The removal of white privilege pursuant to a program of affirmative action would not be implemented under an ideology of subordination, nor would it be situated in the context of the historical or present exploitation of whites. It is thus not a matter of implementing systematic disadvantage to whites or installing mechanisms of group exploitation. Whites are not an oppressed people and are not at risk of becoming so. Those whites who are disadvantaged in society suffer not because of their race but in spite of it. Refusing to implement affirmative action as a remedy for racial subordination will not alleviate the class oppression of poor whites; indeed, failing to do so will reinforce the existing regime of race and class domination which leaves lower-class whites more vulnerable to class exploitation. Affirmative action does not institute a regime of racialized hierarchy in which all whites, because they are white, are deprived of economic, social, and political benefits. It does not reverse the hierarchy; rather, it levels the racial privilege.

Even if one rejects the notion that properly constructed affirmative action policies cause whites no injustice, affirmative action does not implement a set of permanent, never-ending privileges for blacks. Affirmative action does not distort black expectations because it does not naturalize these expectations. Affirmative action can only be implemented through conscious intervention, and it requires constant monitoring and reevaluation—so it does not function behind a mask of neutrality in the realm beyond scrutiny. Affirmative action for blacks does not reify existing patterns of privilege, nor does it produce subordination of whites as a group. If anything, it might fairly be said that affirmative action creates a property interest in true equal opportunity—opportunity and means that are equalized.

B. What Affirmative Action Has Been; What Affirmative Action Might Become

The truncated application of affirmative action as a policy has obscured affirmative action as a concept. The ferocious and unending debate on affirmative action cannot be understood unless the concept of affirmative action is considered and conceptually disengaged from its application in the United States.

As policy, affirmative action does not have a clearly identifiable pedigree; rather, it was one of the limited concessions offered in official response to demands for justice pressed by black constituencies. Despite uneven implementation in the areas of public employment, higher education, and government contracts, it translated into the attainment by blacks of jobs, admissions to universities, and contractual opportunities. Affirmative action programs did not, however, stem the tide of growing structural unemployment and underemployment among black workers, nor did it prevent the decline in material conditions for blacks as a whole. Such programs did not change the subordinated status of blacks, in part because of structural changes in the economy, and in part because the programs were not designed to do so.

However, affirmative action is more than a program: it is a principle, internationally recognized, based on a theory of rights and equality. Formal equality overlooks structural disadvantage and requires mere nondiscrimination or "equal treatment"; by contrast, affirmative action calls for equalizing treatment by redistributing power and resources in order to rectify inequities and to achieve real equality. The current polarized debate on affirmative action and the intense political and judicial opposition to the concept is thus grounded in the fact that, in its requirement of equalizing treatment, affirmative action implicitly challenges the sanctity of the original and derivative present distribution of property, resources, and entitlements, and it directly confronts the notion that there is a protectable property interest in "whiteness." If affirmative action doctrine were freed from the constraint of protecting the property interest in whiteness—if, indeed, it were conceptualized from the perspective of those on the bottom—it might assist in moving away from a vision of affirmative action as an uncompensated taking and inspire a new perspective on identity as well. The fundamental precept of whiteness, the core of its value, is its exclusivity; but exclusivity is predicated not on any intrinsic characteristic, but on the existence of the symbolic Other, which functions to "create an illusion of unity" among whites. Affirmative action might challenge the notion of property and identity as the unrestricted right to exclude. In challenging the property interest in whiteness, affirmative action could facilitate the destruction of the false premises of legitimacy and exclusivity inherent in whiteness and break the distorting link between white identity and property.

Affirmative action in the South African context offers a point of comparison. It has emerged as one of the democratic movement's central demands, appearing in both the constitutional guidelines and draft Bill of Rights issued by the African National Congress. These documents simultaneously denounce all forms of discrimination and embrace affirmative action as a mechanism for rectifying the gross inequities in South African society.

The South African conception of affirmative action expands the application of affirmative action to a much broader domain than has typically been envisioned in the United States. That is, South Africans consider affirmative action a strategic measure to address directly the distribution of property and power, with particular regard to the maldistribution of land and the need for housing. This policy has not yet been clearly defined, but what is implied by this conception of affirmative action is that existing distributions of property will be modified by rectifying unjust loss and inequality. Property rights will then be respected, but they will not be absolute; rather, they will be considered against a societal requirement of affirmative action. In essence, this conception of affirmative action is moving toward the reallocation of power and the right to have a say. This conception is in fact consistent with the fundamental principle of affirmative action and effectively removes the constraint imposed in the American model, which strangles affirmative action principles by protecting the property interest in whiteness.

V. CONCLUSION

Whiteness as property has carried and produced a heavy legacy. It is a ghost that has haunted the political and legal domains in which claims for justice have been inadequately addressed for far too long. Only rarely declaring its presence, it has warped efforts to remediate racial exploitation. It has blinded society to the systems of domination that work against so many by retaining an unvarying focus on vestiges of systemic racialized privilege which subordinates those perceived as a particularized few—the Others. It has thwarted not only conceptions of racial justice but also conceptions of property which embrace more equitable possibilities. In protecting the property interest in whiteness, property is assumed to be no more than the right to prohibit infringement on settled expectations, ignoring countervailing equitable claims predicated on a right to inclusion. It is long past time to put the property interest in whiteness to rest. Affirmative action can assist in that task. If properly conceived and implemented, it is not only consistent with norms of equality but also essential to shedding the legacy of oppression.

NOTES

1. 163 U.S. 537, 538 (1896).
2. N. Gotanda, "A Critique of 'Our Constitution is ColorBlind,'" 44 *Stan L. Rev.*, 1, 34 (1991).
3. D. Roediger, *The Wages of Whiteness,* at 32 (1991).
4. The system of racial oppression grounded in slavery was driven in large measure (although by no means exclusively) by economic concerns. . . .
5. M. Farrand, ed., 2 *The Records of the Federal Convention of 1787,* at 222 (1911).
6. My use of the term "blackwomen" is an effort to use language that more clearly reflects the unity of identity as "black" and "woman," with neither aspect primary or subordinate to the other. It is an attempt to realize in practice what has been identified in theory—that, as Kimberlé Crenshaw notes, blackwomen exist "at the crossroads of gender and race hierarchies"; K. Crenshaw, "Whose Story Is It, Anyway? Feminist and Antiracist Appropriations of Anita Hill," in Toni Morrison, ed., *Race-ing Justice, En-gendering Power: Essays on Anita Hill, Clarence Thomas, and the Construction of Social Reality,* 402, 403 (1992). [. . .]
7. A. L. Higginbotham, Jr., *In the Matter of Color: Race and the American Legal Process,* at 43 (1978). [. . .]
8. Letter from Thomas Jefferson to John Jordan (Dec. 21, 1805), cited in R. Takaki, *Iron Cages: Race and Culture in Nineteenth-Century America,* at 44 (1990).
9. By 1705, Virginia had classified slaves as real property; see Higginbotham, *supra* note 7, at 52. In Massachusetts and South Carolina, slaves were identified as chattel; *id.* at 78, 211.
10. 4 Ky. (1 Bibb) 97 (1815).
11. Jeremy Bentham, "Security and Equality in Property," in C. B. Macpherson, ed., *Property: Mainstream and Critical Positions,* at 51–52 (1978). [. . .]
12. *Id.* at 366.
13. G. Lukacs, *History and Class Consciousness,* 83, trans. R. Livingstone (1971).
14. K. R. Minogue, "The Concept of Property and Its Contemporary Significance," in J. R. Pennock and J. W. Chapman, eds., *Nomos XXII: Property,* at 15 (1980).
15. See J. H. Crabb, "Annotation, Libel and Slander: Statements Respecting Race, Color, or Nationality as Actionable," 46 *A. L. R.,* 2d 1287, 1289 (1956) ("The bulk of the cases have arisen from situations in which it was stated erroneously that a white person was a Negro. According to the majority rule, this is libelous per se").[. . .]
16. *Bowen v. Independent Publishing Co.,* 96 S. E. 2d 564, 565 (S.C. 1957).
17. R. C. Post, "The Social Foundations of Defamation Law: Reputation and the Constitution," 74 *Cal. L. Rev.,* 691, 709 (1986). . . .
18. Gotanda defines "historical-race' as socially constructed formal categories predicated on race subordination that included presumed substantive characteristics relating to "ability, disadvantage, or moral culpability."
19. "Hypodescent" is the term used by anthropologist Marvin Harris to describe the American system of racial classification in which the subordinate classification is assigned to the offspring if there is one "superordinate" and one

"subordinate" parent. Under this system, the child of a black parent and a white parent is black; M. Harris, *Patterns of Race in the Americas,* 37, 56 (1964).

20. It is not at all clear that even the slaves imported from abroad represented "pure negro races." As Gunner Myrdal noted, many of the tribes imported from Africa had intermingled with peoples of the Mediterranean, among them Portuguese slave traders. Other slaves brought to the United States came via the West Indies, where some Africans had been brought directly, but still others had been brought via Spain and Portugal, countries in which extensive interracial sexual relations had occurred. By the mid-nineteenth century it was, therefore, a virtual fiction to speak of "pure blood" as it relates to racial identification in the United States; see G. Myrdal, *An American Dilemma,* at 123 (1944).
21. *People v. Dean,* 14 Mich. 406, 422 (1866).
22. R. T. Diamond and R. J. Cottrol, "Codifying Caste: Louisiana's Racial Classification Scheme and the Fourteenth Amendment," 29 *Loy. L. Rev.,* 255, 281 (1983).
23. See, for example, *Gray v. Ohio,* 4 Ohio 353, 355 (1831).
24. The courts adopted this standard even as they critiqued the legitimacy of such rules and definitions. For example, in *People v. Dean,* 14 Mich. 406 (1886), the court, in interpreting the meaning of the word "white" for the purpose of determining whether the defendant had voted illegally, criticized as "absurd" the notion that a preponderance of mixed blood, on one side or the other of any given standard, has the remotest bearing upon personal fitness or unfitness to possess political privileges"; *id.* at 417. Yet it held that the electorate that had voted for racial exclusion had the right to determine voting privileges. See *id.* at 416.
25. S. J. Gould, *The Mismeasure of Man,* 24 (1981).
26. W. E. B. Du Bois, *Black Reconstruction* (1976) [1935].
27. *Id.* at 700.
28. *Id.* at 700–1.
29. Roediger, *supra* note 3, at 13. [. . .]
30. *Id.* at 13.
31. *Id.* at 9.
32. *Id.* at 118 (quoting Alan W. C. Green, " 'Jim Crow,' 'Zip Coon': The Northern Origin of Negro Minstrelsy," 11 *Mass. Rev.,* 385, 395 (1970)).
33. A. Hacker, *Two Nations,* 155 (1992).
34. See K. W. Crenshaw, "Race, Reform, and Retrenchment: Transformation and Legitimation in Antidiscrimination Law," 101 *Harv. L. Rev.,* 1331, 1381 (1988).
35. Roediger, *supra* note 3, at 5.

41

International News Service v. Associated Press

Supreme Court of the United States (1918). 248 U.S. 215.

MR. JUSTICE PITNEY delivered the opinion of the court.

The parties are competitors in the gathering and distribution of news and its publication for profit in newspapers throughout the United States. The Associated Press, which was complainant in the District Court, is a cooperative organization, incorporated under the Membership Corporations Law of the State of New York, its members being individuals who are either proprietors or representatives of about 950 daily newspapers published in all parts of the United States. . . .

Complainant gathers in all parts of the world, by means of various instrumentalities of its own, by exchange with its members, and by other appropriate means, news and intelligence of current and recent events of interest to newspaper readers and distributes it daily to its members for publication in their newspapers. The cost of the service, amounting approximately to $3,500,000 per annum, is assessed upon the members and becomes a part of their costs of operation, to be recouped, presumably with profit, through the publication of their several newspapers. Under complainant's by-laws each member agrees upon assuming membership that news received through complainant's service is received exclusively for publication in a particular newspaper, language, and place specified in the certificate of membership, that no other use of it shall be permitted, and that no member shall furnish or permit anyone in his employ or connected with his newspaper to furnish any of complainant's news in advance of publication to any person not a member. And each member is required to gather the local news of his district and supply it to the Associated Press and to no one else.

Defendant is a corporation organized under the laws of the State of New Jersey, whose business is the gathering and selling of news to its customers and clients, consisting of newspapers published throughout the United States, under contracts by which they pay certain amounts at stated times for defendant's service. It has wide-spread news-gathering agencies; the cost of its operations amounts, it is said, to more than $2,000,000 per annum; and it serves about 400 newspapers located in the various cities of the United States and abroad, a few of which are represented, also, in the membership of the Associated Press.

The parties are in the keenest competition between themselves in the distribution of news throughout the United States; and so, as a rule, are the newspapers that they serve, in their several districts.

Complainant in its bill, defendant in its answer, have set forth in almost identical terms the rather obvious circumstances and conditions under which their business is conducted. The value of the service and of the news furnished, depends upon the promptness of transmission, as well as upon the accuracy and impartiality of the news; it being essential that the news be transmitted to members or subscribers as early [as] or earlier than similar information can be furnished to competing newspapers by other news services, and that the news furnished by each agency shall not be furnished to newspapers which do not contribute to the expense of gathering it. And further, to quote from the answer: "Prompt knowledge and publication of world-wide news is essential to the conduct of a modern newspaper, and by reason of the enormous expense incident to the gathering and distribution of such news, the only practical way in which a proprietor of a newspaper can obtain the same is, either through cooperation with a considerable number of other newspaper proprietors in the work of collecting and distributing such news, and the equitable division with them of the expenses thereof, or by the purchase of such news from some existing agency engaged in that business."

The bill was filed to restrain the pirating of complainant's news by defendant in three ways:

. . . and Third, by copying news from bulletin boards and from early editions of complainant's newspapers and selling this, either bodily or after rewriting it, to defendant's customers.

* * *

The only matter that has been argued before us is whether defendant may lawfully be restrained from appropriating news taken from bulletins issued by complainant or any of its members, or from newspapers published by them, for the purpose of selling it to defendant's clients. Complainant asserts that defendant's admitted course of conduct in this regard both violates complainant's property right in the news and constitutes unfair competition in business. And notwithstanding the case has proceeded only to the stage of a preliminary injunction, we have deemed it proper to consider the underlying questions, since they go to the very merits of the action and are presented upon facts that are not in dispute. As presented in argument, these questions are: 1. Whether there is any property in news; 2. Whether, if there be property in news collected for the purpose of being published, it survives the instant of its publication in the first newspaper to which it is communicated by the news-gatherer; and 3. Whether defendant's admitted course of conduct in appropriating for commercial use matter taken from bulletins or early editions of Associated Press publications constitutes unfair competition in trade.

The federal jurisdiction was invoked because of diversity of citizenship, not upon the ground that the suit arose under the copyright or other laws of the United States. Complainant's news matter is not copyrighted. It is said that it could not, in practice, be copyrighted, because of the large number of dispatches that are sent daily; and, according to complainant's contention, news is not within the operation of the copyright act. Defendant, while apparently conceding this, nevertheless invokes the analogies of the law of literary property and copyright, insisting as its principal contention that, assuming complainant has a right of property in its news, it can be maintained (unless the copyright act be complied with) only by being kept secret and confidential, and that upon the publication with complainant's consent of uncopyrighted news by any of complainant's members in a newspaper or upon a bulletin board, the right of property is lost, and the subsequent use of the news by the public or by defendant for any purpose whatever becomes lawful.

* * *

In considering the general question of property in news matter, it is necessary to recognize its dual character, distinguishing between the substance of the information and the particular form or collocation of words in which the writer has communicated it.

No doubt news articles often possess a literary quality, and are the subject of literary property at the common law; nor do we question that such an article, as a literary production, is the subject of copyright by the terms of the act as it now stands. . . .

But the news element—the information respecting current events contained in the literary production—is not the creation of the writer, but is a report of matters that ordinarily are *publici juris;* it is the history of the day. It is not to be supposed that the framers of the Constitution, when they empowered Congress "to promote the progress of science and useful arts, by securing for limited times to authors and inventors the exclusive right to their respective writings and discoveries" (Const., Art. I, § 8, par. 8), intended to confer upon one who might happen to be the first to report a historic event the exclusive right for any period to spread the knowledge of it.

We need spend no time, however, upon the general question of property in news matter at common law, or the application of the copyright act, since it seems to us the case must turn upon the question of unfair competition in business. And, in our opinion, this does not depend upon any general right of property analogous to the common-law right of the proprietor of an unpublished work to prevent its publication without his consent; nor is it foreclosed by showing that the benefits of the copyright act have been waived. We are dealing here not with restrictions upon publication but with the very facilities and processes of publication. The peculiar value of news is in the spreading of it while it is fresh; and it is evident that a valuable property interest in the news, as news, cannot be maintained by keeping it secret. Besides, except for matters improperly disclosed, or published in breach of trust or confidence, or in violation of law, none of which is involved in this branch of the case, the news of current events may be regarded as common property. What we are concerned with is the business of making it known to the world, in which both parties to the present suit are engaged. That business consists in maintaining a prompt, sure, steady, and reliable service designed to place the daily events of the world at the breakfast table of the millions at a price that, while of trifling moment to each reader, is sufficient in the aggregate to afford compensation for the cost of gathering and distributing it, with the added profit so necessary as an incentive to effective action in the commercial world. The service thus performed for newspaper readers is not only innocent but extremely useful in itself, and indubitably constitutes a legitimate business. The parties are competitors in this field; and, on fundamental principles, applicable here as elsewhere, when the rights or privileges of the one are liable to conflict with those of the other, each party is under a duty so to conduct its own business as not unnecessarily or unfairly to injure that of the other. . . .

Obviously, the question of what is unfair competition in business must be determined with particular reference to the character and circumstances of the business. The question here is not so much the rights of either party as against the public but their rights as between themselves. . . . And although we may and do assume that neither party has any remaining property interest as against the public in uncopyrighted news matter after the moment of its first publication, it by no means follows (that there is no remaining property interest in it as between themselves). For, to both of them alike, news matter, however little susceptible of ownership or dominion in the absolute sense, is stock in trade, to be gathered at the cost of enterprise, organization, skill, labor, and money, and to be distributed and sold to those who will pay money for it, as for any other merchandise. (Regarding the news, therefore, as but the material out of which both parties are seeking to make profits at the same time and in the same field, we hardly can fail to recognize that for this purpose, and as between them, it must be regarded as *quasi* property, irrespective of the rights of either as against the public.)

In order to sustain the jurisdiction of equity over the controversy, we need not affirm any general and absolute property in the news as such. The rule that a court of equity concerns itself only in the protection of property rights treats any civil right of a pecuniary nature as a property right . . . and the right to acquire property by honest labor or the conduct of a lawful business is as much entitled to protection as the right to guard property already acquired. . . . It is this right that furnishes the basis of the jurisdiction in the ordinary case of unfair competition.

The question, whether one who has gathered general information or news at pains and expense for the purpose of subsequent publication through the press has such an interest in its publication as may be protected from interference, has been raised many times, although never, perhaps, in the precise form in which it is now presented.

Board of Trade v. Christie Grain & Stock Co., 198 U.S. 236, 250, related to the distribution of quotations of prices on dealings upon a board of trade, which were collected by plaintiff and communicated on confidential terms to numerous persons under a contract not to make them public. This court held that, apart from certain special objections that were overruled, plaintiff's collection of quotations was entitled to the protection of the law; that, like a trade secret, plaintiff might keep to itself the work done at its expense, and did not lose its right by communicating the result to persons, even if many, in confidential relations to itself, under a contract not to make it public; and that strangers should be restrained from getting at the knowledge by inducing a breach of trust.

In National Tel. News Co. v. Western Union Tel. Co., 119 Fed.Rep. 294, the Circuit Court of Appeals for the Seventh Circuit dealt with news matter gathered and transmitted by a telegraph company, and consisting merely of a notation of current events having but a transient value due to quick transmission and distribution; and, while declaring that this was not copyrightable although printed on a tape by tickers in the offices of the recipients, and that it was a commercial not a literary product, nevertheless held that the business of gathering and communicating the news—the service of purveying it—was a legitimate business, meeting a distinctive commercial want and adding to the facilities of the business world, and partaking of the nature of property in a sense that entitled it to the protection of a court of equity against piracy.

* * *

Not only do the acquisition and transmission of news require elaborate organization and a large expenditure of money, skill, and effort; not only has it an exchange value to the gatherer, dependent chiefly upon its novelty and freshness, the regularity of the service, its reputed reliability and thoroughness, and its adaptability to the public needs; but also, as is evident, the news has an exchange value to one who can misappropriate it.

The peculiar features of the case arise from the fact that, while novelty and freshness form so important an element in the success of the business, the very processes of distribution and publication necessarily occupy a good deal of time. Complainant's service, as well as defendant's, is a daily service to daily newspapers; most of the foreign news reaches this country at the Atlantic seaboard, principally at the City of New York, and because of this, and of time differentials due to the earth's rotation, the distribution of news matter throughout the country is principally from east to west; and, since in speed the telegraph and telephone easily outstrip the rotation of the earth, it is a simple matter for defendant to take complainant's news from bulletins or early editions of complainant's members in the eastern cities and at the mere cost of telegraphic transmission cause it to be published in western papers issued at least as early as those served by complainant. Besides this, and irrespective of time differentials, irregularities in telegraphic transmission on different lines, and the normal consumption of time in printing and distributing the newspaper, result in permitting pirated news to be placed in the hands of defendant's readers sometimes simultaneously with the service of competing Associated Press papers, occasionally even earlier.

Defendant insists that when, with the sanction and approval of complainant, and as the result of the use of its news for the very purpose for which it is distributed, a portion of complainant's members communicate it to the general public by posting it upon bulletin boards so that all may read, or by issuing it to newspapers and distributing it indiscriminately, complainant no longer has the right to control the use to be made of it; that when it thus reaches the light of day it becomes the common possession of all to whom it is accessible; and that any purchaser of a newspaper has the right to communicate the intelligence which it contains to anybody and for any purpose, even for the purpose of selling it for profit to newspapers published for profit in competition with complainant's members.

The fault in the reasoning lies in applying as a test the right of the complainant as against the public, instead of considering the rights of complainant and defendant, competitors in business, as between themselves. The right of the purchaser of a single newspaper to spread knowledge of its contents gratuitously, for any legitimate purpose not unreasonably interfering with complainant's right to make merchandise of it, may be admitted; but to transmit that news for commercial use, in competition with complainant—which is what defendant has done and seeks to justify—is a very different matter. In doing this defendant, by its very act, admits that it is taking material that has been acquired by complainant as the result of organization and the expenditure of labor, skill, and money, and which is salable by complainant for money, and that defendant in appropriating it and selling it as its own is endeavoring to reap where it has not sown, and by disposing of it to newspapers that are competitors of complainant's members is appropriating to itself the harvest of those who have sown. Stripped of all disguises, the process amounts to an unauthorized interference with the normal operation of complainant's legitimate business precisely at the point where the profit is to be reaped, in order to divert a material portion of the profit from those who have earned it to those who have not; with special advantage to defendant in the competition because of the fact that it is not burdened with any part of the expense of gathering the news. The transaction speaks for itself, and a court of equity ought not to hesitate long in characterizing it as unfair competition in business.

The underlying principle is much the same as that which lies at the base of the equitable theory of consideration in the law of trusts—that he who has fairly paid the price should have the beneficial use of the property. . . . It is no answer to say that complainant spends its money for that which is too fugitive or evanescent to be the subject of property. That might, and for the purposes of the discussion we are assuming that it would, furnish an answer in a common-law controversy. But in a court of equity, where the question is one of unfair competition, if that which complainant has acquired fairly at substantial cost may be sold fairly at substantial profit, a competitor who is misappropriating it for the purpose of disposing of it to his own profit and to the advantage of complainant cannot be heard to say that it is too fugitive or evanescent to be regarded as property. It has all the attributes of property necessary for determining that a misappropriation of it by a competitor is unfair competition because contrary to good conscience.

The contention that the news is abandoned to the public for all purposes when published in the first newspaper is untenable. Abandonment is a question of intent, and the entire organization of the Associated Press negatives such a purpose. The cost of the service would be prohibitive if the reward were to be so limited. No single newspaper, no small group of newspapers, could sustain the expenditure. Indeed, it is one of the most obvious results of defendant's theory that, by permitting indiscriminate publication by anybody and everybody for purposes of profit in competition with the news-gatherer, it would render publication profitless, or so little profitable as in effect to cut off the service by rendering the cost prohibitive in comparison with the return. The practical needs and requirements of the business are reflected in complainant's by-laws which have been referred to. Their effect is that publication by each member must be deemed not by any means an abandonment of the news to the world for any and all purposes, but a publication for limited purposes; for the benefit of the readers of the bulletin or the newspaper as such; not for the purpose of making merchandise of it as news, with the result of depriving complainant's other members of their reasonable opportunity to obtain just returns for their expenditures.

* * *

MR. JUSTICE HOLMES:

When an uncopyrighted combination of words is published there is no general right to forbid other people repeating them—in other words there is no property in the combination or in the thoughts or facts that the words express. Property, a creation of law, does not arise from value, although exchangeable—a matter of fact. Many exchangeable values may be destroyed intentionally without compensation. Property depends upon exclusion by law from interference, and a person is not excluded from using any combination of words merely because someone has used it before, even if it took labor and genius to make it. If a given person is to be prohibited from making the use of words that his neighbors are free to make some other ground must be found. One such ground is vaguely expressed in the phrase unfair trade. This means that the words are repeated by a competitor in business in such a way as to convey a misrepresentation that materially injures the person who first used them, by appropriating credit of some kind which the first user has earned. The ordinary case is a representation by device, appearance, or other in direction that the defendant's goods come from the plaintiff. But the only reason why it is actionable to make such a representation is that it tends to give the defendant an advantage in his competition with the plaintiff and that it is thought undesirable that an advantage should be gained in that way. Apart from that the defendant may use such unpatented devices and uncopyrighted combinations of words as he likes. The ordinary case, I say, is palming off the defendant's product as the plaintiff's, but the same evil may follow from the opposite falsehood—from saying, whether in words or by implication, that the plaintiff's product is the defendant's, and that, it seems to me, is what has happened here.

Fresh news is got only by enterprise and expense. To produce such news as it is produced by the defendant represents by implication that it has been acquired by the defendant's enterprise and at its expense. When it comes from one of the great news-collecting agencies like the Associated Press, the source generally is indicated, plainly importing that credit; and that such a representation is implied may be inferred with some confidence from the unwillingness of the defendant to give the credit and tell the truth. If the plaintiff produces the news at the same time that the defendant does, the defendant's presentation impliedly denies to the plaintiff the credit of collecting the facts and assumes that credit to the defendant. If the plaintiff is later in western cities it naturally will be supposed to have obtained its information from the defendant. The falsehood is a little more subtle, the injury a little more indirect, than in ordinary cases of unfair trade, but I think that the principle that condemns the one condemns the other. It is a question of how strong an infusion of fraud is necessary to turn a flavor into a poison. The dose seems to me strong enough here to need a remedy from the law. But as, in my view, the only ground of complaint that can be recognized without legislation is the implied misstatement, it can be corrected by stating the truth; and a suitable acknowledgment of the source is all that the plaintiff can require. I think that within the limits recognized by the decision of the Court the defendant should be enjoined from publishing news obtained from the Associated Press for hours after publication by the plaintiff unless it gives express credit to the Associated Press; the number of hours and the form of acknowledgment to be settled by the District Court.

MR. JUSTICE MCKENNA concurs in this opinion.

MR. JUSTICE BRANDEIS dissenting.

News is a report of recent occurrences. The business of the news agency is to gather systematically knowledge of such occurrences of interest and to distribute reports thereof. The Associated Press contended that knowledge so acquired is property, because it costs money and labor to produce and because it has value for which those who have it not are ready to pay; that it remains property and is entitled to protection as long as it has commercial value as news; and that to protect it effectively the defendant must be enjoined from making, or causing to be made, any gainful use of it while it retains such value. An essential element of individual property is the legal right to exclude others from enjoying it. If the property is private, the right of exclusion may be absolute; if the property is affected with a public interest, the right of exclusion is qualified. But the fact that a product of the mind has cost its producer money and labor, and has a value for which others are willing to pay, is not sufficient to ensure to it this legal attribute of property. The general rule of law is, that the noblest of human productions—knowledge, truths ascertained, conceptions, and ideas—become, after voluntary communication to others, free as the air to common use. Upon these incorporeal productions the attribute of property is continued after such communication only in certain classes of cases where public policy has seemed to demand it. These exceptions are confined to productions which, in some degree, involve creation, invention, or discovery. But by no means all such are endowed with this attribute of property. The creations which are recognized as property by the common law are literary, dramatic, musical, and other artistic creations; and these have also protection under the copyright statutes. The inventions and discoveries upon which this attribute of property is conferred only by statute, are the few comprised within the patent law. There are also many other cases in which courts interfere to prevent curtailment of plaintiff's enjoyment of incorporeal productions; and in which the right to relief is often called a property right, but is such only in a special sense. In those cases, the plaintiff has no absolute right to the protection of his production; he has merely the qualified right to be protected as against the defendant's acts, because of the special relation in which the latter stands or the wrongful method or means employed in acquiring the knowledge or the manner in which it is used. Protection of this character is afforded where the suit is based upon breach of contract or of trust or upon unfair competition.

The knowledge for which protection is sought in the case at bar is not of a kind upon which the law has heretofore conferred the attributes of property; nor is the manner of its acquisition or use nor the purpose to which it is applied, such as has heretofore been recognized as entitling a plaintiff to relief.

* * *

The great development of agencies now furnishing country-wide distribution of news, the vastness of our territory, and improvements in the means of transmitting intelligence, have made it possible for a news agency or newspapers to obtain, without paying compensation, the fruit of another's efforts and to use news so obtained gainfully in competition with the original collector. The injustice of such action is obvious. But to give relief against it would involve more than the application of existing rules of law to new facts. It would require the making of a new rule in analogy to existing ones. The unwritten law possesses capacity for growth; and has often satisfied new demands for justice by invoking analogies or by expanding a rule or principle. This process has been in the main wisely applied and should not be discontinued. Where the problem is relatively simple, as it is apt to be when private interests only are involved, it generally proves adequate. But with the increasing complexity of society, the public interest tends to become omnipresent; and the problems presented by new demands for justice cease to be simple. Then the creation or recognition by courts of a new private right may work serious injury to the general public, unless the boundaries of the right are definitely established and wisely guarded. In order to reconcile the new private right with the public interest, it may be necessary to prescribe limitations and rules for its enjoyment; and also to provide administrative machinery for enforcing the rules. It is largely for this reason that, in the effort to meet the many new demands for justice incident to a rapidly changing civilization, resort to legislation has latterly been had with increasing frequency.

The rule for which the plaintiff contends would effect an important extension of property rights and a corresponding curtailment of the free use of knowledge and of ideas; and the facts of this case admonish us of the danger involved in recognizing such a property right in news, without imposing upon news-gatherers corresponding obligations. . . .

A legislature, urged to enact a law by which one news agency or newspaper may prevent appropriation of the fruits of its labors by another, would consider such facts and possibilities and others which appropriate enquiry might disclose. Legislators might conclude that it was impossible to put an end to the obvious injustice involved in such appropriation of news, without opening the door to other evils, greater than that sought to be remedied.

* * *

Or legislators dealing with the subject might conclude, that the right to news values should be protected to the extent of permitting recovery of damages for any unauthorized use, but that protection by injunction should be denied, just as courts of equity ordinarily refuse (perhaps in the interest of free speech) to restrain actionable libels, and for other reasons decline to protect by injunction mere political rights; and as Congress has prohibited courts from enjoining the illegal assessment or collection of federal taxes. If a legislature concluded to recognize property in published news to the extent of permitting recovery at law, it might, with a view to making the remedy more certain and adequate, provide a fixed measure of damages, as in the case of copyright infringement.

Or again, a legislature might conclude that it was unwise to recognize even so limited a property right in published news as that above indicated; but that a news agency should, on some conditions, be given full protection of its business; and to that end a remedy by injunction as well as one for damages should be granted, where news collected by it is gainfully used without permission. If a legislature concluded, . . . that under certain circumstances news-gathering is a business affected with a public interest, it might declare that, in such cases, news should be protected against appropriation, only if the gatherer assumed the obligation of supplying it, at reasonable rates and without discrimination, to all papers which applied therefor. If legislators reached that conclusion, they would probably go further, and prescribe the conditions under which and the extent to which the protection should be afforded; and they might also provide the administrative machinery necessary for ensuring to the public, the press, and the news agencies, full enjoyment of the rights so conferred.

Courts are ill-equipped to make the investigations which should precede a determination of the limitations which should be set upon any property right in news or of the circumstances under which news gathered by a private agency should be deemed affected with a public interest. Courts would be powerless to prescribe the detailed regulations essential to full enjoyment of the rights conferred or to introduce the machinery required for enforcement of such regulations. Considerations such as these should lead us to decline to establish a new rule of law in the effort to redress a newly-disclosed wrong, although the propriety of some remedy appears to be clear.

PART 6

CONTRACTS

In modern times, Anglo-American law has been increasingly dominated by the concept of contract rather than the idea of property. According to this concept, law should protect agreements that are freely entered into. Here, more than in any other field of law, we see how the "bindingness" of law is based on the self-binding acts of individuals. A dispute nonetheless continues about why people are bound to perform their contracts and about why the law is justified in intervening in what appear to be the private actions of individuals trying to regulate their own lives. It is often said that contract law is the cornerstone of a free society. Contract law is also criticized as the basis of economic exploitation by the powerful of the poor.

We begin Part 6 with a selection from Thomas Hobbes's seventeenth-century classic, *Leviathan*. Hobbes defines a contract as "mutual transferring of right." One can transfer a right either by delivering a good to another person or by transferring the right with the promise that the good will follow. However, says Hobbes, a mere promise is not a transfer of right: A promise indicates what one will do in the future, but a contract occurs in the present. For a contract to occur, something must be transferred in the present. Hobbes says that it is the right that must transfer, and there must be some clear sign that this has occurred. In legal systems, societies have established rules for the transfer of right that allow someone to distinguish mere promises from a contract. In the Anglo-American tradition, "consideration" is the sufficient sign that a binding contract has been made.

Hobbes provides one of the most widely cited justifications for the institution of contracts. In the state of nature, prior to the formation of societies, people had no constraints on their avaricious behavior. As a result, each person felt that she had a right to do anything to the other. But this created extreme uncertainty and fear, because no one could trust anyone else. Yet, people saw the need for trust and peace in order to prosper. Because of the lack of trust, agreements were impossible; nonetheless, people were naturally driven to seek them to better their lives. People wanted to trust one another, but the first person to do so would take too great a risk. Societies, especially coercive governments, were created to enforce contracts and to make it reasonable for people to enter into and perform their contracts. Without such arrangements, people would all still be in the state of nature, hoping for peace and prosperity but unable to achieve these goals. Without contracts, people's lives would be "solitary, poor, nasty, brutish, and short."[1]

In "The Practice of Promising," P. S. Atiyah expands on Hobbes's analysis, linking the obligation to perform contracts and keep promises to the performer's expected benefit. Atiyah points out that in law a person justifiably fails to perform a contract either if there has already been a breach by the other party or if the expected benefit of performing has greatly diminished. Indeed, the reason to keep contracts and promises has more to do, he suggests, with

[1]Thomas Hobbes, *Leviathan,* Ch. 13.

the idea that someone else has relied on the expected performance to his or her detriment. In those cases where there has been no loss from relying on the promise of another, judges are unlikely to demand that the breaching party suffer any sanction.

Atiyah argues that one cannot ascertain the moral justification of performing contracts or promises unless one determines *why* the promise was made. Promises are made and kept not out of a general concern for morality but because of what the promisor expects to get by performing. Atiyah contends that intentional commitment is not crucial for justifying the legal enforcement of a contract or promise. He points out that a fraudulent promise is still enforceable if it is relied on. Third parties may be bound by contracts as well, which illustrates that philosophers have put too much weight on the intention of the parties in justifying the legal enforcement of contracts.

Charles Fried, in "Contract As Promise," provides a sustained argument against views like those of Atiyah, contending that contract law hinges on the moral doctrine that a person's explicit, intentional act of promising is morally binding and therefore also legally enforceable. Here, commitment is the most important idea, much more important than expected benefit or reliance. Reliance cannot fully account for why the law enforces contracts, for most frequently expectation, not reliance, serves as the basis of compensation for breached contracts. Expectation is simply the position one would have been in had the contract been performed rather than breached. To account for this scheme of legal compensation requires us to look beyond the interests of the parties to what they have actually committed to do.

Fried sees contracts as exemplifying a distinctly liberal principle—namely, that people should be free to live their lives as they see fit. When a person chooses to make a promise or contract, he transforms an act from something that was previously morally neutral into something that is now morally required. Our free choices make a difference in the world, and we should be held responsible for both the good and the bad that occur as a result of our free choices. If we commit ourselves to perform a certain act, then we should be held liable if we do not so perform. Fried is thus led to conclude that contracts derive their moral justification from their intimate relationship to promises.

In "Legally Enforceable Commitments," Michael D. Bayles proposes a set of reasonable limits for determining which contracts should be legally enforced. Specifically, Bayles proposes three principles that should govern the legal enforcement of contracts. First, he argues that involuntary transfers should be disallowed; only voluntary transfers of goods should be legally enforced. Second, zero-sum transactions should be enforced only if doing so is necessary to prevent loss to one of the parties. Contracts should normally be limited to mutually beneficial transactions, and contracts that involve a loss to both parties should not be allowed. Third, the legal enforcement of contracts should be limited to those that are for the "collective good."

A good example of a dispute about the place of law in contractual situations concerns whether a contract can be so lopsided and coercive as to be morally "unconscionable" and considered legally void on that basis alone. The standard account of unconscionability is that it involves unequal bargaining power, where one of the parties will almost surely not benefit from the transaction. In "Unconscionability and Contracts," Alan Wertheimer argues that many contracts involve unequal bargaining power; indeed, the authors of the Uniform Commercial Code say that the purpose of the unconscionability doctrine is not to eliminate the risk of loss in bargaining that people may voluntarily choose to incur but, rather, "to prevent oppression and unfair surprise" (see p. 389).

Concern about unconscionability typically arises when one party uses a standard form contract that allows no room for bargaining. This increasingly prevalent practice in rental agreements and sales contracts, where the landlord or merchant is economically powerful and the tenant or buyer not terribly knowledgeable, smacks of bargaining inequality from the beginning. But what exactly is the problem with standard form contracts? Wertheimer says that many such contracts are perfectly fair. Indeed, he points out that the take-it-or-leave-it character of standard form transactions often does not substantially differ from most other commercial transactions. Wertheimer suggests that the only way to save the idea of unconscionable contracts is to argue that such agreements are ideally bad for society even if no person is specifically harmed.

To illustrate the general idea and the difficulty of applying unconscionability, we have provided two U.S. cases. The first, *Henningsen v. Bloomfield Motors, Inc.*, concerns a newly purchased car that had a severely defective steering mechanism, causing an accident that totaled the car. The original sales contract had ten separate paragraphs on the back of the main page, in extremely small type, purporting to limit liability to replacement parts. Because all auto manufacturers used the same type of form, the court argued that the buyer had no reasonable alternative but to accept the terms, even though the limitation on warranty left the buyer with little protection from injury resulting from certain serious defects, as was true in this case.

The court in the *Henningsen* case was struck by the way that the warranty limitation resulted in a potential loss of rights on the buyer's part that creates a "great potential for harm." The rights in question involved the right to be compensated for personal injuries sustained by defective products, a fundamentally important right. In ruling for Henningsen against the auto dealer, the court said that its main purpose was to "protect the ordinary man against loss of important rights through what, in effect, is the unilateral act of the manufacturer."[2] Here, the grossly disproportionate bargaining power was the key consideration for the court. Contracts signed under such unequal bargaining positions are simply "inimical to the public good."[3]

The second case, *Williams v. Walker-Thomas Furniture Co.,* concerned an installment contract for the purchase of furniture that stipulated that if a payment was missed, the furniture could be repossessed, along with any other furniture purchased from the same company that still had an outstanding balance. There was nothing fraudulent about the agreement. After the buyer defaulted on one payment, the furniture company attempted to repossess all of the furniture that the buyer had purchased over the previous four years. In holding for the buyer, the court stressed the unequal bargaining positions of the parties, saying that in such situations there "is little real choice" on the part of the buyer. For this reason, the court found the terms of the contract to be unconscionable.

In a brief dissenting opinion, Circuit Judge Dahner argues that more caution is needed in this area than the majority evidenced. According to this judge, the buyer "seems to have known precisely where she stood."[4] For this reason there are multiple public policy issues involved in this case. Making this kind of deal may have been the only way for the buyer to be able to afford to buy the furniture she needed. In this respect, the dissenting judge seems to give voice to the position Wertheimer presented earlier. According to this view, courts should always be reluctant to disregard what two parties have in fact agreed to. Since there was no fraud in this case, isn't it the right of the buyer to make a foolish bargain?

In many, especially non-Western parts of the world, unconscionability of contract is not a recognized legal doctrine. South Africa represents a case in point. Even as many Western legal theorists question the usefulness and desirability of unconscionability doctrines, theorists outside the Western legal tradition are beginning to see its value. In "South African Contract Law," Lynn Berat argues that South Africa should embrace the doctrine of unconscionability. South Africa has especially high numbers of both wealthy businesses and people in abject poverty. Law should protect the vulnerable when their interests conflict with those of the powerful.

Berat's essay provides a useful summary of the main differences between systems of law that follow a Roman model and those that follow an Anglo-Saxon model. The Roman model focuses only on whether there has in fact been an agreement. South Africa has a hybrid system of law, part Anglo-Saxon and part Roman. The Roman influence, brought to South Africa by Dutch settlers, predominates in contract law. As a result, contracts are not invalidated unless they are clearly fraudulent or signed under duress. Berat argues that consideration of fraud and duress will help protect some buyers, but many others will not have their economic rights fully protected until South Africa adopts the unconscionability doctrine.

The final essay in this section, "On Surrogacy: Morality, Markets, and Motherhood," concerns the current controversy about whether surrogate parenting contracts should be enforced at law. Michele M. Moody-Adams provides a strong argument that surrogacy contracts should not be legally enforced. In this case, the service that is contracted for is inextricable from the body that is to perform it. Indeed, it is unclear

[2]*Henningsen v. Bloomfield Motors, Inc.,* Supreme Court of New Jersey, 1960, 161 A. 2d 94.
[3]Ibid., at 95.

[4]*Williams v. Walker-Thomas Furniture Co.,* United States Court of Appeals, District of Columbia Circuit, 1960, 350 F.2d 450.

whether the contract really concerns a "service" at all but, rather, the selling of a baby. The couples cannot avoid treating the surrogate as a commodity and hence cannot treat the surrogate with the respect due to all persons. In this sense, the form of treatment in surrogacy contracts resembles the institution of slavery, which also should never have been legally enforced. According to Moody-Adams, the exploitation involved in surrogacy arrangements is so morally pernicious that the contracts should not be legally enforced.

At its most extreme form, unconscionable and exploitative contracts are considered so morally pernicious that they could not be countenanced without somehow morally tainting the law itself, and hence undermining the moral respect for law that is necessary for our sense of obligation to obey the law. When contracts, which are supposed to provide avenues of increased liberty for individuals, clearly infringe on the liberty of one of the parties to the contract, then the moral pillars of the law have been undermined. It is hard to draw a clear line where contracts become so exploitative or unconscionable as to be no longer legally valid, but few deny that such a line needs to be drawn and then not crossed.

For those of you who want to read more on contract law, we have included a list of works that cover the range of topics in Part 6.

SELECTED READINGS

Atiyah, P. S. *Essays on Contract.* New York: Oxford University Press, 1986.

Carbone, June. "The Limits of Contract in Family Law: An Analysis of Surrogate Motherhood." *Logos* 9 (1988): 147–60.

Coleman, Jules. "A Bargaining Theory Approach to Default Provisions and Disclosure Rules in Contract Law." In *Liability and Responsibility,* edited by Jules Coleman. New York: Cambridge University Press, 1991.

Dees, J. Gregory. "Unconscionability and Fairness: Comments on Wertheimer." *Business Ethics Quarterly* 2, no. 4 (October 1992): 497–504.

Deutch, Sinai. "Contract Law and Consumer Protection in Israel." *New York Law School Journal of International and Comparative Law* 14 (1993): 261–92.

Ingram, David. "Legitimation Crisis in Contract Law: A Test Case for Critical Legal Studies and Its Critics." In *Radical Philosophy of Law,* edited by David Caudill. Atlantic Highlands, NJ: Humanities Press, 1995.

Lewis, Mark. "Contract Law in the People's Republic of China—Rule or Tool: Can the PRC's Foreign Economic Contract Law Be Administered According to the Rule of Law?" *Vanderbilt Journal of Transnational Law* 30 (1997): 495–538.

Pateman, Carole. "Women and Consent." *Political Theory* 8 (May 1980): 149–68.

Taylor, Veronica. "Continuing Transactions and Persistent Myths: Contracts in Contemporary Japan." *Melbourne University Law Review* 19 (1993): 352–98.

Unger, Roberto Mangabeira. "Principle and Counter-Principle: Freedom of Contract and Fairness." In *The Critical Legal Studies Movement, 66–68.* Cambridge: Harvard University Press, 1983.

Wagatsuma, Hiroshi, and Arthur Rossett. "Cultural Attitudes towards Contract Law: Japan and the United States Compared." *UCLA Pacific Basin Law Journal* 2 (1983): 76–97.

Webb, Duncan. "Towards a Contract Law of China: Some Salient Features." *Lloyd's Maritime and Commercial Law Quarterly* (1996): 245–67.

Woozley, A. D. "Promises, Promises." *Mind* 90 (April 1981): 289–91.

42

THOMAS HOBBES

From *Leviathan*

CHAPTER 14
OF THE FIRST AND SECOND NATURAL LAWS, AND OF CONTRACTS

Right of nature what. THE RIGHT OF NATURE, which writers commonly call *jus naturale,* is the liberty each man hath, to use his own power, as he will himself, for the preservation of his own nature; that is to say, of his own life; and consequently of doing any thing, which in his own judgment, and reason, he shall conceive to be the aptest means thereunto.

Liberty what. By LIBERTY, is understood, according to the proper signification of the word, the absence of external impediments: which impediments, may oft take away part of a man's power to do what he would; but cannot hinder him from using the power left him, according as his judgment, and reason shall dictate to him.

A law of nature what. Difference of right and law. A LAW OF NATURE, *lex naturalis,* is a precept or general rule, found out by reason, by which a man is forbidden to do that, which is destructive of his life, or taketh away the means of preserving the same; and to omit that, by which he thinketh it may be best preserved. For though they that speak of this subject, use to confound *jus,* and *lex, right* and *law:* yet they ought to be distinguished; because RIGHT, consisteth in liberty to do, or to forbear: whereas LAW, determineth, and bindeth to one of them: so that law, and right, differ as much, as obligation, and liberty; which in one and the same matter are inconsistent.

Naturally every man has right to every thing. The fundamental law of nature. And because the condition of man, as hath been declared in the precedent chapter, is a condition of war of every one against every one; in which case every one is governed by his own reason; and there is nothing he can make use of, that may not be a help unto him, in preserving his life against his enemies; it followeth, that in such a condition, every man has a right to every thing; even to one another's body. And therefore, as long as this natural right of every man to every thing endureth, there can be no security to any man, how strong or wise soever he be, of living out the time, which nature ordinarily alloweth men to live. And consequently it is a precept, or general rule of reason, *that every man, ought to endeavour peace, as far as he has hope of obtaining it; and when he cannot obtain it, that he may seek, and use, all helps, and advantages of war.* The first branch of which rule, containeth the first, and fundamental law of nature; which is, *to seek peace, and follow it.* The second, the sum of the right of nature; which is, *by all means we can, to defend ourselves.*

The second law of nature. From this fundamental law of nature, by which men are commanded to endeavour peace, is derived this second law; *that a man be willing, when others are so too, as far-forth, as for peace, and defence of himself he shall think it necessary, to lay down this right to all things; and be contented with so much liberty against other men, as he would allow other men against himself.* For as long as every man holdeth this right, of doing anything he liketh; so long are all men in the condition of war. But if other men will not lay down their right, as well as he; then there is no reason for any one to divest himself of his: for that were to expose himself to prey, which no man is bound to, rather than to dispose himself to peace. This is that law of the Gospel; *whatsoever you require that others should do to you, that do ye to them.* And that law of all men, *quod tibi fieri non vis, alteri ne feceris.*

What it is to lay down a right. To *lay down* a man's *right* to any thing, is to *divest* himself of the *liberty,* of hindering another of the benefit of his own right to the same. For he that renounceth, or passeth away his right, giveth not to any other man a right which he had not before; because there is nothing to which every man had not right by nature: but only standeth out of his way, that he may enjoy his own original right, without hindrance from him; not without hindrance from another. So that the effect which redoundeth to one man, by another man's defect of right, is but so much diminution of impediments to the use of his own right original.

Renouncing a right, what it is. Transferring right what. Obligation. Duty. Injustice. Right is laid aside, either by simply renouncing it; or by transferring it to another. By *simply* RENOUNCING; when he cares not to whom the benefit thereof redoundeth. By TRANSFERRING; when he intendeth the benefit thereof to some certain person, or persons. And when a man hath in either manner abandoned, or granted away his right; then is he said to be OBLIGED, or BOUND, not to hinder those, to whom such right is granted, or abandoned, from the benefit of it: and that he *ought*, and it is his DUTY, not to make void that voluntary act of his own: and that such hindrance is INJUSTICE, and INJURY, as being *sine jure;* the right being before renounced, or transferred. So that *injury,* or *injustice,* in the controversies of the world, is somewhat like to that, which in the disputations of scholars is called *absurdity*. For as it is there called an absurdity, to contradict what one maintained in the beginning: so in the world, it is called injustice, and injury, voluntarily to undo that, which from the beginning he had voluntarily done. The way by which a man either simply renounceth, or transferreth his right, is a declaration, or signification, by some voluntary and sufficient sign, or signs, that he doth so renounce, or transfer; or hath so renounced, or transferred the same, to him that accepteth it. And these signs are either words only, or actions only; or, as it happeneth most often, both words, and actions. And the same are the BONDS by which men are bound, and obliged: bonds, that have their strength, not from their own nature, for nothing is more easily broken than a man's word, but from fear of some evil consequence upon the rupture.

Not all rights are alienable. Whensoever a man transferreth his right, or renounceth it; it is either in consideration of some right reciprocally transferred to himself; or for some other good he hopeth for thereby. For it is a voluntary act: and of the voluntary acts of every man, the object is some *good to himself.* And therefore there be some rights, which no man can be understood by any words, or other signs, to have abandoned, or transferred. As first a man cannot lay down the right of resisting them, that assault him by force, to take away his life; because he cannot be understood to aim thereby, at any good to himself. The same may be said of wounds, and chains, and imprisonment; both because there is no benefit consequent to such patience; as there is to the patience of suffering another to be wounded, or imprisoned; as also because a man cannot tell, when he seeth men proceed against him by violence, whether they intend his death or not. And lastly the motive, and end for which this renouncing, and transferring of right is introduced, is nothing else but the security of a man's person, in his life, and in the means of so preserving life, as not to be weary of it. And therefore if a man by words, or other signs, seem to despoil himself of the end, for which those signs were intended; he is not to be understood as if he meant it, or that it was his will; but that he was ignorant of how such words and actions were to be interpreted.

Contract what. The mutual transferring of right, is that which men call CONTRACT.

There is difference between transferring of right to the thing; and transferring, or tradition, that is delivery of the thing itself. For the thing may be delivered together with the translation of the right; as in buying and selling with ready-money; or exchange of goods, or lands: and it may be delivered some time after.

Covenant what. Again, one of the contractors, may deliver the thing contracted for on his part, and leave the other to perform his part at some determinate time after, and in the mean time be trusted; and then the contract on his part, is called PACT, or COVENANT: or both parts may contract now, to perform hereafter: in which cases, he that is to perform in time to come, being trusted, his performance is called *keeping of promise*, or faith; and the failing of performance, if it be voluntary, *violation of faith.*

Free gift. When the transferring of right, is not mutual, but one of the parties transferreth, in hope to gain thereby friendship, or service from another, or from his friends; or in hope to gain the reputation of charity, or magnanimity; or to deliver his mind from the pain of compassion; or in hope of reward in heaven; this is not contract, but GIFT, FREE-GIFT, GRACE: which words signify one and the same thing.

Signs of contract express. Promise. Signs of contract, are either *express* or *by inference.* Express, are words spoken with understanding of what they signify: and such words are either of the time *present,* or *past;* as, *I give, I grant, I have given, I have granted, I will that this be yours*: or of the future; as, *I will give, I will grant:* which words of the future are called PROMISE.

Signs of contract by inference. Signs by inference, are sometimes the consequence of words; sometimes the consequence of silence; sometimes the consequence of actions; sometimes the consequence of forbearing an action: and generally a sign by inference, of any contract, is whatsoever sufficiently argues the will of the contractor.

Free gift passeth by words of the present or past. Words alone, if they be of the time to come, and contain a bare promise, are an insufficient sign of a free-gift, and therefore not obligatory. For if they be of the time to come, as *tomorrow I will give,* they are a sign I have not given yet, and consequently that my right is not transferred, but remaineth till I transfer it by some other act. But if the words be of the time present, or past, as, *I have given,* or *do give to be delivered to-morrow,* then is my to-morrow's right given away to-day; and that by the virtue of the words, though there were no other argument of my will. And there is a great difference in the signification of these words, *volo hoc tuum esse cras,* and *cras dabo;* that is, between *I will that this be thine tomorrow,* and, *I will give it thee tomorrow*: for the word *I will,* in the former manner of speech, signifies an act of the will present; but in the latter, it signifies a promise of an act of the will to come: and therefore the former words, being of the present, transfer a future right; the latter, that be of the future, transfer nothing. But if there be other signs of the will to transfer a right, besides words; then though the gift be free, yet may the right be understood to pass by words of the future: as if a man propound a prize to him that comes first to the end of a race, the gift is free: and though the words be of the future, yet the right passeth: for if he would not have his words so be understood, he should not have let them run.

Signs of contract are words both of the past, present, and future. In contracts, the right passeth, not only where the words are of the time present, or past, but also where they are of the future: because all contract is mutual translation, or change of right; and therefore he that promiseth only, because he hath already received the benefit for which he promiseth, is to be understood as if he intended the right should pass: for unless he had been content to have his words so understood, the other would not have performed his part first. And for that cause, in buying, and selling, and other acts of contract, a promise is equivalent to a covenant; and therefore obligatory.

Merit what. He that performeth first in the case of a contract, is said to MERIT that which he is to receive by the performance of the other; and he hath it as *due.* Also when a prize is propounded to many, which is to be given to him only that winneth; or money is thrown amongst many, to be enjoyed by them that catch it; though this be a free gift; yet so to win, or so to catch, is to *merit,* and to have it as DUE. For the right is transferred in the propounding of the prize, and in throwing down the money; though it be not determined to whom, but by the event of the contention. But there is between these two sorts of merit, this difference, that in contract, I merit by virtue of my own power, and the contractor's need; but in this case of free gift, I am enabled to merit only by the benignity of the giver: in contract I merit at the contractor's hand that he should depart with his right; in this case of gift, I merit not that the giver should part with his right; but that when he has parted with it, it should be mine, rather than another's. And this I think to be the meaning of that distinction of the Schools, between *meritum congrui,* and *meritum condigni.* For God Almighty, having promised Paradise to those men, hoodwinked with carnal desires, that can walk through this world according to the precepts, and limits prescribed by him; they say, he that shall so walk, shall merit Paradise *ex congruo.* But because no man can demand a right to it, by his own righteousness, or any other power in himself, but by the free grace of God only; they say no man can merit Paradise *ex condigno.* This I say, I think is the meaning of that distinction; but because disputers do not agree upon the significance of their own terms of art, longer than it serves their turn; I will not affirm any thing of their meaning: only this I say; when a gift is given indefinitely, as a prize to be contended for, he that winneth meriteth, and may claim the prize as due.

Covenants of mutual trust, when invalid. If a covenant be made, wherein neither of the parties perform presently, but trust one another; in the condition of mere nature, which is a condition of war of every man against every man, upon any reasonable suspicion, it is void: but if there be a common power set over them both, with right and force sufficient to compel performance, it is not void. For he that performeth first, has no assurance the other will perform after; because the bonds of words are too weak to bridle men's ambition, avarice, anger, and other passions, without the fear of some coercive power; which in the condition of mere nature, where all men are equal, and judges of the justness of their own fears, cannot possibly be supposed. And therefore he which performeth first, does but betray himself to his enemy; contrary to the right, he can never abandon, of defending his life, and means of living.

But in a civil estate, where there is a power set up to constrain those who would otherwise violate their faith, that fear is no more reasonable; and for that cause, he which by the covenant is to perform first, is obliged so to do.

The cause of fear, which maketh such a covenant invalid, must be always something arising after the covenant made; as some new fact, or other sign of the will not to perform: else it cannot make the covenant void. For that which could not hinder a man from promising, ought not to be admitted as a hindrance of performing.

Right to the end, containeth right to the means. He that transferreth any right, transferreth the means of enjoying it, as far as lieth in his power. As he that selleth land, is understood to transfer the herbage, and whatsoever grows upon it: nor can he that sells a mill turn away the stream that drives it. And they that give to a man the right of government in sovereignty, are understood to give him the right of levying money to maintain soldiers, and of appointing magistrates for the administration of justice.

No covenant with beasts. To make covenants with brute beasts, is impossible; because not understanding our speech, they understand not, nor accept of, any translation of right; nor can translate any right to another; and without mutual acceptation, there is no covenant.

Nor with God without special revelation. To make covenant with God, is impossible, but by mediation of such as God speaketh to, either by revelation supernatural, or by his lieutenants that govern under him, and in his name: for otherwise we know not whether our covenants be accepted, or not. And therefore they that vow anything contrary to any law of nature, vow in vain; as being a thing unjust to pay such a vow. And if it be a thing commanded by the law of nature, it is not the vow, but the law that binds them.

No covenant, but of possible and future. The matter, or subject of a covenant, is always something that falleth under deliberation; for to covenant, is an act of the will; that is to say, an act, and the last act of deliberation; and is therefore always understood to be something to come; and which is judged possible for him that covenanteth, to perform.

And therefore, to promise that which is known to be impossible, is no covenant. But if that prove impossible afterwards, which before was thought possible, the covenant is valid, and bindeth, though not to the thing itself, yet to the value; or, if that also be impossible, to the unfeigned endeavour of performing as much as is possible: for to more no man can be obliged.

Covenants how made void. Men are freed of their covenants two ways; by performing, or by being forgiven. For performance, is the natural end of obligation; and forgiveness, the restitution of liberty; as being a retransferring of that right, in which the obligation consisted.

Covenants extorted by fear are valid. Covenants entered into by fear, in the condition of mere nature, are obligatory. For example, if I covenant to pay a ransom, or service for my life, to an enemy; I am bound by it: for it is a contract, wherein one receiveth the benefit of life; the other is to receive money, or service for it; and consequently, where no other law, as in the condition of mere nature, forbiddeth the performance, the covenant is valid. Therefore prisoners of war, if trusted with the payment of their ransom, are obliged to pay it: and if a weaker prince, make a disadvantageous peace with a stronger, for fear; he is bound to keep it; unless, as hath been said before, there ariseth some new, and just cause of fear, to renew the war. And even in commonwealths, if I be forced to redeem myself from a thief by promising him money, I am bound to pay it, till the civil law discharge me. For whatsoever I may lawfully do without obligation, the same I may lawfully covenant to do through fear: and what I lawfully covenant, I cannot lawfully break.

The former covenant to one, makes void the later to another. A former covenant, makes void a later. For a man that hath passed away his right to one man to-day, hath it not to pass to-morrow to another: and therefore the later promise passeth no right, but is null.

A man's covenant not to defend himself is void. A covenant not to defend myself from force, by force, is always void. For as I have showed before, no man can transfer, or lay down his right to save himself from death, wounds, and imprisonment, the avoiding whereof is the only end of laying down any right; and therefore the promise of not resisting force, in no covenant transferreth any right; nor is obliging. For though a man may covenant thus, *unless I do so, or so, kill me;* he cannot covenant thus, *unless I do so, or so, I will not resist you, when you come to kill me.* For man by nature chooseth the lesser evil, which is danger of death in resisting; rather than the greater, which is certain and present death in not resisting. And this is granted to be true by all men, in that they lead criminals to execution, and prison, with armed men, notwithstanding that such criminals have consented to the law, by which they are condemned.

No man obliged to accuse himself. A covenant to accuse oneself, without assurance of pardon, is likewise invalid. For in the condition of nature, where every man is judge, there is no place for accusation: and in the civil state, the accusation is followed with punishment; which being force, a man is not obliged not to resist. The same is also true, of the accusation of those, by whose condemnation a man falls into misery; as, of a father, wife, or benefactor. For the testimony of such an accuser, if it be not willingly given, is presumed to be corrupted by nature; and therefore not to be received: and where a man's testimony is not to be credited, he is not bound to give it. Also accusations upon torture, are not to be reputed as testimonies. For torture is to be used but as means of conjecture, and light, in the further examination, and search of truth: and what is in that case confessed; tendeth to the ease of him that is tortured; not to the informing of the torturers: and therefore ought not to have the credit of a sufficient testimony: for whether he deliver himself by true, or false accusation, he does it by the right of preserving his own life.

To an end of an oath. The form of an oath. The force of words, being, as I have formerly noted, too weak to hold men to the performance of their covenants; there are in man's nature, but two imaginable helps to strengthen it. And those are either a fear of the consequence of breaking their word; or a glory, or pride in appearing not to need to break it. This latter is a generosity too rarely found to be presumed on, especially in the pursuers of wealth, command, or sensual pleasure; which are the greatest part of mankind. The passion to be reckoned upon, is fear; whereof there be two very general objects: one, the power of spirits invisible; the other, the power of those men they shall therein offend. Of these two, though the former be the greater power, yet the fear of the latter is commonly the greater fear. The fear of the former is in every man his own religion, which hath place in the nature of man before civil society. The latter hath not so; at least not place enough, to keep men to their promises; because in the condition of mere nature, the inequality of power is not discerned, but by the event of battle. So that before the time of civil society, or in the interruption thereof by war, there is nothing can strengthen a covenant of peace agreed on, against the temptations of avarice, ambition, lust, or other strong desire, but the fear of that invisible power, which they every one worship as God; and fear as a revenger of their perfidy. All therefore that can be done between two men not subject to civil power, is to put one another to swear by the God he feareth: which *swearing,* or OATH, is a *form of speech, added to a promise; by which he that promiseth, signifieth, that unless he perform, he renounceth the mercy of his God, or calleth to him for vengeance on himself.* Such was the heathen form, *Let* Jupiter *kill me else, as I kill this beast.* So is our form, *I shall do thus, and thus, so help me God.* And this, with the rites and ceremonies, which every one useth in his own religion, that the fear of breaking faith might be the greater.

No oath but by God. By this it appears, that an oath taken according to any other form, or rite, than his, that sweareth, is in vain; and no oath: and that there is no swearing by any thing which the swearer thinks not God. For though men have sometimes used to swear by their kings, for fear, or flattery; yet they would have it thereby understood, they attributed to them divine honour. And that swearing unnecessarily by God, is but profaning of his name: and swearing by other things, as men do in common discourse, is not swearing, but an impious custom, gotten by too much vehemence of talking.

An oath adds nothing to the obligation. It appears also, that the oath adds nothing to the obligation. For a covenant, if lawful, binds in the sight of God, without the oath, as much as with it: if unlawful, bindeth not at all; though it be confirmed with an oath.

43

P. S. ATIYAH

The Practice of Promising

From time to time I have commented critically on the methodology of various writers who have sought answers to questions about the nature and sources of promissory obligation without any sociological inquiry into the institution of promising as it currently exists in a modern Western society. I have commented that this approach seems particularly odd when it comes from philosophers who argue that promises derive their binding force from the "practice of promising," but make no attempt to inquire into the rules of this practice. In this chapter I propose to make some preliminary inquiry into the "practice of promising" as it exists in modern England. This in no way professes to be a serious sociological study of promising; in particular, my data come mainly (though not exclusively) from the Law Reports and are no doubt unrepresentative for that reason. This is conceded without reservations; but it remains true that much may be learnt about the morality of promising from some acquaintance with the law, and the legal treatment of promises. It is right to stress that, when people's interests are seriously affected by what they regard as a breach of a promise, they can and do have recourse to the Courts for justice; and although judges are not free to do justice precisely as they please, there is no doubt that in most cases of this nature, the justice which the Courts administer is very largely congruent with the moral sense of the community. Although it may differ from the sort of verdict often to be found in philosophical writings, this is, I believe, because lawyers and judges are more aware of the complexity and subtlety of the problems which are involved. The law is thus more sophisticated in its morality than many non-lawyers might think; it is difficult to substantiate this assertion without a substantial treatment of the law of contract and this is obviously not the place for that. But it is a place for a beginning to be made.

THE STRENGTH OF THE PROMISE-KEEPING PRINCIPLE

I want to begin by suggesting that the strength of the principle that promises must be kept is not nearly so great as seems to be assumed by many writers. Neither in the community at large, nor in the law, I suggest, is the principle accorded that sanctity which many philosophers still think is due to it.[1] Historically, it is of course true that in the middle of the last century the sanctity of contract was widely regarded, by lawyers and others, as the keystone of the social and legal edifice. But the law has moved a long way since then, and this movement certainly appears to have been a response to changing social attitudes; philosophers who still write about the duty to keep promises with the high moral tone that one often finds (for example in Ross, Hare, Hart, Warnock, or Rawls[2]) appear to be reflecting the moral attitudes of the last century rather than those of the present day. It is perhaps significant that a philosopher who has recently made a serious attempt to study the law of contract discovered somewhat to his surprise that in the law, "the opprobrium attached to [promise breaking] is not often great."[3]

So far as the rules of law are concerned, it must be stressed that the sanctions for breach of promise, or (contract) are usually very mild by comparison with many of the sanctions at the law's disposal. It is very rare that the law provides for the *punishment* of the contract-breaker. Neither imprisonment nor fines are available as remedies for breach of contract, nor is it customary (except in certain limited categories) for Courts actually to order contracting parties to perform their contracts.[4] In the great majority of contractual actions the law merely provides for the payment of sums which are due, or for damages in default. And damages are almost invariably assessed on purely compensatory principles, that is to say, they are limited by the extent of the promisee's loss. They cannot include an element of "exemplary" or "punitive" damages such as are sometimes allowed in other kinds of actions. It is true (as we have seen) that the promisee's "loss" is understood sufficiently widely to encompass his lost expectations, but that is normally the limit of the promisor's liability.

But this is not all, because (as I have also pointed out) where the promisee has not relied upon the promise, and no payment has been made to the promisor, so that the promisee's claim is purely for the loss of his expectations, it will often happen that no damages are recoverable at all. If the promisee can obtain substitute performance elsewhere at no additional cost, he is expected, as a reasonable man, to do so, and not to insist upon performance by the

[1]A few writers have themselves criticized the general philosophical tradition on this point, e.g. Narveson, *Morality and Utility,* p. 193; John Finnis, *Natural Law and Natural Rights,* p. 308.

[2]Even J. L. Mackie, *Ethics,* p. 123, surprisingly argues that "Hobbe's third law of nature, that men perform their covenants made, is an eternal and immutable fragment of morality."

[3]R. Bronaugh, "Contracting: An Essay in Legal Philosophy" (unpublished Oxford B. Litt. thesis, 1976), p. 29.

[4]In practice, contracts for the purchase and sale of houses, or land, are normally "specifically enforceable" by order of the Court: failure to comply is punishable by imprisonment.

promisor. This explains why, in cases like *Lazenby Garages v. Wright*, . . . a car dealer who is able to resell a car which the buyer has refused to take and pay for, may be unable to claim any damages at all. So in cases like this the sanction for breach of contract is, in fact, nil.

Moreover, empirical studies of business attitudes to contracts and contract-breaking, both in England and in the United States, suggest that business men in fact expect and tolerate a considerable amount of contract-breaking, at all events on matters which they do not regard as of fundamental importance. A leading American contracts scholar has recently been moved to say that "it is perfectly clear that a great deal of promise breaking is tolerated and expected. Indeed, it is so widely tolerated that a realist would have to say that beneath the covers we are firmly committed to the desirability of promises being broken, not just occasionally but quite regularly."[5]

This kind of evidence may not tell us much about social attitudes to the morality of promising. But there is also evidence from other legal cases that public bodies, at least, appear to have less compunction about promise-breaking today than perhaps they would have done a hundred years ago. Promises are frequently made by corporate bodies or other associations of people (such as Governments) as well as by individuals. And when there is a change in those who represent such bodies, personal moral scruples about promise keeping may be non-existent. Thus (for example) where a local council contracted (that is, promised) to sell council houses to certain tenants, and then, following an election, a new council took office pledged to a new policy, the new council declined to fulfil these contracts. They were sued by one tenant and put up a manifestly untenable defence; they appealed to the Court of Appeal where again, they strenuously defended on the flimsiest of grounds; and when they lost again, they sought leave to appeal to the House of Lords—unsuccessfully.[6] And it is, perhaps, not irrelevant to remember also that in 1975 the Labour Government invited the people of Britain to decide, in the Common Market referendum, whether they wished to affirm or repudiate the treaty obligations solemnly entered into by their elected representatives only a few years earlier. One factor which played virtually no part in the public debates[7] was that the country's representatives had actually signed the Treaty of Accession, and thus pledged the nation's word. The public debates treated the whole issue as though the question was one which arose *de novo*, and as though the merits of joining the Community were up for discussion.

When we turn to the actual rules of law for the "enforcement" of promises, we also find (as I have previously mentioned) that there are different degrees of bindingness. As was stressed in a seminal article on the theory of contractual liability, "the 'binding' effect of a promise is a matter of degree, proceeding in an ascending scale which embraces, in order, the restitution, reliance and expectation interests."[8] If this sounds a little cryptic for those unacquainted with this legal terminology, all that it means is that the legal right of a promisee to obtain recompense for value actually rendered to the promisor ranks highest, that his right to be compensated for loss incurred through reliance on a promise, ranks second, and that his right to compensation for his disappointed expectations ranks lowest in the scale. Some philosophers have recognized that the binding force of promises may vary in a similar sort of way,[9] but the implications of this have not (I think) been properly grasped. At the lowest, recognition of these differing degrees of bindingness must involve acceptance that pure expectations are not generally thought deserving of a high degree of protection, and in some cases are not thought worthy of protection at all. On this view, the breach of a promise which has not been paid for or relied upon is a relatively venial wrong, and in some instances (for example where

[5] I. Macneil, "The Many Futures of Contract," 47 *Southern Calif. Law Rev.* 691, 729 (1974). Indeed, Holmes, J. used to argue that a contracting party was *entitled* to break his contract and pay damages in lieu, if he chose. This view did not win many adherents among lawyers, but in particular circumstances it reflects the reality of legal rules.

[6] *Storer v. Manchester City Council* [1974] 1 WLR 1403.

[7] So far as I am aware, the only prominent figure to raise this issue (in a televised debate at the Oxford Union) was Mr Heath, who had personally signed the Treaty.

[8] Fuller and Perdue, "The Reliance Interest in Contract Damages," 46 *Yale Law J.* 52 and 373, 396 (1936); cf. John Finnis, op. cit., pp. 308 ff., for a very different view.

[9] For example, Ross, *The Right and the Good*, p. 100. Warnock (*The Object of Morality*, p. 94) attempts to distinguish *obligations* (which one is *bound* to perform) and other "duties" (which one *ought*, but is not bound, to do). This distinction seems untenable: the bindingness of *all* oughts is surely a matter of degree.

alternative arrangements can readily be made by the promisee), not of sufficient importance to warrant legal protection. But the point may involve deeper implications, as can be seen if we turn to examine some of the generally accepted justifications for breaking promises.

JUSTIFICATIONS FOR PROMISE-BREAKING

Few philosophers have attempted to analyse the circumstances in which a breach of promise may be found morally justifiable. When they discuss this question at all, it is usually in terms of trivial cases such as a social promise to meet or dine with a friend, which is broken because the promisor's son is taken ill. Now in law, by far the most important justification for breaking a promise is that a return promise has itself been broken in whole or in part. It is the breach by one party of his contractual duties which is the principal justification for breach by the second party of *his* duties. This was originally justified by lawyers at the end of the eighteenth century in the same way that they (and the Natural Lawyers) explained why promises induced by fraud or supervening events might be discharged; that is to say, they argued that it was "impliedly" intended that the promises were conditional upon mutual performance. Thus if one party refused to perform, the other party's promise did not have to be performed, because he had not promised to perform in that event. It later came to be felt that this argument from "implication" was too fanciful to explain the many difficult situations which had to be differentiated by law, and that other considerations explained the legal approach. In particular, judges were, and are, much influenced by the belief that it is *unjust* for a party to be compelled to perform a promise if he has not received (or may not receive) substantially the benefits that he has bargained for.[10]

It thus seems that not only is the receipt of a benefit itself one of the principal grounds for holding a promise to be binding, not only that the duty to recompense for benefits is a strong source of legal obligation even in the absence of a promise; but also that the failure to receive an anticipated benefit is a strong ground for treating the duty to perform a promise as no longer binding. So here too there seems confirmation for the idea that perhaps it is not the promise itself which creates the obligation, so much as the accompanying incidents, such as the rendering of benefits, (or in other circumstances, acts of detrimental reliance).

WHY ARE PROMISES MADE AND KEPT, OR BROKEN?

The above discussion serves as a convenient link to some other questions which are little discussed in the philosophical writings about promises. Why do people make promises? Why do they keep them? Why do they break them? It is evident from the previous discussion that one common reason why people break promises is that a return promise has been, or is very likely to be, broken by the promisee. And this itself is some indication of the fact that people who make promises very often—perhaps usually—do so because they want to get something from the promisee which they can only get by doing so. It seems too often to be assumed by philosophers that the paradigm of a promise is the charitable or wholly benevolent promise, the promise which involves no return at all.[11] This is surely wrong. It is of course difficult to be sure, in the absence of empirical research, what are the most common types of promises, and why these are given, but it seems highly probable that they are promises given as the price of something the promisor wants. Promises of this kind do not confer an uncovenanted benefit on the promisee. On the contrary, it is the promisor who often benefits from such a promise, for it is a means of deferring a liability, rather than of creating an obligation. To take a simple illustration, a person wishes to buy goods but has not the cash to pay the price; he asks the seller to give him credit, that is to say, to accept a promise of payment in lieu of actual payment. In a case of this nature, the

[10]Patterson, "Constructive Conditions in Contracts," 42 *Columbia Law Rev.* 903 (1942). In modern English law, it is well established that a breach of contract by one party discharges the other, *either* (1) if that is the effect of the agreement, expressly or by implication, *or* (2) if the breach substantially deprives the other of the benefit he expected to receive under the contract.

[11]Rawls, *A Theory of Justice,* at pp. 344–50, rightly stresses that promises are "often" made to secure something which the promisor wants. I believe this is a major understatement.

buyer's obligation to pay the price surely derives from his purchase of the goods, rather than from his promise; and, as I have previously argued, the implication of a promise to pay the price may be the result, rather than the cause of holding the transaction to be a purchase. Of course, it must be clear that the transaction is not a gift (and that no doubt depends on the intentions and relationship of the parties), but once this possibility is ruled out, the voluntary acceptance or receipt of the goods by the buyer is the necessary and sufficient condition for his liability. An explicit promise alone is neither of these things. If the promise was given and the seller failed to deliver the goods, the buyer (as explained above) would not be bound to perform his promise; and if the buyer requested the seller to supply the goods and voluntarily accepted them when supplied, he would be liable to pay the price even in the absence of an explicit promise. No doubt it would be said that he had "impliedly" promised, but it is not clear why the implication needs to be made, and the buyer's obligation to pay the price would exist even if he promised without any intention of keeping his promise.

Cases of this nature—that is the giving of promises in lieu of immediate performance of a duty—are very common indeed. But there are other similar cases where the promisor's duty is not deferred, and yet he makes the promise to obtain some benefit which he desires. Two parties enter into a contract on 1 January for the purchase and sale of a house on 1 February. Each promises something to the other because he wants what the other is willing to give. The case differs from that discussed in the previous paragraph because the performance of the two promises is intended to be simultaneous; neither party will perform before the other, and no credit is to be given. But this does not alter the fact that each promise is given because of what it brings; and this also is borne out by the rule that prima facie a failure by one party to perform will discharge the other. Thus many promises are given because the promisor expects to derive some benefit from the promise. But it may be possible to put the matter more generally: promises are given to induce people to act upon them. In the cases so far discussed, the action which the promisor *wants* is something beneficial to him. In these cases, the promisor *wants* the promisee to act in reliance on the promise. But there may be cases in which the action will be of little or no benefit to him except in the trivial sense that if he wants it, it must be assumed that it will be *some* benefit to him. Because this case is conceptually wider than the previous one, it is the one which lawyers and philosophers have tended to concentrate upon. Action in reliance is more generally recognized as a "consideration" in the law than conduct beneficial to the promisor; and a parallel is to be found in much philosophical writing. But it is important to appreciate that in a large proportion of cases, perhaps most cases, the action in reliance which the promisor seeks to induce the promisee to undertake, is something beneficial to the promisor, directly or indirectly.

Now it is apparent that where the promisor has not yet actually obtained what he wants at the time when performance of his promise is due, he will (unless he has changed his mind in the interim) normally be motivated to perform his promise for precisely the same reason that he originally gave it—namely, that he wants to induce the promisee to act in some way likely to be beneficial to him. Thus, in the example of the contract for the purchase and sale of the house, both parties will normally be motivated to perform their promises on the day set for performance for the same reason that they originally gave their promises, that is the seller wants money in preference to the house, and the buyer wants the house in preference to the money.

It should, I hope, be apparent now why it seems to me idle to discuss the source of the moral obligation to perform a promise without having some regard to the question *why* promises are given, and *why* they are (normally) performed. If we assume that promises are binding because of some inherent moral power, or even if we assume that they are binding because of the expectations they rouse, or that they are binding because of the existence of a practice of promising, we are in danger of overlooking that *most* promises are performed because it is in the interests of the promisor to perform. The legal and moral sanction thus turns out to be needed for some cases only; and (I would venture to guess) for a small minority of cases. It is needed for those cases where the promisor has obtained credit, or full performance of what he sought to obtain by his promise; and it is needed for those cases where the promisor changes his mind after giving his promise, and before he performs it. Of course, even in these cases, it may be in the long-term interests of the promisor to perform. As many writers have observed, the loss of credit and trustworthiness which results from promise-breaking may make it in the long-term interests of the promisor to perform, even in the two situations I have mentioned.

The importance of this, I suggest, is that it should influence our view of the paradigm case. In much philosophical writing, it seems to be assumed that the paradigmatic case is of a promise which is wholly gratuitous and is given for charitable or benevolent purposes. It seems to me far more likely that the source of both legal and moral obligations concerning the binding force of promises is derived from the more common case where the promisor obtains, or expects to obtain, some advantage from his promise, and that cases of charitable and benevolent promises are the result of extrapolating from the common case. . . .

THE INTENTIONS OF THE PROMISOR

I want now to draw attention to certain difficulties which arise concerning the intention of the promisor. There is, of course, the obvious and initial difficulty arising from promises which the promisor has no intention of performing. Are these to be called genuine promises? Those who believe that the essence of a promise is the intentional commitment, the intentional acceptance of an obligation, plainly have difficulty with the case of the fraudulent or dishonest promise. I have previously pointed out that there would in fact be no insuperable difficulty in arguing that the promisor in such a case is under a duty, not because he has promised, but because he has deceived. However, this is certainly not the legal approach. A lawyer would unhesitatingly say that a dishonest promise was a promise, and that the promisor is liable because he has promised, and not because he has deceived. Hence he is legally liable for disappointing the promisee's expectations, and not just for loss incurred in reliance. If the dishonest party had not made an apparent promise, but a dishonest statement of a different character, this would not be so. I think it probable that current English "positive" morality would broadly agree with the law in regarding a dishonest promisor as bound because he had promised, and not because he had deceived, though obviously that point cannot be settled by general argument.

Nevertheless, the nature of the intention which a promisor must have—even leaving aside this particular problem—is a much more difficult question than seems to be generally assumed. One of the few writers to discuss this issue is Searle,[12] who argues that a promisor must intend that his words "will place him under an obligation" to do what he promises. Thus, he says, Mr Pickwick did not promise to marry Mrs Bardell because "we know that he did not have the appropriate intention."[13] A lawyer's reaction to this would be that although *we* may know that he did not intend to marry Mrs Bardell, (because the author has told us) Mrs Bardell did not know this fact. And since, in everyday life, there is no benevolent author to tell us what other people's intentions are, we are in fact entitled to assume that their intentions are what they appear to be. The jury's verdict in *Bardell v. Pickwick*—if we can assume that they honestly thought that Mrs Bardell had reasonably construed Mr Pickwick's words as an offer of marriage—was thus sound in law.[14] This may be thought to show that a promisor must at least intend to act in such a way as to make it reasonable to construe him as intending to promise, rather than that he should merely intentionally act. But the significance of this distinction depends on what "reasonable construction" involves. It may involve merely implying a promise because the kind of conduct in question usually is accompanied by an intention voluntarily to assume an obligation. But it may, *per contra,* involve "implying" a promise because the neutral, impartial judge thinks that in all the circumstances, an obligation ought to be imposed on the promisor.

No doubt Mr Pickwick's was an extreme case. But there is also no doubt that it is very common for the law to hold a person bound by a promise when he never intended to give one. Sometimes, as in Mr Pickwick's case, this may well be because the promisee has reasonably understood the words and conduct of the putative promisor as indicating that the promisor does mean to make a promise. Even here, of course, if no such intention is actually present, it is not self-evident what is the source of the

---

[12]"What is a Speech Act?," in *The Philosophy of Language,* pp. 50–1.

[13]Searle also says that even an insincere promisor must intend that his words "will make him responsible for intending to do" what he has said he will do. I must confess my inability to understand the state of mind of a promisor who has this intention. . . .

[14]I said as much in my *Introduction to the Law of Contract* (2nd edn., Oxford, 1971), p. 4

obligation. Some moralists, while agreeing that in such circumstances, a duty or obligation may rest on the promisor, would derive the duty from some other source than a promise.[15] And it is perhaps significant also that some legal writers think that the law goes too far in protecting pure expectations when they are the result of a mistake or misunderstanding of this kind. If, for instance, the mistake is discovered before the promisee has acted on the promise, and before any payment has been rendered for it, it is not obviously just that the promise should still be held binding. In legal theory, the promise probably is still binding, but I think it fair to say that a Court would probably find that theory unpalatable, and would strive to avoid it if it could do so. But, in light of what has already been said in this book, this does not show a legal hankering after a subjective theory of liability. What it shows is that—here as elsewhere—the protection of those who have paid for, or relied upon promises, is generally accorded a much higher priority, than the protection of bare disappointed expectations.

It must now be noted that in the law there are many circumstances in which a promise is implied, not only where there is probably no intention to give one, but where it cannot even be said that the words and behaviour of the promisor, reasonably construed, would give rise to the inference that he intended to give one. A simple example arises in the law of sale, where a seller is often treated as "impliedly" promising to supply goods of merchantable quality, goods fit for their purpose, and so on. Obligations of this kind appear to be imposed on sellers as an expression of the sense of justice arising from social policy; they appear to have little to do with the real intentions of most sellers.

Promises with Variable Content

I now want to say a little about a variety of other difficulties which experience with the law shows to be involved in the notion of intention in this particular sphere. Too many writers appear (at least in dealing with promises[16]) to assume that the state of mind of a person who promises to do something is a relatively simple matter; whether he is honest or not, it seems to be widely assumed that sharp lines can be drawn between the person who intends to do something and the person who does not. Unfortunately this is not the case. There are many acutely difficult questions here. For example, a person may sign a written document which contains many printed clauses, and which purports to be a contract. Each clause may even begin by saying "I hereby promise" or words to that effect. The promisor may, or may not read all or part of the document; he probably has some understanding of the general nature of the document, but it is unlikely that he knows in any detail what the clauses contain or what they mean or what is their legal result. I find it very difficult to say what this person's intentions are in relation to such matters. Lawyers have in the past tended to assume (with little articulated justification) that to sign a document is, in a sense, to indicate one's acceptance of all that it contains. The signer, by placing his signature at the foot of the document, *intends* to bind himself to all that it contains.[17] He may thus be said to promise to do whatever the document requires him to do. But this conclusion creates great difficulties. Suppose the document contains some wholly unexpected and grossly unfair clause, such as has never been included in contracts of this nature, would it still be said that the signature amounts to a promise to do whatever the document requires? Or suppose that the document contains clauses which are today declared to be void by Act of Parliament, for the very purpose of protecting unwary customers who sign such documents without reading them? To the lawyer it matters little whether or not one says that the signer has promised to perform the void clause, because in either event, it is not binding. But to the moralist, it may matter whether we say, "there is no promise here at all," or, "there is a promise but the promisor is legally relieved from performance." And surely the moralist needs to be aware of these problems. Can he really assert that clauses made void by Parliament under consumer protection legislation, are still morally binding and ought to be kept? But if such promises are not morally binding, while other promises (of whose content the promisor is equally ignorant) are binding, how can the explanation be sought in the intention of the promisor?

---

15. For example, Sidgwick, *Methods*, p. 304.

16. Of course, in dealing with the criminal law, a considerable literature (both legal and philosophical) has grown up around the question of intention.

17. See for example, Lord Pearson in *Saunders v. Anglia Building Society* [1971] AC 1004 at 1036.

There are other difficulties. Contracts sometimes contain clauses under which one party may vary the duty of the other party. An example only too well known to many householders today, is the power of a building society to alter the terms of a mortgage by increasing the interest rate payable, after due notice given. Suppose a person has entered into a mortgage of this character, at an initial rate of 7 per cent, but ten years later finds himself paying 12 per cent. Would it be said that he has promised to pay 12 per cent? Or that he intended to pay 12 per cent? Certainly, he is legally bound to pay 12 per cent; he is treated as having contracted to pay for it, but it is not clear to me whether one would say that he had *promised* to pay it, still less that he *intended* to pay it. The reality would seem to be that he intentionally entered into a certain transaction and that one of the consequences of that transaction, to which he is committed, is that he is now bound to pay the higher interest rate.

Stronger cases can be found in the law. For example, a person joins a club or society, or takes shares in a company. The association (whatever its form) will have rules which bind the members, and the person joining will be bound by them, even though he does not read them or know anything about them. Thus far the case is no different from the one discussed earlier. But the rules of an association will almost always contain procedures for their own alteration, and frequently these procedures will envisage alteration by some majority vote of the members. Suppose that a person joins a tennis club with an annual subscription of £5; we may readily agree that he has promised to pay £5 a year, and that he fully intends to do so. But suppose now that the club, by majority vote, with our friend dissenting, increases the subscription to £10. Are we to say that, so long as he remains a member, he has promised to pay £10 annually; are we to say that when he joined he intended to pay whatever subscription was due, from time to time, as duly required by the club rules? Of course, a member may resign from a tennis club, and if he does not resign, we may say he must be "assumed" to have acquiesced in the new subscription and so has impliedly promised to pay it. For most practical purposes this is no doubt legitimate enough; but what is not legitimate is to *equate* this person's state of mind with that of the man who says, "I promise to pay £10." Still more difficult cases can be found where the opportunity to escape the consequences of the new rule by resignation does not exist. For example, a member of a company who holds shares of class A is outvoted on a resolution which has the result of reducing the value of class A shares and increasing the value of class B shares. To "resign" or sell his shares is no solution to this person's problems. The reduction in the value of his shares is already an accomplished fact. Is he bound by the result? Are we to say that, when he joined the company, he must be deemed to have accepted the consequences of any change duly passed by appropriate legal procedures?

Now all these cases raise questions as to the precise relationship which subsists between the intentions of the promisor and the content of the promise. These illustrations show that, in law at least, a person who enters into a transaction may be held bound by many consequences of the transaction even though he does not intend those consequences. Obligations of this kind surely cannot be justified by saying that the promisor "intended" to assume them. The reality is that he intends to enter into a transaction, the consequences of which are imposed upon him by the law. It seems difficult to argue that, in principle, the moral solution to these cases differs from the legal solution. No doubt there may be moral dissent from some extreme legal cases; but it surely cannot be doubted that (for example) a mortgagor is morally, no less than legally, bound to pay the interest rate properly required of him, even though it is far higher than the one he originally promised to pay.

One further problem needs mention. In law, breach of a contract often has the result of making the promisor liable to pay damages. The way in which the damages are assessed often depends on a number of legal rules which may, in some situations, involve much complexity. If, in the cases discussed in the previous paragraphs, we are willing to say that all the consequences of the original contract, or promise, must be "deemed" to have been covered by the promise, or by the promisor's intentions, are we now to say the same for the legal consequences? It would seem remarkably odd to say that a person who is guilty of a breach of contract must be deemed to have promised (and intended?) to pay damages for breach, as assessed by the Courts. Yet the total consequences of the promise are an elaborate mesh of the actual words used (particularly written words) and of the law. Some promises are read in by the law which are not explicitly stated; some promises which are explicitly stated are struck out by the law as void; other promises are subject to legal interpretation which may alter their literal or prima-facie import; and the calculation of the damages, as I have said, may involve some complex legal rules.

WHO MAKES PROMISES, TO WHOM, AND WHO IS BOUND BY THEM?

There are further sociological matters about the practice of promising on which the law provides some guidance; and here again, I believe, it will be found that some of the assumptions made in much philosophical writing are too simplistic, for lack of attention paid to these data. Let me begin with the question, Who makes promises? Philosophers nearly always assume that promises are only made by individual human beings. But this is not true. Promises are made by people acting collectively in all manner of institutional groups. Promises are made by companies, associations, schools, hospitals, universities, Governments, and many other institutions. This fact is relevant to the moral issues arising from promising for a number of obvious, and perhaps less obvious reasons. First, it makes it necessary to recognize that one person (the agent) can make a promise which binds another person (the principal), something which many philosophers seem reluctant to recognize. Second, it is much more difficult to attribute a "real" intention to a collective group than to a single individual promisor. For one thing, the intentions of (say) the members of a Board or a Committee, acting on behalf of an institution, may not all be the same. For another thing, institutions often act through agents (in the legal sense) such as executives, directors, secretaries, and so forth. Agents sometimes commit their principals by promises which the principal (or superior agents) did not wish, or intend, to make. Legally, there are rules for determining when a principal can be bound by an agent who thus acts in excess of his authority, but there is no doubt that this is a common legal phenomenon. All this naturally strengthens the legal tendency to ignore "real" intentions, and focus on apparent intentions—on what is said and done, rather than what was "actually" intended.

A second reason why the nature of institutional promisors is often relevant to the moral issues is this. Institutions often have specified formal procedures for making decisions. Boards of directors, College Governing Bodies, Committees of various kinds, normally have formal meetings, and keep records of their decisions. When a body of this kind announces its intentions, or makes a decision which it then communicates to the persons concerned, the line between a mere statement of intent and a promise becomes somewhat blurred. A public announcement in the form "The Committee [Board, Government, etc.] has decided . . ." is much closer to being a promise than a comparable statement by a private individual. Decisions of this character are usually more trustworthy than declarations of intent by a single individual, because the former are so much more difficult to change than the latter. An extreme example of this may, perhaps, be found in legislative procedures. There is a sense in which an Act of Parliament is a declaration of Parliament's will and intention that the persons concerned should behave in the manner laid down in the Act. In the British constitutional system, such a declaration of intent does not preclude Parliament from changing its mind tomorrow and repealing the first Act. But parliamentary procedure is a formal process, governed by many technical rules of procedure, and, in the majority of cases, taking several months to transform a Bill into an Act. It is, in the result, reasonable to assume that laws will remain unchanged, save at longish intervals (except of course after an election!), and the public are generally entitled to adjust their conduct on the assumption that they can rely upon the existing law. Indeed, we can go further, because it is reasonable to say that legislation tells the citizen how he must and also how he may behave. Those who adjust their behaviour in reliance on the legality of a course of conduct are entitled to feel aggrieved if they are not given adequate time to adjust to changes in the law. It would indeed not be wholly fanciful to suggest that the legislature, by laying down the lines of proscribed behaviour, is impliedly promising that those who do *not* cross the lines will not be subject to penalties.[18] The implication of a promise in such a case arises from the nature of decision-making procedures, and the way in which Parliament declares its intent. It may, of course, be said that any such implied promise would be fictitious, but that depends upon the nature and purpose of implied promises. No doubt it

---

[18]L. Fuller, *The Morality of Law* (New Haven, 1964), pp. 61–2.

would be fictitious to impute to Parliament any actual intent to assume a legal obligation not to change the law without adequate notice. But it would not be a fiction to argue that Parliament passes laws in order to tell citizens how to behave in various respects; and that if the citizen complies with these instructions, and assumes that if he observes the law he will not be subject to penalties, it would be morally wrong for Parliament to punish him. If we think that that would be morally wrong, it is because we think that people are justified in relying on the law as from time to time enacted, and that such reliance should be protected. So Parliament may well come under a moral obligation to respect such reliance. It seems to be largely a matter of taste whether we say that such an obligation derives from an "implied promise."

One final point may be made here about the parties to a promise. It is not uncommon in law for a promise to become binding on some third party, other than the promisor. For example, contractual problems may bind the executors of the promisor after his death; in effect the promisor's successors take his property burdened with his liabilities, and these liabilities include promissory, or at least contractual liabilities. Or, again, it is sometimes possible for an owner of a piece of land to burden the land with a promise (for example, not to build on it, or not to build certain types of property), and this promise will bind subsequent owners of the land provided that certain simple formalities as to registration have been complied with. Cases of this nature may be of some importance to the basis of the promissory liability for the moralist as well as the lawyer. For one thing, they illustrate what is often thought to be an impossibility, namely that a promisor can promise that someone else will do something; but they also illustrate cases where it is plain that the liability of a person on a promise must be based on something other than his consent. The third party who succeeds to, or buys, property thus burdened with another's promises, will often know of the burden when he takes the property, and may in some sense be assumed to acquiesce in it; but this is not necessarily the case. The purchaser of land burdened with a registered covenant is bound by it even if he knew nothing of it at all: the onus is on him to discover it by searching the register. Of course, it can be said that the reasons for holding such a third party bound by a promise may be quite different from those affecting the promisor himself. But in practice it will usually be found that, in the absence of consent, there will be present one or both of the other two bases of contractual liability, viz. that the third party has derived some benefit, for which the promise is, in a broad sort of way, the *quid pro quo;* or alternatively that the promisee has acted upon the promise in such a way that it would seem unreasonable and unjust if the third party was not bound by it. So once again, it seems that the duty to recompense benefits and to compensate for losses incurred by actions in reliance may actually embrace liabilities thought to be promissory, and which certainly are promissory in origin. . . .

44

CHARLES FRIED

Contract As Promise

It is a first principle of liberal political morality that we be secure in what is ours—so that our persons and property not be open to exploitation by others, and that from a sure foundation we may express our will and expend our powers in the world. By these powers we may create good things or low, useful articles or luxuries, things extraordinary or banal, and we will be judged accordingly—as saintly or mean, skillful or ordinary, industrious and fortunate or debased, friendly and kind or cold and inhuman. But whatever we accomplish and however that accomplishment is judged, morality requires that we respect the person and property of others, leaving them free to make their lives as we are left free to make ours. This is the liberal ideal. This is the ideal that distinguishes between the good, which is the domain of aspiration, and the right, which sets the terms and limits according to which we strive. This ideal makes what we achieve our own and our failures our responsibility too—however much or little we may choose to share our good fortune and however we may hope for help when we fail.[1]

Everything must be available to us, for who can deny the human will the title to expand even into the remotest corner of the universe? And when we forbear to bend some external object to our use because of its natural preciousness we use it still, for it is to our judgment of its value that we respond, our own conception of the good that we pursue. Only other persons are not available to us in this way—they alone share our self-consciousness, our power of self-determination; thus to use them as if they were merely part of external nature is to poison the source of the moral power we enjoy. But others *are* part of the external world, and by denying ourselves access to their persons and powers, we drastically shrink the scope of our efficacy. So it was a crucial moral discovery that free men may yet freely serve each others' purposes: the discovery that beyond the fear of reprisal or the hope of reciprocal favor, morality itself might be enlisted to assure not only that you respect me and mine but that you actively serve my purposes.[2] When my confidence in your assistance derives from my conviction that you will do what is right (not just what is prudent), then I trust you, and trust becomes a powerful tool for our working our mutual wills in the world. So remarkable a tool is trust that in the end we pursue it for its own sake; we prefer doing things cooperatively when we might have relied on fear or interest or worked alone.[3]

The device that gives trust its sharpest, most palpable form is promise. By promising we put in another man's hands a new power to accomplish his will, though only a moral power: What he sought to do alone he may now expect to do with our promised help, and to give him this new facility was our very purpose in promising. By promising we transform a choice that was morally neutral into one that is morally compelled. Morality, which must be permanent and beyond our particular will if the grounds for our willing are to be secure, is itself invoked, molded to allow us better to work that particular will. Morality then serves modest, humdrum ends: We make appointments, buy and sell, harnessing this loftiest of all forces.

What is a promise, that by my words I should make wrong what before was morally indifferent? A promise is a communication—usually verbal; it says something. But how can my saying something put a moral charge on a choice that before was morally neutral? Well, by my misleading you, or by lying.[4] Is lying not the very paradigm of doing wrong by speaking? But this won't do, for a promise puts the moral charge on a *potential* act—the wrong is done later, when the promise is not kept—while a lie is a wrong committed at the time of its utterance. Both wrongs abuse trust, but in different ways. When I speak I commit myself to the truth of my utterance, but when I promise I commit myself to *act*, later. Though these two wrongs are thus quite distinct there has been a persistent tendency to run them together by treating a promise as a lie after all, but a particular kind of lie: a lie about one's intentions. Consider this case:

> I. I sell you a house, retaining an adjacent vacant lot. At the time of our negotiations, I state that I intend to build a home for myself on that lot. What if several years later I sell the lot to a person who builds a gas station on it? What if I sell it only one month later? What if I am already negotiating for its sale as a gas station at the time I sell the house to you?[5]

If I was already negotiating to sell the lot for a gas station at the time of my statement to you, I have wronged you. I have lied to you about the state of my intentions, and this is as much a lie as a lie about the state of the plumbing.[6] If, however, I sell the lot many years later, I do you no wrong. There are no grounds for saying I lied about my intentions; I have just changed my mind. Now if I had *promised* to use the lot only as a residence, the situation would be different. Promising is more than just truthfully reporting my present intentions, for I may be free to change my mind, as I am not free to break my promise.

Let us take it as given here that lying is wrong and so that it is wrong to obtain benefits or cause harm by lying (including lying about one's intentions). It does not at all follow that to obtain a benefit or cause harm by breaking a promise is also wrong. That my act procures me a benefit or causes harm all by itself proves nothing. If I open a restaurant near your hotel and prosper as I draw your guests away from the standard hotel fare you offer, this benefit I draw from you places me under no obligation to you. I should make restitution only if I benefit *unjustly,* which I do if I deceive you—as when I lie to you about my intentions in example I.[7] But where is the injustice if I honestly intend to keep my promise at the time of making it, and later change my mind? If we feel I owe you recompense in that case too, it cannot be because of the benefit I have obtained through my promise: We have seen that benefit even at another's expense is not alone sufficient to require compensation. If I owe you a duty to return that benefit it must be because of the promise. It is the promise that makes my enrichment at your expense unjust, and not the enrichment that makes the promise binding. And thus neither the statement of intention nor the benefit explains why, if at all, a promise does any moral work.

A more common attempt to reduce the force of a promise to some other moral category invokes the harm you suffer in relying on my promise. My statement is like a pit I have dug in the road, into which you fall. I have harmed you and should make you whole. Thus the tort principle might be urged to bridge the gap in the argument between a statement of intention and a promise: I have a duty just because I could have foreseen (indeed it was my intention) that you would rely on my promise and that you would suffer harm when I broke it. And this wrong then not only sets the stage for compensation of the harm caused by the misplaced reliance, but also supplies the moral predicate for restitution of any benefits I may have extracted from you on the strength of my promise.[8] But we still beg the question. If the promise is no more than a truthful statement of my intention, why am *I* responsible for harm that befalls you as a result of my change of heart? To be sure, it is not like a change in the weather—I might have kept to my original intention—but how does this distinguish the broken promise from any other statement of intention (or habit or prediction of future conduct) of mine of which you know and on which you choose to rely? Should your expectations of me limit my freedom of choice? If you rent the apartment next to mine because I play chamber music there, do I owe you more than an expression of regret when my friends and I decide to meet instead at the cellist's home? And in general, why should my liberty be constrained by the harm you would suffer from the disappointment of the expectations you choose to entertain about my choices?

Does it make a difference that when I promise you do not just happen to rely on me, that I communicate my intention to you and therefore can be taken to know that changing my mind may put you at risk? But then I might be aware that you would count on my keeping to my intentions even if I myself had not communicated those intentions to you. (*You* might have told me you were relying on me, or you might have overheard me telling some third person of my intentions.) It might be said that I become the agent of your reliance by telling you, and that this makes my responsibility clearer: After all, I can scarcely control all the ways in which you might learn of my intentions, but I *can* control whether or not I tell you of them. But we are still begging the question. If promising is no more than my telling you of my intentions, why do we both not know that I may yet change my mind? Perhaps, then, promising is like telling you of my intention and telling you that I don't intend to change my mind. But why can't I change my mind about the latter intention?

Perhaps the statement of intention in promising is binding because we not only foresee reliance, we invite it: We intend the promisee to rely on the promise. Yet even this will not do. If I invite reliance on my stated intention, then that is all I invite. Certainly I may hope and intend, in example I, that you buy my house on the basis of what I have told you, but why does that hope bind me to do more than state my intention honestly? And that intention and invitation are quite compatible with my later changing my mind. In every case, of course, I should weigh the harm I will do if I do change my mind. If I am a doctor and I know you will rely on me to be part of an outing on which someone may fall ill, I should certainly weigh the harm that may come about if that reliance is disappointed. Indeed I should weigh that harm even if you do not rely on me, but are foolish enough not to have made a provision for a doctor. Yet in none of these instances am I bound as I would be had I promised.[9]

A promise invokes trust in my future actions, not merely in my present sincerity. We need to isolate an additional element, over and above benefit, reliance, and the communication of intention. That additional element must *commit* me, and commit me to more than the truth of some statement. That additional element has so far eluded our analysis.

It has eluded us, I believe, because there is a real puzzle about how we can commit ourselves to a course of conduct that absent our commitment is morally neutral. The invocation of benefit and reliance are attempts to explain the force of a promise in terms of two of its most usual effects, but the attempts fail because these effects depend on the prior assumption of the force of the commitment. The way out of the puzzle is to recognize the bootstrap quality of the argument: To have force in a *particular case* promises must be assumed to have force generally. Once that general assumption is made, the effects we intentionally produce by a particular promise may be morally attributed to us. This recognition is not as paradoxical as its abstract statement here may make it seem. It lies, after all, behind every conventional structure: games[10], institutions and practices, and most important, language.

Let us put to one side the question of how a convention comes into being, or of when and why we are morally bound to comply with its terms, while we look briefly at what a convention is and how it does its work. Take the classical example of a game. What the players do is defined by a system of rules—sometimes quite vague and informal, sometimes elaborate and codified. These rules apply only to the players—that is, to persons who invoke them. These rules are a human invention, and their consequences (castling, striking out, winning, losing) can be understood only in terms of the rules. The players may have a variety of motives for playing (profit, fun, maybe even duty to fellow players who need participants). A variety of judgments are applicable to the players—they may be deemed skillful, imaginative, bold, honest, or dishonest—but these judgments and motives too can be understood only in the context of the game. For instance, you can cheat only by breaking rules to which you pretend to conform.

This almost canonical invocation of the game example has often been misunderstood as somehow applying only to unserious matters, to play, so that it is said to trivialize the solemn objects (like law or promises) that it is used to explain. But this is a mistake, confusing the interests involved, the reasons for creating and invoking a particular convention, with the logical structure of conventions in general. Games are (often) played for fun, but other conventions—for instance religious rituals or legal procedures—may have most earnest ends, while still other conventions are quite general. To the last category belongs language. The conventional nature of language is too obvious to belabor. It is worth pointing out, however, that the various things we do with language—informing, reporting, promising, insulting, cheating, lying—all depend on the conventional structure's being firmly in place. You could not lie if there were not both understanding of the language you lied in and a general convention of using that language truthfully. This point holds irrespective of whether the institution of language has advanced the situation of mankind and of whether lying is sometimes, always, or never wrong.

Promising too is a very general convention—though less general than language, of course, since promising is itself a use of language.[11] The convention of promising (like that of language) has a very general purpose under which we may bring an infinite set of particular purposes. In order that I be as free as possible, that my will have the greatest possible range consistent with the similar will of others, it is necessary that there be a way in which I may commit myself. It is necessary that I be able to make nonoptional a course of conduct that would otherwise be optional for me. By doing this I can facilitate the projects of others, because I can make it possible for those others to count on my future conduct, and thus those others can pursue more intricate, more far-reaching projects. If it is my purpose, my will that others be able to count on me in the pursuit of their endeavor, it is essential that I be able to deliver myself into their hands more firmly than where they simply predict my future course. Thus the possibility of commitment permits an act of generosity on my part, permits me to pursue a project whose content is that *you* be permitted to pursue *your* project. But of course this purely altruistic motive is not the only motive worth facilitating. More central to our concern is the situation where we facilitate each other's projects, where the gain is reciprocal. Schematically the situation looks like this:

> You want to accomplish purpose A and I want to accomplish purpose B. Neither of us can succeed without the cooperation of the other. Thus I want to be able to commit myself to help you achieve A so that you will commit yourself to help me achieve B.

Now if A and B are objects or actions that can be transferred simultaneously there is no need for commitment. As I hand over A you hand over B, and we are both satisfied. But very few things are like that. We need a device to permit a trade over time: to allow me to do A for you when you need it, in the confident belief that you will do B for me when I need it. Your commitment puts your future performance into my hands in the present just as my commitment puts my future performance into your hands. A future exchange is transformed into a present exchange. And in order to accomplish this all we need is a conventional device which we both invoke, which you know I am invoking when I invoke it, which I know that you know I am invoking, and so on.

The only mystery about this is the mystery that surrounds increasing autonomy by providing means for restricting it. But really this is a pseudomystery. The restrictions involved in promising are restrictions undertaken just in order to increase one's options in the long run, and thus are perfectly consistent with the principle of autonomy—consistent with a respect for one's own autonomy and the autonomy of others. To be sure, in getting something for myself now by promising to do something for you in the future, I am mortgaging the interest of my future self in favor of my present self. How can I be sure my future self will approve?* This is a deep and difficult problem about which I say more later in this chapter. Suffice it to say here that unless one assumes the continuity of the self and the possibility of maintaining complex projects over time, not only the morality of promising but also any coherent picture of the person becomes impossible.

THE MORAL OBLIGATION OF PROMISE

Once I have invoked the institution of promising, why exactly is it wrong for me then to break my promise?

My argument so far does not answer that question. The institution of promising is a way for me to bind myself to another so that the other may expect a future performance, and binding myself in this way is something that I may want to be able to do. But this by itself does not show that I am morally obligated to perform my promise at a later time if to do so proves inconvenient or costly. That there should be a system of currency also increases my options and is useful to me, but this does not show why I should not use counterfeit money if I can get away with it. In just the same way the usefulness of promising in general does not show why I should not take advantage of it in a particular case and yet fail to keep my promise. That the convention would cease to function in the long run, would cease to provide benefits if everyone felt free to violate it, is hardly an answer to the question of why I should keep a particular promise on a particular occasion.

David Lewis has shown[12] that a convention that it would be in each person's interest to observe if everyone else observed it will be established and maintained without any special mechanisms of commitment or enforcement. Starting with simple conventions (for example that if a telephone conversation is disconnected, the person who initiated the call is the one who calls back) Lewis extends his argument to the case of language. Now promising is different, since (unlike language, where it is overwhelmingly in the interest of all that everyone comply with linguistic conventions, even when language is used to deceive) it will often be in the interest of the promisor *not* to conform to the convention when it comes time to render his performance. Therefore individual self-interest is not enough to sustain the convention, and some additional ground is needed to keep it from unraveling. There are two principal candidates: external sanctions and moral obligation.

David Hume sought to combine these two by proposing that the external sanction of public opprobrium, of loss of reputation for honesty, which society attaches to promise-breaking, is internalized, becomes instinctual, and accounts for the sense of the moral obligation of promise.[13] Though Hume offers a possible anthropological or psychological account of how people feel about promises, his is not a satisfactory *moral* argument. Assume that I can get away with breaking my promise (the promisee is dead), and I am now asking why I should keep it anyway in the face of some personal inconvenience. Hume's account of obligation is more like an argument *against* my keeping the promise, for it tells me how any feelings of obligation that I may harbor have come to lodge in my psyche and thus is the first step toward ridding me of such inconvenient prejudices.

Considerations of self-interest cannot supply the moral basis of my obligation to keep a promise. By an analogous argument neither can considerations of utility. For however sincerely and impartially I may apply the utilitarian injunction to consider at each step how I might increase the sum of happiness or utility in the world, it will allow me to break my promise whenever the balance of advantage (including, of course, my own advantage) tips in that direction. The possible damage to the institution of promising is only one factor in the calculation. Other factors are the alternative good I might do by breaking my promise, whether and by how many people the breach might be discovered, what the actual effect on confidence of such a breach would be. There is no a priori reason for believing that an individual's cal-

*Note that this problem does not arise where I make a present sacrifice for a future benefit, since by hypothesis I am presently willing to make that sacrifice and in the future I only stand to gain.

culations will come out in favor of keeping the promise always, sometimes, or most of the time.

Rule-utilitarianism seeks to offer a way out of this conundrum. The individual's moral obligation is determined not by what the best action at a particular moment would be, but by the rule it would be best for him to follow. It has, I believe, been demonstrated that this position is incoherent: Either rule-utilitarianism requires that rules be followed in a particular case even where the result would not be best all things considered, and so the utilitarian aspect of rule-utilitarianism is abandoned; or the obligation to follow the rule is so qualified as to collapse into act-utilitarianism after all.[14] There is, however, a version of rule-utilitarianism that makes a great deal of sense. In this version the utilitarian does not instruct us what our individual moral obligations are but rather instructs legislators what the best rules are.[15] If legislation is our focus, then the contradictions of rule-utilitarianism do not arise, since we are instructing those whose decisions can *only* take the form of issuing rules. From that perspective there is obvious utility to rules establishing and enforcing promissory obligations. Since I am concerned now with the question of individual obligation, that is, moral obligation, this legislative perspective on the argument is not available to me.

The obligation to keep a promise is grounded not in arguments of utility but in respect for individual autonomy and in trust. Autonomy and trust are grounds for the institution of promising as well, but the argument for *individual* obligation is not the same. Individual obligation is only a step away, but that step must be taken.[16] An individual is morally bound to keep his promises because he has intentionally invoked a convention whose function it is to give grounds—moral grounds—for another to expect the promised performance.[17] To renege is to abuse a confidence he was free to invite or not, and which he intentionally did invite. To abuse that confidence now is like (but only *like*) lying: the abuse of a shared social institution that is intended to invoke the bonds of trust. A liar and a promise-breaker each *use* another person. In both speech and promising there is an invitation to the other to trust, to make himself vulnerable; the liar and the promise-breaker then abuse that trust. The obligation to keep a promise is thus similar to but more constraining than the obligation to tell the truth. To avoid lying you need only believe in the truth of what you say when you say it, but a promise binds into the future, well past the moment when the promise is made. There will, of course, be great social utility to a general regime of trust and confidence in promises and truthfulness. But this just shows that a regime of mutual respect allows men and women to accomplish what in a jungle of unrestrained self-interest could not be accomplished. If this advantage is to be firmly established, there must exist a ground for mutual confidence deeper than and independent of the social utility it permits.

The utilitarian counting the advantages affirms the general importance of enforcing *contracts*. The moralist of duty, however, sees *promising* as a device that free, moral individuals have fashioned on the premise of mutual trust, and which gathers its moral force from that premise. The moralist of duty thus posits a general obligation to keep promises, of which the obligation of contract will be only a special case—that special case in which certain promises have attained legal as well as moral force. But since a contract is first of all a promise, the contract must be kept because a promise must be kept.

To summarize: There exists a convention that defines the practice of promising and its entailments. This convention provides a way that a person may create expectations in others. By virtue of the basic Kantian principles of trust and respect, it is wrong to invoke that convention in order to make a promise, and then to break it.

WHAT A PROMISE IS WORTH

If I make a promise to you, I should do as I promise; and if I fail to keep my promise, it is fair that I should be made to hand over the equivalent of the promised performance. In contract doctrine this proposition appears as the expectation measure of damages for breach. The expectation standard gives the victim of a breach no more or less than he would have had had there been no breach—in other words, he gets the benefit of his bargain.[18] Two alternative measures of damage, reliance and restitution, express the different notions that if a person has relied on a promise and been hurt, that hurt must be made good; and that if a contract-breaker has obtained goods or services, he must be made to pay a fair (just?) price for them.[19] Consider three cases:

II-A. I enter your antique shop on a quiet afternoon and agree in writing to buy an expensive chest I see there, the price being about three times what you paid for it a short time ago. When I get home I repent of my decision, and within half an hour of my visit—before any other customer has come to your store—I telephone to say I no longer want the chest.

II-B. Same as above, except in the meantime you have waxed and polished the chest and had your delivery van bring it to my door.

II-C. Same as above, except I have the use of the chest for six months, while your shop is closed for renovations.

To require me to pay for the chest in case II-A (or, if you resell it, to pay any profit you lost, including lost business volume) is to give you your expectation, the benefit of your bargain. In II-B if all I must compensate is your effort I am reimbursing your reliance, and in II-C to force me to pay a fair price for the use I have had of the chest is to focus on making me pay for, restore, an actual benefit I have received.

The assault on the classical conception of contract, the concept I call contract as promise, has centered on the connection—taken as canonical for some hundred years—between contract law and expectation damages. To focus the attack on this connection is indeed strategic. As the critics recognize and as I have just stated, to the extent that contract is grounded in promise, it seems natural to measure relief by the expectation, that is, by the promise itself. If that link can be threatened, then contract itself may be grounded elsewhere than in promise, elsewhere than in the will of the parties. In his recent comprehensive treatise, *The Rise and Fall of Freedom of Contract,* Patrick Atiyah makes the connection between the recourse to expectation damages and the emerging enforceability of executory contracts—that is, contracts enforced, though no detriment has been suffered in reliance and no benefit has been conferred. (Case II-A is an example of an executory contract.) Before the nineteenth century, he argues, a contractual relation referred generally to one of a number of particular, community-sanctioned relations between persons who in the course of their dealings (as carriers, innkeepers, surgeons, merchants) relied on each other to their detriment or conferred benefits on each other. It was these detriments and benefits that had to be reimbursed, and an explicit promise—if there happened to be one—was important primarily to establish the reliance or to show that the benefit had been conferred in expectation of payment, not officiously or as a gift. All this, Atiyah writes, turned inside out when the promise itself came to be seen as the basis of obligation, so that neither benefit nor reliance any longer seemed necessary and the proper measure of the obligation was the promise itself, that is, the expectation. The promise principle was embraced as an expression of the principle of liberty—the will binding itself, to use Kantian language, rather than being bound by the norms of the collectivity—and the award of expectation damages followed as a natural concomitant of the promise principle.

The insistence on reliance or benefit is related to disputes about the nature of promising. As I have argued, reliance on a promise cannot alone explain its force: There is reliance because a promise is binding, and not the other way around. But if a person is bound by his promise and not by the harm the promisee may have suffered in reliance on it, then what he is bound to is just its performance. Put simply, I am bound to do what I promised you I would do—or I am bound to put you in as good a position as if I had done so. To bind me to do no more than to reimburse your reliance is to excuse me to that extent from the obligation I undertook. If your reliance is less than your expectation (in case II-A there is no reliance), then to that extent a reliance standard excuses me from the very obligation I undertook and so weakens the force of an obligation I chose to assume. Since by hypothesis I chose to assume the obligation in its stronger form (that is, to render the performance promised), the reliance rule indeed precludes me from incurring the very obligation I chose to undertake at the time of promising. The most compelling of the arguments for resisting this conclusion and for urging that we settle for reliance is the sense that it is sometimes harsh and ungenerous to insist on the full measure of expectancy. (This is part of Atiyah's thrust when he designates the expectation standard as an aspect of the rigid Victorian promissory morality.) The harshness comes about because in the event the promisor finds the obligation he assumed too burdensome.

This distress may be analyzed into three forms: (1) The promisor regrets having to pay for what he has bought (which may only have been the satisfaction of promising a gift or the thrill of buying a lottery ticket or stock option), though he would readily do the same thing again. I take it that this kind of regret merits no sympathy at all. Indeed if we gave in to it we would frustrate the promisor's ability to engage in his own continuing projects and so the promisor's plea is, strictly speaking, self-contradictory. (2) The promisor regrets his promise because he was mistaken about the nature of the burdens he was assuming—the purchaser in case II-A thought he would find the money for the antique but in fact his savings are depleted, or perhaps the chest is not as old nor as valuable as he had imagined, or his house has burned down and he no longer needs it. All of these regrets are based on mistaken assumptions about the facts as they are or as they turn out to be. . . . [T]he doctrines of mistake, frustration, and impossibility provide grounds for mitigating the effect of the promise principle without at all undermining it.

Finally there is the most troublesome ground of regret: (3) The promisor made no mistake about the facts or probabilities at all, but now that it has come time to perform he no longer values the promise as highly as when he made it. He regrets the promise because he regrets the value judgment that led him to make it. He concludes that the purchase of an expensive antique is an extravagance. Compassion may lead a promisee to release an obligation in such a case, but he releases as an act of generosity, not as a duty, and certainly not because the promisor's repentance destroys the force of the original obligation. The intuitive reason for holding fast is that such repentance should be the promisor's own responsibility, not one he can shift onto others. It seems too easy a way of getting out of one's obligations. Yet our intuition does not depend on suspicions of insincerity alone. Rather we feel that holding people to their obligations is a way of taking them seriously and thus of giving the concept of sincerity itself serious content. Taking this intuition to a more abstract level, I would say that respect for others as free and rational requires taking seriously their capacity to determine their own values. I invoke again the distinction between the right and the good. The right defines the concept of the self as choosing its own conception of the good. Others must respect our capacity as free and rational persons to choose our own good, and that respect means allowing persons to take responsibility for the good they choose. And, of course, that choosing self is not an instantaneous self but one extended in time, so that to respect those determinations of the self is to respect their persistence over time. If we decline to take seriously the assumption of an obligation because we do not take seriously the promisor's prior conception of the good that led him to assume it, to that extent we do not take him seriously as a person. We infantilize him, as we do quite properly when we release the very young from the consequences of their choices.[20]

Since contracts invoke and are invoked by promises, it is not surprising that the law came to impose on the promises it recognized the same incidents as morality demands. The connection between contract and the expectation principle is so palpable that there is reason to doubt that its legal recognition is a relatively recent invention. It is true that over the last two centuries citizens in the liberal democracies have become increasingly free to dispose of their talents, labor, and property as seems best to them. The freedom to bind oneself contractually to a future disposition is an important and striking example of this freedom (the freedom to make testamentary dispositions or to make whatever present use of one's effort or goods one desires are other examples), because in a promise one is taking responsibility not only for one's present self but for one's future self. But this does not argue that the promise principle itself is a novelty—surely Cicero's, Pufendorf's and Grotius's discussions of it[21] show that it is not—but only that its use has expanded greatly over the years.

REMEDIES IN AND AROUND THE PROMISE

Those who have an interest in assimilating contract to the more communitarian standards of tort law have been able to obscure the link between contract and promise because in certain cases the natural thing to do *is* to give damages for the harm that has been suffered, rather than to give the money value of the promised expectation. But it does not follow from these cases that expectation is not a normal and natural measure for contract damages. First, these are situations in which the harm suffered is the measure of damages because it is hard to find the monetary value of the expectation. A leading case, *Security*

Stove & Mfg. Co. v. American Railway Express Co.,[22] illustrates the type. The plaintiff stove manufacturer had arranged to have a new kind of stove shipped by the defendant express company to a trade convention, at which the plaintiff hoped to interest prospective buyers in his improved product. The president and his workmen went to the convention, but the defendant failed to deliver a crucial part of the exhibit in time, and they had nothing to show. Plaintiff brought suit to recover the cost of renting the booth, the freight charges, and the time and expenses lost as a result of the fruitless trip to the convention. The recovery of these items of damages, which (with the possible exception of the prepaid booth rental) seem typical examples of reliance losses, is generally agreed to have been appropriate. There was no way of knowing what results the plaintiff would have obtained had he succeeded in exhibiting his product at the convention. There was no way of knowing what his expectancy was, and so the court gave him his loss through reliance. But this illustrates only that where expectancy cannot be calculated, reliance may be a reasonable surrogate. It is reasonable to suppose that the plaintiff's expectation in *Security Stove* was at least as great as the monies he put out to exhibit his goods—after all, he was a businessman and is assumed to have been exhibiting his goods to make an eventual profit. If it could somehow be shown that the exhibit would have been a failure and the plaintiff would have suffered a net loss, the case for recovery would be undermined, and most authorities would then deny recovery.*[23]

Second are the cases in which the amount needed to undo the harm caused by reliance is itself the fairest measure of expectation.

> III-A. Buyer approaches manufacturer with the specifications of a small, inexpensive part—say a bolt—for a machine buyer is building. Manufacturer selects the part and sells it to buyer. The bolt is badly made, shears, and damages the machine.

The value of the thing promised, a well-made bolt, is negligible, but to give buyer his money back and no more would be a grave injustice. Here it does seem more natural to say that the manufacturer induced buyer's reasonable reliance and should compensate the resulting harm. But it is equally the case that it is a fair implication of the simple-seeming original transaction that manufacturer not only delivered and promised to transfer good title to the bolt, but promised at the same time that the bolt would do the job it was meant to do.*[24]

It is for the (perhaps wholly innocent) breach of this implied promise that we hold manufacturers liable. The soundness of this analysis is brought home if we vary the facts slightly:

> III-B. Same as above, except buyer purchases the bolt over the counter in a local hardware store, saying nothing about its use.

To make the owner of the hardware store or the manufacturer of the bolt responsible for large damages in this case seems unfair. One can say that this is because they could not *foresee* harm of this magnitude arising out of their conduct. (A tort locution: The man who negligently jostles a package containing a bomb could not *foresee* and is not responsible for harm of the ensuing magnitude when the package explodes.) But one can as well cast the matter again in contractual terms, saying that they did not undertake this measure of responsibility. After all, if in the first version of this example the buyer and manufacturer had agreed that manufacturer would be responsible only up to a certain amount, say ten times the cost of the bolt, such a limitation would generally be respected. So in certain cases tort and contract ideas converge on the same result.[25] In III-A we may say that buyer justifiably relied on manufacturer. He relied in part because of

---

*A case like this may be seen as involving no more than the allocation of the burden of proof as to the expectation. The plaintiff shows his reliance costs and says that prima facie his expectation was at least that great. The burden then shifts to the defendant to show that indeed this was a losing proposition and the expectation was less than the reliance. It seems only fair that since the defendant's breach prevented the exhibition from taking place and thus prevented the drama on which the expectation depended from being played out, the defendant should at least bear the risk of showing that the venture would have been a failure.

*In law the latter promise is called a warranty—a promise not merely that the promisor will do something in the future, but a taking of responsibility over and above the responsibility of well-meaning honesty that something is the case. For instance, a dealer may warrant that a violin is a Stradivarius. This means more than that he in good faith believes it to be one: he is promising that if it is not, he will be responsible. Uniform Commercial Code (hereafter called UCC) §2-714. Cf. Smith v. Zimbalist, 2 Cal. App.2d 324, 38 P.2d 170 (1934), hearing denied 17 Jan. 1935.

the (implied) promise or warranty, and of course it is a primary function of promises to induce reliance.

Consider finally this variation:

> III-C. Manufacturer makes not bolts but tinned goods. Buyer buys a can of peas at a grocer's and serves them to a guest who chips a tooth on a stone negligently included in the can.

Manufacturer promised the guest nothing. (In legal terminology there is between them no privity of contract.) Yet manufacturer should be responsible for the guest's injuries, just as the driver of a car should be responsible for the injuries of a pedestrian whom he negligently hits, though there too privity of contract is lacking.[26] One may say that the guest reasonably relied on the purity of the peas he ate, just as a pedestrian must rely on the due care of motorists. But I never argued that promise is the *only* basis of reliance or that contract is the only basis of responsibility for harms to others.

Third, there are cases in which wrongs are committed and loss is suffered in and around the attempt to make an agreement. In these cases too reliance is the best measure of compensation. A striking example is *Hoffman v. Red Owl Stores:*[27] A prospective Red Owl supermarket franchisee sold his previously owned business and made other expenditures on the assumption that his negotiations to obtain a Red Owl franchise would shortly be concluded. The award of reliance damages was not a case of enforcement of a promise at all, since the parties had not reached the stage where clearly determined promises had been made. Reliance damages were awarded because Red Owl had not dealt fairly with Hoffman. It had allowed him to incur expenses based on hopes that Red Owl knew or should have known were imprudent and that Red Owl was not prepared to permit him to realize. Red Owl was held liable not in order to force it to perform a promise, which it had never made, but rather to compensate Hoffman for losses he had suffered through Red Owl's inconsiderate and temporizing assurances.[28] There is nothing at all in my conception of contract as promise that precludes persons who behave badly and cause unnecessary harm from being forced to make fair compensation. Promissory obligation is not the only basis for liability; principles of tort are sufficient to provide that people who give vague assurances that cause foreseeable harm to others should make compensation. Cases like *Hoffman* are seen to undermine the conception of contract as promise: If contract is really discrete and if it is really based in promise, then whenever there has been a promise in the picture (even only a potential promise) contractual principles must govern the whole relation. To state the argument is to reveal it as a non sequitir. It is a logical fallacy of which the classical exponents of contract as promise were themselves supremely guilty in their reluctance to grant relief for fraud or for mistakes that prevented a real agreement from coming into being. Modern critics of contractual freedom have taken the classics at their word. Justice often requires relief and adjustment in cases of accidents in and around the contracting process, and the critics have seen in this a refutation of the classics' major premise. . . . [C]ontract as promise has a distinct but neither exclusive nor necessarily dominant place among legal and moral principles. A major concern of this book is the articulation of the boundaries and connection between the promissory and other principles of justice.*

The tendency to merge promise into its adjacent concepts applies also to the relation between it and the principle of restitution, which holds that a person who has received a benefit at another's expense should compensate his benefactor, unless a gift was intended. This principle does indeed appeal to a primitive intuition of fairness. Even where a gift was intended, the appropriateness at least of gratitude if not of a vague duty to reciprocate is recognized in many cultures. Aristotle refers the principle to the imperative that some balance be retained among members of a society, but this seems to restate the proposition rather than to explain it.[29] Since restitution, like reliance, is a principle of fairness that operates independently of the will of the parties, the attempt to refer promissory obligation to this principle is another attempt to explain away the self-imposed character of promissory obligation. I have already argued that

---

*There is a category of cases that has become famous in the law under the rubric of promissory estoppel or detrimental reliance. In these cases there has indeed generally been a promise, but the basis for *legal* redress is said to be the plaintiff's detrimental reliance on the promise. Courts now tend to limit the amount of the redress in such cases to the detriment suffered through reliance. But these cases also do not show that reliance and harm are the general basis for contractual recovery. Rather these cases should be seen for what they are: a belated attempt to plug a gap in the general regime of enforcement of promises, a gap left by the artificial and unfortunate doctrine of consideration. . . .

this cannot be done without begging the question. Certainly the restitution principle cannot explain the force of a promise for which no benefit has yet been or ever will be given in return. (The legal recognition of such gift promises is tangled in the confusions of the doctrine of consideration. . . .) The reduction of promise to restitution (or to restitution plus reliance) must fail. There are nevertheless breaches of promise for which restitution is the correct principle of relief.[30]

IV. In a case like *Security Stove*, where the freight charges have been prepaid but the goods never picked up or delivered as agreed, let us suppose the express company could show that the contemplated exhibit would have been a disaster and that the stove company was much better off never having shown at the fair. Perhaps in such a case there should be no award of reliance damages, but should the express company be allowed to keep the prepayment? Should it be able to argue that the stove company is lucky there was a breach?

In terms of both expectation and harm the stove company should get nothing. Its expectation is shown to be negative, and it suffered no harm. And yet it is entirely clear that Railway Express should make restitution. They did nothing for the money and should not keep it. But is this enforcing the promise? Not at all.

V. I owe my plumber ten dollars, so I place a ten-dollar bill in an envelope, which I mistakenly address and send to you.

On what theory can I get my ten dollars back from you? You made no promise to me. You have *done* me no wrong, and so that is not the ground of my demand that you return the money—though you wrong me now if you do not accede to my demand. The principle is a general one: It is wrong to retain an advantage obtained without justification at another's expense. And what justification can you offer for keeping the ten dollars?*[31] What justification can Railway Express offer for keeping the freight charges in case IV? That it has done the stove company a favor by spoiling the exhibit? But this is no favor the stove company asked for and not one that Railway Express had a right to thrust on it. And surely Railway Express cannot say it received the money properly under a contract, since it has utterly repudiated that contract. The contract drops out leaving Railway Express without justification. In this state of affairs the stove company wins.

Promise and restitution are distinct principles. Neither derives from the other, and so the attempt to dig beneath promise in order to ground contract in restitution (or reliance, for that matter) is misconceived. Contract is based on promise, but when something goes wrong in the contract process—when people fail to reach agreement, or break their promises—there will usually be gains and losses to sort out. The *Red Owl* case is one illustration. Here is another:

I. Britton signs on to work for Turner for a period of one year at an agreed wage of $120 to be paid at the end of his service. After nine months of faithful service he quits without justification, and Turner without difficulty finds a replacement for him.

On one hand Britton has not kept his promise; on the other Turner has had substantial benefit at his expense.[32] The promise and restitution principles appear to point in opposite directions in this situation. . . . [I]t is the very distinctness of the principles that causes such questions to arise. Certainly nothing about the promise principle, the conception of contract as promise, entails that all disputes between people who have tried but failed to make a contract or who have broken a contract must be decided solely according to that principle.

*That you thought it was a present, spent it, and would now have to dip into the grocery budget to pay me back? Well, that might be a justification if it were true.

NOTES

1. On the right and the good the critical discussion is John Rawls, *A Theory of Justice* §§68, 83–85 (Cambridge, 1971), which harks back to Immanuel Kant, *Groundwork of the Metaphysics of Morals* (Paton trans., Harper Torchbooks ed. New York, 1964) where the contrast is made between the right and happiness. See also W. D. Ross, *The Right and the Good* (Oxford, 1930); Ronald Dworkin, "Liberalism," in *Public and Private Morality* (S. Hampshire ed. Cambridge, England, 1978). On the relation between liberalism and responsibility,

see Friedrich Hayek, *The Constitution of Liberty* ch. 5 (Chicago, 1960); Charles Fried, *Right and Wrong* 124–126 (Cambridge, 1978); Rawls, supra at 519. For a different view see C. B. Macpherson, *The Political Theory of Possessive Individualism—Hobbes to Locke* (Oxford, 1962).

2. Immanuel Kant, *The Metaphysical Elements of Justice* 54–55 (Ladd trans. Indianapolis, 1965).
3. See Charles Fried, *An Anatomy of Values* 81–86 (Cambridge, 1970); Henry Sidgwick, *Elements of Politics,* quoted in Friedrich Kessler and Grant Gilmore, *Contracts* 4 (2d ed. Boston, 1970).
4. Sissela Bok, *Lying: Moral Choice in Public Life* (New York, 1978); Fried, supra note 1, ch. 3.
5. This example is based on Adams v. Gillig, 199 N.Y. 314, 92 N.E. 670 (1930).
6. See generally Page Keeton, "Fraud: Statements of Intention," 15 *Texas L. Rev.* 185 (1937).
7. See generally Robert Goff and Gareth Jones, *The Law of Restitution* ch. 1 (2d. ed. London, 1978).
8. For a strong statement of the tort and benefit principles as foundations of contract law, see Patrick Atiyah, *The Rise and Fall of Contract* 1–7 (Oxford, 1979). A remarkable article stating the several moral principles implicit in contract law is George Gardner, "An Inquiry into the Principles of the Law of Contracts," 46 *Harv. Law Rev.* 1 (1932).
9. For a review of Anglo-American writing on promise from Hobbes to modern times, see Atiyah, supra note 8, at 41–60, 649–659. There has been a lively debate on the bases for the moral obligation of promise in recent philosophical literature. Some philosophers have taken a line similar to that of Atiyah and Gilmore, deriving the obligation of promise from the element of reliance. The strongest statement is Neil MacCormick, "Voluntary Obligations and Normative Powers," *Proceedings of the Aristotelian Society,* supp. vol. 46, at 59 (1972). See also Pall Ardal, "And That's a Promise," 18 *Phil. Q.* 225 (1968); F. S. McNeilly, "Promises Demoralized," 81 *Phil. Rev.* 63 (1972). G. J. Warnock, *The Object of Morality* ch. 7 (London, 1971), offers an effective refutation along the lines in the text, but his affirmative case proposes that the obligation of a promise rests on the duty of veracity, the duty to make the facts correspond to the promise. For an excellent discussion of this last suggestion and a proposal that accords with my own, see Don Locke, "The Object of Morality and the Obligation to Keep a Promise," 2 *Canadian J. of Philosophy* 135 (1972). Locke's emphasis on trust seems a clearer and sounder version of H. A. Prichard's proposal that the obligation of a Promise rests on a more general "agreement to keep agreements." *Moral Obligation* ch. 7 (Oxford, 1957).
10. A number of the philosophers who disagree with the Atiyah-MacCormick argument emphasize the conventional aspect of the invocation of the promissory form, as well as the self-imposed nature of the obligation. E. g. Joseph Raz, "Voluntary Obligations," *Proceedings of the Aristotelian Society,* supp. vol. 46, at 79 (1972); Raz, "Promises and Obligations," in *Law, Morality, and Society* (Hacker, Raz eds. Oxford, 1977); John Searle, *Speech Acts* 33–42, 175–188 (Cambridge, 1969); Searle "What Is a Speech Act?" in *The Philosophy of Language* (John Searle ed. Oxford, 1971). The locus classicus of this view of promising is John Rawls, "Two Concepts of Rules," 64 *Phil. Rev.* 3 (1955). The general idea goes back, of course, to Ludwig Wittgenstein, *Philosophical Investigations* § 23. For Hume's account of the conventional nature of promissory obligation, see *A Treatise of Human Nature* 516–525 (Selby-Bigge ed. Oxford, 1888).
11. Stanley Cavell's contention in *The Claim of Reason* 293–303 (Oxford, 1979) that promising is not a practice or an institution, because unlike the case of a game one cannot imagine setting it up or reforming it and because promising is not an office, seems to me beside the point. Kant's discussion, supra note 2, shows that morality can mandate that there be a convention with certain general features, as does Hume's discussion supra note 10, though Hume's morality is a more utilitarian one.
12. David Lewis, *Convention* (Cambridge, 1969).
13. Supra note 10.
14. Here I side with David Lyons, *The Forms and Limits of Utilitarianism* (Oxford, 1965) in a continuing debate. For the most recent statement of the contrary position, see Richard Brandt, *A Theory of the Good and Right* (Oxford, 1979). For an excellent introduction, see J. J. C. Smart and Bernard Williams, *Utilitarianism: For and Against* (Cambridge, England, 1973). I argue that it is a mistake to treat Rawls's discussion of promising in "Two Concepts of Rules," supra note 10, as an instance of rule-utilitarianism in my review of Atiyah, 93 *Harv. Law Rev.* 1863n18 (1980). See also Charles Landesman, "Promises and Practices," 75 *Mind* (n.s.) 239 (1966).
15. This was in fact Bentham's general perspective. See also Brandt, supra note 14.

16. Compare Rawls, supra note 1, ch. 6, where it is argued that (*a*) the deduction of the principles of justice for institutions, and (*b*) a showing that a particular institution is just are not sufficient to generate an obligation to comply with that institution. Further principles of natural duty and obligation must be established.
17. See Locke, supra note 9; Prichard, supra note 9; Raz, supra note 10.
18. American Law Institute, *Restatement (1st) of the Law of Contracts* [hereafter cited as *Restatement* (1st) or (2d)], § 329, Comment a: "In awarding compensatory damages, the effort is made to put the injured party in as good a position as that in which he would have been put by full performance of the contract. . . ."; E. Allan Farnsworth, "Legal Remedies for Breach of Contract," 70 *Colum. L. Rev.* 1145 (1970); Gardner, supra note 8; Charles Goetz and Robert Scott, "Enforcing Promises: An Examination of the Basis of Contract," 80 *Yale L. J.* 1261 (1980).
19. See Fuller and Perdue, "The Reliance Interest in Contract Damages," 46 *Yale L. J.* 52, 373 (1936, 1937); Garner, supra note 8.
20. For discussions of these issues see Fried, supra note 3, at 169–177; Rawls, supra note 1, §85; and the essays in *The Identities of Persons* (Amelie Rorty ed. Berkeley, 1976) and *Personal Identity* (John Perry ed. Berkeley, 1975).
21. See Atiyah, supra note 8, at 140–141 for a discussion of these early sources. See my review of Atiyah, 93 *Harv. L. Rev.* 1858, 1864–1865 (1980) for a further discussion of these and other early sources.
22. 227 Mo. App. 175, 51 S.W. 2d 572 (1932).
23. *Restatement* (1st) §333(d).
24. Gardner, supra note 8, at 15, 22–23.
25. This is the problem that is standardly dealt with in contract texts under the rubric of consequential damages, or the principle in *Hadley v. Baxendale* 9 Exch. 341 (1854). See Gardner, supra note 8, at 28–30. Holmes, in Globe Refining v. Landa Cotton Oil Co., 190 U.S. 540 (1903) explained the limitation of liability for consequential damages in terms of the agreement itself: The defendant is liable only for those risks he explicitly or tacitly agreed to assume. This conception has been generally rejected in favor of a vaguer standard by which defendant is liable for any risks of which he had "reason to know" at the time of the agreement. UCC §2–715 comment 2. Holmes's test seems more consonant with the thesis of this work. See Pothier, *The Law of Obligations,* quoted in Lon Fuller and Melvin Eisenberg, *Basic Contract Law* 27 (3rd ed. St. Paul, 1972). The difference between the two positions is not great: first because it is always within the power of the parties to limit or expand liability for consequential damages by the agreement itself, UCC §2–719(3); second, because the "reason to know" standard means that the defendant at least has a fair opportunity to make such an explicit provision.
26. UCC §2–318; William Prosser, *Torts* ch. 17 (4th ed. St. Paul, 1971).
27. 133 N.W. 2d 267, 26 Wis. 2d 683 (1965).
28. See Stanley Henderson, "Promissory Estoppel and Traditional Contract Doctrine," 78 *Yale L. J.* 343, 357–360 (1969); see generally Friedrich Kessler and Edith Fine, "*Culpa in Contrahendo,* Bargaining in Good Faith, and Freedom of Contract: A Comparative Study," 77 *Harv. L. Rev.* 401 (1964).
29. *Nicomachean Ethics,* bk. V, iv–v.
30. See John Dawson, "Restitution or Damages?," 20 *Ohio St. L. J.* 175 (1959); Gardner, supra note 8, at 18–27. . . .
31. Goff and Jones, supra note 7, at 69; the problem raised in the footnote is treated at 88–89.
32. Britton v. Turner, 69 N.H. 281 (1834).

45

MICHAEL D. BAYLES

Legally Enforceable Commitments

Introduction

A continuing issue of contract law is what purported promises, agreements, or contracts should be legally enforced. Classic common-law theory usually addresses this issue through the doctrine of consideration: only those promises for which consideration is given are legally enforceable. The intent to enter contractual relations has also often been mentioned as another factor but its importance is questionable. In the absence of consideration, an intent to enter contractual relations would not suffice; and if a court finds consideration, it will also find an implied intent to contract unless there is a very explicit statement to the contrary.

My aim here is to consider what commitments should be legally enforceable. Although the terms "promisor" and "promisee" will be used, the term "commitment" is used to avoid possible limitations imposed by the concepts of promise and agreement. If one person sells a boat to another representing it as fourteen feet long, it seems odd to say that the seller promises that it is fourteen feet long; however, the seller certainly makes a commitment to its being that long. In other situations the "promisor" might not say anything but the "promisee" reasonably relies on a commitment. Without any linguistic communication, however, one might hesitate to say a promise was made.

Normative Analysis

The purpose herein is to consider what commitments *should* be legally enforced, not to determine which ones have been or will be enforced.[1] Because there is little agreement on methods for establishing such normative claims, it is important to state the method used even though space does not permit a defense of the method.

The central normative question is: What principles would rational persons accept courts using to decide cases in a society in which they expected to live?[2] As acceptable principles could and should vary with the type of society, the society is assumed to be an industrialized Western one with a common-law system. The crucial concepts to clarify are those of principles and rational persons.

Principles and rules can be distinguished from each other.[3] On the one hand, rules apply in an all-or-nothing way; if they apply to a situation, they determine its evaluation. For example, a law requiring two witnesses to a will not in the handwriting of the testator is a rule. If a will has only one witness, it is invalid. In contrast, when principles apply, they do not necessarily determine an evaluation. For example, it might be a principle that people should be free to dispose of their property by devise as they wish. It does not necessarily follow that a freely made will should be upheld because a contrary principle, for example, that a person should make adequate provision for children, might also apply. On the other hand, because principles do not apply in an all-or-nothing way and can conflict, principles have "weight." Conflicting principles must be weighed or balanced against one another, and some have more weight than others. Because rules apply in an all-or-nothing fashion, they do not have to be weighed or balanced against one another.

Some scholars reject this distinction between principles and rules, contending that principles differ from rules only by being more general.[4] In this view, both rules and principles have weight and can be balanced against one another. This contention does not affect the following arguments because the essential features are the possibility of weighing or balancing and different levels of generality. The following discussion presents some principles for different types of commitments.

A rational person uses logical reasoning and all relevant available information in acquiring desires and values, deciding what to do, and accepting legal principles.[5] Logical reasoning is not restricted to deductive logic but also includes inductive logic or scientific method. A rational person considers arguments for and against principles, accepting the sound arguments and rejecting the unsound ones. All relevant available information is all pertinent information that a person in the situation can obtain. It is information, not knowledge, that a rational person has. People are rational if they use the best information available, even if it later turns out to be incorrect; indeed, it would be irrational to use information that, on the basis of presently available evidence, appeared incorrect even if it were later found to be correct. Information is relevant to the acceptability of a legal principle if it indicates that the principle's use by courts has or lacks

[1]See Michael D. Bayles, "Introduction: The Purposes of Contract Law," *Valparaiso University Law Review* 17 (1983): 613–615.

[2]See also Richard B. Brandt, "A Motivational Theory of Excuses in the Criminal Law," in J. Roland Pennock and John W. Chapman (eds.) *Criminal Justice: Nomos XXVII,* (New York: New York University Press, 1985), p. 169.

[3]Ronald Dworkin, *Taking Rights Seriously* (Cambridge: Harvard University Press, 1977), pp. 22–28; Michael D. Bayles, *Principles of Legislation* (Detroit: Wayne State University Press, 1978), pp. 42–44.

[4]Joseph Raz, "Legal Principles and the Limits of Law," *Yale Law Journal* 81 (1972): 823–54.

[5]Richard B. Brandt, *A Theory of the Good and the Right* (Oxford: Clarendon Press, 1979), pp. 10–16; Bayles, *Principles of Legislation,* pp. 51–54.

some normative characteristic, such as fairness, or that the probable consequences of such use, including effects on third parties, would be good or bad.

Some normative basis must be used in determining what legal principles are justifiable or acceptable, but it need not be a moral or legal one. Much legal analysis and justification is in terms of people's interests. There is little reason to believe that these interests or desires (the difference is not important here) are irrational. Herein certain basic desires are assumed to be rational, namely, those for wealth, security, bodily and mental integrity (including life), prestige or reputation, and freedom. Most of these have been justified elsewhere.[6]

Finally, it is assumed that rational persons could be either party to a case. This assumption is implicit in the very question being asked, for it concerns the acceptability of legal principles for a society in which one expects to live. In contract cases, many principles can be used by plaintiff or defendant. In arguing for a legal principle, one must then consider its acceptability from both parties' points of view.[7] This type of argument is common in courts. An example is the following argument by Judge Turnage for the rule that rejection of a purchased option does not terminate the right to accept later unless the other party has materially changed position.

> This rule fully protects the rights of both parties. It extends to the optionor the protection he requires in the event a rejection of the option is communicated to him and he thereafter changes his position in reliance thereon to his detriment. At the same time it protects the right of the option holder to have the opportunity to exercise his option for the full period for which he paid, absent the material change in position.[8]

This argument shows that it is a reasonable rule whichever party one might be. One has no reason to think that people are more likely to have written than purchased an option.

Contract Law

Contracts are often defined as promises or agreements enforceable at law.[9] Contract law might then be taken to be the law pertaining to the enforcement of promises or agreements. However, this narrow conception of contract law is inadequate for material normally included in contract law, let alone for evaluating the law. Many court cases normally included in contract law do not, for one reason or another, involve enforceable agreements or promises. Indeed, often it is found that no contract has been made. In short, contract law concerns more than enforceable contracts and agreements; it also concerns failed attempts to make them. This narrow conception of contract has made possible talk of the death of contract,[10] because nontraditional principles have come to play such an important role in failed attempts to contract.

An extremely broad conception of contract law is the law pertaining to private transfer of property or services. So conceived, contract law includes many subjects not usually thought to belong to it, such as wills and inheritance, gifts, restitution, fraud, and conversion of property. This extremely broad conception of contract law can be subdivided by the use of two distinctions. The first is simply whether an intended transfer is a present or future one. The second distinction is among "plus sum," "zero sum," and "minus sum" interactions. In plus sum interactions, more value exists after the interaction than before; that is, value is increased. The general concept of a plus sum interaction has three subcases. One party might lose but the other gain more than the first loses; one party might remain the same and the other gain; and both parties might gain. If Arnold purchases a watch from a store, then presumably both he and the store benefit and the interaction is a plus sum one of the last type. In zero sum interactions, the same amount of value exists after the interaction as before. If two people each mistakenly take the other's similar umbrella from a stand, the interaction is a zero sum one. An interaction would also be a zero sum one if one party gained precisely what the other lost. In minus sum interactions, less value exists after the interaction than before. If two people have an automobile accident, value is decreased.

---

6 Bayles, *Principles of Legislation*.

7 See also David A. J. Richards, "Human Rights and the Moral Foundations of the Substantive Criminal Law," *Georgia Law Review* 13 (1979): 1414–15, 1436.

8 Ryder v. Wescoat, 535 S.W. 2d 269 (Mo. Ct. App. 1976).

9 Arthur Linton Corbin, *Corbin on Contracts*, 1 Vol. edn. (St. Paul, Minn.: West Publishing Co., 1952), p. 5; G. H. Trietel, *The Law of Contract*, 5th edn. (London: Stevens & Sons, 1979), p. 1.

10 Grant Gilmore, *The Death of Contract* (Columbus, Ohio: Ohio State University Press, 1974).

Either one party is the same and the other worse off or both are worse off.

How one classifies some interactions depends on how value is conceived. For example, gifts are usually treated as zero sum interactions, probably because there is only a one way transfer. But the parties to a gift transfer might think of it as a plus sum interaction. The recipient of a book might value it more than a donor who has already read it. The donor might value the recipient having the book and indicate this by paying to mail the book to the donee. Voluntary gifts can then increase economic value and be plus sum interactions. Gift interactions can also be minus sum ones, for example, when a recipient places less value on a gift than the donor or the market. One often receives gifts that one did not want and puts away in a drawer or closet. Perhaps on average gifts are zero or modest plus sum interactions, the plus sum ones barely offsetting the minus sum ones.

With these two distinctions, transfers of property or services can be classified as follows.

	ZERO SUM	PLUS SUM
PRESENT	gift inter vivos gift causa mortis	barter cash sales
FUTURE	conditional deeds succession	executory contracts

All of the transfers in the zero sum column are considered in property law. Gifts causa mortis and deeds with conditional delivery are placed near the border of present and future, because gifts causa mortis are present transfers with a right to revoke, whereas conditional deeds involve future transfers when the condition is met.

Logically, one might expect contract law to concern all the transfers in the plus sum column. However, there are two main problems with that. First, the concept of a plus sum interaction needed is a special one. Contract law is not limited to interactions which are in fact plus sum ones; it includes cases when something goes wrong and the interaction is not a plus sum one. One must view the interaction from a prospective or *ex ante* perspective; it is expected to be a plus sum interaction. As noted above, one party can lose and the interaction still be a plus sum one if the other party gains more than the first loses. Nonetheless, if the interaction is voluntary, rational parties expect it to be beneficial to them, although they need not expect or even consider whether it will be beneficial to the others. The concept then is of mutually expected beneficial plus sum interactions. Each party hopes to get something that is of more value to it than what is given. Because each party expects to benefit, based on the parties' expectations, *ex ante* the interaction is a plus sum one of the third type—in which both parties gain. Court cases arise when something goes wrong and the transfer does not occur or is for some other reason not mutually beneficial as expected.

Second, many commentators claim that contracts necessarily involve a promise.[11] If promises always relate to the future, then contract law excludes all present transfers such as barter.[12] This creates a problem for cash sales of goods as in purchasing groceries. Of course many sales of goods are partially "executory," for example, one party is to perform at a future date. Moreover, even most present sales involve commitments to the future, for example, warranties. Nonetheless, a cash payment for goods "as is" (no warranties) is included in the Uniform Commercial Code[13] and thus part of what is usually considered contract law. We have placed cash sales of goods in the present category, but near the border because of the future effect of warranties. If one party in a sale is to perform in the future, then sales of goods belong to executory contracts as that term is meant in the table, namely, as all those in which at least one party makes a commitment to something in the future.

Finally, "interaction" rather than the more usual "transaction" has been used because of its durational openness. "Transaction" suggests a discrete event, whereas "interaction" can apply to a long-term relationship. Much traditional contract law focuses on brief interactions between strangers. Yet, in the contemporary world, many contracts, such as employment, franchise, and installment contracts, pertain to a course of dealing between parties.[14] Although many of these long-term or relational contracts are treated

[11]John D. Calamari and Joseph M. Perillo, *The Law of Contracts,* 2d edn. (St. Paul, Minn.: West Publishing Co., 1977), p. 1; Corbin, *Corbin on Contracts,* p. 7.

[12]Corbin, *Corbin on Contracts,* p. 6.

[13]U.C.C. sec. 2-316 (3) (d) (1978).

[14]See generally Ian R. Macneil, *The New Social Contract* (New Haven and London: Yale University Press, 1980).

in special fields, such as labor law, it is desirable to develop contract principles that can cover both them and discrete transactions.

Thus, the main function of contract law is to regulate mutually expected beneficial interactions transferring property or services between private persons[15] and to provide civil remedies when they go wrong. Failed mutually expected plus sum interactions usually become zero sum or minus sum ones. Most minus sum interactions are treated in tort law, but because many failed mutually expected plus sum interactions become minus sum ones, there is an overlap of tort and contract principles, especially for remedies. This does not mean that tort and contract law are the same; they take different perspectives. Tort law takes an *ex post* view of interactions as minus sum ones. Criminal law also regulates plus sum and minus sum interactions, but it can be distinguished by its remedy—punishment.

AIMS

Most theories of contract law adopt a single aim: the enforcement of agreements or promises, maximizing economic value, or fulfilling reasonable expectations. An advantage of this approach is that it provides a unity to the field. However, human beings, and courts composed of them, are not such single-minded machines. People can have more than one purpose for their activities or institutions and reconcile or balance them when they conflict. Consequently, none of these theories alone provides an adequate basis for evaluating the law. Nevertheless, it is useful to briefly examine their claims, and then to bring together the insights they provide.

Agreement and Promise

The classical view is that contract law is to enforce the agreement or promises of the parties. On the agreement version, the purpose of contract law is to carry out the wills of parties who intended to be legally bound by an agreement.[16] On the promise version, the purpose of contract law is to enforce the moral obligation to keep promises when the institution of promising is intentionally invoked.[17] Three claims are central to both versions. (1) The parties intend to bind themselves. (2) The parties freely choose to bind themselves. (3) Legal enforcement increases freedom or autonomy by enabling people to make definite arrangements for the future.[18]

There are problems with this view as the sole purpose of contract law. First, much of contract law concerns situations when, for one reason or another, agreements or valid promises were not made. The purpose of enforcing agreements or promises thus does not reach them. The heroic approach is to call such situations contractual accidents or gaps falling outside of contract law proper.[19] But this is like saying principles of building construction pertain only when they are followed and have no relevance to situations when they are not.

Second, the first two claims are sometimes denied in the law. Parties can be legally bound although they did not intend to bind themselves legally. Indeed, it is not at all unusual for parties to find they have legally binding contracts or promises when they did not so intend. Contrarily, some contracts are not legally enforced even if the parties want and intend them to be, for example, gambling contracts. Whether one is legally bound depends on the rules of law, although often one can avoid legal obligations by explicitly stating that one is not making legal commitments. It follows that parties do not always freely choose to bind themselves. One should distinguish two aspects of freely binding oneself—entering a contract and choosing the terms of a contract. Terms of a contract are often set by law (for example, a marital contract), but one is free to enter it or not. In a few cases, a contract is not even entered freely. Different conceptions of freedom can pertain here, but on almost any of them some contracts are not entered freely, for example, an agreement with a judge not to do some act.[20]

---

[15]See Anthony T. Kronman, "Contract Law and Distributive Justice," *Yale Law Journal* 89 (1980): 472.

[16]G. H. Fridman, "On the Nature of Contract," *Valparaiso University Law Review* 17 (1938): 631.

[17]Charles Fried, *Contract as Promise* (Cambridge: Harvard University Press, 1981), p. 16; see also P.S. Atiyah, *An Introduction to the Law of Contract,* 3rd edn. (Oxford: Clarendon Press, 1981), p. 3.

[18]Fridman, "Nature of Contract," p. 636; Fried, *Contract as Promise*, pp. 20–21.

[19]Fried, *Contract as Promise,* p. 69.

[20]Atiyah, *Law of Contract,* p. 23.

One's overall freedom is increased by being able to make legally binding agreements. One has options to bind oneself in the future. But it is the ability to bind others to one, not the ability to bind oneself, that is the most valuable aspect of contract, although being able to bind oneself and doing so might be necessary to get others to bind themselves. One is freed from worry and actions to ensure the promised performance. Thus, enforcement of agreements or promises cannot be the sole aim of contract law, because it simply fails to cover a multitude of situations arising in it. Nonetheless it, and especially the freedom it provides, can still be purposes of contract law.

Maximizing Economic Value

Economic analysts view law, at least private law, as designed to maximize economic value or wealth.[21] The point or test of legal enforcement (imposition of liability) is to create incentives for value maximizing conduct in the future.[22] A more contract specific and sophisticated aim is to "maximize the net beneficial reliance derived from promise-making activity."[23] "Beneficial reliance" is reliance on commitments that are kept so that one benefits. "Detrimental reliance" is reliance when a commitment is not kept and one loses. A balance must be struck between the benefits from fulfilled commitments and the losses from unfulfilled ones. In reciprocal or bargained for contracts, these two considerations can be balanced by the parties in their negotiations. For example, if Bradford is negotiating a contract to loan Caswell a sum of money, the interest to be charged will reflect Bradford's estimate of the likelihood of Caswell repaying. The greater the risk of nonrepayment (loss), the higher the interest (benefit) will be. In nonreciprocal contracts, the law must be more active, because these considerations are not balanced by the parties adjusting the terms.

On this economic view, freedom is subordinated to increasing wealth. Freedom of parties is not important for its own sake but because value is determined by the free preferences of persons. Free choice in entering contracts and fixing their terms is essential, because it ensures that both parties expect to benefit from them and value is thus increased. If a person did not (freely) intend to make a commitment, then its enforcement is not justified, because there is not reason to believe the person thought it would be beneficial.[24] The economic view supports a freedom the promise theory does not, namely, the freedom to breach contracts. If a party finds that another deal can provide more benefit even if damages are paid, then that party is free to break the contract. Indeed, to maximize value, the party should do so. Similarly, if the original judgment about expected benefit from the contract were incorrect and one would lose from completing the deal, one is free to and should breach if the damages would be less than the costs of performance.

The economic view focuses on the fact that contracts are mutually expected to be beneficial, that is, value increasing interactions. One has good reasons to accept the economic purpose. Laws facilitating mutually expected beneficial plus sum interactions are desirable, since one can expect to benefit whichever party one is. Moreover, one has no reason to object to rules that enable others to break contracts provided one receives benefits equivalent to what one would have received had the contract been performed. However, economic theorists tend to discount the costs of breach by the other party, in particular, the costs of suing for compensation. Possible legal expenses and judicial error are costs of another's breach that must be subtracted from the benefits of the contract. Consequently, one would not accept allowing others to breach whenever, after subtracting one's expected benefits, they gain.

Maximizing beneficial reliance comes close to maximizing the trust which promise theorists see as central. On a promise view, the principles of mutual trust and respect are the basis for enforcing promises.[25] Beneficial reliance amounts to action in trust that promises will be fulfilled. Thus, both views fasten on essentially the same element but describe it in different terminology—mutual trust and beneficial

[21]Richard A. Posner, *The Economics of Justice* (Cambridge: Harvard University Press, 1983), pp. 88–115.

[22]Richard A. Posner, *Economic Analysis of Law*, 2d edn. (Boston: Little, Brown and Co., 1977), p. 68.

[23]Charles J. Goetz and Robert E. Scott, "Enforcing Promises: An Examination of the Basis of Contract," *Yale Law Journal* 89 (1980): 1321.

[24]Anthony T. Kronman and Richard A. Posner, "Introduction: Economic Theory and Contract Law," in Anthony T. Kronman and Richard A. Posner (eds.), *The Economics of Contract Law*, (Boston: Little, Brown and Co., 1979), p. 5.

[25]Fried, *Contract as Promise*, p. 17.

reliance. They have different views as to the ultimate purpose or benefit of enforcement. Promise theorists view the benefit as freedom, while economic theorists view it as material gain. The difference is subtle, because an important point of contractual freedom is to be able to improve one's situation materially by arranging the future. However, freedom to contract includes the freedom to make expected detrimental commitments as well as beneficial ones, although a rational self-interested person would not do so.

Reasonable Expectations

Another view contends that "the fundamental purpose of contract law is the protection and promotion of expectations reasonably created."[26] In a contractual setting, only those reasonable expectations of which the other party was or should have been aware are to be protected.[27] This view emphasizes one being responsible for another reasonably relying on, or having expectations due to, one's words or actions.[28] If one is or should have been aware that one's actions would create expectations in another, then one is responsible for fulfilling (not frustrating) those expectations.

The central problem for this view is to specify when expectations and reliance are reasonable.[29] One might determine reasonableness of contractual expectations and reliance by social practices. Courts often use commercial customs and practices as a basis for interpreting contracts.[30] However, for many contracts no such commercial basis exists. Instead, one has to turn to what the average person would have expected or to a normative theory about reasonable expectations. Using the expectations of the average person will not provide a sound normative basis for contract law. Even if one thinks it valuable to satisfy people's expectations, this will not help. The average person's expectations are often determined, directly or indirectly, by what the law is. Thus, the argument might be circular: the law should be such and such because that complies with what people expect, but they expect that because the law is such and such. A normative basis should thus enable one to evaluate the expectations of people. The concept of a rational person as used here can fulfill that role. But then the view simply amounts to claiming that contracts should be enforced when rational persons have good reasons for doing so. This does not provide an aim for contract law.

The aim of protecting reasonable expectations and reliance is closely related to the aims of the promise and economic views. Reasonable expectations arise from promises, and their protection and promotion largely involves enforcing the promises. Promoting and protecting reasonable reliance is similar to the economic view's concern to maximize beneficial reliance. The economic theory, however, provides a criterion for determining when and how reliance should be protected, thereby specifying what reliance is reasonable. The reasonable expectations view does not provide guidance here.

Specific Aims

With different language and emphasis, each of the views is concerned to promote and protect mutually expected beneficial plus sum interactions involving the transfer of property or services and the interests arising therein. It is possible to pick out specific aims common to these views and to add one that they ignore. Both the promise and economic views emphasize freedom to enter contracts and fix their terms. Although the reasonable expectations view does not emphasize freedom, it does emphasize responsibility for the exercise of freedom, for expectations and reliance voluntarily created. Consequently, the freedom to transfer property and services in mutually expected beneficial interactions is common to each. This aspect is contained in the following principle. *(1) The principle of freedom of transfer: (a) property and services should be voluntarily transferable from one person to another; and (b) involuntary transfers should be not be allowed.* This principle is a very general one, covering gifts and testamentary dispositions as well as contracts.[31]

The expected benefit of entering interactions involving commitments rests on the assurance that they will be fulfilled. The views' emphasis on trust,

---

[26]Barry Reiter and John Swan, "Contracts and the Protection of Reasonable Expectations," in Barry J. Reiter and John Swan (eds.), *Studies in Contract Law* (Toronto: Butterworths, 1980), p. 6.

[27]Reiter and Swan, "Contracts," p. 7.

[28]Barry Reiter, "Contracts, Torts, Relations and Reliance," in Barry J. Reiter and John Swan (eds.), *Studies in Contract Law* (Toronto: Butterworths, 1980), p. 242.

[29]B. S. Atiyah, *Promises, Morals, and Law* (Oxford: Clarendon Press, 1981), p. 68.

[30]*Restatement (Second) of Contracts* secs. 219–22 (1979).

[31]See also Fried, *Contract As Promise,* p. 39.

beneficial reliance, and fulfillment of reasonable expectations all support legal assurance. Promises are more trustworthy if supported by law; beneficial reliance is more likely when the law enforces most commitments; and expectations and reliance are reasonable if the law will protect them. Not all commitments need be or should be legally enforced. Much depends on whether the interaction is expected to be a plus sum, zero sum, or minus sum one. One has good reasons for the promotions and enforcement of commitments in mutually expected beneficial plus sum interactions, because one can expect to benefit from them. This rationale does not apply to zero sum and minus sum interactions. In an expected minus sum interaction, at least one party and often both will lose, so one has no reason to support commitments to them. In zero sum interactions, either both parties will be left as they were or one will gain what the other loses. With an equal chance of being either party, one would be indifferent to them. Again, however, whether an interaction is zero sum depends on what counts as value. If one counts the psychological satisfaction of a donor or the greater value to the donee, then the giving of gifts can be a plus sum interaction. One might thus rationally desire to bind oneself legally to giving a gift in the future. Moreover, as a potential donee in a zero sum interaction, one does not want it turned into a minus sum interaction with oneself the loser.

(2) The principle of enforceable commitments: commitments in transfers of property or services should be supported and enforced (a) in mutually expected beneficial plus sum interactions, and (b) in zero sum interactions if (i) it is necessary to prevent loss due to reasonable reliance by intended beneficiaries or (ii) donors indicate they are enforceable. This principle encapsulates the reasoning of the previous paragraph. It extends to wills and gratuitous conditional deeds, for by making such instruments a donor indicates that they are enforceable. It also protects reasonable reliance on gratuitous promises. This principle assumes that, in accordance with the principle of freedom of transfer, the commitments are voluntary.

Of course, as with all principles, there can be sufficient reasons against complying with it. In law, a crucial concern is not bothering with de minimis or trivial matters. This consideration is largely met by the costs imposed on parties in lawsuits for enforcement of commitments. Although none of the views considered makes note of the point, one also has another good reason to limit enforcement of commitments. *(3) The principle of collective good: enforcement of commitments should be limited by social policies for the collective good.* Courts have always so limited commitments, refusing to enforce contracts contrary to public policy. One stands to benefit from justifiable policies of this sort. Although one might want to enter into an arrangement involving a commitment contrary to such a policy, for most people the chances of this being so are small. Even if one would want to make or receive such a commitment in a particular case, it does not follow that a legal principle of enforcing such commitments would benefit one. One would have to consider the detrimental effects on one as a member of society from their enforcement. Consequently, for almost everyone, the expectable benefits from the principle outweigh the expectable benefits of not having it. However, few policies are likely to restrict enforcement, because mutually beneficial interactions do not usually impose harm on others. The primary instances of this occur when collective restraint from conduct is necessary for some good, for example, refraining from anticompetitive business practices. . . .

46

ALAN WERTHEIMER

Unconscionability and Contracts

ABSTRACT: This article considers the principles that underlie the claim that some contracts are unconscionable and that such contracts should not be enforceable. It argues that it is much more difficult to explain unconscionability than is often supposed, particularly in cases where the contract is mutually advantageous or Pareto superior. Among other things, the article considers whether unconscionability is a defect in process or result, whether the gains in an unconscionable contract are disproportionate, whether there is a strong link between the use of standard forms and unconscionability, and whether the principle of inequality of bargaining power can account for unconscionability. After rejecting several standard explanations of unconscionability, I consider several alternative ways in which it might be explained.

INTRODUCTION

McNamara, a television and stereo dealer, advertised a color television on a "rent to own" plan—a plan that required "no deposit," "no credit," and "no long term obligation."[1] After seeing the advertisement, Carolyn Murphy, a welfare recipient, leased a 25-inch Philco color television from McNamara, agreeing to pay a $20 delivery charge and 78 weekly payments of $16, after which she would own the set, having paid $1,268 for a set which retailed for $499. After paying $436 over a six month period, Ms. Murphy saw a newspaper article criticizing the plan and stopped making payments. McNamara sought to repossess the set and threatened to file criminal charges if Ms. Murphy failed to return it. Ms. Murphy filed for an injunction against repossession, claiming that the agreement was unconscionable and therefore unenforceable. The court granted the injunction: ". . . an agreement for the sale of consumer goods entered into with a consumer having unequal bargaining power, which agreement calls for an unconscionable purchase price, constitutes an unfair trade practice. . . ."[2]

In nullifying Murphy's contract with McNamara, the court seems to say that it will not allow one party to exploit another party even if the parties appear to agree to the transaction and even if the relation is (arguably) mutually advantageous. It is unfairness, not harm, that seems to do the work. But what made this contract unconscionable? And if a contract can be both unconscionable and mutually advantageous, should such contracts be unenforceable? Those are the sorts of questions which I would like to explore in this paper. I hope to use the doctrine of unconscionability in contracts as a lens through which to get a clearer understanding of exploitation—its essential characteristics and its moral force.

At the most general level, contract law can be justified in two principal ways.[3] First, it may be said that contract law facilitates individual autonomy or freedom.[4] To be autonomous is to be able to plan and control one's life, and that includes the ability to form binding relationships with others, an ability which is facilitated by contract law. Second, contract law can also be justified in consequentialist or utilitarian terms. From this perspective, contract law promotes social utility by allowing individuals to put their resources to more valued uses.[5]

The contrast between these background justifications for contract law is (roughly) replicated in the way in which we might evaluate the morality of contracts. We can, it seems, evaluate an agreement or contract in terms of its *process,* that is, the way in which it was formed, and its *substance,* that is, its result or content. On the one hand, we might say that the process is morally legitimate if the parties come to their agreement freely and with (relatively) full information. On the other hand, we might say that the result is morally legitimate if it is mutually advantageous or, as economists would say, Pareto superior.

Yet we can and do ask another question about substance. We can ask whether a contract represents a fair exchange of value. If we assume, for the sake of argument, that it is possible to evaluate contracts in terms of fairness, it is still *another* question as to why enforceable contracts must be fair, assuming they are freely entered into and mutually advantageous. The autonomy view of contract need *not* assume that contracts are an instance of pure procedural justice, and the utilitarian view need not deny that there can be an independent criterion of fairness. These views need only maintain that a contract should be regarded as *binding* if it is voluntary or Pareto superior, not that it is therefore just.

Now on the standard contemporary view of freedom of contract, a valid contract requires (1) parties with capacity, (2) manifested assent, and (3) consideration.[6] The principal common law defenses to a contract—duress, fraud, misrepresentation, incapacity, mistake—focus on capacity and assent, on the "process" or "voluntariness" of the contract, rather than its substance, defenses which are obviously required by the autonomy view. Interestingly, the utilitarian view of contract law emphasizes the same procedural dimensions. Gifts and deliberate self-sacrifice aside, people will not freely enter into an agreement unless they expect it to be advantageous to them. On the consequentialist account of contract law, the principal exceptions to the enforcement of contracts will be those that defeat the assumption that the agreement is (at least *ex ante*) reasonably regarded as Pareto superior. On this view, a contract procured through coercion or fraud should be nullified not because it is involuntary, but because fraud negates the presumption that the contract is beneficial to the defrauded party.

Now it might be thought that whereas capacity and assent refer to "process" criteria, "consideration" has to do with the substance or fairness of the agreement. But that would be a mistake. Consideration must flow between the parties to establish that an agreement or exchange has occurred (rather than a one-sided promise), but the *adequacy* or *amount* of the consideration is irrelevant. The terms of a contract may be harsh, but "the Chancery mends no man's bargain."[7]

This is not the whole truth. For it is also said that when we examine what judges *do* as well as what they *say*, we will find that "relief from contractual obligations is frequently given on the ground of unfairness. . . ."[8] For example, in a famous maritime case, *The Port Caledonia and the Anna*, a vessel in difficulty asked for assistance from a nearby tug. The tugmaster's terms were £1,000 or no rope. The master of the vessel agreed to pay the £1,000. In refusing to uphold the agreement (the court awarded the tugmaster £200 for his efforts) the court said this: "I have to ask myself whether the bargain that was made was so inequitable, so unjust, and so unreasonable that the court cannot allow it to stand."[9] But this sort of case, indeed, the sorts of cases which characterized unconscionability in equity courts, are not much help in contemporary cases of unconscionability, for the traditional equity case involved a claim that one party took advantage of some *special weakness* of the other party in a unique transaction rather than a more impersonal imbalance of economic power, the sort of situation which framed *Murphy v. McNamara*.[10]

CONTEMPORARY UNCONSCIONABILITY

The contemporary doctrine of unconscionability has received its most explicit development in Section 2-302 of the Uniform Commercial Code— "Unconscionable Contract or Clause." It reads as follows:

> (1) If the court as a matter of law finds the contract or any clause of the contract to have been unconscionable at the time it was made the court may refuse to enforce the contract, or it may enforce the remainder of the contract without the unconscionable clause, or it may so limit the application of any unconscionable clause as to avoid any unconscionable result.[11]

By adopting the UCC, state legislatures gave courts a statutory mandate to invalidate unconscionable contracts. But it is less clear what that meant.[12] The text of 2-302 strongly suggests that unconscionability is a matter of result rather than process. Yet the language of the provision notwithstanding, the official *commentary* on 2-302 says that the doctrine of unconscionability is "designed to prevent oppression and unfair surprise . . . and not the disturbance of risks because of superior bargaining power." Here, it seems, process is more important than result. But rather than pursue doctrinal statements, let us instead consider the way in which unconscionability has been understood in some contemporary cases.

Henningsen v. Bloomfield Motors (1960).[13] Mr. Henningsen purchased a Plymouth, manufactured by Chrysler Corporation, from Bloomfield Motors. Ten days later, Mrs. Henningsen was injured while driving the car. According to an insurance adjuster, something went "wrong from the steering wheel down to the front wheels." The Henningsens sued for damages on grounds of negligence and upon breach of express and implied warranties. The trial court dismissed the negligence counts, but an award was granted on the grounds of implied warranty of merchantability. Bloomfield Motors and Chrysler appealed, claiming that the purchase order which Mr. Henningsen signed contained, albeit in fine print, the uniform warranty of the Automobile Manufacturers Association, which disclaimed any responsibility for injuries.

In finding for Henningsen, the Court paid homage to the principle of freedom of contract, but also emphasized that the disclaimer was contained in a "standard form." According to the Court, "freedom of contract" is most at home when a contract is the result of "free bargaining of parties . . . who meet each other on a footing of approximate economic equality" rather than the "standardized mass contract . . . used primarily by enterprises with strong bargaining power and position" and which is presented to the consumer on a take-it-or-leave-it basis.

Williams v. Walker-Thomas Furniture Co. (1965).[14] Williams, who was on welfare, purchased a number of items from Walker-Thomas under an installment agreement, which provided that "all payments now and hereafter made by [purchaser] shall be credited pro rata on all outstanding leases, bills and accounts due the Company by [purchaser] at the time each such payment is made."[15] In effect, the "add-on" provision gave Walker-Thomas the right to repossess old items until the new item was paid off. In 1962, Williams bought a stereo set of stated value of $514.95. She owed $164 on prior purchases. When she defaulted, Walker-Thomas sought to repossess all the items purchased since 1957. On appeal, the U. S. Court of Appeals held that "where the element of unconscionability is present at the time a contract is made, the contract should not be enforced."[16] And an unconscionable contract, said the court, includes "an absence of meaningful choice on the part of one of the parties together with contract terms which are unreasonably favorable to the other party."[17]

Gianni v. Gantos (1986).[18] In June 1980, Gantos, a clothing retailer, submitted to Gianni, a clothing manufacturer, an order for women's holiday clothing to be delivered on October 10, 1980. The back of the purchase order contained this clause: "Buyer reserves the right to terminate by notice to Seller all or any part of this Purchase Order with respect to Goods that have not actually been shipped by Seller. . . ." In late September, 1980, and before any clothing had been shipped, Gantos canceled the order. Faced with the prospect of holding inventory that it could not sell, Gianni subsequently agreed to a 50% price reduction if Gantos would accept the goods. A lower court held the agreement invalid on the grounds that the cancellation clause was unconscionable.

According to the court, the parties did not have equal bargaining power because the "holiday order" comprised about 20% of Gianni's annual business and Ganto's sales were 20 times those of Gianni. A buyer for Gantos testified that such clauses were, in fact, standard in the business because "the buyer in our industry is in the driver's seat."[19]

Lloyds Bank Ltd. v. Bundy (1974).[20] Herbert Bundy, an elderly farmer, and his only son, Michael, had been customers of a branch of Lloyds Bank for many years. Michael formed a company which banked at the same branch. Michael's company was not doing well and, on several occasions, Herbert Bundy gave the bank additional security for the son's overdrafts. In December, 1969, Michael visited Herbert along with Mr. Head, a new assistant manager of the bank. Mr. Head told Herbert that the bank would continue to support his son only if he secured the son's overdrafts with all of his remaining assets—his farm—but it did not offer any additional line of credit. Herbert said that he was 100% behind his son. Without seeking further advice, he signed the papers. When the son's business failed, the bank sought possession of the farm.

The Court of Appeals ruled that the contract was unenforceable, primarily because it resulted from a serious inequality of bargaining power. In addition, it was said that the terms were unfair because neither the father nor the son received adequate consideration, that Herbert's judgment had been impaired by his love for his son, that Herbert did not and was not urged to consult an independent advisor, and that there was a conflict of interest between the bank and the father which the bank failed to acknowledge.

Macaulay v. Schroeder Music Publishing Co. Ltd. (1974).[21] Macaulay, an unknown young song writer, entered into a standard form agreement with Schroeder, whereby Schroeder acquired the right to publish all songs written by Macaulay for a five year period and, if Macaulay earned royalties exceeding £5,000 during the five year period, the agreement would be automatically extended for another five years. By contrast, Schroeder could terminate the contract at any time. Acting as a court of appeals, the House of Lords ruled that the contract was void because the terms of the contract were unreasonably asymmetrical and because the terms were contained in a standard form, rather than having been reached through a process of negotiation or bargaining.[22]

Process and/or Result? With this as background we are now in a (somewhat) better position to consider this question: What *kind* of defect is unconscionability? Is it a defect in process and/or result? There are both textual and conceptual reasons for regarding a defect in *result* as a necessary if not sufficient condition of unconscionability. The textual support can be found in the statute and cases we have considered. I say that there are conceptual reasons for regarding a defect in result as necessary to unconscionability because we can well imagine a relevant defect in voluntariness that would *not* entail unconscionability, as when, for paternalistic reasons, A coerces B to agree to terms that are manifestly in B's interests and (otherwise) eminently fair.

PROCESS

Even if a defect in result is *necessary* for unconscionability, is it *sufficient*? Or is a defect in process also necessary? One thing, I think, is clear. If unconscionability involves a defect in process, it is *not* a straightforward defect of voluntariness. There are three reasons to adopt this view. First, the standard defenses to a contract, such as duress and fraud, not only compromise voluntariness, they constitute reasons to doubt that a contract is advantageous to B as compared with the precontractual baseline. By contrast, the typical modern unconscionability case claims that the contract is *unjust,* and not that it is not advantageous at all. Second, if unconscionable contracts were involuntary, there would be no need to develop a principle of unconscionability. The standard defenses could do all the work. Third, there is no reason to think that freedom of contract was, in fact, violated in the typical case of unconscionability.

Now some disagree with the previous claim. Joel Feinberg, for example, argues that *Henningsen* can be understood as a case of duress because "the weaker party has no reasonable alternative to the terms offered by the stronger party and is thus forced to choose what to him appears the lesser evil. . . ."[23] I disagree. There may be *a* sense in which the offeree is "forced" to contract in some unconscionability cases, but it is quite distinct from the way in which coercion and duress are understood in the law. A contract signed at the point of a gun is made under duress not merely because A has "no reasonable choice" but to sign, but, and this is crucial, because A proposes to do something which is independently wrong—to shoot B—if B refuses to sign.[24] That B agrees to A's terms because B has no better alternative or even a decent alternative has *never* been definitive of coercion or duress. We do not say, for example, that a wage contract is involuntary just because B has to work and has no better alternative or that a patient's consent to surgery is invalid just because B wants to live and the only alternative is death.

Consider some of the other cases we have examined. Even if Murphy could not have purchased a television on more favorable terms, say because she was a poor credit risk and could not make a down-payment, we can hardly say that McNamara coerced her into signing the contract. Indeed, she had a reasonable alternative to this agreement—not to buy a television at all. And much the same could be said about the "add-on" clause in *Williams.* What of *Gianni* and *Macaulay*? Gantos was not proposing to harm Gianni if Gianni did not accept the contract on Gantos' terms. And the same was true for Schroeder. To say "these are my terms—take it or leave it" may be objectionable in certain circumstances, but it hardly seems coercive.

Contrast these cases with *The Port Caledonia.* In this case, we might say that the vessel agreed to pay £1,000 for a rope under duress, not because it had no reasonable alternative, but because the tugmaster had an *obligation* to rescue the vessel on better terms, that it was not morally or legally free to sail away. But in seeing why this case might constitute coercion, we see why the other cases do not. For it seems preposterous to say that McNamara, Walker-Thomas, Gantos and Schroeder had an independent obligation to deal with their respective parties on better terms or that they were not free to walk away from the deal.

If I am right in arguing that unconscionability does not require a defect in voluntariness, it does not follow that unconscionability turns on result alone.[25] Unconscionability might require a different sort of procedural defect, but then we would have to explain just what this procedural defect involves and why—when combined with a defect in result—it deserves a special status.

RESULT

Let us assume that a contract is minimally advantageous to B as compared with the precontractual baseline. There are two ways in which we might regard the *terms* of a contract as unconscionable: (1) *harshness*—the terms may be particularly harsh for B; (2) *disproportionality*—A's benefit from the agreement is exorbitant or disproportionate to B's gain. It is a further question as to whether, as Joel Feinberg suggests, an unconscionable contract must be both harsh *and* disproportionate.

When courts find that a contract is unconscionably harsh, they tend to focus on the non-monetary terms of the contract as contrasted with the monetary price. In principle, of course, there can be no rigid distinction between monetary and non-monetary terms. A contract represents a package of price, quality, financial provisions, and risks. Harsh *terms* may be compensated by a relatively generous *price*. Suppose, for example, that a couple prefers to hire a live-in nanny who will agree not to entertain boy-friends at home.[26] If the couple is prepared to pay a wage premium in order to hire on its preferred terms, then there is hardly anything unconscionable with the arrangement, even if it would otherwise be viewed as excessively demanding.[27] The nanny cannot legitimately complain that the terms are unfair, particularly if she could have secured her preferred terms for a lower wage.

Why do unconscionability cases tend to focus on terms rather than (monetary) price?[28] First, because price is a continuous variable whereas non-monetary terms have a binary quality, it may be easier to make judgments about the unconscionability of contractual terms. Second, although a price may be *exorbitant*, it does not typically establish an *oppressive relation* that endures over time. By contrast, some contractual terms establish just such relations. Third, there may be more explicit bargaining over price than over terms. Henningsen probably did bargain over price with Bloomfield Motors, and, if not, he could easily have taken his business elsewhere if he could get a better deal. On the other hand, he had no opportunity to bargain over the warranty with Bloomfield or anyone else. And so we have the appearance of a harsh result which one party cannot alter.

I say we have the "appearance" of a harsh result because, as we say, appearances can be deceiving. When harsh terms are clearly compensated monetarily, as with the nanny, we are less apt to regard them as unacceptable. But no such comparison is possible when the *same* terms are used among competitors. Nonetheless, it is possible that automobile buyers have, in effect, been compensated (without their asking to be compensated in *this* way) in advance—that, in principle, Chrysler would have been willing to allow Henningsen to purchase a far more inclusive warranty, one which included insurance for injuries, for an added premium. If so, we would need to ask why consumers do not get to choose high price/easy terms over low price/harsh terms, but the fact remains that Henningsen received a price discount for accepting harsh terms.

To put the point slightly differently, what appear to be extremely harsh terms—*ex post*—may not be harsh when considered *ex ante*. Consider *Macaulay*. Macaulay signed on with Schroeder—putting himself at risk for a ten year commitment—when he was an unknown songwriter. It is entirely possible that a music publisher will make a profit on only 10% of their unknown songwriters. Schroeder is willing to lose money on 90% of such clients only because it makes a significant profit on the other 10%.[29] The successful songwriter may feel exploited, but only because his vision is limited. The reasonableness of contractual terms must be evaluated against the background of the risks involved.

And this gives rise to the second point, namely, that what *appear* to be harsh terms may better reflect the buyer's risk than the seller's greed. (Re)consider the "add-on" provision of Williams's agreement with Walker-Thomas.[30] Given the high probability that Williams would default, given that her purchases were likely to depreciate quickly and that repossession of the sole item in case of default would entail a loss for Walker-Thomas, it is possible that the only way for her to have received more favorable *terms* was for her to pay a higher down-payment on the goods involved.[31]

One final point about harshness. It would be a mistake to claim that a contract is unconscionably harsh only when B's utility is not significantly enhanced as contrasted with the pre-contractual position. For some, nay most, allegedly unconscionable contracts are ones in which B's utility is *greatly* enhanced, as when the vessel gained its rescue for £1,000. If this is so, either harshness is not a straightforward function of utility gain or many contracts which have been thought to be unconscionably harsh are, in fact, not unconscionably harsh.

Let us now consider disproportionality. It is commonly thought that an agreement is exploitative or unconscionable when A gets much more value from the exchange than B, that a fair transaction is "one in which the surplus is divided (approximately) equally."[32]

But how should we conceptualize equal gain? A famous example asks how a rich man and a poor man should agree to share $200.

> The rich man could argue for a $150–$50 split in his favor because it would grieve the poor man more to lose $50 than the rich man to lose $150 . . . an arbitrator, keeping in mind the needs of the rich man and the poor man, might suggest the reverse split.[33]

If we measure a party's gain in terms of utility, then the rich man's argument is extremely persuasive. Similarly, in the *Port Caledonia,* there is every reason to think that the vessel gained more utility from being rescued than the tugmaster received from £1,000. So if unconscionability has to do with A's and B's relative gains, we must rely on independent or "objective" criteria for measuring their gains, or claim that A's gain is exorbitant even if A gains *less* than B (because, say, in a normal transaction, B *should* gain much more than A), or conclude that many allegedly unconscionable contracts are not in fact unconscionable.

Suppose we say that A's gain is disproportionate if its profits are—by some general standard—supracompetitive. This standard would not yield unconscionability in cases such as *Henningsen, Gianni,* and *Macaulay,* for despite concerns about the terms of the contracts, there is simply no evidence that these businesses generated supracompetitive profits. But what of businesses which prey on the poor as in *Murphy* and *Williams*? Here, too, there is no reason to think that these contracts generate exorbitant profit margins. Indeed, if these businesses were especially profitable, we would have to explain why potential competitors allow sellers to garner monopoly profits rather than enter the business themselves and, *ex hypothesi,* drive the price down. There are, then, two possibilities: (1) if unconscionability requires supracompetitive profits, then many contracts which are thought to be unconscionable are not; (2) if these contracts are unconscionable, then unconscionability does *not* require exorbitant or disproportionate profits.

STANDARD FORMS

We have seen that allegations of unconscionability often refer to allegedly onerous provisions which are contained in standard form contracts. What *precisely* was the problem in *Macaulay* or *Henningsen* or *Williams*? True, in some cases, the offeror may have known more about the content and effects of the contract than the offeree. And an asymmetry of information may well create an exploitable inequality between the parties. But, and by contrast with claims that are frequently made about the use of standard forms, it is simply *not* true that the "take-it-or-leave-it" character of standard forms typically arises in non-competitive industries. Critics of standard forms have failed to note that virtually *all* transactions occur on a "take-it-or-leave-it" basis in a truly competitive market. In a truly competitive market, *no one* gets to negotiate *anything.*[34] Everyone is a "price taker." The seller must offer the equilibrium price and the buyer must either pay the price or do without.

On this view, the use of standard forms occurs in a competitive market because they reduce transaction costs. To require or even encourage bargaining in individual transactions would be expensive, and the offeree would end up paying some if not all of those costs or would be driven out of the market entirely. In principle, then, the use of standard forms in a competitive market should be beneficial to the *class* of offerees, although not always to particular offerees.

If this is so, how can we also explain the apparently onerous terms to which the courts have objected in *Henningsen, Macaulay, Williams,* and the like? If Mr. Henningsen would have preferred a better warranty, albeit perhaps at a higher price, why was it not offered by Bloomfield Motors or another dealer? If the "add-on" provision in Williams's contract with Walker-Thomas Furniture was, in fact, a bad deal, why wasn't some competitor offering a better deal—not out of kindness, but in order to make a buck?[35]

One possibility is that these markets are not competitive, but there is no evidence that this is so. A second possibility is that market imperfections remain even in a reasonably competitive market, and that a more perfect market would have produced a better package of price and terms. But there is, of course, a third possibility, namely, that when all is said and done the allegedly onerous terms provide the maximum benefit to the offeree—given the risks inherent in contracting with the offeree.[36] If we employ the doctrine of unconscionability to benefit the exploited party, then we need to engage in careful economic analysis to determine whether the allegedly harsh terms actually optimize the weaker party's benefits—given his or her background positions.

INEQUALITY OF BARGAINING POWER

Let us take another tack, by considering the notion of "inequality of bargaining power," the concept that appears to be the *gravamen* of virtually all unconscionability cases, despite the fact that it has received precious little analysis as to its defining characteristics or its normative force. At the broadest level, there are two questions to which we want answers: (1) What constitutes an inequality of bargaining power? (2) What are the normative upshots of such inequalities?

What gives A greater bargaining power than B?[37] We can begin by distinguishing between *bargaining ability,* which is a function of one's personal characteristics (e.g., information, toughness, patience, perceptiveness, etc.) and *bargaining potential,* which is primarily a function of one's external resources or circumstances. Put colloquially, bargaining ability concerns how well one plays one's cards, whereas bargaining potential is a function of the cards themselves.[38]

Now some unconscionability cases appear to involve problems of bargaining ability. Herbert Bundy's agreement was set aside because he made an agreement for which he incurred risks but for which he received virtually nothing in return. To the extent that "inequality of bargaining power" refers to defects in capacity, it is relatively unproblematic. For it represents a defect in voluntariness and efficiency.[39] But what of those "one-sided" contracts which result from an inequality of bargaining *potential*? How can we explain *Henningsen, Gianni,* and *Macaulay*—all of which allegedly involved an inequality of bargaining power? There is no reason to doubt anyone's competence or rationality in these cases. Nonetheless, the courts appear to be claiming that there were gross asymmetries between the parties with respect to bargaining *potential* and that these asymmetries led to an unjust result.

What constitutes inequality in bargaining potential? Two potential candidates—size and necessity—can be set aside. Consider size. Although the image of the lonely individual facing the large corporation seems to have figured in several decisions, this model is quite misleading. I do not think that the contemporary (1991) automobile buyer is at a disadvantage in bargaining (through the dealer) with General Motors.[40] For size is irrelevant when the "larger" party needs the "smaller" party more than the other way around. Necessity is similarly irrelevant. The fact that B needs a good—even in order to live—does not give A any special power over B *if* there is a competitive market among sellers of the good.[41]

It might be thought that the more resources one brings to a bargaining situation, the greater one's bargaining power. But this, too, is incorrect.

> *The Investment Case.* B needs $500 for a venture that will yield $1,000. B is prepared to contribute $400, which is all that he has, but he needs $100 from A, who is quite wealthy.

Although B is contributing more resources, A has more bargaining potential. Suppose that A proposes that the $1,000 be divided thus: A gets $400, B gets $600. This gives A a 300% return on his investment, while B gets a 50% return on his investment. This may look unfair. It may *be* unfair. But A's threat to walk if B does not accept his proposal is credible precisely because a proportional split (where A receives $200 and B receives $800) does *not,* in fact, do much for A—given his current position.

The general point is, then, that bargaining potential is not a function of size or necessity or resource contribution. It is a function of a party's "threat advantage"—his willingness not to contract if his proposal is not accepted. And that is largely a function of a party's utilitarian gain from the precontractual baseline. A has a threat advantage because A stands to lose less if agreement is not reached. Put slightly differently, it is precisely because the stronger party gets *less* utility from a proposed bargain that he is able to get a greater share of objective resources.

Assume that A has greater bargaining potential than B. What follows—normatively speaking? I want briefly to make five points. First, we need a moral principle of fair division. For unless we can say something about how the surplus *ought* to be divided, we cannot say that an agreement is *morally* one sided—however unequal the distribution appears.

Second, although rational choice theory has made important contributions to a special normative problem—what ideally rational bargainers would do in a bargaining situation—there is no reason to think that a rational choice solution to the bargaining problem provides us with the best principle of fair division.

Third, there are no unproblematic solutions to the normative problem. Although this is not the place to probe this question in detail, let me mention but two principles which we might consider. At first glance, equal utility gain is an attractive moral principle. It is frequently said that a contract is just when it benefits both parties to the same extent. Unfortunately, and as we have already seen, equal utility may well prescribe exactly the sorts of distributions that motivated the concern with inequality of bargaining potential.

And so we might look to the proportionality principle—"one that distributes the cooperative surplus in proportion to the contributions of individuals. . . ."[42] Even if this principle were morally attractive, it raises thorny questions as to how to measure a party's contribution. Should a party's contribution be evaluated in "objective" terms or in terms of utility, in which case each $100 from B is worth *more* than $100 from A? And should a party's contribution be understood as its *pre-cooperative* value or its value to the cooperative activity? Is A's contribution of $100 a contribution of $100 (as compared with B's contribution of $400) or is it a contribution which made it possible to realize a $500 gain? In *The Port Caledonia,* for example, should we say that the tug is contributing a rope (which, *ex hypothesi,* is not worth that much) or is he contributing that which *saves a vessel* (which, *ex hypothesi,* is worth a lot)? And what is the vessel contributing? Its needs for rescue?

I do not want to deny that there may be solution(s) to the problem of fair division. I do want to claim that absent some principle of fair division, it is not clear that the alleged injustices that arise from inequalities of bargaining power are, in fact, unjust.

And that gives rise to the fourth point, the problem of background endowments. Even if the parties abide by reasonable principles of fair division, the resulting bargain may be unjust if the background conditions are unjust. Indeed, even scrupulous adherence to principles of fair bargaining may simply pass through unjust background endowments.

The fifth point about inequalities of bargaining power is this. That a bargain results in an unjust distribution does not entail that we should prevent such injustices from occurring. If it is desirable to allow B to improve his situation, and if we assume that the background injustices notwithstanding, A is under no moral requirement to provide that improvement, then it is at least arguable that contract law should uphold bargains that result from inequalities of bargaining potential. It is one thing to disallow contracts in which the strong "push the weak to the wall," as in *Bundy,* and quite another to disallow contracts in which the strong find the weak "*at* the wall," and where the contract will give the weak a little distance.

CONCLUSIONS

So let us take stock.

The first point is this. Some allegedly unconscionable contracts are not only not obviously unconscionable, they may be eminently fair. I see no reason to think that Schroeder took unfair advantage of Macaulay or to doubt that the *ex ante* value of the contract reflected the genuine risks of dealing with unknown songwriters. Similarly, and without knowing more, it is entirely possible that Gantos's contract with Gianni is best understood as an assignment of risk for which Gianni was compensated in the price it receives from retailers to whom it sells. More generally, it is a gross mistake to think that we can assess the fairness of an agreement by simple inspection of its terms. Unlike pornography, we cannot always tell unconscionability when we see it.

But other cases are more troublesome and we may remain concerned about the contract even after engaging in careful analysis. Let us classify putatively unconscionable contracts on two criteria: (1) whether the contract is beneficial to B as contrasted with the precontractual baseline; (2) whether the contract is extremely profitable to A. In principle, then, we can identify four types of unconscionable contracts: (a) harmful/high profit; (b) harmful/low profit; (c) beneficial/high profit; (d) beneficial/low profit.

As we have seen, contracts of type (a) and (b) will occur when B does not understand or lacks the capacity to understand the terms of the contract or the value of the goods that have been purchased or when B is placed under such stress that he cannot resist entering into a non-advantageous transaction (hence rules providing for a "cooling off" period for contracts made with door-to-door salespersons). In these cases, unconscionability is a relatively unproblematic form of paternalism, where we seek to protect B from harming himself because we have reason to doubt the full voluntariness of his decision.

There is, however, no reason to assume that contracts which are harmful to B typically generate high profits for A. There is, for example, no reason to assume that Lloyd's bank was making a high profit in its dealings with Bundy. Rather, its behavior may have been unconscionable precisely because it sought to avoid a loss when it should have swallowed it. Consider *Murphy* as a type (b) contract, say because the cost of the rental plan exceeded the value of the television to Murphy and because "rent to own" plans are not extraordinarily profitable, because many televisions are returned after a short period having depreciated greatly in value. In that case, the contracts were unconscionable not because A's profits are exorbitant, but because we would prefer that *no one* deal with consumers on terms that are likely to prove harmful to them. If one cannot profitably deal with a class of consumers on better terms, it is better that one not deal with them at all.

Let us now consider type (c) cases, where A makes a high profit yet the agreement is beneficial to B. This will typically occur when there is some sort of market imperfection. Consider *The Port Caledonia*. Given the choice between contracting with the tug on "extortionate" terms and not contracting at all, the vessel will prefer the "freedom to choose." But the vessel might prefer to be *prevented* from entering into an "extortionate" agreement with the tug if the tug would then rescue the vessel on better terms. Here the argument for unconscionability is not paternalistic but *strategic*. It is in the vessel's interest (or the class of vessels) to have its bargaining range limited, not because the vessel doesn't *know* what is in its interest, but because limiting its options puts it in a stronger bargaining position.[43] Here the doctrine of unconscionability effectively seeks to replicate the results of a more perfect market. It supplies the price that the tug would have charged had there been a competitive market for rescues.

But the most interesting and difficult cases are the beneficial/low profit contracts. *Henningsen* and *Williams* may both exemplify this situation, but there are important differences between them. In one type of case, perhaps illustrated by *Henningsen,* there is an information and collective action problem which can be solved on Pareto superior terms. In the second type, perhaps illustrated by *Williams,* no Pareto superior moves are available.

Suppose that most car buyers would be better off with a less limited warranty, even if it required them to pay a higher price. For some reason, automobile manufacturers have settled on low price/harsh terms contracts, but they are quite prepared to offer high price/soft terms contracts so long as this does not put them at a competitive disadvantage. If we declare that the low price/harsh terms contracts are void for unconscionability, then most buyers will be better off and the manufacturers will not be worse off. Declaring the contracts unconscionable serves to create a larger social surplus—where the buyer gets virtually all of the increase. This may be an eminently sensible reason to interfere with the market, but it has little to do with inequalities of bargaining power or wrongful exploitation.

There is another type (d) case which deserves to be mentioned. Suppose that some automobile buyers have much greater bargaining ability than others. Because all dealers encounter a comparable mix of good and bad bargainers, they must "take advantage" of the bad bargainers if they are to stay in business. If we prevent dealers from exploiting the bad bargainers, say by reducing price dispersion, then the bad bargainers would gain, but the good bargainers would lose. For the bad bargainers were not actually being exploited by the dealers, they were being exploited by the good bargainers. It may well turn out that many cases of unconscionability are like this: prohibiting people from entering unconscionable contracts shifts the benefits *among* the offerees, but not between the class of offerees and the offerors.

But the most difficult cases arise when contractual terms are minimally beneficial to B, generate only competitive profits to A, and no Pareto superior contracts are available. Suppose (what is probably not quite true) that Williams's contract with Walker-Thomas accurately and fairly reflected the risks of dealing with very poor customers and that Williams did not underestimate the costs involved or overestimate the value of the appliance. This was a problem of poverty, not ignorance. Let us also assume, for the sake of argument, that the background endowments are *unjust,* that Williams would not be (so) poor in a just society.

Should we refuse to enforce such contracts on grounds of unconscionability? Assuming that we could reliably distinguish these contracts from the others, then if the only justification of unconscionability is to protect the exploited party, then the answer seems to be no. There are, however, several additional types of arguments for refusing to enforce unconscionable contracts in such cases which might be mentioned.

The first and welfarist line of argument maintains that unconscionable contracts have negative externalities, they generate psychic disutility for other members of the society. I am inclined to think that these considerations have some *causal* importance in explaining the appeal of unconscionability law, but it is hard to see why they have any moral significance. For it may well be said that if we are not prepared to rectify the unjust background conditions themselves, it would be self indulgent to prevent people from improving on their admittedly unjust situation just because such contracts make us uncomfortable.

A second line of argument takes justice a bit more seriously. This view notes that principles of justice affect social behavior and helps to explain the sorts of transactions that do and do not occur. There is a growth industry in economics dedicated to the proposition that rational actor models do not explain everything, that sellers will often accept less than they would receive if they acted as rational maximizers and that buyers will often refuse to pay an "exorbitant" price even though a rational actor model would predict that they would. On this view, principles of fair division are important social and cultural goods. And from that perspective, the doctrine of unconscionability can be understood as one way that society signals its commitment to principles of fair division. Once again, it is important to note that this line of argument justifies a doctrine of unconscionability by appeal to its effects on third parties.

Thirdly, I wish to mention a class of perfectionist arguments although I shall not defend them here. These arguments maintain that it would be wrong to allow parties to enter into certain forms of relation even though they prefer to do so and even though it would improve their welfare. These arguments could take at least two different forms. First, we could argue that a person is *morally* harmed—degraded—when he enters into an unjust relation that there is a sense in which entering into an unconscionable contract is, in *some* sense, bad for B. The problem here is that absent some argument, there is no reason to believe that this is so.

A second view takes a different tack. On that view, unconscionable agreements may be bad even if they are bad for no one. On this view, unconscionability is "a free-floating evil."[44] It might be said that it is wrong to allow unjust relations to occur, even when (as contrasted with the world in which they do not occur) they are not bad for anyone—just as some versions of retributivism claim that it is good that wrongdoers are punished even when it's not good for anyone. I do not know if one or both of these perfectionist lines of argument can be sustained. But something like them may have to be sustained if we are going to justify prohibiting at least some unconscionable contracts.

NOTES

1. Murphy v. McNamara, 38 Conn. Super. 183, 416 A. 2d 170 (1979). The injunction was granted, but McNamara was permitted to file suit for the difference between the amount Murphy had already paid and the value of the set.
2. *Id.* at 416 A.2d at 177.
3. Some may argue that there is, in the final analysis, no distinction between these justifications. For the purpose of the present argument, I do not need to take a position on that argument.
4. See Charles Fried, *Contract As Promise* (Cambridge, MA: Harvard University Press, 1981).
5. The classic defense of this view is Richard Posner, *Economic Analysis of Law* (Boston: Little Brown, 1977).
6. Arthur Leff, "Unconscionability and the Code—The Emperor's New Clause," 115 *U. Pa. L. Rev.* 485, 486 (1967). These are necessary but not sufficient requirements of a valid contract. An agreement which meets these criteria may be unenforceable on paternalistic grounds, as when a tenant is not permitted to waive a warranty of habitability, because it threatens to harm third parties, or because society has decided that certain goods should not be "commodified"—for example, votes, drugs, or sex. More generally, an agreement which is against "public policy" is not enforceable, even though it may meet the tests of capacity, assent, and consideration.
7. Lord Nottingham in *Maynard v. Moseley* 3 Swans, 651, at 655, 36 Eng. Rep. 1009 (1676), cited in S. M. Waddams, *The Law of Contracts,* 326 (2d ed. 1984).
8. S. M. Waddams, *The Law of Contracts,* 326.
9. *The Port Caledonia and the Anna* (1903), p. 184, 190. Quoted in S. M. Waddams, *Unconscionability in Contracts,* 39 *Mod. L. Rev.* 369, 385 (1976). Also see Lord Goff of Chieveley and Gareth Jones, *The Law of Restitution* 267 (3d ed. 1986).
10. In addition, equity cases typically involved a claim of *specific performance.* Unlike many modern cases of unconscionability, equity cases did not generally involve a dispute about the price of

a transaction or an effort to have the transaction go through on more favorable terms. Rather, the promise demanded transfer of the land and the promisor sought to overturn the transaction in its entirety. See Leff, *supra* note 6.

11. Thomas M. Quinn, et al., *Uniform Commercial Code Commentary and Law Digest* 2-94 (1978).
12. It seems that unconscionability is defined as "a matter of *law*" rather than a matter of *fact* in order to make it easier to appeal a lower court's decision.
13. 32 N. J. 385, 161A2d 69 (1960).
14. 350 F.2d 445 (D.C. Cir. 1965).
15. *Id.,* at 447.
16. *Id.,* at 449.
17. *Id.,* at 450, quoting 1 Corbin, *Contracts* §128 (1963). Although the Court did not claim that the contract was unconscionable in light of these criteria, it concluded that the District Court had a legal basis for considering the question. Judge Danaher, dissenting, maintained that Williams knew just where she stood, that the pricing and credit policies may have been reasonably consistent with the risk of default. *Id.*, at 450.
18. 151 Mich. App. 598, 391 N.W. 2d 760 (1986).
19. *Id.,* at 762.
20. 3 W.L.R. 501 (1974).
21. 1 W.L.R. 1308 (1974).
22. Actually, the Court noted that the agreement had been signed "with a few alterations"—implying that at least some negotiation had, in fact, occurred. *Id.*, at 1309.
23. *Id.,* pp. 251–52.
24. See my *Coercion* (Princeton: Princeton University Press, 1987), Chapter 2.
25. "... despite indications of increasing freedom for courts to manipulate contract terms, the concept of unconscionability still directs judicial inquiry to the bargaining behavior of the parties." Lewis Kornhauser, *Unconscionability in Standard Forms,* 64 *Cal. L. Rev.* 1151, 1162 (1976).
26. I borrow this example from Brian Barry's, "Lady Chatterley's Lover and Doctor Fischer's Bomb Party: Liberalism, Pareto Optimality and the Problem of Objectionable Preferences," in his collection, *Democracy, Power and Justice* (Oxford: Clarendon Press, 1989), p. 374.
27. *Id.*
28. I shall use the term "price" to refer to *monetary* price in what follows although it is obvious that the terms are part of the overall price of a contract.
29. For an interesting analysis of this case, see M. J. Trebilcock, *The Doctrine of Inequality of Bargaining Power in the House of Lords,* 26 *U. Toronto L. J.* 359 (1976).
30. See Richard Epstein, *Unconscionability: A Critical Appraisal,* 18 *J. L. & Econ.* 293 (1975).
31. See *Id.*, at 307.
32. Robert Frank, *Passions within Reason* (New York: W. W. Norton, 1988), p. 164.
33. Duncan Kennedy, "Distributive and Paternalist Motives in Contract and Tort Law With Special Reference to Compulsory Terms and Unequal Bargaining Power," 41 *Md. L. Rev.* 563, 616 (1982).
34. [sic—missing]
35. As Duncan Kennedy puts it, "If there is competition among sellers, and good information about buyer preferences, sellers will offer whatever terms they think buyers will pay for." "Distributive and Paternalistic Motives in Contract and Tort Law," *Id.*
36. Richard Posner, *Economic Analysis of Law,* p. 85.
37. As Thomas Schelling reminds us, we must be very cautious. "'Bargaining power,' 'bargaining strength,' 'bargaining skill' suggest that the advantage goes to the powerful, the strong, or the skillful. It does, of course, if those qualities are defined to mean only that negotiations are won by those who win. But if the terms imply that it is an advantage to be more intelligent . . . or to have more financial resources, more physical strength . . . or more ability to withstand losses, then the term does a disservice. These qualities are by no means universal advantages in bargaining situations; they often have a contrary value." *The Strategy of Conflict* (New York: Oxford University Press, 1963), p. 22.
38. The distinction between bargaining ability and bargaining potential cannot be pressed too far. It appears, for example, that blacks and women pay more for new cars than white males, not because of animus, but because profit-maximizing dealers believe that blacks and women are less likely to shop around. If so, a black or a woman may have less bargaining power not because of some characteristic *qua* individual, but because of other people's perceptions. In this sense, we might count the *perception* of one's bargaining ability as an *external* resource. If this belief were false, and if only some dealers had this belief, then blacks and women would not pay more.

They would go to other dealers. Yet if many dealers have this false belief, then the market will still settle on a higher price for blacks and women. Ian Ayres, "Fair Driving: Gender and Race Discrimination in Retail Car Negotiations," 104 *Harv. L. Rev.* 817, 845 (1991).

39. I say *relatively* unproblematic, because it is not clear whether a contract should be nullified if A neither caused nor knowingly took advantage of B's incapacity.
40. Nor is Bethlehem Steel at a disadvantage in dealing with the (much larger) United States government when the government needs its ship-building capacity during a war.
41. As Duncan Kennedy remarks, "If there are many sellers of a necessity, none of them will be able to charge more than the going package of price and terms without losing all his buyers." *Supra*, note 35 at 618–19.
42. Jody S. Kraus and Jules L. Coleman, "Morality and the Theory of Rational Choice," in Peter Vallentyne (ed.) *Contractarianism and Rational Choice* (New York: Cambridge University Press, 1991), p. 267.
43. "What we have here is a situation in which someone may be better off doing a certain deal than not doing it if he is permitted to do it, but would be better off still if he were not permitted to do it." Brian Barry, "Lady Chatterley's Lover and Doctor Fischer's Bomb Party: Liberalism, Pareto Optimality, and the Problem of Objectionable Preferences," in Jon Elster and Aanund Hylland (eds.) *Foundations of Social Choice Theory* (Cambridge: Cambridge University Press, 1986), p. 21.
44. Joel Feinberg, *Harmless Wrongdoing* (New York: Oxford University Press, 1988).

47

Henningsen v. Bloomfield Motors, Inc.

Supreme Court of New Jersey, 1960.
32 N.J. 358, 161 A.2d 69.

FRANCIS, J. . . . The terms of the warranty are a sad commentary upon the automobile manufacturers' marketing practices. Warranties developed in the law in the interest of and to protect the ordinary consumer who cannot be expected to have the knowledge or capacity or even the opportunity to make adequate inspection of mechanical instrumentalities, like automobiles, and to decide for himself whether they are reasonably fit for the designed purpose. . . . But the ingenuity of the Automobile Manufacturers Association, by means of its standardized form, has metamorphosed the warranty into a device to limit the maker's liability. . . .

[W]hat effect should be given to the express warranty in question which seeks to limit the manufacturer's liability to replacement of defective parts, and which disclaims all other warranties, express or implied? In assessing its significance we must keep in mind the general principle that, in the absence of fraud, one who does not choose to read a contract before signing it, cannot later relieve himself of its burdens. . . . And in applying that principle, the basic tenet of freedom of competent parties to contract is a factor of importance. But in the framework of modern commercial life and business practices, such rules cannot be applied on a strict, doctrinal basis. The conflicting interests of the buyer and seller must be evaluated realistically and justly, giving due weight to the social policy evinced by the Uniform Sales Act, the progressive decisions of the courts engaged in administering it, the mass production methods of manufacture and distribution to the public, and the bargaining position occupied by the ordinary consumer in such an economy. This history of the law shows that legal doctrines, as first expounded, often prove to be inadequate under the impact of later experience. . . .

The traditional contract is the result of free bargaining of parties who are brought together by the play of the market, and who meet each other on a footing of approximate economic equality. In such a society there is no danger that freedom of contract will be a threat to the social order as a whole. But in present-day commercial life the standardized mass contract has appeared. It is used primarily by enterprises with strong bargaining power and position. "The weaker party, in need of the goods or services, is frequently not in a position to shop around for better terms, either because the author of the standard contract has a monopoly (natural or artificial) or because all competitors use the same clauses. His contractual intention is but a subjection more or less voluntary to terms dictated by the stronger party, terms whose consequences are often understood in a vague way, if at all." Kessler, "Contracts of Adhesion—Some Thoughts About Freedom of Contract," 43 Colum. L. Rev. 629, 632 (1943). . . .

The warranty before us is a standardized form designed for mass use. It is imposed upon the automobile consumer. He takes it or leaves it, and he must take it to buy an automobile. No bargaining is engaged in with respect to it. In fact, the dealer through whom it comes to the buyer is without authority to alter it; his function is ministerial—simply to deliver it. The form warranty is not only standard with Chrysler, but, as mentioned above, it is the uniform warranty of the Automobile Manufacturers Association. . . .

The gross inequality of bargaining position occupied by the consumer in the automobile industry is thus apparent. There is no competition among the car makers in the area of the express warranty. Where can the buyer go to negotiate for better protection? Such control and limitation of his remedies are inimical to the public welfare and, at the very least, call for great care by the courts to avoid injustice through application of strict common-law principles of freedom of contract. Because there is no competition among the motor vehicle manufacturers with respect to the scope of protection guaranteed to the buyer, there is no incentive on their part to stimulate good will in that field of public relations. Thus, there is lacking a factor existing in more competitive fields, one which tends to guarantee the safe construction of the article sold. . . .

Although the courts, with few exceptions, have been most sensitive to problems presented by contracts resulting from gross disparity in buyer-seller bargaining positions, they have not articulated a general principle condemning, as opposed to public policy, the imposition on the buyer of a skeleton warranty as a means of limiting the responsibility of the manufacturer. They have endeavored thus far to avoid a drastic departure from age-old tenets of freedom of contract by adopting doctrines of strict construction, and notice and knowledgeable assent by the buyer to the attempted exculpation of the seller. . . . Accordingly to be found in the cases are statements that disclaimers and the consequent limitation of liability will not be given effect if "unfairly procured"; . . . if not brought to the buyer's attention and he was not made understandingly aware of it; . . . or if not clear and explicit. . . .

The rigid scrutiny which the courts give to attempted limitations of warranties and of the liability that would normally flow from a transaction is not limited to the field of sales of goods. Clauses on baggage checks restricting the liability of common carriers for loss or damage in transit are not enforceable unless the limitation is fairly and honestly negotiated and understandingly entered into. If not called specifically to the patron's attention, it is not binding. It is not enough merely to show the form of a contract; it must appear also that the agreement was understandingly made. . . . The same holds true in cases of such limitations on parcel check room tickets, ... and on storage warehouse receipts; . . . on automobile parking lot or garage tickets or claim checks; . . . as to exculpatory clauses in leases releasing a landlord of apartments in a multiple dwelling house from all liability for negligence where inequality of bargaining exists, see Annot., 175 A.L.R. 8 (1948). . . .

It is true that the rule governing the limitation of liability cases last referred to is generally applied in situations said to involve services of a public or semi-public nature. Typical, of course, are the public carrier or storage or parking lot cases. . . . But in recent times the books have not been barren of instances of its application in private contract controversies. . . . Basically, the reason a contracting party offering services of a public or *quasi*-public nature has been held to the requirements of fair dealing, and, when it attempts to limit its liability, of securing the understanding consent of the patron or consumer, is because members of the public generally have no other means of fulfilling the specific need represented by the contract. Having in mind the situation in the automobile industry as detailed above, . . . there would appear to be no just reason why the principles of all of the cases set forth should not chart the course to be taken here.

It is undisputed that [the dealer] with whom Henningsen dealt did not specifically call attention to the warranty on the back of the purchase order. The form and the arrangement of its face, as described above, certainly would cause the minds of reasonable men to differ as to whether notice of a yielding of basic rights stemming from the relationship with the manufacturer was adequately given. The words "warranty" or "limited warranty" did not even appear in the fine print above the place for signature. . . .

But there is more than this. Assuming that a jury might find that the fine print referred to reasonably served the objective of directing a buyer's attention to the warranty on the reverse side, and, therefore, that he should be charged with awareness of its language, can it be said that an ordinary layman would realize what he was relinquishing in return for what he was being granted? Under the law, breach of warranty against defective parts or workmanship which caused personal injuries would entitle a buyer to damages even if due care were used in the manufacturing process. Because of the great potential for harm if the vehicle was defective, that right is the most important and fundamental one arising from the relationship. Difficulties so frequently encountered in establishing negligence in manufacture in the ordinary case, make this manifest. . . . Any ordinary layman of reasonable intelligence, looking at the phraseology, might well conclude that Chrysler was agreeing to replace defective parts and perhaps replace anything that went wrong because of defective workmanship during the first 90 days or 4,000 miles of operation, but that he would not be entitled to a new car. It is not unreasonable to believe that the entire scheme being conveyed was a proposed remedy for physical deficiencies in the car. *In the context* of this warranty, only the abandonment of all sense of justice would permit us to hold that, as a matter of law, the phrase "its obligation under this warranty being limited to making good at its factory any part or parts thereof" signifies to an ordinary reasonable person that he is relinquishing any personal injury claim that might flow from the use of a defective automobile. Such claims are nowhere mentioned. . . .

The task of the judiciary is to administer the spirit as well as the letter of the law. . . . [P]art of that burden is to protect the ordinary man against the loss of important rights through what, in effect, is the unilateral act of the manufacturer. . . . From the standpoint of the purchaser, there can be no arms length negotiating on the subject [of warranties]. Because his capacity for bargaining is so grossly unequal, the inexorable conclusion which follows is that he is not permitted to bargain at all. . . .

Public policy is a term not easily defined. Its significance varies as the habits and needs of a people may vary. It is not static and the field of application is an ever increasing one. A contract, or a particular provision therein, valid in one era may be wholly opposed to the public policy of another. . . . Public policy at a given time finds expression in the Constitution, the statutory law and in judicial decisions. In the area of sale of goods, the legislative will has imposed an implied warranty of merchantability as a general incident of sale of an automobile by description. The warranty does not depend upon the affirmative intention of the parties. It is a child of the law; it annexes itself to the contract because of the very nature of the transaction. . . . The judicial process has recognized a right to recover damages for personal injuries arising from a breach of that warranty. The disclaimer of the implied warranty and exclusion of all obligations except those specifically assumed by the express warranty signify a studied effort to frustrate that protection. True, the Sales Act authorizes agreements between buyer and seller qualifying the warranty obligations. But quite obviously the Legislature contemplated lawful stipulations (which are determined by the circumstances of a particular case) arrived at freely by parties of relatively equal bargaining strength. The lawmakers did not authorize the automobile manufacturer to use its grossly disproportionate bargaining power to relieve itself from liability and to impose on the ordinary buyer, who in effect has no real freedom of choice, the grave danger of injury to himself and others that attends the sale of such a dangerous instrumentality as a defectively made automobile. . . . [W]e are of the opinion that Chrysler's attempted disclaimer of an implied warranty of merchantability and of the obligations arising therefrom is so inimical to the public good as to compel an adjudication of its invalidity. . . . The principles that have been expounded as to the obligation of the manufacturer apply with equal force to the separate express warranty of the dealer. . . .

[W]e conclude that the disclaimer of an implied warranty of merchantability by the dealer, as well as the attempted elimination of all obligations other than replacement of defective parts, are violative of public policy and void. . . . [T]he judgments in favor of the plaintiffs and against the defendants are affirmed.

48

Williams v. Walker-Thomas Furniture Co.

350 F. 2d 445 (1965)

J. SKELLY WRIGHT, Circuit Judge: Appellee, Walker-Thomas Furniture Company, operates a retail furniture store in the District of Columbia. During the period from 1957 to 1962 each appellant in these cases purchased a number of household items from Walker-Thomas, for which payment was to be made in installments. The terms of each purchase were contained in a printed form contract which set forth the value of the purchased item and purported to lease the item to appellant for a stipulated monthly rent payment. The contract then provided, in substance, that title would remain in Walker-Thomas until the total of all the monthly payments made equaled the stated value of the item, at which time appellants could take title. In the event of a default in the payment of any monthly installment, Walker-Thomas could repossess the item.

The contract further provided that "the amount of each periodical installment payment to be made by [purchaser] to the Company under this present lease shall be inclusive of and not in addition to the amount of each installment payment to be made by [purchaser] under such prior leases, bills or accounts; *and all payments now and hereafter made by [purchaser] shall be credited pro rata on all outstanding leases, bills and accounts* due, the Company by [purchaser] at the time each such payment is made." (Emphasis added.) The effect of this rather obscure provision was to keep a balance due on every item purchased until the balance due on all items, whenever purchased, was liquidated. As a result, the debt incurred at the time of purchase of each item was secured by the right to repossess all the items previously purchased by the same purchaser, and each new item purchased automatically became subject to a security interest arising out of the previous dealings.

On May 12, 1962, appellant Thorne purchased an item described as a Daveno, three tables, and two lamps, having total stated value of $391.10. Shortly thereafter, he defaulted on his monthly payments and appellee sought to replevy all the items purchased since the first transaction in 1958. Similarly, on April 17, 1962, appellant Williams bought a stereo set of stated value of $514.95.[1] She too defaulted shortly thereafter, and appellee sought to replevy all the items purchased since December, 1957. The Court of General Sessions granted judgment for appellee. The District of Columbia Court of Appeals affirmed, and we granted appellants' motion for leave to appeal to this court.

Appellants' principal contention, rejected by both the trial and the appellate courts below, is that these contracts, or at least some of them, are unconscionable and, hence, not enforceable. In its opinion in Williams v. Walker-Thomas Furniture Company, 198 A.2d 914, 916 (1964), the District of Columbia Court of Appeals explained its rejection of this contention as follows:

> "Appellant's second argument presents a more serious question. The record reveals that prior to the last purchase appellant had reduced the balance in her account to $164. The last purchase, a stereo set, raised the balance due to $678. Significantly, at the time of this and the preceding purchases, appellee was aware of appellant's financial position. The reverse side of the stereo contract listed the name of appellant's social worker and her $218 monthly stipend from the government. Nevertheless, with full knowledge that appellant had to feed, clothe and support herself and seven children on this amount, appellee sold her a $514 stereo set.

"We cannot condemn too strongly appellee's conduct. It raises serious questions of sharp practice and irresponsible business dealings. A review of the legislation in the District of Columbia affecting retail sales and the pertinent decisions of the highest court in this jurisdiction disclose, however, no ground upon which this court can declare the contract in question contrary to public policy. We note that were the Maryland Retail Installment Sales Act, Art. 83, §§128–153, or its equivalent, in force in the District of Columbia, we could grant appellant appropriate relief. We think Congress should

[1]At the time of this purchase her account showed a balance of $164 still owing from her prior purchases. The total of all the purchases made over the years in question came to $1,800. The total payments amounted to $14,00.

consider corrective legislation to protect the public from such exploitive contracts as were utilized in the case at bar."

We do not agree that the court lacked the power to refuse enforcement to contracts found to be unconscionable. In other jurisdictions, it has been held as a matter of common law that unconscionable contracts are not enforceable.[2] While no decision of this court so holding has been found, the notion that an unconscionable bargain should not be given full enforcement is by no means novel. In Scott v. United States, 79 U.S. (12 Wall.) 443, 445 20 L.Ed. 438 (1870), the Supreme Court stated:

> ". . . If a contract be unreasonable and unconscionable, but not void for fraud, a court of law will give to the party who sues for its breach damages, not according to its letter, but only such as he is equitably entitled to. . . ."[3]

Since we have never adopted or rejected such a rule,[4] the question here presented is actually one of first impression.

Congress has recently enacted the Uniform Commercial Code, which specifically provides that the court may refuse to enforce a contract which it finds to be unconscionable at the time it was made. 28 D. C. Code § 2–302 (Supp. IV 1965). The enactment of this section, which occurred subsequent to the contracts here in suit, does not mean that the common law of the District of Columbia was otherwise at the time of enactment, nor does it preclude the court from adopting a similar rule in the exercise of its powers to develop the common law for the District of Columbia. In fact, in view of the absence of prior authority on the point, we consider the congressional adoption of § 2–302 persuasive authority for following the rationale of the cases from which the section is explicitly derived.[5] Accordingly, we hold that where the element of unconscionability is present at the time a contract is made, the contract should not be enforced.

Unconscionability has generally been recognized to include an absence of meaningful choice on the part of one of the parties together with contract term which are unreasonably favorable to the other party.[6] Whether a meaningful choice is present in a particular case can only be determined by consideration of all the circumstances surrounding the transaction. In many cases the meaningfulness of the choice is negated by a gross inequality of bargaining power.[7] The manner in which the contract was entered is also relevant to this consideration. Did each party to the contract, considering his obvious education or lack of it, have a reasonable opportunity to understand the terms of the contract, or were the important terms hidden in a maze of fine print and minimized by deceptive sales practices? Ordinarily, one who signs an agreement without full knowledge of its terms might be held to assume the risk that he has entered a

---

[2]Campbell Soup Co. v. Wentz, 3 Cir., 172 F.2d 80 (1948); Indianapolis Morris Plan Corporation v. Sparks, 132 Ind.App. 145, 172 N.E.2d 899 (1961); Henningsen v. Bloomfield Motors, Inc., 32 N.J. 358, 161 A.2d 69, 84–96, 75 A.L.R.2d 1 (1960). *Cf.* 1 CORBIN, CONTRACTS § 128 (1963).

[3]See Luing v. Peterson, 143 Minn. 6, 172 N.W. 692 (1919); Greer v. Tweed, N.Y. C.P., 13 Abb.Pr., N.S., 427 (1872); Schnell v. Nell, 17 Ind. 29 (1861); and see generally the discussion of the English authorities in Hume v. United States, 132 U.S. 406, 10 S.Ct. 134, 33 L.Ed. 393 (1889).

[4]While some of the statements in the court's opinion in District of Columbia v. Harlan & Hollingsworth Co., 30 App.D.C. 270 (1908), may appear to reject the rule, in reaching its decision upholding the liquidated damages clause in that case the court considered the circumstances existing at the time the contract was made, see 30 App.D.C. at 279, and applied the usual rule on liquidated damages. See 5 CORBIN CONTRACTS §§ 1054–1075 (1964); *Note,* 72 YALE L.J. 723, 746–755 (1963). Compare Jaeger v. O'Donoghue, 57 App.D.C. 191, 18 F.2d 1013 (1927).

[5]See Comment § 2–302, Uniform Commercial Code (1962). Compare *Note,* 45 VA.L.REV. 583, 590 (1959), where it is predicted that the rule of § 2–302 will be followed by analogy in cases which involve contracts not specifically covered by the section. *Cf.* 1 STATE OF NEW YORK LAW REVISION COMMISSION, REPORT AND RECORD OF HEARINGS ON THE UNIFORM COMMERCIAL CODE 108–110 (1954) (remarks of Professor Llewellyn).

[6]See Henningsen v. Bloomfield Motors, Inc., *supra* Note 2; Campbell Soup Co. v. Wentz, *supra* Note 2.

[7]See Henningsen v. Bloomfield Motors, Inc., supra Note 2, 161 A. 2d at 86, and authorities there cited. Inquiry into the relative bargaining power of the two parties is not an inquiry wholly divorced from the general question of unconscionability, since a one-sided bargain is itself evidence of the inequality of the bargaining parties. This fact was vaguely recognized in the common law doctrine of intrinsic fraud, that is, fraud which can be presumed from the grossly unfair nature of the terms of the contract. See the oft-quoted statement of Lord Hardwicke in Earl of Chesterfield v. Janssen, 28 Eng.Rep. 82, 100 (1751):

> ". . . [Fraud] may be apparent from the intrinsic nature and subject of the bargain itself; such as no man in his senses and not under delusion would make. . . ."

And *cf.* Hume v. United States, *supra* Note 3, 132 U.S. at 413, 10 S.Ct. at 137, where the Court characterized the English cases as "cases in which one party took advantage of the other's ignorance of arithmetic to impose upon him, and the fraud was apparent from the face of the contracts." See also Greer v. Tweed, *supra* Note 3.

one-sided bargain.[8] But when a party of little bargaining power, and hence little real choice, signs a commercially unreasonable contract with little or no knowledge of its terms, it is hardly likely that his consent, or even an objective manifestation of his consent, was ever given to all the terms. In such a case the usual rule that the terms of the agreement are not to be questioned[9] should be abandoned and the court should consider whether the terms of the contract are so unfair that enforcement should be withheld.[10]

In determining reasonableness or fairness, the primary concern must be with the terms of the contract considered in light of the circumstances existing when the contract was made. The test is not simple, nor can it be mechanically applied. The terms are to be considered "in the light of the general commercial background and the commercial needs of the particular trade or case."[11] Corbin suggests the test as being whether the terms are "so extreme as to appear unconscionable according to the mores and business practices of the time and place. " 1 CORBIN, *op. cit. supra* Note 2.[12] We think this formulation correctly states the test to be applied in those cases where no meaningful choice was exercised upon entering the contract.

Because the trial court and the appellate court did not feel that enforcement could be refused, no findings were made on the possible unconscionability of the contracts in these cases. Since the record is not sufficient for our deciding the issue as a matter of law, the cases must be remanded to the trial court for further proceedings.

So ordered.

DANAHER, Circuit Judge (dissenting):

The District of Columbia Court of Appeals obviously was as unhappy about the situation here presented as any of us can possibly be. Its opinion in the *Williams* case, quoted in the majority text, concludes: "We think Congress should consider corrective legislation to protect the public from such exploitive contracts as were utilized in the case at bar."

My view is thus summed up by an able court which made no finding that there had actually been sharp practice. Rather the appellant seems to have known precisely where she stood.

There are many aspects of public policy here involved. What is a luxury to some may seem an outright necessity to others. Is public oversight to be required of the expenditures of relief funds? A washing machine, e. g. , in the hands of a relief client might become a fruitful source of income. Many relief clients may well need credit, and certain business establishments will take long chances on the sale of items, expecting their pricing policies will afford a degree of protection commensurate with the risk. Perhaps a remedy when necessary will be found within the provisions of the "Loan Shark" law, D.C.CODE §§ 26–601 *et seq.* (1961).

I mention such matters only to emphasize the desirability of a cautious approach to any such problem, particularly since the law for so long has allowed parties such great latitude in making their own contracts. I dare say there must annually be thousands upon thousands of installment credit transactions in this jurisdiction, and one can only speculate as to the effect the decision in these cases will have.

I join the District of Columbia Court of Appeals in its disposition of the issues.

---

[8]See RESTATEMENT, CONTRACTS § 70 (1932); *Note,* 63 HARV. L.REV. 494 (1950). See also Daley v. People's Building, Loan & Savings Ass'n, 178 Mass. 13, 59 N.E. 452, 453 (1901), in which Mr. Justice Holmes, while sitting on the Supreme Judicial Court of Massachusetts, made this observation:

> ". . . Courts are less and less disposed to interfere with parties making such contracts as they choose, so long as they interfere with no one's welfare but their own. . . . It will be understood that we are speaking of parties standing in an equal position where neither has any oppressive advantage or power. . . ."

[9]This rule has never been without exception. In cases involving merely the transfer of unequal amounts of the same commodity, the courts have held the bargain unenforceable for the reason that "in such a case, it is clear, that the law cannot indulge in the presumption of equivalence between the consideration and the promise." 1 WILLISTON, CONTRACTS § 115 (3d ed. 1957).

[10]See the general discussion of "Boiler-Plate Agreements" in LLEWELLYN, THE COMMON LAW TRADITION 362–371 (1960).

[11]Comment, Uniform Commercial Code § 2–307.

[12]See Henningsen v. Bloomfield Motors, Inc., *supra* Note 2; Mandel v. Liebman, 303 N.Y. 88, 100 N.E.2d 149 (1951). The traditional test as stated in Greer v. Tweed, *supra* Note 3, 13 Abb.Pr.,N.S., at 429, is "such as no man in his senses and not under delusion would make on the one hand, and as no honest or fair man would accept, on the other."

49

LYNN BERAT

South African Contract Law: The Need for a Concept of Unconscionability

I. INTRODUCTION

Despite a decade of economic difficulties, caused in part by the imposition of sanctions, South Africa remains the economic powerhouse of southern Africa.[1] Now, as the ruling National Party and major opposition groups such as the African National Congress[2] ("ANC") seek to arrive at a new dispensation of the country's wealth, the future shape of the economy is a vexing issue.[3] South Africa's escape from its downward economic spiral requires economic growth. Such growth is especially important if Africans, who for decades have occupied an inferior position in South African society, are to participate fully in South Africa's economic life. To achieve this goal, contract law will have to be altered. In particular, the courts should develop a doctrine of unconscionability to safeguard the interests of the millions of Africans entering into contracts and other business transactions for the first time. As many Africans are disadvantaged by little or no education,[4] and are daunted by the prospect of dealing with an unfamiliar legal system,[5] it is imperative that such a doctrine exist to protect their rights. Currently, South African contract law contains no specific concept of unconscionability. The concept's position is the same as that in the United States in 1952, when jurist Arthur Corbin wrote:

> There is sufficient flexibility in the concepts of fraud, duress, misrepresentation, and undue influence, not to mention differences in economic bargaining power, to enable the courts to avoid enforcement of a bargain that is shown to be unconscionable by reason of gross inadequacy of consideration accompanied by other relevant factors.[6]

Indeed, these doctrines, which reflect South Africa's hybrid legal heritage, form the South African analogue to unconscionability. It now seems imperative that a more explicit concept of unconscionability similar to that found in the United States' Uniform Commercial Code[7] ("U.C.C.") be developed in transformed South Africa. This Article examines South Africa's hybrid legal heritage. It provides an overview of contract formation in South Africa and discusses the concepts of fraud, duress, and undue influence. Finally, this Article suggests that South Africa adopt a commercial code, giving special attention to formulating a concept of unconscionability.

A. The South African Legal Heritage

Scholars have characterized South African law as a hybrid or mixed legal system,[8] consisting mainly of Roman, Roman-Dutch, and English law.[9] Roman law evolved over twelve centuries, from around 753 B.C., the traditional date of Rome's founding, to A.D. 565, the date of Emperor Justinian's death.[10] Continuing

---

[1] *See* Lynn Berat, *Undoing and Redoing Business in South Africa: The Lifting of the Comprehensive Anti-Apartheid Act of 1986 and the Continuing Validity of State and Local Anti-Apartheid Legislation,* 6 CONN. J. INT'L. L. 7 (1991).

[2] The African National Congress is described in TOM LODGE, BLACK POLITICS IN SOUTH AFRICA SINCE 1945 (1983).

[3] *See* Berat, *supra* note 1, at 9–11; Lynn Berat, *The Courts and the Economy in a New South Africa: A Call for an Indexation Model,* 15 B.C. INT'L & COMP. L. REV. 1 (1992).

[4] *See generally* FRANCIS WILSON & MAPHELA RAMPHELE, UPROOTING POVERTY: THE SOUTH AFRICAN CHALLENGE (1988).

[5] The future of customary law, as opposed to the western-based South African national system, remains unresolved. For a discussion of this problem, see Lynn Berat, *Customary Law in the New South Africa: A Proposal,* 15 FORDHAM INT'L. L.J. 92 (1991).

[6] ARTHUR CORBIN, CORBIN ON CONTRACTS 188 (1952).

[7] Section 2-302 provides:

> (1) If the court as a matter of law finds the contract or any clause of the contract to have been unconscionable at the time it was made the court may refuse to enforce the contract, or it may enforce the remainder of the contract without the unconscionable clause as to avoid any unconscionable result.
>
> (2) When it is claimed or appears to the court that the contract or any clause thereof may be unconscionable the parties shall be afforded a reasonable opportunity to present evidence as to its commercial setting, purpose and effect to aid the court in making its determination.

U.C.C. § 2-302 (1990).

[8] Imre Zajtay & W. J. Hosten, *The Permanence of Roman Law Concepts in the Continental Legal System and South African Law,* 2 COMP. & INT'L L.J. S. AFR. 181, 197 (1969).

[9] *See* JOHN DUGARD, HUMAN RIGHTS AND THE SOUTH AFRICAN LEGAL ORDER 8 (1978).

[10] *See* W. J. HOSTEN ET AL., INTRODUCTION TO SOUTH AFRICAN LAW AND LEGAL THEORY 132 (1983) (discussing South Africa's mixed system of law).

through medieval times, Roman law had a major influence upon European institutions.[11] The late thirteenth century through the end of the sixteenth century marked the period of reception of Roman law into the law of the Netherlands. The resulting Roman-Dutch law "is a conglomerate of Roman law, Germanic customary law, feudal law, canon law," and natural law concepts. It enjoyed its classical period from the sixteenth century to the late eighteenth century.

The Dutch East India Company brought this classical Roman-Dutch law to the Cape of Good Hope in 1652, when it took possession of the Cape and founded a station there for its ships traveling the Netherlands to the Dutch East Indies route. Roman-Dutch law continued as the Cape's common law during the period of Dutch East India Company rule from 1652 to 1795. In 1795, Great Britain occupied the Cape, fearing that the French Republic would seize it. The Dutch East India Company formally capitulated to the British on September 16, 1795. The Articles of Capitulation empowered the Raad van Justitie, renamed the Court of Justice, to administer Roman-Dutch law in civil and criminal matters. In 1802, Britain entered into a truce with Napoleon, and, in March of that year, signed the Treaty of Amiens, restoring all of its recent colonial conquests except Ceylon and Trinidad. Thus, Great Britain ceded its authority to the Netherlands, which had become the Batavian Republic by that time. The British, however, remained cautious of Napoleon's colonial designs, and by 1806 again controlled the Cape.

British rule did not signal the end of Roman-Dutch law at the Cape. The Cape Articles of Capitulation of January 10 and 18, 1806, provided that "the Burghers and Inhabitants shall preserve all their Rights and Privileges which they have enjoyed hitherto."[12] Some scholars claim this provision ensured the perpetuation of Roman-Dutch law.[13] The well-established principle of English law that "the laws of a conquered country continue in force, until they are altered by the conqueror" also protected Roman-Dutch law.[14] However, the legal system at the Cape did not escape English influences. Indeed, the British government envisioned English law gradually assimilating Roman-Dutch law. In 1823, the British government appointed a commission to review colony affairs. Reporting in 1826 on judicial matters at the Cape, the commission suggested that the existing procedure should assimilate English procedure, future legislation should follow principles of English jurisprudence, and the courts should gradually adopt English common law.

In the years after 1826, this policy engendered numerous legislative changes that greatly affected procedure, evidence, and succession. For example, Ordinance No. 40 of 1928 restyled Cape criminal procedure in the manner of English criminal procedure. Ordinance No. 72 of 1830 adopted the English law of evidence with minor modifications. Civil procedure also experienced a remodeling along English lines, although some Roman-Dutch procedures remained. In 1833, Ordinance No. 104 replaced the Roman-Dutch law of universal succession of heirs with the English system of executorship. In 1845, Ordinance No. 15 established the English underhand form of will. Additionally, the Law of Inheritance Amendment Act and the Succession Act removed various restrictions on testamentary transfers.

The English legal system greatly influenced mercantile law, company law, and insolvency law. Cape statutes adopted English statutes verbatim by reference or by repromulgation. These included the Merchant Shipping Act of 1855; the General Law Amendment Act of 1879, governing maritime and shipping law, fire, life, and marine insurance, stoppage in transit, and bills of lading; the Joint Stock Companies Limited Liability Act of 1861; and the Companies Act of 1892.

English law also had a non-legislative impact. The English language dominated the courts, English judges occupied the bench, and English legal training was required for advocates. The use of the English system of government also meant the introduction of

---

[11] WOLFGANG KUNKEL, AN INTRODUCTION TO ROMAN LEGAL AND CONSTITUTIONAL HISTORY 168–78 (1966). For more on Roman law, see FRITZ SCHULTZ, HISTORY OF ROMAN LEGAL SCIENCE (1946).

[12] Cape Colony, Articles of Capitulation, Nos. 11, 12 (1806).

[13] *See, e.g.,* H. D. J. Bodenstein, *English Influences on the Common Law of South Africa,* 32 S. AFR. L.J. 337, 339 (1915); N. J. De Wet, *Die Romeins-Hollandse Reg in Suid-Afrika no 1806,* 21 TYDSKRIF VIR HEDENAAGSE ROMEINS-HOLLANDSE REG 239, 239 n.2 (1958).

[14] Campbell v. Hall, [1774] 1 Cowp. 204, 209 (Eng. K.B.); *see* DUGARD, *supra* note 9, at 8.

English principles of constitutional law. Although Roman-Dutch law remained the basic common law of the Cape, by the end of the nineteenth century, it had been thoroughly infused with English law.

Meanwhile, in the nineteenth century, Roman-Dutch law spread from the Cape to the Afrikaner republics of the Transvaal and the Orange Free State and to the British colony of Natal.[15] All three adopted the Roman-Dutch system, but English law, operating through the law of the Cape Colony, soon modified it.[16] After the 1899–1902 South African War,[17] in 1910, the two former Afrikaner republics and the two British colonies formed the Union of South Africa,[18] which remained until the Union transformed itself into the Republic of South Africa in 1961.[19] The pronouncement about the common law notwithstanding, the South African legal system had clearly become a "three-layer cake" of Roman, Roman-Dutch, and English law.[20] These influences continue to manifest themselves in modern South African contract law.

II. CONTRACTS AND THEIR LEGAL EFFECTS

In Roman law, only four types of agreements constituted enforceable contracts. These were (1) *contracts re,* in which a party delivered a thing *(res)* to the other and could, therefore, claim redelivery or counterperformance from the other; (2) *contracts literis,* in which a creditor made an entry in his or her domestic account books relating to a debt owed to the creditor and that entry made the debt enforceable; (3) *contracts verbis,* in which the agreement was made orally in the form of question and answer; such a contract was called a *stipulatio* and was enforceable because of its form; and (4) *contracts consensu,* in which agreement was enough to make a contract of sale, partnership, hire, or mandate binding.

Roman law required agreement and *causa,* or cause, to constitute a valid contract. *Causa* could be found in *contracts re* by delivery of the thing; in *contracts literis* by the entry in the books; in *contracts verbis* by the form of words used; and in *contracts consensu* by the agreement itself. An agreement that did not fall into one of these four classes was not enforceable and was called a *nudum pactum.* The rule appeared in the maxim, *Ex nudo pacto non oritur actio,* meaning no action arises from a bare agreement. Not enforceable by action, a *nudum pactum* gave rise to a natural obligation and could be used as a defense.

The *causa* requirement grew increasingly meaningless because of a European-developed rule that made all serious agreements actionable. By the seventeenth century, this had become the rule in Holland. Nevertheless, some writers still followed the older terminology and insisted that *causa* was necessary for contracts to be valid. In England, the courts did not require *causa* for a valid contract. However, except with regard to sealed covenants, the courts demanded that there be consideration, a counterperformance, or quid pro quo. By the nineteenth century, English ideas had so influenced legal thought at the Cape that many believed Roman-Dutch references to *causa* meant the same thing as consideration did to the English.[21] The courts in the Transvaal dismissed this view.[22] The issue remained controversial until 1919, when the Appellate Division of the South African Supreme Court ("Appellate Division") accepted the Transvaal view.[23]

Under modern South African law, a contract is an agreement between or among persons that gives rise to personal rights and corresponding obligations.[24] Although a contract is an agreement legally binding

[15]For a constitutional history of the Afrikaner Republics, see Leonard Thompson, *Constitutionalism in the South African Republics,* BUTTERWORTH'S S. AFR. L. REV. 49 (1954).

[16]HOSTEN ET AL., *supra* note 10, at 201–03.

[17]*See* Lynn Berat, *Constitutionalism and Mineral Law in the Struggle for a New South Africa: The South African War Revisited,* 15 SUFFOLK TRANSNAT'L L.J. 61 (1992).

[18]*See* LEONARD THOMPSON, THE UNIFICATION OF SOUTH AFRICA 1902–1910, at 459 (1960).

[19]THOMPSON, [A HISTORY OF SOUTH AFRICA (1990)], at 188.

[20]Zajtay & Hosten, *supra* note 8, at 197. One judge wrote:

> Our country has reached a stage in its national development when its existing law can better be described as South African than Roman-Dutch. . . . No doubt its roots are Roman-Dutch, and splendid roots they are. But continuous development has come through adaptation to modern conditions, through case law, through statutes, and through the adoption of certain principles and features of English law. . . . The original sources of the Roman-Dutch law are important, but exclusive preoccupation with them is like trying to return the oak tree to its acorn.

Ex parte de Winnaar, [1959] 1 S.A. 837, 839 (S. Afr. N.P.D.).

[21]*See* [Conradie v. Roussouw, 1919 A.D. 279 (S. Afr.).]

[22]*See e.g.,* Rood v. Wallach, 1904 T.S. 187, 209 (S. Afr.).

[23]*Conradie,* 1919 A.D. at 317.

[24]J.C. DE WET & A.H. VAN WYK, DIE SUID-AFRIKAANSE KONTRAKTEREG EN HANDELSREG 4 (1978).

on the parties,[25] not all agreements bind the parties. Rather, an agreement is a contract only if it has a number of essential elements: (1) the agreement is for future performance or non-performance by one or more of the parties; (2) the parties have the legal capacity to contract; (3) the parties seriously intend to bind themselves; (4) with few exceptions, the agreement is executed with some formality and in writing; and (5) the agreement is not contrary to statutory law, public policy, or good morals in its formation, performance, or purpose.

If these five elements are present, the agreement becomes a legally binding contract. However, "legally binding" does not mean that the law inevitably compels the parties to perform their promises or undertakings, because the law cannot or will not compel certain types of performance. Each party to a contract acquires a right against the other party for the agreed upon performance, as well as for a corresponding obligation. Each party has a duty to perform this obligation, which gives the other party a cause of action for specific performance when the party fails to perform. Should the other party not comply with court-ordered specific performance, then the plaintiff has a cause of action for damages. However, a court will not order specific performance for certain types of contracts, such as unenforceable contracts, contracts void *ab initio,* and voidable contracts.

An unenforceable contract is one on which no action can be brought. No legal obligations may be imposed, but a natural obligation remains. Since 1969, when the South African government passed the Prescription Act,[26] only wagering contracts or bets have constituted unenforceable contracts.

A contract is void *ab initio* if it lacks one or more of the elements necessary to the formation of a contract. Such an agreement has no legal effect from its inception. An agreed upon performance prohibited by law is an example of this kind of contract. Others include contracts lacking a definite agreement on the terms of performance, or contracts involving an insane party. These agreements give no legal rights to either party. One or both of the parties cannot later ratify these agreements. In addition, registration will not validate an agreement that is void *ab initio.* A court order is not necessary to set it aside because the agreement is deemed to be worthless. Although a void contract gives neither side a cause of action, if one party has performed the terms of the agreement, the court may sometimes grant the party redress by restoring the property or by granting monetary compensation.

Unlike contracts void *ab initio,* voidable contracts contain all of the essential elements of an agreement. However, some flaw exists at the time the agreement was made, which entitles the parties to repudiate the contract and ask that both parties be restored, if possible, to their original positions. Such reinstatement is termed *restitutio in integrum.* A flawed contract is voidable at the option of the prejudiced party. Yet, unless and until the prejudiced party justifiably repudiates it, the contract is prima facie valid and binding on the parties. A court order declaring the contract rescinded is not necessary, as it only determines that party's right to end the contract. The flaws that make a contract voidable are of three types: fraudulent or non-fraudulent misrepresentations, duress, and undue influence. These three flaws form the South African equivalent of the doctrine of unconscionability as applied in the United States and elsewhere. The interplay between duress and undue influence evidences the continuing tensions between Roman-Dutch and English law present in South Africa's mixed legal heritage.

III. UNCONSCIONABILITY SOUTH AFRICAN–STYLE: MISREPRESENTATION, DURESS, AND UNDUE INFLUENCE

A. Misrepresentation

In the formation of contracts, a party's mistaken motive is irrelevant and does not prevent the parties to the contract from reaching an agreement.[27] However, an action may lie if the mistake was caused by misrepresentation.[28] A party who has been per-

[25]However, parties can sometimes be bound by a contract even though they are not really in agreement. George v. Fairmead (Pty) Ltd., [1958] 2 S.A. 465 (S. Afr. App. Div.).

[26]Republic of South Africa, Prescription Act No. 68 (1969).

[27]For example, X buys a 1966 Ford Mustang from Y. Both believe the car has a V8 engine, but later determine that it has a V6 engine.

[28]*See* H. R. Hahlo & Ellison Kahn, The Union of South Africa: Development of its Laws and Constitution 463 (1960).

suaded by misrepresentation to enter into a contract or to accept terms to which he or she otherwise would not have agreed is entitled to relief if the representation was intentional, negligent, or innocent.

1. *Fraudulent Misrepresentation*

Fraudulent misrepresentation is a precontractual false statement of fact intentionally made by one party to a contract, that induces the other party to enter into the contract or to agree to terms to which he or she would not have agreed had the truth been known.[29] Fraudulent misrepresentation requires five elements. First, there must be a precontractual false statement of fact. This statement can include the expression of an opinion that is not honestly held.[30] The statement need not be explicit, and conduct can suffice,[31] as can silence, if the silence fails to rectify an incorrect impression.[32] Second, the misrepresentation must be wrongful, meaning unlawful. A fraudulent misrepresentation is a tort, called a *delict,* in South Africa.[33] For tort liability, the act complained of must have been wrongful. Thus, if the misrepresentation was unlawful under the circumstances, liability arises. However, the courts pay particular attention only to cases where the misrepresentation was based on a wrongful omission.[34] Wrongfulness is assumed where misrepresentation by words or other positive conduct induced the contract or led a party to accept terms to which he or she otherwise would not have agreed.[35] Third, the misrepresentation must be made fraudulently. Misrepresentations are made fraudulently when the maker does not honestly believe the truth of his or her statement and intends the other party to act on it.[36] Fourth, the misrepresentation must induce the other party to conclude the contract or to agree to its terms. A court will not find liability for fraudulent misrepresentation unless there is proof of a causal link between the misrepresentation and the act of the misled party in concluding the contract or agreeing to certain terms. Fifth, the misrepresentation must be made by the other party to the contract or by a third party acting in collusion with, or as an agent of, one of the parties to the contract. A fraudulent inducement from an independent third party does not affect the contract.

The parties to a contract cannot agree between themselves to exclude remedies for fraudulent misrepresentation. Furthermore, the misrepresenting party cannot claim that the aggrieved party, as a reasonable person, should not have been misled. A contracting party who has been the victim of a fraudulent misrepresentation has a choice of two remedies: The party may accept the contract or rescind it and receive *restitutio in integrum.* The right to choose a remedy is clear where the party would not have entered into the contract without the misrepresentation. This is *dolus dans causam contractum,* or causal fraud. Incidental fraud, or *dolus incidens in contractum,* is found in situations where no causal fraud occurred. Instead, the party agreed to terms which he or she otherwise would not have agreed. The South African law regarding incidental fraud is unclear.

A party may choose rescission as a defense against the other party's action on the contract or upon filing an action. Whether he or she accepts or rescinds the contract, the aggrieved party has an action in tort for any loss suffered. A party must elect to rescind within a reasonable time after the party learns of the misrepresentation, or lose the right. Once a party elects a remedy, he or she must abide by it. If a party chooses rescission, he or she must restore to the other party that which he or she received under the contract. However, the court may decline to follow this rule if justice requires.

The measure of the injured party's damages is the difference between the party's current financial situation and the financial situation he or she would have been in had the misrepresentation not been made. If

---

[29] *Id.*

[30] A. J. C. Copeling, *Copyright in Ideas?,* 28 TYDSKRIF VIR HEDENDAAGSE ROMEINS-HOLLANDSE REG 3 (1965).

[31] Displaying a used car among new ones is an example of conduct constituting fraudulent misrepresentation.

[32] M. A. Miller, *Fraudulent Non-Disclosure,* 74 S. AFR. L.J. 177, 179–80 (1957).

[33] Trotman v. Edwick, [1951] 1 S.A. 443 (S. Afr. App. Div.); De Jager v. Grunder, [1964] 1 S.A. 446 (S. Afr. App. Div.); Ranger v. Wykerd, [1977] 2 S.A. 976 (S. Afr. App. Div.).

[34] Failing to speak is wrongful if there was a duty to speak. On the duty to speak, see Bodemer v. American Ins. Co., [1961] 2 S.A. 662, 669 (S. Afr. App. Div.) (a contract *uberrimae fidei* imposes duty to speak); Glaston House (Pty) Ltd. v. Inag (Pty) Ltd., [1977] 2 S.A. 846, 867–69 (S. Afr. App. Div.) (duty to speak if seller knows of latent defects in item sold).

[35] The misrepresentation must be related to the material facts. Karroo v. Farr, 1921 A.D. 413, 415 (S. Afr.). Puffing alone is not actionable. DIG 4.3.37 (Ulpian, Sabinus, bk. 44); Voet Commentarius 21.1.3.

[36] Rex v. Myers, [1948] 1 S.A. 375, 382 (S. Afr. App. Div.).

the party chooses rescission and restitution, damages are usually calculated on the basis of wasted costs. However, if the contract is upheld, calculation becomes more difficult, with the method depending upon the circumstances. The court always endeavors to determine the detriment suffered by the aggrieved party because of the misrepresentation. Nevertheless, two generalizations may be made. First, in a causal fraud case, the court typically determines damages by subtracting the value of the performance made by the misrepresenting party from the value of the performance made by the aggrieved party. The court then adds any consequential loss suffered by the aggrieved party. Second, in an incidental fraud case, the court often calculates damages by subtracting the price that would have been paid if there had been no misrepresentation from the price actually paid. The court then adds any consequential loss.

2. *Non-Fraudulent Misrepresentation*

Non-fraudulent misrepresentation is the negligent or innocent misrepresentation by one party to a contract that induces the other party to enter into a contract or to agree to terms to which the party would not have agreed had he or she known the truth. Thus, non-fraudulent misrepresentation has the same elements as fraudulent misrepresentation, except that the misrepresentation is made negligently or innocently[37] rather than intentionally.

Under Roman law, a party could plead the *exceptio doli* to a claim on a contract concluded on the basis of an innocent misrepresentation. Although Roman-Dutch law accepted this rule, neither Roman nor Roman-Dutch law provided a cause of action for innocent misrepresentation. In 1907, South African law departed from this position and allowed the innocent party to sue for rescission and restitution, but did not permit the recovery of damages. Twenty years later, the Appellate Division determined that the parties can, by prior agreement, exclude remedies for non-fraudulent misrepresentation.

In 1959, the Orange Free State Provincial Division held that there was no reason for denying a claim for restitutional damages to a buyer who had entered into a contract of sale as a result of the seller's material, innocent misrepresentation. The courts in the Transvaal and Natal also adopted this position.

Finally, in 1973, the Appellate Division addressed remedies for non-fraudulent misrepresentation in *Phame (Pty) Ltd. v. Paizes.* The court established two rules concerning remedies regarding sales contracts. First, a buyer can claim either rescission or restitution with the *actio redhibitoria.* The buyer can claim restitutional damages, abatement of the purchase price, with the *actio quanti minoris* if he or she has been mislead by a seller's misrepresentation that constituted a *dictum et promissum.*[38] The party to whom the misrepresentation is made may raise the *exceptio redhibitoria* or the *exceptio quanti minoris* as a defense to an action by the seller. Second, if the seller's misrepresentation is not a *dictum et promissum,* or if the representation is made to a party to a contract other than a sales contract, the party to whom the misrepresentation is made may claim rescission and restitution or may raise the *exceptio doli* as a defense to an action by the other party. In such cases, no action for restitution arises.

B. Duress

Duress, which derived from Roman-Dutch law, occurs when a person acts through fear of actual or threatened danger. Three elements must exist to establish a claim of duress. First, there must be a threat of imminent or inevitable harm to the life, person, honor, or property of a person or family member.[39] Threats of criminal prosecution will suffice.[40] Likewise, threats to destroy or forfeit property, known as duress of goods, permit the property owner to repudiate any contract extorted by the threats.[41]

---

[37]According to the South African law of *delict,* negligent misrepresentation gives rise to the *delictual actio legis Aquiliae,* legal action, for damages in the same manner as a fraudulent misrepresentation. *Herschel,* [1954] 3 S.A. at 464.

[38]One example is a material statement by the seller to the buyer during the negotiations that bears on the quality of the thing sold and goes beyond mere praise and commendation.

[39]GROTIUS, INLEIDING 3.48.6; VAN LEEUWEN, CENS FOR 1.4.41.2–3; Broodryk v. Smuts, 1942 Natal L.R. 47 (S. Afr.); Jans Rautenbach Produksies (Edms) Bpk v. Wijma [1970] 4 S.A. 31 (S. Afr. T.P.D.); Shepstone v. Shepstone, [1974] 1 S.A. 411 (S. Afr. D. & C.L.D.).

[40]*See, e.g., Broodryk,* 1942 Natal L.R. at 47; *Jans Rautenbach Produksies (Edms) Bpk,* [1970] 4 S.A. 31; Arend v. Astra Furnishers (Pty) Ltd., [1974] 1 S.A. 765 (S. Afr. C.P.D.).

[41]Hendricks v. Barnett, [1975] 1 S.A. 765 (S. Afr. N.P.D.). For example, if a person in a position of authority unlawfully compels the owner of certain goods to pay or agree to pay him or her money by threatening that failure to pay will result in a forfeiture of the goods, the goods' owner is not bound if he or she protests at the time.

The second element of duress is an unlawful threat.[42] A threat is unlawful if the threatened conduct is unlawful in itself or the purpose of the threat is unlawful, such as attempting to obtain something to which one is not entitled.[43] A creditor's threat to institute civil proceedings to enforce his or her rights is not unlawful as long as the creditor does not try to obtain something to which he or she is not entitled. A party entering into a contract under these circumstances cannot set it aside on the grounds of duress.

It is unlawful to threaten a person with criminal prosecution in order to enforce a private debt if the other party did not commit the crime or if the creditor is using the threat to obtain something to which the creditor is not entitled. A split of authority exists as to whether the same result occurs if the debtor committed the crime and the creditor seeks only that to which he or she is entitled. For example, South African jurist Wessels wrote that "[t]he threat to prosecute a person for a crime involving imprisonment unless he enters into a contract is sufficient mortal violence to justify the setting aside of the contract." In contrast, the Transvaal Provincial Division of the Supreme Court and the Durban and Coast Local Division of the Supreme Court believe that if the debtor committed the crime and the creditor seeks no more than that to which he or she is entitled, the threat of criminal proceedings is lawful. The Cape Provincial Division has not yet decided the issue, but, should the case arise, the court is likely to determine that the threat of criminal procedure is *contra bonos mores* or against public policy, even if the debtor has committed the crime and the creditor seeks no more than that which the creditor is due. All South African courts should adopt this view. It seems inappropriate that the criminal process, aimed at protecting society at large, can be used to enforce private rights. Moreover, irrespective of duress, every threat of criminal prosecution implies that there will not be future prosecution if the desired contract is concluded. All such contracts implicitly are agreements to stop prosecutions or to compound crimes and will be void as against public policy.

The third element of duress is that the threat must have induced the threatened party to enter into the contract or to agree to terms to which he or she otherwise would not have agreed. Hence, the threat and the contract must have a causal link. Many jurisdictions also require the victim's reasonable fear, although the victim's fear does not make the contract voidable. On the other hand, obtaining the victim's consent by improper means does make the contract voidable.[44] Indeed, it is difficult to imagine how the unreasonableness of the victim's fear has inferential value in deciding whether the threats actually induced the formation of the contract. If reasonable fear were required, any distinction made by courts between threats to an individual and duress of goods where the victim can claim duress only if he or she acted under protest, would also relate to proving a causal link between the threat and the victim's subsequent conduct.

With regard to remedies under Roman Law, a duress victim could use the *exceptio quod metus causa* as a defense against an action on the contract into which he or she had entered.[45] A victim could also claim *restitutio in integrum* in cases where he or she had already performed the contractual terms.[46] In addition, a victim could obtain damages with delictual *actio quod metus causa*.[47] Roman-Dutch law followed these precedents,[48] and, following its Roman-Dutch heritage, South African law allows the threatened party to accept the contract or have it set aside.[49] In electing to avoid the contract, the threatened party may either raise duress as a defense or claim *restitutio in integrum*. Regardless of whether the threatened party accepts or rejects the contract, the

---

[42]Voet 4.2.10; *Broodryk,* 1942 Natal L.R. at 47; *Jans Rautenbach Produksies (Edms) Bpk,* [1970] 4 S.A. at 31; *Arend,* [1974] 1 S.A. at 765.

[43]*See* P. J. J. Olivier, *Onregmatige Vreesaanjaging,* 28 Tydskrif Vir Hedendaagse Romeins-Hollandse Reg 187, 203 (1965).

[44]Grotius, De Iure B Ac P 2.11.7; De Wet & Van Wyk, [Die Suid-Afrikanse Kontraktereg en Handelsreg 4 (1978)], at 44.

[45]*See* Mauerberger v. Mauerberger, [1948] 4 S.A. 902, 903–05 (S. Afr. C.P.D.).

[46]Grotius, Inleiding 3.48.6; Grotius, De Iure B Ac P 2.11.7; Van Leeuwen, Cens For 1.1.13.5–7; Voet, Commentarius 4.2.1.

[47]Grotius, Inleiding 3.48.6; Grotius, De Iure B Ac P 2.11.7; Van Leeuwen, Cens For 1.1.13.5–7; Voet, Commentarius 4.2.1.

[48]Grotius, Inleiding 3.48.6; Grotius, De Iure B Ac P 2.11.7; Van Leeuwen, Cens For 1.1.13.5–7; Voet, Commentarius 4.2.1.

[49]*Broodryk,* 1942 Natal L.R. at 47; *Jans Rautenbach Produksies (Edms) Bpk,* [1970] 4 S.A. at 31; *Shepstone,* [1974] 1 S.A. at 411; *Ilanga Wholesalers,* [1974] 2 S.A. at 292; *Arend,* [1974] 1 S.A. at 765.

threatened party may receive delictual damages in compensation for his or her negative interest.

C. Undue Influence

Like English common law, South African law holds that a contract made under duress is voidable.[50] However, the English common law is much narrower than its South African counterpart. The English concept comprises only cases of actual or threatened physical violence to, or unlawful constraint of, the contracting party's person. The narrowness of the English common law concept of duress resulted in intervention by courts of equity, which, through application of the doctrine of constructive fraud, had broader jurisdiction over contracts made without free consent than did the common law courts. The equity courts developed a doctrine of undue influence, which provided relief in cases where a contract was procured through improper pressure that did not rise to the level of duress. It also provided relief in cases where a special relationship existed between the contracting parties. The two types of cases are indistinguishable. Where no special relationship exists between the parties, the party alleging undue influence must prove that the other party imposed improper pressure on him or her. Where a special relationship does exist, a presumption of undue influences arises, which the alleged undue influencer must rebut. Many relationships give rise to the presumption, including those of parent-child, guardian-ward, religious adviser-disciple, physician-patient, attorney-client, and trustee-*cestui que* trust.

After the South African War, the courts in the Cape and Natal, and the Appellate Division first referred to undue influence as a ground for setting aside a contract. Some of the courts accepted unquestioningly the proposition that the doctrine of undue influence formed part of South African law. In 1948, the Cape Provincial Division of the Supreme Court determined that undue influence had a basis in South African law. In reaching its decision, the Court drew on previous decisions of South African courts, the writings of several scholars, the views of various writers on the grounds for *restitutio in integrum,* and on the fact that undue influence prevented true consent. Six years later, in *Preller v. Jordaan,* the Appellate Division accepted the view that undue influence provided a ground for *restitutio in integrum.* That decision marked the unambiguous acceptance in South African law of the rule that a party can avoid a contract if the other party used undue influence to induce him or her to enter into it. The acceptance of this rule diverges from Roman-Dutch practice, which is demonstrated by the minority judgment of Van den Heever in *Preller,* and by the writings of South African jurist De Wet in an examination of the sources the court relied upon in *Preller.*

Despite acceptance of the general rule, the specific elements of undue influence remain unclear. The English courts vaguely define undue influence as "some unfair and improper conduct, some coercion from outside, some overreaching, some form of cheating, and generally, though not always, some personal advantage obtained by" the guilty party. The South African courts have not been more precise. In *Preller,* the court found that the grounds for *restitutio in integrum* were broad enough to include the case

> where one person obtains an influence over another which weakens the latter's powers of resistance and renders his will compliant, and where such person then uses his influence in an unconscionable manner to persuade the other to agree to a prejudicial transaction which he would not have concluded with normal free will.

Then, in *Patel v. Grobbelaar,* the Appellate Division affirmed the Transvaal Provincial Division's decision requiring a plaintiff asserting undue influence to prove three elements: (1) the defendant exerted influence over him or her; (2) the influence weakened his or her resistance and made him or her compliant; and (3) the defendant used his or her influence unscrupulously to induce the plaintiff to agree to a transaction which was prejudicial to him or her and which he or she would not otherwise have entered.

In terms of remedies for undue influence, the injured party may elect to accept the contract or to rescind it and claim *restitutio in integrum.* The courts have not decided whether the party also has an action for damages. However, if undue influence is to be accepted as duress, a plaintiff would have an action for damages.

---

[50] G. C. Cheshire & C. H. S. Fifoot, The Law of Contract 285–90 (1981).

IV. THE NEED FOR A COMMERCIAL CODE WITH EMPHASIS ON UNCONSCIONABILITY

As South Africa struggles to cast off apartheid's sordid legacy, there is much discussion of a new constitution that will guarantee human rights and equality before the law.[51] There is also great debate over whether such a document should guarantee economic rights. This debate, however, centers on land and wealth redistribution, and does not involve contract formation or the sanctity of contracts.

Nevertheless, there are pressing reasons for those crafting a new legal order for the country to pay particular attention to contract law. To create a just society, the South African economy will have to expand dramatically. Expanding the economy will require infusions of foreign capital, but such investment alone will not be enough to undo the underlying problems of high unemployment, poverty, and despair. Domestic economic growth will also have to be fueled by greater African participation, primarily through small business creation and heightened presence in the consumer economy. In such an environment, contracts, whether between businesses, between businesses and individuals, or between individuals, will assume a new importance as the foundations facilitating economic change. Inevitably, contract disputes will arise, particularly because middle class South African blacks starting new businesses will not have established advice networks to rely on for assistance in making deals. Consequently, it seems likely that many contract disputes will find their way to court.

Historically, in South Africa, white judges enforced laws created by whites in courts catering to white interests; hence, it will be important for courts to be responsive to those wronged in contract disputes. This is essential not only for economic stability but also for the creation of much needed respect for the rule of law in general. The courts' responsiveness is even more urgent because whites will continue to dominate the economy, the judiciary, and the bar in the foreseeable future. Therefore, both South African courts and those creating a new legal order for the country should make an effort to define a coherent doctrine of unconscionability that favors the rights of victims.

In terms of case law, courts should adopt a concept of unconscionability that seeks to merge, where possible, the existing doctrines of misrepresentation, duress, and undue influence. The success of this merger will partly depend upon the continuing position of Roman-Dutch law in the South African legal order, an issue not yet decided.[52] Even so, the hybrid legal heritage does not pose too formidable an obstacle to the development of a judicial doctrine of unconscionability.

Looking beyond the case law, any new government should adopt a commercial code, perhaps modeled on the United States' Uniform Commercial Code,[53] that would have explicit provisions on unconscionability. Such provisions, developed in consultation with judges, commercial lawyers, and consumer advocates, would help guide judges in devising their standards. To better serve South Africa's undereducated African population, the code should avoid legal jargon as much as possible. Once adopted, the government should publicize the code by distributing summaries for laypersons published in the official language, which is likely to be English,[54] as well as in Afrikaans and various African languages. The government should mobilize trade unions, consumer groups, and those conducting secondary school street law programs to familiarize people with the code. Both entrepreneurs and consumers alike will then become comfortable with commercial law and enter into transactions that will benefit the economy and, therefore, all South Africans.

V. CONCLUSION

South Africa has a hybrid legal system that combines elements of Roman, Roman-Dutch, and English law. That mixed heritage is readily apparent in South

---

[51]On the constitutional debate, see Lynn Berat, *A New South Africa?: Prospects for an Africanist Bill of Rights and a Transformed Judiciary,* 13 LOY. L.A. INT'L & COMP. L.J. 467, 467–84 (1991).

[52]On the future of Roman-Dutch law, see, e.g., ALBIE SACHS, THE FUTURE OF ROMAN-DUTCH LAW IN A NON-RACIAL DEMOCRATIC SOUTH AFRICA: SOME PRELIMINARY OBSERVATIONS (1989).

[53]U.C.C. (1990).

[54]On the language question, see Neville Alexander, Language Planning in South Africa with Special Reference to the Harmonization of the Varieties of Nguni and Sotho, Paper Presented at the South African Research Program Seminar, Yale University (Feb. 20, 1991); Neville Alexander, The Sociology of Language Planning for a Democratic South Africa, Paper Presented at the South African Research Program Seminar, Yale University (Oct. 17, 1990).

African contract law, which has never developed the concept of unconscionability as found in the law of the United States and other countries, but instead relies upon the doctrines of misrepresentation, duress, and undue influence. As debates rage in South Africa about the post-apartheid legal order, many of the ills besetting the country demand eradication. The post-apartheid order must involve the increased participation of Africans both as business owners and consumers. To encourage that participation, there should be a doctrine of unconscionability that favors the victims of unconscionable contracts. This should be developed in two ways. First, the courts should harmonize existing doctrines and develop a concept of unconscionability. Second, those responsible for commercial law in any new government should adopt a commercial code that employs a concept of unconscionability; such a code must avoid legal jargon and be explained to laypersons through various education programs. Only by encouraging Africans to feel that the economy belongs to them will the growth so necessary to South Africa's stability and survival be able to occur.

50

MICHELE M. MOODY-ADAMS

On Surrogacy: Morality, Markets, and Motherhood

When a surrogate parenting agreement fails the consequences can be extraordinary. Of course, the typical surrogate arrangement would involve just three people: a sperm donor who commissioned artificial insemination, the woman who served as both genetic and gestational mother, and the wife of the sperm donor hoping to adopt the child. But a child born today could be the subject of a dispute with as many as five people claiming to be her parents: a sperm donor, an egg donor, a woman in whose womb gestation takes place (who need not be the egg donor), and a couple planning to raise the child.[1] Traditional conflicts between the claims of adoptive and biological parenthood are thus complicated by the ways in which advances in reproductive technology force us to rethink the notion of biological parenthood. What were once stages in a single biological development can now be separate processes with the potential to generate a bewildering array of claims to biological parenthood.

Yet the problems of surrogacy go far beyond complications in the practice of family law—even in the typical surrogate arrangement—when surrogacy involves the exchange of money. The vehemence with which many defenses of paid surrogacy deny that the practice involves exchanging money for a baby is evidence of how troubling the practice can be. Typical defenses aim to show that paid surrogacy does not violate those features of adoption law that officially prohibit treating babies as marketable commodities. But I show in Section One that such denials not only fail to be compelling, they also commit their proponents to an equally problematic claim that the money is simply payment for the surrogate mother's "services and expenses," not a fee for termination of parental rights or for consent to surrender the child for adoption.[2] For how many couples would be willing to pay for a surrogate's "services," and then allow her to keep the baby? What they want, of course, is *precisely* the surrender of the baby and termination of the surrogate mother's parental rights. Moreover, these demands not only violate moral and legal strictures against exchanging persons for money; they also involve taking a stance toward the surrogate that, if taken towards a building contractor, or a professional athlete, would violate moral and legal prohibitions against slavery.

Of course defenses of paid surrogacy argue that the surrogate's "service" is no ordinary personal service. But I show in Section Two that once we recognize *why* the surrogate mother's service is unique, we become aware of a set of moral and legal principles that condemn as impermissible any attempt to treat that service as a marketable commodity. Section Two also shows that participants in paid surrogacy arrangements accept moral principles governing childbearing that, once acknowledged, would require them to reject the practice as morally impermissible. My discussion does not aim to provide exhaustive justification of these principles (though they help make sense of moral experience), but rather to engage defenders of surrogacy for pay in critical self-reflection on their acceptance of the practice. Indeed, the discussions in Sections One and Two are broadly Socratic in character: critical reflection on one's own unreflective assumptions about a practice is assumed to be a central element of moral reflection on that practice.

Section Three discusses the views of those who would revise those legal practices, and reject those moral principles, that require us to reject paid surrogacy. Two very different but broadly utilitarian considerations—one relying upon the needs of the infertile, the other upon the importance of their desires—have been thought to ground compelling arguments in favor of the practice.[3] But neither argument can override the objections to treating babies, or the capacity to give birth to a baby, as marketable commodities. An important version of the argument from desires—drawing on principles of the "economic analysis of the law"—would reject absolute prohibitions upon the commodification of babies and motherhood. On this view, given considerations of "efficiency," the mere existence of desires justifies allowing a market to satisfy those desires.[4] Yet, as I argue in Section Three, it is ultimately self-defeating for those who value market relations to claim that every human relationship is appropriately treated as a market relationship. Stable market relationships, after all, depend upon the stability, for instance, of promises and contracts, and upon credit and trust. But such phenomena, in turn, depend upon a widespread acceptance that some relationships between persons are not up for sale. It is especially short-sighted to argue for lifting barriers that protect those *family* relationships through which one can most easily, and most fully, learn respect for non-market human relationships. Those who value market relationships ought also to condemn surrogacy for pay.

Thus critical reflection on the presuppositions of paid surrogacy also issues in a concrete policy recommendation. The surrogate parenting agreements that are central to paid surrogacy are not only morally impermissible, but should also be declared legally unenforceable.[5]

I. THE SURROGATE PARENTING AGREEMENT

No defense of surrogacy for pay has clearly distinguished the practice from baby-selling, and if one cannot draw this distinction it will be impossible to show that the practice does not violate standard adoption laws. Many defenders of paid surrogacy insist that any payment promised to the mother is compensation for the mother's services, not payment for the baby. They claim, in effect, that surrogate parenting agreements are personal service contracts. But this claim immediately generates a problem within contract law. Anglo-American courts traditionally have ruled that a person who breaches a personal service contract with another private party is *not* legally bound to render the service she promised to render. That is, even in the event of a breach of a personal contract, courts typically refuse to grant to any private party a remedy of "specific performance." A principal reason for this refusal is the belief that, in general, compelling someone to perform a service she does not want to perform comes dangerously close to violating legal prohibitions of slavery.[6] Further, a person who has been wronged by a breach of a personal service contract may seek other generally satisfactory remedies: first, rescission of the contract (behaving as though the contract never existed, and withholding any payment); second, money damages (where these can be estimated); or, third, an "equitable relief" in the form of an injunction to keep the offending party from performing the service for anyone else, for the duration of the contract. When a service is unique, the law assumes an "implied covenant" not to work for a competitor for the duration of the contract.

But if we conceive of surrogate parenting agreements as personal service contracts, we create a peculiar problem. For defenders of paid surrogacy normally demand precisely what the law says that no private party can be entitled to: specific performance as a remedy for the breach of a personal service contract. Brokers of surrogacy arrangements generally claim that no couple would initiate the arrangements if they believed that the carrying mother could frustrate their expectations at will. Thus they usually insist that the law should give advance assurance that courts will grant specific performance. This insistence, of course, expresses the commissioning couple's conviction that nothing short of the surrender of the baby—not money damages, not preventing the mother from surrendering the baby to someone else—could compensate them for their loss were they to be deprived of the baby. But there is no small irony here: the same people who would insist that nothing can compensate *them* were *they* to be deprived of the baby, are nonetheless willing to argue against a carrying mother in a surrogacy arrangement making precisely the same claim.

Of course, it might be possible to defend the practice despite the objection about specific performance.

First, one might simply deny that surrogacy for pay ever involves a personal service contract; such a denial would certainly avoid the "no specific performance" objection. But to claim that paid surrogacy does not involve a personal service contract is tacitly to agree that it does, after all, involve the direct exchange of money for a baby. Many might find this unsettling, but bolder proponents of the economic analysis of the law might well respond, "What's wrong with that?" Such thinkers would argue that if desires create a market for babies, it may just be old-fashioned to maintain legal prohibitions limiting the exchange of money for the desired "goods."[7] Even in the realm of family law, they argue, we best promote the efficient satisfaction of desires by accepting that nearly everything can be had for a price. Indeed, Richard Posner has measured the "value" of children to a childless couple *solely* in terms of that couple's willingness to pay a certain price for the child.[8]

Other defenders of surrogacy for pay attempt to avoid the "no specific performance"objection by a different means. One commentator on reproductive law has argued that

> "We might . . . want a period between the signing and the insemination or other forms of legal protection. But I believe the contract is valid. Once the child is born, it is no longer a personal services contract."[9]

According to this claim, surrogacy for pay *does* involve a personal service contract up until the time at which the baby is born. But the alleged transformation of the surrogacy agreement from a personal services contract into something altogether different seems almost magical. Of course, the law is full of fictions. When I set up shop to sell vacuum cleaners, the law assumes that every vacuum cleaner I sell comes with an "implied warranty of fitness" for the purpose, even if I never explicitly promise a customer anything of the sort. When an opera singer signs a contract for a season with one opera company, the law assumes the existence of an implied covenant not to work for a competitor, whatever the singer expressly says. But the claim that the birth of a baby transforms one *kind* of contract into a contract of an altogether different *kind* is one fiction too many. If you like this magic, you must then cope with the fact that the personal service contract would have to be magically transformed into a contract to deliver the baby for pay. This alternative, then, provides no refuge from the by now familiar refrain—that it is difficult to see how surrogacy for pay is anything other than the exchange of a baby for money.

Still a third defense of the practice might urge that resistance to the demand for specific performance of surrogate agreements simply rests on a conceptual error: an error embodying a misunderstanding of the nature of the parties involved in the contract. A woman who signs a surrogacy agreement, some have argued, is not a surrogate *mother* at all, but rather, a "surrogate womb" or a "surrogate uterus":

> "In both structural and functional terms, Mr. and Mrs. Stern's role as parents to Baby M was achieved by a surrogate uterus and not a surrogate mother."[10]

This is a vivid and rather chilling example of the power of synedoche, indeed, of figurative language generally. But it is particularly revealing of some crucial assumptions underlying the practice of surrogacy for pay. The claim implies that a woman signing a surrogacy agreement can have no title to press for custody of the child to whom she gives birth since she is simply a "surrogate womb." A womb obviously cannot make legal or moral claims on a child—or any legal or moral claims whatsoever—since a womb is a thing, albeit a living thing. A *person* can object that a demand for specific performance would be an unacceptable instance of forcing her to do something against her will. A *womb*, in contrast, has no will, and therefore cannot complain of being forced to act against it. The implication of this reduction of a surrogate mother to a bodily organ is that a woman who signs a surrogate parenting agreement is not a person, at least not for the duration of the pregnancy. Indeed, it comes dangerously close to suggesting that the woman who signs such an agreement is not a person at all.

Of course the defender of the practice has one very obvious retort. It might be argued that a woman who signs a surrogate agreement is agreeing to be treated as though she *were* just a surrogate womb and thereby agreeing, in advance of the birth, to give up all legal claims to the child. But this suggests some new questions which come to light when we reflect on the laws governing adoption. Adoption laws typically rest on the assumption that a woman cannot possibly predict whether or not she will have an attachment to a child to whom she will give birth. Hence, these laws allow—at least, in principle—that even a woman who has agreed to give a child up for adoption may, in the future, have good reasons to change her mind. Some commentators, curiously, have suggested that this provision assumes that women are frivolous. One commentator on the custody challenge in the Baby M trial argued that

> "Allowing Mrs. Whitehead to get out of the contract would reinforce the stereotype of women being flighty and letting their emotions get in the way."[11]

But in the matter of something as banal as a contract for new kitchen cabinets one is often given a few days after signing the agreement to back out of the contract. Such provisions rest on the assumption that only in what Bishop Butler would have called a "cool hour" can one be sure that one has given truly *informed* consent. The decision to give up a child is surely momentous enough to warrant protection of a time during which one can be sure that the decision represents *informed* consent—namely, after the child is born.

There are good reasons to assume that informed consent is possible only if the mother has had time to reflect *following* the birth of the baby. Circumstances unique to giving birth make the experience rather different from having kitchen cabinets installed. Some would argue that the uniqueness is a function of "instinctive" or "natural" affective ties between a new mother and newborn child. However, such arguments are not very compelling: "natural" and "instinctive" are notoriously slippery terms, and claims about "natural" bonds between mother and child often obscure the importance of affective ties which can develop between a child and *any* people likely to be its principal caretakers. Nonetheless, even if the affective bonds that can exist between a mother and a child are largely—even wholly—social rather than biological in origin, they are worth encouraging. If a mother intends to keep the child to whom she gives birth, obvious benefits accrue to mother and child when the bonds between them are strong. More important, all of our normative expectations concerning child rearing condemn as psychologically unhealthy, or morally unfit, a woman who does not profess strong affective ties to her offspring. By allowing for the possibility that such ties will prove quite powerful, adoption laws thus reiterate the message which every other aspect of social and moral life attempts to convey. What an irony, then, that surrogacy for pay treats as somehow blameworthy, or indicative of poor psychological health, sentiments and behavior which a woman would be blamed for *not* displaying under any other circumstances.[12]

II. MOTHERHOOD AS A SUI GENERIS ACTIVITY

This irony drives home the peculiarly degrading and dehumanizing consequences of a fiction that would equate a pregnant woman with her mere womb. Of course, some basic reflection on rudimentary biological facts could have revealed the shortcomings in the notion that a pregnant woman is just a "surrogate womb." But the notion is more than just bad science. It reflects an attitude embedded very deeply in many cultures, including our own—namely, that the woman's contribution to a child's being is somehow unimportant, or grossly subordinate to the man's contribution. Even in cases of routine pregnancy, certain linguistic conventions may make it difficult to take the woman's contribution to the child very seriously. For instance, in English, it is quite common to use the word "father" as a verb—to describe the consequence of one relatively brief physical act; the verb form of the word "mother," on the other hand, is commonly reserved only for the ongoing activity of actually nurturing the child after it is born.[13] To say that there is an asymmetry here is understatement in the extreme. Moreover, in the extraordinary circumstances of surrogate parenting agreements, this linguistic asymmetry is reproduced in moral and legal asymmetries that are deeply problematic.

Over against this, some critics have offered a contrasting asymmetry. For example, it has been argued that in a custody dispute where the surrogate mother is the genetic mother, the surrogate's claim should have precedence over the claim of someone who "has donated one of his fifty million sperm."[14] The authors of the *Warnock Report,* among others, have made the more provocative claim that even where the carrying mother is not the genetic mother there is still the same kind of presumption in favor of her claim to the child.[15] These claims might seem simply to replace one asymmetry with another. But this new asymmetry can be defended, once we understand that the "service" provided by a surrogate mother (whether genetically related to the baby or not) is no ordinary personal service. It is, in fact, a *sui generis* activity and cannot properly be the subject of a personal service contract.

To see that this is so, we need only try to find an analogy between surrogacy and other activities that are traditionally treated as the subjects of personal service contracts. Consider, for instance, the services of an opera star or a professional athlete. Few people will ever sing like Kathleen Battle, or play basketball like Michael Jordan. Each of these individuals has some special skill, or capacity, which people will pay to enjoy because it is in some important respect unique. So far, the analogy with surrogate motherhood seems to stand up. An infertile couple seems to be paying a surrogate to perform a service which they lack the capacity to perform, and typically her services will be unique in the appropriate way—she is pregnant with a child who bears genetic ties to one, or possibly both, members of the couple. There are, nonetheless, important ways in which carrying a child to term is not analogous to either of these activities.

Now there is clearly no such thing as a disembodied service—a service apart from a body performing it.[16] But the carrying mother in a surrogate agreement performs her embodied labor in a distinctive way. To begin with, she cannot perform the service at all unless she first undergoes a specific medical procedure carried out by an agent of the commissioning couple: usually artificial insemination, and (very rarely) embryo transfer. While a professional athlete, for instance, might be required to undergo a drug test, no such test is a physical prerequisite of performing the contracted skill. Second, the contribution which the surrogate mother's embodied labor makes to the end *result* of that labor differs from that required by the performance of any other task. Surrogate parenting agreements typically spell out, in great detail, regulations to govern the conduct of the surrogate mother during the pregnancy.[17] Moreover, a surrogate mother cannot adequately perform the service without careful attention to the most intricate physiological details, and this attention requires a twenty-four-hour-a-day commitment. Indeed, in some jurisdictions, a surrogate mother who fails to live up to these terms might be subject to a felony charge for some activity (such as consuming alcohol in private) that would not be a felony were she not performing the "service."[18] No analogous circumstances confront the athlete or the opera star. Finally, the surrogate mother's service is of "full value" to the commissioning couple only in virtue of its connection to the end result of the service—namely, the baby. This is not true of the services of a professional athlete or an opera singer: we pay to see these people engaged in a process or an activity, and the relevant interest is met only in this way. But the commissioning couple in a surrogate agreement have no intrinsic interest in watching the surrogate go through the pregnancy. Indeed, their interest in the pregnancy is merely incidental to their interest in the end result. Of course, the "end result" is also unique—the commissioning couple clearly think so. Implicit in what they think, of course, is that a person is a special kind of entity, the loss of which cannot be compensated by money damages, or by legal injunctions against other people. This is no doubt why so many couples vehemently deny that they *intend* to exchange the money for a baby.

One final attempt to deny the *sui generis* character of the surrogate mother's service might involve the suggestion that surrendering a child as part of a surrogate agreement is, in principle, no different from giving blood. One might argue that giving blood is certainly embodied labor, that the full value of the service inheres in the end result, and that the result is in important respects unique (we cannot manufacture an adequate substitute for blood). One might then note that we allow people to exchange blood for money. Many commentators contend, further, that allowing a marketplace in blood and blood products is not only morally acceptable, but also ensures efficient distribution of a needed resource. Why isn't it permissible to treat paid surrogacy in the same way?

Yet at least one writer, Richard Titmuss, has challenged both the efficiency of the marketplace in blood and blood products, and its morality as well.[19] Moreover, Titmuss's arguments against the efficiency of the practice are of particular interest during an era in which an improperly screened blood supply poses serious risks of disease and death to large numbers of people. But his claims about the morally problematic implications of the practice are of special interest in this context. Titmuss has argued quite powerfully that a social policy promoting the selling of blood, among other things, "represses the expression of altruism," and "erodes the sense of community."[20] These effects, in Titmuss's view, result from our refusal to see that human blood is most appropriately regarded not as a commodity but as a gift.

There is much of value in the notion that this fundamental life-preserving human tissue is most appropriately understood as a gift and not as a marketable commodity. Were we to conceive of giving blood as a process of gift-exchange (rather than commodity-exchange) the donation of blood—like any gift—could be understood to create, or sometimes simply affirm, bonds between the giver and the recipient of the gift. The activity might also be seen as part of a process of reciprocal gift-exchange in which the gift creates a duty of gratitude that cannot be discharged by the exchange of money. Many communities already have in place mechanisms for discharging this duty: the most common such mechanism is an agreement to make blood available to the donor (or the donor's immediate family) in an emergency. Finally, as Titmuss suggests, a process of gift-exchange eliminates many pressures encouraging potential sellers of blood to engage in deception or misrepresentation about their health.[21] Thus both efficiency and morality might be better served by construing blood as a gift, and not as a marketable commodity.

But, whether we choose a gift-model or commodity-model of exchange, the attempted analogy between surrogate motherhood and the donation of blood will not stand up. The analogy fails because the good being circulated when one donates blood is qualitatively different from the entity being surrendered when a surrogate mother gives up a baby. First, a baby has interests, while blood and blood products clearly have none. Second, a baby can suffer harms, and has interests in being protected from these harms. While improper storage certainly damages blood and blood products, these products have no interests in being protected from such harms since they have no interests at all. Third, babies have interests in being protected from a variety of *future* harms that have nothing to do with physical damage or abuse, and are typically unintelligible simply as economic losses. Two of the most problematic harms potentially associated with surrogacy for pay (or any practice involving the exchange of a baby for money) are harms of this sort. An older child who discovers that, as a baby, he circulated in a market exchange may suffer a severe loss of self-respect. Such a child may find it difficult to learn respect for others. Alternatively, a child who knows that she has circulated in a market exchange is susceptible to a constant fear that she might be sold to someone else, should she no longer prove "satisfactory." Such a child will find it difficult to learn trust for others. The potential for loss of self-respect, and the inability to trust others, cannot be dismissed as mere "externalities" that have no bearing on whether to allow market considerations to structure the "exchange" of babies.[22] A society that fails to try to protect persons from such harms fails to respect those persons, and also endangers those character traits that enable economic systems to function at all.

Yet while the attempted analogy between surrendering a baby and donating blood breaks down, there are nonetheless important reasons to conceive of a child as a gift. Indeed, this conception helps illuminate the ways in which the moral obligations of parenthood (and the obligations embodied in legal practice) might be imposed. We can view the child as a special kind of gift that creates a custodial, or guardian, relation between parent and child. A custodial relation can be understood to hold between a person and some entity (or entities) with which that person has been entrusted. Moreover, we are not entitled to do just anything with those entities which have been entrusted to us. This is just part of the concept of trust; trust is a moral relation imposing obligations on the person in whom trust has been invested. On this conception, then, giving birth brings with it the obligation to carry out a set of moral responsibilities best described as *custodial.* Further, on this conception of the child as a gift, moral obligations are imposed first and foremost on the mother who gives birth to the child—and, of course, on anyone who has agreed, in advance, to *help* her discharge the moral responsibilities associated with birth.[23] It is also important to stress that on this conception of childbearing, the custodial relation exists—unavoidably—between a newborn child and the woman who gives birth to the child. Once we recognize the existence of such a relation we can immediately understand some of the reasons for which a decision to give a child up for adoption, for instance, is morally such a serious matter.

But assuming the existence of such a relation may also allow us to explain why some surrogate mothers—their agreements notwithstanding—vehemently resist surrendering the babies to whom they give birth. It may even help explain why some surrogates argue, sometimes vehemently, that they "don't do it for the money." A culture in which nearly everything *can* be had for a price may find it difficult to trust or even to understand such claims—particularly when made by women who accept the pay. But like any human action, the actions of a surrogate mother may be the product of several different motives. Most of the fees are so small—for nine months of "service," twenty-four hours a day—that it is unlikely that money could be the only motive. I suggest that a large subset of women who engage in paid surrogacy understand their activity, at least in part, as that of giving the commissioning couple a gift which that couple are unable to give to themselves.

Now, any such belief on the part of a surrogate mother is surely complex. It may be bound up with a different and troubling belief that a woman's worth as a person is inseparable from her capacity to give birth. It is also difficult to justify a surrogate's willingness to participate in a practice that requires her to confuse gift-exchange with commodity-exchange in this way. Yet interviews with some women who have participated in paid surrogacy suggest that they view the practice as an unusual form of gift-exchange, creating complex moral bonds between themselves and the commissioning couple. Some even seem to believe that their activity creates a duty of gratitude that cannot be discharged by the exchange of money; they may even hope to become part of an extended family, taking part in rearing the child.[24] To be sure, the commissioning couples are generally very grateful—even the vast majority who will very likely sever all ties with the surrogate mother, once the child is born. But couples initiate the process because they want to create the conventionally exclusive bonds—emotional and moral—that typically exist between parents and children.

But all parties to surrogate agreements implicitly accept a conception of the child as gift that is morally much richer than my argument has so far suggested. Arguments advanced in custody battles arising out of failed surrogacy arrangements often stress the importance of what is in the "best interests of the child." In fact, surrogate agreements—usually written even before conception takes place—tend to make special appeals to this notion. An excerpt from the agreement in the *Baby M* case is a good example:

> "Mary Beth Whitehead, Surrogate, represents that she is capable of conceiving children. Mary Beth Whitehead understands and agrees that *in the best interest of the child,* she will not attempt to form a parent-child relationship with any child or children she may conceive, carry to term and give birth to, pursuant to the provisions of the Agreement, and shall freely surrender custody to William Stern, Natural Father, immediately upon birth of the child; and terminate all parental rights to said child pursuant to this Agreement [emphasis added]."[25]

But it is not clear why the authors of such agreements would assume that anyone—a surrogate mother, a family court judge—would be moved by such concerns unless they, too, thought that the child is the sort of gift whose birth creates custodial responsibilities. It is true, as the New Jersey Supreme Court pointed out, that this "best interest" clause is barely plausible, and potentially quite unfair to the surrogate: she is asked to decide about the child's *best* interests before she has conceived, and often before she knows very much about the commissioning couple.[26] But the clause is nonetheless important because it reveals that all parties to the agreement accept that the surrogate mother will have custodial obligations with regard to the child she bears.

The problem, however, is that authors of surrogate parenting agreements try to convince a potential surrogate mother that she can best perform her custodial obligations by agreeing, before the child's birth—even in advance of conception—to give the child up. Legal regulations governing adoption suggest that surrogacy agreements get things the wrong way around. These agreements attempt to detach the act of giving birth to a child from the moral obligations which it creates—in advance of the very phenomenon which creates the relevant obligations. That is, they try to sever the connection between giving birth and having full custodial responsibilities. But this connection, as adoption laws provide, cannot rightfully be severed until the birth mother has had a chance to decide whether or not she can live up to the responsibilities imposed upon her by the birth of the child. On this conception, adoption is permissible only because it can be understood as an attempt to live up to one's custodial responsibilities by accepting that someone else is better able, or more willing, to care for the child. On this conception, then, surrendering a baby to someone else is permissible as a last resort. But surrogate parenting agreements attempt to treat the surrender as a first resort, and they attempt to convince the carrying mother to agree to this surrender even before she has conceived. These agreements simply try to *ignore* the moral responsibilities of parenthood which all parties to the agreement believe to be created by giving birth. On the terms of those who sanction the practice—those who accept the morally rich conception of the child as a gift—the practice is indefensible.

III. THE NEEDS AND DESIRES OF THE INFERTILE

Some theorists may insist that despite the potential conflict with legal and moral principles prohibiting the exchange of a baby for money, and despite the failed analogy between surrogacy and activities appropriately considered as marketable personal services, there are still compelling considerations in favor of paid surrogacy. Arguments based upon the claims of the infertile—either their needs or their desires—are sometimes claimed to create a moral presumption in favor of the practice, and to provide reasons for revising laws with which the practice might conflict.

The question of the needs of the infertile couples opens up an important, broadly utilitarian, line of argument in defense of surrogacy. This argument begins with the claim that the couple's inability to have a child is the source of great suffering—an inability said to prove particularly painful because of the dearth of children available for adoption. The suffering of the infertile is then said to have a special moral claim on us because infertility is either a disease, or a handicap, or both. Peter Singer and Deane Wells, for instance, argue that infertility simply *is* "a medical disability."[27] A refusal to allow paid surrogacy, the argument concludes, causes more suffering than would ever be caused by allowing the practice—even with its attendant risks.[28] But I contend that the distress suffered by the infertile grounds a compelling argument for the practice only if that argument embodies a serious conceptual confusion: the notion that infertility is either a disease, or a handicap.[29]

According to a widely accepted definition of infertility, a *marriage* is infertile when no pregnancy has occurred after a year of coitus without contraception.[30] This may sound straightforward—at least until we reflect on the fact that infertility is here being treated as a condition of two people, a married couple. Moreover, what is sometimes described as a single condition is actually quite complex, involving several different kinds of conditions. The problem can be low sperm count in the male; tubal blockage, failure of ovulation, or cervical problems in the female; or some combination of conditions involving the male and the female. Yet on the standard medical model of disease individual persons have diseases, not some union of persons.[31] Treating infertility as a disease thus requires a substantial departure from this model. Further, some conditions included under the label "infertility" are actually the effects of some other disease: they are either "symptoms" or consequences of some disease, rather than themselves diseases. Other conditions described as infertility involve a loss or impairment of functioning which has no obvious medical explanation.[32] None of these conditions fit very comfortably into the category of disease. In short, there is just no clear or convincing argument to support the claim that infertility is a disease. The mental suffering caused by infertility might fall within the scope of mental illness, but this would not show that infertility *itself* is a disease.

If the concept of disease does not illuminate the problem, the notion that infertility is a handicap does not fare any better. In some respects this concept is even more problematic. First, it rests on assumptions not unlike those which encourage some potential surrogate mothers to think that their worth as persons can be affirmed only by being pregnant and giving birth. But there is no merit to the claim that the life of one unable to have children is less worthwhile—sheerly in virtue of that fact—than the life of one who is so able. Second, though Singer and Wells describe infertility as "a medical disability," and insist that infertile couples have a morally compelling *need* for surrogate arrangements, their claim fails to be compelling.[33] There is a very good case for claiming that a disabled person, for instance, has a morally compelling need for a wheel chair, or physical therapy, or a special parking space. Losing one's legs regularly prevents one from carrying out basic life-preserving activities. But being unable to have children clearly does not. Infertility may create a presumption in favor of making some kinds of reproductive technology available to infertile couples. But surrogacy for pay is not just another kind of reproductive technology; a woman who plans to serve as a carrying mother (whether genetically related to the child she carries or not) is not a surrogate womb, but a person. The suffering of infertile couples who want children does not support considerations capable of overriding the moral and legal arguments against the demand for specific performance of surrogate contracts, or against allowing the exchange of babies for money.

Some theorists—drawing on principles of the economic analysis of the law—might argue that a different (also broadly utilitarian) argument, based on the primacy of desires, grounds a compelling case in favor of surrogacy for pay. A defender of the economic analysis of the law need not fear the objection to specific performance of personal service contracts: this theorist would not shrink from the suggestion that surrogacy for pay ultimately involves the exchange of a baby for money. Indeed, this theorist explicitly rejects absolute prohibitions against the commodification of persons as unnecessary obstacles to the efficient satisfaction of desires.[34] However, such a theorist does not recognize that, even though the family is unavoidably an economic institution, not every interaction or relationship between persons *within* the family can be rightly understood on the model of market behavior. For it is typically only within a family (in all of its possible guises) that a child can learn the kind of trust and respect for persons upon which stable economic systems rely. Moreover, families that fail to teach lessons of trust and respect may cause irreparable psychological damage. Complex markets cannot operate independent of promises, contracts, trust, and credit. The very existence of market relationships thus depends upon socially established normative expectations that at least some things—one's word, one's reputation, one's respect for others and their property—will not be up for sale. To argue for the commodification of those relationships best able to develop these expectations (and a readiness to conform to them) is to undermine the very conditions that enable complex commodity exchange.[35]

Equally important, the commissioning couples *cannot* consistently resist absolute prohibitions against treating persons as marketable commodities. They already accept moral principles condemning such treatment, and their acceptance is manifested in the nature of many of their wishes to participate in the practice in the first place. They want a child; and will accept nothing *but* a child from a surrogate mother; no amount of money will compensate them should they be deprived of the child. The economic analyst of the law assumes that the value of the child to the couple can be measured *solely* in terms of the price they would be willing to pay.[36] But this is just mistaken: the couple takes the child to have *intrinsic* worth—a worth that cannot be measured in economic terms. Surrogacy for pay requires the couple to attempt to put a price on the very entity which they believe to be beyond price; thus their own assumptions commit them to rejecting surrogacy for pay as morally indefensible. Importantly, not even the theorist of the economic analysis of the law can show why the moral principles which these couples accept should not govern practice. The relevant moral principles are an important part of a valuable tradition that places at the center of moral reflection an absolute requirement to respect persons as more than mere things. Human history—including American history—reminds us that we have not yet experienced a society that consistently accords respect to all persons.

NOTES

1. Stephen L. Isaacs and Renee J. Holt, "Redefining Procreation: Facing the Issues." *Population Bulletin,* vol. 42, no. 3 (Washington, D.C.: Population Reference Bureau), Sep. 1987.
2. This is the claim insisted upon, unsuccessfully, in the agreement in the "Baby M" case. *In the Matter of Baby M,* 109 N.J. 396, Appendix A, at 471.
3. Arguments about right are less prominent since the New Jersey Supreme Court declared that the "right to procreate" even if constitutionally protected, does not extend to the "custody, care, companionship, and nurturing that follow birth. " *In The Matter of Baby M,* at 447–51.
4. Richard Posner contends that "efficiency" just is "exploiting economic resources in such a way that 'value'—human satisfaction as measured by aggregate consumer willingness to pay for goods and services—is maximized." He argues that resources are employed efficiently when shifted, through voluntary exchange, to "uses in which the value to consumers, as measured by their willingness to pay, is highest." Efficiency in family law, he contends, would be promoted by allowing the sale of babies. Posner, *Economic Analysis of the Law,* 2nd ed. (Boston: Little, Brown and Company, 1977), pp. 10 and 111–16. See also Elizabeth M. Landes and Richard A. Posner, "The Economics of the Baby Shortage," *Journal of Legal Studies,* vol. 7 (1978), pp. 323–48.
5. My argument may support the stronger conclusion that it should be illegal to broker these agreements. I will not make that case, however, since uniformly declaring paid surrogacy agreements legally unenforceable would effectively discourage the practice.
6. Arthur Miller, "Job Contracts: Are They Worth the Paper They're Printed On?", in John Arthur and William H. Shaw, eds., *Readings in Philosophy of Law,* (Englewood Cliffs, New Jersey: Prentice-Hall, Inc. 1984), pp. 294–305.

7. Landes and Posner suggest that a baby is a "complex and durable good," one that "yields services over a substantial period of time," in "Economics of the Baby Shortage," p. 341.
8. By "value" Posner means human satisfaction—as measured by "aggregate consumer willingness to pay for goods and services," *Economic Analysis of the Law,* p. 10. But if willingness to pay a certain price were the only appropriate consideration in paid surrogacy, the couples would accept the return of any money paid to a carrying mother attempting to retain custody.
9. Lori Andrews, specialist in reproductive law, quoted in Ethan Bronner, "Surrogacy: A Child's Fate and a World's Values," *The Boston Globe,* April 5, 1987, 92.
10. Dr. Lee Salk, quoted in Phyllis Chesler, *Sacred Bond: The Legacy of Baby M* (New York: *Times* Books, Random House, 1988), p. 14.
11. Lori Andrews, quoted on Ethan Bronner, "Surrogacy: A Child's Fate and a World's Values," *The Boston Globe,* April 5, 1987; see also, Ethan Bronner, "Legal Specialists Voice Reservations," *The Boston Globe,* April 1, 1987, 7.
12. A witness for the couple in the Baby M case made this claim about the surrogate in the case: "Under Narcissistic Personality Disorders there is noted a sense of self importance and a sense of specialness to the various life problems encountered. Mrs. Whitehead makes an assumption that because she is the mother that the child, Baby M, belongs to her." Quoted in Phyllis Chesler, *Sacred Bond: The Legacy of Baby M,* Appendix C, p. 181.
13. Ann Fehn brought this linguistic peculiarity to my attention.
14. Betty Friedan, quoted in the *New York Times,* April 5, 1987.
15. Mary Warnock, *A Question of Life: The Warnock Report on Human Fertilisation and Embryology* (Oxford: Blackwell, 1984). The report argues, p. 37, that ". . . where a woman donates an egg for transfer to another the donation should be treated as absolute and that, like a male donor, she should have no rights or duties with regard to any resulting child." It is also argued that cases in which an embryo is provided for transfer into a "carrying mother" should be treated like egg donation (p. 47). The report also contends that sperm donors in artificial insemination (independent of surrogacy) should be granted no parental rights or duties, on p. 25.
16. Orlando Patterson, *Slavery and Social Death* (Cambridge: Harvard University Press, 1982), pp. 24–25.
17. The agreement in the Baby M case is an important example. See *In the Matter of Baby M,* 109 N.J. 396. Appendix A.
18. I refer to the much debated charge of "felony abuse of a fetus."
19. Richard Titmuss, *The Gift Relationship: From Human Blood to Social Policy* (New York: Vintage Books, 1971).
20. Titmuss, *Ibid.,* Chs. 5 and 12–14.
21. Titmuss, *Ibid.* See also Kenneth Arrow, "Gifts and Exchange," *Philosophy and Public Affairs,* vol. 1 (1972), pp. 343–62.
22. Landes and Posner, in "The Economics of the Baby Shortage," suggest that we could protect the welfare of children in a baby market *simply* by prosecuting abuse and neglect (p. 345). Further, they ignore the fact that goods that have once circulated on the market may always circulate again—it is not sufficient simply to claim that because most couples desire infants, the question of a market in older children is "largely academic" (p. 345).
23. In non-surrogate pregnancies this most often means that a mother *and* a father have custodial responsibilities. Of course there are important asymmetries between the birth mother and the genetic father: the birth mother is *physically* confronted with custodial responsibilities toward the child while it develops, and often legally liable for ignoring them. She is furthermore *socially,* and *legally,* less able to ignore her custodial responsibilities once the child is born.
24. Studies of surrogates are discussed in Christine Overall, *Ethics and Human Reproduction* (Boston: Allen and Unwin, 1987), pp. 123–24. See also, Ann Taylor Fleming, "Our Fascination with Baby M," *New York Times Magazine,* March 29, 1987, p. 35; and Robert Coles, "So, You Fell in Love with Your Baby," *New York Times Book Review,* June 26, 1988.
25. *In the Matter of Baby M,* 109 N.J. 396, Appendix A, 471.
26. The Court argued that surrogate agreements attempt to do what adoption laws forbid: to hold the mother to an "irrevocable agreement, prior to birth, even prior to conception, to surrender the child. . . . " They found it implausible and unfair

to claim that the surrogate could decide the child's best interests "before she has even conceived, and in some cases before she has the slightest idea of what the natural father and adoptive mother are like." *In the Matter of Baby M,* pp. 421–40.

27. Peter Singer and Deane Wells, *Making Babies: The New Science and Ethics of Conception* (New York: Charles Scribner's Sons, 1985), pp. 46–52 (esp. 48).
28. Singer and Wells, *Ibid.,* pp. 104–16, reject privately arranged surrogacy for pay (arguing that it poses a great risk of abuse), but support creating a public non-profit agency to regulate agreements and fees. However, this simply puts the public in the business of brokering the exchange of babies for money.
29. Overall, *Ethics and Human Reproduction,* pp. 139–44.
30. Isaacs and Holt, "Redefining Procreation," pp. 4–5. See also, Overall, *Ethics and Human Reproduction,* pp. 139–44.
31. See, Overall, *Ethics and Human Reproduction,* pp. 139–44.
32. Isaacs and Holt, "Redefining Procreation," pp. 4–5.
33. Singer and Wells, *Ibid.,* p. 112.
34. Posner, *Economic Analysis of the Law;* cf. Landes and Posner, "The Economics of the Baby Shortage."
35. Kenneth Arrow makes a similar suggestion in "Gifts and Exchanges," pp. 345–46.
36. Posner, *Economic Analysis of the Law,* p. 10 and pp. 114–16.

PART 7

CONSTITUTIONAL LAW

Contemporary disputes in constitutional law center on well-known philosophical topics, such as rights, equality, privacy, fairness, the interpretation of texts. Indeed, a constitution is supposed to provide a grounding for a legal system, and groundings are often drawn in broadly philosophical terms. Constitutions provide the abstract principles that guide judges and legislators. The analysis of abstract principles is, of course, the proper domain of philosophy. Consider the question of what is the proper relationship between a given government and its citizens. Clearly, this question has both constitutional and philosophical implications. It is thus no mystery that philosophy has been more prominent in constitutional-law debates than anywhere else in law.

We begin Part 7 with Ronald Dworkin's "Constitutional Cases." Dworkin focuses our attention on two issues concerning how to interpret a constitution properly. First, how faithful must interpreters be to the intentions of those who wrote and adopted the given constitution? Second, how narrowly should one view "the moral rights that individuals have against society?"(see p. 429). Though both issues are often lumped under the heading of "strict" construction, as opposed to liberal construction, of a constitution, Dworkin argues that we should not confuse these issues. In trying to be faithful to the framers' intent, one can be a strict constructionist but not view moral rights narrowly in the legal context, if it turns out that the framers intended to give a broad construal of moral rights in law.

The distinction between two ways of being strict in interpreting a constitution comes to a head when a constitution includes intentionally vague clauses concerning moral rights, such as the clause in the U.S. Constitution guaranteeing "equal protection of the laws." It would not be faithful to the framer's intentions to conceive this provision of equal rights narrowly if the framers intended a broad moral base for the system of laws that the Constitution grounded. Dworkin argues further that this was the framers' intent in forming the U.S. Constitution. He then argues forcefully for an "activist" court that puts moral concerns high on its agenda. Only in this way will courts be faithful to the founding moral principles of U.S. democracy.

One type of "strict" interpretation of a constitution takes a historical approach, by which one makes the intent of the authors or framers of a constitution definitive when one is deciding how to interpret and apply a constitution to present-day cases. In "Does the Constitution Mean What It Always Meant?" Stephen R. Munzer and James W. Nickel advance several arguments against the historical approach. They argue that changes in government over time, as well as changes in circumstance, make it difficult to adhere strictly to the framers' intent. On the other hand, the authors argue against a complete rejection of *any* attention to the framers' intent. Such a view, Munzer and Nickel argue, presents clearly counterintuitive results—matters clearly mandated by the Constitution can be rejected with impunity. They thus argue for a middle ground on how strictly to interpret the Constitution.

Munzer and Nickel also argue against Dworkin's view of constitutional interpretation. They contend that even the vague clauses of a constitution, such as equal protection of the laws, "have more content than Dworkin allows"(p. 447). These are not mere concepts that the framers intended to have no fixed meaning. As such, we need to pay attention to what the framers intended these concepts to capture. The authors propose a view more faithful to the framers' intent than is Dworkin's view but which also recognizes the U.S. government as interactive, where change is democratically debated over time. How we interpret the Constitution should reflect this democratic deliberation.

The Chinese constitution recognizes an even broader array of people's rights against the government than does the U.S. Constitution. Even so, the United States often criticizes the Chinese government for not respecting the rights of its citizens. One of the reasons for this, according to R. P. Peerenboom, is that the Chinese do not conceive of rights as "trumps" against all other concerns. This view proceeds from China's historical reliance on the philosophy of Confucianism, which does not recognize universally applicable moral norms. Further, Confucian philosophy is community oriented and contextual. As such, the Chinese interpret rights in their constitution according to these values.

Does the lack of universal scope of Chinese constitutional rights make them inferior to Western rights said to be "inalienable" and to extend to all citizens? In "What's Wrong with Chinese Rights?" Peerenboom argues that the Chinese conception of rights is not necessarily inferior. Despite the rhetoric of Western rights theorists, rights are not extended to everyone in every situation in Western countries either. For example, a person has a right of free speech, but no right to yell "fire" in a crowded theater. In addition, when rights are tailored to the particular circumstances of different communities, they will better serve the purposes for which they were designed, namely, to serve the common good.

In India, judges regularly rule that the eradication of poverty is their main mandate, a striking view given that this view is so clearly unsupported by the Indian constitution. Jeremy Cooper, in "Poverty and Constitutional Justice," argues that the Indian Supreme Court is justified in so acting, because such action is necessary for the Court to achieve social justice in their country. Further, Cooper argues, courts must actively support the most downtrodden members of society if the courts are to have any claim for respect. That is, courts cannot both falter in their pursuit of social justice for the poor and also claim justice as their main moral underpinning. Here we have one of the most persuasive arguments for "activism" in judicial decision making. In contrast, the next selection provides a powerful argument for judicial restraint.

In the current debate over constitutional rights, the most controversy centers on so-called privacy rights. We begin a set of readings on this topic with a short but pithy statement of the view of the opponents of the constitutional right to privacy in the United States. In "The Right of Privacy," Robert Bork makes the obvious but important point that there is no mention of privacy in the Bill of Rights of the United States Constitution. For this reason alone, Bork says, we should be very suspicious of talk of the right to privacy, especially because such talk seems to know no bounds. Bork, a strict constructionist, sees the string of court cases starting with *Griswold v. Connecticut* as "nothing more than a warrant judges had created for themselves to do whatever they wished" (p. 484).

When she examines the U.S. Supreme Court's decision in *Bowers v. Hardwick* concerning homosexuality, Judith DeCew takes quite a different position on the constitutional right to privacy. In "Constitutional Privacy, Judicial Interpretation, and *Bowers v. Hardwick*," DeCew criticizes positions like Bork's because, she claims, it is very difficult to ascertain the "true" intent of the framers, especially because the framers were themselves a diverse group of people who came to the constitutional convention with widely varying agendas. Further, because the framers were unlikely to hold views on homosexuality, it is hard to say what was or would have been the framers' intent. We need a middle ground with some flexibility to deal with issues that the framers probably had not considered.

DeCew also points out that "strict" construction of the Constitution is a two-edged sword, especially concerning privacy rights. On the one hand, a narrow construal of the Constitution can thwart attempts to extend privacy rights to increasing numbers of people in the United States. On the other hand, a narrow reading of the Constitution also normally offers a narrow scope in terms of precedent. In *Bowers v. Hardwick*, for instance, the court ruled that the right to engage in sodomy is not protected by privacy rights. According to DeCew, this means that the court has left the door open concerning homosexual rights, because sodomy is not a sexual practice restricted to homosexuals.

Ireland is an interesting example of a country where judges have applied principles of morality to decide questions of sexual privacy, but with very different results from those in the United States. In Ireland, judges refer to conservative, moral principles of natural law in deciding cases about abortion, birth control, and homosexual rights. In the United States, thinkers like Ronald Dworkin urge that liberal principles of morality constrain the law. In "Natural Law: Alive and Kicking?" Rory O'Connell documents how this conception of morality has played itself out in these decisions, and he reminds us that a debate still exists regarding which principles of morality one should apply to law.

O'Connell comments that judicial activism concerning sexual rights will have very different results depending on which conception of morality judges actively apply. U.S. courts "emphasize the 'dignity and freedom of the individual.'" But Irish courts "emphasize the supremacy of God['s]" law (p. 507). In Ireland, God's natural law is held to be superior even to the Irish constitution. In matters of sexual privacy, appeals to dignity and freedom will allow courts to extend privacy rights to protect those seeking abortion and birth control, whereas appeals to natural law will have the opposite result in these cases. Judicial activism fueled by concerns for morality looks very different in Ireland than in the United States. We need to remember that both forms of activism are possible once we move away from strict constructionism.

Another set of constitutional issues concerns racial and sexual discrimination. Charles R. Lawrence III, in "If He Hollers Let Him Go," discusses racist hate speech on campus. He argues that the antidiscrimination principle that arises out of the equal protection clause can be used to attack speech that is racially offensive. According to Lawrence, both racist conduct and racist speech can fall under the antidiscrimination principle, because racism "is both 100 percent speech and 100 percent conduct" (p. 514). The difficulty, as Lawrence admits, is that curtailing racist hate speech risks curtailing other forms of speech that minority members rely on to get their message out.

To counter the worries about censorship that arise when racist hate speech is legally sanctioned, Lawrence reminds us that there has always been an exception to the right of free speech concerning so-called fighting words, or words that aim to inflict suffering on others and instigate a retaliation. He argues that racist hate speech is very similar to "face-to-face insults, a form of speech that is unprotected by the first amendment" (p. 517). The clash between the constitutional principles of freedom of speech and equal protection of the laws can be resolved, he argues. We want to make sure that the words of some do not effectively silence others.

A similar issue arises in the debates about legally sanctioning pornographic writings and pictures. Here we return to Ronald Dworkin, who begins his essay "Do We Have a Right to Pornography?" asking "how far people should have the right to do the wrong thing." Dworkin considers the right to pornography under the larger banner of the right to moral independence. Such a right is not absolute and may be overridden if the exercise of that right causes harm. For such a right to be overridden, there must be more than the suggestion that attitudes engendered by viewing pornography will not be suitable for "human flourishing." Those who seek legal limits on pornography, Dworkin asserts, have mixed motives. They believe that pornographers are people of bad character, not merely purveyors of harmful material. Disentangling the motives of those opposed to pornography makes the case for legally restricting pornography that much harder to defend.

In attempting to defend the right to moral independence, Dworkin claims that rights need to be regarded as trumps against a majority that seeks to advance its happiness. The preferences of a majority of people opposed to pornography should not be given any more weight than the preferences of a majority of people committed to Nazism. Rights function to protect members of the minority. This is not to say that majorities have no rights. Dworkin proposes a compromise: legal restrictions on the "public" display of pornography may be countenanced as long as no grave harm is done. However, banning pornography, especially for "private" consumption, cannot be justified, for it clearly restricts an important right of the minority.

In "Whose Right? Ronald Dworkin, Women, and Pornographers," Rae Langton challenges Dworkin's position by urging that we think of the harm of pornography in terms of the perpetuation of the inequality of the sexes rather than in terms of specific isolated harms. Pornography is a kind of propaganda that expresses a certain view of women. Most importantly, pornography legitimizes such practices as rape and sexual abuse of women. Langton thinks that Dworkin should give this type of harm more weight, because his general view proceeds from the principle of equality. That is, he should have taken more seriously than he did the feminist argument that pornography subordinates women.

We conclude with two famous U.S. Supreme Court cases about racial discrimination and the Constitution. In *Plessy v. Ferguson,* the Supreme Court considered the case of a man who was seven-eighths Caucasian but who was treated by Louisiana as nonwhite. He was accused of sitting in the whites-only section of a train. Plessy challenged the law under which he was arrested as unconstitutional, saying that it violated his Fourteenth Amendment right to equal protection of the laws. The Court decided that equal protection was not envisioned by the framers to "abolish distinctions based on color," but only to make the races equal. Upholding the doctrine of "separate but equal," the majority ruled against Plessy, because he had the opportunity to ride in just as good a train car set aside for nonwhites. Importantly, the dissenting opinion by Justice Harlan states that the law should be color-blind, a position which was used to attack the separate but equal doctrine but which itself was later criticized for supporting more subtle forms of racism.

In *Brown v. Board of Education,* the U.S. Supreme Court overturned the Plessy case. Here the plaintiffs were African-American schoolchildren who claimed to be denied equal protection when they were prohibited from attending whites-only schools. The plaintiffs claimed that segregated schools were inherently unequal and violated the Constitution. The Court held that the "segregation of children in public schools solely on the basis of race, even though the physical facilities and other 'tangible' factors may be equal," (p. 540) deprives the children of equality of opportunity guaranteed by the Constitution. This opinion had far-reaching effects on U.S. society, which are still being felt. *Brown v. Board of Education* is considered a landmark in the battle against racism in constitutional law.

SELECTED READINGS

Arthur, John. *The Unfinished Constitution: Philosophy and Constitutional Practice.* Belmont, CA: Wadsworth, 1989.

Beatty, David. "Protecting Constitutional Rights in Japan and Canada." *American Journal of Comparative Law* 41 (1993): 535–50.

Dahl, Robert. "Thinking About Democratic Constitutions: Conclusions from Democratic Experience." *NOMOS XXXVIII: Political Order*, pp.175–206. New York: New York University Press, 1996.

Diefenbach, Donald. "The Constitutional and Moral Justification for Copyright." *Public Affairs Quarterly* 8, no. 3 (July 1994): 225–35.

Kentridge, Sydney. "Bills of Rights—the South African Experiment." *Law Quarterly Review* 112 (1996): 237–61.

Lyons, David. "Basic Rights and Constitutional Interpretation." *Social Theory and Practice* 16, no. 3 (Fall 1990): 337–57.

Martin, Rex, and Stephen Griffin. "Constitutional Rights and Democracy in America: The Issue of Judicial Review." *Ratio Juris* 8, no. 2 (July 1995): 180–98.

Michaelman, Frank. "Must Constitutional Democracy Be 'Responsive'?" *Ethics* 107, no. 4 (July 1997): 706–23.

Minow, Martha. *Making All the Difference: Inclusion, Exclusion, and American Law.* Ithaca, NY: Cornell, 1990.

Prior, E. J. "Constitutional Fairness or Fraud on the Constitution? Compensatory Discrimination in India." *Case Western Reserve Journal of International Law* 28 (1996): 63–100.

Robinson, John. "Physician Assisted Suicide: Its Challenge to the Prevailing Constitutional Paradigm." *Notre Dame Journal of Law and Ethics* 9, no. 2 (1995): 345–66.

Slinn, Peter. "A Fresh Start for Africa? New African Constitutional Perspectives." *Journal of African Law* 35 (1991): 1–7.

Smith, Patricia. "Constitutional Interpretation by Strict Construction." *Journal of Social Philosophy* 19 (Summer 1988): 43–55.

Sunstein, Cass R. *The Partial Constitution.* Cambridge, MA: Harvard University Press, 1993.

51

RONALD DWORKIN

Constitutional Cases

1

When Richard Nixon was running for President he promised that he would appoint to the Supreme Court men who represented his own legal philosophy, that is, who were what he called "strict constructionists." The nominations he subsequently made and talked about, however, did not all illuminate that legal philosophy; jurisprudence played little part in the nation's evaluation of Haynesworth and Carswell, let alone those almost nominated, Hershell Friday and Mildred Lilly. But the President presented his successful choices, Lewis Powell and William Rehnquist, as examples of his theory of law, and took the occasion to expand on that theory for a national television audience. These men, he said, would enforce the law as it is, and not "twist or bend" it to suit their own personal convictions, as Nixon accused the Warren Court of doing.

Nixon claimed that his opposition to the Warren Court's desegregation decisions, and to other decisions it took, were not based simply on a personal or political distaste for the results. He argued that the decisions violated the standards of adjudication that the Court should follow. The Court was usurping, in his views, powers that rightly belong to other institutions, including the legislatures of the various states whose school systems the Court sought to reform. He was, of course, not alone in this view. It has for some time been part of general conservative attitudes that the Supreme Court has exceeded its rightful authority. Nixon, Ford and many Congressmen and representatives have canvassed ways to limit the Court's authority by legislation. Nixon, for example, asked for a Congressional statute that would have purported to reverse important decisions, including the decision in *Swann v. Charlotte-Mecklenburg Board of Education* which gave federal courts wide powers to use busing orders as a remedy for certain forms of *de facto* segregation, and Senator Jackson and others have for some time campaigned for a constitutional amendment to the same point.

I shall not be concerned with the correctness of any of the Court's controversial decisions, nor with the wisdom of these various attempts, so far unsuccessful, to check its powers by some form of legislation or amendment. I am concerned rather with the philosophy of constitutional adjudication that the politicians who oppose the Court suppose that they hold. I shall argue that there is in fact no coherent philosophy to which such politicians may consistently appeal. . . .

Nixon is no longer president, and his crimes were so grave that no one is likely to worry very much any more about the details of his own legal philosophy. Nevertheless in what follows I shall use the name "Nixon" to refer, not to Nixon, but to any politician holding the set of attitudes about the Supreme Court that he made explicit in his political campaigns. There was, fortunately, only one real Nixon, but there are, in the special sense in which I use the name, many Nixons.

What can be the basis of this composite Nixon's opposition to the controversial decisions of the Warren Court? He cannot object to these decisions simply because they went beyond prior law, or say that the Supreme Court itself seems intent on limiting the liberal decisions of the Warren Court, like *Miranda*. The Constitution's guarantee of "equal protection of the laws," it is true, does not in plain words determine that "separate but equal" school facilities are unconstitutional, or that segregation was so unjust that heroic measures are required to undo its effects. But neither does it provide that as a matter of constitutional law the Court would be wrong to reach these conclusions. It leaves these issues to the Court's judgment, and the Court would have made law just as much if it had, for example, refused to hold the North Carolina statute unconstitutional. It would have made law by establishing, as a matter of precedent, that the equal protection clause does not reach that far.

So we must search further to find a theoretical basis for Nixon's position. It may be silly, of course, to suppose that Nixon has a jurisprudence. He might simply have strung together catch phrases of conservative rhetoric, or he might be recording a distaste for any judicial decision that seems to extend the rights of individuals against constituted authority. But Nixon is, after all, a lawyer, and in any event his conservative views are supported by a great many lawyers and some very distinguished legal scholars. It is therefore important to see how far this conservative position can be defended as a matter of principle and not simply of prejudice.

2

The constitutional theory on which our government rests is not a simple majoritarian theory. The Constitution, and particularly the Bill of Rights, is designed to protect individual citizens and groups against certain decisions that a majority of citizens might want to make, even when that majority acts in what it takes to be the general or common interest. Some of these constitutional restraints take the form of fairly precise rules, like the rule that requires a jury trial in federal criminal proceedings or, perhaps, the rule that forbids the national Congress to abridge freedom of speech. But other constraints take the form of what are often called "vague" standards, for example, the provision that the government shall not deny men due process of law, or equal protection of the laws.

This interference with democratic practice requires a justification. The draftsmen of the Constitution assumed that these restraints could be justified by appeal to moral rights which individuals possess against the majority, and which the constitutional provisions, both "vague" and precise, might be said to recognize and protect.

The "vague" standards were chosen deliberately, by the men who drafted and adopted them, in place of the more specific and limited rules that they might have enacted. But their decision to use the language they did has caused a great deal of legal and political controversy, because even reasonable men of good will differ when they try to elaborate, for example, the moral rights that the due process clause or the equal protection clause brings into law. They also differ when they try to apply these rights, however defined, to complex matters of political administration, like the educational practices that were the subject of the segregation cases.

The practice has developed of referring to a "strict" and a "liberal" side to these controversies, so that the Supreme Court might be said to have taken the "liberal" side in the segregation cases and its critics the "strict" side. Nixon has this distinction in mind when he calls himself a "strict constructionist." But the distinction is in fact confusing, because it runs together two different issues that must be separated. Any case that arises under the "vague" constitutional guarantees can be seen as posing two questions: (1) Which decision is required by strict, that is to say faithful, adherence to the text of the Constitution or to the intention of those who adopted that text? (2) Which decision is required by a political philosophy that takes a strict, that is to say narrow, view of the moral rights that individuals have against society? Once these questions are distinguished, it is plain that they may have different answers. The text of the First Amendment, for example, says that Congress shall make *no* law abridging the freedom of speech, but a narrow view of individual rights would permit many such laws, ranging from libel and obscenity laws to the Smith Act.

In the case of the "vague" provisions, however, like the due process and equal protection clauses, lawyers have run the two questions together because they have relied, largely without recognizing it, on a theory of meaning that might be put this way: If the framers of the Constitution used vague language, as they did when they condemned violation of "due process of law," then what they "said" or "meant" is limited to the instances of official action that they had in mind as violations, or, at least, to those instances that they would have thought were violations if they had had them in mind. If those who were responsible for adding the due process clause to the Constitution believed that it was fundamentally unjust to provide separate education for different races, or had detailed views about justice that entailed that conclusion, then the segregation decisions might be defended as an application of the principle they had laid down. Otherwise they could not be defended in this way, but instead would show that the judges had substituted their own ideas of justice for those the constitutional drafters meant to lay down.

This theory makes a strict interpretation of the text yield a narrow view of constitutional rights, because it limits such rights to those recognized by a limited group of people at a fixed date of history. It forces those who favor a more liberal set of rights to concede that they are departing from strict legal authority, a departure they must then seek to justify by appealing only to the desirability of the results they reach.

But the theory of meaning on which this argument depends is far too crude; it ignores a distinction that philosophers have made but lawyers have not yet appreciated. Suppose I tell my children simply that I expect them not to treat others unfairly. I no doubt have in mind examples of the conduct I mean to discourage, but I would not accept that my "meaning" was limited to these examples, for two reasons. First I would expect my children to apply my instructions to situations I had not and could not have thought about. Second, I stand ready to admit that some particular act I had thought was fair when I spoke was in fact unfair, or vice versa, if one of my children is able to convince me of that later; in that case I should want to say that my instructions covered the case he cited, not that I had changed my instructions. I might say that I meant the family to be guided by the *concept* of fairness, not by any specific *conception* of fairness I might have had in mind.

This is a crucial distinction which it is worth pausing to explore. Suppose a group believes in common that acts may suffer from a special moral defect which they call unfairness, and which consists in a wrongful division of benefits and burdens, or a wrongful attribution of praise or blame. Suppose also that they agree on a great number of standard cases of unfairness and use these as benchmarks against which to test other, more controversial cases. In that case, the group has a concept of unfairness, and its members may appeal to that concept in moral instruction or argument. But members of that group may nevertheless differ over a large number of these controversial cases, in a way that suggests that each either has or acts on a different theory of *why* the standard cases are acts of unfairness. They may differ, that is, on which more fundamental principles must be relied upon to show that a particular division or attribution is unfair. In that case, the members have different conceptions of fairness.

If so, then members of this community who give instructions or set standards in the name of fairness may be doing two different things. First they may be appealing to the concept of fairness, simply by instructing others to act fairly; in this case they charge those whom they instruct with the responsibility of developing and applying their own conception of fairness as controversial cases arise. That is not the same thing, of course, as granting them a discretion to act as they like; it sets a standard which they must try—and may fail—to meet, because it assumes that one conception is superior to another. The man who appeals to the concept in this way may have his own conception, as I did when I told my children to act fairly; but he holds this conception only as his own theory of how the standard he set must be met, so that when he changes his theory he has not changed that standard.

On the other hand, the members may be laying down a particular conception of fairness; I would have done this, for example, if I had listed my wishes with respect to controversial examples or if, even less likely, I had specified some controversial and explicit theory of fairness, as if I had said to decide hard cases by applying the utilitarian ethics of Jeremy Bentham. The difference is a difference not just in the *detail* of the instructions given but in the *kind* of instructions given. When I appeal to the concept of fairness I appeal to what fairness means, and I give my views on that issue no special standing. When I lay down a conception of fairness, I lay down what I mean by fairness, and my view is therefore the heart of the matter. When I appeal to fairness I pose a moral issue; when I lay down my conception of fairness I try to answer it.

Once this distinction is made it seems obvious that we must take what I have been calling "vague" constitutional clauses as representing appeals to the concepts they employ, like legality, equality, and cruelty. The Supreme Court may soon decide, for example, whether capital punishment is "cruel" within the meaning of the constitutional clause that prohibits "cruel and unusual punishment." It would be a mistake for the Court to be much influenced by the fact that when the clause was adopted capital punishment was standard and unquestioned. That would be decisive if the framers of the clause had meant to lay down a particular conception of cruelty, because it would show that the conception did not extend so far. But it is not decisive of the different question the Court now faces, which is this: Can the Court, responding to the framers' appeal to the concept of cruelty, now defend a conception that does not make death cruel?

Those who ignore the distinction between concepts and conceptions, but who believe that the Court ought to make a fresh determination of whether the death penalty is cruel, are forced to argue in a vulnerable way. They say that ideas of cruelty change over time, and that the Court must be free to reject out-of-date conceptions; this suggests that the Court must change what the Constitution enacted. But in fact the Court can enforce what the Constitution says only by making up its own mind about what is cruel, just as my children, in my example, can do what I said only by making up their own minds about what is fair. If those who enacted the broad clauses had meant to lay down particular conceptions, they would have found the sort of language conventionally used to do this, that is, they would have offered particular theories of the concepts in question.

Indeed the very practice of calling these clauses "vague," in which I have joined, can now be seen to involve a mistake. The clauses are vague only if we take them to be botched or incomplete or schematic attempts to lay down particular conceptions. If we take them as appeals to moral concepts they could not be made more precise by being more detailed.[1]

The confusion I mentioned between the two senses of "strict construction" is therefore very misleading indeed. If courts try to be faithful to the text of the Constitution, they will for that very reason be forced to decide between competing conceptions of political morality. So it is wrong to attack the Warren Court, for example, on the ground that it failed to treat the Constitution as a binding text. On the contrary, if we wish to treat fidelity to that text as an overriding requirement of constitutional interpretation, then it is the conservative critics of the Warren Court who are at fault, because their philosophy ignores the direction to face issues of moral principle that the logic of the text demands.

I put the matter in a guarded way because we may *not* want to accept fidelity to the spirit of the text as an overriding principle of constitutional adjudication. It may be more important for courts to decide constitutional cases in a manner that respects the judgments of other institutions of government, for example. Or it may be more important for courts to protect established legal doctrines, so that citizens and the government can have confidence that the courts will hold to what they have said before. But it is crucial to recognize that these other policies compete with the principle that the Constitution is the fundamental and imperative source of constitutional law. They are not, as the "strict constructionists" suppose, simply consequences of that principle.

3

Once the matter is put in this light, moreover, we are able to assess these competing claims of policy, free from the confusion imposed by the popular notion of "strict construction." For this purpose I want now to compare and contrast two very general philosophies of how the courts should decide difficult or controversial constitutional issues. I shall call these two philosophies by the names they are given in the legal literature—the programs of "judicial activism" and "judicial restraint"—though it will be plain that these names are in certain ways misleading.

The program of judicial activism holds that courts should accept the directions of the so-called vague constitutional provisions in the spirit I described, in spite of competing reasons of the sort I mentioned. They should work out principles of legality, equality, and the rest, revise these principles from time to time in the light of what seems to the Court fresh moral insight, and judge the acts of Congress, the states, and the President accordingly. (This puts the program in its strongest form; in fact its supporters generally qualify it in ways I shall ignore for the present.)

The program of judicial restraint, on the contrary, argues that courts should allow the decisions of other branches of government to stand, even when they offend the judges' own sense of the principles required by the broad constitutional doctrines, except when these decisions are so offensive to political morality that they would violate the provisions on any plausible interpretation, or, perhaps, when a contrary decision is required by clear precedent. (Again, this put the program in a stark form; those who profess the policy qualify it in different ways.)

The Supreme Court followed the policy of activism rather than restraint in cases like the segregation cases

[1]It is less misleading to say that the broad clauses of the Constitution "delegate" power to the Court to enforce its own conceptions of political morality. But even this is inaccurate if it suggests that the Court need not justify its conception by arguments showing the connections between its conception and standard cases, as described in the text. If the Court finds that the death penalty is cruel, it must do so on the basis of some principles or groups of principles that unite the death penalty with the thumbscrew and the rack.

because the words of the equal protection clause left it open whether the various educational practices of the states concerned should be taken to violate the Constitution, no clear precedent held that they did, and reasonable men might differ on the moral issues involved. If the Court had followed the program of judicial restraint, it would therefore have held in favor of the North Carolina statute in *Swann,* not against it. But the program of restraint would not always act to provide decisions that would please political conservatives. In the early days of the New Deal, as critics of the Warren Court are quick to point out, it was the liberals who objected to Court decisions that struck down acts of Congress in the name of the due process clause.

It may seem, therefore, that if Nixon has a legal theory it depends crucially on some theory of judicial restraint. We must now, however, notice a distinction between two forms of judicial restraint, for there are two different, and indeed incompatible, grounds on which that policy might be based.

The first is a theory of political *skepticism* that might be described in this way. The policy of judicial activism presupposes a certain objectivity of moral principle; in particular it presupposes that citizens do have certain moral rights against the state, like a moral right to equality of public education or to fair treatment by the police. Only if such moral rights exist in some sense can activism be justified as a program based on something beyond the judge's personal preferences. The skeptical theory attacks activism at its roots; it argues that in fact individuals have no such moral rights against the state. They have only such *legal* rights as the Constitution grants them, and these are limited to the plain and uncontroversial violations of public morality that the framers must have had actually in mind, or that have since been established in a line of precedent.

The alternative ground of a program of restraint is a theory of judicial *deference.* Contrary to the skeptical theory, this assumes that citizens do have moral rights against the state beyond what the law expressly grants them, but it points out that the character and strength of these rights are debatable and argues that political institutions other than courts are responsible for deciding which rights are to be recognized.

This is an important distinction, even though the literature of constitutional law does not draw it with any clarity. The skeptical theory and the theory of deference differ dramatically in the kind of justification they assume, and in their implications for the more general moral theories of the men who profess to hold them. These theories are so different that most American politicians can consistently accept the second, but not the first.

A skeptic takes a view, as I have said, that men have no moral rights against the state and only such legal rights as the law expressly provides. But what does this mean, and what sort of argument might the skeptic make for his view? There is, of course, a very lively dispute in moral philosophy about the nature and standing of moral rights, and considerable disagreement about what they are, if they are anything at all. I shall rely, in trying to answer these questions, on a low-keyed theory of moral rights against the state. . . . Under that theory, a man has a moral right against the state if for some reason the state would do wrong to treat him in a certain way, even though it would be in the general interest to do so. So a black child has a moral right to an equal education, for example, if it is wrong for the state not to provide that education, even if the community as a whole suffers thereby.

I want to say a word about the virtues of this way of looking at moral rights against the state. A great many lawyers are wary of talking about moral rights, even though they find it easy to talk about what is right or wrong for government to do, because they suppose that rights, if they exist at all, are spooky sorts of things that men and women have in much the same way as they have non-spooky things like tonsils. But the sense of rights I propose to use does not make ontological assumptions of that sort: it simply shows a claim of right to be a special, in the sense of a restricted, sort of judgment about what is right or wrong for governments to do.

Moreover, this way of looking at rights avoids some of the notorious puzzles associated with the concept. It allows us to say, with no sense of strangeness, that rights may vary in strength and character from case to case, and from point to point in history. If we think of rights as things, these metamorphoses seem strange, but we are used to the idea that moral judgments about what it is right or wrong to do are complex and are affected by considerations that are relative and that change.

The skeptic who wants to argue against the very possibility of rights against the state of this sort has a difficult brief. He must rely, I think, on one of three general positions: (a) He might display a more pervasive moral skepticism, which holds that even to speak of an act being morally right or wrong makes no sense. If no act is morally wrong, then the government of North Carolina cannot be wrong to refuse to bus school children. (b) He might hold a stark form of utilitarianism, which assumes that the only reason we ever have for regarding an act as right or wrong is its impact on the general interest. Under that theory, to say that busing may be morally required even though it does not benefit the community generally would be inconsistent. (c) He might accept some form of totalitarian theory, which merges the interests of the individual in the good of the general community, and so denies that the two can conflict.

Very few American politicians would be able to accept any of these three grounds. Nixon, for example, could not, because he presents himself as a moral fundamentalist who knows in his heart that pornography is wicked and that some of the people of South Vietnam have rights of self-determination in the name of which they and we may properly kill many others.

I do not want to suggest, however, that no one would in fact argue for judicial restraint on grounds of skepticism; on the contrary, some of the best known advocates of restraint have pitched their arguments entirely on skeptical grounds. In 1957, for example, the great judge Learned Hand delivered the Oliver Wendell Holmes lectures at Harvard. Hand was a student of Santayana and a disciple of Holmes, and skepticism in morals was his only religion. He argued for judicial restraint, and said that the Supreme Court had done wrong to declare school segregation illegal in the *Brown* case. It is wrong to suppose, he said, that claims about moral rights express anything more than the speakers' preferences. If the Supreme Court justifies its decisions by making such claims, rather than by relying on positive law, it is usurping the place of the legislature, for the job of the legislature, representing the majority, is to decide whose preferences shall govern.

This simple appeal to democracy is successful if one accepts the skeptical premise. Of course, if men have no rights against the majority, if political decision is simply a matter of whose preferences shall prevail, then democracy does provide a good reason for leaving that decision to more democratic institutions than courts, even when these institutions make choices that the judges themselves hate. But a very different, and much more vulnerable, argument from democracy is needed to support judicial restraint if it is based not on skepticism but on deference, as I shall try to show.

4

If Nixon holds a coherent constitutional theory, it is a theory of restraint based not on skepticism but on deference. He believes that courts ought not to decide controversial issues of political morality because they ought to leave such decisions to other departments of government. If we ascribe this policy to Nixon, we can make sense of his charge that the Warren Court "twisted and bent" the law. He would mean that they twisted and bent the principle of judicial deference, which is an understatement, because he would be more accurate if he said that they ignored it. But are there any good reasons for holding this policy of deference? If the policy is in fact unsound, then Nixon's jurisprudence is undermined, and he ought to be dissuaded from urging further Supreme Court appointments, or encouraging Congress to oppose the Court, in its name.

There is one very popular argument in favor of the policy of deference, which might be called the argument from democracy. It is at least debatable, according to this argument, whether a sound conception of equality forbids segregated education or requires measures like busing to break it down. Who ought to decide these issues of moral and political theory? Should it be a majority of a court in Washington, whose members are appointed for life and are not politically responsible to the public whose lives will be affected by the decision? Or should it be the elected and responsible state or national legislators? A democrat, so this argument supposes, can accept only the second answer.

But the argument from democracy is weaker than it might first appear. The argument assumes, for one thing, that state legislatures are in fact responsible to the people in the way that democratic theory assumes. But in all the states, though in different degrees and for different reasons, that is not the case. In some states it is very far from the case. I want to pass that point, however, because it does not so much undermine the argument from democracy as call for more democracy, and that is a different matter. I want to fix attention on the issue of whether the appeal to democracy in this respect is even right in principle.

The argument assumes that in a democracy all unsettled issues, including issues of moral and political principle, must be resolved only by institutions that are politically responsible in the way that courts are not. Why should we accept that view of democracy? To say that that is what democracy means does no good, because it is wrong to suppose that the word, as a word, has anything like so precise a meaning. Even if it did, we should then have to rephrase our question to ask why we should have democracy, if we assume that is what it means. Nor is it better to say that that view of democracy is established in the American Constitution, or so entrenched in our political tradition that we are committed to it. We cannot argue that the Constitution, which provides no rule limiting judicial review to clear cases, establishes a theory of democracy that excludes wider review, nor can we say that our courts have in fact consistently accepted such a restriction. The burden of Nixon's argument is that they have.

So the argument from democracy is not an argument to which we are committed either by our words or our past. We must accept it, if at all, on the strength of its own logic. In order to examine the arguments more closely, however, we must make a further distinction. The argument as I have set it out might be continued in two different ways: one might argue that judicial deference is required because democratic institutions, like legislatures, are in fact likely to make *sounder* decisions than courts about the underlying issues that constitutional cases raise, that is, about the nature of an individual's moral rights against the state.

Or one might argue that it is for some reason *fairer* that a democratic institution rather than a court should decide such issues, even though there is no reason to believe that the institution will reach a sounder decision. The distinction between these two arguments would make no sense to a skeptic, who would not admit that someone could do a better or worse job at identifying moral rights against the state, any more than someone could do a better or worse job of identifying ghosts. But a lawyer who believes in judicial deference rather than skepticism must acknowledge the distinction, though he can argue both sides if he wishes.

I shall start with the second argument, that legislatures and other democratic institutions have some special title to make constitutional decisions, apart from their ability to make better decisions. One might say that the nature of this title is obvious, because it is always fairer to allow a majority to decide any issue than a minority. But that, as has often been pointed out, ignores the fact that decisions about rights against the majority are not issues that in fairness ought to be left to the majority. Constitutionalism—the theory that the majority must be restrained to protect individual rights—may be a good or bad political theory, but the United States has adopted that theory, and to make the majority judge in its own cause seems inconsistent and unjust. So principles of fairness seem to speak against, not for, the argument from democracy.

Chief Justice Marshall recognized this in his decision in *Marbury v. Madison,* the famous case in which the Supreme Court first claimed the power to review legislative decisions against constitutional standards. He argued that since the Constitution provides that the Constitution shall be the supreme law of the land, the courts in general, and the Supreme Court in the end, must have power to declare statutes void that offend that Constitution. Many legal scholars regard his argument as a *non sequitur,* because, they say, although constitutional constraints are part of the law, the courts, rather than the legislature itself, have not necessarily been given authority to decide whether in particular cases that law has been violated.[2] But the argument is not a *non sequitur* if we take the principle that no man should judge in his own cause to be so fundamental a part of the idea of legality that Marshall would have been entitled to disregard it only if the Constitution had expressly denied judicial review.

Some might object that it is simple-minded to say that a policy of deference leaves the majority to judge

---

[2]I distinguish this objection to Marshall's argument from the different objection, not here relevant, that the Constitution should be interpreted to impose a legal *duty* on Congress not, for example, to pass laws abridging freedom of speech, but it should not be interpreted to detract from the legal *power* of Congress to make such a law valid if it breaks its duty. In this view, Congress is in the legal position of a thief who has the duty not to sell stolen goods, but retains legal power to make a valid transfer if he does. This interpretation has little to recommend it since Congress, unlike a thief, cannot be disciplined except by denying validity to its wrongful acts, at least in a way that will offer protection to the individuals the Constitution is designed to protect.

its own cause. Political decisions are made, in the United States, not by one stable majority but by many different political institutions each representing a different constituency which itself changes its composition over time. The decision of one branch of government may well be reviewed by another branch that is also politically responsible, but to a larger or different constituency. The acts of the Arizona police which the Court held unconstitutional in *Miranda,* for example, were in fact subject to review by various executive boards and municipal and state legislatures of Arizona, as well as by the national Congress. It would be naïve to suppose that all of these political institutions are dedicated to the same policies and interests, so it is wrong to suppose that if the Court had not intervened the Arizona police would have been free to judge themselves.

But this objection is itself too glib, because it ignores the special character of disputes about individual moral rights as distinct from other kinds of political disputes. Different institutions do have different constituencies when, for example, labor or trade or welfare issues are involved, and the nation often divides sectionally on such issues. But this is not generally the case when individual constitutional rights, like the rights of accused criminals, are at issue. It has been typical of these disputes that the interests of those in political control of the various institutions of the government have been both homogeneous and hostile. Indeed that is why political theorists have conceived of constitutional rights as rights against the "state" or the "majority" as such, rather than against any particular body or branch of government.

The early segregation cases are perhaps exceptions to that generality, for one might argue that the only people who wanted *de jure* segregation were white Southerners. But the fact remains that the national Congress had not in fact checked segregation, either because it believed it did not have the legal power to do so or because it believed it did not want to; in either case the example hardly argues that the political process provides an effective check on even local violations of the rights of politically ineffective minorities. In the dispute over busing, moreover, the white majority mindful of its own interests has proved to be both national and powerful. And of course decisions of the national government, like executive decisions to wage war or congressional attempts to define proper police policy, as in the Crime Control Act of 1968, are subject to no review if not court review.

It does seem fair to say, therefore, that the argument from democracy asks that those in political power be invited to be the sole judge of their own decisions, to see whether they have the right to do what they have decided they want to do. That is not a final proof that a policy of judicial activism is superior to a program of deference. Judicial activism involves risks of tyranny; certainly in the stark and simple form I set out. It might even be shown that these risks override the unfairness of asking the majority to be judge in its own cause. But the point does undermine the argument that the majority, in fairness, must be allowed to decide the limits of its own power.

We must therefore turn to the other continuation of the argument from democracy, which holds that democratic institutions, like legislatures, are likely to reach *sounder* results about the moral rights of individuals than would courts. In 1969 the late Professor Alexander Bickel of the Yale Law School delivered his Holmes Lectures at Harvard and argued for the program of judicial restraint in a novel and ingenious way. He allowed himself to suppose, for purposes of argument, that the Warren Court's program of activism could be justified if in fact it produced desirable results.[3] He appeared, therefore, to be testing the policy of activism on its own grounds, because he took activism to be precisely the claim that the courts have the moral right to improve the future, whatever legal theory may say. Learned Hand and other opponents of activism had challenged that claim. Bickel accepted it, at least provisionally, but he argued that activism fails its own test.

The future that the Warren Court sought has already begun not to work, Bickel said. The philosophy of racial integration it adopted was too crude, for example, and has already been rejected by the more imaginative leaders of the black community. Its thesis of simple and radical equality has proved unworkable in many other ways as well; its simple formula of one-man-one-vote for passing on the fairness of election

[3]Professor Bickel also argued, with his usual very great skill, that many of the Warren Court's major decisions could not even be justified on conventional grounds, that is, by the arguments the Court advanced in its opinions. His criticism of these opinions is often persuasive, but the Court's failures of craftsmanship do not affect the argument I consider in the text. (His Holmes lectures were amplified in his book *The Supreme Court and the Idea of Progress,* 1970.)

districting, for instance, has produced neither sense nor fairness.

Why should a radical Court that aims at improving society fail even on its own terms? Bickel has this answer: Courts, including the Supreme Court, must decide blocks of cases on principle, rather than responding in a piecemeal way to a shifting set of political pressures. They must do so not simply because their institutional morality requires it, but because their institutional structure provides no means by which they might gauge political forces even if they wanted to. But government by principle is an inefficient and in the long run fatal form of government, no matter how able and honest the statesmen who try to administer it. For there is a limit to the complexity that any principle can contain and remain a recognizable principle, and this limit falls short of the complexity of social organization.

The Supreme Court's reapportionment decisions, in Bickel's view, were not mistaken just because the Court chose the wrong principle. One-man-one-vote is too simple, but the Court could not have found a better, more sophisticated principle that would have served as a successful test for election districting across the country, or across the years, because successful districting depends upon accommodation with thousands of facts of political life, and can be reached, if at all, only by the chaotic and unprincipled development of history. Judicial activism cannot work as well as government by the more-or-less democratic institutions, not because democracy is required by principle, but, on the contrary, because democracy works without principle, forming institutions and compromises as a river forms a bed on its way to the sea.

What are we to make of Bickel's argument? His account of recent history can be, and has been, challenged. It is by no means plain, certainly not yet, that racial integration will fail as a long-term strategy; and he is wrong if he thinks that black Americans, of whom more still belong to the NAACP than to more militant organizations, have rejected it. No doubt the nation's sense of how to deal with the curse of racism swings back and forth as the complexity and size of the problem become more apparent, but Bickel may have written at a high point of one arc of the pendulum.

He is also wrong to judge the Supreme Court's effect on history as if the Court were the only institution at work, or to suppose that if the Court's goal has not been achieved the country is worse off than if it had not tried. Since 1954, when the Court laid down the principle that equality before the law requires integrated education, we have not had, except for a few years of the Johnson Administration, a national executive willing to accept that principle as an imperative. For the past several years we have had a national executive that seems determined to undermine it. Nor do we have much basis for supposing that the racial situation in America would now be more satisfactory, on balance, if the Court had not intervened, in 1954 and later, in the way that it did.

But there is a very different, and for my purpose much more important, objection to take to Bickel's theory. His theory is novel because it appears to concede an issue of principle to judicial activism, namely, that the Court is entitled to intervene if its intervention produces socially desirable results. But the concession is an illusion, because his sense of what is socially desirable is inconsistent with the presupposition of activism that individuals have moral rights against the state. In fact, Bickel's argument cannot succeed, even if we grant his facts and his view of history, except on a basis of a skepticism about rights as profound as Learned Hand's.

I presented Bickel's theory as an example of one form of the argument from democracy, the argument that since men disagree about rights, it is safer to leave the final decision about rights to the political process is safer. He argues that the endurance of a political process, safer in the sense that the results are likely to be sounder. Bickel suggests a reason why the political process is safer. He argues that the endurance of a political settlement about rights is some evidence of the political morality of that settlement. He argues that this evidence is better than the sorts of argument from principle that judges might deploy if the decision were left to them.

There is a weak version of this claim, which cannot be part of Bickel's argument. This version argues that no political principle establishing rights can be sound, whatever abstract arguments might be made in its favor, unless it meets the test of social acceptance in the long run; so that, for example, the Supreme Court cannot be right in its views about the rights of black children, or criminal suspects, or atheists, if the community in the end will not be persuaded to recognize these rights.

This weak version may seem plausible for different reasons. It will appeal, for instance, to those who believe both in the fact and in the strength of the ordinary man's moral sense, and in his willingness to entertain appeals to that sense. But it does not argue for judicial restraint except in the very long run. On the contrary, it supposes what lawyers are fond of calling a dialogue between the judges and the nation, in which the Supreme Court is to present and defend its reflective view of what the citizen's rights are, much as the Warren Court tried to do, in the hope that the people will in the end agree.

We must turn, therefore, to the strong version of the claim. This argues that the organic political process will secure the genuine rights of men more certainly if it is not hindered by the artificial and rationalistic intrusion of the courts. On this view, the rights of blacks, suspects, and atheists will emerge through the process of political institutions responding to political pressures in the normal way. If a claim of right cannot succeed in this way, then for that reason it is, or in any event it is likely to be, an improper claim of right. But this bizarre proposition is only a disguised form of the skeptical point that there are in fact no rights against the state.

Perhaps, as Burke and his modern followers argue, a society will produce the institutions that best suit it only by evolution and never by radical reform. But rights against the state are claims that, if accepted, require society to settle for institutions that may not suit it so comfortably. The nerve of a claim of right, even on the demythologized analysis of rights I am using, is that an individual is entitled to protection against the majority even at the cost of the general interest. Of course the comfort of the majority will require some accommodation for minorities but only to the extent necessary to preserve order; and that is usually an accommodation that falls short of recognizing their rights.

Indeed the suggestion that rights can be demonstrated by a process of history rather than by an appeal to principle shows either a confusion or no real concern about what rights are. A claim of right presupposes a moral argument and can be established in no other way. Bickel paints the judicial activists (and even some of the heroes of judicial restraint, like Brandeis and Frankfurter, who had their lapses) as eighteenth-century philosophers who appeal to principle because they hold the optimistic view that a blueprint may be cut for progress. But this picture confuses two grounds for the appeal to principle and reform, and two senses of progress.

It is one thing to appeal to moral principle in the silly faith that ethics as well as economics moves by an invisible hand, so that individual rights and the general good will coalesce, and law based on principle will move the nation to a frictionless utopia where everyone is better off than he was before. Bickel attacks that vision by his appeal to history, and by his other arguments against government by principle. But it is quite another matter to appeal to principle *as* principle, to show, for example, that it is unjust to force black children to take their public education in black schools, even if a great many people *will* be worse off if the state adopts the measures needed to prevent this.

This is a different version of progress. It is moral progress, and though history may show how difficult it is to decide where moral progress lies, and how difficult to persuade others once one has decided, it cannot follow from this that those who govern us have no responsibility to face that decision or to attempt that persuasion.

5

This has been a complex argument, and I want to summarize it. Our constitutional system rests on a particular moral theory, namely, that men have moral rights against the state. The difficult clauses of the Bill of Rights, like the due process and equal protection clauses, must be understood as appealing to moral concepts rather than laying down particular conceptions; therefore a court that undertakes the burden of applying these clauses fully as law must be an activist court, in the sense that it must be prepared to frame and answer questions of political morality.

It may be necessary to compromise that activist posture to some extent, either for practical reasons or for competing reasons of principle. But Nixon's public statements about the Supreme Court suggest that the activist policy must be abandoned altogether, and not merely compromised, for powerful reasons of principle. If we try to state these reasons of principle, we find that they are inconsistent with the assumption of a constitutional system, either because they leave the majority to judge its own cause, or because they rest on a skepticism about moral rights that neither Nixon nor most American politicians can consistently embrace.

So Nixon's jurisprudence is a pretense and no genuine theory at all. It cannot be supported by arguments he can accept, let alone by arguments he has advanced. Nixon abused his legal credentials by endorsing an incoherent philosophy of law and by calling into question the good faith of other lawyers because they do not accept what he cannot defend.

The academic debate about the Supreme Court's power of judicial review must, however, have contributed to Nixon's confusion. The failure to draw the distinctions I have described, between appealing to a concept and laying down a conception, and between skepticism and deference, has posed a false choice between judicial activism as the program of moral crusade and judicial restraint as the program of legality. Why has a sophisticated and learned profession posed a complex issue in this simple and misleading way?

The issue at the heart of the academic debate might be put this way. If we give the decisions of principle that the Constitution requires to the judges, instead of to the people, we act in the spirit of legality, so far as our institutions permit. But we run a risk that the judges may make the wrong decisions. Every lawyer thinks that the Supreme Court has gone wrong, even violently wrong, at some point in its career. If he does not hate the conservative decisions of the early 1930s, which threatened to block the New Deal, he is likely to hate the liberal decisions of the last decade.

We must not exaggerate the danger. Truly unpopular decisions will be eroded because public compliances will be grudging, as it has been in the case of public school prayers, and because old judges will die or retire and be replaced by new judges appointed because they agree with a President who has been elected by the people. The decisions against the New Deal did not stand, and the more daring decisions of recent years are now at the mercy of the Nixon Court. Nor does the danger of wrong decisions lie entirely on the side of excess; the failure of the Court to act in the McCarthy period, epitomized by its shameful decision upholding the legality of the Smith Act in the *Dennis* case, may be thought to have done more harm to the nation than did the Court's conservative bias in the early Roosevelt period.

Still, we ought to design our institutions to reduce the risk of error, so far as this is possible. But the academic debate has so far failed to produce an adequate account of where error lies. For the activists, the segregation decisions were right because they advanced a social goal they think desirable, or they were wrong because they advanced a social goal they dislike. For the advocates of restraint they were wrong, whether they approve or disapprove that social goal, because they violated the principle that the Court is not entitled to impose its own view of the social good on the nation.

Neither of these tests forces lawyers to face the special sort of moral issue I described earlier, the issue of what moral rights an individual has against the state. The activists rest their case, when they argue it at all, on the assumption either that their social goals are self-evidently good or that they will in the long run work for the benefit of everybody; this optimism exposes them to Bickel's argument that this is not necessarily so. Those who want restraint argue that some principle of legality protects constitutional lawyers from facing any moral issues at all.

Constitutional law can make no genuine advance until it isolates the problem of rights against the state and makes that problem part of its own agenda. That argues for a fusion of constitutional law and moral theory, a connection that, incredibly, has yet to take place. It is perfectly understandable that lawyers dread contamination with moral philosophy, and particularly with those philosophers who talk about rights, because the spooky overtones of that concept threaten the graveyard of reason. But better philosophy is now available than the lawyers may remember. Professor Rawls of Harvard, for example, has published an abstract and complex book about justice which no constitutional lawyer will be able to ignore.[4] There is no need for lawyers to play a passive role in the development of a theory of moral rights against the state, however, any more than they have been passive in the development of legal sociology and legal economics. They must recognize that law is no more independent from philosophy than it is from these other disciplines.

---

[4]*A Theory of Justice*, 1972. . . .

52

STEPHEN R. MUNZER
JAMES W. NICKEL

Does the Constitution Mean What It Always Meant?

INTRODUCTION

One does not have to dig very deeply into the literature of American constitutional law to suspect that many constitutional provisions do not mean today what their framers thought they meant.[1] This mutability of constitutional norms is not surprising; the document is nearly two centuries old, has few formal amendments, and was framed in a different social and political age. The Constitution has remained vital largely because its provisions have proved adaptable to the changing needs of a developing society. It does not mean what it always meant.[2] But this phenomenon of constitutional change raises a number of perplexing questions. How can the Constitution change when the text and the intentions of its framers remain static? What are the methods of constitutional change short of formal amendment? When and how should such change occur?

This Article attempts to develop an account of constitutional change that addresses these questions. It presents our Constitution as a text-based institutional practice. It thus is opposed to theories, like the "historical approach,"[3] which see the Constitution simply as an original text together with an accretion of historically correct interpretations, and to theories, like Karl Llewellyn's,[4] which see it as just a complicated institution. No progress can be made in understanding what the Constitution is unless we recognize that our constitutional system is a unique, intricate product of text and institutional practice and that the notions of "meaning," "interpretation," and "fidelity" to the Constitution must reflect that duality.

In Part I, we examine three established theories of constitutional interpretation and change and identify the deficiencies of each. In Part II, we propose a more adequate theory. Analytically, our account tries to explain informally what it is, in terms of the philosophy of language, for the "meaning" of the Constitution to change, and how various models must be used to understand that change. Recognizing such change, the account analyzes patterns of judicial innovation, the nature of constitutional "interpretations" and "fidelity" to the Constitution, and the criteria for being part of our constitutional law. The normative part of our account is an attempt, not to develop a set of principles for generating results in concrete cases, but to show how the functions of the Constitution help establish when constitutional change is proper and who should make it. It thus seeks to locate the boundaries of constitutional argument within that part of political theory referred to as constitutionalism.

I. THREE THEORIES OF THE CONSTITUTION AND ITS DEVELOPMENT

A. The Historical Approach

The historical approach to constitutional interpretation regards the words and intent of the authors of

[1]For discussion of specific areas of constitutional growth, see Grey, *Do We Have an Unwritten Constitution?*, 27 STAN. L. REV. 703, 710–14 (1975).

[2]As used in this Article the word "meaning" does not, save in a few places where the context so indicates, refer to the sense that a word, phrase or sentence bears in a given language ("language meaning"). Nor is it identical with the intention with which a word, phrase or a sentence is uttered by a particular speaker on a particular occasion ("utterance meaning"). The meaning of the Constitution and its clauses is indeed related to utterance meaning, but differs from it in at least two ways. First, their meaning is initially the product, not of a single speaker at a single time, but of a complex of intentions on the part of framers, ratifiers, and perhaps others at different times. Second, while it is often maintained that utterance meaning cannot change, the meaning of the Constitution and its clauses, in our view, is susceptible of being amplified and altered by later authoritative interpretations. The best vehicle for analyzing constitutional meaning as just explained may be one of the speech, act or intentional theories of meaning current among analytic philosophers of language. *See, e.g.*, J. L. AUSTIN, HOW TO DO THINGS WITH WORDS (1962); S. SCHIFFER, MEANING (1972); J. SEARLE, SPEECH ACTS (1969). But we know of no such theory which has been developed to accommodate constitutional meaning, nor are we simply borrowing notions that every philosopher of language would accept. Part II of this Article offers an extended, though still informal and imprecise, account of constitutional meaning and how it can change. A formal and rigorous theory cannot be attempted here.

[3]*See* text accompanying notes 5–15 *infra*.

[4]Llewellyn, *The Constitution as an Institution*, 34 COLUM. L. REV. 1 (1934). *See* text accompanying notes 16–30 *infra*.

the Constitution as the sole source of constitutional law.[5] Under this approach, the Constitution is to be interpreted in the same manner as any other historical text. One looks to the intent of the authors and to the textual language as understood at the time the document was drafted. One may also rely on prior interpretations provided they comport with the words and intent of the framers. Most versions of the historical approach would permit one, in hard cases, to appeal to a broad conception of intent and to conjecture about what the framers would have decided had they faced a certain issue, even though they did not or could not have actually done so. The important point, however, is that the original meaning of a constitutional provision must always be controlling.

The historical approach has several seemingly powerful points in its favor. It explains the preoccupation of lawyers with the language of the document and the prominence of the search for original understandings—two features of our constitutional practice that, for brevity, we shall call the "textual focus." Furthermore, it may seem that since the authors of the Constitution proposed, and the people accepted, a certain document as the supreme law of the land, what was meant at that time should still be legally controlling. Lastly, the idea that a written document can, apart from amendments, change in its meaning or content may seem incoherent.

There are, however, decisive grounds for rejecting the historical approach. Analytically, it cannot account for the actual extent of change in our constitutional law. While it is true that the meaning of a term ("connotation") can remain constant even though the objects to which it applies ("denotation") may change,[6] this simple distinction is not helpful when new items included under a term are significantly dissimilar from those previously recognized.[7] It is also true that conjectures invoking the broad intent of the framers are permitted by the historical approach. But the reliability and fecundity of such conjectures should not be overestimated. Even if we can establish that the goal of the authors of, say, the first amendment, was to ensure that public issues could be fully and freely discussed, this provides us with little guidance in balancing this goal against competing goals such as ensuring public security,[8] or in dealing with nonpolitical literature.[9] Moreover, many important doctrinal developments cannot plausibly be accommodated by this method of analysis. It is, for example, most doubtful that the use of the equal protection clause to bar many forms of nonracial discrimination[10] can be justified by an appeal to the intentions of the authors of that clause.

---

[5]Advocates of this approach include William Crosskey and, most recently, Raoul Berger. *See, e.g.,* 1 & 2 W. CROSSKEY, POLITICS AND THE CONSTITUTION (1953); Berger, *The Imperial Court,* N. Y. TIMES, Oct. 9, 1977, §6 (Magazine), at 38 (article drawn from forthcoming book). Judicial statements abound. *See, e.g.,* Harper v. Virginia Bd. of Elections, 383 U.S. 663, 677–78 (1966) (Black, J., dissenting); West Coast Hotel Co. v. Parrish, 300 U.S. 379, 402–03 (1937) (Sutherland, J., dissenting); South Carolina v. United States, 199 U.S. 437, 448–49 (1905); Dred Scott v. Sandford, 60 U.S. (19 How.) 393, 426 (1857) (Taney, C. J.). There are extensive statements of historical and nonhistorical approaches by justice Sutherland and Chief Justice Hughes, respectively, in Home Bldg. & Loan Ass'n v. Blaisdell, 290 U.S 398 (1934).

[6]For example, the meaning of "house" does not change when houses are built or destroyed. *See generally* J. S. MILL, A SYSTEM OF LOGIC 19–25 (8th ed. 1872). Justice Sutherland used this distinction as a way of allowing for new applications of constitutional provisions: "The provisions of the Federal Constitution, undoubtedly, are pliable in the sense that in appropriate cases they have the capacity of bringing within their grasp every new condition which falls within their meaning. But, their meaning is changeless; it is only their *application* which is extensible." Home Bldg. & Loan Ass'n. v. Blaisdell, 290 U.S. 398, 451 (1934) (dissenting opinion) (emphasis on original; footnote omitted). *See also* Village of Euclid v. Ambler Realty Co., 272 U.S. 365, 687 (1926) (Sutherland, J.).

[7]For example, the power to "regulate Commerce . . . among the several States," U.S. CONST. art. I, § 8, cl. 3, was early held sufficient to authorize Congress to charter corporations for the construction of a railroad, Roberts v. Northern Pac. R.R., 158 U.S. 1, 21 (1895), or a bridge, Luxton v. North River Bridge Co., 153 U.S. 525 (1894). Later concern with national economic problems and "undesirable" local activities gradually led the Supreme Court to accept the commerce clause as support for legislation of widely different sorts. *See, e.g.,* United States v. Darby, 312 U.S. 100 (1941) (wage and hour legislation); NLRB v. Jones & Laughlin Steel Corp., 301 U.S. 1 (1937) (labor practices). Sometimes the economic effect was tangential, as in Wickard v. Filburn, 317 U.S. 111 (1942) (penalty on wheat produced and consumed at home upheld). In addition, legislation was allowed to prohibit "immoral" practices having a fleeting connection, if any, with interstate commercial activity. *See, e.g.,* United States v. Five Gambling Devices, 346 U.S. 441 (1953) (registration of gambling machines); Hoke v. United States, 227 U.S. 308 (1913) (prostitution); The Lottery Case, 188 U.S. 321 (1903) (lottery tickets). The commerce clause was also used to justify civil rights legislation. *See* Heart of Atlanta Motel, Inc. v. United States, 379 U.S. 241 (1964); Katzenbach v. McClung, 379 U.S. 294 (1964).

[8]*See, e.g.,* Dennis v. United States, 341 U.S. 494 (1951); Gitlow v. New York, 268 U.S. 652 (1925).

[9]*See, e.g.,* Virginia State Bd. of Pharmacy v. Virginia Citizens Consumer Council, Inc., 425 U.S. 748 (1979) (first amendment protection of commercial speech).

[10]*See, e.g.,* Sugarman v. Dougall, 413 U.S. 634 (1973); *In re* Griffiths, 413 U.S. 717 (1973); Graham v. Richardson, 403 U.S. 365 (1971) (equal protection clause protects aliens).

If one seeks to avoid this conclusion by appealing to the *very* broad intent of the framers—for example, by imputing to them a desire to create a just society—serious problems arise. One is that claims about such broad goals are apt to be at best weakly supported by the historical evidence. Hence it will be difficult to know whether the justices are carrying out the will of the framers or deciding on other grounds. In addition, such appeals to very broad intent can easily serve as masks for judicial decision-making based solely on judges' perceptions of desirable social goals. It is therefore doubtful that any "historical approach" can produce large amounts of new constitutional doctrine that is any different in practice from a straightforward policy-oriented approach.

The normative deficiencies of the historical approach are even more striking. First, a constitutional system that makes formal amendments very difficult and does not allow for gradual change through interpretation is likely to become rigid and out-of-date. If one accepts that change in governmental structures is inevitable and often desirable, provision must be made for such change.

Second, strict reliance on the historical approach would require us to abandon—or at least to regard as mistaken while continuing to follow—large parts of current constitutional doctrine. As has been argued in detail by Professor Thomas C. Grey,[11] numerous developments in our constitutional law cannot plausibly be justified in terms of original understandings. To many it would be unacceptable, for example, to retrench the protections of privacy and equality afforded by expansive interpretations of the Bill of Rights. And even those not enamoured of the work of the recent Court may perhaps concede that a great deal of doctrinal and social disruption would result if one were to turn back the clock.

Third, the nature of historical materials and the uses judges can make of them create serious problems for the historical approach. Foremost among these is the likelihood that the historical materials will be incomplete, inaccurate, or conflicting.[12] In addition, the intentions of individuals are notoriously difficult to ascertain, and it is especially difficult to identify the intentions of a large *group* such as the authors of the Constitution.[13] Even when there might be sufficient evidence for an expert historian to arrive at a clear result, a judge may not be equipped to do so or to evaluate another's claim to have done so. Moreover, given the difficulty of securing amendments, practitioners of the historical approach may, consciously or subconsciously, be moved to use slanted or fabricated history to justify results they favor on other grounds.[14] This procedure may lead to acceptable results in particular cases, but its misuse of historical materials might hinder critical examination of the real reasons for the decision and lead to doctrinal distortions to be contended with in the future. Of course, any procedure involving the assessment of evidence is vulnerable to error and mishandling; the point is that the risks are exacerbated with historical evidence because judges are not trained historians and operate under pressures that may deflect them from historically generated results. Furthermore, it should be noted that there is a special danger in allowing a controversial case to turn on an historical claim if the claim is not beyond dispute. Since good historical research is not within the competence of most judges, the antecedent probability of mistakes is high. This increases the chances that professional historians will challenge and refute the Court's reading of history, thus undermining the basis, or ostensible basis, for the decision.[15]

A fourth normative difficulty with the historical approach is that the original intent, even when it can be determined by judges, will sometimes be unpersuasive. Because conditions have changed greatly since the Constitution was written, we should expect that some of the results and rationales for decisions generated by a historical interpretation will be unap-

---

[11]Grey, supra note 1, at 710–14.

[12]*See* Wofford, *The Blinding Light: The Uses of History in Constitutional Interpretation,* 31 U. CHI. L. REV. 502, 503–06 (1964).

[13]Wofford offers a useful discussion of the problems of the various intents of the framers, ratifiers, and so on. *Id.* at 507–09. For difficulties concerning intents of groups, see MacCallum, *Legislative Intent,* 75 YALE L.J. 754 (1966). In regard to whether the particular intentions of framers should be considered, Dworkin has suggested—in the related area of statutory construction—that we should not be concerned with the mental state of particular legislators, but instead consider what interpretation of a statute best fits within the legislature's general responsibilities. R. DWORKIN, *Hard Cases,* in TAKING RIGHTS SERIOUSLY 81, 108 (1977) [hereinafter cited as Dworkin, *Hard Cases*].

[14]These matters are ably documented in Kelly, *Clio and the Court: An Illicit Love Affair,* 1965 SUP. CT. REV. 119.

[15]*See* Wofford, *supra,* note 12, at 528.

pealing. It is not clear why the will of the people of two hundred years ago should, aside from the wisdom that will contains, completely control our constitutional practices today. The current authoritativeness of original understandings depends in part on the strength of the framers' reasons for their choices and the applicability of those reasons today.

B. Institutional Theories

When one recognizes the deficiencies of the historical approach, a natural reaction is to view the Constitution as part of the practice of ongoing government. A theory reflecting this view is presented in an important but neglected essay by Karl Llewellyn.[16] It is part of a legal realist program which emphasizes patterns of official behavior and discounts the significance of legal rules or verbal formulations of the law.[17] Llewellyn opposes his theory to what is in effect a version of the historical approach.[18] He argues that although some current practices can trace their roots to the text, many changes in constitutional doctrine since 1789 are so sweeping that it is impossible to represent them as textual interpretations.[19] For him, "[w]hat is left, and living, is not a code, but an *institution*."[20]

Llewellyn's theory is elaborated as follows: An "institution" is a set of patterns of behavior, partly similar and partly complementary and competing, among a group of people. That institution which we call the Constitution involves the activities of interested groups and the general public as well as those directly concerned with governing.[21] The Constitution is not, however, the entirety of this behavior but only its *fundamental* part. More precisely, it consists of those regular practices which resist easy change and which have some important function in governmental operations.[22] Nevertheless, no hard and fast line can be drawn between the Constitution and "mere working government"; there will be penumbral patterns of behavior which cannot be firmly placed on either side. Still, it is possible to say that practices such as political patronage and conference committees in Congress are definitely part of the Constitution, while affairs such as the Inaugural Ball are not.[23] Thus "it is not essential that [a] practice . . . be in any way related to the Document" to be part of the Constitution.

Much in Llewellyn's account is genuinely illuminating. In particular it was an achievement to show how institutional practices could affect our constitutional law. Yet Llewellyn's insights are contaminated by mistaken assumptions in two respects. First, he assumes that if rules or constitutional provisions do not give utterly plain and easily applicable guidance, they give no guidance worth the name.[25] Since few provisions give clear-cut answers to particular problems, he writes off much judicial interpretation as legerdemain.[26] Llewellyn's critique, however, holds only against a very formalistic conception of legal rules, and overlooks the fact that constitutional rules, though rarely completely clear, are as a general matter sufficiently informative to shape behavior.[27] A judge might try to apply the cruel and unusual punishment clause by turning in part to linguistic and conceptual analyses of cruelty as well as by looking at prior decisions. Once constitutional rules and language are seen in this light, it becomes less plausible to assert, as Llewellyn implies, that our constitutional law often has only a fleeting connection with the text and its interpretations.

---

[16]Llewellyn, *supra* note 4. Llewellyn indicates, *id.* at 1–2 & nn. 1–2, that his view is also shared by A. BENTLEY, THE PROCESS OF GOVERNMENT (1908), and H. MCBAIN, THE LIVING CONSTITUTION (1927).

[17]*See, e.g.,* K. LLEWELLYN, THE BRAMBLE BUSH (2d ed. 1951); Llewellyn, *A Realistic Jurisprudence—The Next Step,* 30 COLUM. L. REV. 431 (1930).

[18]He refers to the theory he opposes as "the orthodox theory." Llewellyn, *supra* note 4, at 3–4.

[19]Llewellyn notes that the money and borrowing powers of article I, § 8, cls. 2 & 5, have been held, over time, to allow first a national bank, later the Federal Reserve System, and eventually securities affiliates. The connection of the last with the document, he observes wryly, "escapes my untrained eye; the giddy trapeze-work of constitutional theory is not for mere commercial lawyers." *Id.* at 14 n. 28.

[20]*Id.* at 6 n. 13 (emphasis added).

[21]*Id.* at 17–26.

[22]*Id.* at 26–31.

[23]*Id.* at 26–33.

[24]*Id.* at 30.

[25]Thus he writes: "If rules decided cases, one judge would be as good as another, provided only the cases had been adduced before him." *Id.* at 7.

[26]"Only because the Supreme Court has been so good at three-card monte, has made so much *seem* to be where it was not, have the Document and [the orthodox] Theory been able to survive so long." *Id.* at 17 (emphasis in original; footnote omitted).

[27]As H. L. A. Hart has argued, while legal rules and language do not bind rigidly, and while they exhibit open texture and may have exceptions not exhaustively specifiable in advance, they still provide guidance. H. L. A. HART, THE CONCEPT OF LAW 135–36 (1961).

Llewellyn's second mistaken assumption is that *fundamentality* of institutional practice is the touchstone of what is constitutional, but in fact this criterion spawns several counterintuitive results. One is that some clear mandates of the constitutional text, such as the prohibition of titles of nobility,[28] would not be considered part of the Constitution because they are not basic to the workings of the government. Another is that some matters fundamental to government would be regarded as having constitutional status even though they do not. Examples include political patronage and conference committees as well as major regulatory statutes such as the federal antitrust laws.[29] It is plainly a mistake to elevate these items to the same class as the power to declare war or the guarantee of freedom of speech. A final counterintuitive result is that all fundamental institutional practices are in Llewellyn's account seen as vulnerable to or insulated from change in the same way, namely, through alteration in or maintenance of the behavior patterns of those involved in government. However, matters that we regard as having constitutional status generally exhibit a different sort of entrenchment from other practices. If a matter is constitutional, then its abrogation typically is an appropriate subject for formal amendment and not for statutory change. Thus abolition of Congress's power to declare war could be made by formal amendment, though one might allow that this could be changed in other ways as well. In contrast, the elimination of political patronage or conference committees would not be appropriate for the formal amendment process; for these matters a statute would be ample.[30]

It may be replied that these criticisms of Llewellyn turn merely on different senses of the word "constitution." In Llewellyn's sense, the results detailed above are not counterintuitive but just obvious consequences of his theory. This reply may have some surface plausibility, yet we do not think that the issues posed by constitutional change can be adequately confronted if they are seen as merely involving the proprieties of, or irresolvable differences between, linguistic usage. For what is ultimately at stake is the best way of accounting for and formulating prescriptions in regard to an important range of legal phenomena. If so, it is a disadvantage of Llewellyn's theory that it does little to elucidate the textual focus of our constitutional law and that it seems committed to the normative proposition that there is no particular reason why the text and its meaning should figure importantly in constitutional decision-making.

If the defects of Llewellyn's theory stem in large measure from his rejection of the textual focus, it is in order to consider what might be viewed as an attempt by Professor Charles A. Miller to overcome them by combining the historical and institutional approaches.[31] Miller distinguishes between a *Constitution,* which is "a formal written document describing a pattern of legal rules and institutions that function for political purposes," and a *constitution,* which is "a pattern of political relationships which may be, but need not be, defined in legal instruments."[32] Miller suggests that the United States has both a Constitution and a constitution.[33] The textual focus of our constitutional practice relates to the former,[34] and Miller appears to think that the meaning of the Constitution is static.[35] Nevertheless, growth and development can occur because the United States "Constitution" is narrower than its "constitution," and the political relationships which constitute the latter can change. Thus, "should it be insisted that a written document must stay the same, it is the constitution rather than the Constitution of the United States that changes."[36]

Miller's position is in one respect an improvement on Llewellyn's, since he recognizes the importance of the text in our constitutional practice. But his theory is flawed in that it fails to challenge Llewellyn's unsupported assumption that the meaning of the constitutional document cannot change without formal amendment. Moreover, Miller fails to show how the immutable Con-

---

[28]U.S. CONST. art. I, § 9, cl. 8.

[29]The first two examples may be found in Llewellyn, *supra* note 4, at 29–30. Indeed, since Llewellyn wrote, certain patronage dismissals have been held unconstitutional. *See* Elrod v. Burns, 427 U.S. 347 (1976). The Sherman Act is seen as having constitutional stature in Miller, *Change and the Constitution,* 1970 L. & SOC. ORD. 231, 247–48. Miller's approach to constitutional law—presented also in Miller, *Notes on the Concept of the "Living" Constitution,* 31 GEO. WASH. L. REV. 881 (1963)—has many features in common with Llewellyn's.

[30]These issues are taken up later in our own account of constitution-identity. . . .

[31]C. MILLER, THE SUPREME COURT AND THE USES OF HISTORY 149–69 (1969).

[32]*Id.* at 150 (footnote omitted).

[33]*Id.* at 150–51.

[34]*Id.* at 153.

[35]*Id.* at 150–51. *But see* note 36 *infra.*

[36]C. MILLER, *supra* note 31, at 151 (footnote). Miller seems to suppose that written documents cannot change in meaning. *Id.* at 150–51. However, he subsequently appears to question such an assumption, *Id.* at 151 n. 3, and later says that "since the Constitution was adopted . . . the meaning of the text has

stitution embodied in the document is related to the protean "constitution" comprising our political institutions. Thus it is impossible to be certain which notion would prevail, in Miller's view, when they yielded contradictory results in particular instances. One must suspect, however, that Miller's homage to the textual focus is ultimately mere lip-service, since the rules of our living political institutions would apparently prevail in his eyes over the precepts of an ancient document.

C. Dworkin on Concepts and Conceptions

An attempt to avoid the pitfalls of both the historical and institutional views is found in Professor Ronald Dworkin's theory of legal concepts. The theory rests on a distinction between *concepts* and *conceptions*[37] and is, though highly suggestive, sketchy and imprecise at many points. The statement presented here seems to us the most plausible reading of Dworkin's view, though perhaps he might prefer to develop it differently. The object of the distinction is to justify the claim that the core meaning of the Constitution remains unchanged even when judges diverge from the specific content that the framers would have found there. To appeal to a conception is to appeal to a specific understanding or account of what the words one is using mean. To appeal to a concept is to invite rational discussion and argument about what words used to convey some general idea mean. Concepts are not tied to the author's situation and intentions in the way that conceptions are.[38] Broad phases such as "cruel and unusual punishment," "freedom of speech," "due process," and "equal protection" tend to be vague and abstract. While Dworkin is apparently not committed to thinking of the concepts denoted by these phrases as utterly lacking in content, their content is not usually specific enough to decide troubling cases involving issues such as capital punishment. They are "contested" concepts; their proper content is always disputable.[39] Even though people may agree on some paradigm cases of what is and is not cruel and unusual punishment, the boundaries of this concept are always open to dispute.

Two points should be noted concerning the abstract character of concepts. One is that Dworkin does not suggest that it is impossible to argue rationally about their proper content. He develops elaborate categories to show how an ideal judge would choose among competing conceptions of legal concepts. Briefly stated, Dworkin's idea is that a judge should choose the conception implied by the most coherent account of the principles underlying the legal system and all the nonmistaken legislation and decisions within it.[40] The second point is that concepts alone, because they are abstract, do not generally yield specific results in difficult cases. A conception of the true meaning of the concept must be added. A conception explains why the paradigm cases are instances of the concept and ties

---

changed." *Id.* at 155. Hence it is at least possible that he has no uniform position on this issue. Miller may have fallen into this confusion by failing to distinguish between the meaning of words in a language. One might try to make his position consistent by suggesting that at some points he regards the document to be static in terms of utterance meaning and that at others he is speaking of the language meaning of words used in the text. For further consideration of the distinction between utterance meaning and language meaning in the context of our own theory, see note 2 *supra;* text accompanying note 61 *infra.*

[37]*See* R. DWORKIN, *Constitutional Cases,* in TAKING RIGHTS SERIOUSLY, *supra* note 13, at 131 [hereinafter cited as Dworkin, *Constitutional Cases*].

[38]Dworkin introduces the distinction as follows:

> Suppose I tell my children simply that I expect them not to treat others unfairly. I no doubt have in mind examples of the conduct I mean to discourage, but I would not accept that my "meaning" was limited to these examples, for two reasons. First, I would expect my children to apply my instructions to situations I had not and could not have thought about. Second, I stand ready to admit that some particular act I thought of when I spoke was in fact unfair, or vice versa, if one of my children is able to convince me of that later; in that case I should want to say that my instructions covered the case he cited, not that I had changed my instructions. I might say that I meant the family to be guided by the *concept* of fairness, not by any specific *conception* of fairness that I might have had in mind.

Id. at 134 (emphasis in original).

[39]*See* Dworkin, *Hard Cases, supra* note 13, at 103–07, 126–27, and *passim.* Dworkin, *id.* at 103 n. 1, adopts this notion from Gallie, *Essentially Contested Concepts,* 56 PROC. ARISTOTELIAN SOC'Y 167 (1955–56).

[40]This idea is linked to Dworkin's position that, in virtually all instances, lawsuits have uniquely correct results and judicial decisions declare preexisting rights. *See* Dworkin, *Hard Cases, supra* note 13, at 81, 87, 105; Dworkin, *No Right Answer?*, in LAW, SOCIETY, AND MORALITY: ESSAYS ON HONOUR OF H. L. A. HART, 58 (P. Hacker & J. Raz eds. 1977). This position cannot be discussed here, but it is the subject of Munzer, *Right Answers, Preexisting Rights, and Fairness,* 11 GA. L. REV. 1055 (1977), and the response in Dworkin, *Seven Critics, id.* at 1201, 1241–50. This last essay may modify Dworkin's coherence theory of justifying decisions, as it now appears to be allowed that the best justification may give greater weight to "sound political morality" than to "fit" with institutional history. *Id.* at 1252–55.

their character to some feature of the case at bar, thus generating a particular result.[41]

The authors of our Constitution undoubtedly had conceptions of their own, but in Dworkin's view these are not binding on later interpreters and need not be used in deciding cases now. Dworkin holds that the framers did not intend[42] to give their own conceptions any special weight: "If those who enacted the broad clauses had meant to lay down particular conceptions, they would have found the sort of language conventionally used to do this, that is, they would have offered particular theories of the concepts in question."[43] For example, Dworkin's view is that the authors of the Constitution were not giving, or even trying to give, instructions not to use some particular set of punishments when they prohibited cruel and unusual punishment in the eighth amendment. They were rather telling officials always to consider whether a proposed punishment is compatible with the best current views about what is cruel. It is as if they were saying, "You have to figure out for yourselves what cruelty amounts to in your time and circumstances, but punishments are to be used only if they are not cruel in terms of the conceptions you arrive at." Since the framers were merely offering for guidance the general concepts, and not their own conceptions of them, it is sometimes justifiable to use conceptions different from those the framers used, and so reach results different from those they would have reached. Hence one can arrive at innovative results without being open to the charge of infidelity to the Constitution.[44]

Thus, Dworkin's distinction between concepts and conceptions is used to make the claim that the framers gave their own paradigms and theories of the broad terms they were using "no special standing."[45] This is not merely the innocuous thesis that the framers knew that the exact content of some of their language would be determined as the new government got started and judges began deciding cases. It is the considerably stronger claim that the broad clauses do not have, and were not intended to have, a sufficiently definite content for it to be possible to use them, without the addi-

---

[41]The following passage illustrates Dworkin's view of what is involved in having a moral concept and suggests the nature of a conception:

> Suppose a group believes in common that acts may suffer from a special moral defect which they call unfairness, and which consists in a wrongful division of benefits and burdens, or a wrongful attribution of praise or blame. Suppose also that they agree on a great number of standard cases of unfairness and use these as benchmarks against which to test other, more controversial cases. In that case, the group has a concept of unfairness, and its members may appeal to that concept in moral instruction or agreement. But members of that group may nevertheless differ over a large number of these controversial cases, in a way that suggests that each either has or acts on a different theory of *why* the standard cases are acts of unfairness. They may differ, that is, on which more fundamental principles must be relied upon to show that a particular division or attribution is unfair. In that case, the members have different conceptions of fairness.

Dworkin, *Constitutional Cases, supra* note 37 at 134–35 (emphasis in original).

[42]In general, Dworkin views the "intent of the legislators" as a contested concept. Claims about what was intended are not to be settled exclusively on historical grounds but in terms of which postulated intent would best meet the legislature's constitutional responsibilities. Dworkin, *Hard Cases, supra* note 13, at 108. The authors of the Constitution had no such responsibilities. Hence an account of the background rights they were relying on has to be in terms of what they did and, perhaps, of how the Constitution was subsequently developed. It is unclear whether the claim that they did not intend to give their own conceptions any special standing is to be settled solely on historical grounds, though plainly Dworkin thinks that the kind of language they used is relevant evidence.

[43]Dworkin, *Constitutional Cases, supra* note 37, at 136.

[44]
> Those who ignore the distinction between concepts and conceptions, but who believe that the Court ought to make a fresh determination of whether the death penalty is cruel, are forced to argue in a vulnerable way. They say that ideas of cruelty change over time, and that the Court must be free to reject out-of-date conceptions; this suggests that the Court must change what the Constitution enacted. But in fact the Court can enforce what the Constitution says only by making up its own mind about what is cruel.

Id. Fidelity to the Constitution is therefore compatible with introducing constitutional doctrine that is substantially different from what preceded it and from what the framers would have accepted.

For the application of Dworkin's account to current constitutional issues, see D. RICHARDS, THE MORAL CRITICISM OF LAW (1977). Richards accepts Dworkin's approach to constitutional adjudication and the concepts/conceptions distinction, *id.* at 41–44, 52–53, but gives them a historical twist, and argues that the contract theory of morality in J. RAWLS, A THEORY OF JUSTICE (1971), provides the best conceptions of moral concepts embedded in the Constitution. On the relations between their legal theories, *compare* Richards, *Rules, Policies, and Neutral Principles: The Search for Legitimacy in Common Law, Constitutional Adjudication,* 11 GA. L. REV. 1069 (1977) *with* Dworkin, *Seven Critics, id.* at 1201, 1250–58. Richards' position is critically examined in Munzer, Book Review,—RUTGERS L. REV.—(1978).

[45]*See* Dworkin, *Constitutional Cases, supra* note 37, at 135.

tion of a current conception, in deciding difficult cases now.

Dworkin's theory has the advantage of explaining how change can occur consistent with the textual focus of our constitutional practice. Nevertheless, it seems mistaken in several connected ways.[46] First, even the broad clauses of the Constitution have more content than Dworkin allows, and he gives no adequate reason why that content should not be considered more fully relevant in constitutional argument and decision-making. Ordinarily in interpreting someone's instructions one attends not only to the concepts used but also to the instructor's intentions and situation. In so doing one often finds that an apparently vague word or phrase has a relatively clear meaning in the context. For example, a person may be using a vague phrase in a context where it has a more precise meaning because of a customary or explicit definition. Thus, a vague phrase like "fair hearing" may have a relatively definite meaning within a school system in which there are established customary standards as to what constitutes a fair hearing in dismissal proceedings. Many constitutional commentators have assumed that the phrases of the Constitution can and should be interpreted in the way this example suggests and therefore that, when terms the framers used had a previous legal usage—for example, "bill of attainder,"[47] "cruel and unusual,"[48] or "due process of law"[49]—that usage is relevant. Dworkin has done nothing to criticize this kind of constitutional commentary, or to support his claim that the framers were merely offering concepts and not their own conceptions for guidance, save to note the vagueness of the language they used and the inconvenience of this approach if one wants to reach the conclusion that capital punishment is unconstitutionally cruel. Although such evidence is not decisive[50]—and admittedly becomes less valuable over time—Dworkin does not adequately allow for the *relevance* of historical language, intent, and context. It is true that these are pertinent, in his scheme, to the identification of the concepts the framers were using. But in our view that does not exhaust their relevance. Historical language, intent, and context also bear on the *conceptions* the framers had of those concepts, and hence on the instructions they were giving. If such considerations are to be ignored, this should not in any case be on the weak grounds that Dworkin suggests.

Second, Dworkin claims that whether a person intends to give his own views special standing makes a difference in the "kind of instructions given,"[51] but this is really a matter of degree. It is not easy to classify the clauses of the Constitution into just the two kinds that Dworkin's theory allows. The amount of particular guidance that the framers intended to give seems to vary from provision to provision.[52] There are *many* things that a person using a general concept to give instructions might be doing. He might be offering the general concept and nothing more, while giving no hints as to intended interpretation or scope; he might be using the concept and giving a few indications as to how he wants it generally to be applied (for example, whether he wants it applied broadly or narrowly); or he might be offering a concept and including with it a substantial number of instructions as to how it is to be applied in certain controversial cases.

Third, Dworkin's account of fidelity to the Constitution is insufficiently candid. Dworkin's strategy for making fidelity compatible with substantial constitutional change involves extruding some content from the original document and its amendments.[53] As a result, the very constitutional materials to which new decisions are likely to be unfaithful are conve-

---

[46]We cannot take up here the question, belonging to logical theory and the philosophy of language, of whether it is possible in principle to distinguish concepts from conceptions, and if so how that is to be done.

[47]U.S. Const. art. I, § 9, cl. 3; art. I., § 10, cl. 1.

[48]U.S. Const. amend. VIII.

[49]U.S. Const. amends. V; XIV, § 1.

[50]*See* text accompanying notes 11–15 *supra.*

[51]Dworkin, *Constitutional Cases, supra* note 37, at 135.

[52]For a discussion of theories of the Constitution which emphasize the differences between general and specific clauses, see C. Miller, *supra* note 31, at 162–65. *See also* United States v. Lovett, 328 U.S. 303, 321 (1946) (Frankfurter, J., concurring); Home Bldg. & Loan Ass'n v. Blaisdell, 290 U.S. 398, 426 (1934). A special difficulty for theories that divide all clauses into general (or vague) and specific is that judges sometimes do not agree how a given clause should be classified. *See* Wofford, *supra* note 12, at 515–18.

[53]Dworkin seems to try to have it both ways. He wants particular legal concepts to be empty enough to allow for innovation and development, but the whole of the legal materials to be rich enough to rule out strong discretion. One might wonder whether such poverty of the parts is compatible with such richness of the whole. We would emphasize that we are not questioning Professor Dworkin's candor; only whether his theory allows for as much candor about innovative decisions as do our constitutional practice and any acceptable account of it.

niently absent. Remaining is a framework broad enough to allow for decisions quite different from those generated by original understandings. Dworkin tries to justify this approach by suggesting that it is only what the framers intended, but this suggestion is doubly questionable. First, Dworkin's claim is undefended and implausible. Here two questions about the framers should be carefully distinguished: whether the framers intended that a court should occupy itself with searches for their conceptions, and whether the framers intended that a court should knowingly adopt its own conceptions rather than theirs. We have argued in effect that Dworkin's negative answer to the former question is dubious in many instances.[54] But even if one allowed his answer, it would not follow that Dworkin is right in giving an affirmative response to the latter question. The framers might have anticipated that later their own conceptions would sometimes be unrecoverable but might not have licensed a court to substitute its own conceptions when their conceptions are readily ascertainable. Second, Dworkin's claim puts the focus of argument in the wrong place. The grounds for continued adherence to the basic structure of the Constitution as well as to the framers' conceptions when recoverable should be articulated in terms of current political considerations rather than giving controlling power to the intentions of people who are long dead. The important thing is not what was originally intended, but what has subsequently been done with the document and the role it now plays.

II. TOWARD A MORE ADEQUATE THEORY OF CONSTITUTIONAL CHANGE

Having criticized three theories of constitutional change and development we are now able to identify the central problem that must be confronted in developing a more adequate theory. That problem is the tension between change in constitutional norms and the textual focus. If a new theory is to improve on past efforts, it must account for a changing Constitution while explaining the central role of the text without depleting that text of its original content. The theory offered here attempts to accomplish this task. Analytically, it holds that authoritative interpretations can modify the meaning of the Constitution and that the present content of the document results from the interaction over time of framers, judges, legislators, and executive officials. Change occurs in the meaning of the Constitution itself, not merely in its interpretations or in the meanings of certain words belonging to the English language. Normatively, the theory that constitutional change through interpretation is necessary and desirable, and some guidance as to when such change is in order, can be found in the functions of the Constitution.

A. The Problem of a Written Constitution

The root of the problem of meaning-change stems from the idea that we have a written constitution. That idea is in some sense obviously right. But is it completely right? To grapple with this question it is instructive to consider a syllogism advanced by Justice Brewer: "The Constitution is a written instrument. As such its meaning does not alter. That which it meant when adopted it means now."[55] The conclusion of this argument follows logically from the premises. Thus to deny the conclusion one must deny at least one of the premises. The first premise says that ours is a written constitution; the second says that a written constitution cannot change in its meaning. These premises will be considered in turn.

1. *A Partially Written Constitution.* If our Constitution were simply a body of unwritten customary rules, little difficulty would be encountered in understanding how its meaning could change.[56] Rules without complete canonical formulations can plainly

[54]*See* text accompanying notes 42–50 *supra.*

[55]South Carolina v. United States, 199 U.S. 437, 448 (1905).These premises are the foundation of the historical approach. *See* notes 5–15 and accompanying text *supra.* There we analyzed the operation of a theory based on this foundation. In this section we examine the validity of its underlying premises.

be modified by the informal formulations they receive from time to time. Some may doubt whether this is true of written constitutions, especially since the point of writing down rules may be to limit such change. Reflection reveals, however, that the clauses of the U.S. Constitution are, in at least two ways, only partial formulations of constitutional law. First, these clauses do not give the full or exact scope of all constitutional rules specified in the text; to determine that one must, among other things, read the relevant cases. Second, they do not even mention some constitutional rules, namely those which, like the right to travel and the right of privacy,[57] are not found in any particular provision of the text.

2. *The Need for Change in the Written Constitution.* The conclusion that the Constitution is composed of both a written text and formulations of additional rules does not allow us fully to rebut Justice Brewer's argument. It might still be asserted that the written Constitution has retained precisely the meaning it had when ratified, and that only those constitutional rules which lack a canonical formulation in the original document have undergone a change in meaning or content. This will not do, however, if a phrase from the written Constitution is now to describe a rule that is radically different from the rule that the phrase originally formulated. If a provision *P* of the Constitution originally gave an accurate description of rule *R* of constitutional law, and that rule has changed substantially so that it is now a different rule *R'*, it is hard to imagine how *P* can without change in meaning now be a full and accurate description of *R'*. For *P* to be an accurate description of *R'* it must have a different meaning from that which it had when it was an accurate description of *R*. For example, the freedom of speech and press guaranteed by the first amendment was originally concerned essentially with political speech and perhaps allied forms of communication expressing ideas in science, art, morality, religion, etc. So understood, that amendment did not give any protection to commercial speech such as advertising.[58] Under recent decisions, however, certain forms of advertising receive some shelter under the first amendment.[59] Thus, to state the matter generally, we must either abandon words used in the text as the accurate descriptions of much-modified rules, or admit that the words do not now mean what they meant.

3. *Authoritative Interpretation As the Instrument of Change.* The issue in analyzing Justice Brewer's second premise is not whether something that an authoritative interpreter does can change what a constitutional provision meant; its original meaning is a historical fact not subject to change. It is rather a question of whether the action of an authoritative interpreter can change what the provision will thereafter mean.[60] Now to some an affirmative answer will seem beset by an insuperable difficulty, namely, the fact that philosophers often think of the meaning of an utterance as being fixed for the present and for the future by the author's language and intent. It is not, of course, problematic to say that change occurs in the meanings of words in a language; the meaning of "wonderful," for example, is now somewhat different from what it was prior to the eighteenth century. But it is problematic to say that an utterance which a particular person made at a particular time

[56]Such an approach to constitutional development is suggested by Charles A. Miller's distinction between the *Constitution* as formal written document and the *constitution* as a pattern of political relationships. *See* C. MILLER, *supra* note 31, at 149–69. Miller's analysis is a reaction to the sort of argument Justice Brewer makes, and is critically discussed at text accompanying notes 31–36 *supra*.

[57]*See, e.g.,* Shapiro v. Thompson, 394 U.S. 618 (1969) (constitutional right to travel established); Griswold v. Connecticut, 381 U.S. 479 (1965) (constitutional right of privacy established).

[58]*See, e.g.,* Valentine v. Chrestensen, 316 U.S. 52 (1942).

[59]*See* Bates v. State Bar of Ariz., 97 S.Ct. 2691 (1977) (advertising by lawyers); Virginia State Bd. of Pharmacy v. Virginia Citizens Consumer Council, Inc., 425 U.S. 748 (1976) (advertising by pharmacists). Without merit is the objection that change in meaning need not be invoked if either the earlier or the later decisions are mistaken. For while an authoritative interpretation can sometimes properly be criticized as a mistake, such criticism does not deprive the interpretation of constitutional status unless it quickly leads to the overturning of the interpretation or makes such overturning likely. . . .

[60]We do not take up here how retroactively applied interpretations are to be analyzed. Perhaps some such interpretations can be seen as declarations of the "correct" meaning of a constitutional clause. But often this declaratory analysis of retroactivity will be most implausible, and some different account will be needed of how the legal significance of past events can now be changed. A theory of the appropriate sort, which may be conjoined with our view of constitutional change, is developed in Munzer, *Retroactive Law,* 6 J. LEGAL STUD. 373 (1977).

can have one meaning at that time and another meaning later.[61]

Yet even if utterance meaning in the standard case is unalterable, for two reasons that is no bar to change in the meaning of the constitutional text. The first is that the original document cannot be counted an "utterance" in the usual sense. The standard or paradigm case of an utterance is when one person speaks or writes a sentence on a particular occasion; its meaning is typically a function of the utterer's intentions together with the context and the senses assigned to those words in grammatical combinations in a given language. In contrast, the sentences of the Constitution were products of more than one person (draftsmen, framers, ratifiers) and more than one time (successive drafting, debating, adoption, and ratification stages). No doubt in the process statements were made which are susceptible of being analyzed as standard utterances. But the eventual product is not thus susceptible: if the text of the Constitution is an utterance or set of utterances at all, it is not so in the standard sense. Its original meaning may, it is true, still be a function of the various intentions, contexts, and words that led to it. Yet if so, given the number of persons involved at different times and in different situations, that meaning will be an extraordinarily complex function of those elements.

The second reason is that the original text serves through authoritative interpreters to give ongoing guidance in changing circumstances. Perhaps the idea that the meaning of a text composed of standard utterances cannot change is satisfactory where no one is empowered to make official determinations of its meaning, or where the language is not intended to provide a reason for action, or where directives supplied by the text apply only in a finite number of static situations. But if we turn our attention to law, it does not seem so strange that the current meaning of a constitutional provision should be the result of the activities of both the authors and the officials who applied it. Authoritative interpreters, in their institutional capacity of determining what a provision means in unanticipated situations, supplement or modify the meaning or content of the provision. The institutional practice involved in the use and interpretation of constitutional language is one in which the responsibility for creating the current meaning of a constitutional provision is spread among different people at different times; the power of creating meaning is broken into shares. The original authors of the Constitution determined the meaning it would have unless and until it was changed or developed through amendment or decision, and thereby set out the general direction of its future development. The meaning of the Constitution changes as it is interpreted. Authoritative interpretations of the text often create a new meaning for it, and the original meaning, or whatever had previously replaced it, ceases to be the current meaning. Hence we say that the current meaning of a constitutional provision is the result of interaction over time between the framers and its authoritative interpreters. This interaction is a dynamic process; it may often take the form of cooperation, but there may at times be tug-of-war or outright conflict between different interpreters.

It is now clear that both premises of Justice Brewer's argument must be rejected. Our Constitution is first of all not merely a written instrument. Viewed more accurately it is a text-based institutional practice in which authoritative interpreters can create new constitutional norms. Secondly, the meaning of a written document like the text of the Constitution can intelligibly be said to change. The "meaning" possessed by the text differs from utterance meaning as standardly conceived, and was originally the product of many persons. That initial meaning has subsequently been altered in an interactive institutional process. . . .

[61]As one contemporary philosopher of language has written:

> A speech has a date and duration, not so its meaning. When a speech is over nothing can change what is meant. What has been said cannot be unsaid, though later remarks can contradict it. Even the ambiguities in this evening's speech must remain such forever, though tomorrow's press conference may clarify the speaker's intentions. Though the speech may be differently translated in different countries or different periods, no one could judge the correctness of each new translation unless he assumed the meaning of the original speech to remain the same. Though expositions of what has been said can change they can also be criticized, and the question whether a given exposition is loose or close, fair or biased, accurate or inaccurate, would not arise unless the meaning itself were invariant under exposition.

L. J. Cohen, The Diversity of Meaning 3 (2d ed. 1966).

53

R. P. PEERENBOOM

What's Wrong with Chinese Rights?: Toward a Theory of Rights with Chinese Characteristics

The question "What's wrong with Chinese rights?" implies that there are Chinese rights. A quick glance at the constitution of the People's Republic of China suggests that a Chinese citizen shares the full complement of rights that members of modern, western liberal democracies have come to hold so dear: freedom of speech, press, association, religious belief and practice; inviolability of the person; protection from unlawful arrest and search of person, and so on.[1] Indeed, some claim that Chinese citizens enjoy rights unknown to their American counterparts: job placement and security, free access to medical care, and other "economic rights" are most often cited.[2]

Yet despite this seemingly rosy picture, the cry for human rights in China has grown steadily louder since the Tiananmen tragedy and the collapse of socialism in Eastern Europe and the former USSR. To be sure, qualifications are in order. The cry rises largely from foreigners and a coterie of Chinese dissidents and intellectuals, many now living abroad in exile.[3] As an on-site observer of the 1989 demonstrations, I was particularly struck by the low priority given to human rights by many of the protesters, reports of western journalists notwithstanding. While a few students and intellectuals called for human rights (and even fewer could state what that meant), the vast majority of the demonstrators seemed motivated primarily by economic concerns, with inflation and corruption heading the list.[4] Those rights that the demonstrators did seek—freedom of the press, greater voice in electing officials—were grounded in pragmatic concerns: a free, investigative press would keep tabs on and expose corrupt officials; elections would allow for the expulsion of those exposed.[5]

Further, the call for "human rights" in China tends to elide several issues. The rhetoric of human rights is often that of universal, inalienable, absolute rights—and indeed often that of so-called "natural" rights. But is that actually what Chinese need or want? As rhetoric, rights talk is glorious: all people are created equal, each individual possesses an inviolable right to life, liberty, and the pursuit of happiness.[6] But this is rhetoric—powerful, effective, socially significant rhetoric, but rhetoric nonetheless. As such, it has been criticized, at least in unqualified form, as nonsense on stilts.[7] More importantly, such a conception of human rights is at

---

[1]ZHONGGUO RENMIN GONGHEGUO XIANFA [Constitution of the People's Republic of China] arts. 33–40 (1982) [hereinafter PRC CONST.]. For a discussion of Chinese rights, see Louis Henkin, *The Human Rights Idea in Contemporary China: A Comparative Perspective, in* HUMAN RIGHTS IN CONTEMPORARY CHINA 25–26 (R. Randle Edwards et al. eds., 1986); Andrew J. Nathan, *Political Rights in the Chinese Constitutions, in id.* at 79–80.

[2]*See* PRC CONST., *supra* note 1, arts. 42–46.

[3]In the years since Tiananmen, the topic of human rights has been increasingly debated in China. For a useful overview of current issues and theories, *see* DANGDAI RENQUAN [CONTEMPORARY HUMAN RIGHTS] (The Legal Research Institute of the Chinese Academy of Social Sciences ed., 1992).

[4]Two of the more popular slogans were *dadao guandao* (smash profiteering) and *fandui fubai* (oppose corruption). A poll conducted in early May of 865 Beijing residents found that 71% believed corruption to be the main cause of instability in China. *See* Seth Faison, *Poll Shows Support for Demonstration,* S. CHINA MORNING POST, May 12, 1989, at 1. *See also* Nicholas Kristof, *China Erupts: The Reasons Why,* N.Y. TIMES MAGAZINE, June 4, 1989, at 26, 28 (noting that dissatisfaction stemmed not only from a desire for democracy, but also from economic frustration).

[5]For a similar view, *see* Jane Macartney, *The Students: Heroes, Pawns, or Power-Brokers?,* in THE BROKEN MIRROR: CHINA AFTER TIANANMEN 3, 5, 12, 13 (George Hicks, ed., 1990). Andrew Nathan has noted that intellectuals attempted to limit the movement's agenda to issues of freedom of speech and dialogue with the government. Freedom of speech is, of course, particularly important to academics. *See* Andrew Nathan, *Tiananmen and the Cosmos,* NEW REPUBLIC, July 19, 1991, at 31, 32. *See also* Marsha L. Wagner, *The Strategies of the Student Democracy Movement in Beijing, in* TIANANMEN: CHINA'S STRUGGLE FOR DEMOCRACY 43, 59, 74–76 (Marsha L. Wagner & Winston L.Y. Yang eds., 1990) (students wanted a more honest government but continued to believe the Party and government officials could be reformed through moral suasion).

[6]THE DECLARATION OF INDEPENDENCE (U.S. 1776). In Dworkinian terms, the rights of the individual trump the overall good of society; in Nozickian, "individuals have rights and there are things no person or group may do to them"; in Rawlsian, "each person possesses an inviolability founded on justice that even the welfare of society as a whole cannot override." *See* RONALD DWORKIN, TAKING RIGHTS SERIOUSLY (1977); ROBERT NOZICK, ANARCHY, STATE AND UTOPIA ix (1974); JOHN RAWLS, A THEORY OF JUSTICE 3 (1971).

[7]Jeremy Bentham, *Anarchical Fallacies,* in 2 COLLECTED PAPERS (1843), *reprinted in* HUMAN RIGHTS 32 (A.I. Meldin ed., 1970).

odds with reality in which intuitions about human dignity and individual rights are at odds with equally strong intuitions about utilitarian consequences, the overall social good, and duties to others.[8] The result is a compromise: one has a right to free speech, yet one cannot cry "fire" in a theater, to cite a familiar example.

Notwithstanding the stirring words of the Declaration of Independence and distinguished philosophers, all states impose limits on individual rights in the name of public interest. Indeed, the Universal Declaration of Human Rights explicitly provides:

> In the exercise of his rights and freedoms, everyone shall be subject only to such limitations as are determined by law solely for the purpose of securing due recognition and respect for the rights and freedoms of others and of meeting the *just requirements of morality, public order and the general welfare* in a democratic society.[9]

Rhetoric aside, we constantly perform a complex calculus by which the rights or protected interests of individuals are weighed against the good of the collective (and other rights). Reasonable people differ as to the proper balance to effect; that diverse cultures would reach different conclusions is only natural.[10]

Examining the criticisms of China's human rights record raises three related questions. Are critics calling for a new kind of Chinese right—absolute, inalienable, ahistorical, human cum natural rights—or simply a different calculus where the rights of individuals are not so readily traded off to promote the "collective good"?

Similarly, does the problem lie in the outcome of the calculus or in the manner in which the calculus is made? While the Tiananmen massacre shocks the conscience, the more basic problem may be how the tragic decisions that culminated in tanks rolling through the streets of Beijing were reached: that is, via an authoritarian one-party system rather than a democratic process.

Finally, it is not so much the *how* of the calculus but the *who*. Though some intellectuals call for democracy, one still encounters with alarming frequency the traditional paternalistic attitude that the "masses" are not sufficiently educated to shoulder the responsibilities of democracy.[11] This suggests that in the eyes of many, what is needed is not an institutional change from dictatorship to democracy, but simply a change in dictators: just replace old guard conservatives with free-market reformers and all will be well.[12]

Whatever one's response to these questions, there can be little doubt that individuals in the PRC need some protection against the all-powerful state. There must be real constraints imposed on the government. If we were to impose these constraints through the vehicle of rights, then the PRC needs i) a stronger system of enforceable rights—rights in practice, not just name, and ii) a coherent theory of Chinese rights—a theory of rights justified on Chinese terms.

In Part I, I examine institutional obstacles to a workable system of rights in China. In Part II, I explore some of the philosophical assumptions that underwrite western rights theories. In Part III, I contrast these assumptions with the underlying premises of Confucianism. I do so because I believe Confucianism continues even today to be the basis of the

---

[8]In response to Kant's injunction against treating humans as things, Oliver Wendell Holmes candidly remarked, "If a man lives in society, he is liable to find himself so treated." OLIVER W. HOLMES, THE COMMON LAW 38 (Mark DeWolfe Howe, ed., Belknap Press of Harvard University 1963) (1881). Indeed, "No society has ever admitted that it could not sacrifice individual welfare to its own existence." *Id.* at 37.

[9]Universal Declaration of Human Rights, art. 29(2) U.N. GAOR, U.N. Doc. A/811 (1948) (emphasis added). The U.S. also limits rights in the name of the public good. Our system first distinguishes between rights. Some are classified as "fundamental" or "preferred"—for example, freedom of religion and speech. But even these fundamental rights are not absolute or inalienable; they may be overridden if on strict scrutiny the court finds a compelling state interest. Other rights, for example economic rights, may be infringed on finding nothing more than a minimally rational basis for the trumping legislation. Griswold v. Connecticut, 381 U.S. 479, 486 (1965) (Goldberg, J., concurring); Poe v. Ullman, 367 U.S. 497, 522 (1961) (Harlan, J., dissenting).

[10]The point is not that China may justify or be excused for Tiananmen simply by waving a banner of cultural relativism. Some things—such as the torture of student activists—are clearly not acceptable, *by anyone's standards,* western or Chinese (be they Confucian or socialist). *See Activist Details Human Jail Abuse,* S. CHINA MORNING POST, June 1, 1992, at 10.

[11]*Cf.* Andrew Nathan, *Tiananmen and the Cosmos, supra* note 5, at 32, 35 (noting that intellectuals wanted democracy without the demos). Indeed, in a June 3, 1989 interview, the student leader Wuer Kaixi stated that "the Chinese people lack consciousness of democracy, and do not understand democracy." MING PAO, June 17, 1989; FOREIGN BROADCAST INFORMATION SERVICE, June 20, 1989, at 24–27 [hereinafter FBIS].

[12]Witness the support for so-called new or neo-authoritarianism in the PRC modeled on the economically free-market and politically authoritarian approach of Taiwan, Singapore, and South Korea. *See* XIN QUANWEIZHUYI [NEW AUTHORITARIANISM] (Liu Jun & Li Lin eds., 1989); *see also* Michel Oksenberg et al. eds., BEIJING SPRING, 1989: CONFRONTATION & CONFLICT 123–49 (1990).

Chinese world view, despite the attempts of the socialist government to eradicate such "feudal" thinking. Hence any workable theory of rights justifiable on Chinese terms will in all likelihood emerge out of and be consistent with the basic premises of Confucianism. Of course Confucianism is not the only intellectual influence. Thus I discuss socialism in Part IV. In Part V, I critique China's socialist regime not on the alien terms of western rights theories but from a Chinese perspective on rights. In Part VI, I sketch the contours of a Chinese rights theory and speculate as to the possibilities of its realization.[13]

I. INSTITUTIONAL OBSTACLES

A central obstacle to the protection of rights in China is the primacy of the Party over the rule of law. Party control eviscerates the rule of law, prevents the development of a genuinely independent judiciary, and renders meaningless the concept of constitutional review. According to the constitution, the Party is to follow the law,[14] yet in practice, the Party remains the law.[15] This is to be expected, given the basic premises of socialism. Mao once described law and courts as "instruments with which one class oppresses another. As far as the hostile classes are concerned these are instruments of oppression. They are violent and certainly not 'benevolent things.'"[16] As a tool of socialism, the law must serve the Party rather than individuals. That such ideas retain their currency despite repeated calls for a rule of law independent of Party control is scarcely surprising. What is perhaps somewhat surprising is the articulation of such views by the most senior members of the judiciary. For example, a major newspaper recently quoted Justice Minister Cai Cheng as declaring: "Chinese law must be at the service of class struggle . . . [T]here can be no question of 'the law being supreme'. . . . China must jettison the concept of 'the supremacy of the law' because the judicial code and system must be at the service of the proletariat class."[17]

There will be no way to protect the rights and interests of individuals if political might makes right—as the history of many other countries demonstrates. If rights are to become meaningful in China, limitations on Party power are essential.

To justify state abuse of individual rights, the Party can turn to article 51 of the constitution, itself a major impediment to practicable rights: "The exercise of citizens of the PRC of their freedoms and rights may not infringe upon the interests of the state, of society, and of the collective, or upon the lawful freedoms and rights of other citizens."[18] This manifestly asserts the hierarchy of state over individual, undermining the *raison d'être* of rights as a guarantee that "each person possesses an inviolability founded on justice that even the welfare of society as a whole cannot override."[19]

Another institutional impediment, related to but distinct from the issue of an independent judiciary and rule of law, is the lack of constitutional review. In the United States, the judiciary has emerged as the body that reviews governmental actions for conformity with the Constitution, but other arrangements are possible.[20] What matters is not so much the particular method, but that some agency other than the

[13]The claim is not that Chinese intellectual traditions alone will determine the nature and course of human rights in China. No doubt Chinese rights are and will continue to be influenced by a host of other factors, including domestic and foreign political and economic realities. *But see infra* notes 113–115 and accompanying text. Nor do I claim that Chinese intellectual traditions "lock in" a particular form of rights—or that, for instance, the Chinese cannot escape from the walls of Confucian political philosophy. The thesis is simply that these intellectual traditions, particularly Confucianism, will most likely exert considerable influence on Chinese human rights.

[14]PRC CONST., *supra* note 1, art. 5; *see also Human Rights in China,* 34 BEIJING REV., Nov. 4-10, 1991 at 8, 14 [hereinafter WHITE PAPER]. (This is Beijing's official statement on human rights.)

[15]*See* Nathan, *supra* note 1, at 101-02, 108-12; *see also* Andrew Nathan, *Sources of Chinese Rights Thinking,* in HUMAN RIGHTS IN CONTEMPORARY CHINA, *supra* note 1, at 125, 132–37; SHAO-CHUAN LENG & HUNGDAH CHIU, CRIMINAL JUSTICE IN POST-MAO CHINA 98–104 (1985); Li Maoguan, *Why "Laws Go Unenforced,"* 32 BEIJING REV. 17–18 (1980). While in theory the 1982 Constitution limits Party authority, the ultimate authority of the Party is explicit in the 1975 and 1978 constitutions. Further, during all periods since 1949, the Party has in practice dominated the People's Congresses, courts and other organs of state. For continuing problems in the establishment of a truly independent judiciary, *see* REPORT OF THE AUSTRALIAN HUMAN RIGHTS DELEGATION TO CHINA 14–26, 27-29 (1991).

[16]MAO ZEDONG, ON PEOPLE'S DEMOCRATIC DICTATORSHIP 16–17 (1951).

[17]Willy Wo-lap Lam, *Justice Minister Rejects "Supremacy of the Law,"* S. CHINA MORNING POST, Nov. 12, 1991, at 12.

[18]PRC CONST., *supra* note 1, art. 51.

[19]RAWLS, *supra* note 6. Whether state interest may trump individual interest, and if so, under what conditions, are discussed *infra.* As noted in *supra* notes 6–7 and accompanying text, all states impose limits on individual rights in the name of the public good.

[20]*See* Louis Favoreu, *Constitutional Review in Europe, in* CONSTITUTIONALISM AND RIGHTS 38, 47–54 (Louis Henkin & Albert Rosenthal eds., 1990).

one that created the law be given the power of review. The 1982 PRC constitution gives the power to interpret and enforce the constitution not to the judiciary or an independent constitutional review body but to the standing committee of the supreme legislature, the National People's Congress. Because it is the National People's Congress that drafts and adopts laws in the first place, "[i]t seems unlikely that the standing committee would interpret any statute or amendment as inconsistent with the constitution or the basic principles of the statutes (such as Criminal Law)."[21]

Constitutional review is one element of what some scholars have termed "constitutionalism." Although constitutionalism has not been definitively defined, the lack of it is generally considered fatal to human rights. Noting that variations are possible and no authoritative definition exists, Louis Henkin, a prominent champion of this new *ism,* offers several core elements: government according to the constitution; separation of powers; popular sovereignty and democratic government; constitutional review; independent judiciary; civilian control of the military; individual rights; and limitations on suspension, derogation, or amendment of the constitution by political organs.[22] Obviously China fails several, if not all, of these threshold tests. For example, the government has not only suspended the constitution but regularly promulgated new ones.[23] More importantly, by all accounts the government has disregarded all of its constitutions at one time or another.[24] In addition, separation of powers is nonexistent. As noted, the Party dominates all aspects of government, including the military.

Taken collectively, wholesale violation of these elements is perhaps a good indicator of the absence of a strong commitment to individual rights.[25] More debatable is whether possessing any single element or combination of elements is either necessary or sufficient to ensure human rights. England, for instance, does not even have a written constitution, and many states allow suspension of the constitution during times of crisis.[26] Conversely, the PRC at least nominally provides for separation of powers and functions.[27] How can England, a country without a written constitution, succeed in providing human rights while the PRC, constitution in hand, fails? "In the end," concludes Henkin, "constitutionalism depends on political, social and economic stability and a political culture that is committed to constitutionalism."[28] Perhaps most importantly, for human rights to be respected, there must be rights consciousness, a culture of rights, an attitude among the people that the government cannot do to them as it wishes.[29] The people must learn to stand up to the government and insist on their rights. They must demand that the judiciary and the body responsible for constitutional review perform their designated func-

---

[21]LENG & CHIU *supra* note 15, at 43. PRC CONST., *supra* note 1, at 43. *See also* Nathan, *supra* note 1, at 120.

[22]Louis Henkin, Constitutions and the Elements of Constitutionalism, paper prepared for the American Council of Learned Societies Conference on Constitutionalism and the Transition to Democracy in Eastern Europe, Pecs, Hungary (June 18–20, 1990) (on file at Chinese Legal Studies Center, Columbia University), *passim.*

[23]China has had four constitutions since 1949. The first was promulgated in 1954, followed by new ones in 1975, 1978, and 1982. For a comparison, see Nathan, *supra* note 1, at 80–81.

[24]For abuses of the constitution and the criminal process arising out of the Tiananmen "incident" see Jerome Cohen, *Tiananmen and the Rule of Law,* in THE BROKEN MIRROR, *supra* note 5, at 325–26. Ironically, one important motivation behind the return to a rule of law called for by Deng and other leaders in the late 1970's was personal experience of widespread legal abuse during the Cultural Revolution. *See* LENG & CHIU *supra* note 15, at 35–37 (noting also the importance of rule of law to the "four modernizations" and economic reform).

[25]Simply as an analytical matter, wholesale rejection of constitutionalism necessarily entails rejection of rights because one element of constitutionalism *is* individual rights. Indeed, to the extent that a commitment to rights is a necessary condition of constitutionalism, the argument is circular: constitutionalism is necessary for rights, and rights are necessary for constitutionalism. If individual rights are not a necessary element, one can avoid the apparent circularity by defining constitutionalism without reference to rights for the purpose of the discussion.

[26]Even the *International Covenant on Civil and Political Rights,* U.N. GAOR, 21st Sess., Annex,1496th plen. mtg. at art. 4 (1966), provides that "[i]n time of public emergency which threatens the life of the nation," States may "take measures derogating from their obligations under the present Covenant to the extent strictly required by the exigencies of the situation."

[27]*See e.g.,* PRC CONST., *supra* note 1, art. 126 (providing for an independent judiciary).

[28]Henkin, *supra* note 1, at 19.

[29]As Peter Lin notes, even a consciousness of rights is not sufficient. In addition,

> there must be a widespread, entrenched, and "self-sacrificial" commitment by the elites to act consistently with the values and standard of rationality generally accepted by the people. Such a commitment involves "self-sacrifice" because the governing elites have to forgo the advantage they could otherwise gain by abusing their power, in exchange for a system from which all will benefit.

Peter Lin, *Between Theory and Practice: The Possibility of a Right to Free Speech in the People's Republic of China,* 4 J. CHINESE L. 257, 268 (1990).

tions in the face of opposition from political powers. This attitude is sorely lacking in China.[30]

Many in the United States turn to the judiciary when they feel their rights have been violated. However for historical reasons, many Chinese continue to shy away from and fear the courts.[31] Chinese tradition frowned on judicial resolution of conflicts.[32]

Conflicts were to be resolved through informal, extrajudicial means such as mediation spearheaded by a local elder.[33] To end up in court was shameful and risky. The pitfalls of even successful litigation are enshrined in the Chinese proverb: "Win your lawsuit but lose your money."[34] Traditional distrust of and reluctance to rely on the formal legal system remain an impediment to the development of a rights attitude and culture in China.[35]

Even assuming that these obstacles could be overcome—the influence of the Party diminished, article 51 rewritten (or limited by interpretation), constitutional review established, and the deep-rooted fear of the courts overcome—it is unlikely that a strong theory of individual rights would emerge in China. To understand this, one must examine the philosophical assumptions that lie at heart of the Chinese world view. Perhaps the best way to do this is to begin with a brief overview of the underpinnings of western rights theories.

II. UNDERPINNINGS OF HUMAN RIGHTS THEORIES

Western theories of human or natural rights have as a whole been foundational and universal in character.[36] They tend to be written as if equally applicable to contemporary Asia as to seventeenth-century Europe or twentieth-century United States. For instance, one popular form of expression is that human rights are "self-evident."[37] As Henry Rosemont has noted, "it is a bedrock presupposition of our moral, social, and political thinking that human

---

[30] To be sure, some have stood up and continue to stand up to the government. One need only recall the unforgettable image of the sole demonstrator standing resolutely in front of a row of tanks. Similarly, the existence of underground newspapers and dissidents both in China and living abroad in exile demonstrates that some Chinese are prepared to oppose the government. Even more direct evidence is the recent phenomenon of politically motivated lawsuits against the government. *See* Sheryl WuDunn, *Chinese Bite Back at Beijing with Lawsuits,* N.Y. TIMES, Sept. 13, 1992, at 9 (noting that the government is unlikely to lose a politically sensitive lawsuit).

Nevertheless, such pockets of resistance remain the exception and not the rule. The few people willing to challenge the political authority of the government directly fall far short of the kind of broad-based social support that Henkin sees as necessary to constitutionalism.

[31] *See* Li Maoguan, *supra* note 15, at 18–19.

[32] "In hearing litigation," remarked Confucius, "I am no different from any other man. But if you insist on a difference, it is, perhaps, that I try to get the parties not to resort to litigation in the first place." CONFUCIUS, LUN YÜ [ANALECTS] 12:13 [hereinafter ANALECTS]. For an English translation, see D. C. LAU, CONFUCIUS: THE ANALECTS (1979). Citations to the Analects follow the numbering of Lau.

[33] For informal or "extralegal" methods of conflict resolution in contemporary China, *see* VICTOR H. LI, LAW WITHOUT LAWYERS 14–16, 44–65 (1978); JEROME A. COHEN, THE CRIMINAL PROCESS IN THE PEOPLE'S REPUBLIC OF CHINA 1949–1963 97–199 (1968).

[34] SYBILLE VAN DER SPRENKEL, LEGAL INSTITUTIONS IN MANCHU CHINA 135 (1966). For an excellent "insider's view" of the Chinese legal system of the Qing, see HUANG LIU-HONG, A COMPLETE BOOK CONCERNING HAPPINESS AND BENEVOLENCE (Djang Chu trans. & ed., 1984). Huang describes frankly the corruption plaguing every level of the judicial system.

[35] There is some evidence that the historical stereotypes are losing their validity. In 1989, Chinese brought 1.85 million civil cases. This represented a 24% increase over 1988 and a sevenfold jump over 1978. Edward Epstein, *China's Legal Reforms, in* CHINA REVIEW 9.33 (Kuan Hsin-Chi & Maurice Brosseau eds., 1991) (citing RENMIN ERBAO [PEOPLE'S DAILY], Apr. 10, 1990, at 2). Nevertheless, traditional attitudes continue to exert an influence, as noted by Li Maoguan, *supra* note 15.

[36] More accurately, civil and political rights are understood as universal, abstract, and natural whereas social, economic, and collective rights are understood as contingent, nonuniversal, and decidedly secondary. *See* Ann Kent, *Waiting for Rights: China's Human Rights and China's Constitutions, 1949–1989,* 13 HUM. RTS. Q. 170, 174 (1991). I do not mean to imply that all rights theories, even political rights theories, are universal natural rights theories. Nevertheless, I consider such theories in this section for several reasons. First, the rhetoric of rights theories is often that of universal, natural rights. The claim that China needs human rights is often the claim that China needs universal human rights. Second, such theories have been and remain extremely influential in the western tradition. Third, understanding how assumptions underlying such theories are at odds with Chinese political tradition helps explain why China is more likely to adopt the kind of contingent, communitarian rights theory described in part VI. Of course, westerners may also favor similar theories. Indeed, communitarian theories are currently in vogue. I do not claim that such theories must be unique to China or that no western thinkers have advanced similar views.

[37] The poverty of this "justification" is itself evident from Alasdair MacIntyre's observation that:

> there is no expression in any ancient or medieval language correctly translated by our expression "a right" until near the close of the middle ages: the concept lacks any means of expression in Hebrew, Greek, Latin or Arabic, classical or medieval, before 1400, let alone in Old English, or in Japanese even as late as the mid-nineteenth century.

ALASDAIR MACINTYRE, AFTER VIRTUE 69 (1984).

beings have rights, solely by virtue of being human . . . [T]he concept of human beings as right-bearers is not itself in serious question in contemporary Western moral, social and political philosophy."[38] This, like so many other self-evident axioms of western social and political philosophy, is far from obvious in a Chinese context. The oft-noted late arrival of the concept "right" to China, along with classical Confucianism's emphasis on rites[39] rather than rights, suggests that within a Chinese cultural and philosophical milieu, it is far from self-evident that everyone enjoys rights that even the good of society as a whole cannot override.

A second source of human rights is God. So-called natural rights are often said to be God-given. Many today dismiss such a suggestion as preposterous, truly nonsense on stilts. Rights, they argue, do not rain down from heaven: they are political creations. In any case, the Chinese can hardly be expected to ground a rights theory upon Judeo-Christian religious conceptions.

A third scenario is the Hobbesian/Lockean fable of the ascent of humans from a brutal and savage state of nature to the civilized wonder of a social life where each person's autonomy and dignity is safeguarded by a strong theory of rights. The story begins with atomistic, rational individuals free from any duty to others, who realize the gains in safety and self-protection from cooperation and consent to limit individual freedom. By signing a mythical social compact, one limits one's liberty in exchange for certain rights. Just what these rights are varies from thinker to thinker. The same basic story-line underwrites the minimalist libertarian state of Locke and Nozick;[40] the autocratic, sovereign-dominated Leviathan of Hobbes;[41] the majoritarianism of Rousseau;[42] and, in a slightly altered version, the contemporary liberal democracy of Rawls.[43]

If one allows that society is an arena in which self-interested individuals compete for scarce resources and goods, some set of principles, rules, or laws may be needed to protect the rightful claims of individuals to goods or liberties from invasion by others. By contrast, Confucianism rejects both the atomistic individual and inevitable competition assumptions. But before turning to Confucianism, one further point merits comment. Contemporary rights thinking revolves around the distinction between Kantian deontic principles and utilitarian consequences or social policy.[44] Those who take rights seriously side with Dworkin in privileging principle over policy.[45] Those more concerned with the distributive effects of legal and political decisions give primacy to policy. A third, more pragmatic faction refuses to privilege either side, insisting instead on a situational analysis where one effects justice by balancing the rights of individuals to pursue their own ideals against the social consequences of individual choice.[46]

Confucianism, however, rejects both the atomistic individual and inevitable competition assumptions. Part of my project shall be to argue that the situational character of Confucian ethics and the pragmatism of Chinese leaders make unlikely the pressing concern with deontic principles necessary to underwrite a strong theory of individual rights. Indeed, the context-specificity of Confucian ethics militates against any attempt to pass off historically and cul-

---

[38]Henry Rosemont, *Why Take Rights Seriously? A Confucian Critique,* in HUMAN RIGHTS AND THE WORLD'S RELIGIONS 167 (Leroy Rounder ed., 1988). Some western thinkers have begun to challenge the notion that humans possess rights simply by virtue of birth.

[39]*Li,* conventionally translated as rites, refers to the full range of social customs, ethical norms, and political principles that inform interpersonal relations, social institutions, and normative discourse in China.

[40]JOHN LOCKE, TWO TREATISES OF GOVERNMENT bk. II, chs. VIII-XV, 361–99 (Peter Laslett ed., 1960) (3d ed. 1698); NOZICK, *supra* note 6, at 10–25.

[41]THOMAS HOBBES, LEVIATHAN P. I., chs. 13–15, 17–19, P. II, ch. 26, 183–217, 223–39, 313 (Crawford B. Macpherson ed., 1951) (1651).

[42]JEAN JACQUES ROUSSEAU, ON SOCIAL CONTRACT bk. IV, ch. 2, *in* THE ESSENTIAL ROUSSEAU 88 (Lowell Bair tr., 1974) (1762).

[43]RAWLS, *supra* note 6, at 11–17. The Rawlsian variant adds a twist or two: rational agents in the "original position" now make life-choices from behind a veil of ignorance. *Id.* at 17–22, 136–41. However, the key assumptions remain the same. One is still in a world of atomistic individuals in competition for scarce goods, a world where individual rights and liberties precede obligations to the state and to each other.

[44]*See* Philip Soper, *Dworkin's Domain,* 100 HARV. L. REV. 1166, 1180–81 (1987).

[45]DWORKIN, *supra* note 6, at 219–24.

[46]*See* R. Kent Greenwalt, *Law's Empire,* 84 J. PHIL. 284, 290 (1987) (book review); *see also* R. P. Peerenboom, *A Coup D'Etat in Law's Empire: Dworkin's Hercules Meets Atlas,* 9 LAW & PHIL. 95, 108–11 (1990).

turally contingent political policies and theories as universal, ahistorical absolutes.[47]

III. CONFUCIANISM

In asking how individuals become obligated to the state (and each other), Hobbes achieved the equivalent of a Copernican revolution in social and political thought. Previously the assumption was that the individual was born a member of a state. A human being, in the words of Aristotle, was a political animal, part and parcel of a polis.[48] Few doubted that the interests of the state naturally preceded those of the individual. The question in Plato's Republic was "How can one best serve the state," not "What can the state do for me."[49]

Chinese thinking to this day is dominated by this pre-Hobbesian world view. State interests override the interests and rights of any given individual. The apparent one-sidedness of this relationship is diminished to some extent, however, by a second basic assumption in Chinese thought: that the interests of the state and individual are in, or at least can be brought into, harmony.

One of the primary concerns of Tocqueville and Mill was that individuals and minorities would be overwhelmed by the more powerful majority and state.[50] In contrast, early rights advocates in China saw no contradiction between individual rights and the goals of the state.[51] On the contrary, the belief was that unleashing individual initiative would further the interests of the state. Convinced of the fundamental harmony of state and individual, Chinese leaders and intellectuals never developed a strong theory of rights to protect the individual against the dominant interests of the majority and state.

In fact, Chinese leaders tended to view rights as derivative from the state. As R. Randle Edwards explains, "China's leaders today, like the imperial and bureaucratic rulers of the past, hold that rights flow from the state in the form of a gratuitous grant that can be subjected to conditions or abrogation by the unilateral decision of the state."[52] In contrast, most western theorists maintain that the state is designed to protect rights which derive from one's status as a human being. To override these rights, the state must meet stringent political and legal standards and demonstrate compelling state interests.[53]

---

[47]Of course, not all western ethical theories are foundational and universalist in character. For instance, situational ethics and the normative views of American pragmatists such as Dewey share much in common with Confucianism. *See* RANDALL P. PEERENBOOM, LAW AND MORALITY IN ANCIENT CHINA: THE SILK MANUSCRIPTS OF HUANG-LAO, ch. IV (1993). Similarly, many writers now accept that normative theories and systems are contingent. Indeed, even Rawls has conceded that his arguments for justice as fairness are framed to apply to the "'basic structure' of a modern constitutional democracy." John Rawls, *Justice As Fairness: Political not Metaphysical,* 14 PHIL. & PUB. AFFS. 223, 224 (1985). *See also* John Rawls, *Kantian Constructivism in Moral Theory,* 77 J. PHIL. 515, 518 (1980); John Rawls, *The Idea of an Overlapping Consensus,* 7 OXFORD J. LEGAL STUDIES 1 (1987) ("[T]he aims of political philosophy depend on the society it addresses"). He then proceeds to list seven features of modern constitutional democracies, including "the fact that the political culture of a society with a democratic tradition implicitly contains certain fundamental intuitive ideas from which it is possible to work up a political conception of justice suitable for a constitutional regime." *Id.* at 4–5.

[48]ARISTOTLE, POLITICS, *in* THE COMPLETE WORKS OF ARISTOTLE, bk. I, ch. 2, at 1987 (Jonathan Barnes ed., 1984) ("[M]an is by nature a political animal"). He adds, "([H]e who is unable to live in society, or who has no need because he is sufficient for himself, must be either a beast or a god." *Id.* at 1988. For a similar view, *see* CONFUCIUS, ANALECTS, *supra* note 32, at 18:7 ("One cannot associate with birds and beasts. Am I not a member of this human race? Who, then, is there for me to associate with?") For the Confucian view of the self as a nexus of relations—social, political, cultural, religious, and so forth—*see infra* notes 57–61, 74 and accompanying text.

[49]PLATO, THE REPUBLIC, in PLATO: THE COLLECTED DIALOGUES 575–844 (Edith Hamilton & Huntington Cairns eds., 1961).

[50]Their worries were in part a response to the autocratic, all-powerful sovereign of Hobbes and the majoritarian universal will of Rousseau. *See* ALEXIS DE TOCQUEVILLE, DEMOCRACY IN AMERICA ch. 15, *in* ALEXIS DE TOCQUEVILLE: DEMOCRACY, REVOLUTION, AND SOCIETY, 99–101 (John Stone & Stephen Mennell eds., 1980) (1835) (warning against the "tyranny of the majority"). *See also* JOHN STUART MILL, ON LIBERTY, ch. 4 141–62 (Gertrude Himmelfarb ed., 1982). (1859).

[51]ANDREW NATHAN, CHINESE DEMOCRACY 50–51 (1985).

[52]R. Randle Edwards, *Civil and Social Rights: Theory and Practice in Chinese Law Today,* in HUMAN RIGHTS IN CONTEMPORARY CHINA, *supra* note 1, at 44–45.

[53]The compelling interest standard applies to "fundamental" or "preferred" rights. Non-fundamental rights are measured by a mere minimum rationality test: the legislature must have had some intelligible reason for enacting the rights limiting legislation. *See supra* note 9 and accompanying text. Of course, this points to one of the major conceptual equivocations underlying rights talk. Not all rights are created equal. One must distinguish between explicit constitutional rights, implicit constitutional rights, legislative rights, legal rights, and nonlegal rights (social rights or rights in theory—philosophical rights—and so forth).

By drawing a distinction between human beings *qua* members of a biological species and humans *qua* social beings, classical Confucianism rejects the assumption that individuals are entitled to certain inalienable rights from birth. The well-publicized and much debated distinction between masses (*min*) and persons (*ren*) as well as that between the small person (*xiao ren*) and the exemplary person (*jun zi*)[54] suggests that one must earn rights by achieving some minimal level of personhood, of humanity.[55] That is, entitlement to the privileges and benefits offered by society requires demonstration of credentials as a participating member of society. As David Hall and Roger Ames remark:

> A person is not entitled to political participation because he is born into an exclusive *jen* [human being] class. Rather, he becomes *jen* as a consequence of that personal cultivation and socialization that renders him particular. Being a person is something one does, not something one is; it is an achievement rather than a given.[56]

The achievement, it should be emphasized, is a social one. For Confucius, one *becomes* a human being, a humane person, by virtue of participation in society. Personhood and humanity are functions of socialization. At birth, before the process of enculturation, of becoming humane, we are not different than the other beasts.[57] It is this joining with others, overcoming one's natural conditionality (*ming*) in creating a different and better society, which is distinctive about humans. If one cannot overcome the passions, instincts and desires that human beings share with beasts, then one fails to achieve humanity, to become the kind of person society has an interest in protecting and granting even minimal rights.[58]

The Confucian (and socialist) challenge then is to inspire in members of society the desire to achieve a humane society and to encourage them to direct their energies toward the attainment of a harmonious social order where the interests of individuals and of the state are reconciled. This requires a willingness to participate in collective living, to search for a cooperative solution, to become humane (*ren*). It is in this sense that humanity is not something that can be conferred by law or by right of birth.

Confucianism would consider it a failure for society to aim at securing a minimum level of basic rights for alienated individuals unable or unwilling to participate cooperatively in collective living. If one accepts that there is no way to overcome the self-interested passions and desires of the animal world, then there is no hope for a humane society. Confucius realized that laws cannot force people to be humane.[59] For society to achieve collective humanity, the people that *constitute* it must be willing to put

---

[54]Linguistic distinctions continue to be important. Ann Kent notes that despite the restrictive nature of the 1982 constitution, Chinese citizens experienced in practice an expansion of civil and political rights during the early to mid-1980s. Consonant with greater liberties was a shift from collective to individual consciousness, as symbolized by the increasing use of *gongmin* (citizen) as opposed to the previously dominant *qunzhong* (masses). Kent, *supra* note 36, at 188.

During the 1989 protests, some of the working class demonstrators referred to themselves as *shimin* (urbanites or civilians). Significantly, intellectuals continued to refer to these demonstrators as *qunzhong* (masses) or *laobaixing* (common people), reinforcing the appearance, if not the reality, of anti-democratic elitism. Nathan, *supra* note 5, at 32.

[55]Mary Anne Warren was one of the first in the contemporary western literature to draw a similar distinction between "genetic humans" and "persons." *See* Mary Anne Warren, *On the Moral and Legal Status of Abortion,* 57 MONIST 43–61 (1973).

[56]DAVID L. HALL & ROGER T. AMES, THINKING THROUGH CONFUCIUS 139 (1987).

[57]See ANALECTS, *supra* note 32, at 18:6, 10:17. Humans, of course, have the potential to differentiate themselves from animals. This may provide a justification for extending some degree of moral consideration to children, though it does little for the severely impaired. The relatively high degree of infanticide, the almost non-existence of opposition to abortion, and the fact that in traditional Chinese law children were provided little protection against their parents, suggest that children were not full-fledged members of society and that one's right to consideration was indeed linked to social achievement. In the Qin, for example, the father was permitted to kill or mutilate his son as long as he first petitioned for approval. A. F. P. HULSEWE, REMNANTS OF HAN LAW 8 (1985). If the child was born deformed, infanticide was permitted. *Id.* at 139. Harsh treatment of one's offspring was also permitted in other dynasties. *See* GU TANG LU SHUYI [THE TANG CODE AND COMMENTARIES], arts. 253, 256; for an English translation, *see* WALLACE JOHNSON, THE TANG CODE 21, 31–32 (1979).

[58]The view that some members of society have no claim right on society even to life is not completely alien to the American mind: presumably some such notion underlies the popular appeal of capital punishment in the United States. The difference is that in China one must first earn one's rights whereas in the United States one starts with rights but can forfeit them through socially inappropriate behavior.

[59]"Lead the people by edicts, keep them in line with penal law, and they will avoid punishments but have no sense of shame. Lead them with virtue, keep them in line with the rites, and they will not only have a sense of shame but will order themselves harmoniously." ANALECTS, *supra* note 32, at 2:3.

aside narrow self-interest and see their interests as inextricably tied to societal interests.

The ethical focus, therefore, cannot be on determining and implementing a universal system of laws that establishes a minimum standard of basic rights for individuals alienated from each other and society. Rather, the ethical orientation must be directed to the achievement of the highest quality of life made possible by the joint efforts of humans cooperating in collective living.[60] The call is for realization of excellence in interpersonal relations (*ren*).[61]

Rights may serve well to provide a minimum level of protection for the individual. But rights, particularly as conceived and enforced in the United States, are no panacea: such rights are negative, not positive rights.[62] They are rights against the state, providing freedom *from* state intervention, but they generally do not entitle one *to* substantive benefits.[63] For instance, one has no legal claim to the economic rights enumerated in the Universal Declaration of Human Rights.[64]

Furthermore, rights are but half of the picture—the other half is duties. One indication of the different orientation of Confucian China and the United States is the contrasting conceptions of the relation between, and relative importance of, rights and duties. In the United States, much is made of rights, but duties, if discussed at all, are considered merely as corollaries to rights: in Hohfeldian terms, if one has a claim right, then others, including the state, have a duty not to interfere with that right.[65] There is generally no legal duty to the state or to fellow citizens. There is, for instance, no constitutional obligation to render aid to another;[66] indeed, in all but two states, one need not throw a life-jacket to a drowning person even though the inconvenience would be trivial.[67]

Emphasizing duties rather than rights, Chinese tradition turns Hohfeld on his head: rights are corollaries to duties.[68] For instance, a child has a duty of

---

[60]In a Confucian world, ethical standards—of which rights are one species—serve not so much as aspirational norms as inspirational themes. *See* A. S. CUA, DIMENSIONS IN MORAL CREATIVITY 124 (1978). That is, one is not simply to conform to a particular rule or standard. Rather one is to embody and give expression to the underlying ideal in one's own way, in light of one's own circumstances. To act appropriately in a given circumstance, one must "appropriate" the ethical value—one must make that value one's own. As a consequence, one has a great deal of discretion in how one translates an ethical rule or norm into practice.

The inspirational character of Confucian ethics explains in part an observation of Andrew Nathan, namely, that rights in Chinese constitutions are programmatic—"that is, they are presented as goals to be realized." *See* Nathan, *supra* note 1, at 121. What are minimal ethical and political restraints imposed on the government in the West become in Confucian China ethical ideals through which social beings can realize a humane society. These ideals must be translated into practice and given expression in light of the particular circumstances. Thus, in seeking harmony, one begins but does not end with rights.

[61]Thus, one is transformed from a human being *qua* animal to a social person entitled to deference and respect. As A. S. Cua observes, "concept of ren is the concept of an ideal of moral excellence. . . .The focus is on man himself and what he can morally accomplish in relation to others." CUA, *supra* note 60, at 68.

[62]*See* David Currie, *Positive and Negative Constitutional Rights,* 53 U. CHI. L. REV. 864 (1986).

[63]*See, e.g.,* DeShaney v. Winnebago County Dep't of Social Servs., 489 U.S. 189, 196 (1989).

> [The Due Process Clause's] purpose was to protect the people from the State, not to ensure that the State protected them from each other. . . . Consistent with these principles, our cases have recognized that the Due Process Clauses generally confer no affirmative right to governmental aid, even where such aid may be necessary to secure life, liberty, or property. . . .

[64]Universal Declaration of Human Rights, *supra* note 9, arts. 22–25 (right to work, social security, and an adequate standard of living, including food, clothing, housing, and medical care).

[65]*See* Westley Newcomb Hohfeld, *Fundamental Legal Conceptions as Applied in Judicial Reasoning,* 23 YALE L. J. 16, 31–32 (1913).

[66]U.S. tort law does impose specific duties on some individuals in certain circumstances based on a "special relationship" between the parties. For instance, innkeepers have certain duties toward their guests, as do jailors to their prisoners, and hosts to guests invited onto the premises. *See* RESTATEMENT (SECOND) OF TORTS § 314A (1965). Similarly, one who attempts to aid another but leaves that person worse off or who intentionally prevents a third party from coming to the aid of someone injured may be held liable. *Id.* at §§ 322, 323, 324A, 326, 327. Further, a small number of states have enacted good samaritan laws. *See infra* note 67. Nevertheless, in the vast majority of states, the general rule is that in the absence of a special relation, "the fact that the actor realized or should realize that action on his part is necessary for another's aid or protection does not of itself impose upon him a duty to take such action." RESTATEMENT at § 314.

[67]*See* VT. STAT. ANN. tit. 12, sec. 519 (1973); MINN. STAT. sec. 604.05 (1984). More than a dozen European states have good samaritan laws that impose criminal sanctions for failing to provide aid to one in peril . For good samaritan laws in Europe, see Rudzinski, *The Duty to Rescue: A Comparative Analysis,* in THE GOOD SAMARITAN AND THE LAW 91 (J, Ratcliffe ed., 1966).

[68]Of course, this is largely a matter of rhetorical emphasis. On the Hohfeldian view, claim rights and duties are but two sides of the same coin. Nevertheless, the rhetorical difference is illuminating. *See* Wang Jiafu et al., *Lun Fazhi Gaige [On Reform of the Legal System],* 2 FAXUE YANJIU 1, 8 (1989) (arguing that while rights entail duties and duties entail rights, rights should nonetheless occupy the leading position).

piety to his parents; as a result, parents have a "claim right" to support. Not surprisingly, the current constitution requires children to support their parents.[69] Individuals have legal duties not only to their parents but also to each other and the state.[70]

More broadly, the Confucian concept of *ren* is a duty to act appropriately in relation to others. At first blush, Confucianism appears to promote not natural rights but natural duties. Human beings, born into a family, a society, a state, owe duties to other members by virtue of birth. Some Confucians have even attempted to ground the hierarchial five primary social relations in a hierarchical natural order: just as heaven is above earth and yang superior to yin, so is the ruler above the official, the husband superior to wife,[71] and so on.[72]

Yet at the heart of a duty lies not simply the natural relation but also deference. One becomes an authority, a person to whom others will defer, in part by age and natural relation but, more importantly, by earning the respect of others. To do so, one must show cultural and moral achievement and demonstrate to others that they are better off following one's advice than had they set out on their own.[73] In times of conflict, people turn to the authoritative person (*jun zi*) as the one best able to envision a solution and thereby restore harmony.

In the Confucian world, there are no ahistorical or abstract rational beings. Confucianism concurs in this regard with Edmund Pincoffs, who maintains that "individualism makes sense only against a background of social organization. There is no human situation that consists of an aggregate of unrelated individuals. . . . We come into a world that is already organized; . . . we understand ourselves through our reflection in the perceptions of others. . . ."[74]

The historicized, relational character of the Chinese self/person makes it difficult to isolate the basic ethical unit, the individual, to whom ahistorical, universal rights would attach. Identity constantly changes, varying with the context; duties and, correspondingly, rights/rites are also constantly being redefined as other actors change. A son owes deference and filial piety to his father; the father owes deference and piety to his son. Confucianism requires sensitivity to the particular person and the web of relations that define the person. Whereas Kantian rights are based on the fundamental dignity and equality of every human being, Confucian rites give full play to the relational differences that distinguish each person. Thus, ethical duties radiate out in concentric circles—at the center, oneself, then one's parents, the rest of the nuclear family, relatives, friends, neighbors, state, nation, world—the larger the circle, the lesser the duty. The notion that generic rights or duties attach to individuals *simpliciter* is alien to the more graded and finely tuned rites-oriented mind.

Of central importance to the historically rich Confucian world view and its non-rights based method of conflict resolution are the *li*. The *li*—conventionally translated as rites—may be understood more broadly to include the full range of social customs, ethical norms, and political principles embodied in the complex relations, organizations, and institutions of society. They are culture-specific norms, the contingent, ever-changing values of a particular society. But the *li* are important not merely as the amassed wisdom of the ages, but also because they are the communally-owned repository of shared meaning and value on which people can draw in times of conflict. However different people may be, there are still deep chords of affinity which bind them together as a result of a shared past. By tapping the areas of commonality, one may be able to find the ground upon which to build consensus, to forge new harmony.

---

[69]PRC CONST., *supra* note 1, art. 49 (also providing that parents have a duty to rear and educate their minor children).

[70]*Id.* arts. 42, 46, 49, 54–56.

[71]The issue of Confucianism's role in the historical subordination of women in China is a difficult one. No doubt the traditional hierarchical status relationships of Confucianism contributed to discrimination against women in practice. Nevertheless, Confucian theory does not mandate such a result. As a contextual ethical system, it is able to pay greater heed to women's interests, in keeping with their changed circumstances and status in contemporary society. That said, women's issues will most likely remain a concern.

[72]The five primary relations are ruler/official, husband/wife, parent/child, older brother/younger brother, friend/friend. Only the last is not hierarchical. One of the first to ground the five relations in the natural order was Dong Zhongshu. *See* WING-TSIT CHAN, A SOURCEBOOK IN CHINESE PHILOSOPHY 277–278 (1963).

[73]Thus one condition for deference is that the authority, the person in the superior position, respect the interests of the deferring party. Obviously the leaders in Beijing did not meet this condition in dealing with the students and workers in 1989. Indeed, the failure of creativity resulting in the excessive and unnecessary use of force by the *authoritarian* regime reveals their bankruptcy as *authoritative* Confucian rulers.

[74]EDMUND PINCOFFS, QUANDARIES AND VIRTUES 8 (1986).

Placing the burden of achieving or failing to achieve a humane society on the members of society fosters an environment in which compromise and innovative solutions can occur. The absence of any fixed, external, or privileged standards deprives one of a foundation on which to ground a dogmatic position.

There is then little room for the privileging of deontological principles that underwrite contemporary liberal rights theory. To the pragmatic Chinese mind, to ignore social consequences is sheer folly. Indeed, it is not at all clear that deontic principles make much sense in a Chinese context; to paraphrase Cardozo, rights (or duties) in the air are no rights (or duties) at all:[75] rights and duties can only arise out of a particular context. Consequently, one must approach afresh each new conflict between principle and policy, between rights and consequences.[76]

To insist on one's rights in a Chinese context is a cultural *faux pas*—one must be willing to negotiate, to compromise. Even when the legal system is invoked, the emphasis most often remains on compromise. Most contractual disputes are resolved through mediation or arbitration, in which "the court's judgment is not phrased in terms of a holding or a directive. Rather, after mediation by the court, the record indicates that the parties agreed to the particular resolution."[77] To be sure, court mediation in China may often be considerably less than voluntary.[78] Significantly, however, it seems the court wants to at least maintain the appearance that the parties themselves have come to a harmonious resolution on mutually agreeable terms (just as our courts strive to keep alive the myth of impartial, apolitical justice).[79]

The emphasis placed on compromise, mutual agreement, and harmony even in the legal context suggests that substantive justice tends to take precedence over formal justice. When a mutually acceptable solution cannot be reached, or the interests of the individual and the state cannot be reconciled, then the lack of procedural rights is particularly worrisome, as in the trials of the 1989 student demonstrators.[80]

Indeed, one may object to this picture of a harmonious Confucian society on several fronts. First, extralegal methods of resolving conflict such as informal mediation may not fully respect legal rights and interests. In the absence of formal oversight, abuse and corruption are possible. One side may be able to take advantage of personal connections (*guan xi*) to influence the mediator. Even if the process is not corrupt, the social pressure from neighbors and colleagues to accept a solution that compromises legal rights and interests may be overwhelming.

Second, a key assumption of mediation and the Confucian approach to conflict resolution more generally is that harmony is possible and interests reconcilable. But perhaps Mill was right in posing private

---

[75]Palsgraf v. Long Island Railroad Co., 162 N.E. 99 (N.Y. 1928) (citing FREDERICK POLLOCK, TORTS 455 (1891)) ("Proof of negligence in the air, so to speak, will not do.").

[76]Lest anyone believe that socialist China has succeeded in eradicating Confucian values, consider the government's official statement on human rights:

> China is in favor of strengthening international cooperation in the realm of human rights on the basis of mutual understanding and seeking a common ground while reserving differences. However, no country in its effort to realize and protect human rights can take a route that is divorced from its history and its economic, political and cultural realities. . . . It is also noted in the resolution of the 46th conference on human rights that no single mode of development is applicable to all cultures and peoples. It is neither proper nor feasible for any country to judge other countries by the yardstick of its own mode or to impose its own mode on others. . . . Consideration should be given to the differing views on human rights held by countries with different political, economic and social systems, as well as different historical, religious and cultural backgrounds. International human rights activities should be carried on in the spirit of seeking common ground while reserving differences, mutual respect, and the promotion of understanding and cooperation.

WHITE PAPER, *supra* note 14, at 8. Present are many of the key features of Confucianism: rejection of abstract, universal dogmas and ethical principles; attention to the particular historical context of the parties; attempt to find and build on common ground in order to realize a solution amenable to all parties; belief in multiple possible resolutions to social and political conflicts; focus on persuasion and rejection of force. Indeed, if one had to summarize Confucian teaching in a single sentence, one would be hard pressed to do better than Beijing's twice repeated slogan: seek common ground while reserving differences, maintain mutual respect, and promote understanding and cooperation. Again, by their own self-selected standards, the leaders in Beijing failed utterly in violently oppressing the 1989 demonstrators.

[77]Roderick Macneil, *Contract in China: Law, Practice, and Dispute Resolution,* 38 STAN. L. REV. 303, 333 (1986).

[78]*See* Donald Clarke, *Dispute Resolution in China,* 5 J. CHINESE L. 245, 245–46 (1991).

[79]Macneil, *supra* note 77, at 342. *See also* Economic Contract Law of the People's Republic of China, art. 32 (adopted Dec. 13, 1981) (if both parties have "committed mistakes," they should "share responsibility" according to "actual circumstances").

[80]*See infra* note 102.

and public, individual interest and state interest as fundamental antinomies.[81] Third, even if harmony is theoretically possible, in practice, people must be willing to seek a solution amenable to all. This attitude seems sorely lacking in the present-day China. Today, the number of encounters between strangers is ever increasing; perhaps an inevitable consequence is a breakdown in the kind of cooperative behavior and attitudes required by Confucianism. Fourth, even assuming sufficient altruism and a willingness to compromise, there must be sufficient common ground on which to build a solution acceptable to all. Such common ground may not exist in many instances in China.

A fifth problem is that Confucius' ethical gaze was so trained on the lofty heights attainable by humankind that he neglected to provide for even a minimal level of institutional protection for the individual against the state and others. The emphasis on duty, rather than on rights, leaves the individual vulnerable to the whims of the state. A related objection is that the Confucian system encourages authoritarianism. In the absence of external ethical or internal political constraints, the authoritative Confucian leader all too readily becomes an authoritarian despot. The Confucian system confers great discretionary power on the ruler, relying on the moral character of the ruler and internal monitoring by officials to ensure that the state serves the people. Far from being politically benign, the rhetoric of harmony is easily manipulable in the service of dictators.

IV. SOCIALISM

Socialism may take many forms, some of which are more rights-friendly than others, but Marxism, at least Marx's Marxism, is not an ideology hospitable to rights. Marx viewed rights as an illusion, crumbs thrown to the alienated worker to dupe her or him into accepting the legitimacy of the state and the current economic order. Rights play no role in the ideal communist society, for the state withers away and with it the need for rights as protections from the state. Nor would rights be needed to protect against others, because self-interested individuals coveting the property of others would no longer exist. Once one does away with private property, which leads to class conflict and "the struggle of the isolated individual against the relationship of dominance,"[82] a new socialist human being is created, more other-regarding than the self-interested capitalist ancestor. Similarly, because everyone would be provided for, positive rights would be unnecessary. The result for Marx—as for Confucius—is that harmony would prevail. Each person would achieve full potential in a self-regulating society. Order would emerge from the bottom up, out of the particular historical conditions, rather than being imposed from above in accordance with allegedly universal or natural principles that in fact only represent the interests of the ruling class.[83]

For the present, rights and law may be useful tools to serve socialism's ends. Beyond doubt, law has served as an important tool in the factional power struggles of socialist China.[84] Official attitudes toward the judiciary and law have swung radically. Even so, rights have never been taken seriously in any period. Emphasis on "formal" law has resulted in harsher penalties in practice, with the Party exerting control over the legal process in order to realize its political objectives.[85] On the other hand, the less formal approaches have often been equally detrimental to individual rights.

At one end of the informal spectrum lay mediation, with disputes resolved outside the courts, either with a village elder's assistance or under the guidance of local Party officials, neighborhood committees, or the police.[86] Other informal sanctions during the Maoist years varied from private criticism and education to public criticism, censure, and struggle.[87] There were in fact different forms of struggle. The lesser exposed one to "intense vituperation from those in attendance,

[81] *See* MILL, *supra* note 50.

[82] KARL MARX, THE GERMAN IDEOLOGY, quoted in COHEN, *supra* note 33, at 75.

[83] Unlike Marx, Mao rejected the utopian "theory of no clashes." Instead, he called for permanent revolution to ensure that the bureaucracy remained faithful to the needs of the masses and to prevent the emergence of class conflicts. *See* Mao Tsetung, *The Vision of the Great Leap;* in THE PEOPLE'S REPUBLIC OF CHINA: A DOCUMENTARY HISTORY OF REVOLUTIONARY CHANGE 381, 385–87 (Mark Selden ed., 1979).

[84] For an overview of law in Maoist China, *see* Alice E.-S. Tay, *The Struggle for Law in China,* 21 U. BRIT. COLUM. L. REV. 561 (1987).

[85] *See* Note, *Concepts of Law in the Chinese Anti-Crime Campaign,* 98 HARV. L. REV. 1890 (1985).

[86] As noted earlier, legal rights are often compromised in the mediation process. *See supra* note 78 and accompanying text.

[87] *See* COHEN, *supra* note 33, at 20.

amid shaking fists, shouts, and accusing fingers";[88] the more severe forms often resulted in physical violence.

Political status determined treatment, for Mao distinguished contradictions between the people and the enemy from contradictions among the people.[89] Conflicts among the people were to be handled through "democratic" means—education and persuasion—with formal legal punishment meted out only to those resistant to persuasion and rehabilitation. But severe sanctions and dictatorial methods were to be employed in dealing with enemies such as "reactionaries, exploiters, counterrevolutionaries, landlords, bureaucrat-capitalists, robbers . . . and other scoundrels who disrupt social order."[90] Thus the more serious forms of informal sanction, such as struggle, were reserved for those with bad political backgrounds or guilty of political crimes. The scope of "political" crime, however, could be extraordinarily broad.

In any event, none of these various "informal" means of social control focused particularly on individual rights. To the contrary, insisting upon one's rights would only have subjected a person to greater abuse for maintaining incorrect political views.

On a more theoretical level, throughout the socialist period, rights have been seen as political expedients, granted by the state as needed and revoked when necessary. Furthermore, duties coexist with rights: for example, the duty as well as the right to work and receive education.[91] More ominously, one has the duty to safeguard the security, honor, and interests of the motherland.[92] Indeed, duties are owed primarily to the state rather than to other individuals.[93] Commentators have criticized the tendency in the PRC to emphasize duties at the expense of rights.[94] But the existence of duties *per se* does not account so much for the detriment to the individual as the fact that duties are owed to the *state* and the demands upon the individual in the name of socialism are essentially unlimited, defined primarily by the transitory dictates of the Party.

One positive aspect of socialism, however, is the importance invested in economic and social rights. The PRC constitution provides not only the right to a job, education, and vocational training, but to rest, medical care, and material support for the elderly, ill, or disabled.[95] Indeed, one of Beijing's major complaints has been that international rights organizations have focused myopically on political rights, ignoring China's commitment to economic rights and actual improvements in the basic material living conditions of many citizens. There is some truth to that assertion, but it is far from the whole story.

V. A CRITIQUE, ON CHINESE TERMS

Discussion of China's record on human rights all too often ends up with both sides talking past rather than to each other.[96] Westerners, particularly the United States and its representatives, denounce China for abuse of political freedoms and rights. Chinese retort that the foremost human right is the right to subsistence.[97] By all accounts, China has made remarkable economic progress, given its huge population and history of imperialist exploitation and decades of war with rights-conscious western nations. Indeed, the Chinese may well wonder at the authenticity of western protestations given the severe mistreatment of Chinese citizens by the imperial powers.[98] Even today, states far wealthier than China fail to provide the economic rights mandated by the Universal Declaration and arguably achieved to some extent in the PRC.

[88] *Id.*

[89] MAO TSETUNG, *On the Correct Handling of Contradictions among the People, in* 5 SELECTED WORKS OF MAO TSETUNG 391 (1977).

[90] *Id.* at 393.

[91] PRC CONST., *supra* note 1, arts. 42, 46.

[92] *Id.* art. 54; *see also* art. 33 ("Every citizen enjoys the rights and at the same time must perform the duties prescribed by the Constitution and the law.").

[93] *See id.* arts. 42, 46, 52, 54–56. *But see* art. 49 (duty of parents to rear and educate children and duty of children to support parents).

[94] *See, e.g.,* Wang et al., *supra* note 68, at 8.

[95] PRC CONST., *supra* note 1, arts. 43–45.

[96] If indeed they talk to each other at all. Recently, Britain's Home Office refused to see a human rights delegation from China, fearing that the Chinese group was planning to criticize Britain's human rights record, particularly with respect to Northern Ireland. Under pressure from the Foreign Office, the Home Office relented. Refusal to see the delegation might have jeopardized Prime Minister Major's request to send Britain's own human rights delegation to China. Geoffrey Crothall, *U.K. Averts Incident by Agreeing to See China Team,* S. CHINA MORNING POST, Feb. 14, 1992, at 1.

[97] WHITE PAPER, *supra* note 14, at 9.

[98] For an account of these atrocities and human rights abuses inflicted on Chinese citizens, *see id.* at 10.

Despite the rhetoric of universal human rights, the reality is that different states have different conceptions and practices with respect to rights, reflecting their own cultural, philosophical, political, ethical, and economic traditions. Thus a more productive approach than simply attempting to impose one's own particular rights ideology on another sovereign state is to engage the other on its own terms. To do so is not to endorse an anything-goes cultural relativism or to deny the legitimacy of judging another culture. At minimum, a country must stand up to scrutiny on its own terms: it must be able to withstand criticism of both its theory (or underlying philosophies) and empirical practice. More importantly, many terms are shared terms. One need not be an ethical absolutist to decry the massacre of unarmed students and citizens in and around Tiananmen Square.[99]

To begin with the positive, China may be praised for the progress it has made in its efforts to secure economic rights for citizens. There is, of course, room for improvement. Citizens have a right to a job, but it may not be a job to which they are inclined or suited. In practice, the duty to work means that people are assigned jobs, at times in cities far from their spouse's place of work. In addition, medical care could be improved and a more comprehensive welfare system implemented. But these are to a large measure social policy choices; how one society directs resources will differ from another.[100]

China's most noticeable failure is in the area of political rights. Beijing's assertions that "the people are the real masters of the country with the right to run the country's economic and social affairs"[101] is of course absurd. Nor can one take seriously the government's attempt to portray the current system as one of free elections with politically independent multiple parties, or its claim that "the Party conducts its activities within the framework of the Constitution and the law."[102] The assertion that there is no censorship in China and that the government upholds the principle of "letting a hundred flowers blossom and a hundred schools of thought contend" is patently false.[103] To declare that there are no political prisoners in China (only "counterrevolutionaries") is insulting not only to the courageous demonstrators of 1989 but to those around the world who witnessed the events on television.[104]

Although the constitution and other laws nominally provide various rights, many are not legally enforceable in practice. For instance, while the recently promulgated Administrative Law allows citizens to sue the government,[105] the government has never lost a politically sensitive case.[106] Thus, another reason why citizens often do not pursue their legal rights is their belief that to do so is futile.

Beijing's issuance of a lengthy statement on human rights denying this familiar catalogue of com-

---

[99]The theoretically interesting metaethical issue is whether one may legitimately judge another individual or culture according to values *not* shared by that individual or culture. Because I rely on shared and indigenous Chinese values, I need not address the issue. For a defense of "evaluative universalism," where one judges another culture according to the values one believes in, see Andrew Nathan, *The Place of Values in Cross-Cultural Studies: The Example of Democracy in China,* in IDEAS ACROSS CULTURES 293–317 (Paul A. Cohen & Merle Goldman eds., 1990). Little is to be gained from judging another culture according to exogenous values if the other side refuses to engage in dialogue on those terms or believes its own values to be superior. That such coercive methods would succeed with Beijing is unlikely. *See infra* notes 113–115 and accompanying text.

[100]Ann Kent argues that notwithstanding previous achievements, China in the 1980s experienced several setbacks in the actual realization of economic rights. For instance, the right to work was increasingly out of step with the realities of the fledgling commodity or market economy spawned by reform policies. Further negative developments included: "(1) the commodification of social welfare; (2) the increase of the rural-urban gap in the provision of social services; (3) the devolution of responsibility for social welfare and social security; and (4) the lack of a comprehensive unemployment insurance system." *See* Kent, *supra* note 36, at 193–99.

[101]WHITE PAPER, *supra* note 14, at 13

[102]*Id.* at 14–15. For an account of Beijing's abuse of PRC criminal procedure laws in the treatment of 1989 demonstrators, see Asia Watch, *Rough Justice in Beijing: Punishing the "Black Hands" of Tiananmen Square,* in NEWS FROM ASIA WATCH, Jan. 27, 1991, at 4–7.

[103]WHITE PAPER, *supra* note 14, at 15–16, 19. Witness the treatment of Zhang Yimou's films. *See* Lynn Pan, *A Chinese Master,* N.Y. TIMES MAGAZINE, Mar. 1, 1992, at 30. Foreign reporters are also subject to restrictions. For a discussion of post-Tiananmen suppression of freedom of expression, *see* Asia Watch, *Punishment Season: Human Rights in China After Martial Law,* in THE BROKEN MIRROR, *supra* note 5, at 383–86; for limits on the press, *see* International League for Human Rights & the Ad Hoc Study Group on Human Rights in China, *Winter in Beijing: Continuing Repression Since the Beijing Massacre,* Feb. 18, 1990, at 20–22.

[104]WHITE PAPER, *supra* note 14, at 24. One report based on Chinese documents estimated that, as of 1991, as many as 100,000 people were imprisoned for opposing the government. *See* Charles Lane, *The Last Gulag,* NEWSWEEK, Sept. 23, 1991, at 26.

[105]*See* Zhonghua Renmin Gongheguo Xingzheng Susong Fa (Administrative Litigation Law of the PRC) (promulgated April 4, 1989), RENMIN RIBAO, Apr. 10, 1989, at 2, *trans. in* China Law and Practice, June 5, 1989, at 37–57.

[106]*See supra* note 30.

plaints demonstrates that it is aware of a problem. In many instances, the PRC baldly lied rather than attempt to justify human rights abuses, which indicates a failure according not to alien western principles but to China's own standards. The Chinese Constitution provides for these rights—they are the self-selected goals and commitments of the government itself. Failure to realize them is a failure of the current regime to make good on its own promises.

With rights violations so widespread, Beijing cannot simply attempt to explain away particular instances. One government justification argues that China is a poor country, and economic stability must therefore take priority over all else, including political rights.[107] Though there may be a kernel of truth to this argument, it cannot justify the many specific instances of censorship, suppression of political speech, imprisonment of political activists, and so on. Not every attempt to exercise a political right threatens economic progress, but such attempts threaten the continued rulership of the current regime, and socialism itself.

The problem, therefore, is systemic. As noted, socialism is hostile to genuine political rights. Thus one can scarcely be surprised at the host of institutional impediments to rights discussed previously: Party domination of both the legislature and judiciary (despite constitutional provisions of independence); elevation of the interests of the state over the rights of the individual as sanctioned in article 51; use of the language of duty to override rights, and so on. Enjoyment of genuine rights apparently is incompatible with the continued existence of statist socialism in China. Beijing's only possible remaining justification is that the future benefits of socialism outweigh the present costs of exploiting, lying to, and abusing the people. But the collapse of socialism around the world and the bankruptcy of Communism as a practicable ideal cut against any such justification.

In any event, even if the current regime, or a post-socialist China, decides to take rights seriously, these rights will be rights with Chinese characteristics. That a Chinese rights culture will share western philosophical conceptions is highly doubtful. Many of the basic elements of traditional Chinese thought and practice militate against a strong theory of rights: the historical conception of person where one is born into a family, community, and state rather than the Hobbesian view of rights-bearing individuals preceding the state; the notion that rights are grants from the state rather than manna from heaven; the rejection of deontological and universal principles in favor of contingent, culture-sensitive ethics; the lack of foundational external restraints on authoritarian political rulers; the preference for informal mediation rather than appeal to the courts for enforcement of rights.

What then will rights with a Chinese face look like? Will such a theory provide rights that genuinely protect the individual in practice? Although one cannot be sure, certain guesses may be ventured.

VI. A CHINESE THEORY OF RIGHTS

Given the pragmatic, anti-foundational character of much of Chinese philosophy, and of Confucianism in particular, any rights theory justifiable on Chinese terms will almost assuredly be a contingent one. There will be no attempt to pass off Chinese rights as universal rights—rights in China will be viewed as a product of Chinese culture, traditions, and historical and economic conditions.[108] As such, they may or may not be appropriate for other countries.[109] Further, rights will differ not only between China and other states but within China from one period to the next. This of course is the reality everywhere in the world. What will differ is that in China jurisprudential rhetoric may match reality.[110]

---

[107] *Cf.* WHITE PAPER, *supra* note 14, at 11–12.

[108] In this respect, Marxism's emphasis on historical materialism coincides with Confucianism's sensitivity to the particular conditions of society, reinforcing the view of rights as contingent. Even some scholars who argue for an expansive theory of human rights based on the commonality (*gongtongxing*) of all people reflect the influence of Marxism in maintaining that rights are a product of the particular historical, economic, and material conditions of a society. *See, e.g.,* Li Buyun, *Lun renquan de sanzhong cunzai xingtai [On Three Forms of Existence of Human Rights],* 65 FAXUE YANJIU [STUDIES IN LAW] 11, 13 (1992).

[109] It is true that all state[s] *may* share some similar rights. Such rights, however, would be contingent on political, cultural, and economic factors.

[110] As Nathan points out, a prominent feature of Chinese rights is that they have varied from one constitution to the next. He attributes this to the belief of authors of the Chinese Constitutions that rights are grants from the state, and hence may be added or subtracted at the will of the state. Nathan, *supra* note 1, at 121. The conception of social order as historically contingent and evolving may also explain this phenomenon: as the society changes, so must rights.

Second, Chinese rights will be more communitarian in theory and in practice. The traditional emphasis on social harmony and duties will be manifested in a theory that imposes duties as well as confers rights. Rights will provide a minimum level of protection for the individual against others and the state; duties will point to social solidarity and possibilities for human achievement. One will owe duties to fellow citizens as well as to the state, although not as in statist socialism to the *socialist* state as such. In contrast to PRC practice today, duties will not be used to limit rights in the name of the socialist cause but rather to supplement rights as ethical standards and guideposts.

Third, rights will continue to be looked upon as inspirational ethical themes to be realized in light of the particular situation by individuals seeking a harmonious solution to problems rather than simply as minimalist protections against the state and others.[111] Thus, rights will be one resource, a starting point, for resolving conflicts. The goal will still be to move beyond strident insistence on rights to the detriment of others to creative solutions acceptable to all. Of course, in some cases, such solutions may not be possible. This may be because those involved are unwilling to put aside narrow self-interest—in which case there may yet be hope for persuasion—or it may be because there simply are not sufficient resources to satisfy everyone, or because some issues do not lend themselves to compromise. In such instances, where the ideal of harmony cannot be attained and the best solution is a more modest one, rights will play an important role in ensuring that certain individual interests are afforded at least special consideration and perhaps some minimum level of protection.

Fourth, given the historicized conception of the self in which a person is born into a complex social matrix, one would expect a relational theory of rights. One's rights (and duties) will vary depending on the relation of the parties. Not all rights and duties will be created equal; there will be greater duties to (and claim greater rights from) one's family than fellow citizens. Indeed, there will be greater duties to some citizens than others: for instance, the duty to neighbors or colleagues may be more stringent than those to strangers.

[111] *See supra* note 60 and accompanying text.

One constraint on the full realization of a highly articulated relational model of rights is the limited capacity of the formal legal system to take into account the particulars of the parties. Thus, a fifth aspect of Chinese rights culture will be the continued reliance on informal means for conflict resolution. Although far from perfect, traditional methods such as mediation offer many advantages. Both parties save face, fully participate in the proceeding, and shape the ultimate solution. The process, usually faster and cheaper than more formal methods, allows for a more particularized justice and for the restoration of social harmony, with both sides feeling they have received their due.

A sixth characteristic of Chinese rights and one positive result of socialism will be the continued prominence given to economic rights. Citizens have come to expect certain economic and material benefits from the state. Any regime that assumes power would be hard pressed to justify the elimination of medical care, for instance. The provision of a minimum level of material support is also consistent with the ideals, if not the historical reality, of Chinese traditions. Now that the people have actually observed that it is possible for the state to provide a minimum standard of living for all, they will not accept the old excuse that China is simply too poor.

A seventh characteristic is that rights will continue to be instrumental, construed as political and ethical tools for achieving the ultimate goal of harmony. The extreme deontological position that an individual possesses an inviolability that even the good of society as a whole cannot override is out of step with Chinese ethical traditions.

An eighth characteristic and a corollary of the rejection of the extreme deontological rights position is that the balance between the rights of the individual and the interests of the collective will probably be more inclined toward the latter than in the United States, though to what extent is difficult to predict.

As for whether Chinese rights will continue to be considered grants from the state, that too is uncertain. The idea that humans are born into this world with a full complement of rights as well as duties might take hold in the popular mind—as may the idea that the state is to serve the people rather than the rulers. Surely, greater contact with the world outside China will tend to reinforce such notions. If assimilated, such beliefs will make more likely the development of a viable rights culture in China.[112]

The seeds of a rights culture have already been planted in China, at least to the extent that the litany of rights provided in the constitution is not simply empty rhetoric. International pressure and a desire to enjoy the benefits of membership in the community of civilized nations may push China marginally further in the direction of a more rights-oriented public policy. Arguably, international pressure has already produced results. One can point not only to the government White Paper on rights but also to the release of prisoners tied to visits of foreign diplomats or to congressional votes on key issues such as most-favored nation status.[113]

However, the government will do what is necessary to maintain power—most importantly, maintaining economic progress and a higher standard of living. For this it needs foreign assistance.[114] Thus, in dealing with foreigners, Beijing must play high stakes poker. Whenever possible, the government goes on the attack, citing past imperialist abuses and contemporary rights failures within foreigners' own countries, or it stonewalls, simply denying that there are political prisoners or human rights abuses in China. Only when the potential economic gains are high and the international pressure unrelenting does Beijing make concessions to the international community, releasing a few prisoners here, making a conciliatory statement there. Ultimately, little changes within the Great Wall, as indicated by the recent statements of Justice Minister Cai Cheng rejecting the rule of law for the supremacy of the Party.[115]

Even if post-socialist China implements a contingent, communitarian rights program like the one outlined, the question remains whether it will be of much use. When push comes to shove, will the rights promulgated in the future constitution be worth the paper they are written on? When the interests of the individual conflict with those of the state, will the latter inevitably prevail, as they have throughout much of Chinese history?

The danger of an avowedly contingent theory of rights is that once one allows rights to be compromised to secure other normative considerations, the Pandora's box is open. Powerful political parties may abuse this window of discretionary opportunity to inappropriately override legitimate individual rights. Since absolute power in the hands of the foolhardy—or self-interested—is a real and ominous possibility, there should be many and stringent institutional safeguards. Decisions as to when state interests are sufficiently compelling to override constitutional rights granted to individuals should not be in the hands of a single branch of government, much less a single person. Constitutional review and a truly independent judiciary seem imperative. Whether these institutional adjustments alone or in combination with other changes are sufficient is difficult to predict. At a minimum, a rights culture with a heightened rights consciousness on the part of the people also seems essential. If the people do not stand up for their rights, the courts surely will not.

CONCLUSION

Not all rights theories are theories of natural rights. Nor does taking human rights seriously necessarily entail that rights be considered absolute and inalienable, a trump against any and all interests of the state, or as invariably of greater moral weight than matters of policy or social consequences. Indeed, no system takes human rights that seriously in practice.

There can be little doubt that the calculus as to the proper balance of individual autonomy versus social good will differ between the United States and China,

---

[112]There is no inherent contradiction between an instrumental, harmony-based theory of rights and the view that such rights attach to human beings *qua* human beings. One could believe that one is born with certain rights that protect one against certain intrusions by the state and others and yet do not trump all social consequences.

[113]However, the extent to which the international community can exercise influence over China is limited. Having suffered through 100 years of imperialist oppression, China is highly sensitive to foreign criticism and intrusions in sovereign affairs. One need only reflect on Tiananmen to appreciate Beijing's disdain for world opinion. More importantly, the leaders of the PRC are fully aware that foreign commitment to human rights is not deep. When economic goals conflict with concern for human rights abuse, economics wins out all too often. In light of such short-term self-interest and transitory commitment, the PRC need but stay the course.

[114]It bears noting that even in the immediate days following Tiananmen, Beijing insisted that its open-door policies would continue unabated. *See, e.g.,* Deng Xiaoping's remarks on June 9, 1989, BEIJING REV., June 12–25, 1989, at 4.

[115]*See supra* note 17 and accompanying text.

as it does between the United States and every other country in the world. Although the ultimate ability of a contingent, communitarian rights theory to protect Chinese citizens against their government is uncertain, one thing is clear: the rhetoric of absolute, ahistorical, universal rights is at odds with China's philosophical and cultural traditions. The hope that China will adopt wholesale American rights ideology is misplaced. China may adopt a more rights-oriented public policy, but even then, rights in China will remain rights with Chinese characteristics.

54

JEREMY COOPER

Poverty and Constitutional Justice: The Indian Experience

I. INTRODUCTION

In 1933, the British House of Lords affirmed its view that "poverty is a misfortune for which the law cannot take any responsibility at all."[1] In 1986, Justice Bhagwati, Chief Justice of the Indian Supreme Court, described the function of a Supreme Court, in relation to poverty and oppression, in a somewhat different vein:

> The judges in India have asked themselves the question: Can judges really escape addressing themselves to substantial questions of social justice? Can they simply say to litigants who came to them for justice and the general public that accords them power, status and respect, that they simply follow the legal text when they are aware that their actions will perpetuate inequality and injustice? Can they restrict their enquiry into law and life within the narrow confines of a narrowly defined rule of law? Does the requirement of constitutionalism not make of greater demands on the judicial function?[2]

The history of litigation in the Indian Supreme Court throughout the past decade has demonstrated that the answer to all of the above rhetorical questions has been a clear and unambiguous no, the Judges cannot. Throughout the 1980s, whenever a citizen of India has come to the Indian Supreme Court, seeking relief under the constitution, the court seems consistently to have asked itself the same fundamental question: Will the granting of the relief asked by the plaintiff advance the goal of social justice? If the answer is affirmative, the litigant is granted the relief requested. If the answer is negative, the relief is refused.[3] This Article seeks to describe and explain the background of this phenomenon, and to explore the promises and limitations found in this strategy for poverty lawyers in other jurisdictions.

India has a total area of 3,287,782 square kilometers and a population in excess of 700 million, of whom only 100 million live in cities or towns. Although there are considerable gaps between rich and poor, the vast majority of the Indian population is poor. An enormous variety of races and peoples live within the political boundaries of the state, and despite a large Hindu majority, there are large minorities of other religions, including Moslems, Christians, Sikhs, Buddhists, and Jains. India's legal system is among the oldest in the world.[4] The Constitution of India, created in 1950, gave its Supreme Court the powers to nullify actions of the Executive and the Legislature, when the action breaches fundamental human rights.[5] These powers are as wide ranging as those afforded in 1787 by the United States Constitution's Founding Fathers to the United States Supreme Court, a Court described by one international law expert as "the world's first human rights tribunal."[6] The traditions of the Indian Supreme Court between 1950 and 1980 were proud, with many strong judgements meted from its chambers.[7] However, the primary focus of their judgements was not poverty or social

[1]WOLFGANG FRIEDMAN, LAW IN A CHANGING SOCIETY 122 (1972).
[2]P. Bhagwati, *Chief Justice on What Justices Should Do,* THE TIMES OF INDIA, Sept. 21, 1986, at 9.

[3]B. Agarwala, *The Legal Philosophy of P. N. Bhagwati,* 14 Ind. L. Rev. 136, 140 (1987).
[4]JUDGES AND THE JUDICIAL POWER vi (Rajeev Dhavan et al. eds., 1985).
[5]UPENDRA BAXI, THE INDIAN SUPREME COURT AND POLITICS 10 (1980); S. P. SATHE, CONSTITUTIONAL AMENDMENTS 1950–1988 LAW AND POLITICS (1989).
[6]P. SIEGHART, THE LAWFUL RIGHTS OF MANKIND 29 (1985).
[7]H. SEERVAI, CONSTITUTIONAL LAW OF INDIA (1987); SATHE, *supra* note 5.

justice.[8] Indeed, the contrary was more often the case, as was observed by Dwivedi in 1973, when characterizing the Indian Supreme Court of that period as "an arena of legal quibbling for men with long purses."[9] The legal system had itself been "transplanted from a foreign colonial power based on foreign ideals and values and imposed on a country with vastly different indigenous value systems, traditions and customs."[10] The court tried to follow the arcane methods of the British House of Lords. It is not surprising therefore that during the period from 1950–80, the Indian Supreme Court was frequently accused of obstructing social reform.[11] In the 1980s, however, due largely to the collective philosophy of a group of radical judges who formed the majority view of the court at that time, a primary function of the Indian Supreme Court became "the liberation of the poor and oppressed through judicial initiatives" with the overt assistance of "the social activists and public interest litigators."[12] In a decade, the Indian Supreme Court became the last resort for the oppressed and bewildered.[13]

As part of this process, numerous public interest groups mobilized to take advantage of a likely favourable judicial response to protect a whole range of vulnerable, or victimised groups, including prisoners held without trial, bonded labourers, pavement dwellers, litigants without legal aid, women bought and sold as chattels, children forced into jails for homosexual activities, slave labourers paid wages in the form of toxic drugs causing an incurable disease, tortured young prisoners in state jails, and abused inmates of children's homes.[14] The blend of social and judicial activism allowed the Indian Supreme Court finally to break free from its conservative traditions, and what Dhavan has described as "the conflicts between Nehru's political mandate approach and subsequent affirmations of juridical constitutionalism" were at least temporarily resolved in favour of judge led human rights litigation.[15] In the words of Chief Justice Bhagwati:

> With a legal architecture designed for a colonial administration and a jurisprudence structured around a free-market economy, the Indian judiciary could not accomplish much in fulfilling the constitutional aspirations of the vast masses of underprivileged people during the first three decades of freedom. During the last five or six years however, social activism has opened up a new dimension of the judicial process, and this new dimension is a direct emanation from the basic objectives and values underlying the Indian Constitution.[16]

The next part of this Article traces the background to the above stated period of judicial activism and assesses its achievements.

II. BACKGROUND

The background to the development in India of a Supreme Court committed to pro-active litigation designed to achieve social justice on behalf of the poor is to be found in an influential report on the lack of national judicare published by a high level committee in India in 1977.[17] A crucial section of this report reads as follows:

> In our expensive court system, it is impossible for the lower income groups and the poor to enforce rights. The poor people of a village may be prevented from walking along a public pathway by a feudal chief, immigrant workers may be denied fair wages, women workers as a class may be refused equal wages. Collective wrongs call for class action. The rule of *locus standi* requires to be broad-based and any organisation or individual must be able to start such legal action.[18]

---

[8]RAJEEV DHAVAN, THE SUPREME COURT AND PARLIAMENTARY SOVEREIGNTY: A CRITIQUE OF ITS APPROACH IN RECENT CONSTITUTIONAL CASES (1976); Rajeev Dhavan, *Managing Legal Activism: Reflections on India's Legal Aid Programme,* 15 ANGLO. AM. L. REV. 281, 297 (1986).

[9]Keshavananda Bharati v. State of Kerala, 1973 All India Reporter (A.I.R.) 1461, 1485 (S.C.).

[10]M. Williams, *Increasing Access to Justice: A Search for Alternatives,* THE LAWYERS, Jan. 1990, at 4.

[11]M. Menon, *Public Interest Litigation: A Major Breakthrough in the Delivery of Social Justice,* 9 J. BAR COUNCIL OF INDIA 150, 155 (1982).

[12]P. Singh, *Access to Justice: Public Interest Litigation and the Indian Supreme Court* 10–11 DELHI L. REV. 56 (1981–82).

[13]Upendra Baxi, *Taking Suffering Seriously: Social Action Litigation in the Supreme Court of India,* 29 REVIEW OF THE INTERNATIONAL COMMISSION OF JURISTS 37, 37 (1982).

[14]*Id.* at 42–43.

[15]Letter from Rajeev Dhavan, to Jeremy Cooper (Apr. 4, 1992).

[16]P. N. Bhagwati, *Judicial Activism and Public Interest Litigation,* 23 COLUM. J. TRANSNAT'L L. 561, 568 (1985).

[17]REPORT ON NATIONAL JURIDICARE (Ministry of Law, Justice and Company Affairs, Govt. of India, 1977); DHAVAN, *supra* note 8, at 293.

[18]DHAVAN, *supra* note 8, at 293.

This committee, which included two distinguished Indian Supreme Court Judges, Justice Bhagwati and Justice Krishna Iyer, was committed from the outset to a path of reform that was to be based on high-profile litigation, at a time when governments throughout the world were engaged in similar debates on the broadening of access to justice, but few were seeking the path of group litigation as their chosen priority.[19] However, this particular path was not entirely new to Indian jurisprudence. It had already been seen as an appropriate priority in the Indian context by the Bhagwati Committee of Gujerat on Legal Aid in 1971, by the Krishna Iyer Committee on Processual Justice to the People in 1973, and the Rajasthan Law Reform Committee in 1975.[20] Indeed, the latter committee had gone so far as to proclaim that "public interest litigation can prove to be the glory of our legal and judicial system," and the Krishna Iyer Committee had been happy to expand the concept of public interest litigation to embrace socio-legal research on problems affecting the poor, the initiation of law and judicial reforms, and the auditing of the work of state financed social welfare organisations.[21]

The recommendations contained in the 1977 report were largely accepted by the Bhagwati Committee for Legal Aid Implementation, set up in 1980 to give practical effect to the report. By 1982, a leading Indian jurist could already write that

> today, over a hundred matters being litigated mostly in the Supreme Court and the High Courts relate to problems affecting directly the rights of perhaps a hundred thousand or more people who, in the ordinary course of nature, would never have come before the courts for redressal of their just grievances.[22]

Few, if any other jurisdictions in the world could claim such a radical transformation in such a short period of time. What was it that occurred in India at this time that brought about this change?

Perhaps the most remarkable aspect of this process was the shift that occurred in this period in the Indian Supreme Court's perception of its own function with regard to human rights protection. Far from being a merely defensive fortress for the protection of the traditionally accepted "fundamental" human rights, such as equality before the law and personal liberty, the Indian Supreme Court adopted a highly visible role as the initiator of affirmative action to force national and state governments to accept the existence of a whole range of positive rights, hitherto more or less unrecognised outside the canons of international statements of human rights principles.[23] In the space of a mere five years, the Indian Supreme Court, in a string of dazzling judgements, asserted inter alia, the fundamental right of Indian citizens to speedy trial, against bondage, to livelihood, against environmental pollution, to human dignity, and to legal aid.[24] In their judgements in this period of judicial activism, the Indian Supreme Court Justices deliberately adopted a style of interpretation that they argued "shared the passion of the Constitution for social justice."[25] Their credo was the conviction that "in a developing society judicial activism is essential for participative justice. . . . Justices are the constitutional invigilators and reformers (who) bring the rule of law closer to the rule of life."[26]

III. THE STRATEGIES

At the heart of the reforms that made possible the outgrowth of judicial activism in the 1980s was a two-pronged assault on traditional conceptions of constitutional court practice. The first strategy has involved rethinking judicial interpretation in the con-

---

[19] *See* ACCESS TO JUSTICE (Mauro Cappelletti & B. Garth eds. 1979–81).

[20] DHAVAN, *supra* note 8, at 293–94.

[21] Menon, *supra* note 11.

[22] *Id.* at 151.

[23] The principal international human rights instrument of relevance is The International Bill of Human Rights consisting of The Universal Declaration of Human Rights 1948 (adopted and proclaimed by General Assembly Resolution 217 A (iii)), The International Covenant on Civil and Political Rights 1976, and The International Covenant on Economic, Social and Cultural Rights 1976 (adopted by General Assembly of the United Nations by Resolution 2200).

[24] Hoskot v. State of Maharasta, 1978 A.I.R. 1548, 1553 (S.C.); People's Union for Democratic Rights v. India, 1982 A.I.R. 1473, 1487 (S.C.); Olga Tellis v. Bombay Mun. Corp. 1986 A.I.R. 180, 193 (S.C.); Rural Litigation & Entitlement Kendra, Dehradun v. State of U.P., 1985 A.I.R. 652, 656 (S.C.); Mullin v. Administrator, Union Territory of Delhi, 1981 A.I.R. 746, 753 (S.C.); Barse v. State of Moharoshta, 1983 A.I.R. 378, 382 (S.C.); Suk Das v. Union Territory of Arunchal Pradesh, 2 S.C.C. 401, 408 (1986).

[25] V. Krishna Iyer, *Democracy of Judicial Remedies: A Rejoinder to Hidayatullah,* 4 S.C.C. 1 (1984); A. Bhattacharjee, *Judicial Activism and the World Judges Conference,* 3 S.C.C. 1 (1984); P. Bhagwati, *Unorganised Rural Labour,* 3 S.C.C. 44 (1984); P. Singh, *Judicial Socialism and Promises of Liberation,* 28 J. OF INDIAN LAW INSTITUTE 338 (1988).

[26] Singh, *supra* note 25, at 339.

text of constitutional rights and social justice and the second a dynamic approach to civil procedure. Let us examine each of these in turn.

A. Judicial Interpretation, Constitutional Rights, and Social Justice

Throughout the 1980s, the Indian Supreme Court has argued that it has the social responsibility of imaginatively interpreting constitutional rights to reflect social justice, and to operate neither narrowly nor statically. Rights are dynamic and should be treated as such. Justice Bhagwati developed this philosophy at the Bangalore Judicial Colloquium where reviewing the development of human rights he said:

> Civil and political rights . . . do not exist for the large masses of people in the developing countries who are suffering from poverty, want and destitution. . . . It is only if social and economic rights are ensured to these large masses of people that they will be able to enjoy civil and political rights and become equal participants in the democratic process.[27]

In sharp contrast, the American Professor, Geoffrey Hazard, described the contribution of civil justice to social justice as "diffuse, microcosmic, and dull."[28] He argues that this more or less meets the expectations of the poor that the legal system is supposed to serve, leaving the true resolution of the question of social justice where it belongs: "on the conscience of the community."[29] However, Stephen Sedley, a highly experienced public interest advocate practising in England (now a High Court judge), demonstrates that this "dull function" of the justice system is more complex than it may first appear when he writes, "Left-wing critiques of judicial decision making often fail to grasp the complexity of judicial aims and the divergences that may exist between those aims and the myopic ends of the politicians for whom the judges probably vote."[30] Crucially, Sedley's experience when appearing before the highest judges in the land, in a series of politically and socially embattled cases, lead him to caution that "[t]he judiciary may be reactionary, but it is not the Tory Party in horsehair, and it is eminently capable of biting the hand that feeds it."[31] In another article on the same theme, he states that "there is no defensible simple equation of conservative judges, with conservative law-making. . . . The radicalism of modern political conservatism in Britain has in many respects overtaken that of the judiciary."[32] This view is energetically supported by another leading commentator on the function of British judges, Professor Simon Lee, author of a seminal text, *Judging Judges*.[33] However, a contemporary Australian judge of high status, Justice Michael Kirby, argues from another perspective, one drawn more from a sense of the function of a judge, than the politics he or she may embody, when he states, "The sense of frustration about the overly activist court . . . may in the ultimate cause, and even justify, unrest and the very civic disorder which it has traditionally been a function of the judiciary to avoid and replace."[34]

In the 1980s the justices of the Indian Supreme Court have not shared the scepticism of Hazard, the cautioning balance of Sedley and Lee, nor the pragmatic restraint of Kirby.[35] Furthermore, they have totally rejected in the Indian context the stronger statements of the academic left contained in the conclusions of such writers as Ewing and Gearty, who having investigated the arguments in favour of creating a legally enforceable Bill of Rights in the United Kingdom, conclude "[w]e consider that the arguments against a judicially enforceable Bill of Rights are overwhelming."[36] The Indian judges argue that it is the luxury of the academic to argue such points, and the duty of the courts to prove them wrong.[37]

---

[27]P. Bhagwati, *Inaugural Address by the Convenor, in* COMMONWEALTH SECRETARIAT xx–xix (1988).

[28]Geoffrey C. Hazard, *Social Justice through Civil Justice,* 36 U. CHI. L. REV. 699, 712 (1969).

[29]*Id.*

[30]Stephen Sedley, *Free Speech for Rupert Murdoch,* LONDON REVIEW OF BOOKS, Dec. 19, 1991 at 3, 3.

[31]*Id.*

[32]Stephen Sedley, *Hidden Agendas: The Growth of Public Law in Britain and Canada, in* SOCIALIST LAWYER 12 (1990).

[33]*See generally* SIMON LEE, JUDGING JUDGES (1988).

[34]M. Kirby, *The Role of the Judge in Advancing Human Rights by Reference to Human Rights Norms, in* COMMONWEALTH SECRETARIAT 67 (1988).

[35]*But see* P. Singh, *Thinking about the Limits of Judicial Vindication of Public Interest,* 3 S.C.C 1 (1985).

[36]This brief quotation does not do justice to the serious and trenchant critique put forward by Ewing and Gearty in their analysis of the dangers of a judge enforced Bill of Rights in the United Kingdom. It is submitted, however, that the arguments contained in their excellent paper, are highly specific to the United Kingdom. K. EWING & C. GEARTY, DEMOCRACY OR A BILL OF RIGHTS (1990).

[37]*Id.*

It is clear that the primary function of the Indian Supreme Court in constitutional rights litigation has been to stimulate government and other public bodies to adopt proper practices, under the closer scrutiny of social activist organisations. The results for the parties are ultimately of secondary importance. But a further function of the Indian Supreme Court's work for the poor and oppressed could perhaps be described as the opening of a dialogue on oppression, as an attempt to influence and redefine public opinion.[38] Bickel has observed that in the United States:

> virtually all important decisions in the Supreme Court are the beginnings of a conversation between the Court and the people and their representatives. They are never, at the start, conversations between equals. The Court has an edge, because it initiates things with some immediate action, even if limited. But conversations they are, and to say that the Supreme Court lays down the law of the land is to state the ultimate result, following upon a complex series of events, in some cases and in others it is a form of speech only. The effectiveness of the judgement universalised depends on consent and administration.[39]

Interpreting the Constitution

How then has the Indian Supreme Court set about this dual purpose of regulating public bodies through social activism and opening of further dialogue on the nature of constitutional rights in its judgements?

At the heart of the Indian Supreme Court's judicial activism in the 1980s has been a perception that constitutional interpretation fundamentally differs, almost mystically, from statutory interpretation. Justice Bhagwati expressed this distinction at the Commonwealth Law Conference in Jamaica in 1986, in the following terms:

> It must be remembered that a constitution is a totally different kind of enactment than an ordinary statute. It is an organic instrument defining and regulating the power structure and power relationship: it embodies the hopes and aspirations of the people; it projects certain basic values and it sets out certain objectives and goals. It cannot therefore be interpreted like any ordinary statute. It must be interpreted creatively and imaginatively with a view to advancing the constitutional values and spelling out and strengthening the basic human rights of the large masses of people in the country, keeping in mind all the time that it is the constitution, the basic law of the land, that we are expounding and that ultimately, as one great American judge felicitously said, "the Constitution is what we say it is."[40]

Let us look at this approach in practice by reference to some of the key decisions of the Indian Supreme Court in this period.[41] Perhaps the most celebrated decision of the early 1980s was the case of *People's Union for Democratic Rights v. Union of India*.[42] This case centered on the exposure of illegal employment practices that were being carried out on a grand scale, as the country prepared to host the highly prestigious Asian Games. The practices were first unearthed by social activists, and presented to the Indian Supreme Court by way of an epistolary petition.[43] In order to comply with the exacting international standards necessary to host this prestigious event, the Indian Government had to embark upon a large range of construction projects including the building of flyovers, stadia, swimming pools, hotels, and the Asian Games Village Complex.[44] The Government duly contracted the work out to a number of agencies, some of whom flaunted the labour laws on such matters as minimum wages and equal wages for men and women, and the prohibition on the employment of children under fourteen. In addition, many of the workers were denied proper living conditions and medical and other facilities to which they were entitled by law. The significant point about the case for our purposes, was that it was brought not against the contractors, who were clearly and flagrantly breaching labour laws, but was brought against the Indian Government for failing to uphold various fundamental human rights of its citizens. This was despite the fact that the contractors were already being prosecuted under various criminal acts, for their wrongdoing. Constitutionally, the Indian Supreme

---

[38] DHAVAN, *supra* note 8, at 299.

[39] A. BICKEL, THE SUPREME COURT AND THE IDEA OF PROGRESS (1970).

[40] P. N. Bhagwati, *Fundamental Rights in their Economic, Social, and Cultural Context, in* COMMONWEALTH SECRETARIAT 57 (1988).

[41] M. P. Jain, *Justice Bhagwati and Indian Administrative Law,* 16 THE BANARAS LAW JOURNAL 1 (1980).

[42] 1982 A.I.R. 1473 (S.C.).

[43] *Id.* at 1476.

[44] *Id.* at 1479.

Court could only accept a direct petition of this kind if it could demonstrate a breach of a fundamental right under the Constitution.[45] At this point, the new creativity emerged.

Article 23 of the Indian Constitution enacts the fundamental right prohibiting "traffic in human beings and forced labour."[46] A narrow "statutory interpretation" of this section would not conclude that the facts as presented in this particular case revealed such a breach. The Indian Supreme Court thought otherwise. It argued that:

> in a country like India, where there is so much poverty and unemployment and there is no equality of bargaining power, a contract of service may appear on the face of it voluntary, but it may in reality be involuntary. . . . Where a person is suffering from hunger or starvation, when he has no resources at all to fight disease or to feed his wife and children, or even to hide their nakedness, where utter and grinding poverty has broken his back and reduced him to a state of helplessness and despair and where no other employment is available to alleviate the rigor of his poverty, he would have no choice but to accept any work, that comes his way, even if the remuneration offered to him is less than the minimum wage . . . the labour (thus) provided to him would be "forced labour."[47]

The Indian Supreme Court further justified this decision by reference to what it considered the "broader purposes of the Constitution," which were defined as "ushering in a new socio-economic order."[48] In these circumstances, the Court argued that the word "force" must be construed to include not only physical or legal force, but also force arising from the compulsion of economic circumstances which leaves no choice of alternatives to a person in want.[49]

The Indian Supreme Court's interpretation of Article 21 of the Indian Constitution provides further insight into this new activity in judicial interpretation. Article 21 of the Indian Constitution enacts a further fundamental right that "no person shall be deprived of his life or personal liberty except by procedure established by law."[50] The Indian Supreme Court formed the view, in the course of its deliberations in the early 1980s, that the state was dragging its heels in providing access to justice. In the words of Justice Bhagwati, "large masses of the people were leading a life of destitution . . . on account of a lack of awareness, assertiveness and availability of machinery, and were priced out of the legal system and thus denied access to justice."[51] In a leading case, *M. M. Hoskot v. State of Maharasta 1978,*[52] the Indian Supreme Court held it to be in breach of Article 21 to try a criminal case, imperilling the life or personal liberty of an individual, without giving him proper and adequate legal representation.[53] Furthermore, if a magistrate did not inform the accused of this right, the conviction could be set aside.[54] In another case involving Article 21, the Indian Supreme Court decided that "life" does not mean merely physical existence, but also includes "the use of every limb or faculty through which life is enjoyed."[55] Implicit in this right was the right to "live with basic human dignity and all that goes along with it, including the right to the basic necessities of life and also the right to carry on such functions and activities as constitute the base minimum expression of the human self."[56] Thus, the Court elevated this right to the status of fundamental right. In another Article 21 case, the Court concluded that the "right to life" also included the "right to a livelihood."[57] In another case, Article 21 was said to include the right to be "free from exploitation," and

> at the least, therefore, it must include protection of the health and strength of workers, men and women, and of the tender age of children against abuse, opportunities and facilities for children to develop in a healthy manner and in conditions of freedom and dignity, educational facilities, just and humane conditions of work and maternity relief. These are the minimum requirements which must exist in order to enable a person to live with human dignity.[58]

---

[45] *Id.* at 1476, 1479.
[46] INDIA CONST. art. 23.
[47] P. N. BHAGWATI, OBSERVE LABOUR LAWS: AN HISTORIC JUDGMENT OF SUPREME COURT OF INDIA 28–29 (1982).
[48] *Id.* at 5–6.
[49] *Id.* at 29.

[50] INDIA CONST. art. 21.
[51] Bhagwati, *supra* note 40, at 65.
[52] 1978 A.I.R. 1548 (S.C.).
[53] *Id.* at 1554.
[54] *Id.* at 1556.
[55] Bhagwati, *supra* note 40, at 65.
[56] Olga Tellis v. Bombay Mun. Corp., 1985 A.I.R. 180, 193 (S.C.).
[57] Hoskot v. State of Maharasta, 1978 A.I.R. 1548, 1553 (S.C.).
[58] Morcha v. India, 1983 A.I.R. 802, 811–12 (S.C.); Jamie Cassels, *Judicial Activism and Public Interest Litigation in India: Attempting the Impossible,* 37 AM. J. COMP. L. 495, 503–04 (1989).

B. A Dynamic Approach to Civil Procedure

The relationship between civil procedure and substantive law has always given rise to controversy of interpretation.[59] In 19th and turn of the century jurisprudence, the function of procedure was by and large perceived as neutral, and mechanical, giving rise to such anodyne definitions as that of Jeremy Bentham—"procedure is the course taken for the execution of the laws,"[60] and Collins M.R. "the relation of the rules of practice to the work of justice is intended to be that of handmaid rather than mistress."[61] Later proceduralists have been more willing to assert the dynamic function of civil procedure in promoting or thwarting access to justice. Cappelletti, for example, has described civil procedure as "like a mirror, in which the great issues of liberty and justice, the great themes of the relationship between individuals, groups, and states, are faithfully reflected."[62] The justices of the Indian Supreme Court grasped the dynamic potential of civil procedure to transform the workings and even the basic function of a constitutional court with fortitude, and in several outstanding judgements in the early 1980s made a series of overarching decisions regarding procedure that laid the groundwork for future poverty litigation.

In a major statement of the Indian Supreme Court's philosophy with regard to its encouragement of public interest litigation on behalf of the poor and oppressed, Bhagwati, in a 1982 judgement, summarised the necessary reforms as threefold: (1) *locus standi* should be made available to anybody who can show a bona fide observation of a legal injury or wrong done to any person or group, if that person or group cannot themselves approach a court by reason of poverty, disability, or a socially or economically disadvantaged position; (2) the defendant in a private action can be the state, for failing to protect the constitutional rights of the injured citizen, even though the immediate technical defendant is a private individual or body, such as a private employer; and (3) whatever the status of the parties to the action, the remedy must be appropriate to the social problem involved, and if no enforceable remedy exists, a new one must be invented.

Let us examine each of these three components of the Indian Supreme Court philosophy, as articulated by Bhagwati, in turn, beginning with the momentous changes in *locus standi,* and the collation of evidence thereafter.[63]

Locus Standi

At the heart of the procedural reforms enacted by the Indian Supreme Court in this period was a revolutionary approach to *locus standi.* The approach was in essence more of a revolution in interpretation than in substance, for the traditional common law rider that *locus standi* can only be granted to those with "sufficient interest" in the outcome of the proceedings was retained. The interpretation of what amounts to "sufficient interest" was revolutionary. In a landmark case in 1981, Bhagwati delivered the following judgement for the court:

> Today a vast revolution is taking place in the judicial process; the theatre of law is fast changing and the problems of the poor are coming to the forefront. The Court has to innovate new methods and devise new strategies for the purpose of providing access to justice to the large masses of people who are denied their basic human rights. . . . The only way in which this can be done is by entertaining writ petitions and even letters from public spirited individuals seeking judicial redress for the benefit of persons who have suffered [injuries]. . . . We hope and trust that the High Courts of the country will also adopt this pro-active, goal-oriented approach.[64]

The Provision: Epistolary Jurisdiction The implications contained in this judgement for the future jurisprudence of civil procedure go far beyond the confines of India. Proceduralists throughout the world, should undergo a uniform catching of breath,

---

[59] *See* Hein Kötz, *Civil Litigation and the Public Interest,* 1 Civil Justice Quarterly 237 (1982); J. A. Jolowicz, *On the Nature and Purposes of Civil Procedural Law, in* International Perspectives on Civil Justice 27 (I.R. Scott ed. 1990).

[60] Jeremy Bentham, Principles of Judicial Procedure, Works Vol. 2.

[61] Per Collins M.R. in Re Coles and Ravenshear 1907 1 K.B. at 4.

[62] Mauro Cappelletti, *Some Reflexions on the Role of Procedural Scholarship Today, in* The Eighth World Conference on Procedural Law Justice and Efficiency, General Reports and Discussions 441, 442 (W. Wedekind ed. 1989).

[63] Judges Appointment and Transfer Case, 1982 A.I.R. 149 (S.C.).

[64] Gupta v. President of India, 1982 A.I.R. 149, 189 (S.C.).

if they grasp the full implications of this radical approach to the limits of *locus standi*. Speaking to the Administrative Law Bar Association in London in 1990, Sir Konrad Schiemann, Justice of the English High Court remarked that "neither (England) nor any other (country) has . . . . a legal system under which anyone could obtain a ruling from a court on any subject upon which he or she desired a ruling."[65] But by 1981, India had already opened the doors to such a possibility. What this remarkable judgement meant in practice was as follows:

> Where a legal wrong or a legal injury is caused [or threatened] to a person or to a determinate class of persons . . . and such person[s] . . . [are] by reason of poverty, helplessness or disability or socially or economically disadvantaged position, unable to approach the Court for relief, any member of the public can maintain an application for an appropriate direction, order or writ in the High Court under Article 226 and in case of breach of any fundamental right of such person or determinate class of persons, in [the Supreme Court] under Article 32 seeking judicial redress for the legal wrong or injury caused to such person or determinate class.[66]

What clearly emerges from this statement is the breaking down of the procedural barrier of *locus standi* coupled with the reservation of a fast stream, direct access to the Indian Supreme Court provision for cases involving "fundamental rights" as defined in Part III of the Indian Constitution.[67]

This provision is particularly radical because of the further ruling that a person acting *pro bono publico* can initiate proceedings in the public interest simply by writing a letter (described as the epistolary jurisdiction). A judge may issue public interest proceedings by his own motion, *suo moto*.[68] The court justified this procedure as "a major breakthrough . . . in bringing justice closer to the large masses of people."[69] It was noted that the Court

> for a long time had remained the preserve of the rich and the well-to-do, and had been used only for the purpose of protecting the rights of the privileged classes. As a result of this innovative use of judicial power . . . the portals of the court [were] thrown open to the poor, the ignorant and the illiterate.[70]

The epistolary jurisdiction is more important for its symbolic reaching out to the common man, and to its confirmation that access to justice is upheld as a fundamental right by the Indian Supreme Court itself, than for its extensive practical use. In the first four years of its availability, little more than seventy cases are recorded as having availed of its potential.[71] The epistolary jurisdiction has been particularly welcomed and used by investigative journalists who have written articles about social injustices they have uncovered, which when issues of fundamental rights have been involved have subsequently been translated by social action groups into direct writs to the Indian Supreme Court. [72] One of the first uses of this jurisdiction was by a Supreme Court advocate, who filed a writ in 1980, based on a series of journalistic articles in a national daily, *The Indian Express,* exposing certain nefarious practices in Bihar, involving pre-trial prisoners.[73] In the same year, two professors of law wrote a letter to the same newspaper, exposing barbaric conditions in a protective home for women, which the Indian Supreme Court translated into a writ petition under Article 21 of the Indian Constitution.[74] Following this, a law student and a social worker adopted a similar strategy to expose barbarism in a women's home in Delhi, and three journalists exposed and filed a writ concerning a market in which women were bought and sold as chattels. Other social activist groups, lawyers, social workers, and academics have used the same jurisdiction to similar effect.[75]

Whilst the epistolary jurisdiction allows individuals not directly involved in an injustice to petition the court without incurring the expense of pursuing the

---

[65]Sir Konrad Schiemann, *Locus Standi,* PUBLIC LAW, 342, 342 (1990).

[66]*See supra* note 63.

[67]S. P. Sathe, FUNDAMENTAL RIGHTS AND AMENDMENT OF THE INDIAN CONSTITUTION, 53 (1968); S. P. Sathe, *supra* note 5, at 16–22; P. Tripathi, *Perspectives on the American Constitutional Influence on the Constitution of India, in* CONSTITUTIONALISM IN ASIA: ASIAN VIEWS OF THE AMERICAN INFLUENCE 56 (Beer ed. 1979); Mauro Cappelletti, *The Law Making Power of the Judge, and Its Limits: A Comparative Analysis,* 8 MONASH UNIV. L. REV. 15 (1981-82); DHAVAN, *supra* note 8.

[68]P. JASWAL, PUBLIC INTEREST LITIGATION: SOME NEW DEVELOPMENTS IN INDIA, ADDRESS AT THE HUMAN RIGHTS SEMINAR, SOAS, LONDON UNIVERSITY, February 17, 1992.

[69]Bhagwati, *supra* note 16, at 572.

[70]*Id.* at 571–72.

[71]JASWAL, *supra* note 68.

[72]Bhagwati, *supra* note 16, at 572; Baxi, *supra* note 13, at 39.

[73]Baxi, *supra* note 13, at 39.

[74]Cassels, *supra* note 58, at 495; Baxi, *supra* note 13, at 39.

[75]Baxi, *supra* note 13, at 39–40.

litigation, it alone would be of little value without some subsidiary provision regarding the collection of evidence and financing of the case thereafter. The Indian Supreme Court developed a strategy to cover this difficulty. The Court's strategy has been the appointment of socio-legal commissions of enquiry to visit the sites of alleged injustice and to collect all necessary evidence, at the court's own expense.[76] Such commissions of enquiry may employ social activists, teachers, researchers, journalists, or government and judicial officers.[77] Any evidence thus collected is regarded as prima facie evidence, and is submitted to all interested parties inviting affidavit response. The case will then be adjudicated on the basis of all the "evidence" thus accumulated.[79]

Abuse of Process Dangers of possible abuse of the liberal *locus standi* provisions are also dealt with in the judgement when the court stated that applicants must be acting bona fide.[80] If it appears that applicants are acting "for personal gain or private profit or out of political motivation or other oblique consideration,"[81] the court can reject the application. Herein lies the abuse of process provision that in practice is rarely used in India.[82] A wider range of possible abuses of the open system of access to the jurisdiction of courts, afforded by ultra liberal standing rules, has been canvassed by Schiemann.[83] Schiemann focuses on the negative impact that open access might have upon a cautious administrator who, fearful of litigation from an unknown quarter, might "concentrate less on the quality of his decision, and more on making it 'judge proof.'"[84] Schiemann notes also the problems of paying for the expanded litigation that open access will encourage, and the risk that flamboyant publicists and pressure groups might convert the courts into some form of debating platform, despite the certain knowledge that they will lose their case.[85] Despite raising the disadvantages, however, Schiemann largely answers these criticisms when he muses that

> the undesirability of putting certain actions beyond legal challenge by anyone is self evident. The politically, financially or socially strong can oppress the weak, safe in the knowledge that the courts cannot interfere. This is undesirable not only because oppression is undesirable, but also because if the law is openly flouted without redress in the courts the law is brought into contempt as being a dream without substance.[86]

If this is the conclusion of a judge operating in the relative affluence of English "social injustice," it seems safe to say that in a country operating on a scale of poverty and related economic problems such as India, the abuse of process provisions that are necessary in more affluent jurisdictions seem to be of little relevance or application.

Sufficient Interest

> If no specific legal injury is caused to a person or to a determinate class or group of persons by the act or omission of the State or any public authority and the injury is caused only to *public interest* . . . any member of the public acting bona fide and having *sufficient interest* can maintain an action for redressal of such public wrong. . . . What is *sufficient interest* to give standing to a member of the public would have to be determined by the Court in each individual case. It is not possible for the Court to lay down any hard and fast rule.[87]

It is perhaps in the interpretation of this section of the judgement that the most far-reaching and radical practices have occurred. No universal agreement exists as to the definition of the term "public interest" despite a tremendous amount of scholarship devoted to the subject.[88] What emerges from the Indian case-law is that if the Indian Supreme Court considers that litigation in any particular matter is "in the public interest," the court will grant de facto *locus standi* to the applicant on the basis of a perceived "sufficient interest." The terms "sufficient interest" and "in the

[76] Bhagwati, *supra* note 16, at 574.
[77] *Id.*
[78] *Id.*
[79] *Id.* at 575.
[80] Tripathi, *supra* note 67.
[81] *Id.*
[82] *Id.*
[83] Schiemann, *supra* note 65, at 342.
[84] *Id.* at 348.
[85] *Id.*
[86] *Id.* at 343.
[87] S. P. Gupta v. President of India, 1982 A.I.R. 149, 190, 192 (S.C.) (emphasis added).
[88] J. Cooper, Keyguide to Information Sources in Public Interest Law (1991).

public interest" are effectively merged into one and the same. This is going further than any equivalent court has dared to do elsewhere. Prior to this advance, the concept of sufficient interest had already been given a more liberal hue in a common law setting by Lord Denning, in a 1976 Court of Appeal case in England, *R. v. Greater London Council, ex parte Blackburn*.[89] The Indian Supreme Court have always seen this brilliant, but maverick, English judge as an inspiration, and a man in their own mould. In this case, Mr. Blackburn, a ratepayer, had successfully applied to the court for an order to enforce the council's statutory duty to prohibit the exhibition of pornographic films in the London area, a duty which the council had previously refused to exercise.[90] In granting *locus standi* to Mr. Blackburn, and thereafter the right to enforce the statutory duty, Lord Denning wrote the following:

> I regard it as a matter of high constitutional principle that, if there is good ground for supposing that a government department or a public authority is transgressing the law or is about to transgress it, in a way which offends or injures thousands of Her Majesty's subjects [sic], then any one of those offended or injured can draw it to the attention of the courts of law and seek to have the law enforced, [then] the courts in their *discretion* can grant whatever remedy is appropriate.[91]

This liberal approach to the concept of standing was broadly adopted by the British House of Lords in a landmark case in 1981, *I.R.C. v. The National Federation of Self-Employed & Small Businesses Ltd.*[92] By a curious coincidence, this case was being heard at almost the same time as the Indian Supreme Court was laying down its judgement on the issue of standing and sufficient interest. In the case before the House of Lords, the court had to decide whether a group representing self-employed people had sufficient interest in a decision by the Inland Revenue to grant an "amnesty" to another group of notorious tax defaulters, to be granted *locus standi* to challenge the decision of the Inland Revenue.[93] The House of Lords decided that the group did have sufficient interest. Lord Diplock concluded that

> it would . . . be a grave lacuna in our system of public law if a pressure group, like the federation or even a single public-spirited taxpayer, were prevented by outdated technical rules of locus standi from bringing the matter to the attention of the court to vindicate the rule of law and get the unlawful conduct stopped.[94]

A leading administrative law academic and appeal court judge, Lord Justice Woolf, reflected upon the significance of this judgment in the following terms:

> Since the decision of the House of Lords . . . I know of no case where the court has come to a conclusion that there is a breach of the law being committed by a public body which requires rectifying but because the person making the application has insufficient standing, leave should not be granted.[95]

Subsequent case law in England has, however, cast doubt upon the wisdom of Lord Justice Woolf's unfettered optimism.[96]

Locus Standi and Justiciability

> [T]he Court [has] to bear in mind that there is a vital distinction between locus standi and justiciability and it is not every default on the part of the State or a public authority that is justiciable. The Court must take care to see that it does not overstep the limits of its judicial function and trespass into areas which are reserved to the Executive and the Legislature by the Constitution.[97]

The State As Defendant

Trubek has argued that constitutional rights, rooted in a liberal understanding of society, do less to improve

[89]3 All E.R. 184 (1976).
[90]*Id.* at 186.
[91]*Id.* at 192.
[92]2 All E.R. 93 (1981).
[93]*Id.* at 96.

[94]*Id.* at 107.
[95]H. Woolf, *Locus Standi in Practice, in* INTERNATIONAL PERSPECTIVES ON CIVIL JUSTICE 262 (I. Scott ed. 1990).
[96]I am grateful to my colleague Bill Bowring for bringing to my attention a spate of recent cases in the English Court of Appeal, which have drawn back from further developing the open access of *locus standi,* intimated by Lord Justice Woolf in the quotation, in particular the cases of R. v. Secretary of State for the Environment, ex parte The Rose Theatre Trust Co., 1990 1 All E.R. at 754.
[97]S. P. Gupta v. President of India, 1982 A.I.R. 149, 195 (S.C.); *see* Carol Harlow, *Public Interest Litigation in England: The State of the Art,* PUBLIC INTEREST LAW 90 (J. Cooper & R. Dhavan eds. 1986).

the welfare of the disadvantaged than to entrench the existing maldistribution of wealth and power.[98] This view is sustained and developed by Katz in his study of 100 years of the history of poverty law programmes in Chicago.[99] Katz reaches the disturbing conclusion that the most aggressive and creative of the poverty lawyers have proved to be less successful at eliminating poverty than reorganizing the poor into a formal category.[100] These observations illustrate the danger contained in the second of Bhagwati's philosophical/procedural axioms. Nevertheless, it remains pivotal to the entire system.

In Singh's analysis of the effectiveness of judicial activism as a means of employing rule of law rhetoric as a weapon against both poverty and lawlessness, he has observed that the primary function of such activity, in India, is "to raise the standards of governmental accountability towards . . . human values and not necessarily the widening of the adjudication process to the mass of the people."[101] Herein lies the justification for rights based strategies, that may be the subject of more sceptical scrutiny in the highly developed, and more mechanically administered welfare states operating in more affluent countries than India. Cassels has observed, in this context, that "litigative strategies can never substantially redistribute wealth or power, nor penetrate and affect the economic and cultural conditions which define the reality of Indian life."[102] The fact that these strategies do nevertheless frequently expose the lawlessness of public bodies does serve a useful political function, particularly when that public body is the government.

Galanter has described disputes requiring access to a forum such as the Indian Supreme Court, namely one that is "external to the original social setting of the dispute, at a location at which some specialised learning or expertise will be brought to bear,"[103] as a manifestation of a legal centralist model of justice dispensation, and not, in Galanter's view, a model that is in any way essential to the achievement of justice in a given society.[104] What is important in the Indian context is the fact that the legal centralist model function symbolically and politically, as the embodiment of human rights aspiration, through the mouths of a genuine political elite, the justices of the Indian Supreme Court, and as such can perform the function of the watchdog of governmental accountability referred to above. The history of the Indian Supreme Court has demonstrated unequivocally that it is a political institution.[105]

The separation, both cultural and physical of this powerful political institution from the mass of those whom it seeks to serve, is significant in that "[t]o the foreign observer, one of the most striking aspects of the Indian legal system is the extent to which formal legal arrangements exist in almost metaphysical isolation from social reality."[106] In practical terms, the political and the symbolic function of the court's decisions have exercised a far greater influence on Indian society than the formal decision between the parties. The willingness of the court to concentrate its energies in the field of social justice has opened the door to facilitate what the Trubeks have described as a people's "aspiration for . . . civil justice."[107] They argue that

> when the state seeks to protect interests without groups, it confronts problems very different from those encountered when it seeks to protect the more traditional interests of organised sectors of society. Effective protection of any interest means much more than giving formal guarantees of rights. These rights must be translated into tangible benefits, and this can only occur in the day-to-day operation of government and private entities regulated by government.[108]

This perspective clearly raises serious questions as to what precisely is to be understood by the concept of facilitation. Do the judges create the concept of civic justice in people's minds, or do they merely give a for-

---

[98]D. Trubek, *Public Policy Advocacy: Administrative Government and Representation of Diffuse Interests, in* ACCESS TO JUSTICE, 443–94 (M. Cappelletti, B. Garth, eds. 1979–81).
[99]JACK KATZ, POOR PEOPLE'S LAWYERS IN TRANSITION (1982).
[100]*Id.*
[101]SINGH, *supra* note 25, at 340–41.
[102]Cassels, *supra* note 58, at 515.
[103]Marc Galanter, *Justice in Many Rooms: Courts, Private Ordering, and Indigenous Law,* 19–20 JOURNAL OF LEGAL PLURALISM, 1, 1 (1981–82).
[104]*Id.*
[105]DHAVAN, *supra* note 8, at 296; Baxi, *supra* note 5, at 147; George Gadbois, *The Supreme Court of India As a Political Institution,* in JUDGES AND THE JUDICIAL POWER 250, 250–51 (Rajeev Dhavan et al. eds. 1985).
[106]Cassels, *supra* note 58, at 515.
[107]L. Trubek & D. Trubek, *Civic Justice through Civil Justice: A New Approach to Public Interest Advocacy in the United States, in* ACCESS TO JUSTICE IN THE WELFARE STATE, 119, 119 (Mauro Cappelletti ed. 1981).
[108]*Id.* at 120 (footnote omitted).

mal expression to pre-existent notions? The debate goes far beyond the confines of this Article, and indeed can be said to be the central debate underpinning much political and legal/constitutional discussion that is currently taking place in central and eastern Europe. For our purposes, the function of the epistolary jurisdiction is primarily to permit the people to define for themselves what they perceive as civil injustice, and for the court to exercise its discretion, tempered by practical constraints, in the prioritisation of its treatment of such decisions, as manifest in the petitions that come before it. Set out below are some examples of the operation of this axiom in practice in the Indian context.

In a country in which direct action is constantly on the agenda as the most likely alternative to legal process, and as a means to achieve a solution to a social or political problem, the symbolic function of the Supreme Court in replacing, and thereby diverting the threat of direct action cannot be over-emphasised. One writer suggested in the 1980s in this context that the legalisation of politics threatens to divert, manage, and contain the demands of social activists for a more humane social order.[109] Thus, the Indian Supreme Court allows for a process of "continued and effective participation in the ongoing stream of governmental decisions"[110] in a way that no other organ of the state can achieve. For Indian social activists, it is the best thing available.

Appropriate Remedies

Whatever the strength and originality of the new procedures developed by the Indian Supreme Court in the 1980s to allow greater access for the poor to its chamber, there would have been little point in allowing such access without also evolving new remedies for giving relief. As Bhagwati himself pointed out: "The suffering of the disadvantaged could not be relieved by mere issuance of prerogative writs of certiorari, prohibition or mandamus, or by making orders granting damages or injunctive relief, where such suffering was the result of continuous repression and denial of rights."[111]

The process of developing appropriate remedies involves two aspects. The first aspect is the principle of flexibility, whereby a specific remedy is developed to meet the facts of the injustice uncovered by the court. One case dealt with the discovery of a large scale, illegal debt bondage network, akin to the most primitive form of slavery.[112] The remedy of the courts was to make an order giving various directions for identifying, releasing, and rehabilitating labourers held in debt bondage, and for ensuring thereafter that all labour laws would be observed, that they would all receive a minimum wage, wholesome drinking water, medical assistance, and appropriate schooling facilities for their children, along with legal awareness training.[113]

In another series of cases involving the scandal of people being held pre-trial for longer periods than the maximum possible sentence for their alleged offence, the Supreme Court directed the Bihar state government to prepare an annual census of the prisoners on trial in their state, and to submit it annually to the High Court, which would declare for the early disposal of all cases in which prisoners were being held for an unreasonably long period.[114] In a third case, again in the state of Bihar, in which prisoners under trial had been blinded by the police, the Court ordered that these prisoners should be given vocational training in an institute for the blind, and paid compensation for the rest of their lives.[115] In a fourth case, involving the abuse by male police officers of women in custody, the court directed that there should be a separate lock-up for women, supervised by women police officers, and that a written notice should be placed in each lock-up informing the arrested person of their rights.[116]

The second aspect in the development of effective remedies relates to enforcement. The remedy may be tailor-made to match the problem, but unenforceable and therefore worthless. In the words of Bhagwati:

> The orders made by the Court are obviously not self-executing. They have to be enforced through State agencies; if the State agencies are not enthusiastic in enforcing the Court orders and do not actively cooperate in that task, the object and purpose of the public interest litigation would remain unfulfilled.[117]

[109]*See inter alia* Michael Mandel, *The Rule of Law and Legalisation of Politics in Canada,* 13 INT. JOURNAL OF THE SOCIOLOGY OF LAW 273 (1985).
[110] Trubek & Trubek, *supra* note 107, at 121.
[111]Bhagwati, *supra* note 16, at 575.

[112]Bandhua Mukti Morcha v. Union of India, 1984 A.I.R. 802 (S.C.).
[113]*Id.* at 828.
[114]Upendra Baxi, *The Supreme Court under Trial: Undertrials and the Supreme Court,* S.C.C. 35 (1980).
[115]Khatri v. State of Bihar, 1981 A.I.R. 928, 934 (S.C.).
[116]Sheela Barse v. State of Maharashtra, 1983 A.I.R. 378, 382 (S.C.).
[117]Bhagwati, *supra* note 16, at 576–77.

The main device adopted by the Court to try to ensure enforcement of their orders has been the creation of special monitoring agencies, who report back to the court on the effectiveness of the ordered enforcement procedure. Thus in the case concerning the protection of women in police custody, the Court instructed a woman judicial officer to make regular visits to the police stations in question and to report to the High Court on whether the directives were being obeyed.[118] In the case involving bonded labourers, the Supreme Court appointed the Joint-Secretary in the Ministry of Labour to visit the quarries where the bonded labour network had existed, after three months, with a similar purpose.[119] In a case involving environmental pollution caused by a gas leak from a chemical plant, an even more stringent monitoring system was set up by the Court.[120]

> On the basis of recommendations of four separate court-appointed technical teams the court ordered specific technical, safety and training improvements. It required the allocation of trained staff to defined safety functions. To monitor the plant the court set up an independent committee to visit the plant every two weeks, and also ordered the government inspector to make surprise visits once a week. . . . [It] "suggested" that the government establish an Ecological Sciences Resource Group to assist the court. . . . [It] required the company and its managers to deposit security to guarantee compensation to any who might be injured as a result of the enterprise's activity.[121]

The remedies are thus an imaginative and bold step down the road of constitutional court activism and enforcement of rights. Their effectiveness is challenged by some, and is in any event piecemeal, and under-researched.[122] The Indian Supreme Court has accepted that unless and until the attitudes of public administrators change significantly, the vigilance and dedication of social activists on the ground will remain of greater importance than any Supreme Court eloquence in protecting the poor.[123] They have not yet proved Hazard wrong.[124]

IV. CONCLUSION

> I often wonder whether we do not rest our hopes too much upon constitutions, upon laws and upon courts. These are false hopes; believe me, they are false hopes. Liberty lies in the hearts of men and women; where it dies there is no constitution, no law, no court can save it; no constitution, no law, no court can even do much to help it. While it lies there it needs no constitution, no law, no court to save it.[125]

The words of Judge Learned Hand ring as true today as they did when he first uttered them in 1953. And they are just as true in India, as they are anywhere else. In particular, it would be misleading to assume that the "Indian Experiment" in public interest litigation has been an unmitigated success. Some quarters are especially critical: "The Indian legal system, in its current condition, is far from meeting its constitutional obligation of promoting justice. In fact, it actually operates to deny justice to a majority of the Indian population, the rural and the urban poor."[126] "Public Interest Litigation is failing in India in more ways than one."[127] Specifically, the number of cases using the epistolary jurisdiction has been relatively small,[128] and has served to clog up the court dockets. The time taken to bring public interest cases to the Supreme Court is inordinate, and has been heavily criticised.[129] The leading exponents of public interest judicial activism, Justices Bhagwati and Krishna Iyer, are no longer in the court, and their replacements are more cautious and conservative; epistolary litigants are normally allocated a legal aid lawyer, not the lawyer of their choice; and litigants are not able to select the judge that might be more sympathetic to their cause.[130] Nevertheless, these cautionary statements remain cautionary, not debilitating. These statements certainly do not undermine the tremendous achievements of the Indian Supreme Court over the past decade in demonstrating the potential possessed by any constitutional court to bring about significant improvements in the general level of social justice at any

[118]*Sheela Barse,* 1983 A.I.R. at 382.
[119]Bandhua Mukti Morcha v. Union of India, 1984 A.I.R. 802, 831 (S.C.).
[120]Mehta v. India, 2 S.C.C. 176, 196–200 (1986).
[121]Cassels, *supra* note 58, at 506.
[122]*Id.* at 517.
[123]Sheela Barse v. State of Maharashtra, 1983 A.I.R. 378, 379–80 (S.C).
[124]Hazard, *supra* note 28, at 699.
[125]LEARNED HAND, SPIRIT OF LIBERTY: PAPERS AND ADDRESSES OF LEARNED HAND, *cited in* J. MCCLUSKEY, LAW, JUSTICE AND DEMOCRACY, REITH LECTURES 1987, at 60.
[126]Williams, *supra* note 10, at 4.
[127]Dhavan, *supra* note 15.
[128]Jaswal, *supra* note 68.
[129]B. Pande, *The Food Petitions: Is There the Right to Basic Human Needs?,* THE LAWYERS, September 1989, at 4.
[130]JASWAL, *supra* note 68.

one time, nor do they undermine the continuing symbolic function of the Supreme Court, to lead the way as champions of simple concepts of justice.

Extrapolation of policy for one country from the experiences of another is never a wise philosophy, particularly when the social, political, and economic differences are as great as they are between India and the Western countries in which constitutional courts make at least a pretence of asserting fundamental human rights through the process of judicial decision making. Nevertheless, some of the clear conclusions that emerge from the recent Indian experience are of such universality that they bear discussion and debate "in fora" far wider than the Indian sub-continent.[131] First, it is clear that the same words in constitutions can be interpreted in widely differing ways, according to the desire of the judges to make them work in a particular way. Second, procedural restraints on access to the courts are by and large, judge-made, and the potential to open up access rests in large part with the same judges. Wherever debates on *locus standi* take place, at least in the common law world, the terms of reference are remarkably similar. The judges take it upon themselves to decide whether a particular party should, or should not, be heard. Third, if judges have the personal, social, or political will to do so, they have enormous scope to expand the type of remedies they wish to see operating in their courts, and the types of evidence that they wish brought before them. Fourth, as history comes full circle, and critics, echoing contemporary debates in the United States, intimate that public interest litigation in India is not today what it was three years ago, the words of John Curran in 1790, are as true today as they were when uttered in those fomenting years of revolutionary politics some 200 years ago: "The condition upon which God hath given liberty to man is eternal vigilance; which condition if he break, servitude is at once the consequence of his crime, and the punishment of his guilt."[132]

It has been shown in the course of this Article that to use its public interest function effectively, a court must not only be fearless in stating its objectives, but set out a reform agenda designed to achieve those objectives. This agenda will involve a willingness to see and use the creative potential of civil procedure as a tool for reform rather than technical barrier to justice. It will require bold and imaginative initiatives to create enforcement mechanisms and procedures appropriate to the problem in hand. It will require the appointment of the right judges, bearing in mind that in developing countries "judges will frequently be among the very few highly educated citizens available for leadership."[133] Above all, it will involve a conscious and overt acceptance by constitutional court justices, wherever they may sit, that theirs is the power to make law,[134] and this is a power that they should not squander negatively. In the words of one of the British House of Lords judges, Lord Reid: "There was a time when it was thought almost indecent to suggest that Judges make law—they only declare it. . . . But we do not believe in fairy tales any more."[135]

[131]It is significant however that in the past twelve months, activists in Bangladesh and in Pakistan are starting to group together with a view to encouraging their own Supreme Courts to adopt a similar stance to that of India.

[132]John Philpot Curran, from his speech on The Right of Election of Lord Mayor of Dublin, made on 10th July, 1790, in the City of Dublin, Ireland.

[133]Kirby, *supra* note 34, at 71.

[134]Cappelletti, *supra* note 67; K. ROHL, THE JUDGE AS MEDIATOR (University of Wisconsin-Madison Disputes Processing Research Program Working Paper, 1988–89).

[135]Lord Reid, *The Judge As Law Maker,* 12 JOURNAL OF THE SOCIETY OF PUBLIC TEACHERS OF LAW 22, 22 (1972–73).

55

ROBERT BORK

The Right of Privacy: The Construction of a Constitutional Time Bomb

The 1965 decision in *Griswold* v. *Connecticut* was insignificant in itself but momentous for the future of constitutional law. Connecticut had an ancient statute making it criminal to use contraceptives. The state also had a general accessory statute allowing the punishment of any person who aided another in committing an offense. On its face, the statute criminalizing the use of contraceptives made no distinction between married couples and others. But the statute also had never been enforced against anyone who used contraceptives, married or not. There was, of course, no prospect that it ever would be enforced. If any Connecticut official had been mad enough to attempt enforcement, the law would at once have been removed from the books and the official from his office. Indeed, some Yale law professors had gotten the statute all the way to the Supreme Court a few years previously, and the Court had refused to decide it precisely because there was no showing that the law was ever enforced. The professors had some difficulty arranging a test case but finally managed to have two doctors who gave birth control information fined $100 apiece as accessories.

Such enforcement in the area as there was consisted of the occasional application of the accessory statute against birth control clinics, usually clinics that advertised. The situation was similar to the enforcement of many antigambling laws. They may cover all forms of gambling on their faces, but they are in fact enforced only against commercial gambling. An official who began arresting the priest at the church bingo party or friends having their monthly poker game at home would have made a most unwise career decision and would be quite unlikely to get a conviction. There are a number of statutes like these in various state codes, such as the statutes flatly prohibiting sodomy and other "unnatural practices," which apply on their faces to all couples, married or unmarried, heterosexual or homosexual. The statutes are never enforced, but legislators, who would be aghast at any enforcement effort, nevertheless often refuse to repeal them.

There is a problem with laws like these. They are kept in the codebooks as precatory statements, affirmations of moral principle. It is quite arguable that this is an improper use of law, most particularly of criminal law, that statutes should not be on the books if no one intends to enforce them. It has been suggested that if anyone tried to enforce a law that had moldered in disuse for many years, the statute should be declared void by reason of desuetude or that the defendant should go free because the law had not provided fair warning.

But these were not the issues in *Griswold*. Indeed, getting off on such grounds was the last thing the defendants and their lawyers wanted. Since the lawyers had a difficult time getting the state even to fine two doctors as accessories, it seems obvious that the case was not arranged out of any fear of prosecution, and certainly not the prosecution of married couples. *Griswold* is more plausibly viewed as an attempt to enlist the Court on one side of one issue in a cultural struggle. Though the statute was originally enacted when the old Yankee culture dominated Connecticut politics, it was now quite popular with the Catholic hierarchy and with many lay Catholics whose religious values it paralleled. The case against the law was worked up by members of the Yale law school faculty and was supported by the Planned Parenthood Federation of America, Inc., the Catholic Council on Civil Liberties, and the American Civil Liberties Union. A ruling of unconstitutionality may have been sought as a statement that opposition to contraception is benighted and, therefore, a statement about whose cultural values are dominant. Be that as it may, the upshot was a new constitutional doctrine perfectly suited, and later used, to enlist the Court on the side of moral relativism in sexual matters.

Justice Douglas's majority opinion dealt with the case as if Connecticut had devoted itself to sexual fascism. "Would we allow the police to search the sacred precincts of marital bedrooms for telltale signs of the use of contraceptives? The very idea is repulsive to the notions of privacy surrounding the marriage relationship." That was both true and entirely irrelevant to the case before the Court. Courts usually judge statutes by the way in which they are actually enforced, not by imagining horrible events that have never happened, never will happen, and could be stopped by courts if they ever seemed about to happen. Just as in *Skinner* he had treated a proposal to sterilize three-time felons as raising the specter of racial genocide, Douglas raised the stakes to the sky here by treating Connecticut as though it was threatening the institution of marriage. "We deal with a right of privacy older than the Bill of Rights—older than our political parties, older than our school system." The thought was incoherent. What the right of privacy's age in comparison with that of our political parties and school system had to do with anything was unclear, and where the "right" came from if not from the Bill of Rights it is impossible to understand. No court had ever invalidated a statute on the basis of the right Douglas described. That makes it all the more perplexing that Douglas in fact purported to derive the right of privacy not from some pre-existing right or law of nature, but from the Bill of Rights. It is important to understand Justice Douglas's argument both because the method, though without merit, continually recurs in constitutional adjudication and because the "right of privacy" has become a loose cannon in the law. Douglas began by pointing out that specific guarantees in the Bill of Rights have penumbras, formed by emanations from those guarantees that help give them life and substance." There is nothing exceptional about that thought, other than the language of penumbras and emanations. Courts often give protection to a constitutional freedom by creating a buffer zone, by prohibiting a government from doing something not in itself forbidden but likely to lead to an invasion of a right specified in the Constitution. Douglas cited *NAACP* v. *Alabama,* in which the Supreme Court held that the state could not force the disclosure of the organization's membership lists since that would have a deterrent effect upon the members' first amendment rights of political and legal action. That may well have been part of the purpose of the statute. But for this anticipated effect upon guaranteed freedoms, there would be no constitutional objection to the required disclosure of membership. The right not to disclose had no life of its own independent of the rights specified in the first amendment.

Douglas named the buffer zone or "penumbra" of the first amendment a protection of "privacy," although, in *NAACP* v. *Alabama,* of course, confidentiality of membership was required not for the sake of individual privacy but to protect the public activities of politics and litigation. Douglas then asserted that other amendments create "zones of privacy." These were the first, third (soldiers not to be quartered in private homes), fourth (ban on unreasonable searches and seizures), and fifth (freedom from self-incrimination). There was no particularly good reason to use the word "privacy" for the freedoms cited, except for the fact that the opinion was building toward those "sacred precincts of marital bedrooms." The phrase "areas of freedom" would have been more accurate since the provisions cited protect both private and public behavior.

None of the amendments cited, and none of their buffer or penumbral zones, covered the case before the Court. The Connecticut statute was not invalid under any provisions of the Bill of Rights, no matter how extended. Since the statute in question did not threaten any guaranteed freedom, it did not fall within any "emanation." *Griswold* v. *Connecticut* was, therefore, not like *NAACP* v. *Alabama.* Justice Douglas bypassed that seemingly insuperable difficulty by simply asserting that the various separate "zones of privacy" created by each separate provision of the Bill of Rights somehow created a general but wholly undefined "right of privacy" that is independent of and lies outside any right or "zone of privacy" to be found in the Constitution. Douglas did not explain how it was that the Framers created five or six specific rights that could, with considerable stretching, be called "privacy," and, though the Framers chose not to create more, the Court could nevertheless invent a general right of privacy that the Framers had, inexplicably, left out. It really does not matter to the decision what the Bill of Rights covers or does not cover.

Douglas closed the *Griswold* opinion with a burst of passionate oratory. "Marriage is a coming together for better or for worse, hopefully enduring, and intimate to the degree of being sacred. It as an association that promotes a way of life, not causes; a harmony in living, not political faiths; a bilateral loyalty, not commercial or social projects. Yet it is an association for as noble a purpose as any involved in our prior decisions." It is almost a matter for regret that Connecticut had not threatened the institution of marriage, or ever attempted to prevent anyone from using contraceptives, since that left some admirable sentiments, expressed with rhetorical fervor, dangling irrelevantly in midair. But the protection of marriage was not the point of *Griswold.* The creation of a new device for judicial power to remake the Constitution was the point.

The *Griswold* opinion, of course, began by denying that any such power was being assumed. "[W]e are met with a wide range of questions that implicate the Due Process Clause of the 14th Amendment. Overtones of some arguments suggest that [*Lochner* v. *New York*] should be our guide. But we decline that invitation. . . . We do not sit as a super-legislature to determine the wisdom, need, and propriety of laws that touch economic problems, business affairs, or social conditions." *Griswold,* as an assumption of judicial power unrelated to the Constitution is, however, indistinguishable from *Lochner.* And the nature of that power, its lack of rationale or structure, ensured that it could not be confined.

The Court majority said there was now a right of privacy but did not even intimate an answer to the question, "Privacy to do what?" People often take addictive drugs in private, some men physically abuse their wives and children in private, executives conspire to fix prices in private, Mafiosi confer with their button men in private. If these sound bizarre, one professor at a prominent law school has suggested that the right of privacy may create a right to engage in prostitution. Moreover, as we shall see, the Court has extended the right of privacy to activities that can in no sense be said to be done in private. The truth is that "privacy" will turn out to protect those activities that enough Justices to form a majority think ought to be protected and not activities with which they have little sympathy.

If one called the zones of the separate rights of the Bill of Rights zones of "freedom," which would be more accurate, then, should one care to follow Douglas's logic, the zones would add up to a general right of freedom independent of any provision of the Constitution. A general right of freedom—a constitutional right to be free of regulation by law—is a manifest impossibility. Such a right would posit a state of nature, and its law would be that of the jungle. If the Court had created a general "right of freedom," we would know at once, therefore, that the new right would necessarily be applied selectively, and, if we were given no explanation of the scope of the new right, we would know that the "right" was nothing more than a warrant judges had created for themselves to do whatever they wished. That . . . is precisely what happened with the new, general, undefined, and unexplained "right of privacy."

Justice Black's dissent stated: "I like my privacy as well as the next one, but I am nevertheless compelled to admit that government has a right to invade it unless prohibited by some specific constitutional provision." He found none. "The Court talks about a constitutional 'right of privacy' as though there is some constitutional provision or provisions forbidding any law ever to be passed which might abridge the 'privacy' of individuals. But there is not." He pointed out that there are "certain specific constitutional provisions which are designed in part to protect privacy at certain times and places with respect to certain activities." But there was no general right of the sort Douglas had created. Justice Stewart's dissent referred to the statute as "an uncommonly silly law" but noted that its asininity was not before the Court. He could "find no such general right of privacy in the Bill of Rights, in any other part of the Constitution, or in any case ever before decided by this Court." He also observed that the "Court does not say how far the new constitutional right of privacy announced today extends." That was twenty-four years ago, and the Court still has not told us.

56

JUDITH DeCEW

Constitutional Privacy, Judicial Interpretation, and *Bowers v. Hardwick*

Constitutional law is on the brink of a new era. Three Supreme Court justices are in their eighties, those who have been the staunchest defenders of civil liberties and rights during the last two decades. The most recent right recognized by the Court, constitutional privacy, is also one of the most controversial. It has been used to gain powerful protection for individuals, but has also been criticized as the worst instance of subjective judicial decision-making.

My goal is to examine alternative views on constitutional interpretation to help assess the majority and minority arguments in a recent constitutional privacy case, *Bowers v. Hardwick,* in which the Supreme Court reversed the Eleventh Circuit Court decision and upheld Georgia's anti-sodomy laws.[1] I strongly criticize the *Bowers* decision, but show why it need not be very significant for the development of privacy and why it suggests unexpected positive perspectives for the future of constitutional privacy protection.

1. CONSTITUTIONAL INTERPRETATION

There are a variety of views describing the role of judges in constitutional decision-making, and it will be helpful if we distinguish a few of these very roughly. A dominant theme in the American constitutional tradition is originalism, "the familiar approach to constitutional adjudication that accords binding authority to the text of the Constitution or the intentions of its adopters."[2] One widely accepted justification for originalism is that the Constitution is the supreme law of the land and expresses the will of the citizens; hence the judge's task is to ascertain their will through a strict interpretation of the document. Originalism is often associated with legal positivism, and it underlies the view described by members of the Reagan administration, such as ex-Attorney General Edwin Meese,[3] that judges must apply the law as it is stated to the facts presented to deduce the judgment. The goal of originalism is to constrain judicial discretion and to avoid judicial activism so that unelected officials are not usurping the legislative function.

One version of originalism focuses on strict interpretation of the constitutional text, construing words and phrases narrowly and precisely. Defenders of this sort of view might well be concerned to articulate the intentions of the framers of the Constitution, yet believe the text is the surest guide for doing so.

Unfortunately most scholars agree that, despite the appeal of the rhetoric in defense of such a view, a strict interpretation of the Constitution is problematic or impossible in many cases. One major concern with strict textualism is that it is too historically dependent. It requires and relies on an historical inquiry to understand how phrases such as "cruel and unusual punishment" were used at the time the Constitution was drafted, and to determine the perspective of the adopters themselves.

More worrisome, there are many open-ended or vague phrases in the Constitution that cannot merely be applied straightforwardly. For example, what conduct counts as "free speech"? Does "equal protection of the law" grant Bakke admission to medical school, or exclude him to generate equal opportunity for minorities? And what is protected as "due process" under the Fourteenth Amendment? In none of these cases can the words merely be applied to facts to generate a decision. Even given historical information about terminological usage in the text, reading a provision without regard to its current social context may yield irresolvable indeterminacies, and the consistency hoped for may be elusive.

An alternative narrow view of constitutional interpretation, suggested by Robert Bork, Raoul Berger, and others,[4] urges basing decisions in difficult cases on the intentions of the framers of the Constitution. There are a number of serious analogous difficulties with this view. Again, it is a substantial historical project to ascertain the relevant intentions. The legal history of legislation drafting often yields indecisive or inconsistent testimony and evidence, making it difficult or sometimes impossible to discern the "true" intention of the framers. And new historical evidence can shed light on or actually alter an understanding of their "real" intent. Moreover, the task is a complex one if we recall that the adopters were a diverse group including some delegates to the Philadelphia convention and majorities in ratifying conventions. Perhaps some members had clear intentions about certain constitutional provisions, yet others may have held different views or may have had no clear intent. Hence it is not at all obvious how, or whether it is even possible, to determine their collective intent with any reliability.

In addition, this view of adjudication requires ascertaining the adopter's intentions not only about the meaning of various provisions, but also about their scope, and what the adopters intended future interpreters to do. Such difficulties lead one to wonder, then, why an historian's judgment about what was intended 200 years ago should determine the legitimacy of a current interpretation. It is even more difficult to see how to project the adopters' concepts and attitudes onto a future they didn't or couldn't have envisioned. When a case involves an issue that was not or could not have been anticipated by the framers, perhaps because of technological or medical advancement, there may be no information to rely on to determine their intentions. Did the framers intend First Amendment protection for the mass media, for example? In such cases the theory either cannot be applied at all or cannot be immune to the possibility of subjective judicial decision-making it is aimed to avoid.

Most other legal theorists believe, then, that these methods are unrealistic and often impossible to put into practice. In order to give content to the ambiguous and vague language of the Constitution and to allow the Constitution and governmental process to adapt to technological and social changes, some more active judicial interpretation of the law is necessary.

Yet this generates a slippery slope worry. If judges have some discretion in interpreting the law, what constraints are they bound by? A genuine concern is that allowing some judicial discretion will lead to free-wheeling judicial innovation, as described and defended by American legal realists in the early twentieth century. One characterization of their view is that all law is judge-made law, that the judicial decision is the law, and that legal rules are merely sources of law, not binding on judges. On this account judges not only do, but should, make law.[5] The most extreme version of this view, that judicial decisions are wholly subjective and personal, and that written opinions are merely rationalizations, is intuitively jarring. Moreover, realism seems contrary to two democratic ideals: (a) that subjective legislative policy-making is an inappropriate role for unelected officials on courts, and (b) that *ex post facto* law is illegitimate because citizens deserve fair warning when their behavior is beyond the bounds of law.

Clearly, a more acceptable view on the decision-making role of the judge will fall somewhere between originalism and extreme realism. There are a wide range of alternative views on the proper domain of judicial intervention. One requires judicial interpretation to appeal to some set of evolving principles as a guide, such as those suggested by Lon Fuller, principles that can be defended as embodied in the Constitution and its history because they focus on the goals and purposes of the provisions.[6] John Hart Ely has advocated a process-oriented approach defending unrepresented minorities,[7] for example, and Ronald Dworkin has defended a rights-based constitutional theory.[8] Alexander Bickel appeals to broad "fundamental values,"[9] and Paul Brest defends a "nonoriginalism" view according to which the text and original history of the Constitution get presumptive weight but are not treated as authoritative or binding; the presumption is defeasible over time in light of experience and perceptions."[10]

These views may be more or less deferential to the legislature, more or less interventionist, but all expect judges to be constrained by rationality and consistency as far as possible and all place weight on the Constitution as well as subsequent precedents. All endorse the view that "the principles of the Constitution should not be frozen in time, but should grow in meaning as the country evolves."[11] My purpose in this section has not been to defend a particular mediating view on constitutional interpretation, but to stress the implausibility of rejecting the legitimacy of constitutional privacy on the grounds that it is not explicitly mentioned in the Constitution or was not intended by the framers.

2. CONSTITUTIONAL PRIVACY PRIOR TO *BOWERS*

The constitutional right to privacy was first announced in *Griswold v. Connecticut,* when the Court overturned convictions of the Director of Planned Parenthood in Connecticut and a doctor from Yale Medical School for violating a statute which banned dispersement of contraceptive information, instruction, and even medical advice to married persons.[12] Given that the offense was disbursement of information, not contraceptive devices in this case, it is interesting that the Court did not invoke any free speech justifications for their decision. In any case, controversy began almost immediately because there were four different justifying opinions written in defense of the judgment.

In his opinion for the Court, Douglas defended a "penumbral" right to privacy "emanating" from the Constitution and its amendments. He claimed the right to privacy protects a "zone" of privacy including the sexual relations of married persons. Others on the Court thought, to the contrary, that the same judgment could be defended using the due process clause or the concept of liberty of the Fourteenth Amendment, or by the Ninth Amendment.

Soon after the *Griswold* decision, the right to privacy was cited in *Loving v. Virginia* as justification to overturn a Virginia statute against interracial marriage,[13] in *Stanley v. Georgia* as defense of one's right to view pornography in one's home,[14] and in *Eisenstadt v. Baird* as the reason to allow distribution of contraceptive devices.[15] In *Moore v. City of East Cleveland*[16] privacy was extended to decisions concerning family composition and living arrangements. The constitutional privacy right is also associated with earlier decisions striking down a law requiring students to be educated at public schools,[17] and banning Oklahoma's practice of mandatory sterilization for recidivists.[18] Although the constitutional right to privacy played a central role in the famous and controversial abortion decision *Roe v. Wade,* and subsequent decisions on third party consent for minors,[19] it has been less successful protecting funding for abortions,[20] protecting computer records of patients who have prescriptions for dangerous but lawful drugs,[21] and protecting the privacy of intimate sexual behavior in the *Bowers* case.

Douglas's vague language in *Griswold* and wide variety of constitutional appeals to defend it, as well as the diversity of claims protected under the term "privacy," have all contributed to making constitutional privacy vulnerable to attack. Furthermore, Justice Blackmun, author of the most controversial of the constitutional privacy cases, the abortion decision *Roe v. Wade,* has said on several occasions during the past year that he believes that decision will be overturned.

Apart from political reasons for this possibility, there are at least two ways in which the wording of Blackmun's opinion can be said to invite (undoubtedly unintentionally) replies such as the Human Life Amendments or Human Life Bills which have been submitted as attempts to overturn the *Roe* decision. In his opinion Blackmun says,

> We need not resolve the difficult question of when life begins. When those trained in the respective disciplines of medicine, philosophy, and theology are unable to arrive at any consensus, the judiciary, at this point in the development of man's knowledge, is not in a position to speculate as to the answer.[22]

Even if *at that point in the development of man's knowledge,* namely 1973, such a determination could not be expected, the invitation left was that at some future time philosophical, medical, or other technological development or information might make such a determination possible. And so it was hardly surprising that during the Human Life Bill hearings nearly ten years later, testimony abounded from such experts about when life begins.

Blackmun also wrote in *Roe v. Wade,* "in view of all this, we do not agree that, by adopting one theory of life, Texas may override the rights of the pregnant woman that are at stake."[23] Again the wording was less careful than it might have been. For even though the Court held that Texas could not adopt a certain theory of life in this way, it was at least not ruled out that the federal government could. This lack of foresight or sloppiness may impact the *Roe* decision in the future. Nevertheless, it is narrow and specific enough to the issue of the status of the fetus that it need not undermine constitutional privacy protection in general.

It might still seem, however, that this combination—*Roe* being in jeopardy and the Court's recent refusal to allow privacy as a defense for consenting homosexuality in one's home in *Bowers*—seals the fate of constitutional privacy as a species soon to be extinct. I shall argue, to the contrary, that the reasoning in *Bowers* shows the future of privacy may not be so bleak after all.

3. THE ARGUMENTS IN *BOWERS V. HARDWICK*

The Supreme Court's decision in *Bowers v. Hardwick* was handed down during the summer of 1986. In a 5–4 decision the Court refused to strike down Georgia's anti-sodomy laws. In all there are four main sets of arguments and counter-arguments.

i. The Constitutional Question. The first arguments concern the nature and scope of the question at issue in the *Bowers* case. According to Justice White's majority opinion, "[t]he issue presented is whether the Federal Constitution confers a fundamental right upon homosexuals to engage in sodomy and hence invalidates the laws of the many states that still make such conduct illegal and have done so for a very long time."[24] By constructing the question this narrowly it is not difficult to see how the majority could defend their view that the clear answer is no. Certainly no right to homosexual sodomy is explicitly mentioned in the Constitution, and at least in the past two hundred years it is unlikely to have been endorsed in this country. We have seen, however, the inadequacies of originalist views of constitutional decision-making. The essential issue, then, is whether the majority asked the appropriate constitutional question and whether a moderate theory of judicial adjudication supports the right at stake.

The Georgia law states in part, "[a] person commits the offense of sodomy when he performs or submits to any sexual act involving the sex organs of one person and the mouth or anus of another. . . ."[25] Although Michael Hardwick was caught by Atlanta police in a homosexual relationship in his bedroom, no distinction is made in the wording of the statute between homosexual and heterosexual behavior, or married and unmarried partners. Thus it seems the minority is clearly correct to charge that a fair reading of the statute reveals that the majority has distorted the question presented. To the extent evidence of any legislative purpose for the 1968 enactment of the statute can be discerned, it seems to have been to broaden coverage to reach both homosexual and heterosexual activity, since laws against homosexuality had been on the books in Georgia for years. Yet the majority does not justify their selective application of the law.

ii. The Relevance of Privacy. Some commentators have held that "the Supreme Court failed to consider many of the issues Hardwick raised, such as privacy. . . ."[26] A careful reading of the decision shows, to the contrary, that the Court did consider the privacy claim, however summarily, and rejected it. Thus the second argument made by the majority is that privacy protection does not extend to the *Bowers* case. Their justification that privacy is irrelevant is that this case has no resemblance to past constitutional privacy cases.

> No connection between family, marriage, or procreation on the one hand and homosexual activity on the other has been demonstrated . . . [and] any claim that these cases nevertheless stand for the proposition that any kind of private sexual conduct between consenting adults is constitutionally insulated from state proscription is unsupportable.[27]

This argument goes to the heart of the controversy over what a right to privacy can and should mean. Certainly on narrow and specific grounds it is true that intimate sexual behavior is not the particular issue in any of the previous constitutional privacy cases, although choices about sexual behavior are hardly unrelated to choices about the use of contraceptives. If one thought that constitutional privacy encompasses a broad right to sexual self-determination, then *Bowers* shatters that illusion. Moreover, the majority says little to clarify the confusion or give guidelines for what is covered by privacy.

Nevertheless, privacy was judged to be at stake in protecting the right to choose one's marriage partner, one's decision whether to use contraception, to have a child, or even to send one's child to private school. The Court dismisses the relevance to these past constitutional privacy cases by distinguishing them as involving rights related to "family, marriage, or procreation." The minority worries that the Court cites family values as important, but chooses to protect only the stereotypical family. They argue, against the majority, that utilitarian concerns whether preservation of the family enhances general welfare are irrelevant. By focusing on "marriage, family, and procreation," the majority ignores a second dominant theme in past defenses of constitutional privacy, namely whether a decision or action is fundamental to one's self-identity. The main point is that these rights have in the past been protected because of their importance in the individual's life. They touch central concerns that help define oneself as a person. These minority claims are bolstered by the Court's constitutional doctrine that privacy is a "fundamental value" so that state legislation involving privacy deserves a higher level of assessment, called "strict scrutiny."

Moreover, neither access to contraception nor abortion rights are limited to married couples. Indeed, the Court declared in *Eisenstadt v. Baird,* allowing distribution of contraceptives, that such a distinction is unconstitutional, and the plaintiff in *Roe v. Wade* was unmarried. So it is difficult to see how these decisions can be characterized as focusing on "marriage" and "family." The Court's attempt to distinguish *Bowers* from cases concerning procreation may seem on firmer ground. Yet the Court stressed in *Carey v. Population Services International*[28] that the contraception cases protect the decision to engage in sex without bearing or begetting a child.

In addition, the Court has repeatedly stated in earlier cases that privacy protects decisions on "fundamental" and "personal" matters, indicating a far closer relationship between the precedents and the *Bowers* case than the majority admits. Citing *Paris Adult Theatre I. v. Slaton,* the minority scolds, "Only the most willful blindness could obscure the fact that sexual intimacy is 'a sensitive, key relationship of human experience, central to family life, community welfare, and the development of human personality.'"[29]

Even if we acknowledge that the scope of constitutional privacy protection is as yet insufficiently clarified, it is extremely difficult to distinguish *Bowers* from cases where constitutional privacy was upheld if we rely on the Court's own language in previous privacy decisions. Whatever else might or might not be protected by privacy, Justice Blackmun argues that "the right of an individual to conduct intimate relationships in the intimacy of his or her own home seems to me to be at the heart of the Constitution's protection of privacy."[30] It is interesting that philosophers recognize a similar point in contexts unrelated to law. Consider Stuart Hampshire's remarks, "We know that in the average life nothing is more important in moral consciousness than family and sexual relations, and than love and friendship, and their accepted manners of expression also. . . . That which is very variable in human relations, . . . may have profound moral importance. . . ."[31]

iii. The Slippery Slope Argument. The majority attempts to distinguish *Bowers* from earlier privacy cases on marriage, family, and procreation, yet claims it is *not* differentiable from other cases introduced in its slippery slope argument. The Court could not strike down the Georgia statute and allow consenting homosexual conduct, they argue, while leaving exposed to prosecution adultery, incest, and other sexual crimes, even though they are committed within the home. According to the majority opinion no distinction between homosexual intimacy and incest can be made except by fiat. Sensing danger, they say they are unwilling to travel down that road.

We cannot say the location of behavior is irrelevant to a privacy decision. The Fourth Amendment protects the "right of the people to be secure in their . . . houses," and there is significance in the view that one's home is one's castle and governmental interference there is at least *prima facie* illegitimate. In addition, the holding in *Stanley v. Georgia,* that obscene matter may be viewed in one's own home, not only rested on a First Amendment argument, but was also anchored on respect for the privacy of one's home, since the Court has acknowledged that the conduct would not be protected outside the home. *Stanley* even protected behavior not accepted by the majority.

Nevertheless, the outcome in *Bowers* did not, and the majority is correct that it cannot, rest solely on the location of the behavior. We do not condone child abuse or wife-battering, in ethics or the law, even if it is done within the confines of the home. And examination of these cases shows clear ground for distinguishing incest and adultery from consenting homosexual relations between adults, namely that incest and (usually) adultery harm someone, as does child abuse and wife-battering, while the consenting behavior at stake does not. The Constitution does not enact Mill's harm principle, of course, but harm is clearly a compelling state interest that can override privacy rights.

We may well want to require more justification for governmental intrusion into the home as opposed to other locations. That does not mean, however, that *Bowers* must lead us down the slippery slope feared by the majority. As the Court's reference to other "sexual crimes" indicates, considerations of harm and consent provide important and reasonable ways of making a non-arbitrary distinction the Court claimed was impossible.

iv. The Enforcement of Morals. A final set of arguments focus not merely on the particulars of this case, but on more general issues surrounding morals legislation. In a brief concluding paragraph Justice White considers the respondents' argument that state legislation must at least pass the rational basis test and the only basis for the statute is the presumed belief that a majority of the electorate in Georgia find homosexual sodomy to be immoral. White replies for the Court that "[t]he law, however, is constantly based on notions of morality, and if all laws representing essentially moral choices are to be invalidated under the Due Process Clause, the courts will be very busy indeed."[32]

This brief dismissal raises two main concerns. First, it is of course true that the law is infused with morality in may senses. Moral wrongs are often legal wrongs, and moral arguments are made to defend or criticize legislation. Many moral offenses, thefts and murders, for example, are legal offenses. But not every moral wrong is a legal wrong. One is not held liable for every lie or broken promise. Furthermore, saying that the law is "based on" morality does not establish whether or not majority moral views on controversial cases should in every, or even most cases, be enacted as legislation. It is surely worrisome if White's comment implies that the anti-sodomy law needed nothing more than *some* basis in morality, even a false or dubious majority belief. Second, White is making a common legal argument about the possible flood of litigation arising from a decision. It is often a major practical concern that some decisions invite more lawsuits which fill court calendars. Yet *Bowers* does not invite *all* moral choices to be questioned. Legislative statutes are often justified in a variety of ways. Thus it is unrealistic to believe that the particular facts of the *Bowers* case, had it been decided differently, would have generated a flood of litigation from others believing they have been prosecuted unfairly under laws with *no* justification beyond the majority moral beliefs of the electorate.

Chief Justice Burger, in his concurring opinion, reiterates the enforcement of morality argument even more forcefully. "To hold that the act of homosexual sodomy is somehow protected as a fundamental right would be to cast aside a millennia of moral teaching."[33] On one interpretation, Burger is claiming that in light of traditional condemnation of homosexuality, it is hard to claim there is a fundamental right to engage in it. He is perhaps appealing to Frankfurter's traditions of ordered liberty, and saying a fundamental right to privacy regarding homosexuality is not in that tradition. But then we might wonder why arguments for a fundamental right encompassing homosexual conduct have to be "traditionalistic" rather than, say, "rationalistic." Indeed, Justice Stevens argues in his dissent that "the fact that the governing majority in a State has traditionally viewed a practice as immoral is not a sufficient reason for upholding a law prohibiting the practice; neither history nor tradition could save a law prohibiting miscegenation from constitutional attack."[34]

According to another interpretation, Burger's assumption is that if a moral view is taught or strongly held for a long time, then it is legitimate for the state to codify that moral conviction. Yet the Court's privacy precedents do not uphold this view. Although he found the statute in *Griswold* "uncommonly silly" and "obviously unenforceable," Justice Stewart dissented from the decision to override the doctors' convictions by deferring to the legislature to change the statute. Nevertheless, he cautioned "it is not the function of this Court to decide cases on the basis of community standards"[35] whatever those standards may be. Philosophers have countered similarly in totally general terms unrelated to the issue in *Bowers*,

> It evidently does not follow from the fact that a way of life has survived, and that it has some hold over men's sentiments and loyalties, that that way of life, with the moral claims which are a necessary element of it, ought for these reasons to be protected and prolonged: there may well be overriding reasons of a rational kind against these claims—that they are unfair or that they destroy happiness.[36]

Blackmun's retort for the minority is more scathing: "I cannot agree that either the length of time a majority has held its convictions or the passions with which it defends them can withdraw legislation from this Court's scrutiny."[37]

Arguments for and against the legitimacy of enforcing moral views dominated the debate between Oxford professor of jurisprudence H. L. A. Hart and Judge Sir Patrick Devlin over the 1965 British Wolfenden report recommending decriminalization of laws against adult consenting homosexuality and prostitution.[38] Devlin worried that such decriminalization would result in the ultimate moral collapse and destruction of society analogous to that resulting from treason and sedition. Courts must always weigh individual rights to privacy against public security and in this case the balance tipped, on Devlin's view, in favor of public welfare.

Hart countered by doubting the grave harm Devlin envisioned in his analogies with sedition and treason, and by pointing out that the only test Devlin had for determining which "immoralities" should be legislated against was the deep disgust of the average citizen. Most persuasively, he urged that at the very least such strong feelings, even if popular, should be subjected to the most rigorous scrutiny in order to rule out misinformation, bias and other prejudice before enacting legislation. Issues raised in this debate are taught in many introductory college philosophy courses and one would think that we could learn from the wisdom of a scholar such as Hart. However his concerns about scrutinizing majority moral opinions were not rebutted by Devlin nor were they anywhere even mentioned by the majority in the *Bowers* case.

Equally telling is the minority's argument that there is a special need to be careful to protect the rights of those who are in a minority. This need is reflected in the Court's past adoption of a policy of tougher scrutiny for legislation that affects a "suspect classification." The constitutional doctrine would dictate more careful scrutiny of the goals of the legislation and the extent to which its means are likely to accomplish those goals, neither of which are addressed by the majority in *Bowers*. Suspect classifications that have been granted this strict scrutiny focus on racial minorities, but not women. The conditions enumerated by the Court for determining the existence of a suspect classification are that (i) the group be stigmatized from a history of prejudice,[39] (ii) the class must suffer from unequal treatment,[40] (iii) the classification must be based on some immutable trait that all members share,[41] and (iv) the group must be a discrete and insular minority unable to protect its interests through ordinary political means.[42] It is difficult to deny that homosexuals comprise a true minority in numbers as well as being a group that has borne the burden of vehement negative public feelings and discriminatory treatment in public schools, the military, child custody, the legal profession, and private employment. Though not part of established law, it is at least arguable on accepted constitutional principles that the Court should be especially careful, as they were not, in assessing legislation that affects them.

4. CONCLUSIONS ON THE FUTURE OF PRIVACY

My analysis of the arguments in *Bowers* has led to at least four conclusions. First, I have shown that the majority drew the constitutional question more narrowly than can be defended by the wording of the statute. Second, I argued that they rejected appeals to privacy in a way that is inconsistent with their earlier statements in constitutional privacy cases. Third, the majority argued that a contrary decision in this case would lead down a slippery slope to disaster allowing crimes such as incest, whereas there are ample and reasonable grounds to deny any such slide. Finally, they have endorsed arguments on the enforcement of morals almost uniformly rejected by legal theorists and philosophers, without so much as even mentioning those alternative positions, or the inconsistency of failing to afford special protection to threatened minorities. Each of these is a serious criticism of the case, and taken together they form a powerful argument that the majority decision in *Bowers* was logically flawed and inadequately justified.

For those directly affected by the case, the consequences are devastating. It is a blow to all human beings, not only gays, that all plausible constitutional bases for striking down the anti-sodomy laws were rejected. It is not surprising, therefore, that more recent cases have relied on different arguments concerning the discrimination against gays as a class, sometimes restricting identification of the respondent as one professing to be gay only, so there is no issue concerning violation of sodomy laws.[43]

"The Court is most vulnerable and comes nearest to illegitimacy when it deals with judge-made law having little or no cognizable roots in the language or design of the Constitution,"[44] announces White in his majority opinion in *Bowers*. He is clearly referring to worries that constitutional privacy was insufficiently defended as a constitutional guarantee when it was announced in *Griswold*. Apparently his argument is that defending Hardwick's rights under constitutional privacy will be equally problematic more than twenty years later. But the twenty years of cases add a powerful set of precedents that, I have argued, an acceptable and non-originalist theory of constitutional adjudication cannot ignore.

The majority gives no explanation for narrowing the constitutional question posed in *Bowers*, and even appears to go out of its way to restrict the issue, giving the impression of procedural manipulation. Because, in addition, the majority opinion contains a tone of disapproval and language strongly condemning homosexuality, it reads as if the majority made up its mind to deny homosexuals constitutional protection, and then applied traditional moral views to defend its position, ignoring the Court's own contrary arguments and authority of precedent. Sadly, Justice Stevens suggests just that in his conclusion that the majority excludes homosexuals from the Constitution's protection simply because it dislikes them.[45]

If *Bowers* rests on nothing but the collective distaste and emotional response of five judges predisposed against Hardwick, then given the precedents on privacy and their links to *Bowers* it is *at least as plausible* to judge *Bowers* as a case which is vulnerable, as judge-made law approaching illegitimacy. Critics of the Warren court have shown that judges do abuse their power when they depart from explicit rules and consistency with precedent to achieve a result they find desirable on other grounds. Courts should take logic, precedent, and consistency seriously.[46] But then, I have argued, it is the majority opinion in *Bowers*, not the minority, that is least well justified constitutionally.

There is a further major concern, that constitutional decision-making will change dramatically if the Court continues in other cases to draw the question narrowly as it did in *Bowers*. If they do so, they can undermine, restrict, and even retrench many individual rights, not merely privacy. Narrow question-drawing is potentially even more threatening to individual rights if it is combined with on originalist view of constitutional decision-making, because new technology brings issues the framers of the Constitution did not and could not have foreseen. This is a second sense in which *Bowers* is a particularly troubling decision.

It has been argued, however, that there is a glimmer of hope in the *Bowers* judgment. Because the constitutional question was drawn so narrowly the majority opinion need not be read to extend to heterosexuals.[47] Consensual sodomy statutes aimed at heterosexuals have been held, and should remain, unconstitutional. This is not to support the *Bowers* decision, but to point out that sexual self-determination is not totally jettisoned by the Court and to acknowledge that protecting the privacy interests of some is better than protecting none at all. An important response is that it would be preferable to enforce the statute as written, making no distinction between heterosexual and homosexual behavior, because that would force a greater degree of political responsibility on the legislature. Legislators would then have to face the majority for restricting their rights as well.

Another view is that *Bowers* can be read as drawing the far boundary of the privacy right in sexual matters.[48] That interpretation may be correct, even if the wrong boundary was drawn. The Court refused to expand privacy protection and may continue to resist further expansion in other areas.

Nevertheless, it does not follow that *Bowers* significantly narrows the scope of privacy rights, as some commentators have suggested.[49] Taking that view obscures a very positive, but perhaps ironic, side to the decision. Given (1) that *Bowers* was decided on such narrow grounds, solely on the question whether or not there is a constitutional right to homosexual sodomy, and (2) that privacy was deemed irrelevant to the case, and (3) that the case was ardently distinguished from previous constitutional privacy cases, then the judgment does not pose the threat to constitutional privacy that it might have. I have argued that the Court erred seriously in their decision. Nevertheless, privacy may profit from their error. Having announced that *Bowers* has no link to previous privacy cases, it cannot be consistently and rationally used to overturn those privacy rights.[50]

NOTES

1. *Bowers v. Hardwick,* 103 S. Ct. 2841 (1986).
2. Paul Brest, "The Misconceived Quest for the Original Understanding," *Boston University Law Review* 60 (1980): 204–38. This section was strongly influenced by Brest's articulate paper.
3. Edwin Meese, "Construing the Constitution," *University of California Davis Law Review* 19 (1985): 22–30.
4. Robert Bork, "Neutral Principles and Some First Amendment Problems," *Indiana Law Journal* 47 (1971): 1–35; Raoul Berger, *Government by the Judiciary,* (Cambridge: Harvard University Press, 1977); Henry Monaghan, "Our Perfect Constitution," *New York University Law Review* 56 (1981): 353–96.
5. Theodore Benditt, *Law As Rule and Principle,* (Sussex: Harvester Press, 1978). See also DeCew, "Realities About Legal Realism," *Law and Philosophy* 4 (1985): 405–22.
6. With characteristic vision, Fuller charged that "our courts' piece-meal and backward-looking system of legislating frequently proves inadequate to meet the need for legal control in fields where social practices are changing rapidly," "American Legal Realism," 82 *University of Pennsylvania Law Review* 439 (1934), cited in Kenneth I. Winston, "Is/Ought Redux: The Pragmatist Context of Lon Fuller's Conception of Law," *Oxford Journal of Legal Studies* 8 (1988): 331.
7. *Democracy and Distrust: A Theory of Judicial Review,* (Cambridge: Harvard University Press, 1980).
8. *Taking Rights Seriously,* (Cambridge: Harvard University Press, 1977), and *Law's Empire,* (Cambridge: Harvard University Press, 1986).
9. *The Least Dangerous Branch,* (Indianapolis: Bobbs-Merrill, 1962).
10. Brest, p. 205.
11. Thomas B. Stoddard, "*Bowers v. Hardwick:* Precedent by Personal Predilection," *The University of Chicago Law Review* 54 (1987): 648.
12. *Griswold v. Connecticut,* 381 U.S. 479 (1965).
13. *Loving v. Virginia,* 388 U.S. 1 (1967).
14. *Stanley v. Georgia,* 394 U.S. 557 (1969).
15. *Eisenstadt v. Baird,* 405 U.S. 438 (1972).
16. *Moore v. East Cleveland,* 431 U.S. 494 (1977).
17. *Pierce v. Society of Sisters,* 268 U.S. 510 (1925).
18. *Skinner v. Oklahoma,* 316 U.S. 535 (1942).
19. *Roe v. Wade,* 410 U.S. 113 (1973).
20. *Harris v. McRae,* 488 U.S. 297 (1980).
21. *Whalen v. Roe,* 429 U.S. 589 (1977).
22. *Roe v. Wade,* reprinted in James Rachels, ed., *Moral Problems,* (New York: Harper & Row, 1979), p. 113.
23. *Moral Problems,* p. 114.
24. 54 *The U.S. Law Week* 4920. Edited versions of the arguments in this section are reprinted in "The Future of Privacy: Assessing the Supreme

Court's Antisodomy Decision," *Radcliffe Quarterly* 75 (1989): 14–18.
25. Georgia Code Ann. S. 16-6-2 (1984).
26. Joseph R. Thornton, "*Bowers v. Hardwick:* An Incomplete Constitutional Analysis, *North Carolina Law Review* 65 (1987): 1101.
27. 54 *U.S.L.W*. 4920.
28. *Carey v. Population Services International,* 431 U.S. 678 (1977).
29. *Paris Adult Theatre I v. Slaton,* 413 U.S. 49 (1973). Cited at 54 *U.S.L.W.* 4924.
30. 54 *U.S.L.W*. 4925.
31. Stuart Hampshire, *Morality and Conflict,* (Cambridge: Harvard University Press, 1983), p. 153.
32. 54 *U.S.L.W.* 4922.
33. 54 *U.S.L.W*. 4922.
34. I thank an anonymous referee for suggesting this interpretation. Justice Stevens' reply is at 54 *U.S.L.W.* 4927.
35. Quoted in Richard Wasserstrom, ed., *Today's Moral Problems,* (New York: Macmillan, 1979), pp. 414 and 416.
36. Hampshire, p. 137.
37. 54 *U.S.L.W.* 4926.
38. Lord Patrick Devlin, "Morals and the Criminal Law," from *The Enforcement of Morals* (Oxford: Oxford University Press, 1965); H. L. A. Hart, "Immorality and Treason," *The Listener,* (July 1959).
39. *San Antonio Independent School District v. Rodriguez,* 411 U.S. 1 (1973), (on school financing systems).
40. *Matthews v. Lucas,* 427 U.S. 495 (1976), (on illegitimate children).
41. *Rodriguez,* op. cit.
42. *Rodriguez and U.S. Carolene Products* 304 U.S. 144 (1938).
43. For example, in 1988 a panel of judges of the U. S. Ninth Circuit Court of Appeals in California ordered openly gay Sergeant Perry Watkins reinstated in the Army. They won by relying on showing unjust discrimination against the class of gays, and distinguished this case on the grounds that it only involved professed sexual orientation, no charge of a specific act of sodomy. See *Time,* February 22, 1988. The New York Court of Appeals expressly extended constitutional protection to homosexual conduct in *People v. Onofre,* 51 N.Y. 2d 476 (at 485), cert denied 451 U.S. 987 (1981), but this is the overwhelming exception.
44. 54 *U.S.L.W.* 4921.
45. Compare Thornton, p. 1122. See Stevens's dissent at 54 *U.S.L.W.* 4928.
46. Stoddard, p. 648.
47. Mitchell L. Pearl, "Chipping Away at *Bowers v. Hardwick:* Making the Best of an Unfortunate Decision," *New York University Law Review* 63 (1988): 154–90. I am grateful to an anonymous referee for the response below.
48. See Julia K. Sullens, "Thus Far and No Further: The Supreme Court Draws the Outer Boundary of the Right to Privacy," *Tulane Law Review* 61 (1987): 907–29.
49. Daniel J. Langin, "*Bowers v. Hardwick:* The Right of Privacy and the Question of Intimate Relations," *Iowa Law Review* 70 (1987): 1443.
50. An earlier version of this paper was presented at Hampshire College. I am indebted to Ilona Bell, Jay Garfield, Marlene Fried, and two anonymous referees from this journal for helpful comments on earlier drafts of the paper. I am also grateful for support from the Bunting Institute at Radcliffe College.

57

RORY O'CONNELL

Natural Law: Alive and Kicking? A Look at the Constitutional Morality of Sexual Privacy in Ireland

1. INTRODUCTION

Whilst for two centuries, the paradigm of legal discussion had been the separation of law and morality, there are those who wish to return to pre-Kantian, pre-Benthamite days of a unity, or at least a connection, of law and morality. Roland Dworkin, Carlos Nino and Robert Alexy are but three of the theorists who dispute the paradigm of separation. They dismiss the title "natural law" for their theories, but in so far as the term designates the belief that law includes a strong moral element, the term applies. How does a system of law which recognizes a strong connection between the two, actually work? Here I examine the issue of sexual morality in Irish constitutional law, where judges operate with a very moralized conception of law.

The reader should look for three elements in this article. First, the actual role played by moral reasoning in the decisions of the courts. Second, the nature of the decisions as a debate between different judges and different philosophies. Third, the judicial contribution of two sorts to the ongoing public debate on the same issues. Judges both demonstrate the concrete effects of the existing rules and principles of law, and offer visions of different underlying justifications which may serve to either re-interpret or revise those rules and principles.

Please note two elements of Irish law. The Irish system is a common law one, with all the trappings: a Supreme Court cum Constitutional Court, a unified court system, a moderate doctrine of precedent, and multiple Supreme Court opinions. Second, the courts have, since 1965, asserted the power to deem certain human rights to be fully fledged constitutional rights, even though nowhere mentioned in the text (*Ryan v. Ireland,* [1965] I.R. 294). This they have done invoking Art. 40, section 3, sub-section 1 (Art. 40.3.1) of the Constitution, which implies that the Constitution protects all personal rights, not merely those specifically mentioned.

2. THE BIRTH OF CONSTITUTIONAL PRIVACY: *M'GEE*

One finds no mention of the right of privacy in the Irish Constitution. Nevertheless, it is a constitutional right, born of a confrontation between personal circumstances and the blunt prohibition of the positive law, and finding its solution in a piece of moral–legal reasoning at the highest level.

Mrs. Mary M'Gee was a young married woman with four children. At least one of those births had been a complicated one, and her doctor advised her that any more pregnancies would seriously harm her. She decided, with her husband, that they should use some form of contraception. Customs officers seized the spermicidal jelly she sought to import relying on section 17 of the 1935 Criminal Law (Amendment) Act, which banned the sale or importation (but not the use or manufacture) of contraceptives. This section was enacted, by an overwhelming majority, two years before the adoption of the 1937 Constitution. Since no one manufactured contraceptives in the Ireland of 1973, there was no legal means to acquire them. Mrs. M'Gee argued in the High Court that section 17 violated her enumerated constitutional right to marital privacy. The judge disagreed. According to him, to determine whether a right was protected, one had to determine what was the will of the people in 1937, when they adopted the Constitution. The constitutional principles of 1973 must not differ too much from the morality of traditional 1937 society. The section must not have violated the beliefs of the people of 1937, because only two years before, Parliament had adopted the law almost unanimously. So the section did not conflict with the Constitution. Now Mrs. M'Gee had but one recourse—to appeal to the Supreme Court (*M'Gee v. Ireland,* [1974] I.R. 284).

Four (of five) judges agreed that the provision violated the hitherto unknown right of marital privacy (though they disagreed on the reasoning). Perhaps none of them realized the implications their decision would have on the lives of many people, from gay men to fourteen year old rape victims, and more generally on Irish public life. (I consider here only two main judgements.)

Henchy J., like two other judges, based his opinion on Art. 40.3.1. Henchy J. stresses that the purpose of s. 17 was to protect the communal notion of sexual morality (ibid., 324). The "totality of the prohibition aims at nothing less" than to prohibit *in effect* the use of contraceptives, given the absence of any manufacturer of contraceptives in Ireland. Henchy J. then sets out the unenumerated rights doctrine. A particular right has constitutional status if it "inheres" in the citizen "by virtue of his human personality" (ibid., 325). This must be shown considering the Constitution as a whole, and in light of the constitutional social order, and the concrete conditions of the person involved. It is not possible to list fully these rights.

The section subjects the couple to the criminal law because of their decision. It condemns them "to a way of life . . . fraught with worry, tension, and uncertainty" (ibid., 326). Henchy J. continues:

> And this in the context of a Constitution which in its preamble proclaims as one of its aims the dignity and freedom of the individual; which in sub. s. 2 of s. 3 of Article 40 casts on the State a duty to protect

> as best it may from unjust attack and in the case of injustice done to vindicate the life and person of every citizen; which in Article 41 . . . guarantees to protect it [the family] in its constitution and authority as the necessary basis of social order and as indispensable to the welfare of the nation and the State; and which also in Article 41, pledges the State to guard with special care the institution of marriage, . . . (*M'Gee v Ireland,* [1974] I.R. 284, 326)

The objection to s. 17 is that "the law, by prosecuting her, will reach into the privacy of her marital life in seeking to prove her guilt" (ibid., 326). The section violates both Art. 40.3.1's guarantee of privacy in marriage, and Art. 41's protection of the family (ibid., 328).

For Walsh J. the central issue is whether the legislature can make contraceptives absolutely unavailable (ibid., 308). He explains that the Constitution places justice over law. Rights are not created by law; the Constitution merely "confirms their existence and gives them protection" (ibid., 310). When it comes to fundamental rights, the courts may review Parliament's determination of the common good.

Walsh J. bases his decision on Art. 41 which requires the State to protect the family. It is of the essence that the couple be allowed to determine for themselves the number of children to have, if any (ibid., 311). The religion of other parties, and the moral beliefs of the citizens do not amount to an exigency justifying intervention:

> The private morality of its citizens does not justify intervention by the State into the activities of those citizens unless and until the common good requires it. (*M'Gee v. Ireland,* [1974] I.R. 284, 312)

There can be no imposition of a code of morality on a married couple (ibid., 313). Interference would only be justified as the only possible means to prevent such an effect on public morality that amounts to the subversion of the common good (ibid., 314). The ban on importation is invalid.

Walsh J. comments on the nature of the Constitution and the judiciary. The Constitution envisages that "we are a religious people" (Preamble, Art. 6). So human rights are part of the natural law "of God promulgated by reason" which is "the ultimate governor of all the laws of men." Art. 44 insists that we live in a pluralist state, where all religions are entitled to Constitutional protection (ibid., 317). In a pluralist society, judges cannot turn to religious experts or churches for an explanation of the natural law. This is a task for the judiciary, guided by the structure of the Constitution, and the "Aristotelian" and "Christian" virtues of justice, prudence and charity (ibid., 318–19). Any judicial interpretation may be reviewed in the light of developing values (ibid., 319).

Walsh amplifies his view in several articles. The Constitution represents the fundamental values of the sovereign people, which they have reserved from the political process and entrusted to the judiciary (Walsh 1987a, 87, 108). It is written in the present tense and judges must so interpret it—it is not "concerned with what has been, but with what may be" (Walsh 1987b, 195). Of course it is a law which includes "social and political objectives . . . [and] certain moral concepts" and thus embroils judges in contemporary "social, economic, philosophical and political debates" (ibid., 192). The judge must explore questions of justice, so he must rely on "instinct or intuition, . . . his own moral sense and his own intelligence." Both judges and law makers must act according to "prevailing ideas of justice" with which they are imbued "by training and experience" (Walsh 1987a, 106. Cf. Dworkin 1986, 249–50, 257–58, 398).

He regards the 1937 Constitution as endorsing a natural law approach first seen in *State (Ryan) v. Lennon,* ([1935] I.R. 370), where Kennedy C. J., dissenting, argued that Art. 2a of the 1922 Constitution was invalid because the creation of a special military court violated the natural law (ibid., 89–91). Walsh J. notes the disasters of positivism in Nazi Germany and South Africa and the importance of natural law values in international human rights law. So far this leaves open the question as to whether he is talking of secular (e.g., Lockean) or religious (e.g., Thomistic) natural law. He then states that the Constitutional version of natural law is theological, but not Catholic (ibid., 94). According to Walsh J. all democracies reject the idea that "the state of God or that state power is right"—they are committed to defending rights (ibid., 95). Given the role of judges as defenders of the Constitution, they may deploy any remedy they deem necessary to defend a fundamental right (Walsh 1987b, 193; *State (Quinn) v. Ryan,* [1965] I.R. 70).

What are we to make of the role of moral or political argument in this case? First the Supreme Court rejects the High Court claim that the Constitution is limited by the morals of 1937, either those embraced by the people who drafted or who adopted it. The Constitution must be given a present tense interpretation, in the light of today's values. From whence are those values to be derived? Clearly Parliament's conception of justice is not decisive. Yet it would appear that even the conceptions of justice of the people of today, and of the judges are not to be chosen simply because of who believes in them. Rather:

> The judges must, therefore . . . interpret these rights in accordance with their ideas of prudence, justice and charity. . . . no interpretation of the Constitution is intended to be final for all time. It is given in the light of prevailing ideas and concepts. (*M'Gee v. Ireland,* [1974] I.R. 294, 319)

Judges must interpret the *Constitution's* conception of justice—during which they must rely on their own and others' ideas on the question (cf. Dworkin 1986, 254–58).

A second point is whether the right to marital privacy is founded on Art. 40.3.1 or Art. 41. Article 40.3.1 is inspired by secular rationalist thought, and Art. 41 by Aquinian thought (Costello 1956, 1962). Art. 41 states that the family exists as an institution prior to positive law and has "inalienable and imprescriptible" rights, which the State must protect. Divorce is forbidden. Furthermore the State recognizes the value of woman's work in the home, and guarantees that mothers shall not be forced to work outside the home. Article 40.3.1 requires the State to respect, and in so far as is practicable, defend and vindicate personal rights in general.

Walsh J. chooses Art. 41, and emphasises the value of marriage, whilst the other three members of the majority invoke Art. 40.3.1 which protects all personal rights (Henchy J. agrees that Art. 41 is also violated). Walsh J. specifies that the statute violates Art. 41's guarantee of marital privacy, Art. 40.1's guarantee of equality, and Art. 40.3.1's guarantee of a right to protection of health, but not any personal right of privacy in Art. 40.3.1.

In basing the decision on Art. 41, Walsh J. makes it impossible for anyone to use that part of his reasoning to found a right to privacy outside of marriage. The majority, by basing the decision on Art. 40.3.1, makes it clear that it is a personal right which inheres in every citizen, and leaves open for consideration whether it extends beyond a right to privacy in marital relations. As M'Carthy J. (who was State counsel in *M'Gee*) later noted, the majority upheld the *right of (personal) privacy in a case involving marriage (Norris).* That is, the right to privacy should not be limited to marriage. The three judge majority chose a basis for the right to privacy which left no doubt that it was personal, not marital right. Possibly this difference reflects differing philosophical visions: one an approach centering on individual autonomy, one centering on perfectionist or communitarian beliefs of the importance of family.

When considering the doctrine of unenumerated rights, the judges dramatically reject several less radical conceptions of rights. They reject the pre-1965 judicial belief that it is for Parliament to protect rights. They assert that the state does not merely protect positive rights, whether explicitly mentioned or necessarily implied. Rather it protects rights which derive from a synthesis between the Constitution and justice. There is no clear-cut technical reason to opt for one or other of these approaches to rights. The soundest argument in favour of each relies on a vision of political morality. Those who believe that the value of the law rests in clear terms being applied by non-political judges worry about the unenumerated rights doctrine, those who believe that some rights are more important than legal certainty endorse the doctrine (Kelly 1967, Introduction; Chubb 1991, ch. 6). The majority makes it clear that the Constitution has outgrown the mindset of its drafters, and embraces the notion that law and state must first pay homage to justice. Walsh J. explicitly states that the Constitution places justice above the law (*M'Gee v. Ireland,* [1974] I.R. 284, 310). Henchy J. stresses that the Constitution protects those rights which inhere "in the citizen in question by virtue of his human personality" (ibid., 325), not simply because of a term of the Constitution. The judges pursue a synthesis of justice and the Constitution, which is required by the Constitution itself, as interpreted (ibid., 318, 325).

Which view of justice should be relied on in determining personal rights: theological, liberal, perfectionist, communitarian? Do the judges accept Kenny J's assertion in *Ryan* ([1965] I.R. 294), that rights are rooted in the "Christian and democratic nature of the State" and if so what do they mean by it?

Henchy J. believes that personal rights are rooted in the human personality, which gives rights in certain social situations. In this case a wife and mother made a conscientious decision, about an important area of her life. The State was not entitled to frustrate that decision, even indirectly. Behind this argument is a conception of justice which centers on individual autonomy. The individual may effectuate decisions about intimate matters, even if society disapproves.

Walsh J.'s opinion poses a dilemma for Irish jurists. He asserts that justice is superior to the law, and that "the individual has natural and human rights over which the State has no authority" (*M'Gee v. Ireland,* [1974] I.R. 284, 310). On this basis, Art. 41 recognizes the right of a married couple to decide whether to have children and how many (ibid., 311). The State cannot interfere with this decision simply because the private morality of some or most people disapproves (ibid., 312–13). This argument would seem more appropriate in the context of an Art. 40 personal right. Why should a right not to have a moral rule imposed on one, be particularly connected with a familial right? In other parts, the emphasis on the family may suggest a communitarian or other perfectionist approach: The marital couple (not the individual) is the most important entity, and so valued is it, that it is exempt from the restrictions which apply outside marriage. However this seems contrary to the strongly anti-perfectionist streak just referred to.

After disposing of the case, Walsh J. made several comments on religion which might be misinterpreted. He refers to his own statement in *Quinn's Supermarket,* ([1972] I.R. 1, a religious freedom case), that the Constitution recognizes that the people are religious, but also that they live in a pluralist State (*M'Gee v. Ireland,* [1974] I.R. 294, 317). However the super constitutional status of rights is founded on their being part of the natural law, whose superiority to positive law is implicit in the Preambular reference to Christianity and the constitutionally recognized authority of God (ibid., 318). Nevertheless pluralism requires that judges determine the contents of these rights in accordance with the virtues of prudence, justice and charity (ibid., 318–319).

There are two possible interpretations of this argument. The first is that constitutional rights must be interpreted according to Christian or Judao-Christian concepts of justice. The second is that the argument recognizes that our notions of justice and natural rights have their genesis in religious concepts, but that these concepts have now been bequeathed to the Constitution (and liberal tradition). The concepts of justice and rights are therefore the property of the Constitution, and must be interpreted by judges with respect for the contemporary views of these concepts, with respect for the Constitutional text, and the pluralist nature of the State.

Which interpretation later judges would accept, of course depends on their own normative outlook. This debate would have far reaching reverberations in Irish public life, which would only climax in 1992. But now I turn to the second stage of this debate.

3. AND THE DEATH OF PRIVACY?

Dr. (now Senator) David Norris, was a man with a serious problem. A congenital homosexual, he was seriously oppressed by laws penalizing homosexual acts. Sections 61 and 62 of the 1861 Offence Against the Person Act punished sodomy (anal intercourse) and attempts to commit it (whether between a man and a man or between a man and a woman), and section 11 of the 1885 Criminal Law (Amendment) Act punished "gross indecency" between men. The penalty for the latter was a jail sentence of up to two years. Someone convicted of the first could be jailed for any period up to life.

Mr. Norris had not been prosecuted under either section when he sought a declaration in the High Court of their unconstitutionality. However as a congenital homosexual, and gay rights activist, he had suffered psychological trauma, and discrimination. It was impossible for him to develop a homosexual relationship. At one stage his psychiatrist advised him to leave the country. Instead he publicly campaigned for an end to the Victorian era in Ireland.

Norris argued that the laws violated his unenumerated right to individual privacy (*Norris,* [1984] I.R. 36). He called 10 witnesses to show that the effects of such laws on homosexual people were severely negative. The State did not adduce any evidence to show that homosexuality was a threat to society's morals, health or any other significant interest. Nevertheless the State won.

According to M'William J., the role of the court is to determine whether there exist reasonable grounds for the legislature to believe that principles of morality, order and social policy require a particular legislative provision. If such grounds exist, then the legislation is valid (ibid., 46, 48). M'William J. interprets Walsh J, in *M'Gee,* as saying that constitutional morality is associated with the morality of the Irish

Christian churches (ibid., 48). M'William J. says, referring to Christian dogma, that since the function of the sexual organs is reproduction, it is reasonable to believe "that sexuality outside marriage should be condemned, and that sexuality between people of the same sex is wrong" (ibid., 45).

Norris appealed to a Supreme Court composed of O'Higgins C. J., Finlay P., Henchy, Griffin, M'Carthy JJ. The judges gave two different answers to the question left unresolved by Walsh J.'s comments in *M'Gee*. The Chief Justice delivered the majority judgement, with which Finlay P. and Griffin JJ. agreed. The other two saved the pride of Irish jurists.

For O'Higgins C. J., the court's role is not to reform the law, but merely to interpret it "with objectivity and impartiality" (ibid., 53). He notes that the laws concern conduct of a kind usually regarded . . . as abnormal and unnatural" (ibid., 51) and considers the development of the law in the UK. He describes as "understandable" the reluctance of the UK legislature to change the law on a matter involving "deep religious and moral beliefs" (ibid., 61). The Chief Justice emphasizes that organized religions have despised homosexuality as "a perversion of the biological function of the sexual organs and an affront both to society and to God." St. Paul and all Christian churches have condemned it (ibid., 61). O'Higgins C. J. thus endorses the sectarian interpretation of Walsh J. in *M'Gee*.

The Chief Justice, citing a book by a Prof. West, describes a homosexual lifestyle as being "sad, lonely, and harrowing," promiscuous, frustrating, unstable, depressing and leading to a high incidence of suicide attempts (ibid., 62). O'Higgins C. J. did not mention that Prof. West was called as a witness by Mr. Norris, and had said that the *statutes* had these "prejudicial effects" for homosexuals, without achieving any significant social interest (ibid., 74, per Henchy J.). O'Higgins C. J. also said that the book mentions that the effect of decriminalisation was an increase in homosexual behavior and an increase in sexually transmitted diseases (ibid., 62). He did not mention Prof. West's comment on oath, that decriminalisation in England had not led to either result (ibid., 74).

O'Higgins C. J. then considers the effect of decriminalization of homosexual behaviour on marriage. He notes that the 1957 English Wolfenden Committee, which recommended decriminalisation in England and Wales, thought that there might be adverse effects for marriage, as homosexual behavior by the husband might lead to marital breakdown. The report also thought that decriminalisation might discourage moderately inclined homosexual people from marrying. In other words, "homosexual behavior and this encouragement may not be consistent with respect and regard for marriage" and it is reasonable to assume that permitting such behaviour harms marriage (ibid., 63).

O'Higgins C. J. rejects the notion that the right to privacy means that the law has no business interfering with private morality.

> The preamble to the Constitution proudly asserts the existence of God in the Most Holy Trinity and recites that the people of Ireland humbly acknowledge their obligation to "our Divine Lord, Jesus Christ." It cannot be doubted that the people, . . . were proclaiming a deep religious conviction and faith and an intention to adopt a Constitution consistent with . . . Christian beliefs. (*Norris,* [1984] I.R. 36, 64)

O'Higgins rejects as unreasonable the idea, that the people, in 1937 thought they were sweeping away anti-homosexual laws which had enforced Christian morality for centuries. In 1937 such conduct was prohibited in all parts of the United Kingdom and Ireland. So the right to privacy does not set up an area of exclusion. The State has an:

> . . . Interest in the general moral well-being of the community and [is] . . . entitled, where it is practicable to do so, to discourage conduct which is morally wrong and harmful to a way of life and to values which the State wishes to protect. (*Norris,* [1984] I.R. 36, 64)

Thus among the immoral acts which the State can forbid, even when done in private, are abortion, incest, suicide pacts, suicide attempts, mercy killing. These can be prohibited even when no harm is done to anyone else. And in fact, homosexual practices may cause harm, at least to oneself, for they may lead one into a homosexual existence, the horrors of which O'Higgins C. J. believes he has described. And such conduct may lead to an increase in venereal disease, which is a threat to the public health. Also homosexual practices are harmful to marriage, or at least potentially so and marriage is an institution the state is sworn to uphold (Art. 41) (ibid., 65). For these reasons, the State may punish homosexual practices.

Henchy J. dissented. After noting the "Christian" nature of the state, the reference to "prudence, justice and charity," "dignity and freedom of the individual," and "democratic State" in the Preamble and Art. 5, he explains that the "vital human component" in the Constitutional order must be accorded:

> . . . Such a range of personal freedoms or immunities are necessary to ensure his dignity and freedom as an individual in the type of society envisaged. (*Norris,* [1984] I.R. 36, 71)

These rights inhere in the human personality and include a complex of rights which create a zone of privacy:

> A secluded area of activity or non-activity which may be claimed as necessary for the expression of an individual personality, for purposes not always necessarily moral or commendable, but meriting recognition in circumstances which do not engender considerations such as State security, public order or morality, or other essential components of the common good. (*Norris,* [1984] I.R. 36, 72)

As in *M'Gee* the condemnation of the activity by religious groups is constitutionally irrelevant.

The court must decide whether there are reasons of public order and morality which require the intrusion into the zone of privacy with such disastrous effects for the plaintiff. Given that the statute was passed by a Parliament unaware of the Constitution, and that it indiscriminatingly criminalises all homosexual acts between males, there is a heavy onus on the State to justify that intervention into the private zone.

Henchy J. spends five pages examining the testimony of eminent Irish, British and US psychiatrists, sociologists, theologians (ibid., 72–76). The State called no witnesses; it introduced no evidence at all. All of the testimony was to the effect that: Criminalisation severely hurt homosexuals; there was no harm to society by its decriminalisation; decriminalisation would have beneficial effects for homosexuals and society generally. He observes that the case turns on one issue: Are the harmful effects to society of decriminalising homosexual behaviour less significant than the harmful effects to homosexuals of maintaining the Victorian statutes? If the latter harms are demonstrated by evidence to be significant, and the former harms are shown to be negligible, then the decision must be for the plaintiff (ibid., 77). Since "the unrebutted consensus of the evidence was against" any justification of the laws, the judge was bound to give judgement for Norris. He should not substitute his own beliefs on homosexuality to justify such an extreme law (ibid., 77). The trial judge went astray in not relying on the evidence, but on the attitude of the Irish Christian Churches in determining the constitutionality of the law. Acts condemned by religious bodies might undermine the common good, and so merit punishment. However even then the State could not seek to eliminate them by the criminal law.

> To do so would upset the necessary balance which the Constitution posits between the common good and the dignity and freedom of the individual. What is deemed necessary to his dignity and freedom by one man may be abhorred by another as an exercise in immorality. The pluralism necessary for the preservation of constitutional requirements in the Christian democratic State envisaged by the Constitution means that sanctions of the criminal law may be attached to immoral acts only when the common good requires their proscription as a crime. (*Norris,* [1984] I.R. 36, 78)

He notes that decriminalisation is not synonymous with approval of certain acts, but rather indicates that the common good does not require such a severe encroachment into the private sphere. At the very least, the law would have to make an exception for homosexual people.

M'Carthy J. also forcefully dissented. He argues that the courts must use a "present tense" and not a historical approach when interpreting the Constitution:

> . . . The Constitution is a living document, its life depends not merely upon itself but upon the people from whom it came and to whom it gives varying rights and duties. (*Norris,* [1984] I.R. 36, 96)

M'Carthy J. then examines several cases relating to unenumerated rights.[1] He insists that rights are not

---

[1]In *Ryan* ([1965] I.R. 294, right to health), Kenny J. describes unenumerated rights as being justified by the "Christian and democratic nature of the State." In *G. v. An Bord Uchtála* ([1980] I.R. 32, rights of unmarried mothers, and children born outside of marriage), Walsh J. cites approvingly the opinion of Henchy J. in *M'Gee* that unenumerated rights vest in people as a consequence of their human personality. In *State (C.) v. Frawley* ([1976] I.R. 365, the right not to be subject to torture or inhuman and degrading treatment) and *State (M.) v. Attorney General* ([1979] I.R. 73, the right to leave the State), Finlay P. refers to the phrase of Kenny J. in *Ryan* about the Christian ethos of the State.

based on Christianity, though they are related to Christ's "great doctrine of charity" which the Irish Constitution has inherited (ibid., 99). They are rooted in the human personality, and the State must treat them "with due observance of prudence, justice and charity, so that the dignity and freedom of the individual may be assured" (Preamble) (ibid., 100).

The right to privacy was identified by the majority in *M'Gee*. There are many examples of privacy in the Constitution (e.g., secret ballot, property, inviolability of dwelling). These are but aspects of the general right to personal privacy, rooted in Art. 40.3.1 (ibid., 100). In *M'Gee,* the majority upheld the *personal* right of privacy *in marriage,* not simply the right of a married couple to privacy: Their decision was based on Art. 40.3.1 not Art. 41 (Family).

Here that right is infringed by law which says that one man may masturbate in private, a man and a woman may masturbate in private, a woman may masturbate in private, an entire society of women may do so—but two men may not (ibid., 101). Unlike issues of protecting others, or of maintaining military discipline, there is no compelling state interest involved in preventing two consenting men from masturbating in private. The State has not justified "state interference of a most grievous kind (the policeman in the bedroom)" (ibid., 102).

Again in this decision, we find the strong impact of moral reasoning. I start with the Chief Justice. The exact basis of his opinion is unclear. There are several rationales which might justify his decision, but only two of these merit serious attention.

The first argument is a communitarian/historicist one. This would suggest that the Constitution is founded on the community's vision of the good life, which the 1937 generation bequeathed to its successors. To maintain the continuity of that tradition, one must not change the constitutional requirements too much from the values of 1937. If the 1937 community regarded certain activities as so abhorrent that it punished them with life imprisonment, and if, in its communal charter it included references to philosophies which condemned those practices, then judges may not extend the protection of the Constitution to them.

There is a significant flaw with this approach. The majority do not state that *M'Gee* is overruled. *M'Gee* is one of many cases where judges gave the Constitution a "present tense interpretation." It must not be shackled to the consciences of an earlier generation. The 1937 generation accepted laws banning the importation or sale of contraceptives. They accepted that accused persons could be subject to preventive detention,[2] that a special criminal status could be created for homeless persons,[3] and that women could be exempt from jury service.[4] All these provisions had been declared unconstitutional. Such an approach in *Norris* would have required the judges to explain why they were departing from the present tense approach of so many cases.

The more likely argument is a perfectionist one asserting the natural inferiority of homosexuality to heterosexuality. O'Higgins C. J. starts his discussion by referring to homosexual acts as "abnormal and unnatural." He notes that organized Christian religion has condemned homosexual acts consistently through history. He then examines the alleged harms caused by homosexual behaviour. There is no evidence of these harms, and the majority's willingness to accept their reality underscores their attitude to the worth of homosexuals.

O'Higgins C. J. then explains that homosexual acts are not covered by the right to privacy. Why not? First, because the Constitution acknowledges the supremacy of Christian values. Second, the State may protect the "general moral well-being of the community" and punish what is "morally wrong." Thus homosexual acts are the same as other victimless acts such as abortion, incest, suicide, and mercy killing, which the State may punish because they are wrong. Other than the reference to traditional condemnation as a "perversion of the biological functions" and an insult to God and society, O'Higgins C. J. does not give concrete substantiated examples of the harms caused by homosexuality.

The majority says that homosexual acts are to be condemned even if they take place in private, and harm no one. They may be condemned even though that has seriously harmful effects on gay men, without achieving any benefit for society, simply because they are morally wrong. The tenor of O'Higgins' argument is similar to Finnis' natural law approach. Homosexuality, like masturbation, is a form of sexu-

---

[2]Declared unconstitutional in *People v. O'Callaghan* ([1966] I.R. 501).

[3]Declared unconstitutional in *King v. Attorney General* ([1981] I.R. 223).

[4]Declared unconstitutional in *DeBúrca v. Attorney General* ([1976] I.R. 38).

ality which cannot substantiate two basic goods (friendship and procreation). This choice to use oneself for purposes not related to these goods is "disintegrative manipulation" of oneself, and has been condemned by all reasonable societies (Finnis, 1985, 1993). The choice is always wrong regardless of its concrete effects on health or marriage. And the choice to do something immoral can be punished regardless of the absence of a concrete harm to the common good. The majority accepts the sectarian interpretation of Walsh J.'s *M'Gee* decision, and repudiates his comments on pluralism.

The dissenters are loyal to the vision of constitutional morality in *M'Gee*. They insist that the Constitution must be interpreted in the present tense; that respect for individual autonomy precludes invading the bedroom because of a conventional social morality; that the beliefs of no church forms any part of constitutional law. They refer to Christianity only as the historical tradition which bequeathed to modern liberalism certain core values (*Norris,* [1984] I.R. 36, 99).

There are three elements to the dissenting opinions. First, there is the close attention to the concrete facts, which is tied into the second element, the emphasis that the individual counts. The minority say that *the State, through means direct and indirect, has seriously hurt the plaintiff; it must now justify its actions to him.* The focus on the reality of a situation is a key element of post 1970s liberal thought (Dworkin, 1993; Dworkin, 1985, 353–59).

The dissenters believe that the individual, as a "vital human" in a democratic society, must be accorded a zone of non-interference where she can develop. As Rawls puts it: "Each person possesses an *inviolability* founded on justice that even the welfare of society as a whole cannot override" (Rawls 1971, 3. Italics added). The State must not interfere in this zone, even though what takes place within is immoral. To interfere on this ground would violate the pluralism envisaged by the Constitution, endorsed by the Supreme Court in *M'Gee* and *Quinn's Supermarket* ([1972] I.R. 1). The State may only interfere if it can prove that there is a sufficiently weighty requirement of State security, public order or public morality which requires such intervention, and that such weighty requirement counterbalances the serious harm caused to gay men.

The third element is an anti-perfectionist approach (neutrality), rooted in human equality. Each person is an equal; to respect this the State may not regard some conceptions of the good as superior or inferior to others (Dworkin, 1985, 181–213). This is what the dissenters insist, when they deny the people of the State to interfere simply because it objects strongly to the individual's practices within the confines of her constitutionally protected domain. It is also found in earlier decisions of the Supreme Court, most notably in *Quinn's Supermarket,* ([1972] I.R. 1), and *M'Gee* ([1974] I.R. 294). Such is the requirement of pluralism which runs as a "golden thread" through the decisions of Walsh, Henchy and M'Carthy JJ. in the triad of decisions.

The Irish State did eventually end its persecution of homosexuality, but only after the European Court of Human Rights reminded it of its duty (*Norris,* [1991] 13 E.H.R.R. 186; 1993 Criminal Law (Sexual Offences) Act). The 1993 debate on the amendment of the laws included contributions from some conservative groups who explicitly relied on the perfectionist vision proposed by the *Norris* majority in their opposition to the reform. The then Prime Minister argued for reform, insisting, as had Henchy and M'Carthy JJ., that the principle of equality demands respect for the orientation of the gay minority. So the competing visions of the Court found their way into the political dialogue, with the dissenting view (eventually) winning out.

The visionary conflict continued in other areas. *Norris* did not establish a particular vision even in the courts of the 1980s. Three years after *Norris,* the High Court decision of Hamilton P. (now Chief Justice) in *Kennedy v. Ireland,* ([1987] I.R. 587, a telephone tapping case), seemed to resurrect the liberal opinions of the dissenters. Hamilton P. held that the right to privacy was a constitutional right, founded on the duty to assure the dignity and freedom of the individual in a democratic state. Certainly his opinion suggests that the anti-perfectionist liberal vision of *M'Gee* and the *Norris* dissenters is not buried. However he himself gives us ground to think otherwise.

4. LIFE VERSUS PRIVACY

We turn now to the most explosive issue in any discussion of the right of privacy—abortion. The *M'Gee* vision provoked public debate on the right to privacy. Some activists were concerned that some judge, relying on US precedent (*Roe v. Wade,* [1973] 410 US 113), might discover a right to an abortion lying within the right to privacy and invalidate sections 58, 59 of the 1861 Offences Against the Person Act, which prohibit abortion. This fear led to a decisive political debate on the amendment of the Constitution.

At one stage, someone tried to argue that the proposed amendment was invalid. The courts refused to get involved in the debate on the amendment: *Finn* ([1983] I.R. 154). The people may enact any wording as part of the Constitution. The judicial role is limited to elaborating on the effects of past decisions, or proposing new underlying visions to existing rules and principles. Judges do not debate on the formation of the sovereign will itself. (But see O'Hanlon 1992, 1993.)

Following this debate, the people approved the Eighth Amendment of the Constitution in 1983. This inserted Art. 40.3.3 immediately after Art. 40.3.2 (Personal Rights):

> The State acknowledges the right to life of the unborn and, with due regard to the equal right to life of the mother, guarantees in its law to respect, and as far as practicable, by its laws to defend and vindicate the right. (Art. 40.3.3)

In the 12 years which followed Parliament ignored its constitutional duty to legislate on this topic and instead the judges strove to elaborate the meaning of the sub-section in practice.

In 1986, a private organization, the Society for the Protection of the Unborn Child (SPUC), sought to prevent two agencies assisting women who wished to go to England for an abortion (*Att. Gen. (SPUC) v. Open Door,* [1987] I.R. 477). (The English 1967 Abortion Act is more liberal than the Irish Law.)

SPUC sought three remedies: First, a declaration that the activities of the defendants were unlawful in view of Art. 40.3.3; second, a declaration that the defendants were engaged in a conspiracy to corrupt public morals; third, an injunction prohibiting the defendants from assisting pregnant women to obtain an abortion.[5]

The case went before Hamilton P. He notes that the right to life of the unborn is one of the rights of the natural law. The Constitution does not create the right; it recognizes it and guarantees to protect it (ibid., 481). The courts must protect it, whether the threat comes from the state or private individuals (ibid., 483). Courts can protect such rights even if the legislature had not given them a statutory form (ibid., 488–89; *State (Quinn) v. Ryan,* [1965] I.R. 70). Should no procedure exist to protect adequately a right, then the courts will create one (*Open Door,* [1987] I.R. 477, 489). Although the courts may go to great lengths to protect rights, Hamilton P. decided not to create what might amount to a new crime, that of assisting someone to commit an abortion abroad.

Hamilton P. considered a "crime" allegedly existing at common law, the unwritten law laid down by Superior Courts as binding: conspiracy to corrupt public morals (a conspiracy is a simple agreement by two or more people to do something; one may be guilty of conspiracy even if one has done nothing). In fact this "crime" was invented by the English House of Lords in the 1960s in *Shaw v. DPP,* ([1962] Appeal Cases 220). Further, the House of Lords held that people may be convicted of conspiracy to corrupt public morals, *even where the conduct they were promoting was not itself a crime* (*Knuller,* [1973] A.C. 446).

Hamilton P. accepted that conspiracy to corrupt public morals was a crime in Irish law (*Open Door,* [1987] I.R. 477, 494). Furthermore, it was not necessary that the conduct promoted itself be criminal (ibid., 495). However, he refused to grant a declaration saying that the defendants were guilty of the crime. That would usurp the function of a criminal court sitting with a jury (ibid., 497).

Hamilton P. then considered whether the plaintiff was entitled to a declaration that the activities were unlawful, as a violation of the right to life. He observes that the defendant agencies are assisting women in obtaining an abortion in England (ibid., 499). Abortion is a violation of a right, and it is not rendered constitutional by committing it abroad (ibid., 493). Every citizen must obey the law and not interfere with constitutional rights (ibid., 496). The right to life must be protected, and no other lesser right (to privacy, to expression or to information) may interfere with it (ibid., 500). He granted an injunction, prohibiting the defendants from assisting women to obtain an abortion. There was an unsuccessful appeal to the Supreme Court (*Open Door,* [1988] I.L.R.M. 18, 27).

There are two issues in the decision of Hamilton P.: the recognition of the crime of conspiracy to corrupt public morals, and the use of an injunction to restrain the provision of information relating to abortion. I treat here only of the first.

---

[5] An injunction is a court order backed up with the threat of summary punishment in the event of non-compliance.

When discussing *Norris,* I argued that the dissenters were moved by a belief that the individual is important, and that there is a heavy onus on the State to justify its interventions into her zone of autonomy. In *Kennedy,* Hamilton P. apparently accepted this. Yet when importing a crime of conspiracy he attaches no weight to the rights of privacy or expression. Consider this novel crime. In this case, Hamilton P. suggests that it strikes into a private conversation between a pregnant woman and her counsellor concerning a most intimate matter. The justification for this intrusion is that they may be discussing the promotion of immorality. The crime is not limited to conspiracy to attack fundamental rights. It is not limited to conspiracy to do something unlawful. It is not limited to conspiracy to do something immoral. It applies to conspiracies to *promote* immorality. This is a blunt rejection of the proposition in *M'Gee* ([1974] I.R. 284) and the dissent in *Norris* ([1984] I.R. 36), that something may not be condemned as illegal simply because it is perceived as immoral. It might be legitimate for Parliament to punish conspiracy to attack fundamental rights, or to do something unlawful. But if Hamilton P. is saying that one can punish conspiracy to do or promote something immoral, he is saying that *M'Gee* should be overruled. For in *M'Gee,* the court said that Parliament could not criminalise the intention of Mrs. M'Gee and her husband to do something perhaps immoral. Indeed *M'Gee* goes further: Parliament could not, even by indirect means, punish the effectuation of the intention. This new crime is far more extensive in scope than the law in *M'Gee:* It covers the joint intention to advocate something, not only the doing of something.

Furthermore the invasion of the private sphere is done in a very vague manner. It is unconstitutional for any crime to be so vague that someone does not know whether she is within its terms or not (*King,* [1981] I.R. 223). This applies with even greater force when the activity punished may well be the exercise of a right (*King*). The phrase "conspiracy to corrupt public morals" gives no indication as to what sort of conduct or expression is covered. It thus violates the proscription of vague criminal laws. Suppose that two people admit in public that they are homosexual lovers. Is this conspiracy to corrupt public morals? Suppose that two men hold hands in public. Is this conspiracy to corrupt public morals? There is no precision as to whether this offence, never considered by an Irish legislature or executive, or judge prior to this case, may strike in the zone of privacy upheld in *M'Gee* and *Kennedy,* ([1987] I.R. 587). It is an arbitrary criminalisation of potentially large areas of expression and private conduct. The recognition of this crime is support for the perfectionist element of *Norris,* ([1984] I.R. 36).

In other cases in the 1980s, the courts confirmed these rules: No one is allowed to give information which will assist a woman to obtain an abortion abroad. This applies at least to counselling groups, and student unions (*Coogan,* [1989] I.R. 734: *Grogan,* [1989] I.R. 753). The right to life cannot be defeated by any lesser right, such as privacy, or expression. However debate on the merits of abortion was permitted. And, apparently, travel abroad was also permitted.

So by 1990 it appears that the judges had put a particular interpretation on the Constitution—one which subordinated the rights to privacy and expression to one particular right. Furthermore the solution was socially acceptable in that it simultaneously expressed public disapproval of abortion, while allowing women (those who could afford it) to have abortions in England.

5. LIFE VERSUS LIFE

This is not the conclusion of the story. In a case combining a tragic personal situation, and abstract Constitutional principles, a different evaluation emerges. In *Attorney General v. X,* ([1992] 1 I.R. 1) the Government's legal adviser sought an injunction restraining a fourteen year old rape victim from leaving the State to have an abortion. The girl was inclined towards suicide due to the pressures of the pregnancy.

Costello J. in the High Court, granted the injunction. He reiterated that constitutional rights are judicially enforceable even if not regulated by statute (ibid., 10). He held that the threat to the life of the foetus was more serious than the threat to the life of the girl, which was declared by Art. 40.3.3 to be equal to the life of the foetus. There was evidence that the girl would commit suicide if the abortion did not take place. Costello J. considered that this threat was different from the threat to the life of the foetus: If an abortion took place, the foetus would certainly die, whereas if it did not, it was not certain the young girl would kill herself (ibid., 12).

Costello J. rejected an argument rooted in the Constitutional right against preventive detention (*People v. O'Callaghan,* [1966] I.R. 510). He also rejected a challenge based on the EC right to travel abroad to receive services (*Luisi and Carbone,* [1984] 1 E.C.R. 377, case 286/82), arguing that the injunction was justified by a public policy exception to that right, which he derived from an analogy with the case of free movement of workers (*R. v. Bouchereau,* [1977] 2 E.C.R. 1999, case 30/77). The judge also considers that such an injunction would be a proportional limit on rights under the European Convention on Human Rights.

The High Court prohibited the girl or her family from arranging an abortion, and prohibited the girl from leaving the state for nine months. Costello J. provided a reasoned explanation of what the constitutional principles required in the case. In affirming those principles, he also laid down a challenge to those who stood by them.

Seven days later, the Supreme Court heard an appeal. After two days, amidst the largest amount of publicity ever to attach to any case, the Court granted the appeal. A week later the judges explained why.

Finlay C. J. spoke first. He reviews the facts, and refers to the judicial duty to protect fundamental rights even in the absence of legislation (*Att. Gen. v. X,* [1992) 1 I.R. 1, 50–51). He refers to the statements of Walsh J. in *M'Gee,* about the superiority of justice, to the remarks of O'Higgins C. J. in *State (Healy) v. O'Donoghue,* ([1976] I.R. 325) on the duty to judge according to developing notions of prudence, justice, and charity (*Att. Gen. v. X,* [1992] 1 I.R. 1, 52–53). He emphasises that judges must construe the constitution harmoniously. He says that the appropriate test to apply in this case was:

> . . . If it is established as a matter of probability that there is a real and substantial risk to the life, as distinct from the health, of the mother, which can only be avoided by the termination of her pregnancy, such termination is permissible, . . . (*Att. Gen v. X,* [1992], 1 I.R. 1, 54)

In this case, the young girl was suicidal. Since suicide is something which it is not possible to guard against, this constitutes such a real and substantial risk, and the girl was entitled to an abortion, and to leave the State to obtain one. Egan and O'Flaherty JJ. concur with most of the Chief Justice's reasoning on the right to life.

Finlay C. J. then considers the unenumerated right to travel abroad. He observes that, if the protection of fundamental rights cannot be reconciled one with the other, then the courts must protect the most important right (ibid., 57). The right to life clearly prevails over the right to travel abroad, and the courts may suspend the right to travel abroad, to protect the right to life. Egan J. agrees (ambiguously) with Finlay C. J. on this issue (ibid., 92).

M'Carthy J. also granted the appeal. He dislikes the notion of a hierarchy of rights (ibid., 78). Even the right to life is not absolute: The Constitution apparently allows the death penalty. He rejects a hierarchical approach: The real question is how to defend and vindicate the two rights as far as practicable (Art. 40.3.3 only imposes the duty to defend and vindicate rights as far as practicable). In his opinion, where there is a real and substantial risk to the life of the mother, then defending the right of the unborn may not be practicable (ibid., 80).

M'Carthy J. then considers the right to travel. He rejects the balancing exercise. One does not balance rights but ascertains whether citizens have them or not. If they do, then they may exercise them, regardless of their purpose (ibid., 38). The mere fact that someone intended to do something when abroad (even murder) cannot be invoked to curtail the right to travel. So only M'Carthy J. defends the position of Henchy J. in *Norris,* that persons may exercise rights even though for an immoral purpose.

Hederman J. delivered a thoughtful, indeed forceful dissent. He emphasises that the State has a far-ranging duty to protect life "which is the essential value of every legal order and essential to the enjoyment of all other rights." This duty includes positive duties: For instance, the right to life may be invoked to require the State to deal with life-threatening pollution. Indeed, Hederman J. says that not only may all persons invoke the right to life, but further, people may invoke it on others' behalf (ibid., 71).

Art. 40.3.3 of the Constitution makes it clear that the foetus is entitled to live. Hederman J. allows one exception—an operation, "the sole purpose of which is to save the life of the mother" cannot be considered "a direct killing of the foetus" even if the inevitable consequence of the operation is the death of the foetus (ibid.,

72). However the mother may not invoke her right to privacy in abortion cases, for "the unborn life is an autonomous human being protected by the Constitution" (ibid., 72). The right to self-determination does not include the right to end life.

In this case, the State's duties extend to restricting the right to travel of the young girl. Such a restriction, though offensive to the Constitution, is not so offensive as the "irrevocable step of the destruction of life" (ibid., 73). Before an abortion may be permitted to save the life of a pregnant woman, it must be shown, by weighty, cogent evidence, that it is the only way to save her life. In this case the threat to the girl's life is the threat of suicide. The appropriate response is to put the girl under supervision. It is not acceptable to destroy one human life to dissuade someone else from taking a life, even her own (ibid., 76).

This case carries forward themes from earlier cases. I draw your attention to the dissent of Hederman J., with its emphasis on the value of life as overriding other concerns, and the overall role of perfectionist–sectarian reasoning in the opinions.

Hederman J.'s dissenting opinion is interesting for its reliance on what appears to be some form of secularized Catholic beliefs, rather similar to the approach promoted by Finnis (1980). He describes life as first and foremost a value to which the Constitution is dedicated. This recalls Finnis' theory which is a value not a rights based theory. For Finnis (and apparently Hederman J.) rights and duties flow from the supreme values. Secondly, Hederman J. is clearly of the opinion that one has a duty never to act against a basic value. Third, Hederman J., like Finnis, relies on the Catholic doctrine of "double effect" to describe some actions which result in the death of the foetus as not being an abortion even though the death is the natural and probable consequence. And, of course, like Finnis, he believes that the foetus is entitled to the protection of the right to life. In drawing these comparisons, I do not suggest that Hederman J.'s library includes the collected works of the Oxford scholar. Rather I note that he relies on certain contested moral theories, which happen to have been expressed by Finnis. In considering the acceptability of Hederman's opinion, we are surely allowed to consider the debate surrounding the most sophisticated defender of that view.

The second point is the more important. In *Norris,* there were strong suggestions of a perfectionist, even sectarian, underpinning to the reasoning of the judges. *Open Door* seemed to confirm that vision (even though *Kennedy* disputed it). The most striking feature of the *X* case, is that the reasoning of the judges is secular; even Hederman J. does not rely on religious arguments to bolster his dissent. Furthermore, the majority judges do not seem to rely on any perfectionist theory (or at least not any perfectionist theory with a strong concept of the good). They rely on a discussion of the rights involved. No one suggests that abortion may be prohibited because it is immoral or unpopular, or violates God's law. Rather it is prohibited because it violates the right to life of the unborn. Indeed the majority upheld a *right* to an abortion, that is a right to do something perceived as immoral. Again, the argument of some of the judges that the right to life could be limited to protect the right to life, is not one which relies on any perfectionist theory. Clearly the type of reasoning found in *Norris* is no longer acceptable (for the moment).[6]

The Supreme Court provided a controversial concretisation of the moral legal principles of Irish abortion law. They did not simply say (as many would have said) that the girl was free to go, even though abortion is a violation of a human right. Nor did they say, as Finnis and the Catholic church, that the termination of a pregnancy to save the life of the girl, is not an abortion. Either view would have played mere lip service to the constitutional doctrine of a hierarchy of rights, the constitutional right of the foetus, and the constitutional supremacy of life.

The decision posed many questions which Parliament tried to avoid answering by proposing referenda to the People. Although some people demanded the abolition of any right to abortion, the Government proposed three amendments to the people. These amendments provided that Art. 40.3.3 did not limit either the right to travel or the right to receive information about services lawfully available abroad, and provided that an abortion was not justified to prevent a suicide. If all these had been accepted, it would

[6]This is confirmed by *F. v. F.,* ([1994] 2 I.L.R.M. 401), where the High Court refused to hear evidence from moral theologians, insisting that it is for judges, not religious experts to determine the meaning of the Constitution, in the light of evolving values. The judge thus dismisses the degree of importance attached to beliefs claiming a religious provenance, in *Norris,* ([1984] I.R. 36). Indeed he describes Walsh J.'s opinion in *M'Gee,* ([1974] I.R. 284), as decisively rejecting any influence by theology or religion or constitutional development.

mean that a judge in an *X* type case would have to say to a suicidal woman—"you have no right to an abortion—but you may go to have one anyway." This solution the people rejected; rather they voted in favour of the first two proposals, and against the third. The right to abortion in limited cases remains, but now judges and legislators must reconsider the abortion rules developed in *Open Door.*[7] So the dialogue originating in *M'Gee* continues.

6. CONCLUSION

I have now presented some key cases of Irish constitutional law, where law interacts with morality. What is the moral of the story?

The first thing to note is that the cases form, not merely a narrative but a debate. In *M'Gee,* ([1974] I.R. 284) the majority judges of the Supreme Court upheld the claim to an unenumerated right to privacy, on the basis of a moral approach which stressed the autonomy of the individual. The majority rejected the notion that the conventional morality of society (of 1937 or 1973) could define the limits of individual freedom, at least in certain important areas of human life.

However, we then came to *Norris,* ([1984] I.R. 36) where the opposite occurs. A three judge majority rely on a perfectionist theory of morality, to limit the right to sexual freedom of gay men and others wishing to have anal intercourse. This despite the serious damage inflicted on those who were affected, despite the failure of the State to adduce any evidence that such stern prohibitions were necessary.

One should not conclude that this perfectionist approach swept all before it. In *Kennedy,* ([1987] I.R. 587) Hamilton P. relied on the moral vision presented by the dissenters in *Norris,* to condemn a violation by the State of individual privacy. But then in *Open Door,* ([1987] I.R.477), he goes to the opposite extreme. Without any discussion of its roots in Irish law, he imports the "crime" of conspiracy to corrupt public morals. This "crime" is entirely contrary to the spirit of a legal system which respects the right to privacy. Like the *Norris* majority, it surrenders individual autonomy to the whim of conventional morality.

The decision in the *X* case, ([1992] 1 I.R. 1) suggests a different solution to the debate. The majority judgements of the Supreme Court make it clear that it is the nature of rights, and their relationship with the constitutional text, and not conventional (or religious) morality, which is determinative. The Supreme Court recognized a limited right to an abortion, not conceded by conventional morality. The perfectionist reasoning of *Norris* is nowhere to be found.

However the debate is not just a legal one between judges. It is also a public one, to which the judiciary contribute. The right to privacy protected the decision to use contraceptives. At the time there was a serious public debate, with many people demanding the decriminalisation of the sale and importation of contraception. Parliament declined to deal with the issue. It was left to the Court to decide, and establish the State's commitment to pluralism and autonomy.

However that decision, and its reasoning, led some people to launch a public campaign to give constitutional protection to the foetus. This issue was publicly debated, and the sovereign people made known its decision in 1983. (As noted above the courts declined to review the legality of a procedurally correct amendment proposal: *Finn,* [1983] I.R. 154; *Abortion Information,* [1995] 2 I.L.R.M. 81.) Normally one would expect the public debate to continue, with Parliament fleshing out the guidelines left vague by the new amendment. However Parliament did nothing.

Instead the issue was thrown back to the courts, to resolve weighty public problems in the context of specific cases. The courts produced some answers, which Parliament left undisturbed. The general acceptance of society was ruptured when Costello J. produced a thoroughly reasoned decision, which demonstrated how the principles perceived to be underpinning the abortion laws led to a result no one wanted—the confinement of a 14 year old rape victim in the State. The general acceptance was shattered this time—with public demands that the girl be let free. The Supreme Court perceived the principles to be applied differently from Costello J. Unlike many members of the public, the judges did not advocate a thoroughly hypocritical solution. Constrained by notions of legal consistency, the judges ended the injunction, and explained that the

[7] The Supreme Court rejected the opportunity to do so in *Att. Gen. (SPUC) v. Open Door,* ([1994] I.L.R.M. 256), for procedural reasons. In 1995 Parliament finally enacted the Regulation of Information Act, which the Supreme Court upheld as valid: *Abortion Information,* ([1995] 2 I.L.R.M. 81) in a decision much criticized by conservative interest groups.

wording of the people's amendment created a right (albeit in limited circumstances) to an abortion. They thus provided a consistent elaboration of the public rules.

The debate did not thereby terminate. As explained above, the elaboration provided by the Court led to a major debate on the amendment of the Constitution, during which the people rejected one change to the solution in *X*, but accepted two changes to the Constitution, which overruled *Open Door*. In 1995 Parliament enacted the Regulation of Information Act to implement the amendments. In a key decision the Supreme Court upheld its validity, giving it a reading favourable to the free flow of information (*Abortion Information,* [1995] 2 I.L.R.M. 81).

The contributions of the judiciary seem to be of two types: the visionary and the elaboratory. In some decisions, judges consider the specific rules available to them, and the principles which underpin them, and try to elaborate the requirements and impact of these in a concrete case. Thus they provide an example of what the political decisions of the people lead to. For instance, in *Open Door*, the courts say in effect: "If you believe in the right to life of the foetus, you are committed to restricting the rights of women." Costello's judgement in *X,* ([1992] 1 I.R. 1), is a particularly good instance. If you accept that there is a hierarchy of rights topped by life (*Shaw,* [1982] I.R. 1), that the foetus has the right to live equal to the rights of others (Art. 40.3.3), and that courts may do anything to protect the hierarchically superior right (ibid.), then you must accept Costello's application in the concrete case.

Yet other decisions involve visionary debates: What view of political morality should inspire our interpretations of the Constitution? In *M'Gee* a strongly liberal theory was defended, which also found expression in the dissenting opinions in *Norris*. Yet *Norris* and *Open Door* offer a more perfectionist vision. Although *X* does not revert to the liberal vision of an earlier age, it also does not embrace the perfectionism of *Norris*. Regarding the issue in *Norris,* the dissenters' vision won out in the political debate.

So our judges both implement and suggest. They solve present problems with reasoning rooted in the past, but with an eye to the future (Dworkin 1986, 225, ch.11).

However we must sometimes reconstruct the reasoning of the judges, where they do not make it transparent or fully coherent. When we do reconstruct that reasoning, we better understand the vision and its implications for concrete cases. And such reconstruction forces us to pose other questions not adequately treated of in the judges' reasoning. For instance, most people agree that it makes an important difference whether the right to life is considered to be rooted in a value, or a right properly so-called (Dworkin 1993, 11–13). Yet the judges in the abortion cases do not seem to be entirely aware of the need to answer this question.

The notion of moralized constitutionalism as a legal debate and a contribution to a public debate on political morality, is the central point of this article. However there are other questions to note. Clearly the majority judges in *Norris* and *M'Gee* relied on very different notions of political morality in reaching their decisions. The judges in *M'Gee* paid great respect to the principles of autonomy and pluralism; those in the later case, to more perfectionist notions.

This poses a question to those who argue for a moralized conception of law. Exactly what criteria are to be used to decide which vision of political morality is to guide interpretation? Should judges decide in a practical discourse what is the most appropriate morality, and then present it to the rest of us? Or should they opt for the theory closest to the wording and tenor of the text? Or should they defer to the perceived conventional morality of the society? How would such philosophers have advised the judges in *Norris* who had to decide between those provisions of the Constitution which emphasize the "dignity and freedom of the individual" and those sections which emphasize the supremacy of God?

A final point to note is that the Irish example demonstrates that judicial activism and judicial moralization of the law cut both ways. One may not simply applaud moralization when liberals carry the day *(M'Gee)* and complain when conservatives do *(Norris)*. A more nuanced theory which specifies the criteria for judging the acceptability of either vision is needed. On the issue of activism, do defenders of activism wish to stand over *Open Door;* do defenders of deference to legislative judgement wish to praise *Norris?* Where does this issue even fit in when Parliament simply ignores a problem *(Open Door, X)?*

With this article I have tried to give a vivid picture of how law develops in a system accepting a moralized conception of law. The reader may be amused, horrified, or impressed. But the question of law and morality is, for Irish lawyers at least, no academic distraction, but a practical reality. The final word I leave to Hamilton C. J. in the recent *Abortion Information* case, of which regrettably considerations of space and time preclude a full consideration. Although denying that there was a "natural law" superior to the Constitution, the Chief Justice continued:

> . . . The courts . . . in determining . . . the rights which are *superior to positive law or which are imprescriptible or inalienable* . . . must interpret them in accordance with *their ideas of prudence, justice and charity*." (*Abortion Information*, [1995] 2 I.L.R.M. 81, 107, italics added)

REFERENCES

Chubb, Basil. 1991. *The Politics of the Irish Constitution*. Dublin: Institute of Public Administration.

Costello, Declan. 1956. The Natural Law and the Constitution. *Studies* 45:403.

———.1962. Book Review. *Studies* 51:201.

Dworkin, Ronald. 1985. *A Matter of Principle*. Cambridge: Harvard University Press.

———.1986. *Law's Empire*. London: Fontana.

———.1993. *Life's Dominion*. London: Harper and Collins.

Finnis, John. 1980. *Natural Law and Natural Rights*. Oxford: Oxford University Press.

———.1985. Personal Integrity, Sexual Morality and Responsible Parenthood. *Anthropos* 1:43.

———.1993. Is Homosexual Conduct Wrong? Disintegrity. *The New Republic,* 15th November.

Kelly, John. 1967. *Fundamental Rights in the Irish Law and Constitution*. Dublin: Figgis.

Kelly, John, Gerald Hogan and Gerry Whyte. 1994. *The Irish Constitution*. Dublin: Jurist.

O'Hanlon, Roderick. 1992. Natural Rights and the Irish Constitution. *Irish Law Times* 8.

———. 1993. The Judiciary and the Moral Law. *I.L.T.* 129.

Rawls, John. 1971. *A Theory of Justice*. Oxford: Oxford University Press.

Walsh, Brian. 1987a. The Constitution and Constitutional Rights. In *The Constitution of Ireland*. Ed. Litton. Dublin: Institute of Public Administration.

———.1987b. The Constitution: A View from the Bench. In *DeValera's Constitution and Ours*. Ed. Farrell. Dublin: Gill and MacMillan.

58

CHARLES R. LAWRENCE III

If He Hollers Let Him Go: Regulating Racist Speech on Campus

Racist incidents occur at the University of Michigan, University of Massachusetts-Amherst, University of Wisconsin, University of New Mexico, Columbia University, Wellesley College, Duke University, and University of California-Los Angeles.

—MS. MAGAZINE, OCTOBER 1987

The campus ought to be the last place to legislate tampering with the edges of first amendment protections.

University of Michigan:
"Greek Rites of Exclusion": Racist leaflets distributed in dorms; white students paint themselves black and place rings in their noses at "jungle parties."

—THE NATION, JULY 1987

Silencing a few creeps is no victory if the price is an abrogation of free speech. Remember censorship is an ugly word too.

Northwest Missouri State University:
White Supremacists distribute flyers stating: "The Knights of the Ku Klux Klan are Watching You."

—KLANWATCH INTELLIGENCE REPORT NO. 42, FEBRUARY 1988 [KLANWATCH]

Kansas University:
KKK members speak.

—KLANWATCH

Temple University:
White Student Union formed.

—KLANWATCH

Stanford University:
Aryan Resistance literature distributed.

—KLANWATCH

The title of this chapter was inspired by the novel of Chester Himes, *If He Hollers Let Him Go* (1945).

Stockton State College (New Jersey):
Invisible Empire literature distributed.

—KLANWATCH

Memphis State University:
Bomb threats at Jewish Student Union.

—KLANWATCH

Arizona State University:
Shot fired at Hillel Foundation building.

—KLANWATCH

The harm that censors allege will result unless speech is forbidden rarely occurs.

Dartmouth College:
Black professor called "a cross between a welfare queen and a bathroom attendant" and the *Dartmouth Review* purported to quote a Black student, "Dese boys be sayin' that we be comin' here to Dartmut an' not takin' the classics."

—THE NATION, FEBRUARY 27, 1989)

Yes, speech is sometimes painful. Sometimes it is abusive. That is one of the prices of a free society.

Purdue University:
Counselor finds "Death Nigger" scratched on her door.

—THE NATION, FEBRUARY 27, 1989

More speech, not less, is the proper cure for offensive speech.

Smith College:
African student finds message slipped under door that reads, "African Nigger do you want some bananas? Go back to the Jungle."

—NEW YORK TIMES, OCTOBER 19, 1988

Speech cannot be banned simply because it is offensive.

University of Michigan:
Campus radio station broadcasts a call from a student who "joked": "Who are the most famous black women in history? Aunt Jemima and Mother Fucker."

—THE NATION, FEBRUARY 27, 1989

Those who don't like what they are hearing or seeing should try to change the atmosphere through education. That is what they will have to do in the real world after they graduate.

University of Michigan:
A student walks into class and sees this written on the blackboard: "A mind is a terrible thing to waste—especially on a nigger."

—CHICAGO TRIBUNE, APRIL 23, 1989

People of color, women, and gays and lesbians owe their vibrant political movements in large measure to their freedom to communicate. If speech can be banned because it offends someone, how long will it be before the messages of these groups are themselves found offensive?

Stanford University:
"President Donald Kennedy refused yesterday to consider amnesty for students who took over his office last week. . . . Kennedy insisted that the probe of violations of the Stanford code go forward. The students [who were demanding more minority faculty and ethnic studies reforms] consider the prospect of disciplinary action unfair in view of Stanford's decision earlier this year not to punish two white students who defaced a poster of 19th century composer Ludwig von Beethoven to portray a stereotypical black face, then tacked it up in a predominantly black dormitory. The two incidents differ sharply, Kennedy said. The poster was admittedly racially offensive. But its defacement probably was protected by constitutional freedoms. However, the office takeover was clearly a violation of Stanford's policy against campus disruption."

—SAN FRANCISCO CHRONICLE, MAY 25, 1989

Now it's the left that is trying to restrict free speech. Though the political labels have shifted, the rationale is the same: Our adversaries are dangerous and therefore should not be allowed to speak.

In recent years, university campuses have seen a resurgence of racial violence and a corresponding rise in the incidence of verbal and symbolic assault and harassment to which blacks and other traditionally subjugated groups are subjected. The events listed above were gathered from newspaper and magazine reports of racist incidents on campuses. The accompanying italicized statements criticizing proposals to regulate racism on campus were garnered from conversations, debates, and panel discussions at which I was present. Some were recorded verbatim and are exact quotes; others paraphrase the sentiment expressed. I have heard some version of each of these arguments many times over. These incidents are but a small sampling of the hate speech to which minorities are subjected on a daily basis on our nation's college campuses. There is a heated debate in the civil liberties community concerning the proper response to incidents of racist speech on campus. Strong disagreements have arisen between those individuals who believe that racist speech such as that described above should be regulated by the university or some public body and those individuals who believe that racist expression should be protected from all public regulation. At the center of the controversy is a tension between the constitutional values of free speech and equality. Like the debate over affirmative action in university admissions, this issue has divided old allies and revealed unrecognized or unacknowledged differences in the experience, perceptions, and values of members of long-standing allies. It also has caused considerable soul searching by individuals with longtime commitments to both the cause of political expression and the cause of racial equality.

I write this chapter from within the cauldron of this controversy. I make no pretense of dispassion or objectivity, but I do claim a deep commitment to the values that motivate both sides of the debate. I have spent the better part of my life as a dissenter. As a high school student I was threatened with suspension for my refusal to participate in a civil defense drill, and I have been a conspicuous consumer of my first amendment liberties ever since. I also have experienced the injury of historical, ubiquitous, and continuous defamation of American racism. I grew up with Little Black Sambo and Amos and Andy, and I continue to receive racist tracts in the mail and shoved under my door. As I struggle with the tension between these constitutional values, I particularly appreciate the experience of both belonging and not belonging that gives to African Americans and other outsider groups a sense of duality. W. E. B. DuBois—scholar and founder of the National Association for the Advancement of Colored People (NAACP)—called the gift and burden inherent in the dual, conflicting heritage of all African Americans their "second-sight."

The double consciousness of groups outside the ethnic mainstream is particularly apparent in the context of this controversy. Blacks know and value the protection the first amendment affords those of us who must rely upon our voices to petition both government and our neighbors for redress of grievances. Our political tradition has looked to "the word," to the moral power of ideas, to change the system when neither the power of the vote nor that of the gun were available. This part of us has known the experience of belonging and recognizes our common and inseparable interest in preserving the right of free speech for all. But we also know the experience of the outsider. The framers excluded us from the protection of the first amendment. The same Constitution that established rights for others endorsed a story that proclaimed our inferiority. It is a story that remains deeply ingrained in the American psyche. We see a different world than that seen by Americans who do not share this historical experience. We often hear racist speech when our white neighbors are not aware of its presence.

It is not my purpose to belittle or trivialize the importance of defending unpopular speech against the tyranny of the majority. There are very strong reasons for protecting even racist speech. Perhaps the most important reasons are that it reinforces our society's commitment to the value of tolerance, and that by shielding racist speech from government regulation, we are forced to combat it as a community. These reasons for protecting racist speech should not be set aside hastily, and I will not argue that we should be less vigilant in protecting the speech and associational rights of speakers with whom most of us would disagree.

But I am deeply concerned about the role that many civil libertarians have played, or the roles we have failed to play, in the continuing, real-life struggle through which we define the community in which we live. I fear that by framing the debate as we have—as one in which the liberty of free speech is in conflict with the elimination of racism—we have advanced the cause of racial oppression and placed the bigot on the moral high ground, fanning the rising flames of racism. Above all, I am troubled that we have not listened to the real victims, that we have shown so little empathy or understanding for their injury, and that we have abandoned those individuals whose race, gender, or sexual orientation provokes others to regard them as second-class citizens. These individuals' civil liberties are more directly at stake in the debate. In this chapter I focus on racism. Although I will not address violent pornography and homophobic hate speech directly, I will draw on the experience of women and gays as victims of hate speech where they operate as instructive analogues.

I have set two goals in constructing this chapter. The first goal is limited and perhaps overly modest, but it is nonetheless extremely important: I will demonstrate that much of the argument for protecting racist speech is based on the distinction that many civil libertarians draw between direct, face-to-face racial insults, which they think deserve first amendment protection, and all other fighting words, which they find unprotected by the first amendment. I argue that the distinction is false, that it advances none of the purposes of the first amendment, and that the time has come to put an end to the ringing rhetoric that condemns all efforts to regulate racist speech, even narrowly drafted provisions aimed at racist speech that results in direct, immediate, and substantial injury.

I also urge the regulation of racial epithets and vilification that do not involve face-to-face encounters—situations in which the victim is part of a captive audience and the injury is experienced by all members of a racial group who are forced to hear or see these words. In such cases, the insulting words are aimed at an entire group with the effect of causing significant harm to individual group members.

My second goal is more ambitious and more indeterminate. I propose several ways in which the traditional civil liberties position on free speech does not take into account important values expressed elsewhere in the Constitution. Further, I argue that even those values the first amendment itself is intended to promote are frustrated by an interpretation that is acontextual and idealized, by presupposing a world characterized by equal opportunity and the absence of societally created and culturally ingrained racism.

This chapter is divided into four parts: The first part explores whether our Constitution already commits us to some regulation of racist speech. I argue that it does; that this is the meaning of *Brown v. Board of Education*. For the time being, I would ask only that the reader be open to considering this interpretation of *Brown*. This interpretation is useful even for those who believe the censorship of any expression cannot ultimately be condoned: *Brown* can help us better understand the injury of racist speech, an understanding that is vital to our discussion.

I also consider the implications of the state action doctrine in understanding *Brown* and argue that the public/private ideology promoted by that doctrine plays a critical role in advancing racism and clouding our vision of the appropriate role for the community in disestablishing systematic, societal group defamation.

The second part considers the debate over regulation of racial harassment on campus. I argue that carefully drafted regulations can and should be sustained without significant departures from existing first amendment doctrine. The regulation of racist fighting words should not be treated differently from the regulation of garden-variety fighting words, and captive audiences deserve no less protection when they are held captive by racist speakers. I also suggest that rules requiring civility and respect in academic discourse encourage rather than discourage the fullest exchange of ideas. Regulation that require minimal civility of discourse in certain designated forums are not incursions on intellectual and political debate.

The third part explores the nature of the injury inflicted by racist hate speech and examines the unstated assumptions that lie at the core of first amendment theory. In this part, I urge reconsideration of the history of racism in the United States; the ubiquity and continued vitality of culturally engendered conscious and unconscious beliefs about the inferiority of non-whites, and the effect of inequities of power on the marketplace of ideas.

In the last part, I argue that civil libertarians must examine not just the substance of our position on racist speech but also the ways in which we enter the debate. The way the debate has been framed makes heroes out of bigots and fans the flames of racial violence. I also consider the reasons for some civil libertarians' resistance to even minimal and narrowly drafted regulations of racist harassment.

BROWN V. BOARD OF EDUCATION: A CASE ABOUT REGULATING RACIST SPEECH

The landmark case of *Brown v. Board of Education* is not one we normally think of as concerning speech. As read most narrowly, the case is about the rights of Black children to equal educational opportunity. But *Brown* can also be read more broadly to articulate a principle central to any substantive understanding of the equal protection clause, the foundation on which all anti-discrimination law rests. This is the principle of equal citizenship. Under that principle, "Every individual is presumptively entitled to be treated by the organized society as a respected, responsible, and participating member." The principle further requires the affirmative disestablishment of societal practices that treat people as members of an inferior or dependent caste, as unworthy to participate in the larger community. The holding in *Brown*—that racially segregated schools violate the equal protection clause—reflects the fact that segregation amounts to a demeaning, case-creating practice. The prevention of stigma was at the core of the Supreme Court's unanimous decision in *Brown* that segregated public schools are inherently unequal. Observing that the segregation of Black pupils "generates a feeling of inferiority as to their status in the community," Chief Justice Earl Warren recognized what a majority of the Court had ignored almost sixty years earlier in *Plessy v. Ferguson.* The social meaning of racial segregation in the United States is the designation of a superior and an inferior caste, and segregation proceeds "on the ground that colored citizens are . . . inferior and degraded."

The key to this understanding of *Brown* is that the practice of segregation, the practice the Court held inherently unconstitutional, was *speech. Brown* held that segregation is unconstitutional not simply because the physical separation of Black and white children is bad or because resources were distributed unequally among Black and white schools. *Brown* held that segregated schools were unconstitutional primarily because of the *message* segregation conveys—the message that Black children are an untouchable caste, unfit to be educated with white children. Segregation serves its purpose by conveying an idea. It stamps a badge of inferiority upon Blacks, and this badge communicates a message to others in the community, as well as to Blacks wearing the badge, that is injurious to Blacks. Therefore, *Brown* may be read as regulating the content of racist speech. As a regulation of racist speech, the decision is an exception to the usual rule that regulation of speech content is presumed unconstitutional.

The Conduct/Speech Distinction

Some civil libertarians argue that my analysis of *Brown* conflates speech and conduct. They maintain that the segregation outlawed in *Brown* was discriminatory conduct, not speech, and the defamatory message conveyed by segregation simply was an incidental by-product of that conduct. This position is often stated as follows: "Of course segregation conveys a message, but this could be said of almost all conduct. To take an extreme example, a murderer conveys a message of hatred for his victim. But we would not argue that we cannot punish the murder—the primary conduct—merely because of this message, which is its secondary by-product." The Court has been reluctant to concede that the first amendment has any relevance whatsoever in examples like this one, because the law would not be directed at anything resembling speech or at the views expressed. In such a case the regulation of speech is truly incidental to the regulation of the conduct.

These same civil libertarians assert that I suggest that all conduct with an expressive component should be treated alike—namely, as unprotected speech. This reading of my position clearly misperceives the central point of my argument. I do not contend that *all* conduct with an expressive component should be treated as unprotected speech. To the contrary, my suggestion that *racist* conduct amounts to speech is premised upon a unique characteristic of racism—namely its reliance upon the defamatory message of white supremacy to achieve its injurious purpose. I have not ignored the distinction between the speech and conduct elements of segregation, although, as the constitutional scholar Lawrence Tribe explained, "Any particular course of conduct may be hung almost randomly on the 'speech' peg or the 'conduct' peg as one sees fit." Rather, my analysis turns on that distinction; I ask the question of whether there is a purpose to outlawing segregation that is unrelated to its message and conclude that the answer is no.

If, for example, John W. Davis, counsel for the Board of Education of Topeka, Kansas, had been asked during oral argument in *Brown* to state the board's purpose in educating Black and white children in separate schools, he would have been hard pressed to answer in a way unrelated to the purpose of designating Black children as inferior. If segregation's primary goal is to convey the message of white supremacy, then *Brown*'s declaration that segregation is unconstitutional amounts to a regulation of the message of white supremacy. Properly understood, *Brown* and its progeny require that the systematic group defamation of segregation be disestablished. Although the exclusion of Black children from white schools and the denial of educational resources and association that accompany exclusion can be characterized as conduct, these particular instances of conduct are concerned primarily with communicating the idea of white supremacy. The nonspeech elements are by-products of the main message rather than the message being simply a by-product of unlawful conduct.

The public accommodations provisions of the Civil Rights Act of 1964 illuminate why laws against discrimination also regulate racist speech. The legislative history and the Supreme Court's opinions upholding the act establish that Congress was concerned that Blacks have access to public accommodations to eliminate impediments to the free flow of interstate commerce, but this purpose could have been achieved through a regime of separate but equal accommodations. Title II of the Civil Rights Act goes farther; it incorporates the principle of the inherent inequality of segregation and prohibits restaurant owners from providing separate places at the lunch counter for "whites" and "coloreds." Even if the same food and the same service are provided, separate but equal facilities are unlawful. If the signs indicating separate facilities remain in place, then the statute is violated despite proof that restaurant patrons are free to disregard the signs. Outlawing these signs graphically illustrates my point that antidiscrimination laws are primarily regulations of the content of racist speech.

In the summer of 1966, Robert Cover and I were working as summer interns with C. B. King in Albany, Georgia. One day we stopped for lunch at a take-out chicken joint. The establishment was housed in a long diner-like structure with an awning extending from each of two doors in the side of the building. A sign was painted at the end of each awning. One said White, the other Colored. Bob and I entered the "white" side together, knowing we were not welcome to do so. When the proprietor took my order, I asked if he knew that the signs on his awnings were illegal under Title II of the Civil Rights Act of 1964. He responded, "People can come in this place through any door they want to." What this story makes apparent is that the signs themselves violate the antidiscrimination principle even when the conduct of denial of access is not present.

Another way to understand the inseparability of racist speech and discriminatory conduct is to view individual racist acts as part of a totality. When viewed in this manner, white supremacists' conduct or speech is forbidden by the equal protection clause. The goal of white supremacy is not achieved by individual acts or even by the cumulative acts of a group, but rather it is achieved by the institutionalization of the ideas of white supremacy. The institutionalization of white supremacy within our culture has created conduct on the societal level that is greater than the sum of individual racist acts. The racist acts of millions of individuals are mutually reinforcing and cumulative because the status quo of institutionalized white supremacy remains long after deliberate racist actions subside.

Professor Kendall Thomas describes the way in which racism is simultaneously speech (a socially constructed meaning or idea) and conduct by asking us to consider the concept of "race" not as a noun but as a verb. He notes that race is a social construction. The meaning of "Black" or "white" is derived through a history of acted-upon ideology. Moreover, the cultural meaning of race is promulgated through millions of ongoing contemporaneous speech/acts. Thus, he says, "We are raced." The social construction of race is an ongoing process.

It is difficult to recognize the institutional significance of white supremacy or how it *acts* to harm, partially because of its ubiquity. We simply do not see most racist conduct because we experience a world in which whites are supreme as simply "the world." Much racist conduct is considered unrelated to race or regarded as neutral because racist conduct maintains the status quo, the status quo of the world as we have known it. Catharine MacKinnon has observed that "To the extent that pornography succeeds in constructing social reality, it becomes invisible as harm." Thus, pornography "is more act-like than thought-like." This truth about gender discrimination is equally true of racism.

Just because one can express the idea or message embodied by a practice such as white supremacy does not necessarily equate that practice with the idea. Slavery was an idea as well as a practice, but the Supreme Court recognized the inseparability of idea and practice in the institution of slavery when it held the enabling clause of the thirteenth amendment clothed Congress with the power to pass "all laws necessary and proper for abolishing all badges and incidents of slavery in the United States." This understanding also informs the regulation of speech/conduct in the public accommodations provisions of the Civil Rights Act of 1964 discussed above. When the racist restaurant or hotel owner puts a Whites Only sign in his window, his sign is more than speech. Putting up the sign is more than an act excluding Black patrons who see the sign. The sign is part of the larger practice of segregation and white supremacy that constructs and maintains a culture in which nonwhites are excluded from full citizenship. The inseparability of the idea and practice of racism is central to *Brown*'s holding that segregation is inherently unconstitutional.

Racism is both 100 percent speech and 100 percent conduct. Discriminatory conduct is not racist unless it also conveys the message of white supremacy—unless it is interpreted within the culture to advance the structure and ideology of white supremacy. Likewise, all racist speech constructs the social reality that constrains the liberty of nonwhites because of their race. By limiting the life opportunities of others, this act of constructing meaning also makes racist speech conduct.

The Public/Private Distinction

There are critics who would contend that *Brown* is inapposite because the equal protection clause only restricts government behavior, whereas the first amendment protects the speech of private persons. They say, "Of course we want to prevent the state from defaming Blacks, but we must continue to be vigilant about protecting speech rights, even of racist individuals, from the government. In both cases our concern must be protecting the individual from the unjust power of the state."

At first blush this position seems persuasive, but its persuasiveness relies upon the mystifying properties of constitutional ideology. In particular, I refer to the state action doctrine. Roughly stated,

> The [state action] doctrine holds that although someone may have suffered harmful treatment of a kind that one might ordinarily describe as a deprivation of liberty or a denial of equal protection of the laws, that occurrence excites no constitutional concern unless the proximate active perpetrators of the harm include persons exercising the special authority or power of the government of a state.

By restricting the application of the fourteenth amendment to discrimination implicating the government, the state action rule immunizes private discriminators from constitutional scrutiny. In so doing, it leaves untouched the largest part of the vast system of segregation in the United States. The *Civil Rights Cases* in which this doctrine was firmly established stands as a monument preserving American racial discrimination. Although the origin of state action is textual, countervailing values of privacy, freedom of association, and free speech all have been used to justify the rule's exculpation of private racism.

For example, it is argued that a white family's decision to send its children to private school or to move to a racially exclusive suburb should be accorded respect in spite of the fourteenth amendment's requirement of nondiscrimination because these decisions are part of the right to individual familial autonomy. In this way, the state action rule's rather arbitrary limit on the scope of the antidiscrimination principle is transformed into a right of privacy—which is presented as the constitutional embodiment of an affirmative, neutral, and universally shared value. A new and positive image emerges—an image that has been abstracted from its original context.

In the abstract, the right to make decisions about how we will educate our children or with whom we will associate is an important value in American society. But when we decontextualize by viewing this privacy value in the abstract, we ignore the way it operates in the real world. We do not ask ourselves, for example, whether it is a value to which all people have equal access. And we do not inquire about who has the resources to send their children to private school or move to an exclusive suburb. The privacy value, when presented as an ideal, seems an appropriate limitation on racial justice because we naively believe that everyone has an equal stake in this value.

I do not mean to suggest that privacy or autonomy has no normative value; there is some point at which the balance ought to be struck in its favor *after full consideration of the inequities that might accompany that choice.* What is objectional about the privacy language that I am discussing here is that is ignores inequities and assumes we all share equally in the value being promoted.

The Supreme Court's treatment of the abortion controversy provides the most striking example of the fact that the right of autonomous choice is not shared by rich and poor alike. In *Roe v. Wade,* the Court declared in no uncertain terms that the right of privacy "is broad enough to encompass a woman's decision whether or not to terminate her pregnancy." Yet, in *Harris v. McRae,* the Court with equal certainty asserted, "It simply does not follow that a woman's freedom of choice carries with it a constitutional entitlement to the financial resources to avail herself of the full range of protected choices."

The argument that distinguishes private racist speech from the government speech outlawed by *Brown* suffers from the same decontextualizing ideology. If the government is involved in a joint venture with private contractors to engage in the business of defaming Blacks, should it be able to escape the constitutional mandate that makes that business illegal simply by handing over the copyright and the printing presses to its partners in crime? I think not. And yet this is the essence of the position that espouses first amendment protection for those partners.

In an insightful article considering the constitutional implications of government regulation of pornography, the legal scholar Frank Michelman observed that the idea of state action plays a crucial, if unspoken, role for judges and civil libertarians who favor an absolute rule against government regulation of private pornographic publications (or racist speech), even when that expression causes "effects fairly describable . . . as deprivations of liberty and denials of equal protection of the laws." He noted that judges and civil libertarians would not balance the evils of private subversions of liberty and equal protection against the evils of government censorship because "the Constitution, through the state action doctrine, in effect tells them not to." Michelman suggests that the state action doctrine, by directing us to the text of the fourteenth amendment, diverts our attention from the underlying issue—whether we should balance the evils of private deprivations of liberty against the government deprivations of liberty that may arise out of state regulations designed to avert those private deprivations.

A person who responds to the argument that *Brown* mandates the abolition of racist speech by reciting the state action doctrine fails to consider that the alternative to regulating racist speech is infringement of the claims of Blacks to liberty and equal protection. The best way to constitutionally protect these competing interests is to balance them directly. To invoke the state action doctrine is to circumvent our value judgment as to how these competing interests should be balanced.

The deference usually given to the first amendment values in this balance is justified using the argument that racist speech is unpopular speech, that like the speech of civil rights activists, pacifists, and religious and political dissenters, it is in need of special protection from majoritarian censorship. But for over three hundred years, racist speech has been the liturgy of the leading established religion of the United States, the religion of racism.

Racist speech remains a vital and regrettably popular characteristic of the U.S. vernacular. It must be noted that there has not yet been satisfactory retraction of the government-sponsored defamation in the slavery clauses, the *Dred Scott* decision, the Black codes, the segregation statutes, and countless other group libels. The injury to Blacks is hardly redressed by deciding the government must no longer injure our reputation if one then invokes the first amendment to ensure that racist speech continues to thrive in an unregulated private market.

Consider, for example, the case of *McLaurin v. Oklahoma State Regents,* in which the University of Oklahoma graduate school, under order by a federal court to admit McLaurin, a Black student, designated a special seat, roped off from other seats, in each classroom, the library, and the cafeteria. The Supreme Court held that this arrangement was unconstitutional because McLaurin could not have had an equal opportunity to learn and participate if he was humiliated and symbolically stigmatized as an untouchable. Would it be any less injurious if all McLaurin's classmates had shown up at class wearing blackface? Should this symbolic speech be protected by the Constitution? Yet, according to a *Time* magazine report, in the fall of 1988 at the University of Wisconsin, "Members of the Zeta Beta Tau fraternity staged a mock slave auction, complete with some pledges in blackface." More recently, at the same university, white male students trailed Black female students shouting, "I've never tried a nigger before." These young women were no less severely injured than was McLaurin simply because the university did not directly sponsor their assault. If the university fails to protect them in their right to pursue their education free from this kind of degradation and humiliation, then surely there are constitutional values at stake.

It is a very sad irony that the first instinct of many civil libertarians is to express concern for possible infringement of the assailants' liberties while barely noticing the constitutional rights of the assailed. Shortly after *Brown,* many Southern communities tried to escape the mandate of desegregation by closing public schools and opening private (white) academies. These attempts to avoid the fourteenth amendment through the privatization of discrimination consistently were invalidated by the courts. In essence, the Supreme Court held that the defamatory message of segregation would not be insulated from constitutional proscription simply because the speaker was a nongovernment entity.

The Supreme Court also has indicated that Congress may enact legislation regulating private racist speech. In upholding the public accommodations provisions of Title II of the Civil Rights Act of 1964 in *Heart of Atlanta Motel v. United States,* the Court implicitly rejected the argument that the absence of state action meant that private discriminators were protected by first amendment free speech and associational rights. Likewise in *Bob Jones University v. United States,* the Court sustained the Internal Revenue Service decision to discontinue tax-exempt status for a college with a policy against interracial dating and marriage. The college framed its objection in terms of the free exercise of religion, arguing its policy was religiously motivated, but the Court found that the government had "a fundamental, overriding interest in eradicating racial discrimination in education" that "substantially outweighs whatever burden denial of tax benefits" placed on the college's exercise of its religious beliefs. It is difficult to believe that the university would have fared any better under free speech analysis or if the policy had been merely a statement of principle rather than an enforceable disciplinary regulation. Regulation of private racist speech also has been held constitutional in the context of prohibition of race-designated advertisements for employees, home sales, and rentals.

Thus *Brown* and the antidiscrimination law it spawned provide precedent for my position that the content regulation of racist speech is not only permissible but may be required by the Constitution in certain circumstances. This precedent may not mean that we should advocate the government regulation of all racist speech, but it should give us pause in assuming absolutist positions about regulations aimed at the message or idea such speech conveys. If we understand *Brown*—the cornerstone of the civil rights movement and equal protection doctrine—correctly, and if we understand the necessity of disestablishing the system of signs and symbols that signal Blacks' inferiority, then we should not proclaim that all racist speech that stops short of physical violence must be defended.

RACIST SPEECH AS THE FUNCTIONAL EQUIVALENT OF FIGHTING WORDS

Much recent debate over the efficacy of regulating racist speech has focused on the efforts by colleges and universities to respond to the burgeoning incidents of racial harassment on their campuses. At Stanford, where I teach, there has been considerable controversy over whether racist and other discriminatory verbal harassment should be regulated and what form any regulation should take. Proponents of regulation have been sensitive to the danger of inhibiting expression, and the current regulation (which was drafted by my colleague Tom Grey) manifests that sensitivity. It is drafted somewhat more narrowly than I would have preferred, leaving unregulated hate speech that occurs in settings where there is a captive audience, but I largely agree with this regulation's substance and approach. I include it here as one example of a regulation of racist speech that I would argue violates neither first amendment precedent nor principle. The regulation reads as follows:

Fundamental Standard Interpretation: Free Expression and Discriminatory Harassment

1. Stanford is committed to the principles of free inquiry and free expression. Students have the right to hold and vigorously defend and promote their opinions, thus entering them into the life of the University, there to flourish or wither according to their merits. Respect for this right requires that students tolerate even expression of opinions which they find abhorrent. Intimidation of students by other students in their exercise of this right, by violence or threat of violence, is therefore considered to be a violation of the Fundamental Standard.

2. Stanford is also committed to principles of equal opportunity and nondiscrimination. Each student has the right to equal access to a Stanford education, without discrimination on the basis of sex, race, color, handicap, religion, sexual orientation, or national and ethnic origin. Harassment of students on the basis of any of these characteristics tends to create a hostile environment that makes access to education for those subjected to it less than equal. Such discriminatory harassment is therefore consid-

ered to be a violation of the Fundamental Standard.

3. This interpretation of the Fundamental Standard is intended to clarify the point at which protected free expression ends and prohibited discriminatory harassment begins. Prohibited harassment includes discriminatory intimidation by threats of violence, and also includes personal vilification of students on the basis of their sex, race, color, handicap, religion, sexual orientation, or national and ethnic origin.
4. Speech or other expression constitutes harassment by vilification if it:
   a. is intended to insult or stigmatize an individual or a small number of individuals on the basis of their sex, race, color, handicap, religion, sexual orientation, or national and ethnic origin; and
   b. is addressed directly to the individual or individuals whom it insults or stigmatizes; and
   c. makes use of "fighting" words or non-verbal symbols. In the context of discriminatory harassment, "fighting" words or non-verbal symbols are words, pictures or symbols that, by virtue of their form, are commonly understood to convey direct and visceral hatred or contempt for human beings on the basis of their sex, race, color, handicap, religion, sexual orientation, and national and ethnic origin.

This regulation and others like it have been characterized in the press as the work of "thought police," but the rule does nothing more than prohibit intentional face-to-face insults, a form of speech that is unprotected by the first amendment. When racist speech takes the form of face-to-face insults, catcalls, or other assaultive speech aimed at an individual or a small group of persons, then it falls within the "fighting words" exception to first amendment protection. The Supreme Court has held that words that "by their very utterance inflict injury or tend to incite an immediate breach of the peace" are not constitutionally protected.

Face-to-face racial insults, like fighting words, are undeserving of first amendment protection for two reasons. The first reason is the immediacy of the injurious impact of racial insults. The experience of being called "nigger," "spic," "Jap," or "kike" is like receiving a slap in the face. The injury is instantaneous. There is neither an opportunity for intermediary reflection on the idea conveyed nor an opportunity for responsive speech. The harm to be avoided is both clear and present. The second reason that racial insults should not fall under protected speech relates to the purpose underlying the first amendment. The purpose of the first amendment is to foster the greatest amount of speech. Racial insults disserve that purpose. Assaultive racist speech functions as a preemptive strike. The racial invective is experienced as a blow, not a proffered idea, and once the blow is struck, it is unlikely that dialogue will follow. Racial insults are undeserving of first amendment protection because the perpetrator's intention is not to discover truth or initiate dialogue, but to injure the victim.

The fighting words doctrine anticipates that the verbal slap in the face of insulting words will provoke a violent response, resulting in a breach of the peace. When racial insults are hurled at minorities, the response may be silence or flight rather than a fight, but the preemptive effect on further speech is the same. Women and minorities often report that they find themselves speechless in the face of discriminatory verbal attacks. This inability to respond is not the result of oversensitivity among these groups, as some individuals who oppose protective regulation have argued. Rather it is the product of several factors, all of which evidence the nonspeech character of the initial preemptive verbal assault. The first factor is that the visceral emotional response to personal attack precludes speech. Attack produces an instinctive, defensive psychological reaction. Fear, rage, shock, and flight all interfere with any reasoned response. Words like "nigger," "kike," and "faggot" produce physical symptoms that temporarily disable the victim, and the perpetrators often use these words with the intention of producing this effect. Many victims do not find words of response until well after the assault, when the cowardly assaulter has departed.

A second factor that distinguishes racial insults from protected speech is the preemptive nature of such insults—words of response to such verbal attacks may never be forthcoming because speech is usually an inadequate response. When one is personally attacked with words that denote one's subhuman status and untouchability, there is little, if anything, that can be said to redress either the emotional or reputational injury. This is particularly true when the message and meaning of the epithet resonates with beliefs widely held in society. This preservation of widespread beliefs is what makes the face-to-face racial attack more likely to preempt speech than other fighting words do. The racist name caller is accompanied by a cultural chorus of equally demeaning speech and symbols. Segregation and other forms of racist speech injure victims because of their dehumanizing and excluding message. Each individual message gains its power because of the cumulative and reinforcing effect of countless similar messages that are conveyed in a society where racism is ubiquitous.

The subordinated victims of fighting words also are silenced by their relatively powerless position in society. Because of the significance of power and position, the categorization of racial epithets as fighting words provides an inadequate paradigm; instead one must speak of their functional equivalent. The fighting words doctrine presupposes an encounter between two persons of relatively equal power who have been acculturated to respond to face-to-face insults with violence: The fighting words doctrine is a paradigm based on a white male point of view. It captures the "macho" quality of male discourse. It is accepted, justifiable, and even praiseworthy when "real men" respond to personal insult with violence. (Presidential candidate George Bush effectively emulated the most macho—and not coincidentally most violent—of movie stars, Clint Eastwood, when he repeatedly used the phrase, "Read my lips!" Any teenage boy will tell you the subtext of this message: "I've got nothing else to say about this and if you don't like what I'm saying we can step outside.") The fighting words doctrine's responsiveness to this male stance in the world and its blindness to the cultural experience of women is another example of how neutral principles of law reflect the values of those who are dominant.

Black men also are well aware of the double standard that our culture applies in responding to insult. Part of the culture of racial domination through violence—a culture of dominance manifested historically in thousands of lynchings in the South and more recently in the racial violence at Howard Beach and Bensonhurst—is the paradoxical expectation on the part of whites that Black males will accept insult from whites without protest, yet will become violent without provocation. These expectations combine two assumptions: First, that Blacks as a group—and especially Black men—are more violent; and second, that as inferior persons, Blacks have no right to feel insulted. One can imagine the response of universities if Black men started to respond to racist fighting words by beating up white students.

In most situations, minorities correctly perceive that a violent response to fighting words will result in a risk to their own life and limb. This risk forces targets to remain silent and submissive. This response is most obvious when women submit to sexually assaultive speech or when the racist name caller is in a more powerful position—the boss on the job or a member of a violent racist group. Certainly, we do not expect the Black woman crossing the Wisconsin campus to turn on her tormentors and pummel them. Less obvious, but just as significant, is the effect of pervasive racial and sexual violence and coercion on individual members of subordinated groups, who must learn the survival techniques of suppressing and disguising rage and anger at an early age.

One of my students, a white, gay male, related an experience that is quite instructive in understanding the fighting words doctrine. In response to my request that students describe how they experienced the injury of racist speech, Michael told a story of being called "faggot" by a man on a subway. His description included all of the speech-inhibiting elements I have noted previously. He found himself in a state of semishock, nauseous, dizzy, unable to muster the witty, sarcastic, articulate rejoinder he was accustomed to making. He was instantly aware of the recent spate of gay bashing in San Francisco and that many of these incidents had escalated from verbal encounters. Even hours later when the shock subsided and his facility with words returned, he realized that any response was inadequate to counter the hundreds of years of societal defamation that one word—"faggot"—carried with it. Like the word "nigger" and unlike the word "liar," it is not sufficient to deny the truth of the word's application, to say, "I am not a faggot." One must deny the truth of the word's meaning, a meaning shouted from the rooftops by the rest of the world a million times a day. The complex response "Yes, I am a member of the group you despise and the degraded meaning of the word you use is one that I reject" is not effective in a subway encounter. Although there are many of us who constantly and in myriad ways seek to counter the lie spoken in the meaning of hateful words like "nigger" and "faggot," it is a nearly impossible burden to bear when one is ambushed by a sudden, face-to-face hate speech assault.

But there was another part of my discussion with Michael that is equally instructive. I asked if he could remember a situation when he had been verbally attacked with reference to his being a white male. Had he ever been called a "honkey," a "chauvinist pig," or "mick"? (Michael is from a working-class Irish family in Boston.) He said that he had been called some version of all three and that although he found the last one more offensive than the first two, he had not experienced—even in that subordinated role—the same disorienting powerlessness he had experienced when attacked for his membership in the gay community. The question of power, of the context of the power relationships within which speech takes place, and the connection to violence must be considered as we decide how best to foster the freest and fullest dialogue within our communities. Regulation of face-to-face verbal assault in the manner contemplated by the proposed Stanford provision will make room for more speech than it chills. The provision is clearly within the spirit, if not the letter, of existing first amendment doctrine.

The proposed Stanford regulation, and indeed regulations with considerably broader reach, can be justified as necessary to protect a captive audience from offensive or injurious speech. Courts have held that offensive speech may not be regulated in public forums such as streets and parks where listeners may avoid the speech by moving on or averting their eyes, but the regulation of otherwise protected speech has been permitted when the speech invades the privacy of unwilling listeners' homes or when unwilling listeners cannot avoid the speech. Racist posters, flyers, and graffiti in dorms, classrooms, bathrooms, and other common living spaces would fall within the reasoning of these cases. Minority students should not be required to remain in their rooms to avoid racial assault. Minimally, they should find a safe haven in their dorms and other common rooms that are a part of their daily routine. I would argue that the university's responsibility for ensuring these students receive an equal educational opportunity provides a compelling justification for regulations that ensure them safe passage in all common areas. Black, Latino, Asian, or Native American students should not have to risk being the target of racially assaulting speech every time they choose to walk across campus. The regulation of vilifying speech that cannot be anticipated or avoided would not preclude announced speeches and rallies where minorities and their allies would have an opportunity to organize counter-demonstrations or avoid the speech altogether. . . .

59

RONALD DWORKIN

Do We Have a Right to Pornography?

It is an old problem for liberal theory how far people should have the right to do the wrong thing. Liberals insist that people have the legal right to say what they wish on matters of political or social controversy. But should they be free to incite racial hatred, for example? British and American law now give different answers to that specific question. The United Kingdom Race Relations law makes it a crime to advocate racial prejudice, but the First Amendment to the United States Constitution forbids Congress or any of the states from adopting any such law.

Pornography in its various forms presents another instance of the same issue. The majority of people in both countries would prefer (or so it seems) substantial censorship, if not outright prohibitions, of "sexually explicit" books, magazines, photographs, and films, and this majority includes a considerable number of those who are themselves consumers of whatever pornography is on offer. (It is part of the complex psychology of sex that many of those with a fixed taste for the obscene would strongly prefer that their children, for example, not follow them in that taste.) If we assume that the majority is correct, and that people who publish and consume pornography do the wrong thing, or at least display the wrong sort of character, should they nevertheless have the legal right to do so?

Some lawyers and political philosophers consider the problem of pornography to be only an instance of the first problem I mentioned, the problem of freedom to speak unpopular or wicked thoughts. But we should be suspicious of that claim, because the strongest arguments in favor of allowing *Mein Kampf* to be published hardly seem to apply in favor of the novel *Whips Incorporated* or the film *Sex Kittens*. No one, I think is denied an equal voice in the political process, however broadly conceived, when he is forbidden to circulate photographs of genitals to the public at large, or denied his right to listen to argument when he is forbidden to consider these photographs at his leisure. If we believe it wrong to censor these forms of pornography, then we should try to find the justification for that opinion elsewhere than in the literature celebrating freedom of speech and press. . . .

Consider the following suggestion. People have the right not to suffer disadvantage in the distribution of social goods and opportunities, including disadvantage in the liberties permitted to them by the criminal law, just on the ground that their officials or fellow-citizens think that their opinions about the right way for them to lead their own lives are ignoble or wrong. I shall call this (putative) right the right to moral independence, and in this part I shall consider what force this right would have on the law of pornography if it were recognized. . . .

The right to moral independence is a very abstract right (or, if you prefer, the statement of the right I gave is a very abstract statement of the right) because this statement takes no account of the impact of competing rights. It does not attempt to decide whether the right can always be jointly satisfied for everyone, or how conflicts with other rights, if they arise, are to be settled. These further questions, along with other related questions, are left for more concrete statements of the right. Or (what comes to the same thing) for statements of the more concrete rights that people have in virtue of the abstract right. Nevertheless, the questions I wish to put may usefully be asked even about the abstract statement or the abstract right.

Someone who appeals to the right of moral independence in order to justify a permissive legal regime of obscenity does not suppose that the community will be better off in the long run (according to some description of what makes a community better off like. . .) if people are free to look at obscene pictures in private. He does not deny this. His argument is in the conditional mood: even if conditions will not then be so suitable for human flourishing as they might be, for example, nevertheless the right must be respected. But what force does the right then have? When does the government violate that right?

It violates the right, we may say, at least in this case: when the only apparent or plausible justification for a scheme of regulation of pornography includes the hypothesis that the attitudes about sex displayed or nurtured in pornography are demeaning or bestial or otherwise unsuitable to human beings of the best sort, even though this hypothesis may be true. It also violates that right when that justification includes the proposition that most people in the society accept that hypothesis and are therefore pained or disgusted when other members of their own community, for whose lives they understandably feel special responsibility, do read dirty books or look at dirty pictures. The right is therefore a powerful constraint on the regulation of pornography, or at least so it seems, because it prohibits giving weight to exactly the arguments most people think are the best arguments for even a mild and enlightened policy of restriction of obscenity. What room is left, by the apparently powerful right, for the government to do anything at all about pornography?

Suppose it is discovered that the private consumption of pornography does significantly increase the danger of crimes of violence, either generally or specifically crimes of sexual violence. Or suppose that private consumption has some special and deleterious effect on the general economy, by causing great absenteeism from work, for example, as drink or breakfast television is sometimes said to do. Then government would have, in these facts, a justification for the restraint and perhaps even for the prohibition of pornography that does not include the offending hypothesis either directly, by the assumption that the hypothesis is true, or indirectly, in the proposition that many people think it true. After all (as is often pointed out in discussions of obscenity, including the Williams Report), the Bible or Shakespeare might turn out to have these unfortunate consequences, in which case government would have a reason for banning these books that did not require a comparable hypothesis about them.

This possibility raises a slightly more subtle point. Suppose it were discovered that all forms of emotionally powerful literature (including Shakespeare, the Bible, and many forms of pornography) contributed significantly to crime. But the government responded to this discovery selectively, banning most examples of pornography and other literature it considered worthless, but allowing Shakespeare and the Bible nevertheless, on the ground that these were of such literary and cultural value that it was worth the crime they caused to preserve them. Nothing in this selection and discrimination (as so far stated) violates the right to moral independence. The judgment in question—that pornography does not in fact contribute enough of literary value, or that it is not sufficiently informative or imaginative about the different ways in which people might express themselves or find value in their lives, to justify accepting the damage of crime as the cost of its publication—is not the judgment that those who do enjoy pornography have worse character on that account. Any judgment of literary or cultural value will be a judgment about which honest and reasonable people will disagree. But this is true of many other kinds of judgments that government must nevertheless make. The present judgment is no doubt special because it may be used as a screen to hide a different judgment that would offend the right to independence, the judgment that pornography should be treated differently from the Bible because the people who prefer it are worse people. That danger might be sufficiently strong so that a society jealous of the right of moral independence will, for prophylactic reasons, forbid officials to make the literary judgment that would distinguish *Sex Kittens* from *Hamlet* if both were found to provoke crime. That does not touch the present point, that the literary judgment is different, and does not itself threaten the right of independence; and it is worth adding that very few of the people who do admit to enjoying pornography claim distinct literary merit for it. They claim at most the kind of merit that others, with more conventional ideas about amusement, claim for thrillers.

But this is, in any case, only academic speculation, because there is no reason to suppose a sufficiently direct connection between crime and either *Sex Kittens* or *Hamlet* to provide a ground for banning either one as private entertainment. But what about public display? Can we find a plausible justification for restricting the display of pornography that does not violate the right of moral independence? We can, obviously, construct a certain argument in that direction, as follows. "Many people do not like to encounter genital displays on the way to the grocer. This taste is not, nor does it necessarily reflect, any adverse view of the character of those who do not mind such encounters. Someone who would not like to find pornography in his ordinary paths may not even object to finding it elsewhere. He may simply have tastes and preferences that reject certain combinations in his experience, like someone who likes pink sunsets but not pink houses in Belgravia, who does not object to neon in Leicester Square but would hate it in the Cotswolds. Or he may have a more structured or more consequentialist scheme of preferences about his environment. He may find or believe, for example, that his own delight in other peoples' bodies is lessened or made less sharp and special if nakedness becomes either too familiar to him or less peculiar to those occasions in which it provides him special pleasure, which may be in museums or his own bedroom or both. Or that sex will come to be different and less valuable for him if he is too often or too forcefully reminded that it has different, more commercial or more sadistic, meaning for others. Or that his goal that his children develop certain similar tastes and opinions will be thwarted by the display or advertising that he opposes. None of these different opinions and complaints *must* be the product of some conviction that those with other opinions and tastes are people of bad character, any more than those who hope that state-supported theater will produce the classics exclusively must think that those who prefer experimental theater are less worthy people."

This picture of the motives people might have for not wanting to encounter pornography on the streets is a conceivable picture. But I suspect, as I suggested earlier, that it is far too crude and one-dimensional as a picture of what these motives actually are. The discomfort many people find in encountering blatant nudity on the hoardings is rarely so independent of their moral convictions as these various descriptions suggest. It is at least part of the offense, for many people, that they detest themselves for taking the interest in the proceedings that they do. It is a major part of the offense, for others, that they are so forcefully reminded of what their neighbors are like and, more particularly, of what their neighbors are getting away with. People object to the display of naked men and women in erotic poses, that is, even when these displays occur (as for commercial reasons they inevitably do) in those parts of cities that would be in no sense beautiful or enlightening even without the pornography. Even if we took the descriptions of peoples' motives in the argument I set out at face value, moreover, we should be forced to recognize the substantial influence of moral convictions just in those motives, for someone's sense of what he wants his own attitudes toward sex to be, and certainly his sense of what attitudes he hopes to encourage in his children, are not only influenced by, but constitute, his moral opinions in the broad sense.

We therefore encounter, in people's motives for objecting to the advertising or display of pornography, at least a mix and interaction of attitudes, beliefs, and tastes that rule out any confident assertion that regulation justified by appeal to these motives would not violate the right to moral independence. We do not know whether, if we could disentangle the different strands of taste, ambition, and belief, so as to winnow out those that express moral condemnation or would not exist but for it, the remaining strands would justify any particular scheme of regulation of display. This is not just a failure of information that would be expensive to obtain. The problem is more conceptual than that: the vocabulary we use to identify and individuate motives—our own as well as those of others—cannot provide the discrimination we need.

A society anxious to defend the abstract right to moral independence in the face of this complexity, has two options at least. It might decide that if popular attitudes toward a minority or a minority practice are mixed in this way, so that the impact of adverse moral convictions can be neither excluded nor measured, then these attitudes should all be deemed to be corrupted by such convictions, and no regulation is permissible. Or it might decide that the case of mixed attitudes is a special kind of case in the administration of the abstract right, so that more concrete statements of what people are entitled to have under the right must take the fact of mixed attitudes into account. It might do this, for example, by stipulating, at the more concrete level, that no one should suffer *serious* damage through legal restraint when this can only be justified by the fact that what he proposes to do will frustrate or defeat preferences of others that we have reason to believe are mixed with or are consequences of the conviction that people who act in that way are people of bad character. This second option, which defines a concrete right tailored to the problem of mixed preferences, is not a relaxation or compromise of the abstract right, but rather a (no doubt controversial) application of it to that special situation. Which of the two options (or which further option) provides the best response to the problem of mixed motives is part of the more general problem of justification that I postponed to the next section. The process of making an abstract right successively more concrete is not simply a process of deduction or interpretation of the abstract statement but a fresh step in political theory.

If society takes the second option just described in the case of pornography (as I think it should . . .), then its officials must undertake to decide what damage to those who wish to publish or read pornography is serious and what is trivial. Once again reasonable and honest officials will disagree about this, but we are trying to discover, not an algorithm for a law of obscenity, but rather whether a plausible concrete conception of a plausible abstract right will yield a sensible scheme of regulation. We should therefore consider the character of the damage that would be inflicted on consumers of pornography by, say, a scheme of zoning that requires that pornographic materials be sold and films shown only in particular areas, a scheme of advertising that prohibits in public places advertisements that would widely be regarded as indecent, and a scheme of labeling so that those entering cinemas or shops whose contents they might find indecent would be warned. There are three main heads of damage that such a regime might inflict on consumers: inconvenience, expense, and embarrassment. Whether the inconvenience is serious will depend on the details of, for example, the zoning. But it should not be considered serious if shoppers for pornography need travel on average only as far as, say, shoppers for stereo equipment or diamonds or secondhand books need travel to find the centers of such trade. How far this scheme of restriction would increase the price of pornography is harder to predict. Perhaps the constraint on advertising would decrease the volume of sales and therefore increase unit costs. But it seems unlikely that this effect would be very great, particularly if the legal ban runs to the character not to the extent of the advertising, and permits, as it should, not only stark "tombstone" notices, but the full range of the depressingly effective techniques through which manufacturers sell soap and video cassette recorders.

Embarrassment raises a more interesting and important question. Some states and countries have required people to identify themselves as belonging to a particular religion or holding certain political convictions just for the sake of that identification, and for the sake of the disadvantage it brings in its train. The Nazi's regime of yellow armbands for Jews, for example, or the registry of members of civil rights groups that some southern states established and the Supreme Court ruled unconstitutional in *NAACP v. Alabama ex rel Patterson*. Since in cases like these identification is required just as a mark of public contempt, or just to provide the social and economic pressure that follows from that contempt, these laws are ruled out by even the abstract form of the right. But the situation is rather different if identification is a by-product rather than the purpose of a scheme of regulation, and is as voluntary as the distinct goals of regulation permit. It would violate the right of moral independence, plainly, if pornography houses were not allowed to use plain-brown-wrapper mail for customers who preferred anonymity, because embarrassment would be the point of that restriction, not a by-product. Also, I think, if the law forbade pornography shops from selling anything but pornography, so that a shy pornographer could not walk out of the shop with a new umbrella as well as a bulge in his coat pocket. But the right of moral independence does not carry with it any government obligation to insure that people may exercise that right in public places without its being known by the public that they do. Perhaps the government would be obliged to take special measures to guard against embarrassment in a society in which people actually were likely to suffer serious economic harm if they were seen leaving a shop carrying the wrong sign. But that is unlikely to be true about shy pornographers in this country now, who might sensibly be required to bear the social burden of being known to be the kind of people they are.

I conclude that the right to moral independence, if it is a genuine right, requires a permissive legal attitude toward the consumption of pornography in private, but that a certain concrete conception of that right nevertheless permits a scheme of restriction rather like the scheme that the Williams Report recommends. It remains to consider whether that right and that conception can themselves be justified in political theory. But I might first observe that nothing in my conclusion collides with my . . . claim that the Williams strategy, on which the Report relies, cannot support either its permissive attitude or its restrictive scheme. For I did not argue, in support of that claim, that the restrictive scheme would impose great damage on individuals. I said only that the Williams strategy as a whole, which based its arguments not on the interests of pornographers but on the contribution they might make to a beneficial exchange of communication, failed to provide the necessary distinction. Nor do I now appeal to the ideal that is the nerve of that strategy—that the community be free to develop the best conditions for human flourishing—in support of my own conclusions about the law of pornography. I argue rather that, whether or not the instrumental claims of the Williams Report are sound, private liberty is required and public constraint permitted by an appealing conception of an important political right.

The rest of this essay considers the question of how the right to moral independence might be defended, both in its abstract form and in the more concrete conception we discussed in considering public display of pornography. This question is important beyond the relatively trivial problem of obscenity itself: the right has other and more important applications, and the question of what kinds of arguments support a claim of right is an urgent question in political theory.

Rights, . . . are best understood as trumps over some background justification for political decisions that states a goal for the community as a whole. If someone has a right to moral independence, this means that it is for some reason wrong for officials to act in violation of that right, even if they (correctly) believe that the community as a whole would be better off if they did. There are many different theories in the field about what makes a community better off on the whole; many different theories, that is, about what the goal of political action should be. One prominent theory (or rather group of theories) is utilitarianism in its familiar forms, which suppose that the community is better off if its members are on average happier or have more of their preferences satisfied. Another, and in certain ways different, theory is the theory we found in the Williams strategy, which argues that the community is better off if it provides the most desirable conditions for human development. There are of course many other theories about the true goal of politics, many of them much more different from either of these two theories than these are from each other. To some extent, the argument in favor of a particular right must depend on which of these theories about desirable goals has been accepted; it must depend, that is, on what general background justification for political decisions the right in question proposes to trump. In the following discussion I shall assume that the background justification with which we are concerned is some form of utilitarianism, which takes, as the goal of politics, the fulfillment of as many of people's goals for their own lives as possible. This remains, I think, the most influential background justification, at least in the informal way in which it presently figures in politics in the Western democracies.

Suppose we accept then that, at least in general, a political decision is justified if it promises to make citizens happier, or to fulfill more of their preferences, on average, than any other decision could. Suppose we assume that the decision to prohibit pornography altogether does meet that test, because the desires and preferences of publishers and consumers are outweighed by the desires and preferences of the majority, including their preferences about how others should lead their lives. How could any contrary decision, permitting even the private use of pornography, then be justified?

Two modes of argument might be thought capable of supplying such a justification. First, we might argue that, though the utilitarian goal states one important political ideal, it is not the only important ideal, and pornography must be permitted in order to protect some other ideal that is, in the circumstances, more important. Second, we might argue that further analysis of the grounds that we have for accepting utilitarianism as a background justification in the first place—further reflection of why we wish to pursue that goal—shows that utility must yield to some right of moral independence here. The first form of argument is pluralistic: it argues for a trump or utility on the ground that though utility is always important, it is not the only thing that matters, and other goals or ideals are sometimes more important. The second supposes that proper understanding of what utilitarianism is, and why it is important, will itself justify the right in question.

I do not believe that the first, or pluralistic, mode of argument has much prospect of success, at least as applied to the problem of pornography. But I shall not develop the arguments now that would be necessary to support that opinion. I want instead to offer an argument in the second mode, which is, in summary, this. Utilitarianism owes whatever appeal it has to what we might call its egalitarian cast. (Or, if that is too strong, would lose whatever appeal it has but for that cast.) Suppose some version of utilitarianism provided that the preferences of some people were to count for less than those of others in the calculation how best to fulfill most preferences overall either because these people were in themselves less worthy or less attractive or less well loved people, or because the preferences in question combined to form a contemptible way of life. This would strike us as flatly unacceptable, and in any case much less appealing than standard forms of utilitarianism. In any of its standard versions, utilitarianism can claim to provide a conception of how government treats people as equals, or, in any case, how government respects the fundamental requirement that it must treat people as equals. Utilitarianism claims that people are treated as equals when the preferences of each, weighted only for intensity, are balanced in the same scales, with no distinctions for persons or merit. The corrupt version of utilitarianism just described, which gives less weight to some persons than to others, or discounts some preferences because these are ignoble, forfeits that claim. But if utilitarianism in practice is not checked by something like the right of moral independence (and by other allied rights), it will disintegrate, for all practical purposes, into exactly that version.

Suppose a community of many people including Sarah. If the Constitution sets out a version of utilitarianism which provides in terms that Sarah's preferences are to count for twice as much as those of others, then this would be the unacceptable, nonegalitarian version of utilitarianism. But now suppose that the constitutional provision is the standard form of utilitarianism, that is, that it is neutral toward all people and preferences, but that a surprising number of people love Sarah very much, and therefore strongly prefer that her preferences count for twice as much in the day-to-day political decisions made in the utilitarian calculus. When Sarah does not receive what she would have if her preferences counted for twice as much as those of others, then these people are unhappy, because their special Sarah-loving preferences are unfulfilled. If these special preferences are themselves allowed to count, therefore, Sarah will receive much more in the distribution of goods and opportunities than she otherwise would. I argue that this defeats the egalitarian cast of the apparently neutral utilitarian Constitution as much as if the neutral provision were replaced by the rejected version. Indeed, the apparently neutral provision is then self-undermining because it gives a critical weight, in deciding which distribution best promotes utility, to the views of those who hold the profoundly un-neutral (some would say anti-utilitarian) theory that the preferences of some should count for more that those of others.

The reply that a utilitarian anxious to resist the right to moral independence would give to this argument is obvious: utilitarianism does not give weight to the truth of that theory, but just to the fact that many people (wrongly) hold that theory and so are disappointed when the distribution the government achieves is not the distribution they believe is right. It is the fact of their disappointment, not the truth of their views, that counts, and there is no inconsistency, logical or pragmatic, in that. But this reply is too quick. For there is a particularly deep kind of contradiction here. Utilitarianism must claim (as I said earlier, any political theory must claim) truth for itself, and therefore must claim the falsity of any theory that contradicts it. It must itself occupy, that is, all the logical space that its content requires. But neutral utilitarianism claims (or, in any case, presupposes) that no one is, in principle, any more entitled to have any of his preferences fulfilled than anyone else is. It argues that the only reason for denying the fulfillment of one person's desires, whatever these are, is that more and more intense desires must be satisfied instead. It insists that justice and political morality can supply no other reason. This is, we might say, the neutral utilitarian's *case* for trying to achieve a political structure in which the average fulfillment of preferences is as high as possible. The question is not whether a government can achieve that political structure if it counts political preferences like the preferences of the Sarah-lovers or whether the government will then have counted any particular preference twice and so contradicted utilitarianism in that direct way. It is rather whether the government can achieve all this without implicitly contradicting that case.

Suppose the community contains a Nazi, for example, whose set of preferences includes the preference that Aryans have more and Jews less of their preferences fulfilled just because of who they are. A neutral utilitarian cannot say that there is no reason in political morality for rejecting or dishonoring that preference, for not dismissing it as just wrong, for not striving to fulfill it with all the dedication that officials devote to fulfilling any other sort of preference. For utilitarianism itself supplies such a reason: its most fundamental tenet is that people's preferences should be weighed on an equal basis in the same scales, that the Nazi theory of justice is profoundly wrong, and that officials should oppose the Nazi theory and strive to defeat rather than fulfill it. A neutral utilitarian is barred, for reasons of consistency, from taking the same politically neutral attitude to the Nazi's political preference that he takes toward other sorts of preferences. But then he cannot make the case just described in favor of highest average utility computed taking that preference into account.

I do not mean that endorsing someone's right to have his preference satisfied automatically endorses his preference as good or noble. The good utilitarian, who says that the pinball player is equally entitled to satisfaction of that taste as the poet is entitled to the satisfaction of his, is not for that reason committed to the proposition that a life of pinball is as good as a life of poetry. Only vulgar critics of utilitarianism would insist on that inference. The utilitarian says only that nothing in the theory of justice provides any reason why the political and economic arrangements and decisions of society should be any closer to those the poet would prefer than those the pinball player would like. It is just a matter, from the standpoint of political justice, of how many people prefer the one to the other and how strongly. But he cannot say that about the conflict between the Nazi and the neutral utilitarian opponent of Nazism, because the correct political theory, his political theory, the very political theory to which he appeals in attending to the fact of the Nazi's claim, does speak to the conflict. It says that what the neutral utilitarian prefers is just and accurately describes what people are, as a matter of political morality, entitled to have, but that what the Nazi prefers is deeply unjust and describes what no one is entitled, as a matter of political morality, to have. But then it is contradictory to say, again as a matter of political morality, that the Nazi is as much entitled to the political system he prefers as is the utilitarian.

The point might be put this way. Political preferences, like the Nazi's preference, are on the same level—purport to occupy the same space—as the utilitarian theory itself. Therefore, though the utilitarian theory must be neutral between personal preferences like the preferences for pinball and poetry, as a matter of the theory of justice, it cannot, without contradiction, be neutral between itself and Nazism. It cannot accept at once a duty to defeat the false theory that some people's preferences should count for more than other people's and a duty to strive to fulfill the political preferences of those who passionately accept that false theory, as energetically as it strives for any other preferences. The distinction on which the reply to my argument rests, the distinction between the truth and the fact of the Nazi's political preferences, collapses, because if utilitarianism counts the fact of these preferences, it has denied what it cannot deny, which is that justice requires it to oppose them.

We could escape this point by distinguishing two different forms or levels of utilitarianism. The first would be presented simply as a thin theory about how a political constitution should be selected in a community whose members prefer different kinds of political theories. The second would be a candidate for the constitution to be so chosen; it might argue for a distribution that maximized aggregate satisfaction of personal preferences in the actual distribution of goods and opportunities, for example. In that case, the first theory would argue only that the preferences of the Nazi should be given equal weight with the preferences of the second sort of utilitarian in the choice of a constitution, because each is equally entitled to the constitution he prefers, and there would be no contradiction in that proposition. But of course the neutral utilitarian theory we are now considering is not a thin theory of that sort. It proposes a theory of justice as a full political constitution, not just a theory about how to choose one, and so it cannot escape contradiction through modesty.

Now the same argument holds (though perhaps less evidently) when the political preferences are not familiar and despicable, like the Nazi theory, but more informal and cheerful, like the preferences of the Sarah-lovers who think that her preferences should be counted twice. The latter might, indeed, be Sarahocrats who believe that she is entitled to the treatment they recommend by virtue of birth or other characteristics unique to her. But even if their preferences rise from special affection rather than from political theory, these preferences nevertheless invade the space claimed by neutral utilitarianism and so cannot be counted without defeating the case utilitarianism provides. My argument, therefore, comes to this. If utilitarianism is to figure as part of an attractive working political theory, it must be qualified so as to restrict the preferences that count by excluding political preferences of both the formal and informal sort. One very practical way to achieve this restriction is provided by the idea of rights as trumps over unrestricted utilitarianism. A society committed to utilitarianism as a general background justification which does not in terms disqualify any preferences might achieve that disqualification by adopting a right to political independence: the right that no one suffer disadvantage in the distribution of goods or opportunities on the ground that others think he should have less because of who he is or is not, or that others care less for him than they do for other people. The right of political independence would have the effect of insulating Jews from the preferences of Nazis, and those who are not Sarah from the preferences of those who adore her.

The right of moral independence can be defended in a parallel way. Neutral utilitarianism rejects the idea that some ambitions that people might have for their own lives should have less command over social resources and opportunities than others, except as this is the consequence of weighing all preferences on an equal basis in the same scales. It rejects the argument, for example, that some people's conception of what sexual experience should be like, and of what part fantasy should play in that experience, and of what the character of that fantasy should be, are inherently degrading or unwholesome. But then it cannot (for the reasons just canvassed) count the moral preferences of those who do hold such opinions in the calculation whether individuals who form some sexual minority, including homosexuals and pornographers, should be prohibited from the sexual experiences they want to have. The right of moral independence is part of the same collection of rights as the right of political independence, and it is to be justified as a trump over an unrestricted utilitarian defense of prohibitory laws against pornography, in a community of those who find offense just in the idea that their neighbors are reading dirty books, in much the same way as the latter right is justified as a trump over a utilitarian justification of giving Jews less or Sarah more in a society of Nazis or Sarah-lovers.

It remains to consider whether the abstract right to moral independence, defended in this way, would nevertheless permit restriction of public display of pornography in a society whose preferences against that display were backed by the mixed motives we reviewed in the last part. This is a situation in which the egalitarian cast of utilitarianism is threatened from not one but two directions. To the extent to which the motives in question are moral preferences about how others should behave, and these motives are counted, then the neutrality of utilitarianism is compromised. But to the extent to which these are the rather different sort of motives we reviewed, which emphasize not how others should lead their lives, but rather the character of the sexual experience people want for themselves, and these motives are disregarded, the neutrality of utilitarianism is compromised in the other direction, for it becomes unnecessarily inhospitable to the special and important ambitions of those who then lose control of a crucial aspect of their own self-development. The situation is therefore not an appropriate case for a prophylactic refusal to count any motive whenever we cannot be sure that that motive is unmixed with moralism, because the danger of unfairness lies on both sides rather than only on one. The alternative I described in the preceding section is at least better than that. This argues that restriction may be justified even though we cannot be sure that the preferences people have for restriction are untinged by the kind of preferences we should exclude, provided that the damage done to those who are affected adversely is not serious damage, even in their own eyes. Allowing restrictions on public display is in one sense a compromise; but it is a compromise recommended by the right of moral independence, once the case for that right is set out, not a compromise of that right. . . .

60

RAE LANGTON

Whose Right? Ronald Dworkin, Women, and Pornographers

Amidst the heated and often acrimonious controversies about pornography and government policy, the answer to one question at least has always seemed obvious. Should liberal theorists be in favor of permitting pornography? As champions of our basic liberties, and as champions especially of free speech, liberals have found it easy to answer this question with a simple "yes." They are of course accustomed to viewing their opponents in this debate as conservatives, who want pornography prohibited because it is immoral; liberals view moralistic motives of this kind with deep (and doubtless justified) suspicion. But there are other voices in the debate, too, voices arguing that we have reason to be concerned about pornography, not because it is morally suspect, but because we care about equality and the rights of women. This aspect of the debate between liberals and their opponents can begin to look like an argument about liberty and equality—freedom of speech versus women's rights—and so, apparently, it has been regarded by the courts.[1]

Ronald Dworkin is one liberal theorist who has defended a right to pornography, addressing the topic in "Do We Have a Right to Pornography?"[2] He is, in addition, a liberal who thinks that there can be no real conflict between liberty and equality.[3] Given that the pornography issue can be seen as apparently posing just such a conflict, it is natural to wonder whether Dworkin is right. In this article I put to Dworkin the question raised at the outset: Should liberals, or should Dworkin, at any rate, be in favor of permitting pornography? In the light of Dworkin's general theoretical commitments, the answer is not as obvious as it might appear.

In commenting elsewhere on the topical relevance of the argument he presented in "Do We Have a Right to Pornography?" Dworkin remarks that the controversy it deals with is one that has been given "fresh shape and importance" by recent history. "Old wars over pornography and censorship have new armies," he writes, " in radical feminists and the Moral Majority."[4] The recent history here alluded to presumably includes the controversy over a feminist antipornography ordinance that was passed in 1984 by the Indianapolis City Council, was swiftly challenged, and

[1]American Booksellers, Inc. v. Hudnut, 598 F. Supp. 1327 (S.D. Ind. 1984) (hereafter Hudnut).

[2]Ronald Dworkin, "Do We Have a Right to Pornography?" *Oxford Journal of Legal Studies* 1 (1981): 177–212: repr. in *A Matter of Principle* (Cambridge, Mass.: Harvard University Press, 1985), pp. 335–72. Page references are to the reprint in *A Matter of Principle*.

[3]Ronald Dworkin, "What Is Equality? Part 3: The Place of Liberty," *Iowa Law Review* 73 (1987): 9.

[4]Dworkin, *A Matter of Principle,* p. 1.

was judged by the district court to be unconstitutional.[5]

One modest aim of this article is to show that, whatever success Dworkin's argument may have against the armies of the Moral Majority, it does not even begin to address the approach he labels "radical feminist." A second and more substantial aim is to show that the latter "feminist" argument is not only consistent with Dworkin's liberalism, but is, so far as I can tell, demanded by it. My strategy here will be to work entirely within the Dworkinian theoretical system, and to show how that system yields a conclusion about pornography that is radically at odds with Dworkin's own, as expressed in his article on this topic. I argue that Dworkin's principle of equal concern and respect requires a policy about pornography that conflicts with commonly held liberal views about the subject, and that coincides instead with the restrictive or prohibitive policy favored by his feminist foes. In the course of my argument I restrict my attention to pornography of a certain kind, and I make use of certain empirical claims that Dworkin does not consider. But, granted these not overly controversial claims, Dworkin's theoretical commitments appear to supply ample resources for the justification of a prohibitive strategy. Dworkin, of course, agrees that some empirical premises would be sufficient to support a prohibitive argument. If, for example, there were conclusive evidence linking pornography to violence, one could justify a prohibitive strategy on the basis of a simple harm principle. However, the prohibitive arguments advanced in this article do not require empirical premises as strong as this, nor do they rely on a simple harm principle. They rely instead on the notion of equality that forms the linchpin of Dworkinian liberal theory. . . .

DWORKIN ON PORNOGRAPHY

In "Do We Have a Right to Pornography?" Dworkin considers a question that has attracted attention from many political theorists, from liberals at one end of the spectrum to the redoubtable "new armies" of conservatives and feminists at the other. What might we expect Dworkin's approach to be? On the one hand, Dworkin is first and foremost a liberal theorist, and the freedom to produce and consume pornography has long been a liberal cause. But he is at the same time a writer famous for taking the principle of equality to be the starting point for sound political thinking; a writer whose sensitivity in dealing with the complex issues surrounding prejudice against an oppressed group we have already witnessed; and a writer who begins his discussion of the pornography question by drawing an analogy between laws concerning pornography and laws concerning racist speech. "Should we be free to incite racial hatred?" he asks his readers in the opening paragraph—an interesting question and one whose implications seem worth pursuing.

Given this hopeful start, and given also that the feminist "armies" had already begun to mass at the time of his writing,[6] we might reasonably expect that a rights-based argument *against* pornography would merit at least some brief mention in the essay. Such hopes, as it turns out, are disappointed, and Dworkin's question in the opening paragraph is not pursued in any detail. He considers, at various points throughout the essay, a vast number of ways in which pornography might more or less plausibly be construed as a harm. The sample that follows is by no means exhaustive, but I can assure my reader that there is one construal that is conspicuous by its absence, namely, that women as a group might be harmed by pornography.

Here is the quick sample. Since most people would prefer censorship, permitting pornography harms general utility by leaving the majority of preferences unsatisfied.[7] Pornography damages the cultural environment.[8] It upsets and disgusts people.[9] It limits people's ability to lead the kind of lives they would want for themselves and their children.[10] It makes sex seem less valuable.[11] People find discomfort in encountering blatant nudity because they detest themselves for

[5]See Hudnut; see also 771 F.2d 323 (7th Cir. 1985), affirmed 106 S.Ct. 1172 (1986).

[6]As demonstrated, for example, in the classic collection of essays *Take Back the Night: Women on Pornography* (New York: William Morrow, 1980), containing essays published earlier.

[7]Dworkin, "Right to Pornography?" p. 335.

[8]Ibid., pp. 337, 340.

[9]Ibid., pp. 344–45.

[10]Ibid., p. 349.

[11]Ibid., p. 356.

[12]Ibid.

taking an interest in the proceedings, and they are forcefully reminded of what their neighbors are like and of what their neighbors are getting away with.[12]

To be fair Dworkin does indeed raise the issue of whether pornography ever presents a "special danger of personal harm narrowly conceived,"[13] and although he usually takes this to be a question about people's responses when directly confronted with pornography, he, along with the Williams Committee, "concedes . . . the relevance of the question whether an increase in the amount of pornography in circulation in the community is likely to produce more violence or more sexual crimes of any particular sort. . . ."[14] This is as close as Dworkin ever gets to considering whether or not it may be women who are, in the end, the ones hurt by the pornography industry. As a rule, when he raises the possibility of any link between pornography and harm to women of a concrete and familiar sort, he fails to take it seriously. Indeed, were it not for the evidence we already have of Dworkin's awareness of the subtle complexities surrounding questions of group oppression, the reader might be tempted to suppose that Dworkin's chief interest is to lampoon the idea. Imagining that pornography might be violence is like imagining that reading *Hamlet* might lead to violence.[15] Or, in another passage, he wonders whether pornography might be like "breakfast television": both might be found to encourage absenteeism from work, and thereby have (perish the thought!) "some special and deleterious effect on the general economy."[16] But as he continues with such comparisons, we begin to discover that he thinks that questions about concrete harm are mere "academic speculation";[17] the pornography issue is itself a "relatively trivial" problem.[18] By contrast, embarrassment—that is, embarrassment on the part of the shy pornographer"—he describes as raising an "interesting and important question."[19] When it comes to the plight of the shy pornographer, Dworkin displays a touching concern; he suggests that legislators should make sure that the consumer can, should he so desire, buy an umbrella at his favorite adult bookstore, so as to disguise his secret and perhaps shameful habits.

Readers may have gathered by now that Dworkin and I do not share exactly the same view about what is and what is not an important question. Embarrassment is not, all things considered, a very important question; the well-being of women is. Leaving such sympathies aside, there are of course some relevant empirical questions to be addressed here. And on certain questions of this kind Dworkin accepts the findings of the Williams Committee, namely, that there is no persuasive evidence that pornography causes violent crime.[20] On other empirical questions—for example, questions about pornography's possible role in a society in which women happen to be widely oppressed—Dworkin is comfortably silent. One wonders whether he would have been as comfortable had Sweatt's opponents cited, in support of their case, similar findings that had reached a similarly happy conclusion that there was no persuasive evidence that the practice of racial segregation causes violent crime. One does not always need conclusive evidence about crime to have cause for concern, nor is violence the only worry in situations in which there is widespread prejudice and discrimination against a particular group. In such situations, as Dworkin has already taught us, our investigation must take special care.

Readers of "Do We have a Right to Pornography?" may be a little puzzled at this point. Why, we may be forgiven for asking, does Dworkin consider this "relatively trivial" issue to be worthy of serious attention, worthy in fact of a full forty-five pages of sophisticated political analysis? If we look again at the first of Dworkin's suggestions about the harm pornography brings about, we will find our answer. Most people, he says, would *prefer* censorship; if, in spite of this, we permit pornography, *general utility* will be harmed, since the majority preferences will be left unsatisfied.

This is enough to give us a fair idea of Dworkin's special interest in the question. We have the starting point for a familiar Dworkinian recipe for identifying rights, where one begins by noting that there is a good utilitarian argument for a certain policy, and that certain individuals will suffer as a result of this policy; investigates the preferences upon which the utilitarian argument is based; shows that they are

[13]Ibid., p. 340.
[14]Ibid., p. 338.
[15]Ibid., p. 335.
[16]Ibid., p. 354.
[17]Ibid., p. 355.
[18]Ibid., p. 359.
[19]Ibid., p. 358. Note that Dworkin uses the term *pornographer* to mean "consumer of pornography"; I follow his usage for the purposes of this article.

[20]Ibid., p. 338. As we will see later, this finding did not prevent the Williams Committee from making prohibitive recommendations with respect to pornography of certain kinds.

external preferences; and finally concludes that the individuals concerned have rights that must defeat the policy in question. This was Dworkin's response to *Sweatt;* and this is his response to pornography also.

Before offering this analysis in any detail, however, Dworkin is anxious to show the inadequacies of competing attempts to argue for the permission of pornography.[21] The Williams Committee, says Dworkin, attempted to do so by invoking a certain goal-based strategy, according to which free expression is a means to an important social end. Free expression is necessary if we are to have "a society that is most conducive to human beings' making intelligent decisions about what the best lives for them to lead are, and then flourishing in those lives."[22] Given the value of free expression, we should accept a presumption against any prohibition of it. Dworkin goes on to argue that a goal-based strategy of this kind, however admirable, simply does not have the resources to support an argument for permitting pornography; what one needs, instead of this argument of policy, is an argument of principle, that is, an argument that uses the concept of a right.

Dworkin's verdict on the Williams Report is not vital to our present inquiry, but it strikes me that he may have mischaracterized the difference between his own approach and that of the Williams Committee. Rather than presenting a contrast between goal-based and rights-based strategies for the defense of free expression, a more plausible analysis of the difference might be that it consists in a contrast between two rights-based strategies, Dworkin seeing a need to derive the right in question from a basic right to equality, and the Williams Committee seeing no such need. The following passage from the Williams Report can surely be read as an explicit rejection of the merely goal-based strategy that Dworkin attributes to the committee: "The value of free expression *does not lie solely in its consequences.* . . . It is rather that *there is a right to free expression* . . . and weighty considerations in terms of harm have to be advanced by those who seek to curtail it."[23]

Dworkin proceeds to show how it is possible to mount an argument of principle against a prohibitive policy. Suppose, he says, that the policy of prohibiting pornography would satisfy the preferences of the majority,[24] and that the opportunities of the consumers of pornography would be curtailed as a result. Our next step, if we are interested in finding out whether pornographers might have rights against this policy, is to consider the character of the preferences upon which the policy relies, since the right to equality demands that certain preferences be disregarded. Does the prohibitive policy rely on any external preferences? Remember that external preferences can be of two broad types: one can prefer that another person receive fewer goods and opportunities because one thinks that that person is worth less concern, or, alternatively, because one thinks that that person's conception of the good life deserves less respect. The external preferences involved in the *Sweatt* argument were of the former variety; in the case of pornography I take it that Dworkin thinks they are of the latter. People want pornography to be prohibited chiefly because they think that it is ignoble or wrong, and that a conception of the good life that holds otherwise deserves less respect. "Moralistic" preferences of this kind must, says Dworkin, be defeated by a corresponding "right to moral independence," which he describes as "the right not to suffer disadvantage in the distribution of social goods and opportunities, including disadvantage in the liberties permitted to them by the criminal law, just on the ground that their officials or fellow citizens think that their opinions about the right way for them to lead their own lives are ignoble or wrong."[25] Insofar as the utilitarian argument hinges on moralistic preferences, the consumers of pornography have rights that trump the prohibitive policy, and our policy should be permissive.[26]

It is crucial to note that pornographers are said to have rights not because there is something special about speech per se, and pornography is speech; nor because there is something special about the private domain in

---

[21]Home Office, *Report of the Committee on Obscenity and Film Censorship.* Cmnd. 7772 (London: Her Majesty's Stationery Office, 1979) (hereafter Williams Report). The Williams Report recommended, in brief, that some kinds of pornography (including live sex shows and child pornography) be banned and that other kinds of pornography be permitted on a restricted basis. Dworkin's chief, but by no means exclusive, concern is with its permissive aspect.

[22]Dworkin, "Right to Pornography?" p. 338.

[23]Williams Report, p. 56; italics mine.

[24]Dworkin, "Right to Pornography?" pp. 335, 360.

[25]Ibid., p. 353.

[26]Insofar as this permissive policy would in turn constrain the ability of other people to lead the lives of their choice, we have an argument for restriction of some form. So what Dworkin ends up with, balancing these conflicting considerations, is an endorsement of the compromise solution offered by the Williams Report, i.e., that most pornography should be permitted but restricted through measures such as zoning (ibid., p. 358).

which pornography is often consumed; but simply because they are vulnerable to the effects of the external preferences of others, and equality demands that such preferences be ignored. This essay provides a good illustration of Dworkin's strategy of deriving traditional liberties from the principle of equality alone. It is also worth pointing out that Dworkin claims that his own strategy, as illustrated here, does justice to deeply held liberal convictions about the value of free speech in a way that competing theoretical strategies cannot hope to do.[27]

PORNOGRAPHY AND CIVIL RIGHTS: A FEMINIST RESPONSE

The purpose of this section is to review briefly a certain feminist civil rights argument about pornography, in the hope of showing how the question is transformed once it is placed in a civil rights context. . . . The reader should be aware that the argument reviewed in this section is one of a variety of feminist responses, many of which disagree with both the analysis and the course of action advocated by this one.[28]

In contrast to the argument discussed in Dworkin's paper on the topic, this feminist argument against pornography sets aside questions about "morality" and focuses instead on the civil status of women. The argument has been put very forcefully by Catherine Mac Kinnon,[29] who has written widely on the subject, and who was involved in the drafting of the Indianapolis ordinance. In that ordinance pornography is defined as a civil rights violation:[30] "We define pornography as the graphic sexually explicit subordination of women through pictures or words that also includes women dehumanized as sexual objects, things or commodities; enjoying pain or humiliation or rape; being tied up, cut up, mutilated, bruised, or physically hurt; in postures of sexual submission or servility or display; reduced to body parts, penetrated by objects or animals, or presented in scenarios of degradation, injury, torture; shown as filthy or inferior; bleeding, bruised or hurt in a context which makes these conditions sexual."[31] The ordinance distinguished pornography from erotica, taking erotica to be sexually explicit material other than that covered by the above definition. It should be emphasized that according to this argument, and in contrast to "moralistic" arguments, there is nothing

[27]Ibid., p. 352.

[28]For a range of views other than MacKinnon's, see, e.g., Gail Chester and Julienne Dickey, eds., *Feminism and Censorship: The Current Debate* (Bridport, Eng.: Prism Press, 1988); Nan D. Hunter and Sylvia A. Law, "Brief Amici Curiae of Feminist Anti-Censorship Taskforce, *et al.*," in American Booksellers, Inc. v. Hudnut, 771 F.2d 323 (1985); Andrea Dworkin, *Pornography: Men Possessing Women* (London: The Women's Press, 1981); Varda Burstyn, ed., *Women Against Censorship* (Vancouver: Douglas and MacIntyre, 1985); and Edward Donnerstein, Daniel Linz, and Steven Penrod, *The Question of Pornography: Research Findings and Policy Implications* (New York: Free Press; London: Collier Macmillan, 1987), chaps. 7, 8.

[29]See MacKinnon, *Feminism Unmodified,* esp. "Francis Biddle's Sister." There are many important aspects of MacKinnon's argument that I do not take time to consider in any detail here—for example, the claim that pornography constitutes a form of subordination (which has been considered by Melinda Vadas in "A First Look at the Pornography/Civil Rights Ordinance: Could Pornography Be the Subordination of Women?" *Journal of Philosophy* [1987]: 487–511), and the claim (in answer to the champions of free speech) that pornography silences women, preventing women's exercise of free speech. The latter claim, if developed, might lead to an argument of a rather different kind, which saw the issue as presenting a conflict, not between liberty and equality, but between the liberty of men and the liberty of women.

[30]It should be noted that the ordinance made pornography civilly actionable, rather than a criminal offense. The definition used here is one that raises many difficult legal and philosophical questions in its own right, but I am afraid that such questions, while admittedly important, lie beyond the scope of this paper. A further question related to the definitional problems is that of the "slippery slope," a question that rightly concerned Dworkin (and the Williams Committee) and again deserves more attention than I give it here. While the "slippery slope" problem raises many difficulties, one should not, I take it, assume that it is insoluble; I proceed on the assumption that the problem is not so daunting that it rules out the possibility of discussion.

[31]MacKinnon, "Francis Biddle's Sister," p. 176.

[32]To give the reader some idea of the kind of pornography that might be covered by the above definition, I offer the following description of a relatively soft-core example, which appeared on the cover of an issue of *Hustler:* "The photograph is captioned 'Beaver Hunters.' Two white men, dressed as hunters, sit in a black Jeep. The Jeep occupies almost the whole frame of the picture. The two men carry rifles. The rifles extend above the frame of the photograph into the white space surrounding it. The men and the Jeep face into the camera. Tied onto the hood of the black Jeep is a white woman. She is tied with thick rope. She is spread-eagle. Her pubic hair and crotch are the dead center of the car hood and the photograph. Her head is turned to one side, tied down by rope that is pulled taut across her neck, extended to and wrapped several times around her wrists, tied around the rearview mirrors of the Jeep, brought back across her arms, crisscrossed under her breasts and over her thigh, drawn down and wrapped around the bumper of the Jeep, tied around her ankles. . . . The text under the photograph reads: 'Western sportsmen report beaver hunting was particularly good throughout the Rocky Mountain Region during the past season. These two hunters easily bagged their limit in the high country. They told HUSTLER that they stuffed and mounted their trophy as soon as they got her home.'" (Description given in Andrea Dworkin, *Pornography: Men Possessing Women,* pp. 25–26.)

wrong whatsoever with materials that are simply sexually arousing and explicit; the focus of concern lies elsewhere.[32] Insofar as the ordinance is not concerned with explicit material per se, it departs of course from a more traditional or popular conception that simply equates pornography with the sexually explicit, a conception I take Dworkin to have been using. Pornography as defined above is a subset, though, of pornography as it is popularly conceived, and Dworkin's remarks about the relevance of his own argument to the "radical feminist" case[33] indicate that he views pornographers as having a right to this kind of pornography as well.

The distinctive feature of the MacKinnon argument is that it views pornography—as defined in the ordinance—as having implications for sexual equality: pornography is seen as a practice that contributes to the subordinate status of women, just as certain other practices (segregation among them) contribute to the subordinate status of blacks. The argument seeks to establish at least two things: one is that women do not, as a matter of fact, currently have equal status; and the other is that pornography does, as a matter of fact, contribute significantly to the continuing subordinate position of women.

The first claim is, I think, not very controversial, and a cursory glance at sociological facts about the distribution of income and power should be enough to confirm it. One dimension to the inequality is the economic; women earn substantially less then men, and a disproportionate number of women live in poverty.[34] A further dimension to the inequality is to be found in the scale of the sexual abuse, including but not confined to rape, that women suffer and that men, as a rule, do not.[35] The advent of feminism has brought with it a new and more acute awareness of the conditions of women, says MacKinnon. I well let her continue:

> Rape, battery, sexual harassment, forced prostitution, and the sexual abuse of children emerge as common and systematic. . . . Sexual harassment of women by men is common in workplaces and educational institutions. Based on reports in one study of the federal workplace, up to 85 percent of women will experience it, many in physical forms. Between a quarter and a third of women are battered in their homes by men. Thirty-eight percent of little girls are sexually molested inside or outside the family. . . . We find that rape happens to women in all contexts, from the family, including rape of girls and babies, to students and women in the workplace, on the streets, at home, in their own bedrooms, by men they do not know and by men they do know, by men they are married to, men they have had social conversation with, and, least often, men they have never seen before. Overwhelmingly, rape is something that men do or attempt to do to women (44 percent of American women according to a recent study) at some point in our lives.[36]

What is different about MacKinnon's approach to facts like these is that she sees sexual violence not simply as "crime" (as Dworkin seemed apt to do), but rather as a dimension to the inequality of the sexes, and one that calls for an explanation. These things are done to women; they are not, by and large, done to men. To call such violence simply "crime," says MacKinnon, without remarking upon the interesting fact that the perpetrators are nearly always members of one class of citizens, and the victims members of another, would be to disguise its systematically discriminatory nature.

Turning now to the second claim, the feminist argument can be seen as offering a hypothesis about the explanation for this pattern of sexual abuse: part of the explanation lies in the fact that certain kinds of pornography help to form and propagate certain views about women and sexuality. Such pornography is said to work as a kind of propaganda, which both expresses a certain view about women and sexuality and perpetuates that view; it sexualizes rape, battery, sexual harassment,

---

[33]Dworkin, *A Matter of Principle,* p. 1.

[34]"What women do is seen as not worth much, or what is not worth much is seen as something for women to do," comments MacKinnon about women's pay, which at the time of her writing was 59 cents to the man's dollar ("Francis Biddle's Sister," p. 171). According to more recent figures, women in the United States who work full time now earn 66 cents to the man's dollar and constitute more than 60 percent of adults living below the federal poverty line (Claudia Wallis, "Onward Women!" *Time,* 4 December 1989, 85).

[35]This is not, of course, to say that it is only women who suffer sexual abuse, or to underrate the extent of the sexual violence suffered by children of both sexes, or by men in prisons. It is only to say that, as a pervasive phenomenon, sexual violence seems to be directed mainly against women.

[36]MacKinnon, "Francis Biddle's Sister," p. 169. (I have taken some liberties with the order of these passages.) MacKinnon cites a formidable array of studies in support of these claims; the constraints of space dictate that I cannot reproduce all of her sources here, so I refer the reader to the notes in her work (*Feminism Unmodified,* pp. 277–79). Joel Feinberg cites 1980 FBI Uniform Crime statistics, according to which "a twelve-year-old girl in the United States has one chance in three of being raped in her lifetime" (*Offense to Others* [New York: Oxford University Press, 1985], p. 149).

prostitution, and child sexual abuse; it thereby celebrates, promotes, authorizes and legitimizes them."[37] To back up this claim, a substantial amount of empirical evidence was cited by those supporting the ordinance (in the form of both social science studies and testimony of people whose lives had been directly affected by pornography) which pointed to the conclusion that pornography influences behavior and attitudes, and does so in ways that undermine both the well-being of women and sexual equality.[38] In the light of evidence of this kind, the Indianapolis City Council issued the following findings:

> Pornography is a discriminatory practice based on sex which denies women equal opportunities in society. Pornography is central in creating and maintaining sex as a basis for discrimination. Pornography is a systematic practice of exploitation and subordination based on sex which differentially harms women. The bigotry and contempt it promotes, with the acts of aggression it fosters, harm women's opportunities for equality of rights in employment, education, access to and use of public accommodations, and acquisition of real property; promote rape, battery, child abuse, kidnaping and prostitution and inhibit just enforcement of laws against such acts; and contribute significantly to restricting women in particular from full exercise of citizenship and participation in public life.[39]

The case was viewed by the district court as presenting a conflict between First Amendment guarantees of free speech and the Fourteenth Amendment right to be free from sex-based discrimination.[40] The ordinance would survive constitutional scrutiny only if the state's interest in sex-based equality were "so compelling as to be fundamental," for "only then can it be deemed to outweigh interest of free speech."[41] And the court concluded, as a matter of law, that the state's interest in sex-based equality was not so compelling.[42]

It is worth noting that the empirical findings were not disputed; in fact, when the case went to the court of appeals, Judge Frank Easterbrook went so far as to say, "We accept the premises of this legislation. Depictions of subordination tend to perpetuate subordination. The subordinate status of women in turn leads to affront and lower pay at work, insult and injury at home, battery and rape on the streets." His conclusion, however, is that "this simply demonstrates the powers of pornography as speech."[43] . . .

61

Plessy v. Ferguson

163 U.S. 537; 41 L. Ed. 256;
16 S. Ct. 1138 (1896)

JUSTICE BROWN *delivered the opinion of the Court.*

This case turns upon the constitutionality of an act of the general assembly of the State of Louisiana,

---

[37]MacKinnon, "Francis Biddle's Sister," pp. 171–72.

[38]The question of what is involved in making a causal claim of this kind is an important one. No one is claiming, of course, that there is a simple link; one can agree with Feinberg that "pornography does not cause normal decent chaps, through a single exposure, to metamorphose into rapists" (*Offense to Others,* p. 153). For an interesting discussion of the notions of causality that bear on questions of this kind, see Frederick Schauer, "Causation Theory and the Causes of Sexual Violence," *American Bar Foundation Research Journal* 1987, no. 4 (Fall 1987): 737–70. Questions about the empirical evidence are also important, and deserve more attention than I can give them here, but in brief: The social science studies seem to suggest that pornography, especially some kinds of violent pornography, can increase aggression against women in certain circumstances, and that it can change attitudes in the following ways. Subjects who are exposed to it can become more likely to view women as inferior, more disposed to accept "rape myths" (e.g., that women enjoy rape), more callous about sexual violence, more likely to view rape victims as deserving of their treatment, and more likely to say that they would themselves rape if they could get away with it. The personal testimony cited at the original Minneapolis Public Hearings (with reference to an ordinance nearly identical to that passed at Indianapolis, which did not, however, become law) included, among other things, testimony of women who had been victims of "copycat" rapes inspired by pornography. See the transcript of the 1983 Minneapolis Public Hearings, published as *Pornography and Sexual Violence: Evidence of the Links* (London: Everywoman, 1988); see also Eva Feder Kittay, "The Greater Danger—Pornography, Social Science and Women's Rights: Reply to Brannigan and Goldenberg." *Social Epistemology* 2 (1988): 117–33; for a more comprehensive discussion of the social science evidence, see Donnerstein et al., *The Question of Pornography.*

[39]Hudnut 1320.

[40]Hudnut 1327.

[41]Hudnut 1316. The case also raised constitutional problems in connection with the "due process" requirements of the Fifth and Fourteenth Amendments. The ordinance was judged to be vague and to establish prior restraint of speech and would therefore have been unconstitutional on those grounds alone.

[42]Hudnut 1326.

[43]771 F.2d 392 (7th Cir. 1985).

passed in 1890, providing for separate railway carriages for the white and colored races. . . .

The first section of the statute enacts "that all railway companies carrying passengers in their coaches in this state shall provide equal but separate accommodations for the white and colored races, by providing two or more passenger coaches for each passenger train, or by dividing the passenger coaches by a partition so as to secure separate accommodations: *Provided,* That this section shall be construed to apply to street railroads. No person or persons shall be permitted to occupy any coaches other than the ones assigned to them, on account of the race they belong to."

By the second section it was enacted "that the officers of such passenger trains shall have power and are hereby required to assign each passenger to the coach or compartment used for the race to which such passenger belongs: any passenger insisting on going into a coach or compartment to which by race he does not belong, shall be liable to a fine of $25 or in lieu thereof to imprisonment for a period of not more than twenty days in the parish prison." . . .

The information filed in the criminal district court charged in substance that Plessy, being a passenger between two stations within the State of Louisiana, was assigned by officers of the company to the coach used by the race to which he belonged, but he insisted upon going into a coach used by the race to which he did not belong. Neither in the information nor plea was his particular race or color averred.

The petition for the writ of prohibition averred that petitioner was seven-eighths Caucasian and one-eighth African blood; that the mixture of colored blood was not discernible in him, and that he was entitled to every right, privilege, and immunity secured to citizens of the United States of the white race; and that, upon such theory, he took possession of a vacant seat in a coach where passengers of the white race were accommodated, and was ordered by the conductor to vacate said coach and take a seat in another assigned to persons of the colored race, and having refused to comply with such demand he was forcibly ejected with the aid of a police officer, and imprisoned in the parish jail to answer a charge of having violated the above act.

The constitutionality of this act is attacked upon the ground that it conflicts both with the Thirteenth Amendment of the Constitution, abolishing slavery, and the Fourteenth Amendment, which prohibits certain restrictive legislation on the part of the States.

1. That it does not conflict with the Thirteenth Amendment, which abolished slavery and involuntary servitude, except as a punishment for crime, is too clear for argument. . . .

   A statute which implies merely a legal distinction between the white and colored races—a distinction which is founded in the color of the two races, and which must always exist so long as white men are distinguished from the other race by color—has no tendency to destroy the legal equality of the two races, or reestablish a state of involuntary servitude. Indeed, we do not understand that the Thirteenth Amendment is strenuously relied upon by the plaintiff in error in this connection.

2. By the Fourteenth Amendment, all persons born or naturalized in the United States, and subject to the jurisdiction thereof, are made citizens of the United States and of the State wherein they reside; and the States are forbidden from making or enforcing any law which shall abridge the privileges or immunities of citizens of the United States, or shall deprive any person of life, liberty, or property without due process of law, or deny to any person within their jurisdiction the equal protection of the laws. . . .

The object of the Amendment was undoubtedly to enforce the absolute equality of the two races before the law, but in the nature of things it could not have been intended to abolish distinctions based upon color, or to enforce social, as distinguished from political, equality, or a commingling of the two races upon terms unsatisfactory to either. Laws permitting and even requiring their separation in places where they are liable to be brought into contact do not necessarily imply the inferiority of either race to the other, and have been generally, if not universally, recognized as within the competency of the state legislatures in the exercise of their police power. The most common instance of this is connected with the establishment of separate schools for white and colored children, which have been held to be a valid exercise of the legislative power even by courts of States where the political rights of the colored race have been longest and most earnestly enforced.

One of the earliest of these cases is that of *Roberts v. Boston,* 5 Cush. 198, in which the supreme judicial court of Massachusetts held that the general school committee of Boston had power to make provision for the instruction of colored children in separate schools established exclusively for them, and to prohibit their attendance upon the other schools. . . . It was held that the powers of the committee extended to the "establishment of separate schools for children of different ages, sexes, and colors.". . . Similar laws have been enacted by Congress under its general power of legislation over the District of Columbia . . . as well as by the legislatures of many of the States, and have been generally, if not uniformly, sustained by the courts. . . .

Laws forbidding the intermarriage of the two races may be said in a technical sense to interfere with the freedom of contract, and yet have been universally recognized as within the police power of the State, *State v. Gibson,* 36 Ind. 389 (10 Am. Rep. 42).

The distinction between interfering with the political equality of the negro and those requiring the separation of the two races in schools, theaters, and railway carriages, has been frequently drawn by this court. Thus in *Strauder v. West Virginia,* 100 U.S. 303, it was held that a law of West Virginia limiting to white male persons, twenty-one years of age and citizens of the State, the right to sit upon juries, was a discrimination which implied a legal inferiority in civil society, which lessened the security of the right of the colored race, and was a step towards reducing them to a condition of servility. . . .

Much nearer, and, indeed almost directly in point, is the case of the *Louisville, N.O. & T.R. Co. v. Mississippi,* 133 U.S. 587, wherein the railway company was indicted for a violation of a statute of Mississippi, enacting that all railroads carrying passengers should provide equal, but separate, accommodations for the white and colored races, by providing two or more passenger cars for each passenger train, or by dividing the passenger cars by a partition, so as to secure separate accommodations. The case was presented in a different aspect from the one under consideration, inasmuch as it was an indictment against the railway company for failing to provide the separate accommodations, but the question considered was the constitutionality of the law. In that case, the supreme court of Mississippi, 66 Miss. 662, had held that the statute applied solely to commerce within the State, and, that being the construction of the state statute by its highest court, was accepted as conclusive. "If it be a matter," said the court, "respecting commerce wholly within a state, and not interfering with commerce between the states, then, obviously, there is no violation of the commerce clause of the Federal Constitution. . . . No question arises under this section as to the power of the state to separate in different compartments interstate passengers, or to affect in any manner, the privileges and rights of such passengers. All that we can consider is, whether the state has the power to require that railroad trains within her limits shall have separate accommodations for the two races; that affecting only commerce within the states is no invasion of the powers given to Congress by the commerce clause.". . .

[I]t is . . . suggested by the learned counsel for the plaintiff in error that the same argument that will justify the state legislature in requiring railways to provide separate accommodations for the two races will also authorize them to require separate cars to be provided for people whose hair is of a certain color, or who are aliens, or who belong to certain nationalities, or to enact laws requiring colored people to walk upon one side of the street, and white people upon the other, or requiring white men's houses to be painted white, and colored men's black, or their vehicles or business signs to be of different colors, upon the theory that one side of the street is as good as the other, or that a house or vehicle of one color is as good as one of another color. The reply to all this is that every exercise of the police power must be reasonable, and extend only to such laws as are enacted in good faith for the promotion of the public good, and not for the annoyance or oppression of a particular class. . . .

So far, then, as a conflict with the Fourteenth Amendment is concerned, the case reduces itself to the question whether the statute of Louisiana is a reasonable regulation, and with respect to this there must necessarily be a large discretion on the part of the legislature. In determining the question of reasonableness it is at liberty to act with reference to the established usages, customs, and traditions of the people, and with a view to the promotion of their comfort, and the preservation of the public peace and good order. Gauged by this standard, we cannot say that a law which authorizes or even requires the separation of the two races in public conveyances is unreasonable or more obnoxious to the Fourteenth Amendment than the acts of

Congress requiring separate schools for colored children in the District of Columbia, the constitutionality of which does not seem to have been questioned, or the corresponding acts of state legislatures.

We consider the underlying fallacy of the plaintiff's argument to consist in the assumption that the enforced separation of the two races stamps the colored race with a badge of inferiority. If this be so, it is not by reason of anything found in the act, but solely because the colored race chooses to put that construction upon it. The argument necessarily assumes that if, as has been more than once the case, and is not unlikely to be so again, the colored race would become the dominant power in the state legislature, and should enact a law in precisely similar terms, it would thereby relegate the white race to an inferior position. We imagine that the white race, at least, would not acquiesce in this assumption. The argument also assumes that social prejudices may be overcome by legislation, and that equal rights cannot be secured to the negro except by an enforced commingling of the two races. We cannot accept this proposition. If the two races are to meet on terms of social equality, it must be the result of natural affinities, a mutual appreciation of each other's merits and a voluntary consent of individuals. . . . Legislation is powerless to eradicate racial instincts or to abolish distinctions based upon physical differences, and the attempt to do so can only result in accentuating the difficulties of the present situation. If the civil and political rights of both races be equal, one cannot be inferior to the other civilly or politically. If one race be inferior to the other socially, the Constitution of the United States cannot put them upon the same plane.

It is true that the question of the proportion of colored blood necessary to constitute a colored person, as distinguished from a white person, is one upon which there is a difference of opinion in the different States, some holding that any visible admixture of black stamps the person as belonging to the colored race (*State v. Chavers,* 5 Jones, L. II); others that it depends upon the predominance of blood (*Gray v. State,* 4 Ohio 354; *Monroe v. Collins,* 17 Ohio St. 665); and still others that the predominance of white blood must only be in the proportion of three fourths (*People v. Dean* 14 Mich. 406; *Jones v. Com.* 80 Va. 544). But these are questions to be determined under the laws of each State and are not properly put in issue in this case. Under the allegation of his petition it may undoubtedly become a question of importance whether, under the laws of Louisiana, the petitioner belongs to the white or colored race.

The judgment of the court below is therefore affirmed.

[JUSTICE BREWER did not hear the argument or participate in the decision of this case.]

JUSTICE HARLAN, *dissenting.* . . .

[W]e have before us a state enactment that compels, under penalties, the separation of the two races in railroad passenger coaches, and makes it a crime for a citizen of either race to enter a coach that has been assigned to citizens of the other race.

Thus the State regulates the use of a public highway by citizens of the United States solely upon the basis of race.

However apparent the injustice of such legislation may be, we have only to consider whether it is consistent with the Constitution of the United States. . . .

In respect of civil rights, common to all citizens, the Constitution of the United States does not, I think, permit any public authority to know the race of those entitled to be protected in the enjoyment of such rights. Every true man has pride of race, and under appropriate circumstances, when the rights of others, his equals before the law, are not to be affected, it is his privilege to express such pride and to take such action based upon it as to him seems proper. But I deny that any legislative body or judicial tribunal may have regard to the race of citizens when the civil rights of those citizens are involved. Indeed such legislation as that here in question is inconsistent, not only with that equality of rights which pertains to citizenship, national and state, but with the personal liberty enjoyed by everyone within the United States. [The Thirteenth, Fourteenth and Fifteenth Amendments] removed the race line from our governmental systems. They had, as this Court has said, a common purpose, namely, to secure "to a race recently emancipated, a race that through many generations have [*sic*] been held in slavery, all the civil rights that the superior race enjoys." They declared, in legal effect, this court has further said, "that the law in the states shall be the same for the black as for the white: that all persons, whether colored or white, shall stand equal before the laws of the states, and, in regard to the colored race, for whose protection that amendment was primarily designed, that no discrimination shall be made against them by law because of their color." We also said; "The words of the Amendment, it is true, are prohibitory, but they contain a necessary implication of a positive immunity, or right, most valuable to the colored race—the right to exemption from unfriendly legislation against them distinctively as colored—exemption from legal discriminations, implying inferiority in civil society, lessening the security of their enjoyment of the rights which others enjoy, and discrimination which are steps towards reducing them to the condition of a subject race."...

It was said in argument that the statute of Louisiana does not discriminate against either race, but prescribes a rule applicable alike to white and colored citizens. But this argument does not meet the difficulty. Everyone knows that the statute in question had its origin in the purpose, not so much to exclude white persons from railroad cars occupied by blacks, as to exclude colored people from coaches occupied or assigned to white persons. Railroad corporations of Louisiana did not make discrimination among whites in the matter of accommodation for travelers. The thing to accomplish was, under the guise of giving equal accommodation for whites and blacks, to compel the latter to keep to themselves while traveling in railroad passenger coaches. No one would be so wanting in candor to assert the contrary. The fundamental objection, therefore, to the statute is that it interferes with the personal freedom of citizens. "Personal liberty," it has been well said, "consists in the power of locomotion, of changing situation, or removing one's person to whatsoever place one's own inclination may direct, without imprisonment or restraint, unless by due course of law," 1 B1. Com. 134. If a white man and a black man choose to occupy the same public conveyance on a public highway, it is their right to do so, and no government, proceeding alone on grounds of race, can prevent it without infringing the personal liberty of each.

It is one thing for railroad carriers to furnish, or to be required by law to furnish, equal accommodations for all whom they are under a legal duty to carry. It is quite another thing for government to forbid citizens of the white and black races from traveling in the same public conveyance, and to punish officers of railroad companies for permitting persons of the two races to occupy the same passenger coach. If a State can prescribe as a rule of civil conduct, that whites and blacks shall not travel as passengers in the same railroad coach, why may it not so regulate the use of the streets of its cities and towns as to compel white citizens to keep on one side of the street and black citizens to keep on the other? Why may it not, upon like grounds, punish whites and blacks who ride together in street cars or in open vehicles on a public road or street? Why may it not require sheriffs to assign whites to one side of the courtroom and blacks to the other? And why may it not also prohibit the commingling of the two races in the galleries of legislative halls or in public assemblages convened for the political questions of the day? Further, if this statute of Louisiana is consistent with the personal liberty of citizens, why may not the State require the separation in railroad coaches of native and naturalized citizens of the United States, or of Protestants and Roman Catholics?

The answer given at the argument to these questions was that regulations of the kind they suggest would be unreasonable, and could not, therefore, stand before the law. Is it meant that the determination of questions of legislative power depends upon the inquiry whether the statute whose validity is questioned is, in the judgment of the courts, a reasonable one, taking all the circumstances into consideration? A statute may be unreasonable merely because a sound public policy forbade its enactment. But I do not understand that the courts have anything to do with the policy or expediency of legislation. A statute may be valid, and yet upon grounds of public policy may well be characterized as unreasonable. Mr. Sedgwick correctly states the rule when he says that the legislative intention being clearly ascertained, "the courts have no other duty to perform than to execute the legislative will, without any regard to their views as to the wisdom or justice of the particular enactment." Sedgw. Stat. & Const. L. 324....

The white race deems itself to be the dominant race in this country. And so it is, in prestige, in achievements, in education, in health, and in power. So, I doubt not that it will continue to be for all time, if it remains true to its great heritage and holds fast to the principles of constitutional liberty. But in view of the Constitution, in the eye of the law, there is in this country no superior, dominant, ruling class of citizens. There is no caste here. Our Constitution is color-blind, and neither knows nor tolerates classes among citizens. In respect of civil rights, all citizens are equal before the law. The humblest is the peer of the most powerful. The law regards man as man, and takes no account of his surroundings or of his color when his civil rights as guaranteed by the supreme law of the land are involved. It is therefore to be regretted that this high tribunal, the final expositor of the fundamental law of the land, has reached the conclusion that it is competent for a state to regulate the enjoyment by citizens of their civil rights solely upon the basis of race.

In my opinion, the judgment this day rendered will, in time, prove to be quite as pernicious as the decision made by this tribunal in the *Dred Scott Case*. . . . The recent amendments of the Constitution, it was supposed, had eradicated the principles (announced in that decision) from our institutions. But it seems that we have yet, in some of the states, a dominant race, a superior class of citizens, which assumes to regulate the enjoyment of civil rights, common to all citizens, upon the basis of race. The present decision, it may well be apprehended, will not stimulate aggressions, more or less brutal and irritating, upon the admitted rights of colored citizens, but will encourage the belief that it is possible, by means of state enactments, to defeat the beneficent purposes which the people of the United States had in view when they adopted the recent amendments of the Constitution. . . . Sixty millions of whites are in no danger from the presence here of eight millions of blacks. The destinies of the two races in this country are indissolubly linked together, and the interests of both require that the common government of all shall not permit the seeds of race hate to be planted under the sanction of law. What can more certainly arouse race hate, what more certainly create and perpetuate a feeling of distrust between these races, than state enactments which in fact proceed on the ground that colored citizens are so inferior and degraded that they cannot be allowed to sit in public coaches occupied by white citizens? That, as all will admit, is the real meaning of such legislation as was enacted in Louisiana.

The sure guaranty of the peace and security of each race is the clear, distinct, unconditional recognition by our governments, national and state, of every right that inheres in civil freedom, and of the equality before the law of all citizens of the United States without regard to race. State enactments, regulating the enjoyment of civil rights, upon the basis of race, are cunningly devised to defeat legitimate results of the war, under the pretense of recognizing equality of rights, and can have no other result than to render permanent peace impossible and to keep alive a conflict of races, the continuance of which must do harm to all concerned. . . .

The arbitrary separation of citizens, on the basis of race, while they are on a public highway, is a badge of servitude wholly inconsistent with the civil freedom and the equality before the law established by the Constitution. It cannot be justified upon any legal grounds.

If evils will result from the commingling of the two races upon public highways established for the benefit of all, they will be infinitely less than those that will surely come from state legislation regulating the enjoyment of civil rights upon the basis of race. We boast of the freedom enjoyed by our people above all other peoples. But it is difficult to reconcile that boast with a state of the law which, practically, puts the brand of servitude and degradation upon a large class of our fellow citizens, our equals before the law. The thin disguise of "equal" accommodations for passengers in railroad coaches will not mislead anyone, or atone for the wrong this day done. . . .

I am of opinion that the statute of Louisiana is inconsistent with the personal liberty of citizens, white and black, in that State, and hostile to both the spirit and letter of the Constitution of the United States. If laws of like character should be enacted in the several States of the Union, the effect would be in the highest degree mischievous. Slavery as an institution tolerated by law would, it is true, have disappeared from our country, but there would remain a power in the States, by sinister legislation, to interfere with the full enjoyment of the blessings of freedom: to regulate civil rights, common to all citizens, upon the basis of race; and to place in a condition of legal inferiority a large body of American citizens, now constituting a part of the political community, called the people of the United States, for whom and by whom, through representatives, our government is administered. Such a system is inconsistent with the guarantee given by the Constitution to each state of a republican form of government, and may be stricken down by Congressional action, or by the courts in the discharge of their solemn duty to maintain the supreme law of the land anything in the Constitution or laws of any State to the contrary notwithstanding.

For the reasons stated, I am constrained to withhold my assent from the opinion and judgment of the majority.

62

Brown v. Board of Education of Topeka, Kansas I

347 U.S. 483; 98 L. Ed. 873;
74 S. Ct. 686 (1954)

CHIEF JUSTICE WARREN *delivered the opinion of the Court.*

These cases came to us from the States of Kansas, South Carolina, Virginia, and Delaware. They are premised on different facts and different local conditions, but a common legal question justified their consideration together in this consolidated opinion.

In each of the cases, minors of the Negro race, through their legal representatives, seek aid of the courts in obtaining admission to the public schools of their community on a non segregated basis. . . . In each of the cases other than the Delaware case, a three-judge federal district court denied relief to the plaintiffs on the so-called "separate but equal" doctrine, announced by the Court in *Plessy v. Ferguson*. . . . In the Delaware case, the Supreme Court of Delaware adhered to that doctrine, but ordered that the plaintiffs be admitted to the white schools because of their superiority to the Negro schools.

The plaintiffs contend that segregated public schools are not "equal" and cannot be made "equal," and that hence they are deprived of the equal protection of the laws. Because of the obvious importance of the question presented, the Court took jurisdiction. Argument was heard in the 1952 Term, and reargument was heard this Term on certain questions propounded by the Court.

Reargument was largely devoted to the circumstances surrounding the adoption of the Fourteenth Amendment in 1868. It covered exhaustively consideration of the Amendment in Congress, ratification by the States, then existing practices in racial segregation, and the views of proponents and opponents of the Amendment. This discussion and our own investigation convince us that, although these sources cast some light, it is not enough to resolve the problem with which we are faced. At best, they are inconclusive. The most avid proponents of the post-War Amendments undoubtedly intended them to remove all legal distinctions among "all persons born or naturalized in the United States." Their opponents as certainly were antagonistic to both the letter and spirit of the Amendments and wished them to have the most limited effect. What others in Congress and the state legislatures had in mind cannot be determined with any degree of certainty.

An additional reason for the inconclusive nature of the Amendment's history, with respect to segregated schools, is the status of public education at that time. In the South, the movement toward free common schools, supported by general taxation, had not yet taken hold. Education for white children was largely in the hands of private groups. Education for Negroes was almost nonexistent, and practically all of the race was illiterate. In fact, any education of Negroes was forbidden by law in some States. Today, in contrast, many Negroes have achieved outstanding success in the arts and sciences as well as in the business and professional world. It is true that public education had already advanced further in the North, but the effect of the Amendment on Northern States was generally ignored in the Congressional debates. Even in the North, the conditions of public education did not approximate those existing today. The curriculum was usually rudimentary; ungraded schools were common in rural areas; the school term was but three months a year in many States; and compulsory school attendance was virtually unknown. As a consequence, it is not surprising that there should be so little in the history of the Fourteenth Amendment relating to its intended effect on public education.

In the first cases in this Court construing the Fourteenth Amendment, decided shortly after its adoption, the Court interpreted it as proscribing all state-imposed discriminations against the Negro race. The doctrine of "separate but equal" did not make its appearance in the Court until 1896 in the case of *Plessy v. Ferguson,* . . . involving not education but transportation. American courts have since labored with the doctrine for over half a century. In this Court, there have been six cases involving the "separate but equal' doctrine in the field of public education. In *Cumming v. Board of Education of Richmond County* and *Gong Lum v. Rice,* the validity of the doctrine itself was not challenged. In more recent cases, all on the graduate school level, inequality was found in that specific benefits enjoyed by white students were denied to Negro students of the same educational qualifications *(State of Missouri ex. rel. Gaines v. Canada, Sipuel v. Board of Regents of University of Oklahoma, Sweatt v. Painter,* and *McLaurin v. Oklahoma State Regents).* In none of these cases was it necessary to reexamine the doctrine to grant relief to the Negro plaintiff. And in *Sweatt v. Painter,* . . . the Court expressly reserved decision on the question whether *Plessy v. Ferguson* should he held inapplicable to public education. . . .

In approaching this problem, we cannot turn the clock back to 1868 when the Amendment was adopted, or even to 1896 when *Plessy v. Ferguson* was written. We must consider public education in the light of its full development and its present place in American life throughout the Nation. Only in this way can it be determined if segregation in public schools deprives these plaintiffs of the equal protection of the laws.

Today, education is perhaps the most important function of state and local governments. Compulsory school attendance laws and the great expenditures for education both demonstrate our recognition of the importance of education to our democratic society. It is required in the performance of our most basic public responsibilities, even service in the armed forces. It is the very foundation of good citizenship. Today it is a principal instrument in awakening the child to cultural values, in preparing him for later professional training, and in helping him to adjust normally to his environment. In these days, it is doubtful that any child may reasonably be expected to succeed in life if he is denied the opportunity of an education. Such an opportunity, where the State has undertaken to provide it, is a right which must be made available to all on equal terms.

We come then to the question presented: Does segregation of children in public schools solely on the basis of race, even though the physical facilities and other "tangible" factors may be equal, deprive the children of the minority group of equal educational opportunities? We believe that it does.

In *Sweatt v. Painter* . . . in finding that a segregated law school for Negroes could not provide them equal educational opportunities, this Court relied in large part on "those qualities which are incapable of objective measurement but which make for greatness in a law school." In *McLaurin v. Oklahoma State Regents* . . . the Court, in requiring that a Negro admitted to a white graduate school be treated like all other students, again resorted to intangible considerations: ". . . his ability to study, to engage in discussion and exchange views with other students and, in general, to learn his profession." Such considerations apply with added force to children in grade and high schools. To separate them from others of similar age and qualifications solely because of their race generates a feeling of inferiority as to their status in the community that may affect their hearts and minds in a way unlikely ever to be undone. The effect of this separation on their educational opportunities was well stated by a finding in the Kansas case by a court which nevertheless felt compelled to rule against the Negro plaintiffs:

> Segregation of white and colored children in public schools has a detrimental effect upon the colored children. The impact is greater when it has the sanction of the law; for the policy of separating the races is usually interpreted as denoting the inferiority of the negro group. A sense of inferiority affects the motivation of a child to learn. Segregation with the sanction of law, therefore, has a tendency to retard the educational and mental development of negro children and to deprive them of the benefits they would receive in a racially integrated school system.

Whatever may have been the extent of psychological knowledge at the time of *Plessy v. Ferguson,* this finding is amply supported by modern authority. Any language in *Plessy v. Ferguson* contrary to this finding is rejected.

We conclude that in the field of public education the doctrine of "separate but equal" has no place. Separate educational facilities are inherently unequal. Therefore, we hold that the plaintiffs and others similarly situated for whom the actions have been brought are, by the reason of the segregation complained of, deprived of the equal protection of the laws guaranteed by the Fourteenth Amendment. This disposition makes unnecessary any discussion whether such segregation also violates the Due Process Clause of the Fourteenth Amendment.

Because these are class actions because of the wide applicability of the decision, and because of the great variety of local conditions, the formulation of decrees in these cases presents problems of considerable complexity. . . . In order that we may have the full assistance of the parties in formulating decrees, the cases will be restored to the docket, and the parties are requested to present further argument on [the appropriate decree]. The Attorney General of the United States is again invited to participate. The Attorneys General of the States requiring or permitting segregation in public education will also be permitted to appear as *amici curiae* upon request to do so by September 15, 1954, and submission of briefs by October 1, 1954.

Cases ordered restored to docket for further argument on question of appropriate decrees.

It is so ordered.

PART 8

FAMILY LAW

Recently, philosophers have displayed increasing interest in the area of family law, for several reasons. Two reasons stand out in particular. First, in recent decades, philosophers have shown both a renewed interest in ethical theory overall and a new interest in applied ethics. This attention has instigated debate on topics such as the potential foundations for rights, abortion, euthanasia, and same-sex marriage, to name only a few. Second, the emergence of philosophy influenced by political movements such as feminism and the gay and lesbian rights movement has motivated concern for exploring such issues as gender equality within family law.

The writings that follow illustrate the diversity of issues found within family law. One main issue concerns the very definition of family. How is a family formed? Can the way a family is formed limit whom the state considers to be a family? The answers to such questions particularly affect one current topic of public debate, namely, the legalization of same-sex marriage. Another issue concerns the rights of unwed mothers and fathers in adoption proceedings. Does gender equality mean giving both access to the same rights? Or does one of the parties deserve special status? As important as these questions are, they only hint at the complexity of issues in family law.

Given the variety of issues within family law, we begin this chapter with a discussion of the structure of the family. In "Relational Rights and Responsibilities: Revisioning the Family in Liberal and Political Theory and Law," Martha Minow and Mary Lyndon Shanley explore a variety of views of the family in discussing the principles that ought to govern family law. The first view stems from contract-based theories. Some feminists argue that marriage contracts could potentially allow for greater freedom and autonomy by allowing spouses to decide how to order all aspects of familial life. Additionally, the state could readily allow same-sex marriage contracts. Contracting out childbearing through surrogate mothers could also increase autonomy. Though contracts may allow such benefits, Minow and Shanley believe that contracts are too crude to deal with a complex relationship like a marriage, in part because they lack flexibility. Minow and Shanley go on to explore community-based theories of the family. Such theories view families as public, not private, entities that help to compose civil society and the polity. Some feminists see this theory as recognizing the true construction of the self, a view that focusing on autonomy can distort. While this theory may allow a more comprehensive view of the self, it may promote increasingly deep divisions on a variety of topics. For example, a community might not endorse same-sex marriage because its members hold so many different views of the family and therefore cannot reach a consensus. Third, Minow and Shanley discuss rights-based theories of the family. In such theories, society extends particular individual rights to families. Although this theory respects freedom by limiting government action within the family, questions arise concerning conflicts between rights. For example, the state might need to enter the home to protect individual rights such as the right to be free from abuse. Although such conflicts exist, the theory does not clarify which rights ought to receive priority.

Given the strengths and weaknesses of these theories, Minow and Shanley focus on two paradoxes that principles governing family law must recognize. First, such principles must present each person as both a distinct individual and a person in relationships. Second, the principles must acknowledge that family relationships are both outside of and shaped by the political order. Minow and Shanley believe that relational rights, those rights that arise from and are grounded in human relationships, best answer the two paradoxes. A concept of relational rights will expand our understanding of individuals by focusing on relationships and recognizing the interdependence among all family members and that between the family and the larger polity. Additionally, Minow and Shanley see this expansion as invigorating both private and public discussion of family issues. For example, the community must address questions of justice within both the family and the larger polity before we achieve justice in either arena. These discussions will eventually reform both family law and the processes that lead to its creation.

In "Beyond Lesbian and Gay 'Families We Choose,'" William N. Eskridge, Jr., focuses on the issues surrounding same-sex families. Currently, gays and lesbians have what Eskridge terms "families of choice," but they lack the options and securities of heterosexual families. This is because the law restricts whom gays and lesbians can marry and limits their parenting options. More important, Eskridge finds families of choice objectionable because these families lead to the neglect of the relational features of the self. Because the state does not allow gays and lesbians to marry, they turn to other options. They can, for example, adopt contracts that capture many aspects of marriage, have a web of friendships that replaces traditional marriage, or have domestic partnerships. While this variety of choices might sound appealing, Eskridge finds it problematic because, although heterosexuals can have fractured selves, gays and lesbians have even more choices, fewer well-defined roles, and less security. This leads to an increased potential for fracture on the part of gays and lesbians. For Eskridge, relationships shape identity; therefore, parent-child or partner-partner relationships deserve special protection because they are critical to identity. Partnerships allow individuals to transcend the self and deepen their identities. This ability to transcend and deepen leads to a stable sense of self. By limiting same-sex relationships, Eskridge argues that the state limits the flourishing of personhood and discriminates unfairly against gays and lesbians.

In a selection from *Economic Analysis of Law*, Richard A. Posner offers an economic analysis of the family and its various aspects. Posner speculates that the persistence of the family means it must have important economizing properties, such as playing a role in the division of labor. Yet, falling marriage rates and increasing divorce rates suggest that the benefits of marriage are failing relative to costs. Although Posner uses free-market principles to explore marriages, he does point out differences between marriage and contract law, especially before the institution of no-fault divorce. First, the spouses cannot alter or terminate a marriage contract by mutual consent, unlike a business contract. Second, sanctions for breaches are more severe for marriages. Third, courts do not intervene to settle disputes in marriages. Posner suggests that a return to some of these limitations might help marriage partners. For example, if society banned divorce, people would be more careful in entering it, would have longer courtships, and would have incentive to work out problems in the marriage. However, because such a system would have its costs, Posner recognizes there is no proof that limiting divorce is the better system.

Posner next explores the impact of a marriage's dissolution. When marriages dissolve, they create a situation much more difficult than that created when businesses dissolve. In a marriage, the wife may have little market income, but she might have helped the family, and potentially helped increase the husband's income, by focusing exclusively on the work of the home. Nevertheless, Posner argues that community property laws are too arbitrary; as an alternative, he suggests using a hypothetical prenuptial agreement as a benchmark. If the parties gained the wealth after marriage, they should think about what split they would have agreed to if one party exclusively held the wealth before marriage. Posner also offers several ways to view alimony. First, it could be a form of damages for breach of contract. Second, it could be a form of paying the wife for her share of the marital partnership assets. Third, it could be a form of severance pay or unemployment benefits.

Posner explores a variety of other familial issues. For example, parents' fear of underinvestment in their children drives social responses such as compulsory and free public schooling. Additionally, Posner argues that the state should allow any parents who do not wish to invest in their children to put them up for adoption and be paid for surrendering their parental rights. Allowing such payment will not, in Posner's opinion, lead to any greater harms than those that already exist in the adoption system. Similarly, society should allow surrogate motherhood contracts, but with restrictions that make the contract more certain and less easy to break. As for laws regarding sexual behavior, such as homosexuality, Posner claims that society should allow these laws if they make economic sense. Given the high cost of prohibiting victimless crimes, such laws are likely unjustified.

On another front, Jacqueline Krikorian explores women's marital rights in "A Different Form of Apartheid? The Legal Status of Married Women in South Africa." Krikorian first focuses on marital rape. In South Africa, the common law held that marital rape is not a criminal offense, because the husband is entitled under law to have sexual relations with his wife. Krikorian identifies two reasons for this practice that arise out of Roman-Dutch common law. First, married spouses have reciprocal and irrevocable mutual obligations, with the right to have sex being one of them. Second, wives are to submit to their husband's sexual demands, because South African society views wives as inferior beings, with the husband controlling their bodies and possessions. Recently, there has been conflict in the South African judicial system over this practice, and the courts have accepted two limitations. First, if a wife's physical health is at risk, she can refuse. Second, there cannot be excessive force by the husband, but if force arises, the state will charge him with assault, not rape. In 1985, the South African Law Commission recommended that the marital rape exemption be eliminated, but this recommendation was rejected. The National Party Government reexamined this issue in 1993 and, after several attempts, they eventually abolished it. Nevertheless, Krikorian argues that wives still have to convince an unwilling police force and judiciary a rape occurred. The corroboration rule of evidence makes this more difficult, because under this rule the court does not take a woman's testimony at face value; instead, the court must corroborate her testimony for fear she is lying under oath.

Next, Krikorian explores the impact of the community property laws on the women of South Africa. Asian, coloured,[1] and white women married before 1984 were governed by the "common law community of property system" (see p. 589). First, this system allowed community of property, making spouses co-owners of all property. Second, it gave marital power to the husband in controlling all property, all finances, and the person of his wife. Women could not contract without their husband's consent, except for household necessities. Women also had no legal standing in court, except in matrimonial actions. One could opt out of this system with an antenuptual contract, which gave the spouses separate estates. Under this system, wives could not inherit, unless specified to in a will, and husbands remained head of household. Black South African women married before 1988 were autonomically married out of community of property and were subject to marital power, but they could opt out with an antenuptual contract.

The government changed this system for Asian, coloured, and white women with the passage of the Matrimonial Property Act of 1984 and for black women in 1988. Under this policy, the state retained community of property, but it abolished the marital power consequences. Men remained head of household but had to share the administration of joint estates. Also, the government changed aspects of the opting out of community of property. For example, women could inherit without a will, but a prior agreement could limit this. In 1993, the government further changed the law to eliminate men's marital powers and head-of-household status. While these policies govern all marriages after 1984 or 1988, the old rules still govern all marriages before then unless the marriage partners petition the court for a change to the new rules.

In "The Tragedy of Bride Burning in India: How Should the Law Address It?" Anshu Nangia explores the issues surrounding dowry murders in India. Often in India, when a husband receives a dowry deemed too small, he or a relative will murder his wife, with the death generally caused by burning or by driving her to suicide. To limit these dowry deaths, the government of India now presumes that any death occurring within seven years of the marriage, when combined with cruelty or harassment by the husband or in-laws, is a dowry death. The burden of proof is on

---

[1] "Coloured" here means having one black parent.

the accused to demonstrate that the death was not a dowry death. This presumption is critical, because the death usually occurs in the home and is done by burning, a method that destroys evidence. Although this presumption is beneficial, the government must also demonstrate cruelty or harassment, which is also difficult to prove, because it can be subtle and private. Additionally, the seven-year limit allows for the postponement of dowry death. The assumption is that the seven years will bring stability and children that together ease tension; yet, Nangia argues, this is not always the case. Further, given the high cost of divorce and maintenance, killing the wife is often cheaper.

The court system also allows cognizance of the offense in several ways: the court's own knowledge, a police report, or a complaint by the spouse, parent of the spouse, or welfare organization. This allows women's organizations to work with the court to help women by reporting crimes they or their parents might not report. Even so, Nangia argues, this system depends on the discretion of the court and often leads to dismissal. When the police arrest a spouse for a dowry murder, the offense is both nonbailable and noncompoundable. Unfortunately, many courts do allow bail and most cases result in acquittals. The government has also instituted complementary provisions designed to help the victim. Cruelty and breach of trust are both criminal offenses punishable by imprisonment for up to three years. Again, Nangia illustrates that the criminal often covers up such crimes or the police ignore them. Thus, while the government has instituted statutory reform, Nangia points to problems with the system that allow dowry murders to continue.

Deborah L. Forman, in "Unwed Fathers and Adoption: A Theoretical Analysis in Context," focuses on the case law that has come to define the rights of unwed biological fathers. Historically, these fathers have had no rights to custody, visitation, or recognition. The mother had sole custody and could put the child up for adoption without the biological father's consent. *Stanley v. Illinois*[2] began the erosion of this policy. Forman argues this case was relatively easy to decide because Stanley was both the biological and social father of the children.

Quilloin v. Walcott[3] was the first Supreme Court decision to consider the rights of unwed fathers in the case of adoption. Here, Quilloin sought to block the adoption of his illegitimate child to the stepfather. The Supreme Court rejected his claim for two reasons. First, the family unit that already exists receives full recognition. Second, Quilloin had never shouldered any responsibility for his child previously. This ruling made "simple biology" not enough to block adoptions; instead, there must be some kind of social relationship. In a similar case, *Caban v. Mohammed,*[4] the biological father had lived with the mother for several years and continued to see the child. Both biological parents had married and both wanted to adopt the child. The Supreme Court ruled that there was no fundamental difference between paternal and maternal rights that justified maternal privilege. Yet, the Court limited this finding to cases where the father is known and has expressed an interest in his child, and the child is not a newborn. Again, the existence of a social relationship is crucial to the recognition of an unwed father's right to veto an adoption. *Lehr v. Robertson*[5] further clarified the Court's view. Here, Lehr had never lived with the mother after the birth of the child, been named the father, or filed to receive notice of the adoption. The Supreme Court rejected his claim, stating that fatherhood depends on social fatherhood and an assumption of paternal responsibilities. Biology is not enough to stop an adoption; instead, "biology plus" is necessary. *Michael H. v. Gerald D.*[6] complicates the Court's prior rulings. Here, the husband of the mother, Gerald D., was not the biological father of the child; Michael H. was. Michael lived with the mother for one and one-half years; after her return to her husband, the father filed for paternity and visitation, thereby satisfying the biology-plus formula. Although he satisfied the criterion, the Court denied his motion for paternity and visitation, because the Court found that the law protects the marital family.

These rulings illustrate two principles: biology is not enough, and biology plus is necessary but not sufficient, for exercising the rights of the father. Given the problems with biology plus, many states now use the "substantial commitment standard," where the father must demonstrate a commitment to assuming parental responsibilities before his rights

[2]405 U.S. 645 (1972).
[3]434 U.S. 246 (1978).

[4]441 U.S. 380 (1979).
[5]463 U.S. 248 (1983).
[6]491 U.S. 110 (1989).

are granted, but this standard is still vague and difficult to apply. *In re Raquel Marie X,*[7] the New York Court of Appeals struck down a requirement that the father live with the mother for six months before the adoption in order for him to exercise his rights. In *Baby Girl S,*[8] a similar case, the New York Court of Appeals stated that the six-month statute failed to serve adequately any valid state interest. Forman claims these rulings initially appear to be pleasing to multiple factions. Men receive more rights, but they must earn those rights. Some have argued, however, that problems remain. For example, the state treats children as property and focuses on individuals, not the family. Forman argues that this view assumes that parental rights cannot incorporate the child's interests, but this is an incorrect assumption.

In "Fathers' Rights, Mothers' Wrongs? Reflections on Unwed Fathers' Rights and Sex Equality," Mary L. Shanley focuses on the basis and nature of an unwed biological father's right to veto an adoption decision of the mother. When a biological father vetoes the adoption and receives custody of the child, the court often grounds this right in both the idea that parenthood is a good and a commitment to gender equality. Yet, such decisions assume that once a mother has surrendered custody her wishes are no longer relevant. Shanley argues that such assumptions ignore the mother's preference as to who will raise her child. In fact, she may have compelling reasons for not making the father a custodial parent, such as not knowing the father well or suspicion of abuse. Given these potential problems, Shanley argues that there are reasons to weigh the mother's wishes more heavily than the father's. Because the mother has borne the child for nine months, the relationship of the father and the mother to the child is not symmetrical. The activity of carrying the child for nine months affects the mother by allowing her to establish caregiving before birth in a way that is unique to women. Given that the relationships are not symmetrical, with the mother having a stronger relationship to the child based on nurturance, many have argued that the law should give the mother the right to decide custody. Also, giving the unwed biological father custody could potentially ignore the circumstances surrounding the conception of the child. For example, they could have conceived the child through abuse or rape.

Shanley argues that, rather than focusing on the parents' status as autonomous rights bearers, custody law must begin to recognize the social relationships between the parties. The father must establish his relationship by behavior that expresses his intention to parent. The mother demonstrates her relationship by the very fact of carrying the pregnancy to term. Shanley explores several conditions she thinks ought to be required before the law allows a father to exercise his right to veto an adoption: The father must have paid or offered to pay reasonable child support; the father must have initiated judicial proceedings to establish paternity and to obtain custody within the specified time limit; the court must hear the mother's objections, if any, to the father having custody; the court must listen to the reasons why the mother opposes the father's custody; the law must require that the mother inform the father in writing early in the pregnancy; the law must require that the father act soon after the receipt of notification; and, if the father can veto an adoption, the mother must be able to negate her consent to adoption and retain custody of the child, if she so desires. Such guidelines, according to Shanley, will better regulate child custody. The only case left out is when the mother lies to the father about paternity. In such cases, Shanley suggests jail terms for the offender, which in this case is the mother of the child.

Finally, *Stanley v. Illinois* serves as an example of family law. Stanley lived with the mother of his three children sporadically for eighteen years. When she died, the state presumed him unfit because he had not married the mother. The state did not grant him a hearing, and he lost his children to the state. Stanley sued to recover his children, lost the initial claim, but appealed to the Illinois Supreme Court. He claimed that, given the lack of a hearing, the state did not show that he was unfit, and it violated the equal protection clause. The Illinois Supreme Court rejected the claim that the state had violated the equal protection clause. Further, the court did agree the state had not shown that he was unfit, but found that fitness was irrelevant. Stanley appealed to the Supreme Court, still claiming Illinois had violated the equal protection clause in refusing him a fitness hearing. The Supreme Court found that Stanley was entitled to a fitness hearing, and, by denying him, the state had violated the equal

[7]559 N.E.2d 418, 423 (N.Y.), *cert denied sub nom.* Robert C. v. Miguel T., 498 U.S. 984 (1990).
[8]535 N.Y.S.2d 678, 678 (Sur. Ct. 1988).

protection and due process clauses. The Court recognized that Illinois' goal of focusing on the fitness of parents is to ensure that it protects children. Yet, by removing the children from a fit father, as Stanley was, the state only harms the children and works against its own interests. Additionally, the state cannot simply assume that all unmarried fathers are bad. This assumption might increase efficiency, but the Court found that there are values that are more important than efficiency. In assuming unfitness, the state harmed both the father and the children. The Court found that all parents are entitled to a hearing to establish unfitness; thus, Illinois violated Stanley's rights of due process and equal protection.

Clearly, family law presents a wide scope of often controversial issues. Please see the selected readings that follow if you wish to learn more about these timely concerns.

SELECTED READINGS

Caudill, David S., and Steven Jay Gold, eds. *Radical Philosophy of Law.* Atlantic Highlands, NJ: Humanities Press, 1995.

Dolgin, Janet. "Just a Gene: Judicial Assumptions about Parenthood." *UCLA Law Review* 40 (1993): 637–94.

Eskridge, William. "A History of Same-Sex Marriage." *Virginia Law Review* 79 (1993): 1419–513.

Fineman, Martha. *The Illusion of Equality: The Rhetoric and Reality of Divorce Reform.* Chicago: University of Chicago Press, 1991.

———. *The Neutered Mother, the Sexual Family, and Other Twentieth-Century Tragedies.* New York: Routledge, 1995.

Kaganas, Felicity. "Rape in Marriage: Developments in South African Law." *International and Comparative Law Quarterly* 35 (1986): 456–61.

Lazarus, Keri. "Adoption of Native Americans and First Nations' Children: Are the United States and Canada Recognizing the Best Interests of the Children?" *Arizona Journal of International and Comparative Law* 14 (1987): 255–84.

Menon, Nivedita. "Abortion and the Law: Questions for Feminism." *Canadian Journal of Women and the Law* 6 (1993): 103–18.

Pateman, Carole. *The Sexual Contract.* Stanford, CA: Stanford University Press, 1988.

Posner, Richard. *Sex and Reason.* Cambridge, MA: Harvard University Press, 1992.

Romany, Celina. "Black Women and Gender Equality in a New South Africa: Human Rights Law and the Intersection of Race and Gender." *Brooklyn Journal of International Law* 21(1996): 857–98.

Srivastava, Suresh. "Women in India: Law and Practice." *Law Institute Journal* 64 (1990): 524–26.

Weston, Kathy. *Families We Choose: Lesbians, Gays, Kinship.* New York: Columbia University Press, 1991.

Zinman, Daniel. "Father Knows Best: The Unwed Father's Right to Raise His Infant Surrendered for Adoption." *Fordham Law Review* 60 (1992): 971–1001.

63

MARTHA MINOW
MARY LYNDON SHANLEY

Relational Rights and Responsibilities: Revisioning the Family in Liberal Political Theory and Law

Family policy issues in the late twentieth century magnetically collect concerns about the quality of both intimate and civic life. What do people owe one another as family members and as citizens? What are the prospects for sexual equality within the family, and what does such equality have to do with other areas of life? What constellations of people should count as families in the eyes of the law? Should family members be entrusted with life and death decisions such as abortion and euthanasia, and if not, then who should be? Does anyone outside the family, including government, bear responsibility for the health and welfare of children, people with disabilities, and the elderly? These questions have arisen due to changing social mores and practices, new developments in medical and reproductive technologies, and shifting macroeconomic patterns. In addition, the collapse of the common law paradigm of the patriarchal family has left political and legal theory with a plethora of competing accounts about the nature of family relationships and of the family's relation to the state. This article examines some of those accounts, and tries to set forth what we see as principles that should guide a family law that respects sexual equality and diversity of family forms, takes seriously the responsibilities generated by family relationships, and recognizes the role of the larger society in sustaining viable and vibrant families. . . .

ALTERNATIVE VIEWS OF "THE FAMILY" IN CONTEMPORARY LIBERAL THEORY AND LAW

Contract-based Theories: The Primacy of Individual Volition

Ever since Sir Henry Maine characterized the development of modern law as a movement from status to contract, these concepts have been juxtaposed as competing bases for legal regimes: one must choose between ascriptive roles and obligations, on the one hand, or freely chosen roles and obligations, on the other. Hence proponents of a contractual ordering of family life point out the consistency between their views and many of the deepest aspirations of liberal society: the right of individuals to have their freedom limited only by self-assumed obligations.

Given the burdens that ascriptive notions about women's "nature" and proper roles have placed on women seeking equality in both the family and public life, it is not surprising that some feminists see contract as an instrument to provide women greater freedom, self-determination, and equality without subjecting either women or men to traditional sex roles (Fineman 1995; Kymlicka 1991; Shalev 1989; Shultz 1982, 1990; Weisbrod 1994; Weitzman 1974, 1981, 1985). Unlike traditional marriage law's assumptions about the sexual division of labor in both household and larger society, contractual ordering could allow spouses to decide for themselves how to order their personal as well as their financial relationship during their marriage and in the event of divorce. Contracts could also provide for pluralism and diversity in family life impossible to achieve under a uniform domestic relations law. If marriage were regulated by contract, for example, there would seem to be no reason why two individuals of the same sex should be prohibited from entering such a contract. Arguing both for contractual ordering and for legal recognition of same-sex marriage, Lenore Weitzman asserts that "there is a serious question as to whether the state has any legitimate interest interfering with contracts regarding non-commercial sexual relations between consenting adults," although she acknowledges that legal recognition of same-sex marriages might be hampered by the fact that homosexual relations are "still prohibited by the criminal codes of most states" (Weitzman 1974, 1275 and n. 479). Marjorie Shultz finds that the repeated refusals by the states to formalize unions of same-sex couples by legal marriage "reflect a hesitancy to pursue fully the implications of pluralism and privacy. Where diverse individual outcomes are valued and pluralism is necessary, some form of private ordering of conduct and values is the appropriate regulatory structure" (Shultz 1982, 248). The point of marriage is to create clear expectations and binding obligations to promote stable interpersonal relationships. It is reasonable to ask the state to enforce agreements that would underpin the material aspects of such relationships, but it is not a legitimate concern of the state who may marry whom, or how they should order the personal and material aspects of their relationship.

Proponents of contractual ordering of reproduction see it, like contract marriage, as a way of breaking down gender stereotypes and increasing the scope of human choice in establishing families. Contracts could facilitate diverse ways of bringing children into a family, including children born through contract pregnancies ("surrogate mother" arrangements) and through sperm donation from known donors; a contract might regulate the degree of contact between biological parent(s) and offspring in open adoptions; and in some accounts, it would make adoption a market transaction (Shalev 1989; Robertson 1989; Caplan 1990; Posner 1992). Some feminists welcome contract pregnancy as a way to illustrate that childbearing and child rearing are quite distinct human functions and that child rearing need not be and should not be assigned exclusively to the woman who bears the child (or to women rather than men, for that matter) (Shultz 1990, 304; Shalev 1989, 121). From this perspective, contract pregnancy seems to expand choice for both the woman who bears the child and for the commissioning parent(s). Carmel Shalev argues that one aspect of autonomy is "the deliberate exercise of choice with respect to the individual's reproductive capacity," and that pregnancy contracts should be strictly enforced out of respect for women's decision-making capacity (Shalev 1989, 103).

Contract pregnancy also would allow women who cannot bear children to become parents either alone or with a partner. They could also become parents through foster care and adoption, of course, but a contract pregnancy would allow a couple to become parents without relying on adoption agencies and state departments of social services, to take responsibility for a child even before conception, and sometimes for one or both of them to have a genetic relationship to the child (Shalev 1989; Shultz 1990). Contract pregnancy might also enable a gay couple to have a child to which one of them was biologically related. A contract might allow a lesbian couple wishing to have a child with a known sperm donor to stipulate the nature and degree of his involvement with the child. Contracts could also permit adults who were not in a sexual relationship to share responsibility for child rearing (Young 1995).

While private ordering has liberating aspects, it also entails more worrisome implications. The assumption that bargains will be freely struck masks configurations of social power that provide the backdrop to any contracts. Generations of labor leaders have pointed out the fallacy of assuming that workers and employers were equally free bargaining agents. With respect to the marriage contract, one of John Stuart Mill's great insights in *The Subjection of Women* was his observation that the decision to marry for the vast majority of women could scarcely be called "free." Given women's low wages, scarcity of jobs, and lack of opportunity for higher or even secondary education, marriage was for them a "Hobson's choice": that or none (Mill [1969]). Even the "I do" of someone very much in love and desirous of marriage does not in-and-of-itself guarantee freedom. With respect to contract pregnancy, the notion that the "labor" of pregnancy and childbirth can be sold like any other bodily labor sweeps away "any intrinsic relation between the female owner, her body, and reproductive capacities" (Pateman 1988, 216). As Pateman points out, this objectification of women's bodies and reproductive labor could be more alienating than liberating for many. Furthermore, to depict a woman who agrees to bear a child because it is the only way to bring her household income above the poverty line as exercising her "freedom" ignores the restraints or compulsions of economic necessity.

If contract provides no advantage over public law with respect to enhancing the freedom of parties to either marriage or pregnancy contracts, it similarly offers no guarantee of an equal relationship between the parties to the contract. Leaving decisions about property distribution to contracts between the marriage partners carries no guarantee that such agreements will be more fair than statutory stipulations regarding equitable distribution. Similarly, descriptions of contract pregnancy as nothing more than womb rental in a supposedly neutral market masks the profoundly gendered nature of the structures that surround such transactions. Contractual ordering does not alter those background economic and social conditions that curtail the freedom of some and enhance that of others, that create relationships of domination and subordination between men and women as well as between rich and poor.

Contractual ordering also fails to deal with the fact that certain dependencies that develop in intimate relationships cannot be adequately addressed by contract. Persons who may be considered independent actors at the time a contract is signed make whole series of decisions—not only career decisions but other life choices as well—the consequences of which can neither be anticipated nor allocated between the parties when they occur. "Surrogate" mothers who attempt to revoke their agreements often describe the emergence of an unanticipated sense of relationship that emerged unbidden during the course of pregnancy. To speak of the "freedom" of the contracting woman as residing in her intention as an "autonomous" agent misunderstands the relationship between woman and fetus, and the influence of that relationship on the woman's sense of herself (Young 1990, 167; Rich 1976, 47).

The model of the individual on which proposals for contracts-in-lieu-of-marriage and contract pregnancy rests—that of a self-possessing individual linked to others only by agreement—fails to do justice to the complex interdependencies involved in family relations and child rearing. Proposals to replace family law by private ordering reflect the serious limitations of a version of liberalism that understands freedom as the ability to determine and pursue one's goals without interference from government or other individuals, and obligation as arising only from specific acts of the will. It also does away with any recognition of a public interest in the ordering of family relationships. Contractual ordering regards individuals as what Hegel called "immediate self-subsistent persons," abstracted from their social relationships (quoted in Pateman 1983, 95). The bases of marriage, reproductive activity, and family life thus become indistinguishable from those of civic and economic association. From this perspective, as Carole Pateman has pointed out, "Marriage and the family are . . . treated as if they were an extension of civil society and so constituted by, and their relationships exhausted by, contract" (Pateman 1983, 82). Contractual ordering is not so much a movement away from status as its negation or mirror image: "The undifferentiated social bonds of a hierarchy of ascription are replaced by the undifferentiated, universal bond of contract" (Pateman 1983, 95).

In its capacity to replace the outmoded, hegemonic, and frequently oppressive understandings of gender norms of traditional statutory and common law rules infusing family law, contract seems to many advocates of gender equality and pluralism of family forms a tool of liberation. But this tool is too crude to deal with the complex relationships of family life. Although persons may freely decide to marry, marriage itself is a social practice; stipulations governing the rights and responsibilities of spouses and parents reflect shared understandings of propriety and fairness which may be subject to debate, but should not be set aside by idiosyncratic agreements. Too often other people are deeply affected by the contracts over whose terms they have no say. Rejecting the contractarians' notion of marriage as a partnership to be shaped by the wills of the parties, genetic material and babies as marketable resources, and gestation as comparable to any other waged labor, other legal and political theorists emphasize the socially constructed nature of both families and their individual members.

Community-based Theories: The Importance of Social Norms and Traditions of the Good

Unlike contract-based theorists, who leave family definition and responsibilities to the private ordering of individuals, community-based theorists regard families as expressions of personal and social relationships larger than individuals and not resting primarily on agreement (Elshtain 1991, 1995; Galston 1991; Glendon 1987, 1991; Regan 1993; Sandel 1982; Walzer 1983). Community-based theorists reject the picture of the self adopted by contractarians, who start with the autonomous individual and neglect both the context of larger social relationships and "communal notions of equity and responsibility" in relationships (Regan 1993, 42, 168, 125). These theorists all emphasize that families are not simply private associations but also crucial institutions that help compose civil society and the polity.

Some community-based theorists turn to traditional sources to articulate the content of social norms and the shape of relationships endorsed by the community (Glendon 1987, 1991; *Michael H. v. Gerald D.,* opinion for the Court by Justice Antonin Scalia). Others stress a commitment by the society to pursue the common good rather than a regime of entirely private, individual choices (Selznick 1994, 26–28). Some expressly embrace the title "communitarian" in search of public values larger than the preferences of individuals and more than a mere aggregation of those preferences (Galston 1991; Etzioni 1993). They value civil society and criticize liberalism's tendency to ignore or reject history, tradition, or collective decisions about the good life.

Community-based theorists stress that no person becomes autonomous without first going through an extended period of dependency. "Selves" are formed through the intense relationships of infancy and childhood. Community-based theorists also remind us that individuals are shaped by membership in particular ethnic, regional, and religious communities whose values may depart from the values of society's majority. Where contract-based theories would urge freedom for individuals to embrace their own values under a state neutral about all values except individuals' freedom to contract, community-based theories regard it as neither possible nor desirable "that the state should refrain from coercive public judgments about what constitutes the good life for individuals" (Galston 1991, 14).

Many feminists endorse at least parts of the community-based critiques of contractarian versions of liberal individualism. They agree with the critique of autonomous individualism that neglects or distorts how human identities are formed; they add that this picture is deeply gendered in both imagining a male self and neglecting historically female work in nurturing children and dependents (Benhabib and Cornell 1987, 12; Held 1987, 113). In a moving essay on family life Jean Elshtain points out the way in which the notion of the autonomous individual has not only denied the importance of community but has also denigrated women's traditional sphere of activity and ignored the contribution "women's work" has made to sustaining both families and civil society. Any viable human community, she notes, must include persons "devoted to the protection of vulnerable human life. That, historically, has been the mission of women. The pity is not that women reflect an ethic of social responsibility but that the public world has, for the most part, repudiated such an ethic" (Elshtain 1995, 268).

Feminist community-based theorists agree that political life should hold more than the fulfillment of ends chosen independently by individuals (Weiss 1995, 176), and that more than calculated self-interest can and should bind together the political community (Friedman 1993, 285). But while they join other communitarians in the critique of marriage as merely a contract, they are skeptical about turning to traditional articulations of "shared norms about how spouses should act toward one another" as a basis for understanding spousal responsibilities (Regan 1993, 143). These shared norms have been too thoroughly permeated by gender inequality to act as a model for contemporary marriage law. In such discussions, feminists no less than other community-based theorists face difficult disagreements about which norms and values the community should endorse and law should enforce.

These disagreements do not simply track debates over tradition versus change, or social control versus private individual choice. William Galston rejects the assumption that the only political alternatives are liberal neutrality and antiliberalism. There is, he argues, "a third way: a nonneutral, substantive liberalism committed to its own distinctive conception of the good, broadly (though not boundlessly) respectful of diversity, and supported by its own canon of the virtues" (Galston 1991, 44). For Galston, these values include self-restraint, self-transcendence, tolerance, the work ethic, a capacity for moderate delay of gratification, adaptability, the "disposition and the capacity to engage in public discourse," and the "disposition to narrow the gap between principles and practices in liberal society" (Galston 1991, 213–27).

Yet once the topic for debate is the content of values deserving public endorsement and enforcement, disagreements can grow intense even among people who share a critique of the excesses of individualism. Elshtain, for example, argues not only that "the family is a prerequisite for any form of social life" but also that "a particular ideal of the family is imperative to create a more humane society" (Elshtain 1995, 268). Much contemporary debate over families involves disagreements about what precisely the terms of that particular ideal should be, and whose intimate relationships should be excluded from public support or even punished.

Consider the question whether same-sex couples should be allowed to marry. Community-based theorists join in agreeing that this is not a question to be left to the parties themselves, as contractarians would have it. Nor do community-based theorists ask, as rights-based theorists do, whether individuals regardless of sexual orientation should enjoy a right against state control over intimate relationships. Community-based theorists instead view questions such as same-sex marriage as questions for the community to decide, based on tradition, normative theories of the good, or other collective judgments. The result is considerable disagreement.

Jean Elshtain opposes gay and lesbian marriage. She argues that maintaining marriage as a heterosexual union crucially emphasizes the link between sexual expression and procreative activity. The commitments entailed in marriage stand, and should stand, in contrast to unrestrained, public, and commercial sex and the ethos of the "'wanting' self" so familiar in the world of contract. Although not all families will raise children, "the symbolism of marriage-family as social regenesis is fused in our centuries-old experience with marriage ritual, regulation, and persistence." Because there is great social value in preserving the family as an institution "framed within a horizon of intergenerationality," Elshtain is willing to privilege "a restrictive ideal of sexual and intimate relations" (Elshtain 1991, 686). She would not leave same-sex couples unprotected; she favors ordinances that allow unmarried couples to register as domestic partners and to assume mutual financial responsibility for each other and receive recognition as a couple for certain purposes such as certain insurance and housing. She would, nonetheless, restrict marriage to heterosexual couples in order to emphasize that "marriage is not, and never has been, primarily about two people . . . [but] about the possibility of generativity" (Elshtain 1991, 686).

In contrast, other community-based theorists argue in favor of legalizing marriage for same-sex couples. To do so, they argue, would express the value to society of stable, committed adult relationships, particularly where children are involved. Michael Sandel argues that legal recognition of same-sex marriage would reaffirm the state's interest in protecting the social institution of marriage. Homosexual marriage would reinvigorate "failing public norms of monogamy, loyalty, and mutual care." It would "cultivat[e] the disposition to cooperation rather than competition without which democratic community is unthinkable" (Sandel 1989). Milton Regan favors legalizing gay and lesbian marriage because doing so would recognize "the role of marriage in promoting a relational sense of identity," that is, it would emphasize society's commitment to a noncontractarian view of commitment and responsibility (Regan 1993, 121). Theorists with this perspective would endorse the substantive ends of intimate relationships rather than merely a right of choice in intimate settings.

The arguments on both sides refer to values, traditions, and substantive ends, many of which overlap and converge; nothing internal to this debate can resolve it. Community-based theorists invite and indeed prescribe such debates given their commitment to the substantive good. They further present conflicts over how to ground the values that should prevail and even how to justify critiques of the excesses of individualism. Some, such as Glendon, would combat excessive individualism by norms of individual responsibility and state obligation to protect families (Glendon 1987, 134). Others, such as Galston, pursue community-based norms from a functional or instrumental perspective; social power should be deployed to reduce divorce, for example, in order to lessen the chances that children of divorce fail to grow into independent and contributing members of the society, economic community, and polity (Galston 1991, 287). Still others focus on the violation of traditions of human integrity presented by market approaches, such as contract pregnancy (Rhode 1989, 225), or on the need to revitalize traditions such as the centrality of status (Regan 1993, 151–53).

Having embraced as a political task the substantive choices about families and intimate roles and duties, community-based theorists have to confront deep divisions about policy choices and the values implicated by them. Religious and cultural views and practices vary regarding what kind of family form is desirable, who is a good parent, what range of choice should be granted over reproduction and to whom, and what duties adult children owe their parents. The community-based theories lack the easy accommodation for pluralism afforded by contract-based theories that leave many such matters to private agreement; they also lack a similar accommodation for pluralism afforded by rights-based theories that endorse individual freedoms.

The community-based theories proceed instead with the view that one way of life is to be preferred or some are to be disfavored. Not only does this view run counter to the liberty and tolerance usually advocated in pluralist societies, it also invites potentially unresolvable and intense conflicts about what should and should not be preferred. By forcing authoritative decisions about the issues that contract-based and rights-based theorists would reserve to private individuals, community-based theorists may exacerbate social and political divisions along religious and cultural lines. A response to similar conflicts prompted the development of individual rights frameworks in eighteenth-century Europe, and many legal and political theorists seize the vision of individual freedoms and equality in a third, rights-based approach to family law.

Rights-based Theories: The Tension between Individualism and Family Relationship

Community-based theories seem to invite disputes over what kinds of families and family values society should endorse, whereas contract-based approaches seem to promote pluralism of family forms and intimate choices yet simultaneously fail to protect individuals against oppressive bargains and ongoing patterns of social inequality. Advocates of rights-based approaches to family law seem to hope that they will be able to promote pluralism while also putting forward as societal values certain basic freedoms guaranteed to each individual. Such approaches are rooted both in classical liberalism and in U.S. constitutionalism.

Extending individual rights to the realm of families is a relatively new phenomenon: prior to the mid-twentieth century, the Supreme Court seldom confronted disputes claiming constitutionally protected rights associated with family formation or dissolution, definitions of kinship or affiliation, and obligations of care and support based on family ties. Instead, those matters remained subject to state regulation, and often the states in turn relied on traditions, religious or otherwise. The states did define terms for family formation and dissolution but also tended to exempt families from otherwise prevailing rules of contract, tort, and criminal law. In these respects, U.S. courts followed a tradition of noninterference in family lives, at least when that tradition coincided with state purposes and values. Notable exceptions required parents to comply with compulsory school laws for their children, and subjected, in particular, poor, immigrant, African American, and Native American families to surveillance, which at times led to the removal of children from their family homes.

In the mid-twentieth century, litigation involving various "rights" of family members began to impart a federal, constitutional dimension to family law. The Supreme Court pronounced constitutional bases for a right to marry (*Loving v. Virginia* 1967); the right to procreate (*Skinner v. Oklahoma* 1942; *Griswold v. Connecticut* 1965); the right not to procreate (*Griswold v. Connecticut* 1965; *Eisenstadt v. Baird* 1972; *Roe v. Wade* 1973); the right to retain or establish parental ties (*Stanley v. Illinois* 1972; *Lehr v. Robertson* 1983). The Court rejected claims for a right to engage in consensual homosexual activity (*Bowers v. Hardwick* 1986), and restricted claims of parental status outside of marriage (*Lehr v. Robertson* 1983; *Michael H. v. Gerald D.* 1989). The Court also recognized as worthy of constitutional protection certain claims of parental decision-making power (*Wisconsin v. Yoder* 1972; *Parham v. J.R.* 1979) and family privacy (*Moore v. City of East Cleveland* 1977).

Two fundamental conceptions of rights undergird these decisions. The first views the family as a unitary entity, entitled to protection from state scrutiny or interference; the second locates rights in distinct individuals who should be guarded from state obstruction in intimate choices and behaviors (Hearst 1995; Minow 1988). Both approaches offer a critical purchase on otherwise prevailing governmental actions, but the second in particular begins to challenge legal assumptions about proper family relationships. Elizabeth Schneider has documented efforts to marshal individual rights against assault by spouses, and against the screen of family privacy that had shielded such practices from arrest, prosecution, and punishment (Schneider 1985, 1992). Nan Hunter, Sylvia Law, and more recently William Eskridge have asserted individual rights to marry that should extend to couples of the same sex, in part to counter gender hierarchies that hurt women even in heterosexual marriages (Hunter 1991; Law 1988; Eskridge 1993). The prevalence of constitutional theories about marriage prompts one commentator to label his criticism of such theories a "dissenting view" (Maltz 1992). Nancy Polikoff argues that courts should recognize that both partners in a lesbian couple should have parental rights with regard to children living in their household (Polikoff 1990).

Commentators using rights discourse are not always in agreement over what rights are relevant and which should prevail in any particular case. John Robertson advocates recognition of a right to use medical technology and to purchase genetic and gestational services from others (Robertson 1983, 1989). In contrast, Margaret Jane Radin invokes rights of individuals to resist the incursions of the market especially in the context of genetic material and "surrogate," or contract mother arrangements (Radin 1987, 1995).

The most pronounced conflict, however, pits the vision of individuals enjoying rights against the picture of the family as a unitary entity entitled to rights against state intrusion. Many of the asserted individual rights specifically prevail upon the state to pry behind closed doors to family homes either to protect individuals from harm or to enable them to alter the otherwise prevailing pattern of relationships. Thus, the right to be free from abuse in marriage brings the state into the household by justifying actual police investigations and more basically by instituting a norm of mutual respect between spouses. The right to choose contraception or abortion enables not just a couple but an individual to make choices without the interference of others, including the intimate partner.

Although John Rawls notably neglects the internal ordering of families, his work has strengthened the intellectual resources for rights-based theories. *A Theory of Justice* develops a strong foundation for notions of individual rights even when they challenge traditions and conventions. Rawls's work has also led to debates about what the rights pertaining to family members might be, and whether a rights-based discourse is, in the end, adequate for a political or legal theory of the family. Notably, Susan Okin criticizes Rawls for failing to take gender seriously in formulating the principles of justice and for failing to carry these principles fully into the context of families (Okin 1989, 89–109). Attacking the common law notion that the family is a unitary entity that should be shielded from the state's prying eye, Okin argues that the traditional liberal defense of family privacy has made it difficult to recognize the gender inequality that permeates social and legal arrangements affecting women's lives in both families and civil society. Okin maintains further that when Rawls identifies "the monogamous family" as one of the major social institutions that is to be guided by his two principles of justice, he fails to acknowledge that most families violate the principle of equal liberty and the principle that any inequalities should work to the benefit of the least well-off. No one uncertain about what sex he or she will have, Okin argues, would accept the prevailing gender structures of society and the family as just.

This argument by Okin makes tremendous strides toward a theory of justice addressing families. It demands that such a theory explore the ways that gender-based practices affect the distribution of power and goods both in families and in larger social institutions, and in the interaction between both realms. Similarly, Okin opens the way toward consideration of state recognition for relationships between same-sex couples as part of a larger effort to eliminate the significance of gender roles (Okin 1996).

Eva Kittay similarly sets forth grounds for rejecting Rawls's assumptions about families. Like Okin, she rejects his assumption that heads-of-households can be understood as mutually disinterested decision-makers except regarding intergenerational ties (Okin 1989; Kittay 1995, 13). Missing from Rawls's view is attention to those relationships of care-giving and dependency that exist not simply between generations, but among those living at the same time. Dependency may arise from youth or age, disability or illness, or mutual reliance; neither dependent people nor those who care for them conform to the model of the self-sufficient, autonomous individual presumed by liberal theorists such as Rawls (Kittay 1995, 14–16).

In this respect, Kittay, along with others, criticizes the very conception of liberal rights insofar as it neglects the significance of care and relationships of care to both a theory of justice and an ideal way of life. Kittay joins others such as Annette Baier, Carol Gilligan, Virginia Held, Sara Ruddick, and Joan Tronto who regard it as a moral imperative that all people should benefit from conditions for continuous care and connection (Baier 1985; Gilligan 1982; Held 1987; Ruddick 1989; Tronto 1993). An ethic of care that values the efforts of continuous attention and help must find a place in any adequate account of family lives and in any just family law. The work of theorists who explore an ethic of care tends to expose a conceptual limitation in rights, conventionally conceived, as a basis of thinking about families: whether assigned to individuals or to families as entities, rights may fail to highlight, protect, or define relationships of moral connection. Yet so many rights associated with family life—the rights to marry, to divorce, to receive child support, to procreate—involve not individuals per se but the claims, responsibilities, and boundaries of particular human relationships. Defining such rights requires articulation of the moral predicates and scope of such relationships (Minow 1990; Kiss forthcoming).

In their rejection of the model of the self-sufficient and self-interested individual, community-based theorists critical of the liberal tradition do not distinguish contractarian from rights-based approaches in political theory and law. We agree that a political theory inattentive to the connections between and among people can never adequately address themes and issues facing families, but we think it important to distinguish contractarian and rights-based views. Contractarian views acknowledge human relationships but treat them all as chosen and susceptible to market or market-like bargains. Little scope for public articulation of values persists in a contract-based regime beyond preservation of the institution of contract and perhaps rejection of extreme bargains. Rights-based views instead require public articulation of the kinds of freedoms that deserve protection and the qualities of human dignity that warrant societal support.

Moreover, whether acknowledged or not, rights articulate relationships among people. Every freedom of action guaranteed to an individual demands as a correlate constraints of respect by other individuals. (Minow 1990; Kiss forthcoming). In the context of family matters, rights-based theories need to acknowledge more fully their relational dimensions and draw on the insights of those who study caretaking.

This route—enriching rights-based theories with strong attention to relationships and their preconditions—holds more promise for family law than the other approaches surveyed here. Contract-based theories promote individual freedoms but neglect social values and concerns about inequality and dignity; community-based theories articulate shared values but risk constraining individual freedoms and social pluralism while prompting greater social conflict. Rights-based theories invigorate as social values respect for certain individual freedoms, but they historically lack a rich understanding of relationships, including their preconditions, their responsibilities, and their consequences. In the next section we consider whether and how a notion of relational rights, informed by theories of caretaking and moral relationships, might address a variety of difficult issues confronting family policy and law.

ELEMENTS OF AN ADEQUATE THEORY OF FAMILY LAW: RELATIONAL RIGHTS AND RESPONSIBILITIES

This discussion of three contemporary approaches to family law illuminates the difficulty of framing family law in the face of both vast social changes and the collapse of the common law paradigm of the family as a unitary, hierarchical, and indissoluble entity. Difficult policy issues demand answers and simultaneously reveal the inadequacy of current normative resources undergirding family law. Among these issues are those concerning:

- the place of biology in reproduction: What, if any, claims should those with biological ties have regarding the conception, gestation, birth, and custody of a child?
- sexual orientation: What relations between adult homosexual partners, and among homosexual parents and minor children, should the state permit or promote?
- the preference or privilege that might attach to families formed according to legal formalities compared with families formed informally: Should those in legally executed marriage and adoption receive benefits denied to those in informal arrangements?
- the role of the market in forming family relationships: Should people be able to contract for the conception and/or gestation of a child? for a child available for adoption? for sexual services? for spouses?
- the role of government money in providing support for families: Should government subsidize child care, respite care, care of ill or disabled family members?

- the relationship of the workplace to family life: Should workplaces be structured to favor or support one or more types of families? Should work loads in the paid labor force be rendered more flexible to accommodate demands of children, elderly relatives, or other family duties?
- the relative power of family members in family-related decision-making: Is there any legal or philosophical basis for granting greater power to one member of an adult partnership, such as in decisions over abortion and child custody? In decisions about custody, how (if at all) should decision-making power be allocated between parents and children? In medical treatment decisions, how should the views of patients, spouses, and other relatives be collected and given force?
- racial and religious identities: Is there any place for racial or religious identity as a basis for decision-making by the state in disputes over child custody or rules governing foster care, adoption, marriage, divorce, and medical treatment?
- dependency, disability, and illness: Who is responsible for the daily care and financial support of dependents such as children, elderly people, and people with severe disabilities or illnesses? What degree of family relationship establishes such responsibilities?

Each of these issues has arisen because of new technologies, changing social practices, and conflicts among normative or ethical perspectives. The hard choices each poses for policymakers indicate the extent to which family law and family policy reflect both human social practices and institutions, and conscious political choices. These choices require argument, debate, and continual assessment and reassessment in light of experience and values.

But to say that family law is properly the product of political discussion and negotiation is not to say that it cannot be based on principle. It is, rather, to say that in a world in which social and material conditions change over time, the way in which law reflects fundamental principles will change too.

We believe that any adequate family law must be based on principles that take account of two paradoxical characteristics of family life and the family's relationship to the state. First, the individual must be seen simultaneously as a distinct individual and as a person, fundamentally involved in relationships of dependence, care, and responsibility. For example, a woman who agrees to bear a child for someone else must be viewed both as a responsible agent and as someone who, after bearing a fetus to term, has established some relationship to the child. A court deciding who shall have custody of the child she has borne and now wishes to keep must neither reduce the case to the enforcement of a contract nor regard the fact of childbearing alone as determining parental claims (Shanley 1993; see also Shanley 1995). Similarly, when either same-sex or heterosexual couples who share custody of children separate or divorce, rulings determining financial support and child custody or visitation must consider each party to such actions both as separate adults and as individuals-in-relationship. The law must allow parents to resume their independence and to remarry or form new relationships if they wish, but the law must also enforce the continuing obligations each has to their children. Those obligations are not only for financial support, but may also include requirements that one parent not take actions that would jeopardize the possibility of a continuing relationship between the other parent and the child.

Second, family law and political theory must take account of the additional paradox that family relationships are simultaneously outside of and yet shaped by the political order. Even confining our view to Western societies, the forms family associations take are clearly affected by law. People's views of who might be a possible marriage partner are shaped by the prohibited degrees of kinship and bans on same-sex and polygamous marriages. Laws also have affected who were regarded as parents and children; legal adoption allowed the creation of nonbiological family ties, while bastardy statutes denied any legal significance whatsoever to the biological tie between offspring and parents (Grossberg 1985). Yet families were clearly not creatures of the state like joint-stock companies and limited partnerships. With the exception of bastardy statutes, the biological tie between an adult and his or her offspring has been taken to establish prima facie parental rights and obligations; few have proposed that children, at birth, be assigned to the best possible caretaker, rather than to their biological parents.

Moreover, peoples' lives as family members are importantly framed and influenced by practices and decisions of the larger society. Some of those practices and decisions impose burdens and allocate benefits according to generally held views about acceptable family and public behaviors; for example, nepotism laws both reflected and enforced norms against married women's working outside the home. Others reflect matters including but not limited to macroeconomic policies that set the acceptable level of unemployment, and therefore the availability of jobs; resources devoted to public transportation; and employment practices that affect equal opportunity regardless of gender, race, or other characteristics. The current practice of contract pregnancy in the United States, for example, is shaped by cultural norms that link maternity and womanhood very closely and that regard biological ties to the children one raises as highly desirable, and by economic structures that have made paid gestational labor an attractive job relative to other available options for some women and couples.

We have argued that neither a contract-based approach nor a community-based approach takes adequate account of these two paradoxical aspects of family life. While a contractarian view of marriage emphasizes the need to accommodate differences among individuals and within relationships, it encompasses only the first part of each paradox, ignoring responsibilities that may not be readily dealt with by contract and the social and economic contexts that influence the choices made by family members. While community-based theories understand the importance of tradition and social context in shaping individuals and their relationships, they risk marginalizing perspectives of members of nontraditional groups that have not historically had strong political representation. A conception of relational rights and responsibilities, we believe, would not regard "rights" as belonging to individuals and arising from the imperative of self-preservation, but rather would view rights as claims grounded in and arising from human relationships of varying degrees of intimacy, what Kenneth Karst has called "intimate associations" (Karst 1980).

Relational rights and responsibilities should draw attention to the claims that arise out of relationships of human interdependence. Those claims entitle people to explore a range of relationships and in so doing to draw sustenance from the larger community. A focus on relational rights and responsibilities might examine the legality of same-sex marriage by considering the place of such proposed relationships in the lives of those immediately involved and those in the surrounding community. Similarly, in thinking about cases in which a gestational mother who is party to a pregnancy contract wishes to keep the child rather than turn him or her over to the other contracting party, attention to relational rights and responsibilities requires consideration of the relationship between the gestational mother and the baby, the potential relationship between the commissioning parent(s) and the baby, and the baby's need for ongoing relationships with adults who assume full parental responsibilities. The issues for resolution thus are not simply the rights of adults who entered a contract, nor of community standards about contracts in such circumstances, but the moral and psychological dimensions of persons whose claims arise out of actual and potential relationships. In other disputes concerning child custody, a focus on relational rights and responsibilities would give great weight to preserving some continuity of relationships.

An adequate theory of family law would also have to recognize the relationship between family life and the political and economic order. Here again a vital conception of relationships and responsibilities would help. Each intimate relationship is in turn embedded in relationships of neighbors, religious and ethnic groups, and even relationships of strangers, all deeply affected but not entirely determined by the political system and economic circumstances. Connecting these relationships to a vibrant sense of responsibility would engage wide circles of people, including even public-policymakers and voters who would need to consider what social and economic structures are necessary to permit continuous, caring human relationships especially responsive to those most dependent on such care. As Kittay argues, "A society cannot be well-ordered, that is, it cannot be one in which all its members are sustained and included within the ideal of equality, if it fails to be a society characterized by care" (Kittay 1995, 24). The polity cannot presuppose the contribution made by caregivers to maintaining the social and political order, but "must take upon itself the primary responsibility of maintaining structures that will support the principles of care" (Kittay 1993, 7b).

Expanding our understanding of the individual to encompass relationships of interdependency would invigorate private and public responses to family issues. Acknowledging the interdependence of family members and the larger polity itself is crucial, although this is simply a beginning, not an end, of the analysis. For then the society, whether through law or other means, must still address what criteria should be used to resolve disputes over what should count within the very definition of "family" and what constellation of intimate relations should receive the special resources of public approval and recognition. The resolution of such issues, we argue, requires not only reasoned deliberation but also politics and a political practice revised along the principles of justice aimed to produce participation by the full variety of human being in the society.

A satisfactory theory of family law would thus have to reach the operations of the political and legal systems that generate and implement family law. The theory would need to justify reforms so that people who are presently marginalized could come to participate effectively in the debates and decisions that frame entitlements essential to sustaining viable family lives.

This last point connects families and politics more directly than the familiar but still important point that families prepare new generations of political actors (Tocqueville 1954; Mill [1969]; Chodorow 1978; Okin 1989; Sennett 1977). That important fact does justify greater public attention to the work of families and greater public resources to support that work. More basically, however, families cannot fully teach justice in the absence of a just family law. The creation of a just family law requires reform not only of family law itself but also of the larger political and legal processes by which family law is created and applied. If the political process employed to explore and debate the nature and status of family life itself does not redress the structures of hierarchy that have permeated the family, then the resulting political choices about family are suspect. Exclusions and disadvantages on the basis of gender, race, ethnicity, religion, and class have rendered problematic the conventional conception of family in political and legal discourse. If those same exclusions and disadvantages characterize the political process intended to rectify these shortcomings, political constructions of the family cannot be deemed legitimate according to the criteria of a liberal democracy. For this reason, an adequate political and legal theory of the family must include attention to the political process through which choices about family status and family relations are produced. In particular, an adequate political theory of the family cannot presuppose equality and full and fair representation in the political process. We suggest that the United States cannot claim to have a legitimate family policy unless and until the political process that produces it is more inclusive and trustworthy than it is at present.

A political and legal theory that took into account the two paradoxical aspects of family membership in a liberal society to which we have called attention here would not provide ready, easy, or generally acceptable answers to difficult questions such as those we raise at the beginning of this section. It would, however, provide the analytic, intellectual, and rhetorical resources for approaching such questions. It would help to ensure that the contractarian models of economic life do not take over all other areas of public life or of family relationships, and that a search for common norms does not eliminate pluralism or curtail privacy. It would also put the prerequisites of relationships of care at the center of concern, rather than treat them as incidental effects of individual choices or needs. A theory of relational rights and responsibilities would encompass not only individual freedoms but also rights to enter and sustain intimate associations consistent with public conceptions of the responsibilities those associations entail, underscoring the connection between families and the larger community. Progress in thinking about and addressing the complex issues concerning family life that have arisen from the demise of the common law model of the patriarchal family, sociological changes in family structures, and developments in reproductive technology seems most likely to develop from a political and legal theory that focuses on the relationships that constitute family life and the preconditions necessary to sustain such relationships.

REFERENCES

Baier, Annette. 1985. Caring about caring. In *Postures of the mind: Essays on mind and morals.* Minneapolis: University of Minnesota Press.

Bartlett, Katharine. 1984. Rethinking parenthood as an exclusive status: The need for legal alternatives when the premise of the nuclear family has failed. *Virginia Law Review* 70(5): 879–963.

Becker, Gary S. 1981. *A treatise on the family.* Cambridge: Harvard University Press.

Benhabib, Seyla, and Drucilla Cornell. 1987. Introduction: Beyond the politics of gender. In *Feminism as critique,* ed. Seyla Benhabib and Drucilla Cornell. Minneapolis: University of Minnesota Press.

Burnham, Margaret. 1987. An impossible marriage: Slave law and family law. *Journal of Law and Inequality* 5(2): 187–225.

Burtt, Shelley. 1994. Reproductive responsibilities: Rethinking the fetal rights debate. *Policy Science* 27(2–3): 179–96.

Caplan, Lincoln. 1990. *An open adoption.* New York: Farrar, Straus and Giroux.

Chodorow, Nancy. 1978. *The reproduction of mothering: Psychoanalysis and the sociology of gender.* Berkeley: University of California Press.

Cohen, Joshua. 1992. Okin on justice, gender, and the family. *Canadian Journal of Philosophy* 22(2): 263–86.

Elshtain, Jean Bethke. 1991. Accepting limits. *Commonweal* 18(20) (22 November): 685–86.

———. [1982] 1995. Feminism, family, and community. In *Feminism and Community,* ed. Penny Weiss and Marilyn Friedman. Philadelphia: Temple University Press.

Elshtain, Jean Bethke et al. 1993. A communitarian position on the family. *National Civic Review* (Winter): 25–35.

Eskridge, William. 1993. A history of same-sex marriage. *Virginia Law Review* 79(7):1419–1513.

Etzioni, Amitai. 1993. *The spirit of community: Rights, responsibilities, and the communitarian agenda.* New York: Crown Publishers.

Fineman, Martha Albertson. 1991. *The illusion of equality: The rhetoric and reality of divorce reform.* Chicago: University of Chicago Press.

———. [sic] Review of *Justice, gender, and the family.* Ethics 102 (3): 647–49.

———. 1995. *The neutered mother, the sexual family, and other twentieth-century tragedies.* New York: Routledge.

Friedman, Marilyn. 1993. Feminism and modern friendship: Dislocating the community. In *Friendship: A philosophical reader,* ed. Neera Kapur Badhwar. Ithaca: Cornell University Press.

Galston, William. 1991. *Liberal purposes: Goods, virtues, and diversity in the liberal state.* Cambridge: Cambridge University Press.

Gilligan, Carol. 1982. *In a different voice.* Cambridge: Harvard University Press.

Glendon, Mary Ann. 1987. *Abortion and divorce in Western law.* Cambridge: Harvard University Press.

———. 1991. *Rights talk: The impoverishment of politics.* Cambridge: Harvard University Press.

Grossberg, Michael. 1985. *Governing the hearth: Law and family in nineteenth-century America.* Chapel Hill: University of North Carolina Press.

Hartog, Hendrick. 1991. Marital existence and marital expectations in 19th century America. *Georgetown Law Journal* 80(October):95–129.

Hearst, Alice. 1995. Domesticating reason: Families and good citizens. Paper presented at Law and Society Association Conference, Toronto, Ontario, 3 June.

Held, Virginia. 1987. The non-contractual family: A feminist view. *Canadian Journal of Philosophy.* Supplementary 13.

Holmes, Stephen. 1993. *The anatomy of anti-liberalism.* Cambridge: Harvard University Press.

Horsburgh, Beverly. 1992. Redefining the family: Recognizing the altruistic caregiver and the importance of relational needs. *University of Michigan Journal of Law Reform* 25(2): 423–564.

Hunter, Nan. 1991. Marriage, law, and gender: A feminist inquiry. *Law and inequality*(1): 9–ff.

Karst, Kenneth L. 1980. The freedom of intimate association. *Yale Law Journal* 89(4): 624–92.

Kiss, Elizabeth. forthcoming. Alchemy or fool's gold? Assessing feminist doubts about rights. *Contentious concepts: feminist perspectives on political theory,* ed. Mary Lyndon Shanley and Uma Narayan. Cambridge: Polity Press.

Kittay, Eva Feder. 1993. Taking dependency seriously: Equality, social cooperation, and The Family and Medical Leave Act considered in light of the social organization of dependency work. Paper delivered at Conference on Feminism and Social Action, University of Pittsburgh. November.

———. 1995. Taking dependency seriously: The Family and Medical Leave Act considered in the light of the social organization of work and gender equality. *Hypatia* 10(1): 8–30.

Kymlicka, Will. 1991. Rethinking the family. *Philosophy and Public Affairs* 20(1): 77–98.

Law, Sylvia. 1988. Homosexuality and the social meaning of gender. *Wisconsin Law Review* 2: 187–235.

Littleton, Christine. 1987. Equality across difference: A place for rights discourse? *Wisconsin Women's Law Journal* 3: 189–212.

Locke, John. [1690] 1980. *Second treatise of government,* ed. C. B. Macpherson. Indianapolis: Hackett.

Maltz, Earl M. 1992. Constitutional protection for the right to marry: A dissenting view. *George Washington Law Review* 60(4): 949–68.

May, Elaine Tyler. 1980. *Great expectations: Marriage and divorce in post-Victorian America.* Chicago: University of Chicago Press.

Mill, John Stuart. [1869] 1988. *The subjection of women,* ed. Susan Moller Okin. Indianapolis: Hackett.

Minow, Martha. 1985. "Forming under everything that grows": Toward a history of family law. *Wisconsin Law Review* 4: 819–98.

———. 1988. We, the family: Constitutional rights and American families. In *The Constitution and American life,* ed. David Thelen. Ithaca: Cornell University Press.

———. 1990. *Making all the difference: Inclusion. exclusion, and American law.* Ithaca: Cornell University Press.

Okin, Susan Moller. 1989. *Justice, gender, and the family.* New York: Basic Books.

———. 1996. Sexual orientation, gender, and families: Dichotomizing differences. *Hypatia* 11(1): 30–48.

Pateman, Carole. 1983. The shame of the marriage contract. In *Women and men's wars,* ed. Judith Stiehm. New York: Pergamon Press.

———. 1988. *The sexual contract.* Stanford: Stanford University Press.

Pateman, Carole, and Teresa Brennan. 1979. "Mere auxiliaries to the commonwealth": Women and the origins of liberalism. *Political Studies* 27(2): 183–200.

Polikoff, Nancy. 1990. This child does have two mothers: Redefining parenthood to meet the needs of children in lesbian-mother and other non-traditional families. *Georgetown Law Review* 78(3): 459–575.

Posner, Richard. 1992. *Sex and reason.* Cambridge: Harvard University Press.

Radin, Margaret J. 1987. Market inalienability. *Harvard Law Review* 100(8): 1849–1937.

———. 1995. What, if anything, is wrong with baby-selling? *Pacific Law Journal* 135–45.

Rawls, John. 1971. *A theory of justice.* Cambridge: Harvard University Press.

Regan, Milton C. 1993. *Family law and the pursuit of intimacy.* New York: New York University Press.

Rhode, Deborah. 1989. *Justice and gender: Sex discrimination and the law.* Cambridge: Harvard University Press.

Rich, Adrienne. 1976. *Of woman born: Motherhood as experience and as institution.* New York: Norton, Bantam.

Robertson, John. 1983. Procreative liberty and the control of contraception, pregnancy, and childbirth. *Virginia Law Review* 69(3): 405–62.

———. 1989. Embryos, families, and procreative liberty. *Southern California Law Review* 59(5): 939–1041.

Ruddick, Sara. 1989. *Maternal thinking.* Boston: Beacon Press.

Sandel, Michael J. 1982. *Liberalism and the limits of justice.* Cambridge: Cambridge University Press.

———. 1989. Moral argument and liberal toleration: Abortion and homosexuality. *California Law Review* 77(3): 521–38.

Schneider, Elizabeth M. 1986. The dialectic of rights and politics: Perspectives from the women's movement. *New York University Law Review* 61: 589–ff.

———. 1992. Particularity and generality: Challenges of feminist theory and practice in work on woman-abuse. *Brooklyn Law Review* 67(3): 520–68.

Selznick, Philip. 1994. Foundations of communitarian liberalism. *The responsive community* 4(4) (Fall): 16–28.

Sennett, Richard. 1977. *The fall of public man.* New York: Knopf.

Shalev, Carmel. 1989. *Birth power.* New Haven: Yale University Press.

Shanley, Mary Lyndon. 1995. Fathers' rights, mothers' wrongs? Reflections on unwed fathers' rights and sex equality. *Hypatia* 10(1): 74–103.

———. 1993. "Surrogate mothering" and women's freedom: A critique of contracts for human reproduction. *Signs* 18(3): 618–39.

———. 1989. *Feminism, marriage, and the law in Victorian England,* 1850–1895. Princeton: Princeton University Press.

Shultz, Marjorie Maguire. 1982. Contractual ordering of marriage: A new model for state policy. *California Law Review* 70(2): 204–334.

———. 1990. Reproductive technology and intention-based parenthood: An opportunity for gender neutrality. *Wisconsin Law Review* 2: 297–398.

Tocqueville, Alexis de. 1954. *Democracy in America.* New York: Vintage Books.

Tronto, Joan. 1993. *Moral boundaries: A political argument for an ethic of care.* New York: Routledge.

Walzer, Michael. 1983. *Spheres of justice: A defense of pluralism and equality.* New York: Basic Books.

Weisbrod, Carol. 1980. *The boundaries of utopia.* New York: Pantheon.

———. 1994. The way we live now: A discussion of contracts and domestic relations. *Utah Law Review* 2: 777–815.

Weiss, Penny A. 1995. Feminism and contractarianism: Comparing critiques of liberalism. In *Feminism and community,* ed. Penny A. Weiss and Marilyn Friedman. Philadelphia: Temple University Press.

Weitzman, Lenore. 1974. Marriage contracts. *California Law Review* 62(4): 1169–1258.

———. 1981. *The marriage contract: Spouses, lovers, and the law.* New York: Free Press.

———. 1985. *The divorce revolution: Unexpected social and economic consequences for women and children in America.* New York: Free Press.

Weston, Kath. 1991. *Families we choose: Lesbians, gays, kinship.* New York: Columbia University Press.

Williams, Patricia. 1991. *The alchemy of race and rights.* Cambridge: Harvard University Press.

Yellin, Jean F. 1989. *Women and sisters: The antislavery feminists in American culture.* New Haven: Yale University Press.

Young, Iris. 1995. Mothers, citizenship, and independence: A critique of pure family values. *Ethics* 105(3): 535–56.

———. 1990. Pregnant embodiment: Subjectivity and alienation. In *"Throwing like a girl" and other essays in feminist philosophy and social theory.* Bloomington: Indiana University Press.

Zainaldin, Jamil S. 1979. The emergence of a modern American family law: Child custody, adoption, and the courts, 1796–1851. *Northwestern University Law Review* 73(6): 1038–89.

64

WILLIAM N. ESKRIDGE, JR.

Beyond Lesbian and Gay "Families We Choose"

Modern family law in this century has been characterized by a shift in emphasis from status to choice, from the status-based roles imposed by communal tradition to the consensual duties created by contract. This shift reflects a progressive adoption in the family law context of the consequences of a "liberal" conception of self. The liberal self is an autonomous actor whose liberty is constrained only to the extent the actor agrees (contract) or harms others (tort and crimes). Hence, the liberal self is free to enter into, and exit from, family arrangements largely at will, uninhibited by social custom or old-fashioned status rules. Lesbians and gay men have been among the avant-garde of this shift, for we do not usually follow the traditional husband-wife-kids model of family formation. Instead, we have turned to "families we choose"[1]—circles of consent-based intimacy among friends, partners, former lovers, children, and others.

On the other hand, the law still retains many requirements founded on traditional status-based understandings about family. As a consequence, lesbian and gay families of choice lack many of the options and securities enjoyed by heterosexual families. For example, the status of being a married "spouse" entitles one to mutual emotional and financial support, priority as representative in the event of the other spouse's incapacity or death, and presumptive inheritance and property rights. Also, the status of being "parents" to children assures enormous control over those children, even if they are not biologically related to the parents. Adhering to traditional status ideas, no state (as of 1995) permits lesbian or gay people to be spouses to one another, and most states offer barriers to their being parents. The gaylesbian response is that such limitations are outdated, in light of family law's embrace of the liberal self and its freedom to negotiate the terms of intimate relationships in so many other areas (such as no-fault divorce). Under a rigorously liberal jurisprudence, gaylesbian families we choose would not be discouraged, indeed, they would be accorded legal recognition.

This libertarian jurisprudence is an insufficient response to antihomosexual status-based rules, in part because status is resurgent in family law, and properly so. Liberalism's insistence upon an autonomous self is more appropriate for the market (where it has nonetheless been repeatedly compromised) than for the family. The liberal construct of the acontextual self is not only at war with antihomosexual limitations on family formation, but also with the prohomosexual need for human interconnection that impels people to form families in the first place. A risk of conceiving our interhuman relationships as nothing more than families we choose—a marketplace of intimacies—is to neglect or even sacrifice the advantages of relational features that are constitutive of self.

Libertarian arguments can and should be important for criticizing antihomosexual traditions, but status-based arguments ought not be ignored. By excluding us from the legal status of spouse and parent, law denies us possibilities for human interconnection routinely afforded other people and frustrates opportunities for lesbians, gay men, and bisexuals to foster their "relational selves." These exclusions constitute a denial of citizenship. The whole web of excluding practices is unjustified because sexual orientation is an irrational organizing principle for creating family statuses. I shall conclude by applying status-based arguments to argue that the gaylesbian movement should seek recognition of same-sex marriage, or its equivalent.

FAMILIES WE CHOOSE, FRACTURING OF SELF

American family law in the twentieth century has shown a general shift from status to contract, and this shift rests on the apparent acceptance of the liberal view of the self as autonomous and self-regarding, constructing patterns of intimacy on its own terms rather than the terms dictated by traditional institutions and the roles they impose.[2] Out of necessity, same-sex couples have been the shock troops of the liberated family. For example, "Boston marriages" between pairs of women and legal marriages between a woman and another woman "passing" as a man flourished during the Victorian era, the rhetorical apex of status-based intimacy.[3] Because homosexual relations have been illegal in most of the United States until recently, same-sex intimacy has been both closeted as well as socially constructed in modern American history. Today, such intimacy is no longer necessarily closeted, but it remains constructed: lesbians and gay men must rely on our own devices, instead of those off-the-rack rules offered by the state to heterosexuals, to form and cement families we choose.

When people started "coming out" in significant numbers after the Stonewall riots of June 1969, more gay people were able to form what can be called "families we choose." Professor Kath Weston, the anthropologist who coined the term, associates such families with the coming out process itself. Such an association reflects the fundamentally liberal assumptions of most gaylesbian thinking about families and relationships. Coming out has thus been conceptualized as a classic liberal move: the self asserts its acontextual identity as "gay"—in defiance, if need be, of disapproval by society, family, and friends. For the "out" gay person, family is much less likely to be defined by either blood or marriage than is the case for the closeted gay or the straight person because some members of the blood family will not accept the gay person's identity and the gay person does not have the formal option of getting married to the person she or he loves. Lacking the marriage option and often losing some ties of blood, the gay person is left to construct—to choose—her own family. Such families of choice both complement the traditional family and transcend it. Consider the following range of choices:

1. *The Functional Equivalent of the Victorian Family.* Although lesbian and gay couples cannot marry as a matter of law and cannot procreate with one another as a matter of biology, they can create the functional equivalent of the Victorian family or its recent exemplars, the Ward and June Cleavers and the Ozzie and Harriet Nelsons.[4] Some religions in America will conduct a marriage ceremony for same-sex couples if so desired, and most of the accoutrements of marriage (such as community property, joint obligations, and legal capacity to act for one another) can be created by contract, albeit at substantial trouble and expense. Same-sex couples can and often do have children: lesbian couples through artificial insemination from a male donor and (less often) male couples through surrogacy contracts with a female donor. Thus June and Harriet don't need Ward and Ozzie to have a family; like generations of Boston marriages, June and Harriett can construct their own relationship and, unlike such unions in the past, can come by children as well.
2. *A Web of Friendships.* Replicating the Victorian family is not Professor Weston's vision. Her families we choose are webs of friendships, with or without children and typically without formal commitments. Your family might consist of the partner with whom you live, as well as her child by a prior marriage; your former lover with whom you own and run a business; your best friend from college who was the first person you came out to (and whom you had a crush on); a

person with AIDS whom you and your partner have agreed to help support; and your hang-out buddies on the local women's softball team, the same team where you met your current partner. The family might well consist of blood relatives (such as your child and your own mother who loves you even though she does not completely understand your sexuality) and even of legally imposed relationships (such as your former husband with whom you share custody of your child), but it often does not.

3. *Something of Each.* There are, of course, variations falling between the two patterns. For example, a gay man may marry a woman who is or becomes his best friend and the mother of his children, but still may have one or more men as his primary sexual lovers.[5] In most major cities today, same-sex couples can quasi-formalize their relationships by registering as "domestic partners," something of a rhetorical way station between relationship and marriage. In an increasing number of states, same-sex couples can adopt one another's children through the process of a "cross-parent adoption."[6]

These developments are usually represented in gay-friendly accounts as positive ones. Lesbians and gay men can have just as rich a personal life as straight people, and that life can and usually does include intimate relationships. Such positivity is all but dictated by the conventional liberal script: once a person discovers her "true" acontextual self and rationally pursues strategies that fulfill the needs and desires of that self, the person will do well. I subscribe to this script, as far as it goes, but the lesbian and gay experience suggests the cogency of Professor Milton Regan's argument that this conventional understanding of self is insufficiently rich.[7] For gays and lesbians more than for most straight people, the self is fractured by the variety of contexts into which it is tossed. The families we choose expose and perhaps even contribute to such a fractured self. Lesbian and gay experience with families we choose illustrates the way in which the technologically advanced global community plays on the liberal conception of personhood: the openness of the acontextual self to a variety of experiences undermines the possibility that there will be a stable self.

Consider the case of Sharon Lynne Bottoms.[8] Ms. Bottoms married Dennis Doustou in 1989 and became pregnant the next year. Being a wife was not a role that she desired for long. In 1991, before her child, Tyler Doustou, was born, Ms. Bottoms left Mr. Doustou and began dating women, initiating a dramatically different script for her life. Ms. Bottoms retained her role as a mother, but the need to support her family impelled her to rely on her own mother, Kay Bottoms, to care for Tyler most of the time. In 1992, Sharon Bottoms began living with April Wade, her partner with whom she shares a bed. In January 1993, Ms. Bottoms informed her mother that Tyler would spend less time at his grandmother's house because of the presence of Tommy Conley, whom Sharon Bottoms considered an undesirable influence on her son.

The foregoing account illustrates both the libertarian efflorescence of families we choose and the antilibertarian implications once self is turned loose. However much different the "liberated" Sharon Bottoms is from the married Sharon Bottoms, I doubt that the latter is the "final" or the "real" Sharon Bottoms, for she will continue to change as she continues to have new experiences and relationships. Thus, there is no assurance that she will be in a relationship with Ms. Wade ten years from now. Nor is it guaranteed that Ms. Bottoms will consider herself a lesbian ten years from now, even if she is still partnered with Ms. Wade. Examples could be multiplied for the following proposition: the liberal aspiration that the person be open to her desires and to new experiences assures that the person will change and, hence, that there will be no "core" or acontextual person the liberal can call "the real Sharon Bottoms."

Even at one point in time, there will be no acontextual Sharon Bottoms. Consider the following (plausible but hypothetical) scenario. In the morning, Ms. Bottoms may be warm and nurturing as she prepares lunches for her child and takes him to day care. At her job, she will act in a different context, where she must take orders and respond to problems that arise; she is delighted to be employed, after a period of unemployment and reliance on AFDC [Assistance to Families with Dependent Children] payments to support her family. Hence, Ms. Bottoms shows eagerness and gritty determination to do well in this job, and the nurturing mother becomes a serious nose-to-the-grindstone worker. During the day, she calls her mother and engages in a conversation about the bad influence Mr. Conley is on her son; Sharon Bottoms is passionately judgmental and curses Mr. Conley as she hangs up in pique at what she considers her mother's folly. When she returns home to cook dinner, she is creative and animated as she devotes herself to domestic chores and she beams with parental approval when her son brings home fingerpainting from school (which Ms. Bottoms tapes to the refrigerator door). Ms. Wade receives a hug and a kiss when she returns home, and Ms. Bottoms discusses with her the AA meeting they plan to attend the next evening (Ms. Wade is a recovering alcoholic).

Who is the real Sharon Bottoms: the decisive decision maker, the chef, the cursing daughter, the devoted parent, the domestic partner, the former wife? The Ms. Bottoms I have hypothesized is all of these and a great deal more. While there are recurring themes in the various contextual Sharon Bottoms, her self is "protean," shifting from one situation to another.[9] This contextualized protean self is also a fractured self, never revealing more than a few of its potentialities or features in any one situation. Such fractures are particularly apparent in the current lesbian version of Sharon Bottoms. The lesbian Sharon Bottoms is more fluid than the housewife of old (or the employee of today) because her role is less well-defined and less secure. Notwithstanding the precedents of Boston marriages and an increasing number of open lesbian relationships, same-sex couples like Ms. Bottoms and Ms. Wade are making up the roles as they go along, which is both exciting and exhausting. The relative absence of traditions requires the exercise of choice constantly, but the constant need to exercise choice envelops the self in a gyre of reaction and rebirth—a process by which the self evolves. The liberal paradigm of an acontextual self open to new experiences is undermined by its practice in a dynamic world.

Families we choose are also less than secure legal constructions. The next section will examine how this is so and the legal arguments for and against this insecurity. The final section will argue that this insecurity is not desirable. From that argument, I shall develop a status-based case for legal recognition of same-sex marriages that complements the libertarian case. I shall insist that, for reasons of personhood and identity, it is important for gays and lesbians to seek this controversial goal.

RESPONSES TO STATUS-BASED ARGUMENTS AGAINST LESBIAN AND GAY FAMILIES

The choice of same-sex couples to form relationships and to raise children is fraught with a great deal more uncertainty than different-sex couples face. That uncertainty is directly (albeit not exclusively) connected with the legal regime for same-sex relationships, which rejects the liberal perspective of choice and pervasively discriminates against same-sex couples by reason of status-based arguments.

For the leading example, consider the right to marry. Marriage is one of the least exclusive institutions in the United States, but it is a club that still excludes homosexuals in every state of the union.[10] The reasoning of these decisions has been status based. The following, from the Kentucky Supreme Court, is typical:

> Marriage has always been considered as the union of a man and a woman and we have been presented with no authority to the contrary.
>
> It appears to us that the [same-sex couple appealing the denial of their marriage license] are prevented from marrying, not by the statutes of Kentucky or the refusal of the County Court Clerk of Jefferson County to issue them a license, but rather by their own incapability of entering into a marriage as that term is defined.[11]

A few courts have gone one step further in reasoning from the status of gay men and lesbians as "outlaws": "[L]egislative authorization of homosexual, same-sex marriages would constitute tacit approval or endorsement of the sexual conduct, to wit, sodomy, commonly associated with homosexual status—conduct deemed by society to be so morally reprehensible as to be a criminal offense in the District of Columbia."[12]

Similar status-grounded arguments have been raised to deny lesbian and gay parents custody of their children. Some states permit denial of custody based on nothing more than pure status. Florida's adoption law, for example, states that "[n]o person eligible to adopt under this statute may adopt if that person is a homosexual."[13] Other states will permit homosexual activity to justify denial of custody if a sufficient factual showing is made. In a particularly antihomosexual version of this approach, Virginia presumes a parent involved in a same-sex relationship to be unfit if there is a custody dispute with the other parent.[14] In the Sharon Bottoms case, a Virginia trial judge extended this rule to deny custody to a lesbian mother, in favor of the child's grandmother:

> Sharon Bottoms has . . . admitted . . . that she is living in an [sic] homosexual relationship. . . . She is sharing . . . her bed with . . . her female lover. . . . Examples given were kissing, patting, all of this in the presence of the child. . . . I will tell you first that the mother's conduct is illegal. . . . I will tell you that it is the opinion of the court that her conduct is immoral. And it is the opinion of this court that the conduct of Sharon Bottoms renders her an unfit parent. However, I also must recognize, and do recognize, that there is a presumption in the law in favor of the custody being with the natural parent. And I ask myself are Sharon Bottoms' circumstances of unfitness . . . of such an extraordinary nature as to rebut this presumption. My answer to this is yes. . . .[15]

Although this judge's explanation was unusually discriminatory even under Virginia law (and has been reversed on intermediate appeal), judges throughout the country accomplish surreptitiously what this Virginia judge did openly: deny child custody to lesbian or gay parents essentially because of their status.

The liberal response to these arguments has been to emphasize their inconsistency with the libertarian view of the family as a construction of free choice by autonomous agents. Indeed, the United States Supreme Court has held that the due process clauses in the Constitution assure individuals both a right to marry[16] and a liberty interest in their biological children.[17] Under such a libertarian approach, the state must allow people to do what they want, so long as they cause no harm to others. Resting on an incomplete understanding of personhood, this has been an incomplete response to the arguments just noted.

As an initial matter, there is the problem that arguments of status cannot easily be separated from arguments of choice, for one's status and the status of those affected will influence the normative evaluation of one's choices. If two parents choose to end their marriage, the existence of children—and their status as parents—will constrain their choices. Because of the children's status as vulnerable persons, their "best interests" will override parental preferences to the contrary, and each parent will be saddled with financial and other obligations by reason of their parental status. When the Virginia Supreme Court created a presumption against custody to lesbian and gay parents, it cited the "intolerable burden upon [the child] by reason of the social condemnation attached to [the gay parent], which will inevitably afflict her relationships with her peers and with the community at large."[18] The connection between status and choice is fainter but still discernible in the context of marriage. For many heterosexuals, to give state sanction to gay and lesbian marriages would be to diminish their own, which is a third-party effect of such recognition, and an effect that sometimes assumes hysterical proportions. The context in which one's choice is assessed is infinitely elastic, and there is not much a libertarian can say to impose one context (what I want) over another (the effect on my bigoted neighbor).

More importantly, status arguments have not disappeared from family law, nor should they disappear. Consider the issue of surrogacy contracts, in which a woman (usually one needing money) agrees to bear a stranger's child and to relinquish her parental rights to the child. Such contracts and other forms of "baby selling" are a logical consequence of one form of libertarian thinking,[19] subject to the just-noted objection that the third-party effects on the child must be explored and considered. Notwithstanding the libertarian appeal of surrogacy arrangements, they are explicitly prohibited in about a dozen states[20] and are heavily regulated in other jurisdictions.[21] Proponents of such laws reject a simple libertarian conception of family in this setting, either because the conditions for free choice are not present or (perhaps much the same idea) because status-based concerns are overriding. Thus, surrogacy laws serve either to prevent women from making decisions they will likely regret (the libertarian conception is inappropriate) or to express society's valorization of the parent-child connection as inalienable (a status-based idea).[22] Although I am sympathetic to the libertarian position generally, in this particular situation it does not unequivocally support a laissez-faire approach and is overshadowed by status-based concerns.

Indeed, the surrogacy issue suggests a status-based argument for overturning the family law presumptions and prohibitions based on sexual orientation. Why would moral thinkers consider the mother-child connection close to inalienable? It is inalienable for precisely the same reason that Sharon

Bottoms ought not to lose her child, either to her own mother or to her former husband, and for much the same reason why Sharon Bottoms and April Wade ought to be able to get married on the same terms as Sharon Bottoms and Dennis Doustou. The parent-child and partner-partner connections receive and ought to receive special legal protection because they are critical to identity. They are critical to identity because the self is relational both in its formation and in its expressions.[23]

Recall the earlier argument that liberalism cannot maintain its conception of the acontextual self in the face of experience in an increasingly mobile world; one's identity is shaped and reshaped by the many different contexts in which one finds one self. I now maintain that individual identity is shaped and reshaped through relationships. It is inhumane to seize a newborn baby from the arms of a surrogate mother because even outside of the womb that baby remains a part of her, and she remains with him. Her personhood becomes tied up with his. The familiar willingness of a mother to sacrifice her life for her child is a rational response of one whose self is inextricably intertwined with the self of the child. A similar even if less intense phenomenon infuses committed partnerships, whereby the partner's aches are my aches, the partner's joy, mine as well.

Human selves are from birth relational. Our early identity is interconnected with (and for a while dominated by) our parent(s) and other caretakers.[24] If adolescence is a period where we declare emotional independence from our parents, it is also one where begins the deep emotional bonding with our peers. Becoming an adult—achieving a flourishing personhood—typically involves one or more intimate relationships. Sharon Bottoms's personhood cannot be understood without reference to her relationships with her mother, Kay Bottoms; her former husband, Dennis Doustou; her son, Tyler; and her lover, April Wade. By initially denying her custody of her son and by denying her the opportunity to marry Ms. Wade, the state of Virginia is trying to discourage Ms. Bottoms from pursuing a flourishing personhood. The security the state offers heterosexual partners and parents, and denies to homosexual ones, is an invidious discrimination, a denial of Ms. Bottoms's citizenship.[25]

Under any fair constitutional system, the discrimination posed by these state prohibitions requires a justification beyond mere prejudices.[26] Does the discrimination against lesbian and gay marriages and custody protect innocent children, for example? Every respectable study I have seen concludes that lesbian and gay parents are just as responsible, loving, and capable as heterosexual parents and that there is no basis to believe that children of gay households will be adversely affected by the experience.[27] Does the discrimination foster a healthy and thriving society? I strongly doubt it because it channels people's energies into unproductive quarrels about features of one's personhood that are not easily alterable and that have little if any bearing on other people or their own entitlement for citizenship.

STATUS-BASED REFLECTIONS ON FEMINIST AND LESBIAN ARGUMENTS ABOUT SURROGACY, INSEMINATION, AND MARRIAGE

Feminist critiques of family law have reintroduced status concerns but with a decidedly different twist from traditional status-based arguments. Liberal feminists have argued against status in family law: the wife should be treated just like the husband for purposes of alimony, custody, and the like. Reflecting developments within feminist thought and within family law as well, other feminist theorists have strongly differentiated women from men in matters of domestic relations. Such theorists have introduced new status-based arguments, and their arguments have relevance for thinking about gay and lesbian families. I shall focus on issues of surrogacy, insemination, and marriage.

Professor Robin West maintains that women have distinctive "selves" because they are, or potentially are, mothers who will bear and nurture children.[28] Their relational selves are particularly constituted by the connection with a child. West's theory is at least in part status based, for it maintains that being a mother—or even potentially being a mother—ought to have consequence because of the centrality of childbearing to a woman's self. A variety of interesting legal corollaries might follow from such a claim.

For example, West's theory provides a robust defense for state laws prohibiting or heavily regulating surrogacy contracts. To allow a woman to precontract to give up her child and her parental rights to the purchasing family in return for money is objectionable in part because the woman would "regret" this earlier contract once the child is born. Liberal theory would justify regulation on the ground that the regret is a predictable cognitive dysfunction: people often underestimate future costs (losing the baby) and overvalue present satisfactions (the friendship of the purchasing family, up-front gifts, and the promise of money). This is not a completely satisfying justification, as our polity routinely enforces such irrational behavior (extravagant credit arrangements, for example). West's theory offers a richer, and I think better, defense for surrogacy laws: what the woman is selling in a surrogacy contract is part of herself, and that relational feature of selfhood should be either inalienable (the child cannot be sold any more than the surrogate can sell a limb or an organ) or alienable only in the best interests of the child (the traditional family law approach).

I embrace this corollary of Professor West's theory but am skeptical of another possible corollary (neither of which is discussed by Professor West). While about half the states stringently regulate or prohibit a woman from giving up her parental rights before the birth of the child (surrogacy), almost all of the states freely allow a man to give up his parental rights before the birth of the child (insemination). Discrimination between women and men can be justified on status grounds: the surrogate mother is much more connected to or invested in the child than the sperm donor, who can easily be anonymous to the child. This rationale does, in my view, justify different treatment of surrogacy and insemination. Does it justify the drastically different way our policy treats surrogacy (heavily regulated) and insemination (unregulated)? I am more skeptical. What the sperm donor is giving up is an important relational opportunity, a fundamental part of his future self. The state that protects surrogate mothers ought also to provide some protection for sperm donors—surely informed-consent rules would be appropriate and perhaps also a short period after the child's birth in which the biological father can change his mind about giving up parental rights.[29]

A more celebrated venue for feminist status-based concerns has been the institution of marriage. Several generations of feminist theorists have criticized the institution as patriarchal, and lesbian feminist theorists have criticized gay and lesbian lawyers and litigants seeking recognition of same-sex marriages. The leading critic, lawyer Paula Ettelbrick, maintains that lesbians, gay men, and bisexuals should reject marriage, and its patriarchy, and should instead seek to form their own families.[30] In other words, by rejecting the roles of "husband" and "wife," gays and lesbians can undermine an institution that contributes to preserving the underclass status of women generally, and lesbians in particular. Ms. Ettelbrick also argues that if gays and lesbians are able to marry, their rebel status will be ended, leaving nonmarried lesbians as a group of permanently subordinated outsiders.[31] Her ultimate position is consistent with liberalism for she is skeptical about marriage for anyone, and presumably she would support the same rights for homosexual couples as for heterosexual couples. Nevertheless, her arguments strike me as ultimately status- rather than choice-based arguments: we should refrain from expanding our range of choices because some of us outsiders would become insiders, leaving the rest out in the cold. This kind of argument is different in kind from those made by traditional moralists or by Professor West, but they are also status-based justifications for narrowing choice.

Not surprisingly, the primary response to Ms. Ettelbrick by promarriage gay and lesbian activists is unabashedly liberal and speaks in the argot of choice. Lawyer Thomas Stoddard and Professor Nan Hunter, for example, believe that there is no inherent patriarchal consequence arising from the status of being married and, indeed, that same-sex marriage would destabilize gender-based status arrangements in traditional marriages.[32] I am open to this argument, though the historical evidence does not much support Mr. Stoddard's and Professor Hunter's position.[33] A better argument is a status-based one that appeals to another feature of the institution of marriage: commitment.

A decision to marry is a decision to limit one's future choices, a commitment to consider the interests of another person (and often children as well) in the future. This is in part a consequence of law, which treats the partners as an interdependent legal team and makes it difficult and costly for the team to break up. The promise and the reasonable expectation of partnership and commitment are valuable for a variety of reasons, including the personal security that comes from knowing that one can depend on someone else, for better or for worse (with an emphasis on the latter). What I should like to emphasize, however, is the importance such partnership and commitment potentially have for a relational conception of identity.

Partnership is important because it provides an intense focal point for one to transcend one's "self" and to deepen one's identity through intimate interaction with another self. This is, of course, a status-based argument for families we choose—a series of open-ended partnerships more closely analogous to friendships than to marital relationships. I think this is good, but not complete, for there is an additional value to the partnership's being committed.

We are all products of our relationships with our parents, and I think the healthiest parent-child relationships are ones where the child feels secure about the parent's unconditional love, her unquestioning commitment to the child and the child's well-being. Although the mutual love between parent and child is complicated, involving biological as well as emotional connections, I would hypothesize that the love is as much a consequence as a cause of the mutual expectation that the relationship will be a lasting one. An analogous point can be made about partnership relations; they will be different, and in my view deeper, if they are conducted within a mutual understanding of lasting commitment.

As Professor Regan has indicated, status—including the status of spousehood—protects people's capacity for intimacy and thereby fosters a stable sense of self over time. The stable sense of self is at risk in a society of nothing but choice because such a world fractures self, as argued above. A stable sense of self is a worthwhile aspiration for both negative and positive reasons. As to the former, recall the parable of Buridan's ass. Finding itself equidistant from two equally attractive haystacks, the animal starved because it could not choose between them. Buridan's ass may be an early example of the fractured personality, torn apart by too many choices. Similarly, the protean individual of the late twentieth century risks being torn apart by too many roles.

While a world of nothing but choice risks the fracturing of self, a world of nothing but status risks the ossification or subordination of self. Hence, I am quite comfortable with the current plasticity of marriage as an institution where exit is merely hard and not impossible. Moreover, commitment may carry a precious tariff if one rational self exploits the other, as has too frequently been the case not only in marriages but also in families we choose. Nonetheless, I would insist on the value of commitment for many couples, and if commitment is valuable, it ought to be available to lesbians and gay couples, on the same terms it is offered to heterosexual ones.

CONCLUSION

A thriving society is one that accommodates the needs of its productive citizens. A worthy polity is one that contributes to the personal flourishing of its citizens. In light of these goals, our country at the turn of a new century faces these important and complementary challenges: on the one hand, to construct flexible safe harbors for citizens to form lasting intimate relationships that minimize risks of interpersonal exploitation and, on the other hand, to reconcile the citizenry to opening up these constructions to previously excluded persons, particularly lesbians, bisexuals, and gay men.

NOTES

1. Kathy Weston, *Families We Choose: Lesbians, Gays, Kinship* (1991).
2. See Milton C. Regan, Jr., *Family Law and the Pursuit of Intimacy* (1993); Marjorie M. Schultz, "Contractual Ordering of Marriage: A New Model for State Policy," 70 *California Law Review* 204 (1982); Jana B. Singer, "The Privatization of Family Law," 1992 *Wisconsin Law Review* 1443. See generally Mary Ann Glendon, *The Transformation of Family Law: State, Law, and Family in the United States and Western Europe* (1989).
3. See Lilian Faderman, *Surpassing the Love of Men: Romantic Friendship and Love Between Women from the Renaissance to the Present* (1981).
4. Surveys of do-it-yourself Victorian family formation can be found in Hayden Curry, Denis Clifford, and Robin Leonard, *A Legal Guide for Lesbian and Gay Couples* (8th ed., 1994); Barbara J. Cox, "Alternative Families: Obtaining Traditional Family Benefits through Litigation, Legislation, and Collective Bargaining," 2 *Wisconsin Women's Law Journal* 1 (1986).

5. See Catherine Whitney, *Uncommon Lives: Gay Men and Straight Women* (1990).
6. For leading cases, see Adoption of Tammy, 619 N.E.2d 315 (Mass. 1993); Matter of Adoption of Child by J. M. G., 632 A.2d 550 (N.J. Ch. 1993); *In re* B.L.V.B., 628 A.2d 1271 (Vt. 1993); *In re* L.S., 119 WLR 2249 (D.C. Super. Ct. 1991). See generally Nancy D. Polikoff, "This Child Does Have Two Mothers: Redefining Parenthood to Meet the Needs of Children in Lesbian-Mother and Other Nontraditional Families," 78 *Georgetown Law Journal* 459 (1990).
7. See Regan, *Pursuit of Intimacy,* supra note 2, at ch. 3.
8. The facts in the account that follows are taken from Judge Coleman's opinion in Bottoms v. Bottoms, 444 S.E.2d 276 (Va. Ct. App. 1994), *revised,* 457 S.E.2d 102 (Va. 1993), and from a law review article by Sharon Bottoms's attorney in the case. See Stephen B. Pershing, "'Entreat Me Not To Leave Thee'; *Bottoms v. Bottoms* and the Custody Rights of Gay and Lesbian Parents," 3 *William and Mary Bill of Rights Journal* 289 (1994).
9. Robert Jay Lifton, *The Protean Self: Human Resilience in an Age of Fragmentation* (1993); see Kenneth J. Gergen, *The Saturated Self: Dilemmas of Identity in Contemporary Life* (1991); Anthony Giddens, *Modernity and Self-Identity: Self and Society in the Late Modern Age* (1991).
10. The main decisions rejecting same-sex marriage are Jones v. Hallahan, 501 S.W.2d 588 (Ky. 1973); Baker v. Nelson, 191 N.W.2d 185 (Minn. 1971); Singer v. Hara, 522 P.2d 1187 (Wash. Ct. App. 1974); Dean v. District of Columbia, Civ. No. 90-13892 (D.C. Super. Ct. Dec. 30, 1991), *affirmed,* 653 A.2d 307 (D.C. Ct. App. 1995); DeSanto v. Barnsley, 476 A.2d 952 (Pa. Super. Ct. 1984). As of 1995, there is a good chance that the Supreme Court of Hawaii will invalidate that state's prohibition of same-sex marriage. Its opinion in Baehr v. Lewin, 852 P.2d 44 (Haw. 1993), found the prohibition to be sex discrimination and remanded to the trial court for a hearing to determine whether the state has a compelling justification for the discrimination. See William N. Eskridge, Jr., *The Case for Same-Sex Marriage* (1996).
11. Hallahan, 501 S.W.2d at 589; see G. Sidney Buchanan, "Same-Sex Marriage: The Linchpin Issue," 10 *University of Dayton Law Review* 541 (1985).
12. Dean, Civ. No. 90-13892, Slip opinion, 9 (D.C. Super. Ct. Dec. 30, 1991). The district's sodomy law repealed soon after this opinion was issued.
13. Fla. Stat. Ann. sec. 63.042 (West 1985). See also N.H. Rev. Stat. Ann. sec. 170-B:4 (Butterworth 1994)("any individual not a minor and not a homosexual may adopt . . .").
14. Roe v. Roe, 324 S.E.2d 691 (Va.1985).
15. Bottoms v. Bottoms, No. CH93JA0517-00 (Va. Cir. Ct. Henrico County, Sept. 7, 1993), *rev'd,* No. 1930-93-1 (Va. Ct. App. June 21, 1994). See Pershing, "Custody Rights," supra note 8.
16. See Turner v. Safley, 482 U.S. 78 (1987) (state cannot deny prisoners [!] the right to marry); Zablocki v. Redhail, 434 U.S. 374 (1978) (state cannot deny dead-beat dads the right to remarry); Loving v. Virginia, 388 U.S. 1 (1967) (state cannot deny different-race couples the right to marry).
17. See Lassiter v. Department of Social Services of Durham County, N.C., 449 U.S. 819 (1981). But see Michael H. v. Gerald D., 491 U.S. 110 (1989)(upholding statute establishing conclusive evidence of paternity in the husband of the woman who bears the child).
18. Roe v. Roe, 324 S.E.2d at 694.
19. See Lori B. Andrews, *Between Strangers: Surrogate Mothers, Expectant Fathers, and Brave New Babies* (1989); Richard A Posner, *Sex and Reason,* 409–29 (1992).
20. As of 1995, statutes prohibit surrogacy contracts in Arizona, the District of Columbia, Indiana, Louisiana, Maryland, Michigan, Nebraska, New York, North Dakota, Oregon, Utah, and Washington. A court decision rendered them illegal in New Jersey.
21. As of 1995, statutes regulating permissible surrogacy contracts have been adopted in Florida, Illinois, Kentucky, Maryland, Nevada, New Hampshire, and Virginia.
22. Commentators supporting regulation of surrogacy include Martha A. Field, *Surrogate Motherhood* (1990) (libertarian-based arguments on the whole); Judith Areen, "Baby M Reconsidered," 76 *Georgia Law Journal* 1741 (1988) (criticizing libertarianism as a partial perspective and raising status-based arguments; Alexander M. Captron and Margaret J. Radin,

"Choosing Family Law over Contract Law As a Paradigm for Surrogate Motherhood," in *Surrogate Motherhood: Politics and Privacy* 59 (Larry Gostin, ed., 1990) (status-based arguments); Lisa Sowle Cahill, "The Ethics of Surrogate Motherhood: Biology, Freedom, and Moral Obligation," in id. at 151 (status-based arguments).

23. This concept is associated with postmodernism, see Regan, *Pursuit of Intimacy,* supra note 2, at ch. 4, but I am using the term in ways consistent with, even if subversive of, liberal or modernist premises. See Anthony Giddens, *The Consequences of Modernity* (1990). See also William N. Eskridge, Jr., and Brian Weimer, "The Economics Epidemic from an AIDS Perspective," 61 *University of Chicago Law Review* 733, 753–60 (1994), drawing the idea of "relational preferences" from Amartya Sen, "Behavior and the Concept of Preference," 40 *Economica* 241 (1973).
24. See Erik Erikson, *Childhood and Society* (1953).
25. For legal indictments of these discriminations, see William N. Eskridge, Jr., "A History of Same-Sex Marriage," 79 *Virginia Law Review* 1419 (1993); Pershing, "Custody Rights," supra note 8; "Note, Custody Denials to Parents in Same-Sex Relationships: An Equal Protection Analysis," 102 *Harvard Law Review* 617 (1989).
26. See Palmore v. Sidoti, 466 U.S. 429 (1984)(court making custody determination cannot consider race of either parent; "private biases and the possible injury they might inflict" are not "permissible considerations for removal of an infant child from the custody of its natural mother"); see also Robinson v. California, 370 U.S. 660 (1962)(state cannot punish status of being an addict). See generally Kenneth L. Karst, *Belonging to America: Equal Citizenship and the Constitution* (1989).
27. For examples of such studies, see Mary E. Hotvedt and Jane Barclay Mandel, "Children of Lesbian Mothers," in *Homosexuality: Social, Psychological, and Biological Issues* 275 (William Paul et al., eds., 1982); Sharon L. Huggins, "A Comparative Study of Self-Esteem of Adolescent Children of Divorced Lesbian Mothers and Divorced Heterosexual Mothers," in *Homosexuality and the Family* 123 (Frederick W. Bozett, ed., 1989); Charlotte J. Patterson, "Children of Lesbian and Gay Parents," 63 *Child Development* 1025 (1992) (surveying the social science literature). See also Gregory M. Herek, "Myths about Sexual Orientation: A Lawyer's Guide to Social Science Research," 1 *Law and Sexuality* 133, 156 (1991).
28. Robin West, "Jurisprudence and Gender," 55 *University of Chicago Law Review* 1 (1988).
29. If the latter proposal were adopted, it would necessitate modification of presumptive parenthood rules in many states. Most states conclusively presume that the husband of the biological mother—and therefore not the biological father—is the legal father of the child. I recognize that such modification raises important issues of status and do not maintain that the husband or the partner of the biological mother is without interest that should be protected. I am only questioning the one-sidedness of current law.
30. Paula L. Ettelbrick, "Since When Is Marriage a Path to Liberation?" in *Lesbian and Gay Marriage* 20 (Suzanne Sherman, ed., 1992).
31. Ibid., at 26; see Nancy D. Polikoff, "We Will Get What We Ask for: Why Legalizing Gay and Lesbian Marriage Will Not 'Dismantle the Legal Structure of Gender in Marriage,'" 79 *Virginia Law Review* 1535 (1993); Ruthan Robson and S. E. Valentine, "Lov(h)hers: Lesbians as Intimate Partners and Lesbian Legal Theory," 63 *Temple Law Review* 511 (1990).
32. See Nan Hunter, "Marriage, Law and Gender: A Feminist Inquiry," 1 *Law and Sexuality* 9, 18–19 (1991); Thomas B. Stoddard, "Why Gay People Should Seek the Right to Marry," in *Lesbian and Gay Marriage,* supra note 30, at 13.
33. See Polikoff, supra note 31.

65

RICHARD A. POSNER

From *Economic Analysis of Law*

CHAPTER 5 / FAMILY LAW AND SEX LAW[1]

The central institution of the family is marriage, a relationship that hovers uneasily at the border of contract. So a chapter on family law is a natural sequel to one on contract law, and the role of marriage law in channeling sexual and procreative activity makes economic analysis of the regulation of sexual activity a natural extension of economic analysis of the family. However, several topics within this broad area—rape, inheritance (which is largely familial), and sex discrimination (a topic inseparable from the family)—are deferred to later chapters.

§5.1 THE THEORY OF HOUSEHOLD PRODUCTION

The economic analysis of the family is founded on the perception that the household is not merely a consuming, but more importantly a producing, unit in society. The food, clothing, furniture, medicines, and other market commodities that the household purchases are inputs into the production of nourishment, warmth, affection, children, and the other tangible and intangible goods that constitute the output of the household. A critical input into this productive process is not a market commodity at all; it is the time of the household members, in particular—in the traditional family—of the wife.

The persistence of the family as a social institution suggests to an economist that the institution must have important economizing properties. What might these be? Economies of scale (for instance, from sharing a kitchen)? But these could be, and often are, achieved outside of marriage and in any event are often smaller than the costs of having to adapt one's tastes, schedule, etc., to another person's. A more important factor is that the family facilitates the division of labor, yielding gains from specialization. In the traditional family the husband specializes in some market employment (for example, engineering) that yields income that can be used to purchase the market commodities needed as inputs into the final production of the household, while the wife devotes her time to processing market commodities (for example, groceries) into household output (for example, dinner). By specializing in production for the market the husband maximizes the family's money income with which to buy the market commodities that the family needs. By specializing in household production the wife maximizes the value of her time as an input into the production of the household's output. The division of labor—the husband working full-time in the job market, the wife full-time in the household—operates to maximize the total real income of the household by enabling husband and wife to specialize in complementary activities. It is the same principle that leads us to expect a person who works half-time as a doctor and half-time as a lawyer to produce less than one-half the total output of medical and legal services of two people of equal ability to his, one of whom is a full-time doctor and the other a full-time lawyer. People who do the same thing all the time tend to do it better than people who divide their time between unrelated tasks.

Only a tendency is involved, however, as we can see by restating the point in the useful economic terminology of economies of scale. If the average cost of some output, which might be a household's nonmarket production or a doctor's output of medical services, falls as output increases, production is said to exhibit economies of scale. Economies of scale are not unlimited; otherwise there would be only one producer of each type of good or service. The doctor or lawyer who tried to work 24 hours a day would experience grave diseconomies of scale; and for many women full-time housework entails a degree of tedium that offsets their greater efficiency at housework than their husband's.

---

[1] See Judith Areen, Cases and Materials on Family Law (3d ed. 1992); Homer H. Clark, Jr. & Carol Glowinsky, Domestic Relations: Cases and Problems (5th ed. 1995); Carl E. Schneider & Margaret F. Brinig, An Invitation to Family Law: Principles, Process and Perspective (1996).

The gains from specialization are realized through trade. This is seen most clearly in the marriage setting by focusing on the major "commodity" that marriage produces: children. Although many marriages are childless, only a few are childless by choice; and it is hard to believe that marriage would be a common institution if most people didn't want children. Raising children requires, especially in their early years, an enormous amount of parental (traditionally maternal) time, and a woman who is busy raising a child will not have time to work in the market for the money she needs for complementary inputs (food, clothing, shelter, etc.). So she "trades" her work in the home for the husband's work in the market; he "buys" her care of children that are his as well as hers.

Although analysis is simplified by the assumption that each spouse is fully employed in his or her respective sphere, it does not depend on the assumption. Indeed, the earlier mention of the tedium factor, and the broader point that economies of scale in both market and household production are limited, suggests that the optimal division of labor within marriage may involve one spouse working full time in the market and part time at home and one spouse working part time in the market and full time at home. We shall see that it is important today for women to hedge their bets on marriage by becoming established in the labor market, notwithstanding the resulting sacrifice of gains from specialization, both the woman's and her husband's.

Must the primary market producer be the man and the primary household producer the woman? No. The plausible reasons why the woman is more likely, even today, to be the primary household producer are twofold. First, to the extent that sex discrimination in the labor market depresses women's market earnings relative to men's, it makes household work relatively more attractive to the wife than to the husband. Second, insofar as women bear the children and are better adapted to child (especially infant) care, the wife's costs of household production will be lower than the husband's. Women who take time off from work to bear children and to take care of them as infants, even if they do this because it is efficient, will have lower average wages, even if there is no sex discrimination, when they return to the labor market (why?).

While marriage is a "partnership," there are important differences between business and familial organization. For example, the division of the marital income may not be determined by the relative value of each spouse's contribution, as it would be in a business partnership. A related point (can you see why?) is that specific tasks within the household are not directed and monitored in a hierarchical, bureaucratic, or even contractual manner. There is a substitute in marriage for the control mechanisms within a business firm. Economists naturally do not call this factor "love," but describe it as a form of altruism. Altruism is the condition in which the welfare of one person is a positive function of the welfare of another. If H loves W, then an increase in W's happiness or utility or welfare (synonyms) will be felt by H as an increase in his own happiness or utility or welfare. Altruism facilitates cooperation; it is a cheap and efficacious substitute for (formal) contracting. But it would be a mistake to think that altruism is the solvent for every conflict or exploitation in the marriage relationship.[2] Even if H values W's utility, he may not value it as highly as he values his own utility. Suppose the cost to W of doing one more hour of housework is 10 and the benefit is 8. And suppose that W's utility enters into H's with a discount factor of 50 percent, so the cost of that extra hour to him is only 5, and let us assume that the value of it to him is 9. So H has a net gain of 4 from the extra hour of her work and W a net loss of 2. In the market we would expect H to compensate W by paying W between 2 (the minimum price she would demand) and 4 (the maximum price H would pay). What determines within a marriage where in the bargaining range the deal will be struck? Is it certain that H will have to pay *anything* to induce W to work the extra hour?

The declining marriage rate and rising divorce rate suggest that the benefits of marriage have been falling relative to the costs. The value of having many children has declined with the decline in infant mortality; it requires fewer births to have reasonable confidence of reaching one's target number of grown children. And the cost of children has increased. Among other things, the advent of cheap household

---

[2]As emphasized in Gillian K. Hadfield, Households at Work: Beyond Labor Market Policies to Remedy the Gender Gap, 82 Geo. L.J. 89, 96–98 (1993).

labor-saving devices and the increasing fraction of jobs that do not require great physical strength have reduced the cost to women of working in the market and increased the demand for their services by employers. The resulting rise in the net income that women can earn in the market (wages minus costs of work, those costs including loss of time for household production) has raised the opportunity cost of being a housewife, for that cost is the net market income forgone by staying home. Since the household commodity that places the greatest demands on the wife's time is rearing children, an increase in the opportunity cost of that time is immediately translated into an increase in the shadow price of children to the household.

We have treated children as an ultimate "commodity," but it is possible to treat them instead as an input into other commodities. The economist speculates that children are produced (1) as an unintended by-product of sexual activity, (2) as an income-producing investment, (3) as a source of other services to the parents, and (4) (really a subset of (3)) out of an instinct or desire to preserve the species or perpetuate the genetic characteristics, the name, or the memory of the parents. In an age of widely available contraception and abortion, (1) has become relatively unimportant; it was never very important, except where law or custom confined sexual activity to marriage. (2) was once important in our society (as it is in very poor societies today). At common law, the parents owned the child's market earnings until his majority and were entitled to support from the child in their old age. The outlawing of child labor, and the prevalence of public and private pension schemes, have obsoleted (2) and prompted a search for less tangible services that parents might derive from a child (for example, respect). (3) and (4) are the most plausible explanations for the desire to have children in contemporary society. Liking children is a subset of (3): The pleasure we get from our children's presence is the result of "consuming" the intangible "services" that they render us.

§5.2 FORMATION AND DISSOLUTION OF MARRIAGE

Commercial partnerships are voluntary contractual associations, and so, up to a point, are marriages. The "marriage market" is an apt metaphor for the elaborate process of search by which individuals seek marital partners with whom to form productive households. The market is rational. For example, bright men tend to marry bright women; an agricultural analogy will reveal why. Suppose there are two farms, and the soil of one is (untreated) twice as productive as the soil of the other (untreated). A chemical will double the yield of whichever farm it is applied to, but there is only enough chemical for one farm. Should it be applied to the farm with the poorer soil, on the theory that that farm needs it more? Should it be divided between the two farms? (Half the chemical will increase the output of a farm by 50 percent.) Or should it all be applied to the farm with the better soil? The last. Suppose the output of the farm with the richer soil is (before treatment with the chemical) 2, and the output of the other farm 1. If the chemical is applied all to the poorer farm, the total output of the two farms will be 4 (2 + 2); if applied half and half, $4\frac{1}{2}$ ($3 + 1\frac{1}{2}$); but if applied all to the better farm, 5 (4 + 1). Coming a little closer to home, we would also expect that law firms that had the best partners would hire the best associates to work with them, that law schools with the best students would have the best teachers, and that business firms in thriving markets would have better executives on average than firms in declining ones. And so in marriage as well if the positive qualities of spouses are related multiplicatively as in the farm, law firm, law school, and corporate examples, and not just additively.

Might the proper analogy to marriage instead be the international trade in unlike commodities—say, wheat for aircraft—where there is no presumption that the best of one is being exchanged for the best of the other, the second best for the second best, and so on? These goods are not used together, as are land and fertilizer in our first example; so the potential multiplicative effect, which might in the marriage example include the production of children of superior intelligence or beauty, is missing. There is another reason for "positive assortative" mating of humans besides the potential multiplicative effect of the parents' qualities: It reduces friction, and therefore transaction costs, within the household.

Despite the resemblance of marriage to a business partnership, the marital relationship is not—or at least was not before no-fault divorce (about which more later)—an unalloyed example of free-market principles. Three features in particular, which seem at once odd . . . and incompatible with one another, mark off traditional marriage law from contract law.

First, the parties are not free to set the term of the contract or even to terminate the contract by mutual consent; the term is life, subject to termination for cause.

Second, despite the long term, the sanction for breach is more severe than in the case of a regular contract. If the husband abandons the wife (or vice versa), he not only must continue to support her (which is analogous to his having to pay damages) but may not marry anyone else. It is as if a contract breaker could be enjoined from making a substitute contract for the one he had broken—and for the rest of his life.[3]

Third, despite the locked-in nature of their relationship, if spouses have a dispute during the course of the marriage the courts generally will not intervene to settle the dispute, even if the spouses have a signed contract allocating rights and duties that one spouse alleges has been broken; the spouses will be compelled to work it out for themselves.

Marriage law is thus a puzzling amalgam of intrusiveness (in regard to the term of the contract and the sanctions for breach) and hands-off-ness. The explanation may be that the marriage "contract" affects nonconsenting third parties, the children of the marriage. Of course, even in a system of consensual divorce, parents who love their children will take the cost of divorce to the children into account in deciding whether to divorce; but unless they are completely selfless they will not fully internalize the cost to the children and thus may decide to divorce even though the total costs to all concerned exceed the total benefits.[4] It might seem that locking parents into a miserable marriage, by making divorce impossible, would condemn the children to misery too. But this ignores the fact that forbidding divorce will induce more careful search for a marriage partner in the first place. The more costly a mistake is, the less likely it is to be committed; and a mistake in choosing a spouse is more costly in a system that forbids divorce (or makes it very difficult) than in one that permits it. A related point is that the longer the marriage search, the higher the average age of spouses at marriage; and more mature, experienced people are less likely to make mistakes than greenhorns. So there is the curious paradox that making divorce more difficult may actually foster happy marriages! Moreover, if people know they are locked into a relationship, they have an incentive to create methods of working out their differences, so there is less need for judicial remedies such as divorce.

This is not a complete analysis, of course. The additional marital search that a rule of no (or hard-to-obtain) divorce fosters is neither costless nor, since we are dealing with a long-term contract, totally efficacious in preventing mismatches. Spouses may change over their lifetimes in ways that they could not have foreseen and that drive the benefits of continued marriage below the costs. The happiness of the spouses is part of the total welfare to be maximized, not just the happiness of the children. So the analysis does not prove that divorce should be made difficult. It may, however, explain the law's reluctance—so at variance with the corresponding rule of contract law—to recognize fraud as a ground for annulling a marriage, unless the fraud involves sex (typically, the husband failed to disclose before the marriage that he was impotent). In a system where divorce is very difficult, prospective marriage partners (or their parents or other intermediaries) conduct a careful investigation into the qualities of the most promising prospect; and a lengthy courtship provides an opportunity for each prospective spouse to unmask the deceptions by which people try to represent themselves in personal relationships as having better qualities and prospects than they really do. (Where have we seen these deceptions before?) The greater the precontractual search, the fewer legal remedies are necessary. But fraud as to sex goes to the heart of the marriage contract, and dissolution of a childless marriage involves minimum social costs.

The refusal of English law until well into the nineteenth century to recognize any grounds for

---

[3]In fact, breaches of contracts for personal services are enjoinable only if the promisor's services are unique, which would make the promisee's remedy in damages inadequate.

[4]Well, but are there any "costs" to the children, in an economic sense? If as in the usual case they have no money, doesn't this mean that their welfare should have no weight in the social calculus, except insofar as they are valued by others (mainly their parents)? Then there would be no externality. But children are "poor" only because they cannot borrow against their future earnings (why not, besides the obvious point that they may lack the knowledge and experience to negotiate a loan?). As we are about to see, society undertakes a variety of measures to compensate for this failure of the capital markets, such as public education, child labor laws, and, arguably, restrictions on divorce and custody. These measures can be explained and evaluated as measures to approximate the results that would obtain if children could borrow against their future earnings.

divorce may actually have protected the weaker spouse (invariably the wife) more effectively than allowing divorce for cause would have done. In a system that allows divorce for cause, a husband who wants "out" of the marriage will have an incentive to so mistreat his wife that she will be driven to sue for divorce, provided that alimony or other remedies would not visit the full costs of the mistreatment on him, as often they would not in a system where litigation was slow, costly, and uncertain. But if the remedial difficulties can be overcome, then allowing divorce for cause makes economic sense, as it enables at least a rough comparison between the costs to the children of divorce and the cost to a severely wronged spouse of remaining married. Moreover, the traditional grounds of divorce, with one partial and very interesting exception (adultery), seem to have been limited to cases where the husband's misconduct was likely to hurt the children as well as the wife: cases of insanity, extreme cruelty, and criminality.

Regarding adultery, one notes with interest that traditionally a single act of adultery by the wife was grounds for divorce, while the husband had to be a habitual adulterer in order to entitle the wife to a divorce. The economic explanation is that the wife's adultery is more costly to the husband than the husband's adultery to the wife, even if the purely emotional cost of adultery—the shame or fury that it engenders in the dishonored spouse when he or she discovers the adultery—is the same to both spouses (but will it be?). An adulterous wife may conceive a child who is not the child of her husband; and since the capacity of women to bear children is distinctly finite, the benefits of the marriage to the husband will be significantly impaired, assuming he wants to have children of his blood. The husband's adultery, in contrast, need not reduce the number of children that his wife will bear or the support he will give each of them; the benefits of the marriage to her, at least in terms of children, may not be impaired at all (though it may be, if he sires and supports illegitimate children). If, however, the husband is a *habitual* adulterer, he may be so distracted from his wife's and (legitimate) children's needs as to impose on her a cost as high as a wife's isolated adultery would impose on the husband.

The problem with recognizing *any* grounds for divorce is that it erodes the policy, plausibly designed for the protection of the children of the marriage, against voluntary dissolutions of marriage. An agreement to dissolve a marriage involves only two people; although there is a bilateral-monopoly problem, transaction costs should not be prohibitive. Once the parties have arrived at mutually agreeable terms, they need only manufacture evidence of a breach that provides legal grounds for divorce in order to get around a law against consensual divorce. The manufacture of evidence is not costless, so a stringent divorce law will preserve some marriages by increasing the costs of dissolution. But were society determined to preserve marriages, it would at least prevent the parties from controlling the evidence; it would allow divorce only when the public prosecutor, or some other third party, had proved the commission of a breach of the marriage contract. The "fault" system is tantamount to confining the enforcement of laws punishing such "victimless" crimes as bribery and dope peddling to the bribed official and the narcotics purchaser. And as the gains from marriage have declined, the pressure for divorce has risen. This has made enforcing a policy against consensual divorce increasingly costly, which may help explain the trend toward more liberal divorce laws.

If spouses want to regulate their relationship by means of a legally enforceable contract specifying, say, how much housework each will do, is there any reason why courts should (as they generally do) refuse to enforce the contract? Should it make a difference whether the contract was made before or during the marriage? Whether the marriage dissolved before enforcement of the contract was sought? Does "commodification" of marital services, that is, treating them as services bought and sold in the marketplace, weaken or strengthen the woman's bargaining position in marriage?

§5.3 CONSEQUENCES OF DISSOLUTION

When a conventional partnership is dissolved, the assets of the partnership must be distributed among the partners, and it is the same with marriage. But determining the spouses' respective shares of the assets acquired by the household during the marriage is difficult. If the wife has had very little market income, all or most of the household's tangible assets will have been bought with the husband's money. Yet his earning capacity may owe much to her efforts. She may have supported him while he was a student in law school or medical school, reducing her own consumption and also forgoing opportunities to increase her own earning capacity, through advanced training. Having invested in his earning capacity, she is entitled to repayment out of his assets or earnings, as the courts are beginning to understand.[5] Even if the couple was married after the man completed his professional training, and the wife specialized exclusively in household production, it would be error to attribute all the household's assets to the husband's production. The value of the wife's nonpecuniary contribution may have been as great as the husband's[6] and in any event is unlikely to have been negligible. If the husband had had to devote substantial time to household production, his market income would have been lower and fewer assets would have been accumulated; some of those assets were thus bought by the wife's labor in the household.

However, the rule in community-property states that 50 percent of the assets accumulated during the marriage are deemed the wife's property upon dissolution is arbitrary, especially when applied to the increasing number of superrich people in the United States. Suppose two people marry when they are very young, and they bring no financial assets to the marriage. H becomes a fabulously successful businessman. By the time he is 50, he has accumulated a net worth of $50 million. W stays home and raises the couple's children. If H and W now divorce (let us assume without fault on either side), what should W's entitlement be?

One can approach this question by asking how much H would have had to pay to hire someone (or ones) to provide the services that W provided. That's the right question from an economic standpoint, but how to answer it? The question can be sharpened a bit by asking how H and W would have agreed to divide their assets (in the event of divorce) when they got married had they thought about the possibility of H's becoming fabulously successful and made provision for this contingency in a prenuptial agreement. While H's succeeding in business might well be due in significant part to W's contributions, even if she never worked in the market, it is unlikely that the *fabulous* dimension of his success was, and this would argue against giving her anything near $25 million. Such an entitlement would overpay her, and H presumably would not have agreed to this *ex ante*. This hypothetical-contract approach to the issue of valuation might be operationalized by examining the terms of prenuptial agreements to see what provision they typically make for unexpected financial success by either spouse. This would provide a market benchmark for use in cases in which there was no prenuptial agreement.[7]

Besides prescribing the division of the marital assets, the divorce decree may order the husband to pay the wife (1) a fixed amount periodically unless and until she remarries (alimony) and (2) a part of the cost of raising the children of the marriage, of whom she will ordinarily have custody (child support).[8] Alimony is analytically complex. It appears to serve three distinct economic functions:

1. It is a form of damages for breach of the marital contract. But if this were all there was to alimony one would expect it to be paid in a lump sum, like other forms of damages, in order to minimize the costs of judicial supervision; and it would never be awarded to the spouse who was at fault, as it often is.

2. Alimony is a method of repaying the wife (in the traditional marriage) her share of the marital partnership's assets. Often the principal asset to which the wife will have contributed by her labor in the household or in the market—as in our example of the wife who supported her husband while he was in graduate school—is the husband's earning capacity.

---

[5]See, e.g., In re Marriage of Francis, 442 N.W.2d 59 (Iowa 1989); In re Marriage of Haugan, 343 N.W.2d 796 (Wis.1984); O'Brien v. O'Brien, 489 N.E.2d 712 (N.Y. 1985); and for discussion, Daniel D. Polsby & Martin Zelder, Risk-adjusted Valuation of Professional Degrees in Divorce, 23 J. Leg. Stud. 273 (1994). Should the wife be treated as a lender or an equity-type investor? And what if the divorce occurs many years after the marriage—might she not in that case have been fully repaid during the marriage?

[6]It has been estimated that, on average, the value of the wife's household production is equal to more than 70 percent of the household's money (i.e., market) income after taxes, which implies that the wife's household production generates 40 percent of the household's full income. Reuben Gronau, Home Production—A Forgotten Industry, 62 Rev. Econ. & Stat. 408 (1980).

[7]Should the wife's share of the marital assets be reduced if the dissolution of the marriage was due to fault on her part?

[8]Joint custody has become common. Can you think of an economic reason why?

This is an asset against which it is difficult to borrow money (why?). So it might be infeasible for the husband to raise the money necessary to buy back from the wife, in a lump sum, as much of the asset as she can fairly claim is hers by virtue of her contributions; instead he must pay her over time out of the stream of earning that the asset generates. But this is not a complete explanation of alimony either, because if it were the law would not terminate alimony when the wife remarries.

3. The most important economic function of alimony may be to provide the wife with a form of severance pay or unemployment benefits. In the traditional family, where the wife specializes in household production, any skills she may have had in market production depreciate, and eventually her prime employment possibilities—should the present marriage dissolve—will narrow down to the prospect of remarrying and forming a new household where she can ply her trade. Because the search for a suitable spouse is often protracted and because age may depreciate a person's ability (especially if a woman) to form a new marriage that will yield her as much real income as the previous one did, it makes sense to include as a standard term in the implicit marriage contract a form of severance pay or unemployment compensation that will maintain the divorced wife at her previous standard of living during the search for a new husband. Consider an analogy to law practice. By agreeing to work for a law firm that specialized exclusively in negotiating oil-tanker mortgages, a lawyer might make it very difficult for himself, in the event he was ever laid off, to find an equally remunerative position (why?). But that is all the more reason why he might demand, as a condition of working for such a firm, that it agree that should it ever lay him off it will continue to pay his salary until he finds equally remunerative work, even if the search is protracted.

An alternative in both the housewife's and the lawyer's case would be a higher wage, to compensate for the risk of prolonged unemployment in the event of layoff. But in the case of marriage, the husband may be incapable of making the necessary transfer payments to the wife, especially during the early years of the marriage, when the household may not have substantial liquid assets. Also, to calculate in advance the appropriate compensation for a risk as difficult to quantify as that of divorce would be costly, especially since the relevant probability is really a schedule of probabilities of divorce in each year of the marriage. This is a reason for awarding alimony on a periodic basis even when it is awarded as a form of damages.

Just as severance pay is generally independent of whether the employer was at fault in discharging the worker, so alimony, viewed as a form of severance pay, is not dependent on notions of fault. But just as an employee might forfeit his entitlement to severance pay by having quit in breach of his employment contract, so alimony should be denied or reduced (and sometimes it is) if the wife was seriously at fault in procuring dissolution of the marriage. Better, any damages she caused the family by walking out on the marriage could be subtracted from her alimony payments if her share of the marital assets was insufficient to cover them.

§5.4 THE LEGAL PROTECTION OF CHILDREN

To realize their potential as adults—in economic terms, to achieve a high level of lifetime utility—children require a considerable investment of both parental time and market inputs (food, clothing, tuition, etc.). Since costs as well as benefits must be considered in any investment decision, the optimal level of investment in a particular child is the level that maximizes the combined welfare of the child, his parents, and other family members. That level will vary from family to family depending on such factors as the child's aptitudes, the parents' wealth, and how much the parents love the child; the more they love it, the higher will be the optimal investment, because the costs of the investment will be felt very lightly, even not at all, by the parents (can you see why?). Parents who make great "sacrifices" for their children are not worse off than those of the same income who make few sacrifices, any more than people who spend a large fraction of their income on housing or travel are worse off than people who spend a smaller fraction of the same income on those things.

Even when parents love their children very much, there is a danger of underinvestment in children. Suppose a child is born to very poor parents. The child has enormous potential earning power if properly fed, clothed, housed, and educated, but his parents can't afford these things. This would not matter if either the child or the parents could borrow against the child's future earning capacity. But the costs of borrowing against a highly uncertain future stream of earnings, and also the difficulty (given the constitutional prohibition of involuntary servitude) of collateralizing a loan against a person's earning capacity (you cannot make him your slave if he defaults), make such loans an infeasible method of financing a promising child.

This problem, plus the fact that some parents love their children little or not at all[9] and the existence of widespread altruism toward children in general (i.e., not just one's own children), may explain why legal duties are imposed on parents to provide care and support, including education, for their children. Other social responses, besides the compulsory schooling laws, to the problem of underinvestment in children's human capital include child labor laws and the public provision of education to the children of the poor at no charge.[10] But this does not explain why the children of the rich should also be entitled to a free public education. One argument for such a subsidy is that educated people are a source of external benefits. They reduce the costs of communication, and they produce ideas that confer benefits that the producer cannot fully appropriate. For example, the patent laws do not permit an inventor to capture the full social benefits of his invention (explain), and therefore he and his family may underinvest in his human capital. Of course, even if there are good reasons for an education subsidy, they may not be the cause of it. The provision of free public schooling, coupled with the requirement of school attendance, benefits teachers, and also workers who would otherwise have to compete with children and teenagers.[11]

A serious practical problem with laws forbidding neglect is what to do with the child if the threat of fine or imprisonment fails to deter the parents from neglecting it. The law's answer has been to place the neglected child either with foster parents or in a foster home. Both solutions are unsatisfactory because of the difficulty of monitoring the custodian's performance. The state can pay foster parents a subsidy sufficient to enable them to invest optimally in the care and upbringing of the child, but who is to know whether they have made that investment? The state cannot *trust* the foster parents. Because they have no property rights in the child's lifetime earnings, they have no incentive to make the investment that will maximize those earnings.[12]

Another solution to the problem of the neglected or unwanted child is to allow the parents (or mother, if the father is unknown or uninterested) to put up the child for adoption, preferably before they begin to neglect it. Adoption enables the child to be transferred from the custody of people unlikely to invest optimally in its upbringing to people much more likely to do so. But effective contraception and the decline in the stigma of being an unwed mother have reduced to a trickle the supply of children for adoption. Recent advances in the treatment of fertility (perhaps spurred in part by the decline in the supply of babies for adoption) may have capped the demand for babies for adoption, but the demand remains much greater than the supply. The waiting period to obtain a baby from an adoption agency has lengthened to several years, and sometimes the agencies have no babies for adoption. The baby shortage would be considered an intolerable example of market failure if the commodity were telephones rather than babies.

In fact the shortage appears to be an artifact of government regulation, in particular the state laws forbidding the sale of parental rights. Since many

[9]Even in an age of universal availability of contraceptive methods and a constitutional right to abortion, some children are produced as an undesired by-product of sexual activity, and in addition parents may have second thoughts once they begin coping with a baby. As a matter of fact, the ready availability of contraceptive methods need not, at least in theory, significantly reduce the number of unwanted children that are born. Contraception reduces an expected cost of sex (the cost in unwanted children) and hence increases the incidence of sex; the fraction of unwanted births is thus smaller, but the number of sexual encounters, by which that fraction must be multiplied to yield the *number* of unwanted births, is larger.

[10]There is a rich economic literature on human capital. See, e.g., Gary S. Becker, Human Capital: A Theoretical and Empirical Analysis, With Special Reference to Education (3d ed. 1993). . . .

[11]Linda Nasif Edwards, An Empirical Analysis of Compulsory Schooling Legislation, 1940–1960, 21 J. Law & Econ. 203 (1978).

[12]Would you expect the problem of mistreatment of foster children to be more serious in foster *homes* (i.e., where the child lives with foster parents) or in foster *institutions* (i.e., where the child is taken care of by a professional staff)?

people who are capable of bearing children do not want to raise them, many other people who cannot produce their own children want to raise children, and the costs of production to natural parents are much lower than the value that many childless people attach to children, a *market* in babies for adoption would be feasible. As a matter of fact, there is already a black market in babies. Its necessarily clandestine mode of operation imposes heavy information costs on the market participants as well as expected punishment costs on the middlemen (typically lawyers and obstetricians). The result is higher prices and smaller quantities sold than would be the case in a legal market.

This is shown in Figure 5.1, where p_0 is the free market price of parental rights and q_0 the free market quantity, and government regulation places a ceiling on price at p_r, well below p_0 (p_r is not shown as zero both because adoption agencies and other legal suppliers do charge fees to adoptive parents and because children are expensive to raise). The price ceiling causes a reduction in the quantity supplied to q_{rs}, creating excess demand of $q_{rd} - q_{rs}$. A black market springs up, but such a market is much more costly to operate than a free market would be (because of punishment costs, poor information, and lack of enforceable warranties), and clears at price p_b (where D intersects S_b, the higher, black market supply curve), which is higher than the free market price. So only q_b babies are supplied, compared to q_0 at the free market price.

Not all babies are adopted through the black market, of course: only $q_b - q_{rs}$. Adoption agencies—private, nonprofit organizations licensed by the state—use queuing and various nonmarket criteria (some highly intrusive and constitutionally questionable, such as requiring that the adoptive parents have the same religion as the natural parents) to ration the inadequate supply of babies that they control. The principal objection to the agencies is not the criteria they use to ration their supply of babies but their monopoly of legal adoptions, which ensures (given their profit function) that the supply will remain inadequate.

Many states also permit independent adoption of babies; the natural parents (normally just the mother) arrange for the adoption without using the facilities of an adoption agency. This avoids the sometimes irrelevant and demeaning criteria of the agencies, but

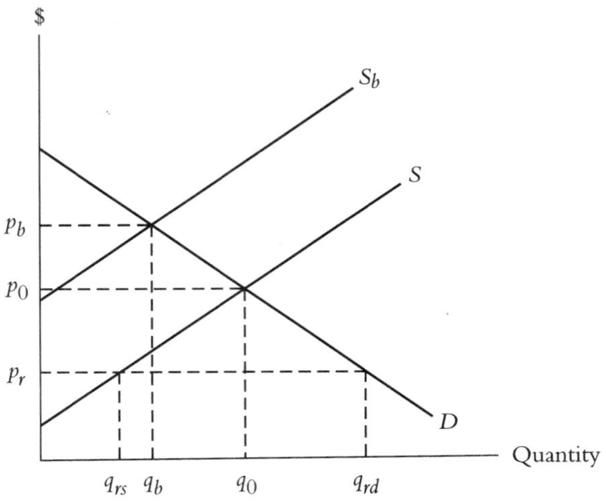

Figure 5.1

since the mother is not permitted to *sell* her parental rights, independent adoption does not create a real market. The lawyer who arranges the adoption, however, is permitted to exact a fee for his services plus payment for the mother's hospital and related child-bearing expenses, and since these charges are difficult to police, in practice they will often conceal a payment for the parental right itself. Also close to outright sale is the "family compact." The mother agrees to give up the child to a close relative in exchange for financial consideration running to the child. Such contracts have been enforced where the court was satisfied that the arrangement benefited the child.[13]

The economist's standard response to a black market is to propose abolition of the price control that has brought it into existence. Applied here, this would mean allowing pregnant women to make binding contracts to give up their child for adoption, with no limit on the price specified in the contract. The objections are, for the most part, the standard objections to free markets. For example, it is argued that there is no assurance that the adoptive parents who are willing to pay the most money for a child will provide it with the best home. But the persons who value a child the most are likely to give it the

[13]Enders v. Enders, 164 Pa. 266, 30 A. 129 (1894); Clark v. Clark, 122 Md. 114, 89 A. 405 (1913); In re Estate of Shirk, 186 Kan. 311, 350 P.2d 1 (1960).

most care,[14] and at the very least the sacrifice of a substantial sum of money to obtain a child attests to the seriousness of the purchaser's desire to have the child. The reply to this is that the high-paying adoptive parents may value the child for the wrong reasons: to subject it to sexual abuse or otherwise to exploit it. But the laws forbidding child neglect and abuse would apply fully to the adoptive parents (as they do under present law, of course). Naturally one would want to screen adoptive parents for possible criminal proclivities—just as is done today.

Well, but couldn't the payment of a large sum to obtain parental rights exhaust the adoptive parents' financial ability to support the child? Or, more realistically, reduce their investment in the child's upbringing? This assumes, however, that a free market would generate high prices. That is an unusual objection to free markets, and is misplaced here. The market price might not exceed the opportunity costs (mainly the mother's time and medical expenses) that the adoptive parents would have incurred had they produced the child themselves rather than bought parental rights to it. For that would be the competitive price. The net cost to the adoptive parents would thus be close to zero, except that the adoptive parents would incur some costs in locating and trying to ascertain the qualities of the child that they would not have incurred had they been its natural parents. The black market price is high because it must cover the sellers' expected punishment costs for breaking the law and because the existence of legal sanctions prevents the use of the most efficient methods of matching up sellers and buyers.[15]

Opponents of the market approach also argue that the rich would end up with all the babies, or at least all the good babies. (Recall the parallel argument against permitting the sale of radio and television frequencies.) Such a result might of course be in the children's best interest, but it is unlikely to materialize. People with high incomes tend to have high opportunity costs of time, and child rearing is a time-intensive activity. The total demand for children on the part of wealthy childless couples must be very small in relation to the supply of children that would be generated in a system where there were economic incentives to produce children for childless couples.

The poor may actually do worse under present adoption law than they would in a free market. Most adoptions are channeled through adoption agencies, which in screening prospective adoptive parents attach great importance to the applicants' income and employment status. People who may flunk the agencies' criteria on economic grounds might, in a free market with low prices, be able to adopt children, just as poor people are able to buy color television sets. The point can be generalized: a disfavored group (the poor, homosexual, members of a racial minority, and so forth) can often do better in a private market regulated by contract law than in the public or nonprofit arenas. Courts that would not grant special protection to the members of such a group might nevertheless enforce their contracts.[16] Profit-making enterprises care more for the color of a person's money, and less for the person's color or other personal characteristics, than do nonprofit organizations.

Although the condition of the market for adopting infants is one of chronic excess demand, the condition of the market for adopting children who are no longer infants is one of chronic oversupply (why?). An impediment to their adoption is the fact that foster parents are paid for foster care, but not for adopting a foster child, so that if they do adopt their foster child they incur even higher costs than other adoptive parents, since, as we know, forgone income is a cost. Can you think of any practical measure for overcoming this problem?

§5.5 SURROGATE MOTHERHOOD

The sale of parental rights is illegal in all states, but a closely related practice—surrogate motherhood—is

[14] The existence of a market in parental rights would also increase the natural mother's incentive to produce a healthy baby and would reduce the demand for abortion.

[15] In one respect, however, the black market price is lower than a legal free market price would be. The buyer in the black market does not receive any legally enforceable warranties (of health, genealogy, or whatever), comparable to those that buyers receive in legal markets. The buyer in a legal market would receive a more valuable package of rights, and it should cost more, because the seller would demand compensation for bearing risks formerly borne by the buyer. But the resulting price increase would be nominal rather than real (can you see why?). How might Figure 5.1 be redrawn to reflect this point?

[16] As emphasized in Martha M. Ertman, Contractual Purgatory for Sexual Marginorities: Not Heaven, But Not Hell Either, 73 Denver U. L. Rev. 1107 (1997).

not. Suppose H is fertile but W is not. H and W hire S, a fertile woman, to bear a child for the couple at an agreed price. S is then artificially inseminated with H's sperm. When the child is born, S surrenders her parental right to W in accordance with the contract. This is the practice known as surrogate motherhood. It is intensely controversial. In the *Baby M* case,[17] the Supreme Court of New Jersey held that the enforcement of surrogate motherhood contracts was contrary to the public policy of the state.

The court gave a number of reasons for this conclusion that demonstrate a lack of economic sophistication . . . "A child," the court said, "instead of starting off its life with as much peace and security as possible, finds itself immediately in a tug-of-war between contending mother and father."[18] But this tug-of-war is an artifact of legal uncertainty. Were the enforceability of surrogate contracts settled, the surrogate mother would have had no grounds for challenging the contract. "The whole purpose and effect of the surrogacy contract was to give the father the exclusive right to the child by destroying the rights of the mother." An obvious point is overlooked: no contract, no child. It is not as if there had been a baby in being when the contract was signed, and the mother was being asked to give up her rights to it. The purpose of the contract was not to extinguish the mother's rights but to induce a woman to become a mother for the sake of another woman. The court does not understand the productive function of contracts. It mistakenly believes that contracts merely rearrange the consequences of accomplished facts, as the court regards the birth of Baby M.

"In surrogacy," the court continues, "the highest bidders will presumably become the adoptive parents regardless of suitability." The implication is of a fixed supply, such as the paintings of Van Gogh, being auctioned off. But the supply is not fixed, and competition among would-be surrogate mothers can be expected to force price down to cost, placing surrogacy within the reach of infertile couples of modest means. The court is worried about "the highest paying, ill-suited, adoptive parents." But as wealthy people invariably jump to the head of the queue in a system of regulated adoption, surrogate motherhood will improve the prospects for infertile couples of limited financial means. "The demand for children is great and the supply small. The availability of contraception, abortion, and the greater willingness of single mothers to bring up their children has led to a shortage of babies offered for adoption. The situation is ripe for the entry of the middleman who will bring some equilibrium into the market by increasing the supply through the use of money." Precisely. But this is an argument for, not against, middlemen. The person who does something about an imbalance between demand and supply is blamed by the court because his motivation is financial. "It is unlikely that surrogacy will survive without money. . . . That conclusion contrasts with adoption; for obvious reasons, there remains a steady supply, albeit insufficient, despite the prohibitions against payment." That "albeit insufficient" is the giveaway that the court does not understand the market system. The supply is insufficient *because* of the prohibitions against payment, and its insufficiency induces infertile couples to turn to market alternatives, such as surrogate motherhood. The market failure is in adoption, not in surrogate motherhood.

"We doubt that infertile couples in the low-income bracket will find upper-income surrogates." This is the jurisprudence of envy. Infertile low-income couples, even if one supposes incorrectly that they could never afford the price of a surrogate-motherhood contract, are not helped by policies that limit the options of infertile high-income couples. "There are, in short, values that society deems more important than granting to wealth whatever it can buy, be it labor, love, or life." How, though, are those values served by refusing to enforce contracts of surrogate motherhood? The court does not explain.

§5.6 LAW AND POPULATION

We have seen that the production of children involves potential externalities, but our focus has been on the quality rather than on the quantity of children—that is, on the optimal level of investment in the human capital of a given child rather than on the optimal number of children. But of course the number of children can, by affecting the size of the population,

---

[17] In re Baby M, 109 N.J. 396, 537 A.2d 1227 (1988).

[18] This and the following quotations are from 109 N.J. at 435–441, 537 A.2d at 1247–1249.

affect the welfare of society as a whole.[19] In a densely populated country a further increase in population may exacerbate already serious problems of congestion (e.g., on highways) and pollution (actually a form of congestion—can you see why?), imposing costs on other people which neither the new child nor his parents will ever be asked to defray.[20] Conversely, in a sparsely populated country threatened by external enemies, the production of an additional child may confer a benefit over and above any private gains to the child and his parents, by (eventually) strengthening the country militarily. And maybe external enemies aren't necessary. An increase in population will (up to a point) enable a greater division of labor, causing costs to fall. The result will be an increase in the nation's average as well as total wealth.[21]

Birth rates in wealthy countries today are very low, but since these countries are also crowded and since military technology has shifted against large armies, it is not clear that a low birth rate—even one below replacement level—should be a cause for concern. If it is, the problem is easily rectified by reducing the barriers to immigration—more easily than by subsidizing births. A subsidy will require additional taxes, which may drive women out of the home and into the market in even greater numbers. . . .

Some Asian countries are so concerned with overpopulation that they have tried to limit every family to a fixed number of children—in China, only one. Such an approach is clearly inefficient, because families differ in their efficiency in producing children. It might cost family A less to produce a second child than it would cost B to produce a first child of the same quality. The same total growth (positive or negative) in the Chinese population could thus be produced at less cost by giving every couple one child permit and allowing the permits to be sold than by making such permits nontransferable (the present policy).

Current population policy in the United States is a confusing, perhaps accidental, mixture of subsidies and penalties for child production. The exemption from income taxation of nonpecuniary income from household production subsidizes the production of children relative to market uses of the woman's time, as does of course the exemption for dependents. The common rule that child-support payments required by a divorce decree will be reduced if the father remarries and produces children of the new marriage reduces the private cost to the father of having more children below the social cost.[22] Cutting in the opposite direction is easy divorce, which reduces the incentive to make long-term marital investments, such as child rearing, and hence reduces the birth rate. But a rule absolutely forbidding divorce may have a similar effect by increasing the optimal length of premarital search and so increasing the average age of marriage and reducing the number of children produced.

§5.7 WHY REGULATE SEXUAL BEHAVIOR?

Especially in Christian and Muslim societies, the state takes it upon itself not merely to regulate marriage, but to regulate—or to try to regulate—sexual behavior directly, even when it is consensual behavior between competent adults. For example, many U.S. states continue to make fornication, adultery, and homosexual intercourse crimes (though the laws are rarely enforced); prostitution is a crime everywhere in the U.S. except for a few counties in Nevada; and the sale of hard-core pornography is nominally illegal.

Do these prohibitions make any economic sense, or are they unjustifiable interferences with freedom of contract?[23] The answer may depend on whether the regulated activities impose significant cost on third parties. For example, adultery imposes costs on the adulterer's spouse.[24] Fornication may impose social costs in the form of an abandoned or neglected child. Any form of intercourse other than monogamous

---

[19]The study of population (demography) is a field to which economists have made distinguished contributions since Malthus—whose gloomy outlook led contemporaries to dub economics "the dismal science." For modern treatments, see, e.g., Gary S. Becker, An Economic Analysis of Fertility, in his book The Economic Approach to Human Behavior 171 (1976); Becker & Kevin M. Murphy, The Family and the State, 31 J. Law & Econ. 1 (1988).

[20]What assumption is being made here about property rights in highways?

[21]Explain how this conclusion is affected by tariffs.

[22]Can you distinguish the case in which parents reduce the investments in their existing children because a new child is born?

[23]See Richard A. Posner, Sex and Reason (1992), esp. chs. 6, 7.

[24]Is there an externality? . . .

intercourse between persons who were virgins when their relationship began creates a risk of spreading disease—AIDS has made us all very conscious of the dangers of sexually transmitted epidemics. Yet, odd as this may seem, the externality created by sexually transmitted diseases is spread primarily by *voluntary* contact, implying (to the economist) that a person is compensated (how?) for assuming the risk of contracting the disease. Hence the number of cases of sexually transmitted diseases may be closer to the optimum than in the usual airborne or water-borne or insect-borne epidemics. Closer to, but not at: The person who voluntarily assumes a risk of infection imposes an expected cost on his future sexual partners (and often on his and their future children) without their consent.

Unwanted births are a small risk of prostitution and none at all of homosexual intercourse, but sexually transmitted disease is a large risk of these activities, though the exact weight of this point in economic policy is, for the reason just stated, uncertain. In the case of bisexuals and also of men who patronize (female) prostitutes, there is an external cost to spouses—maybe; for it is arguable that if these outlets were closed to married men, such men would be more likely to seek sexual variety in forms more threatening to marriage—for example, long-term liaisons that might lead to divorce and remarriage. To put this in economic terms, prostitution may be both a substitute for and a complement to marital intercourse, in much the same way that pornography may be both a substitute for and a complement to rape—the former, to the extent that pornography makes masturbation a more satisfactory substitute for sexual intercourse; the latter, to the extent that it stimulates desire for sexual intercourse, of which rape of course is one form.

Supposing that society wants to reduce the amount of sexually transmitted disease, should it try to prohibit promiscuous intercourse, heterosexual or homosexual? The costs of repressing victimless (in the sense of consensual) crimes that are committed in private are immense. They include, besides the direct costs, the disincentive that criminalization creates to undergo medical tests, seek treatment, cooperate in studies, learn about methods of prevention, etc.—all measures that may be important in the control of an epidemic. Note that forbidding homosexual marriage raises the cost of monogamous homosexual relationships (and so increases promiscuity), because marriage is a subsidy to monogamy; and, speaking of marriage, studies show that in societies that are intolerant of homosexuals, a higher percentage of male homosexuals marry women,[25] which increases the danger of spreading AIDS to the heterosexual population. Another cost of repression is the reduction in utility that is brought about by deterring people from engaging in practices that they enjoy—but that reduction might be offset, at least in part, by an increase in utility to those people who abhor the practices.

Laws forbidding fornication and adultery are quixotic in today's society because the costs of nonmarital intercourse have fallen. Effective contraception has reduced the costs of sex, especially of nonmarital sex (why?). Since women increasingly work outside the home, the costs to their husbands of maintaining surveillance over them have risen, implying a fall in the probability of detection. In addition, nonmarital search costs have fallen because women mingle with men at work. With the decline in the benefits of marriage, more women are unmarried for a longer time, so the pool of unmarried sexual partners is larger. Even the costs of single parenthood have declined for women, because women now have market income with which to purchase the market commodities that they need to raise a child. With women less dependent economically on men, they are less willing to surrender their sexual freedom in exchange for economic support (why do men desire such a trade?). Hence the value of virginity declines. Virginity, a demonstration of self-control, is a signal of probable marital chastity.

When laws cannot be explained as measures for correcting externalities or otherwise promoting economic efficiency, the economist is inclined to consider next the possibility that they are designed to redistribute wealth, perhaps at the behest of some interest group. . . . Some of our sex laws may be of this kind. An example is the prohibition of bigamy (polygamy), which by limiting competition of men for women increases the sexual and marital opportunities of younger, poorer men. The prohibition is in effect a tax on wealth, for only wealthy men can afford multiple wives. The tax does not generate revenue directly, but

---

[25]Michael W. Ross, The Married Homosexual Man: A Psychological Study 110–111 and Tab. 11.1 (1983). For example, the percentage of male homosexuals in the U.S. who marry is roughly twice as high as in Sweden. Id.

by reducing the cost of a wife it transfers wealth from the more affluent to the less affluent (and more numerous) men.

Similarly, the gradual decriminalization of homosexual activity may be due less to an exogenous growth of tolerance among the heterosexual population than to the fact that growing urbanization has increased the number of homosexuals who, being geographically concentrated, can organize more effectively for political action than if they were dispersed. Why are homosexuals concentrated in cities? There is a good economic reason. The cost of matching (a form of search cost) is higher, the thinner the market in which the search takes place. Homosexuals are only a small fraction of the population, so in a small town or a rural area the market for homosexual matches is apt to be exceedingly thin. Homosexuals can reduce the cost of matching (specifically the travel cost) by moving to cities, where they will in consequence form a larger fraction of the population than they do in the nation as a whole.

This is to speak of the supply side of political influence. There is a demand side, and in recent years it too has encouraged political action by homosexuals. For since the advent of AIDS, homosexuals have had more to gain from enlisting government on their side than was formerly the case—massive financial and research aid to fight the scourge.

Finally, the anti-abortion movement in the second half of the nineteenth century, which produced the laws struck down in *Roe v. Wade*,[26] was powered to a significant degree by physicians who, wanting licensed professionals to have a monopoly of medical practice, made abortionists—who were not regular physicians—the symbol of the moral and medical hazards of allowing nonregulars to provide medical services.

The social issues presented by AIDS, abortion, and births out of wedlock (and hence adoption) are interrelated in a way that economic analysis can illuminate.[27] Condoms are much more effective at preventing the transmission of disease than the birth control pill, which isn't effective at all, but the pill is more reliable in preventing pregnancy than condoms are. Therefore the AIDS epidemic, by increasing the expected cost of sexually transmitted disease, can be expected to induce a substitution away from the birth control pill and toward the condom. This substitution will be retarded, and hence the spread of the disease accelerated, if the law restricts abortion. Abortion backs up contraception as a method of avoiding a birth. If the back-up is removed or made significantly more costly, the cost of imperfect contraception (e.g., the condom) will rise, making it more likely that sexual partners will choose the better contraceptive (e.g., the pill) over the better disease-preventive. Social conservatives hope that AIDS will discourage the pill and restricting abortion [sic] the condom, leaving as the only alternative abstinence—the perfect contraceptive and disease-preventive. In economic terms, they hope that the demand for sex is highly elastic with respect to disease and pregnancy risks, so that measures to prevent reducing those risks will cause a big drop in the amount of sexual activity, at least outside of marriage.

[26] 410 U.S. 113 (1973).

[27] See Tomas J. Philipson & Richard A. Posner, Sexual Behaviour, Disease, and Fertility Risk, 1 Risk Decision & Policy 91 (1996).

66

JACQUELINE KRIKORIAN

A Different Form of Apartheid? The Legal Status of Married Women in South Africa

I. THE LEGAL STATUS OF WOMEN IN A CIVIL MARRIAGE

The rules governing the legal status of married women in South Africa are both complex and confusing. In general, a married woman's rights and legal capacity have been determined by her race, the year in which she was married, and the type of marriage—a civil or customary union. Despite certain differences in the various statutes and case-law, there are strong similarities which cut across these classifications. The majority of married women have been limited or restricted in their proprietary, contractual, and legal capacities, in their ability to obtain guardianship of their children, and in their bodily integrity.

A. The Marital Rape Exemption under Common Law

In South Africa, the common law sanctioned a husband's sexual control over his wife through the use of the marital rape exemption rule. The judiciary has held repeatedly that the common law does not recognize rape between a husband and wife as a criminal offence.[1] Until recently, the legislature has been unwilling to alter this finding. A husband has been "entitled" to have sexual relations with his wife; her consent was both irrelevant and unnecessary.

Modern South African legal observers have provided two explanations for the existence of the marital rape exemption rule. Both originate in seventeenth century Roman-Dutch common law. The first justification is based on *consortium omnis vitae,* an abstract concept "comprising the totality of a number of rights, duties and advantages accruing to spouses of a marriage."[2] Once married, spouses were deemed to have reciprocal and irrevocable mutual obligations toward one another.

> Flowing from the marital relationship are the duties of cohabitation, loyalty, fidelity, mutual assistance and support. Spouses are under a duty to live together, to afford each other the marital privileges, and to be faithful to each other.[3]

The Ciskei General Division Court in *S. v. Ncanywa* postulated that as a consequence of *consortium omnis vitae* "both the husband and the wife were under a duty to submit to the right of coition of the other party."[4] Grotius, a seventeenth century Roman-Dutch legal jurist, noted that marriage conferred "the lawful use of each other's bodies."[5]

While the first explanation of the Roman-Dutch origins of the marital rape exemption law underscores the mutual rights and duties of the spouses, the second emphasizes the power of a husband over his wife. Women were supposed to submit to their spouse's sexual demands because they were considered inferior beings.[6] Upon marriage, a husband gained control over his wife's "person," which was interpreted as a right to sexual intercourse,[7] as well as over her property.[8] This position was supported by early Roman-Dutch legal authorities, who held that a man could not rape his wife because he had the right to her person.[9] The conclusion was that the marital rape exemption prevented a man being charged with the rape of his wife.

These historical explanations for the marital rape exemption were accepted by South African courts throughout the twentieth century. In defining the crime of rape, members of the judiciary have expressly held that a husband cannot rape his wife. In 1958, Appeal Justice Schreiner noted that the established definition of the offence of rape "consists of having connection with a woman, other than the man's wife, without her consent."[10] The rationale for this position was explained by Justice Nienaber in *S. v. H.:*

> [I]f the wife is indeed obliged in law to submit to intercourse by her husband, then the actual physical act of intercourse can as such never [be] unlawful. And since unlawful sexual intercourse is the very centrepiece of a charge of rape, there can, generally speaking, be no rape between husband and wife.[11]

While the common law marital rape exemption had wide acceptance, one court did deny its existence. In *S. v. Ncanywa,* Justice Heath of the Ciskei General Division[12] sharply criticized the rule and held that there was no justification for the old marital rape exemption.[13] The defendant was subsequently convicted of

---

[1] *H.R. Hahlo, The South African Law of Husband and Wife,* 5th ed. (Cape Town: Juta, 1985) at 132.

[2] *Grobbelaar v. Havenga* (1964), 3 S.A. 522 at 522D (N).

[3] Hahlo, *supra* note 1 at 130.

[4] *S v. Ncanywa* (1992), 2 S.A. 182 at 187 (Ck GD) rev'd (1993), 2 S.A. 567 (Ck AD) [hereinafter *Ncanywa* cited to (1992) 2 S.A.]; Hahlo, *ibid.* at 132.

[5] Grotius 1.5.1., *The Introduction to Dutch Jurisprudence,* trans. A.F.S. Maasdorp (1878), cited in *Ncanywa, ibid.,* at 187. Also noted in F. Kaganas & C. Murray, "Rape in Marriage—Conjugal Right or Criminal Wrong?" (1983) Aota Juridica 125 at 126.

[6] See Kaganas & Murray, *ibid.*

[7] For a discussion of the following sources for this proposition see Voet, *Commentarius and Pandectas* 23.2.41, 62, Van Leeuwen, *Rooms-Hollands* Reg 1.6.3, 7, Huber, *Heedendaegse Rechtsgeleertheyt* 1.9.10, 11, 13; 1.10.1, 4, 6, 7 and *Grotius, Inleiding tot de Hollandsche Rechtsgeleertheyt,* 1.3.8; 1.5.19, 20, 21, 22 [hereinafter *Inleiding*], see *ibid.*

[8] *Ibid.*

[9] *See Ncanywa, supra* note [4] at 186 where Heath J. examines the marital powers of the husband with regard to the various aspects of the marriage including conjugal right, and cites both Damhouder, *Pracktycke in Crimineele Sake* (1650) 95.16 and Moorman, *Verhandelinge over de Misdaden en der Selver Straffen* (1764) C 88 as authority for this principle. See also *ibid.* at 127.

[10] *R. v. K.* (1958), 3 S.A. 420 at 421F (A.D.).

[11] *S. v. H.* (1985), 2 S.A. 750 at 753E (N).

[12] Until the April 1994 election, the Ciskei was an "independent" state within South Africa.

[13] *Ncanywa, supra* note 4 at 211–212.

the rape of his spouse. On appeal, the conviction was set aside on the grounds that there was authority for the marital rape exemption rule in South African law.[14] Moreover, it was held that any changes to the common law rule had to be left up to the legislators as it would "be difficult for this Court to decide whether in the Ciskei the rule should be varied or totally rejected."[15]

Some courts have accepted, however, that there were at least two "limitations" to the marital rape exemption rule. First, if a woman's physical health was at risk, she was entitled to refuse to have intercourse with her husband.[16] Second, a husband could not use excessive force when compelling his wife to have sexual intercourse with him.[17] Even early Roman-Dutch observers acknowledged that a man's rights were restricted "to the extent that he was expected to refrain from beating her or ill-treating her."[18] As a result, unnecessary force or violence in the context of marital intercourse could result in common assault charges, but not rape charges. This was recognized specifically in *S. v. H.*

> [R]ape in our law today is not, of course, intercourse with force; it is sexual intercourse without consent. Not every rape, therefore, "contains" the element of physical force or violence. Although violence will frequently be the means to accomplish copulation, violence as such is not an element of the crime of rape. The [marital rape] immunity may cover the end; it does not follow that it should therefore also cover the means.[19]

The court found that although marital rape or attempted marital rape could not be deemed unlawful, "any force beyond that inherent in the physical act of intercourse itself will amount to an assault . . . regardless of whether the force is exerted in pursuit of sexual intercourse or not."[20] Despite the strong condemnation of the actions of the accused in this case, however, the court recognized that in assault charges of this nature, "all sorts of defenses may be open to the husband—not the least of which will be the absence of any *dolus* [intent] if he genuinely believed that he was acting within his rights."[21]

In 1985, the South African Law Commission recommended that the marital rape exemption rule be abolished. It argued that a husband's immunity from prosecution in marital rape cases was "nothing else than a legal fiction of consent by the wife."[22] In September 1987, this recommendation was put before Parliament in the form of a draft bill, stating that "notwithstanding anything to the contrary contained in the common law, a man may be held criminally responsible for raping his lawful wife."[23] The Bill was fiercely resisted and eventually rejected by the Joint Parliamentary Committee investigating the issue. Instead, it was amended only to require courts to consider marital rape as an aggravating circumstance for men charged with assault of their wives.[24]

The Parliamentary Committee justified its departure from the South African Law Commission's proposal on a number of policy considerations:

> (a) [t]he proposal . . . [was] of an emotional and sensitive nature. It [was] clear there [was] a wide divergence of opinion in South Africa regarding any reform in this regard . . .
> (b) [abolishing the marital rape exemption would] give rise to an increase in the already high divorce rate. The mere threat of a charge of rape will probably, in the light of the grave consequences and the social implications and sanctions involved, lead to the termination of a marriage relationship . . .
> (c) [i]t [was] undesirable to intrude in the realm of marriage relationship and family-related matters by means of the criminal law . . .
> (d) [the proposal would] give rise to evidential problems since it [would] be very difficult to prove the crime of rape in view of the marriage relationship . . .

---

[14] *S. v. Ncanywa* (1993), 2 S.A. 567 at 575–576.
[15] *Ibid.* at 576.
[16] P.M.A. Hunt, *South African Law and Procedure,* Vol 2 (Cape Town: Juta, 1982) at 438. See also *Ainsbury v. Ainsbury* (1929), A.D. 109 at 117–118, noted in J.R.L. Milton, *South African Criminal Law and Procedure,* 2nd ed. (Cape Town: Juta, 1982) at 438. . . . It should be noted that a woman's health was considered to be at risk if her husband had a venereal disease.
[17] The South African Law Commission Report. *Women and Sexual Offences in South Africa.* (Project 45) (April 1985) at 29 [hereinafter *Women and Sexual Offences*].
[18] *Inleiding, supra* note [7] at 1.5.20.
[19] *S. v. H., supra* note [11] at 755.
[20] *Ibid.* at 756.
[21] *Ibid.*
[22] *Women and Sexual Offences, supra* note [17] at 36.
[23] B106-87, *The Criminal Law and Criminal Procedure Act Amendment Bill.* See also J.R.L. Milton, "Comments on Law Reform: Marital Rape" (1989) 2 South African Criminal J. at 79–82.
[24] The amended bill was passed into law in March of 1989 as the *Criminal Law and the Criminal Procedure Act Amendment Act,* No. 39 of 1989.

> (e) The crime of rape is a very serious offence . . . [making it] unacceptable for an offender within the marriage context to be threatened or visited with such a severe penalty . . . [25]

Finally, while expressing a need for Legislative "condemnation of the use of violence in marriage, especially violence which is coupled with sexual intercourse," the Parliamentary Committee noted that alternative remedies existed in the civil and criminal law.[26]

The issue was re-examined by the National Party Government on 2 February, 1993. In its proposed *Charter of Fundamental Rights,* it appeared to express the intention to abolish the marital rape exemption rule:

> 33 (3) . . . every woman shall have the right . . .
> c) not to be discriminated against solely by reason of her marital status or pregnancy; . . .
> e) to her physical and mental integrity and in particular to legal protection against rape and sexual harassment.[27]

Two weeks later, however, the government introduced draft legislation retaining the marital rape exemption, while narrowing its application to husbands and wives who lived together. Husbands separated from their wives could be charged with rape if they had non-consensual intercourse.[28] Justice Minister Kobie Coetsee explained that "a man who lives with his wife should be in a position to say that he has certain privileges."[29]

The Democratic Women's Forum argued that the "proposal to provide marital immunity against rape was a relic of an era when wives were equivalent to goods and chattels."[30] Similarly, Catherine O'Regan of the University of Cape Town, Faculty of Law expressed her disappointment with the decision of the government not to adhere to the recommendations of the South African Law Commission, which the Government itself had established. She stated that all this new draft legislation did was to "move the chairs around but not [change] the fundamental principle."[31]

Five months later the National Party government re-introduced the draft legislation, this time proposing to abolish the marital rape exemption.[32] However, s. 5 stated that a husband could not be prosecuted for the rape of his wife "without the written authority of an Attorney-General."[33] Thus the draft legislation still distinguished between a husband raping his wife and a man raping a woman who was not his spouse.

Finally, in December 1993, the marital rape exemption rules were completely abolished with the passage of the *Prevention of Family Violence Act*[34] s. 5 of which reads: "Notwithstanding anything to the contrary contained in any law or in the common law, a husband may be convicted of the rape of his wife."[35]

The practical effectiveness of this provision may be limited by the difficulties women still face in convincing the police and the judiciary of the seriousness of the violation of their person. Not only do women face a credibility issue in the courtroom in matters involving domestic violence,[36] but the corroboration rule of evidence makes it difficult to prove that such violence has occurred. The rule requires that members of the judiciary exercise caution in using the uncorroborated evidence of women in sexual assault cases. Judges and magistrates are required to show awareness of the special dangers of convicting upon the evidence of a complainant in a sexual case,[37] since:

> the bringing of the charge may have been motivated by spite, sexual frustration or other unpredictable

---

[25] *Report of the Joint Parliamentary Committee,* 7 February 1989, cited in Milton, supra note [23] at 80.
[26] *Ibid.*
[27] *Government's Proposals on a Charter of Fundamental Rights,* 2 February 1993 at 20 [hereinafter *Government's Proposals*].
[28] *Draft Bill on Prevention of Family Violence,* s.6. *Government Gaz.* 332, No. 14,591 at 46.
[29] Justice Minister Kobi Coetsee quoted in Phillip van Niekerk, "Crossing Party Lines to Lure Unlikely Votes." *The [Toronto] Globe and Mail* (8 February 1993) A9. On questioning by the press, Justice Minister Coetsee added, "with consent, of course."
[30] Barry Streek, "New Family Bill Makes Marital Rape Illegal" *The [Cape Town] Cape Times* (3 June 1993) 2.
[31] Catherine O'Regan on "Insights," a radio talk show on the Government's Proposed Legislation Regarding Women. April of 1993, South Africa.
[32] B114-93, *Prevention of Family Violence Bill,* s. 5(1). Introduced 24 June 1993.
[33] *Ibid.* s 5(2).
[34] No. 133 of 1993. Section 2 stipulates that any party can apply to a court for an interdict to prevent threats or assault against himself or herself, or a child living with the parties. Although it is a welcome change, this section will not substantially change the status quo. Few women will have the knowledge or trust, let alone the resources, to apply to the courts for interdicts.
[35] *Ibid.* It may be more than just coincidence that the common law rule was overridden by statute just as the all white government was trying to broaden its electoral base for the first all-race elections.
[36] K. Ross, "Battered Women: An Invisible Issue" at 12–14. This is a paper available in the Institute of Criminology, University of Cape Town. [Editor's Note: We have been unable to verify the accuracy of this source.]
[37] L.H. Hoffmann & D. Zeffertt, *The South African Law of Evidence,* 4th ed. (Durban: Butterworths, 1988) at 579.

> emotional cause . . . Certain sexual offences such as indecent assault and criminal injuria are difficult charges to refute because they are usually alleged to have taken place in private, leave no outward traces, and proof depends entirely upon the word of the complainant against that of the accused. In particular, the demeanor of the complainant in the witness box or her apparent social standing should never be relied upon as substitute for caution.[38]

As one writer has argued, this position is based on "a traditional suspicion of women's testimony and an imputation of female propensity to lie."[39] There is a general belief that women would use assault and rape complaints "as a weapon of vindictiveness against their innocent husbands" and these men would be left "vulnerable under these circumstances since a rape complaint is easy to make but difficult to rebut."[40] The misguided and conservative belief that only women would lie under oath in a sexual assault case is little more than a crude stereotype. One observer notes, "the so-called cautionary rule has no other purpose than to discriminate against women complainants."[41] It is clear that the practical effectiveness of legislation abolishing the marital rape exception will be limited by the corroboration rule.

While the marital rape exemption rule has had effects across the racial lines, legislative changes pertaining to women have generally been dealt with on a "race-by-race" basis, with the needs of white women being addressed before those of black women. For example, all white, coloured, and Asian women who had entered into a civil marriage after 1984 had their status and rights strengthened through statutory intervention. This same position however, was attained by black women only in 1988. Currently, issues and concerns that affect women of all races who have a civil marriage are being addressed, while the needs of women married under customary law are to be addressed at a later date.

B. Asian, Coloured and White Women Married before 1984

Asian, coloured and white women married before 1984 were governed automatically by a regime known as the "common law community of property system," in which the husband retained the "marital power."[42] Until December 1993, about two-thirds of women married before 1984 fell under this marital regime.[43] As will be examined, the other one-third opted out of this system through an antenuptial agreement.

There were two inter-related components in this system. One involved "community of property." This term refers to a system in which both "the husband and wife [became] co-owners in undivided half-shares of all the assets they both possess at the moment of their marriage, as well as all of the assets acquired by them" during the marriage.[44] Their joint estate was held responsible for any debts or liabilities legally incurred by either of them.[45]

The other component of this regime was "marital power," which consisted of two main elements. First, the husband had the legal power to control the family's property and finances. It was the husband, not the wife, who had the power to administer the estate, since he could buy and sell assets, pledge assets or burden them with a mortgage, and bind the credit of the joint estate—all this without the wife's consent or even knowledge.[46]

The wife's rights and powers in this area were thus strictly limited. Without the consent of her husband, she could not enter into a binding contract that incurred any obligation. In the event this happened, the husband had the right to repudiate any contract entered into by his wife, and could "recover from the other contracting party . . . whatever the wife [had] paid or delivered."[47]

As a result, a woman subject to her husband's marital power could not conduct a business or profession

---

[38]*Ibid.* For case-law discussion of the need for corroboration, *see R. v. M.* (1947) 4 S.A. 489 (N.)

[39]N. Pillay, "Judges and Gender: Wife Battery and Child Abuse" (1993) 16 Agenda at 64.

[40]*Women and Sexual Offences, supra* note [17] at 32.

[41]*S. v. D. and Another* (1992) 1 S.A. 513 at 516C-F (Namibia High Court). While the case is not South African, the court posited that such interpretations of women's behaviour are based on the conclusions that they are all *prima facie* deceitful and act with hidden motives. See "Judges and Gender: Caution Please Women Approaching the Bench" (1992) 13 Agenda 75 at 75 for a discussion of the case's application in South Africa.

[42]Hahlo, *supra* note [1] at 153.

[43]J. Segar & C. White, "Constructing Gender: Discrimination and the Law in South Africa" (1989) 4 Agenda 95 at 104. This figure is based upon the 1981 Census compiled on 1956 data.

[44]D.S.P. Cronjé, *The South African Law of Persons and Family Law,* 2nd ed. (Durban: Butterworths, 1990) at 238.

[45]*Ibid.*

[46]See *Estate Sayle v. Commissioner of Inland Revenue* (1945) A.D. 388, 396 as noted in *ibid.* at 253.

[47]Rodenburg *De Jure Conj Prael* 186–187 and Voet 12.6.19 as noted in Hahlo *supra* note [1] at 192.

without his written or implied authorization. With his approval she could engage in public transactions because she was considered to be her husband's agent and the administrator of their estate with respect to her profession,[48] but the husband retained the power to withdraw his consent at any time.[49] Furthermore, if he was deemed insane, her agency rights would be terminated automatically.[50]

There were some general exceptions to this rule. For example, a wife was entitled to enter into contracts to purchase any household necessities.[51] What was considered a household necessity depended on the family's particular circumstances; the courts found that engaging a plumber and purchasing food, clothes, and small items of furniture were "necessities," while buying a piano, renting an apartment or booking a holiday were not.[52]

The second aspect of the husband's marital power was power over the person of his wife. This entitled him to represent her in any legal action involving a third party.[53] In short, without her husband's consent, a woman had no standing in a court of law.

> [A wife] may not conduct civil legal proceedings unassisted, whether as plaintiff or defendant. Actions concerning the joint estate must be instituted by or against the husband, in his capacity as its administrator, and actions concerning the wife personally must be instituted by or against him in his capacity as her guardian. He may bring or defend an action even against her will.[54]

Any proceedings without the husband's approval would have no legal effect, since a judgment against the wife could be set aside.[55] An important exception to this general rule permitted a wife to bring matrimonial actions against her husband.[56]

Clearly, the effect of marital power on married women was to relegate their rights and legal status to an inferior position as compared to their male partners. In fact, the South African Law Commission was of the view that their position was worse than that of a minor:

> There is no general rule that the husband must exercise his marital power in the interests of his wife; he is, in principle, entitled to exercise the marital power to his own advantage. The opposite applies in the relationship between the guardian and his ward; the guardian must exercise his guardianship in the exclusive interests of the ward.[57]

As a result of the woman's inferior legal status under marital power, the system was open to abuse. Therefore, both the legislature and the courts adopted some measures in an attempt to protect women from husbands who misused their marital power.

The *Matrimonial Affairs Act,* 1953, limited the ability of the husband to use his marital power "to alienate, mortgage, burden with a servitude or confer any real right," in the wife's immovable property without her consent, unless a judge was satisfied that "such consent was unreasonably held."[58] The wife's movable property also received some limited protection in the legislation.[59]

The common law also provided the wife with some remedies against her husband. If she could show that her husband's conduct was seriously prejudicial to her interests, she could obtain a court order to prevent him from further actions involving their joint assets.[60] A wife also had a remedy at common law to protect herself "if the husband [abused] his power of administration by squandering or dealing recklessly" with their assets.[61]

In practice, however, these general safeguards were of little value. The *Matrimonial Affairs Act* did "very little to improve the position of a wife married in community of property" because of its limited applica-

[48] *Ibid.* at 215.
[49] *Chenille Industries v. Vorster* (1953) 2 S.A. 691 (O). See also *ibid.* at 215.
[50] *Tucker's Fresh Meat Supply (Pty) Ltd. v. Echakowitz* (1958) 1 S.A. 505 (A).
[51] Cronjé, *supra* note [44] at 258; Hahlo, *supra* note [1] at 203–207.
[52] Hahlo, *ibid.* at 204 and accompanying text.
[53] *Ibid.* at 232.
[54] *Ibid.* at 232, 233ff.
[55] Cronjé, *supra* note [44] at 275; *ibid.* at 234.
[56] Cronjé, *ibid.* at 276; Hahlo, *ibid.* at 237.
[57] *Report Pertaining to the Matrimonial Property Law with Special Reference to the Matrimonial Affairs Act, 1953.* South African Law Commission Report. (February, 1982) at 34 [hereinafter *Report Pertaining to the Matrimonial Property Law*] [Editor's Note: We have been unable to verify the accuracy of this source].
[58] *Matrimonial Affairs Act,* no. 37 of 1953, s. 1.
[59] *Ibid.* s. 2.
[60] Such prejudice, however, had to be more than economic prejudice, it had to be fraudulent. See Cronjé, *supra* note [44] at 253–254; Hahlo, *supra* note [1] at 198.
[61] Hahlo, *ibid.* at 133.

tion.[62] Similarly, in the words of the South African Law Commission, the common law remedies were of "little significance" because they offered "scant consolation where the husband has already abused his marital power"[63]

The concept of marital power has had a pervasive influence in the lives of married women in non-legal matters:

> Women requiring necessary surgical procedures such as a hysterectomy, mastectomy, ligation or legal abortions have reported that hospitals have declined to perform the operations unless the husband's consent has been obtained. This has resulted in great hardship, especially for women in rural areas and informal settlements whose husbands or guardians are inaccessible.[64]

There was, and most likely still is, "a great deal of misconception of the husband's marital power over his wife."[65] Even though a woman's consent alone is required, misguided notions concerning marital power have thus limited a married woman's rights, despite there being no foundation in law for such actions.

In addition to marital power, there were some further "invariable" powers that the husband retained over the wife. A husband was deemed to be the "head of the household," and as a result, he "had the decisive say in all matters concerning the common life" of the family.[66] For example, he had the right to determine their standard of living, and had the "superior" rights in regard to the guardianship of the children of the marriage.[67] In this respect, "he [had] the decisive say in the exercise of parental power."[68]

As previously noted, two-thirds of Asian, coloured or white women came under this marital system. Through the use of an antenuptial agreement, the other one-third generally opted out of both the community of property and the marital power regime. Under such agreements, each spouse retained control of her or his separate estate, and in general was not liable for the other's debts.[69] At the same time, wives were not entitled to any assets their husbands accumulated during the marriage. Even upon the death of their husbands, they did not have a legal claim to part of the estate if they were left out of the will.[70] Recent legislation, however, has provided that a wife can claim financial assistance against the husband's estate until her death or remarriage, if she cannot ensure her own maintenance from her own means or earnings.[71] The original bill proposed by Parliament had deemed that a disinherited spouse be given a fixed portion of the estate, but this was rejected as being contrary to the ideal of freedom of testation.

Contracting out of marital power meant that women were the sole administrators of their estates. They retained the right to enter into contracts and financial transactions and engage in civil litigation independently of their husbands. Nevertheless, husbands always retained the rights of the head of the household, as referred to above, because this was deemed to be an invariable consequence of marriage.[72]

C. Black Women Married before 1988

Black women married before 1988 were automatically married *out* of community of property, but were still subject to marital power. The consequences of this marital regime were harsh:

> [A] black woman married according to civil rites faces disadvantages without compensatory benefits: she has no right to share in the property of her husband, and is deprived of the power to administer her own property, has limited contractual capacity, and has no *locus standi in iudicio*.[73]

---

[62] *Report Pertaining to the Matrimonial Property Law, supra* note [57] at 40.
[63] *Ibid.* at 35.
[64] N. Pillay, "Judges and Gender" (1992) 15 Agenda 47 at 47–48.
[65] *Ibid.* at 48.
[66] Hahlo, *supra* note 5 at 133.
[67] *Ibid.* at 148.
[68] *Ibid.*

[69] *Ibid.* at 260.
[70] These women did not have a legal claim to part of the estate if they were left out of the will at *common law.* Statutorily, they were entitled to some portion of the estate. See the *Intestate Succession Act,* no. 13 of 1934 as rep. by Act No. 81 of 1987, s. 1(1)(a) as am. by Act No. 43 of 1992. See also *ibid.,* s. 1 (1)(c), as am. by Act No. 139 of 1987. These sections permitted recovery dependent upon the status of other members of the family still surviving.
[71] *Maintenance of Surviving Spouse Act,* No. 27 of 1990, s. 2.
[72] Hahlo, *supra* note [1] at 267–268.
[73] J. Julyan, "Women, Race and the Law" in A. Rycroft et al., eds., *Race and the Law in South Africa* (Cape Town: Juta, 1987) 139 at 143.

This marital regime could be altered if both spouses declared their alternative preference to a magistrate, or through the use of an antenuptial contract.[74]

D. Asian, Coloured and White Women Married after 1984, and Black Women Married after 1988

The passage of the *Matrimonial Property Act* of 1984,[75] altered the marital regime for any Asian, coloured or white women married after 1 November 1984, but was not retroactive. Couples married before its enactment, however, were allowed to change the system that governed their marriage by applying to the court.

The legislation retained the community of property aspect of the marriage, but abolished the marital power consequences for women married after 1984. Section 12 clarified the effect of the abolition:

> S. 12 Subject to the provisions of this Act, the effect of the abolition of the marital power is to do away with restrictions which the marital power places on the capacity of a wife to contract and to litigate.[76]

However, s. 13 provided that:

> S. 13 The provisions of this Chapter do not affect the law relating to the position of the husband as head of the family or the law relating to domicile and guardianship.[77]

Surprisingly, some hailed this new act as the end of "two thousand years of male domination in marriage."[78]

Under the *Act,* both spouses had an equal right to administer their joint estate, enter into commercial transactions or engage in civil litigation with third parties.[79] However, each was limited in his or her ability to enter into matters of significant financial consequence without the other's written consent.[80] Similarly, a "spouse married in community of property shall not without the written consent of the other spouse, institute legal proceedings against another person or defend legal proceedings instituted by another person."[81]

The legislation also altered some of the harsh financial consequences of marrying out of community of property. Section 21(2) provided that the court would have some discretion to order that assets accumulated by one spouse could be redistributed to the other spouse. However, the overall impact of this section was restricted. The court's discretion was limited to marriages entered into before the passage of the Act and only to those where one spouse had contributed directly or indirectly to the maintenance or increase of the estate of the other party.[82] Moreover, any previous agreement between the parties regarding the division of property would remove the court's discretionary powers to intervene in the matter.[83] However, this legislation did not apply to black women married under the civil regime until the passage of the *Marriage and Matrimonial Property Law Amendment Act,* 1988.[84] It provided that black women married after 2 December 1988 were to fall under the marital regime established by the *Matrimonial Property Act* "to bring Black marriages in accordance with those of Whites."[85] The legislation was, once again, not retroactive, but women married before this period could petition the court to come under this system.[86]

E. Recent Statutory Reforms

The outdated statutory regime governing civil marriages was in desperate need of reform. In December 1993, the National Party Government proclaimed legislation abolishing marital power over all married women in the *General Law Fourth Amendment Act*:[87]

> 29 (1) The common law rule in terms of which a husband obtains the marital power over the person

[74]Cronjé, *supra* note [44] at 226, 239–240.
[75]No. 88 1984 [hereinafter *Matrimonial Property Act*].
[76]*Ibid.*, s. 12.
[77]*Ibid.*, s. 13.
[78]Hahlo, *supra* note [1] at 248.
[79]*Matrimonial Property Act, supra* note [75], ss. 12 and 14. See discussion in J.D. Sinclair, *An Introduction to the Matrimonial Property Act* (Cape Town: Juta, 1984) at 15–16.
[80]*Matrimonial Property Act, supra* note [75], s. 15; Sinclair, *ibid.* at 17–19.
[81]*Matrimonial Property Act, ibid.,* s. 17(1). Exceptions exist where the proceedings are in respect of separate property or regarding the profession or trade or business of only one spouse. See also *Sinclair, ibid.* at 24.
[82]*Matrimonial Property Act, ibid.,* s.21(2). Sinclair, *ibid.* at 48.
[83]Sinclair, *ibid.*
[84]No. 3 1988 [hereinafter *Marriage and Matrimonial Property Act*].
[85]Cronjé, *supra* note [44] at 240.
[86]*Ibid.* at 226–227; *Marriage and Matrimonial Property Act, supra* note [84], s. 25(3).
[87]*General Law Fourth Amendment Act,* No. 132 1992.

and property of his wife is hereby repealed.
(2) Any marital power which a husband has over the person and property of his wife immediately prior to the date of coming into operation of this subsection, is hereby abolished.[88]

A further section of this legislation abolished the powers and authority associated with the husband's role as "head of the household."[89]

These provisions, enacted by the white government shortly before the all-race elections, dramatically altered the common and statutory regime governing women in a civil marriage. Unfortunately, this is not the situation for women married under customary law. . . .

67

ANSHU NANGIA

The Tragedy of Bride Burning in India: How Should the Law Address It?

INTRODUCTION

Within a week of marriage, Savita Sharma's in-laws made demands for a refrigerator, scooter, television set, and cash.[1] Her mother-in-law verbally abused her, did not give her enough food to eat or soap to bathe with, and locked up all her clothes.[2] Both her mother-in-law and her husband beat her.[3] On one occasion, she overheard her mother-in-law tell a tenant. "I will burn her and then give money to the police to hush up the case."[4] Savita Sharma's emotional and physical suffering at the hands of her husband and in-laws is typical of what many young married women experience in India if their husband and in-laws are dissatisfied with the amount of dowry[5] that the women bring to the marriage.

Frequently, the violence escalates and results in either the young bride's murder or in her suicide.[6] Sudha Jain's case is typical; her husband, her mother-in-law, and her brother-in-law caught hold of her, poured kerosene on her body, and set her on fire.[7]

The National Crimes Record Bureau of India recorded in 1995 that an average of seventeen dowry deaths take place every day in India.[8] In 1994, the official number of recorded dowry deaths totaled 4935, and in 1993 the figures reached almost 6000.[9] Unless India aggressively addresses the problem of dowry and dowry violence, innocent young women will continue to die in alarming numbers. . . .

---

[88] *Ibid.* s. 29.
[89] *Ibid.* s. 30.
[1] *See* Raka Sinha, *Seven Dowry Victims Go to the Supreme Court,* EVE'S WEEKLY, Nov. 26–Dec. 2 1983, at 16.
[2] *See id.*
[3] *See id.*
[4] *Id.*
[5] Dowry usually refers to gifts given during the marriage to the son-in-law or his parents in cash or kind. *See* RANJANA KUMARI, BRIDES ARE NOT FOR BURNING 1 (1989). However, from the point of view of women's status, dowry has to be looked at as constituting: 1) gifts given to the bride but usually not considered her exclusive property; often the content and value of these gifts are settled before the marriage and announced openly or discreetly; 2) gifts given to the bridegroom before and at marriage; 3) gifts presented to the bride's in-laws. *See id.* "The settlement often includes the enormous expenses incurred on travel and entertainment of the bridegroom's party. The gift-giving often continues through the first few years of marriage. . . ." *Id.* (footnote omitted).
[6] *See* S.C. Sahu, *Marriage—Why Dowryless?—A Medicologist's Considerations,* in DOWRY: DIAGNOSIS & CURE 1, 2 (Bibekananda Das ed., 1989).
[7] *See* V. Kumar, *Death for Bride-Killers,* EVE'S WEEKLY, July 30–Aug. 5, 1983, at 14. Sudha Jain was found dead in her in-laws' home. When the police reached the scene of the crime, they found a stove with a pot of milk on it, a match-box, and some burnt, wet pieces of cloth which smelt of kerosene. *See id.* The in-laws claimed that Sudha had accidentally caught fire while heating milk on the stove. *See id.* In dowry-related murders, pouring kerosene over the woman and setting her alight is the most common method of killing her because kerosene is readily available in almost every household. *See* Sahu, *supra* note 6, at 2. Furthermore, the murder can easily be made to look like a kitchen accident since burning the woman is the surest way of destroying evidence of foul play. *See id.*
[8] *See* Rani Jethmalani, *Introduction* TO KALI'S YUG: EMPOWERMENT, LAW AND DOWRY DEATHS 13, 14 (Rani Jethmalani ed., 1995). The National Crimes Record Bureau is a division of the Ministry of Home Affairs of the Government of India. It maintains data on national crime and publishes it in its annual publication, *Crime in India. See, e.g.* NATIONAL CRIMES RECORDS BUREAU, CRIME IN INDIA 1994 (1996) [hereinafter CRIME IN INDIA 1994].
[9] *See* CRIME IN INDIA 1994, *supra* note 8, at 212.

The Definition of Dowry

The current version of the Dowry Prohibition Act defines "dowry" as:

> [A]ny property or valuable security given or agreed to be given either directly or indirectly—
> (a) By one party to a marriage to the other party to the marriage; or
> (b) By the parents of either party to a marriage or by any other person to either party to the marriage to any other person,
> At or before or any time after the marriage in connection with the marriage. . . .[10]

The words "in connection with the marriage," added in 1984, replace the words "as consideration for the marriage,"[11] which appeared in the original Dowry Prohibition Act of 1961.

On its face, this definition is comprehensive because dowry includes not only what the bridegroom and his family demand or take, or agree to take, but also includes that which the bride and her family demand or take, or agree to take.[12] The words "in connection with the marriage" further suggest that dowry includes any transfer of property or consumer goods that flows from one side to the other in order to complete the marriage transaction or to sustain the marriage arrangement. As such, the definition of dowry suggests that anything given before, after, or at the time of marriage may constitute dowry. . . .[13]

The Dowry Death Offense

The Dowry Prohibition (Amendment) Act of 1986 introduced section 304B into the Indian Penal Code, which defines and punishes perpetrators for the crime of dowry death:

> Where the death of a woman is caused by any burns or bodily injury or occurs otherwise than under normal circumstances within seven years of her marriage and it is shown that soon before her death she was subjected to cruelty or harassment by her husband or any relative of her husband for, or in connection with, any demand for dowry, such death shall be called "dowry death," and such husband or relative shall be deemed to have caused her death.[14]

If all the above conditions are present, then there is a presumption that the accused has committed the crime of dowry death; the operative part of section 113B of the Indian Evidence Act inserted by the Dowry Prohibition (Amendment) Act of 1986 states that the "Court shall presume that such person had caused the dowry death."[15] If the individual is unable to meet the burden of proof that he or she did not commit the dowry death offense, that individual is convicted and subject to "imprisonment for a term which shall not be less than seven years but which may extend to imprisonment for life."[16]

The most important aspect of section 304B is section 113B of the Evidence Act because the accused is presumed to have committed the dowry death, regardless of whether the accused has any direct connection with it.[17] The prosecution need only provide direct evidence of cruelty and harassment for or in connection with the demand for dowry in order for the presumption to apply.[18]

This presumption is especially critical because the death normally occurs in the in-laws' home and the woman is frequently burned to death. By burning the woman to death, the husband and in-laws usually destroy the evidence connecting them to the crime.[19] Moreover, they can easily manipulate the evidence in their favor by claiming that the woman died as a result of a kitchen accident. Consequently, shifting the burden to the husband and in-laws to prove that they did not murder the woman or assist in her suicide strengthens the prosecution for dowry death offenses.

Nevertheless, section 304B is problematic because before any presumption of dowry death can be made, the prosecution has to overcome the hurdle of establishing that the husband and in-laws subjected the

---

[10]Dowry Prohibition Act, No. 28, § 2, 6 INDIA CODE 40E (1961), *as amended by* Dowry Prohibition (Amendment) Act, No. 63, § 2 (1984) and Dowry Prohibition (Amendment) Act, No. 43, § 2, 1986 A.I.R. 73 (Nag.) 188.
[11]Dowry Prohibition (Amendment) Act, No. 63, § 2(a) (1984).
[12]*See* PARAS DIWAN & PEEYUSHI DIWAN, WOMEN AND LEGAL PROTECTION 161 (1995).
[13]*See id.* at 150.
[14]Dowry Prohibition (Amendment) Act, No. 43, § 10, 1986 A.I.R. 73 (Nag.) 190 (amending INDIA PEN. CODE § 304B).
[15]*Id.* § 12, 1986 A.I.R. 73 (Nag.) 191 (amending Indian Evidence Act, No. 1, § 113B, 4 INDIA CODE 11 (1872)).
[16]*Id.* § 10, 1986 A.I.R. 73 (Nag.) 190 (amending INDIA PEN. CODE § 301B(2)).
[17]*See* [D. N. Sandanshiv & Jolly Mathew, "Legal Reform in Dowry Laws" in KALI'S YUG., *supra* note 8], at 86.
[18]*See id.*
[19]*See supra* note 7 and accompanying text.

woman to cruelty. Cruelty to a married woman means:

> (a) any wilful conduct which is of such a nature as is likely to drive the woman to commit suicide or to cause grave injury or danger to life, limb or health (whether mental or physical) of the woman; or
>
> (b) harassment of the woman where such harassment is with a view to coercing her or any person related to her to meet any unlawful demand for any property or valuable security or is on account of failure by her or any person related to her to meet such demand.[20]

The definition of cruelty is very broad and includes both physical and mental cruelty. It recognizes that the physical and the emotional abuse of the woman is intimately related to the dowry demands of the husband and in-laws.

Despite this expansive definition of cruelty, the prosecution bears a heavy burden to prove that the husband and in-laws subjected the woman to cruelty before death. Cruelty takes subtle forms, and generally the only witnesses to the abuse are the husband and in-laws.[21] The husband and in-laws have control over the evidence and can easily manipulate it in their favor. Consequently, the prosecution encounters similar problems in procuring physical evidence to establish cruelty as it does in establishing murder or assisted suicide.

Another problem with section 304B is that charges for the dowry death offense can be brought against the husband and in-laws only where the woman died under unnatural circumstances "within seven years of her marriage."[22] The seven-year limitation enables offenders to escape penalty under the dowry death provision by postponing the woman's murder until the limitation has expired. For instance, on March 8, 1995, Babulal burned his twenty-two-year-old wife Vimala Devi to death after having waited for seven years to realize his plan.[23] He had told Vimala Devi that he would kill her when the seven years were up.[24] Nevertheless, the police refused to register a case against him because the seven-year limitation had expired.[25]

Vimala Devi's murder calls for a reassessment of the seven-year limitation. The assumption behind the seven-year limitation is that it is "believed to be ample time to manage and ascertain a potentially abusive relationship. Dowry abuse is thought to be lessened with the arrival of children and time for the marriage to stabilize."[26] However, this assumption disregards the social reality that some families will go to great lengths to secure more dowry.[27] Babulal was willing to sustain a marriage and terrorize his wife for seven years in order to satisfy his greed for more money.[28] The seven-year limitation did not protect Vimala Devi and it will not protect other women, because "[i]t is cheaper for a man to kill his spouse and obtain a new one with another dowry than [it is] to divorce his wife and pay her maintenance."[29] For this reason, section 304B should be amended to eliminate the seven-year limitation.

Furthermore, the presumption of dowry death should be applied to any death that "occurs otherwise than under normal circumstances."[30] In other words, if a woman is found burned to death under suspicious circumstances in the privacy of her husband's or in-laws' home, the presumption should be that the husband and the in-laws murdered her or caused her to commit suicide. The current burden on the prosecution to prove that the husband and in-laws subjected the woman to cruelty before the woman's death should be removed. It is an onerous requirement and poses a practical obstacle to the conviction of offenders.

---

[20] INDIA PEN. CODE § 498A, *as amended by* Criminal Law (Second Amendment) Act of 1983, No. 46, § 2, 1984 A.I.R. 71 (Nag.) 68. Although no explanation for cruelty is given under § 304B, the Supreme Court of India has held that "cruelty" under § 304B has the same meaning as "cruelty" under INDIA PEN. CODE § 498A, under which cruelty, by itself, is a punishable offense. *See* Shanti v. State of Haryana, [1991] 1 S.C.C. 271; Sandanshiv & Mathew, *supra* note [17], at 84.

[21] *See* DIWAN & DIWAN, *supra* note [12], at 119 (noting the difficulty in proving events which take place "within the four walls of the home"); Sandanshiv & Mathew, *supra* note [17], at 80.

[22] INDIA PEN. CODE § 304B(1), *as amended by* Dowry Prohibition (Amendment) Act, No. 43, § 10, 1986 A.I.R. 73 (Nag.) 190.

[23] *See Police Refuse to Register Dowry Death Case against Husband,* INDIAN EXPRESS (Del.), Mar. 13, 1995, Metro sec., at 2 [hereinafter *Police Refuse*].

[24] *See id.*

[25] *See id.*

[26] Ritu Banerjee, *Bride-Burning and the Law: Vimala Devi's Tragedy,* in [*Souvenir of the First International Conference on Dowry and Bride-Burning in India* (1995)], at 4–1, 4–4 [hereinafter DOWRY CONFERENCE SOUVENIR].

[27] *See id.*

[28] *See id.*

[29] *Id.*

[30] INDIA PEN. CODE § 304B(1), *as amended by* Dowry Prohibition (Amendment) Act, No. 43, § 10, 1986 A.I.R. 73 (Nag.) 190.

Cognizance of Offenses

Section 7(1)(b) of the current Dowry Prohibition Act states:

> [N]o court shall take cognizance of an offence under this Act except upon—
> (i) its own knowledge or a police report of the facts which constitute such offence, or
> (ii) a complaint by the person aggrieved by the offence or a parent or other relative of such person, *or by any recognized welfare institution or organisation.*[31]

The strength of this provision lies in the court's competence to hear a case that comes to it based on a complaint made to the court or to the police by women's organizations that are knowledgeable about the victim's plight.

The role of women's organizations in bringing to the court's attention offenses committed in relation to the taking of or demand for dowry is especially critical to the enforcement of the Act, because women's organizations work directly with victims. Women's organizations provide women with counseling, legal advice, and placement in shelters,[32] and therefore the organizations are likely to be most knowledgeable when violations of the Act occur.

Furthermore, giving women's organizations the authority to make complaints on behalf of victims enables the court to hear cases that otherwise would not come before it because women and their parents are unlikely to report violations of the Act out of social pressures and fear.[33] First, they are generally interested in preserving the marriage, and not in punishing offenders despite excessive and unlawful demands for dowry.[34] Second, the woman and her parents view dowry as a necessary price to pay for a married life, which they equate with the woman's happiness.[35] Once the woman gets married, the decision to complain against dowry becomes much more difficult since compliance with the demand controls the maintenance of the marriage.[36] As a result, the woman or her relatives file a complaint "only when harassment for dowry increases beyond endurance."[37]

Despite the legal authority of women's organizations to make complaints about violations under the Dowry Prohibition Act, the major weakness to the effectiveness of this provision is the discretion given to courts to hear dowry cases. Since judges vary in the sensitivity and the seriousness with which they regard the dowry problem, they may dismiss cases with or without serious investigation, depending on their dispositions and views. Therefore, section 7 should be amended to reduce the discretion of judges in taking cognizance of offenses under the Act and to mandate serious investigation of all dowry complaints. Perhaps, separate family courts should be established to handle all dowry cases so that they can be resolved justly, efficiently, and expeditiously.

Discipline for Offenses under the Act

Section 8 of the Dowry Prohibition Act[38] makes all offenses non-bailable[39] and non-compoundable.[40] This

[31]Dowry Prohibition Act, No. 23, § 7(1)(b)(i)–(ii), 6 INDIA CODE 40F (1961), *as amended by* Dowry Prohibition (Amendment) Act, No. 63, § 6 (1984) (emphasis added).

[32]*See Police Refuse, supra* note [23], at 2; KUMARI, *supra* note 5, at 86. *See generally* D. N. Sandanshiv, *Bride Burning: Perspective of Interveners, in* KALI'S YUG, *supra* note 8, at 94, 94–104.

[33]*See* . . . KUMARI, *supra* note 5, at 86–87 (noting the "significant role" that women's organizations play in the anti-dowry movement, and their ability to change prevailing social norms).

[34]*See* . . . [Ved Kumari, "State's Response to the Problem of Rape and Dowry," in *Women & Law: Contemporary Problems* (Lotika Sarkar & B. Sivaramayya eds., 1994)], at 119.

[35]*See* KUMARI, *supra* note 5, at 15.

[36]*See* KUMARI, *supra* note [34], at 120.

[37]*Id.* at 119.

[38]Dowry Prohibition Act, No. 28, § 8, 6 INDIA CODE 40G (1961), *as amended by* Dowry Prohibition (Amendment) Act, No. 63, § 7 (1984) *and* Dowry Prohibition (Amendment) Act, No. 43, § 7, 1986 A.I.R. 73 (Nag.) 189.

[39]*Id.* § 8(2) (as amended 1986). A non-bailable offense is one that prohibits a convicted individual from posting bail as a matter of right. The defendant must petition the court for bail, and give reasons why bail is appropriate in his case. For instance, a defendant could argue that his release on bail would not in any way contaminate evidence. Generally, the court has exercised great discretion in granting bail and has awarded it in many cases. *See* Sandanshiv & Mathew, *supra* note [17], at 90–91. In *Amarnath Gupta v. State of Madhya Pradesh,* 1990 Crim. L.J. 2163 (India), the High Court issued an order granting bail "on the ground that the victim's diary contained a letter written by her stating that nobody was to be blamed for her suicide." Sandanshiv & Mathew, *supra* note [17], at 90. The High Court rationalized the decision by noting that nothing in the record indicated that the defendants would misuse the liberty granted to them. *See id.* The Supreme Court reversed the High Court decision, but in doing so noted that "sentimentalism has no place in the judicial process." *Id.* at 90–91. Despite the Supreme Court's stance in exercising caution in the grant of bail, both the high courts and courts of sessions continue to grant bail in dowry death cases. *See id.* at 90.

[40]Under the Indian law, a non-compoundable offense is one that does not allow the parties to compromise once the case goes to court. *See* Letter From Subhadra Chaturvedi, Advocate, Supreme Court and High Courts, New Delhi, to author (Dec. 7, 1996) (on file with the *Brooklyn Journal of International Law*).

section is desirable because convicted offenders are not entitled to bail as a matter of right, and they must petition the court in order to be considered for bail. Unfortunately, this provision has not been effective in deterring the grant of bail in dowry death cases because the Sessions Courts and the High Courts continually grant bail in cases of domestic violence and dowry deaths despite the Supreme Court's repeated pleas of caution.[41]

Since courts are liberal in granting bail to offenders, offenders are free to tamper with and hamper investigations, and to influence witnesses.[42] For this provision to be more effective as a deterrent to dowry crimes and as a method of ensuring unhampered investigation, courts will have to take dowry crimes more seriously and to restrict bail to exceptional cases.

Currently, the liberal grant of bail by courts only serves as an incentive for the husbands and in-laws to commit dowry crimes and then to cover up the evidence. Furthermore, the non-compoundability of offenses under the Act does not deter families from taking dowry, demanding dowry, or killing for dowry. Preventing parties from compromising once the case goes to court does not necessarily allow the conclusion that husbands and in-laws will think twice before committing the crime for fear of a long-drawn-out battle in court. Husbands and in-laws can easily avoid this provision by compromising with the woman's family before the case goes to court. According to Public Prosecutor Renuka: "Seventy per cent of dowry death cases are ending in acquittals due to compromises between the in-laws and the victim's parents. Sometimes, for as small a sum as 5,000 Rupees, the dowry victim's parents are withdrawing the complaint. And such compromises are increasing alarmingly.[43] Consequently, the penal provisions under the Act are not a deterrent to dowry crimes because the husband and in-laws know that they can escape penalty by paying off the victim's parents with a nominal sum of money.

In this context, parents are playing an active role in perpetuating dowry crimes against their daughters. Therefore, to protect women and to ensure that offenders are punished for their crimes, section 8 of the Act should be amended to take away the discretion of the woman's parents and relatives to withdraw the complaint.

COMPLEMENTARY PROVISIONS IN THE INDIAN PENAL CODE

Protection against Cruelty

The Criminal Law (Second Amendment) Act of 1983 inserted section 498A into the Indian Penal Code, which criminalizes physical and emotional abuse by the husband or his relatives, and specifically characterizes the wife's harassment for the unlawful demand for dowry as an offense of cruelty.[44] The legislature introduced this section in response to the "increasing number of dowry deaths."[45] It recognized that cruelty by the husband and his relatives "culminate[s] in suicide by, or murder of, the hapless woman concerned,"[46] and that these cases "constitute only a small fraction of the cases involving such cruelty."[47] Section 498A defines the offense of cruelty as follows:

> (a) any wilful conduct which is of such a nature as is likely to drive the woman to commit suicide or to cause grave injury or danger to life, limb or health (whether mental or physical) of the woman; or
>
> (b) harassment of the woman where such harassment is with a view to coercing her or any person related to her to meet any unlawful demand for any property or valuable security or is on account of failure by her or any person related to her to meet such demand.[48]

Cruelty is punishable with a term of imprisonment which may extend to three years and a fine.[49]

The strength of section 498A is that it specifically deals with the situation where the husband and in-laws

---

[41]*See* Sandanshiv & Mathew, *supra* note [17], at 90. Courts of Sessions are trial courts; high courts are the intermediate appellate courts. The Supreme Court is the highest court and its determination is final.

[42]*See* [Daksha Hathi, "Bride Burning & After: Making a Farce of Tragedy," *Deccan Herald* (Bangalore, India), Sept. 24, 1994, Society sec.], at 8.

[43]*Id.*

[44]INDIA PEN. CODE § 498A, *as amended by* Criminal Law (Second Amendment) Act of 1983, No. 46 § 2, 1984 A.I.R. 71 (Nag.) 68.

[45]R. DAYAL, LAW RELATING TO DOWRY 1157 (1995) (citing legislative history of the Criminal Law (Second Amendment) Act of 1983, No. 46, 1984 A.I.R. 71 (Nag.) 68).

[46]*Id.*

[47]*Id.*

[48]INDIA PEN. CODE § 498A(a)–(b), *as amended by* Criminal Law (Second Amendment) Act of 1983, No. 46, § 2, 1984 A.I.R. 71 (Nag.) 68.

[49]*See id.*

demand dowry from the woman after the marriage and where the dowry falls short of the expectations of the husband and in-laws. Section 498A links this unlawful demand with the social reality of the harassment that many women face when the dowry falls short of the demand or expectation. This provision can be used for criminal redress by women against their husbands or in-laws for depriving them of food and clothing, for locking them up in dingy rooms, or for beating them.

Furthermore, section 498A makes the husband and in-laws liable for cruelty any time after the marriage. There is no requirement that the harassment occur within seven years of marriage like the one found in the dowry death offense created by the Dowry Prohibition Act.[50] This is beneficial for women because they may tolerate years of abuse before they decide to leave the violent home.

Section 498A also recognizes that the level of abuse may be so intense that it may endanger the woman's life or drive her to suicide. Nevertheless, the level of punishment this section imposes on the offender does not reflect that greater levels of abuse should warrant stricter penalties. Therefore, section 498A should be amended to remove the three-year maximum imprisonment term and to allow for stricter penalties that coincide with the level of abuse.

Section 498A presents the same problems of burden and proof as does section 304B. This problem of evidence and proof should be addressed by creating a presumption of cruelty whenever any form of wealth is transferred from the woman's family to the husband and in-laws. The burden of proof would then be on those who have control over the evidence—the husband and in-laws—to prove that they did not physically or emotionally harass the woman or her family for dowry.

Since cruelty in the marriage is normally intimately linked with the demand for dowry, section 498A should also be amended to allow the return of the woman's dowry to her or her heirs when cruelty is established and the husband and in-laws are convicted. This provision should be amended along the lines of section 6(3A) of the Dowry Prohibition Act, which requires the court to transfer the dowry to the woman even after the conviction of the husband and in-laws for the failure to transfer dowry.[51] Such a provision would allow for the usual criminal remedy of imprisonment, and additionally would mandate the return of the woman's dowry to her without her having to institute a separate civil action for a civil remedy. It would, in effect, increase the cost of punishment to the husband and in-laws for inflicting physical and emotional abuse on the woman.

Furthermore, such a provision would protect the woman because she often encounters great difficulties in a civil suit for the return of her personal property or *strīdhan*. *Kamini Sahuami v. Purna Chandra Sahoo*[52] illustrates this difficulty. In *Kamini Sahuami,* the husband thrashed his wife, burned her with a hot rod, and threw her out of the house because her parents were unable to meet additional demands for dowry.[53] The wife instituted a civil suit for the return of the property that she left behind in the husband's home.[54] But the trial court ignored the wife's averment that she gave her ornaments to her husband; it held that the woman took her ornaments with her when she left her husband's home.[55]

The trial court's judgment ignored the social reality that a wife may allow her husband to hold on to her valuable possessions since the continuation of a dowry-based marriage depends on the amount of wealth that the husband and in-laws can extract from the wife and her parents.[56] The court also did not consider the fact that a wife who was beaten could not reasonably be expected to take or be allowed to take her gold ornaments with her.[57]

The wife experiences severe constraints on her ability to prove her averments because the court must

---

[50]*See* [INDIA PEN. CODE § 304B, *as amended by* Dowry Prohibition (Amendment) Act, No. 43 § 10, 1986 A.I.R. 73 (Nag.) 188].

[51]Dowry Prohibition Act, No. 28, § 6(3A), 6 INDIA CODE 40F (1961) (as amended 1984 and 1986).

[52]1987 A.I.R. 74 (Ori.) 134.

[53]*Id.* at 135.

[54]*See id.*

[55]*See id.* at 137.

[56]*See* [Rani Jethmalani & P. K. Dey, "Dowry Deaths & Access to Justice," in KALI'S YUG, *supra* note 8 at 36, 38; *see also* Kumarin, *supra* note 5, at 43–46. . .].

[57]On appeal in *Kamini Sahuami,* the High Court of Orissa did consider this fact and overturned the trial court's ruling because it recognized the validity of the wife's claim. *See Kamini Sahuami,* 1987 A.I.R. at 137–138. The High Court also recognized that it would be impossible for the wife to prove that she was severely beaten up and thrown out of the home in light of the fact that her in-laws were the only witnesses. *See id.* A realistic evaluation of the wife's plight enabled the High Court to accept the wife's averment that her husband held her gold ornaments. Consequently, the court ordered the husband to return her gold ornaments or their monetary equivalent. *See id.*

weigh her statements against those of her husband. Frequently, the only witnesses to her statements and the violent circumstances that force her out of the home are the husband and in-laws. Amending section 498A to order the return of the woman's dowry to her would remove the discretion of judges to decide whether the level of cruelty in the marriage is sufficient to make it impossible for the woman to exercise control over her property. Under the scheme of a presumption of cruelty, the husband and in-laws would have the burden of proving that the physical and emotional abuse of the woman is not linked to the demand for dowry. If they are unable to meet this burden of proof, the court would convict the husband for the physical and emotional abuse as well as order the return of the woman's dowry to her.

After such an amendment, the woman would not have to bear the burden of proof to establish cruelty as she would have to in the civil suit in order to prevail on her dowry claim. If amended as suggested, section 498A could offer her protection not only from physical and mental cruelty, but also from the extortion and misappropriation of her personal property by the husband and in-laws.

Criminal Breach of Trust

Section 405 of the Indian Penal Code states that:

> Whoever, being in any manner entrusted with property, or with any dominion over property, dishonestly misappropriates or converts to his own use that property, or dishonestly uses or disposes of that property in violation of any direction of law prescribing the mode in which such trust is to be discharged, or of any legal contract, express or implied, which he has made touching the discharge of such trust, or wilfully suffers any other person so to do, commits "criminal breach of trust."[58]

Section 406 provides for punishment of imprisonment of up to three years, a fine, or both for any person who commits criminal breach of trust.[59]

The Supreme Court precedents on the criminal breach of trust indicate that in order to establish "entrustment of dominion" over property to an accused person, it must be shown that the person's dominion over the property was the result of entrustment.[60] The requirements of entrustment are: (a) that the person handing over any property or on whose behalf that property is handed over to another, continues to be its owner; and (b) the person handing over the property must have confidence in the person taking the property to create a fiduciary relationship between them.[61] Moreover, the accused must hold the property for the benefit of its owner.[62]

Nevertheless, section 405 does not require the creation of trust with all the technicalities of the law of trust, such as a special agreement between the parties.[63] It contemplates that a relationship of trust is created by the transfer of the owner's property to a third party for the purpose of retaining it until a certain contingency arises or disposing it on the happening of a certain event.[64]

Thus, the Supreme Court has interpreted the term "trust" creatively and broadly, in order to give a criminal remedy to dowry victims against their husbands and in-laws for misappropriating their personal property.[65] In *Pratibha Rani v. Suraj Kumar,* the Supreme Court approved the Calcutta High Court's holding that a woman does not lose ownership of her ornaments in handing them over to her husband and in-laws; but rather, she trusts them to return her property to her after using it for the purpose for which she handed it over.[66]

Despite the Supreme Court's extension of trust to include the relationship of husband and wife, many lower courts are reluctant to find a husband guilty under section 405. In the Supreme Court opinion of *Pratibha Rani,* Justice Ali Fazl stated: "[E]ven when clear and specific allegations are made in the complaint that [*strīdhan*] properties were entrusted to the husband, [lower courts] refuse to believe these hard

[58] India Pen. Code § 405.
[59] *Id.* § 406.

[60] *See* Velji Raghavji v. State of Maharashtra, A.I.R. 1965 S.C. 1433, 1435.
[61] *See* Pratibha Rani v. Suraj Kumar, A.I.R. 1985 S.C. 628, 640 (citing State of Gujarat v. Jaswantlal Nathalal, (1968) 2 S.C.R. 408).
[62] *See* Narayan Ittiravi v. State of Tra.-Co., A.I.R. 1953 S.C. 478, 484.
[63] *See* Harihar Prasad v. Tulsi Das Mundhra, A.I.R. 1981 S.C. 81, 82 (citing Jaswantrai Manilal v. State of Bombay, (1956) S.C.R. 483).
[64] *See id.*
[65] *See* Pratibha Rani, A.I.R. 1985 S.C. at 640 (citing Sushil Kumar Gupta v. Joy Shanker Bhattacharjee A.I.R. 1971 S.C. 1543).
[66] *See id.* (citing Basudeb Patra v. Kanai Lal Haldar, A.I.R. 1949 (Cal.) 207).

facts and brush them aside on the ground[s] that they are vague."[67]

In *Pratibha Rani,* Pratibha Rani's husband threw her out of the house because her parents failed to meet the additional dowry demands of the husband and in-laws.[68] They also refused to return her *strīdhan* or personal property, including her clothes and jewelry.[69] The High Court concluded that the husband and her in-laws did not violate section 405 because Pratibha Rani did not entrust her *strīdhan* to her husband.[70] The High Court's conclusion rested on the premise that *strīdhan* of the wife is joint property, and consequently that spouses do not stand in formal relationship to one another in such a way that each possesses exclusive property and entrusts the other with that property or with dominion over that property.[71] Marriage, the High Court reasoned, is a union between two people and implies joint ownership over even movable properties exclusively owned by each.[72]

On appeal, the Supreme Court rejected these arguments because the High Court built its conclusion on the incorrect premise that *strīdhan* is joint property rather than the woman's absolute property.[73] The husband's or in-laws' possession of the *strīdhan* does not in and of itself indicate that the woman owns it with them jointly or that she transferred her rights of ownership to them.[74] The Court stated that:

> [S]o far as the jewellery and clothes, blouses, nighties and gowns are concerned they could be used only by the wife and were her stridhan. By no stretch of imagination could it be said that the ornaments and sarees and other articles mentioned above could also be used by the husband. If, therefore, despite demands these articles were refused to be returned to the wife by the husband and his parents, it amounted to an offence of criminal breach of trust.[75]

The Court reasoned that the realities of married life in India indicate that the wife entrusts her husband and her in-laws with her personal property.[76] A newly married woman is unlikely to "keep her personal property or belongings like jewellery, clothing, etc., under her own lock and key, thus showing a spirit of distrust to the husband at the very behest."[77]

Pratibha Rani reflects the aggressive stand that the Supreme Court has taken to ensure that women have a criminal remedy in addition to a civil remedy for the misappropriation of their personal property by their husband and in-laws. Underlying the *Pratibha Rani* decision is the recognition that most of the dowry wealth is handed directly to the husband and in-laws and that women have little or no access to it. The Court displays an understanding of dowry as property given by the woman's parents to the husband and in-laws for the benefit of the bride, regardless of whether in actual practice the woman possesses it. Even clothes and jewelry that, in ancient times, were given directly to the bride in the form of *strīdhan,* are more likely today to be given to the husband and in-laws. Even if they are given directly to the woman, the husband and in-laws are more likely than not to take her clothes and jewelry from her.

This assumption that the Court makes is critical to its conclusion that the husband misappropriated the woman's jewelry and clothes in criminal breach of trust. Since dowry is given by the woman's parents for her benefit, the husband and in-laws do not rightfully own it. If they do not own this property, then they can only hold it in trust for the bride. Thus, the conclusion follows that any time the husband and in-

[67] *Id.* at 643.
[68] *Id.* at 630, 632.
[69] *See id.* at 630.
[70] *See id.* at 632, 634.
[71] *See id.* at 634.
[72] *See id.*
[73] *See id.* The Supreme Court chided the High Court in no uncertain terms, and was shocked that the lower court could:

> permit the husband to cast his covetous eyes on the absolute and personal property of his wife merely because it is kept in his custody, thereby reducing the custody to a legal farce. . . [I]t seems to us even if the personal property of his wife is jointly kept, it would be deemed to be expressly or impliedly kept in the custody of the husband and if he dishonestly misappropriates or refuses to return the same, he is certainly guilty of criminal breach of trust, and there can be no escape from this legal consequence.

Id. at 634–35.
[74] *See id.*
[75] *Id.* at 633. The Court left open in its list of articles the status of furniture and utensils, which could possibly be characterized as joint property as opposed to the woman's *strīdhan*—her absolute property. The court reasoned that an argument could be made that the husband and wife held these items in joint possession since they were meant for the joint use of husband and wife. *See id.*
[76] *See id.* at 633, 635.
[77] *Id.* at 634.

laws use or dispose the property without the woman's permission or refuse to return it to her upon her request, they have misappropriated her property.

This interpretation of criminal breach of trust in the context of the marital relationship is in line with the use of the term "trust" in section 6 of the Dowry Prohibition Act. Section 6 of the Act states that: "Where any dowry is received by any person other than the woman in connection with whose marriage it is given, that person shall transfer it to the woman . . . and pending such transfer, shall hold it in trust for the benefit of the woman."[78]

The use of the term "trust" here indicates that the legislature understood the meaning of "trust" to encompass the relationship between the husband or in-laws and the wife. Any dowry that passes to the husband or in-laws is the woman's property and can only be held in trust until it is transferred to the woman.

If this definition of "trust" is imported into section 405, then it invites the conclusion that the husband and in-laws violate this trust when they refuse the woman access to property that was given for her benefit. This conclusion is consistent with the legislative intent of the Parliament to protect the woman's control over her property, when it created the offense of the failure to transfer dowry under the Dowry Prohibition Act. Therefore, the Supreme Court furthered the legislative intent of Parliament in construing the general provisions of sections 405 and 406 to afford a criminal remedy to dowry victims for the misappropriation of their property by their husbands or in-laws.

Nevertheless, lower courts remain an obstacle to dowry victims who seek a criminal remedy under section 405. The legislature should respond to the judicial reluctance at the lower levels by clarifying that section 405 extends to women who seek a criminal remedy for the misappropriation of their personal property by their husbands and in-laws.

The Role of Law Enforcement Agencies in Hampering the Effectiveness of Dowry and Dowry Violence Legislation

Law enforcement agencies disregard the complaints of many dowry victims, their families, and women's organizations about the unlawful demands for dowry by husbands and in-laws and dowry-related violence and death.[79] They frequently fail to register offenses and carelessly or dishonestly investigate and prosecute cases. As a result, in many cases, the guilty go free.

The Supreme Court decision of *Lichhamadevi v. State of Rajasthan*[80] is one such case. In *Lichhamadevi,* a bride's brother-in-law escaped punishment for burning the young bride to death because the police failed to prosecute him, despite the mother-in-law's statement that the brother-in-law might have burned the bride and despite the neighbors' claims that they saw the brother-in-law behind the kitchen and running down the stairs while the bride was in flames inside.[81]

In the same case, the police also failed to charge the husband for abetting in the murder even though there was sufficient evidence to support the charge.[82] The husband silently watched his wife as she was aflame, made no effort to take her to the hospital, and took no action to secure blood for her.[83] The police's failure to take initial action against the brother-in-law and husband allowed two of the three participants in the dowry murder to go free; only the mother-in-law was convicted.[84]

The police have also been guilty of delaying and hindering justice by manipulating crucial evidence in the case against perpetrators. *Sudha Goel's* case[85] illustrates the difficulty that courts face in resolving contradictions in the evidence when the police tamper with a dying declaration,[86] often the most crucial

[78]Dowry Prohibition Act, No. 28, § 6(1), 6 INDIA CODE 40F (1961).

[79]*See* KUMARI, *supra* note 5, at 81–85; Jethmalani & Dey, *supra* note [56] at 49–50.

[80]A.I.R. 1988 S.C. 1785.

[81]*Id.* at 1787.

[82]*See id.*

[83]*See id.*

[84]*See id.* at 1788.

[85]State (Delhi Admin.) v. Kumar, A.I.R. 1986 S.C. 250; *see* Jethmalani & Dey, *supra* note [56], at 51–60 (discussing *Kumar*). Twenty-year-old Sudha Goel was subjected to ill-treatment by her husband, his mother, and his brother within the first month of marriage for bringing in insufficient dowry. *See* Jethmalani & Dey, *supra* note [56], at 52. She was pregnant, and a week before her delivery she was murdered. *See id.*

[86]Under Indian law, a dying declaration is a statement made by a person who is under a sense of impending death and who, after making the statement, dies. *See* Sandanshiv & Mathew, *supra* note [17], at 87. Such a statement is an exception to the general rule that hearsay evidence is not admissible, unless such evidence is tested by cross-examination. *See id.* The rationale for the dying declaration exception to the hearsay rule is that a person on the verge of death is most unlikely to make an untrue statement. *See id.*

evidence leading to the conviction of the perpetrator. Sudha's oral dying declaration to the neighbor-witnesses who saw her in flames when she was brought out of the house differed from the written, unsigned version recorded by the Investigation Officer at the hospital.[87] The oral declaration reflected that the mother-in-law burned the wife, while the written version portrayed the incident as an accident.[88] Since written declarations are normally more reliable than oral declarations by virtue of their form, inconsistency in the oral and written declarations is problematic for courts, as it was in this case. The trial court and the high court reached different conclusions, depending on the weight they each attributed to the oral and written declarations.[89]

In addition to revealing dishonest investigations by police, the *Sudha Goel* case also shows how police collusion can delay justice even after the Supreme Court's conviction of the husband. The police did not promptly arrest the husband upon conviction as proper procedure required.[90] When the police finally arrested the husband to complete a term for life, the husband (during his time out on bail) had married a second time and had two children as well.[91]

Since police misconduct is pervasive at all stages, from the filing of the complaint to investigation of the case and acquisition of evidence to arrest of the offender, the law should take a heavy-handed approach against law enforcement agencies. It should classify such a crime as an obstruction of justice and impose strict penalties. Specifically, the role of the police in the manipulation of evidence in collusion with the husband's family or the doctor should be condemned as a crime for the suppression of evidence. With strict penalties in place, law enforcement agents would take dowry cases more seriously and have greater incentives to follow proper procedure. With more exigent enforcement, bribes by husbands and their families may look less attractive. Further, dowry and dowry violence legislation could be more effectively enforced.

CONCLUSION

India must strengthen its dowry and dowry violence legislation to take into account the social acceptance of dowry at all levels of society, including the acceptance by the woman's parents, the woman herself, the husband and his family, law enforcement agents, and lower courts. Dowry and dowry violence are as much an outgrowth of consumer greed and a decline in moral values as they are a reflection of a patriarchal society that discourages the education and economic self-sufficiency of women. Within this context, the bridegroom's family has the superior position in the marriage transaction and can structure it in ways to avoid criminal penalties under the legislation. In addition, it has the social support of law enforcement agents who are reluctant to enforce violations of dowry and dowry violence provisions. The bridegroom's family also has the social support of lower courts that are reluctant to give a woman property rights over the dowry, and to acknowledge the role of the violence of husbands and in-laws in denying these rights to her.

The legislation must be strengthened to increase the cost to the husband and in-laws of taking dowry and abusing the woman. It should ensure that the woman has property rights over the wealth that passes from her parents to the bridegroom's family. Stricter penalties need to be in force to punish the misappropriation of property by the husband and in-laws, and any violence perpetrated with the intent to do so.

Moreover, a presumption of cruelty should be legislated in cases where there is evidence that dowry passed to the husband or in-laws. This would make it easier for women and their families to seek a criminal remedy for abuse at all levels of severity, not just in cases where it leads to the death of the woman. Such legislation could protect women and essentially could increase the cost to husbands and in-laws for engaging in this conduct.

For legislation in these areas to be effective, however, the police must be held accountable for their misconduct, and must actively enforce the law. Therefore, strict penalties should be imposed on the police for failure to follow proper procedure.

---

[87] *See* Jethmalani & Dey, *supra* note [56], at 53–55.
[88] *See id.*
[89] *See Kumar*, A.I.R. 1986 S.C. at 253–254. The trial court accepted the oral declaration and convicted the husband. *See id.* at 253. The high court reversed the conviction, as it accepted the written declaration of the investigating officer. *See id.* at 258. On appeal, the Supreme Court convicted the husband. *See id.* at 266. It accepted Sudha Goel's oral declaration on the ground that it was corroborated by the reliable testimony of neighbors who witnessed the statement. *See id.* at 259.
[90] *See* Jethmalani & Dey, *supra* note [56], at 60.
[91] *See id.*

And, finally, the legislature should clear ambiguities in the legislation in order to guide courts in interpreting and applying the law to reach just results in dowry and dowry violence cases. Fortunately, the Supreme Court's realistic and innovative approach toward recognizing the rights of women over their property provides a glimmer of hope.

68

DEBORAH L. FORMAN

Unwed Fathers and Adoption: A Theoretical Analysis in Context

INTRODUCTION

Few family law cases have captured national attention like the story of "Baby Jessica."[1] A nation watched transfixed as she was dragged, sobbing, from the arms of her prospective adoptive mother, Roberta DeBoer, bound for a new home with her biological parents, Dan and Cara Schmidt. The nightmare began in Iowa when Cara, twenty-eight and unmarried, discovered she was pregnant.[2] Shortly after giving birth on February 8, 1991, she signed a consent form relinquishing her parental rights and allowing the DeBoers, a Michigan couple, to take custody of her daughter and petition to adopt her. Scott Seefeldt, named by Cara as the father of the child, also signed a consent form. Six days after the birth, Cara regretted her decision and sought to regain custody of her daughter. She began by informing Dan Schmidt that she believed *he* was the father of her child. Cara and Dan had been dating at the time she became pregnant. Although they continued to work for the same employer, Cara had never told Dan she was pregnant with his child.[3]

Cara and Dan immediately instituted proceedings in Iowa to reclaim their child. When Jessica was not yet one month old, Cara filed a request to revoke her consent to custody, confessing to the court that she had lied about the identity of the biological father. Shortly thereafter, Dan filed an affidavit of paternity and a petition to vacate the termination of paternal rights and to intervene in the adoption.[4] After hearing five courts affirm their right to Jessica, and some two years after they first sought relief, Dan and Cara finally got their child back. But the Schmidts' long-delayed victory appeared to many to be a defeat for Baby Jessica. Having lived virtually her entire life with the DeBoers, Jessica faced the task of adjusting at the age of two-and-a-half to life with parents who were essentially strangers to her.[5]

The media blitz that surrounded this case was unprecedented. An overwhelming majority of the public believed the courts erred in returning Jessica to the Schmidts.[6] Much of the attention focused on the biological father, Dan Schmidt. The Iowa courts based their decision denying the DeBoers' petition for adoption and requiring the return of Jessica on the protection of Dan Schmidt's rights.[7] Because his consent to the adoption had never been obtained, his parental rights could not be terminated absent a showing of abandonment or unfitness, neither of which was established by the evidence.[8]

Although the DeBoers failed to establish that Dan was an unfit father, neither was he a candidate for

---

[1]She is now called Anna Jacqueline Schmidt. Michele Ingrassia & Karen Springen, *She's Not Baby Jessica Anymore,* NEWSWEEK, Mar. 21, 1994, at 60, 60.

[2]The facts that follow are set forth in the various legal opinions issued in the case, specifically *In re* B.G.C., 496 N. W. 2d 239 (Iowa 1992), and DeBoer v. Schmidt (*In re* Baby Girl Clausen), 501 N. W. 2d 193 (Mich. Ct. App.), *aff'd,* 502 N. W. 2d 649 (Mich.), *stay denied sub nom.* DeBoer v. DeBoer, 114 S. Ct. 1, *and stay denied,* 114 S. Ct. 11 (1993).

[3]*In re B.G.C.,* 496 N. W. 2d at 247 (Snell, J., dissenting).

[4]*Id.* at 246

[5]Fortunately, the concerns about Jessica's welfare appear at this point to have been unfounded. She has apparently made a surprisingly smooth transition to her new home. . . .

[6]A USA Today/CNN Gallup Poll indicated that 78% of those polled believed the DeBoers should have retained custody. Sandra Sanchez, *Sentiment Strong against Jessica Ruling,* USA TODAY, Aug. 4 1993, *available in* LEXIS, Nexis Library, PAPERS File, at 1A; *Americans Think Jessica Sent to Wrong Home, Poll Finds,* S.F. CHRON., Aug. 5 1993, at A3, *available in* Westlaw, SF-CHRON Database; *Poll: Jessica Should Stay with DeBoers,* ROCKY MOUNTAIN NEWS, Aug. 5, 1993 at 38A, available in Westlaw, RM-NEWS Database.

[7]*See In re B.G.C.,* 496 N. W. 2d at 246 ("The parental rights of this father may not be dismissed without compliance with our termination statute, and the court correctly ordered that the petition for adoption be dismissed.").

[8]Dan had not "abandoned" Jessica because he took immediate legal action as soon as he learned he might be the father. *Id.* at 245–46.

"Father of the Year." He had had two other children out of wedlock whom he had failed to support and with whom he had only sporadic contact.[9] Dan was an easy target. He fit the classic public and legal image of the unwed father—irresponsible, unavailable, and unconcerned—and that is how the media portrayed him. The decision protecting his "rights" at the expense of Baby Jessica and the DeBoers seemed a travesty and prompted a public outcry in favor of amending the law to prevent such a miscarriage of justice from occurring again.[10]

Admittedly, the Baby Jessica case was a disaster, but it was caused less by the decision to protect an unwed father's rights than by procedural problems with the case. More fundamentally, the case reflected the complexity of interpersonal relationships and our societal confusion about what it means to be a parent, particularly a father. It may be tempting to read this case simply as an example of the court's reflexive recognition of a man's patriarchal "right" to retain his child as a form of property. To do so, however, is to vastly underestimate the complexity of the case and misconstrue the meaning of the decision and others like it.

During the course of the proceedings, Dan and Cara married and had another child. Dan now appears to be the kind of father our society venerates. Moreover, Dan is not unique. In the last decade, numerous cases have considered the rights of unwed fathers seeking to obtain custody of children relinquished for adoption by the mother. In doing so, they have both reflected and promulgated notions of fatherhood that carry substantive as well as symbolic content. Taken as a whole, these judicial decisions and the statutes they interpret reveal a profound ambivalence about fatherhood and a striking inability of the legal system to understand, respond to, and resolve complex family disputes.

This Article attempts to uncover the theoretical framework underlying the law's treatment of unwed fathers' rights in adoption and to explore alternative theories so that we may better approach the daunting task of doing justice in these troubling cases. I begin . . . by analyzing the theoretical and doctrinal basis for defining unwed fathers' rights as set forth in the Supreme Court's jurisprudence of fatherhood. [Later,] I explore the range of theoretical options for constructing fatherhood in these cases. At one end of the spectrum stands the historical view, which defines fatherhood exclusively in terms of marital status and declares that unwed fathers have few, if any, legal rights concerning their children. Although the Supreme Court has forced a shift away from this approach, . . . proponents of this theory persist. At the other end of the spectrum stands a theory of fatherhood that would grant men the same rights as women regarding adoption based solely on their biological relationship to the child. Finally, a third position has emerged that recognizes unwed men as fathers once they have met certain threshold requirements. Most commonly, the requirement is that the man have shown a willingness to assume his parental responsibilities.

This "substantial commitment" theory recognizes the ability and desire of fathers to assume their parental responsibilities, and it has the potential to encourage them to do so. In this respect, it captures the essence of parenting and embodies the basic values that should define that endeavor. Unfortunately, reflecting the societal and judicial ambivalence that surrounds the concept of fatherhood, courts have had great difficulty applying this standard in a meaningful way. Instead, they have tended to categorize unwed fathers reflexively, often in ways that ignore the reality of the interpersonal circumstances before them. . . .

THE SUPREME COURT'S JURISPRUDENCE OF FATHERHOOD

Historically, unwed fathers had no rights to custody, visitation, or recognition of their children.[11] Many state statutes recognized only the mother as the par-

[9] *Id.* at 245.

[10] Maryanne George & Tina Lam, *Jessica's Case May Spur New Adoption Laws: Bills Could Make Michigan a Model State*, Detroit Free Press, Aug. 4, 1993, at 1B, available in Westlaw, DET-FP Database.

[11] *See* Phillips v. Horlander, 535 S.W. 2d 72, 73 (Ky. 1975) (noting that, at common law, the putative father had support obligations, but "had no rights whatsoever of custody, visitation or support," and asserting that "[i]n all other respects the child, vis a vis the putative father, was a non person"); John R. Hamilton, Note, *The Unwed Father and the Right to Know of His Child's Existence*, 76 Ky. L.J. 949, 950 (1988) (explaining that "courts and legislatures traditionally have been openly hostile to the recognition of parental rights of unwed fathers").

ent of an illegitimate child.[12] She was presumed to have custody, and she alone could consent to making the child available for adoption.[13] In most states, the law did not even require that notice of the adoption be provided to an unwed father.[14]

A series of cases decided by the United States Supreme Court beginning in 1972 with *Stanley v. Illinois*[15] dramatically altered this longstanding doctrine and the legal meaning of fatherhood. In *Stanley,* Peter Stanley challenged the automatic termination of his parental rights upon the death of his children's mother. Peter Stanley had lived with Joan Stanley "intermittently" for eighteen years, and he was the father of her three children.[16] When she died, the children became wards of the state in a dependency proceeding instituted by the State of Illinois on the ground that they had "no surviving parent or guardian."[17] Unlike mothers and married fathers, Stanley was never afforded an individualized hearing to determine if he was unfit before losing custody of his children. Stanley was presumed unfit because he had not married Joan.[18]

Stanley appealed, claiming that Illinois had violated the Equal Protection Clause by depriving him of his children without holding an individualized hearing on his parental fitness.[19] The Supreme Court agreed, holding that to deny Stanley a hearing violated equal protection and due process.[20] In doing so, the Court placed unwed fathers in the same constitutional context as other parents. Peter Stanley, like any parent, had a "cognizable and substantial" interest in the care and custody of his children.[21] The Court eschewed reliance on formal family structure and acknowledged that bonds in nonmarital families "were often as warm, enduring, and important as those arising within a more formally organized family unit."[22]

Stanley was a relatively easy case.[23] Peter Stanley had lived with and acted as a father to his children for some eighteen years. He was thus both a biological father *and* a social father.[24] Because he played both these roles, the Court did not need to make clear whether Stanley's rights flowed from his biological connection to his children, from his social relationship with the children, from a quasi-marital relationship with Joan, or from the presence of a "family unit."[25] Subsequent cases would shed some light on this issue.

Quilloin v. Walcott[26] was the first Supreme Court decision to consider unwed fathers' rights in an adoption case. The petitioner, Leon Quilloin, sought to block adoption of his illegitimate child. The mother had married Randall Walcott and petitioned to allow him to adopt the child.[27] Under Georgia law, Quilloin's consent was not required for the adoption unless he had married the mother or had obtained a court order legitimating the child.[28] The Georgia court denied Quilloin's request for legitimation of the child and visitation and granted the adoption in the best interest of the child.[29] On appeal, the Supreme Court rejected Quilloin's claim that he was entitled to a parental veto of the adoption unless he was found unfit.[30]

Two facts appeared central to the Court's conclusion. First, allowing the adoption would "give full recognition to a family unit already in existence."[31]

---

[12]*See, e.g.,* Hamilton, *supra* note [11], at 980 n. 273 (describing an Illinois statute defining "parent" as "the father and mother of a legitimate child . . . or the natural mother of an illegitimate child" (quoting Illinois Adoption Act § 1 (E), 1959 Ill. Laws 1270 (repealed 1987))).

[13]2 Homer H. Clark, Jr., The Law of Domestic Relations In The United States § 21.2, at 572 (2d ed. 1987); *see also* Caban v. Mohammed, 441 U.S. 380, 390 n. 8 (1979) (noting that "[c]onsent of the unmarried father has never been required for adoption under New York law, although parental consent otherwise has been required at least since the late 19th century").

[14]*See* Hamilton, *supra* note [11], at 982 & n. 289 (discussing different statutory schemes that specify classes of unwed fathers who are entitled to receive notice).

[15]405 U.S. 645 (1972). The other cases include Quilloin v. Walcott, 434 U.S. 246 (1978); *Caban,* 441 U.S. at 380; Lehr v. Robertson, 463 U.S. 248 (1983); and Michael H. v. Gerald D., 491 U.S. 110 (1989).

[16]*Stanley,* 405 U.S. at 646.

[17]*Id.* at 649.

[18]*Id.* at 650.

[19]*Id.* at 646.

[20]*Id.* at 658.

[21]*Id.* at 652.

[22]*Id.* The Court also pointed out that when the state's procedure "explicitly disdains present realities in deference to past formalities, it needlessly risks running roughshod over the important interests of *both parent and child.*" *Id.* at 657 (emphasis added).

[23]*But see id.* at 665–66 (Burger, C.J. , dissenting) (arguing that the distinction between mothers and married fathers on the one hand and unwed fathers like Stanley on the other was justified).

[24]Janet L. Dolgin, *Just a Gene: Judicial Assumptions About Parenthood,* 40 UCLA L. Rev. 637, 650 (1993).

[25]*Id.* at 650–51.

[26]434 U. S. 246 (1978).

[27]*Id.* at 247.

[28]*Id.* at 249.

[29]*Id.* at 251.

[30]*Id.* at 255.

[31]*Id.*

This was not a case in which the state was "forc[ing] the breakup of a natural family" or in which the child was being placed with strangers.[32] Second, unlike married fathers, Quilloin had "never shouldered any significant responsibility with respect to the daily supervision, education, protection, or care of the child," and indeed did "not even now seek custody."[33] By contrast, a married father would have "borne full responsibility for the rearing of his children," at least while the marriage lasted.[34]

Clearly, biology alone did not entitle an unwed father to rights coequal with those of mothers or married fathers. Nor, apparently, did the existence of a social relationship between the father and child. Quilloin had visited the child on numerous occasions and had brought him gifts and toys; further, the child had expressed a desire to maintain contact with the father.[35] Perhaps the Court viewed these interactions as insufficiently substantial to constitute a social relationship worthy of constitutional protection. More likely, as Janet Dolgin argues, the Court was troubled by Quilloin's failure to form a "family unit" with the mother and child.[36]

Caban v. Mohammed,[37] decided the following year, supports this view. *Caban,* like *Quilloin,* involved an unwed father's attempt to veto a stepparent adoption. This time, the father, Abdiel Caban, unlike Leon Quilloin, had lived with the mother and their two children for several years.[38] Caban continued to see the children after the mother left him and married Kazim Mohammed in 1974.[39] The Mohammeds subsequently petitioned to adopt the children, and Caban and his new wife did the same.[40] The trial court granted the Mohammeds' adoption petition, severing all of Caban's parental rights.[41] Caban appealed, claiming that the operative statute, section 111 of the New York Domestic Relations Law,[42] violated equal protection by granting an unwed mother, but not an unwed father, the right to withhold consent to an adoption.[43] Caban also claimed the statute violated his due process right "to maintain a parental relationship" with his children absent a finding that he was unfit.[44]

Finding the statute to be a gender-based classification, the Court applied intermediate scrutiny.[45] While the Court recognized that the state's interest in ensuring the welfare of illegitimate children through adoption was "an important one," it rejected the state's contention that "a fundamental difference between maternal and paternal relations" justified the difference in treatment.[46] In the Court's view, "maternal and paternal roles are not invariably different in importance. . . . The present case demonstrates that an unwed father may have a relationship with his children fully comparable to that of the mother."[47] The Court did limit its holding, however, to cases in which the identity of the unwed father is known and he has "manifested a significant paternal interest in the child."[48] The Court expressly left open the question of whether a state could apply more stringent requirements for recognizing a paternal veto in cases involving newborns.[49] The language of *Caban* strongly suggests that the existence of a social father-child relationship is crucial to recognizing an unwed father's

---

[32]*Id.* (quoting Smith v. Organization of Foster Families for Equality & Reform, 431 U. S. 816, 862–63 (1977) (Stewart, J., concurring)).
[33]*Id.* at 256.
[34]*Id.* If the Court was suggesting that shouldering parental responsibility means daily caretaking, it is questionable whether many fathers in intact families, let alone divorced fathers, would qualify under that definition. Women do the vast majority of household work and day-to-day caretaking of children. ROBERT L. GRISWOLD, FATHERHOOD IN AMERICA 227 (1993).
[35]*Quilloin,* 434 U.S. at 251 & n. 11. In typical fashion, the Court discounted the child's desire to maintain a relationship with the biological father. The Court stated in the text that "[t]he child himself expressed a desire to be adopted," but relegated to a footnote the child's expressed desire to continue to visit with his biological father after the adoption. *Id.* at 251, 251 & n. 11.
[36]Dolgin, *supra* note [24], at 655.
[37]441 U. S. 380 (1979).
[38]*Id.* at 382.
[39]*Id.*
[40]*Id.* at 382–83.
[41]*Id.* at 383–84.
[42]N.Y. DOM. REL. LAW § 111 (McKinney 1977) (declared unconstitutional in *Caban,* 441 U.S. at 380) (amended 1980).
[43]*Caban,* 441 U.S. at 383–84.
[44]*Id.* at 385.
[45]To withstand intermediate scrutiny, "[g]ender-based distinctions 'must serve important governmental objectives and must be substantially related to achievement of those objectives.'" *Id.* at 388 (quoting Craig v. Boren, 429 U.S. 190, 197 (1976)).
[46]Id. at 388, 391.
[47]*Id.* at 389.
[48]*Id.* at 394; *see also id.* at 409 (Stevens, J. , dissenting) (emphasizing that "[the Court] confines its holding to cases such as the one at hand involving the adoption of an *older* child against the wishes of a natural father who previously has participated in the rearing of the child and who admits paternity" (emphasis in original)).
[49]*Id.* at 392 n. 11.

equal right to veto an adoption.[50] However, the prior existence of a family unit composed of Caban, the children, and the children's mother undoubtedly influenced the Court as well.[51]

The Court made even clearer its view of who qualifies as a father in yet another case involving an attempt by an unwed father to block a stepparent adoption. In *Lehr v. Robertson,*[52] Jonathan Lehr was the unwed father of a daughter, Jessica. Jessica's mother, Lorraine, married Richard Robertson a few months after Jessica's birth.[53] When Jessica was two years old, the Robertsons sought to adopt her. The trial court subsequently granted the adoption even though Lehr had never received notice of the proceeding.[54] Lehr had never filed with the putative father registry, which would have entitled him to notice of any adoption proceedings, nor did he meet any of the other statutory criteria for receiving notice.[55] Although he and Lorraine had lived together prior to Jessica's birth and he had visited her at the hospital, he had never lived with Lorraine or Jessica after the birth, nor was he named the father on the birth certificate or identified as such by Lorraine in a sworn statement.[56]

Lehr had, however, filed a paternity petition shortly after the adoption proceeding commenced. The court hearing the adoption petition was aware of the pending paternity petition, but did not believe notice was required.[57] Lehr challenged the granting of the adoption, claiming that he was entitled to notice and an opportunity to be heard under the Due Process and Equal Protection Clauses.[58] The Court rejected Lehr's claim. In doing so, the court set forth its clearest explication of fatherhood. "Fatherhood" depends on the existence of an actual social relationship with the child and particularly on the man's assumption of parental responsibilities.[59] According to the Court:

> When an unwed father demonstrates a full commitment to the responsibilities of parenthood by "com[ing] forward to participate in the rearing of his child," . . . his interest in personal contact with his child acquires substantial protection under the Due Process Clause. At that point it may be said that he "act[s] as a father toward his children." . . . But the mere existence of a biological link does not merit equivalent constitutional protection.[60]

The biological connection merely provides the man with a unique "opportunity" to develop a relationship with his child. This opportunity interest becomes a fully protected constitutional interest only if the father grasps it by developing an actual relationship with the child. The advent of this "biology plus" formula led many to conclude that the Court had ushered in a new era recognizing the rights of fathers based on the parent-child relationship.[61]

The Court's most recent pronouncement on the subject, *Michael H. v. Gerald D.,*[62] however, casts considerable doubt on that interpretation. In *Michael H.,* a plurality of the Court upheld a California statute that applied a conclusive presumption of paternity to the mother's husband if the child was conceived and born during the marriage.[63] The child's mother in this case, Carol, was married to Gerald D. at the time the child, Victoria, was conceived and born, but blood tests proved that Michael H. was Victoria's biological father.[64] Michael had lived with Carol and Victoria on and off for about a year and a half. During that time, Michael filed a filiation action to establish paternity and obtain visitation.[65] Carol signed a stipulation that Michael was Victoria's natural father, but she never filed it because soon thereafter she returned to Gerald. Gerald then moved to intervene in Michael's suit

---

[50]*See id.* at 393 (stating that "in cases such as this, where the father has established a substantial relationship with the child," there is no difficulty in determining paternity and thus no justification for disparate treatment).
[51]Dolgin, *supra* note [24], at 657–59.
[52]463 U.S. 248 (1983).
[53]*Id.* at 250.
[54]*Id.*
[55]*Id.* at 250–52.
[56]*Id.* at 252.
[57]*Id.* at 253.
[58]*Id.* at 250.
[59]*Id.* at 261.
[60]*Id.* (citations omitted) (quoting Caban v. Mohammed, 441 U.S. 380, 392, 389 n. 7 (1979)).
[61]*E.g.,* Hamilton, *supra* note [11], at 950, 960; Daniel C. Zinman, Note, *Father Knows Best: The Unwed Father's Right to Raise His Infant Surrendered for Adoption,* 60 FORDHAM L. REV. 971, 980 (1992).
[62]491 U.S. 110 (1989).
[63]*Id.* at 119–20.
[64]*Id.* at 114.
[65]A few months later, a court-appointed guardian ad litem filed a cross-complaint on behalf of Victoria "asserting that if she had more than one psychological or *de facto* father, she was entitled to maintain her filial relationship, with all of the attendant rights, duties, and obligations, with both." *Id.* at 114. The Court rejected her argument. *Id.* at 130–31.

and filed a motion for summary judgment based on the marital presumption.[66] The trial court ruled that Gerald was conclusively presumed to be Victoria's father and denied Michael paternity and visitation.[67]

The facts of *Michael H.* clearly satisfied the biology plus formula ostensibly established by the previous Supreme Court cases. Michael had lived with Victoria and held her out as his child.[68] Nonetheless, in a fragmented opinion, the Court held that denying Michael H. recognition as the child's father pursuant to the statute did not violate his substantive[69] or procedural[70] due process rights. In the plurality opinion, Justice Scalia conceded that Michael H. met the biology plus formula.[71] He concluded, however, that the *Stanley* line of cases did not rest on that rationale.[72] Justice Scalia rejected Michael's claim to a fundamental liberty interest in his relationship with Victoria on the grounds that history and tradition had never protected an adulterous father's relationship with his child. To the contrary, he noted that historically "our traditions have protected the marital family . . . against the sort of claim Michael asserts."[73]

The Supreme Court's definition of fatherhood after *Michael H.* is far from clear[74] and undoubtedly reflects the ambivalence society and the individual Justices feel about unwed fathers.[75] Janet Dolgin argues that *Michael H.* merely made explicit what was already implicit in the earlier fathers' rights cases—that to become a father, a man must do more than create a social relationship with the *child;* he must create a family, and that depends on maintaining an "appropriate" relationship with the mother.[76] While Justice Scalia certainly placed great emphasis on the "unitary," or marital, family to deny Michael recognition as a father, he left open the possibility that the Court might reach a different conclusion about an adulterous father's rights when the marital parents did not wish to raise the child themselves.[77] This reservation arguably undercuts Dolgin's interpretation; it would recognize a liberty interest in a man in Michael's position even though he had never formed a more traditional family with the mother and child than Michael did with Carol and Victoria.

Despite the confusion generated by this line of cases, some principles underlying the Court's theory of fatherhood can be discerned. First, the biological connection itself does not make a man a father.[78] To qualify as a father, the man must also establish a social relationship with the child.[79] Second, the satisfaction of

---

[66]*Id.* at 115; *see* CALIF. EVID. CODE ANN. § 621 (West 1966) (providing a conclusive presumption that the issue of a wife cohabitating with her husband is legitimate), *repealed by* 1992 Cal. Stat. ch. 162, § 8. This presumption of legitimacy was reenacted nearly verbatim subject to rebuttal through the administration of blood tests. 1992 Cal. Stat. ch. 162, § 10, codified at CAL. FAM. CODE ANN. §§ 7500–7501 (West 1993).

[67]*Michael H.,* 491 U.S. at 115–16.

[68]*Id.* at 114. Victoria's efforts through her guardian ad litem to maintain her relationship with Michael further evidence the existence of a developed father-child relationship. *E.g., id.* at 130–31; *supra* note [65].

[69]*Michael H.,* 491 U.S. at 129–30.

[70]*Id.* at 121.

[71]*Id.* at 123 ("Michael reads the landmark case of *Stanley v. Illinois* . . . and the subsequent cases . . . as establishing that a liberty interest is created by biological fatherhood plus an established parental relationship—factors that exist in the present case as well.").

[72]*Id.*

[73]*Id.* at 124. Justice O'Connor, in a concurring opinion joined by Justice Kennedy, agreed with all of Justice Scalia's opinion except footnote six, in which he adopted "a single mode of historical analysis" to identify liberty interests. *Id.* at 132 (O'Connor, J., concurring). Justice Stevens agreed with the result because § 4601 of the California Civil Code gave Michael H. an opportunity to obtain visitation rights. *Id.* at 133–34 (Stevens, J., concurring). However, Stevens disagreed with Scalia's substantive due process analysis and was willing to assume that Michael had a liberty interest in his relationship with Victoria. *Id.* at 133. The remaining Justices would have recognized Michael's liberty interest and found that the conclusive marital presumption violated that interest. *Id.* at 136, 151 (Brennan, J., dissenting); *id.* at 163 (White, J., dissenting).

[74]*See* Linda R. Crane, *Family Values and the Supreme Court,* 25 CONN. L. REV. 427, 453 n. 171 (1993) (discussing the varying levels of judicial scrutiny applied by the Court in the cases involving unwed fathers); David L. Batty, Note, Michael H. v. Gerald D.: *The Constitutional Rights of Putative Fathers and a Proposal for Reform,* 31 B.C. L. REV. 1173, 1203–04 (1990) (asserting in the wake of the decision that "the law of putative father's rights has been further confused and remains fraught with numerous unanswered questions"); Elizabeth A. Hadad, Note, *Tradition and the Liberty Interest: Circumscribing the Rights of the Natural Father*—Michael H. v. Gerald D., 56 BROOK. L. REV. 291, 314, 314–23 (1990) (criticizing the plurality opinion as "marked by confusion").

[75]*See generally* Crane, *supra* note [74] (exploring the extent to which public opinion and moral judgments affect judicial decisions regarding unwed fathers).

[76]*Dolgin, supra* note [24], at 669.

[77]*Michael H.,* 491 U.S. at 129 n. 7. This situation was considered in John E. v. Doe, 564 N.Y.S.2d 439, 442 (App. Div. 1990), *appeal denied,* 577 N.E.2d 1058 (N.Y. 1991). . . .

[78]In an oft-quoted passage, Justice Stewart wrote: "Parental rights do not spring full-blown from the biological connection between parent and child. They require relationships more enduring." Caban v. Mohammed, 441 U.S. 380, 397 (1979) (Stewart, J., dissenting) (adopted in Lehr v. Robertson, 463 U. S. 248, 260 (1983)).

[79]*Lehr,* 463 U.S. at 262–63. *But see* Hamilton, *supra* note [11] at 979 (arguing that under Lehr, the biological connection alone gives rise to a constitutional interest).

the biology plus formula is necessary but not sufficient to establish fatherhood. Whether a man will be recognized as a father will depend to a great extent on the nature of the relationship he has maintained with the mother and whether his recognition would disrupt any existing formal family units.[80] . . .

THE SUBSTANTIAL COMMITMENT STANDARD

. . . Many states today base recognition of unwed fathers' rights on a demonstrated commitment to assuming parental responsibilities. Some states express this idea through statutes that define certain acts that qualify an unwed man as a father.[81] Other states, often in interpreting such statutes, have adopted a more open-ended standard: If the father shows a substantial commitment to assuming the role of a parent, he will be considered a father and he will have all the rights of mothers and married fathers with respect to adoption of his child.[82] While the standard appears simple enough, in fact, it has proved quite difficult to apply in a manner consistent with its purposes and theoretical underpinnings. The discussion that follows will center largely on New York, because it has one of the most developed bodies of case law in this area.[83]

In the landmark case of *In re Raquel Marie X.,*[84] the New York Court of Appeals took an important step to ensure that genetic fathers would be able to grasp their "opportunity interest" and thereby achieve full constitutionally protected status as fathers. The court of appeals struck down a statute that required an unwed father to live with the child's mother for six continuous months prior to placement for adoption in order for his consent to be required for the adoption.[85]

The constitutionality of the statute had been challenged in two cases that were ultimately consolidated

[80]In *Michael H.,* Justice Scalia criticized Justice Brennan for viewing the relationship between Michael and Victoria in isolation when considering Michael's liberty interest. Michael H. v. Gerald D., 491 U.S. 110, 124 n. 4 (1989). For Scalia, Michael's relationship with Victoria's mother and the mother's relationship with her husband were valid considerations, *id.,* and the potential disruption of the formal family unit could also not be ignored, *see id.* at 129 ("Where . . . the child is born into an extant marital family, the natural father's unique opportunity [to develop a relationship with the child] conflicts with the similarly unique opportunity of the husband of the marriage; and it is not unconstitutional for the State to give categorical preference to the latter.").

[81]For example, South Carolina requires the consent of an unwed father if he has maintained substantial and continuous contact with the child, has lived with the child or the mother and held himself out to be the father, or has paid reasonable birth and pregnancy expenses. S.C. CODE ANN. § 20-7-1690 (Law. Co-op. Supp. 1992); *see* Abernathy v. Baby Boy, 437 S.E.2d 25, 29 (S.C. 1993) (holding that an unwed father "is entitled to constitutional protection not only when he meets the literal requirements" of the statute but also "when he undertakes sufficient prompt and good faith efforts to assume parental responsibility and to comply with the statute"). Other states require different acts to qualify an unwed man as a father. *See* MICH. COMP. LAWS ANN. § 710.39(2) (West 1993) (requiring court action to terminate a father's rights if the father "has established a custodial relationship with" or cared for the mother or child after the child's birth); N.C. GEN. STAT. § 48-6 (1992) (requiring consent if the putative father has "provided substantial financial support or consistent care with respect to the child and mother"); OKLA. STAT. tit. 10, § 60.6 (1991) (requiring consent unless the putative father failed to acknowledge or establish paternity, exercise parental rights and duties over the child, and provide financial support during pregnancy).

[82]Satisfaction of this standard generally means that the father's consent is required for adoption of his child or that his parental rights cannot be terminated absent a showing of unfitness. In some cases, the courts describe this as protecting the father's "opportunity interest" in developing a relationship with his child. *E.g.,* Steven A. v. Rickie M. (*In re* Adoption of Kelsey S.), 823 P.2d 1216, 1236 (Cal. 1992) (en banc); *Appeal of* H.R. (*In re* Baby boy C.), 581 A.2d 1141, 1177 (D.C. 1990); *In re* Baby Girl Eason, 358 S.E.2d 459, 462 (Ga. 1987); Steve B.D. v. Swan (*In re* Steve B.D.), 730 P.2d 942, 945–46 (Idaho 1986); *In re* Adoption of B.G.S., 556 So. 2d 545, 558–59 (La. 1990); *In re* Raquel Marie X., 559 N.E.2d 418, 423 (N.Y.), *cert. denied sub nom.* Robert C. v. Miguel T., 498 U.S. 984 (1990); Nale v. Robertson, 871 S.W. 2d 674, 680 (Tenn. 1994); *In re* Baby Girl K., 335 N.W.2d 846, 852 (Wis. 1983), *appeal dismissed,* 465 U.S. 1016 (1984); BDR v. BEB (*In re* Adoption of BBC), 831 P.2d 197, 199–201 (Wyo. 1992).

In other cases, the courts look for manifestation of commitment (or lack thereof) to evaluate whether the father has "abandoned" the child, making his consent to the adoption unnecessary. *E.g.,* Doe v. Roe (*In re* Adoption of Doe), 543 So. 2d 741, 745–46 (Fla.), *cert.denied,* 493 U.S. 964 (1989); *In re* B.G.C., 496 N.W.2d 239, 246 (Iowa 1992); *In re* Adoption of Klonowski, 622 N.E.2d 376, 378 (Ohio Ct. App. 1993).

In some states, an unwed father's demonstration of commitment will only earn him a right to notice and an opportunity to be heard on the child's best interests. *See, e.g.,* Hiskey v. Hamilton, 824 P.2d 1170, 1174 (Or. Ct. App.), *review denied,* 832 P.2d 455 (Or. 1992).

In determining whether to terminate a putative father's parental rights in an adoption proceeding, the Uniform Putative and Unknown Fathers Act provides for a multifactor analysis to ascertain whether the potential for developing a father-child bond should be protected. UNIF. PUTATIVE & UNKNOWN FATHERS ACT § 5, 98 U.L.A. 43 (Supp. 1993).

[83]California has also developed a considerable body of law that in many respects parallels New York's. *See infra* note [112].

[84]559 N.E.2d at 418.

[85]*Id.* at 419.

on appeal.[86] In *Raquel Marie,* the mother, Louise, and father, Miguel, had met in high school and had a child together. They lived together sporadically but frequently returned to their parents' homes during the course of their "tumultuous" relationship.[87] On May 26, 1988, Louise gave birth to Raquel Marie. On July 22, she relinquished the child for adoption.[88] Meanwhile, Miguel had instituted custody proceedings on July 19; he obtained an order of filiation on August 19. Miguel and Louise subsequently married on November 4, and Louise joined in opposing the adoption.[89] The family court denied the adoption, but the decision was reversed on appeal.[90]

In *Baby Girl S.,* the mother, Regina, was married but estranged from her husband when she became involved with the child's father, Gustavo.[91] Upon learning that Regina might be pregnant, Gustavo offered to marry her, but she declined, concerned that she might lose custody of her daughter.[92] Regina later lied to Gustavo that she was not pregnant, broke off their relationship, and began planning for the adoption of the baby.[93] Gustavo learned in January 1988 that Regina was pregnant after all.[94] In a phone conversation with Gustavo, she again denied that he was the father, and told him she planned to place the child for adoption.[95] He "begged her not to," then went to see her.[96] At this meeting, he told her he loved her and offered $8000 to help with expenses.[97] She again denied his paternity.

On March 2, 1988, approximately two months before the birth of the baby, Gustavo filed a petition in family court to establish paternity and obtain custody.[98] The judge in this proceeding entered a temporary restraining order prohibiting Regina from removing the child from the county and directed her to appear in court with the child on June 14.[99] On that day, she finally revealed she had placed the child for adoption.[100] Gustavo filed with the putative father registry the following day.[101] Meanwhile, on May 4, the adoptive parents had petitioned in the surrogate's court to adopt the child.[102] The court hearing the adoption case learned of Gustavo's petition on June 15.[103] After a trial in September 1989, the petition to adopt was denied,[104] and the adoptive parents appealed.[105]

The court held that neither Miguel nor Gustavo had a right to veto the adoptions under the terms of section 111(1)(e) of New York's Domestic Relations Law.[106] According to this section, the consent of an unwed father of a newborn was required only if he and the mother had lived together continuously for the full six months prior to placement of the child.[107]

On appeal, the court of appeals held that the "living together" requirement was unconstitutional because it failed to serve adequately any valid state interest.[108] The court recognized that the state had legitimate and substantial interests in protecting the

[86] *In re* Raquel Marie X., 545 N.Y.S.2d 379 (App. Div. 1989), *appeal dismissed,* 552 N. E.2d 168 (N.Y.), *and rev'd,* 559 N.E.2d 418 (N.Y.), *cert. denied sub nom.* Robert C. v. Miguel T., 498 U.S. 984 (1990): *In re* Adoption of Baby Girl S., *published in part at* 535 N.Y.S.2d 676 (Sur. Ct. 1988), *aff'd without opinion,* 543 N.Y.S.2d 602 (App. Div.), *appeal dismissed,* 547 N.E.2d 104 (N.Y. 1989), and *aff'd sub nom. In re* Raquel Marie X., 559 N.E.2d 418 (N.Y.), *cert. denied sub nom.* Robert C. v. Miguel T., 498 U.S. 984 (1990).

[87] *Raquel Marie,* 545 N.Y.S.2d at 380.

[88] *Id.*

[89] *Id.* at 381.

[90] *Id.*

[91] *In re* Adoption of Baby Girl S., 535 N.Y.S.2d 678, 678 (Sur. Ct. 1988), *aff'd without opinion,* 543 N.Y.S.2d 602 (App. Div.), *appeal dismissed,* 547 N.E.2d 104 (N.Y. 1989), *and aff'd sub nom. In re* Raquel Marie X., 559 N.E.2d 418 (N.Y.), *cert. denied sub nom.* Robert C. v. Miguel T., 498 U.S. 984 (1990).

[92] *Id.*

[93] *Id.* at 678. Much of the lower court's opinion concerned the fraudulent activities of the lawyer who arranged for the adoption and the adoptive couple. *See id.* at 678–80. The attorney had instructed Regina to lie at the adoption hearing about how she met the adoptive parents, because he had actually served as the "go-between." *Id.* at 678. He also advised Regina to use her maiden name on the consent form to prevent Gustavo from receiving notice of the proceeding if he had filed with the putative father registry. *Id.* at 679. When asked at the hearing to identify the father, she named her estranged husband. *Id.* at 677.

[94] *Id.* at 678.

[95] *Id.*

[96] *Id.*

[97] *Id.*

[98] *Id.* at 677.

[99] *Id.* at 677–78.

[100] *Id.* at 678.

[101] *Id.*

[102] *Id.* at 677.

[103] *Id.*

[104] *Id.* at 685.

[105] *In re* Raquel Marie X., 559 N.E.2d 418, 418 (N.Y.), *cert. denied sub nom.,* Robert C. v. Miguel T., 498 U. S. 984 (1990).

[106] *Id.* at 419.

[107] N.Y. Dom. Rel. Law § 111(1)(e) (McKinney 1988) (amended 1993). Section 111(1)(e) also required the father to make a public acknowledgment of paternity within the six months preceding placement and to pay pregnancy and birth expenses. *Id.*

[108] *Raquel Marie,* 559 N.E.2d at 427.

integrity of the adoption process and in distinguishing whether the unwed father's commitment was sufficient to warrant constitutional protection.[109] But the court viewed the "living together" requirement as "only tangentially related to the parental relationship" and so impermissible.[110]

In striking down this law, the court rejected a scheme that effectively based paternal rights on the mother's consent and began moving away from a vision of fatherhood defined by the man's relationship to the mother. *Raquel Marie* stressed that the proper focus for whether to recognize a father's rights should be on the relationship between the father and the child, not the father and the mother.[111] The court disconnected the father's rights from the quality of the father-mother relationship; the mother would no longer have exclusive control over the father's ability to assume a parental role. The New York court sent a message that genetic fatherhood was more than a mere biological link by giving real meaning and protection to the opportunity created by the genetic connection. So long as the father demonstrates his willingness and desire to assume all parental responsibilities, the court said, he should be treated as a father and have the right to veto an adoption.[112]

The application of the standard to Gustavo, the father in *In re Baby Girl S.,* one of the two cases consolidated on appeal in *Raquel Marie,* demonstrates how the standard worked. Gustavo had proposed marriage to the mother, repeatedly expressed concern for mother and child, offered support, and taken legal action to obtain custody.[113] The court rightly concluded that he had done "everything possible" to demonstrate his parental responsibility and thus was entitled to custody of his child.[114]

On the surface, the *Raquel Marie* decision looks like a crowd-pleaser. Men can feel gratified that they have acquired more "rights" and have moved a step closer to equality under family and adoption law. Feminists, too, can take heart that the court has taken an enlightened view of rights in this context. Rather than granting fathers rights as entitlements, the court insisted that these fathers earn their rights by demonstrating responsibility and commitment to parenting. In this respect, the court achieves the feminist goal persuasively articulated by Katharine Bartlett of transforming rights claims based on property and exchange notions into "a responsibility-based standard."[115] Also, by encouraging paternal responsibility and caretaking, the court facilitates the demise of oppressive sex-role stereotypes.

Not everyone supports the decision, however. Barbara Woodhouse argues that the *Raquel Marie* approach "reflect[s] a legal tradition of possessive individualism" that treats children as property.[116] She states that the overemphasis on individualism protects an adult's abstract "rights" at the expense of the child's experience and welfare.[117] Standards like *Raquel Marie* foster family atomization and focus on individual family members, rather than on an "interdependent" family system.[118] In Woodhouse's view,

---

[109] *Id.* at 425.
[110] *Id.* at 426.
[111] *Id.*
[112] *Id.* The California Supreme Court adopted a similar standard in Steven A. v. Rickie M. (*In re* Adoption of Kelsey S.), 823 P. 2d 1216, 1236 (Cal. 1992). In this case the court held unconstitutional a statute that granted presumed father status (a necessary qualification if an unwed father wished to veto an adoption) only if the unwed father, among other criteria, received the child into his home and held the child out as his natural child. *Id.* at 1219–20. As in *Raquel Marie,* the court struck down the statute because it allowed the mother unilaterally to prevent the father from achieving presumed status and thus enabled the state to terminate his rights merely on a "best interest" showing. *Id.* at 1236.
[113] *In re* Adoption of Baby Girl S., *published in part at* 535 N.Y.S.2d 676, 678 (Sur. Ct. 1988), *aff'd without opinion,* 543 N.Y.S.2d 602 (App. Div.), *appeal dismissed,* 547 N.E.2d 104 (N.Y. 1989), and *aff'd sub nom. In re* Raquel Marie X., 559 N.E.2d 418 (N.Y.), *cert. denied sub nom.* Robert C. v. Miguel T., 498 U.S. 984 (1990).

[114] *Raquel Marie,* 559 N.E.2d at 428.
[115] [Katherine T. Bartlett, "Re-Expressing Parenthood," 98 Yale L. J. (1988)], at 324, 339–40. Indeed, the *Raquel Marie* court cites Bartlett. *Raquel Marie,* 559 N.E.2d at 423–24. Bartlett recognizes that some may view her position on this issue as not feminist because it does not explicitly enhance women's rights and power. She provides an eloquent response to this potential charge:

> The criticism that my approach is inadequate in advancing the empowerment of women reflects, in large part, a disagreement over tactics and vision. Like other feminists, I object to the genderized hierarchy that oppresses women. But I am not indifferent to the means by which we seek to end that oppression. Rules explicitly designed to allow women to win custody disputes on their own terms for the sake of enhancing the power of women would perpetuate the male norms of power and advantage, while doing nothing to further a transformation and reordering of values associated with childrearing that is critical to any credible progressive vision of a better world.

Bartlett . . . at 339–40. . . .
[116] [Barbara B. Woodhouse, "Hatching the Egg: A Child-Centered Perspective on Parents' Rights," *14 Cardozo L. Review* (1993)], at 1809.
[117] *Id.* at 1810.
[118] *Id.* at 1800, 1852–55.

this approach "isolates" the child "from its contextual surroundings."[119]

The problem with Woodhouse's critique is that she fails to recognize that, in many of these cases, at the time of the adoption no interdependent *family* really exists. The court's emphasis on individual rights does not cause the breakdown of these families or prevent them from forming; real interpersonal conflicts do. While Woodhouse aptly recognizes that the courts in these cases regularly ignore the children's experience, she overlooks an important point.

The jurisprudential emphasis on the father's "rights" hides an assumption that underlies the constitutional, common-law, and statutory doctrine in this area: The preference for biological parents is an expression of our belief, however misguided, that parents are inclined naturally to best take care of their children.[120] This premise underlies the law that protects parents from having their children taken by the state or private parties because others may be "better" parents. It is not simply a question of vindicating adult desires.

This inability to recognize that the "parental rights" perspective can incorporate the child's interests has led to increasing polarization of the positions, epitomized by the debate waged by the majority and dissenting Presiding Justice Tully in *In re Doe*.[121] The majority consciously and vociferously styled itself as the savior and protector of Baby Richard, the child who was the subject of this custody dispute between a biological father, now married to the child's biological mother, and the adoptive parents. According to the majority:

> [T]he time has long past [sic] when children in our society were considered the property of their parents. Slowly, but finally, when it comes to children even the law has rid itself of the *Dred Scott* mentality that a human being can be considered a piece of property "belonging" to another human being. . . . Thus, . . . we start with the premise that Richard is not a piece of property with property rights belonging to either his biological or adoptive parents. Richard "belongs" to no one but himself.
>
> . . . [I]t is his best interest . . . that come[s] before anything else, including the interests and rights of biological and adoptive parents.[122]

While the majority's rhetoric has a certain appeal, it leads to a questionable result based on a skewed presentation of the facts and a seriously strained application of the law. As the dissent pointed out, "[t]he majority, in its misguided fervor to champion 'injustice,' has patently distorted and slanted the actual facts of this case."[123] Presiding Justice Tully's rhetoric is equally dramatic. He writes:

> We are so overwrought by "pop culture" values in our society that we can allow, without hesitating, the concept now being promulgated, without a loud cry of "Something is wrong here." This child should be reunited with his biological parents. The mish-mash that society has somehow created in the year 1993 goes against core Judeo-Christian principles, which for thousands of years have supported the family unit above all else. Moreover, this concept is universal and transcends all national, ethnic and religious lines. We are now elevating social workers, attorneys and media reaction above familial rights to determine the best interests of children. . . .

The flaw in the *Raquel Marie* analysis lies not in the standard—which recognizes paternal rights based on demonstrated commitment to the child—but in the application of the standard. As Woodhouse astutely observes, courts deciding these cases have an amazing ability to ignore children's experiences,[124] but she fails to see that the courts often ignore the experiences of the adults involved as well. The courts' relentless need to put fathers and mothers into some neat niche leads them to create distorted factual stories and legal constructs divorced from the reality of people's lives. . . .

---

[119] *Id.* at 1852.

[120] *See Appeal of* H.R. (*In re* Baby Boy C.), 581 A.2d 1141, 1184 (D.C. 1990) (Rogers, C. J., concurring) (suggesting that the biological parent presumption "merely reflects the wisdom of human experience that children ordinarily will be best cared for by those bound to them by the ties of nature").

[121] 627 N.E.2d 648 (Ill. App. Ct.), *rev'd,* No. 76063, 1994 WL 265086 (Ill. June 16, 1994). . . .

[122] *John Doe,* 726 N.E.2d at 651–52.

[123] *Id.* at 656 (Tully, P. J., dissenting).

[124] Woodhouse, *supra* note [116], at 1855.

69

MARY L. SHANLEY

Fathers' Rights, Mothers' Wrongs? Reflections on Unwed Fathers' Rights and Sex Equality

The recent case of *Baby Girl Clausen,* involving a custody dispute between the biological parents, Cara Clausen and Daniel Schmidt of Iowa, and the adoptive parents, Roberta and Jan DeBoer of Michigan, over who should be recognized as the legal parents of baby Jessica, focused national attention on the issue of what rights biological unwed fathers may have to custody of their infant offspring. When Cara Clausen, at the time unmarried, gave birth to a baby girl, she gave her irrevocable consent to the child's adoption two days after its birth, as did the man she named as the child's father on the birth certificate. Within weeks, however, Clausen regretted her decision and informed Daniel Schmidt that he was the baby's father. Schmidt responded by filing a petition to establish paternity, and initiating legal action to block the adoption. Schmidt contended that a biological father has a right to custody of his child unless it is shown that he is "unfit" to be a parent. After some two years of litigation, Michigan declared it did not have jurisdiction in the matter and Iowa proceeded to enforce its decree that Schmidt's parental rights had never properly been terminated and the child had to be returned to his physical custody.[1]

Many of those who commented on the case asked whether Daniel Schmidt's alleged rights should be enforced in the face of the trauma Jessica, now a toddler, would suffer in being removed from the only family she had known. While this matter merits serious attention, I focus on a different issue raised by the case, namely the basis and nature of an unwed biological father's right to veto an adoption decision of an unwed mother. This question was obscured in the case of *Baby Girl Clausen* because Daniel Schmidt initiated his action with the full cooperation of Cara Clausen, who had come to regret her decision. But it was *his* rights that the Iowa courts upheld, holding that an unwed biological father had a right to preclude an adoption initiated by the biological mother or the state.

There have been a significant number of cases in which an unwed biological father has sought to reverse the biological mother's decision to allow a child to be adopted, statutory provisions stipulating under what conditions an unwed biological father's consent is necessary vary greatly from state to state, and legal thinking on the matter is quite unsettled.[2] Many courts continue to apply the traditional rule that they must consider the "best interest" of the child in making any decision about custody. Supporters of biological fathers' rights, by contrast, argue that when the biological mother does not wish to retain custody, the biological father's claim automatically takes precedence over that of some "stranger" or potential adoptive parent (Boyd 1990; Buchanan 1984; Eveleigh 1989; Hamilton 1987–88; Raab 1984; Serviss 1991; Steward 1990; Zinman 1992).[3] Interestingly, some advocates of women's rights have also criticized the best interest standard as too subject to the biases of individual judges but have argued that women's unique role in human gestation and childbirth, as well as various aspects of their social and economic vulnerability, dictate that an unwed biological mother must be able to make the decision to have her child adopted without interference by the father or the state (Becker 1989; Erickson 1984; Erickson 1990, 39 n. 22; Rothman 1989). According to this view, neither the biological mother nor the state has an obligation to seek the biological father's consent to the adoption decision, or even to inform him of his paternity. From such a perspective, statutes that require biological mothers, but not biological fathers, to consent to the adoption of their newborn infant do not deny men equal protection. The debate between advocates of these two perspectives takes us to the difficult issue of what, indeed, should be the grounding of *anyone's* claim to parental rights.

From my perspective, neither the "fathers' rights" nor the "maternal autonomy" position provides a fully satisfactory basis for thinking about the custodial claims of unwed biological parents. I am persuaded by considerations advanced by advocates in both camps that the best interest standard is unsuitable for cases involving newborns surrendered by their mothers for adoption, in part because that standard does not adequately recognize the claims of biological paternity, and in part because it is difficult to guard adequately against the biases of individual judges . . .

FIT FATHERS AND COMPETENT MOTHERS: WHO SHALL DECIDE WHEN BIOLOGICAL PARENTS DISAGREE?

An Unwed Father's Right to "Grasp the Opportunity" to Become a Parent: The Pursuit of Abstract Equality

In recent years some biological fathers have claimed that, because of the mother's lack of cooperation, they have not found any way to meet the Court's demand, articulated in *Lehr,* that a biological father who wants to retain his parental rights and "enjoy the blessings of the parent-child relationship" act to "grasp the opportunity" to develop a relationship with his offspring by assuming some "responsibility for the child's future" (463 U.S. 248 at 262). Should a biological father have the opportunity to veto an adoption regardless of the wishes of the mother? Should adoption proceedings be precluded until the father has been heard? What considerations should guide us as we try to evaluate such issues? To answer these questions we need to think about both the basis of claims for custodial rights and the relative claims of biological mothers and fathers outside of marriage.

The argument that the biological father must be given custody when the biological mother chooses not to raise the child is grounded first of all in the conviction that parenthood is a significant good in the lives of men as well as women. Fathers might wish to raise their children for the same reasons mothers do—sharing intimacy and love, nurturing a child to adulthood, seeing one's genetic inheritance survive into the next generation, and passing on ethnic and religious traditions. A commitment to gender neutrality led most states to abandon an automatic maternal preference if mother and father, married or unmarried, each sought custody, and the same commitment would suggest that the law presume that the law must require the consent of *both* parents before the child can be adopted.

Various commentators support an unwed biological father's right to veto the adoption of his child on the grounds that fathers have a fully comparable interest to that of mothers in exercising parental rights and responsibilities. Claudia Serviss says all parents have "a constitutionally-protected opportunity interest in developing a parent-child relationship" (Serviss 1991, 788). John Hamilton argues that all unwed fathers have a right to be notified by the state of the existence of their offspring and be heard before any adoption can proceed, and that the state may therefore require the biological mother to identify the biological father (Hamilton 1987–88), while Daniel Zinman insists that the state must allow a biological father to take custody of his child when the biological mother has relinquished her rights, unless he is shown to be unfit (Zinman 1992). In a recent California case, *In the Matter of Kelsey S.,* the California Supreme Court appeared to agree that a gender-neutral standard should prevail. It held unconstitutional a statute that gave unwed mothers and legally recognized or "presumed" fathers a greater say in preadoption proceedings to terminate parental rights than it gave to unwed biological fathers. The court declared that the statute rested on a "sex-based distinction" that bore no relationship to any legitimate state interest once the child was outside the mother's body and she had decided to relinquish custody.[4]

The presumption of fitness for biological parents also avoids the dangers of subjective judgment and cultural prejudice that seem unavoidable in attempts to determine the child's best interest (Bartlett 1988, 303). One supporter of an unwed father's right to custody argues that a best interest determination "is subject to abuse and may lead to paternalistic infringement on the parent-child relationship in the name of the child's welfare. Given the long waiting list of adoptive parents that exists today and the traditional preference for rearing a child in a two-parent home, a best interest test is a no-win situation for the unwed father of a newborn with whom he has not yet had the opportunity to develop an emotional tie."[5] In 1987, the Georgia Supreme Court explicitly rejected the best interest test in favor of a fitness standard on the grounds that it was presumptively unfair to compare the putative father with adoptive parents with whom the child had never lived. It held that "If [the father] has not abandoned his opportunity interest, the standard which must be used to determine his rights to legitimate the child is his fitness as a parent to have custody of the child. If he is fit he must prevail" (*In re Baby Girl Eason,* 257 Ga. 292 at 297, 358 S.E. 2d 459 at 463 [1987], qtd. in Zinman 1992, 993–94).

Use of the best interest test in cases of an infant who has lived with no adult care-giver for any appreciable period of time should be changed not only in the interests of sex equality but of family diversity as well. The best interest standard invites the court to make judgments about the relative merit of a whole array of "lifestyle" issues that are not subject to scrutiny when an unwed biological father does not contest a biological mother's wish to retain custody of her child. A "fitness" standard applied to unwed biological fathers would avoid the possibility that an adoption decision might rest on a judge's preference that a child be raised in a two-parent household rather than by a single male, or a judge's prediction that middle-class professionals will give a child more "advantages" than the child would receive in a working-class home. If no action (or failure to act) by the biological father shows that he should not be entrusted with custody, then value judgments concerning different lifestyles and household arrangements should be precluded from inappropriately influencing the custody decision concerning the placement of a newborn infant.

To argue that the courts should abandon the best interest standard when an unwed biological father wishes to raise an infant does not, however, imply that the only relevant consideration is the biological father's "fitness." The question of whether an unwed biological father shall have a right to custody of his newborn infant is not about parental rights *tout court,* but also or alternatively about an unmarried woman's authority to decide who shall take custody of her newborn child. For the biological father to assume custody, the biological mother's expressed wishes concerning the child's placement will of necessity be overridden. Arguments that a biological father should be able to veto the adoption decision of the biological mother and assume custody unless proven to be unfit run up against counter arguments that the courts should defer to an unwed biological mother with respect to placement of her child. It is to these considerations that I now turn.

An Unwed Mother's Claim to Decisional Autonomy: Taking Context Seriously

Arguments in favor of the "fitness" standard for unwed biological fathers falsely assume that once a biological mother has surrendered the child for adoption she has no further relevant wishes with respect to custody. Defenders of an unwed biological father's right to veto an adoption often contrast what they portray as his laudable desire to assume custody and to care for the child with the biological mother's uncaring decision not to raise the child herself. The image of the "bad mother," and the assumption that if the mother chooses not to raise the child, she must be indifferent to its fate, hover just beneath the surface of such depictions. The notion that once a mother decides to relinquish her child for adoption she can have no further relevant concerns distorts and denigrates both her experience of pregnancy and the nature of her decision.[6] But relinquishment of the newborn for adoption may reflect any of a wide array of circumstances: lack of money or job prospects, youth or immaturity, feelings of inadequacy or isolation. While some women may be indifferent to the placement of their children, in most cases relinquishment is not a sign that the biological mother does not care for the child; in most cases women agonize over the adoption decision and try to make certain to do what is best for their offspring (Sweeney 1990; Erickson 1984, 459 and n. 65; Erickson 1990, 38 n. 44).

A woman's decision to place her biological child for adoption also does not mean that she is indifferent about the question of who raises the child. The argument that an unwed biological father should be preferred to adoptive parents because they are "strangers" to the child inappropriately ignores the biological mother's preference that the child be adopted through an agency or private placement rather than placed with a guardian or in the father's custody. If the mother has had very little contact with the father beyond the act of intercourse that led to her pregnancy, the father may be as much a *social* "stranger" to her and the child as the adoptive parents, and his claim rests on genetics alone. Contrasting the biological father's rights to those of strangers obscures the fact that the fundamental or precipitating disagreement about custody is not between the adoptive parents and the biological father, but between the two biological parents. And if the mother has known the father over a considerable period of time, her unwillingness to make him the custodial parent needs to be examined to see why she feels as she does, just as it would be if the parents were married.

Are there any reasons to weigh the biological mother's wishes about who shall (or shall not) take custody of the child more heavily than those of the biological father ? At the time of birth the relationship of biological father and mother to the child is neither biologically nor socially symmetrical. She has borne the child for nine months, activity for which there is no precise male analog; indeed, no one else can perform functions analogous to those of gestation.[7] The biological mother's "expectant" state has affected both her own physiological experience and the ways in which others view and interact with her.[8] The Supreme Court has recognized the significance of this asymmetry between mother and father during pregnancy by holding that a wife is not required to notify her husband or obtain his consent before getting an abortion (*Planned Parenthood of Southeastern Pennsylvania v. Casey,* 112 S. Ct. 2791 [1992]). To what extent should asymmetry of biological function during gestation affect the right to make custodial decisions concerning a newborn?

Some theorists argue that the fact that only the woman is engaged in the physical gestation of the human fetus should make a decisive difference in the rights to be accorded unwed mothers and fathers in deciding on the custody of their offspring. According to sociologist Barbara Katz Rothman, parenting is a social relationship and parental rights are established by care-giving. In her view, the biological difference between mother and father is crucial and conclusive in establishing their respective claims for custody of newborns: "Infants belong to their mothers at birth because of the unique nurturant relationship that has existed between them up to that moment. That is, birth mothers have full parental rights, including rights of custody, of the babies they bore" (Rothman 1989, 254). By the same token, other persons with a genetic tie to the child do not have such rights: "We will not recognize genetic claims to parenthood, neither as traditional 'paternity' claims nor as genetic maternity in cases of ovum donation" (254). Rothman would have the gestational mother's absolute claim last for six weeks after giving birth, and so the adoption decision would rest solely in the mother's hands during that period. After six weeks, "Custody would go to the nurturing parent in case of dispute" (255). Rothman emphasizes that her preference for the gestational mother rests on her understanding of pregnancy as "a social as well as a physical relationship," and that "*any* mother is engaged in a social interaction with her fetus as the pregnancy progresses" (97). Neither the physical interdependence nor the social relationship between mother and fetus can be fully shared by any other adult, no matter how attentive. Actual care-giving, not genetic connection, creates familial bonds and, in this case, Rothman argues, custodial rights.

Others also have argued that parental rights usually are not symmetrical and that the social or biological bonds (or both) between mothers and children should give mothers the authority to decide who should have custody of their offspring. Nancy Erickson argues that the liberty interest that a parent has "to control the care, custody, and upbringing of the child" pertains only to the mother (not the father) of a newborn. At birth the mother is "not only the 'primary caretaker parent,' she is the only caretaker parent" because of her role during pregnancy (Erickson 1984, 461–62). Thinking about custody of older children of parents who divorce, Mary Becker argues that mothers are so frequently the primary caregivers of their children that it makes sense to adopt an automatic "maternal deference" standard rather than hold a hearing to try to determine what arrangement would be in the child's best interest: "When the parents cannot agree on a custody outcome, the judge should defer to the mother's decision on custody provided that she is fit, using the 'fitness' standard applicable when the state is arguing for temporary or permanent separation of parents and children in intact families" (Becker 1992, 971). Becker is not terribly worried that giving primacy to the mother's wishes might in some instances permit a woman to deprive a caring father of custody: "A maternal deference standard would recognize that mothers, as a group, have greater competence and standing to decide what is best for their children . . . than judges, fathers, or adversarial experts. . . . Mothers will sometimes make wrong decisions, but in the aggregate they are likely to make better decisions than the other possible decision makers" (972). Becker's reasoning applied to custodial decisions affecting newborns suggests that courts should defer to a biological mother, both because the woman has provided direct nurture to the fetus during pregnancy, and because, on average, biological mothers' decisions are likely to be as good as or better than those of anyone else.

Martha Fineman, similarly very critical of the best interest standard, would replace it with a "primary care-giver" standard (Fineman 1991). Fineman argues that the best interest of the child standard frequently disadvantages mothers by looking to the likely future financial resources of father and mother. It would be more appropriate (both in terms of fairness to the parents and of the child's emotional well-being), Fineman asserts, to look instead at who has actually given the child physical and emotional care up to the present. In most, but not all, instances, this will be the mother. Although Fineman does not discuss custody of newborns, if courts were to apply the primary care-giver standard to the kinds of disputes I am discussing, it would suggest that the mother who has borne and given birth should make the custody decision concerning the infant.

Many arguments for giving an unwed biological father custody of an infant child whom a biological mother wishes to have adopted not only ignore the physical and social experiences of pregnancy but also invite no inquiry at all into the conditions under which the woman became pregnant. Just as inquiry into the biological father's actions during the mother's pregnancy is permissible to encourage paternal nurturance and to counter notions of male ownership of children, so attention to the circumstances under which conception took place is reasonable to ensure that the child was not conceived as the result of abusive behavior toward the mother.[9] In trying to determine which parent's wishes concerning adoption should prevail, it would not be unreasonable for the law to regard an unmarried biological father who had been in a long-term relationship with the mother or shared living expenses with her and their offspring differently than one who engaged in casual or coercive sex (perhaps a "date rape" that the woman did not prosecute) or deceived the woman (perhaps saying he was single when he was in fact married) or willfully ignored the fact that the girl was under the age of consent.

While they refute the patriarchal premise of many fathers' rights arguments that a father has a right to custody of his biological offspring unless he is proven to be "unfit," many arguments that mothers should have the exclusive right to decide to place their offspring for adoption run the risk of treating some men unjustly and of locking both women and men into traditional gender roles. If parental claims are properly grounded in the first instance in a *combination* of biological ties and nurturance, then while a father's genetic link per se does not give him parental rights, it becomes a reason *to look to see* if he has attempted to assume responsibility for the child, and has done so without interfering with the mother's well-being. If, and only if, he has acted accordingly, should a court recognize his claim to custody.

RETHINKING THE BASES OF PARENTAL RIGHTS: RESPONSIBILITY, RELATIONSHIP, AND CARE

If unwed biological fathers should have some custodial claim to their children but not the extreme claim qualified only by "fitness," what standards should define the extent of their rights? The law needs to adopt stringent criteria for assessing the biological father's intention to take responsibility for and act as a parent to his child even prior to birth. Such criteria will require us to shift our thinking and mode of argumentation away from an emphasis on parents as owners to parents as stewards, from parental rights to parental responsibilities, and from parents viewed as individuals to parents as persons-in-relationship with a child.[10]

Many discussions of the "rights" of biological mothers and fathers reveal the inherent tension in liberal theory and legal practice between protecting individuals and their freedoms and protecting and fostering those relationships which in fundamental ways constitute every individual.[11] The language of parental rights emphasizes the parent's status as an autonomous rights-bearer, and invoking individual rights has proved useful in minimizing the role of the state in people's procreative and child-rearing decisions. For example, begetting, bearing, and raising children are for many people part of the good or fulfilling life that the liberal state is obligated to protect. No one seriously proposes that children should simply be assigned at birth to the best possible or next available parents without regard to who begot and bore them. Courts have recognized the importance of intergenerational ties for many people and protected the liberty to procreate and parent a child not only in custody cases like *Stanley* and *Caban,* but in decisions prohibiting forced sterilization, such as *Skinner v. Oklahoma* (316 U.S. 535 [1942]).[12] And since biological parents have a variety of incentives to care for their children to the best of their ability, assigning custody to them simultaneously protects children's rights as well as those of adults and sets important bounds to the exercise of state power.[13]

Yet in other contexts, use of the language of parental rights inappropriately focuses on the individual parent rather than on the relationships that are inherent in being a "parent." Katharine Bartlett has advocated recasting many legal disputes that involve parents and children in such a way that the language used does not pit one "right" against another, but emphasizes the view that parenthood implies deep and sustained human connection and must be grounded in adult responsibility for children: "The law should force parents to state their claims . . . not from the competing, individual perspectives of either parent or even of the child, but from the perspective of each parent-child relationship. And in evaluating (and thereby giving meaning to) that relationship, the law should focus on parental responsibility rather than reciprocal 'rights.'" Bartlett suggests that language based more explicitly on open-ended responsibility toward children would capture the nature of the parent-child relationship better than discussions framed in terms of parental rights (Bartlett 1988, 295).[14]

When someone is considered in the role of parent, he or she cannot be viewed apart from the child that makes him or her a parent; an "autonomous" (in the sense of unfettered or atomistic) individual is precisely what a parent is *not*. A "parental right" should not be viewed as pertaining to an individual per se, but only to an individual-in-relationship with a dependent child. It is therefore entirely appropriate for the law to require that efforts be made to establish a relationship before a parental right can be recognized.

Asking a court to determine whether a man or woman has made efforts to establish a parental relationship with a newborn is, however, fraught with difficulties that involve the different physical relationship of biological father and mother to the fetus during pregnancy, the social relationships between biological father and mother, and the need to minimize both intrusiveness by the courts and subjectivity in their judgments. Indeed, part of the attraction of both the paternal fitness test and the maternal deference standard is that each of these provides a fixed criterion for determining an unwed biological father's custodial claim. Unfortunately, however, the efficiency and clarity of each of these criteria are purchased at the cost of reducing legal discourse about family relationships to an assertion of either fathers' or mothers' rights.

My proposal that an unwed biological father have an opportunity to establish through his behavior his intention to parent his offspring tries to minimize the legal effects of biological asymmetry without ignoring altogether the relevance of sexual difference. I assume that an unwed biological mother has demonstrated a parental relationship with her newborn by virtue of having carried the fetus to term, while an unwed biological father may be required to show actual involvement with prenatal life if he wishes to have custody of the child. The model or norm of "parent" in this case, therefore, is established not by the male who awaits the appearance of the child after birth, but by the pregnant woman (Eisenstein 1988, 79–116).

Some people might object that assuming maternal care simply by the fact of pregnancy is invalid, especially in cases in which the mother has taken drugs or engaged in other behavior that might have a harmful effect on the fetus. As Cynthia Daniels has pointed out, the image of the pregnant drug addict is deeply disturbing, "representing as it does the paradox of a woman simultaneously engaged in the destruction of life (addiction) and the perpetuation of life (pregnancy)" (Daniels 1993, 98). In such cases, should the mother forfeit either her claim to custody or her claim to make the decision to place the child for adoption?[15]

It is tempting to blame, and to seek to punish, the pregnant addict when confronted by the needs of children who are physically or mentally impaired as a result of their exposure to harmful substances during gestation. It is important, however, to ascertain just what the drug-dependent mother is guilty of, and whether punishment or taking away her right to be heard concerning custody of her child is an appropriate response to her behavior.[16] In cases of maternal drug use, it is sometimes difficult to distinguish whether damage to a newborn resulted from drugs taken by the mother or from other factors such as drugs taken by the father, environmental pollutants (particularly high in poor neighborhoods), and malnutrition.[17] What is the degree of a woman's culpability if, like many drug-addicted pregnant women, she sought treatment for her addiction, but was turned away?[18] Even if in a particular case it could be ascertained that fetal damage was uniquely caused by drugs the mother took, it does not follow that she was so indifferent to the well-being of her child that she should be deprived of her right to be heard with respect to placing the child for adoption. The care the pregnant woman has given the fetus through bearing it to term and the harm her actions have caused it cannot be separated; both involve the biology and chemistry of gestation, the passage of materials across the placenta through the bloodstream. To see the pregnant drug addict as a child abuser rather than a person who is herself in need of medical treatment is to ignore the inseparability of mother and fetus during pregnancy (see Young 1994). The mother's decision to place the child for adoption will often be made in an effort to protect the child from harm now that it can be cared for outside her body.

The different biological roles of men and women in human reproduction make it imperative that law and public policy "recognize that a father and mother must be permitted to demonstrate commitment to their child in different ways."[19] What actions might a court accept as indications that an unwed biological father had made every effort to act as a parent to the child? Recent legislative efforts in New York State show that this question is not easily answered. In 1990, in *In re Raquel Marie X.* (76 NY 2d387 [1990]), the New York Court of Appeals struck down a statute that stipulated that only a father who had established a home with the mother for six months prior to her relinquishment of the child for adoption could veto the mother's adoption decision. The court held that the provision imposed "an absolute condition . . . only tangentially related to the parental relationship" and allowed a woman who would not live with a man the power unilaterally to cut off his constitutionally protected interest in parenting his child (76 NY2d at 405, 559 N.E. 2d at 426, 559 N.Y.S. 2d at 863). It instructed the legislature to find some other way to gauge a father's commitment to his unborn child's welfare, and set forth certain standards that lower courts were to follow in the meantime when judging an unwed father's parental commitment. "The father must be willing to assume full custody, not merely attempt to prevent the adoption, and he must promptly manifest parental responsibility both before and after the child's birth."[20] In assessing the father's demonstration of responsibility, judges should look at such matters as "public acknowledgment of paternity, payment of pregnancy and birth expenses, steps taken to establish legal responsibility for the child, and other factors evincing a commitment to the child" (76 NY2d at 428, 559 N.E. 2d at 428, 559 N.Y.S. 2d at 865).

Although courts in New York have used these guidelines in resolving a number of cases involving unwed fathers' efforts to block mothers' adoption decisions in the years since *In re Raquel Marie X.*,[21] four years have gone by without the New York legislature passing a new statute governing an unwed father's right to veto an adoption. Three recent bills introduced in the legislature (two in the Assembly, one in the Senate) have differed strikingly in their underlying approaches to unwed fathers' rights. Both the variety of provisions in these bills and the fact that none has been enacted into law reflect a widely shared uncertainty over what considerations should be brought to bear to determine the nature and extent of an unwed biological father's custodial rights. I discuss these bills in the order of what each requires for a father to establish his right to consent to the adoption of his offspring, from the weakest to the strongest stipulations.

The first of two bills (A. 8028) introduced in the Assembly during the 1993 and 1994 legislative sessions, listed a number of actions an unwed father of an infant under six months might take to establish his right to consent to the adoption. The bill would make his consent necessary if he openly lived with the child or the child's mother prior to the placement of the child for adoption; *or* held himself out to be the father of such child during such period; *or* paid or offered to pay a reasonable sum, consistent with his means, for the medical expenses of pregnancy and childbirth; *or* initiated judicial proceedings to obtain custody of the child; *or* married the child's mother.[22] Since the father needs to have taken only one of these actions and may have initiated judicial proceedings after the child was born, this bill applies a simple "fitness" test and requires no showing of interest prior to the child's birth.

By contrast with the minimal expectations put on unwed fathers by A. 8028, the Senate bill (S. 3776) introduced in the Senate during the 1991 and 1992 legislative sessions requires that a father have demonstrated his commitment to his offspring in a number of ways both prior to and after the birth of the child.[23] It does so by replacing most "or"s in the Assembly bill with the conjunctive "and," thus insisting that a biological father have supported the mother or baby financially, held himself out as the father, and taken steps to initiate legal proceedings to assume custody of the child.

The second Assembly bill (A. 8319) introduced during the 1993 and 1994 legislative sessions would exact an even stronger commitment from the father. It stipulates that the father have paid or offered to pay a reasonable part of the medical expenses of pregnancy and childbirth and the child's living expenses, and that he have initiated judicial proceedings to establish paternity and to obtain sole custody of the child within clearly specified time limits. The bill further stipulates that "'ability to assume sole custody' shall mean ability to assume guardianship and custody of the child and become the primary caretaker of the child for the foreseeable future."[24] This bill clearly means to grant the right to consent to an adoption only to unwed fathers who demonstrate that they have been and will be actively engaged in the care and upbringing of their offspring; the stipulations rest on an image of father as caretaker and nurturer, not simply as progenitor.

A. 8319 goes a long way to enact the spirit of the principles set forth in this essay, but a fully adequate statute would go further. A court should be required to hear a mother's objections, if she has any, to a father's assuming custody of the child, both because the birth of a child has resulted from a web of social interactions and relationships, and because the mother's relinquishment of the child for adoption should be viewed as the last in a series of actions meant to provide care for the child, not as an act of abandonment that gives her no interest in the child's placement. In cases in which the mother objects to the father's assumption of custody, a court should listen to the *reasons* the mother opposes placing the child in the biological father's custody. Because parental rights must be grounded in the provision of care and the assumption of responsibility, if an unwed mother could demonstrate that her pregnancy was a result of force, coercion, or deception, or that she had been under the age of consent when intercourse occurred, the father would be held to be "unfit." This still might not meet the possibility that a man who desired children might impregnate a woman whom he knew would neither abort nor raise a child, provide care and financial support throughout the pregnancy, and petition for paternity and custody—a kind of inexpensive "surrogacy." I am convinced that such intentional instrumental use of any woman's body is morally abhorrent, but I am not certain how to ensure that such a man could not assume custody of his offspring under such circumstances.

Finally, a statute should provide that a pregnant woman who wishes to make plans for her child should be able to ascertain early in the pregnancy whether or not the father will step forward later to oppose the adoption. The law should provide that she be able to notify him in writing of the pregnancy and preclude him from a veto if he fails to act soon after receipt of such notification. Similarly, if a father is found to be entitled to veto an adoption, a mother should be able to negate her consent to the child's adoption and be put back in the same position she was in prior to her consent, that is, as one of two unwed parents each of whom seeks custody (Erickson 1991).

One purpose of spelling out what actions the father needs to take to establish his claim would be to ascertain as early as possible during the pregnancy or after birth whether or not he wished custody, so that infants could be definitively freed for adoption. Where the mother objected to the father's assuming custody, a hearing would be necessary. A hearing would, of course, take more time than assigning custody based on a rule that any "fit" biological father prevail or that a mother be able to make the decision to place her child for adoption unimpeded by the biological father. But a hearing to ascertain whether an unwed biological father has grasped the opportunity to parent his newborn should not cause more delay than a best interest hearing. Such a hearing would be to ascertain facts about the unwed father's behavior and the mother's considered opinion concerning custody, not to try to project what custodial arrangement might be in the child's best interest.

These considerations leave unresolved the thorny issue of how the law should deal with cases in which a biological mother lies to the biological father about his paternity or otherwise hides her pregnancy, making it impossible for him to take any action to signal his willingness to take care of his offspring. In 1992 the New York Court of Appeals addressed the question of what effect a lack of knowledge of a woman's pregnancy should have on a biological father's right to seek custody after learning of the child's existence. In *Matter of Robert O. v. Russell K.*, an unwed biological father sought to overturn the adoption of his son on the grounds that either the mother or the State had a duty to ensure that he knew of the child's birth, and that their failure to inform him denied him his constitutional rights. The New York court acknowledged that "the unwed father of an infant placed for adoption immediately at birth faces a unique dilemma should he desire to establish his parental rights." His opportunity to "shoulder the responsibility of parenthood may disappear before he has a chance to grasp it." But although the father, Robert O., acted as soon as he knew of the child's existence, the adoption had been finalized ten months previously. "Promptness," said the court, "is measured in terms of the child's life, not by the onset of the father's awareness." Robert O., having failed to determine in a timely fashion whether the woman with whom he had lived was pregnant, lost the right he would have had to an opportunity to manifest his "willingness to be a parent" (*Matter of Robert O. v. Russell K.,* 80 NY2d 252 [1992] at 262). The responsibility to know of a child's existence should fall on the man who would assume responsibility for raising the child. By contrast, one defender of unwed fathers' rights proposes a jail sentence of up to two years for a woman who refuses to name the father of her child when surrendering the infant for adoption! (Hamilton 1987–88, 1103 n. 406).[25] A biological father aware of a woman's pregnancy should be required to act prior to birth and soon after he suspects his paternity; a biological father who is actively kept ignorant might be allowed to step forward for some specified period after birth (probably not less than eight weeks nor longer than six months), but thereafter the importance of establishing a firm parent-child relationship would preclude his advancing a parental claim. The child's need for such a relationship should also lead to requirements that courts hear and decide disputes concerning the adoption of infants expeditiously.

Although the reflections set forth in this essay suggest various reforms in the laws governing the custody of nonmarital children, they do not in and of themselves answer the question of whether the case of *Baby Girl Clausen* was decided correctly. I find that very hard to do because neither side grounded its position in the kinds of principles I have put forward here. The Iowa statute that Daniel Schmidt invoked to claim that the adoption could not be finalized required the biological father's consent, but no showing that he demonstrate his commitment to the child prior to (or even subsequent to) birth. The father's mere opposition to the adoption was a sufficient basis upon which to grant him custody. The DeBoers, for their part, based their claim that they should be allowed to adopt Jessica on the best interest standard. Placing the child with the Schmidts reinforced the notion that a biological tie between man and child automatically creates a custodial claim. On the other hand, favoring the DeBoers would not only have reinforced the best interest standard but might have been viewed as rewarding them for prolonging legal proceedings after Schmidt raised his claim.

The outcome consonant with the principles advanced here would have granted a hearing to Schmidt, recognizing that while his biological tie alone did not guarantee him custodial rights, the fact that he acted immediately after learning that he was Jessica's biological father and within four weeks after her birth established grounds for a hearing and, provided that Cara Clausen did not object, for custody. Had Clausen objected, the hearing would not have attempted to determine whether the child's best interest would be better served by granting custody to Schmidt or the DeBoers, but whether Schmidt's actions were sufficient to establish a claim to custody. To establish his right to consent to the adoption, he would have to demonstrate that he had good reason to believe that the child Cara Clausen was carrying was not his offspring, that he acted immediately and decisively to assume full custody after learning that he was Jessica's biological father, and that he had done so within the statutory limit for advancing such a claim. It seems to me likely both that Schmidt's claim would have been recognized and that the likelihood of a ruling in his favor would have been much clearer to the DeBoers and their lawyer than was the case under the law then in effect.

The main lesson to be drawn from cases like *Baby Girl Clausen* is that it is imperative that states formulate adoption laws that will reflect the principle that parental rights are established in the first instance by a combination of biology and the provision of care, a principle already articulated by the Supreme Court. Another lesson may be that in certain instances it would make sense to allow some form of legal recognition to the fact that a child may have multiple "parents": genetic parents (sperm and egg donors), biological parents (the gestational mother and genetic father), stepparents, adoptive parents, social parents (that is, those who actually provide care), and legal guardians.[26] The possibility of some such recognition might avoid some cases in which unwed biological fathers who have not married the mothers of their offspring seek to block the adoption of the infant. Some of these cases seem motivated not so much by the man's desire to raise the child as by his fear of losing all opportunity to know the child he has sired. There may be ways of dealing with this fear short of blocking the adoption. Adoption registries that allow adopted children and birth parents to contact one another by mutual consent when the child has reached his or her majority seem to have been helpful to biological parents, adoptive parents, and children alike. They allow for the simultaneous recognition of the importance of both biological and social parenting, and in doing so undercut the suggestion that something about adoption is shameful and best kept hidden. Such registries also take into account the perspective of children who want to know their biological forebears, without weakening either the legal rights and responsibilities of the social (adoptive) parents or the primacy of the emotional bonds between adoptive parents and children.

Beyond these legal changes, cases such as *Matter of Robert O. v. Russell K.* and *Baby Girl Clausen* should also lead us to try to understand the circumstances that might lead an unwed mother to lie about or conceal the paternity of her child, such as fear of violence or harassment, or shame over an unwanted sexual relationship. Working toward justice in family relationships requires struggling to eliminate the social conditions that give rise to such fear and shame, and also requires making sure that all citizens have access to the resources that allow family relationships to survive and flourish, so that no biological parent will be forced by economic factors to relinquish custody of children they would prefer to raise themselves had they the resources to do so.

CONCLUSION

This analysis of disputes over paternal custody of nonmarital newborns makes it abundantly clear that the language of individual rights, so central to liberal political theory, and to the due process and equal protection guarantees of the U.S. Constitution, is not well-suited to dealing with complex issues of parent-child relationships. Although notions of maternal or paternal rights are not useless (for example, they allow us to think about limits to state intervention), they tend to focus attention on an adult *individual,* whereas parental issues involve two adults and a child, and the relationships among them.[27] Legal and social discourse alike must put the lived relationship between parents and between parent and child, not the rights of individuals alone, at the center of the analysis of parental claims. In particular the language of a father's "right" to custody of his infant child based on his genetic tie obscures the complexity of the relationships involved in human reproductive activity.

Because parenting involves being in a relationship with another dependent person, a parental "right" cannot properly be conceived of as something independent of the relationship. An individual can exercise a parental right, but the existence or the nature of the right cannot be explained by reference to that individual alone. Only by taking account of the interpersonal dependency, reciprocity, and responsibility involved in family relationships will we be able to approach a world dedicated to achieving both lived equality between men and women and committed parents for every child.

NOTES

1. *In the Interest of B.G.C.,* Supreme Court of Iowa, No. 207/91-476, 92–49, September 23, 1992, and *In the Matter of Baby Girl Clausen,* Michigan Court of Appeals, No. 161102, March 29, 1993.
2. A summary of the different statutory provisions in all fifty states regarding who must give consent to an adoption and under what conditions is found in *Adoption Laws: Answers to the Most-Asked Questions* (Rockville, MD: National Adoption Information Clearinghouse, n.d.).
3. Hirczy (1992) and Hamilton (1987–88) argue that the law should insist that the paternity of every child be established at birth, a necessary prerequisite for an unwed father's assertion of paternal rights.
4. See Goldberg (1992).
5. "Recent Developments: Family Law—Unwed Fathers' Rights—New York Court of Appeals Mandates Veto Power over Newborn's Adoption for Unwed Father Who Demonstrates Parental Responsibility—*In re Raquel Marie X.*" *Harvard Law Review* 104 (January 1991): 807. Fineman (1988, 770) and Eveleigh (1989) also express strong reservations about the best interest test in custody adjudication.
6. For a discussion of the many ways legal and social discourses label women as "bad mothers" see Roberts (1992). By contrast, Eveleigh (1989) writes

as if the biological mother who has relinquished custody has no further relevant interest in her child; when a biological father seeks custody of his newborn offspring, the relevant interests, she says, are those of the state, the father, and the child.

7. The uniqueness of pregnancy has implications for the custodial claims not only of unwed fathers but also for those of a lesbian partner who had planned to co-parent a child, as well as those of a genetic mother who might turn to a "surrogate" to bear a child on her behalf.
8. On the social construction of the experience of pregnancy and childbirth see Martin (1987) and Rothman (1982).
9. It is not necessary to accept Catharine MacKinnon's view that fully consensual sexual relations between men and women are virtually impossible to achieve in our society in order to acknowledge that the context in which sexual relations take place—including great disparities of social and economic resources—-can make sexual relationships more or less consensual or coercive. See MacKinnon (1989, 174) and (1987, 88). For an opposing view see Roiphe (1993), which sees many feminist challenges to social structures of inequality that affect relationships between men and women as contributions to an ideology not of female empowerment but of female weakness and need for protection.
10. Smith (1983) argues against the "property model" of parenting and family relationships.
11. Excellent discussions of the ways in which classical liberal theory pays insufficient attention to the ways in which individuals are constituted in and by their relationships to others are found in Held (1993); Nedelsky (1989) and (1990); Ruddick (1989); and Tronto (1993).

    Issues involving children raise in a particularly acute manner the tension between protecting people as individuals and protecting family associations or family ties. On the dilemmas inherent in using privacy language to afford protection to both individuals and families see Karst (1980).
12. Although see also cases that permitted sterilization of the mentally retarded, *Buck v. Bell,* 274 U.S. 200 (1927) and *Sterilization of Moore,* 289 N.C. 95, 221 S.E. 2d 307 (1976).
13. See Okin (1989) and Olsen (1985) for a clear analysis of the impossibility of complete state neutrality toward the family.
14. For an interesting critique of Bartlett that is flawed by its failure to recognize the deeply individualistic as well as the patriarchal characteristics of contemporary family law, see Dolgin (1990).

    The idea that parental rights depend on the fulfillment of parental duties receives one of its classic expressions in John Locke's argument against the patriarchal ideas of Sir Robert Filmer. Filmer held that the very act of begetting a child gave a father sovereignty over his offspring. By contrast, Locke asserts that not procreation but only providing care for a child bestows parental authority and that by nature (although not necessarily by law) mothers share such authority. But despite Locke's rejection of patriarchal reasoning with respect to both polity and family, patriarchal notions crept back into much liberal political theory and law because these used the language of the rights of autonomous individuals to talk about or characterize the relationship between parent and child. To some extent, when nineteenth-century feminists began their assault on the common law doctrine of coverture, they used Lockean notions of individual freedom and equality to argue that mothers should have equal rights over marital children. Even these reforms, however, did not subvert the notion of parental autonomy or of parental rights to custody. See Locke ([1690] 1980, 2.6.58). On patriarchalism see Schochet (1975); on Locke's antipatriarchalism see Shanley (1979).
15. I leave aside the question of whether the mother should be subject to prosecution for fetal abuse, although I do not think she should be.
16. This is not to deny responsibility to drug-dependent pregnant women. As Cynthia Daniels writes, "Clearly, race, class, and gender inequality limit an individual's access to a full range of options, but they do not negate all choice. The behavior of poor addicted women may be 'determined' in the historical sense that they are born into conditions which they did not create and cannot control, and which set strict limits on their lives, but this does not mean that they lose all power to shape their own destinies" (Daniels 1993, 125).

    Dorothy Roberts has written with great insight about the ways in which issues of equality and privacy arise in prosecutions of drug-addicted women of color who have babies (Roberts 1991).

17. Studies have shown that the consequences for offspring of poor women who used alcohol and drugs during pregnancy were much more severe than for offspring of upper-income women, chiefly because of differences in nutrition (Nesrin Bingol et al. 1987. "The Influence of Socioeconomic Factors on the Occurrence of Fetal Alcohol Syndrome" *Advances in Alcohol and Substance Abuse* 6(4): 117; cited in Daniels 1993, 125).
18. Two-thirds of the major hospitals in fifteen cities surveyed by the House Select Committee on Children, Youth, and Families in 1989 reported that they had no place to which to refer drug-addicted pregnant women for treatment (Karol L. Kumpfer. 1991. "Treatment Programs for Drug-Abusing Women" *The Future of Children* I[1]: 52; cited in Daniels 1993, 126). In the same year, there were 135 treatment beds available for the more than four thousand pregnant drug-dependent women in the state of Florida (*Johnson v. State of Florida,* Petitioners' Initial Brief, Appeal from the District Court of Appeal, Fifth District 77, 831 Sup. Ct. of Fla. [1990], p. 31; cited in Daniels 1993, 126). Many drug treatment programs do not accept pregnant women for fear that they will be sued if the woman loses the pregnancy as a result of treatment (Chavkin 1991, 1556).
19. "Recent Developments: Family Law—Unwed Fathers' Rights—. . . *In re Raquel Marie X . . . ,*" p. 805 (footnote omitted).
20. "Recent Developments: Family Law . . .—*In re Raquel Marie X . . . ,*" p. 803.
21. For example, *Matter of Kiran Chandini S.,* 166 A.D. 2d 599, 560 N.Y.S. 2d 886 (1990); In the *Matter of John E. v. John Doe,* 564 N.Y.S. 2d 439 (1990); *Matter of Stephen C.,* 566 N.Y.S. 2d 178 (1991); *Matter of Robert O. v. Russell K.,* 80 NY2d 252 (1992).
22. New York State Legislature, Assembly, A. 8028, May 17, 1993; introduced by Member of the Assembly Vito Lopez and referred to the Committee on the Judiciary.
23. New York State Legislature, Senate, S. 3776-B, March 11, 1991; introduced by Senator Mary Goodhue.
24. New York State Legislature, Assembly, A. 8319A, June 4, 1993; introduced by Member of the Assembly Vito Lopez (at the request of the Governor) and referred to the Committee on Children and Families.

    If the father needs to work to support the child, he clearly cannot provide uninterrupted childcare. The stipulation that he be the primary caretaker of the child is meant to preclude men who intend to turn the care of their offspring over to other family members from blocking adoptions. This raises very hard issues about how the law might recognize the roles of members of extended families in raising children, and this aspect of any proposed bill needs further deliberation.
25. Less drastically, Justice Titone, concurring in *Robert O. v. Russell K.,* also felt it unreasonable to require that a man who wishes to assert paternal rights know of the pregnancy of his sexual partner.
26. See interesting suggestions for ways in which the law might recognize more than two parents in Bartlett (1984). See also Bartholet (1993).
27. I leave aside cases of contract parenthood, artificial insemination by donor, and embryo transfer, for example, in all of which issues involving distinctions between genetic, biological, and "intentional" parents arise, and in all of which there may be more than two adults claiming the status of "parent." . . .

REFERENCES

Adoption laws: Answers to the most-asked questions. N.d. Rockville, MD: National Adoption Information Clearinghouse.

Bartholet, Elizabeth. 1993. *Family bonds: Adoption and the politics of parenting.* Boston: Houghton Mifflin.

Bartlett, Katharine. 1984. Rethinking parenthood as an exclusive status: The need for legal alternatives when the premise of the nuclear family has failed. *Virginia Law Review* 70(5): 879–963.

———. 1988. Re-expressing parenthood. *Yale Law Journal* 98(2): 293–340.

Becker, Mary. 1989. The rights of unwed parents: Feminist approaches. *Social Service Review* 63(4): 496–518.

———. 1992. Maternal feelings: Myth, taboo, and child custody. *Review of Law and Women's Studies* 1: 901–92.

Blackstone, William. [1783] 1978. *Commentaries on the laws of England.* 4 vols. 9th ed. Ed. Berkowitz and Throne. Oxford: Clarendon Press.

Boyd, Jeffrey S. 1990. The unwed father's custody claim in California: When does the parental preference doctrine apply? *Pepperdine Law Review* 17: 969–1010.

Buchanan, Elizabeth. 1984. The constitutional rights of unwed fathers before and after *Lehr v. Robertson. Ohio State Law Journal* 45: 311–82.

Buck v. Bell. 1927. 274 U.S. 200.

Caban v. Mohammed. 1979. 441 U.S. 380.

Callahan, Joan C., ed. 1995. *Reproduction, ethics and the law: Feminist perspectives.* Bloomington: Indiana University Press.

Chavkin, Wendy. 1991. Mandatory treatment for drug use during pregnancy. *Journal of the American Medical Association* 266(11): 1556–61.

Daniels, Cynthia R. 1993. *At women's expense: State power and the politics of fetal rights.* Cambridge: Harvard University Press.

Dolgin, Janet L. 1990. Status and contract in feminist legal theory of the family: A reply to Bartlett. *Women's Rights Law Reporter* 12: 103–13.

Eisenstein, Zillah. 1988. *The female body and the law.* Berkeley: University of California Press.

Erickson, Nancy S. 1984. The feminist dilemma over unwed parents' custody rights: The mother's rights must take priority. *Journal of Law and Inequality* 2: 447–72.

———. 1990. Neither abortion nor adoption: Women without options. Paper presented at the American Association of Law Schools (AALS), San Francisco, 6 January.

———. 1991. Proposal for a model law on unwed fathers' adoption rights. Unpublished paper. Brooklyn, N.Y.

Eveleigh, Laurel J. 1989. Certainly not child's play: A serious game of hide and seek with the rights of unwed fathers. *Syracuse Law Review* 40: 1055–88.

Fineman, Martha Albertson. 1988. Dominant discourse, professional language, and legal change in child custody decisionmaking, *Harvard Law Review* 101(4): 727–74.

———. 1991. *The illusion of equality: The rhetoric and reality of divorce reform.* Chicago: University of Chicago Press.

Glendon, Mary Ann. 1991. *Rights talk: The impoverishments of political discourse.* New York: Free Press.

Goldberg, Stephanie B. 1992. Having my baby. *ABA Journal* 78: 84–86.

Gomez v. Perez. 1973. 409 U.S. 535.

Grossberg, Michael. 1985. *Governing the hearth: Law and the family in nineteenth-century America.* Chapel Hill: University of North Carolina Press.

Hamilton, John R. 1987–88. The unwed father and the right to know of his child's existence. *Kentucky Law Journal* 76: 949–1009.

Hartog, Hendrick. 1993. Breaking the marital bond. Princeton University. Unpublished manuscript.

Held, Virginia. 1993. *Feminist morality: Transforming culture, society, and politics.* Chicago: University of Chicago Press.

Hirczy, Wolfgang. 1992. The politics of illegitimacy: A cross-national comparison. Paper presented at the Annual Meeting of the American Political Science Association, Chicago, 3–6 September.

In the Interest of B.G.C. September 23, 1992. Supreme Court of Iowa, No. 207/91-476, 92–49.

In the Matter of Baby Girl Clausen. March 29, 1993. Michigan Court of Appeals, No. 161102.

In re Raquel Marie X. 1990. 76 NY2d 387.

In re Baby Girl Eason. 1987. 257 Ga. 292, 358 S.E. 2d 459.

Johnson, Sally. 1994. Helping fathers become parents. *New York Times,* 24 February, metropolitan edition, C1.

Karst, Kenneth L. 1980. The freedom of intimate association. *Yale Law Journal* 89(4): 624–92.

Lehr v. Robertson. 1983. 463 U.S. 248.

Locke, John. [1690] 1980. *Second treatise of government.* Ed. C. B. Macpherson. Indianapolis: Hackett.

MacKinnon, Catharine A. 1987. *Feminism unmodified: Discourses on life and law.* Cambridge: Harvard University Press.

———. 1989. *Toward a feminist theory of the state.* Cambridge: Harvard University Press.

Martin, Emily. 1987. *The woman in the body: A cultural analysis of reproduction.* Boston: Beacon Press.

Matter of Robert O. v. Russell K. 1992. 80 NY2d 252.

Michael H. v. Gerald D. 1989. 491 U.S. 110.

Nedelsky, Jennifer. 1989. Reconceiving autonomy: Sources, thoughts, and possibilities. *Yale Journal of Law and Feminism* 1 (1): 7–36.

———. 1990. Law, boundaries, and the bounded self. *Representations* 30: 162–189.

New York State Assembly. A. 8028. May 17, 1993.

New York State Assembly. A. 8319A. June 4, 1993.

New York State Senate. S. 3776-B. March 11, 1991.

Okin, Susan M. 1989. *Justice, gender, and the family.* New York: Basic Books.

Olsen, Frances. 1985. The myth of state intervention in the family. *University of Michigan Journal of Law Reform* 18(4): 835–64.

Planned Parenthood of Southeastern Pennsylvania v. Casey. 1992. 112 S. Ct. 2791.

Raab, Jennifer J. 1984. *Lehr v. Robertson:* Unwed fathers and adoption—How much process is due? *Harvard Women's Law Journal* 7: 265–87.

Recent developments: Family law—Unwed fathers' rights—New York Court of Appeals mandates veto power over newborn's adoption for unwed father who demonstrates parental responsibility—In re Raquel Marie X. . . . 1991. *Harvard Law Review* 104(3): 800–807.

Roberts, Dorothy E. 1991. Punishing drug addicts who have babies: Women of color, equality, and the right of privacy. *Harvard Law Review* 104(7): 1419–82.

———. 1992. Racism and patriarchy in the meaning of motherhood. Paper presented at the Feminism and Legal Theory Project Workshop on Motherhood, Columbia Law School, New York, 4–5 December.

Roiphe, Katie. 1993. *The morning after: Sex, fear, and feminism on campus*. Boston: Little Brown and Co.

Rothman, Barbara Katz. 1982. *In labor: Women and power in the birthplace*. New York: Norton.

———. 1989. *Recreating motherhood: Ideology and technology in a patriarchal society*. New York: W. W. Norton.

Ruddick, Sara. 1989. *Maternal thinking: Towards a politics of peace*. Boston: Beacon.

Schochet, Gordon. 1975. *Patriarchalism in political thought*. New York: Basic Books.

Serviss, Claudia. 1991. *Lehr v. Robertson*'s "Grasp the opportunity": For California's natural fathers, custody may be beyond their grasp. *Western State University Law Review* 18: 771–90.

Shanley, Mary L. 1979. Marriage contract and social contract in seventeenth-century English political thought. *Western Political Quarterly* 32(1): 79–91.

———. 1989. *Feminism, marriage, and the law in Victorian England*. Princeton: Princeton University Press.

———. 1993. "Surrogate mothering" and women's freedom: A critique of contracts for human reproduction. *Signs* 18(3): 618–39.

———. 1995. Unwed fathers' rights, adoption, and sex equality: Gender-neutrality and the perpetuation of patriarchy. *Columbia Law Review* 95(1): [60–103].

Smith, Janet Farrell. 1983. Parenting and property. In *Mothering: Essays in feminist theory,* ed. Joyce Trebilcot. Totowa, N.J.: Rowman & Allanheld.

Stanley v. Illinois. 1972. 405 U.S. 645.

Stanton, Elizabeth Rose. 1990. The rights of the biological father: From adoption and custody to surrogate motherhood. *Vermont Law Review* 12: 87–121.

Sterilization of Moore. 1976. 289 N.C. 95, 221 S.E. 2d 307.

Steward, Rebecca L. 1990. Constitutional rights of unwed fathers: Is equal protection equal for unwed fathers? *Southwestern University Law Review* 19:1087–1111.

Sweeney, Maureen A. 1990. Between sorrow and happy endings: A new paradigm of adoption. *Yale Journal of Law and Feminism,* 329–70.

Thomas S. v. Robin Y. 1993. 599 N.Y.S. 377.

Trimble v. Gordon. 1977. 430 U.S. 762.

Tronto, Joan C. 1993. *Moral boundaries: A political argument for an ethic of care*. New York: Routledge.

Weber v. Aetna Casualty & Surety Co. 1972. 406 U.S. 164.

Young, Iris Marion. 1994. Punishment, treatment, empowerment: Three approaches to policy for pregnant addicts. *Feminist Studies* 20(1): 33–58.

Zainaldin, Jamil S. 1979. The emergence of a modern American family law: Child custody, adoption, and the courts, 1796–1851. *Northwestern University Law Review* 73: 1038–1089.

Zinman, Daniel C. 1992. Father knows best: The unwed father's right to raise his infant surrendered for adoption. *Fordham Law Review* 60: 971–1001.

70

Stanley v. Illinois

92 S.Ct. 1208 (1972)

Mr. Justice White delivered the opinion of the Court.

Joan Stanley lived with Peter Stanley intermittently for 18 years, during which time they had three children.[1] When Joan Stanley died, Peter Stanley lost not only her but also his children. Under Illinois law, the children of unwed fathers become wards of the State upon the death of the mother. Accordingly, upon Joan Stanley's death, in a dependency proceeding instituted

[1]Uncontradicted testimony of Peter Stanley, App. 22.

[2]Only two children are involved in this litigation.

by the State of Illinois, Stanley's children[2] were declared wards of the State and placed with court-appointed guardians. Stanley appealed, claiming that he had never been shown to be an unfit parent and that since married fathers and unwed mothers could not be deprived of their children without such a showing, he had been deprived of the equal protection of the laws guaranteed him by the Fourteenth Amendment. The Illinois Supreme Court accepted the fact that Stanley's own unfitness had not been established but rejected the equal protection claim, holding that Stanley could properly be separated from his children upon proof of the single fact that he and the dead mother had not been married. Stanley's actual fitness as a father was irrelevant. In re Stanley, 45 Ill.2d 132, 256 N.E.2d 814 (1970).

Stanley presses his equal protection claim here. The State continues to respond that unwed fathers are presumed unfit to raise their children and that it is unnecessary to hold individualized hearings to determine whether particular fathers are in fact unfit parents before they are separated from their children. We granted certiorari, 400 U.S. 1020, 91 S.Ct. 584, 27 L.Ed.2d 631 (1971), to determine whether this method of procedure by presumption could be allowed to stand in light of the fact that Illinois allows married fathers—whether divorced, widowed, or separated—and mothers—even if unwed—the benefit of the presumption that they are fit to raise their children.

I

At the outset we reject any suggestion that we need not consider the propriety of the dependency proceeding that separated the Stanleys because Stanley might be able to regain custody of his children as a guardian or through adoption proceedings. The suggestion is that if Stanley has been treated differently from other parents, the difference is immaterial and not legally cognizable for the purposes of the Fourteenth Amendment. This court has not, however, embraced the general proposition that a wrong may be done if it can be undone. Cf. Sniadach v. Family Finance Corp. of Bay View, 395 U.S. 337, 89 S.Ct. 1820, 23 L.Ed.2d 349 (1969). Surely, in the case before us, if there is delay between the doing and the undoing petitioner suffers from the deprivation of his children, and the children suffer from uncertainty and dislocation.

It is clear, moreover, that Stanley does not have the means at hand promptly to erase the adverse consequences of the proceeding in the course of which his children were declared wards of the State. It is first urged that Stanley could act to adopt his children. But under Illinois law, Stanley is treated not as a parent but as a stranger to his children, and the dependency proceeding has gone forward on the presumption that he is unfit to exercise parental rights. Insofar as we are informed, Illinois law affords him no priority in adoption proceedings. It would be his burden to establish not only that he would be a suitable parent but also that he would be the most suitable of all who might want custody of the children. Neither can we ignore that in the proceedings from which this action developed, the "probation officer," see App. 17, the assistant state's attorney, see *id.*, at 29–30, and the judge charged with the case, see *id.*, at 16–18, 23, made it apparent that Stanley, unmarried and impecunious as he is, could not now expect to profit from adoption proceedings.[3] The Illinois Supreme Court apparently recognized some or all of these considerations, because it did not suggest that Stanley's case was undercut by his failure to petition for adoption.

Before us, the State focuses on Stanley's failure to petition for "custody and control"—the second route by which, it is urged, he might regain authority for his children. Passing the obvious issue whether it would be futile or burdensome for an unmarried father—without funds and already once presumed unfit—to petition for custody, this suggestion overlooks the fact that legal custody is not parenthood or adoption. A person appointed guardian in an action for custody and control is subject to removal at any time without such cause as must be shown in a neglect proceeding against a parent. Ill.Rev.Stat., c. 37, § 705–8. He may not take the children out of the jurisdiction without the court's approval. He may be required to report to the court as to his disposition of the children's affairs. Ill.Rev.Stat., c. 37, § 705–8. Obviously then, even if Stanley were a mere step away from "custody and control," to give an unwed father only "custody and con-

---

[3]The Illinois Supreme Court's opinion is not at all contrary to this conclusion. That court said: "[T]he trial court's comments clearly indicate the court's willingness to consider *a future* request by the father for *custody and guardianship*." 45 Ill.2d 132, 135, 256 N.E.2d 814, 816. (Italics added.) See also the comment of Stanley's counsel on oral argument: "If Peter Stanley could have adopted his children, we would not be here today." Tr. of Oral Arg. 7.

trol" would still be to leave him seriously prejudiced by reason of his status.

We must therefore examine the question that Illinois would have us avoid: Is a presumption that distinguishes and burdens all unwed fathers constitutionally repugnant? We conclude that, as a matter of due process of law, Stanley was entitled to a hearing on his fitness as a parent before his children were taken from him and that, by denying him a hearing and extending it to all other parents whose custody of their children is challenged, the State denied Stanley the equal protection of the laws guaranteed by the Fourteenth Amendment.

II

Illinois has two principal methods of removing nondelinquent children from the homes of their parents. In a dependency proceeding it may demonstrate that the children are wards of the State because they have no surviving parent or guardian. Ill.Rev.Stat., c. 37, §§ 702–1, 702–5. In a neglect proceeding it may show that children should be wards of the State because the present parent(s) or guardian does not provide suitable care. Ill.Rev.Stat., c. 37, §§ 702–1, 702–4.

The State's right—indeed, duty—to protect minor children through a judicial determination of their interests in a neglect proceeding is not challenged here. Rather, we are faced with a dependency statute that empowers state officials to circumvent neglect proceedings on the theory that an unwed father is not a "parent" whose existing relationship with his children must be considered.[4] "Parents," says the State, "means the father and mother of a legitimate child, or the survivor of them, or the natural mother of an illegitimate child, or the survivor of them, or the natural mother of an illegitimate child, and includes any adoptive parent," Ill.Rev.Stat., c. 37, § 701–14, but the term does not include unwed fathers.

Under Illinois law, therefore, while the children of all parents can be taken from them in neglect proceedings, that is only after notice, hearing, and proof of such unfitness as a parent as amounts to neglect, an unwed father is uniquely subject to the more simplistic dependency proceeding. By use of this proceeding, the State, on showing that the father was not married to the mother, need not prove unfitness in fact, because it is presumed at law. Thus, the unwed father's claim of parental qualification is avoided as "irrelevant."

In considering this procedure under the Due Process Clause, we recognize, as we have in other cases, that due process of law does not require a hearing "in every conceivable case of government impairment of private interest." Cafeteria and Restaurant Workers Union etc. v. McElroy, 367 U.S. 886, 894, 81 S.Ct. 1743, 1748, 6 L.Ed.2d 1230 (1961). That case explained that "[t]he very nature of due process negates any concept of inflexible procedures universally applicable to every imaginable situation" and firmly established that "what procedures due process may require under any given set of circumstances must begin with a determination of the precise nature of the government function involved as well as of the private interest that has been affected by governmental action." *Id.*, at 895, 81 S.Ct., at 1748; Goldberg v. Kelly, 397 U.S. 254, 263, 90 S.Ct. 1011, 1018, 25 L.Ed.2d 287 (1970).

The private interest here, that of a man in the children he has sired and raised, undeniably warrants deference and, absent a powerful countervailing interest, protection. It is plain that the interest of a parent in the companionship, care, custody, and management of his or her children "come[s] to this Court with a momentum for respect lacking when appeal is made to liberties which derive merely from shifting economic arrangements." Kovacs v. Cooper, 336 U.S. 77, 95, 69 S.Ct. 448, 458, 93 L.Ed. 513 (1949) (Frankfurter, J., concurring).

The Court has frequently emphasized the importance of the family. The rights to conceive and to raise one's children have been deemed "essential," Meyer v. Nebraska, 262 U.S. 390, 399, 43 S.Ct. 625, 626, 67 L.Ed. 1042 (1923), "basic civil rights of man," Skinner v. Oklahoma, 316 U.S. 535, 541, 62 S.Ct. 1110, 1113, 86 L.Ed. 1655 (1942), and "[r]ights far more precious . . . than property rights," May v. Anderson, 345 U.S. 528, 533, 73 S.Ct. 840, 843, 97 L.Ed. 1221 (1953). "It is cardinal with us that the custody, care and nurture of the child reside first in the parents, whose primary function and freedom include preparation for obligations the state can neither supply nor hinder." Prince v. Massachusetts, 321 U.S. 158, 166, 64 S.Ct. 438, 442,

[4]Even while refusing to label him a "legal parent," the State does not deny that Stanley has a special interest in the outcome of these proceedings. It is undisputed that he is the father of these children, that he lived with the two children whose custody is challenged all their lives, and that he has supported them.

88 L.Ed. 645 (1944). The integrity of the family unit has found protection in the Due Process Clause of the Fourteenth Amendment, Meyer v. Nebraska, *supra,* 262 U.S. at 399, 43 S.Ct. at 626, the Equal Protection Clause of the Fourteenth Amendment, Skinner v. Oklahoma, *supra,* 316 U.S., at 541, 62 S.Ct., at 1113, and the Ninth Amendment, Griswold v. Connecticut, 381 U.S. 479, 496, 85 S.Ct. 1678, 14 L.Ed.2d 510 (1965) (Goldberg, J., concurring).

Nor has the law refused to recognize those family relationships unlegitimized by a marriage ceremony. The Court has declared unconstitutional a state statute denying natural, but illegitimate, children a wrongful-death action for the death of their mother, emphasizing that such children cannot be denied the right of other children because familial bonds in such cases were often as warm, enduring, and important as those arising within a more formally organized family unit. Levy v. Louisiana, 391 U.S. 68, 71–72, 88 S.Ct. 1509, 1511, 20 L.Ed.2d 436 (1968). "To say that the test of equal protection should be the 'legal' rather than the biological relationship is to avoid the issue. For the Equal Protection Clause necessarily limits the authority of a State to draw such 'legal' lines as it chooses." Glona v. American Guarantee & Liability Ins. Co., 391 U.S. 73, 75–76, 88 S.Ct. 1515, 1516, 20 L.Ed.2d 441 (1968).

These authorities make it clear that, at the least, Stanley's interest in retaining custody of his children is cognizable and substantial.

For its part, the State has made its interest quite plain: Illinois has declared that the aim of the Juvenile Court Act is to protect "the moral, emotional, mental, and physical welfare of the minor and the best interests of the community" and to "strengthen the minor's family ties whenever possible, removing him from the custody of his parents only when his welfare or safety or the protection of the public cannot be adequately safeguarded without removal . . ." Ill.Rev.Stat., c. 37, § 701–2. These are legitimate interests, well within the power of the State to implement. We do not question the assertion that neglectful parents may be separated from their children.

But we are here not asked to evaluate the legitimacy of the state ends, rather, to determine whether the means used to achieve these ends are constitutionally defensible. What is the state interest in separating children from fathers without a hearing designed to determine whether the father is unfit in a particular disputed case? We observe that the State registers no gain towards its declared goals when it separates children from the custody of fit parents. Indeed, if Stanley is a fit father, the State spites its own articulated goals when it needlessly separates him from his family.

In Bell v. Burson, 402 U.S. 535, 91 S.Ct. 1586, 29 L.Ed.2d 90 (1971), we found a scheme repugnant to the Due Process Clause because it deprived a driver of his license without reference to the very factor (there fault in driving, here fitness as a parent) that the State itself deemed fundamental to its statutory scheme. Illinois would avoid the self-contradiction that rendered the Georgia license suspension system invalid by arguing that Stanley and all other unmarried fathers can reasonably be presumed to be unqualified to raise their children.[5]

---

[5]Illinois says in its brief, at 21–23,

> "[T]he only relevant consideration in determining the propriety of governmental intervention in the raising of children is whether the best interests of the child are served by such intervention.
>
> "In effect, Illinois has imposed a statutory presumption that the best interests of a particular group of children necessitates some governmental supervision in certain clearly defined situations. The group of children who are illegitimate are distinguishable from legitimate children not so much by their status at birth as by the factual differences in their upbringing. While a legitimate child usually is raised by both parents with the attendant familial relationships and a firm concept of home and identity, the illegitimate child normally knows only one parent—the mother. . . .
>
> ". . . The petitioner has premised his argument upon particular factual circumstances—a lengthy relationship with the mother . . . a familial relationship with the two children, and a general assumption that this relationship approximates that in which the natural parents are married to each other.
>
> ". . . Even if this characterization were accurate (the record is insufficient to support it) it would not affect the validity of the statutory definition of parent. . . . The petitioner does not deny that the children are illegitimate. The record reflects their natural mother's death. Given these two factors, grounds exist for the State's intervention to ensure adequate care and protection for these children. This is true whether or not this particular petitioner assimilates all or none of the normal characteristics common to the classification of fathers who are not married to the mothers of their children."

See also Illinois' Brief 23 ("The comparison of married and putative fathers involves exclusively factual differences. The most significant of these are the presence or absence of the father from the home on a day-to-day basis and the responsibility imposed upon the relationship"), *id.,* at 24 (to the same effect), *id.,* at 31 (quoted below in n. 6), *id.,* at 24–26 (physiological and other studies are cited in support of the proposition that men are not naturally inclined to childrearing), and Tr. of Oral Arg. 31 ("We submit that both based on history or [*sic*] culture the very real differences . . . between the married father and the unmarried father, in terms of their interests in children and their legal responsibility for their children, that the statute here fulfills the compelling governmental objective of protecting children . . .").

It may be, as the State insists, that most unmarried fathers are unsuitable and neglectful parents.[6] It may also be that Stanley is such a parent and that his children should be placed in other hands. But all unmarried fathers are not in this category; some are wholly suited to have custody of their children.[7] This much the State readily concedes, and nothing in this record indicates that Stanley is or has been a neglectful father who has not cared for his children. Given the opportunity to make his case, Stanley may have been seen to be deserving of custody of his offspring. Had this been so, the State's statutory policy would have been furthered by leaving custody in him.

Carrington v. Rash, 380 U.S. 89, 85 S.Ct. 775, 13 L.Ed.2d 675 (1965), dealt with a similar situation. There we recognized that Texas had a powerful interest in restricting its electorate to bona fide residents. It was not disputed that most servicemen stationed in Texas had no intention of remaining in the State; most therefore could be deprived of a vote in state affairs. But we refused to tolerate a blanket exclusion depriving all servicemen of the vote, when some servicemen clearly were bona fide residents and when "more precise tests," *id.*, at 95, 85 S.Ct., at 779, were available to distinguish members of this latter group. "By forbidding a soldier ever to controvert the presumption of nonresidence," *id.*, at 96, 85 S.Ct., at 780, the State, we said, unjustifiably effected a substantial deprivation. It viewed people one-dimensionally (as servicemen) when a finer perception could readily have been achieved by assessing a serviceman's claim to residency on an individualized basis.

> "We recognize that special problems may be involved in determining whether servicemen have actually acquired a new domicile in State for franchise purposes. We emphasize that Texas is free to take reasonable and adequate steps, as have other States, to see that all applicants for the vote actually fulfill the requirements of bona fide residence. But [the challenged] provision goes beyond such rules. '[T]he presumption here created is . . . definitely conclusive—incapable of being overcome by proof of the most positive character.'" *Id.*, at 96, 85 S.Ct., at 780.

"All servicemen not residents of Texas before induction," we concluded, "come within the provision's sweep. Not one of them can ever vote in Texas, no matter" what their individual qualifications. *Ibid.* We found such a situation repugnant to the Equal Protection Clause.

Despite *Bell* and *Carrington*, it may be argued that unmarried fathers are so seldom fit that Illinois need not undergo the administrative inconvenience of inquiry in any case, including Stanley's. The establishment of prompt efficacious procedures to achieve legitimate state ends is a proper state interest worthy of cognizance in constitutional adjudication. But the Constitution recognizes higher values than speed and efficiency.[8] Indeed, one might fairly say of the Bill of Rights in general, and the Due Process Clause in particular, that they were designed to protect the fragile values of a vulnerable citizenry from the overbearing concern for efficiency and efficacy that may charac-

---

[6]The State speaks of the "general disinterest of putative fathers in their illegitimate children" (Brief 8) and opines that "[i]n most instances the natural father is a stranger to his children." Brief 31.

[7]See In re T., 8 Mich.App. 122, 154 N.W. 2d 27 (1967). There a panel of the Michigan Court of Appeals in unanimously affirming a circuit court's determination that the father of an illegitimate son was best suited to raise the boy, said:

> "The appellants' presentation in this case proceeds on the assumption that placing Mark for adoption is inherently preferable to rearing by his father, that uprooting him from the family which he knew from birth until he was a year and a half old, secretly institutionalizing him and later transferring him to strangers is so incontrovertibly better that no court has the power even to consider the matter. Hardly anyone would even suggest such a proposition if we were talking about a child born in wedlock.
>
> "We are not aware of any sociological data justifying the assumption that an illegitimate child reared by his natural father is less likely to receive a proper upbringing than one reared by his natural father who was at one time married to his mother, or that the stigma of illegitimacy is so pervasive it requires adoption by strangers and permanent termination of a subsisting relationship with the child's father." *Id.*, at 146, 154 N.W.2d, at 39.

[8]Cf. Reed v. Reed, 404 U.S. 71, 76, 92 S.Ct. 251, 254, 30 L.Ed.2d 225 (1971). "Clearly the objective of reducing the workload on probate courts by eliminating one class of contests is not without some legitimacy. . . . [But to] give a mandatory preference to members of either sex over members of the other, merely to accomplish the elimination of hearings on the merits, is to make the very kind of arbitrary legislative choice forbidden by the Equal Protection Clause of the Fourteenth Amendment." Carrington v. Rash, 380 U.S. 89, 96, 85 S.Ct. 775, 780 (1965), teaches the same lesson. ". . . States may not casually deprive a class of individuals of the vote because of some remote administrative benefit to the State. Oyama v. [State of] California, 332 U.S. 633, 68 S.Ct. 269, 92 L.Ed. 249. By forbidding a soldier ever to controvert the presumption of nonresidence, the Texas Constitution imposes an invidious discrimination in violation of the Fourteenth Amendment."

terize praiseworthy government officials no less, and perhaps more, than mediocre ones.

Procedure by presumption is always cheaper and easier than individualized determination. But when, as here, the procedure forecloses the determinative issues of competence and care, when it explicitly disdains present realities in deference to past formalities, it needlessly risks running roughshod over the important interests of both parent and child. It therefore cannot stand.[9]

Bell v. Burson held that the State could not, while purporting to be concerned with fault in suspending a driver's license, deprive a citizen of his license without a hearing that would assess fault. Absent fault, the State's declared interest was so attenuated that administrative convenience was insufficient to excuse a hearing where evidence of fault could be considered. That drivers involved in accidents, as a statistical matter, might be very likely to have been wholly or partially at fault did not foreclose hearing and proof in specific cases before licenses were suspended.

We think the Due Process Clause mandates a similar result here. The State's interest in caring for Stanley's children is *de minimis* if Stanley is shown to be a fit father. It insists on presuming rather than proving Stanley's unfitness solely because it is more convenient to presume than to prove. Under the Due Process Clause that advantage is insufficient to justify refusing a father a hearing when the issue at stake is the dismemberment of his family.

III

The State of Illinois assumes custody of the children of married parents, divorced parents, and unmarried mothers only after a hearing and proof of neglect. The children of unmarried fathers, however, are declared dependent children without a hearing on parental fitness and without proof of neglect. Stanley's claim in the state courts and here is the failure to afford him a hearing on his parental qualifications while extending it to other parents denied him equal protection of the laws. We have concluded that all Illinois parents are constitutionally entitled to a hearing on their fitness before their children are removed from their custody. It follows that denying such a hearing to Stanley and those like him while granting it to other Illinois parents is inescapably contrary to the Equal Protection Clause.[10]

The judgment of the Supreme Court of Illinois is reversed and the case is remanded to that court for proceedings not inconsistent with this opinion. It is so ordered.

Reversed and remanded.

Mr. Justice POWELL and Mr. Justice REHNQUIST took no part in the consideration or decision of this case.

Mr. Justice DOUGLAS joins in Partsz I and II of this opinion.

Mr. Justice BURGER, with whom Mr. Justice BLACKMUN concurs, dissenting.

The only constitutional issue raised and decided in the courts of Illinois in this case was whether the Illinois statute that omits unwed fathers from the definition of "parents" violates the Equal Protection Clause. We granted certiorari to consider whether the Illinois

---

[9]We note in passing that the incremental cost of offering unwed fathers an opportunity for individualized hearings on fitness appears to be minimal. If unwed fathers, in the main, do not care about the disposition of their children, they will not appear to demand hearings. If they do care, under the scheme here held invalid, Illinois would admittedly at some later time have to afford them a properly focused hearing in a custody or adoption proceeding.

Extending opportunity for hearing to unwed fathers who desire and claim competence to care for their children creates no constitutional or procedural obstacle to foreclosing those unwed fathers who are not so inclined. The Illinois law governing procedure in juvenile cases, Ill.Rev.Stat., c. 37, § 704–1 et seq., provides for personal service, notice by certified mail, or for notice by publication when personal or certified mail service cannot be had or when notice is directed to unknown respondents under the style of "All whom it may Concern." Unwed fathers who do not promptly respond cannot complain if their children are declared wards of the State. Those who do respond retain the burden of proving their fatherhood.

[10]Predicating a finding of constitutional invalidity under the Equal Protection Clause of the Fourteenth Amendment on the observation that a State has accorded bedrock procedural rights to some, but not to all similarly situated, is not contradictory to our holding in Picard v. Connor, 404 U.S. 270, 92 S.Ct. 509, 30 L.Ed.2d 438 (1971). In that case a due process, rather than an equal protection, claim was raised in the state courts. The federal courts were, in our opinion, barred from reversing the state conviction on grounds of contravention of the Equal Protection Clause when that clause had not been referred to for consideration by the state authorities. Here, in contrast, we dispose of the case on the constitutional premise raised below, reaching the result by a method of analysis readily available to the state court.

For the same reason the strictures of Cardinale v. Louisiana, 394 U.S. 437, 89 S.Ct. 1161, 22 L.Ed.2d 398 (1969), and Hill v. California, 401 U.S. 797, 91 S.Ct. 1106, 28 L.Ed.2d 484 (1971), have been fully observed.

Supreme Court properly resolved that equal protection issue when it unanimously upheld the statute against petitioner Stanley's attack.

No due process issue was raised in the state courts; and no due process issue was decided by any state court. As Mr. Justice Douglas said for this Court in State Farm Mutual Automobile Ins. Co. v. Duel, 324 U.S. 154, 160, 65 S.Ct. 573, 577, 89 L.Ed. 812 (1945), "Since the [state] Supreme Court did not pass on the question, we may not do so." We had occasion more recently to deal with this aspect of the jurisdictional limits placed upon this Court by 28 U.S.C. § 1257 when we decided Hill v. California, 401 U.S. 797, 91 S.Ct. 1106, 28 L.Ed.2d 484 (1971). Having rejected the claim that Chimel v. California, 395 U.S. 752, 89 S.Ct. 2034, 23 L.Ed.2d 685 (1969), should be retroactively applied to invalidate petitioner Hill's conviction on the ground that a search incident to arrest was overly extensive in scope, the Court noted Hill's additional contention that his personal diary, which was one of the items of evidence seized in that search, should have been excluded on Fifth Amendment grounds as well. Mr. Justice White, in his opinion for the Court, concluded that we lacked jurisdiction to consider the Fifth Amendment contention:

> "Counsel for [the petitioner] conceded at oral argument that the Fifth Amendment issue was not raised at trial. Nor was the issue raised, briefed or argued in the California appellate courts. [Footnote omitted.] The petition for certiorari likewise ignored it. In this posture of the case, the question, although briefed and argued here, is not properly before us." 401 U.S., at 805, 91 S.Ct., at 1111.

In the case now before us, it simply does not suffice to say, as the Court in a footnote does say, that "we dispose of the case on the constitutional premise raised below, reaching the result by a method of analysis readily available to the state court." *Ante,* at 1216 n. 10. The Court's method of analysis seems to ignore the strictures of Justices Douglas and White, but the analysis is clear: the Court holds *sua sponte* that the Due Process Clause requires that Stanley, the unwed biological father, be accorded a hearing as to his fitness as a parent before his children are declared wards of the state court; the Court then reasons that since Illinois recognizes such rights to due process in married fathers, it is required by the Equal Protection Clause to give such protection to unmarried fathers. This "method of analysis" is, of course, no more or less than the use of the Equal Protection Clause as a shorthand condensation of the entire Constitution: a State may not deny *any* constitutional right to some of its citizens without violating the Equal Protection Clause through its failure to deny such rights to *all* of its citizens. The limits on this Court's jurisdiction are not properly expandable by the use of such semantic devices as that.

Not only does the Court today use dubious reasoning in dealing with limitations upon its jurisdiction, it proceeds as well to strike down the Illinois statute here involved by "answering" arguments that are nowhere to be found in the record or in the State's brief—or indeed in the oral argument. I have been unable, for example, to discover where or when the State has advanced any argument that "it is unnecessary to hold individualized hearings to determine whether particular fathers are in fact unfit parents before they are separated from their children." *Ante,* at 1210. Nor can I discover where the State has "argu[ed] that Stanley and all other unmarried fathers can reasonably be presumed to be unqualified to raise their children." *Ante,* at 1213. Or where anyone has even remotely suggested the "argu[ment] that unmarried fathers are so seldom fit that Illinois need not undergo the administrative inconvenience of inquiry in any case, including Stanley's." *Ante,* at 1215. On the other hand, the arguments actually advanced by the State are largely ignored by the Court.[11]

---

[11]In reaching out to find a due process issue in this case, the Court seems to have misapprehended the entire thrust of the State's argument. When explaining at oral argument why Illinois does not recognize the unwed father, counsel for the State presented two basic justifications for the statutory definition of "parents" here at issue. See Tr. of Oral Arg. 25–26. First, counsel noted that in the case of a married couple to whom a legitimate child is born, the two biological parents have already "signified their willingness to work together" in caring for the child by entering into the marriage contract; it is manifestly reasonable, therefore, that both of them be recognized as legal parents with rights and responsibilities in connection with the child. There has been no legally cognizable signification of such willingness on the part of unwed parents, however, and "the male and female . . . may or may not be willing to work together towards the common end of child rearing." To provide legal recognition to both of them as "parents" would often be "to create two conflicting parties competing for legal control of the child."

The second basic justification urged upon us by counsel for the State was that, in order to provide for the child's welfare, "it is necessary to impose upon at least one of the parties legal responsibility for the welfare of [the child], and since necessarily the female is present at the birth of the child and identifiable as the mother," the State has elected the unwed mother, rather than the unwed father, as the biological parent with that legal responsibility.

All of those persons in Illinois who may have followed the progress of this case will, I expect, experience no little surprise at the Court's opinion handed down today. Stanley will undoubtedly be surprised to find that he has prevailed on an issue never advanced by him. The judges who dealt with this case in the state courts will be surprised to find their decisions overturned on a ground they never considered. And the legislators and other officials of the State of Illinois, as well as those attorneys of the State who are familiar with the statutory provisions here at issue, will be surprised to learn for the first time that the Illinois Juvenile Court Act establishes a presumption that unwed fathers are unfit. I must confess my own inability to find any such presumption in the Illinois Act. Furthermore, from the record of the proceedings in the Juvenile Court of Cook County in this case, I can only conclude that the judge of that court was unaware of any such presumption, for he clearly indicated that Stanley's asserted fatherhood of the children would stand him in good stead, rather than prejudice him, in any adoption or guardianship proceeding. In short, far from any intimations of hostility toward unwed fathers, that court gave Stanley "merit points" for his acknowledgment of paternity and his past assumption of at least marginal responsibility for the children.[12]

In regard to the only issue that I consider properly before the Court, I agree with the State's argument that the equal Protection Clause is not violated when Illinois gives full recognition only to those father-child relationships that arise in the context of family units bound together by legal obligations arising from marriage or from adoption proceedings. Quite apart from the religious or quasi-religious connotations that marriage has—and has historically enjoyed—for a large proportion of this Nation's citizens, it is in law an essentially contractual relationship, the parties to which have legally enforceable rights and duties, with respect both to each other and to any children born to them. Stanley and the mother of these children never entered such a relationship. The record is silent as to whether they ever privately exchanged such promises as would have bound them in marriage under the common law. See Cartwright v. McGown, 121 Ill. 388, 398, 12 N.E. 737, 739 (1887). In any event, Illinois has not recognized common-law marriages since 1905. Ill.Rev.Stat., c. 89, § 4. Stanley did not seek the burdens when he could have freely assumed them.

Where there is a valid contract of marriage, the law of Illinois presumes that the husband is the father of any child born to the wife during the marriage; as the father, he has legally enforceable rights and duties with respect to that child. When a child is born to an unmarried woman, Illinois recognizes the readily identifiable mother, but makes no presumption as to the identity of the biological father. It does, however, provide two ways, one voluntary and one involuntary, in which that father may be identified. First, he may marry the mother and acknowledge the child as his own; this has the legal effect of legitimating the child and gaining for the father full recognition as a parent. Ill.Rev.Stat., c. 3, § 12, subd. 8. Second, a man may be found to be the biological father of the child pursuant to a paternity suit initiated by the mother; in this case, the child remains illegitimate, but the adjudicated father is made liable for the support of the child until the latter attains age 18 or is legally adopted by another. Ill.Rev.Stat., c. 106¾, § 52.

Stanley argued before the Supreme Court of Illinois that the definition of "parents," set out in Ill.Rev.Stat., c. 37, § 701–14, as including "the father and mother of a legitimate child, or the survivor of them, or the natural mother of an illegitimate child, [or] . . . any adoptive

---

It was suggested to counsel during an ensuing colloquy with the bench that identification seemed to present no insuperable problem in Stanley's case and that, although Stanley had expressed an interest in participating in the rearing of the children, "Illinois won't let him." Counsel replied that, on the contrary, "Illinois encourages him to do so if he will accept the legal responsibility for those children by a formal proceeding comparable to the marriage ceremony, in which he is evidencing through a judicial proceeding his desire to accept legal responsibility for the children." Stanley, however, "did not ask for custody. He did not ask for legal responsibility. He only objected to someone [else] having legal control over the children." Tr. of Oral Arg. 38, 39–40.

[12]The position that Stanley took at the dependency proceeding was not without ambiguity. Shortly after the mother's death, he placed the children in the care of Mr. and Mrs. Ness, who took the children into their home. The record is silent as to whether the Ness household was an approved foster home. Through Stanley's act, then, the Nesses were already the *actual* custodians of the children. At the dependency proceeding, he resisted only the court's designation of the Nesses as the legal custodians; he did not challenge their suitability for that role, nor did he seek for himself either that role or any other role that would have imposed legal responsibility upon him. Had he prevailed, of course, the *status quo* would have obtained: the Nesses would have continued to play the role of actual custodians until either they or Stanley acted to alter the informal arrangement, and there would still have been no living adult with any legally enforceable obligation for the care and support of the infant children.

parent,"[13] violates the Equal Protection Clause in that it treats unwed mothers and unwed fathers differently. Stanley then enlarged upon his equal protection argument when he brought the case here; he argued before this Court that Illinois is not permitted by the Equal Protection Clause to distinguish between unwed fathers and any of the other biological parents included in the statutory definition of legal "parents."

The Illinois Supreme Court correctly held that the State may constitutionally distinguish between unwed fathers and unwed mothers. Here, Illinois' different treatment of the two is part of that State's statutory scheme of protecting the welfare of illegitimate children. In almost all cases, the unwed mother is readily identifiable, generally from hospital records, and alternatively by physicians or others attending the child's birth. Unwed fathers, as a class, are not traditionally quite so easy to identify and locate. Many of them either deny all responsibility or exhibit no interest in the child or its welfare; and, of course, many unwed fathers are simply not aware of their parenthood.

Furthermore, I believe that a State is fully justified in concluding, on the basis of common human experience, that the biological role of the mother in carrying and nursing an infant creates stronger bonds between her and the child than the bonds resulting from the male's often casual encounter. This view is reinforced by the observable fact that most unwed mothers exhibit a concern for their offspring either permanently or at least until they are safely placed for adoption, while unwed fathers rarely burden either the mother or the child with their attentions or loyalties. Centuries of human experience buttress this view of the realities of human conditions and suggest that unwed mothers of illegitimate children are generally more dependable protectors of their children than are unwed fathers. While these, like most generalizations, are not without exceptions, they nevertheless provide a sufficient basis to sustain a statutory classification whose objective is not to penalize unwed parents but to further the welfare of illegitimate children in fulfillment of the State's obligations as *parens patriae*.[14]

Stanley depicts himself as a somewhat unusual unwed father, namely, as one who has always acknowledged and never doubted his fatherhood of these children. He alleges that he loved, cared for, and supported these children from the time of their birth until the death of their mother. He contends that he consequently must be treated the same as a married father of legitimate children. Even assuming the truth of Stanley's allegations, I am unable to construe the Equal Protection Clause as requiring Illinois to tailor its statutory definition of "parents" so meticulously as to include such unusual unwed fathers, while at the same time excluding those unwed, and generally unidentified, biological fathers who in no way share Stanley's professed desires.

Indeed, the nature of Stanley's own desires is less than absolutely clear from the record in this case. Shortly after the death of the mother, Stanley turned these two children over to the care of a Mr. and Mrs. Ness; he took no action to gain recognition of himself as a father, through adoption, or as a legal custodian, through a guardianship proceeding. Eventually it came to the attention of the State that there was no living adult who had any legally enforceable obligation for the care and support of the children; it was only then that the dependency proceeding here under review took place and that Stanley made himself known to the juvenile court in connection with these

[13]The Court seems at times to ignore this statutory definition of "parents," even though it is precisely that definition itself whose constitutionality has been brought into issue by Stanley. In preparation for finding a purported similarity between this case and Bell v. Burson, 402 U.S. 535, 91 S.Ct. 1586, 29 L.Ed.2d 90 (1971), the Court quotes the legislatively declared aims of the Juvenile Court Act to "strengthen the minor's family ties whenever possible, removing him from the custody of his *parents* only when his welfare or safety or the protection of the public cannot be adequately safeguarded without removal." (Emphasis added.) The Court then goes on to find a "self-contradiction" between that stated aim and the Act's nonrecognition of unwed fathers. *Ante,* at 1213. There is, of course, no such contradiction. The word "parent" in the statement of legislative purpose obviously has the meaning given to it by the definitional provision of the Act.

[14]When the marriage between the parents of a legitimate child is dissolved by divorce or separation, the State, of course, normally awards custody of the child to one parent or the other. This is considered necessary for the child's welfare, since the parents are no longer legally bound together. The unmarried parents of an illegitimate child are likewise not legally bound together. Thus, even if Illinois did recognize the parenthood of both the mother and father of an illegitimate child, it would, of consistency with its practice in divorce proceedings, be called upon to award custody to one or the other of them, at least once it had by some means ascertained the identity of the father.

two children.[15] Even then, however, Stanley did not ask to be charged with the legal responsibility for the children. He asked only that such legal responsibility be given to no one else. He seemed, in particular, to be concerned with the loss of the welfare payments he would suffer as a result of the designation of others as guardians of the children.

Not only, then, do I see no ground for holding that Illinois' statutory definition of "parents" on its face violates the Equal Protection Clause; I see no ground for holding that any constitutional right of Stanley has been denied in the application of that statutory definition in the case at bar.

As Mr. Justice Frankfurter once observed, "Invalidating legislation is serious business. . . ." Morey v. Doud, 354 U.S. 457, 474, 77 S.Ct. 1344, 1354, 1 L.Ed.2d 1485 (1957) (dissenting opinion). The Court today pursues that serious business by expanding its legitimate jurisdiction beyond what I read in 28 U.S.C. § 1257 as the permissible limits contemplated by Congress. In doing so, it invalidates a provision of critical importance to Illinois' carefully drawn statutory system governing family relationships and the welfare of the minor children of the State. And in so invalidating that provision, it ascribes to that statutory system a presumption that is simply not there and embarks on a novel concept of the natural law of unwed fathers that could well have strange boundaries as yet undiscernible.

---

[15]As the majority notes, *ante,* at 1210, Joan Stanley gave birth to three children during the 18 years Peter Stanley was living "intermittently" with her. At oral argument, we were told by Stanley's counsel that the oldest of these three children had previously been declared a ward of the court pursuant to a neglect proceeding that was "proven against" Stanley at a time, apparently, when the juvenile court officials were under the erroneous impression that Peter and Joan Stanley had been married. Tr. of Oral Arg. 19.

PART 9

EMPLOYMENT LAW

Legal issues concerning employment have always generated controversy. In the United States during the late nineteenth century, labor unions began organizing workers into groups. Despite opposition from business and setbacks by Supreme Court decisions, unions made inroads.[1] Eventually, labor unions changed the nature of many employment relations, which had previously been governed by the employment-at-will doctrine. Before unions, employees were hired and fired at the will of their employers. Labor unions wrought dramatic changes. The collective bargaining strength of organized workers forced management to issue contracts to workers and provide them with benefits, such as safer working conditions, pensions, sick pay, and severance pay. Employment in the United States changed again during World War II, when women entered the workforce in droves. Another transformation resulted from the Civil Rights movement of the 1960s, when people of color, especially African Americans, began agitating for equal employment opportunities and affirmative action programs. The Civil Rights Act of 1964, a landmark, dramatically altered hiring, promotion, and firing practices. Yet another dramatic shift was brought about by the feminist movement of the 1970s. Feminist lawyers, especially Catherine A. MacKinnon, forged a new area of law—sexual harassment law. Over the years, sexual harassment cases have come to be litigated as sex discrimination cases under the Civil Rights Act of 1964 and subsequent federal antidiscrimination laws. Developments in this area of law have had profound effects on employment practices.

The essays in Part 9 focus on affirmative action debates and on sexual harassment law and sex discrimination law. This emphasis is not meant to deny the importance of other issues in employment law, but rather to underscore how profoundly and pervasively the emergence of women and people of color in the workplace has affected employment law.

The first two selections are essays from *Affirmative Action: Social Justice or Unfair Preference?* by Albert G. Mosley and Nicholas Capaldi. Mosley argues for affirmative action; Capaldi, against. Affirmative action programs have been defended by two kinds of arguments. Forward-looking arguments claim that affirmative action is necessary for fully integrating minorities and women into the workplace. Backward-looking arguments maintain that affirmative action will compensate groups or individuals for injustices suffered from past discrimination. In "Affirmative Action: Pro," Mosley gives a review of recent case law and considers backward-looking arguments for affirmative action—that is, defenses of affirmative action on grounds of compensatory justice.

The crystallizing moment in the history of affirmative action legislation was the passage of the Civil Rights Act of 1964. Title VII of the act prohibits discrimination based on race, color, religion, sex, or national origin. Title VII did not specify the definition

[1]See, for example, Lawrence M. Friedman, *Crime and Punishment in American History* (New York: Basic Books, 1993): 104–6.

of discrimination, but the courts have delineated three forms it can take. *Disparate treatment* occurs when one either classifies people who are similar, in some relevant respect, as different or classifies people who are different as similar. *Adverse impact* occurs when an apparently neutral procedure, such as testing or interviewing, or any educational or other prerequisite not directly relevant to a given position or occupation disproportionately eliminates a particular group from holding that position or occupation. A third form of discrimination is *perpetuating the effects of past discrimination into the present,* as occurs when a particular group is excluded from training, promotion, or retention benefits.

Legal rulings on allegedly discriminatory practices have been complex and controversial. For example, in *Griggs v. Duke Power Company,*[2] the Court ruled that the burden of proof rested with the employer to show that practices that have a disparate impact on protected minorities are justified by business necessity. The Court reversed itself on this point in more recent cases, such as *Watson v. Fort Worth Bank and Trust* and *Wards Cove Packing v. Antonio.*[3] In these later cases, the Court maintained that the burden of proof rests with the plaintiff to show that a specific employment practice discriminates against a protected group. However, as Mosley notes, the Civil Rights Bill of 1990 reversed the Supreme Court's rulings in these cases, shifting the burden of proof back to the employer to show that an employment practice with adverse impact on a protected group is justified by business necessity.

Reverse discrimination has also raised much controversy. Reverse discrimination claims are usually brought by white male plaintiffs who believe they have been unjustly discriminated against as a result of affirmative action programs. Does affirmative action in employment invidiously discriminate on the basis of race? In *United Steelworkers v. Weber,*[4] the Supreme Court held that it does not. Here, a majority of the Court argued that the purpose of Title VII is to open employment opportunities to African Americans in areas denied them by discrimination. This purpose, the Court held, could justify using race-conscious policies.

The use of race-based classifications has been an ongoing bone of contention in the affirmative action debate. Critics of affirmative action argue that any use of race-based classifications or policies is an invidious means of achieving a color-blind society that violates the equal protection clause of the Fourteenth Amendment. Proponents maintain that it is possible to distinguish invidious from benign uses of racial categories, and that racial classifications must be used to undo the present and past effects of racism. In cases such as *Richmond v. J. A. Croson Company* and *Adarand Constructors Inc. v. Pena,*[5] a majority of the Supreme Court held that, to be constitutional, the use of racial classifications must be subjected to strict scrutiny. *Strict scrutiny* means that a court must review the use of racial classifications to determine whether they redress specific instances of discrimination and are thus narrowly tailored to advance a compelling state interest.

Backward-looking arguments, such as those used by the Supreme Court in *Croson* and *Adarand,* defend affirmative action on the ground that if someone is unjustly deprived of a good or an opportunity, corrective justice requires that the good be restored or that the person be placed in the situation he or she would have occupied had the opportunity not been denied. Mosley observes that most critics of preferential treatment acknowledge the force of backward-looking arguments in cases of unjust discrimination against individuals. These critics object, however, when preferential treatment programs are used to provide group reparations for past harms. The objection is twofold: first, that individuals who benefit from present affirmative action programs are not the ones who have been harmed by past discrimination; second, that qualified applicants who are presently denied positions filled by affirmative action hires are paying a price that should have been borne by those who benefited from past discriminatory practices.

In response, Mosley argues that neither the harms of racism nor its benefits are confined to those individuals directly hurt or helped by discriminatory practices. Racism has pervasive and negative effects on all members of a disadvantaged group. Moreover, because privileged groups benefit from racism through unjust enrichment, one ongoing result of past and present racism is that members of privileged groups develop morally unfounded expectations

[2]401 U.S. 424 (1971).

[3]487 U.S. 977 (1988); 490 U.S. 692 (1989).

[4]443 U.S. 193 (1979).

[5]488 U.S. 469 (1989); 515 U.S. 200 (1995).

about the societal advantages they can and should enjoy. Affirmative action programs, Mosley argues, are fully justified in addressing these wider effects.

In "Affirmative Action: Con," Capaldi argues that affirmative action is illegal and immoral. He begins with the assertion that there is no generally accepted definition of affirmative action. He then lists five possible definitions and contends that two of them delineate senses of affirmative action that are illegal: (1) backward-looking policies designed to rectify the effects of past discrimination and (2) forward-looking preferential treatment programs aimed at achieving some social goal, such as a color-blind society. According to Capaldi, backward-looking policies seek to place victims of past discrimination in positions they would have occupied had it not been for discrimination. They rely on a contrary-to-fact condition: they seek to identify what would have happened if something else had not happened. Forward-looking policies, according to Capaldi, rely on the use of quotas for group representation.

He gives five reasons for thinking that affirmative action in these senses is illegal. First, the Constitution makes clear that individuals, not groups, have rights. Second, two separate provisions of Title VII of the Civil Rights Act of 1964 specifically outlaw the use of preference in employment practices. Capaldi bolsters this claim by referring to the legislative record concerning these provisions. Third, the Supreme Court rejected preferential treatment in *Griggs*. Fourth, in *Bakke,*[6] the Supreme Court attacked and rejected the backward-looking, quota-based approach to affirmative action. Finally, in *Adarand,* the Court considered the Minority Business Enterprise provision of the Public Works Employment Act of 1977. This provision required that a certain percentage of federal funds allocated to state and local governments be used to purchase goods and services from minority-owned businesses, even if other firms offered a lower bid, on the ground that minority-owned businesses had suffered from discrimination in the past and were owed compensation. As you know, in *Adarand,* the Court ruled that the use of racial classifications is subject to strict scrutiny. Capaldi argues that the Court in *Adarand* thereby invalidates affirmative action in the two senses he describes, though it upholds as legal another sense of affirmative action, that in which affirmative action programs are court ordered and narrowly fashioned in order to redress proven specific instances of discrimination.

Is affirmative action immoral? Capaldi argues that it is. He seeks to show that affirmative action violates the fundamental principles that we, as a society, are committed to. He enumerates six such principles that articulate a commitment to two overarching values: individual freedom and equal opportunity. Drawing on quotes from court cases and political leaders, Capaldi makes the case that these values imply a commitment to a color-blind society, in which the worth and rights of individuals—not the histories and treatment of groups—are paramount. Affirmative action programs that promote compensatory and preferential treatment for groups violate the rights of specific individuals to freedom and equality of opportunity. In a deeper sense, these programs offend the moral principles to which the United States as a nation is committed. Consequently, Capaldi claims, affirmative action programs are immoral.

The United States is not the only nation with a history of racial oppression in which debates about affirmative action rage. Wiseman Nkuhlu's piece, "Affirmative Action for South Africa in Transition: From Theory to Practice," gives a glimpse of affirmative action in the new South Africa. Apartheid was a tool for the political exclusion and economic oppression of blacks in South Africa. However, Nkuhlu points out that, since the past is gone, there is little to be gained from using affirmative action as a means of obtaining compensatory justice. More pressing, in his view, is the use of affirmative action as a forward-looking instrument for empowering blacks in South African society. In a society in which 86 percent of the population is black, future economic prosperity depends crucially on enabling blacks to gain the skills and knowledge needed to contribute fully to society. Not only is this essential for future economic well-being, it is also key to restoring blacks' sense of self-worth and their pride in African culture, which apartheid sought to destroy.

Nkuhlu advances a subtle analysis of the pros and cons of affirmative action. He identifies five key issues to be addressed by affirmative action, on the basis of which he offers a range of practical suggestions for

---

[6]*Regents of the University of California v. Bakke,* 438 U.S. 265 (1978).

implementing affirmative action in South Africa. First, blacks must have the preferential support needed to enable them to achieve higher levels of technological and managerial competence. Second, they must be allowed access to economic resources and appropriate support. Third, they must be given space and opportunities to contribute. Affirmative action efforts will be futile, Nkuhlu contends, if blacks cannot attain positions of leadership. Fourth, black trainees in affirmative action programs should not be the only people willing to change; white managers and organizations must change their approach to black advancement. The viability of affirmative action in South Africa depends on the cooperation and contributions of all participants in these programs. Finally, Nkuhlu stresses that affirmative action must address the negative mind-set of black people. Years of apartheid have fostered a host of negative feelings among black South Africans. Fear, anger, resentment, mistrust of government and of white people, and feelings of inadequacy and low self-esteem must be overcome if blacks are to participate fully and equally in South African society. Affirmative action can and should be viewed as a kind of therapy for blacks—as an affirmation of black self-worth and moral and social value.

How is affirmative action in the new South Africa to be achieved? Nkuhlu offers a range of practical suggestions. Their salient feature is their comprehensiveness. Affirmative action must be implemented in all aspects and at all levels of South African life. Complementing these suggestions is the next selection, "Extracts from a Working Document Entitled 'A Bill of Rights for a New South Africa' As Compiled by the Constitutional Committee of the ANC" (African National Congress). Four articles from that document are included here. Articles 13 and 14 specify a commitment to affirmative action and to the positive actions that should be taken to achieve it. Articles 7 and 8 articulate a commitment to gender equality and the rights of disabled people.

The ANC's proposals to eliminate discrimination are not uncontroversial. Indeed, they are sweeping. Of special interest are points three and four under Article 14. Point three provides in part that the State has a duty "to dismantle all structures and do away with all practices that compulsorily divide the population on grounds of race, colour, language, or creed" (see p. 664). Point four empowers the State to "enact legislation to prohibit the circulation or possession of materials which incite racial, ethnic, religious, gender or linguistic hatred" (p. 664). Of course, point four falls foul of the First Amendment of the United States Constitution. However, similar but less extensive proposals in the United States have been made in the form of campus speech codes.

In contrast to the breadth of the ANC's proposals, see the next selection—Article 1, Section 31 of the California State Constitution. This is the descendant of the famous "Proposition 209," approved by California voters in 1996, which effectively ended state-sponsored affirmative action programs in California. Provision (a) is clear: "The state shall not discriminate against, or grant preferential treatment to, any individual or group on the basis of race, sex, color, ethnicity, or national origin in the operation of public employment, public education, or public contracting" (p. 665). Provision (a) is qualified by subsequent provisions, but its impact is evident. This legislation reflects the growing dissatisfaction that many U.S. citizens, both black and white, feel for affirmative action programs.

Sexual harassment is another large and controversial topic affecting employment law. In "Sexual Harassment and Solidarity," Larry May, a philosopher and co-editor of this anthology, analyzes the harms of sexual harassment and examines male reactions to sexual harassment. May examines the harms involved in the two kinds of sexual harassment case the Supreme Court has recognized: *quid pro quo* and hostile environment. A landmark case of harassment in academia, *Alexander v. Yale University,*[7] provides a focal point for discussing the harms of *quid pro quo.* In *Alexander,* a female student alleged that a male professor threatened to lower her grade on a term paper from a B to a C unless she slept with him. Given these facts, the harm of sexual harassment is fairly clear. A coercive threat was made which, if refused, would have worsened the student's post-offer situation in comparison with her pre-offer situation. However, the professor denied the student's version of the story, claiming instead that he had offered to raise her grade from a C to a B if she slept with him. She declined the offer, and did not thereby

[7] 459 F. Supp. 1 (D. Conn. 1977), 631 F. 2d 178 (2d Cir. 1980).

worsen her post-offer situation relative to her pre-offer situation. Consequently, no harm was done.

May argues, however, that moral wrongs can occur even in cases of sexual offers or innuendos with no apparent coercion. A moral wrong can occur when a woman's options are restricted undeservedly and against her will. In these kinds of case, the moral wrong is an illegitimate restriction of the woman's autonomy. This wrong occurs even if the restriction does not actually harm the woman. Consequently, even if the facts in *Alexander* were as the professor claimed, his offer morally wronged the student because it restricted her autonomy undeservedly and against her will.

Had the professor prevailed in *Alexander,* the student's grade would have been determined on the basis of sexual characteristics irrelevant to academic performance. As such, another kind of harm occurred in *Alexander*—hostile environment. A *hostile environment* occurs when sexual remarks, displays, photos, or depictions are so severe and pervasive that they alter the conditions of employment and create an abusive atmosphere. This leads men to view their female colleagues in terms of sexual characteristics and not solely in terms of job-related attributes. In hostile environments, men become free not to take women seriously as full and equal workplace participants. Hostile environments signal to women that they will be viewed as sexual objects and their contributions not taken as seriously as those of men, who are not viewed in sexual terms. Thus, the chief harm of hostile environments is that they create an atmosphere of discrimination in which women are not viewed as full and equal workplace participants. Sexual harassment in hostile environments thereby demeans women. Even when the harassment is subtle, such as an occasional off-color joke, it effectively demeans women and excludes them from full and equal participation. Similar arguments apply to the harassment of gay men by heterosexual men in the workplace.

May links the harassment and exclusion of women and gay men from full and equal workplace participation to male bonding processes that foster solidarity and inclusiveness. "Putting down" women and gays is one traditional way heterosexual men have maintained their position as a dominant group in society. But group solidarity and inclusiveness, May argues, are goods that should not be purchased at the price of excluding and demeaning nonmembers of the group. Men have positive qualities that can foster healthier forms of inclusiveness. Traditional male strengths, he claims, include the practical skills of achieving compromise and building consensus. Consequently, men can and should see themselves as consensus seekers, concerned with building solidarity in mixed groups. Further positive modeling for men in mixed groups comes from team sports, which require collaboration, coordination, and an ability to work with players of different skill levels. May's insights contribute greatly to our understanding of sexual harassment law, for they address the emotional and psychological sources of the behavior that the law is intended to punish and suppress.

Employment law is an evolving discipline. The last two selections explore recent developments that affect sexual harassment law. In "Sexual Character Evidence in Civil Actions: Refining the Propensity Rule," Jane Harris Aiken examines the implications of the rules of evidence for the success or failure of plaintiffs in civil suits for sexual misconduct. At first glance, the rules of evidence might seem abstract and enigmatic, far removed from the realities of workplace interaction. But these rules are crucial to the outcomes of sexual misconduct litigation, for they regulate the facts and allegations that one can admit as evidence in a court of law.

Sexual misconduct cases, Aiken claims, often revolve around two central questions: "Did she invite it?" and "Has he done it before?" In 1995, Congress adopted two significant changes to the rules of evidence that affect whether these questions can be raised in civil cases in federal court, including cases of alleged sexual harassment. New rule 412 extends rape shield protections to plaintiffs in sexual misconduct cases. Rape shield laws prevent information about the plaintiff's sexual history from being introduced as evidence in rape cases, subject to enumerated restrictions. New rule 415 allows plaintiffs to present evidence of a defendant's prior similar acts of sexual misbehavior in order to show that he or she is the kind of person who engages in sexual misconduct. This facilitates the implication that the defendant engaged in the alleged sexual misconduct in the present case.

The more dramatic change, according to Aiken, is new rule 415. Prior to its adoption, the rules of evidence prevented plaintiffs from introducing evidence of a defendant's past sexual misconduct. This permitted juries to assume that the defendant was "Mr. Clean." Allowing the admissibility of evidence of past sexual misconduct thus has the potential to create significant changes in the outcomes of sexual misconduct cases.

However, dramatic changes have not occurred. One reason for this, Aiken contends, is that evidence of a defendant's prior acts to prove character has traditionally been inadmissible. In spite of new rule 415, federal judges have been reluctant to challenge the character bar. Judges are charged with determining the relevance of evidence, as well as with deciding whether the probative value of evidence outweighs its possible prejudicial effects. Despite the fact that rule 415 seems to leave judges with little discretion in determining admissibility, judges have nonetheless excluded evidence introduced in accordance with rule 415 on the grounds that its possible prejudicial effects outweigh its probative value. Aiken discusses several cases that illustrate this.

Should character evidence be admitted in civil sexual misconduct cases? Aiken argues that it should. Her argument rests on the claim that it is permissible for rules of evidence to be fashioned to facilitate the truth-finding process. Given that human beings are imperfect and frequently bring their biases and misconceptions into the courtroom, rules of evidence can be drafted and used to prevent bias from operating in the fact-finding process. Sexual misconduct cases often take the form of "he said, she said" contests. In such cases, juries are often disposed to believe the male defendant, unless the plaintiff's story is corroborated by independent evidence, such as the testimony of other victims of harassment. Rule 415 "levels the playing field" for the lone female plaintiff. Viewed in this way, rule 415 is an antidote that is necessary to combat a common bias found among jurors in sexual misconduct cases.

Essential as it is, in its current form rule 415 is not perfect. It is, Aiken claims, both over- and underinclusive. It is overinclusive insofar as it currently allows too much evidence of a defendant's prior sexual misconduct to be admissible in specific cases. It thereby risks inviting the inference that the defendant is a "bad man" who deserves to be convicted. The rule needs to be narrowed to permit only evidence of prior sexual misconduct that is relevantly similar to the alleged conduct. Rule 415 is underinclusive insofar as its current definition of sexual misconduct does not include a class of nonphysical sexual behavior that constitutes sexual harassment, such as verbal threats or propositions that do not involve sexual touching. If the rule can be amended to remedy these defects, it can, Aiken believes, achieve Congress's goal of protecting victims of sexual misconduct while preserving procedural fairness in trials.

Our discussion of sexual harassment law concludes with excerpts from one of the Supreme Court's most recent decisions, *Faragher v. City of Boca Raton*. Between 1985 and 1990, while going to college, Beth Ann Faragher worked part-time and during the summers as an ocean lifeguard for the city of Boca Raton, Florida. In 1992, she brought suit under Title VII of the Civil Rights Act of 1964 and Florida law against two of her immediate supervisors and the city of Boca Raton. She alleged that the supervisors, both men, had repeatedly engaged in sexually offensive behavior and made sexually offensive remarks that had created a hostile work environment.

The United States District Court for the Southern District of Florida accepted Faragher's hostile work environment claim, and found the city liable for the harassment perpetrated by its supervisory employees. Applying different principles, the Eleventh Circuit Court of Appeals rejected Faragher's Title VII claim against the city. A majority (seven to two) of the United States Supreme Court reversed the decision of the Court of Appeals and held in Faragher's favor. Writing for the majority, Justice David Souter frames the issue before the Court as the task of identifying circumstances under which an employer can be held liable under Title VII of the Civil Rights Act of 1964 for the acts of a supervisory employee whose harassment of subordinates creates a hostile work environment.

Souter uses a previous Supreme Court case, *Meritor Savings Bank v. Vinson*,[8] as the foundation for the Court's decision in *Faragher*. Two holdings from *Meritor* are relevant. First, *Meritor* invokes traditional principles of agency law to hold that employers can be held vicariously liable for the harassing acts of their employees. Second, the vicarious liability of employers for employees' harassing actions is not automatic. *Faragher* extends these holdings and adds that when no tangible employment action is taken, for example,

[8]477 U.S. 57 (1986).

an employee is not demoted or fired, a defending employer can mount an affirmative defense to the charge of liability or claims for damages. The defense consists of two elements. First, a preponderance of the evidence must show that (1) the employer exercised reasonable care to prevent and promptly correct sexually harassing behavior and (2) the plaintiff employee unreasonably failed to take advantage of preventive or corrective opportunities provided by the employer or otherwise failed to avoid harm. The Court stresses that such an affirmative defense is not available to employers if a tangible employment action, such as discharge or demotion, was taken against the plaintiff employee. Applying these principles in *Faragher*, the Court found in Faragher's favor.

No doubt, employment law will continue to develop. Interested readers are invited to consult the selected readings list following for more information.

SELECTED READINGS

Americans With Disabilities Cases. Washington, DC: Bureau of National Affairs, 1993.

Banta, William F. *AIDS in the Workplace: Legal Questions and Practical Answers*. New York: Lexington Books, 1993.

Colker, Ruth. *American Law in the Age of Hypercapitalism: The Worker, the Family, and the State*. New York: New York University Press, 1998.

Collier, Rohan. *Combatting Sexual Harassment in the Workplace*. Buckingham, PA: Open University Press, 1995.

Discrimination in the Workplace: A Legal Survey. New York: National Employment Law Project, 1997.

Eglit, Howard C. *Age Discrimination*. 2d. ed. New York: McGraw-Hill, 1994.

Gould, William B. *Agenda for Reform: The Future of Employment Relationships and the Law*. Cambridge, MA: MIT Press, 1993.

Greene, Katherine W. *Affirmative Action and Principles of Justice*. New York: Greenwood Press, 1989.

Hart, Vivien. *Bound By Our Constitution: Women, Workers, and the Minimum Wage*. Princeton, NJ: Princeton University Press, 1994.

Larson, Lax U. *Civil Rights Act of 1991*. New York: Bender, 1992.

Lindgren, J. Ralph, and Nadine Taub. *The Law of Sex Discrimination*. Minneapolis/St. Paul, MN: West, 1988.

MacKinnon, Catherine. *Sexual Harassment of Working Women*. New Haven, CT: Yale University Press, 1979.

Mills, Jeffrey A. *AIDS and the Law of Workplace Discrimination*. Boulder, CO: Westview Press, 1995.

Mills, Nicolaus. *Debating Affirmative Action: Race, Gender, Ethnicity, and the Politics of Inclusion*. New York: Delta, 1994.

Perritt, Henry H. *Civil Rights in the Workplace*. 2d ed. New York: Wiley Law Publications, 1995.

71

ALBERT G. MOSLEY

Affirmative Action: Pro

Title VII explicitly prohibits the use of race, color, religion, sex, or national origin by employers (of at least fifteen people), employment agencies, and labor organizations to exclude individuals from the full benefits offered by those agencies unless such use serves a bona fide occupational qualification. It also prohibits employment practices that perpetuate the effects of past discrimination, except where such is the result of a bona fide seniority or merit system. Moreover, section 703j explicitly denies that Title VII requires preferential treatment or a racial balance.

Title VII did not specify the definition of discrimination, and the courts have distinguished three forms it may take: (1) *disparate treatment,* classifying people as different who are similar in the relevant respects or classifying people as similar who are different in the relevant respects; (2) *adverse impact,* when a seemingly neutral procedure such as testing, interviewing, or educational requirements disproportionately eliminates a particular group from certain opportunities without those procedures being relevant to fulfilling the requirements of that opportunity; and (3) *perpetuating the effects of past discrimination into the present,* as when an agreement between management and union effectively excludes a particular group from training, promotion, and retention benefits.

Adverse impact might indicate discrimination even though the discriminatory effect was produced by "practices, procedures, or tests neutral on their face, and even neutral in terms of intent" but which were not necessary for the proper performance of the position in question.[1] Adverse impact occurs when a practice produces an underrepresentation of a race, sex, or ethnic group in a given workforce. According to the 1978 Uniform Guidelines on Employee Selection Procedures (for compliance with Revised Order No. 4 of the Carter administration), a practice has an adverse impact on a group if it resulted in a selection rate from that group that was less than four-fifths the selection rate of the group with the highest selection rate.[2] Where there is a pattern of exclusion, the remedy seeks to correct the resulting underrepresentation through special recruitment efforts, goals, and timetables, and, in the most egregious cases, strict numerical quotas until a certain level of representation is reached.[3]

Thus, as in *Griggs v. Duke Power Co.* (1971), requiring a high school diploma or passing score on an intelligence test for jobs that could be performed without need of such would disproportionately affect Blacks and other groups who historically had been denied equal educational benefits. Such "color-blind" qualifications would also exclude many Whites from jobs for which they would otherwise qualify. By outlawing irrelevant requirements and recruitment based on personal networks, affirmative action has made it possible for more people in general to have opportunities that otherwise would have been reserved for a privileged few.[4] This has led Derrick Bell to argue that, contrary to popular opinion, marginalized Whites (women and less well-connected males) have benefited more from affirmative action than Blacks.[5]

Illegal discrimination would also be indicated in practices that perpetuate the effects of past discrimination into the present. Title VII explicitly excluded bona fide seniority systems from this category. On the other hand, the Court held that other practices (e.g., collective bargaining agreements that locked Blacks into lower paying job categories) were not excluded.[6] Agreements requiring union apprenticeships for certain jobs, where Blacks had been denied union membership, reinforced and perpetuated the effects of past discrimination, even if the agreements were not instituted with the intent of adversely affecting Blacks.

Remedies required by a finding of discrimination included hiring, reinstatement, backpay, retroactive seniority, and promotion. Such remedies were meant to correct a finding of discrimination by placing specific victims in the position they would have been in were it not for the discriminatory action of the defendant. And where a policy of discrimination deterred members of an underrepresented minority from even applying for opportunities, relief was to be granted if specific individuals could show that they would have applied but for their knowledge of the operation of the discriminatory policy.[7] . . .

UNITED STEELWORKERS V. WEBER (1979)

In 1978, a union (the United Steelworkers of America) and a corporation (Kaiser Aluminum and Chemical Corporation) tacitly acknowledging that each had engaged in years of racial discrimination against Black workers, entered into a "voluntary" agreement to correct the discrepancy between the percentage of Blacks in skilled craft positions (0 percent) and the percentage of Blacks in the local labor force (39 percent) by reserving 50 percent of the openings in a training program sponsored by the corporation until the discrepancy was eliminated. Workers in skilled positions were paid substantially higher wages and, traditionally, admittance to such training programs was based on union membership and seniority. However, in accordance with the agreement, several Black workers were admitted over Brian Weber and other White workers with greater seniority. Weber brought suit, claiming that his rights (and those of others similarly situated) under Title VII were being violated.

Section 703j of Title VII stated that employers and unions could not be required to correct racial imbalances without a finding of discrimination, but Title VII encouraged voluntary agreements to correct such imbalances.[8] Without an official finding of past discrimination, specific percentages in hirings and promotions could not be viewed as remedial. Nonetheless, it was argued that the imbalance in the proportion of Blacks in skilled positions relative to their proportion in the local workforce was sufficient indication of past discrimination, and that Title VII was intended to redress such by redistributing resources and opportunities from Whites as a group to Blacks as a group. This was made clear in the Kaiser brief, which interpreted the intent of Title VII to be

> not only to compensate or make whole individuals, but also to achieve equality of employment opportunities and remove barriers that have operated in the past to favor . . . White employees over other employees. . . . This "prophylactic" objective . . . reaches beyond the person to the class. Compensation of an individual for harm he suffered does not assure persons of his race equal access to employment opportunities. Disadvantages to the group linger long after the injury to the individual has been enjoined and paid for.

Continuing with this point, the brief contended that "overcoming conditions that operate to the disadvantage of an identifiable group or class frequently requires the presence of that group in the workforce in significant numbers. Until that situation exists others may be deterred from applying or even seriously considering the possibility of doing so."[9]

On the other hand, the brief for Weber contended that the intent of the 50 percent quota was not to redress identifiable instances of discrimination against identifiable individuals, for none of those chosen for the training program were chosen because they were victims of past discrimination by the employer and union. Rather, the intent of the quota was to achieve a racially balanced workforce, and this was being done by discriminating against Whites, who had become the new victims of governmental policies to redistribute advancement opportunities to Blacks, irrespective of merit or seniority. Weber's brief argued that such policies would lead to greater (rather than less) racial animosity by fostering White resentment and Black stereotyping.

In deciding for the defendant (United Steelworkers), the Court held that the purpose of Title VII was to bring Blacks into the mainstream by opening employment opportunities in areas traditionally closed to them because of societal discrimination, and that this purpose could legitimately require using race-conscious policies. If Congress had wished to exclude such means, it could easily have worded 703j to read that Title VII would not "require or permit" preferential treatment, instead of merely stating that Title VII did not "require" preferential treatment. Justice Brennan concluded that the Kaiser-Steelworkers plan

> does not unnecessarily trammel the interests of White employees. The plan does not require the discharge of White workers and their replacement with new Black hires . . . Nor does the plan create an absolute bar to the advancement of White employees . . . Moreover, the plan is a temporary measure; it is not intended to maintain a racial balance, but simply to eliminate a manifest racial imbalance. . . .[10]

Title VII should not be interpreted in such a way as to justify perpetuating the effects of prior discrimination, concurred Justice Blackmun. In dissent, Judge Rehnquist denied that it was the intent of Congress to interpret racial imbalance as sufficient to indicate discrimination and thereby justify compensatory measures.

Exploiting the sentiments expressed in the brief for Weber, Ronald Reagan made opposition to affirmative action a central part of his presidential campaign. Upon taking office in 1981, he proceeded to appoint executives (William Bradford Reynolds, Justice Department; Clarence Pendelton, Jr. and Clarence Thomas, Equal Employment Opportunities Commission) and Supreme Court justices (Antonin Scalia, Anthony Kennedy) who were hostile to the direction that affirmative action had taken. The budgets and staff of the EEOC and the Office of Federal Contract Compliance were cut, curtailing their ability to pursue cases of overt discrimination and affirmative action compliance.[11] . . .

RECENT RULINGS

An important shift in Supreme Court rulings occurred in *Watson v. Fort Worth Bank and Trust* (1988) and *Wards Cove Packing Co. v. Antonio* (1989). In these cases, the Court reversed the *Griggs v. Duke Power Co.* (1973) ruling that the burden of proof rested with the employer to demonstrate the business necessity of employment practices that had a disparate impact on "protected minorities." Instead, the Court placed the burden of proof on the plaintiff to show that a specific employment practice caused discrimination against a "protected group."[12] The Civil Rights Bill of 1990 reversed the Supreme Court rulings in *Watson* and *Wards Cove,* and shifted the burden of proof back to the employer to show that an employment practice with a disparate impact on protected groups was job related and "consistent with business necessity." It also allowed women and minorities to collect damages up to $300,000 if it were proven that they were the victims of intentional discrimination.[13]

Croson and *Adarand* continued the trend of Supreme Court rulings placing greater restrictions on affirmative action measures. In *City of Richmond v. Croson* (1989), the Court held that state and local governments did not have the authority to use set-asides to remedy broad societal discrimination, as did the Congress in *Fullilove*. As of 1983, minority business enterprises (MBEs) received only 0.67 percent of the contracting funds spent by the city government of Richmond, Virginia, although the city was 50 percent Black. Acting to attenuate the effects of Richmond's long history of legally sanctioned segregation and preference for Whites, the city adopted the Minority Business Utilization Plan, which required at least 30 percent of the dollar value of construction contracts to go to MBEs.

Writing for the majority, Justice O'Connor argued that the city of Richmond had not demonstrated that the low percentage of awards to MBEs was the result of past racial discrimination. Rather, she cited nonracial factors such as "deficiencies in working capital, inability to meet bonding requirements, unfamiliarity with bidding procedures, and disability caused by an insufficient track record" as equally probable reasons accounting for the low participation rate. Nor, she continued, had the city eliminated the possibility that Black entrepreneurs simply preferred industries other than construction. All such factors could be addressed by means other than minority set-asides. Thus, minority set-asides had not been demonstrated to be necessary to eliminating the low participation rate.

The Court held that in order to pass the test of strict scrutiny, a direct causal link had to be established between a specific present injury and specific past or present acts of racial discrimination. O'Connor admitted that government had a compelling interest in preventing the use of government funds to support and perpetuate private discrimination. But, she held for the majority, there was no demonstration that lack of Black participation in city construction work was the specific effect of racial discrimination.

In his dissent from the majority, Justice Marshall argued that the city had a compelling interest in intervening so as not to allow the effects of past discrimination to continue into the present and future, both in terms of the costs to the Black community and the benefits channeled to the White community. Lack of working capital and business experience were all traceable to legally sanctioned discrimination that denied Blacks these resources. The fact that there were so few minority construction firms was much more likely the result of reluctance to enter a field in which there was such pronounced racial hostility rather than the result of Blacks' antipathy to that kind of business.

In *Adarand Constructors, Inc. v. Pena* (1995) a contractor claimed that the federal government's practice of using race to identify "socially and economically disadvantaged individuals" for preferential treatment in the granting of highway construction contracts violated his constitutional rights of due process and equal protection. In deference to Congress's lawmaking powers, previous courts had applied only an intermediate level of scrutiny to federal policies involving racial classifications. However, in *Croson,* the Supreme Court required that state and local government policies using racial classifications be subject to strict scrutiny. In *Adarand,* the Court extended this requirement to the federal government.

The Court held that benign as well as invidious uses of racial classifications must satisfy the requirements of strict scrutiny, that is, be necessary for the achievement of a compelling government interest and be narrowly tailored to accomplish this end. This decision overturned the opinion in *Metro Broadcasting Inc. v. F.C.C.,* in which benign uses of racial classifications were required to meet only an intermediate level of scrutiny (i.e., be rationally related to accomplishing an important government end). Writing for the majority, Justice O'Connor applied the reasoning in *Croson* to federal initiatives:

> Absent searching judicial inquiry into the justification for such race-based measures, there is simply no way of determining what classifications are "benign" or "remedial" and what classifications are in fact motivated by illegitimate notions of racial inferiority or simple racial politics. Indeed, the purpose of strict scrutiny is to "smoke out" illegitimate uses of race by assuring that the legislative body is pursuing a goal important enough to warrant use of a highly suspect tool. The test also ensures that the means chosen "fit" this compelling goal so closely that there is little or no possibility that the motive for the classification was illegitimate racial prejudice or stereotype.[14]

In O'Connor's opinion, any local, state, or federal use of race to treat persons differently imposes an injury that must be necessary to achieve a compelling governmental interest. She held open the possibility, however, that there might in fact be policies using racial classifications that might be necessary to respond to the effects of racism (past and present): "we wish to dispel the notion that strict scrutiny is 'strict in theory, but fatal in fact.' . . . The unhappy persistence of both the practice and the lingering effects of racial discrimination against minority groups in this country is an unfortunate reality, and government is not disqualified from acting in response to it."[15]

Justice Scalia rejected even this possibility, however, arguing that "government can never have a 'compelling interest' in discriminating on the basis of race in order to make up for past racial discrimination." While individuals wronged by racial discrimination should be made whole, Scalia concluded that this does not apply to groups. "To pursue the concept of racial entitlement even for the most admirable and benign of purposes is to reinforce and preserve for future mischief the way of thinking that produced race slavery, race privilege and race hatred. In the eyes of government, we are just one race here. It is American."[16]

Justice Clarence Thomas advanced a similar view: "I believe that there is a moral and constitutional equivalence between laws designed to subjugate a race and those that distribute benefits on the basis of race in order to foster some current notion of equality."[17] Despite the good intentions of those who propose benign racial policies, Justice Thomas considered their use harmful because of the resentment they produce and the suspicions they feed that minorities are incapable of achieving without the "patronizing indulgence" of well-wishers.

Writing for the minority in dissent, Justice Stevens dismissed as ridiculous the suggestion that invidious and benign uses of racial classifications are indistinguishable. Such a view, he wrote, "would equate a law that made black citizens ineligible for military service with a program aimed at recruiting black soldiers."[18] He agreed that affirmative action programs may have some stigmatic costs to beneficiaries, but he pointed out that beneficiaries who felt such costs prohibitive could decline to be considered under affirmative action programs.

We see that one basic disagreement in the debate on affirmative action is the means by which a past of racist injuries is to be confronted. Critics of affirmative action argue that we should refuse to use racial classifications hereafter, in fear that such use may lead us to the very horrors we wish to leave behind. Defenders argue that we must use racial classifications in order to confront and undo the present effects of past and present manifestations of racism. In *Croson* and *Adarand,* the majority held that "the Fifth and Fourteenth Amendments to the Constitution protect persons, not groups." The following section will examine the claim implicit in this position, namely, that group disparities in the award of educational, employment, and entrepreneurial opportunities are to be allowed so long as specific victims cannot be identified. . . .

"Backward looking" arguments defend affirmative action as a matter of *corrective justice,* where paradigmatically the harmdoer is to make restitution to the harmed so as to put the harmed in the position the harmed most likely would have occupied had the harm not occurred. An important part of making restitution is the acknowledgment it provides that the actions causing injury were unjust and such actions will be curtailed and corrected. . . .

Most critics of preferential treatment acknowledge the applicability of principles of restitution to individuals in specific instances of discrimination. The strongest case is where y was as [qualified as] or more qualified than z in the initial competition, but the position was given to z because y was Black and z was White.[19] Subsequently, y may not be as qualified for an equivalent position as some new candidate z′, but is given preference because of the past act of discrimination by F that deprived y of the position he or she otherwise would have received.

Some critics have suggested that, in such cases, z′ is being treated unfairly. For z′, as the most qualified applicant, has a right not to be excluded from the position in question purely on the basis of race; and y has a right to restitution for having unjustly been denied the position in the past. But the dilemma is one in appearance only. For having unjustly excluded y in the past, the current position that z′ has applied for is not one that F is free to offer to the public. It is a position that is already owed to y, and is not available for open competition. Judith Jarvis Thompson makes a similar point:

> suppose two candidates [A and B] for a civil service job have equally good test scores, but there is only one job available. We could decide between them by coin-tossing. But in fact we do allow for declaring for A straightway, where A is a veteran, and B is not. It may be that B is a non-veteran through no fault of his own. . . . Yet the fact is that B is not a veteran and A is. On the assumption that the veteran has served his country, the country owes him something. And it is plain that giving him preference is not an unjust way in which part of that debt of gratitude can be paid.[20]

In a similar way, individual Blacks who have suffered from acts of unjust discrimination are owed something by the perpetrator(s) of such acts, and this debt takes precedence over the perpetrator's right to use his or her options to hire the most qualified person for the position in question.

Many White males have developed expectations about the likelihood of their being selected for educational, employment, and entrepreneurial opportunities that are realistic only because of the general exclusion of women and non-Whites as competitors for such positions. Individuals enjoying inflated odds of obtaining such opportunities because of racist and sexist practices are recipients of an "unjust enrichment."

Redistributing opportunities would clearly curtail benefits that many have come to expect. And given the frustration of their traditional expectations, it is understandable that they would feel resentment. But blocking traditional expectations is not unjust if those expectations conflict with the equally important moral duties of restitution and just distribution. It is a question, not of "is," but of "ought": not "Do those with decreased opportunities as a result of affirmative action feel resentment?" but "Should those with decreased opportunities as a result of affirmative action feel resentment?"

White males who are affected by such redistributions may be innocent in the sense that they have not practiced overt acts of racial discrimination, have developed reasonable expectations based on the status quo, and have exerted efforts that, given the status quo, would normally have resulted in their achieving certain rewards. Their life plans and interests are thus thwarted despite their having met all of the standards "normally" required for the achievement of their goals. Clearly, disappointment is not unnatural or irrational. Nonetheless, the resentment is not sufficiently justified if the competing moral claims of restitution and fair distribution have equal or even greater weight.

Since Title VII protects bona fide seniority plans, it forces the burden of rectification to be borne by Whites who are entering the labor force rather than Whites who are the direct beneficiaries of past discriminatory practices. Given this limitation placed on affirmative action remedies, the burden of social restitution may, in many cases, be borne by those who were not directly involved in past discriminatory practices. But it is generally not true that those burdened have not benefited at all from past discriminatory practices. For the latent effects of acts of invidious racial discrimination have plausibly bolstered and encouraged the efforts of Whites in roughly the same proportion as it inhibited and discouraged the efforts of Blacks. Such considerations are also applicable to cases where F discriminated against y in favor of *z*, but the make-whole remedy involves providing compensation to y′ rather than y. This suggests that y′ is an *undeserving beneficiary* of the preferential treatment meant to compensate for the unjust discrimination against y, just as z′ above appeared to be the innocent victim forced to bear the burden that z benefited from. Many critics have argued that this misappropriation of benefits and burdens demonstrates the unfairness of compensation to groups rather than individuals. But it is important that the context and rationale for such remedies be appreciated.

In cases of "egregious" racial discrimination, not only is it true that F discriminated against a particular Black person y, but F's discrimination advertised a general disposition to discriminate against any other Black person who might seek such positions. The specific effect of F's unjust discrimination was that y was refused a position he or she would otherwise have received. The latent (or dispositional) effect of F's unjust discrimination was that many Blacks who otherwise would have sought such positions were discouraged from doing so. Thus, even if the specific y actually discriminated against can no longer be compensated, F has an obligation to take affirmative action to communicate to Blacks as a group that such positions are indeed open to them. After being found in violation of laws prohibiting racial discrimination, many agencies have disclaimed further discrimination while in fact continuing to do so.[21] In such cases, the courts have required the discriminating agencies to actually hire and/or promote Blacks who may not be as qualified as some current White applicants until Blacks approach the proportion in F's labor force they in all likelihood would have achieved had F's unjust discriminatory acts not deterred them. . . .

Racist acts excluding Blacks affected particular individuals, but were directed at affecting the behavior of the group of all those similar to the victim. Likewise, the benefits of affirmative action policies should not be conceived as limited in their effects to the specific individuals receiving them. Rather, those benefits should be conceived as extending to all those identified with the recipient, sending the message that opportunities are indeed available to qualified Black candidates who would have been excluded in the past. . . .

We should conceive of the purpose of preferential treatment as being to benefit, not only the specific individuals directly affected by past racist acts, but also those counterfactually indicated in such acts. Affirmative action communicates not only to the specific Blacks and Whites involved in a particular episode, but to all Blacks and Whites that invidious racial discrimination is no longer the order of the day. Unless this is recognized, the purpose of preferential treatment will not be understood. . . .

NOTES

1. Chief Justice Burger, *Griggs v. Duke Power Co.,* 401 US at 429, 230; Greene, *Affirmative Action,* 64.
2. Suppose the practice selects 75 percent of applicants from group B and 50 percent of the applicants from group A. Since 4/5 of 75 percent is 60 percent and the practice only selects 50 percent of applicants from A, the practice has an adverse impact on group A.
3. Nicolaus Mills, ed., *Debating Affirmative Action* (New York: Dell Publishing, 1994), 14.
4. Derrick Bell, *And We Are Not Saved,* (New York: Basic Books, 1987); see also, Gertrude Ezorsky's *Racism and Justice* (Ithaca, N.Y.: Cornell University Press, 1991) [on recruitment by personal networks] and John Larew's "Who's the Real Affirmative Action Profiteer" in *The Washington Monthly,* June 1991 [admission to elite schools based on parental alumni status].
5. Bell, *And We Are Not Saved,* chap. 2, "The Benefits to Whites of Civil Rights Litigation."
6. As in *Albermarle Paper Co. v. Moody* (1975); see Greene, *Affirmative Action,* 67ff.
7. *Franks v. Bowman Transportation Co.* (1976); *International Brotherhood of Teamsters v. United States* (1977); Greene, *Affirmative Action,* 65–70.
8. See Drew Days III (1987), "Fullilove" in *Yale Law Journal,* 96: 461–62 for past history of discrimination by Kaiser and United Steelworkers. By entering into a voluntary agreement to end discriminatory practices, both union and employer could avoid costly suits for back pay and promotions that might result from an official finding of discrimination.
9. Brief for Kaiser, No. 78-432: 40–42; Greene, *Affirmative Action,* 88–89.

10. 443 US at 208; Greene, *Affirmative Action*, 92.
11. Mills, *Debating Affirmative Action*, 19.
12. Mills, *Debating Affirmative Action*, 20.
13. Mills, *Debating Affirmative Action*, 25–26.
14. *New York Times*, 13 June 1995, D24.
15. Excerpts from *Adarand Constructors v. Pena* in *New York Times*, 13 June 1995, D24.
16. *New York Times*, 13 June 1995, D24; As to whether we are all "one race" in America, see Andrew Hacker, *Two Nations: Black and White, Separate, Hostile, Unequal* (New York: Ballantine Books, 1995).
17. *New York Times*, 13 June 1995, D24.
18. *New York Times*, 13 June 1995, D24.
19. Even in the case where y was only as qualified as z, a fair method of choice between candidates should produce an equitable distribution of such positions between Blacks and Whites in the long run if not in the short.
20. Judith Jarvis Thompson, *Philosophy and Public Affairs* 2, (Summer 1973):379–380.
21. *Sheet Metal Workers v. EEOC* (1986); *United States v. Paradise* (1987).

72

NICHOLAS CAPALDI

Affirmative Action: Con

WHAT IS AFFIRMATIVE ACTION?

There is no generally accepted definition of affirmative action. This tells us a number of things. First, any discussion of whether it is a good or a bad thing will turn on what one understands this expression to mean.

Let us take one example of a definition. "Affirmative action is the name given to a number of policies designed to overcome past and present discrimination and provide opportunity for those traditionally denied it."[1] In this sample definition we can distinguish among (1) the policy or set of practices to be instituted—none of which are specifically mentioned; (2) the intention behind the policy—the quite laudable one of expanding opportunities for those who have not had them; and (3) the explicit diagnosis of why those opportunities were not there—the presumption that discrimination is the exclusive or major reason for the lack of opportunity.

Any debate about whether one is for or against affirmative action must specify whether one agrees or disagrees with (2) the intention or goal, (1) policies designed to achieve that goal, and (3) the definition and diagnosis of the problem to which one is applying both the goal and the policies. There are at least three major responses to the foregoing definition:

One might approve of the intention but believe that the policies will not achieve the intention. This becomes a debate about the best means of achieving a commonly agreed upon goal.

One might approve of the intention but believe that although the policies will achieve their goal, the policies will also conflict with and undermine other socially important goals. This becomes a debate about prioritizing our goals in a world where it is not possible to have everything.

One might approve of the intention but disapprove of the policies because we disagree with the diagnosis. This becomes a debate about what is the nature and source of the problem to which affirmative action as a policy is addressed.

Lack of a generally agreed upon definition also reflects a lack of consensus on the legal and moral status of the concept. The use of the expression is now so widespread that many are apt to presume that there is some firm foundation in law, in morality, or in public policy for it. Among the things that the ongoing debate about affirmative action has revealed are both the ignorance of and the disagreement about the moral, legal, and political principles that inform or should inform public policy. Perhaps the most useful thing that will come out of a debate about affirmative action is that it will require us, as a society, to refocus on our fundamental principles.

Five major definitions of affirmative action exist:

- *Definition 1 (open-search):* Affirmative action consists of those policies designed to advertise all openings as widely as possible and to monitor appointments and promotion processes in order to insure that the process is open, nondiscriminatory, and promotes excellence.
- *Definition 2 (punitive):* Affirmative action consists of any policy, private or public, *ordered by the court* to redress proven cases of individual

discrimination. The remedy may involve a specific *numerical objective,* but the numerical objective is limited to a specific time and place.

- *Definition 3 (minority set-asides):* Affirmative action refers to congressionally mandated rules concerning federal contracts and involving a specific percentage of contracts to be set aside for minority contractors.
- *Definition 4 (backward-compensation):* Affirmative action covers any policy designed to redress alleged cases of discrimination against a group by placing members of the group in the positions they would have allegedly held if the alleged discrimination had not taken place. This is a *contrary-to-fact conditional:* it claims to identify what would happen *if* something else had *not* happened.
- *Definition 5 (forward-preferential):* Affirmative action designates any policy in social planning, without any causal claim of what would have been, designed to produce a society or institution that reflects some stated goal and invokes *quotas* of group representation.[2]

AFFIRMATIVE ACTION IS ILLEGAL

Affirmative action in anything other than the most innocuous sense is illegal. Affirmative action in the senses of definitions 1, 2, and 3 (in a highly limited version) is legal. Affirmative action in the senses of definitions 4 and 5 is illegal. There are five reasons for this.

First, according to the Fourteenth Amendment to the United States Constitution, no state can "deprive any person of life, liberty, or property without due process of law; nor deny to any person within its jurisdiction, the equal protection of the laws." This amendment makes clear that it is individuals, not groups, who have rights.

The first relevant use of the expression "affirmative action" appears in an executive order issued in September 1965 by then President Lyndon B. Johnson requiring federal contractors to take "affirmative action to ensure that applicants are employed, and that employees are treated during employment, without regard to their race, creed, color, or national origin." This is an executive order, not a legislative decision and not a decision of the United States Supreme Court; what it makes explicit is the anti-discrimination principles that are already in the law (thereby encompassing definition 1); curiously, sex and gender are not mentioned.

Second, Titles VI and VII of the Civil Rights Act of 1964 unequivocally outlaw preference (definition 5). Two provisions spell this out:

> 703 (h) it shall not be unlawful employment practice . . . for an employer to give and act upon the results of any professionally developed ability test provided that such test, its administration or action upon the results is not designed, intended or used to discriminate because of race, color, religion, sex or national origin. . . .
>
> 703 (j) Nothing contained in this title shall be interpreted to require any employer . . . to grant preferential treatment to any individual or to any group because of the race, color, religion, sex, or national origin of such individual or group on account of an imbalance which may exist with respect to the total number or percentage of persons of any race, color, religion, sex or national origin employed by any employer.

Lest there be any misunderstanding about these provisions, it is useful to cite the legislative record concerning them. As then Senator Hubert H. Humphrey put it, "Title VII does not require an employer to achieve any sort of racial balance in his work force by giving preferential treatment to any individual or group."[3] Senator Harrison Williams noted that Title VII "specifically prohibits the Attorney General or any agency of the government, from requiring employment to be on the basis of racial or religious quotas. Under this provision an employer with only white employees could continue to have only the best qualified persons even if they were all white."[4] Senator Joseph Clark stated, "Quotas are themselves discriminatory."[5] If anyone still has any doubts, then recall the words of Representative Emanuel Celler, Chairman of the House Judiciary Committee and the congressman responsible for introducing the legislation:

> It is likewise not true that the Equal Employment Opportunity Commission would have power to rectify existing "racial or religious imbalance" in employment by requiring the hiring of certain people without regard to their qualifications simply because they are of a given race or religion. Only actual discrimination could be stopped.[6]

Third, in *Griggs v. Duke Power Co.* (1971), the U.S. Supreme Court went out of its way to disclaim preference.

> Congress did not intend . . . to guarantee a job to every person regardless of qualifications . . . [Title VII] does not command that any person be hired simply because he was formerly the subject of discrimination, or because he is a member of a minority group. Discriminatory preference for any group, minority or majority, is precisely and only what Congress has proscribed. . . . Congress has not commanded that the less qualified be preferred over the better qualified simply because of minority origins. Far from disparaging job qualifications as such, Congress has made such qualifications the controlling factor, so that race, religion, nationality, and sex become irrelevant.[7]

Fourth, in the pivotal *Alan Bakke* case (1978), Justice Powell, in the plurality opinion, specifically attacked and rejected the backward-looking argument for compensation (what I have called definition 4). To begin with, Justice Powell reiterated that the law and previous U.S. Supreme Court decisions were directed toward overt instances of discrimination: "we have never approved preferential classification in the absence of proven constitutional or statutory violations." In addition, the overt instances of discrimination can only be recognized as directed toward individuals: "We have never approved a classification that aids persons perceived as members of relatively victimized groups at the expense of other innocent individuals." In specifically rejecting the contrary-to-fact conditional hypothesis, Powell responded to the minority opinion justices who upheld it as follows:

> I disagree with much that is said in their opinion. They would require as a justification for a program . . . only two findings: (i) that there has been some form of discrimination against the preferred minority groups "by society at large" . . . and (ii) that "there is reason to believe" that the disparate impact sought to be rectified by the program is the "product" of such discrimination.
>
> The breadth of this hypothesis is unprecedented in our constitutional system. The first step is easily taken. . . . The second step, however, involves a speculative leap: but for this discrimination by society at large, Bakke "would have failed to qualify for admission" because Negro applicants . . . would have made better scores. *Not one word in the record supports this conclusion.* [italics added] . . . [it] offers no standards for courts to use in applying such a presumption of causation to other racial or ethnic classifications. . . .
>
> There is no principled basis for deciding which groups would merit "heightened judicial solicitude" and which would not. . . . This kind of variable sociological and political analysis necessary to produce such rankings simply does not lie within the judicial competence. . . . isolated segments of our vast governmental structures are not competent to make those decisions at least in the absence of legislative mandates and legislatively determined criteria.[8]

The final and most important case to substantiate the claim that affirmative action in any interesting sense is illegal is *Adarand Contractors, Inc. v. Pena* (1995). Congress had, in the Minority Business Enterprise provision of the Public Works Employment Act of 1977, required that 10 percent of the federal funds allocated to state and local governments for public works projects must be used to purchase goods and services from minority-owned businesses even if nonminority-owned firms offered a lower bid. The reasoning behind this legislation was that minorities had been discriminated against in the past and were due redress. This is a case of punitive action (definition 2). Some had suggested that it constituted legislative endorsement of either compensation (definition 4) or preference (definition 5).

The Adarand decision effectively reduced this policy to the punitive version (definition 2). One reason this decision is so important is that it clarified a somewhat bewildering series of previous decisions.[9]

As Justice O'Connor expressed it in *Adarand:*

> The Court's failure to produce a majority opinion in Bakke, Fullilove, and Wygant left unresolved the proper analysis for remedial race-based governmental action. See *United States v. Paradise,* 480 U.S., at 166 [43 FEP Cases, at 7] (plurality opinion of Brennan, J.) ("[A]lthough this court has consistently held that some elevated level of scrutiny is required when a racial or ethnic distinction is made for remedial purposes, it has yet to reach consensus on the appropriate constitutional analysis"); *Sheet Metal Workers v. EEOC,* 478 U.S. 421, 480 [41 FEP Cases 107, 130] (1986) (plurality opinion of Brennan, J.). Lower courts found this lack of guidance unsettling. See, e.g., *Kromnick v. School District of Philadelphia,* 739 F.2d 894, 901 [35 FEP Cases 538, 544] (CA3 1984) ("The absence of an Opinion of the Court in either Bakke or Fullilove and the concomitant failure of the Court to articulate an analytic framework supporting the judgments makes the position of the lower federal courts considering the constitutionality

of affirmative action programs somewhat vulnerable"). . . . The Court resolved the issue, at least in part, in 1989. . . . A majority of the court in *Croson* held that "the standard of review under the Equal Protection Clause is not dependent on the race of those burdened or benefitted by a particular classification," and that the single standard of review for racial classifications should be "strict scrutiny."

"Strict scrutiny" means that previous discrimination must be established, that is, we are dealing with definition 2, and that the redress must be carefully limited in time and place.

Justice O'Connor continues:

> Accordingly, we hold today that all racial classification, imposed by whatever federal, state, or local government actor, must be analyzed by a reviewing court under strict scrutiny. In other words, such classifications are constitutional only if they are narrowly tailored measures that further compelling governmental interests.
>
> Our action today makes explicit what Justice Powell thought implicit in the Fullilove lead opinion: federal racial classifications, like those of a State, must serve a compelling governmental interest, and must be narrowly tailored to further that interest.[10]

Affirmative action as either compensation or preference is illegal. If such policies are so pervasive, this reflects the illegal and unauthorized activities of government bureaucracies (a widespread problem that goes way beyond affirmative action); it reflects those activist judges who confuse the judicial process with the legislative process and who confuse their own values with the true moral foundations of the United States; it reflects the ideological agenda of many academics; it reflects the unscrupulous activities of politicians whose careers are predicated on maintaining voting blocks based upon racial clientage; and it reflects fear in the business community of endless litigation.

AFFIRMATIVE ACTION IS IMMORAL

As a society the United States is committed to six major normative premises:

1. We are committed to the belief in a *cosmic order* ("In God We Trust").
2. We are committed to the belief in the sanctity of the *individual*.

The *Declaration of Independence* declares:

> We hold these truths to be self-evident, that all men are created equal, that they are endowed by their Creator with certain unalienable Rights, that among these are Life, Liberty, and the pursuit of Happiness. That to secure these rights, Governments are instituted among Men, deriving their just powers from the consent of the governed.

In his dissent in the *Plessy v. Ferguson* case (1896), Justice Harlan enunciated the fundamental principle of individuality in a specific way, namely that the U.S. Constitution is and ought to be *color-blind*.[11] This reiterates the point that it is the individual as such and not membership in a group that defines who we are. "Our constitution is color-blind, and neither knows nor tolerates classes among citizens. . . . The law regards man as man, and takes no account of his surroundings or of his color."[12]

In arguing against the then majority view, Harlan warned that the separate but equal doctrine "will, in time prove to be quite as pernicious as the decision made by this tribunal in the Dred Scott case."[13] The point of Harlan's observation is that invidious comparisons or classifications deny individuals the equal protection of the laws. Finally, Harlan reiterated that "the destinies of the two races, in this country, are indissolubly linked together, and the interests of both require that the common government of all shall not permit the seeds of race hate to be planted under the sanction of law."[14]

In his famous "I have a dream" speech on the steps of the Lincoln Memorial in 1964, Dr. Martin Luther King, Jr., looked forward to when his children would "live in a nation where they will not be judged by the color of their skin but by the content of their character."

Harlan's view has also been echoed in a recent statement by Justice Scalia:

> government can never have a "compelling interest" in discriminating on the basis of race in order to "make up" for past racial discrimination in the opposite direction. . . . Individuals who have been wronged by unlawful racial discrimination should be made whole; but under our constitution there can be no such thing as either a creditor or debtor race. That concept is alien to the constitution's focus upon the individual. . . . To pursue the concept of racial entitlement—even for the most admirable and benign of purposes—is to reinforce and preserve for future mischief the way of thinking that produced

> race slavery, race privilege, and race hatred. In the eyes of government, we are just one race here. It is American.[15]

The sanctity of the individual has to be understood in a special moral way.

The Sanctity of the individual means:

> a. that human beings possess the rational capacity to recognize a universal cosmic order;
> b. that human beings have the internal capacity to be unconstrained in their decision to act in accordance with the cosmic order, that is, *free will;*
> c. that true freedom and dignity consist in the inner or self-discipline that comes with the exercise of these capacities; and
> d. that these capacities can only be discovered retrospectively by their exercise; limited government and a free market economy are the only political and economic institutions compatible with individual dignity; the justification of such institutions is not their efficiency but their efficacy for the exercise of personal autonomy.

The continuous Western meaning of freedom is self-government; the modern version of freedom is the self-government of the individual (not the classical notion of a self-governing polis).

This special moral understanding of individuality has most recently been enunciated by Justice Clarence Thomas in his condemnation of affirmative action (understood in the preferential sense).

> I believe that there is a moral [and] constitutional equivalence . . . between laws designed to subjugate a race and those that distribute benefits on the basis of race in order to foster some current notion of equality. Government cannot make us equal; it can only recognize, respect, and protect us as equal before the law. That these programs may have been motivated, in part, by good intentions cannot provide refuge from the principles that under our Constitution, the government may not make distinctions on the basis of race. As far as the Constitution is concerned, it is irrelevant whether a government's racial classifications are drawn by those who wish to oppress a race or by those who have a sincere desire to help those thought to be disadvantaged. There can be no doubt that the paternalism that appears to lie at the heart of this program is at war with the principle of inherent equality that underlies and infuses our Constitution. . . . These programs not only raise grave constitutional questions, they also undermine the moral basis of the equal protection principle. Purchased at the price of immeasurable human suffering, the equal protection principle reflects our Nation's understanding that such classifications ultimately have a destructive impact on the individual and our society . . . there can be no doubt that racial paternalism and its unintended consequences can be as poisonous and pernicious as any other form of discrimination.[16]

3. We are committed to the belief that the communal good is not something over and above the good of the individuals who make up the community.
4. We are committed to the belief that the *rule of law* means due process and equality before the law (i.e., equality of opportunity and not equality of result).

The popular understanding of these principles is reflected in a poll conducted by *USA Today* (24 March, 1995, 3A). In this survey, 73 percent favor "special efforts to find qualified minorities and women and then encouraging them to apply for jobs with that company," and at the same time 84 percent of the public oppose "favoring a minority who is less qualified than a white applicant, when filling a job in a business that has few minority workers."

5. We subscribe to a *republican* or limited form of government and not a democracy. It is a system in which liberty is established by restraining government through checks and balances of power.
6. We embrace a *free market economy*. The only real good is the good of the individual. Free market economies are especially important because they combine efficiency and morality.

The wealth created in a free market economy is a good thing because: (a) It enhances the human condition. Income is not merely a means to consumer satisfaction, nor merely an incentive. Rather, income is a *means to accomplishment.* (b) Wealth liberates us from the culture of poverty. Whereas in the medieval world it was wealth that created a scandal, the scandal of the modern world is the existence of poverty. (c) Private wealth provides a check on the power of the government, and leads to the expansion of individual liberties. (d) Finally, wealth provides the dynamic of social reform.

Every one of these points is invoked in one of President Abraham Lincoln's speeches:

> I beg you to remember this, not merely for my sake, but for yours. I happen, temporarily, to occupy the White House. I am a living witness that any one of your children may look to come here as my father's child has. It is in order that each one of you may have, through this free government which we have enjoyed, an open field and a fair chance for your industry, enterprise, and intelligence; that you may all have equal privileges in the race of life, with all its desirable human aspirations. It is for this the struggle should be maintained. . . . The nation is worth fighting for, to secure such an inestimable jewel.[17]

Most of the participants in the affirmative action debate subscribe to these fundamental moral principles. Even those who have actively supported the implementation of preferential programs agree that these are the fundamental principles. What they have urged is that the programs of preference are a temporary means to achieve the fundamental values. Joseph Califano, former Secretary of Health, Education, and Welfare under President Carter, wrote in 1989 that affirmative action was intended "only as a temporary expedient to speed blacks' entry into the social and economic mainstream. . . . it was never conceived as a permanent program and its time is running out."[18] Even in his dissent in *Bakke,* Justice Blackmun stated that "in order to get beyond racism, we must first take account of race," thereby acknowledging that affirmative action at best is a temporary expedient. What is at issue is whether we can temporarily suspend these principles for a desirable end, that is, whether the end justifies the means. . . .

One last thing we want to note about our fundamental moral principles is their logical status. In calling these our fundamental norms, we are not describing how people actually behave but how they ought to behave. Having these as norms permits us to identify those cases where we have failed to live up to them. Too many proponents of affirmative action fail to understand the logical status of norms, thinking that they have either invalidated the norms (e.g., color-blindness) or they have invalidated our claim to have identified the norm as norm because of our failure to live up to it. In practice, the United States has failed in part and continues to fail to live up to the ideal of a color-blind society—but these are grounds for trying harder, not for adopting race consciousness as a norm.

There are two moral arguments routinely presented in favor of affirmative action. One reflects definition 4 (compensation) and one reflects definition 5 (preference). We turn now to those arguments and my rebuttal of them.

The compensation argument maintains that slavery and discrimination practiced over a long period of time have disadvantaged the present generations of African Americans so that they (1) cannot compete effectively, and (2) therefore, should be awarded positions and promotions in a manner consistent with the punitive principles as enunciated in definition 2. This is not a strictly legal argument because the law demands that overt and provable practices of discrimination against specific individuals must be the basis of redress and remediation.

The argument makes two assumptions. The first is the statistical assumption that every group possesses the same talents and interests in the same proportion as their percentage in the population. The second assumption is that it is possible to construct a contrary-to-fact conditional argument of an historical-causal kind to substantiate this claim of what might have been.

The compensation argument can be rebutted on the following grounds:

1. It misconstrues the legal nature of compensation.[19] In order for "compensation" to be invoked, we must (a) show that the injury—in this case failure to achieve—was caused by discrimination (or analogous phenomenon), (b) identify the party at fault, and (c) calculate a relevant benefit to be paid by the party at fault. Item (a) is never established in a direct causal fashion; with regard to item (b) the perpetrating parties are either long dead or identified in a hopelessly amorphous fashion as "society at large"; with regard to item (c), there is no way to extract a benefit given what we have said about item (b), and any relevant benefit would be monetary, not a position that the alleged injured party is unable to hold if injured.

2. The punitive redress that the courts have imposed never involves giving positions to people who cannot compete effectively but to people who can compete but were never given the opportunity to compete.

3. There is absolutely no evidence for the extraordinary statistical assumption; moreover, if you believe that some groups are underrepresented then it follows as a matter of logical truth that some groups are overrepresented. Who is willing to point the finger at allegedly overrepresented groups?

4. To put such a policy into action leads to *reverse discrimination,* that is, penalizing innocent individuals by denying them opportunities; this amounts to believing that the end justifies the means.

5. There is no way to substantiate the contrary-to-fact conditional argument (Justice Powell's point in *Bakke*): (a) That a significant number of African Americans fully participate is counterevidence—Why were they, unlike their brethren, not harmed to the point of being unable to compete effectively? (b) We can construct equally plausible (or implausible) contrary-to-fact scenarios, for example, the African American descendants of slaves are beneficiaries of slavery in that they have better lives (or even are alive in greater numbers) than they would have been if slavery had not existed. (c) We can reverse the reverse-discrimination with the following equally plausible (or implausible) scenario—African Americans actually owe compensation to the United States! The failure of present generations of African Americans to participate fully is not the result of slavery and discrimination but of other factors, for some of which they bear responsibility (a point to be expanded upon later). Moreover, this failure to participate fully has actually harmed non-African Americans more than helped them because it has wasted enormous resources and thereby limited the number of opportunities available to everybody else.

I think this last scenario deserves to some extent to be considered seriously. Many who argue for affirmative action see the economy as a zero-sum game with a constant pie, so that in order to gain a bigger slice of pie one has to take a piece from someone else. This is a fundamental misperception of both economics and of the fundamental values of the United States. They misunderstand—hence, they have the wrong diagnosis of the problems at issue.

The incorrect diagnosis (based on faulty economics) is that Whites have taken too much of something and thereby denied access to it by African Americans. The correct diagnosis, I suggest, is that by failing to embody certain values, African Americans have deprived themselves of opportunities. Because they have the wrong diagnosis, they propose the wrong (and counterproductive) remedies such as affirmative action, which is a form of redistribution. A useful analogy is to recall that in the 1950's it was fashionable for intellectuals in Latin America to diagnose their economic underdevelopment as a consequence of capitalist exploitation, specifically the notion that Latin America and the Third World in general were condemned to be providers of raw materials. The recent explosive growth of their economies coincided with the acceptance of a new diagnosis that Latin America had not been capitalist enough.

Let us now turn to the preference argument. This argument maintains that because of the history of slavery and discrimination, African Americans have never been made to feel that they belong. This is especially problematic in a democratic society. Affirmative action is a way to help African Americans realize the basic values of the United States.

This argument rests upon a number of misconceptions. First of all, it is conceptualizing the problem in terms of the notion of a "democratic society." This is incorrect for two reasons. The United States is not a democracy but a republic. In a republic, government is limited to serving other interests because those interests reflect the basic rights of individuals. That is, political institutions are subordinate to moral preconceptions. James Madison argued that it was a utopian decision to expect unanimity; factions were inevitable; the instrument for avoiding factional strife was checks and balances. Democracy is not an intrinsic end but a quite limited institutional arrangement that reflects more fundamental values. There is a serious confusion here of normative priority. Politicizing U.S. society and politicizing the issue of why African Americans do not participate as much as we would all wish is the wrong way to approach this issue.

Second, conceptualizing the problem from the point of view of groups (that is, African Americans conceived of as a voting block) is symptomatic of the failure to develop a sense of individuality. The question is not whether my group participates fully, the question is whether "I" or "you" participate fully.

Third, part of the reason that so many African Americans feel that they do not belong is that they have failed to embrace, much less understand, the fundamental values that animate our society. . . .

NOTES

1. G. Horne, *Reversing Discrimination: The Case for Affirmative Action.* New York: International Publishers, 1992, 1.

2. See M. Rosenfeld, *Affirmative Action and Justice: A Philosophical and Constitutional Inquiry*. New Haven: Yale University Press, 1991, 47–48. . . .
3. Humphrey (110 Cong. Rec. 12723).
4. Williams (110 Cong. Rec. 1433).
5. Clark (110 Cong. Rec. 7218).
6. Celler (110 Cong. Rec. 1518).
7. *Griggs v. Duke Power Co.,* 401 U.S. 424 (1971).
8. Powell, 1978, 2751, note #36, *Supreme Court Reporter,* 98A.
9. Controversial intervening cases included: (a) *United Steelworkers of America v. Weber* (1979). Under pressure from the Labor Department, Kaiser Aluminum and the United Steelworkers agreed to a training program which imposed a 50 percent quota for African Americans. The agreement was temporary; there was no commitment to maintaining racial balance; and no decision on defining what is permissible affirmative action. Most notable in this case is Justice Rehnquist's dissent in which he argued that even the "voluntary" policy is inconsistent with Title VII, and his critique of Justice Brennan in which Rehnquist denounced the idea that Title VII does not require but permits preference as an "Orwellian" interpretation of the law. (b) *Fullilove v. Klutznick* (1980). Here, the majority upheld minority set-asides as a version of our definition 2. (c) *Wygant v. Jackson Board of Education* (1986). The Board of Education of Jackson, Michigan, and the local teacher's union had entered into an agreement whereby layoffs were determined not simply by seniority but in order to maintain racial balance. The majority's view, as expressed by Justice Powell, reasserted that group classifications are suspect and justified only if they serve a compelling state interest and must be tailored so as not to burden innocent parties. (d) *Richmond v. Croson* (1989). The City of Richmond, Virginia, itself had adopted a 30 percent set-aside provision for minority contractors. Here the majority held that racial classifications are suspect categories.
10. O'Connor (1995, *Adarand*), 1839–41.
11. See L. D. Weeden, "Just Say No to Race Exclusive College Scholarships: From an Afrocentric Perspective," *Thurgood Marshall Law Review,* xx, 1995, 205–241.
12. Harlan, 163 U.S. 537, 16 S. Ct. 1146. See Charles A. Lofgren, *The Plessy Case: A Legal-Historical Interpretation*. New York: Oxford University Press, 1987.
13. 163 U.S. 537, 559 (1896) (Harlan, J., dissenting).
14. 163 U.S. 537, 1147.
15. Scalia (1995, *Adarand*) 1844.
16. Thomas (1995, *Adarand*) 1845.
17. Lincoln, 1864 address to 166th Ohio Regiment (1907), 206.
18. Califano quoted in P. C. Roberts and L. M. Stratton, "Proliferation of Privilege," *National Review* (November 6, 1995), 41. See L. Pojman, "The Moral Status of Affirmative Action," *Public Affairs Quarterly,* vi, 1992, 181–206.
19. Randy E. Barnett, "Compensation and Rights in the Liberal Conception of Justice," *Nomos,* xxxiii, 1991, 311–329, has made an even stronger case by pointing out that compensation in Anglo-American common law is tied to a liberal conception of justice that is rights-based not injury based. . . .

73

WISEMAN NKUHLU

Affirmative Action for South Africa in Transition: From Theory to Practice

INTRODUCTION

The liberation struggle is about both political and economic power and control. The many years of apartheid marginalized blacks not only from political power but from economic participation as well. Successive governments used legislation to inhibit the economic advancement of blacks and state budgetary allocations to promote the development of whites through better education, health facilities and housing. Black access to jobs and to economic resources—land, capital and technology—was severely restricted through a plethora of laws and regulations.

Added to this was the demeaning of African culture and values and the adoption of white values and patterns of behaviour as the accepted norm. This made it extremely difficult for blacks to penetrate the centres of power in the country. The dominance of white values and patterns of behaviour in places of leadership made blacks foreigners in their own land. Racial prejudice and the degradation of everything African eroded the black sense of self-esteem, stifled creativity and undermined the long tradition of self-reliance.

It is this history and its legacy that militates against blacks at the work place and in the corridors of power in government and elsewhere. Legislative exclusion, discriminatory state budgetary allocations and the lack of an inclusive culture places blacks at a considerable disadvantage. It therefore follows that if nothing is done to change social relations and to provide blacks with access to resources and means to overcome the economic marginalization of the past, the patterns of economic control, ownership and management that have been produced by the apartheid system will remain unchanged even in a non-racial, non-sexist democratic South Africa. The call for Affirmative Action is a call to prevent this from happening. It is a call to ensure that conditions are created to enable blacks to overcome the disadvantages of the past and to make a positive contribution to the future.

In a way Affirmative Action would be futile if the only aim was to compensate for the wrongs of the past. The past is gone and it cannot be retrieved. It is the present and the future that we can change. Therefore Affirmative Action must be aimed at making the future better not only for this generation, but for future generations as well. This leads to the second and possibly the most potent rationale for Affirmative Action, namely that future prosperity depends on the economic productivity, management and technological capability of blacks. Blacks constitute an overwhelming majority of the country's population—86%. It therefore follows that, unless they are enabled to contribute meaningfully to economic progress, the country's economic potential will not be realized. For this reason, it is imperative that steps be taken not only to create equal opportunities but also to enable blacks and women to make their fair contribution to economic prosperity. This is necessary not only for improving the material conditions of all South Africans but also for strengthening the sense of self worth of those that apartheid sought to dehumanize.

KEY ISSUES TO BE ADDRESSED BY AFFIRMATIVE ACTION

The most obvious issue is the removal of all forms of discrimination, formal and informal, and all obstacles to equality of opportunity. This is possibly the least contentious aspect of Affirmative Action. There is wide support for the principle of equality of opportunity. Therefore one would expect white males in this country to support the adoption of an Equal Opportunity Policy. The increasing support for a non-racial, non-sexist democratic system of government by all South Africans is a clear indication that the formal adoption of an Equal Opportunity Policy is no longer an issue. The real challenge is to change the behaviour of people. South Africans have been conditioned by apartheid over many decades to see people not as individuals but as members of different racial groups and as a result racism is ingrained in the minds and hearts of many South Africans. It is very important that this fact be understood and taken into account in formulating strategies to promote an equal-opportunity environment. Changing the laws and establishing formal equality of opportunity is not enough. There must be ways and means to tackle the more subtle and informal forms of discrimination. Otherwise attempts to achieve equal opportunities will be frustrated.

Affirmative Action becomes contentious when pro-active programmes aimed at advantaging those who have been disadvantaged in the past are proposed. Some people perceive such measures as reverse discrimination and others criticize them for creating a new form of dependency. The first position is associated mainly with liberal whites and the second with conservative blacks who have made it in the world of the white males. Both positions are unacceptable as they are based on assumptions that are difficult to defend. Maphai (1989) points out that the criticism of preferential support aimed at enabling blacks to overcome the disadvantages of the past is based on a false assumption, which is that white males were entitled to all the preferential advantages they have enjoyed over the decades. On the question of dependency there is no evidence to show that Affirmative Action inevitably leads to lower performance as argued by conservative black writers like Prof. Shelby Steele of the United States of America. Innes (1992) rebuts Steele's argument by asking the question: Why have other groups like women who are also beneficiaries of Affirmative Action done so well in the USA? My own conclusion is that the weight of evidence does not support the assertion that Affirmative Action inevitably leads to lower performance. What is clear is that in situations where affirmative action strategies fail to address all the essential factors, positive results are not achieved. We should therefore not waste time arguing about the merits and demerits of Affirmative Action, but we should focus our creative minds on formulating comprehensive affirmative action strategies.

It is self-evident that in order to achieve effective equality of opportunity, blacks have to be afforded preferential support to enable them to attain a higher level of technological and managerial capability. Secondly, they must be enabled to gain access to economic resources and provided with appropriate support. Thirdly, they must be given space and opportunities to make a contribution. All the efforts would be futile if they are not able to access positions of leadership and decision-making.

The fourth issue that Affirmative Action must address is changing the mind-set of white managers and the manner in which most organizations approach black advancement. The focus of most managers and of most progressive organizations is to help the black person to overcome his/her deficiencies. Hence the emphasis on education, training and evaluation of the black candidates. It is assumed that it is the black trainee who must change, the managers must continue managing as they have always done and the organization must maintain its structures and systems. It is the new people who must adapt. If they fail they are condemned and in extreme cases kicked out and this becomes another confirmation of a stereotype about blacks.

It is this type of thinking that is behind the failure of a number of affirmative action initiatives. For Affirmative Action to work it must be realized that the managers must also change. Most white managers do not expect blacks to succeed in managerial positions. This negative expectation demoralizes the black trainees. The expectation affects the approach of the white manager as well as the morale of the black trainees. In addition, most managers have poor people management skills. Both points are highlighted by Linda Human in *Educating and Developing Managers for a Changing South Africa* (1991):

> Development is rather a process in which ability can increase through the dynamic and complex interaction between the individual's perceived ability, his or her motivation and the way in which the person is managed. If the person is managed badly, either because the manager has not been shown how to manage people or because the manager has preconceived notions concerning the ability of members of other race groups . . . or if the manager is not assessed and rewarded or sanctioned in terms of his/her own performance appraisal on the development of people, then it is highly unlikely that the subordinate will develop to the extent that he/she otherwise might.

She views poor people management as a major contributory factor to the failure of a number of affirmative action initiatives.

The need to change the mind-set of managers and social relations in most organizations cannot be overemphasized. The integration of blacks in all spheres of South African life and the enhancement of their contribution to socio-economic development is a process. It cannot happen successfully by changing blacks only and leaving all other things unchanged. Employers must understand this and accept that they need help to make the transformation in the same way that blacks need help. Ramphele (1992) puts it this way:

> Blacks and women are not just aspiring to access what has been denied them, but are demanding a fundamental redefinition of the values, norms and practices of existing social relations . . . a fundamental transformation of social relations so that they would reflect the diversity of our society.

The last key issue that Affirmative Action must address is changing the mind-set of the black people. Blacks must overcome the feelings of anger, alienation and even inferiority produced by the excruciating, dehumanizing experiences under apartheid. Although the past cannot be forgotten, it must not be allowed to detract attention from the challenges of today and of tomorrow. The challenge is to affirm the dignity and sense of self-worth of black people. This has been the aim of the liberation struggle throughout the decades. The African National Congress Youth

League (ANCYL) in 1944 articulated the ultimate goal of the struggle as follows: "to free Africa as a whole and South Africa in particular from foreign domination and leadership, and to make it possible for Africa to make her contribution to human progress and happiness." The Pan Africanist Congress has steadfastly upheld the position taken by the ANCYL in 1944. The Black Consciousness movement was inspired by the same concern; Motlhabi (1984) puts it as follows: "Black Consciousness was seen by its proponents as some form of re-awakening of Black people in South Africa to their value as human beings and their dignity as God's children and creatures."

Focus on the core purpose of the liberation struggle has a very sobering effect. It reminds blacks in particular of the fact that the real issue is freedom to contribute to human progress and happiness. Therefore black people will have their dignity and sense of self-worth affirmed only through attaining standards of democracy and human rights, economic productivity, technological and managerial competence, and accountability that are comparable to other developed communities of the world. These are the kind of accomplishments that contribute to human progress and happiness.

The logical inference is that for Affirmative Action to work, blacks must be positive and determined to overcome all the obstacles. They must be willing and motivated to work hard and to make the sacrifices that are necessary for success. This means overcoming alienation, the culture of entitlement and distrust of systems and standards which have been used to marginalize and exclude them from positions of leadership and responsibility.

The question is how to make this happen. How do you nurture a spirit of enterprise and of seeking challenges? How do you generate motivation and diligence? The first thing is to make people believe that the new system is fair. The laws of the country and those of individual organizations must be accepted as fair by all concerned. The unhappy experiences under apartheid have made black people very suspicious. Secondly, linked to increased support to ensure effective equal opportunity, outstanding achievements must be rewarded and young men and women motivated to seek new challenges. In this way creativity, self-reliance and excellence will develop and over time supersede the victim mentality and the entitlement syndrome. The black leadership has a duty to inspire black people to strive for achievements that will enable them to take full responsibility for their well-being and to earn the respect of other peoples of the world.

AFFIRMATIVE ACTION IN PRACTICE

Meaningful implementation of Affirmative Action requires a national commitment to a policy of effective equal opportunity and to measures aimed at facilitating and supporting the participation of previously disadvantaged groups. Currently the country is in transition from apartheid to a non-racial, non-sexist democracy and because of this there is talk about Affirmative Action but no coherent policy.

What is encouraging is the growing realization that as part of the normalization process in the country, Affirmative Action is inevitable. Business leaders and academics are acknowledging openly the need for Affirmative Action and the subject has become a regular feature at conferences and workshops. The release of the ANC Policy Guidelines for a Democratic South Africa has also highlighted the need for business in particular to bring forward viable options. The ANC states the case for Affirmative Action as follows: "Unless special interventions are made, the patterns of structured advantage and disadvantage created by apartheid and patriarchy will replicate themselves from generation to generation." The Pan Africanist Congress and the Azanian People's Organization also have affirmative action proposals in their economic policy positions.

The other very strong proponents of Affirmative Action are black labour, business, and professional organizations. The National African Federated Chamber of Commerce and Industry (NAFCOC) in particular has made far-reaching policy demands. At its annual conference in 1990 it announced that the corporate sector had to meet the following demands by the year 2000:

- 30% of all board members of companies listed on the Johannesburg Stock Exchange (JSE) have to be black,
- 40% of all shares on the JSE should be black-owned,
- 50% of the value of all outside purchases by companies listed on the JSE should come from black suppliers,

- 60% of top management in JSE listed companies should be black.

These are the targets that NAFCOC is proposing. Business may dismiss them as irresponsible or may be more constructive and view them as a challenge to start the process of determining targets for itself or in conjunction with NAFCOC and other interested organizations. NAFCOC and the Black Management Forum have launched a joint project for the training of black directors. The aim is to tackle the issues in a pro-active manner rather than to simply say they are not achievable.

From the above it is very clear that the pressure for Affirmative Action is growing. It cannot be resisted by continuing to do business as usual or offering the non-availability of blacks with the right education and experience as an excuse. The time for excuses is over. If major employers fail to come up with meaningful proposals, then a future democratic government will be obliged to impose affirmative action policy and guidelines.

This brings us to the discussion of substantive affirmative action measures; what they should seek to achieve and how they should be structured. It needs to be stressed that Affirmative Action is about human dignity and development. It is about removing obstacles that inhibit the realization of human potential and the provision of support systems to ensure that development actually takes place. Because development is a complex process, it follows that the desired results will not be achieved through focusing on single issues like the job-advancement of blacks and women in the public service and big business. In order to achieve sustainable progress a comprehensive strategy is essential. The strategy should encompass all major areas like sports, culture, politics and the economy. It is important that all barriers to entry be removed and appropriate support be provided to enable those who have been disadvantaged to compete on an equal footing. The management structures should be de-racialized and democratized and special measures taken to ensure meaningful representation of blacks and women at all levels. Access to resources must also receive attention. Restricted access to land, capital and technology remains a major constraint to black economic advancement.

The most crucial element in the whole process of Affirmative Action is the role played by the State in the development of people. The State must support the development of blacks by directing government expenditure towards meeting the basic needs of the poor through the provision of basic education, health, housing, water, electricity, etc. Expenditure on such programmes reaches the majority of disadvantaged people and enables them to enjoy a better quality of life.

Development institutions have a very important role to play in extending basic infrastructure in areas traditionally reserved for blacks and in extending access to resources to disadvantaged groups. Therefore their role in Affirmative Action needs to be understood and strengthened. It must always be borne in mind that the majority of disadvantaged people are poor and unemployed. Affirmative Action must include these people as well. They must be empowered through the creation of structures that enable them to be involved in decisions affecting their lives and through increased access to economic resources and income-generating activities.

The transformation of the public service is, for obvious reasons, the most important condition for black advancement. Senior public service officials are responsible for implementing government policies and for managing the delivery of services. This gives them power over what the government does. If they do not support the policies they simply hold back implementation, in other words they are in a position to frustrate reform initiatives. Therefore, to change the orientation of the government, there is a need to replace a substantial number of senior public service officials, not only with blacks and women but also with other competent South Africans who have a different orientation and no loyalty to the apartheid past. Transformation is also necessary in order to change the image of certain government departments that have become symbols of oppression and humiliation to blacks. I am referring to the Department of Education and Training, the police and defence forces. Unless competent blacks with good political credentials are appointed to key positions in these departments it is going to be very difficult to turn them into the symbols of nation-building that they should be. It therefore follows that black advancement in the public service must not only come gradually from the bottom, but that there must also be appointments to strategic positions at senior levels.

The question of standards must be addressed through vigorous training. All available training facilities and overseas offers of assistance must be utilized to prepare the ground for an integrated public service.

The private sector has a very important role to play through business and/or professional associations. It must increase its support of black advancement through the promotion of blacks in business and through special projects like the Chartered Accountants Education Endowment Trust (CA's Eden Trust). The Trust provides bursaries and mentorship to blacks aspiring to become professional accountants. It is time for business associations like the South African Chamber of Business to either have their own programmes for the promotion of blacks in business or develop joint projects with either NAFCOC or FABCOS or both. Organizations like the Black Management Forum are very keen to cooperate with established businesses in their programmes, but interest remains restricted to a few progressive companies.

Regarding black management advancement, it has to be stressed that the absence of blacks at the general manager/executive director level has become the focus of attention. This is true of all types of institutions including private sector corporations and development institutions. Most black leaders accept that the process of black advancement has to take time but the virtual absence of blacks at this level is a matter of concern.

What is really required very urgently from the private sector is an act of statesmanship—something that rivals what Mr. N Mandela and Mr. FW de Klerk are struggling to achieve at the political level—a new beginning that clearly demonstrates the commitment of business to justice and equity. An example of an action that would have the desired impact is the initiation of a credible programme directed at increasing black ownership and control in selected major companies within an agreed time span of say three to five years.

This is an attainable objective. Financial resources are available and raw material for management is available. We have a core of black university graduates in this country who can be trained locally and overseas. What is lacking is goodwill and vision on the part of business and the black leadership.

A programme of this type would serve as a model for economic integration and would go a long way in changing perceptions. The long-term benefit would be increased goodwill and trust. It would be a small step for business, but a giant leap for South Africa in the direction of unity and economic stability.

Finally a few remarks about individual employers. It is important that every organization start its own affirmative action programme. Each and every employer must have a clearly formulated affirmative action policy, which must be communicated to all employees. Affirmative Action must be integrated in the corporate strategy and be an integral part of the responsibilities of line managers. The commitment of the chief executive and the governing board or council should not be in doubt and managers must be rewarded for achievements in Affirmative Action in the same way that they are rewarded for achieving other corporate objectives.

Given the urgent need to increase the number of blacks in key positions in both government and the private sector it is strongly recommended that in recruiting for junior and middle management positions preference be given to blacks. This position is supported by a number of researchers including Ramphele, Human and Innes. Employers must of course set minimum requirements for each position and preference be given to blacks who meet the minimum requirements.

The adoption of an affirmative action recruitment policy must be supported by the introduction and improvement of development programmes that are tailor-made to the needs of each individual. This point is emphasized by Human (1991). According to her, many affirmative action initiatives fail because of poor people management skills of managers and poor support systems to trainees. To ensure that there is no lowering of standards, promotion must be based on performance. Under no circumstances must individuals be promoted because of their skin colour. The emphasis must be on facilitating access and providing adequate, appropriate individualized support.

Communication of support services available to staff is cited as another very important factor by Ramphele (1992). Black managers/professionals sometimes fail to achieve the same level as their white counterparts because they are denied access to information which the white males easily get from other white males during social/informal interactions.

Organizations that are serious about Affirmative Action must have appropriate monitoring/evaluation structures and processes. Ideally monitoring must be assigned to committees with meaningful representation of disadvantaged groups—blacks and women—and must be given appropriate status by management.

Reports by outside consultants are just not enough. There are issues that are subtle and difficult to detect unless you actually experience them. An outside consultant may fail to capture such issues.

The last word on the subject is that many studies show that human resource development is crucial to economic growth and sustained prosperity. Therefore, extending human resource development to include all South Africans is without doubt in the long-term interests of the country as a whole. It is strongly argued that in this process Affirmative Action is in the interest of business as well. Extending the supply of high-level manpower benefits business by removing a bottleneck to future growth. It is acknowledged that there are significant costs in the short term, but in the long term Affirmative Action will have positive returns for business and for the country in terms of improved political and business stability, higher productivity and better availability of high-level manpower.

Because of the importance of Affirmative Action to the country, it is recommended that a national forum on the issue be convened. The subject is too vital to be left to business and labour. It requires a more inclusive process.

CONCLUSION

In the final analysis it is the responsibility of all South Africans to shape a future that is better than the present. Blacks cannot be expected to accept that the power relations established during the apartheid era have to continue. Whites cannot claim that they are entitled to the advantages they now have. But the real crux is addressing the obstacles to effective equal opportunities without creating distortions that are going to undermine creativity, productivity and equity in future. In other words the affirmative action initiatives must be compatible with long-term economic growth and prosperity.

REFERENCES

ANC (1992) *ANC Policy Guidelines for a Democratic South Africa*. Johannesburg; Policy Unit of the African National Congress

Human, L. (1990) Empowerment through Development: The Role of Affirmative Action and Management Development in the Demise of Apartheid. *Management Education and Development* Vol. 21, Part 4, 1990

Human, L. (1991) *Educating and Developing Managers for a Changing South Africa*. Cape Town; Juta

Innes, D. (1992) *Affirmative Action: Issues and Strategies*. The Innes Labour Brief. Vol. 3(3)

Maphai, V.T. (1989) Affirmative Action in South Africa: A Genuine Option? *Social Dynamics* 15(2): 1–24

Motlhabi, M. (1984) *The Theory and Practice of Black Resistance to Apartheid*. Johannesburg; Skotaville Publishers

Ramphele, M. (1992) Affirmative Action in Employment. UDUSA National Conference 1–3 July, University of Durban-Westville (unpublished)

74

Extracts from a Working Document Entitled "A Bill of Rights for a New South Africa" As Compiled by the Constitutional Committee of the ANC

ARTICLE 13

Affirmative Action

1. Nothing in the Constitution shall prevent the enactment of legislation, or the adoption by any public or private body of special measures of a positive kind designed to procure the advancement and the opening up of opportunities, including access to education, skills, employment and land, and the general advancement in social, economic and cultural spheres, of men and women who in the past have been disadvantaged by discrimination.
2. No provision of the Bill of Rights shall be construed as derogating from or limiting in any way the general provisions of this Article.

ARTICLE 14

Positive Action

1. In its activities and functioning, the State shall observe the principles of non-racialism and non-sexism, and encourage the same in all public and private bodies.
2. All benefits conferred and entitlements granted by the State shall be distributed on a non-racial and a non-sexist basis.
3. The State and all public and private bodies shall be under a duty to prevent any form of incitement to racial, religious or linguistic hostility and to dismantle all structures and do away with all practices that compulsorily divide the population on grounds of race, colour, language, or creed.
4. With a view to achieving the above, the State may enact legislation to prohibit the circulation or possession of materials which incite racial, ethnic, religious, gender or linguistic hatred, which provoke violence, or which insult, degrade, defame or encourage abuse of any racial, ethnic, religious, gender or linguistic group.
5. All organs of the State at the national, regional and local levels shall pursue policies and programmes aimed at redressing the consequences of past discriminatory laws and practices, and at the creation of a genuine non-racial democracy in South Africa.
6. Such policies shall include the implementation of programmes aimed at achieving speedily the balanced structuring in non-racial form of the public service, defence and police forces and the prison service.
7. Without interfering with its independence, and with a view to ensuring that justice is manifestly seen to be done in a non-racial way and that the wisdom, experience and judicial skills of all South Africans are represented on the bench, the judiciary shall be transformed in such a way as to consist of men and women drawn from all sectors of South African society.
8. In taking steps to correct patterns or practices of discrimination, special attention shall be paid to rectifying the inequalities to which women in South Africa have been subjected, and to ensuring their full, equal, effective and dignified participation in the political, social, economic and cultural life of the nation.
9. Legislation may be enacted requiring non-governmental organizations and private bodies to conduct themselves in accordance with the above principles.

ARTICLE 7

Gender Rights

1. Men and women shall enjoy equal rights in all areas of public and private life, including employment, education and within the family.
2. Discrimination on the grounds of gender, single parenthood, legitimacy of birth or sexual orientation shall be unlawful.
3. Positive action shall be undertaken to overcome the disabilities and disadvantages suffered on account of past gender discrimination.
4. The law shall provide remedies for sexual harassment, abuse and violence.
5. Educational institutions, the media, advertising and other social institutions shall be under a duty to discourage sexual and other types of stereotyping.

ARTICLE 8

Disabled Persons

1. There shall be no discrimination against disabled persons.
2. Legislation shall provide for the progressive opening up of employment opportunities for disabled men and women, for the removal of obstacles to their enjoyment by them of public amenities and for their integration into all areas of life.

75

California Constitution

Article 1, Section 31, a–h

§ 31. DISCRIMINATION BASED ON RACE, SEX, COLOR, ETHNICITY, OR NATIONAL ORIGIN; GENDER-BASED QUALIFICATIONS IN PUBLIC EMPLOYMENT, EDUCATION, OR CONTRACTING

Sec. 31. a. The state shall not discriminate against, or grant preferential treatment to, any individual or group on the basis of race, sex, color, ethnicity, or national origin in the operation of public employment, public education or public contracting.

b. This section shall apply only to action taken after the section's effective date.

c. Nothing in this section shall be interpreted as prohibiting bona fide qualifications based on sex which are reasonably necessary to the normal operation of public employment, public education, or public contracting.

d. Nothing in this section shall be interpreted as invalidating any court order or consent decree which is in force as of the effective date of this section.

e. Nothing in this section shall be interpreted as prohibiting action which must be taken to establish or maintain eligibility for any federal program, where ineligibility would result in a loss of federal funds to the state.

f. For the purposes of this section, "state" shall include, but not necessarily be limited to, the state itself, any city, county, city and county, public university system, including the University of California, community college district, school district, special district, or any other political subdivision or governmental instrumentality of or within the state.

g. The remedies available for violations of this section shall be the same, regardless of the injured party's race, sex, color, ethnicity, or national origin, as are otherwise available for violations of then-existing California antidiscrimination law.

h. This section shall be self-executing. If any part or parts of this section are found to be in conflict with federal law or the United States Constitution, the section shall be implemented to the maximum extent that federal law and the United States Constitution permit. Any provision held invalid shall be severable from the remaining portions of this section.

(Added by Initiative Measure (Prop. 209, approved Nov. 5, 1996).)

76

LARRY MAY

Sexual Harassment and Solidarity

Sexual harassment, like rape, seems obviously wrong. Yet, many men are not as willing to condemn it as they are willing to condemn rape. In part, this is no doubt due to the fact that it is less clear what are the boundaries of the concept of harassment, where some putative forms of harassment are not easily distinguished from "horse play" or pranksterism.[1] But it may also be due to the fact that men are reluctant to condemn practices which have for so long functioned to build solidarity among men.[2] The *Playboy* centerfold pinned to the bulletin board at a workplace has at least two functions. It is a constant source of erotic stimulation for the men who work there; and it is a constant source of embarrassment and annoyance for many of the women, a clear sign that this is not the kind of place for them, but that it is a place for men.

In this chapter I wish to examine sexual harassment in its various forms, seeking a basis for moral criticism of it. In addition to more standard criticisms, largely parallel to those developed in law, I offer a new critique that calls attention to the way that sexual harassment promotes male solidarity and also thereby often excludes women from full and equal participation in various practices and contexts. At the end of the chapter I discuss positive aspects of male solidarity and indicate why sexual harassment is not a good basis for such solidarity. Men need to feel good about who they are as men, not on the model of little boys retreating to a clubhouse with a "no girls allowed" sign on the door, but on the model of reformed alcoholics who are now so changed that they are not afraid to discuss their past problems with others as well as among themselves.

I. SEXUAL INTIMIDATION

The case of *Alexander v. Yale University* was the first sexual harassment lawsuit to concern an educational rather than a workplace setting.[3] The case concerned a female student at Yale University who alleged that one of her male political science professors threatened to *lower* her grade on a term paper (from a B to a C) unless she slept with him. The student, who was hoping to go to law school, felt intimidated by the proposal but did not capitulate. After her initial accusation, other women came forward with similar stories about this particular political science professor. The professor denied these other charges but admitted discussing grades with the student who sued. He claimed that he had offered to *raise* the student's grade (from a C to a B) if she slept with him, but that she had simply declined his offer. Since, on his view, the grade had remained what the student had earned, no harm had been done to the student. No foul, no harm.

This case raised difficulties with the way that sexual harassment had been previously understood. Previously, sexual harassment was thought by the courts to involve five elements:

1. a sexual advance
2. by a person in a more powerful position
3. made to a person in a less powerful position
4. against the second person's will
5. which adversely affected
    - a. retention of job
    - b. evaluation
    - or c. promotion.

At least according to the version of the story told by the political science professor, the student had not been adversely affected, and so the fifth element of sexual harassment was not present.

Sexual harassment was understood to be harmful in that it constituted an unjustified form of intimidation, much like blackmail. But the attorneys who defended the Yale student felt that a different model was needed given the group-oriented nature of the offense. So they seized on the idea that sexual harassment like that directed at the student was a form of sex discrimination and thus harmful as a form of degradation. But what if the facts were as alleged by the professor, was there any discrimination against or degradation of the student? This seemed not to be like blackmail, since there was no clear indication that she would be rendered worse off if she turned down the professor's proposal.

If the facts were as the student alleged, then this was an egregious case of sexual intimidation. No one who understands the purpose of educational institutions would countenance the idea of a male professor threatening to give a student less than she deserved unless the student did something so utterly outside the realm of academic achievement as providing sexual favors. Worse than this is the idea of a male professor abusing his power and authority over often naive students for his own personal gain. And worse yet is the idea that a man could extort sex from an otherwise unwilling female by threatening to do something undeserved to harm her career prospects. For all these reasons, sexual harassment of the sort alleged by the student is clearly morally wrong.

If we believe the male political science professor, something morally wrong has occurred as well, although somewhat less clearly so. On his version he offered to give the student a grade better than she deserves, and so he seemingly did not threaten to harm her undeservedly. But there was an indication that the female student may have been harmed which can be seen in that she would not have wanted to have such proposals made in the first place. The student was put in the position of having her sexuality count as a basis of academic achievement. This had a negative impact on the educational environment in which the student resided.[4] I have elsewhere argued that this was indeed a form of sex discrimination which effectively coerced the student, even though there was no direct threat to her, at least if we believe the professor's story.[5]

The professor's "offer" changes the range of options that the student previously had in a way which makes her post-offer situation worse than it was in the pre-offer state. The student could no longer proceed as before, thinking of her options in a purely academic way. And in this sense she is disadvantaged, perhaps even coerced, in that she is made to accept a set of options that she would not otherwise choose. When such proposals get made, the well is poisoned, and it is no longer possible for the student to think of herself as merely a student and not also as a sex object.[6] In the case of sexual harassment, seen as either a direct threat or as a seemingly innocent sexual offer, harm has occurred.

Laurence Thomas has challenged my analysis of sexual harassment in offer situations. He contends that not all examples of sexual offers contain veiled threats or can be characterized as situations that the woman would prefer not to be in. He gives an example: "Deborah is Peter's secretary. Peter offers to pay Deborah so many dollars per week, in addition to her present salary, if she would be his exclusive sexual partner. The money would come out of his own pocket."[7] Thomas stipulates that there is no veiled threat here, and no one is under psychological duress. In the case in question, Thomas "is not inclined to think that there is a moral wrong here."[8] His rationale is expressed in this blunt statement: "It simply cannot be the case that we should not enter into any interaction if there is the possibility that it might become morally explosive."[9]

It seems to me, however, that Peter has done something morally suspect by introducing sex into the workplace. Even though Deborah can take the offer or leave it, she cannot, on her own, return to a situation where her relationship with Peter was strictly professional. By turning the offer down, she does not return to the previous state of affairs because of the way that Peter's offer has changed the relationship between them and set the stage for abuses of Peter's authority.[10] This much Thomas admits; yet he claims that we cannot stop acting just because it might turn out that abuse could occur. But he has focused on only one aspect of the problem, the possibility that things might turn ugly. What he has missed is that the relationship has changed, nearly irrevocably, in a way that is out of Deborah's control.

In some cases of sexual offers, or sexual innuendos, nothing straightforwardly coercive occurs, but there may be reason nonetheless to think that a moral wrong has occurred. The moral wrong concerns the way that a person's options are restricted against that person's will. It is morally wrong not only to make a person's options worse than they were before, but also to limit them undeservedly if this is against the person's will. In this latter case, it is not the worsening of the situation but rather the way that it is undeservedly taken out of the control of the woman which makes it morally suspect. To put the point starkly, sexual harassment normally involves a restriction of options which also restricts autonomy.[11] In the straightforwardly coercive cases of sexual harassment, autonomy is restricted because a woman is forced to accede to a man's wishes or risk harm to herself. In some subtler cases of sexual harassment, autonomy is restricted in that a change in relationship is effected against the wishes of the woman, possibly to her detriment. But even if it is not to her detriment, she has been undeservedly forced into a situation that she has not chosen. In the next sections I will explore in more detail the moral harms of some of the subtle cases of sexual harassment.

II. HOSTILE ENVIRONMENTS

In 1993 the United States Supreme Court gave its clearest support to a relatively new basis for understanding the harm of sexual harassment which is closer to the basis I have just suggested than is the intimidation model, although with several important differences. The Court carefully enunciated a doctrine that held that sexual harassment can be harmful in that it produces a hostile or abusive work environment for a person because of her gender.[12] I want to explore various theoretical issues that are implicated in this new approach to sexual harassment, where the older model of intimidation and blackmail is by and large abandoned. I am especially interested in how this new model affects our understanding of male behavior in educational and workplace settings.

Here are some of the relevant facts of the case of *Harris v. Forklift Systems, Inc.*

> Teresa Harris worked as a manager at Forklift Systems, Inc., an equipment rental company, from April 1985 until 1987. Charles Hardy was Forklift's president. The magistrate found that, throughout Harris's time at Forklift, Hardy often insulted her because of her gender and often made her the target of unwanted sexual innuendos. Hardy told Harris on

> several occasions, in the presence of other employees, "You're a woman, what do you know" and "We need a man as the rental manager"; at least once, he told her she was "a dumb ass woman." Again, in front of others, he suggested that the two of them "go to the Holiday Inn to negotiate [Harris's] raise." Hardy occasionally asked Harris and other female employees to get coins from his front pants pocket. He threw objects on the ground in front of Harris and other women, and asked them to pick them up. He made sexual innuendos about Harris's and other women's clothing.[13]

This pattern of harassment was not aimed at extracting a particular form of behavior, such as a sexual favor. It was not straightforwardly coercive, but nonetheless something seems morally wrong about Hardy's actions.

What Hardy did was to create an environment in which it was very difficult for his female employees to be taken seriously as equals to their male counterparts. Justice Sandra Day O'Connor, delivering the opinion of the court, considered this case an example of a "discriminatorily abusive work environment." This new standard "takes a middle path between making actionable any conduct that is merely offensive, and requiring the conduct to cause a tangible psychological injury." A hostile environment is, according to O'Connor, not something that can be defined with mathematical precision, but it can be determined by "looking at . . . the frequency of the discriminatory conduct; its severity; whether it is physically threatening or humiliating, or a mere offensive utterance; and whether it unreasonably interferes with an employee's work performance."

The harm of a hostile work environment is relatively clear. Again, according to O'Connor, a "discriminatorily abusive work environment, even one that does not seriously affect employees' psychological well-being, can and often will detract from employees' job performance, discourage employees from remaining on the job, or keep them from advancing in their careers." Even without a showing of these specific harms, O'Connor rightly pointed to the denial of "workplace equality" which is broadly guaranteed by Title VII of the Civil Rights Act of 1964.[14] The key here is that this form of behavior treats men differently from women, subjecting only the women to these risks.

The chief harm of sexual harassment is indeed that it discriminates against women by subjecting women to "run a gauntlet of sexual abuse in return for the privilege of being allowed to work and make a living"[15] and thereby demeans them. Sexual harassment, even of the more subtle variety, normally changes the work environment against the wishes of the women. And this creates a difference between male and female employees. Women are forced to be seen as both workers and sexual objects, while men are free either to be seen as only workers or to be seen as workers and sexual objects. The environmental change effected by sexual harassment discriminates against women, generally to their detriment.

What if the changes in the work environment are welcome? What if a particular woman wishes to be able to advance by the use of sexual favors? To go back to Thomas's example, what if Deborah wishes to be able to supplement her income by doing sexual favors, on the side, for her boss? Does it still make sense to say that the environment is discriminatory? I believe the answer to this question is yes. But I'm not so sure that the environment is always hostile or abusive. In order to see this one needs to think about the way that women in the workplace, or in an educational setting, will be affected as a group. The environment is discriminatory because of the way that only women have had their options restricted in respect to the kind of relationships they can have with their male bosses. Normally only women, not men, are the ones whose appearance and sexual characteristics matter and who will be judged according to non-work-related, sexual criteria.

In my view the court has done well to focus on the discriminatory environment, rather than intimidation, created by even subtle examples of sexual harassment. But it has potentially led us astray by calling that environment hostile or abusive. Surely in the most egregious cases, such as that of Charles Hardy and Teresa Harris at Forklift Systems, Inc., the discriminatory work environment does become abusive. But in the more subtle cases, this is not necessarily so, and yet the environment is still discriminatory, and morally suspect for that reason. When more subtle forms of sexual harassment occur, such as when a *Playboy* centerfold is displayed in a common room, women are treated in a way that men are not, and even if some women find this to be welcome it still puts them at a competitive disadvantage in terms of being taken as seriously as their male counterparts with regard to job performance. Their sexuality is considered, illegitimately, to be relevant to job performance, and other, legitimate, bases of job performance are put on the same level as this illegitimate basis, thereby tainting the legitimate bases. This situation has been forced upon them and is, generally speaking, contrary to the autonomy of the women in question.

Sex discrimination can be morally wrong on at least three counts: women are degraded; they are treated unfairly; or they are denied a certain amount of autonomy over their lives. When women seem to welcome differential status in a given context, as in the case of Deborah welcoming the opportunity to make more money by sleeping with her boss, it can appear that women are gaining autonomy rather than losing it. But this is not the case. For what is being lost is the choice of whether to be treated only as a worker and not also as a sex object. In most contexts this loss of control brings more harm to the woman's autonomy than the possible gain from being given more attention or allowed to use one's sexuality to gain certain advantages. What counts as "job related" or "meritorious" has undergone a sometimes subtle shift, to the detriment of women workers.

III. FEMALE EXCLUSION FROM FULL PARTICIPATION

One of the things often ignored in discussions of sexual harassment is how it promotes male solidarity, especially a solidarity that keeps women in an inferior position and excludes them from full and equal participation in a practice. Think of a very minor form of sexual harassment, at least as compared to that suffered in the *Harris* or *Alexander* cases, namely, a *Playboy* centerfold placed on a locker door in an employee work area. Such an act is not likely to cause serious psychological distress to female employees, and it is not some kind of quid pro quo attempt to extort sexual favors. Nevertheless it resembles these more egregious acts in excluding women from full and equal participation in a work environment with their male colleagues, as we will see.

How is it that even such seemingly innocuous acts as posting the *Playboy* centerfold in a common area can contribute to a form of male bonding and solidarity that is aimed at, or at least has the known effect of, making females feel unwelcome?[16] My analysis is explicitly group oriented. The various forms of sexual harassment share, it seems to me, the effect of creating an environment in which women feel excluded. In this respect sexual harassment is best understood as a harm perpetrated by men against women. To see why this is a group-based problem as well as an interpersonal problem, one needs to recognize that putting the poster on the wall is a signal to any woman who enters the room that women are to be viewed as comparable to the woman in the centerfold picture—to be gawked at, drooled over, and reduced to the measurements of their breasts and buttocks—not welcome here as equals to men.

Even in the most egregious cases, sexual harassment often appears to be merely an interpersonal problem. One party, typically a male, is proposing sex to another party, typically a female, and the female does not welcome such a proposal. But again, one needs to realize that in many of these cases, including *Alexander v. Yale* and *Harris v. Forklift Systems, Inc.*, the woman who sues is normally not the only one being harassed. Other female students or employees often come forward to allege the same behavior toward them by the same male. The multiple victims of sexual harassers make it unlikely that theirs is only an interpersonal problem between an individual male and an individual female.

The type of behavior characteristic of sexual harassment rarely relates to the differences of individual women. The underlying attitudes of the men in question are contempt or at least condescension toward all or most women, not merely toward the one who is currently being harassed. In the next section we will see in more detail how this works when we examine the case of a heterosexual male who harasses a homosexual male. The thing that links the two cases is that exclusion is occurring because a person fails to occupy a certain category, not because of one's unique characteristics. A group-based harm has occurred whenever there is harm directed at a person because of features that that person shares with other members of a group.[17]

Indeed, it is common for sexual harassment to promote male solidarity in educational or employment contexts. Think again of the *Playboy* centerfold displayed in a prominent place in an auto mechanic's work area. If a woman should stray into the work area by mistake or in order to find the mechanic working on her car, she will be alerted right away that this is a male-only domain. Indeed, it may be the practice of the fellow mechanics to touch the breasts of the woman in the picture or to pat her buttocks as they enter or leave the work area, especially when women are present. Here is a good example of how pornographic images can be used to isolate women and separate them from men, but this image also solidifies bonds of men with men. Such a practice is obviously much less morally offensive than actually touching the breasts or patting the buttocks of real women in the workplace. But these practices serve as a reminder that the same thing could happen to women who stumble into the wrong place at the wrong time.

Here is another case.[18] A male graduate student displays a *Playboy* centerfold on a bulletin board in an office that houses half a dozen teaching assistants in philosophy, some of whom are women. The male students gather and comment on the physical dimensions of the centerfold woman's breasts and buttocks, laughing and joking and comparing the dimensions of the centerfold woman to those of their fellow female graduate students. The women find this behavior either annoying or humiliating or both. One woman finds it increasingly difficult to go into the office, knowing that her male colleagues may be discussing the dimensions of her breasts and buttocks. Another woman who complains finds herself the subject of ridicule for her lack of camaraderie.

In both of these cases male bonding and solidarity are furthered by excluding women from full and equal participation. Of course, it is not necessarily the intention of these men or of these practices to exclude women, although this is at least a reasonable thing to expect. The exclusion is by and large the unintended, but foreseen, consequence of the practices that build solidarity. But this is not a necessary result of building male solidarity, as we will see in the final section of this chapter. Indeed, men often find themselves today under siege because their practices of bonding have so publicly excluded women in ways that have deprived women of opportunities to advance, compete, and cooperate in the larger society. Men have been challenged in this domain, both in the courts and in various other public forums. It is not male solidarity that is the culprit, but the forms of harassment that have both supported the bonding between men, and also excluded women from full and equal participation with males.

One may wonder if it is always wrong for one group to adopt practices that have the effect of excluding another group. To answer this question one needs to think seriously about the moral principles that would be implicated in such exclusion. Exclusion is not always morally wrong or even suspect. But when exclusion affects a whole category of people and there is no reasonable basis for it, then it is morally suspect. The principle of moral equality is implicated whenever like cases are not treated alike. Excluding one group of people from a domain without good reason is a paradigmatic example of morally suspicious treatment. While it is obviously quite common for one group of people to exclude another group, moral criticism is appropriate when the exclusion is done for arbitrary reasons, especially if it perpetuates a pattern of exclusion in the larger society.

Is it necessary that there be a past pattern of exclusion for a current particular instance of sexual harassment to constitute group-based harm to women? This is a complex question that cannot be easily answered. Implicated here is the question whether harassment of a man by a female superior would constitute harm to men as a group. In part the answer could be obvious. If the man is sexually harassed merely for being a man, where other men have been similarly treated, then the man is clearly harmed in a discriminatory way and, in some sense, so are men as a group. But without the pattern of adverse treatment it is unclear that men as a group are *significantly* harmed by this seemingly isolated act by a woman. What makes sexual harassment a form of morally harmful sexual discrimination is that it contributes to a particular pattern of subordination.

If we are discussing these issues in a legal context, it is probably a mistake to say that a past pattern of exclusion is necessary for legally actionable harm, because on this construal a judge who does not see the pattern of past behavior will be entitled to disregard any current harm. But in the moral context, where we are not relying on judges who must decide whether to allow a suit to go forward, it is more reasonable to think that patterns of past discrimination are relevant to the assessment of harmfulness of what one man does to a female subordinate. While sexual harassment is often a form of group-based harm, it is not always so, and the harms involved in sexual harassment are not completely captured by focusing on the group. This point will become clearer, I hope, in light of some nonstandard examples of sexual harassment in the next section.

IV. DISCRIMINATION AND HARASSMENT

I wish to investigate two cases of harassment that complicate the preceding analysis because of the sexual orientation of the people involved. I begin with a brief examination of a hypothetical case, then move on to a more developed treatment of an actual case and a variation on that case. The first case involves a bisexual man who harasses both men and women indifferently. The second case is that of a heterosexual man who harasses another man whom he believes to be a homosexual. A consideration of these cases will allow us to achieve a more adequate understanding of the moral harm involved in excluding someone on grounds of sexuality. A variation on the latter case, where the supervisee is actually a homosexual, is especially interesting for even though it does not involve harassment by a man of a woman, it nonetheless involves harassment of one person whose group, homosexual males, is subordinated on grounds of sexuality, by another person whose group, heterosexual males, is dominant. A consideration of this case also relates to the previous section's discussion of how sexual harassment contributes to male solidarity.

In the case of a bisexual man who sexually harasses both men and women indifferently, we can begin to see whether it matters morally that the harassment is based on men's historical dominance of women.[19] This harasser does not treat women differently from men, so there is no disparate treatment of women and therefore it appears that there is no sex discrimination occurring either. This case contrasts with the case of the male boss who simply harasses (in the sense of "gives a hard time to") every one of his employees equally; the harassment itself may be morally problematic, but not because of its connection with sexuality. The male bisexual harasser seemingly harasses men and women indiscriminately, but the harassment is on sexual grounds and takes a sexual form, either making sexual propositions or engaging in sexual jokes and ridicule that change the workplace environment.

It seems fair to say that the male bisexual harasser is engaging in sexual harassment since his behavior places both men and women in uncomfortable, and unwanted, positions, undeservedly restricting their autonomy. His propositions indicate that he views sexual favors as appropriate criteria in judging job performance. Insofar as the employees wish that this were not the case, the work environment has been rendered hostile. But the hostility is muted by the fact that this does not appear to be part of a larger pattern of hostile treatment by bisexuals in the larger society. What makes sexual harassment so problematic morally is that it contributes to a larger social problem, namely, the discriminatory treatment of women by men.

The male bisexual harasser does engage in sexual harassment, which creates a hostile work environment, but he does not engage in sex discrimination. Even though he sexually harasses women in the workplace, creating a hostile work environment for them, even sexually intimidating them in some cases, his behavior does not necessarily contribute to a society-wide pattern of sex discrimination. The main reason for this, of course, is that he does not treat the men in his employ any differently. This is not to deny that the women may respond quite differently from their male colleagues to his propositions, because of differential socialization. And this socialization may make things worse for the women, who find it harder to resist the propositions than the men. But the acts of the bisexual harasser are not themselves instances of sex discrimination and hence do not violate the moral principle of equal treatment and equal respect.[20]

Now consider a case of a heterosexual male who harasses a male supervisee. A recent case arose in Springfield, Illinois.

> The suit alleges that the supervisor, John Trees, created "a sexually offensive and hostile work environment" at a Transportation Department facility in Springfield, repeatedly making comments in front of other workers indicating he believed that [Jim] Shermer was a homosexual. . . . Shermer isn't gay, the suit says. He alleges he "suffered emotional distress to his reputation, embarrassment, humiliation and other personal injuries," as a result of Tree's behavior. . . . A federal judge in Springfield dismissed the suit in August [1996], in part because of the state's novel argument: As a man on an all-male work crew, it was intrinsically impossible for Shermer to prove he was the victim of sexual discrimination, a necessary component of sexual harassment.[21]

I am inclined to agree with the judge in this case. There is no sex discrimination here because not all, or any other, men are being treated similarly by the supervisor, and there is no indication that the supervisee is being harassed because he is male.

In a variation of the above case, where the heterosexual male supervisor was harassing a homosexual male, we can begin to see whether it matters morally that harassment is directed at women for it to be pernicious. Here the history of the discriminatory treatment of homosexual men by the larger society makes the act of sexual harassment of a homosexual man more like the standard cases of men harassing women than like the original case, one heterosexual male harassing another, or like the hypothetical case of the male bisexual harasser. But even in this case, sexual harassment is not a form of sex discrimination, because it is not directed at someone by virtue of being a member of a certain gender group. As long as heterosexual men are not subjected to the same mistreatment, then it is not clear that the mistreatment is based on belonging to a gender group. But it may be discriminatory nonetheless if it turns out that the harasser only mistreats homosexual men, and no others, and such mistreatment is arbitrary.

Illegal discrimination occurs whenever one group is arbitrarily and adversely treated differently from another. Harassment of homosexual men is a clear example of discrimination even though it is not a form of sex discrimination. Discrimination against homosexuals is still in the stage of being quite blatant in most of Western society. The acts of gay bashing and ridicule of gay lifestyles occur largely unabated and unchallenged. In this sense discrimination against homosexuals is in a different stage, and perhaps a worse stage, from that of discrimination against women. The main way to see that it is, is to think about discrimination as a form of exclusion from full and equal participation in social practices. Discrimination against homosexuals, especially men, is so virulent that it virtually excludes this group from mainstream society in ways that are not now true for the way discrimination against women works.

Discrimination against women and discrimination against homosexual men share this much: they are both instances of dominant males excluding from full and equal participation those who are different from them and thereby building solidarity within the dominant group. But such solidarity is morally problematic, especially when it is purchased by virulent antihomosexual behavior and attitudes. When solidarity is purchased by strong exclusion, two sorts of moral wrong occur. First, of course, there is harm to the excluded group, and its members. Second, the group that does the excluding is also morally harmed and, in this sense, harms itself by its irrational aggression and anger, emotional responses that make it much harder for its members to know and do what is right and hence to attain certain moral virtues.

Aggression and anger often block one's ability to perceive a moral situation correctly. Indeed, the kind of exclusion-oriented aggression and anger characteristic of discrimination against homosexual men have made it very difficult for heterosexual men to recognize their behavior as discriminatory and their attitudes as displaying a lack of respect for fellow humans. Exclusion of one group by another is not always, but quite often, associated with characterizing the excluded group as one which is deserving of its exclusion. In the case of discrimination against homosexual men in Western society, and also in many areas of the non-Western world, the exclusion has been joined by strong emotional reactions directed against the "pernicious" lifestyles of gay men. These strong emotional reactions have created moral harms both for those harassed but also, interestingly, for those who do the harassing.

What would it take for a society to restructure itself so that women and homosexuals were not excluded and vilified for failing to conform to heterosexual male standards? It is beyond the scope of my project to attempt to give a full answer to this question. But one thing does seem clear to me. If heterosexual men could find alternative mechanisms for building solidarity which did not rely on exclusion, then a major part of the motivation for discrimination might be eliminated. I next turn my attention to such alternative bases for building solidarity among heterosexual men, some of which seem promising and some of which do not. I will be chiefly interested in examining a group which calls itself the Promise Keepers, and also groups of men which have chosen non-competitive athletic activities.

V. INCLUSION AND MALE SOLIDARITY

Can solidarity be built around nonexclusionary practices and ideologies? Is it likely that men will be able to maintain solidarity by stressing inclusiveness rather than exclusiveness? Male athletes and soldiers have often formed strong bonds of inclusion. In some contexts they have managed to do so without also excluding women, but this has not often happened by chance. Instead, it takes planning and imagination for men to find methods of solidarity building that do not also exclude women. . . . After providing some conceptual background considerations, I will here focus on an athletic example and one drawn from a quasi-religious context.

As I have argued elsewhere, solidarity involves the following overlapping components:

conscious group identification,
bonds of sentiment,
interest in the group's well-being,
shared values and beliefs, and
a readiness to show moral support.[22]

The first component, conscious group identification, requires some sense that one's own group is different from other groups, and so there is some conceptual exclusivity built into the notion of solidarity from the start. But the kind of exclusivity here required for solidarity does not entail the kind of exclusivity that is involved in sexual harassment. One can distinguish oneself from others without needing to exclude from full and equal participation those others or needing to demean these others in order to boost oneself.

The second component, bonds of sentiment, and the fourth, shared values and beliefs, certainly put a premium on one's own group and what is shared therein. But this does not begin to rule out also having bonds of sentiment with non-group members or sharing values and beliefs with members of a larger unit, such as a society or nation, or even with other groups of which one is also a member or to which one feels some loose kinship. To feel bonds of sentiment with my family members does not mean that I cannot also feel bonds of sentiment with my neighbors, or with the members of another family half a world away. Bonds of sentiment do not necessarily compete with each other; one bond does not rule out another.

The third component, an interest in the group's well-being, may also be thought to require exclusivity, since having such an interest seems to preclude having an interest in the well-being of others, or at least it cannot countenance the kind of indiscriminate interestedness I have suggested. But this is also mistaken. Well-being is not always, or even often, a zero-sum game. This should be obvious but if it is not consider one's own health. In order to enjoy good health it is important that one eat in moderation and exercise regularly. One can garner these two essential ingredients of good health without denying them to anyone else. In some limited contexts, if food is in very short supply, then my continued good health is in competition with yours, and I suppose the same may be true if there is a limited amount of available space for us to exercise. But given the wide variety of acceptable foodstuffs available in most societies and the wide range of possible exercise regimens, it is not very often that one person's pursuit of his or her good health is at odds with anyone else's. Indeed, my good health requires that others remain relatively healthy as well so that they do not infect me.

The fifth component of solidarity, a readiness to show moral support, is perhaps the most problematic for my analysis, for surely a person's time is limited, so that if one shows moral support for a person in one's group, one will be less likely to have time to show moral support for someone not in one's group. But there is no reason to think that not having time to show moral support for members of another group than one's own means that one needs to show contempt for or to demean these folks. Indeed, showing contempt for someone is itself time-consuming, whereas not doing so is not time-consuming. Those who actively exclude others by deriding, defaming, or harassing them surely take time away from displaying moral support for their own group, unless showing contempt for another group just is showing support for one's own group. But this is simply not true except in limited contexts. Booing another team may be seen as showing support for one's own team. But acting hostilely toward a woman cannot be conceived as showing support for one's maleness without a very special, and extremely odd, set of circumstances, since men and women, as members of their respective gender groups, are generally not engaged in a zero-sum game in the workplace or educational setting.[23]

The movement called the Promise Keepers is an attempt to provide men with a sense of pride in being men and a sense of solidarity that is explicitly aimed at dissuading men from being intimidating, contemptuous, or hostile toward women. The idea behind the "promise" is explicitly that men have made commitments to those women with whom they are in relationships, and their main duty is to keep these commitments. But in addition, the men are looking for a group to join to provide them with support and motivation to help them become "men" in some positive sense of that term, especially good Christian men, men who follow the example of Jesus Christ in their daily lives. It is no accident that this group has held rallies that look like sports events, often actually held in large sports arenas.

The chief positive image of men which the Promise Keepers use to build solidarity is the image of men as providers and protectors of women and children. In this revitalized vision of the traditional male role, men are asked to put wife and children ahead of careers and to become the true spiritual leaders of their families. The men who have taken this route report that they have better relations with their children, that their marriages are revitalized, that they have surrendered themselves to God. Indeed, the whole point of the movement is best expressed as a call for each man to become less of "an independent person."[24] This call is successful evidently because while it criticizes certain aspects of traditional male roles, it also provides a positive model for change which draws on other aspects of traditional male roles.

The image of men as providers and protectors of women will not necessarily diminish the exclusivity of the male domain, especially if men still see themselves as the leaders or heads of the family unit. The Promise Keepers have left themselves open to the criticism that they are reinstilling in men the idea that they are superior to women as leaders, in both spiritual and nonspiritual ways, and this could function to restrict women from full and equal participation in the decision-making domain of family life. It is clear that what many men find attractive here is that they have found a new way that they can assert themselves, and draw on their traditional strengths, and not feel guilty about doing it. Much of this seems right to me. But we must be wary of this new movement merely reinforcing the prevalent cultural view that men should be in charge and women should be excluded from major decision-making roles. This already seems evident in the way the leaders of this group often talk about the role of women, and exclusionary practices are also evident in the sometimes hostile way this group has tried to exclude gay men from its ranks.[25]

To overcome some of these potential problems, I propose that we think about a different movement, perhaps called "Consensus Seekers," which would be more inclusive than the Promise Keepers, and not so closely tied to a particular religious creed. Here the idea would be that men can draw strength from their traditional roles as those who are good at practical tasks such as compromise and consensus building in the political and business arenas. Alongside the tradition of men acting independently and aggressively, there is also a tradition of men being good team players and facilitators. Men could use these consensus-building skills to find solutions to social, familial, and small-group problems, especially concerning mixed-sex situations, which allow both gender groups to feel as if their interests have been well respected. The model for such groups is the sports arena, where men have often excelled at finding a common basis for fellow members to draw strength from the team and to put their best efforts into the common goals of the group.

Men can find strength, support, and solidarity from interacting with other men to create new patterns of socialization for younger men which stress these traditional male virtues but downplay the aggressiveness and combativeness that also often accompany all-male groups in sports and other domains.[26] But unlike the Promise Keepers, the idea is not that men need to do something for women that women cannot do for themselves. Rather, the idea is that men can facilitate the greater participation of both sexes by exercising some traditional male virtues. And it should be apparent that these virtues can be exercised effectively only in a nonexclusionary way that does not express hostility toward any other group, be they women or homosexuals.

In some sports contexts we can find the rudimentary basis for a model of nonaggressive and nonexclusionary masculinity which I wish to defend. Pre-high school, and some informal adult, sports such as soccer, volleyball, and softball are often conducted with mixed teams of men and women. And in some of these cases, the boys or men manage to become true team players, adapting themselves to the variable range of skills of the players, rather than becoming disdainful of the girls or women on the team. Here is an example of the kind of non-zero-sum game I mentioned earlier. Males can feel good about what they accomplish as males in a way that enhances rather than diminishes the status of females. If these same men try to exclude women or demean them, they make it far less likely that they themselves can excel and display virtue, whether on the sports field or as moral agents.

Sexual harassment in employment and educational contexts is similarly situated with rancor or exclusion in the gender-mixed team. The man who expresses rancor toward female teammates lowers team morale and makes it generally less likely that these women will want to cooperate with him down the road. This reaction will adversely affect his own ability to display excellence and virtue, both on and off the field. In a very real sense the sexist diminishes himself. The solidarity built upon sexual harassment will often alienate those who are excluded, even though men may have to depend on the cooperation of those they have just alienated. Sexual harassment is morally suspicious and also practically problematic. Men should come to see sexual harassment as wrong on both of these counts, just as many men currently see rape as wrong.

NOTES

1. I do not mean to dismiss the difficulty of distinguishing innocent pranks from those that constitute harassment. But I will sidestep this question and employ examples that seem clearly to be more than innocent pranks.
2. Throughout this chapter I use the term "solidarity" to refer to the phenomenon first discussed theoretically by Emil Durkheim as "cohesiveness within a group." See chap. 2, "Solidarity and Moral Support," in May, *The Socially Responsive Self* [Chicago: University of Chicago Press, 1996].
3. *Alexander v. Yale University,* 459 F.Supp. 1 (D. Conn. 1977), 631 F.2d 178 (2d Cir. 1980). The courts ruled the case moot since the student had already graduated and other students were not clearly adversely affected by the harassment of one of their friends.
4. I am assuming that female students generally do not want to have their sexuality become a basis for academic success. Cynics might dispute this assumption, but I have never met a female student who took such a cynical view.
5. John C. Hughes and Larry May, "Sexual Harassment," *Social Theory and Practice 6* (Fall 1980).
6. See Larry May and John C. Hughes, "Is Sexual Harassment Coercive?" in *Moral Rights in the Workplace,* ed. Gertrude Ezorsky (Albany: State University of New York Press, 1987). One of the main problems is that the woman no longer has at least one choice she had before, namely, to be regarded just as a student. Even if she doesn't mind being seen as a sex object, there is a problem in that her position in an academic community is being defined in a way over which she has no control.
7. Laurence Thomas, "On Sexual Offers and Threats," in *Moral Rights in the Workplace,* ed. Ezorsky, p. 125.
8. Ibid., p. 126.
9. Ibid.
10. For instance, Peter may be motivated to look more or less favorably on Deborah's job performance based on how well they are getting along sexually. There is another way to view this whole business that I also find helpful. It might be that the mutually trusting relationship that Peter and Deborah had is now shattered because neither can now trust the other to be "objective" about work-related matters. I am grateful to Ed Soule for providing this complementary way of seeing the damage that is done merely by Peter making the offer.
11. See my discussion of the harm that occurs when options are restricted in section II: Conceptualizing Harm, in Chapter 4 [*Masculinity and Morality* (Ithaca, NY: Cornell University Press, 1998)].
12. This doctrine was first embraced, by a unanimous Supreme Court, in *Meritor Savings Bank v. Vinson,* 477 U.S. 57, 106 S.Ct. 2399, 91 L.Ed.2d 49 (1986).
13. *Harris v. Forklift Systems, Inc.* 114 S.Ct. 367 (1993).
14. Ibid.
15. This is a quotation from the Eleventh Circuit Court of Appeals ruling in *Henson v. Dundee,* quoted by Chief Justice William Rehnquist in *Meritor Savings Bank v. Vinson.*
16. Esther Nevarez, who counsels employers for the New Jersey Division of Civil Rights, put the

point quite well when she said that such behavior "affects the esprit de corps in an office because it eliminates certain groups of people from participating." She was quoted in Trip Gabriel, "New Issue at Work: On-Line Sex Sites," *New York Times,* June 27, 1996, B4.

17. See my discussion of this point in May, *The Morality of Groups* [Notre Dame, IN: University of Notre Dame Press, 1987].
18. Both the case of the mechanic and that of the graduate student are based on examples of which I have had personal experience.
19. This hypothetical case is loosely based on several actual cases I have heard about in the last ten years.
20. This is not to say that nothing morally suspicious has occurred here. The case I have described clearly involves an abuse of power by the bisexual harasser.
21. Kevin McDermott, "Same-Sex Suit Pits Man vs. Male Boss," *St. Louis Post-Dispatch,* October 13, 1996, D1, 11.
22. I explain why each of these components is an important element of solidarity in May, *The Socially Responsive Self,* chap. 2.
23. There may indeed be competition for various goods, such as rewards or raises, but the main goods at stake in workplace and educational contexts are like health in that they are best garnered through cooperative methods since the size and extent of the good is dependent on working together.
24. Carol McGraw and Mike Eisenbath, "God's Guys," *St. Louis Post-Dispatch,* June 28, 1995, E1, 5.
25. For a rich account of this movement, and a devastating critique of their practices, see Clatterbaugh, *Contemporary Perspectives on Masculinity,* chap. 9.
26. I take up this theme in greater detail in the next chapter, Chapter 7: "Socialization and Separatism" [*Masculinity and Morality*].

77

JANE HARRIS AIKEN

Sexual Character Evidence in Civil Actions: Refining the Propensity Rule

Who will believe thee, Isabel?
My unsoiled name, th' austereness of my life,
My vouch against you, and my place i' th' state,
Will so your accusation overweigh
That you shall stifle in your own report
And smell of calumny. . . .
Say what you can, my false o'erweighs your true.[1]

"With only one accuser . . . and everyone else saying something contrary, the public is doubtful. But with two accusers, no matter what the second's credibility, the public really listens."[2]

I. INTRODUCTION

When claims of sexual misconduct are made, two threads are often seen in the kinds of questions raised: Did she "invite it," and has he ever done it before? The way these questions are handled can determine the outcome of a sexual misconduct case. In 1995, Congress weighed in on whether these questions could be asked in civil cases in federal court and adopted two significant changes to the rules of evidence. One, revised Rule 412,[3] extends "rape shield" protection to civil actions that claim sexual misconduct, including sexual harass-

---

[1]William Shakespeare, *Measure for Measure* act 2, sc. 4, in *William Shakespeare: The Complete Works* 414 (Alfred Harbage ed., Penguin Books, 1969) (Angelo's response to Isabella, a nun who pleads with Angelo not to execute her brother, when she claims that she will tell the world that Angelo has proposed she have sex with him to buy her brother's life).

[2]Jane Mayer & Jill Abramson, *Strange Justice: The Selling of Clarence Thomas* 324 (1994) (quoting David Demarest, White House Communications Director throughout the Clarence Thomas hearings, during a Republican strategy meeting in which the participants discussed ways to prevent another woman from testifying about Clarence Thomas's alleged sexually harassing behavior toward her).

[3]The portion of Rule 412 governing civil actions reads as follows:

ment. The other, new Rule 415,[4] allows plaintiffs to offer evidence of a defendant's commission of prior similar acts to prove that he is the kind of person who engages in such sexual misconduct, and thus to imply that he engaged in it on the occasion in question.[5]

If courts follow the rules and the Advisory Committee Notes interpreting Rules 412 and 415, a plaintiff's sexual misconduct case today will look very different than it would have just three years ago. Instead of voluminous testimony regarding the plaintiff's dress and personal fantasies, the record might include testimony about the defendant's prior misconduct. Instead of broad discovery into the plaintiff's sex life, discovery might be directed toward prior sexual misconduct by the defendant. The evidence might instead give the trier of fact a very different picture of the plaintiff as a victim, the defendant as a perpetrator, and, if offered under a theory of respondeat superior, might significantly affect the corporate entity's financial liability for the defendant's behavior.

Of the two changes, the more dramatic by far is new Rule 415. Previously, the question of whether the defendant had engaged in prior sexual misconduct could not be asked to corroborate the plaintiff's story. This left jurors free to assume that the defendant was "Mr. Clean." The Rules of Evidence made it virtually impossible for a plaintiff to correct this assumption. New Rule 415 purports to lift that restriction, at least to some extent. Under this rule, evidence of certain types of prior acts may be "considered for its bearing on any matter to which it is relevant." Thus, in theory, the plaintiff may offer evidence of such acts to show that the defendant is the sort of person who would engage in sexual misconduct, and argue that conclusion to the jury.

Despite this potential for dramatic change, revised Rules 412 and 415 have not had such an impact. An analysis of how Rule 412 has been applied in civil cases reveals a mixed response to the goals of the rule. Courts are more willing to be suspicious of broad inquiries into a plaintiff's sexual history even at discovery. At the same time, they are finding new relevance for such evidence when evaluating damage claims. Case law after the implementation of amended Rule 412 suggests that if the plaintiff asserts a claim for mental or emotional damages, her sexual history and predisposition are likely to be discoverable and perhaps admissible.

While Rule 412 has thus achieved, at best, inconsistent results, Rule 415 has encountered especially blunt resistance. Judges simply are not admitting sexual character evidence offered to show general propensity. When they encounter such evidence in civil cases, courts invoke discretionary authority to exclude it. This approach runs counter to the plain meaning of the rule and substantially limits its impact. This Article explores the reach of Rule 415, analyzes how courts have limited its effect, and suggests how the rule can be modified to ensure it provides the corroboration necessary for achieving justice in sexual misconduct cases. [The next part] assesses the potential impact of Rule 415. . . [The following part] discusses how courts are assessing probative value and prejudice when evidence of general propensity to engage in sexual misconduct is admitted. Together, these parts of the analysis demonstrate the need for a fresh look at the problem addressed by Rule 415. [The next part] provides that look. It develops a

---

a. Evidence generally inadmissible.—The following evidence is not admissible in any civil or criminal proceeding involving alleged sexual misconduct except as provided in subdivisions (b) and (c):
   1. Evidence offered to prove that any alleged victim engaged in other sexual behavior.
   2. Evidence offered to prove any alleged victim's sexual predisposition.

b. Exceptions.—
   1. . . . .
   2. In a civil case, evidence offered to prove the sexual behavior or sexual predisposition of any alleged victim is admissible if it is otherwise admissible under these rules and its probative value substantially outweighs the danger of harm to any victim and of unfair prejudice to any party. Evidence of an alleged victim's reputation is admissible only if it has been placed in controversy by the alleged victim.

c. . . . .

FED. R. EVID. 412.

[4]Rule 415 states in relevant part:

a. In a civil case in which a claim for damages or other relief is predicated on a party's alleged commission of conduct constituting an offense of sexual assault or child molestation, evidence of that party's commission of another offense or offenses of sexual assault or child molestation is admissible and may be considered as provided in Rule 413 and Rule 414 of these rules.

FED. R. EVID. 415. The Rule deals with *sexual assault* but the definition includes a broad range of activities not commonly thought to be sexual assault. *See infra* [section: "Rule 415's Expansive Coverage"].

[5]The bar to this prior act evidence is codified in Rule 404(a) which states:

a. Character evidence generally. Evidence of a person's character or a trait of character is not admissible for the purpose of proving action in conformity therewith on a particular occasion, except: . . .

FED. R. EVID. 404(a).

principled way of approaching the refinement of Rule 415, addressing concerns about lack of symmetry (the notion that evidence of a defendant's sexual character is admissible but comparable evidence about a plaintiff is not) and demonstrating that those concerns are misplaced. The discussion concludes with a proposed revision to Rule 415 which would continue to make evidence of a defendant's sexual character admissible—indeed, would allow it in a wider array of civil cases—while providing some needed guidance about when such evidence should be admitted.

RULE 415

The Character Bar

. . . The Federal Rules' overriding principle is that probative evidence is normally admissible unless there is a good reason not to admit it. Like the common-law courts, the Federal Rules incorporate a suspicion of general propensity evidence. Rule 404 generally will not allow a proponent to introduce evidence in any form (opinion, reputation or specific acts) showing that a person has a particular character trait if the reason for introducing it is to argue that the person acted in conformity with the trait.[6] This said, however, the character bar is not absolute. The rules allow admission of character evidence when sound policy demands it.

Rule 415 states in part:

> In a civil case in which a claim for damages or other relief is predicated on a party's alleged commission of conduct constituting an offense of sexual assault or child molestation, evidence of that party's commission of another offense or offenses of sexual assault or child molestation is admissible and may be considered [for its bearing on any matter to which it is relevant]. . . .

Rule 415 is thus a stark departure from the Anglo-Saxon evidentiary principle that we evaluate people on the basis of what they do, not who they are. As Senator Biden observed, it goes against "800 years of experience" about what evidence should be admitted as relevant. Rule 415, by its terms, allows blanket admission of certain prior acts even if offered to show the defendant's character. Prior to Rule 415's enactment, courts struggled to find a non-character reason to admit a defendant's prior acts of sexual misconduct. They would typically rely on Rule 404(b), which enacts the common law exceptions to the ban against evidence of prior acts.[7] Though courts have been increasingly willing to admit evidence to show motive, opportunity, intent, plan, or absence of mistake, character evidence has not been allowed. However, following the adoption of Rule 415, the proponent of prior acts evidence need not be concerned about the niceties of framing it to conform to the character bar. In cases that include sexual assault and child molestation, the new rules presumably allow plaintiffs to argue that "because he did this before, he probably did it this time."

Rule 415's Expansive Coverage

Rule 415's definition of sexual assault determines what actions will open the door to this kind of evidence, as well

---

[6]Rule 404 states in part: "Evidence of a person's character or a trait of character is not admissible for the purpose of proving action in conformity therewith on a particular occasion. . . ." FED. R. EVID. 404(a). The concern that underlies the rules is the risk the fact finder will rule against a party because he or she is a "bad person," regardless of the facts of the instant case. McCormick explains this concern:

> [E]vidence that an individual is the kind of person who tends to behave in certain ways almost always has some value as circumstantial evidence as to how he acted . . . in the matter in question. . . . Yet, evidence of character in any form—reputation, opinion from observation, or specific acts—generally will not be received to prove that a person engaged in certain conduct. . . .

EDWARD W. CLEARY, MCCORMICK ON EVIDENCE § 188, at 554 (3d ed. 1984).

[7]Rule 404(b) states in part:

> Evidence of other crimes, wrongs, or acts is not admissible to prove the character of a person in order to show action in conformity therewith. It may, however, be admissible for other purposes, such as proof of motive, opportunity, intent, preparation, plan, knowledge, identity, or absence of mistake or accident. . . .

FED R. EVID. 404(b). Some courts have used "lustful disposition" as a supposedly non-character reason for admitting prior acts of sexual molestation. *See, e.g.,* State v. Lachterman, 812 S.W.2d 759, 768 (Mo. Ct. App. 1991) (affirming lower court's admission of prior sexual acts on a "depraved sexual instinct" theory), *cert. denied,* 503 U.S. 983 (1992). But see Lannan v. State, 600 N.E.2d 1334 (Ind. 1992) (abolishing Indiana's "depraved sexual instinct" exception to character evidence).

David Bryden and Roger Park discuss how courts manipulate Rule 404(b) to admit prior uncharged sexual offenses. They conclude that courts generally do not treat evidence of uncharged sex offenses differently from other crimes. They do note, however, that courts in a number of states are less likely to admit uncharged misconduct in acquaintance rape cases than in stranger rape or child abuse cases. David P. Bryden & Roger C. Park, *"Other Crimes" Evidence in Sex Offense Cases,* 78 MINN L. REV. 529, 560 (1994).

as what evidence can be used. The definition includes all crimes under federal or state law that involve:

> [C]ontact, without consent, between any part of the defendant's body or an object and the genitals or anus of another person; . . . contact, without consent, between the genitals or anus of the defendant and any part of another person's body; . . . deriving sexual pleasure or gratification from the infliction of death, bodily injury, or physical pain on another person. . . .

The definition appears to limit the rule to what is traditionally thought to be rape or felony sexual assault.

However, the definition of "sexual assault" also includes "any conduct proscribed by chapter 109A of title 18, United States Code." This substantially expands the range of behavior that will be admissible. Besides including aggravated sexual abuse, it also includes non-aggravated sexual abuse: causing or attempting to cause another to engage in a sexual act by placing the person in fear. In the "non-aggravated" situation, it encompasses the fear of being fired or receiving disadvantageous treatment for failure to comply. The Code also criminalizes abusive sexual contact. Sexual contact is defined as "the intentional touching, either directly or through the clothing, of the genitalia, anus, groin, breast, inner thigh, or buttocks of any person with an intent to abuse, humiliate, harass, degrade, or arouse or gratify the sexual desire of any person." Wright and Graham describe this definition as "so broad that it includes conduct not often thought of as criminal in some quarters; e.g., horseplay in which one co-worker 'gooses' another." The definition notably does not include behavior that might result in a sexually hostile work environment such as sexual comments and propositions. Attempts and conspiracy to commit such acts would also be admissible.

The Code's definition of sexual assault increases the breadth of Rule 415 and its potential impact. It greatly enlarges the number of claims in which sexual character evidence could be offered because the rule applies to more cases than just damage suits over criminal acts of sexual assault. Typical tort actions arising from sexual misconduct include claims of assault, battery, intentional infliction of emotional distress, false imprisonment, seduction, sexual harassment, transmission of sexually transmitted disease, negligent entrustment and negligent supervision. Sexual harassment suits often include allegations of unwanted sexual touching (pinching bottoms, hands on breasts), thus invoking the possibility of admission of other similar acts against harassers and their employers. Because Rule 415 will apply in sexual harassment cases in which there has been physical contact, it is likely to have a greater impact on the admission of evidence in federal courts than its companion rules 413 and 414. Federal jurisdiction, so elusive for a damage action brought by the victim of rape, is readily available to victimized employees because Title VII confers such jurisdiction. Sexual harassment cases are a substantial part of the federal docket. Further, because a sexual harassment action can reach the deeper pocket of the employer, there may be more incentive to pursue the case. . . .

. . . In addition to its expansive definition of covered acts, Rule 415 multiplies the sources for such evidence. There is no time limit on the uncharged conduct. In the past, sexual character evidence in the form of prior bad acts was restricted to acts in the workplace and often restricted to the time frame in which the plaintiff's complaints were made. Rule 415 does not require a workplace nexus for prior acts of sexual assault brought in as evidence. Courts have looked outside the workplace to minimize the effect of sexual behavior in the workplace. In *Rabidue v. Osceola Refining Co.,* the court dismissed complaints of sexual harassment that included vulgar and pornographic poster displays within the workplace. One poster showed a woman with a golf ball between her breasts and a man with a golf club standing over her and yelling "fore!" The court characterized the impact of such displays on the environment as "de minimis . . . when considered in the context of a society that condones and publicly features and commercially exploits open displays of written and pictorial erotica at the newsstands, on prime-time television, at the cinema, and in other public places."

Using this logic, a plaintiff could argue that the outside behavior of the alleged harasser is useful to determine whether his likely workplace behavior is socially acceptable. If 415 evidence is introduced, the defendant's prior behavior constitutes, by the terms of the rules, a criminal offense, and is presumptively socially unacceptable. This assists plaintiffs because a witness to sexual assault behavior outside the workplace can testify without fear of retaliation on the job. A plaintiff might garner evidence from the defendant's former place of employment or establish potential evidence of the defendant's behavior in social settings. For example, the plaintiff might offer testimony of waitresses from a local bar who say the defendant is a customer and regularly attempts to fondle the buttocks or breasts of waitresses while they are serving him. Domestic assault might also meet the federal definition. A supervisor's ex-wife might be willing to testify to sexual abuse during the marriage that caused her to seek a protection order.

The above examples appear to fall within Rule 415's definition of sexual assault. As a preliminary step, the plaintiff must then argue that such evidence is relevant to the claim. Rule 415 requires only that the evidence be relevant. Rule 401, governing relevance, is an extremely low threshold: it encompasses all "evidence having *any tendency* to make the existence of any fact that is of consequence to the determination of the action more probable or less probable than it would be without the evidence." Whether the defendant engaged in the alleged acts is certainly a fact of consequence, and his sexual character adds an inferential link in determining that fact. Because Rule 415 specifically allows a general propensity argument, the plaintiff might be able to show sufficiently similar circumstances to suggest that this is the kind of man who responds toward women in sexually inappropriate ways when in a position of relative power. The possibility of such explicit character arguments, formerly unheard in courts, demonstrates the potential significance of the change that Congress has wrought. . . .

JUDICIAL RESPONSES TO ELIMINATION OF THE CHARACTER BAR

A basic axiom of evidence law is that the judge is charged with determining relevance. The judge also weighs probative value against prejudicial effect. Nowhere is the concern about unfair prejudice greater than when the admission of evidence risks luring the fact finder into arriving at a decision based on improper considerations. General propensity arguments are certain to draw objections that the evidence is more prejudicial than probative.[8] . . .

. . . When asked about Rule 415, federal judges have responded that they will not admit such general propensity evidence, and that they would readily sustain Rule 403 objections. Congress drafted Rule 415 in such a way that arguably leaves a court very little discretion when determining admissibility. Even if the rule does not limit judicial discretion entirely, at least it requires the court to be more circumscribed when finding prejudice. The sponsors of this legislation were aware that judges might resist. As Susan Molinari, the principal House sponsor, pointed out:

> the practical efficacy of these rules will depend on faithful execution by judges of the will of Congress in adopting this critical reform. To implement the legislative intent, the courts must liberally construe these rules to provide the basis for a fully informed decision of sexual assault and child molestation cases, including assessment of the defendant's propensities and questions of probability in light of the defendant's past conduct.

Applying Rule 403 to sexual character evidence is complicated by two aspects of Rule 415: first, the probative value of such evidence might be inflated by Rule 415's allowance that evidence of this type is admissible for *any* relevant purpose; and second, one traditional source of unfair prejudice, that the evidence might be used to show general propensity, can no longer be considered in the balance. Rule 415 is not affected by Rule 404's character bar: inferring present behavior from past bad acts is allowed under Rule 415. Therefore, if the objection to Rule 415 evidence is based on alleged unfairness caused by the possibility that the jury would find the defendant liable based on a general propensity theory, a Rule 403 objection should fail because Rule 415 specifically allows the jury to draw those conclusions.

The effect of broadening the basis for establishing probative value and narrowing the basis for finding unfair prejudice should weaken a Rule 403 objection. Yet, other than stranger rape or child molestation cases, in every reported case where the proponent has offered evidence that relies on the broad definition of sexual assault, the courts have sustained 403 objections. Similarly, although the rule specifically permits "bad character" evidence, judges resist, and

---

[8]Rule 403 states:

> Although relevant, evidence may be excluded if its probative value is substantially outweighed by the danger of unfair prejudice, confusion of the issues, or misleading the jury, or by considerations of undue delay, waste of time, or needless presentation of cumulative evidence.

FED R. EVID. 403.

most do not allow sexual character evidence offered for general propensity purposes in civil cases. Rule 415 is meaningless if it cannot be used to allow admission of character evidence.

In *Frank v. County of Hudson,*[9] a sexual harassment action brought by employees of the Sheriff's Office against the County of Hudson, the Sheriff's Office and several officials, the defendants sought a protection order to preclude the plaintiffs from using the statement of a defendant supervisor's stepdaughter that he had sexually abused her for nearly ten years.[10] The plaintiffs, whose allegations against this supervisor included claims that he forced them to view him masturbating, and that he sexually touched the plaintiffs' buttocks, made gratuitous sexual comments, and intimidated them through the use of a shotgun,[11] offered a number of theories of relevance for the stepdaughter's statement. These included the general propensity of the supervisor to engage in sexual assaults, the supervisor's motive and intent, and his supervisors' prior knowledge of his conduct.[12] The court assigned a low degree of probative value to these theories[13] and stated there was a great risk of unfair prejudice.[14] The prejudice that the court identified was the emotional response that child sexual abuse is likely to elicit in a trier of fact. In issuing the protective order, the court said, "And the potential for unfair prejudice if the evidence were admitted at trial is great. The purpose of the evidence rules' general prohibition against propensity evidence is to address the danger that a jury might convict the defendant not for the offense charged but for the extrinsic offense presented.[15]

This court's reasoning is inconsistent with the mandates of Rule 415. Instead of crediting the use of character evidence in its analysis of probative value, the court discounts those theories. It also heightens Rule 403 concerns by focusing on the prejudicial effect of the prior acts evidence. The court's analysis suggests that evidence of prior sexual assault must be relevant on some other ground than character. This is the underlying reasoning for Rule 404(b), and would add little, if anything, to that traditional analysis. The court's interpretation effectively eviscerates Rule 415. However, the legislative history of Rules 413 and 414 indicates that Congress decided that the risks of generally allowing sexual character evidence were overshadowed by the need to crack down on crimes of sexual abuse. Congress adopted the rule despite being warned by the Judicial Conference that this was an ill-advised and fundamental alteration of traditional principles and standards.

Another example of a court negating the intent of Rule 415 is found in *United States v. Guardia,*[16] a criminal case against a physician charged with criminal sexual penetration and simple battery arising from gynecological examinations of two patients. The government sought to introduce the testimony of four other women who alleged similar acts of inappropriate touching during their gynecological examinations.[17] The defense maintained that no such sexual activity occurred. The prosecution argued that such evidence was admissible under Rule 413 to show that the defendant has "'an on-going disposition to commit sexual assaults against his female patients.'"[18] The court granted the defendant's motion in limine stating:

> [T]he Court believes it is more appropriate to interpret Rule 413, like the other Rules of Evidence, to "secure fairness in administration, elimination of unjustifiable expense and delay, and promotion of growth and development of the law of evidence to the end that the truth may be ascertained and proceedings justly determined." Fed. R. Evid. 102. These goals would not be served by allowing six rather than two witnesses to testify as to how they believe Defendant sexually assaulted them and, more importantly, subjecting the jury to the expert testimony necessary for it to determine the legal significance of such testimony by each 413 witness.[19]

The court's reasoning appears to undercut the purpose of Rule 413 (the criminal analogue of Rule 415). Here the prosecution was offering prior acts of the defendant substantially similar to the acts alleged.

---

[9]924 F. Supp. 620 (1996).
[10]*Id.* At 622.
[11]*Id.*
[12]*Id.* at 625–26.
[13]*Id.* at 626.
[14]924 F. Supp. at 626–27.
[15]*Id.* at 627.

[16]955 F. Supp. 115 (D.N.M. 1997).
[17]*Id.* at 116.
[18]*Id.* at 119 (quoting the Government's Response to Defendant's Motion in Limine).
[19]*Id.* at 119–120.

The defense contended that inappropriate acts never occurred. The court did not specifically argue that it would not admit character evidence because it offends the character bar but rather alluded to the potential for confusion and delay. Such an argument might have more force if the evidence were dissimilar, but here the evidence was of the same sort as that alleged in the criminal complaint. Given Rule 413's broad mandate of admissibility, as well as the similarity of the prior acts, their proximity in time, and repetitive nature, the required showing under Rule 403—that the unfair prejudice outweigh the probative value—was not satisfied. The court's concern about confusion appeared to be grounded in the fear that the trier of fact might use the other acts to determine whether the defendant engaged in the present act, in other words, to show general propensity under Rule 413.

Finally, in *Cleveland v. KFC National Management Co.,*[20] a sexual harassment case, the defendant moved that the plaintiff be precluded from admitting any evidence of prior sexual misconduct of her former manager, an employee of KFC.[21] The defendant argued that the evidence was inadmissible under Rule 415, and that even if it were admissible, its prejudicial effect substantially outweighed its probative value.[22] After finding that Rule 415 did apply to these facts and that it was admissible against the company through respondeat superior,[23] the court turned to the Rule 403 analysis. The evidence the plaintiff sought to introduce was not described in specific detail but was characterized as "inflammatory."[24] The court instructed the plaintiff that if she wished to admit the evidence of the agent's misconduct, the evidence "must be both probative in that it proves corporate knowledge of similar misconduct and it must corroborate plaintiff's story; otherwise, the prejudicial effect on the jury is not substantially outweighed."[25] Evidence of "notice" to the employer would be admissible under Rule 404(b). Corroboration, on the other hand, would not be admissible unless under Rule 415 since it would be character evidence. By using the conjunction "and" in its instruction to the parties regarding the effect of Rule 403, the court required the evidence to be used for non-propensity purposes, thereby gutting Rule 415.

In each of these cases, the court's interpretation of how 403 balancing affects Rules 413 and 415 is inconsistent with the plain meaning of the rule. Congress can enact rules of evidence that deprive judges of discretionary authority. The fact that such rules can result in what otherwise might be "unfair prejudice" does not invalidate the rule. In *Green v. Bock Laundry Machine,*[26] for example, an injured worker brought a products liability action against a manufacturer after the worker's arm was severed while he was working at a car wash. The plaintiff was employed while on work release from the county prison. The defendant cross-examined the plaintiff about prior felony convictions for burglary under then-rule 609(a)(1), which allowed impeachment with prior convictions without any balancing of unfair prejudice against probative value. After a judgment for the defendant, the plaintiff appealed. The plaintiff argued that Rule 609 should be subject to the Rule 403 balancing test. He cited as unfair prejudice the fact that the jury might use the burglary convictions to decide he was a "bad man," not worthy of compensation, rather than to assess veracity. The Court recognized that such mandatory admission might produce some unjust results, but held that mandating admission was the plain meaning of the rule.[27] The Advisory Committee responded to the concerns raised in *Green* by amending Rule 609 to ensure that there would be traditional Rule 403 balancing when determining admissibility of prior convictions for impeachment purposes.[28]

When judicial decisions applying Rule 415 find their way to the Supreme Court, the Court could find that the plain meaning of Rule 415 precludes the application of any other rule, and thus that Rule 403 balancing is inappropriate. It is not likely the Court will go that far. It could find that Rule 403 balancing is allowed when applying Rule 415 but that general propensity concerns are, by the terms of the rule, not

[20] 948 F. Supp. 62 (N.D. Ga. 1996).
[21] *Id.* at 62–63.
[22] *Id.* at 64.
[23] *Id.* at 65.
[24] *Id.* at 66.
[25] 948 F. Supp. at 66.

[26] 490 U.S. 504 (1989).
[27] *Id.* at 527.
[28] Rule 609(a) as amended now reads, "For the purpose of attacking the credibility of a witness, (1) evidence that a witness other than the accused has been convicted of a crime shall be admitted, *subject to Rule 403,* if the crime was punishable by death or imprisonment in excess of one year. . . ." FED R. EVID. 609(a) (emphasis added).

necessarily unfairly prejudicial. Any finding that Rule 403 prevents admission must be based on more limited concerns of waste of time or confusion. This would have the probable effect of forcing judges to admit the evidence despite their reservations about the fairness of using sexual character evidence. Any change in that outcome would have to come from Congress. . . .

REFINING THE PROPENSITY RULE

Policy Considerations

The Need for Character Evidence in Civil Cases

There are compelling reasons to admit sexual character evidence. Critics of character evidence in general suggest that juries tend to overvalue it, thereby inappropriately shifting the balance against the defendant. However, plaintiffs in sexual misconduct cases face the opposite problem: jurors tend not to believe the plaintiff's story unless they have evidence the defendant has behaved that way before. If the plaintiff is prohibited from introducing character evidence, juries make the "Mr. Clean" assumption and are less willing to credit her claims. Without Rule 415, plaintiffs can be hamstrung by being prohibited from introducing evidence to counter jury bias.

Congress singled out sexual assault and child molestation cases because, unlike other crimes, they often turn on difficult credibility determinations. The need for victim corroboration particularly arises in sexual misconduct cases when the parties have known one another. Unlike other offenses, sexual misconduct cases raise the question of whether the victim consented or welcomed the behavior. Sexual character evidence in such cases provides corroboration for the complainant. The need for corroboration springs from the belief that if there is a swearing contest between a man and a woman about whether sexual misconduct occurred, the man will be believed.

The need for corroboration does not arise only in sexual assault cases. Sexual harassment cases also frequently turn on an assessment of whether the plaintiff welcomed the behavior. Moreover, the plaintiff is making a charge against a more powerful party: she is frequently a subordinate bringing a claim against a superior. The alleged harasser often comes to the lawsuit with the "Mr. Clean" presumption plus the added respectability of a supervisory or managerial position, increasing his apparent social desirability and credibility. The result is a jury predisposed to favor the defendant. If evidence of prior acts of sexual assault is admitted, it will likely cause the jury to rethink its assessment of the individual.

In sexual harassment cases, the third or fourth woman to experience the harassment is often the one who brings the case, and it takes those other women's testimony to make the plaintiff's story believable. If jurors learn the alleged perpetrator engaged in similar unwelcome acts in the past, they still might not believe the plaintiff; they may even find problems with the stories of other alleged victims. But if no reason exists to suggest collusion among the accusers, such corroborating evidence has a synergistic effect. The fact that such acts all occurred is independent evidence that confirms the plaintiff's complaint.

It is often asked in high profile sexual misconduct cases: if what she says is true, where are all the other women? The common wisdom is that if a person has harassed someone on the job, then he has done it frequently. Despite juries' biases that the single report of one victim is insufficient, prior to Rule 415 a plaintiff in a sexual harassment case could not present evidence of other acts by the defendant because of the bar on character evidence. Rule 415 removes the character-evidence bar for sexual assault cases because such a barrier does not make sense in the context of sexual misconduct. The rule opens the door to evidence that can counterbalance biased responses about victim credibility, and thereby even out the jury's credibility assessment.

It is not a new idea to use the rules of evidence to remedy bias in the fact finding process. Rule 412 bars the admission of evidence of an alleged victim's past sexual behavior or sexual predisposition, subject to a balancing test provided in the rule, in sexual misconduct civil cases. The inclusion of "harm to the victim" as part of the balancing test is perhaps the key to the effective implementation of amended Rule 412. It focuses the court on the impact of evidence on the victim. This assessment is less concerned with increasing the ability of the court to arrive at the truth than with the social policy determination that a victim of sexual assault should not be subject to harassment. If the proponent of the evidence can demonstrate that the proposed evidence is otherwise admissible under the rules and its probative value substantially outweighs the harm to any victim or of unfair prejudice to any party, the evidence is admissible. By requiring the evidence to be "otherwise admissible," the evidence must also meet the strictures of Rule 404, which precludes the use of evidence as inference of character to prove conduct in conformity with that character. The Advisory Committee made clear that its goal was to use the rules of evidence to "remedy stereotypical thinking in the fact-finding process." As drafted, Rule 412 substantially limits what had become a typical defense used in sexual harassment cases. The rule thwarts the attempt to imply, "she invited it." Juries will no longer be treated to lurid stories about the plaintiff's alleged sexual exploits. Without such tales, juries can evaluate a claim of sexual misconduct unhampered by that bias. Thus the same concerns that motivated the exclusion of character evidence under Rule 412 justify the need to admit character evidence under Rule 415.

If the primary purpose of the fact finding process is to arrive at the truth, the law must assume that judges and juries act as they are, with all their inherent biases, not as one would wish them to be. Rule 415's goal is to counter the biases that make it difficult for the fact finder to follow the law. In enacting Rule 412, Congress specifically stated that it will help in resisting pervasive stereotypes. Once rules of evidence can be used to combat societal stereotypes, it should not matter whether the purpose is to preclude the introduction of arguably relevant evidence, as in 412, or to mandate the inclusion of other evidence, as in 415.

Symmetry

It will undoubtedly be argued that Rules 412 and 415 stack the deck in the plaintiff's favor. Rule 415 says that prior sexual misconduct is relevant and probative of behavior on the present occasion. That determination seems to directly contradict the rationale in Rule 412 that a woman's sexual history is not a good predictor of her present behavior. The apparent inconsistency of these premises could be claimed to render the rules asymmetrical. This perceived lack of symmetry may have an impact on the judicial decisionmaker. If a plaintiff seeks to introduce the defendant's history of sexual assault, a court might be less willing to exclude the plaintiff's sexual history out of a sense of perceived fairness. A plaintiff might therefore choose not to seek this kind of information for fear that it will increase the likelihood of a wholesale attack on her background. The potential that Rule 415 might undermine Rule 412 could be the most persuasive justification for abandoning this foray into character evidence. There needs to be a compelling reason for this apparent asymmetry.

Indeed, there is. Both Rule 412 and Rule 415 are geared toward reducing fact finder bias. Rule 412 does not rest on the assumption that sexual character evidence is irrelevant in predicting present behavior. It is premised on the idea that courts should not tolerate wholesale attacks on the sexual character of a person to encourage the fact finder not to believe that person. It is designed to undercut bias that jurors bring to the fact finding process. Rule 415 is an important companion to Rule 412. It is also concerned with fact finder bias. Instead of precluding evidence that invites such bias, Rule 415 ensures that the rules of evidence do not preclude evidence that would counteract that bias. Rules 412 and 415 can be used to cleanse the fact finding process of biases that have reinforced the asymmetry of power and powerlessness in matters of sex. Both of these rules assist the trier of fact in focusing on the behavior of the alleged perpetrator, rather than indulging in stereotypic beliefs that women cannot be believed when making claims of sexual misconduct. The result is a potentially powerful tool to combat long-held stereotypes that have infected sexual misconduct cases: that the victim either invited the treatment, or deserved it, or is not to be believed without sufficient corroboration.

While most of the criticism of these new and revised rules has focused on the potential harm of admitting prior acts evidence, the real problem with Rule 415 is that it imposes inadequate limits on the admission of such evidence. The plain meaning of the rule suggests that a plaintiff can introduce any sexual character evidence minimally relevant to the issues before the court, as long as that behavior meets the broad definition of sexual assault. In essence, a plaintiff is invited to paint the defendant as a "bad man" in hope of enticing a jury to find the facts of the present case in her favor. So construed, Rule 415 goes too far.

Proposed Coverage of Rule 415

Prior Conduct

No change in Rule 415 is necessary to allow the admission of prior acts of offensive sexual touching.

Nevertheless, unless the rule is construed more narrowly, Rule 415 evidence suffers from the same problems that prompted the need for Rule 412: it is overinclusive. Instead of making sexual character evidence admissible for any relevant purpose, admissibility should be limited to evidence offered to corroborate the plaintiff's story. Concomitant with that narrowing, the evidence must also *be* corroborating—that is, the sexual character evidence must be substantially similar to the act alleged.

Courts could look to several factors to determine the probative value of the evidence. These factors include:

- similarity in type between the alleged events and prior events;
- similarity in relationship between alleged perpetrator and alleged victim in each circumstance;
- similarity in settings in which the events took place;
- proximity in time; and
- frequency of other acts.

Such a construction of Rule 415 would reap the benefits of propensity evidence without undermining Rule 412. Although still relying on general propensity, using this kind of evidence to corroborate a victim's story is considerably narrower than admitting sexual character evidence merely to imply that this is a bad person who should be found liable because he is so bad. For example, thirty-year-old allegations of statutory rape or more recent allegations of child molestation would not be usable in a present case of sexual harassment if these factors are used.

The suggested refinement of Rule 415 would limit evidence of corroboration to substantially similar behavior by the alleged perpetrator. This requirement of similarity not only provides useful evidence of corroboration but it also has considerably more probative value than any general evidence that the defendant is a "bad guy." Social science evidence suggests that the predictive value of behavior depends on its similarity to the alleged activity. This modification of Rule 415 draws on that insight. For example, given the similarity in circumstances and situation, a plaintiff should be able to show a defendant's character as a sexual harasser through the testimony of other employees in other workplaces who also experienced offensive touching. She might also draw parallels between the defendant as a customer in a bar fondling his server and the defendant's and plaintiff's relationships within the office. The testimony would be probative of his tendency to assume sexual access to subordinate females, thus corroborating the plaintiff's assertion that he sexually harassed her on the claimed occasion.

The application of the factors allows room for argument. For example, domestic violence could at first appear to lack similarity to charges of sexual harassment. However, an argument could be made, depending on the factual circumstances, that the defendant's power relationship to his subordinate shares many of the characteristics of the power relationship between a husband and wife, and therefore, the domestic violence may corroborate an alleged sexual harassment victim's claims. These factors help guide the courts in identifying whether the evidence can be used to corroborate the plaintiff's claim. In addition, courts can exercise their supervisory power to exclude evidence under Rule 403. The mere fact that the evidence is offered for general propensity purposes should not be deemed unfair prejudice. However, other Rule 403 considerations may still arise.

Sexual Misconduct Claims

If Rule 415 evidence is limited to the defendant's prior acts that corroborate, it is underinclusive in its definition of sexual misconduct. At present, Rule 415's definition of covered acts, though broader than perhaps its drafters anticipated, does not include the vast array of non-physical sexual misconduct that constitutes sexual harassment. For example, as presently drafted, Rule 415 would not allow evidence that the defendant had propositioned or made sexual comments to other women because that does not involve sexual touching. The better solution is to narrow Rule 415 so sexual character evidence could only be used for corroborative or credibility purposes, while expanding the list of behaviors admissible under Rule 415 to include nonphysical sexual misconduct such as comments and propositions. Rule 412 applies in cases involving alleged sexual misconduct. Deciding whether an act constitutes sexual misconduct under Rule 412 has not proven to be too obscure for the courts. Expanding the definition of corroborating evidence would make Rule 415 more consistent with the purpose of countering the "one charge of sexual misconduct is not enough" biases found in a jury.

Many substantive claims in sexual harassment cases hinge on credibility. To prove sexual harassment under Title VII, a plaintiff must either prove that a sexually harassing work environment exists or that submission to sexual conduct was made a condition of receiving a tangible employment benefit. To prove hostile environment, the plaintiff must prove that sexual harassment within the workplace is sufficiently severe or pervasive that it alters the conditions of employment and creates an abusive working environment. The plaintiff's credibility necessarily affects a juror's assessment of these issues.[29] Rule 415 evidence might be useful to bolster the plaintiff's credibility when she attempts to show that the offense was:

- *objectionable to a reasonable person.*[30] A plaintiff's assertion that she was offended may be undermined by the jury's bias. She may be assumed to be unbelievable or hypersensitive. Evidence of the defendant's prior sexual misconduct lends credibility to her claims.
- *gender-based.*[31] A defendant might argue his acts were not motivated by the plaintiff's sex but were merely horseplay directed toward everyone, male or female, in the workplace. This essentially is an argument that she is overreacting to workplace pranks and "reading in" a gender motivation. The defendant's prior acts of sexual misconduct might be offered to show a gender-specific sexual motivation under Rule 404(b). Such acts may also undercut the implication that the plaintiff was hypersensitive.
- *unwelcome.*[32] The claim that the plaintiff welcomed the conduct is usually bolstered by evidence of the plaintiff's prior sexual conduct (now limited by revised Rule 412). If that proof implies the plaintiff sought the attention and is now "crying foul," or that the defendant misunderstood her purported "invitation," the defendant could be inviting the jury to indulge in impermissible stereotypes. Sexual character evidence offered against the defendant might undermine the jury's tendency to embrace the suggestion that the plaintiff is prevaricating.
- *pervasive.*[33] An aspect of the pervasiveness measure dovetails with the assessment of offensiveness. In each, the fact finder is asked to evaluate a plaintiff's assertion that workplace behavior affected her ability to work. Using Rule 415, a plaintiff could show other acts of sexual assault by the defendant within the workplace that occurred prior to her employment, and thereby bolster her assertion that such activity was pervasive enough to affect the conditions of her employment.

In addition, sexual character evidence can be used to combat traditional defenses to sexual harassment complaints. Often it is the third or fourth woman to be harassed who brings the suit. She may succeed because she has the corroboration of the others. Prior acts within the workplace before the plaintiff was employed undermine the defendant's implied assertion that he does not engage in sexually harassing activity. The behavior outside of the workplace may also be relevant. A person who engaged in sexual misconduct outside of the workplace undermines his claims that he is an "angel" in the office. For example, a frequently seen attack is to suggest that a plaintiff's delay in complaining or failure to complain suggests she concocted the whole story. The absence of a prompt complaint reinforces the fact finder's bias to disbelieve the complainant. Sexual character evidence regarding the defendant corrobo-

---

[29]*See* Harris v. Forklift Sys., Inc., 510 U.S. 17 (1993).

[30]The plaintiff bears the burden of proving that the conduct was offensive. *Id.;* Robinson v. Jacksonville Shipyards, 760 F. Supp. 1486, 1499–1501 (M.D. Fla. 1991); EEOC v. Gurness Inn Corp., 48 Fair Empl. Prac. Cas. (BNA) 871, 878 (N.D. Ill. 1988), *aff'd,* 914 F.2d 815(7th Cir. 1990).

[31]Courts have allowed the use of prior acts evidence under Rule 404(b) to prove motive. *See* Wendorf v. Metropolitan Life Ins. Co., 47 Empl. Prac. Dec. (CCH) 38, 316 (E.D.N.Y. 1988); Turley v. Union Carbide Corp., 618 F. Supp. 1438 (S.D. W. Va. 1985); Walter v. KEGO Radio, 518 F. Supp. 1309 (D.N.D. 1981); Halpert v. Wertheim & Co., 27 Fair Empl. Prac. Cas. (BNA) 21 (S.D.N.Y. 1980); Bennett v. Corroon & Black Corp., 517 So. 2d 1245 (La. Ct. App. 1987). That evidence would continue to be admissible under that theory.

[32]*See, e.g.,* Horn v. Duke Homes, 755 F.2d 599, 602 (7th Cir. 1985) (three women came forward to testify the same supervisor had harassed them); Priest v. Rotary, 634 F. Supp. 571, 574–76 (N.D. Cal. 1986) (other women testified to show that the restaurant owner had engaged in a pattern of sexual harassment).

[33]To prevail in a claim of a sexually harassing work environment, the plaintiff must demonstrate that the harassment is pervasive. Pervasiveness is extremely difficult to prove. The plaintiff must show that the harassment is sufficient "to alter the conditions of [her] employment and create an abusive working environment." Henson v. City of Dundee, 682 F.2d 897, 904 (11th Cir. 1982). Even though courts have allowed such evidence prior to the adoption of Rule 415 to show pattern or practice, the new rule expands admissibility.

rates the plaintiff's story and helps counteract credibility damage caused by the absence of prompt complaint.

As with all rules that attempt to cope with how things are rather than how one wishes them to be, using the rules to show corroboration might risk reinforcing the biases the rules purport to cure. Advocating the admission of such evidence is not without its problems. For example, courts might come to expect such evidence. At this point, there is no data on how many alleged sexual harassers have histories of engaging in similar behavior. Defendants might attempt to argue the lack of corroborating evidence to the fact finder. After such an argument, juries might consider its absence significant. Courts could begin to look for prior evidence of sexual assault as a part of the proof of the case, thus raising the threshold that plaintiffs have to meet to survive a summary judgment motion. The need for corroboration might be intensified by a rule that specifically allows such evidence to be admitted on that theory of relevance.

There may come a time when such evidence is not needed, but that time has not yet arrived. Sexual assault and harassment are such pervasive and debilitating aspects of women's lives that one cannot afford to ignore the substantial obstacle to achieving justice caused by a jury's need for corroboration. As long as one can anticipate that a juror will not believe the plaintiff unless she is backed by others with similar stories, then if such evidence is available, it should be freely admissible.

CONCLUSION

In its zeal to convict child molesters and rapists, Congress has created a civil rule that might have far more impact than the criminal rules upon which it is premised. If courts follow the law as passed by Congress, Rules 412 and 415 will shift the balance of power in civil actions arising from sexual misconduct. A victim of sexual misconduct may invoke the shield of the amended Rule 412, thus precluding in greater measure than previously possible the introduction of the victim's prior sexual conduct or evidence of sexual predisposition to imply that she apparently invited, consented to, or welcomed the alleged sexual misconduct. But the alleged perpetrator of sexual misconduct may also find himself confronted with his own sexual history if the offered evidence constitutes sexual assault under the rules, which includes sexual touching permitted through fear. Under the rules as presently constructed, such evidence can be offered for whatever purpose is relevant, including general propensity: the alleged victim may offer evidence against the alleged perpetrator of prior sexual acts to show that he engages in such acts, and therefore probably engaged in those acts this time.

An analysis of recent case law suggests, however, that these changes have begun to cause a backlash. Courts are resisting character evidence and exercising their supervisory powers under Rule 403 to preclude sexual character evidence under Rule 415. Yet victims of sexual misconduct suffer now under a legal system that treats their story as unbelievable unless corroborated. Although Rule 415 is flawed, it levels the playing field for victims of sexual misconduct by allowing plaintiffs to introduce evidence to bolster their credibility. The rule should be narrowed so that relevance is limited to similar-acts evidence offered as corroboration to combat jury bias. At the same time, it should be expanded to include a wider array of sexual misconduct cases. In this way, Congress could achieve its goal of protecting the victims of sexual offenses while preserving basic fairness in the administration of trials.

78

Faragher v. City of Boca Raton

524 US —, 141 L Ed 2d 662, 118 S Ct—
[No. 97-282]

ARGUED MARCH 25, 1998. DECIDED JUNE 26, 1998.

Decision: Employer held (1) subject to vicarious liability, under Title VII of Civil Rights Act of 1964, for supervisor's actionable sexual harassment, but (2) able to raise affirmative defense looking to reasonableness of conduct of employer and victim.

SUMMARY

After resigning from her employment by a city as a lifeguard, a woman brought, in the United States District Court for the Southern District of Florida, against two of her immediate male supervisors and the city an action asserting sexual harassment claims under Title VII of the Civil Rights Act of 1964 (42 USCS §§ 2000e et seq.). The lifeguard, asserting that the two supervisors were agents of the city and that their conduct, which allegedly had created a sexually hostile atmosphere, constituted discrimination in the lifeguard's terms, conditions, and privileges of employment, in violation of 42 USCS § 2000e-2(a)(1), sought a judgment against the city for nominal damages. The District Court, concluding that the harassment was pervasive enough to support an inference of knowledge or constructive knowledge by the city and that the city was liable to the lifeguard under traditional agency principles, awarded the lifeguard nominal damages of one dollar on her Title VII claim (864 F Supp 1552). After a panel of the United States Court of Appeals for the Eleventh Circuit reversed the District Court's judgment against the city (76 F3d 1155), the Court of Appeals, en banc, again reversing the judgment against the city, concluded that (1) in harassing the lifeguard, the supervisors had acted outside the scope of their employment and had not been assisted by their agency relationship with the city, and (2) the city lacked constructive knowledge of the harassment (111 F3d 1530).

On certiorari, the United States Supreme Court reversed the judgment of the Court of Appeals and remanded the case for reinstatement of the judgment of the District Court. In an opinion by SOUTER, J., joined by REHNQUIST, Ch. J., and STEVENS, O'CONNOR, KENNEDY, GINSBURG, and BREYER, JJ., it was held that (1) an employer is subject to vicarious liability under Title VII to a victimized employee for an actionable sexually hostile environment created by a supervisor with immediate or successively higher authority over the employee; (2) when no tangible employment action is taken, a defending employer may raise an affirmative defense to liability or damages, subject to proof by a preponderance of the evidence; (3) this defense comprises the two necessary elements that (a) the employer exercised reasonable care to prevent and correct promptly any sexually harassing behavior, and (b) the plaintiff employee unreasonably failed to take advantage of any preventive or corrective opportunities provided by the employer or to avoid harm otherwise; and (4) under the circumstances in the case at hand, (a) as a matter of law, the city could not be found to have exercised reasonable care to prevent the supervisors' harassing conduct, and (b) there was no reason to remand for consideration of the lifeguard's efforts to mitigate her own damages, since her award was nominal.

THOMAS, J., joined by SCALIA, J., dissenting, expressed the view that (1) absent an adverse employment consequence, an employer cannot be held vicariously liable if a supervisor creates a hostile work environment, and (2) thus the city was not vicariously liable for the conduct of the two supervisors, as the lifeguard suffered no adverse employment consequence from such conduct. . . .

OPINION OF THE COURT

Justice **Souter** delivered the opinion of the Court.

This case calls for identification of the circumstances under which an employer may be held liable under Title VII of the Civil Rights Act of 1964, 78 Stat. 253, as amended, 42 USC § 2000e *et seq.* [42 USCS §§ 2000e *et seq.*], for the acts of a supervisory employee whose sexual harassment of subordinates has created a hostile work environment amounting to employment discrimination. We hold that an employer is vicariously liable for actionable discrimination caused by a supervisor, but subject to an affirmative defense looking to the reasonableness of the employer's conduct as well as that of a plaintiff victim.

I

Between 1985 and 1990, while attending college, petitioner Beth Ann Faragher worked part time and during the summers as an ocean lifeguard for the Marine Safety Section of the Parks and Recreation Department of respondent, the City of Boca Raton, Florida (City). During this period, Faragher's immediate supervisors were Bill Terry, David Silverman, and Robert Gordon. In June 1990, Faragher resigned.

In 1992, Faragher brought an action against Terry, Silverman, and the City, asserting claims under Title VII, 42 USC § 1983 [42 USCS § 1983], and Florida law. So far as it concerns the Title VII claim, the complaint alleged that Terry and Silverman created a "sexually hostile atmosphere" at the beach by repeatedly subjecting Faragher and other female lifeguards to "uninvited and offensive touching," by making lewd remarks, and by speaking of women in offensive terms. The complaint contained specific allegations that Terry once said that he would never promote a woman to the rank of lieutenant, and that Silverman had said to Faragher, "Date me or clean the toilets for a year." Asserting that Terry and Silverman were agents of the City, and that their conduct amounted to discrimination in the "terms, conditions, and privileges" of her employment, 42 USC § 2000e-2(a)(1) [42 USCS § 2000e-2(a)(1)], Faragher sought a judgment against the City for nominal damages, costs, and attorney's fees.

Following a bench trial, the United States District Court for the Southern District of Florida found that throughout Faragher's employment with the City, Terry served as Chief of the Marine Safety Division, with authority to hire new lifeguards (subject to the approval of higher management), to supervise all aspects of the lifeguards' work assignments, to engage in counseling, to deliver oral reprimands, and to make a record of any such discipline. 864 F Supp 1552, 1563–1564 (1994). Silverman was a Marine Safety lieutenant from 1985 until June 1989, when he became a captain. *Id.,* at 1555. Gordon began the employment period as a lieutenant and at some point was promoted to the position of training captain. In these positions, Silverman and Gordon were responsible for making the lifeguards' daily assignments, and for supervising their work and fitness training. *Id.,* at 1564.

The lifeguards and supervisors were stationed at the city beach and worked out of the Marine Safety Headquarters, a small one-story building containing an office, a meeting room, and a single, unisex locker room with a shower. *Id.,* at 1556. Their work routine was structured in a "paramilitary configuration," *id.,* at 1564, with a clear chain of command. Lifeguards reported to lieutenants and captains, who reported to Terry. He was supervised by the Recreation Superintendent, who in turn reported to a Director of Parks and Recreation, answerable to the City Manager. *Id.,* at 1555. The lifeguards had no significant contact with higher city officials like the Recreation Superintendent. *Id.,* at 1564.

In February 1986, the City adopted a sexual harassment policy, which it stated in a memorandum from the City Manager addressed to all employees. *Id.,* at 1560. In May 1990, the City revised the policy and reissued a statement of it. *Ibid.* Although the City may actually have circulated the memos and statements to some employees, it completely failed to disseminate its policy among employees of the Marine Safety Section, with the result that Terry, Silverman, Gordon, and many lifeguards were unaware of it. *Ibid.*

From time to time over the course of Faragher's tenure at the Marine Safety Section, between 4 and 6 of the 40 to 50 lifeguards were women. *Id.,* at 1556. During that 5-year period, Terry repeatedly touched the bodies of female employees without invitation, *ibid.,* would put his arm around Faragher, with his hand on her buttocks, *id.,* at 1557, and once made contact with another female lifeguard in a motion of sexual simulation, *id.,* at 1556. He made crudely demeaning references to women generally, *id.,* at 1557, and once commented disparagingly on Faragher's shape, *ibid.* During a job interview with a woman he hired as a lifeguard, Terry said that the female lifeguards had sex with their male counterparts and asked whether she would do the same. *Ibid.*

Silverman behaved in similar ways. He once tackled Faragher and remarked that, but for a physical characteristic he found unattractive, he would readily have had sexual relations with her. *Ibid.* Another time, he pantomimed an act of oral sex. *Ibid.* Within earshot of the female lifeguards, Silverman made frequent, vulgar references to women and sexual matters, commented on the bodies of female lifeguards and beachgoers, and at least twice told female lifeguards that he would like to engage in sex with them. *Id.,* at 1557–1558.

Faragher did not complain to higher management about Terry or Silverman. Although she spoke of their behavior to Gordon, she did not regard these discussions as formal complaints to a supervisor but as conversations with a person she held in high esteem. *Id.,* at 1559. Other female lifeguards had similarly informal talks with Gordon, but because Gordon did not feel that it was his place to do so, he did not report these complaints to Terry, his own supervisor, or to any other city official. *Id.,* at 1559–1560. Gordon responded to the complaints of one lifeguard by saying that "the City just [doesn't] care." *Id.,* at 1561.

In April 1990, however, two months before Faragher's resignation, Nancy Ewanchew, a former lifeguard, wrote to Richard Bender, the City's Personnel Director, complaining that Terry and Silverman had harassed her and other female lifeguards. *Id.,* at 1559. Following investigation of this complaint, the City found that Terry and Silverman had behaved improperly, reprimanded them, and required them to choose between a suspension without pay or the forfeiture of annual leave. *Ibid.*

On the basis of these findings, the District Court concluded that the conduct of Terry and Silverman was discriminatory harassment sufficiently serious to alter the conditions of Faragher's employment and constitute an abusive working environment. *Id.,* at 1562–1563. The District Court then ruled that there were three justifications for holding the City liable for the harassment of its supervisory employees. First, the court noted that the harassment was pervasive enough to support an inference that the City had "knowledge, or constructive knowledge" of it. *Id.,* at 1563. Next, it ruled that the City was liable under traditional agency principles because Terry and Silverman were acting as its agents when they committed the harassing acts. *Id.,* at 1563–1564. Finally, the court observed that Gordon's knowledge of the harassment, combined with his inaction, "provides a further basis for imputing liability on *[sic]* the City." *Id.,* at 1564. The District Court then awarded Faragher one dollar in nominal damages on her Title VII claim. *Id.,* at 1564–1565.

A panel of the Court of Appeals for the Eleventh Circuit reversed the judgment against the City. 76 F3d 1155 (1996). Although the panel had "no trouble concluding that Terry's and Silverman's conduct . . . was severe and pervasive enough to create an objectively abusive work environment," *id.,* at 1162, it overturned the District Court's conclusion that the City was liable. The panel ruled that Terry and Silverman were not acting within the scope of their employment when they engaged in the harassment, *id.,* at 1166, that they were not aided in their actions by the agency relationship, *id.,* at 1166, n 14, and that the City had no constructive knowledge of the harassment by virtue of its pervasiveness or Gordon's actual knowledge, *id.,* at 1167, and n 16.

In a 7-to-5 decision, the full Court of Appeals, sitting en banc, adopted the panel's conclusion. 111 F3d 1530 (1997). Relying on our decision in *Meritor Savings Bank, FSB v Vinson,* 477 US 57, 91 L Ed 2d 49, 106 S Ct 2399 (1986), and on the Restatement (Second) of Agency § 219 (1957) (hereafter Restatement), the court held that "an employer may be indirectly liable for hostile environment sexual harassment by a superior: (1) if the harassment occurs within the scope of the superior's employment; (2) if the employer assigns performance of a nondelegable duty to a supervisor and an employee is injured because of the supervisor's failure to carry out that duty; or (3) if there is an agency relationship which aids the supervisor's ability or opportunity to harass his subordinate." *Id.,* at 1534–1535.

Applying these principles, the court rejected Faragher's Title VII claim against the City. First, invoking standard agency language to classify the harassment by each supervisor as a "frolic" unrelated to his authorized tasks, the court found that in harassing Faragher, Terry and Silverman were acting outside of the scope of their employment and solely to further their own personal ends. *Id.,* at 1536–1537. Next, the court determined that the supervisors' agency relationship with the City did not assist them in perpetrating their harassment. *Id.,* at 1537. Though noting that "a supervisor is always aided in accomplishing hostile environment sexual harassment by the existence of the agency relationship with his employer because his responsibilities include close proximity to and regular contact with the victim," the court held that traditional agency law does not employ so broad a concept of aid as a predicate of employer liability, but requires something more than a mere combination of agency relationship and improper conduct by the agent. *Ibid.* Because neither Terry nor Silverman threatened to fire or demote Faragher, the court concluded that their agency relationship did not facilitate their harassment. *Ibid.*

The en banc court also affirmed the panel's ruling that the City lacked constructive knowledge of the supervisors' harassment. The court read the District Court's opinion to rest on an erroneous legal conclusion that any harassment pervasive enough to create a hostile environment must *a fortiori* also suffice to charge the employer with constructive knowledge. *Id.,* at 1538. Rejecting this approach, the court reviewed the record and found no adequate factual basis to conclude that the harassment was so pervasive that the City should have known of it, relying on the facts that the harassment occurred intermittently, over a long period of time, and at a remote location. *Ibid.* In footnotes, the court also rejected the arguments that the City should be deemed to have known of the harassment through Gordon, *id.,* at 1538, n 9, or charged with constructive knowledge because of its failure to disseminate its sexual harassment policy among the lifeguards, *id.,* at 1539, n. 11.

Since our decision in *Meritor,* Courts of Appeals have struggled to derive manageable standards to govern employer liability for hostile environment harassment perpetrated by supervisory employees. While following our admonition to find guidance in the common law of agency, as embodied in the Restatement, the Courts of Appeals have adopted different approaches. . . .

. . . We granted certiorari to address the divergence, 522 US ——, 139 L Ed 2d 337, 118 S Ct 438 (1997), and now reverse the judgment of the Eleventh Circuit and remand for entry of judgment in Faragher's favor.

II

A

Under Title VII of the Civil Rights Act of 1964, "[i]t shall be an unlawful employment practice for an employer . . . to fail or refuse to hire or to discharge any individual, or otherwise to discriminate against any individual with respect to his compensation, terms, conditions, or privileges of employment, because of such individual's race, color, religion, sex, or national origin." 42 USC § 2000e-2(a)(1) [42 USCS § 2000e-2(a)(1)]. We have repeatedly made clear that although the statute mentions specific employment decisions with immediate consequences, the scope of the prohibition "'is not limited to "economic" or "tangible" discrimination,'" *Harris v Forklift Systems, Inc.,* 510 US 17, 21, 126 L Ed 2d 295, 114 S Ct 367 (1993) (quoting *Meritor Savings Bank, FSB v Vinson,* 477 US, at 64, 91 L Ed 2d 49, 106 S Ct 2399), and that it covers more than "'terms' and 'conditions' in the narrow contractual sense." *Oncale v Sundowner Offshore Services, Inc.,* 523 US ——, ——, 140 L Ed 2d 201, 118 S Ct 998 (1998). Thus, in *Meritor* we held that sexual harassment so "severe or pervasive" as to "'alter the conditions of [the victim's] employment and create an abusive working environment'" violates Title VII. 477 US, at 67, 91 L Ed 2d 49, 106 S Ct 2399 (quoting *Henson v Dundee,* 682 F2d 897, 904 (CA11 1982)).

In thus holding that environmental claims are covered by the statute, we drew upon earlier cases recognizing liability for discriminatory harassment based on race and national origin, . . . just as we have also followed the lead of such cases in attempting to define the severity of the offensive conditions necessary to constitute actionable sex discrimination under the statute. . . .

So, in *Harris,* we explained that in order to be actionable under the statute, a sexually objectionable environment must be both objectively and subjectively offensive, one that a reasonable person would find hostile or abusive, and one that the victim in fact did perceive to be so. 510 US, at 21–22, 126 L Ed 2d 295, 114 S Ct 367. We directed courts to determine whether an environment is sufficiently hostile or abusive by "looking at all the circumstances," including the "frequency of the discriminatory conduct; its severity; whether it is physically threatening or humiliating, or a mere offensive utterance; and whether it unreasonably interferes with an employee's work performance." *Id.,* at 23, 126 L Ed 2d 295, 114 S Ct 367. Most recently, we explained that Title VII does not prohibit "genuine but innocuous differences in the ways men and women routinely interact with members of the same sex and the opposite sex." *Oncale,* 523 US, at ——, 140 L Ed 2d 201, 118 S Ct 998. A recurring point in these opinions is that "simple teasing," *id.,* at ——, 140 L Ed 2d 201, 118 S Ct 998, offhand comments, and isolated incidents (unless extremely serious) will not amount to discriminatory changes in the "terms and conditions of employment."

These standards for judging hostility are sufficiently demanding to ensure that Title VII does not become a "general civility code." *Id.,* at ——, 140 L Ed 2d 201, 118 S Ct 998. Properly applied, they will filter out complaints attacking "the ordinary tribulations of the workplace, such as the sporadic use of abusive language, gender-related jokes, and occasional teasing." B. Lindemann & D. Kadue, Sexual Harassment in Employment Law 175 (1992) (hereinafter Lindemann & Kadue) (footnotes omitted). We have made it clear that conduct must be extreme to amount to a change in the terms and conditions of employment, and the Courts of Appeals have heeded this view. . . .

While indicating the substantive contours of the hostile environments forbidden by Title VII, our cases have established few definite rules for determining when an employer will be liable for a discriminatory environment that is otherwise actionably abusive. Given the circumstances of many of the litigated cases, including some that have come to us, it is not surprising that in many of them, the issue has been joined over the sufficiency of the abusive conditions, not the standards for determining an employer's liability for them. There have, for example, been myriad cases in which District Courts and Courts of Appeals have held employers liable on account of actual knowledge by the employer, or high-echelon officials of an employer organization, of sufficiently harassing action by subordinates, which the employer or its informed officers have done nothing to stop. . . .

Nor was it exceptional that standards for binding the employer were not in issue in *Harris, supra.* In that case of discrimination by hostile environment, the individual charged with creating the abusive atmosphere was the president of the corporate employer, 510 US, at 19, 126 L Ed 2d 295, 114 S Ct 367, who was indisputably within that class of an employer organization's officials who may be treated as the organization's proxy. . . .

Finally, there is nothing remarkable in the fact that claims against employers for discriminatory employment actions with tangible results, like hiring, firing, promotion, compensation, and work assignment, have resulted in employer liability once the discrimination was shown. See *Meritor,* 477 US, at 70–71, 91 L Ed 2d 49, 106 S Ct 2399 (noting that "courts have consistently held employers liable for the discriminatory discharges of employees by supervisory personnel, whether or not the employer knew, should have known, or approved of the supervisor's actions"); *id.,* at 75, 91 L Ed 2d 49, 106 S Ct 2399, 91 L Ed 2d 49, 106 S Ct 2399. . . .

A variety of reasons have been invoked for this apparently unanimous rule. Some courts explain, in a variation of the "proxy" theory discussed above, that when a supervisor makes such decisions, he "merges" with the employer, and his act becomes that of the employer. . . .

. . . Other courts have suggested that vicarious liability is proper because the supervisor acts within the scope of his authority when he makes discriminatory decisions in hiring, firing, promotion, and the like. . . .

. . . Others have suggested that vicarious liability is appropriate because the supervisor who discriminates in this manner is aided by the agency relation. . . .

The soundness of the results in these cases (and their continuing vitality), in light of basic agency principles, was confirmed by this Court's only discussion to date of standards of employer liability, in *Meritor, supra,* which involved a claim of discrimination by a supervisor's sexual harassment of a subordinate over an extended period. In affirming the Court of Appeals's holding that a hostile atmosphere resulting from sex discrimination is actionable under Title VII, we also anticipated proceedings on remand by holding agency principles relevant in assigning employer liability and by rejecting three *per se* rules of liability or immunity. 477 US, at 70–72, 91 L Ed 2d 49, 106 S Ct 2399. We observed that the very definition of employer in Title VII, as including an "agent," *id.,* at 72, 91 L Ed 2d 49, 106 S Ct 2399, expressed Congress's intent that courts look to traditional principles of the law of agency in devising standards of employer liability in those instances where liability for the actions of a supervisory employee was not otherwise obvious, *ibid.,* and although we cautioned that "common-law principles may not be transferable in all their particulars to Title VII," we cited the Restatement §§ 219-237, with general approval. *Ibid.*

We then proceeded to reject two limitations on employer liability, while establishing the rule that some limitation was intended. We held that neither the existence of a company grievance procedure nor the absence of actual notice of the harassment on the part of upper management would be dispositive of such a claim; while either might be relevant to the liability, neither would result automatically in employer immunity. *Ibid.* Conversely, we held that Title VII placed some limit on employer responsibility for the creation of a discriminatory environment by a supervisor, and we held that Title VII does not make employers "always automatically liable for sexual harassment by their supervisors," *ibid.,* contrary to the view of the Court of Appeals, which had held that "an employer is strictly liable for a hostile environment created by a supervisor's sexual advances, even though the employer neither knew nor reasonably could have known of the alleged misconduct," *id.,* at 69–70, 91 L Ed 2d 49, 106 S Ct 2399.

Meritor's statement of the law is the foundation on which we build today. Neither party before us has urged us to depart from our customary adherence to *stare decisis* in statutory interpretation, *Patterson v McLean Credit Union,* 491 US 164, 172–73, 105 L Ed 2d 132, 109 S Ct 2363 (1989) (*stare decisis* has "special force" in statutory interpretation). And the force of precedent here is enhanced by Congress's amendment to the liability provisions of Title VII since the *Meritor* decision, without providing any modification of our holding. Civil Rights Act of 1991, § 102, 105 Stat. 1072, 42 USC § 1981a (42 USCS § 1981a); see *Keene Corp. v United States,* 508 US 200, 212, 124 L Ed 2d 118, 113 S Ct 2035 (1993) (applying the "presumption that Congress was aware of [prior] judicial interpretations and, in effect, adopted them"). . . .

B

2 The Court of Appeals also rejected vicarious liability on the part of the City insofar as it might rest on the concluding principle set forth in § 219(2)(d) of the Restatement, that an employer "is not subject to liability for the torts of his servants acting outside the scope of their employment unless . . . the servant purported to act or speak on behalf of the principal and there was reliance on apparent authority, or he was aided in accomplishing the tort by the existence of the agency relation." Faragher points to several ways in which the agency relationship aided Terry and Silverman in carrying out their harassment. She argues that in general offending supervisors can abuse their authority to keep subordinates in their presence while they make offensive statements, and that they implicitly threaten to misuse their supervisory powers to deter any resistance or complaint. Thus, she maintains that power conferred on Terry and Silverman by the City enabled them to act for so long without provoking defiance or complaint.

The City, however, contends that § 219(2)(d) has no application here. It argues that the second qualification of the subsection, referring to a servant "aided in accomplishing the tort by the existence of the agency relation," merely "refines" the one preceding it, which holds the employer vicariously liable for its servant's abuse of apparent authority. Brief for Respondent 30–31, and n 24. But this narrow reading is untenable; it would render the second qualification of § 219(2)(d) almost entirely superfluous (and would seem to ask us to shut our eyes to the potential effects of supervisory authority, even when not explicitly invoked). The illustrations accompanying this subsection make clear that it covers not only cases involving the abuse of apparent authority, but also to cases in which tortious conduct is made possible or facilitated by the existence of the actual agency relationship. . . .

We therefore agree with Faragher that in implementing Title VII it makes sense to hold an employer vicariously liable for some tortious conduct of a supervisor made possible by abuse of his supervisory authority, and that the aided-by-agency-relation principle embodied in § 219(2)(d) of the Restatement provides an appropriate starting point for determining liability for the kind of harassment presented here. Several courts, indeed, have noted what Faragher has argued, that there is a sense in which a harassing supervisor is always assisted in his misconduct by the supervisory relationship. . . .

. . . The agency relationship affords contact with an employee subjected to a supervisor's sexual harassment, and the victim may well be reluctant to accept the risks of blowing the whistle on a superior. When a person with supervisory authority discriminates in the terms and conditions of subordinates' employment, his actions necessarily draw upon his superior position over the people who report to him, or those under them, whereas an employee generally cannot check a supervisor's abusive conduct the same way that she might deal with abuse from a co-worker. When a fellow employee harasses, the victim can walk away or tell the offender where to go, but it may be difficult to offer such responses to a supervisor, whose "power to supervise—[which may be] to hire and fire, and to set work schedules and pay rates—does not disappear . . .

when he chooses to harass through insults and offensive gestures rather than directly with threats of firing or promises of promotion." Estrich, Sex at Work, 43 Stan. L. Rev. 813, 854 (1991). Recognition of employer liability when discriminatory misuse of supervisory authority alters the terms and conditions of a victim's employment is underscored by the fact that the employer has a greater opportunity to guard against misconduct by supervisors than by common workers; employers have greater opportunity and incentive to screen them, train them, and monitor their performance.

In sum, there are good reasons for vicarious liability for misuse of supervisory authority. That rationale must, however, satisfy one more condition. We are not entitled to recognize this theory under Title VII unless we can square it with *Meritor*'s holding that an employer is not "automatically" liable for harassment by a supervisor who creates the requisite degree of discrimination, and there is obviously some tension between that holding and the position that a supervisor's misconduct aided by supervisory authority subjects the employer to liability vicariously; if the "aid" may be the unspoken suggestion of retaliation by misuse of supervisory authority, the risk of automatic liability is high. To counter it, we think there are two basic alternatives, one being to require proof of some affirmative invocation of that authority by the harassing supervisor, the other to recognize an affirmative defense to liability in some circumstances, even when a supervisor has created the actionable environment.

There is certainly some authority for requiring active or affirmative, as distinct from passive or implicit, misuse of supervisory authority before liability may be imputed. That is the way some courts have viewed the familiar cases holding the employer liable for discriminatory employment action with tangible consequences, like firing and demotion. See *supra,* at —— - ——, 141 L Ed 2d, at 678. And we have already noted some examples of liability provided by the Restatement itself, which suggests that an affirmative misuse of power might be required. See *supra,* at —— - ——, 141 L Ed 2d, at 685 (telegraph operator sends false messages, a store manager cheats customers, editor publishes libelous editorial).

But neat examples illustrating the line between the affirmative and merely implicit uses of power are not easy to come by in considering management behavior. Supervisors do not make speeches threatening sanctions whenever they make requests in the legitimate exercise of managerial authority, and yet every subordinate employee knows the sanctions exist; this is the reason that courts have consistently held that acts of supervisors have greater power to alter the environment than acts of co-employees generally, see *supra,* at —— - ——, 141 L Ed 2d, at 685–686. How far from the course of ostensible supervisory behavior would a company officer have to step before his orders would not reasonably be seen as actively using authority? Judgment calls would often be close, the results would often seem disparate even if not demonstrably contradictory, and the temptation to litigate would be hard to resist. We think plaintiffs and defendants alike would be poorly served by an active-use rule.

The other basic alternative to automatic liability would avoid this particular temptation to litigate, but allow an employer to show as an affirmative defense to liability that the employer had exercised reasonable care to avoid harassment and to eliminate it when it might occur, and that the complaining employee had failed to act with like reasonable care to take advantage of the employer's safeguards and otherwise to prevent harm that could have been avoided. This composite defense would, we think, implement the statute sensibly, for reasons that are not hard to fathom.

Although Title VII seeks "to make persons whole for injuries suffered on account of unlawful employment discrimination," *Albemarle Paper Co. v Moody,* 422 US 405, 418, 45 L Ed 2d 280, 95 S Ct 2362 (1975), its "primary objective," like that of any statute meant to influence primary conduct, is not to provide redress but to avoid harm. *Id.,* at 417, 45 L Ed 2d 280, 95 S Ct 2362. As long ago as 1980, the Equal Employment Opportunity Commission (EEOC), charged with the enforcement of Title VII, 42 USC § 2000e-4 [42 USCS § 2000e-4], adopted regulations advising employers to "take all steps necessary to prevent sexual harassment from occurring, such as . . . informing employees of their right to raise and how to raise the issue of harassment." 29 CFR § 1604.11(f) (1997), and in 1990 the Commission issued a policy statement enjoining employers to establish a complaint procedure "designed to encourage victims of harassment to come forward [without requiring] a victim to complain first to the offending supervisor." . . .

. . . It would therefore implement clear statutory policy and complement the Government's Title VII enforcement efforts to recognize the employer's affirmative obligation to prevent violations and give credit here to employers who make reasonable efforts to discharge their duty. Indeed, a theory of vicarious liability for misuse of supervisory power would be at odds with the statutory policy if it failed to provide employers with some such incentive.

The requirement to show that the employee has failed in a coordinate duty to avoid or mitigate harm reflects an equally obvious policy imported from the general theory of damages, that a victim has a duty "to use such means as are reasonable under the circumstances to avoid or minimize the damages" that result from violations of the statute. . . .

. . . An employer may, for example, have provided a proven, effective mechanism for reporting and resolving complaints of sexual harassment, available to the employee without undue risk or expense. If the plaintiff unreasonably failed to avail herself of the employer's preventive or remedial apparatus, she should not recover damages that could have been avoided if she had done so. If the victim could have avoided harm, no liability should be found against the employer who had taken reasonable care, and if damages could reasonably have been mitigated no award against a liable employer should reward a plaintiff for what her own efforts could have avoided.

In order to accommodate the principle of vicarious liability for harm caused by misuse of supervisory authority, as well as Title VII's equally basic policies of encouraging forethought by employers and saving action by objecting employees, we adopt the following holding in this case and in *Burlington Industries, Inc. v Ellerth, ante,* p ——, 141 L Ed 2d 633, 118 S Ct ——, also decided today. An employer is subject to vicarious liability to a victimized employee for an actionable hostile environment created by a supervisor with immediate (or successively higher) authority over the employee. When no tangible employment action is taken, a defending employer may raise an affirmative defense to liability or damages, subject to proof by a preponderance of the evidence, see Fed. Rule. Civ. Proc. 8(c). The defense comprises two necessary elements: (a) that the employer exercised reasonable care to prevent and correct promptly and sexually harassing behavior, and (b) that the plaintiff employee unreasonably failed to take advantage of any preventive or corrective opportunities provided by the employer or to avoid harm otherwise. While proof that an employer had promulgated an antiharassment policy with complaint procedure is not necessary in every instance as a matter of law, the need for a stated policy suitable to the employment circumstances may appropriately be addressed in any case when litigating the first element of the defense. And while proof that an employee failed to fulfill the corresponding obligation of reasonable care to avoid harm is not limited to showing an unreasonable failure to use any complaint procedure provided by the employer, a demonstration of such failure will normally suffice to satisfy the employer's burden under the second element of the defense. No affirmative defense is available, however, when the supervisor's harassment culminates in a tangible employment action, such as discharge, demotion, or undesirable reassignment. See *Burlington, ante,* at ——, 141 L Ed 2d 633, 118 S Ct ——.

Applying these rules here, we believe that the judgment of the Court of Appeals must be reversed. The District Court found that the degree of hostility in the work environment rose to the actionable level and was attributable to Silverman and Terry. It is undisputed that these supervisors "were granted virtually unchecked authority" over their subordinates, "directly controll[ing] and supervis[ing] all aspects of [Faragher's] day-to-day activities." 111 F3d, at 1544 (Barkett, J., dissenting in part and concurring in part). It is also clear that Faragher and her colleagues were "completely isolated from the City's higher management." *Ibid.* The City did not seek review of these findings.

While the City would have an opportunity to raise an affirmative defense if there were any serious prospect of its presenting one, it appears from the record that any such avenue is closed. The District Court found that the City had entirely failed to disseminate its policy against sexual harassment among the beach employees and that its officials made no attempt to keep track of the conduct of supervisors like Terry and Silverman. The record also makes clear that the City's policy did not include any assurance that the harassing supervisors could be bypassed in registering complaints. App. 274. Under such circumstances, we hold as a matter of law that the City could not be found to have exercised reasonable care to prevent the supervisors' harassing conduct. Unlike the employer of a small workforce, who might expect that sufficient care to prevent tortious behavior could be exercised informally, those responsible for city operations could not reasonably have thought that precautions against hostile environments in any one of many departments in far-flung locations could be effective without communicating some formal policy against harassment, with a sensible complaint procedure.

We have drawn this conclusion without overlooking two possible grounds upon which the City might argue for the opportunity to litigate further. There is, first, the Court of Appeals' indulgent gloss on the relevant evidence: "There is some evidence that the City did not effectively disseminate among Marine Safety employees its sexual harassment policy." *Id.,* at 1539, n 11. But, in contrast to the Court of Appeals's characterization, the District Court made an explicit finding of a "complete failure on the part of the City to disseminate said policy among Marine Safety Section employees." 864 F Supp, at 1560. The evidence supports the District Court's finding and there is no contrary claim before us.

The second possible ground for pursuing a defense was asserted by the City in its argument addressing the possibility of negligence liability in this case. It said that it should not be held liable for failing to promulgate an antiharassment policy, because there was no apparent duty to do so in the 1985–1990 period. The City purports to rest this argument on the position of the EEOC during the period mentioned, but it turns out that the record on this point is quite against the City's position. Although the EEOC issued regulations dealing with promulgating a statement of policy and providing a complaint mechanism in 1990, see *supra,* at ——, 141 L Ed 2d, at 688, ever since 1980 its regulations have called for steps to prevent violations, such as informing employees of their rights and the means to assert them. *Ibid.* The City, after all, adopted an antiharassment policy in 1986.

The City points to nothing that might justify a conclusion by the District Court on remand that the City had exercised reasonable care. Nor is there any reason to remand for consideration of Faragher's efforts to mitigate her own damages, since the award to her was solely nominal. . . .

III

The judgment of the Court of Appeals for the Eleventh Circuit is reversed, and the case is remanded for reinstatement of the judgment of the District Court.

It is so ordered.

SEPARATE OPINION

Justice **Thomas,** with whom Justice **Scalia** joins, dissenting.

For the reasons given in my dissenting opinion in *Burlington Industries v Ellerth, ante,* absent an adverse employment consequence, an employer cannot be held vicariously liable if a supervisor creates a hostile work environment. Petitioner suffered no adverse employment consequence; thus the Court of Appeals was correct to hold that the City is not vicariously liable for the conduct of Chief Terry and Lieutenant Silverman. Because the Court reverses this judgment, I dissent.

As for petitioner's negligence claim, the District Court made no finding as to the City's negligence, and the Court of Appeals did not directly consider the issue. I would therefore remand the case to the District Court for further proceedings on this question alone. I disagree with the Court's conclusion that merely because the City did not disseminate its sexual harassment policy, it should be liable as a matter of law. See *ante,* at ——, 141 L Ed 2d, at 690. The City should be allowed to show either that: (1) there was a reasonably available avenue through which petitioner could have complained to a City official who supervised both Chief Terry and Lieutenant Silverman, see Brief for United States and EEOC as *Amici Curiae* in *Meritor Savings Bank, FSB v Vinson,* O.T. 1985, No. 84–1979, p 26, or (2) it would not have learned of the harassment even if the policy had been distributed. Petitioner, as the plaintiff, would of course bear the burden of proving the City's negligence.

PART 10

REMEDIES, SENTENCING, AND PUNISHMENT

What happens when a law has been broken? Most people assume that, in a criminal case, the culprit will be charged, brought to trial, and convicted, if guilty. Then, appropriate punishment will ensue. In a civil case, we assume that the injured party will sue the perpetrator for damages, and, if appropriate, a monetary penalty will be assessed that rectifies the harm that was caused. In many cases, our assumptions are correct. But what kinds of punishments should be meted out to offenders, and for what offenses? What are the standards for deciding the kinds and severity of punishments? Why do we as a society embrace some punishments, such as imprisonment, and reject others, such as corporal punishment? What is the rationale for using alternative sanctions, such as community service or shaming? Is the death penalty appropriate in a modern, civilized society? When, if ever, should we refrain from punishing to the full extent the law allows and, instead, dispense mercy? When, if ever, should the impact of crimes on victims influence sentencing? These and related questions are the subject of Part 10.

The first two selections, by Immanuel Kant and Jeremy Bentham, outline the two major traditional theories of punishment found in the Western philosophical tradition—retributivism and deterrence theory. Retributivism, as presented by Kant in "On the Right to Punish and to Grant Clemency," is a backward-looking theory of punishment. It looks back to a crime the offender has committed and makes a desert claim: Because the offender has committed a crime, he or she deserves to be punished. Besides the moral judgment of desert, other moral contentions lie at the heart of retributivism. For example, the slogans "let the punishment fit the crime" and "an eye for an eye, a tooth for a tooth" capture another central feature of this theory. Retributivists think that punishment should in some way be proportionate to the crime committed. By virtue of having committed a specific crime, an offender deserves to be punished in a specific way—no more and no less. Thus, the proportionality of punishments to crimes places moral constraints on the practice of punishment. Moreover, the fact that an offender has committed a crime is the sole justification for punishment. Because Kant does not subscribe to the central principle of utilitarian morality, which enjoins us to maximize happiness in society, he does not believe that the aim of punishment is to maximize happiness in society. Though he is willing to admit that crime prevention, or utility maximization, or some other social benefit might ensue as a consequence or by-product of punishing an offender, these factors cannot be used as justifications for punishing someone.

Kant's moral theory heavily influences his idea of retributivism. For Kant, human persons are complex. On one hand, a person is a moral agent's and can be held morally responsible for her actions in virtue of being rationally autonomous. To be rationally autonomous is to be rationally self-governing, or capable of freely making one's own moral choices and decisions. Kant calls this aspect of persons the "noumenal self."

On the other hand, persons are subject to nonmoral and immoral inclinations that do not stem from the noumenal self. Kant calls this feature of persons the "phenomenal self." As phenomenal selves, we are capable of criminal actions that violate the moral law. These two aspects of persons loom large in Kant's contractarian justification of laws and punishments. As noumenal persons, we form civil society, and agree to laws and punishments by means of a social contract. In this respect we are self-legislating; we give the laws of society, both civil and criminal, to ourselves. Yet, as phenomenal persons, we are potential criminals. In forming the social contract, we agree to abide by the laws we have chosen, thereby agreeing to legitimate punishment by the state if we transgress.

The implications of Kant's view for the death penalty are especially interesting. Kant believes that rational persons would agree to capital punishment. He argues that it is the only fitting punishment for some crimes, such as murder. Life imprisonment, he says, is not an adequate substitute for the death penalty. The state is given the right to exact the death penalty for specified crimes by the consent of rational persons in the original social contract whereby civil society is formed. Interestingly, the state also has the duty or obligation to execute convicted offenders for these crimes. For Kant assumes that rational persons are morally responsible for the crimes they commit, including murder. To fail to punish an offender in strict accordance with the dictates of proportionality would be to disrespect that person's rational autonomy. Consequently, for the state not to execute a convicted murderer would be for it to fail in its duty to respect the rational humanity of the offender. Failing to respect persons is not a morally legitimate option for the state.

In many respects, the view of Jeremy Bentham opposes Kant's theory. One of the founders of utilitarianism, Bentham endorsed the principle of utility as an overarching moral and social principle. The principle urges us to maximize happiness in society, and Bentham equated happiness with pleasure. He believed that humans are motivated to seek pleasure and to avoid pain. According to Bentham, the goal of punishment is deterrence, or crime prevention. Following the dictates of utility, we should punish—that is, inflict pain—in order to deter criminals from committing crimes. Such crimes reduce overall happiness in society. In contrast to retributivists, utilitarians espouse a forward-looking view of punishment. They look ahead to crime prevention or deterrence as the desired consequences to be gained from punishing offenders. Ultimately, punishment appeals to the rationality of offenders through their senses, for the goal of punishment should be to inflict enough pain on lawbreakers to outweigh the pleasure or benefit they gain from crime.

Bentham believed that a science of pain infliction is possible; that is, that it is possible to scientifically determine the quantity of pain to be administered to an offender. His relentlessly analytic approach is aptly reflected in the reading selection, taken from *An Introduction to the Principles of Morals and Legislation.* Here, he identifies four different kinds of cases that are unfit ("unmeet") for punishment: (1) cases where punishment is groundless, because there is no harm ("mischief") to prevent; (2) cases where it is inefficacious, that is, unable to prevent harm from being caused; (3) cases where it is unprofitable or too expensive, because the harm the punishment would produce outweighs the harm it would prevent; and (4) cases where punishment is needless, because harm can be prevented more cheaply than by punishing. Within each of these categories, further distinctions are made. In addition, Bentham articulates fourteen rules (depending on how one counts) expounding proportions between crimes and punishments.

Despite their evident differences, Kant's and Bentham's theories are similar in two noteworthy respects. Both theories incorporate the view that punishments should in some way be proportionate to crimes, and both can be seen as attempts to justify punishment by appealing to the rationality of offenders. The first similarity, that both theories hold that punishments should be proportionate to crimes, is superficial. For Kant, proportionality is motivated by the moral conviction that offenders may be punished only on grounds of desert. The severity of the punishment criminals deserve depends on the enormity of the crime they've committed. For Bentham, proportionality is motivated by other concerns, most notably, by the aim of maximizing social utility, which requires that punishment be administered as efficiently as possible. If observing proportionality between crimes and punishments would fail to maximize utility, Bentham would, presumably, abandon it. In contrast, Kant's commitment to proportionality is rooted in a central and permanent moral feature of retributivism.

The second respect in which the theories are similar is less superficial. Both theories try to justify punishment by appealing to the rationality of offenders. However, the conceptions of rationality presupposed by each theorist differ markedly. According to Bentham, persons are rational calculators, able to add up the pleasures and pains of crime and punishment and adjust their plans according to the outcome. According to Kant, persons can choose their actions rationally and freely and deserve respect in virtue of that capacity. Punishment is therefore justified as a necessary show of respect for the rational humanity of offenders.

Retributivism and deterrence are not the only justifications for punishment. Incapacitation, or the need to prevent criminal behavior from occurring, and rehabilitation, the goal of restoring offenders to wholeness as functioning members of society, have also been cited as goals of punishing. Yet another function of punishment, its expressive dimension, is explored in the next selection, Dan M. Kahan's "What Do Alternative Sanctions Mean?" Kahan's aim here is twofold: to explain and defend the expressive theory of punishment and to make a case for shaming penalties as alternatives to imprisonment, which is currently the punishment of choice in the United States.

Kahan views the expressive theory of punishment as a specific instance of a general theory of expressive rationality. According to the general theory, being rational consists in choosing actions that, against a background of social norms, express meanings appropriate to our goals and purposes. Punishment is no exception. Punishments express society's moral condemnation of an offender's behavior. Alternatives to imprisonment, such as fines and community service, have not won widespread public acceptance as criminal sanctions because, Kahan suggests, they do not adequately express society's moral censure of criminal wrongdoing.

Kahan's defense of the expressive theory of punishment focuses on the charge that it cannot stand on its own as an independent theory of punishment. Critics claim that, to be effective, expressivism must be completed by either retributivism or deterrence theory. Kahan accepts this claim but argues that neither retributivism nor deterrence theory are complete theories of punishment without expressivism. For example, the expressive theory is needed to give content to retributivism's central claim that offenders should be punished because they deserve it. Criminals deserve punishment because their behavior denies some important moral value, such as the victim's moral worth. Punishing criminals expresses society's condemnation of the offender's denial of the victim's moral value. The expressive theory thus clarifies the moral claims that lie at the heart of retributivism. Further, expressivism contributes to deterrence theory in several respects. For example, by expressing society's moral condemnation of certain forms of behavior, expressivism enables society to identify which choices and consequences merit punishment. Expressivism also influences people's preferences. Knowing that a behavior is against the law and is socially condemned instills in people an aversion to engaging in it. Thus, Kahan claims, both retributivism and deterrence theory rely heavily on expressive dimensions of punishment.

In the last part of his article, Kahan identifies an alternative to imprisonment that he believes satisfies contemporary sensibilities with respect to punishment's expressive function—shaming penalties. He lists four kinds. Stigmatizing publicity tries to magnify the offenders' humiliation by publicizing their misdeeds. Examples include publishing offenders' names in newspapers or broadcasting them on the radio. Literal stigmatization stamps offenders with a mark that invites ridicule. Being made to wear a T-shirt advertising the offense, or requiring drunk drivers to use special license plates or to attach revealing bumper stickers to their cars, are two examples. Self-debasement penalties involve rituals or ceremonies that publicly humiliate offenders. Finally, contrition penalties require public confessions and self-debasement or involve apology rituals. According to Kahan, thorough analysis shows that criticisms of shaming penalties can be answered and that such penalties have many advantages. Because shaming punishments aptly express society's moral condemnation of criminal behavior, we should add them to our repertoire of punishments. Moreover, we should make other sanctions, such as fines and community service, more shameful to bring them more in line with contemporary expressive sensibilities.

The ultimate punishment—the death penalty—is the subject of the next selection, "Representing the Condemned: A Critique of Capital Punishment," by Christine M. Wiseman. Wiseman recounts her experiences representing a condemned death row inmate in

Texas—Billy Conn Gardner. Her strategy throughout is to identify aspects of Gardner's case that undermined the fairness of criminal procedure and to argue that, because these features were not peculiar to his case, they threaten the fairness of capital cases in general.

She points out that 250 executions have taken place since the United States Supreme Court reinstated the death penalty in *Gregg v. Georgia* in 1976. During the same period, fifty-three capital defendants were released from death row due to probable innocence. This represents nearly 2 percent of the people on the nation's death rows. Wiseman admits that this is a triumph of justice at the appellate level. However, as with Gardner's case, these facts do not speak well of the justice dispensed by lower courts in capital cases.

Shoddy police procedure and ineffective court-appointed trial counsel contributed to Gardner's demise. Regarding the latter point, prison records indicate that trial counsel interviewed Gardner in jail for a maximum of fifteen minutes before jury selection. In addition, Gardner was a victim of child abuse—his father injected him with heroin at age nine to make him a cooperative drug runner. This and other facts of child abuse could have been introduced as mitigating factors during sentencing hearings. They were not.

Gardner's case is not unique. Among other evidence, Wiseman cites a comprehensive study conducted by the *National Law Journal* in 1990 of the quality of legal defense in capital cases in the "Death Belt"—Alabama, Georgia, Florida, Louisiana, Mississippi, and Texas. The study concluded that in capital cases in these states, "fairness is more like the random flip of a coin than a delicate balancing of the scales of justice" (see p. 729). One horror story is especially instructive. When Aden Harrison, Jr., was tried for murder in Alabama in 1986, his family, who are African-American, chose former attorney James Venable because of his low fees. At the time, Venable was eighty-three years old and tended to sleep in court. The family did not know that Venable was a former imperial wizard of the Ku Klux Klan.

This story raises the specter of racism in the imposition of the death penalty. Several studies show that racial bias infects capital prosecutions and sentencing. For example, a study by David C. Baldus looked at over 2,000 cases and considered 230 nonracial variables in the Georgia capital sentencing system between 1973 and 1979. Baldus found that a defendant charged with killing a white victim was 4.3 times more likely to receive the death penalty than was someone charged with killing an African-American victim, and that African-American defendants who kill white victims have the greatest chance of getting the death penalty. Another study conducted for the *Dallas Times Herald* and a synthesis of twenty-eight studies by the General Accounting Office reveal similar trends in other states. Moreover, evidence indicates that federal prosecutors seek the death penalty for African-Americans more often than for whites in drug-related murders.

In addition to racism in the imposition of the death penalty, Wiseman discusses the "economics" and the moral "costs" of capital punishment. Common opinion holds that the death penalty is more economical than life imprisonment. However, Wiseman marshals statistics to show that life imprisonment is less costly than capital punishment. If, as she argues, deterrence, and not retribution, is the primary objective of criminal law, this, too, counts against the death penalty. For statistics show that murder rates are higher in states with the death penalty than in states without it. Finally, in discussing the moral "costs" of capital punishment, Wiseman raises two hard questions about the death penalty. As a society, we currently allow the execution of juveniles and the mentally impaired. But should we? In societal debates, tough normative questions about the legitimacy of the death penalty itself as well as about its application to particular classes of offenders remain unresolved.

The issues raised in Wiseman's piece lead naturally to larger philosophical questions. For example, what is just punishment, and how should it be determined? When, if ever, are we justified in showing mercy to a convicted criminal, and which factors should lead us to do so? These larger philosophical questions are explored in "Equity and Mercy," by Martha C. Nussbaum. In the excerpt given here, she draws on classical Greek and Roman thinkers to develop a doctrine of mercy; she then examines its implications for two Supreme Court cases involving the death penalty.

By the fifth century, justice or *dike* is, Nussbaum tells us, a venerated moral norm, associated with giving to each person his or her due. Aristotle makes a major contribution to our understanding of justice through the development of the notion of *epieikeia,* or equity. As elaborated in the *Nicomachean Ethics,* equity is judgment that is responsive to the particular features of each individual case. It is thus more finely tuned or nuanced than strict legal justice or *dike,* more flexible and less rigid. Strict legal justice supplies broad normative guidelines, and equity fills in spaces left by *dike* with judgments that are sensitive to the particularities of each case. Thus, equitable judgments correct and complete those based on strict legal justice, and they even bend the dictates of strict legal justice for a better fit with the particular circumstances of each case. Is equity opposed to justice? Aristotle thinks not. He views equity as a particular kind of justice superior to strict legal justice. Another element is added to equity in the *Rhetoric.* Here, Aristotle suggests that equitable judgment is a kind of "judging with," or *suggnome,* that incorporates a sympathetic understanding of human affairs.

Though many of the elements of a doctrine of mercy are present in Aristotle's notion of the equitable, we are not yet there, Nussbaum claims. This is because Aristotle insists on a place for retribution and retributive anger where circumstances demand it. We must let go of these to arrive at a doctrine of mercy. The Roman Stoic, Seneca, offers a way for us to do this. He urges us to "cultivate humanity," to adopt an attitude of gentleness, and to "give a pardon to the human species" (p. 740). Mercy, or *clementia,* adopts a sympathetic participatory attitude as central to good judgment. Our warrant for embracing a merciful attitude lies in Seneca's diagnosis of the origins of human wrongdoing. We are, he contends, all weak and vulnerable. We depend on external accommodations—food, shelter, human love—for our very survival. Yet, our access to these is often threatened. We inevitably react to these threats with aggression, violence, and anger. These observations have implications both for personal morality and for the moral norms associated with judging. Angry passions destroy the soul. They can be overcome by two kinds of self-discipline: the close regulation of our attachments to externals, and the extirpation of negative passions. This self-discipline requires honest self-examination, including scrutiny of one's own wrongdoings. The acknowledgment of one's own wrongdoings is essential for good judging, for it engenders the sympathetic participatory attitude that is appropriate to judging. Once we see that wrongdoing stems from human weakness, and that we are all weak and, in some respects, wrongdoers, we have all we need to justify a merciful attitude toward others who do wrong.

In the excerpt offered here, Nussbaum pursues the implications of this doctrine of mercy for two Supreme Court cases involving the death penalty—*Walton v. Arizona* and *California v. Brown.*[1] At issue in both is the role of juror discretion in the sentencing phase of capital cases. *Walton* raises questions about the respective roles to be played by aggravating and mitigating circumstances, whereas *Brown* queries the proper role to be played by jurors' emotions. The mercy tradition has implications for both issues. For example, Justice Scalia believes that mitigating criteria should be listed in advance, to parallel lists of aggravating circumstances. This treats mitigating factors as discrete, isolated units. The mercy tradition argues against this treatment, on the ground that we can get a true understanding of an individual's circumstances in a particular case only by regarding her or his life as a whole—by "getting the big picture." Treating mitigating factors as isolated units does not allow us to appreciate the entire panoply of influences that might affect a person's behavior. The mercy tradition also comments on *California v. Brown,* where the Supreme Court evaluated a state jury instruction that jurors in the sentencing phase of capital cases are not to be swayed by emotion, sympathy, public opinion, or public feeling. The mercy tradition does not see emotion, in particular sympathy, as the enemy of reason, but as its informant. In short, Nussbaum, along with Wiseman, has serious doubts about retributivist justifications of capital punishment and believes that the case for its deterrent value has not fully been made.

Whereas Nussbaum argues that a sympathetic understanding of the criminal gives rise to mercy, proponents of the victim's rights movement have sought greater concern for the plight of victims. The last selection in the criminal law section is an excerpt from a U.S. Supreme Court case, *Payne v. Tennessee.* Decided in 1991, it overturns two previous Supreme Court decisions, *Booth v. Maryland* and *South Carolina v. Gathers,*[2] thus allowing victim-impact statements to be read at the penalty phase of capital trials.

A Tennessee court convicted Pervis Payne of the murders of Charisse Christopher and her two-year-old daughter, Lacie, and of the assault with intent to commit murder in the first degree of her three-year-old son, Nicholas. Payne was sentenced to death for

---

[1]110 S. Ct. 3047 (1990); 479 U.S. 538 (1987).
[2]482 U.S. 496 (1987); 490 U.S. 805 (1989).

each of the murders and to thirty years in prison for the assault. At the penalty phase of Payne's trial, the state presented the testimony of Charisse's mother, portions of which dealt with the effects of Payne's crime on her grandson, Nicholas. The prosecutor's closing argument for the death penalty also discussed these effects. Payne's claim in *Payne v. Tennessee* is that the admission of this material violates his Eighth Amendment rights, as applied in *Booth* and *Gathers.* Those cases held that the Eighth Amendment prohibits a capital-sentencing jury from considering victim-impact evidence relating to the personal characteristics of the victim and the emotional impact of the crime on the victim's family.

In *Payne,* the Court reconsiders its holdings in *Booth* and *Gathers.* Writing for a majority of the Court, Chief Justice Rehnquist argues for the admissibility of victim-impact evidence at the penalty phase of capital trials. His argument is two-pronged. First, evidence relating to the harms caused to the victim's family is part of the evidence required to determine the offense as well as the appropriate punishment. Second, evidence relating to the personal characteristics of the victim is required to prevent unfairness at the sentencing phase of capital trials, because sentencers are allowed to consider mitigating evidence relating to the personal characteristics of the defendant.

Rehnquist begins by addressing two premises on which *Booth* relies: (1) Evidence relating to a particular victim or to the harm caused to a victim's family does not in general bear on the blameworthiness of a criminal. (2) Evidence relating only to blameworthiness is relevant to the capital sentencing decision. He shifts the focus from blameworthiness to harm, contending that the assessment of harm has been an important concern of the criminal law, both in determining the elements of an offense and in meting out punishment. Two equally blameworthy defendants, he claims, can be guilty of different offenses solely because their acts cause different amounts of harm. Though the principles that have guided criminal sentencing have varied, judges in recent years who have had discretion in sentencing in criminal cases have been guided by assessments of harm. Moreover, the sentencing authority has been free to consider a wide range of relevant material. Indeed, the Supreme Court has held that the sentencer in capital cases cannot be precluded from considering any relevant mitigating evidence that might argue in favor of a lesser penalty than death. Some of this evidence can relate to the personal characteristics of the defendant. In Payne's case, Rehnquist points out, the court heard evidence from his girlfriend that they met at church and that he was kind and affectionate. The potential for unfairness exists, he contends, if courts are prevented from hearing similar evidence about the victim(s).

What about Payne's concern, also raised in *Booth,* that the admission of victim-impact evidence invites sentencers to decide penalties based on the social worth of the victims? By claiming that victim-impact evidence is not generally offered to encourage comparative judgments of this kind, Rehnquist rejects this possibility. Payne also invokes the doctrine of *stare decisis;* that is, adherence to precedent requires that *Booth* and *Gathers* be respected. In reply, Rehnquist claims that respect for precedent is a flexible principle, not a formula for mechanical adherence to past decisions. *Booth* and *Gathers* are overruled.

A last look at *Payne* is found in Justice Stevens's dissent. Stevens finds two reasons why the use of victim-impact evidence violates the Eighth Amendment's ban on arbitrary and capricious punishment. First, aspects of the victim's character that are unforeseeable to the defendant at the time the crime is committed are irrelevant to determining the defendant's personal responsibility and moral guilt and therefore cannot justify the death penalty. Second, the quantity and quality of victim-impact evidence sufficient to persuade a sentencer to opt for death instead of life imprisonment cannot be determined until after a crime has been committed and therefore cannot be consistently applied in different cases. In addition, Stevens points out that, although legislatures may justly evaluate the harms caused by different kinds of wrongful conduct in distinguishing among kinds of offenses and suitable punishments and that they may even, in capital cases, list aggravating factors that can justify imposing the death penalty, the majority provides no basis for including unforeseeable and indirect harms to the victim's family as aggravating factors on a case by case basis. Though the majority is correct in asserting that sentencers have been free to consider a wide range of relevant information, Stevens contends that victim-impact evidence is irrelevant because it includes harms that defendants could not have reasonably foreseen. Admitting victim-impact evidence encourages reliance on emotion and thereby risks distracting the sentencer with irrelevant and prejudicial considerations. Under these conditions, life or death decisions may stem from whim or caprice.

Crime and punishment have fascinated the human mind for centuries. The following selections are a small fraction of the philosophical and legal material available on remedies, sentencing, and punishment. The interested reader is invited to consult the selected readings list for further sources on these subjects.

SELECTED READINGS

Coleman, Jules L., ed. *In Harm's Way.* New York: Cambridge University Press, 1994.

Davis, Michael. *To Make the Punishment Fit the Crime: Essays in the Theory of Criminal Justice.* Boulder, CO: Westview, 1992.

Duff, Antony. *Philosophy and the Criminal Law: Principle and Critique.* New York: Cambridge University Press, 1998.

Ellis, Anthony. "Recent Works on Punishment," *Philosophical Quarterly* 45, no. 179 (April 1995): 225–33.

Friedman, Lawrence M. *Crime and Punishment in American History.* New York: BasicBooks, 1993.

Griffin, Stephen M., and Robert C. L. Moffat, eds. *Radical Critiques of the Law.* Lawrence: University Press of Kansas, 1997.

Hart, H. L. A. *Punishment and Responsibility: Essays in the Philosophy of Law.* New York: Oxford University Press, 1968.

Hay, Douglas, Peter Limbaugh, John G. Rule, E. P. Thompson, and Cal Winslow. *Albion's Fatal Tree: Crime and Society in Eighteenth-Century England.* New York: Pantheon Books, 1975.

Ignatieff, Michael. *A Just Measure of Pain: The Penitentiary in the Industrial Revolution 1750–1850.* London: Penguin Books, 1978.

Montagne, Philip. *Punishment or Societal Self-Defense.* Lanham, MD: Rowman and Littlefield, 1995.

Murphy, Jeffrie G. *Punishment and Rehabilitation.* 3d ed. Belmont, CA: Wadsworth, 1995.

Pojman, Louis P. *The Death Penalty: For and Against.* Lanham, MD: Rowman and Littlefield, 1998.

Sistare, Christine, ed. *Punishment: Social Control and Coercion.* New York: Peter Long, 1996.

Tam, Henry, ed. *Punishment, Excuses and Moral Development.* Aldershot, England: Avebury, 1996.

Young, David, trans. *Cesare Beccaria: On Crimes and Punishments.* Indianapolis, IN: Hackett, 1986.

79

IMMANUEL KANT

On the Right to Punish and to Grant Clemency

I

The *right to punish* is the right a ruler has against a subject to inflict pain upon him because of his having committed a crime. The head of a state can therefore not be punished; one can only withdraw from his dominion. —A transgression of public law that makes someone who commits it unfit to be a citizen is called a *crime (crimen)* simply but is also called a public crime *(crimen publicum);*[1] so the first (private crime) is brought before a civil court, the latter before a criminal court. —*Embezzlement,* that is, misappropriation of money or goods entrusted for commerce, and fraud in buying and selling, when committed in such a way that the other could detect it,[2] are private crimes. On the other hand, counterfeiting money or bills of exchange, theft and robbery, and the like are public crimes, because they endanger the commonwealth and not just an individual person. —They can be divided into crimes arising from a *mean* character *(indolis abiectae)* and crimes arising from a *violent* character *(indolis violentae).*

Punishment by a court (poena forensis)—that is distinct from *natural punishment (poena naturalis),* in which vice punishes itself and which the legislator does not take into account—can never be inflicted merely as a means to promote some other good for the criminal himself or for civil society. It must always be inflicted upon him only *because he has committed a crime.* For a human being can never be treated merely as a means to the purposes of another or be put among the objects of rights to things: his innate personality protects him from this, even though he can be condemned to lose his civil personality. He must previously have been found *punishable* before any thought can be given to drawing from his punishment something of use for himself or his fellow citizens. The law of punishment is a categorical imperative, and woe to him who crawls through the windings of eudaemonism in order to discover something that releases the criminal from punishment or even reduces its amount by the advantage it promises, in accordance with the pharisaical saying, "It is better for *one* man to die than for an entire people to perish."[3] For if justice goes, there is no longer any value in human beings' living on the earth. —What, therefore, should one think of the proposal to preserve the life of a criminal sentenced to death if he agrees to let dangerous experiments be made on him and is lucky enough to survive them, so that in this way physicians learn something new of benefit to the commonwealth? A court would reject with contempt such a proposal from a medical college, for justice ceases to be justice if it can be bought for any price whatsoever.

But what kind and what amount of punishment is it that public justice makes its principle and measure? None other than the principle of equality (in the position of the needle on the scale of justice), to incline no more to one side than to the other. Accordingly, whatever undeserved evil you inflict upon another within the people, that you inflict upon yourself. If you insult him, you insult yourself; if you steal from him, you steal from yourself; if you strike him, you strike yourself; if you kill him, you kill yourself. But only the *law of retribution (ius talionis)*—it being understood, of course, that this is applied by a court (not by your private judgment)—can specify definitely the quality and the quantity of punishment; all other principles are fluctuating and unsuited for a sentence of pure and strict justice because extraneous considerations are mixed into them. —Now it would indeed seem that differences in social rank would not allow the principle of retribution, of like for like;[4] but even when this is not possible in terms of the letter, the principle can always remain valid in terms of its effect if account is taken of the sensibilities of the upper classes. —A fine, for example, imposed for a verbal injury has no relation to the offense, for someone wealthy might indeed allow himself to indulge in a verbal insult on some occasion; yet the outrage he

---

[1]Natorp suggests that, here again, something is apparently missing from the text, regarding the first kind of crime.
[2]*bei sehenden Augen des Anderen*

[3]John 11:50
[4]*Gleiches mit Gleichem*

has done to someone's love or honor can still be quite similar to the hurt done to his pride if he is constrained by judgment and right not only to apologize publicly to the one he has insulted but also to kiss his hand, for instance, even though he is of a lower class. Similarly, someone of high standing given to violence could be condemned not only to apologize for striking an innocent citizen socially inferior to himself but also to undergo a solitary confinement involving hardship; in addition to the discomfort he undergoes, the offender's vanity would be painfully affected, so that through his shame like would be fittingly repaid with like. —But what does it mean to say, "If you steal from someone, you steal from yourself?" Whoever steals makes the property of everyone else insecure and therefore deprives himself (by the principle of retribution) of security in any possible property. He has nothing and can also acquire nothing; but he still wants to live, and this is now possible only if others provide for him. But since the state will not provide for him free of charge, he must let it have his powers for any kind of work it pleases (in convict or prison labor) and is reduced to the status of a slave for a certain time, or permanently if the state sees fit. —If, however, he has committed murder he must *die*. Here there is no substitute that will satisfy justice. There is no *similarity* between life, however wretched it may be, and death, hence no likeness between the crime and the retribution unless death is judicially carried out upon the wrongdoer, although it must still be freed from any mistreatment that could make the humanity in the person suffering it into something abominable. —Even if a civil society were to be dissolved by the consent of all its members (e.g., if a people inhabiting an island decided to separate and disperse throughout the world), the last murderer remaining in prison would first have to be executed, so that each has done to him what his deeds deserve and blood guilt does not cling to the people for not having insisted upon this punishment; for otherwise the people can be regarded as collaborators in this public violation of justice.

This fitting of punishment to the crime, which can occur only by a judge imposing the death sentence in accordance with the strict law of retribution, is shown by the fact that only by this is a sentence of death pronounced on every criminal in proportion to his *inner wickedness* (even when the crime is not murder but another crime against the state that can be paid for only by death). —Suppose that some (such as Balmerino[5] and others) who took part in the recent Scottish rebellion believed that by their uprising they were only performing a duty they owed the House of Stuart, while others on the contrary were out for their private interests; and suppose that the judgment pronounced by the highest court had been that each is free to make the choice between death and convict labor. I say that in this case the man of honor would choose death, and the scoundrel convict labor. This comes along with the nature of the human mind; for the man of honor is acquainted with something that he values even more highly than life, namely *honor,* while the scoundrel considers it better to live in shame than not to live at all *(animam praeferre pudori. Iuven.).*[6] Since the man of honor is undeniably less deserving of punishment than the other, both would be punished quite proportionately if all alike were sentenced to death; the man of honor would be punished mildly in terms of his sensibilities and the scoundrel severely in terms of his. On the other hand, if both were sentenced to convict labor the man of honor would be punished too severely and the other too mildly for his vile action. And so here too, when sentence is pronounced on a number of criminals united in a plot, the best equalizer before public justice is *death.* —Moreover, one has never heard of anyone who was sentenced to death for murder complaining that he was dealt with too severely and therefore wronged; everyone would laugh in his face if he said this. —If his complaint were justified it would have to be assumed that even though no wrong is done to the criminal in accordance with the law, the legislative authority of the state is still not authorized to inflict this kind of punishment and that, if it does so, it would be in contradiction with itself.

Accordingly, every murderer—anyone who commits murder, orders it, or is an accomplice in it—must suffer death; this is what justice, as the idea of judicial authority, wills in accordance with universal laws that are grounded *a priori.* —If, however, the number of accomplices *(correi)* to such a deed is so great that the state, in order to have no such criminals

---

[5]Arthur Elphinstone, 6th Baron Balmerino, who took part in the attempt of 1745–6 to put Prince Charles Edward Stuart on the British throne, was captured in the defeat of the Scots forces at Culloden and subsequently beheaded.

[6]Juvenal, *Satires,* III.viii.83.

in it, could soon find itself without subjects; and if the state still does not want to dissolve, that is, to pass over into the state of nature, which is far worse because there is no external justice at all in it (and if it especially does not want to dull the people's feeling by the spectacle of a slaughterhouse), then the sovereign must also have it in his power, in this case of necessity *(casus necessitatis),* to assume the role of judge (to represent him) and pronounce a judgment that decrees for the criminals a sentence other than capital punishment, such as deportation, which still preserves the population.[7] This cannot be done in accordance with public law but it can be done by an executive decree that is, by an act of the right of majesty which, as clemency, can always be exercised only in individual cases.

In opposition to this the Marchese Beccaria,[8] moved by overly compassionate feelings of an affected humanity *(compassibilitas),* has put forward his assertion that any capital punishment is wrongful because it could not be contained in the original civil contract; for if it were, everyone in a people would have to have consented to lose his life in case he murdered someone else (in the people), whereas it is impossible for anyone to consent to this because no one can dispose of his own life. This is all sophistry and juristic trickery.

No one suffers punishment because he has willed *it* but because he has willed a *punishable action;* for it is no punishment if what is done to someone is what he wills, and it is impossible *to will* to be punished. —Saying that I will to be punished if I murder someone is saying nothing more than that I subject myself together with everyone else to the laws, which will naturally also be penal laws if there are any criminals among the people. As a co-legislator in dictating the *penal law,* I cannot possibly be the same person who, as a subject, is punished in accordance with the law; for as one who is punished, namely as a criminal, I cannot possibly have a voice in legislation (the legislator is holy). Consequently, when I draw up a penal law against myself as a criminal, it is pure reason in me *(homo noumenon),* legislating with regard to rights, which subjects me, as someone capable of crime and so as another person *(homo phaenomenon),* to the penal law, together with all others in a civil union. In other words, it is not the people (each individual in it) that dictates capital punishment but rather the court (public justice), and so another than the criminal; and the social contract contains no promise to let oneself be punished and so to dispose of oneself and one's life. For, if the authorization to punish had to be based on the offender's *promise,* on his *willing* to let himself be punished, it would also have to be left to him to find himself punishable and the criminal would be his own judge. —The chief point of error (πρωτον ψευδοζ) in this sophistry consists in its confusing the criminal's own judgment (which must necessarily be ascribed to his *reason*) that he has to forfeit his life with a resolve on the part of his *will* to take his own life, and so in representing as united in one and the same person the judgment upon a right[9] and the realization of that right.[10]

There are, however, two crimes deserving of death, with regard to which it still remains doubtful whether *legislation* is also authorized to impose the death penalty. The feeling of honor leads to both, in one case the *honor of one's sex,* in the other *military honor,* and indeed true honor, which is incumbent as duty on each of these two classes of people. The one crime is a mother's *murder of her child (infanticidium maternale);* the other is *murdering a fellow soldier (commilitonicidium)* in a *duel.* —Legislation cannot remove the disgrace of an illegitimate birth any more than it can wipe away the stain of suspicion of cowardice from a subordinate officer who fails to respond to a humiliating affront with a force of his own rising above fear of death. So it seems that in these two cases people find themselves in the state of nature, and that these acts of *killing (homocidium),* which would then not even have to be called murder *(homocidium dolosum),* are certainly punishable but cannot be punished with death by the supreme power. A child that comes into the world apart from marriage is born outside the law (for the law is marriage) and therefore outside the protection of the law. It has, as it were, stolen into the com-

---

[7]Kant is apparently referring to deportation to a province as distinguished from exile. . . .

[8]Cesare Bonesana, Marchese Beccari, whose influential *Dei delitti e della pene* (1764) argued for a reform of the harsh penal codes of the time. Kant's interest in Beccaria may well have arisen from Beccaria's reliance on a text from Rousseau's *Social Contract,* which had been published in 1762: "All laws must be regarded as if they proceeded from the unanimous will of the people."

[9]*Rechtsbeurteilung*

[10]*Rechtsvollziehung*

monwealth (like contraband merchandise), so that the commonwealth can ignore its existence (since it was not right[11] that it should have come to exist in this way), and can therefore also ignore its annihilation; and no decree can remove the mother's shame when it becomes known that she gave birth without being married. —So too, when a junior officer is insulted he sees himself constrained by the public opinion of the other members of his estate to obtain satisfaction for himself and, as in the state of nature, *punishment* of the offender not by law, taking him before a court, but by a *duel,* in which he exposes himself to death in order to prove his military courage, upon which the honor of his estate essentially rests. Even if the duel should involve *killing* his opponent, the killing that occurs in this fight which takes place in public and with the consent of both parties, though reluctantly, cannot strictly be called *murder (homocidium dolosum).* ——What, now, is to be laid down as right in both cases (coming under criminal justice)? —Here penal justice finds itself very much in a quandary. Either it must declare by law that the concept of honor (which is here no illusion) counts for nothing and so punish with death, or else it must remove from the crime the capital punishment appropriate to it, and so be either cruel or indulgent. The knot can be undone in the following way: the categorical imperative of penal justice remains (unlawful killing of another must be punished by death); but the legislation itself (and consequently also the civil constitution), as long as it remains barbarous and undeveloped, is responsible for the discrepancy between the incentives of honor in the people (subjectively) and the measures that are (objectively) suitable for its purpose. So the public justice arising from the state becomes an *injustice* from the perspective of the justice arising from the people.

II

Of all the rights of a sovereign, *the right to grant clemency* to a criminal *(ius aggratiandi),* either by lessening or entirely remitting punishment, is the slipperiest one for him to exercise; for it must be exercised in such a way as to show the splendor of his majesty, although he is thereby doing injustice in the highest degree. —With regard to crimes of *subjects* against one another it is absolutely not for him to exercise it; for here failure to punish *(impunitas criminis)* is the greatest wrong against his subjects. He can make use of it, therefore, only in case of a wrong done *to himself (crimen laesae maiestatis).* But he cannot make use of it even then if his failure to punish could endanger the people's security. —This right is the only one that deserves to be called the right of majesty. . . .

[11] *billig*

80

JEREMY BENTHAM

From *An Introduction to the Principles of Morals and Legislation*

CHAPTER I / OF THE PRINCIPLE OF UTILITY

1. Nature has placed mankind under the governance of two sovereign masters, *pain* and *pleasure.* It is for them alone to point out what we ought to do, as well as to determine what we shall do. On the one hand the standard of right and wrong, on the other the chain of causes and effects, are fastened to their throne. They govern us in all we do, in all we say, in all we think: every effort we can make to throw off our subjection, will serve but to demonstrate and confirm it. In words a man may pretend to abjure their empire: but in reality he will remain subject to it all the while. The *principle of utility* recognises this subjection, and assumes it for the foundation of that system, the object of which is to rear the fabric of felicity by the hands of reason and of law. Systems which attempt to question it, deal in sounds instead of sense, in caprice instead of reason, in darkness instead of light.

But enough of metaphor and declamation: it is not by such means that moral science is to be improved.

2. The principle of utility is the foundation of the present work: it will be proper therefore at the outset to give an explicit and determinate account of what is

meant by it. By the principle of utility is meant that principle which approves or disapproves of every action whatsoever, according to the tendency which it appears to have to augment or diminish the happiness of the party whose interest is in question: or, what is the same thing in other words, to promote or to oppose that happiness. I say of every action whatsoever; and therefore not only of every action of a private individual, but of every measure of government.

3. By utility is meant that property in any object, whereby it tends to produce benefit, advantage, pleasure, good, or happiness, (all this in the present case comes to the same thing) or (what comes again to the same thing) to prevent the happening of mischief, pain, evil, or unhappiness to the party whose interest is considered: if that party be the community in general, then the happiness of the community: if a particular individual, then the happiness of that individual.

4. The interest of the community is one of the most general expressions that can occur in the phraseology of morals: no wonder that the meaning of it is often lost. When it has a meaning, it is this. The community is a fictitious *body,* composed of the individual persons who are considered as constituting as it were its *members.* The interest of the community then is, what?—the sum of the interests of the several members who compose it.

5. It is in vain to talk of the interest of the community, without understanding what is the interest of the individual. A thing is said to promote the interest, or to be *for* the interest, of an individual, when it tends to add to the sum total of his pleasures: or, what comes to the same thing, to diminish the sum total of his pains.

6. An action then may be said to be comformable to the principle of utility, or, for shortness sake, to utility, (meaning with respect to the community at large) when the tendency it has to augment the happiness of the community is greater than any it has to diminish it.

7. A measure of government (which is but a particular kind of action, performed by a particular person or persons) may be said to be conformable to or dictated by the principle of utility, when in like manner the tendency which it has to augment the happiness of the community is greater than any which it has to diminish it. . . .

CHAPTER III / OF THE FOUR SANCTIONS OR SOURCES OF PAIN AND PLEASURE

1. It has been shown that the happiness of the individuals, of whom a community is composed, that is their pleasures and their security, is the end and the sole end which the legislator ought to have in view: the sole standard, in conformity to which each individual ought, as far as depends upon the legislator, to be *made* to fashion his behaviour. But whether it be this or any thing else that is to be *done,* there is nothing by which a man can ultimately be *made* to do it, but either pain or pleasure. Having taken a general view of these two grand objects (viz. pleasure, and what comes to the same thing, immunity from pain) in the character of *final* causes; it will be necessary to take a view of pleasure and pain itself, in the character of *efficient* causes or means.

2. There are four distinguishable sources from which pleasure and pain are in use to flow: considered separately, they may be termed the *physical,* the *political,* the *moral,* and the *religious:* and inasmuch as the pleasures and pains belonging to each of them are capable of giving a binding force to any law or rule of conduct, they may all of them be termed *sanctions.*

3. If it be in the present life, and from the ordinary course of nature, not purposely modified by the interposition of the will of any human being, nor by any extraordinary interposition of any superior invisible being, that the pleasure or the pain takes place or is expected, it may be said to issue from or to belong to the *physical sanction.*

4. If at the hands of a *particular* person or set of persons in the community, who under names correspondent to that of *judge,* are chosen for the particular purpose of dispensing it, according to the will of the sovereign or supreme ruling power in the state, it may be said to issue from the *political sanction.* . . .

CHAPTER XIII / CASES UNMEET FOR PUNISHMENT

§ i. GENERAL VIEW OF CASES UNMEET FOR PUNISHMENT

1. The general object which all laws have, or ought to have, in common, is to augment the total happiness of the community; and therefore, in the first place, to

exclude, as far as may be, every thing that tends to subtract from that happiness: in other words, to exclude mischief.

2. But all punishment is mischief: all punishment in itself is evil. Upon the principle of utility, if it ought at all to be admitted, it ought only to be admitted in as far as it promises to exclude some greater evil.

3. It is plain, therefore, that in the following cases punishment ought not to be inflicted.

1. Where it is *groundless;* where there is no mischief for it to prevent; the act not being mischievous upon the whole.
2. Where it must be *inefficacious:* where it cannot act so as to prevent the mischief.
3. Where it is *unprofitable,* or too *expensive;* where the mischief it would produce would be greater than what it prevented.
4. Where it is *needless:* where the mischief may be prevented, or cease of itself, without it: that is, at a cheaper rate.

§ ii. CASES IN WHICH PUNISHMENT IS GROUNDLESS

These are,

4. (1) Where there has never been any mischief: where no mischief has been produced to any body by the act in question. Of this number are those in which the act was such as might, on some occasions, be mischievous or disagreeable, but the person whose interest it concerns gave his *consent* to the performance of it. This consent, provided it be free, and fairly obtained, is the best proof that can be produced, that, to the person who gives it, no mischief, at least no immediate mischief, upon the whole, is done. For no man can be so good a judge as the man himself, what it is gives him pleasure or displeasure.

5. (2) Where the mischief was *outweighed:* although a mischief was produced by that act, yet the same act was necessary to the production of a benefit which was of greater value than the mischief. This may be the case with any thing that is done in the way of precaution against instant calamity, as also with any thing that is done in the exercise of the several sorts of powers necessary to be established in every community, to wit, domestic, judicial, military, and supreme.

6. (3) Where there is a certainty of an adequate compensation: and that in all cases where the offence can be committed. This supposes two things: 1. That the offence is such as admits of an adequate compensation: 2. That such a compensation is sure to be forthcoming. Of these suppositions, the latter will be found to be a merely ideal one: a supposition that cannot, in the universality here given to it, be verified by fact. It cannot, therefore, in practice, be numbered amongst the grounds of absolute impunity. It may, however, be admitted as a ground for an abatement of that punishment, which other considerations, standing by themselves, would seem to dictate.

§ iii. CASES IN WHICH PUNISHMENT MUST BE INEFFICACIOUS

These are,

7. (1) Where the penal provision is *not established* until after the act is done. Such are the cases, 1. Of an *ex-post-facto* law; where the legislator himself appoints not a punishment till after the act is done. 2. Of a sentence beyond the law; where the judge, of his own authority, appoints a punishment which the legislator had not appointed.

8. (2) Where the penal provision, though established, is *not conveyed* to the notice of the person on whom it seems intended that it should operate. Such is the case where the law has omitted to employ any of the expedients which are necessary, to make sure that every person whatsoever, who is within the reach of the law, be apprized of all the cases whatsoever, in which (being in the station of life he is in) he can be subjected to the penalties of the law.

9. (3) Where the penal provision, though it were conveyed to a man's notice, *could produce no effect* on him, with respect to the preventing him from engaging in any act of the *sort* in question. Such is the case, 1. In extreme *infancy;* where a man has not yet attained that state or disposition of mind in which the prospect of evils so distant as those which are held forth by the law, has the effect of influencing his conduct. 2. In *insanity;* where the person, if he has attained to that disposition, has since been deprived of it through the influence of some permanent though unseen cause. 3. In *intoxication;* where he has been deprived of it by the transient influence of a visible cause: such as the use of wine, or opium, or other

drugs, that act in this manner on the nervous system: which condition is indeed neither more nor less than a temporary insanity produced by an assignable cause.

10. (4) Where the penal provision (although, being conveyed to the party's notice, it might very well prevent his engaging in acts of the sort in question, provided he knew that it related to those acts) could not have this effect, with regard to the *individual* act he is about to engage in: to wit, because he knows not that it is of the number of those to which the penal provision relates. This may happen, 1. In the case of *unintentionality;* where he intends not to engage, and thereby knows not that he is about to engage, in the *act* in which eventually he is about to engage. 2. In the case of *unconsciousness;* where, although he may know that he is about to engage in the *act* itself, yet, from not knowing all the material *circumstances* attending it, he knows not of the *tendency* it has to produce that mischief, in contemplation of which it has been made penal in most instances. 3. In the case of *mis-supposal;* where, although he may know of the tendency the act has to produce that degree of mischief, he supposes it, though mistakenly, to be attended with some circumstance, or set of circumstances, which, if it had been attended with, it would either not have been productive of that mischief, or have been productive of such a greater degree of good, as has determined the legislator in such a case not to make it penal.

11. (5) Where, though the penal clause might exercise a full and prevailing influence, were it to act alone, yet by the *predominant* influence of some opposite cause upon the will, it must necessarily be ineffectual; because the evil which he sees himself about to undergo, in the case of his *not* engaging in the act, is so great, that the evil denounced by the penal clause, in case of his engaging in it, cannot appear greater. This may happen, 1. In the case of *physical danger;* where the evil is such as appears likely to be brought about by the unassisted powers of *nature*. 2. In the case of a *threatened mischief;* where it is such as appears likely to be brought about through the intentional and conscious agency of *man*.

12. (6) Where (though the penal clause may exert a full and prevailing influence over the *will* of the party) yet his *physical faculties* (owing to the predominant influence of some physical cause) are not in a condition to follow the determination of the will insomuch that the act is absolutely *involuntary*. Such is the case of physical *compulsion* or *restraint,* by whatever means brought about; where the man's hand, for instance, is pushed against some object which his will disposes him *not* to touch; or tied down from touching some object which his will disposes him to touch.

§ iv. CASES WHERE PUNISHMENT IS UNPROFITABLE

These are,

13. (1) Where, on the one hand, the nature of the offence, on the other hand, that of the punishment, are, *in the ordinary state of things,* such, that when compared together, the evil of the latter will turn out to be greater than that of the former.

14. Now the evil of the punishment divides itself into four branches, by which so many different sets of persons are affected. 1. The evil of *coercion* or *restraint:* or the pain which it gives a man not to be able to do the act, whatever it be, which by the apprehension of the punishment he is deterred from doing. This is felt by those by whom the law is *observed.* 2. The evil of *apprehension:* or the pain which a man, who has exposed himself to punishment, feels at the thoughts of undergoing it. This is felt by those by whom the law has been *broken,* and who feel themselves in *danger* of its being executed upon them. 3. The evil of *sufferance:* or the pain which a man feels, in virtue of the punishment itself, from the time when he begins to undergo it. This is felt by those by whom the law is broken, and upon whom it comes actually to be executed. 4. The pain of sympathy, and the other *derivative* evils resulting to the persons who are in *connection* with the several classes of original sufferers just mentioned. Now of these four lots of evil, the first will be greater or less, according to the nature of the act from which the party is restrained: the second and third according to the nature of the punishment which stands annexed to that offence.

15. On the other hand, as to the evil of the offence, this will also, of course, be greater or less, according to the nature of each offence. The proportion between the one evil and the other will therefore be different in the case of each particular offence. The cases, therefore, where punishment is unprofitable on this ground, can by no other means be discovered, than by an examination of each particular offence; which is what will be the business of the body of the work.

16. (2) Where, although in the *ordinary state* of things, the evil resulting from the punishment is not greater than the benefit which is likely to result from the force with which it operates, during the same space of time, towards the excluding the evil of the offence, yet it may have been rendered so by the influence of some *occasional circumstances.* In the number of these circumstances may be, 1. The multitude of delinquents at a particular juncture; being such as would increase, beyond the ordinary measure, the *quantum* of the second and third lots, and thereby also of a part of the fourth lot, in the evil of the punishment. 2. The extraordinary value of the services of some one delinquent; in the case where the effect of the punishment would be to deprive the community of the benefit of those services. 3. The displeasure of the *people;* that is, of an indefinite number of the members of the *same* community, in cases where (owing to the influence of some occasional incident) they happen to conceive, that the offence or the offender ought not to be punished at all, or at least ought not to be punished in the way in question. 4. The displeasure of *foreign powers;* that is, of the governing body, or a considerable number of the members of some *foreign* community or communities, with which the community in question, is connected.

§ v. CASES WHERE PUNISHMENT IS NEEDLESS

These are,

17. (1) Where the purpose of putting an end to the practice may be attained as effectually at a cheaper rate: by instruction, for instance, as well as by terror: by informing the understanding, as well as by exercising an immediate influence on the will. This seems to be the case with respect to all those offences which consist in the disseminating pernicious principles in matters of *duty;* of whatever kind the duty be; whether political, or moral, or religious. And this, whether such principles be disseminated *under,* or even *without,* a sincere persuasion of their being beneficial. I say, even *without:* for though in such a case it is not instruction that can prevent the writer from endeavouring to inculcate his principles, yet it may the readers from adopting them: without which, his endeavouring to inculcate them will do no harm. In such a case, the sovereign will commonly have little need to take an active part: if it be the interest of *one* individual to inculcate principles that are pernicious, it will as surely be the interest of *other* individuals to expose them. But if the sovereign must needs take a part in the controversy, the pen is the proper weapon to combat error with, not the sword.

CHAPTER XIV / OF THE PROPORTION BETWEEN PUNISHMENTS AND OFFENCES

1. We have seen that the general object of all laws is to prevent mischief; that is to say, when it is worth while; but that, where there are no other means of doing this than punishment, there are four cases in which it is *not* worth while.

2. When it *is* worth while, there are four subordinate designs or objects, which, in the course of his endeavours to compass, as far as may be, that one general object, a legislator, whose views are governed by the principle of utility, comes naturally to propose to himself.

3. (1) His first, most extensive, and most eligible object, is to prevent, in as far as it is possible, and worth while, all sorts of offences whatsoever: in other words, so to manage, that no offence whatsoever may be committed.

4. (2) But if a man must needs commit an offence of some kind or other, the next object is to induce him to commit an offence *less* mischievous, *rather* than one *more* mischievous: in other words, to choose always the *least* mischievous, of two offences that will either of them suit his purpose.

5. (3) When a man has resolved upon a particular offence, the next object is to dispose him to do *no more* mischief than is *necessary* to his purpose: in other words, to do as little mischief as is consistent with the benefit he has in view.

6. (4) The last object is, whatever the mischief be, which it is proposed to prevent, to prevent it at as *cheap* a rate as possible.

7. Subservient to these four objects, or purposes, must be the rules or canons by which the proportion of punishments to offences is to be governed.

8. The first object, it has been seen, is to prevent, in as far as it is worth while, all sorts of offences; therefore,

The value of the punishment must not be less in any case than what is sufficient to outweigh that of the profit[1] *of the offence.*

If it be, the offence (unless some other considerations, independent of the punishment, should intervene and operate efficaciously in the character of tutelary motives) will be sure to be committed notwithstanding: the whole lot of punishment will be thrown away: it will be altogether *inefficacious.*

9. The above rule has been often objected to, on account of its seeming harshness: but this can only have happened for want of its being properly understood. The strength of the temptation, *cæteris paribus,* is as the profit of the offence: the quantum of the punishment must rise with the profit of the offence: *cæteris paribus,* it must therefore rise with the strength of the temptation. This there is no disputing. True it is, that the stronger the temptation, the less conclusive is the indication which the act of delinquency affords of the depravity of the offender's disposition. So far then as the absence of any aggravation, arising from extraordinary depravity of disposition, may operate, or at the utmost, so far as the presence of a ground of extenuation, resulting from the innocence or beneficence of the offender's disposition, can operate, the strength of the temptation may operate in abatement of the demand for punishment. But it can never operate so far as to indicate the propriety of making the punishment ineffectual, which it is sure to be when brought below the level of the apparent profit of the offence.

The partial benevolence which should prevail for the reduction of it below this level, would counteract as well those purposes which such a motive would actually have in view, as those more extensive purposes which benevolence ought to have in view: it would be cruelty not only to the public, but to the very persons in whose behalf it pleads: in its effects, I mean, however opposite in its intention. Cruelty to the public, that is cruelty to the innocent, by suffering them, for want of an adequate protection, to lie exposed to the mischief of the offence: cruelty even to the offender himself, by punishing him to no purpose, and without the chance of compassing that beneficial end, by which alone the introduction of the evil of punishment is to be justified.

10. But whether a given offence shall be prevented in a given degree by a given quantity of punishment, is never any thing better than a chance; for the purchasing of which, whatever punishment is employed, is so much expended in advance. However, for the sake of giving it the better chance of outweighing the profit of the offence,

The greater the mischief of the offence, the greater is the expense, which it may be worth while to be at, in the way of punishment.

11. The next object is, to induce a man to choose always the least mischievous of two offences; therefore

Where two offences come in competition, the punishment for the greater offence must be sufficient to induce a man to prefer the less.

12. When a man has resolved upon a particular offence, the next object is, to induce him to do no more mischief than what is necessary for his purpose: therefore

The punishment should be adjusted in such manner to each particular offence, that for every part of the mischief there may be a motive to restrain the offender from giving birth to it.

13. The last object is, whatever mischief is guarded against, to guard against it at as cheap a rate as possible: therefore

The punishment ought in no case to be more than what is necessary to bring it into conformity with the rules here given.

14. It is further to be observed, that owing to the different manners and degrees in which persons under different circumstances are affected by the same exciting cause, a punishment which is the same

---

[1](Profit). By the profit of an offence, is to be understood, not merely the pecuniary profit, but the pleasure or advantage, of whatever kind it be, which a man reaps, or expects to reap, from the gratification of the desire which prompted him to engage in the offence.

It is the profit (that is, the expectation of the profit) of the offence that constitutes the *impelling* motive, or, where there are several, the sum of the impelling motives, by which a man is prompted to engage in the offence. It is the punishment, that is, the expectation of the punishment, that constitutes the *restraining* motive, which, either by itself, or in conjunction with others, is to act upon him in a *contrary* direction, so as to induce him to abstain from engaging in the offence. Accidental circumstances apart, the strength of the temptation is as the force of the seducing, that is, of the impelling motive or motives. To say then, as authors of great merit and great name have said that the punishment ought not to increase with the strength of the temptation, is as much as to say in mechanics, that the moving force or *momentum* of the *power* need not increase in proportion to the momentum of the *burthen.*

in name will not always either really produce, or even so much as appear to others to produce, in two different persons the same degree of pain: therefore,

That the quantity actually inflicted on each individual offender may correspond to the quantity intended for similar offenders in general, the several circumstances influencing sensibility ought always to be taken into account.

15. Of the above rules of proportion, the four first, we may perceive, serve to mark out the limits on the side of diminution; the limits *below* which a punishment ought not to be *diminished:* the fifth, the limits on the side of increase; the limits *above* which it ought not to be *increased.* The five first are calculated to serve as guides to the legislator: the sixth is calculated, in some measure, indeed, for the same purpose; but principally for guiding the judge in his endeavours to conform, on both sides, to the intentions of the legislator.

16. Let us look back a little. The first rule, in order to render it more conveniently applicable to practice, may need perhaps to be a little more particularly unfolded. It is to be observed, then, that for the sake of accuracy, it was necessary, instead of the word *quantity* to make use of the less perspicuous term *value.* For the word *quantity* will not properly include the circumstances either of certainty or proximity: circumstances which, in estimating the value of a lot of pain or pleasure, must always be taken into the account. Now, on the one hand, a lot of punishment is a lot of pain; on the other hand, the profit of an offence is a lot of pleasure, or what is equivalent to it. But the profit of the offence *is* commonly more *certain* than the punishment, or, what comes to the same thing, *appears* so at least to the offender. It is at any rate commonly more *immediate.* It follows, therefore, that, in order to maintain its superiority over the profit of the offence, the punishment must have its value made up in some other way, in proportion to that whereby it falls short in the two points of *certainty* and *proximity.* Now there is no other way in which it can receive any addition to its *value,* but by receiving an addition in point of *magnitude.* Wherever then the value of the punishment falls short, either in point of *certainty,* or of *proximity,* of that of the profit of the offence, it must receive a proportionable addition in point of *magnitude.*

17. Yet farther. To make sure of giving the value of the punishment the superiority over that of the offence, it may be necessary, in some cases, to take into the account the profit not only of the *individual* offence to which the punishment is to be annexed, but also of such *other* offences of the *same sort* as the offender is likely to have already committed without detection. This random mode of calculation, severe as it is, it will be impossible to avoid having recourse to, in certain cases: in such, to wit, in which the profit is pecuniary, the chance of detection very small, and the obnoxious act of such a nature as indicates a habit: for example, in the case of frauds against the coin. If it be *not* recurred to, the practice of committing the offence will be sure to be, upon the balance of the account, a gainful practice. That being the case, the legislator will be absolutely sure of *not* being able to suppress it, and the whole punishment that is bestowed upon it will be thrown away. In a word (to keep to the same expressions we set out with) that whole quantity of punishment will be *inefficacious.*

18. These things being considered, the three following rules may be laid down by way of supplement and explanation to Rule 1.

To enable the value of the punishment to outweigh that of the profit of the offence, it must be increased, in point of magnitude, in proportion as it falls short in point of certainty.

19. *Punishment must be further increased in point of magnitude, in proportion as it falls short in point of proximity.*

20. *Where the act is conclusively indicative of a habit, such an encrease must be given to the punishment as may enable it to outweigh the profit not only of the individual offence, but of such other like offences as are likely to have been committed with impunity by the same offender.*

21. There may be a few other circumstances or considerations which may influence, in some small degree, the demand for punishment: but as the propriety of these is either not so demonstrable, or not so constant, or the application of them not so determinate, as that of the foregoing, it may be doubted whether they be worth putting on a level with the others.

22. *When a punishment, which in point of quality is particularly well calculated to answer its intention, cannot exist in less than a certain quantity, it may sometimes be of use, for the sake of employing it, to stretch a little beyond that quantity which, on other accounts, would be strictly necessary.*

23. *In particular, this may sometimes be the case, where the punishment proposed is of such a nature as to be particularly well calculated to answer the purpose of a moral lesson.*

24. The tendency of the above considerations is to dictate an augmentation in the punishment: the following rule operates in the way of diminution. There are certain cases (it has been seen) in which, by the influence of accidental circumstances, punishment may be rendered unprofitable in the whole: in the same cases it may chance to be rendered unprofitable as to a part only. Accordingly,

In adjusting the quantum of punishment, the circumstances, by which all punishment may be rendered unprofitable, ought to be attended to.

25. It is to be observed, that the more various and minute any set of provisions are, the greater the chance is that any given article in them will not be borne in mind: without which, no benefit can ensue from it. Distinctions, which are more complex than what the conceptions of those whose conduct it is designed to influence can take in, will even be worse than useless. The whole system will present a confused appearance: and thus the effect, not only of the proportions established by the articles in question, but of whatever is connected with them, will be destroyed. To draw a precise line of direction in such case seems impossible. However, by way of memento, it may be of some use to subjoin the following rule.

Among provisions designed to perfect the proportion between punishments and offences, if any occur, which, by their own particular good effects, would not make up for the harm they would do by adding to the intricacy of the Code, they should be omitted.

26. It may be remembered, that the political sanction, being that to which the sort of punishment belongs, which in this chapter is all along in view, is but one of four sanctions, which may all of them contribute their share towards producing the same effects. It may be expected, therefore, that in adjusting the quantity of political punishment, allowance should be made for the assistance it may meet with from those other controlling powers. True it is, that from each of these several sources a very powerful assistance may sometimes be derived. But the case is, that (setting aside the moral sanction, in the case where the force of it is expressly adopted into and modified by the political) the force of those other powers is never determinate enough to be depended upon. It can never be reduced, like political punishment, into exact lots, nor meted out in number, quantity, and value. The legislator is therefore obliged to provide the full complement of punishment, as if he were sure of not receiving any assistance whatever from any of those quarters. If he does, so much the better: but lest he should not, it is necessary he should, at all events, make that provision which depends upon himself.

27. It may be of use, in this place, to recapitulate the several circumstances, which, in establishing the proportion betwixt punishments and offences, are to be attended to. These seem to be as follows:

I. *On the part of the offence:*

1. The profit of the offence;
2. The mischief of the offence;
3. The profit and mischief of other greater or lesser offences, of different sorts, which the offender may have to choose out of;
4. The profit and mischief of other offences, of the same sort, which the same offender may probably have been guilty of already.

II. *On the part of the punishment:*

5. The magnitude of the punishment: composed of its intensity and duration;
6. The deficiency of the punishment in point of certainty;
7. The deficiency of the punishment in point of proximity;
8. The quality of the punishment;
9. The accidental advantage in point of quality of a punishment, not strictly needed in point of quantity;
10. The use of a punishment of a particular quality, in the character of a moral lesson.

III. *On the part of the offender:*

11. The responsibility of the class of persons in a way to offend;
12. The sensibility of each particular offender;
13. The particular merits or useful qualities of any particular offender, in case of punishment which might deprive the community of the benefit of them;
14. The multitude of offenders on any particular occasion.

IV. *On the part of the public,* at any particular conjuncture:

15. The inclinations of the people, for or against any quantity or mode of punishment;
16. The inclinations of foreign powers.

V. *On the part of the law:* that is, of the public for a continuance:

17. The necessity of making small sacrifices, in point of proportionality, for the sake of simplicity.

28. There are some, perhaps, who, at first sight, may look upon the nicety employed in the adjustment of such rules, as so much labour lost: for gross ignorance, they will say, never troubles itself about laws, and passion does not calculate. But the evil of ignorance admits of cure: and as to the proposition that passion does not calculate, this like most of these very general and oracular propositions, is not true. When matters of such importance as pain and pleasure are at stake, and these in the highest degree (the only matters, in short, that can be of importance) who is there that does not calculate? Men calculate, some with less exactness, indeed, some with more: but all men calculate. I would not say, that even a madman does not calculate. Passion calculates, more or less, in every man: in different men, according to the warmth or coolness of their dispositions: according to the firmness or irritability of their minds: according to the nature of the motives by which they are acted upon. Happily, of all passions, that is the most given to calculation, from the excesses of which, by reason of its strength, constancy, and universality, society has most to apprehend: I mean that which corresponds to the motive of pecuniary interest: so that these niceties, if such they are to be called, have the best chance of being efficacious, where efficacy is of the most importance.

81

DAN M. KAHAN

What Do Alternative Sanctions Mean?

. . . The singularity of American criminal punishments has been widely lamented. Imprisonment is harsh and degrading for offenders and extraordinarily expensive for society. Nor is there any evidence that imprisonment is more effective than its rivals in deterring various crimes. For these reasons, theorists of widely divergent orientations—from economics-minded conservatives to reform-minded civil libertarians—are united in their support for alternative sanctions.

The problem is that there is no political constituency for such reform. If anything, the public's commitment to imprisonment has intensified in step with the theorists' disaffection with it. In the last decade, prison sentences have been both dramatically lengthened for many offenses and extended to others that have traditionally been punished only with fines and probation.

What accounts for the resistance to alternative sanctions? The conventional answer is a failure of democratic politics. Members of the public are ignorant of the availability and feasibility of alternative sanctions; as a result, they are easy prey for self-interested politicians, who exploit their fear of crime by advocating more severe prison sentences. The only possible solution, on this analysis, is a relentless effort to educate the public on the virtues of the prison's rivals.

I want to advance a different explanation. The political unacceptability of alternative sanctions, I will argue, reflects their inadequacy along the expressive dimension of punishment. The public rejects the alternatives not because they perceive that these punishments won't work or aren't severe enough, but because they fail to express condemnation as dramatically and unequivocally as imprisonment.

This claim challenges the central theoretical premise of the case for alternative sanctions: that all forms of punishment are interchangeable along the dimension of severity or "bite." The purpose of imprisonment, on this account, is to make offenders suffer. The threat of such discomfort is intended to deter criminality, and the imposition of it to afford a criminal his just deserts. But liberty deprivation, the critics point out, is not the only way to make criminals uncomfortable. On this account, it should be possible to translate any particular term of imprisonment into an alternative sanction that imposes an equal amount of suffering. The alternatives, moreover, should be preferred whenever they can feasibly be imposed and whenever they cost less than the equivalent term of imprisonment.

This account is defective because it ignores what different forms of affliction mean. Punishment is *not* just a way to make offenders suffer; it is a special social convention that signifies moral condemnation. Not all modes of imposing suffering express condemnation or express it in the same way. The message of condemnation is very clear when society deprives an offender of his liberty. But when it merely fines him for the same act, the message is likely to be different: you may do what you have done, but you must pay for the privilege. Because community service penalties involve activities that conventionally entitle people to respect and admiration, they also fail to express condemnation in an unambiguous way. This mismatch between the suffering that a sanction imposes and the meaning that it has for society is what makes alternative sanctions politically unacceptable.

The importance of the expressive dimension of punishment should be evident. It reveals, for one thing, that punishment reformers face certain objective constraints. The social norms that determine what different forms of suffering mean cannot be simply dismissed as the product of ignorance or bias; rather, they reflect deeply rooted public understandings that mere exhortation is unlikely to change. But there are also more hopeful implications. If we can understand the expressive dimension of punishment, we should be able to perceive not only what kinds of punishment reforms won't work but also which ones will. Careful attention to social norms might allow us to translate alternative sanctions into a punitive vocabulary that makes them a meaningful substitute for imprisonment. . . .

THE EXPRESSIVE DIMENSION OF PUNISHMENT

Does it make sense to conceive of punishment as a language? Many observers in many different places and at many different times have concluded that it does. Durkheim seems to have had this idea in mind, for example, when he characterized punishment as a "sign indicating [ ] the sentiments of the collectivity," as did Hegel, when he described it as the "annul[ment of a] crime, which otherwise would have been held valid." James Fitzjames Stephen, the nineteenth-century English political theorist and judge, understood punishment to be the means by which "law gives definite expression and a solemn ratification . . . to the hatred which is excited by the commission of an offence. . . ." Various contemporary philosophers, including Jean Hampton, Joel Feinberg, and Robert Nozick, have also emphasized the expressive dimension of punishment.

But theirs is not the orthodox view. "Deterrence" and "retributivism" dominate mainstream theorizing. The proponents of these accounts frequently deride the expressive theory or, even more contemptuously, ignore it altogether.

Disrespect for the expressive theory can be attributed to two causes. The first is its obscurity. The writings of Hegel and Durkheim are filled with dense abstractions, like "annulment," "negation," and "collective conscience." Contemporary philosophers, while more precise in their terminology, still fail to connect their accounts to actual institutions and practices.

Focusing on the abstract quality of such theorizing, critics assail the expressive position as either incoherent or derivative. Crimes, as historical events, are not genuinely "annulled" or "negated" by punishment, they point out. And if expression of condemnation were the salient ingredient of punishment, why wouldn't society be content simply to criticize the criminal verbally? Maybe annulment can be understood less literally as a "righting of the moral balance" upset by the criminal's acts; and maybe expression of disapproval through hard treatment can be defended as discouraging criminality. But if this is how we must reformulate the expressive theorists' arguments, then their account dissolves into conventional retributive and deterrence theories and thus need not be independently taken into account. Or so it is claimed.

The second difficulty for the expressive theory is that it appears strikingly illiberal. Deterrence justifies punishment to prevent harm to others; retributivism confines it to those who voluntarily choose to inflict such harm. The expressive theory, by contrast, appears to emphasize neither consequences nor choices, but rather the enforcement of society's moral values. In his famous rejoinder to Lord Devlin, who had used the expressive theory to criticize proposals to decriminalize homosexuality, H. L. A. Hart assailed this justification for punishment as "belong[ing] to the prehistory of morality." "The idea that we may punish offenders against a moral code, not to prevent harm or suffering or even the repetition of the offence but simply as a means of venting or emphatically expressing moral condemnation, is uncomfortably close to human sacrifice as an expression of religious worship."

I believe that the conventional disregard for the expressive view is ill-considered. The expressive theory, properly understood, is less imperial than the conventional deterrence and retributive theories; it doesn't purport to explain everything of significance in criminal law and may, in fact, be constrained by other important considerations. Nonetheless, theorizing that excludes the expressive dimension of punishment generates incomplete explanations of what the criminal law is and unreliable prescriptions of what it should be.

That is what I will try to show; but what I offer in this Part is only a first step. I will set forth a conception of the expressive theory in simple and concise terms. Although this exposition might at least suggest why the charges typically made against this account are inadequate, I don't intend my discussion to be a complete theoretical defense of the expressive position. Indeed, I want to defend the expressive view without recourse to deep theorizing. I will ultimately seek to demonstrate the utility of the expressive view not by establishing its conceptual coherence in the abstract, but rather by *using* it . . . to account for public sensibilities and to identify desirable institutional reforms.

What Punishment Says and How

Actions have *meanings* as well as consequences. Part of being rational consists in selecting actions that, against the background of social norms, express meanings appropriate to our purposes and goals. Along some dimension, for example, five thousand dollars might be equivalent in value to everything I would do with and for a friend during a certain period of time. But if my goal is to be her *friend,* then giving her the money and sharing my time with her are not interchangeable; giving money in lieu of time fails to convey the respect and affection that being a good friend requires.

This is a general account of expressive rationality; the expressive theory of punishment can be viewed as a special instance of this account. Under this view, we can give a satisfactory account of crime and punishment only if we pay close attention to their social meaning.

The distinctive meaning of criminal wrongdoing is its denial of some important value, such as the victim's moral worth. Along one dimension—say, personal wealth—theft might hurt a person as much as being outperformed by a business competitor. The reason that theft but not competition is a crime, on this account, is that against the background of social norms theft expresses disrespect for the injured party's worth, whereas competition (at least ordinarily) does not. In effect, the thief's behavior says to the victim, "you matter so little, relative to me, that I can take your property without your consent." The theory of meaning here, moreover, is objective: so long as we understand his act to be theft, the wrongdoer's behavior conveys disrespect for the victim regardless of whether the thief meant to make any particular statement.

The expressive theory also explains the relative seriousness of different forms of wrongdoing. A rape, for example, is often more reprehensible than an ordinary assault—even if the assault results in greater physical injury—because the violation of a woman's sexual autonomy conveys greater disrespect for her worth than do most other violations of her person. Or compare the actions of a white supremacist who kills an African-American out of racial hatred and a mother who in anger kills a man who has sexually abused her child. Both acts are wrong, and their consequences are in some sense equivalent—there is one dead person in each case. Nevertheless, the racist's killing is more worthy of condemnation precisely because his hatred expresses a more reprehensible valuation than does the mother's anger.

Under the expressive view, the signification of punishment is moral condemnation. By imposing the proper form and degree of affliction on the wrongdoer, society says, in effect, that the offender's assessment of whose interests count is wrong. It follows, moreover, that when society deliberately forgoes answering the wrongdoer through punishment, it risks being perceived as endorsing his valuations; hence the complaint that unduly lenient punishment reveals that the victim is worthless in the eyes of the law.

These considerations suggest at least one possible response to the charge that the expressive theory is illiberal. The critics assert that the expressive view is dangerous because it concerns itself with values rather than with consequences and choices. A modest proponent of the expressive view might agree that it is inappropriate to punish values *simpliciter*, but still note the difficulty of identifying which choices and consequences to punish, and how much, if they are considered apart from the values that they express. As the rape and theft examples illustrate, attention to social meaning is ubiquitous in the definitions and gradations of criminal offenses. It would be a mistake, moreover, to think that no appropriately robust conception of liberalism can justify this central feature of the law.

The contention that the expressive theory supports illiberal results is based on a specious form of generalization. Expressive arguments *can* be used to justify the criminalization of homosexuality, but the expressive theory *entails* neither this nor any other form of intolerance. Indeed, the expressive theory illuminates a critical part of what is wrong with such laws. The injustice of a prohibition on same-sex sodomy, for example, consists at least as much in the disrespect it expresses toward gays as it does in the impingement of anyone's liberty to engage in particular sexual acts. From an expressive point of view, hate crime legislation can be used to criticize the devaluation of gays just as effectively as sodomy laws can be used to entrench it.

The expressive theory also underscores the importance of form and convention in punishment. Military service might in some sense be equivalent to imprisonment if we consider their effects on a person's liberty. But the reason that only imprisonment and not conscription is regarded as punishment is that against the background of social norms only imprisonment expresses society's authoritative moral condemnation.

The formal and conventional underpinnings of what different forms of affliction signify constrain society's options for expressing condemnation. Just as it would be irrational for a person who wishes to express respect and affection for a friend to offer her money rather than shared experiences, so would it be irrational for society to attempt to condemn a wrongdoer by imposing an affliction that does not signify condemnation within that society. Punishment, as a language, has a vocabulary uniquely suited for getting its meaning across.

This point should emerge more completely in my examination of the political unacceptability of fines and community service; but it is useful at this stage to consider how it relates to another of the standard criticisms of the expressive theory—namely, that if punishment were genuinely expressive it would suffice to condemn a wrongdoer verbally. This argument disregards what convention and form contribute to meaning. In a certain community, the accepted way for a husband to show love and commitment to his wife on their twenty-fifth wedding anniversary might be to give her a ring (or some other gift); if so, just *telling* her that he feels such love and commitment wouldn't be sufficient to express his meaning against the background of this social norm. The question put by the conventional criticism of the expressive view, then, is whether social norms make words an adequate substitute for hard treatment in expressing condemnation.

The answer is obviously no. In some societies, and even in ours at an earlier time, public denunciation by itself might have been sufficient to convey condemnation of a wrongdoer, but such is clearly not true today. Imagine that a judge proposed only to denounce a brutal rapist rather than to sentence him to prison. Such a sentence would no doubt be regarded as inadequate for purposes of deterrence and retribution. But even beyond that, mere verbal denunciation would be understood to trivialize the offense: the way for society to show that it takes rape seriously, and to show that it genuinely condemns a particular rapist, is to make him suffer in an appropriate way. For inflicting punishment—as for many other purposes—actions speak louder than words.

Expressive Condemnation vs. Retributivism and Deterrence

According to its critics, the expressive theory can be saved from incoherence only at the expense of its analytical independence. Clarifying the theory inevitably merges the expressive account into deterrence or retributivism, making independent study of the expressive view unnecessary.

A defender of the expressive theory might respond in one of two ways. First, she could attempt to develop an abstract conception of the expressive position that is in fact analytically independent of either deterrence or retributivism. She could then show that this account either is or should be the basis of criminal law. This strategy attacks the claim of derivativeness head-on.

A second strategy is less ambitious. It essentially demurs to the claim of analytical interdependence. It might be the case that any plausible conception of the expressive view can be fit into the framework of deterrence or retributivism, but it would be fallacious to conclude that the expressive theory can therefore be ignored; that conclusion would follow only if it were possible to develop plausible conceptions of deterrence and retributivism that make no reference to the expressive function of criminal law. And that, the defender of the expressive view would try to show, cannot be done.

I want to pursue this second strategy in the next part of this essay. To set it up, I will consider how retributivism and deterrence theories can be analytically related to and distinguished from the expressive theory.

Start with very basic conceptions of retributivism and deterrence. "Retributivism is the view that punishment is justified by the moral culpability of those who receive it. A retributivist punishes because, and only because, the offender deserves it." Deterrence, in contrast, asserts that punishment is justified because it averts future harm. Society should punish, on this view, only if the expected benefits of a particular penalty exceed the expected costs of imposing it.

The core idea of retributivism—that an individual should be punished "because, and only because, [he] deserves it"—is vague. It is possible to give content to this notion without reference to expressive condemnation; one might say, for example, that an individual deserves punishment when "he renounces a burden which others have voluntarily assumed and thus gains an advantage which others . . . do not possess," or when human beings naturally intuit that the individual has engaged in "a wrong action [that] . . . calls for the infliction of suffering or deprivation on the agent." But it is also possible to use the expressive view to inform desert. On this account, an individual deserves punishment when he engages in behavior that conveys disrespect for important values. The proper retributive punishment is the one that appropriately expresses condemnation and reaffirms the values that the wrongdoer denies.

The expressive theory can also be used to inform deterrence. One way in which it might do so is by supplying a consequentialist theory of value. Without a theory for identifying which outcomes are socially disvalued and how much, it is impossible to know what to deter or how to allocate limited punishment resources among different forms of wrongdoing. Again, one could attempt to specify a consequentialist theory of value—perhaps wealth-maximization—that is indifferent to expressive sensibilities. Or one could overtly draw on these sensibilities to identify preferred outcomes. To return to an earlier example, one might conclude that a white man who kills an African-American out of racial hatred should be punished more severely than a woman who kills the abuser of her child in anger, even if equal punishment would maximize social wealth; when expressive considerations are taken into account, racist killings are deemed to harm society more than are impassioned killings of child molesters.

Another way that the expressive theory might reinforce deterrence is through preference formation. The law can discourage criminality not just by "raising the cost" of such behavior through punishments, but also through instilling aversions to the kinds of behavior that the law prohibits. The latter is often referred to as the "moralizing" or "moral educative" effect of punishment.

The moralizing effect of criminal law depends on a variety of mechanisms, all of which are reinforced by the expressive character of the law. The first is preference adaptation. To avoid cognitive dissonance, citizens form aversions to the kinds of behavior—whether rape, theft, or insider trading—that the law tells them are unworthy of being valued. This sort of preference adaptation is most likely to take place when citizens perceive the law as expressing society's moral condemnation of such conduct.

The law also moralizes by shaping relevant "belief-dependent" preferences. Empirical studies show that the willingness of persons to obey various laws is endogenous to their beliefs about whether others view the law as worthy of obedience: if compliance is perceived to be widespread, persons generally desire to obey; but if they believe that disobedience is rampant, their commitment to following the law diminishes. Even a strong propensity to obey the law, in other words, can be undercut by a person's "desire not to be suckered." When the law effectively expresses condemnation of wrongdoers, however, it reassures citizens that society does indeed stand behind the values that the law embodies.

Finally, the law moralizes through goodwill. Individuals are more disposed to obey particular laws, whether or not those laws accord with their moral beliefs, when they perceive the criminal law as a whole to be basically just. They are more likely to have this perception when criminal punishment confirms, rather than disappoints, shared expectations about what behavior is worthy of moral condemnation.

Theorists who dismiss the expressive theory can't draw on it to support retributivism or deterrence reasoning in any of these ways. Thus, the question should not be whether expressive condemnation can be successfully disconnected from deterrence and retribution, but whether it's possible to develop sensible conceptions of the latter theories without reference to the expressive view. I believe that it isn't; punishment theorizing that disregards the expressive view is necessarily incomplete. It is exactly this inattention to meaning, I will argue, that has blinded conventional theorists to the political unacceptability of alternative sanctions. . . .

ENRICHING OUR PUNITIVE VOCABULARY: THE REDISCOVERY OF SHAME

So far I have concentrated on showing how the social meaning of alternative sanctions, in the form in which they are conventionally proposed, makes them politically unacceptable. I will now examine how the expressive dimension of punishment can be used to identify politically acceptable reforms.

To begin, nothing I've said shows that there is not a problem worth solving with alternative sanctions. The expressive dimension of punishment helps to describe how deep-seated sensibilities inform a society's institutional choices. But nothing in that phenomenon commits us to accept uncritically either the sensibilities or the institutions that happen to satisfy them. All else equal, a society is certainly better off if it can substitute a cheaper pairing of sensibilities and institutions for a costly pairing.

Thus, American jurisdictions would be better off if they could either reform the expressive sensibilities that make cheaper alternatives to imprisonment unacceptable or identify additional cheaper alternatives that satisfy those sensibilities.

Of these two options, the first is a nonstarter. Wholly apart from whether it is appropriate for a liberal society to concern itself with the quality of its citizens' values, a project to reform expressive sensibilities through self-conscious engineering would be extraordinarily complicated. Our knowledge of how to create and alter social norms is relatively primitive. It's unclear how a legislature would even start to transform the understandings that make corporal punishment express inequality, fines moral indifference, and community service public-spiritedness.

The second option—identifying alternative sanctions that satisfy extant expressive sensibilities—has considerably more promise. Expressive modes of valuation resist quantitative metrics, but ordinarily accommodate a wide range of actions that embody appropriate meanings in different contexts. A person who sets out to produce the same amount of "pleasure" in his children, or who insists on mechanically treating all of them "the same," is unlikely to be a good parent; if he is properly attuned to social meaning, however, the incommensurability of his children's well-being will not prevent him from identifying actions that appropriately express his love for each. Likewise, from an expressive point of view, what is critical is not that society inflict the same amount of pain on all wrongdoers or impose the same form of deprivation on all, but that it select afflictions that unambiguously express condemnation against the background of social norms. It would be strange if imprisoning all serious offenders were the only way to do that.

My goal in this Part is to show that it isn't. Social norms permit the construction of a rich array of shaming practices, all of which unambiguously convey moral condemnation. By using these practices, either alone or in combination with conventional sanctions such as fines and community service, American jurisdictions can fashion politically acceptable alternative sanctions.

The Shaming Alternative

Early Americans turned to imprisonment in large part because they believed that existing criminal penalties had lost the power to shame. It is perfectly fitting, then, that contemporary Americans are rediscovering shaming penalties as they attempt to extricate themselves from their excessive reliance on imprisonment. In this Part, I offer an overview of what those penalties are and why they are more likely to be embraced by the public than conventional alternative sanctions.

What Shaming Penalties Are

The last decade has witnessed the advent of a wide variety of shaming sanctions. Although categorizing them risks understating their diversity and richness, these penalties can be grouped into four classes: stigmatizing publicity, literal stigmatization, self-debasement, and contrition.

Stigmatizing publicity is the most straightforward. Penalties in this class attempt to magnify the humiliation inherent in conviction by communicating the offender's status to a wider audience. Some municipalities, for example, publish offenders' names in newspapers or even on billboards, a disposition that is especially common for men convicted of soliciting prostitutes. Other jurisdictions broadcast the names of various types of offenders on community-access television channels.

Literal stigmatization is just that—the stamping of an offender with a mark or symbol that invites ridicule. Some judges order petty thieves to wear t-shirts announcing their crimes. Others achieve the same effect with brightly colored bracelets that read "DUI Convict," "I Write Bad Checks," and the like. One judge ordered a woman to wear a sign declaring "I am a convicted child molester."

Less dramatic but even more common are penalties that attach stigmatizing marks to property. Some jurisdictions now require persons guilty of drunk driving to display special license plates or bumper stickers. Courts have also ordered those convicted of sexual assaults and other crimes to post signs at their residences warning others to steer clear.

Self-debasement penalties involve ceremonies or rituals that publicly disgrace the offender. In a contemporary version of the stocks, for example, some communities require offenders simply to stand in public spaces, such as the local courthouse, with signs describing their offenses. More imaginative forms of self-debasement attempt to match the penalty to the character of the offense. A judge in Tennessee orders convicted burglars to permit their victims to enter their homes and remove items of their choosing. In New York, a slumlord was sentenced to house arrest in one of his rat-infested tenements (where tenants greeted him with the banner, "Welcome, You Reptile!"). Hoboken, New Jersey, requires Wall Street brokers and others who urinate in public to clean the city's streets. This is only a small sample; self-debasement sanctions are as diverse and particular as the crimes that they are used to punish.

Contrition penalties come in two forms. The first requires offenders to publicize their own convictions, describing their crimes in first-person terms and apologizing for them. These penalties combine stigmatizing publicity with an element of self-debasement; the sincerity of the offenders' remorse seems largely irrelevant.

Another form of contrition is the apology ritual. In Maryland, for example, juvenile offenders must apologize on their hands and knees and are released from confinement only if they persuade their victims that their remorse is sincere. Other jurisdictions use community-based sanctions that include public apologies and appropriate reparations. Because many of these penalties contemplate genuine rapprochement, apology rituals seem to be used primarily in cases in which the offender is connected to the victim by family or close community ties.

What Shaming Penalties Mean

The proponents of alternative sanctions shouldn't be entirely surprised by the growing popularity of shaming penalties. Much of their appeal is simply that they are cheaper than imprisonment. Not all offenders who receive shaming penalties would otherwise have been incarcerated, but many of them would have. Courts use shaming penalties to punish a wide array of offenses, including drunk driving, larceny, embezzlement, assault (sexual and nonsexual), burglary, perjury, toxic-waste dumping, and drug distribution. When imposed for crimes such as these, shaming penalties free up imprisonment resources for offenders who more urgently demand incapacitation.

But shaming penalties are also emerging as a serious rival of imprisonment because they do something that conventional alternative sanctions don't do: express appropriate moral condemnation. Such penalties, one court explained, "inflict[ ] disgrace and contumely in a dramatic and spectacular manner." This dimension of meaning sets shaming penalties apart from fines and community service, which seem unsatisfactory precisely because they condemn the offender's acts only equivocally.

In fact, the expression of condemnation is at least as central to shaming penalties as the infliction of shame itself. Shame is the emotion that a person experiences when she believes that she has been disgraced in the eyes of persons whom she respects. Most offenders punished by shaming penalties are likely to feel shame. But some probably do not, just as some offenders do not view imprisonment as vitiating the respect of their peers. The public's realization that not all offenders view such punishments as disgraceful, however, does not diminish the resonance of either shaming penalties or imprisonment as symbols of the community's moral disapproval. If anything, the perception that the offender is not shamed by what is commonly understood to be shame*ful* would reinforce onlookers' conclusion that he is depraved and worthy of condemnation.

Shaming penalties might even more accurately be described as *degradation* penalties. All of them satisfy what Harold Garfinkel identifies as the "conditions of successful status degradation ceremonies": they are imposed by an agent invested with the moral authority of the community; they denounce the wrongdoer and his conduct as contrary to shared moral norms; and they ritualistically separate the wrongdoer from those who subscribe to such norms. It is not a condition of a successful degradation ceremony that it induce any particular belief or emotion on the part of the offender. We might expect the ceremony to cause shame—particularly if the offender identifies with the community that is denouncing him. But to lower the offender's social status within that community, it is enough that the affliction convey disapproval in terms that its members understand.

Whether particular afflictions have this effect obviously depends on the conventional signification of different actions within particular communities. Such understandings, moreover, are richly variant. This is part of the reason that shaming penalties assume such diverse forms.

Insofar as shaming penalties do successfully convey condemnation, substituting them for imprisonment does not invariably offend widespread expressive sensibilities. Accordingly, it should be politically acceptable to punish a wide array of offenses with shaming alone.

Indeed, the political acceptability of shaming penalties as an alternative sanction is nearly an established fact. Public opinion studies suggest that the public is prepared to endorse such penalties with enthusiasm, provided it can be shown that they really work. The actual behavior of judges and other democratically accountable officials backs up this finding. The use of such sanctions can only be expected to widen as their notoriety grows. . . .

82

CHRISTINE M. WISEMAN

Representing the Condemned: A Critique of Capital Punishment

Christine, this won't be an easy letter to write, but it's one I feel I must write. . . . I thank you for calling my family and talking to them. I am very concerned about my Mother and Barbara. I know it's not much, but all I can do is thank you for being there for them this next week. . . .

Love & respect,
Billy[1]

On Thursday, January 25, and Friday, January 26, 1996, the states of Delaware and Utah executed two more death row inmates. News accounts signaling the events opened with the gambit, "[j]ust as capital punishment was becoming somewhat routine, two unusual executions [are] set for this week—one by hanging, the other by firing squad. . . ."[2] I thought back once again to the early morning hours of February 16, 1995, when the State of Texas executed our client.[3] To us, it was anything but routine. Unfortu-

1Excerpt from the final letter written by Billy Conn Gardner to the author on February 11, 1995, shortly before his death. In our final meeting before his death, Billy Gardner waived his attorney-client privilege with respect to the matters discussed in this essay. This essay is dedicated to Nettie Gardner and Barbara Gray, Billy Gardner's mother and sister, two of the forgotten victims of capital punishment.

2Tony Mauro, *Hanging, Firing Squad Executions Set for This Week,* USA TODAY, Jan. 22, 1996, News, at 3A.

3Billy Conn Gardner was represented by Professor Wiseman from February, 1988, until his death on February 16, 1995. After he graduated from law school, Attorney David Bourne of the Milwaukee law firm Quarles & Brady remained with her as co-counsel on the case. Eventually, the firm adopted Gardner as its client as well.

nately, in the circus-like race to execute death row inmates, neither was it unusual.

We stood in the black rainy mist across the walkway from the Walls Unit in Huntsville, staring at the oldest prison in Texas. Pictures of it were plastered on the walls of local bars and on the silkscreened sweatshirts worn by their customers. We stared at the barbed wire, eerie yellow lights and girded towers manned by armed guards, and we wondered what purpose had been served by the execution of this fifty-one year old man. Governor George W. Bush had denied the petition for executive clemency six hours earlier.[4] Like others before him, he followed the ranks of those governors increasingly unwilling to suffer the political ramifications of extending clemency to death row inmates.[5]

There was nothing more we could do as lawyers so we stayed to do what we could as human beings. We stood in the rain, waiting for Billy Gardner's family to reappear from the Execution Chamber, our purpose now to lend a quiet dignity to the end of his life. As the moments ticked by, we stood side by side, saying nothing. The Walls Unit chaplain had told us that "it always rains in Texas when there's an execution." I wondered why no one got the picture. I thought with bitter regret about a criminal justice system which had failed miserably to protect another of its poor and powerless. It was a system in which we had played a pivotal role for seven years, but it was too little too late.

Billy Conn Gardner stood convicted of the capital murder of a cafeteria worker in Dallas, Texas on May 16, 1983.[6] The bullet punctured the worker's liver and she died eleven days later. Before she died, the victim, Thelma Catherine (Caty) Rowe, identified her assailant as a man over 6 feet in height with medium-length reddish-blond hair and a two-inch

---

[4]In Texas, the Governor, acting in concert with the State Board of Pardons and Parole, has the ability to commute a death sentence by act of executive clemency. *See* Daniel T. Kobil, *The Quality of Mercy Strained: Wresting the Pardoning Power from the King,* 69 TEX. L. REV. 569, 605 n. 233 and accompanying text (1991). Since 1976, however, not one appeal for executive clemency on grounds of innocence has succeeded in Texas. As described by one reporter, the process is one "where decisions are meted out by the governor and a parole board consisting of political appointees who follow no fixed set of procedures, are reluctant to second-guess the courts, and are accountable to no one." Susan Blaustein, *Witness to Another Execution,* HARPER'S MAGAZINE, May 1994, at 57. *See also,* Hugo Adam Bedau, *The Decline of Clemency in Capital Cases,* 18 N.Y.U. REV. L. & SOC. CHANGE 255, 257(1990–91)(Despite the diversity in clemency procedures among the states, all "are standardless in procedure, discretionary in exercise, and unreviewable in result.").

[5]During her term of office, Governor Ann W. Richards (1990–94) had granted a clemency hearing only twice. The first such hearing was ordered for Gary Graham, who is still alive. The second hearing was ordered for Vietnam Veteran Robert Black in response to a telephone call from the Vatican. Mr. Black's stay of execution was granted for only 30 days, however. He was later executed in 1992. *See* Joan M. Cheever, *An Appointment in the Death House: A Lawyer's Voyage on a Capital Case Comes to an End on an October Night in Texas,* NAT'L. L.J., Nov. 14, 1994, at A16. National data available from the Department of Justice's Bureau of Justice Statistics suggests that executive clemency has become a rarity. In the decade 1960 through 1970, for example, when statistics were first collected, death sentences numbered 1155, and commutations 182. In the decade 1979 through 1988, death sentences numbered 2535, but there were only 63 commutations. *See* Bedau, *supra* note 4, at 264.

Among the reasons offered to explain the decline in grants of clemency in capital cases is the observation that a governor might commit "political suicide" by granting clemency in a capital case. *See id.* at 268. Although there exist some notable exceptions, e.g., Governor Tony Anaya of New Mexico, who granted commutations to all six persons on death row in 1986, and Governor Richard Celeste of Ohio, who granted clemency in 1991 to 68 individuals, including eight death row inmates, both were serving final terms in office. *See* RANDALL COYNE & LYN ENTZEROTH, CAPITAL PUNISHMENT AND THE JUDICIAL PROCESS 644 (1994).

More recently, when Governor Jim Edgar of Illinois commuted the death sentence to life imprisonment without possibility of parole for Guinevere Garcia on Tuesday, January16, 1996, just fourteen hours before her scheduled execution, he realized that political fallout. In a statement read by his attorney, Governor Edgar reasoned that commutation was justified, not because Garcia "was a woman, or a battered and sexually abused woman. . . . It was just that it was not right, . . . as long as other people convicted of more heinous crimes have eluded the death penalty in Illinois." *See* Ted Gregory & Christi Parsons, *Edgar's Power Halts Execution of Garcia,* CHI. TRIB., Jan. 17, 1996, § 1, at 1. His announcement was met with "shock" by many Republicans in the Illinois General Assembly, who feared "Edgar's move could undercut the GOP's tough-on-crime campaign efforts in key legislative elections this fall that will determine which party will run the legislature for the next two years." Some Republicans even sought to distance themselves from Edgar, commenting publicly that it was "'his decision and his alone'" and signaled no "'red-letter day'" for death penalty opponents. *See* Rick Pearson, *Edgar's '94 Election Ad Echoes after Clemency,* CHI. TRIB., Jan. 17, 1996, § 2, at 1, 7. *See also,* Ted Gregory & Christi Parsons, *Garcia's Clemency Stirs Calls for New Laws,* CHI. TRIB., Jan. 18, 1996. § 2, at 1, 4.

[6]Trial transcripts supporting the facts recounted in this essay are on file with the author and in the Dallas County Courthouse under the case name, *State of Texas v. Billy Conn Gardner,* No. F-83-93161-JLR (265th Judicial District Court, Dallas County, Texas). The trial transcripts were filed on April 26, 1984. Other facts are supported by the transcripts of the Evidentiary Hearing conducted on October 20, 1988 and continued on December 12 and 13, 1988, before the Honorable John Ovard, 265th Judicial District Court, Dallas County, Texas, and filed on December 13, 1988.

red goatee. Billy Gardner stood 5 feet, 11 inches tall, but he had coal black hair and piercing black eyes. He had never worn facial hair, and no one at trial had been asked to explain the reddish-blond hair or the red goatee. The only disinterested eyewitness to the crime was a diminutive custodian from the high school who saw the assailant for two to four seconds standing outside the back door of the cafeteria. He stood six to ten feet away and testified that he took no particular note of the assailant since he thought the man was a school district worker—"out there with the yard pool or something." He also described the assailant as having sandy reddish hair and a little red goatee. His in-court identification of Billy Gardner was based on his personal assessment of what Gardner would look like with red hair and a red goatee. Yet he first identified Billy Gardner's picture from a photographic lineup some three months after the robbery. The police had shown him the photos while he was lying in a hospital bed suffering from a sickle cell crisis.

I thought again about all the arguments I had raised—legal arguments designed to get the state court, the federal district court and eventually the United States Supreme Court to focus on the fact that the wrong man stood convicted of Caty Rowe's murder. As defense counsel, we were well aware of the Texas courts' reluctance to deal with post-conviction claims of actual innocence.[7]

The damning evidence in Gardner's case, as in all too many which have preceded his,[8] was provided by the state's "star" witness, Melvin Sanders. In reality, of course, Sanders had few if any stellar qualities.

Melvin Sanders had fingered our client. Melvin Sanders testified at trial that the robbery was his idea since his wife Paula worked at the targeted cafeteria. He knew when and where the day's receipts would be counted. But he testified that he waited in the car while Billy went in to do the job. In fact, Melvin Sanders cut himself quite a deal before naming his accomplice. After police successfully prevented Sanders from getting probation on a pending forgery charge, prompted federal firearms authorities to file a case against him, convinced the district attorney in a nearby community to prosecute him for a distinct robbery, and threatened to file an action against his wife Paula in the matter, Sanders capitulated. And he named Billy Gardner because he owed Billy Gardner about $700 following a drug deal gone bad. In return for accusing Gardner of murder, Sanders was given testimonial immunity in the capital murder case, probation on the robbery charge, and dismissal of the firearms charge. In addition, his wife Paula was never charged in connection with Caty Rowe's murder. Billy's sister swore before the court that following Sanders' testimony at trial, she had overheard him at a restaurant during an adjournment laughing for her benefit about the fact that he had "pulled off" his testimony.[9] Sources tell us Sanders has since killed himself in a shootout with a bounty hunter because he had snitched on so many people that he figured he would "buy it" in prison anyhow.

The other "star" prosecution witness was Sanders' wife Paula, who worked at the targeted cafeteria. She had testified at trial that she simply could not identify the assailant because she only saw the back of the assailant's hand. Moreover, she was unaware that her husband Melvin Sanders was planning the robbery. Mr. Gardner's trial counsel never knew that Paula Sanders, who had worked at the cafeteria for only three to four months, had run to the cafeteria phone half a dozen times that afternoon, grabbing the phone before anyone else could answer it—that she was nervous and upset the whole day of the burglary—*and* that she sat for the entire encounter facing the assailant—because they never questioned *any* of Paula's co-workers who were present at the scene and who were listed on the police incident report. Instead they hired an investigator who talked with police and simply figured Billy

---

[7]Four death-row inmates in the last four years were found to be innocent and were released; at least four more have presented to the courts compelling claims of innocence. But their pleadings have been dismissed repeatedly because Texas law requires an inmate to produce new evidence of his innocence within thirty days of his conviction—an impossibly short time for a newly condemned person to procure trial transcripts (just preparing these often takes the court as long as thirty days), hire a new lawyer to reinvestigate the case, and file a motion for a new trial. *Blaustein, supra* note 4, at 57.

[8]*See* MICHEAL L. RADELET ET AL., IN SPITE OF INNOCENCE 43–59, 60–76 (1992). In Chapters 1 and 2 of their book, the authors illustrate both how false testimony which is deliberately fabricated by witnesses who are coached by the prosecution can convict an innocent man and how perjured testimony provided by the real assailant can lead to a defendant's wrongful conviction.

[9]*See* Aff. of Barbara Gray, dated July 7, 1988, filed as Exhibit D in *State of Texas v. Billy Conn Gardner,* No. F-83-93161-R. *See also,* Evidentiary Hr'g Tr., Oct. 20, 1988, at 288–89.

Gardner was "good for" the offense. The investigator never contacted any witnesses listed on the police incident report because he "only did what the attorney instructed me to do," and they had given him no instructions regarding such witnesses. In fact, the investigator never contacted the fact witnesses at all during the entire course of the trial, even when it became apparent that they would be called by the State of Texas. That investigator has since died.

And so, Billy Gardner went to his death proclaiming his innocence of a crime for which he was "justly" convicted.

THE RECURRING PROBLEM OF INNOCENCE

During this century alone, more than 7,000 men and women have been legally executed in the United States.[10] Two hundred fifty of those executions have occurred since the United States Supreme Court reinstated the death penalty[11] in *Gregg v. Georgia*.[12] Of those, at least seventy-three (including our client) were executed in Huntsville.[13] More to the point, however, during that same interim, some fifty-three capital defendants have been released from death row because of probable innocence.[14] That number represents nearly 2% of the people sitting on this nation's death rows.[15]

In October 1994, *Life Magazine* detailed five of the more recent occurrences. They included: Andrew Golden, who was released in November 1993 after spending 26 months on Florida's death row for the 1989 murder of his wife—the Florida Supreme Court eventually concluded that the prosecution had

---

[10] RADELET, *supra* note 8, at 19.

[11] Jack Hayes, et al., *Stolen Lives*, LIFE, Oct. 1994, at 64.

[12] 428 U.S. 153 (1976).

[13] When the numbers were tallied by a reporter in 1994, Texas had executed seventy-two men at Huntsville since 1976. That number represented twice as many executions as Florida, "the next most productive state in the execution market, and more than three times as many as in Virginia and Louisiana, which rank third and fourth." The author continued: "In the last two years, the rate of Texas executions has more than tripled, and the seventeen men executed in 1993 alone constitute nearly a fourth of those put to death since executions resumed in Texas in 1982." *Blaustein, supra* note 4, at 54. *See also,* David Margolick, *Texas Death Row Is Growing, But Fewer Lawyers Will Help,* N.Y. TIMES, Dec. 31, 1993, § b, at 1, 13. "For as long as anyone can remember, Texas's death row was the nation's largest; it lost that distinction only because it executed 17 prisoners in 1993—more than three times as many as any other state, and the most here since 1938." *Id.*

By 1995, statistics indicate that Texas had executed ninety-two persons. The southern states of Arkansas, Alabama, Florida, Georgia, Louisiana, Missouri, North Carolina, Texas, and Virginia account for 226 of the 266 people executed in the United States since 1976. *See* Tama Lewin, *Who Decides Who Will Die? Even within States, It Varies,* N.Y. TIMES, Feb. 23, 1995, at A1, A13.

[14] Hayes, *supra* note 11. *See also,* RADELET, *supra* note 8, at 282–356. While there have always been erroneous convictions, some of which resulted in executions, the authors factually document some thirty-nine situations since 1975–76 where a capital defendant, sentenced to death, has been released on grounds of innocence. Among those cases inventoried (including the state of conviction and year of release) were Randall Dale Adams (Texas, 1989); Jerry Banks (Georgia, 1980); Gary L. Beeman (Ohio, 1979); Jerry D. Bigelow (California, 1988); Clarence Lee Brandley (Texas, 1990); Anthony Silah Brown (Florida, 1986); Joseph Green Brown (Florida, 1987); Willie A. Brown and Larry Troy (Florida, 1987); Earl Patrick Charles (Georgia, 1978); James Creamer (Georgia, 1975); Perry Cobb and Darby Williams (a/k/a Darby Tillis) (Illinois, 1987); Robert Craig Cox (Florida, 1989); Henry Drake (Georgia, 1987); Neil Ferber (Pennsylvania, 1986); Charles Ray Giddens (Oklahoma, 1982); Thomas V. Gladish, Richard Wayne Greer, Ronald B. Keine, Clarence Smith (New Mexico, 1975); Timothy B. Hennis (North Carolina, 1989); Larry Hicks (Indiana, 1980); Anibal Jaramillo (Florida, 1981); William Riley Jent and Earnest Lee Miller (Florida, 1988); Lawyer Johnson (Massachusetts, 1982); Wilbert Lee and Freddie Pitts (Florida, 1975): Ralph W. Lobaugh (Indiana, 1977); Gordon Morris (Texas, 1976); Anthony Ray Peek (Florida, 1987); Juan F. Ramos (Florida, 1987); James Richardson (Florida, 1989); Johnny Ross (Louisiana, 1981); Bradley P. Scott (Florida, 1991); Charles Smith (Indiana, 1991); Delbert Tibbs (Florida, 1982); Jonathan Charles Treadaway, Jr. (Arizona, 1976).

In addition to this documentation, the National Coalition to Abolish the Death Penalty in Washington, D.C., listed 51 death row inmates who were freed between 1973 and May, 1994. One of those prisoners, also listed among the Radelet chronicles, was Delbert (the Reverend) Darby Tillis, a minister who frequently works in the Chicago offices of the Illinois Coalition Against the Death Penalty. Tillis had been convicted in 1979 for a double murder and robbery. He protested his innocence at trial, claiming perjured testimony. Eventually, he was released following a fourth retrial in 1987. Amid the testimony which exonerated him was that provided by a former assistant Cook County State's Attorney. *See* James Rowen, *Saved from Execution, He Saves Others,* MILWAUKEE JOURNAL SENTINEL, May 3, 1995, § A, at 1, 8.

Another of those prisoners was Joseph Green Brown, now known as Shabaka WaQlimi, who was released in 1987 after spending fourteen years on Florida's death row. *Id.* at 8. The latter appeared with the author at a community brainstorming conference on April 22, 1995 at St. Matthew's CME Church in Milwaukee, Wisconsin.

[15] Statistics demonstrate that as of April, 1994, there were 2804 men and 44 women awaiting execution in the United States. *See* COYNE & ENTZEROTH, *supra* note 5, at 55 (citing "Decisions of Death" by David Bruck, as updated by the publication Death Row, U.S.A. (NAACP Legal Defense and Educational Fund, Inc.)).

failed to prove her death was anything but an accident,[16] Walter McMillian, who spent six years on death row in Alabama for the murder of a dry cleaning store clerk in 1987—he was released on March 2, 1993 when all three prosecution witnesses finally recanted;[17] Sonia Jacobs, released from prison in 1992—she spent five years on death row in Florida before her sentence of execution by electrocution was commuted to life in 1981;[18] Muneer Deeb, a Jordanian immigrant who spoke little English and spent eight years on death row in Texas for the murder of three teenagers—he was eventually released on January 12, 1993;[19] and finally, there was Kirk Bloodsworth—after spending ten years on death row in Maryland, Bloodsworth was released by order of a circuit judge when DNA tests demonstrated that semen found in the underclothing of the dead child could not have been his.[20]

Since October 1994, when *Life* published its expose, those numbers have increased yet again. After spending five years on death row in Illinois for the 1988 slaying of William Dulin, Joseph Burrows was released from prison on September 8, 1994.[21] Although no physical evidence had linked Burrows to the crime, he was convicted on the testimony of two state witnesses who had received lighter sentences in exchange for their testimony. Later, one of the witnesses confessed that she alone had killed Dulin, and the other witness recanted his testimony, claiming he had been coerced by prosecutors and police officers.[22]

Likewise, Adolph Munson, first sentenced to Oklahoma's death row in 1984, was acquitted on April 5, 1995 after an appeals court ordered him retried amid allegations that the police had withheld hundreds of pages of exculpatory reports and photographs.[23] More recently, *The Chicago Tribune* detailed the travails of Rolando Cruz, a man who was finally released from Illinois' death row on Friday, November 3, 1995, after having spent 11 years on death row for the murder of a ten-year-old child which he did not commit. Prosecutors had ignored the conclusion of the Illinois State Police that another man committed the crime, had ignored the results of their own DNA tests excluding the defendant, and were finally taken to task when a sheriff's lieutenant admitted that he and other law enforcement officers had perjured themselves on the witness stand.[24]

That these persons were released is a triumph of appellate justice for them, but an unmistakable sign that the criminal justice system in this country has not been able to foreclose the inevitability of wrongful conviction. And, as defense counsel, the inevitability of wrongful conviction is my nightmare. My client Billy Gardner was not as fortunate as these, however, and the inevitability of wrongful conviction has now become my curse.

These people are not just anonymous numbers on someone's tally sheet of death row inmates; they are victims—every bit as much as the people whom they were accused of killing. These inmates are people who should never have been tried or people whose cases were plagued by reasonable doubt, but who did not have the resources to raise that reasonable doubt at trial. As I have stated to those persons aghast at the acquittal of O. J. Simpson, the tragedy is not that the criminal justice system works as it should for the rich man; the tragedy is that so often it does not work as it should for the poor. For Billy Gardner and a whole host of poor defendants, the system has collapsed. Visit this nation's death rows; you may spot one or

---

[16] *See* Golden v. State, 629 So.2d 109 (Fla. 1993).
[17] Hayes, *supra* note 11, at 66.
[18] *Id.* at 68.
[19] *Id.* at 70.
[20] *Id.* at 72–3.
[21] *After 5 Years, Death Row Inmate Is Freed by Another's Confession,* N.Y. Times, Sept. 12, 1994, § A, at 16.
[22] *Id.*
[23] *See* Richard L. Fricker, *State Falters in Retrial of Escaped Con,* ABA J., June 1995 at 38, 40. An earlier *ABA Journal* investigation of the Munson case discovered that information which pointed to another suspect had never been turned over to the defense. *See* Richard L. Fricker, *Reasonable Doubts,* ABA J., December 1993, at 38, 39. Among the evidence withheld from defense counsel were statements given by three individuals who said they had seen a white man in the store and a pickup truck parked outside shortly before the victim disappeared (Munson is black); 165 photographs taken by state investigators, one of which depicted a bullet hole larger than the .22 caliber slug both the police and the pathologist identified in the victim's body; and tires removed from Munson's car after he was arrested in California which were never returned to Oklahoma. Police indicated that a problem with a commercial airline had made it impossible to return the tires, even though Munson was flown back to Oklahoma in a private airplane. More importantly, however, photographs and tire-tread measurements taken at the crime scene clearly suggested the assailants used a pickup truck. *Id.* at 39–40.
[24] Maurice Possley, *The Nicarico Nightmare: Admitted Lie Sinks Cruz Case,* Chi. Trib., Nov. 5, 1995, § 1, at 1, 13. *See also,* Gera-Lind Kolarik, *DNA, Changed Testimony Gain Acquittal,* ABA J., Jan. 1996, at 34–5.

two monied people in Arizona or Illinois, but they are a rarity. This nation's thirty-eight death rows[25] are populated instead by people like Billy Gardner, whose father and cousin injected him with heroin at the age of nine to make him a pliant drug runner, whose father raped his younger sister, and whose mother was simply too poor to keep the man away from the home or obtain the necessary rehabilitative help for her son. But there is one other thing to note as well: the people on death row are disproportionately people of color. Statistics disclose, for example, that while only 12% of the United States population is African American, 46% of the death row population is African American.[26]

Moreover, nationwide studies reflect overall patterns of racial discrimination in capital sentencing. One of the most sophisticated studies was conducted by Professor David C. Baldus, who examined the Georgia capital sentencing process between 1973 and 1979. He examined over 2,000 cases and considered 230 non-racial variables. He found that Georgia defendants who were charged with killing white persons received the death penalty in 11% of the cases, but that defendants charged with killing black victims received the death penalty in only 1% of the cases. Put another way, a Georgia defendant charged with killing a white victim was 4.3 times more likely to receive a death sentence than a defendant charged with killing a black victim. Thus, the Baldus study concluded that black defendants who kill white victims have the greatest likelihood of receiving the death penalty.[27]

Beyond the Baldus study, there have been numerous others,[28] including a nationwide study conducted by Jim Henderson and Jack Taylor, reporters for the *Dallas Times Herald*. That study examined 11,425 capital murders from 1977 to 1984 and concluded that "the killer of a white is nearly three times more likely to be sentenced to death than the killer of a black in the 32 states where the death penalty has been imposed."[29] The study also disclosed that in Maryland, killers of white victims were eight times more likely to receive the death sentence than killers of black victims; that in Arkansas, killers of white victims were six times more likely to receive a sentence of death; and that in Texas, killers of white victims were five times as likely to be sentenced to death than killers of blacks.[30] Even more compelling, the General Accounting Office synthesized 28 different studies and found "a pattern of evidence indicating racial disparities in the charging, sentencing, and imposition of the death penalty after the *Furman* decision" in its February 1990 report.[31]

---

[25]As of April, 1994, 36 states had enacted capital punishment. *See* Coyne & Entzeroth, *supra* note 5, at 87–90. *See also,* State of Wisconsin Legislative Reference Bureau, Informational Bulletin 95–1, *Capital Punishment in Wisconsin and the Nation,* Apr. 1995, at 26–7 (prepared by A. Peter Cannon, Senior Research Analyst). Since 1994, that number has grown by two. The state of Kansas authorized capital punishment by lethal injection in 1994 when its governor allowed a bill to become law without her signature. In March 1995, the state of New York enacted legislation permitting capital punishment by lethal injection for the murder of a police officer, judge, or other criminal justice official; for contract and serial killings, torture killings or intentional murder during the course of a felony. *See id.* at 25. Alaska, Hawaii, Iowa, Maine, Massachusetts, Michigan, Minnesota, North Dakota, Rhode Island, Vermont, West Virginia, and Wisconsin have yet to follow suit, although legislation is currently pending in Wisconsin. *See e.g.,* S.B.1, 1995–96 Legislature, 1995 Wis. Laws 11.

[26]According to the NAACP Legal Defense and Educational Fund, Inc. statistics on the death row population in this country as of April, 1994, there were 1131 black inmates and 287 inmates who were classified as either Asian, Latino, Native American or "Unknown." These figures compare with the 1427 white inmates on death row and do not account for the death row inmates in the United States military (8) or in federal prisons (5). *See* Coyne & Entzeroth, *supra* note 5, at 87–90. Justice Marshall also noted this disparity: "A total of 3,859 persons have been executed since 1930, of whom 1,751 were white and 2,066 were Negro. Of the executions, 3,334 were for murder, 1,664 of the executed murderers were white and 1,630 were Negro; 455 persons, including 48 whites and 405 Negroes, were executed for rape. It is immediately apparent that Negroes were executed far more often than whites in proportion to their percentage of the population. Studies indicate that while the higher rate of execution among Negroes is partially due to a higher rate of crime, there is evidence of racial discrimination." Furman v. Georgia, 408 U.S. 238, 364 (Marshall, J., concurring).

[27]McCleskey v. Kemp, 481 U.S. 279, 286–87 (1987). *See also,* Ronald J. Tabak, *Is Racism Irrelevant? Or Should Fairness in Death Sentencing Act Be Enacted to Substantially Diminish Racial Discrimination in Capital Sentencing?,* 18 N.Y.U. Rev. L. & S. Change 777, 780–81 (1990–91).

[28]*See id.* at 780 n. 9.

[29]Jim Henderson & Jack Taylor, *Killers of Dallas Blacks Escape the Death Penalty,* Dallas Times Herald, Nov. 17, 1985, at 1. *See also,* Tabak, *supra* note 27, at 780 n. 10.

[30]*Id.*

[31]*See* U.S. General Accounting Office, Death Penalty Sentencing: Research Indicates Pattern of Racial Disparities 5 (Feb. 1990). The Report concluded that "[i]n 82 percent of the studies, race of victim was found to influence the likelihood of being charged with capital murder or receiving the death penalty, i.e., those who murdered whites were found to be more likely to be sentenced to death than those who murdered blacks. This finding was remarkably consistent across data sets, states, data collection methods, and analytic techniques." *Id.* (footnote omitted).

Furthermore, it appears that federal prosecutions reflect this same racial disparity in that federal prosecutors target blacks far more often than whites when seeking the death penalty for drug-related murders.[32] The House Judiciary Committee's civil and constitutional rights subcommittee reported in March 1994, that in the thirty-seven cases where federal prosecutors had sought the death penalty, twenty-nine were against blacks. Four other were against whites and four were against Hispanic defendants.[33] It is for these same reasons that Justices Brennan,[34] Marshall,[35] and most recently Justice Blackmun of the United States Supreme Court have rejected the constitutionality of capital punishment. Despite judicial efforts to devise legal formulae and procedural rules, the death penalty remains "fraught with arbitrariness, discrimination, caprice, and mistake."[36] Justice Blackmun has therefore termed capital punishment "an experiment that has failed."[37] (And lest you argue death to all first-degree murderers, like other hapless individuals who betray their own ignorance,[38] the Supreme Court struck that down in *Woodson v. North Carolina* as violative of individualized sentencing in 1976).[39]

INEFFECTIVE ASSISTANCE OF COUNSEL

There are other, equally compelling inequities that account for many of these egregious errors. As noted above, they are in large measure the product of a lack of resources, including those resources necessary to hire competent counsel. In Billy Gardner's case, his trial counsel had visited with him for fifteen minutes at most before jury selection in this capital case. Gardner informed us of that fact during our initial interview with him, but trial counsel had countered that the visits were much longer and more frequent. When we subpoenaed the jail records, we knew Billy had told us the truth. Those records reflected but one brief visit between the date of Gardner's arrest and the date of jury selection. Nor did trial counsel bother to interview witnesses at the scene who were listed on the police incident report.

Furthermore, although trial counsel knew that Billy Gardner was a drug addict, they were not aware prior to trial that he was a victim of what one doctor has since termed "catastrophic" child abuse, having been injected with heroin by his father at the age of nine to make him a pliant drug runner. There was no mental health expert and no opportunity to investigate the impact of those mitigating circumstances on Gardner's moral culpability for the offense. Gardner's sister responded to the family's dissatisfaction with trial counsel by investigating the costs of retaining private counsel. Yet she stopped her efforts when told that the minimum fee for a capital case like her brother's was $30,000.[40] But, of course, Billy Gardner is not alone.

The stories of ineffective assistance in capital cases are legion. While awaiting our client's execution

---

[32]*Report: Blacks Suffer Federal Death Penalty Bias,* CHI. TRIB., Mar. 16, 1994, § 1 at 8.

[33]*Id.*

[34]*See* Furman v. Georgia, 408 U.S. 238, 305 (1972) (Brennan, J., concurring) ("Death is an unusually severe and degrading punishment; there is a strong probability that it is inflicted arbitrarily; its rejection by contemporary society is virtually total; and there is no reason to believe that it serves any penal purpose more effectively than the less severe punishment of imprisonment."). *See also,* Gregg v. Georgia, 428 U.S. 153, 229–31 (1976) (Brennan. J., dissenting).

[35]*See Furman,* 408 U.S. at 364–66 (Marshall, J., concurring). *See also, Gregg,* 428 U.S. at 240–41 (Marshall, J., dissenting).

[36]Callins v. Collins, 114 S. Ct. 1127, 1129 (1994) (Blackmun, J., dissenting).

[37]
> From this day forward, I no longer shall tinker with the machinery of death. For more than 20 years I have endeavored—indeed, I have struggled—along with a majority of this Court, to develop procedural and substantive rules that would lend more than the mere appearance of fairness to the death penalty endeavor. Rather than continue to coddle the Court's delusion that the desired level of fairness has been achieved and the need for regulation eviscerated, I feel morally and intellectually obligated simply to concede that the death penalty experiment has failed. It is virtually self-evident to me now that no combination of procedural rules or substantive regulations ever can save the death penalty from its inherent constitutional deficiencies.

Id. at 1130 (Blackmun, J., dissenting).

[38]Rock County Assistant District Attorney Gerald A. Urbik, in a letter to the editor of the WISCONSIN LAWYER criticized the death row advocacy of this author as follows: "Wiseman contends that the death penalty cannot be administered in a nondiscriminatory manner. This is untrue, however. If every murderer convicted of first-degree intentional homicide was executed, there would be little if any room for discriminatory enforcement." *See This Prosecutor Wants the Death Penalty Reinstated,* 69 WISCONSIN LAWYER 2 (June 1995). One would hope that prosecutors who seek the reinstatement of capital punishment in Wisconsin would at least know the law.

[39]Woodson v. North Carolina, 428 U.S. 280, 303–05 (1976) (respect for human dignity underlying the Eighth Amendment requires judicial consideration of individual aspects of the defendant's character and the circumstances of the particular offense as a constitutionally indispensable part of the process of imposing the penalty of death; because the North Carolina statute impermissibly treats all persons convicted of a designated offense as members of a faceless, undifferentiated mass, it is unconstitutional).

in the wee morning hours of February 16, the chaplain at the Walls Unit in Huntsville told us that one Texas lawyer had ten clients currently facing execution in Huntsville. The *Wall Street Journal,* on September 7, 1994, reported that the strategy of Texas lawyer Joe Frank Cannon in capital cases was simple: "Work fast."[41] Mr. Cannon told reporter Paul Barrett that "[j]uries don't like a lot of questioning, all these jack-in-the-box objections, going into every detail, so I've never done it."[42] Instead, he boasts of hurrying through trials "like greased lightning."[43] Appointed by the Texas courts to represent defendants in capital cases at state expense, Cannon has defended eight men who are currently awaiting execution. His collection of ten death sentences is reportedly one of the largest among active defense lawyers.[44] Apparently proud that he spends little time at his office or the law library, Mr. Cannon also boasted, "'I'm not the sort of lawyer who takes a lot of notes.'"[45] A 1995 CNN televised presentation entitled, "On Penalty of Death," reported that in Harris County, Texas, the same county where Mr. Cannon has practiced law for 44 years,[46] fifteen people were sentenced to death in 1994. In each of those cases, the defendant was represented by court-appointed counsel. In another fifteen capital cases where the defendants had privately retained counsel, the district attorney never sought the death penalty in any one of them.[47]

Texas, however, is not the only state to have problems with incompetent lawyers in capital cases. Take the case of former lawyer James Venable in Alabama, reported in the February 1991 issue of the *ABA Journal.* When Aden Harrison Jr. was tried for murder in March 1986, he was represented by Mr. Venable, who was then 83 years old. According to the Fulton County Superior Court, Mr. Venable "slept a 'good deal' of the time."[48] Harrison's family, which is black, chose Venable because of his low fees. What they did *not* know was that James Venable was a former imperial wizard of the Ku Klux Klan. Asked by a reporter to confirm the allegation, Venable remarked, "I've been in the Klan since 1923, when it was over 10 million strong."[49]

In order to assess the quality of legal defense in capital cases in the nation's Death Belt, i.e., Alabama, Georgia, Florida, Louisiana, Mississippi and Texas, the *National Law Journal* in 1990 conducted a comprehensive study.[50] Incident to this investigation, reporters examined thousands of transcript pages in nearly 100 trials; interviewed scores of attorneys who had tried and lost capital cases; and questioned judges, prosecutors, and experts in capital law. Its key findings include the following: (1) trial lawyers who represented death row inmates in the particular six states have been disbarred, suspended or otherwise disciplined at a rate 3 to 46 times the discipline rates for those states; (2) more than half the defense counsel surveyed were handling their first capital case when their clients were convicted; (3) unrealistic statutory fee limits on defense representation act as disincentives to thorough trial investigation and preparation; (4) there are inadequate or non-existent standards for appointment of counsel which sometimes result in widely varying levels of experience in capital cases; (5) extant statutory standards for appointment of counsel are routinely ignored by trial judges and violations are viewed on appeal as "harmless error;" (6) capital trials are often completed in one to two days; (7) penalty phases of capital trials commence immediately after the guilt phase and last several hours at best; (8) little effort is expended to present mitigating evidence at the penalty phase; and (9) the Supreme Court test for effective assistance of counsel as articulated in *Strickland v. Washington*[51] is applied in meaningless fashion to capital cases.[52] The

---

[40]Texas has some public defenders, but for the most part, counsel in capital cases are appointed by the individual trial judges. *See* Marcia Coyle, et al., *Trial and Error in the Nation's Death Belt: Fatal Defense,* 12 NAT'L. L.J. 29, 32 (June 11, 1990). *See also,* Lewin, *supra* note 13, at A13. Texas requires no special training or qualification for capital defense lawyers and provides no counsel beyond the first appeal. *Id.*

[41]*See* Paul M. Barrett, *On the Defense: Lawyer's Fast Work on Death Cases Raises Doubts about System,* WALL STREET J., Sept. 7, 1994, § A, at 1.

[42]*Id.*

[43]*Id.*

[44]*Id.*

[45]*Id.* at A4.

[46]*Id.*

[47]Harris County, which includes the city of Houston, accounted for 113 of the 397 inmates on Texas' death row in 1995. Of the Texas inmates executed since 1976, 37 were from Harris County, where District Attorney Johnny B. Holmes, Jr., pronounces himself a "proud supporter of the death penalty." Lewin, *supra* note 13, at A1, A13.

[48]Paul Marcotte, *Snoozing, Unprepared Lawyer Cited,* ABA J., Feb. 1991, at 14.

[49]*Id.*

[50]*See* Coyle, *supra* note 40, at 29–42.

[51]466 U.S. 668 (1984).

[52]Coyle, *supra* note 40, at 30.

study concluded that "fairness is more like the random flip of a coin than a delicate balancing of the scales of justice."[53]

Moreover, at a time when Congress and the states are expanding their efforts to implement capital punishment, they are also cutting back on defense costs. For example, Congress has voted now to defund the Resource Centers across this country which operated in twenty of the death penalty states. These centers not only represented death row inmates directly, they also trained private lawyers to do the same.[54] In the state of Wisconsin, a growing number of legislators want to reinstate capital punishment, yet they sought to reduce funding for the office of the State Public Defender by $22 million. Whom do they expect will represent the bulk of the capital defendants? Politicized legislatures seek to reduce defense costs but only at the expense of justice for the poor and the innocent. And how many "innocent" death row inmates will it take before the public's lust for blood is sated? . . .

THE "ECONOMICS" OF CAPITAL PUNISHMENT

Beyond the powerful evidence which suggests that the death penalty cannot be meted out fairly as between black and white, rich and poor, there are other concerns. When the United States Supreme Court reinstated capital punishment in *Gregg v. Georgia,* it recognized that contemporary values reflected in public attitudes toward a given punishment played a role in Eighth Amendment analysis and application.[55] However, public perceptions of standards of decency do not conclude the constitutional analysis.[56] The penalty for an offense also must accord with "the dignity of man."[57] That is, a punishment may not be excessive;[58] it may not involve the unnecessary and wanton infliction of pain, nor may it be grossly disproportionate to the severity of the crime.[59] Furthermore, in order to obviate the "unnecessary and wanton infliction of pain," the sanction or penalty imposed cannot be so totally devoid of penological justification that it results in the gratuitous infliction of suffering.[60] It is at this juncture that deterrence becomes significant.

The Supreme Court responded to the issue of penological justification by suggesting two purposes for the death penalty: retribution and deterrence. However, while retribution is not a forbidden objective, nor one which is inconsistent with prevailing constitutional standards, it is no longer the dominant objective of American criminal law.[61] Considered in light of this legitimate objective, capital punishment has been viewed as an expression of society's outrage at particularly offensive conduct.[62] The constitutional question as yet unresolved is whether retribution alone suffices to bring a particular punishment in compliance with the Eighth Amendment. Thus, the proponents' insistence on deterrence. If indeed capital punishment serves no deterrent function or is no more a deterrent to violent crime than life imprisonment without possibility of parole, it may not withstand constitutional scrutiny. As Justice Marshall wrote in *Furman:*

> The fact that the State may seek retribution against those who have broken its laws does not mean that retribution may then become the State's sole end in punishing. Our jurisprudence has always accepted deterrence in general, deterrence of individual recidivism, isolation of dangerous persons, and rehabilitation as proper goals of punishment. Retaliation, vengeance, and retribution have been roundly condemned as intolerable aspirations for a government in a free society.
>
> *Punishment as retribution has been condemned by scholars for centuries, and the Eighth Amendment itself*

---

[53] *Id.*

[54] *See* Henry J. Reske, *The Politics of Death: Dispute over Defender Organizations Mirrors Debate over Death Penalty,* ABA J., Nov. 1995, at 20.

[55] Gregg v. Georgia, 428 U.S. 153, 173 (1976).

[56] *Id.* ("[O]ur cases also make clear that public perceptions of standards of decency with respect to criminal sanctions are not conclusive.").

[57] In *Furman v. Georgia,* the Supreme Court had concluded that the cruel and unusual punishments clause of the eighth amendment "'must draw its meaning from the evolving standards of decency that mark the progress of a maturing society.'" *Furman* 408 U.S. 238, 269–70 (1971) (Brennan, J., and Marshall, J. concurring) (quoting Trop v. Dulles, 356 U.S. 86, 100–101 (1958)). "The Clause 'may be therefore progressive, and is not fastened to the obsolete but may acquire meaning as public opinion becomes enlightened by a humane justice.'" *Id.* at 270 n. 10 (Brennan, J., concurring) (quoting Weems v. United States, 217 U.S. 349, 378 (1910)).

[58] *Gregg,* 428 U.S. at 173.

[59] *Id.*

[60] *Id.* at 183.

[61] *Id.* (citing Williams v. New York, 337 U.S. 241, 248 (1949)).

[62] *Gregg,* 428 U.S. at 184.

> *was adopted to prevent punishment from becoming synonymous with vengeance.*[63]

Indeed, Justice Marshall's sentiments are also reflected in the determination of the newly-created South African Supreme Court, which abolished capital punishment on June 6, 1995.[64] Announcing the unanimous decision of the court, Mr. Arthur Chaskalson, President of the Constitutional Court, stated:

> Retribution cannot be accorded the same weight under our Constitution as the right to life and dignity. . . It has not been shown that the death sentence would be materially more effective to deter or prevent murder than the alternative sentence of life imprisonment.[65]

As noted by Mr. Chaskalson, there is serious question whether capital punishment acts as a deterrence, either to society in general or to the individual criminal. The F.B.I. publication *Crime in the United States* demonstrates that 1994 murder rates in states which do not have the death penalty averaged 3.85 murders per 100,000 of population, while states which use the death penalty averaged 8.07 murders.[66]

Furthermore, capital punishment is more costly than any other option, including life imprisonment. North Carolina conducted a comprehensive study on the issue which was published in 1993. According to that study, North Carolina taxpayers pay $163,000 more to convict and execute an inmate than they do to convict and imprison an inmate for twenty years.[67] Estimates are that each execution in North Carolina costs the state approximately $2.16 million.[68] The *Miami Herald* has similarly reported that the State of Florida spends $3.2 million per execution.[69] Likewise, the Kansas Legislative Research Department has concluded that capital trials can last up to three-and-one-half times as long as non-capital trials, and in California, capital trials cost nearly six times more than other murder trials.[70] Texas taxpayers similarly spend an estimated $2.3 million for each capital prosecution, which is three times the cost of incarcerating an inmate in a maximum security prison for forty years.[71] As of 1993, Maryland has followed suit at a cost of approximately $2 million each year.[72] And finally, the State of New York estimates that costs incurred for attorneys' fees, investigators, experts and other trial and appellate costs would equal nearly $1.7 million per capital case.[73]

Comparable estimates for the cost of life imprisonment are much reduced. A 1985 California study estimated that sentencing a murderer to life imprisonment would cost approximately $440,000, whereas the New York State Defenders Association in 1982 estimated the cost of life imprisonment for forty years at just over $600,000.[74]

THE MORAL "COSTS" OF CAPITAL PUNISHMENT

With the abolition of capital punishment in South Africa on June 6, 1995,[75] the United States stands as one of only two industrialized nations which execute their citizens.[76] In this regard, the United States is allied with such stalwarts as China, Egypt, Iraq, Iran, Russia, and Singapore.[77] Most damning of all, however, we execute our children[78] and we execute our mentally infirm.

---

[63]*Furman,* 408 U.S. at [343] (Marshall, J., concurring) (emphasis added) (footnotes omitted).

[64]Howard W. French, *South Africa's Supreme Court Abolishes Death Penalty,* N.Y. TIMES, International Section A, at 3.

[65]*Id.*

[66]*See* Crime in the United States 1994 (Uniform Crime Reports) 60–67 (Nov. 19, 1995), published by the United States Department of Justice, Federal Bureau of Investigation. Statistics were calculated by averaging the 1994 murder rates per 100,000 population of those states which have the death penalty and the 1994 murder rates per 100,000 population of those states which do not have capital punishment.

[67]COYNE & ENTZEROTH, *supra* note 5, at 84.

[68]*Id.*

[69]D. Von Drehl, *Bottom Line: Life in Prison One-sixth As Expensive,* MIAMI HERALD, July 10, 1988, § A, at 12.

[70]*See* Wisconsin Department of Justice Fiscal Estimate, LRB 0270/1 SB1 (Jan. 26, 1995), at p. 3.

[71]COYNE & ENTZEROTH, *supra* note 5, at 84.

[72]*Id.* at 85.

[73]Wisconsin Department of Justice Fiscal Estimate, *supra* note [70], at 3.

[74]STATE OF WISCONSIN LEGISLATIVE REFERENCE BUREAU, *supra* note 25, at 18.

[75] French, *supra* note 78.

[76]*See* COYNE & ENTZEROTH, *supra* note 5, at 685, 703.

[77]*Id.* Even Russia, however, has only about 400 death row prisoners. That is one for every 370,000 Russians. By contrast, the United States has more than 2,700 death row prisoners. This represents one death row prisoner for every 97,000 Americans. *See On Death Row, It's Wait, Wait, Wait,* THE MILWAUKEE J., Dec. 28, 1992, § A, at 5.

[78]For an excellent discussion of the issues surrounding the juvenile death penalty, *see* Suzanne D. Strater, *The Juvenile Death Penalty: In the Best Interests of the Child?,* 26 LOY. U. CHI. L.J. 147 (1995).

Of the thirty-eight states which endorse capital punishment, sixteen authorize imposition of the death penalty as against juvenile offenders below the age of eighteen.[79] Nine states express no minimum age for the imposition of capital punishment, and three permit executions for offenders as young as fourteen or fifteen.[80]

The United States Supreme Court first confronted the constitutionality of executing juveniles in *Eddings v. Oklahoma*.[81] Although the Court there was able to avoid considering the issue of the defendant's age because the trial court had refused as a matter of law to consider other relevant mitigating evidence,[82] it faced the issue squarely six years later in *Thompson v. Oklahoma*.[83] In Thompson, a five-member plurality of the Court reversed the death penalty as assessed against a fifteen-year-old defendant, but only four members of the majority found that the execution of anyone under the age of sixteen was unconstitutional as against contemporary values.[84]

The Oklahoma statute at issue authorized capital punishment for murder, but did not specify any minimum age at which the commission of murder might lead to the imposition of death.[85] The plurality reasoned that evolving standards of decency, as reflected by state statutes and the sentencing patterns of capital juries, prohibited the execution of a person under the age of sixteen at the time of his or her offense.[86] Its conclusion in this regard was supported by the juvenile's reduced culpability and the failure of the penological purposes of retribution or deterrence when the penalty of death is exacted against such young offenders.[87]

However, at least one justice who joined in reversing the sentence was reserved about the breadth of the *Thompson* holding. Justice Sandra Day O'Connor noted that because Oklahoma's statutes did not specify a minimum age for capital punishment, yet separately provided that fifteen-year-old murder defendants might be treated as adults in some circumstances, there existed a risk that the Oklahoma legislature did not intend that the waiver of a juvenile into adult court should also expose the juvenile to capital punishment.[88] Under such circumstances, the execution of a fifteen-year-old could not be constitutional. She intimated, however, that where that risk is obviated by a statute which specifies a minimum age for the imposition of capital punishment, the execution of younger offenders might yet be constitutional.[89] Moreover, in *Stanford v. Kentucky*,[90] decided less than two years later, the Supreme Court used the same factors delineated in *Thompson* to arrive at a determination that there exists no national consensus against sentencing to death juveniles who are sixteen or seventeen years of age at the time of the offense.

According to statistics compiled by Amnesty International in 1994, only seven countries had executed persons under the age of eighteen for capital crimes within the previous five years. These included Iran, Iraq, Nigeria, Pakistan, Saudi Arabia, Yemen—and the United States.[91] Moreover, although the United Nations General Assembly had passed the *Convention on the Rights of the Child* on November 20, 1989,[92] the United States did not sign the Convention until February 16, 1995.[93] Among the Convention's provisions is Article 37(a), which provides

[79]These are Alabama, Arkansas, Delaware, Georgia, Indiana, Kentucky, Louisiana, Mississippi, Missouri, Nevada, New Hampshire, North Carolina, Oklahoma, Texas, Virginia, and Wyoming. *See* STATE OF WISCONSIN LEGISLATIVE REFERENCE BUREAU, BULL. 95-1, *supra* note 25, at 26–7.

[80]*Id.* The latter group includes Arkansas (14), Louisiana (15) and Virginia (15).

[81]455 U.S. 104 (1982).

[82]*Id.* at 112–13. The court ruled that the trial judge had violated the constitutional premise of Lockett v. Ohio, 438 U.S. 586 (1978), when it refused as a matter of law to consider Eddings' turbulent family history and serious emotional disturbance.

[83]487 U.S. 815 (1988).

[84]These were Justices Stevens, Brennan, Marshall and Blackmun.

[85]*Thompson,* 487 U.S. at 857 (O'Connor, J., concurring).

[86]*Id.* at 821–33.

[87]*Id.* at 833–38.

[88]*See id.* at 857 (O'Connor, J., concurring).

[89]*See id.* at 857–58 (O'Connor, J., concurring). ("In this unique situation, I am prepared to conclude that petitioner and others who were below the age of 16 at the time of their offense may not be executed under the authority of a capital punishment statute that specifies no minimum age at which the commission of a capital crime can lead to the offender's execution.").

[90]492 U.S. 361 (1989).

[91]*See* Robert A. Jordan. *A Cry for Death—To the Death Penalty,* BOSTON GLOBE, Jan. 23, 1994, Focus, at 71. Amnesty International had argued that "the USA is one of only seven countries worldwide to have executed people in the last five years for crimes committed while they were still minors under 18—the others are Iran, Iraq, Nigeria, Pakistan, Saudi Arabia and Yemen."

[92]G.A. Res. 44/25, U.N. Doc. A/Res/44/25 (1989), *reprinted in* 28 I.L.M. 1448, 1456–76 (1989), *addendum* in 29 I.L.M. 1340 (1990).

[93]Madeleine Albright, United States designate to the United Nations signed the Convention on Thursday, February 16, 1995. *U.S. Finally Signs Pact on Rights for Children,* SAN DIEGO UNION-TRIB., Feb. 17, 1995, at A12.

that "[n]either capital punishment nor life imprisonment without possibility of release shall be imposed for offenses committed by persons below eighteen years of age. . . ."[94] Although 181 other nations have done so, the United States Senate has yet to ratify the Convention,[95] which has been opposed by various senators who cite the death penalty prohibition, among others.[96]

The United States' stance on the execution of juveniles has also subjected it to criticism from international human rights experts. When it acceded to the International Covenant on Civil and Political Rights in 1992, the United States reserved, as against Article 6 of the Covenant, the right to impose capital punishment on "persons below 18 years of age."[97] The United States Government had argued that its reservation expressed the will of the majority and was constitutional. When filing its responsive report before members of the United Nations Human Rights Committee, however, committee member P. N. Ghagwati of India chastened John Shattuck, Assistant United States Secretary of State. Ghagwati argued that defending the death penalty as a democratic expression of the majority was "an explanation but not a justification."[98] Similar objections to the United States report were lodged by representatives from Chile, Australia, Cyprus and Venezuela. The latter cautioned that the United States "should not end up being the last country to ensure the fundamental right to life."[99]

Consistent with its ambivalence toward juvenile executions, the United States Supreme Court refused to ban the execution of mentally disabled persons in *Penry v. Lynaugh.*[100] Rejecting public opinion polls conducted in Florida and Georgia as well as the arguments of the American Association on Mental Retardation, the Supreme Court concluded that there existed insufficient evidence of a national consensus against executing mentally retarded people convicted of capital offenses. Thus, such executions could not be categorically prohibited by the Eighth Amendment on that ground.[101] Fearful that any such determination would have a disempowering effect if applied in other areas of the law,[102] the Court instead left to a case-by-case determination whether individual mentally retarded defendants lacked "the cognitive, volitional and moral capacity to act with the degree of culpability associated with the death penalty."[103] It is thus possible, under the American scheme, to execute a person who is mentally retarded by clinical standards but who is deemed by a jury to act with a legal degree of culpability.

SOME TOUGH FINAL QUESTIONS

Society has a moral right to protect itself, but if it can do so by imprisoning its most dangerous members for life, the principle of nonmaleficence certainly precludes it from doing any more. Though some would argue that life without possibility of parole is less merciful than death,[104] I have yet to converse with a death row inmate who would trade the continued hope of a claim of innocence for the opportunity to end it all. And somehow, a moral society must find a way to deal with its "problems," particularly its "problem children," short of exterminating them.

A person with far more experience than I has cogently expressed these sentiments. Sister Helen Prejean, author of *Dead Man Walking*[105] and consultant for the movie of the same name,[106] responded during an interview that capital punishment is an act of murder which contributes to the moral deterioration of society. In her words, it "let[s] the behavior of the criminal be the norm which we imitate."[107] She also reserves a just anger for the politicians who pander to the public's fear of crime by "celebrating" a

[94] *See supra* note [93].
[95] *See* David L. Rubin, *Helping Children,* CHI. TRIB., Jan. 19, 1996, Commentary, at 18.
[96] *See* Jessie Helms, Senator, Senate Foreign Relations, Congressional Press Release, June 14, 1995. Sixteen other senators joined Senator Helms calling on President Clinton not to send the United Nations Convention on the Rights of the Child to the Senate.
[97] *See* Frank Ching, *U.S. Role on Rights Reversed: UN Committee Members Criticize Washington's Record,* FAR E. ECON. REV., June 22, 1995, at 40.
[98] *Id.*
[99] *Id.*
[100] 492 U.S. 302 (1989).
[101] *Id.* at 335.
[102] *Id.* at 340.
[103] *Id.* at 338.
[104] *See* Peter Kendall & Paul Galloway, *The Quality of Mercy: Life Sentence Strains Meaning of Clemency*, CHI. TRIB., § 1 at 1.
[105] SISTER HELEN PREJEAN, DEAD MAN WALKING (1993).
[106] James Rowen, *Hope and the Condemned,* MILWAUKEE J. SENTINEL, Jan. 23, 1996, at E1.
[107] *Id.* at E4.

few cases when they know capital punishment is void of any deterrent value.[108] "'It keeps them from having to deal with the real sources of crime [such as poverty], which are complex and long-term.'"[109]

With the increased public fervor to kill criminals and kill them sooner after conviction, we clearly run the increased risk of executing the wrongfully convicted. To my Christian brethren, I offer this analogy:

> He stood before Pontius Pilate, accused of high treason and blasphemy — proclaiming Himself a King in derogation of Caesar and of Herod. The State had its laws, and the people of Judea agreed that they were just laws. After all, it was important to the survival of those people that they be protected from profligate kings who might form sinister groups of zealots and threaten the welfare of the State. Some might argue that treason to such a society was as significant a crime as murder is to us. And so evidence was taken before the Sanhedrin and before the Procurator Pilate. And the public sought its just sentence under the law—death.
>
> Was it a legitimate exercise of state power under the Law? Of course. Was it carried out according to the technicality demanded by the Law? Absolutely. Was there evidence to support the conviction? Beyond a reasonable doubt. Did the people of Judea act within their rights to demand His death to assuage the outrage committed against their society? Surely. Just as our society purports to act within its legal and moral rights when it demands the death of one person to avenge another. Just as Judean society demanded the death of Christ to avenge the treason He had committed under their laws. It is fair for us; it was fair for them.

Under these circumstances, it seems to me there is only one relevant question to ask: would we kill Him again?

And to those for whom that message holds no particular significance but who are yet willing to risk sacrificing a few innocents to bring justice to the guilty, I have this challenge. If you are indeed willing to take the risk of killing an innocent, then you take it. You substitute your son, your daughter, your brother, your innocent, for my client. Because his mother and sister were not willing to take that risk.

---

[108] *Id.*
[109] *Id.*

83

MARTHA C. NUSSBAUM

Equity and Mercy

(PPA, 191.)

. . . There is a puzzle in the evidence for ancient Greek thought about legal and moral reasoning. Two concepts that do not appear to be at all the same are treated as so closely linked as to be aspects of the same concept, and introduced together by one and the same moral term. The moral term is *epieikeia.*[1] The concepts are the two that I have already identified as my theme: the ability to judge in such a way as to respond with sensitivity to all the particulars of a person and situation, and the "inclination of the mind" toward leniency in punishing—equity and mercy.[2] From the beginning, the idea of flexible particularized judgment is linked with leniency. *Epieikeia,* which originally designated the former, is therefore said to be accompanied by the latter; it is something mild and gentle, something contrasted to the rigid or harsh. The Herodotean father, . . . contrasts the notion of strict retributive justice with *epieikeia,* at a time when that word was already clearly associated with situational appropriateness.[3] The orator Gorgias, praising the civic character of soldiers fallen in battle, says of them that "on many occasions they preferred the gentle equitable *(to praon epieikes)*

---

[1] For an excellent discussion of the term and its philosophical and legal history in Greece and Rome, see Francesco D'Agostino, *Epieikeia: Il Tema Dell'Equità nell'Antichità Greca* (Milan: A. Giuffre, 1973). An excellent study that focuses on fourth-century B.C. oratory and its relationship to Aristotle is John Lawless, *Law, Argument and Equity in the Speeches of Isaeus,* Ph.D. diss., Brown University, 1991. Both D'Agostino and Lawless have extensive bibliographies. *Epieikeia* is usually translated into Latin by *clementia* (see below). Modern scholars generally render it into German with "Billigkeit," Italian by "equità," French by "équité" or (translating the Latin) "clémence."

[2] Both equity and mercy can be spoken of as attributes of persons, as features of judgments rendered by a person, or as moral abstractions in their own right. Thus a person may be praised as *epieikês;* his or her judgments or decisions display *to epieikes,* or show a respect for *to epieikes.*

[3] Hdt. III.53; for discussion, see D'Agostino, *Epieikeia,* p. 7. See also Soph. fr. 770 (Pearson), which contrasts "simple justice" *(tên haplôs dikên)* with both equity and grace *(charis).* All translations from the Greek are my own.

to the harshly stubborn just *(tou authadous dikaiou)*, and appropriateness of reasoning to the precision of the law, thinking that this is the most divine and most common law, namely to say and not say, to do and to leave undone, the thing required by the situation at the time required by the situation."[4] He too, then, links the ability to do and say the right thing in the situation with a certain mildness or softness; opposed to both is the stubborn and inflexible harshness of law. By this time, the original and real etymology of the word *epieikeia*—from *eikos*, the "plausible" or "appropriate,"[5]—is being supplemented by a popular derivation of the term from *eikô*, "yield," "give way." Thus even in writing the history of the term, Greek thinkers discover a connection between appropriate judgment and leniency.[6]

The puzzle lies, as I have said, in the unexplained connection between appropriate situational judgment and mercy. One might well suppose that a judgment that gets all the situational particulars correct will set the level of fault sometimes high up, sometimes low down, as the situation demands. If the judgment is a penalty-setting judgment, it will sometimes set a heavy penalty and sometimes a light one, again as the situation demands. If the equitable judgment or penalty are being contrasted with a general principle designed beforehand to fit a large number of situations—as is usually the case—then we might expect that the equitable will sometimes be more lenient than the generality of the law, but sometimes harsher. For, as that not-very-merciful philosopher Plato puts it in the *Laws*, sometimes the offender turns out to be unusually good for an offender of that sort, but sometimes, too, unusually bad.[7] Plato has a modern ally in Justice Scalia, who feels that it is absurd that aggravation and mitigation should be treated asymmetrically in the law. The very same requirements should hold for both; presumably, once we begin looking at the specific circumstances, we will be about as likely to find grounds for the one as for the other.[8]

But this is not what many Greek and Roman thinkers seem to think. They think that the decision to concern oneself with the particulars is connected with taking up a gentle and lenient cast of mind toward human wrongdoing. They endorse the asymmetry that Justice Scalia finds absurd and incoherent. We must now ask on what grounds, and with what rationality and coherence of their own, they do so. . . .

So far we have been dealing only with a contrast between the equitable and the just. Justice itself is still understood as strict retribution, and therefore the equitable, insofar as it recognizes features of the particular case that the strict law does not cover, stands in opposition to the just. But justice or *dikê* is by the fifth century a venerated moral norm, associated in general with the idea of giving to each his or her due. We would expect, then, as the conflict between equity and strict retributive justice assumed prominence, an attempt to forge a new conception of justice, one that incorporates the insights of equity. This project was pursued to some extent by Plato, in his late works the *Statesman* and the *Laws*.[9] Even more significant for our purposes, it was pursued, albeit unsystematically, by the Attic orators in their

---

[4]Gorgias, *Epitaphios*, fragment Diels-Kranz 82B6. The passage has occasioned much comment and controversy: see D'Agostino, *Epieikeia*, p. 28ff. for some examples. It seems crucial to understand the passage as pertaining to the civic virtue of the fallen, not their military attributes.

[5]See P. Chantraine, *Dictionnaire etymologique de la langue grecque: Histoire des mots*, vol. 2 (Paris: Klinksieck, 1970), p. 355. For other references, see D'Agostino, *Epieikeia*, pp. 1–2, n. 3. *Eikos* is the participle of *eoika*, "seems." (The English word "seemly" is an instructive parallel.) In early poetry, the opposite of *epieikes* is *aeikes*, "outrageous," "totally inappropriate," "horrible."

[6]In addition to the passages discussed below, see Pseudo-Plato, *Definitiones* 412A, the first known definition of *epieikeia*, which defines it as "good order of the reasoning soul with respect to the fine and shameful," as "the ability to hit on what is appropriate in contracts," and also as "mitigation of that which is just and advantageous."

[7]Plato, *Laws* 867d, on regulations concerning the recall of an exiled homicide.

[8]Justice Scalia, in *Walton v. Arizona:* "Our cases proudly announce that the Constitution effectively prohibits the States from excluding from the sentencing decision *any* aspect of a defendant's character or record or *any* circumstance surrounding the crime: [for example] that the defendant had a poor and deprived childhood, or that he had a rich and spoiled childhood" (at 3062).

[9]See *Statesman* 294A–95A, *Laws* 757E, 867D, 876A–E, 925D–26D. Like Aristotle, Plato recognizes the importance of *epieikeia* both in the judgment of whether a certain offense was committed and in the assessment of penalties. He suggests that laws are written deliberately in such a way as to leave gaps to be filled in by the judgment of judges or juries. He compares the prescriptions of law to the general instructions that an athletic trainer has to give when he cannot deal with each pupil one by one and also to a trainer or a medical doctor who has to go out of town and therefore leaves instructions that cannot anticipate all the circumstances that may arise. This being so, it is in the spirit of law that when one *does* look into the particular case, one will modify the prescription to suit the differing conditions.

arguments over particular cases in front of citizen juries."[10] But it was Aristotle who made the major contribution.

Aristotle's discussion of the equitable in the *Nicomachean Ethics* occurs within his account of justice. It begins with an apparent dilemma. The *epieikes,* he says, is neither strictly the same as the just nor altogether different in kind (*EN* 1137a33–4). On the one hand, it looks as if it would be strange to separate *epieikeia* from justice, for we praise both people and their judgments for the quality of *epieikeia,* recognizing it as a normatively good thing. But in that case it will be odd if *epieikeia* turns out to be altogether opposed to the just. Then we would either have to say that justice is not a normatively good quality, or withdraw our normative claims for *epieikeia* (1137a34–b8).[11] Aristotle's solution to the dilemma is to define equity as a kind of justice, but a kind that is superior to and frequently opposed to another sort, namely strict legal justice (1137b8ff.). Equity may be regarded as a "correcting" and "completing" of legal justice.[12]

The reason for this opposition, he continues, is that the law must speak in general terms, and therefore must err in two ways, both leaving gaps that must be filled up by particular judgments, and sometimes even getting things wrong. Aristotle says that this is not the fault of the lawgiver, but is in the very nature of human ethical life; the "matter of the practical" can be grasped only crudely by rules given in advance, and adequately only by a flexible judgment suited to the complexities of the case. He uses the famous image of the good architect who does not measure a complicated structure (for example a fluted column) with a straightedge. If he did, he would get a woefully inadequate measurement. Instead he uses a flexible strip of metal that "bends to the shape of the stone and is not fixed" (1137b30-32). Exactly in this way, particular judgments, superior in flexibility to the general dictates of law, should bend round to suit the case.[13]

[10]See Lawless, *Law, Argument and Equity,* with comprehensive bibliography; for some particulars, see below.

[11]Strictly speaking, there is another possibility: that they are both valuable norms that pervasively conflict in their requirements. Aristotle does recognize contingent conflicts of obligation, but not this more deep-seated value conflict.

[12]*Epanorthôma* suggests both things: the image is of straightening up something that has fallen over or gone crooked a bit. Equity is putting law into the condition to which it aspires in the first place.

Aristotle ends the discussion with some remarks that seem ill-suited to their context, but by now we should be prepared to understand how they fit in:

> It is also clear from this [account of the equitable] what sort of person the equitable person is. For a person who chooses and does such things, and who is not zealous for strict judgment in the direction of the worse, but is inclined to mitigation, even though he can invoke the law on his side—such a person is equitable, and this trait of character is equity, being a kind of justice and not a distinct trait of character. (1137b34–1138a3)

Here Aristotle alludes to and endorses the tradition that links perception of the particular with mitigation, and by now we can see on what grounds he does so. But Aristotle makes a new contribution, for he insists that this is the way a truly *just* person is. In keeping with his insistence throughout his ethical and political writings that justice, as a virtue of character, is a peculiarly human virtue, one that gods neither possess nor comprehend, and indeed would think "ridiculous" (*EN* 1178b11), he now gives the just a definition suited to an imperfect human life.[14]

In the *Rhetoric* discussion of *epieikeia,* having given a very similar account of the equitable as that which corrects or supplements—and thereby fulfills—the written law, Aristotle adds a somewhat more detailed account of equitable assessment, telling us that the equitable person is characterized by a sympathetic understanding of "human things." He uses the word *suggnômê,* "judging with." He links this ability with particular perception, and both of these with the ability to classify actions in accordance with the agent's motives and intentions (1374b2–10).[15]

The logic of these connections seems to be as follows. To perceive the particular accurately, one must "judge *with*" the agent who has done the alleged

[13]On the role of this passage in Aristotle's ethical theory generally, see my essay "The Discernment of Perception: An Aristotelian Model for Public and Private Rationality," in *Love's Knowledge: Essays on Philosophy and Literature* (New York: Oxford University Press, 1990). There I discuss in greater detail Aristotle's reasons for thinking that general rules cannot be sufficient for the complexities of particular cases.

[14]See *EN* VII.1 on ethical excellence in general; *Pol.* I.1 on the social excellences, and *EN* X.8, 1178a9–b18 on virtue and justice as purely human and not divine.

[15]Cf. also *EN* 1143a19–20, connecting *suggnômê* and equity, and both with perception of the particular; cf. also *EN* 1110a24–25, 1111a1–2, on *suggnômê* in tragic situations.

wrong. One must, that is, see things from that person's point of view, for only then will one begin to comprehend what obstacles that person faced as he or she acted. In this sense, it takes *suggnômê* to deliver a "correct discrimination" of the equitable. When one looks at the person's case with *suggnômê,* certain distinctions that do not play a part in the archaic conception of *dikê* assume a remarkable salience. Equity, like the sympathetic spectatorship of the tragic audience, accepts Oedipus's plea that the ignorant and nonvoluntary nature of his act be acknowledged; it acknowledges, too, the terrible dilemmas faced by characters such as Agamemnon, Antigone, and Creon, and the terrible moral defectiveness of all their options. Recognizing the burden of these "human things," the equitable judge is inclined not to be "zealous for strict judgment in the direction of the worse," but to prefer merciful mitigation.

I have already illustrated Aristotle's argument by alluding to tragedy and tragic spectatorship. And since I shall go on to develop my own account of the equitable with reference to literature, it seems well worth pointing out that Aristotle's account of *suggnômê* and *epieikeia* in these passages has close links with his theory of tragedy. For in his theory the spectator forms bonds of both sympathy and identification with the tragic hero.[16] This means that "judging with" is built into the drama itself, into the way in which the form solicits attention. If I see Oedipus as one whom I might be, I will be concerned to understand how and why his predicament came about; I will focus on all those features of motive and agency, those aspects of the unfortunate operations of chance, that I would judge important were I in a similar plight myself. I would ask *how* and *why* all this came about, and ask not from a vantage point of lofty superiority, but by seeing his tragedy as something "such as might happen" in my own life.[17] Tragedy is thus a school of equity, and therefore of mercy. If I prove unable to occupy the equitable attitude, I will not even enjoy tragedy, for its proper pleasure requires emotions of pity and fear that only *suggnômê* makes possible.

Aristotle's attitude to law and equity was not simply a theoretical fiction. There is evidence that it both shaped legal practice and, even more clearly, built upon an already developed and developing tradition of Athenian legal thought.[18] We have, of course, almost no records of the actual outcomes of jury trials, and no record at all of the deliberations of jurors. The process did not encourage lengthy or communal deliberation, as each juror cast a separate vote after hearing the various arguments, apparently without much mutual consultation.[19] We do, however, have many examples of persuasive speeches delivered to such juries. Since the orator's reputation rested on his ability to persuade a jury of average citizens chosen by lot, we can rely on these speeches for evidence of widespread popular beliefs about legal and ethical concepts. These speeches show the orators relying on a concept of law and even of justice that is very much like the one that Aristotle renders explicit and systematic. Thus litigants frequently call for a justice tailored to the circumstances of their own case, and frequently use the expression *ta dikaia* ("those things that are just") in that sense.[20] They often proceed as if the written law is understood to be a set of guidelines with gaps to be filled in or corrected by arguments appealing to the notion of equity.[21] In this

[16]See Stephen Halliwell, *Aristotle's Poetics* (London: Duckworth, 1986), and "Pleasure, Understanding, and Emotion in Aristotle's Poetics," in *Essays on Aristotle's Poetics,* ed. A. Rorty (Princeton: Princeton University Press, 1992), 241–60.

[17]See *Poetics,* ch. 9, and the excellent discussion in Halliwell, "Pleasure." Aristotle remarks that neither pity nor fear will be experienced by a person who believes that he or she is above the uncertainties of life and can suffer no serious reversal. See *Rhet.* 1382b30ff., 1385b21–22, 31: he calls this state of mind a *hubristikê diathesis,* an "overweening disposition."

[18]Among the legal and rhetorical figures mentioned, Lysias predates Aristotle and is active in the late fifth century, while both Isaeus and Isocrates are contemporaries of Aristotle; their period of activity overlaps with the likely period of composition of Aristotle's *Rhetoric,* which is prior to Aristotle's first departure from Athens in 347. Isaeus's earliest and latest works, for example, can be dated approximately to 389 and 344/3 B.C.

[19]On all this, see Lawless, *Law, Argument and Equity,* with copious references to sources ancient and modern.

[20]See Michael Hillgruber, *Die zehnte Rede des Lysias: Einleitung, Text und Kommentar mit einem Anhang über die Gesetzesinterpretation bei den attischen Rednern* (Berlin and New York: Walter de Gruyter, 1988), 116–17. Hillgruber cites passages in the orators where an appeal to *ta dikaia* is used to persuade the jurors that obedience to the letter of the law is not required by their oath. These passages are: Andocides 1.31, Lysias 15.8, Demosthenes 21.4, 21.212, 23.194, 24.575, [Dem.] 58.61. Lawless, *Law, Argument and Equity,* p. 78, discusses this material and adds Isaeus 1.40 to the list.

[21]See K. Seeliger, "Zur Charackteristik des Isaios," *Jahrb. für Philologie* 113 (1876): 673–79, translated in Lawless, *Law, Argument and Equity:* "The principle of equity is almost always maintained, while the letter of the law is not infrequently circumvented, however much the orator is accustomed to holding his opponents to it."

process, frequent appeal is made to the jurors' sense of fairness, as if, once the particular circumstances of the case are understood, they can be expected to see that justice consists in an equitable determination.

This is a deep insight, one that I support. For it seems wrong to make a simple contrast between justice and equity, suggesting that we have to choose between the one and the other.[22] Nor, in a deep sense, do we have to choose between equity and the rule of law as understandings of what justice demands. The point of the rule of law is to bring us as close as possible to what equity would discern in a variety of cases, given the dangers of carelessness, bias, and arbitrariness endemic to any totally discretionary procedure. But no such rules can be precise or sensitive enough, and when they have manifestly erred, it is justice itself, not a departure from justice, to use equity's flexible standard.

We are still not all the way to a doctrine of mercy. For what Aristotle recommends is precise attention to the circumstances of offense and offender, both in ascertaining whether or not there is any guilt and in assessing the penalty if there is. He is prepared to let people off the hook if it can be shown that their wrongdoing is unintentional, or to judge them more lightly if it is the result of something less than fully deliberate badness. But the point of this is to separate out the fully and truly guilty from those who superficially resemble them. In effect, we are given a more precise classification of offenses, a classification that takes intention and motive into account. But once a particular offense is correctly classified, the offender is punished exactly in proportion to the actual offense.

By contrast to the archaic conception of justice, this is indeed merciful, but it does not suffice, I think, for all that we mean by mercy, which seems to involve a gentleness going *beyond* due proportion, even to the deliberate offender. With his emphasis on sympathetic understanding, Aristotle is on his way to this idea. And he insists that the virtuous disposition in the area of retributive anger is best named "gentleness" (using the same word that Gorgias had used in connection with *epieikeia*). He stresses that "the gentle person is not given to retribution [*timôrêtikos*], but is rather inclined to sympathetic understanding [*suggnômonikos*]" (*EN* 1126a2–3). But retribution will still play an important role, where the circumstances demand it. For "people who do not get retributively angry[23] at those at whom they should look like fools. . . . For they seem to have no perception and no feeling of pain . . . and to allow oneself and one's loved ones to be kicked around, and overlook it, is slavish" (1126a4–8). The demand to avoid the slavish is certain to play a role in the public world of the law, as well as in the private world of the family. This demand makes Aristotelian *suggnômê* stop short of mercy. For the full development of that idea, we must wait for Roman Stoicism and for Seneca.[24]

Stoic moral theory accepts and builds on the Aristotelian insight that rules and precepts are useful only as guidelines in both private and public thought. Any fully adequate moral or legal judgment must be built upon a full grasp of all the particular circumstances of the situation, including the motives and intentions of the agent. Like Aristotle, Stoics are fond of using an analogy between medicine and ethics to illustrate this point: general ethical or legal rules are about as useful as medical rules and precepts—which is to say, useful as outlines, but no substitute for a resourceful confrontation with all the circumstances of the case. Both the Greek and the later Roman Stoics stress that an act is fully correct and moral, what they call a *katorthôma,* only if it is done with the appropriate motives and the appropriate knowledge; a *kathêkon* or (in Latin) *officium* is an act of (merely) the right general type, without consideration of the agent's thoughts and motivations. Rules can tell you what the *kathêkonta* are, but to get all the way to a full *katorthôma* you need to become a certain sort of person. The same goes in reverse for bad actions. This means that the Aristotelian idea of justice as equity is already built into the moral schema from the beginning, and it will automatically influence the classification of offenses in public reasoning and in the law.[25]

The Greek Stoics stop there, and in their moral rigor they explicitly reject any application of *epieikeia*

---

[22]For examples of such contrasts, see Richard Posner, *Law and Literature* (Cambridge, Mass.: Harvard University Press, 1988), 108ff. . . .

[23]I am translating *orgizesthai* this way because Aristotle defines *orgê* as a desire for retribution, on account of the pain of a believed slight.

[24]I have discussed Seneca's views on mercy in "Seneca on Anger in Public Life," chapter II of *The Therapy of Desire: Theory and Practice in Hellenistic Ethics* (Princeton: Princeton University Press, forthcoming 1994).

that goes beyond the careful classification of offenses. The soul of the good Stoic judge is a hard soul that protects itself from all impulses that might sway it from the strict path of virtue and duty. "All wise men," they announce, "are harshly rigorous [*austêroi*]."[26] They "never permit their soul to give way or to be caught by any pleasure or pain."[27] This hardness cordons them off from any yielding response to the defects of another person. The wise man, they announce, does not forgive those who err, and he never waives the punishment required in the law. An unyielding judge, the Stoic will do exactly what strict justice requires. In this connection, *epieikeia* is explicitly rejected: the Stoic will never waive the punishment that is mandated for that particular type of offense.[28]

Many Greek Stoic texts show us this attitude of detachment and hardness to offenders, an attitude far removed from the Aristotelian norm of *suggnômê*. One can see this emerge with particular clarity in the treatment of tragedy, which Stoics are permitted to watch, so long as they watch it from a vantage point of secure critical detachment (like Odysseus, they say, lashed to the mast so that he can hear, but not be swayed by, the sirens' song).[29] From this secure vantage point they view the disasters and vulnerabilities of ordinary mortals with amusement and even scorn, defining tragedy as what happens "when chance events befall fools."[30] To Oedipus, the wise man says, "Slave, where are your crowns, where your diadem?" To Medea, the wise man says, "Stop wanting your husband, and there is not one of the things you want that will fail to happen."[31] There is no inevitability in tragedy, for if one has the proper moral views there is no contingency in the world that can bring one low.[32]

Here Seneca steps in, perceiving a serious tension in the Greek Stoic position. On the one hand, Stoicism is deeply committed to the Aristotelian position that good moral assessment, like good medical assessment, is searchingly particular, devoted to a deep and internal understanding of each concrete case. On the other hand, the Stoic norm of critical detachment withholds psychological understanding, treating deep and complex predicaments as easily avoidable mistakes, simply refusing to see the obstacles to good action from the erring agent's own viewpoint.

Seneca opts for the medical side of this dilemma, offering a complex account of the origins of human wrongdoing that leads to a new view of the proper response to it. Seneca begins his argument in *De ira* as an Aristotelian would, asking the judge to look at all the circumstances of the offense (1.19.5–8). At this point he still seems to be a symmetrist, urging that sometimes a closer look makes the person look better, sometimes worse. But he then continues his reflections, in the second book, in a manner that makes our asymmetry open up. People who do bad things—even when they act from bad motives—are not, he insists, simply making a foolish and easily corrigible error. They are yielding to pressures—many of them social—that lie deep in the fabric of human life. Before a child is capable of the critical exercise of reason, he or she has internalized a socially taught scheme of values that is in many ways diseased, giving rise to similarly diseased passions: the excessive love of money and honor, angers connected with slights to one's honor, excessive attachment to sex (especially to romanticized conceptions of the sexual act and the sexual partner), anger and violence connected with sexual jealousy; the list goes on and on.[33]

These cultural forces are in error, and in that sense someone who is in their grip is indeed a "fool," as Epictetus holds. But there is not much point in giving a little sermon to Medea as to a docile child; such

---

[25]One possible difference: Aristotle's ethical schema makes a big distinction between *adikêmata,* for which it is necessary to have a bad *character,* and lesser wrongdoings that will be classified as among the blameworthy *hamartêmata.* The latter class will include bad acts done from weakness of will with respect to some passion. Stoic moral theory is harsher toward the passions, treating them as types of false judgment that are always in an agent's power to refuse. Thus the distinction between *akrasia* and wrongdoing from bad character is significantly weakened, if not altogether eroded.

[26]Diogenes Laertius VII.117 = *Stoicorum Veterum Fragmenta (SVF)* III.637.

[27]Clement, *Strom.* VII.7 = *SVF* III.639.

[28]SVF III.640.

[29]Plutarch, *On How the Young Person Should Listen to Poetry* 15CD. I argue that this work represents some of the contents of Chrysippus's lost work of the same title, in my "Poetry and the Passions: Two Stoic Views." *In Passions & Perceptions,* ed., J. Brunschwig and M. Nussbaum (Cambridge: Cambridge University Press, 1993), 97–149.

[30]Epictetus, *Diss.* 2.26.31. Though a Roman Stoic, Epictetus is loyal to the original views of the Greek Stoics.

[31]Epictetus 1.24.16–18, 2.17.19–22.

[32]The proper view is that virtue by itself is sufficient for *eudaimonia.*

[33]Most of my argument in this passage is based on the *De ira (On Anger),* though there are many similar passages in other works.

errors, taught from an early age, take over the soul and can be eradicated, if at all, only by a lifetime of zealous and obsessive self-examination. And, furthermore, Seneca suggests that anger and the desire to inflict pain—the worst, in his opinion, of the errors of the soul—are not in any simple way just the result of a corrigible error, even at the social level. He repeatedly commits himself to the view that they do not result from innate instinct. On the other hand, they "omit no time of life, exempt no race of human beings" (*De ira* III.22).

In a crucial passage, Seneca says that the wise person is not surprised at the omnipresence of aggression and injustice, "since he has examined thoroughly the circumstances of human life" (*condicio humanae vitae,* II.10). Circumstances, then, and not innate propensities, are at the origins of vice. And when the wise person looks at these circumstances clearly, he finds that they make it extremely difficult not to err. The world into which human beings are born is a rough place, one that confronts them with threats to their safety on every side. If they remain attached to their safety and to the resources that are necessary to protect it—as is natural and rational—that very attachment to the world will almost certainly, in time, lead to competitive or retaliatory aggression. For when goods are in short supply and people are attached to them, they compete for them. Thus aggression and violence grow not so much inside us as from an interaction between our nature and external conditions that is prior to and more deeply rooted than any specific form of society.

Seneca now uses this view as the basis for his argument against retributive anger and in favor of mercy. Given the omnipresence of aggression and wrongdoing, he now argues, if we look at the lives of others with the attitudes typical of the retributive tradition of justice—even in its modified particularist form—if, that is, we are determined to fix a penalty precisely proportionate to the nature of the particular wrongdoing, then we will never cease to be retributive and to inflict punishment, for everything we see will upset us. But this retributive attitude, even when in some sense justified, is not without its consequences for the human spirit. A person who notes and reacts to every injustice, and who becomes preoccupied with assigning just punishments, becomes, in the end, oddly similar to the raging ungentle people against whom he reacts. Retributive anger hardens the spirit, turning it against the humanity it sees. And in turning against humanity, in evincing the rage and hardness of the angry, one then becomes perilously close to the callous wrongdoers who arouse rage in the first place. Thus in Seneca's examples we find acts of horrifying vindictiveness and cruelty committed by people whose anger is initially justified, according to a precise assessment of the nature of the crime. Sulla's acts of retribution were first directed against legitimate enemies; they ended in the murder of innocent children (II.34). Caligula was justified in his anger over the imprisonment of his mother, and yet this led him to cruelty and destruction. Cambyses had just cause of battle against the Ethiopians, but in his obsession with revenge be led his men on a fatal campaign that ended in cannibalism (III.20). . . .

Seneca's famous counterproposal, announced at the very end of *De ira,* is that we should "cultivate humanity" (*colamus humanitatem,* III.43). He elsewhere describes this as the proposal to "give a pardon to the human species" (II.10). It is this attitude that he now calls by the name of mercy, translating Greek *epieikeia* with the Latin word *clementia.* Rejecting the austerity and rigor of the Greek Stoic, he makes a sympathetic participatory attitude central to the norm of good judging. Senecan *clementia* does not fail to pass judgment on wrongdoing; this is continually stressed. Seneca does not hold that the circumstances of human life remove moral and legal responsibility for bad acts. We may still convict defendants who fulfill some basic conditions of rationality in action. But, looking at the circumstances of human life, one comes to understand how such things have happened, and this "medical" understanding leads to mercy.

Clementia, mercy, is even defined in a manner that makes its difference from Greek Stoic harshness evident: it is an "inclination of the soul to mildness in exacting penalties," and also, "that which turns its course away this side of that which could be justly determined" (*De clem.* II.3). The Greek Stoic soul, by contrast, never bends aside, never inclines away from hardness. The somewhat more gentle Aristotelian soul does bend, but inconstantly, conscious always that it is slavish to allow oneself and one's loved ones to be kicked around. Given that Seneca defines mercy as the opposite of cruelty, and given that cruelty is held to be a frequent outgrowth of retributive anger, we can say, putting all this together, that mercy, *clementia,* is opposed at one and the same time both to strictness in exacting penalties and also to retributive anger, as if that strictness does indeed lie very close to anger in the heart. As Seneca says, "It is a fault to punish a fault in full" (*culpa est totam persequi culpam, De clem.* II.7, fr.).[34]

One might, of course, adopt this attitude as a practical strategy to keep the self pure from anger without endorsing it as just or correct toward the offender. Seneca sometimes appears to oscillate between these two positions, since he can commend the practical strategy even to those who do not accept his position about correctness. But in the end his position is clearly that it is right and correct to assign punishments in accordance with mercy, both because of what it means for oneself and because of what it says about and to the offender.

The merciful attitude, as Seneca develops it, entails regarding each particular case as a complex narrative of human effort in a world full of obstacles. The merciful judge will not fail to judge the guilt of the offender, but she will also see the many obstacles this offender faced as a member of a culture, a gender, a city or country, and, above all, as a member of the human species, facing the obstacles characteristic of human life in a world of scarcity and accident. The starting point is a general view of human life and its difficulties, but the search for mitigating factors must at every point be searchingly particular. The narrative-medical attitude asks the judge to imagine what it was like to have been that particular offender, facing those particular obstacles with the resources of that history. Seneca's bet is that after this imaginative exercise one will cease to have the strict retributive attitude to the punishment of the offender. One will be inclined, in fact, to gentleness and the waiving of the strict punishment mandated in the law. The punishments that one does assign will be chosen, on the whole, not for their retributive function, but for their power to improve the life of the defendant.[35]

This merciful attitude requires, and rests upon, a new attitude toward the self. The retributive attitude has a we/them mentality, in which judges set themselves above offenders, looking at their actions as if from a lofty height and preparing to find satisfaction in their pain. The good Senecan judge, by contrast, has both identification and sympathetic understanding. Accordingly, a central element in Seneca's prescription for the judge is that he should remind himself at every turn that he himself is capable of the failings he reproves in others. "If we want to be fair judges of all things, let us persuade ourselves of this first: that none of us is without fault. For it is from this point above all that retributive anger arises: 'I did nothing wrong,' and 'I did nothing.' No, rather, you don't admit to anything" (II.28).

This part of Seneca's argument reaches its conclusion in a remarkable passage in which Seneca confronts himself with the attitude of merciful judgment that he also recommends, describing his own daily practice of self-examination in forensic language that links it to his public recommendations:

> A person will cease from retributive anger and be more moderate if he knows that every day he has to come before himself as judge. What therefore is more wonderful than this habit of unfolding the entire day? How fine is the sleep that follows this acknowledgment of oneself, how serene, how deep and free, when the mind has been either praised or admonished, and as its own hidden investigator and assessor has gained knowledge of its own character? I avail myself of this power, and plead my cause daily before myself. When the light has been removed from sight, and my wife, long since aware of this habit of mine, has fallen silent, I examine my entire day and measure my deeds and words. I hide nothing from myself, I pass over nothing. For why should I fear anything from my own errors, when I can say, "See that you don't do that again, this time I pardon you." (III.36)

Seeing the complexity and fallibility of his own acts, seeing those acts as the product of a complex web of highly particular connections among original impulses, the circumstances of life, and the complicated psychological reactions life elicits from the mind, he learns to view others, too, as people whose errors emerge from a complex narrative history. Seneca's claim is that he will then moderate his retributive zeal toward the punishment of their injustices and intensify his commitment to mutual aid.

[34]Unlike Aristotle, Seneca does not endorse pity or compassion as a correct response to the misfortunes of human life. In his view, to do so would be to give too little credit to the person's own will and dignity and, frequently, too much importance to external events.

[35]Some ameliorative punishments, according to Seneca, can be extremely harsh. Indeed, in a peculiar move, he defends capital punishment itself as in the interest of the punished, given that a shorter bad life is better than a longer one; he compares it to merciful euthanasia.

This part of Seneca's work seems very private. But there is no doubt that the primary aim of this work, and of the later *De clementia* as well, is the amelioration of public life and public judgment. The *De ira* was written at the start of the reign of the emperor Claudius. It responds to a well-known speech by Claudius on the subject of anger and irascibility, and obviously contains advice for the new regime.[36] Moreover, its explicit addressee and interlocutor is Novatus, Seneca's own brother, an aspiring orator and public man. Thus its entire argumentative structure is built around the idea of showing a public judge that the retributive attitude is unsuitable for good judging. As for the *De clementia*, its explicit addressee is none other than the new emperor Nero Caesar himself, and its explicit task is to persuade this young man to use his immense power in merciful, rather than retributive, ways. The private material provides the basis for a new sort of public and judicial life. . . .

Now to contemporary implications. Up until now, I have been talking about a moral ideal, which has evident implications for publicly promulgated norms of human behavior and for public conduct in areas in which there is latitude for judicial discretion. I have suggested that in many ways this norm fulfills and completes a conception of justice that lies itself at the basis of the rule of law; it was to prevent incomplete, defective, and biased discretionary reasoning that the rule of law was introduced and defended. But at this point and for this reason caution is in order, for the moral ideal should not be too simply converted into a norm for a legal system. First of all, a legal system has to look out for the likelihood that the moral ideal will not always be perfectly realized, and it should protect against abuses that moral arbitrariness and bias can engender. This suggests a large role for codified requirements in areas in which one cannot guarantee that the equity ideal will be well implemented. The equity tradition supports this. Second, a system of law must look to social consequences as well as to the just judgment on particular offenders. Thus it may need to balance an interest in the deterrent role of punishments against the equity tradition's interest in punishments that suit the agent. Both the balance between codification and discretion and the balance between equity and deterrence are enormously complex matters, with which my analysis here cannot fully grapple. What I do wish to offer here are some representative suggestions of what the equity tradition has to offer us as we think about these issues. . . .

I have already begun to speak about the criminal law, since the focus in mercy is on wrongdoing and the wrongdoer. The implications of the mercy tradition for issues in the criminal law are many and complex, and I can only begin here to suggest what some of them might be. I shall do this by focusing on a pair of examples: two recent Supreme Court cases involving the death penalty which raise issues of mitigation and aggravation in connection with discretionary sentencing. One is *Walton v. Arizona;* the other is *California v. Brown.* At stake are the roles to be played by discretion in deciding capital cases and the criteria to be used in analyzing the aggravating and mitigating features of the case. Walton was convicted by a jury of first-degree murder and sentenced to death, in accordance with an Arizona statute that requires the judge first to ascertain whether at least one aggravating circumstance is present—in this case two were found[37]—and then to consider all the alleged mitigating circumstances advanced by the defendant, imposing a death sentence if he finds "no mitigating circumstances sufficiently substantial to call for mercy." The defendant is required to establish a mitigating circumstance by the preponderance of the evidence, and it was this that was the central issue in Walton's appeal. Since previous Supreme Court decisions had rejected a requirement of unanimity for mitigation, Walton contended that the preponderance of the evidence test was also unconstitutional.[38] His claim was rejected by a plurality of the court. My concern is not so much with the result as with some interesting issues that emerge from the opinions.

First, it is plain that the Arizona system, which the decision in effect upholds, establishes a lexical ordering, in which a finding of aggravation—which must be based upon criteria explicitly enumerated in the law—is used to classify an offense as a potential death-penalty offense; mitigation is then considered afterwards, in a discretionary manner. In other words,

[36]See J. Fillion-Lahille, *Le De era de Séneque* (Paris: 1984), and the summary of the evidence in Nussbaum, *Therapy,* ch. 11.

[37]The murder was committed in an "especially heinous, cruel or depraved manner," and it was committed for pecuniary gain. Note that even here, in the nondiscretionary and codified portion of the judgment, intentional notions are prominently used.

[38]*Mills v. Maryland,* 486 U.S. 367 (1988), and *McKoy v. North Carolina,* 110 S. Ct. 1229 (1990).

the whole range of potentially mitigating circumstances will be brought forward only when it has already been established that an offense falls into a certain class of extremely serious offenses. Discretionary concern for the entirety of the defendant's history will enter the picture only in the mitigation phase. Justice Stevens comments on this feature in his dissenting opinion, arguing that once the scope of capital punishment is so reduced, the risk of arbitrariness in sentencing is sufficiently reduced as well to permit very broad discretion and individuated decision making with the remaining class. This seems to be a correct and valuable observation. Indeed, the mercy tradition stresses that merciful judgment can be given only when there is time to learn the whole complex history of the life in question and also inclination to do so in a sympathetic manner, without biases of class or race. The tradition wholeheartedly endorses decision making by codified requirement where these requirements cannot be met. (Here Posner's warnings about arbitrariness in equity seem perfectly appropriate, and they are reflected in the move away from unguided discretion represented by the federal sentencing guidelines.)[39] We should not, however, say, as Stevens seems to, that the main function of such criteria is to reduce the number of cases that are eligible for the death penalty. What they do is, of course, more substantial: they eliminate from the death-eligible group many cases for which death would clearly not be an *appropriate* penalty, leaving the judge free to turn his or her attention to those that are more problematic, requiring a more fine-tuned deliberation.[40]

A second significant feature, and a more problematic one, is the plurality's unquestioning acceptance of the preponderance of the evidence test, which, as Allen has shown here and elsewhere, has grave defects when we are dealing with a case having multiple relevant features.[41] Suppose a defendant advances three grounds for mitigation, each of which is established to a .25 probability, and therefore to be thrown out under Arizona's rule. The probability that at least one of the factors is true, assuming they are independent, is, as Allen shows, .58.[42] If each of three factors is proved to a probability of .4, the probability that at least one is true is .78. On the other hand, if the defendant proves just one of the mitigating factors with a probability of .51 and the others with probability 0, he is successful, even though the probability that the decision is correct is in fact lower here than in the previous cases.[43] The law asks the judge to treat each feature one by one, in total isolation from any other. But human lives, as the literary judge would see, consist of complex webs of circumstances, which must be considered as wholes.

This same problem is present in Justice Scalia's scathing attack on the whole notion of mitigation. For Scalia thinks it absurd that we should have codified criteria for aggravation, apply these, and *then* look with unguided discretion to see whether a mitigating factor is present. If the criteria for aggravation are enumerated in the law, so too should be the criteria for mitigation. Only this explicitness and this symmetry can prevent total irrationality. Scalia here ignores the possibility—which Stevens recognizes—that the functions of aggravation-criteria and of mitigation are not parallel: aggravation serves to place the offense in the class to which mitigation is relevant.[44]

---

[39]I have not committed myself here on the ideal scope for discretion in other areas of the law. This is an issue I feel I need to study further before making concrete claims. I focus on the capital cases because they have been the focus of an especially interesting debate about mercy, in which the penalty-setting phase has a special weight. I do think that a similar approach could be tried in another group of cases to which a finding of aggravation is pertinent, namely hate crimes. Here I think one would want to describe the grounds for aggravation very explicitly and systematically, either by setting up a special class of crimes or in the guidelines for sentencing. Once one had determined that particular offense was of this particularly severe kind, one could then consider whether the defendant's youth, family background, and so forth gave any grounds for mitigation.

[40]See Allen, "*Walton,*" p. 741. I agree with this point against Stevens, but disagree with an earlier one. On p. 736, Allen argues that "the primary thrust of [Stevens's] argument . . . is for categorical rather than discretionary sentencing." This seems to me inaccurate: it is, instead, a statement about the conditions under which discretionary sentencing can be well done.

[41]See also Allen, "A Reconceptualization of Civil Trials," *B.U. Law Review* 66 (1986): 401ff.

[42]See Allen, "*Walton,*" pp. 734–35. This is the assumption that the current test in effect makes. If they are not independent, this probabilistic analysis does not follow, but there is also, then, no justification at all for treating them in isolation from one another. In either case, then, the conclusion for which I am arguing follows: the life must be considered as a whole.

[43]One might also point out that different jurors might be convinced by different factors, so long as they are treated as isolated units. One could have a situation in which all jurors agree that there is at least one mitigating factor present but, if they disagree enough about which one it is, the defendant's attempt fails. I owe this point to Cy Wasserstrom.

[44]Here the similarity to the ancient tradition is striking, especially to Seneca's insistence on separating the determination of guilt and its level from the assignment of (merciful) punishment.

Furthermore, in ridiculing the entire notion of discretionary mercy, Scalia adamantly refuses the forms of perception that we have associated with the literary attitude. That is, he treats mitigating factors as isolated units, unconnected either to one another or to the whole of a life. It is in this way that he can arrive at the conclusion that unbridled discretion will (absurdly) be permitted to treat traits that are polar opposites as, both of them, mitigating: for example, "that the defendant had a poor and deprived childhood, or that he had a rich and spoiled childhood."[45] Scalia's assumption is that both of these cannot be mitigating, and that it is a sign of the absurdity of the current state of things that they might both be so treated. But the alleged absurdity arises only because he has severed these traits from the web of circumstances in which they actually figure. In connection with other circumstances either a trait or its opposite might, in fact, be mitigating.[46] This, in Allen's argument and in mine, is the reason why categories for mitigation should not be codified in advance: it will be impossible for such a code to anticipate adequately the countless ways in which factors interweave and bear upon one another in human reality.[47] Telling the whole story, with all the particulars, is the only way to get at that.[48]

In reality, of course, the mercy tradition has serious reservations about the whole idea of capital punishment. Although some of its major exponents, including Seneca, endorsed it, they did so on the basis of very peculiar arguments comparing it to euthanasia (n. 43 above). If we reject these arguments we are left, I think, with no support for capital punishment from within that tradition, and strong reasons to reject retributivist justifications. Indeed, the tradition strongly suggests that such punishments are always cruel and excessive. The question would then have to be whether the deterrence value of such punishments by itself justifies their perpetuation, despite their moral inappropriateness. Furthermore, the deterrence-based argument has never yet been made out in a fully compelling way.

California v. Brown raises a different issue: that of jury instruction, where emotion is concerned. The Court reviewed a state jury instruction stipulating that the jury in a capital case (in the sentencing phase) "must not be swayed by mere sentiment, conjecture, sympathy, passion, prejudice, public opinion or public feellng."[49] From the point of view of our account of literary judging, this instruction is a peculiar and inappropriate mixture. For the juror as "judicious spectator" and merciful reader would indeed disregard conjecture, prejudice, public opinion, and public feeling. On the other hand, sentiment, passion, and sympathy would be a prominent part of the appropriate (and rational) deliberative process, where those sentiments are based in the juror's "reading" of the defendant's history, as presented in the evidence. It would of course be right to leave aside any sentiment having to do with one's own involvement in the outcome, but we assume that nobody with a personal interest in the outcome would end up on the jury in any case. It would also be correct to leave aside any mere gut reaction to the defendant's appearance, demeanor, or clothing, anything that could not be made a reasoned part of the "story" of the case. But the vast majority of the passional reactions of a juror hearing a case of this kind will be based on the story that is told; in this sense, the law gives extremely bad advice.[50] The Court, however, approved the instruc-

---

[45]110 S. Ct. at 3062.

[46]See Allen, *"Walton,"* p. 739; also p. 742: "Any particular fact is of very little consequence standing alone. The web of facts is what matters." In *David Copperfield* we see a very clear example of a rich and spoiled childhood as a mitigating factor: Steerforth has no opportunity to learn moral self-restraint, and is encouraged to use his talent and charm in a reckless manner.

[47]I am not claiming that knowledge of the whole story should never give rise to aggravation of punishment. By focusing on capital cases I have left undiscussed a number of lesser cases in which such thinking might figure. One is a very interesting case recently heard by the Seventh Circuit, in which Posner defends an upward departure from the sentencing guidelines in a case of blackmail, on the ground that the blackmailer's victim, a married homosexual, fit the category of "unusually vulnerable victim" that justifies such aggravation. Detailed consideration of the whole story, and of American homophobia, was required in order to establish that this victim was really more vulnerable than other types of people with sexual secrets to conceal (*U.S. v. Sienky Lallemand,* Seventh Circuit, March 29, 1993).

[48]Another point against Scalia is the structure of the pardon power: a governor can pardon a criminal, but not increase a criminal's sentence or condemn someone who was acquitted. Indeed, asymmetry is built into the entirety of the criminal justice system, in the requirement to prove guilt beyond a reasonable doubt, in the safeguards surrounding the admissibility of confessions, and so forth.

[49]Note that for a juror the case at issue is likely to be a rare event, and thus there is reason to think that jury deliberations will be free from at least some of the problems of callousness and shortness of time that may limit the advisability of discretion in cases involving judges. On the other hand, the limits of juror sympathy with people who are unlike themselves remains a clear difficulty. This is why I sympathize, to the extent that I do, with parts of the warning in the California juror instruction.

tion, concluding that "[A] reasonable juror would . . . understand the instruction . . . as a directive to ignore only the sort of sympathy that would be totally divorced from the evidence adduced during the penalty phase."[51] On the one hand, this seems to me a perfectly reasonable way of articulating the boundaries of appropriate and inappropriate sympathy. On the other hand, the likelihood is so high that the sentiments of the juror would be of the appropriate, rather than the inappropriate, sort—for what else but the story told them do they have to consider?—that approving the regulation creates a misleading impression that some large and rather dangerous class of passions are being excluded.[52] The other opinions in the case confirm the general impression of confusion about and suspicion of the passions. Thus Justice O'Connor argues that "the sentence imposed at the penalty stage should reflect a reasoned *moral* response to the defendant's background, character, and crime rather than mere sympathy or emotion." She goes on to state that "the individualized assessment of the appropriateness of the death penalty is a moral inquiry into the culpability of the defendant, and not an emotional response to the mitigating evidence."[53] This contrast between morality and sympathy is a nest of confusions, as my argument by now should have shown. Justice Brennan, too, holds that "mere sympathy" must be left to one side—though he does hold (dissenting) that the instruction prohibits the juror from considering exactly what he or she should consider.[54] Justice Blackmun does somewhat better, defending the juror's ability to respond with mercy as "a particularly valuable aspect of the capital sentencing procedure." But he, too, contrasts rationality with mercy, even in the process of defending the latter: "While the sentencer's decision to accord life to a defendant at times might be a rational or moral one, it also may arise from the defendant's appeal to the sentencer's sympathy or mercy, human qualities that are undeniably emotional in nature."[55] The confusion persists: in a more recent case, the Court now speaks even more suspiciously and pejoratively of the juror's emotions, contrasting them with the "actual evidence regarding the crime and the defendant"[56]—as if these were not the source of and basis for these emotions.[57]

In short, the insights of the mercy tradition can take us a long way in understanding what is well and not well done in recent Supreme Court writings about sentencing. It can help us to defend the asymmetry between mitigation and aggravation that prevailed in *Walton,* as well as *Walton*'s moderate defense of discretion. But it leads to severe criticism of the categories of analysis deployed in the juror-instruction cases, which employ defective conceptions of the rational. . . .

[50]Compare the advice given to the prospective juror in the state of Massachusetts, in the "Juror's Creed" printed in the Trial Juror's Handbook: "I am a JUROR. I am a seeker of truth . . . I must lay aside all bias and prejudice. I must be led by my intelligence and not by my emotions."

[51]479 U.S. 542–43 (1987).

[52]Thus I agree in part with Allen, *"Walton,"* p. 747, although I do think it reasonable to stipulate this restriction on sentiment and believe that it is possible to think of cases where sentiments would be of the inappropriate sort.

[53]479 U.S. at 545.

[54]*Ibid.* at 548–50.

[55]*Ibid.* at 561–63. Thus I do not agree with Allen that Blackmun "gets it right" (*"Walton,"* p. 750). Allen, like Blackmun, is willing to give the normative term "rational" to the opposition, granting that merciful sentiment is not rational. But why not? Such merciful sentiments are based on judgments that are (if the deliberative process is well executed) both true and justified by the evidence.

[56]*Saffle v. Parks,* 110 S. Ct. 1257 (1990) at 1261.

[57]One might think that my view entails admitting victim impact statements, for they are certainly part of the whole story, even though the victim is often no longer around to tell it. I am dubious. A criminal trial is about the defendant and what will become of him or her. The question before the court is what the defendant did, and the function of narrative is to illuminate the character and origins of that deed. What has to be decided is not what to do about the victim, but what to do about the defendant. Now of course the victim's experience may be relevant to ascertaining the nature of the offense, and to that extent it is admissible anyway. But the additional information imported by victim impact statements seems primarily to lie in giving vent to the passion for revenge, and the emotions they seek to arouse are those associated with that passion.

84

Payne v. Tennessee

501 U.S. 808 (1990)

OPINION OF THE COURT

Chief Justice Rehnquist delivered the opinion of the Court.

In this case we reconsider our holdings in *Booth v. Maryland,* 482 U.S. 496 (1987), and *South Carolina v. Gathers,* 490 U.S. 805 (1989), that the Eighth

Amendment bars the admission of victim impact evidence during the penalty phase of a capital trial.

Petitioner, Pervis Tyrone Payne, was convicted by a jury on two counts of first-degree murder and one count of assault with intent to commit murder in the first degree. He was sentenced to death for each of the murders and to 30 years in prison for the assault.

The victims of Payne's offenses were 28-year-old Charisse Christopher, her 2-year-old daughter Lacie, and her 3-year-old son Nicholas. The three lived together in an apartment in Millington, Tennessee, across the hall from Payne's girlfriend, Bobbie Thomas. On Saturday, June 27, 1987, Payne visited Thomas' apartment several times in expectation of her return from her mother's house in Arkansas, but found no one at home. On one visit, he left his overnight bag, containing clothes and other items for his weekend stay, in the hallway outside Thomas' apartment. With the bag were three cans of malt liquor.

Payne passed the morning and early afternoon injecting cocaine and drinking beer. Later, he drove around the town with a friend in the friend's car, each of them taking turns reading a pornographic magazine. Sometime around 3 p.m., Payne returned to the apartment complex, entered the Christophers' apartment, and began making sexual advances towards Charisse. Charisse resisted and Payne became violent. A neighbor who resided in the apartment directly beneath the Christophers heard Charisse screaming, "'Get out, get out,' as if she were telling the children to leave." Brief for Respondent 3. The noise briefly subsided and then began, "'horribly loud.'" *Ibid.* The neighbor called the police after she heard a "blood curdling scream" from the Christophers' apartment. *Ibid.*

When the first police officer arrived at the scene, he immediately encountered Payne, who was leaving the apartment building, so covered with blood that he appeared to be "'sweating blood.'" The officer confronted Payne, who responded, "'I'm the complainant.'" *Id.*, at 3–4. When the officer asked, "'What's going on up there?'" Payne struck the officer with the overnight bag, dropped his tennis shoes, and fled. 791 S.W. 2d 10, 12 (Tenn. 1990).

Inside the apartment, the police encountered a horrifying scene. Blood covered the walls and floor throughout the unit. Charisse and her children were lying on the floor in the kitchen. Nicholas, despite several wounds inflicted by a butcher knife that completely penetrated through his body from front to back, was still breathing. Miraculously, he survived, but not until after undergoing seven hours of surgery and a transfusion of 1,700 cc's of blood—400 to 500 cc's more than his estimated normal blood volume. Charisse and Lacie were dead.

Charisse's body was found on the kitchen floor on her back, her legs fully extended. She had sustained 42 direct knife wounds and 42 defensive wounds on her arms and hands. The wounds were caused by 41 separate thrusts of a butcher knife. None of the 84 wounds inflicted by Payne were individually fatal; rather, the cause of death was most likely bleeding from all of the wounds.

Lacie's body was on the kitchen floor near her mother. She had suffered stab wounds to the chest, abdomen, back, and head. The murder weapon, a butcher knife, was found at her feet. Payne's baseball cap was snapped on her arm near her elbow. Three cans of malt liquor bearing Payne's fingerprints were found on a table near her body, and a fourth empty one was on the landing outside the apartment door.

Payne was apprehended later that day hiding in the attic of the home of a former girlfriend. As he descended the stairs of the attic, he stated to the arresting officers, "'Man, I ain't killed no woman.'" *Id.*, at 13. According to one of the officers, Payne had "'a wild look about him. His pupils were contracted. He was foaming at the mouth, saliva. He appeared to be very nervous. He was breathing real rapid.'" *Ibid.* He had blood on his body and clothes and several scratches across his chest. It was later determined that the blood stains matched the victims' blood types. A search of his pockets revealed a packet containing cocaine residue, a hypodermic syringe wrapper, and a cap from a hypodermic syringe. His overnight bag, containing a bloody white shirt, was found in a nearby dumpster.

At trial, Payne took the stand and, despite the overwhelming and relatively uncontroverted evidence against him, testified that he had not harmed any of the Christophers. Rather, he asserted that another man had raced by him as he was walking up the stairs to the floor where the Christophers lived. He stated that he had gotten blood on himself when, after hearing moans from the Christophers' apartment, he had tried to help the victims. According to his testimony, he panicked and fled when he heard police sirens and noticed the blood on his clothes. The jury returned guilty verdicts against Payne on all counts.

During the sentencing phase of the trial, Payne presented the testimony of four witnesses: his mother and father, Bobbie Thomas, and Dr. John T. Hutson, a clinical psychologist specializing in criminal court evaluation work. Bobbie Thomas testified that she met Payne at church, during a time when she was being abused by her husband. She stated that Payne was a very caring person, and that he devoted much time and attention to her three children, who were being affected by her marital difficulties. She said that the children had come to love him very much and would miss him, and that he "behaved just like a father that loved his kids." She asserted that he did not drink, nor did he use drugs, and that it was generally inconsistent with Payne's character to have committed these crimes.

Dr. Hutson testified that based on Payne's low score on an IQ test, Payne was "mentally handicapped." Hutson also said that Payne was neither psychotic nor schizophrenic, and that Payne was the most polite prisoner he had ever met. Payne's parents testified that their son had no prior criminal record and had never been arrested. They also stated that Payne had no history of alcohol or drug abuse, he worked with his father as a painter, he was good with children, and he was a good son.

The State presented the testimony of Charisse's mother, Mary Zvolanek. When asked how Nicholas had been affected by the murders of his mother and sister, she responded:

> "He cries for his mom. He doesn't seem to understand why she doesn't come home. And he cries for his sister Lacie. He comes to me many times during the week and asks me, Grandmama, do you miss my Lacie. And I tell him yes. He says, I'm worried about my Lacie." App. 3.

In arguing for the death penalty during closing argument, the prosecutor commented on the continuing effects of Nicholas' experience, stating:

> "But we do know that Nicholas was alive. And Nicholas was in the same room. Nicholas was still conscious. His eyes were open. He responded to the paramedics. He was able to follow their directions. He was able to hold his intestines in as he was carried to the ambulance. So he knew what happened to his mother and baby sister." *Id.,* at 9.

> "There is nothing you can do to ease the pain of any of the families involved in this case. There is nothing you can do to ease the pain of Bernice or Carl Payne, and that's a tragedy. There is nothing you can do basically to ease the pain of Mr. and Mrs. Zvolanek, and that's a tragedy. They will have to live with it the rest of their lives. There is obviously nothing you can do for Charisse and Lacie Jo. But there is something that you can do for Nicholas.
>
> "Somewhere down the road Nicholas is going to grow up, hopefully. He's going to want to know what happened. And he is going to know what happened to his baby sister and his mother. He is going to want to know what type of justice was done. He is going to want to know what happened. With your verdict, you will provide the answer." Id., at 12.

In the rebuttal to Payne's closing argument, the prosecutor stated:

> "You saw the videotape this morning. You saw what Nicholas Christopher will carry in his mind forever. When you talk about cruel, when you talk about atrocious, and when you talk about heinous, that picture will always come into your mind, probably throughout the rest of your lives. . . .
>
> . . . .
>
> " . . . No one will ever know about Lacie Jo because she never had the chance to grow up. Her life was taken from her at the age of two years old. So, no there won't be a high school principal to talk about Lacie Jo Christopher, and there won't be anybody to take her to her high school prom. And there won't be anybody there—there won't be her mother there or Nicholas' mother there to kiss him at night. His mother will never kiss him good night or pat him as he goes off to bed, or hold him and sing him a lullaby.
>
> . . . .
>
> "[Petitioner's attorney] wants you to think about a good reputation, people who love the defendant and things about him. He doesn't want you to think about the people who love Charisse Christopher, her mother and daddy who loved her. The people who loved little Lacie Jo, the grandparents who are still here. The brother who mourns for her every single day and wants to know where his best little playmate is. He doesn't have anybody to watch cartoons with him, a little one. These are the things that go into why it is especially cruel, heinous, and atrocious, the burden that that child will carry forever." *Id.,* at 13–15.

The jury sentenced Payne to death on each of the murder counts.

The Supreme Court of Tennessee affirmed the conviction and sentence. 791 S. W. 2d 10 (1990). The court rejected Payne's contention that the admission of the grandmother's testimony and the State's closing argument constituted prejudicial violations of his rights under the Eighth Amendment as applied in *Booth v. Maryland,* 482 U.S. 496 (1987), and *South Carolina v. Gathers,* 490 U.S. 805 (1989). The court characterized the grandmother's testimony as "technically irrelevant," but concluded that it "did not create a constitutionally unacceptable risk of an arbitrary imposition of the death penalty and was harmless beyond a reasonable doubt." 791 S.W. 2d, at 18.

The court determined that the prosecutor's comments during closing argument were "relevant to [Payne's] personal responsibility and moral guilt." *Id.,* at 19. The court explained that "[w]hen a person deliberately picks a butcher knife out of a kitchen drawer and proceeds to stab to death a twenty-eight-year-old mother, her two and one-half year old daughter and her three and one-half year old son, in the same room, the physical and mental condition of the boy he left for dead is surely relevant in determining his 'blameworthiness.'" The court concluded that any violation of Payne's rights under *Booth* and *Gathers* "was harmless beyond a reasonable doubt." *Id.*

We granted certiorari, 498 U.S. 1080 (1991), to reconsider our holdings in *Booth* and *Gathers* that the Eighth Amendment prohibits a capital sentencing jury from considering "victim impact" evidence relating to the personal characteristics of the victim and the emotional impact of the crimes on the victim's family.

In *Booth,* the defendant robbed and murdered an elderly couple. As required by a state statute, a victim impact statement was prepared based on interviews with the victims' son, daughter, son-in-law, and granddaughter. The statement, which described the personal characteristics of the victims, the emotional impact of the crimes on the family, and set forth the family members' opinions and characterizations of the crimes and the defendant, was submitted to the jury at sentencing. The jury imposed the death penalty. The conviction and sentence were affirmed on appeal by the State's highest court.

This Court held by a 5-to-4 vote that the Eighth Amendment prohibits a jury from considering a victim impact statement at the sentencing phase of a capital trial. The Court made clear that the admissibility of victim impact evidence was not to be determined on a case-by-case basis, but that such evidence was *per se* inadmissible in the sentencing phase of a capital case except to the extent that it "relate[d] directly to the circumstances of the crime." 482 U.S., at 507, n. 10. In *Gathers,* decided two years later, the Court extended the rule announced in *Booth* to statements made by a prosecutor to the sentencing jury regarding the personal qualities of the victim.

The *Booth* Court began its analysis with the observation that the capital defendant must be treated as a "'uniquely individual human bein[g],'" 482 U.S., at 504 (quoting *Woodson v. North Carolina,* 428 U.S. 280, 304 (1976)), and therefore the Constitution requires the jury to make an individualized determination as to whether the defendant should be executed based on the "'character of the individual and the circumstances of the crime.'" 482 U.S., at 502 (quoting *Zant v. Stephens,* 462 U.S. 862, 879 (1983)). The Court concluded that while no prior decision of this Court had mandated that only the defendant's character and immediate characteristics of the crime may constitutionally be considered, other factors are irrelevant to the capital sentencing decision unless they have "some bearing on the defendant's 'personal responsibility and moral guilt.'" 482 U.S., at 502 (quoting *Enmund v. Florida,* 458 U.S. 782, 801 (1982)). To the extent that victim impact evidence presents "factors about which the defendant was unaware, and that were irrelevant to the decision to kill," the Court concluded, it has nothing to do with the "blameworthiness of a particular defendant." 482 U.S. at 504, 505. Evidence of the victim's character, the Court observed, "could well distract the sentencing jury from its constitutionally required task [of] determining whether the death penalty is appropriate in light of the background and record of the accused and the particular circumstances of the crime." The Court concluded that, except to the extent that victim impact evidence relates "directly to the circumstances of the crime," *id.,* at 507, and n. 10, the prosecution may not introduce such evidence at a capital sentencing hearing because "it creates an impermissible risk that the capital sentencing decision will be made in an arbitrary manner," *id.,* at 505.

Booth and *Gathers* were based on two premises: that evidence relating to a particular victim or to the harm that a capital defendant causes a victim's family do not in general reflect on the defendant's "blameworthiness," and that only evidence relating to "blameworthiness" is relevant to the capital sentencing decision. However, the assessment of harm caused by the defendant as a result of the crime charged has understandably been an important concern of the criminal law, both in determining the elements of the offense and in determining the appropriate punishment. Thus, two equally blameworthy criminal defendants may be guilty of different offenses solely because their acts cause differing amounts of harm. "If a bank robber aims his gun at a guard, pulls the trigger, and kills his target, he may be put to death. If the gun unexpectedly misfires, he may not. His moral guilt in both cases is identical, but his responsibility in the former is greater." *Booth,* 482 U.S., at 519 (SCALIA, J., dissenting). The same is true with respect to two defendants, each of whom participates in a robbery, and each of whom acts with reckless disregard for human life; if the robbery in which the first defendant participated results in the death of a victim, he may be subjected to the death penalty, but if the robbery in which the second defendant participates does not result in the death of a victim, the death penalty may not be imposed. *Tison v. Arizona,* 481 U.S. 137, 148 (1987).

The principles which have guided criminal sentencing—as opposed to criminal liability—have varied with the times. The book of Exodus prescribes the *Lex talionis,* "An eye for an eye, a tooth for a tooth." Exodus 21:22–23. In England and on the continent of Europe, as recently as the 18th century, crimes which would be regarded as quite minor today were capital offenses. Writing in the 18th century, the Italian criminologist Cesare Beccaria advocated the idea that "the punishment should fit the crime." He said that "[w]e have seen that the true measure of crimes is the injury done to society." J. Farrer, Crimes and Punishments 199 (1880).

Gradually the list of crimes punishable by death diminished, and legislatures began grading the severity of crimes in accordance with the harm done by the criminal. The sentence for a given offense, rather than being precisely fixed by the legislature, was prescribed in terms of a minimum and a maximum, with the actual sentence to be decided by the judge. With the increasing importance of probation, as opposed to imprisonment, as a part of the penological process, some States such as California developed the "indeterminate sentence," where the time of incarceration was left almost entirely to the penological authorities rather than to the courts. But more recently the pendulum has swung back. The Federal Sentencing Guidelines, which went into effect in 1987, provided for very precise calibration of sentences, depending upon a number of factors. These factors relate both to the subjective guilt of the defendant and to the harm caused by his acts.

Wherever judges in recent years have had discretion to impose sentence, the consideration of the harm caused by the crime has been an important factor in the exercise of that discretion:

> "The first significance of harm in Anglo-American jurisprudence is, then, as a prerequisite to the criminal sanction. The second significance of harm—one no less important to judges—is as a measure of the seriousness of the offense and therefore as a standard for determining the severity of the sentence that will be meted out." S. Wheeler, K. Mann, & A. Sarat, Sitting in Judgment: The Sentencing of White-Collar Criminals 56 (1988).

Whatever the prevailing sentencing philosophy, the sentencing authority has always been free to consider a wide range of relevant material. *Williams v. New York,* 337 U.S. 241 (1949). In the federal system, we observed that "a judge may appropriately conduct an inquiry broad in scope, largely unlimited either as to the kind of information he may consider, or the source from which it may come." *United States v. Tucker,* 404 U.S. 443, 446 (1972). Even in the context of capital sentencing, prior to *Booth* the joint opinion of Justices Stewart, Powell, and STEVENS in *Gregg v. Georgia,* 428 U.S. 153, 203–204 (1976), had rejected petitioner's attack on the Georgia statute because of the "wide scope of evidence and argument allowed at presentence hearings." The joint opinion stated:

> "We think that the Georgia court wisely has chosen not to impose unnecessary restrictions on the evidence that can be offered at such a hearing and to approve open and far-ranging argument. . . . So long as the evidence introduced and the arguments made at the presentence hearing do not prejudice a defendant, it is preferable not to impose restrictions.

> We think it desirable for the jury to have as much information before it as possible when it makes the sentencing decision."

The Maryland statute involved in *Booth* required that the presentence report in all felony cases include a "victim impact statement" which would describe the effect of the crime on the victim and his family. *Booth, supra,* at 498. Congress and most of the States have, in recent years, enacted similar legislation to enable the sentencing authority to consider information about the harm caused by the crime committed by the defendant. The evidence involved in the present case was not admitted pursuant to any such enactment, but its purpose and effect were much the same as if it had been. While the admission of this particular kind of evidence—designed to portray for the sentencing authority the actual harm caused by a particular crime—is of recent origin, this fact hardly renders it unconstitutional. *Williams v. Florida,* 399 U.S. 78 (1970) (upholding the constitutionality of a notice-of-alibi statute, of a kind enacted by at least 15 States dating from 1927); *United States v. DiFrancesco,* 449 U.S. 117, 142 (1980) (upholding against a double jeopardy challenge an Act of Congress representing "a considered legislative attempt to attack a specific problem in our criminal justice system, that is, the tendency on the part of some trial judges 'to mete out light sentences in cases involving organized crime management personnel' ").

We have held that a State cannot preclude the sentencer from considering "any relevant mitigating evidence" that the defendant proffers in support of a sentence less than death. *Eddings v. Oklahoma,* 455 U.S. 104, 114 (1982). See also *Skipper v. South Carolina,* 476 U.S. 1 (1986). Thus we have, as the Court observed in *Booth,* required that the capital defendant be treated as a " 'uniquely individual human bein[g],' " 482 U.S., at 504 (quoting *Woodson v. North Carolina,* 428 U.S., at 304). But it was never held or even suggested in any of our cases preceding *Booth* that the defendant, entitled as he was to individualized consideration, was to receive that consideration wholly apart from the crime which he had committed. The language quoted from *Woodson* in the *Booth* opinion was not intended to describe a class of evidence that *could not* be received, but a class of evidence which *must* be received. Any doubt on the matter is dispelled by comparing the language in *Woodson* with the language from *Gregg v. Georgia,* quoted above, which was handed down the same day as *Woodson.* This misreading of precedent in *Booth* has, we think, unfairly weighted the scales in a capital trial; while virtually no limits are placed on the relevant mitigating evidence a capital defendant may introduce concerning his own circumstances, the State is barred from either offering "a quick glimpse of the life" which a defendant "chose to extinguish," *Mills v. Maryland,* 486 U.S. 367, 397 (1988) (REHNQUIST, C. J., dissenting), or demonstrating the loss to the victim's family and to society which has resulted from the defendant's homicide.

The *Booth* Court reasoned that victim impact evidence must be excluded because it would be difficult, if not impossible, for the defendant to rebut such evidence without shifting the focus of the sentencing hearing away from the defendant, thus creating a " 'mini-trial' on the victim's character." *Booth, supra,* at 506–507. In many cases the evidence relating to the victim is already before the jury at least in part because of its relevance at the guilt phase of the trial. But even as to additional evidence admitted at the sentencing phase, the mere fact that for tactical reasons it might not be prudent for the defense to rebut victim impact evidence makes the case no different than others in which a party is faced with this sort of a dilemma. As we explained in rejecting the contention that expert testimony on future dangerousness should be excluded from capital trials, "the rules of evidence generally extant at the federal and state levels anticipate that relevant, unprivileged evidence should be admitted and its weight left to the factfinder, who would have the benefit of cross-examination and contrary evidence by the opposing party." *Barefoot v. Estelle,* 463 U.S. 880, 898 (1983).

Payne echoes the concern voiced in *Booth*'s case that the admission of victim impact evidence permits a jury to find that defendants whose victims were assets to their community are more deserving of punishment than those whose victims are perceived to be less worthy. *Booth, supra,* at 506, n. 8. As a general matter, however, victim impact evidence is not offered to encourage comparative judgments of this kind—for instance, that the killer of a hardworking, devoted parent deserves the death penalty, but that the murderer of a reprobate does not. It is designed to show instead *each* victim's "uniqueness as an individual human being," whatever the jury might think the loss to the community resulting from his death might be. The facts of *Gathers* are an excellent illustration of this: The evidence showed that the victim was an out of work, mentally handicapped individual, perhaps not, in the eyes of most, a significant contributor to society, but nonetheless a murdered human being. . . .

The present case is an example of the potential for such unfairness. The capital sentencing jury heard testimony from Payne's girlfriend that they met at church; that he was affectionate, caring, and kind to her children; that he was not an abuser of drugs or alcohol; and that it was inconsistent with his character to have committed the murders. Payne's parents testified that he was a good son, and a clinical psychologist testified that Payne was an extremely polite prisoner and suffered from a low IQ. None of this testimony was related to the circumstances of Payne's brutal crimes. In contrast, the only evidence of the impact of Payne's offenses during the sentencing phase was Nicholas' grandmother's description—in response to a single question—that the child misses his mother and baby sister. Payne argues that the Eighth Amendment commands that the jury's death sentence must be set aside because the jury heard this testimony. But the testimony illustrated quite poignantly some of the harm that Payne's killing had caused; there is nothing unfair about allowing the jury to bear in mind that harm at the same time as it considers the mitigating evidence introduced by the defendant. The Supreme Court of Tennessee in this case obviously felt the unfairness of the rule pronounced by *Booth* when it said: "It is an affront to the civilized members of the human race to say that at sentencing in a capital case, a parade of witnesses may praise the background, character and good deeds of Defendant (as was done in this case), without limitation as to relevancy, but nothing may be said that bears upon the character of, or the harm imposed, upon the victims." 791 S.W. 2d, at 19.

In *Gathers,* as indicated above, we extended the holding of *Booth* barring victim impact evidence to the prosecutor's argument to the jury. Human nature being what it is, capable lawyers trying cases to juries try to convey to the jurors that the people involved in the underlying events are, or were, living human beings, with something to be gained or lost from the jury's verdict. Under the aegis of the Eighth Amendment, we have given the broadest latitude to the defendant to introduce relevant mitigating evidence reflecting on his individual personality, and the defendant's attorney may argue that evidence to the jury. Petitioner's attorney in this case did just that. For the reasons discussed above, we now reject the view—expressed in *Gathers*—that a State may not permit the prosecutor to similarly argue to the jury the human cost of the crime of which the defendant stands convicted. We reaffirm the view expressed by Justice Cardozo in *Snyder v. Massachusetts,* 291 U.S. 97, 122 (1934): "[J]ustice, though due to the accused, is due to the accuser also. The concept of fairness must not be strained till it is narrowed to a filament. We are to keep the balance true."

We thus hold that if the State chooses to permit the admission of victim impact evidence and prosecutorial argument on that subject, the Eighth Amendment erects no *per se* bar. A State may legitimately conclude that evidence about the victim and about the impact of the murder on the victim's family is relevant to the jury's decision as to whether or not the death penalty should be imposed. There is no reason to treat such evidence differently than other relevant evidence is treated.

Payne and his *amicus* argue that despite these numerous infirmities in the rule created by *Booth* and *Gathers,* we should adhere to the doctrine of *stare decisis* and stop short of overruling those cases. *Stare decisis* is the preferred course because it promotes the evenhanded, predictable, and consistent development of legal principles, fosters reliance on judicial decisions, and contributes to the actual and perceived integrity of the judicial process. See *Vasquez v. Hillery,* 474 U.S. 254, 265–266 (1986). Adhering to precedent "is usually the wise policy, because in most matters it is more important that the applicable rule of law be settled than it be settled right." *Burnet v. Coronado Oil & Gas Co.,* 285 U.S. 393, 406 (1932) (Brandeis, J., dissenting). Nevertheless, when governing decisions are unworkable or are badly reasoned, "this Court has never felt constrained to follow precedent." *Smith v. Allwright,* 321 U.S. 649, 665 (1944). *Stare decisis* is not an inexorable command; rather, it "is a principle of policy and not a mechanical formula of adherence to the latest decision." *Helvering v. Hallock,* 309 U.S. 106, 119 (1940). This is particularly true in constitutional cases, because in such cases "correction through legislative action is practically impossible." *Burnet v. Coronado Oil &*

Gas Co., supra, at 407 (Brandeis, J., dissenting). Considerations in favor of *stare decisis* are at their acme in cases involving property and contract rights, where reliance interests are involved, . . . the opposite is true in cases such as the present one involving procedural and evidentiary rules.

Applying these general principles, the Court has during the past 20 Terms overruled in whole or in part 33 of its previous constitutional decisions. *Booth* and *Gathers* were decided by the narrowest of margins, over spirited dissents challenging the basic underpinnings of those decisions. They have been questioned by Members of the Court in later decisions and have defied consistent application by the lower courts. See *Gathers,* 490 U.S., at 813 (O'CONNOR, J., dissenting); *Mills v. Maryland,* 486 U.S., at 395–396 (REHNQUIST, C. J., dissenting). See also *State v. Huertas,* 51 Ohio St. 3d 22, 33, 553 N. E. 2d 1058, 1070 (1990) ("The fact that the majority and two dissenters in this case all interpret the opinions and footnotes in *Booth* and *Gathers* differently demonstrates the uncertainty of the law in this area") (Moyer, C. J., concurring). Reconsidering these decisions now, we conclude, for the reasons heretofore stated, that they were wrongly decided and should be, and now are, overruled. We accordingly affirm the judgment of the Supreme Court of Tennessee.

It is so ordered

[STEVENS, J., dissenting.]

. . . Victim impact evidence, as used in this case, has two flaws, both related to the Eighth Amendment's command that the punishment of death may not be meted out arbitrarily or capriciously. First, aspects of the character of the victim unforeseeable to the defendant at the time of his crime are irrelevant to the defendant's "personal responsibility and moral guilt" and therefore cannot justify a death sentence. See *Enmund v. Florida,* 458 U.S., at 801: see also *id.,* at 825 (O'CONNOR, J., dissenting) ("[P]roportionality requires a nexus between the punishment imposed and the defendant's blameworthiness"); *Tison v. Arizona,* 481 U.S. 137, 149 (1987) ("The heart of the retribution rationale is that a criminal sentence must be directly related to the personal culpability of the criminal offender"); *California v. Brown,* 479 U.S. 538, 545 (1987) (O'CONNOR, J., concurring).

Second, the quantity and quality of victim impact evidence sufficient to turn a verdict of life in prison into a verdict of death is not defined until after the crime has been committed and therefore cannot possibly be applied consistently in different cases. The sentencer's unguided consideration of victim impact evidence thus conflicts with the principle central to our capital punishment jurisprudence that, "where discretion is afforded a sentencing body on a matter so grave as the determination of whether a human life should be taken or spared, that discretion must be suitably directed and limited so as to minimize the risk of wholly arbitrary and capricious action." *Gregg v. Georgia,* 428 U.S. 153, 189 (1976) (joint opinion of Stewart, Powell, and STEVENS, JJ.). Open-ended reliance by a capital sentencer on victim impact evidence simply does not provide a "principled way to distinguish [cases], in which the death penalty [i]s imposed, from the many cases in which it [i]s not." *Godfrey v. Georgia,* 446 U.S. 420, 433 (1980) (opinion of Stewart, J.).

The majority attempts to justify the admission of victim impact evidence by arguing that "consideration of the harm caused by the crime has been an important factor in the exercise of [sentencing] discretion." *Ante,* at 820. This statement is misleading and inaccurate. It is misleading because it is not limited to harm that is foreseeable. It is inaccurate because it fails to differentiate between legislative determinations and judicial sentencing. It is true that an evaluation of the harm caused by different kinds of wrongful conduct is a critical aspect in legislative definitions of offenses and determinations concerning sentencing guidelines. There is a rational correlation between moral culpability and the foreseeable harm caused by criminal conduct. Moreover, in the capital sentencing area, legislative identification of the special aggravating factors that may justify the imposition of the death penalty is entirely appropriate. But the majority cites no authority for the suggestion that unforeseeable and indirect harms to a victim's family are properly considered as aggravating evidence on a case-by-case basis.

The dissents in *Booth* and *Gathers* and the majority today offer only the recent decision in *Tison v. Arizona,* 481 U.S. 137 (1987), and two legislative examples to support their contention that harm to the victim has traditionally influenced sentencing discretion. *Tison* held that the death penalty may be imposed on a felon who acts with reckless disregard for human life if a death occurs in the course of the felony, even though capital punishment cannot be imposed if no one dies as a result of the crime. The first legislative example is that attempted murder and murder are classified as two different offenses subject to different punishments. *Ante,* at 819. The second legislative example is that a person who drives while intoxicated is guilty of vehicular homicide if his actions result in a death but is not guilty of this offense if he has the good fortune to make it home without killing anyone. See *Booth,* 482 U.S., at 516 (WHITE, J., dissenting).

These three scenarios, however, are fully consistent with the Eighth Amendment jurisprudence reflected in *Booth* and *Gathers* and do not demonstrate that harm to the victim may be considered by a capital sentencer in the ad hoc and post hoc manner authorized by today's majority. The majority's examples demonstrate only that harm to the victim may justify enhanced punishment if the harm is both foreseeable to the defendant and clearly identified in advance of the crime by the legislature as a class of harm that should in every case result in more severe punishment.

In each scenario, the defendants could reasonably foresee that their acts might result in loss of human life. In addition, in each, the decision that the defendants should be treated differently was made prior to the crime by the legislature, the decision of which is subject to scrutiny for basic rationality. Finally, in each scenario, every defendant who causes the well-defined harm of destroying a human life will be subject to the determination that his conduct should be punished more severely. The majority's scenarios therefore provide no support for its holding, which permits a jury to sentence a defendant to death because of harm to the victim and his family that the defendant could not foresee, which was not even identified until after the crime had been committed, and which may be deemed by the jury, without any rational explanation, to justify a death sentence in one case but not in another. Unlike the rule elucidated by the scenarios on which the majority relies, the majority's holding offends the Eighth Amendment because it permits the sentencer to rely on irrelevant evidence in an arbitrary and capricious manner.

The majority's argument that "the sentencing authority has always been free to consider a wide range of *relevant* material," *ante,* at 820–821 (emphasis added), thus cannot justify consideration of victim impact evidence that is *irrelevant* because it details harms that the defendant could not have foreseen. Nor does the majority's citation of *Gregg v. Georgia* concerning the "wide scope of evidence and argument allowed at presentence hearings," 428 U.S., at 203 (joint opinion of Stewart, Powell, and STEVENS, JJ.), support today's holding. See *ante,* at 821. The *Gregg* joint opinion endorsed the sentencer's consideration of a wide range of evidence "[s]o long as the evidence introduced and the arguments made at the presentence hearing do not prejudice a defendant." 428 U.S., at 203–204. Irrelevant victim impact evidence that distracts the sentencer from the proper focus of sentencing and encourages reliance on emotion and other arbitrary factors necessarily prejudices the defendant.

The majority's apparent inability to understand this fact is highlighted by its misunderstanding of Justice Powell's argument in *Booth* that admission of victim impact evidence is undesirable because it risks shifting the focus of the sentencing hearing away from the defendant and the circumstances of the crime and creating a "'mini-trial' on the victim's character." 482 U.S., at 507. *Booth* found this risk insupportable not, as today's majority suggests, because it creates a "tactical" "dilemma" for the defendant, see *ante,* at 823, but because it allows the possibility that the jury will be so distracted by prejudicial and irrelevant considerations that it will base its life-or-death decision on whim or caprice. See 482 U.S., at 506–507. . . .

PART 11

LEGAL ETHICS

Within the United States, the public does not hold lawyers in high esteem. Not only do "lawyer jokes" abound, but many believe that the behavior of all lawyers is so offensive that we should call *legal ethics* an oxymoron.[1] Quite simply, they believe that being both "a good lawyer and a good person" is impossible.[2] Part 11 explores some of the issues that generate such feelings toward lawyers and attempts to illustrate that it is possible to be a good lawyer and a good person at the same time.

Numerous potential ethical conflicts can arise for an individual lawyer on a day-to-day basis. Conflict of interest can undermine the lawyer-client relationship. Truth telling can become problematic when a lawyer's client is willing to commit perjury. Additionally, the adversarial system itself can force the lawyer to separate her roles in a way that might be personally uncomfortable. These overwhelming conflicts are only a few of the possible ethical dilemmas that surround lawyers. In examining such conflicts, the following essays illustrate that being both a lawyer and a "regular person" can be difficult and that this difficulty does not mean that every good lawyer is automatically a bad person.

Charles Fried begins "The Lawyer As Friend: The Moral Foundations of the Lawyer-Client Relation" by exploring the question underlying our discussion: Is the lawyer who subscribes to the traditional conception of the lawyer's role worthy of our—or even his own—respect? While Fried ultimately claims that such a lawyer is doing what is morally right, he acknowledges two harms that seem to contradict such a claim. First, social harm is caused by giving all one's attention to one client while other needy, and potentially more worthwhile, individuals and causes remain unrepresented. Further, lawyers spend their time showing clients how to get around the law—for example, how to avoid paying a tax although the tax is fair. Second, individual harm is caused by tactics that end up harming the opposing party. For example, although a lawyer might personally and professionally disagree with the tactic, he may question a rape victim, who the lawyer knows is telling the truth, about her sex life in order to undermine her potentially damaging testimony.

Given these potential harms, Fried nevertheless claims that favoring her client can be morally right for a lawyer. This is possible, in Fried's opinion, if we reject the utilitarian view that supports the specified harms. Fried argues that we should use the language of rights and describe the lawyer-client relationship as similar to friendship, although one with a "special purpose." Much like a friend, the client can be considered to have a special claim to the lawyer's concern. This claim is largely due to the special role of lawyers within our complex legal system. Because the legal system must allow individuals to exercise their autonomy, a lawyer's purpose is simply to help her client in that exercise. Without a lawyer, given the very complexity of the law, the exercise of autonomy would be

[1] Charles Wolfram, *Modern Legal Ethics* (St. Paul, MN: West, 1986): 76.
[2] Ibid.

slight or nonexistent. Thus, the system itself positions the lawyer as a "legal friend." Fried recognizes that this relationship appears one-sided, but he claims we should not view this as problematic. In her role as legal friend, the lawyer ensures that the judicial system does not violate her client's legal rights. As such, Fried finds this action to be a morally worthy cause.

In contrast to Fried, David Luban, in "Why Have an Adversary System?" argues that it is not the system of laws, but rather the adversarial system itself, that provides the context for lawyers' behavior. Moreover, Luban contends that a "pragmatic justification" supports the adversarial system. Luban argues that the current adversarial system works well at finding the truth and protecting legal rights. Additionally, no other system is better than the adversarial method. Because some system is necessary and ours is based on the adversarial system, we ought to keep it in place. Luban offers a straightforward cost-benefit analysis of the present system: because the costs of replacement would outweigh the benefits, we ought not replace our current adversarial system.

After acknowledging that some might find this argument weak, Luban offers an analysis of the German inquisitorial system to further advance his claim. If the United States were to implement an inquisitorial system, the judges and therefore the state would play a greater role, while lawyers would play a diminished role. Moreover, given that judges under this system decide what evidence to consider, individuals would not be able to present "their" cases. This is an ability that Luban believes we value too much to abandon. Additionally, such a system requires more trust in officials and government overall than we would be willing to countenance. Given these practical arguments against changing systems, Luban believes that the adversarial system is justified, because changing the system would require too much of us as participants.

The selection by Kenneth Kipnis, "Conflict of Interest and Conflict of Obligation," focuses not on the adversarial system in general, but on a more specific problem. Kipnis identifies three distinct situations that can result in a conflict of interest. According to Kipnis, the first situation is most accurately called a *conflict of obligation,* a situation in which a lawyer has, or will come to have, conflicting obligations. The second scenario, which Kipnis specifically labels a "conflict of interest," comprises the cases where some fact has called the loyalty of a lawyer into question. Finally, Kipnis recognizes a type of conflict of interest where there are two interests and the satisfaction of any one of the interests precludes the satisfaction of the other.

Kipnis discusses several cases designed both to illustrate the potential conflicts that a lawyer might face and to outline what makes these cases ethically interesting. One general ethical problem occurs when a lawyer's obligations to one client conflict with his obligations to another. Kipnis identifies two varieties of this general example. First, when a lawyer attempts to represent divergent interests simultaneously, a conflict of interest may arise. For example, a lawyer who represents multiple parties may have to decide whether or not to appeal a verdict that harms some of the parties while satisfying others. Second, successive representations can also present a conflict of interest. For example, confidentiality to a former client still binds the lawyer who is approached to bring suit against that former client. Another general ethical problem occurs when the lawyer herself has an interest that might result in a conflict with her client. For example, a lawyer may refer a case to a colleague who pays her a referral fee. In these examples, Kipnis argues that the lawyer is under an obligation to disclose the potential conflict and then offer some alternative that will prevent the dilemma. No matter if the lawyer believes she can reasonably avoid a conflict, she must avoid even the appearance of improper activity, so that trust in the system as a whole is not eroded.

In "Conflict of Interest," Larry May further elaborates on such problems. May argues that, despite popular views to the contrary, a lawyer cannot exercise total loyalty to a client. Lawyers often see the law as a business, they view particular cases as potentially advancing their careers, and they have political opinions that hold sway over them. Given these and other potential conflicts, May argues that lawyers have an obligation to disclose to their clients those beliefs, values, and so forth that might create a conflict of interest. May claims that lawyers must, above all else, never infringe a client's autonomy or deceive a client. Once a lawyer has fully disclosed any potential for conflicts, the client can examine the options and either accept the potential for conflict or reject the lawyer as too problematic and begin a new search for representation.

While such disclosure might be difficult, May argues that it is no more difficult than what the traditional view demands. Lawyers must engage in honest, critical self-reflection to discover their own values, but such self-reflection is necessary under the traditional view that calls for complete loyalty. Additionally, while some argue that conflict creates the temptation for wrongdoing, May argues that this need not always be the case. Such a view discounts the potential for genuine conflict that wrongdoing has not tainted. While May argues that no lawyer can ever be totally loyal to a client, he does demand that if any harm occurs because of a conflict, then the lawyer must regret her actions.

The next selection, *Wheat v. United States,* is provided as an example of a potential conflict of interest. Here, Mark Wheat and several codefendants had been charged in a drug conspiracy. Attorney Eugene Iredale represented two of the codefendants. One client, Juvenal Gomez-Barajas, was acquitted on drug charges and, rather than face another trial on additional charges, pled guilty to tax evasion and illegal importation of merchandise. The second client, Javier Bravo, decided to plead guilty to one count of transporting marijuana. Iredale notified the court that Wheat had contacted him and requested that Iredale represent his case also. The government objected to this representation on the grounds of a serious conflict of interest for two reasons. First, the plea entered by Gomez-Barajas was not finalized. If the plea were withdrawn, the government would likely call Wheat to testify against Gomez-Barajas, in which case Iredale could not cross-examine him and thus could not effectively represent Gomez-Barajas. Second, the government would likely call Bravo to testify against Wheat in his pending case, in which case Iredale could not cross-examine him and thus could not effectively represent Wheat. The Supreme Court upheld the lower court's ruling for the government's objection. The Court ruled that the original ruling had not violated Wheat's Sixth Amendment rights. Although all three men had signed waivers of conflict-of-interest, the Court found that there was a substantial risk of such conflict and consequently the waivers could not be upheld.

In the next selection, Monroe H. Freedman focuses specifically on the role of the criminal defense lawyer and explores what he finds to be the "three hardest questions" a criminal defense lawyer will face. While Freedman claims that criminal defense lawyers must have the whole truth from their clients, he acknowledges that such knowledge can lead to ethical dilemmas for the lawyer. First, is it proper to cross-examine a truth-telling witness with the intention of discrediting the witness for the sake of the client? Freedman argues that a criminal defense lawyer must attempt to destroy such testimony because to fail to do so might keep clients from full disclosure. For example, to ensure a vigorous attack on witness testimony, a client might not choose to disclose facts of the case; but this could allow disastrous results if the lawyer is unprepared for evidence that the opposing counsel possesses.

Second, is it proper to place a witness on the stand who the lawyer knows will commit perjury? Again, Freedman argues that doing so is proper for a lawyer. If the potential perjurer is the client, the lawyer must allow her client to take the stand, because failure to do so greatly increases the chance of conviction, which violates the lawyer's duty of zealous advocacy. Additionally, the lawyer cannot withdraw from the case without seriously damaging the client's case. Freedman argues that the lawyer should remain on the case, allow the witness to testify, but attempt to dissuade the witness from committing perjury.

Finally, should the lawyer give legal advice that she believes will lead the client to commit perjury? Freedman says yes. The lawyer must give the client all legal information related to the case. After that, the client must decide how to use the information. The lawyer cannot make this judgment for the client, because doing so would penalize those who are less educated about the law and could limit truth telling by the client. Freedman concludes by claiming that, though some might reject his answers to these three difficult questions, such answers are necessary if the system is to function well.

In the final essay, "Breaking the Law: Lawyers and Clients in Struggles for Social Change," Martha Minow explores the need for lawyers to understand the client's point of view when the client is interested in using the law to achieve social change. Minow is especially interested in cases where a client has decided to break the law as a strategy for achieving such change. While a client may choose this strategy for many reasons, Minow focuses on what ought to affect a lawyer's decision to accept such a client. According to Minow, individual lawyers need to represent lawbreakers; additionally, the legal system needs the type of individual who wants to break the law for social reasons. Specifically, Minow claims that those who protest the laws by violating them serve as a check on a system that generally acts to curb social change. First, these lawbreakers expose and remind legal officials of their biases, both real and potential. Second, they illustrate the limited ability of the law to serve as a moral authority. This illustration can motivate others to challenge the law when other circumstances warrant such action.

While a lawyer should support her socially motivated client for these reasons, Minow cautions lawyers against potential conflicts. First, lawyers must be careful not to focus on winning at the expense of the client's beliefs. Though some clients may agree to such a focus, others may not be so willing to give up their beliefs. Second, a lawyer must be sure not to degrade his client's commitments. A lawyer ought not to argue in a way that does not reflect his client's values and commitments, especially if this means violating the very commitments at stake. For example, a lawyer may argue for a gay client that, although gay sexuality is offensive, sodomy statutes are unconstitutional. Finally, a lawyer must be sure to serve the client's interests. For example, a lawyer should refrain from seeking press attention if her client does not desire such attention. Taken as a whole, Minow's position requires a lawyer to take on her client's perspective, no matter how difficult a lawyer might find that action.

Though we merely begin to represent the scope of problems in legal ethics, we hope you have gained a better understanding of the dilemmas lawyers face. Please see the selected readings that follow.

SELECTED READINGS

American Bar Association. *Code of Professional Responsibility.* Chicago: American Bar Association, 1970.

Auerbach, Jerold. *Unequal Justice: Lawyers and Social Change in Modern America.* New York: Oxford University Press, 1976.

Bayles, Michael. *Professional Ethics.* Belmont, CA: Wadsworth, 1981.

D'Amato, Anthony, and Eberle, Edward J. "Three Models of Legal Ethics." *Saint Louis University Law Journal* 27 (1983): 761–99.

Davis, Michael. "Conflict of Interest." *Business and Professional Ethics Journal* 1 (1982): 17–28.

Freedman, Monroe. *Understanding Lawyers' Ethics.* New York: Matthew Bender, 1990.

Fried, Charles. *Right and Wrong.* Cambridge, MA: Harvard University Press, 1978.

Goldman, Alan H. *The Moral Foundation of Professional Ethics.* Totowa, NJ: Rowman and Littlefield, 1980.

Green, Mark. *The Other Government: The Unseen Power of Washington Lawyers.* New York: Grossman, 1975.

Hazard, Geoffrey C., Jr. *Ethics in the Practice of Law.* New Haven, CT: Yale University Press, 1978.

Hoffer, Peter. *The Law's Conscience.* Chapel Hill: University of North Carolina, 1990.

Kipnis, Kenneth. *Legal Ethics.* Englewood Cliffs, NJ: Prentice-Hall, 1986.

Kronman, Anthony. *The Lost Lawyer.* Cambridge, MA: Harvard University Press, 1993.

Luban, David, ed. *The Good Lawyer: Lawyers' Roles and Lawyers' Ethics.* Totowa, NJ: Rowman and Allanheld, 1984.

———. *Lawyers and Justice.* Princeton, NJ: Princeton University Press, 1988.

Martin, Mike W. "Rights and the Meta-Ethics of Professional Morality." *Ethics* 91(1981): 619–25.

Meltsner, Michael, and Philip Schrag. *Public Interest Advocacy: Materials for Clinical Legal Education.* Boston: Little, Brown, 1974.

Morgan, Thomas D. "The Evolving Concept of Professional Responsibility." *Harvard Law Review* 90 (1977): 702–43.

Schrader, Donald, ed. *Ethics and the Practice of Law.* Englewood Cliffs, NJ: Prentice-Hall, 1988.

Wasserstrom, Richard A., ed. *Morality and the Law.* Belmont, CA: Wadsworth, 1971.

Wolfram, Charles. *Modern Legal Ethics.* St. Paul, MN: West, 1986.

85

CHARLES FRIED

The Lawyer As Friend: The Moral Foundations of the Lawyer–Client Relation

Advocatus sed non ladro, Res miranda populo ....
—MEDIEVAL ANTHEM HONORING ST. IVES

Can a good lawyer be a good person? The question troubles lawyers and law students alike. They are troubled by the demands of loyalty to one's client and by the fact that one can win approval as a good, maybe even great, lawyer even though that loyalty is engrossed by overprivileged or positively distasteful clients. How, they ask, is such loyalty compatible with that devotion to the common good characteristic of high moral principles? And whatever their views of the common good, they are troubled because the willingness of lawyers to help their clients use the law to the prejudice of the weak or the innocent seems morally corrupt. The lawyer is conventionally seen as a professional devoted to his client's interests and as authorized, if not in fact required, to do some things (though not anything) for that client which he would not do for himself.[1] In this essay I consider the compatibility between this traditional conception of the lawyer's role and the ideal of moral purity—the ideal that one's life should be lived in fulfillment of the most demanding moral principles, and not just barely within the law. So I shall not be particularly concerned with the precise limits imposed on the lawyer's conduct by positive rules of the law and by the American Bar Association's *Code of Professional Responsibility*[2] except as these provide a background. I assume that the lawyer observes these scrupulously. My inquiry is one of morals: Does the lawyer whose conduct and choices are governed only by the traditional conception of the lawyer's role, which these positive rules reflect, lead a professional life worthy of moral approbation, worthy of respect—ours and his own?

I. THE CHALLENGE TO THE TRADITIONAL CONCEPTION

A. The Two Criticisms

Two frequent criticisms of the traditional conception of the lawyer's role attack both its ends and its means. First, it is said that the ideal of professional loyalty to one's client permits, even demands, an allocation of the lawyer's time, passion, and resources in ways that are not always maximally conducive to the greatest good of the greatest number.[3] Interestingly, this criticism is leveled increasingly against doctors[4] as well

---

[1]*See, e.g.,* J. Auerbach, *Unequal Justice* (1976); M. Green, *The Other Government* (1975).

Lord Brougham stated the traditional view of the lawyer's role during his defense of Queen Caroline:

> [A]n advocate, in the discharge of his duty, knows but one person in all the world, and that person is his client. To save that client by all means and expedients, and at all hazards and costs to other persons, and, among them, to himself, is his first and only duty; and in performing this duty he must not regard the alarm, the torments, the destruction which he may bring upon others. Separating the duty of a patriot from that of an advocate, he must go on reckless of consequences, though it should be his unhappy fate to involve his country in confusion.

2 *Trial of Queen Caroline* 8 (J. Nightingale ed. 1821). A sharply contrasting view was held by law professors at the University of Havanna who said that "the first job of a revolutionary lawyer is not to argue that his client is innocent, but rather to determine if his client is guilty and if so, to seek the sanction which will best rehabilitate him." Berman, "The Cuban Popular Tribunals," 69 *Colum. L. Rev.* 1317, 1341 (1969). And a Bulgarian attorney has been quoted as saying, "'In a Socialist state there is no division of duty between the judge, prosecutor and defense counsel ... the defense must assist the prosecution to find the objective truth in a case.'" J. Kaplan, *Criminal Justice: Introductory Cases and Materials* 264–65 (1973).

[2]The American Bar Association approved a revised *Code of Professional Responsibility* in 1969. In part that revision was a response to the criticism that the legal profession, by failing to make legal services more widely available, had not met its public responsibilities. J. Auerbach, *supra* note 1, at 285–86. *See also Preface,* ABA Code of Professional Responsibility.

[3]*See* M. Green, *supra* note 1, at 268–69, 285–89.

[4]*See* V. Fuchs, *Who Shall Live?* 60 (1974); Havighurst and Blumstein, "Coping with Quality/Cost Trade-Offs in Medical Care: The Role of PSROs," 70 *Nw. U. L. Rev.* 6, 25–28 (1975). *But see* Fried, "Equality and Rights in Medical Care," 6 *Hastings Center Rep.* 29, 33–34 (1976).

as lawyers. Both professions affirm the principle that the professional's primary loyalty is to his client,[5] his patient. A "good" lawyer will lavish energy and resources on his existing client, even if it can be shown that others could derive greater benefit from them. The professional ideal authorizes a care for the client and the patient which exceeds what the efficient distribution of a scarce social resource (the professional's time) would dictate.

That same professional ideal has little or nothing to say about the initial choice of clients or patients. Certainly it is laudable if the doctor and lawyer choose their clients among the poorest or sickest or most dramatically threatened, but the professional ideal does not require this kind of choice in any systematic way—the choice of client remains largely a matter of fortuity or arbitrary choice. But once the client has been chosen, the professional ideal requires primary loyalty to the client whatever his need or situation. Critics contend that it is wasteful and immoral that some of the finest talent in the legal profession is devoted to the intricacies of, say, corporate finance or elaborate estate plans, while important public and private needs for legal services go unmet. The immorality of this waste is seen to be compounded when the clients who are the beneficiaries of this lavish attention use it to avoid their obligations in justice (if not in law) to society and to perpetuate their (legal) domination of the very groups whose greater needs these lawyers should be meeting.[6]

The second criticism applies particularly to the lawyer. It addresses not the misallocation of scarce resources, which the lawyer's exclusive concern with his client's interests permits, but the means which this loyalty appears to authorize, tactics which procure advantages for the client at the direct expense of some identified opposing party. Examples are discrediting a nervous but probably truthful complaining witness[7] or taking advantage of the need or ignorance of an adversary in a negotiation. This second criticism is, of course, related to the first, but there is a difference. The first criticism focuses on a social harm: the waste of scarce resources implicit in a doctor caring for the hearts of the sedentary managerial classes or a lawyer tending to the estates and marital difficulties of the rich. The professional is accused of failing to confer benefits wisely and efficiently. By the second criticism the lawyer is accused not of failing to benefit the appropriate, though usually unidentified, persons, but of harming his identified adversary.[8]

B. Examples

Consider a number of cases which illustrate the first criticism: A doctor is said to owe a duty of loyalty to his patient, but how is he to react if doing his very

[5]*See* ABA Code of Professional Responsibility Canon 7.

[6]For a description of the growth of such criticisms, see J. Auerbach, *supra* note 1, at 275–88.

[7]For a defense of an attorney's use of such tactics, see M. Freedman, *Lawyers' Ethics in an Adversary System* 43–49 (1975). *See also* Curtis, "The Ethics of Advocacy,"[11] 4 *Stan L. Rev.* 3 (1951).

[8]The point really carries further than the distinction between benefit and harm. In the former case, though some particular person may have benefited had the distribution been efficient, it does not seem correct to say that for that reason this person had a right to the benefit which he was denied, or that this person was wronged by not receiving the benefit. Individuals do not acquire rights under policies which are dictated purely by considerations of efficiency. *See generally* Dworkin, "Hard Cases," 88 *Harv. L. Rev.* 1057, 1058–78 (1975).

Professor Anscombe makes the following suggestive argument: If saving the life of one patient requires a massive dose of a drug that could be divided up and used to save five other people, not one of those five can claim that he has been wronged, that the smaller dose of the drug was owed to him.

> Yet all can reproach me if I gave it to none. It was there, ready to supply human need, and human need was not supplied. So any one of them can say: you ought to have used it to help us who needed it; and so all are wronged. But if it was used for someone, as much as he needed it to keep him alive, no one has any ground for accusing me of having wronged *himself*.—Why, just because he was one of five who could have been saved, is he wronged in not being saved, if someone is supplied with it who needed it? What is *his* claim, except the claim that what was needed go to him rather than be wasted? But it was not wasted. So he was not wronged. So who was wronged? And if no one was wronged, what injury did I do?
>
> . . . .
>
> I do not mean "because they are more" isn't a good reason for helping these and not that one, or these rather than those. It is a perfectly intelligible reason. But it doesn't follow from that that a man acts badly if he doesn't make it his reason. He acts badly if human need for what is in his power to give doesn't work in him as a reason. He acts badly if he chooses to rescue rich people rather than poor ones, having ill regard for the poor ones because they are poor. But he doesn't act badly if he uses his resources to save X, or X, Y and Z, *for no bad reason,* and is not affected by the consideration that he could save a larger number of people. For, once more: who can say he is wronged? And if no one is wronged, how does the rescuer commit any wrong?

Anscombe, "Who is Wronged?" 5 *Oxford Rev.* 16, 16–17 (1967) (emphasis in original).

best for his patient would deplete the resources of the patient's family, as in the case of a severely deformed baby who can only be kept alive through extraordinarily expensive means? Should a doctor prescribe every test of distinct but marginal utility for every patient on public assistance, even if he knows that in the aggregate such a policy will put the medical care system under intolerable burdens?[9] Should he subject his patients to prudent testing of new remedies because he knows that only in this way can medicine make the strides that it has in the past?[10]

These problems are analogous to problems which are faced by the lawyer. The lawyer who advises a client how to avoid the effects of a tax or a form of regulation, though it is a fair tax or a regulation in the public interest, is facing the same dilemma and resolving it in favor of his client. So does the public defender who accedes to his client's demands and takes a "losing" case to trial, thereby wasting court time and depleting the limited resources of his organization. We tolerate and indeed may applaud the decision of a lawyer who vigorously defends a criminal whom he believes to be guilty and dangerous.[11] And I for one think that a lawyer who arranges the estate of a disagreeable dowager or represents one of the parties in a bitter matrimonial dispute must be as assiduous and single-minded in fulfilling his obligation to that client as the lawyer who is defending the civil liberties case of the century.

Illustrative of the second criticism (doing things which are offensive to a particular person) are familiar situations such as the following: In a negotiation it becomes clear to the lawyer for the seller that the buyer and his lawyer mistakenly believe that somebody else has already offered a handsome price for the property. The buyer asks the seller if this is true, and the seller's lawyer hears his client give an ambiguous but clearly encouraging response.[12] Another classic case is the interposition of a technical defense such as the running of the statute of limitations to defeat a debt that the client admits he owes.[13]

There is another class of cases which does not so unambiguously involve the lawyer's furthering his client's interests at the direct expense of some equally identified, concrete individual, but where furthering those interests does require the lawyer to do things which are personally offensive to him. The conventional paradigms in the casuistic literature deal with criminal defense lawyers who are asked improper questions by the trial judge ("Your client doesn't have a criminal record, does he?" or "Your client hasn't offered to plead guilty to a lesser offense, has he?"), a truthful answer to which would be damningly prejudicial to the client, but which the lawyer must lie in defense of his client's interests even though lying is personally and professionally offensive to him.[14] The defense lawyer who cross-examines a complaining rape victim (whom he knows to be telling the truth) about her chastity or lack thereof in order to discredit her accusing testimony faces a similar moral difficulty. In some respects these cases might be taken to illustrate both principal criticisms of the traditional conception. On the one hand, there is harm to society in making the choice to favor the client's interests: a dangerous criminal may escape punishment or an appropriately heavy sentence. On the other hand, this social harm is accomplished by means of acting towards another human being—the judge, the complaining witness—in ways that seem demeaning and dishonorable.

---

[9]*See generally* V. Fuchs, *supra* note 4, at 94–95; Fried, "Rights and Health Care—Beyond Equity and Efficiency," 293 *New England J. Medicine* 241, 244 (1975).

[10]For discussions of this dilemma, see A. Cochrane, *Effectiveness and Efficiency* (1972); C. Fried, *Medical Experimentation: Personal Integrity and Social Policy* (1974).

[11]*See* M. Freedman, *supra* note 7, at 43–49.

[12]DR 7-102(A)(5) of the *Code of Professional Responsibility* states that a lawyer shall not knowingly make a false statement of law or fact in his representation of a client. The issue is how to apply this admonition in the context of negotiation, where deception is commonplace. *See* M. Meltsner and P. Schrag, *Public Interest Advocacy: Materials for Clinical Legal Education* 231–39 (1974).

[13]For a striking example, see *Zabella v. Pakel*, 242 F.2d 452 (7th Cir. 1957), where the debtor asserting the technical defenses was a savings and loan association president, and the creditor was a man who had worked for him as a carpenter and had lent him money in earlier, less fortunate days.

[14]Although Charles Curtis explicitly denounces lying to the court, his observation that the propriety of lying might depend on whether the question is asked "by someone who has a right to ask it" at least implies a possible qualification in the case of improper questioning by the court. Curtis, *supra* note 7, at 7–9. Monroe Freedman does not specifically address this problem, but his argument that an attorney's duty to safeguard the attorney-client privilege requires the attorney to introduce his client's perjurious testimony would seem to extend to this situation. M. Freedman, *supra* note 7, at 27–41. *Cf.* ABA Comm. on Professional Ethics, Opinions No. 287 (1967) (if attorney for defendant learns of previous criminal record through his communications with his client, he has no duty to correct misapprehension on part of court that client has no record).

II. THE LAWYER AS FRIEND

A. The Thesis

In this essay, I will consider the moral status of the traditional conception of the professional. The two criticisms of this traditional conception, if left unanswered, will not put the lawyer in jail, but they will leave him without a moral basis for his acts. The real question is whether, in the face of these two criticisms, a decent and morally sensitive person can conduct himself according to the traditional conception of professional loyalty and still believe that what he is doing is morally worthwhile.

It might be said that any one whose conscience is so tender that he cannot fulfill the prescribed obligations of a professional should not undertake those obligations. He should not allow his moral scruples to operate as a trap for those who are told by the law that they may expect something more. But of course this suggestion merely pushes the inquiry back a step. We must ask then not how a decent lawyer may behave, but whether a decent, ethical person can ever be a lawyer. Are the assurances implicit in assuming the role of lawyer such that an honorable person would not give them and thus would not enter the profession? And, indeed, this is a general point about an argument from obligation:[15] It may be that the internal logic of a particular obligation demands certain forms of conduct (e.g., honor among thieves), but the question remains whether it is just and moral to contract such obligations.

I will argue in this essay that it is not only legally but also morally right that a lawyer adopt as his dominant purpose the furthering of his client's interests—that it is right that a professional put the interests of his client above some idea, however valid, of the collective interest. I maintain that the traditional conception of the professional role expresses a morally valid conception of human conduct and human relationships, that one who acts according to that conception is to that extent a good person. Indeed, it is my view that, far from being a mere creature of positive law, the traditional conception is so far mandated by moral right that any advanced legal system which did not sanction this conception would be unjust.

The general problem raised by the two criticisms is this: How can it be that it is not only permissible, but indeed morally right, to favor the interests of a particular person in a way which we can be fairly sure is either harmful to another particular individual or not maximally conducive to the welfare of society as a whole?[16]

The resolution of this problem is aided, I think, if set in a larger perspective. Charles Curtis made the perspicacious remark that a lawyer may be privileged to lie for his client in a way that one might lie to save one's friends or close relatives.[17] I do not want to underwrite the notion that it is justifiable to lie even in those situations, but there is a great deal to the point that in those relations—friendship, kinship—we recognize an authorization to take the interests of particular concrete persons more seriously and to give them priority over the interests of the wider collectivity. One who provides an expensive education for his own children surely cannot be blamed because he does not use those resources to alleviate famine or to save lives in some distant land. Nor does he blame himself. Indeed, our intuition that an individual is authorized to prefer identified persons standing close to him over the abstract interests of humanity finds its sharpest expression in our sense that an individual is entitled to act with something less than impartiality to that person who stands closest to him—the person that he is. There is such a thing as selfishness to be sure, yet no reasonable morality asks us to look upon ourselves as merely plausible candidates for the distribution of the attention and resources which we command, plausible candidates whose entitlement to our own concern is no greater in principle than that of any other human

---

[15]That one assumes obligations to persons which cannot always be overridden by the benefits which would accrue from aiding some third person is a standard objection to utilitarianism. *See, e.g.,* W. Ross, *The Right and the Good* 17–19 (1930).

[16]I have discussed this problem elsewhere. C. Fried, *An Anatomy of Values* 207–36 (1970); C. Fried, *supra* note 10, at 132–37. *Cf.* Schelling, "The Life You Save May Be Your Own," in *Problems in Public Expenditure Analysis* 127, 129–30 (S. Chase ed. 1968) (also discussing our greater concern for known, as opposed to unknown, individuals).

[17]Curtis, *supra* note 7, at 8. Analogizing the lawyer to a friend raises a range of problems upon which I shall not touch. These have to do with the lawyer's benevolent and sometimes not so benevolent tyranny over and imposition on his client, seemingly authorized by the claim to be acting in the client's interests. Domineering paternalism is not a normal characteristic of friendship. This point is due to Jay Katz.

being. Such a doctrine may seem edifying, but on reflection it strikes us as merely fanatical.

This suggests an interesting way to look at the situation of the lawyer. As a professional person one has a special care for the interests of those accepted as clients, just as his friends, his family, and he himself have a very general claim to his special concern. But I concede this does no more than widen the problem. It merely shows that in claiming this authorization to have a special care for my clients I am doing something which I do in other contexts as well.

B. The Utilitarian Explanation

I consider first an argument to account for fidelity to role, for obligation, made most elaborately by the classical utilitarians, Mill[18] and Sidgwick.[19] They argued that our propensity to prefer the interests of those who are close to us is in fact perfectly reasonable because we are more likely to be able to benefit those people. Thus, if everyone is mainly concerned with those closest to him, the distribution of social energies will be most efficient and the greatest good of the greatest number will be achieved. The idea is that the efforts I expend for my friend or my relative are more likely to be effective because I am more likely to know what needs to be done. I am more likely to be sure that the good I intend is in fact accomplished. One might say that there is less overhead, fewer administrative costs, in benefiting those nearest to us. I would not want to ridicule this argument, but it does not seem to me to go far enough. Because if that were the sole basis for the preference, then it would be my duty to determine whether my efforts might not be more efficiently spent on the collectivity, on the distant, anonymous beneficiary. But it is just my point that *this* is an inquiry we are not required, indeed sometimes not even authorized, to make. When we decide to care for our children, to assure our own comforts, to fulfill our obligations to our clients or patients, we do not do so as a result of a cost–benefit inquiry which takes into account the ease of producing a good result for our friends and relations.

Might it not be said, however, that the best means of favoring the abstract collectivity is in certain cases not to try to favor it directly but to concentrate on those to whom one has a special relation? This does not involve tricking oneself, but only recognizing the limitations of what an individual can do and know. But that, it seems to me, is just Mill's and Sidgwick's argument all over again. There is no trickery involved, but this is still a kind of deliberate limitation of our moral horizon which leaves us uncomfortable. Do I know in a particular case whether sticking to the narrow definition of my role will *in that case* further the good of all? If I know that it will not further the general good, then why am I acting as the role demands? Is it to avoid setting a bad example? But for whom? I need not tell others—whether I tell or not could enter into my calculation. For myself then? But that begs the question, since if short-circuiting the role-definition of my obligation and going straight for the general good is the best thing to do in that case, then the example I set myself is not a bad example, but a good example. In short, I do not see how one can at the same time admit that the general good is one's only moral standard, while steadfastly hewing to obligations to friends, family, and clients. What we must look for is an argument which shows that giving some degree of special consideration to myself, my friends, my clients is not merely instrumentally justified (as the utilitarians would argue) but to some degree intrinsically so.[20]

I think such an argument can be made. Instead of speaking the language of maximization of value over all of humanity, it will speak the language of rights. The stubborn ethical datum affirming such a preference grows out of the profoundest springs of morality: the concepts of personality, identity, and liberty.

C. Self, Friendship, and Justice

Consider for a moment the picture of the human person that would emerge if the utilitarian claim were in fact correct. It would mean that in all my choices I must consider the well-being of all humanity—actual and potential—as the range of my concern. Moreover, every actual or potential human being is absolutely equal in his claims upon me. Indeed, I myself am to

[18]Mill, "Utilitarianism," in *The Philosophy of John Stuart Mill* 321, 342–44 (M. Cohen ed. 1961).

[19]H. Sidgwick, *The Methods of Ethics* 252 (7th ed. 1907).

[20]*See generally* D. Lyons, *Forms and Limits of Utilitarianism* (1965); J. Smart and B. Williams, *Utilitarianism: For and Against* (1973); Harrod, "Utilitarianism Revised," 45 *Mind* 137 (1936); Mabbott, "Punishment," 48 *Mind* 152 (1939).

myself only as one of this innumerable multitude. And that is the clue to what is wrong with the utilitarian vision. Before there is morality there must be the person. We must attain and maintain in our morality a concept of personality such that it makes sense to posit choosing, valuing entities—free, moral beings. But the picture of the moral universe in which my own interests disappear and are merged into the interests of the totality of humanity is incompatible with that,[21] because one wishes to develop a conception of a responsible, valuable, and valuing agent, and such an agent must first of all be dear to himself. It is from the kernel of individuality that the other things we value radiate. The Gospel says we must love our neighbor as ourselves and this implies that any concern for others which is a *human* concern must presuppose a concern for ourselves.[22] The human concern which we then show others is a concern which first of all recognizes the concrete individuality of that other person just as we recognize our own.

It might be objected that the picture I sketch does not show that each individual, in order to maintain the integral sense of himself as an individual, is justified in attributing a greater value to his most essential interests than he ascribes to the most essential interests of all other persons. Should not the individual generalize and attribute in equal degree to all persons the value which he naturally attributes to himself? I agree with those who hold that it is the essence of morality for reason to push us beyond inclination to the fair conclusion of our premises.[23] It *is* fair conclusion that as my experience as a judging, valuing, choosing entity is crucial to me, I must also conclude that for other persons their own lives and desires are the center of their universe. If morality is transcendent, it must somehow transcend particularity to take account of this general fact. I do not wish to deny this. On the contrary, my claim is that the kind of preference which an individual gives himself and concrete others is a preference which he would in exactly this universalizing spirit allow others to exhibit as well. It is not that I callously overlook the claim of the abstract individual, but indeed I would understand and approve were I myself to be prejudiced because some person to whom I stood in a similar situation of abstraction preferred his own concrete dimensions.

Finally, the concreteness which is the starting point of my own moral sensibility, the sense of myself, is not just a historical, biographical fact. It continues to enter into and condition my moral judgments because the effects which I can produce upon people who are close to me are qualitatively different from those produced upon abstract, unknown persons. My own concreteness is important not only because it establishes a basis for understanding what I and what all other human beings might be, but because in engaging that aspect of myself with the concrete aspects of others, I realize special values for both of us. Quite simply, the individualized relations of love and friendship (and perhaps also their opposites, hatred and enmity) have a different, more intense aspect than do the cooler, more abstract relations of love and service to human-

---

[21] *See generally* C. Fried, *An Anatomy of Values,* 203–06; Rawls, "The Independence of Moral Theory," 48 *Am. Phil. Ass'n* 17–20 (1975) (Kantian theory, as compared to utilitarianism, takes seriously basic moral fact of primacy of notion of individual personality).

[22] . . . It is written (Lev. xix. 18, Matth. xxii. 39); *Thou shalt love thy neighbor* (Lev. *loc. cit.,—friend*) *as thyself.* Whence it seems to follow that man's love for himself is the model of his love for another. But the model exceeds the copy.

Therefore, out of charity, a man ought to love himself more than his neighbor.

. . . .

> We must, therefore, say that, even as regards the affection we ought to love one neighbor more than another. The reason is that, since the principle of love is God, and the person who loves, it must needs be that the affection of love increases in proportion to the nearness to one or the other of those principles.
>
> . . . .
>
> . . . As stated above . . . , we ought out of charity to love those who are more closely united to us more, both because our love for them is more intense, and because there are more reasons for loving them. . . .
>
> Accordingly we must say that friendship among blood relations is based upon their connection by natural origin, the friendship of fellow-citizens on their civic fellowship, and the friendship of those who are fighting side by side on the comradeship of battle. Wherefore in matters pertaining to nature we should love our kindred most, in matters concerning relations between citizens, we should prefer our fellow-citizens, and on the battlefield our fellow-soldiers. . . .
>
> . . . .
>
> If however we compare union with union, it is evident that the union arising from natural origin is prior to, and more stable than, all others, because it is something affecting the very substance, whereas other unions supervene and may cease altogether.

II *Thomas Aquinas, Summa Theologica* 1297–1301 (Fathers of the English Dominican Province trans. 1947).

[23] *See* G. Warnock, *The Object of Morality* 79–80 (1971); Nagel, Book Review, 85 *Yale L.J.* 136, 140 (1975).

ity in general. The impulse I describe, therefore, is not in any sense a selfish impulse. But it does begin with the sense of self as a concrete entity. Those who object to my thesis by saying that we must generalize it are not wholly wrong; they merely exaggerate. Truly I must be ready to generalize outward all the way. That is what justice consists of. But justice is not all of morality; there remains a circle of intensity which through its emphasis on the particular and the concrete continues to reflect what I have identified as the source of all sense of value—our sense of self.

Therefore, it is not only consonant with, but also required by, an ethics for human beings that one be entitled first of all to reserve an area of concern for oneself and then to move out freely from that area if one wishes to lavish that concern on others to whom one stands in concrete, personal relations. Similarly, a person is entitled to enjoy this extra measure of care from those who choose to bestow it upon him without having to justify this grace as either just or efficient. We may choose the individuals to whom we will stand in this special relation, or they may be thrust upon us, as in family ties. Perhaps we recognize family ties because, after all, there often has been an element of choice, but also because—by some kind of atavism or superstition—we identify with those who share a part of our biological natures.

In explicating the lawyer's relation to his client, my analogy shall be a friendship, where the freedom to choose and to be chosen expresses our freedom to hold something of ourselves in reserve, in reserve even from the universalizing claims of morality. These personal ties and the claims they engender may be all-consuming, as with a close friend or family member, or they may be limited, special-purpose claims, as in the case of the client or patient.[24] The special-purpose claim is one in which the beneficiary, the client, is entitled to all the special consideration *within* the limits of the relationship which we accord to a friend or a loved one. It is not that the claims of the client are less intense or demanding; they are only more limited in their scope. After all, the ordinary concept of friendship provides only an analogy, and it is to the development of that analogy that I turn.

D. Special-Purpose Friends

How does a professional fit into the concept of personal relations at all? He is, I have suggested, a limited-purpose friend. A lawyer is a friend in regard to the legal system. He is someone who enters into a personal relation with you—not an abstract relation as under the concept of justice. That means that like a friend he acts in your interests, not his own; or rather he adopts your interests as his own. I would call that the classic definition of friendship. To be sure, the lawyer's range of concern is sharply limited. But within that limited domain the intensity of identification with the client's interests is the same. It is not the specialized focus of the relationship which may make the metaphor inapposite, but the way in which the relation of legal friendship comes about and the one-sided nature of the ensuing "friendship." But I do insist upon the analogy, for in overcoming the arguments that the analogy is false, I think the true moral foundations of the lawyer's special role are illuminated and the utilitarian objections to the traditional conception of that role overthrown.

1. *The Professional Role As Socially Defined: The Content of the Relation*

The claims that are made on the doctor or lawyer are made within a social context and are defined, at least in part, by social expectations. Most strikingly, in talking about friendship the focus of the inquiry is quite naturally upon the free gift of the donor; yet in professional relationships it is the recipient's need for medical or legal aid which defines the relationship. So the source of the relationship seems to be located at the other end, that of the recipient. To put this dis-

[24]This argument is, of course, just a fragment which must be fitted into a larger theory. This larger theory would have to explain, among other things, what the precise contents of the various personal roles might be and how conflicts between personal roles are to be resolved. My later discussion of permissible and impermissible tactics in legal representation deals with this conflict in one context. A complete theory would also have to spell out the relation between personal roles and duties to the larger collectivity. These latter duties to man in the abstract as opposed to concrete persons are the subject of principles of justice. I have no doubt that such abstract duties exist and that they can be very demanding. Roughly, I would adopt something like the principles put forward in J. Rawls, *A Theory of Justice* 54–117 (1971). I would require, however, that these principles of justice leave sufficient scope for the free definition and inviolability of personal relations—to a greater extent perhaps than Rawls allows. These systematic concerns are the subject of a larger work from which the present essay is drawn. The relation of principles of justice to other aspects of right and wrong is a principal concern of that larger work.

quiet another way, we might ask how recognizing the special claims of friendship in any way compels society to allow the doctor or the lawyer to define his role on the analogy of those claims. Why are these people not like other social actors designated to purvey certain, perhaps necessary, goods? Would we say that one's grocer, tailor, or landlord should be viewed as a limited-purpose friend? Special considerations must be brought forward for doctors and lawyers.[25]

A special argument is at hand in both cases. The doctor does not minister just to any need, but to health. He helps maintain the very physical integrity which is the concrete substrate of individuality. To be sure, so does a grocer or landlord. But illness wears a special guise: it appears as a critical assault on one's person. The needs to which the doctor ministers usually are implicated in crises going to one's concreteness and individuality, and therefore what one looks for is a kind of ministration which is particularly concrete, personal, individualized. Thus, it is not difficult to see why I claim that a doctor is a friend, though a special purpose friend, the purpose being defined by the special needs of illness and crisis to which he tends.

But what, then, of the lawyer? Friendship and kinship are natural relations existing within, but not defined by, complex social institutions. Illness too is more a natural than social phenomenon. The response here requires an additional step. True, the special situations—legal relations or disputes—in which the lawyer acts as a limited-purpose friend are themselves a product of social institutions. But it does not follow that the role of the lawyer, which is created to help us deal with those social institutions, is defined by and is wholly at the mercy of the social good. We need only concede that at the very least the law must leave us a measure of autonomy, whether or not it is in the social interest to do so. Individuals have rights over and against the collectivity.[26] The moral capital arising out of individuals' concrete situations is one way of expressing that structure of rights, or at least part of it. It is because the law must respect the rights of individuals that the law must also create and support the specific role of legal friend. For the social nexus—the web of perhaps entirely just institutions—has become so complex that without the assistance of an expert adviser an ordinary layman cannot exercise that autonomy which the system must allow him. Without such an adviser, the law would impose constraints on the lay citizen (unequally at that) which it is not entitled to impose explicitly. Thus, the need which the lawyer serves in his special-purpose friendship may not be, as in the case of the doctor, natural, pre-social. Yet it is a need which has a moral grounding analogous to the need which the physician serves: the need to maintain one's integrity as a person. When I say the lawyer is his client's legal friend, I mean the lawyer makes the client's interests his own insofar as this is necessary to preserve and foster the client's autonomy within the law. This argument does not require us to assume that the law is hostile to the client's rights. All we need to assume is that even a system of law which is perfectly sensitive to personal rights would not work fairly unless the client could claim a professional's assistance in realizing that autonomy which the law recognizes.

2. *The Asymmetry of Motive and Duty: The Form of the Relation*

The institutional origin of the lawyer-client relationship is not its only characteristic which suggests that the analogy to natural friendship is vulnerable. In natural friendship the ideal relation is reciprocal; in legal friendship it is not. The lawyer is said to be the client's friend insofar as he is devoted to his client's interests, but it is no part of the ideal that the client should have any reciprocal devotion to the interests of his lawyer. Furthermore, I have argued that our right to be a friend to whomever we choose is a product of our individual autonomy. But in legal friendship the emphasis has been on the autonomy of the client, and it is the client who chooses the lawyer;[27] yet it is the

[25]This question might be more troubling in a socialist system in which the profit motive is theoretically subordinated to the service of the general good. But my argument is that the needs for which lawyers and doctors provide are significantly different in kind from those met by other economic agents. Therefore, my argument about doctors and lawyers should be general enough to apply in either a free enterprise or a socialist system.

[26]For a recent forceful statement of this conception of rights, see Dworkin, *Taking Rights Seriously,* in *Is Law Dead?* 168 (E. Rostow ed. 1971). *See generally* Dworkin, *The Original Position,* 40 *U. Chi. L. Rev.* 500, 522–28 (1973).

[27]The lawyer is generally free to decline to serve for any or no reason. But even that freedom is qualified; there will be times when there may be a duty to serve, as when a court appoints the lawyer to serve or when his declining may leave a person unrepresented. . . .

lawyer who acts as a friend in the relation. And as a final contrast to natural friendship, the usual motive for agreeing or refusing to provide legal services is money. Indeed, when we speak of the lawyer's right to represent whomever he wishes, we are usually defending his moral title to represent whoever pays.

But recall that the concept of legal friendship was introduced to answer the argument that the lawyer is morally reprehensible to the extent that he lavishes undue concern on some particular person. The concept of friendship explains how it can be that a particular person may rightfully receive more than his share of care from another: he can receive that care if he receives it as an act of friendship. Although in natural friendship I emphasized the freedom to bestow, surely that freedom must imply a freedom to receive that extra measure of care. And it is the right of the client to receive such an extra measure of care (without regard, that is, to considerations of efficiency or fairness) as much as the lawyer's right to give it, that I have been trying to explicate. Thus, the fact that the care in legal friendship systematically runs all one way does not impair the argument.

Yet the unease persists. Is it that while I have shown that the lawyer has a right to help the "unworthy" client, I have not shown that whenever the lawyer exercises this right he does something which is morally worthy, entitling him to self-respect? I may have shown that the law is obliged to allow the "unworthy" client to seek legal help and the lawyer to give it. But have I also shown that every lawyer who avails himself of this legal right (his and the client's legal right) performs a *morally worthy* function? Can a good lawyer be a good person?

The lawyer acts morally because he helps to preserve and express the autonomy of his client vis-à-vis the legal system. It is not just that the lawyer helps his client accomplish a particular lawful purpose. Pornography may be legal, but it hardly follows that I perform a morally worthy function if I lend money or artistic talent to help the pornographer flourish in the exercise of this right. What is special about legal counsel is that whatever else may stop the pornographer's enterprise, he should not be stopped because he mistakenly believes there is a legal impediment. There is no wrong if a venture fails for lack of talent or lack of money—no one's rights have been violated. But rights *are* violated if, through ignorance or misinformation about the law, an individual refrains from pursuing a wholly lawful purpose. Therefore, to assist others in understanding and realizing their legal rights is always morally worthy. Moreover, the legal system, by instituting the role of the legal friend, not only assures what it in justice must—the due liberty of each citizen before the law—but does it by creating an institution which exemplifies, at least in a unilateral sense, the ideal of personal relations of trust and personal care which (as in natural friendship) are good in themselves.

Perhaps the unease has another source. The lawyer does work for pay. Is there not something odd about analogizing the lawyer's role to friendship when in fact his so-called friendship must usually be bought? If the lawyer is a public purveyor of goods, is not the lawyer–client relationship like that underlying any commercial transaction? My answer is "No." The lawyer and doctor have obligations to the client or patient beyond those of other economic agents. A grocer may refuse to give food to a customer when it becomes apparent that the customer does not have the money to pay for it. But the lawyer and doctor may not refuse to give additional care to an individual who cannot pay for it if withdrawal of their services would prejudice that individual.[28] Their duty to the client or patient to whom they have made an initial commitment transcends the conventional quid pro quo of the marketplace. It is undeniable that money is usually what cements the lawyer–client relationship. But the content of the relation is determined by the client's needs, just as friendship is a response to another's needs. It is not determined, as are simple economic relationships, by the mere coincidence of a willingness to sell and a willingness to buy. So the fact that the lawyer works for pay does not seriously undermine the friendship analogy. . . .

CONCLUSION

I do not imagine that what I have said provides an algorithm for resolving some of these perennial difficulties. Rather, what I am proposing is a general way of looking at the problem, a way of understanding not so much the difficult borderline cases as the central

[28] *See* ABA Comm. on Professional Ethics, Opinions 56 (1967) (Informal Opinion No. 334); ABA Code of Professional Responsibility EC 2-31, 2-32. *Compare id.* DR 2-110(C)(l)(f) *with id.* DR 2-110(A)(2).

and clear ones, in the hope that the principles we can there discern will illuminate our necessarily approximate and prudential quest for resolution on the borderline. The notion of the lawyer as the client's legal friend, whatever its limitations and difficulties, does account for a kind of callousness toward society and exclusivity in the service of the client which otherwise seem quite mysterious. It justifies a kind of scheming which we would deplore on the part of a lay person dealing with another lay person—even if he were acting on behalf of a friend.

But these special indulgences apply only as a lawyer assists his client in his legal business. I do not owe my client my political assistance. I do not have to espouse his cause when I act as a citizen. Indeed, it is one of the most repellent features of the American legal profession—one against which the barrister–solicitor split has to some extent guarded the English profession—that many lawyers really feel that they are totally bought by their clients, that they must identify with their clients' interests far beyond the special purpose of advising them and operating the legal system for them. The defendants' antitrust lawyer or defendants' food and drug lawyer who writes articles, gives speeches, and pontificates generally about the evils of regulation may believe these things, but too often he does so because it is good for business or because he thinks that such conduct is what good representation requires.[29] In general, I think it deplorable that lawyers have specialized not only in terms of subject matter—that may or may not be a good thing—but in terms of plaintiffs or defendants, in terms of the position that they represent.[30]

There is a related point which cuts very much in the opposite direction. It is no part of my thesis that the *client* is not morally bound to avoid lying to the court, to pay a just debt even though it is barred by the statute of limitations, to treat an opposite party in a negotiation with humanity and consideration for his needs and vulnerability, or to help the effectuation of policies aimed at the common good. Further, it is no part of my argument to hold that a lawyer must assume that the client is not a decent, moral person, has no desire to fulfill his moral obligations, and is asking only what is the minimum that he must do to stay within the law. On the contrary, to assume this about anyone is itself a form of immorality because it is a form of disrespect between persons. Thus in very many situations a lawyer will be advising a client who wants to effectuate his purposes within the law, to be sure, but who also wants to behave as a decent, moral person. It would be absurd to contend that the lawyer must abstain from giving advice that takes account of the client's moral duties and his presumed desire to fulfill them. Indeed, in these situations the lawyer experiences the very special satisfaction of assisting the client not only to realize his autonomy within the law, but also to realize his status as a moral being. I want to make very clear that my conception of the lawyer's role in no way disentitles the lawyer from experiencing this satisfaction. Rather, it has been my purpose to explicate the less obvious point that there is a vocation and a satisfaction even in helping Shylock obtain his pound of flesh or in bringing about the acquittal of a guilty man.[31]

Finally, I would like to return to the charge that the morality of role and personal relationship I offer here is almost certain to lead to the diversion of legal services from areas of greatest need. It is just my point, of course, that when we fulfill the office of friend—legal, medical, or friend *tout court*—we do right, and thus it would be a great wrong to place us under a general regime of always doing what will "do the most good." What I affirm, therefore, is the moral liberty of a lawyer to make his life out of what personal

---

[29]The implications of this idea are particularly important for the so-called Washington lawyer (wherever he might be) who is hired to represent his client before agencies and legislatures contemplating new law. This may put us on one of the borderlines I do not pretend to resolve definitively, yet I think we can get an idea of how to think about these cases too. To the extent that such representation involves participation in a formal proceeding in which laws or regulations are drafted and technical competence is required, the task is *closer* to the traditional task of the lawyer as I have sketched it, and the legal friend concept is more appropriate. To the extent that the representation involves (wholly lawful) deployment of political pressures, inducements, and considerations, it is closer to being political action, and thus to requiring the kind of overriding concern for the common good that should motivate all political actors. Certainly it is absurd that a man should seek to be insulated from moral judgment of his accomplishments as a political string-puller or publicist by the defense that he was only doing it for money.

[30]In England barristers are regularly hired by the government in all manner of litigation, thereby accomplishing the many-sidedness I call for here. *See* Q. Johnstone and D. Hopson, *Lawyers and Their Work* 374–75 (1967). Why should this not be done in the United States? Perhaps there is a fear that this might simply become the occasion for a suspect form of patronage.

[31]This point is due to Albert Sacks and Richard Stewart.

scraps and shards of motivation his inclination and character suggest: idealism, greed, curiosity, love of luxury, love of travel, a need for adventure or repose; only so long as these lead him to give wise and faithful counsel. It is the task of the social system as a whole, and of all its citizens, to work for the conditions under which everyone will benefit in fair measure from the performance of doctors, lawyers, teachers, and musicians. But I would not see the integrity of these roles undermined in order that the millennium might come sooner. After all, it may never come, and then what would we be left with?

86

DAVID LUBAN

Why Have an Adversary System?

ADVERSARY ADVOCACY AS INTRINSICALLY GOOD

When we seek out the services of a professional we seek more than a mere *quid pro quo.* Perhaps this is because the *quo* may be of vital importance to us; perhaps it is because a lot of *quid* may be required to hire those services. In any event, we have the sense of entrusting a large chunk of our life to this person, and the fact that she takes on so intimate a burden and handles it in a trustworthy and skillful manner when the stakes are high seems commendable in itself. Nor does the fact that the professional makes a living by providing this service seem to mitigate the praiseworthiness of it. The business aspect moves along a different moral dimension: it explains how the relationship came about, not what it involves.[1] Finally, our being able to bare our weaknesses and mistakes to the professional and receive assistance without condemnation enhances our sense that beneficence or moral graciousness is at work here. Our lawyer, *mirabile dictu,* forgives us our transgressions.

Feelings such as these are quite real; the question is whether they are more than feelings. If they are, that may show that Schwartz's two principles and thus the adversary system and the behavior it countenances are themselves positive moral goods.

Such arguments are, in fact, frequently made: they are based on the "service ethic," the idea that providing service is intrinsically good. No finer statement of this ideal exists than Mellinkoff's. He sees the paradigm client as the "man-in-trouble":

> Cruelty, oppression, deception, unhappiness, worry, strain, incomprehension, frustration, bewilderment—a sorcerer's bag of misery. These become the expected. Then the saddest of all human cries: "Who will help me?" Try God, and politics, and medicine, and a soft shoulder, sooner or later a lawyer. Too many do.
>
> The lawyer, as lawyer, is no sweet kind loving moralizer. He assumes he is needed, and that no one comes to see him to pass the time of day. He is a prober, an analyzer, a scrapper, a man with a strange devotion to his client. Beautifully strange, or so it seems to the man-in-trouble; ugly strange to the untroubled onlooker.[2]

Charles Fried thinks of the lawyer as a "special-purpose friend" whose activity—enhancing the client's autonomy and individuality—is an intrinsic moral good.[3] This is true even when the lawyer's "friendship" consists in assisting the profiteering slumlord to evict an indigent tenant, or enabling Pakel to run the statute of limitations to avoid an honest debt to Zabella.

I mention Mellinkoff's and Fried's arguments together because, it seems to me, they express similar ideas, while the unsavory conclusion of the latter exposes the limitations of the former. Both arguments are attempts to show that a lawyer serving a client constitutes an intrinsic moral good. Mellinkoff's depiction of this service, however, really shows something much weaker, that a lawyer serving a man-in-trouble is (or even more cautiously, can be) engaged in an intrinsic moral good. If the client is a company laying off workers a few at a time to blackmail the FTC into permitting a merger we are confronted with no man-in-trouble and

[1][Charles Fried, "The Lawyer As Friend: The Moral Foundations of the Lawyer-Client Relation," *Yale Law Journal* 85 (1976)], p. 1075.

[2][David Mellinkoff, *The Conscience of a Lawyer* (St. Paul, MN: West, 1973)], p. 270.

[3][Fried, "The Lawyer As Friend"], pp. 1068–73.

the intuitions to which Mellinkoff's argument appeals disappear. Indeed, if Pakel or the profiteering slumlord were the typical clients, then the real men-in-trouble—the victims of these predators—might be better off taking their chances in the war of all against all rather than seeking to have their "autonomy" vindicated legally. The trouble with Mellinkoff's argument is that he makes all clients look more pitiable than they often are.

Fried, on the other hand, is willing to bite the bullet and argue that it is morally good to represent the man-in-no-trouble-in-particular, the man-who-troubles-others. Fried's idea is that the abstract connection between a remote person (even a person-in-trouble) and the agent exercises too slight a claim on the agent to override the agent's inclination to promote the interests of concrete others such as friends, family, or clients. This argument justifies lavishing special care on our friends, even at the expense of "abstract others," and since lavishing care is morally praiseworthy, once we swallow the notion that a lawyer is a special-purpose friend, we are home free and can guarantee the intrinsic moral worth of the lawyer-client relationship.

Several of Fried's critics focus on the fact that the friendship analogy is question-begging: Fried builds enough lawyerly qualities into his concept of friendship that the rest of the argument virtually writes itself.[4] It does seem to me, however, that the analogy captures some of the legitimacy of the notion of professionals as devoted by the nature of their calling to the service of their clients. Fried's analogy contains a grain of truth.

This grain does not, however, vindicate the adversary system. The friendship analogy undercuts rather than establishes the principle of nonaccountability. We are not—except for the Gordon Liddys of the world—willing to do grossly immoral things to help our friends, nor should we be. Lord Brougham's apology may be many things, but it is not a credo of human friendship in any form. Fried realizes the danger, for he confesses that

> not only would I not lie or steal for . . . my friends, I probably also would not pursue socially noxious schemes, foreclose the mortgages of widows or orphans, or assist in the avoidance of just punishment. So we must be careful lest the whole argument unravel on us at this point.[5]

The method for saving the argument, however, is disappointing. Fried distinguishes between personal wrongs committed by a lawyer, such as abusing a witness, and institutional wrongs occasioned by the lawyer, such as foreclosing on widows. The latter are precisely those done by the lawyer in her proper role of advancing the client's legal autonomy and—a preestablished harmony?—they are precisely the ones that are morally okay. That is because the lawyer isn't really doing them, the system is.

This last distinction has not been very popular since the Second World War, and Fried takes pains to restrict it to "generally just and decent" systems, not Nazi Germany. With this qualification, he can more comfortably assert: "We should absolve the lawyer of personal moral responsibility for the result he accomplishes because the wrong is wholly institutional."[6]

This last sentence, however, is nothing but the assertion that institutional excuses work for lawyers, and this should tip us off that Fried's argument will be useless for our purposes. For consider: our whole line of argument has been an attempt to justify the adversary system by showing that the traditional lawyer-client relation is an intrinsic moral good. Now it seems that this can be established by Fried's argument only if we are permitted to cancel the moral debit column by means of an institutional excuse; but that can work only if the institution is justified, and we are back where we started.

Part of the problem is that Fried bases the institutional excuse on the wrong institution: the context of the lawyer's behavior is not simply the system of laws in general, which he assumes to be just and decent, but the adversary system in particular, with its peculiar requirement of one-sided zeal at the margin of the legal and the moral. It is the adversary system and not the system of laws that shapes the lawyer-client relationship.

The more fundamental problem, however, is that Fried takes the lawyer to be the mere occasion, rather than the agent, of morally-bad-but-legally-legitimate outcomes. The system did it; in the words of a

---

[4]See [Edward Dauer and Arthur Leff, "Correspondence: The Lawyer As Friend," *Yale Law Journal* 86 (1977)], pp. 577–78; [William H. Simon, "The Ideology of Advocacy: Procedural Justice and Professional Ethics," *Wisconsin Law Review* 1978 (1978)], pp. 108–09.

[5][Charles Fried, *Right and Wrong* (Cambridge, MA: Harvard University Press, 1978)], p. 191.

Galway Kinnell poem, it "was just one of those things difficult to pre-visualize—like a cow, say, getting hit by lightning."[7] This is false in three respects: first, because it discounts the extent to which the lawyer has had a creative hand in advocating the outcome, at times even in reversing the law—a skilled lawyer, after all, argues, advocates, bargains, and persuades. Second, it is false because the system is not an abstract structure of propositions but a social structure of interacting human beings, so that the actions of its agents are the system. Third, it is false because the lawyer is indeed acting *in propria persona* by "pulling the levers of the legal machinery."[8] Fried's image seems to trade on a Rube Goldberg insight: if the apparatus is complex enough, then the lever-puller doesn't really look like the agent. But that cannot be right. I produce the outcome, whether I do it by hand or merely pull the levers. The legal levers are pulled by the lawyer: no one else can do it. . . .

ADVERSARY SYSTEM

So far the course of argument has been purely negative, a persecution and assassination of the adversary system. By this time you are entitled to ask what I propose putting in its place. The answer is: nothing, for I think the adversary system is justified.

I do not, let me quickly say, have an argumentative novelty to produce. It would be strange indeed for a social institution to be justified on the basis of virtues other than the tried and true ones, virtues that no one had noticed in it before. My justification is a modest one, carrying no ideological freight: I shall call it the "pragmatic justification" or "pragmatic argument," to suggest its affinity with the relaxed, problem-oriented, and historicist notion of justification associated with American pragmatism. The justification is this: first, the adversary system, despite its imperfections, irrationalities, loopholes, and perversities, seems to do as good a job as any at finding truth and protecting legal rights. None of its existing rivals, in particular the inquisitorial system and the socialist system, are demonstrably better, and some, such as trial by ordeal, are demonstrably worse. Indeed, even if one of the other systems were slightly better, the human costs—in terms of effort, confusion, anxiety, disorientation, inadvertent miscarriages of justice due to improper understanding, retraining, resentment, loss of tradition, you name it—would outweigh reasons for replacing the existing system.

Second, some adjudicatory system is necessary.

Third, it's the way we have always done things.

These propositions constitute a pragmatic argument: if a social institution does a reasonable enough job of its sort that the costs of replacing it outweigh the benefits, and if we need that sort of job done, we should stay with what we have.

A cynic might say that the insight underlying a pragmatic justification is twofold: first, what has been called the "law of conservation of trouble," and second, the principle that the devil you know is better than the devil you don't. The suspicion is that even if the adversary system murders truth (and legal rights, and morality) in its characteristic way, whatever we replace it with will do so in new and unexpected ways. Why, then, go through the trauma of change?

That this is a very relaxed sort of justification may be seen from the fact that it works equally well for the inquisitorial system in France and the socialist system in Bulgaria. A pragmatic justification is weak as well because it crumbles in the face of a demonstration that, contrary to what we believe, the institution is awful enough to replace. The argument, in other words, does not really endorse an institution—it only advocates enduring it.

Accepting a pragmatic justification for the adversary system does not, of course, commit one to a blanket conservatism: one can believe that our society should be drastically changed or that our legal system is hopelessly unjust and still accept that a changed society or overhauled legal system should utilize adversary adjudication. Thus, while the argument leads to a conservative conclusion, it does so in a nonideological way, and the conclusion extends no further than the institution for which the justification is offered.

In my opinion, many of our social institutions are like the adversary system in that they admit only of pragmatic justifications. Some are not intended to serve any positive moral good; some serve it badly. That these institutions are not worth replacing may be a measure of nothing more than social lethargy

---

[6]Ibid., p. 192.

[7][Galway Kinnell, *The Book of Nightmares* (Boston: Houghton Mifflin, 1971)], p. 43.

[8][Slightly paraphrased from Fried, *Right and Wrong*], p. 192, and [Fried, "The Lawyer As Friend"], p. 1085.

and our inability to come up with a better idea; my point is that this is a real reason. A pragmatic argument is logically weak—it justifies institutions without showing that they are better than their rivals, or even that they are particularly good—but in practice it is overwhelmingly powerful. Institutions, like bodies, obey Newton's first law.

AN EXAMPLE: THE WEST GERMAN PROCEDURAL SYSTEM

The reader may at this point feel that my "pragmatic justification" amounts to sending her away hungry. An argument that is logically weak but practically strong seems more like resignation than justification.

The problem, of course, is that the abstract assertion that the adversary system "does a reasonable enough job of its sort that the costs of replacing it outweigh the benefits" inevitably arouses the suspicion that it is simply a whitewash designed to justify the status quo. To make the argument more convincing, I propose to make it more concrete. Let us compare the American adversary system with one so-called "inquisitorial" system, that of the German Federal Republic.

The label "inquisitorial" is quite misleading, of course. It evokes images of the auto-da-fé and the Iron Maiden, the Pit and the Pendulum. In fact, the term refers simply to the much greater role played by the court in a trial. As one scholar describes it:

> The central idea behind the common-law [i.e., adversarial] trial is that of a party contest; the idea behind a criminal trial on the Continent is that of an official inquiry. The common-law trial is the main act of a dispute between two theoretically equal parties who enjoy considerable leeway to determine themselves, through pleadings and stipulations, the limits and outcome of their dispute. The adjudicator plays a largely passive, neutral role until the parties ask him to render a decision. . . .
>
> In a civil-law [i.e., inquisitorial] system, on the other hand, the trial culminates in an official inquiry whose object is to determine whether the defendant is guilty and, if so, what sanction to impose. The court is responsible for presenting the proofs and is not bound by the parties' positions when it formulates issues and reaches an ultimate decision. Trial procedures in this nonadversary model are simpler, less technical, and less lawyer dominated than in the adversary model.[9]

It is the expanded role of the court, and, correspondingly, the diminished role of the lawyers that make German procedure "inquisitorial."

In a German felony *(Verbrechen)* trial, a presiding judge is joined by both professional and lay judges.[10] All cases are tried, because the guilty plea does not exist. The presiding judge studies a dossier prepared by the prosecutor and plays the major role in conducting the case—in effect, the presiding judge absorbs the role of the lawyers. She decides the sequence of proof-taking and conducts the bulk of the questioning of witnesses. The presiding judge decides whether witnesses other than those nominated by the parties should be called; in her hands also lies the decision whether to call expert witnesses, and if so, the choice of experts. The presiding judge can change the charge, increasing or diminishing it. She also authenticates the record of the trial. (In civil cases, the judge dictates a summary of the evidence that serves as the record of the proceedings; no stenographic record exists for either criminal or civil proceedings.)

Few exclusionary rules exist in German procedure. In particular, rules such as the exclusion of hearsay evidence, which exist in common law countries because of the fear that lay jurors would be unable to evaluate it, are unheard of. In Germany the lay "jurors" deliberate together with the professional judges, and it is assumed that the latter will be able to explain the value of evidence to the lay participants.

---

[9][Edward Tomlinson, "Nonadversarial Justice: The French Experience," *Maryland Law Review* 42 (1983)], p. 134.

[10]Here and in the ensuing discussion, I am relying on my own observation of German trials and on three major sources: [John Langbein, *Comparative Criminal Procedure: Germany* (St. Paul, MN: West, 1977)] and [John Langbein, "The German Advantage in Civil Procedure," *University of Chicago Law Review* 52 (1985): 823–66], and [Benjamin Kaplan, Arthur T. Von Mehren, and Rudolph Schaefer, "Phases of German Civil Procedure," Part I *Harvard Law Review* 71 (1958): 1193–268; Part II *Harvard Law Review* 71 (1958): 1443–72]. For a summary of German civil procedure, see [Benjamin Kaplan, "Civil Procedure: Reflections on the Comparison of Systems," *Buffalo Law Review* 9 (1959–60): 409–32], 409–14. The major comparative work on the German and American legal professions is [Dietrich Rueschemeyer, *Lawyers and Their Society: A Comparative Study of the Legal Profession in Germany and the United States* (Cambridge, MA: Harvard University Press, 1973)].

After the judge has questioned witnesses, the lawyers and the defendant may ask further questions. Except in political trials, however, it is rare for them to exercise this option, and almost unheard of that a lawyer would ask more than one or two questions. In part, this is because German judges are thought to do a very good job; in part, it is because a lawyer who asked a lot of questions would be implying that the judge had not done a good job, a dangerous tactic, to say the least. The lawyers also submit written pleadings and make closing arguments. Beyond that, they do nothing.

In civil cases, there is no jury. A judge or panel of judges engages in a series of conferences with the parties and their lawyers. The object of these conferences is to clarify the issues of the case. To this end the lawyers submit written pleadings—shockingly informal ones by American standards—which are continually revised and updated as the case develops. As in criminal trials, the parties themselves often participate directly, without speaking through their lawyers. When it becomes clear that proofs must be taken or witnesses examined, the court takes proofs and examines witnesses—once again, conducting the examination itself and appointing experts of its own choice when it believes they are necessary. Then the conferences resume. Because the trial is divided into discrete sessions, and the parties may modify their pleadings almost without restriction, they do not need the device of civil discovery to avoid unpleasant surprises.

As in a criminal trial, the court decides issues of law on its own, on the principle "the court knows the law" *(jura novit curia)*. It is facilitated in deciding the law, of course, because in civil law countries such as Germany, law is statutory rather than precedential (though precedent is coming to play an increasingly important role in German law), which simplifies legal research considerably. It is often surprising to Americans that the authoritative role played by higher court decisions in the United States is to a large degree exercised by academic commentaries in Germany. If a German judge is unsure how to interpret a statute in the civil code, she simply reads the discussion in Palandt's one-volume desk commentary (updated annually and distributed gratis to judges by the publisher). For harder questions, longer commentaries are available; all the commentaries will in any event cite relevant cases and journal articles. And that is that: no muss, no fuss, no Shepherd's, no Lexis, no digests.

Of course, a procedural system such as the German one requires that lawyers will not engage in large-scale obfuscations after the fashion of their American brothers and sisters, since the courts hardly have the resources or time to discover them. This is one function of the official code of legal ethics. Its basic principle defines the lawyer's status as an "independent organ of the administration of justice" *(unabhängiges Organ der Rechtspflege)*; and the commentaries make clear that this means independence from the client as well as from the state.

Indeed, when politicized defense lawyers for the left-radical Red Army Faction engaged in "procedural sabotage" in Germany in the mid-1970s, public and professional outrage was so great that the code of criminal procedure was amended to prevent multiple representation of criminal defendants. But in fact, the "stonewalling" tactics that the defense lawyers employed are routinely used in the United States by the white-collar defense bar with scarcely a blink of the eyelash on the part of either the public or the courts. The German trial process is simply not conducted with the rock-'em-sock-'em zeal that it is in the United States. . . .

Finally, let us recall that a key to inquisitorial procedure is that the court decides what evidence to take. The court, however, has limited time and resources, and so in complex cases many stones will of necessity be left unturned. This does not mean, of course, that the inquisitorial court is less likely to find out the facts of the matter: the "total war" litigation tactics employed by large American law firms representing rich clients (and that is mostly what we are talking about when we speak of complex litigation) often call to mind giant squids squirting the ink of obfuscation in each others' direction—these tactics consist of delay, endless discovery, vexatious motions, and the complementary shenanigans needed to parry such thrusts. Nevertheless, our ideology of "getting one's day in court"—or perhaps one's half-year—means being able to present the case that one's lawyers want, more or less as they want to present it. We would have to think that our judges were awfully good to let them stage-manage that day in court. Even Judge Wapner does not get that kind of deference.

Let me summarize. Hegel thought of the civil service or bureaucracy as a "universal class" that would realize common interests against particularistic ones; he also (mis)quoted Goethe, saying "the masses are respectable hands at fighting, but miserable hands at judging."[11] Some such antipopulist views, if I am right, undergird the German inquisitorial system. My guess is that, despite the many attractive features of the system, Americans would find the imperatives of inquisitorial procedure unacceptable. These imperatives center around the need to repose a great trust in a large, self-consciously *lebensfremd* officialdom and auxiliary governmental agencies.

One never knows, of course—perhaps the transition could be accomplished without much dislocation. But I am inclined to doubt it. Even if it could—say, by introducing inquisitorial elements into adversary procedures very gradually—the fact remains that by so doing we would be sacrificing some important elements of popular control over the legal system.

And, if I am right about this, we see why a pragmatic justification of the adversary system makes sense. Let me emphasize that I am not arguing that the changes required to switch to inquisitorial procedure are bad—the point is simply that they are trade-offs rather than clear-cut improvements. The argument should work equally well to explain to Germans why they should not rush to abandon a more efficient, competent, and professional inquisitorial system in favor of expensive and theatrical adversarial procedure. The adversary and inquisitorial systems have more-or-less complementary pluses and minuses; why, then, look for greener grass on the other side of the fence?

[11][G. W. F. Hegel, *The Philosophy of Right*, translated by T. M. Knox (London: Oxford University Press, 1952)], § 317, p. 204.

87

KENNETH KIPNIS

Conflict of Interest and Conflict of Obligation

The term "conflict of interest" has its characteristic applications in settings in which formal responsibilities are assumed by individuals occupying certain more or less well-defined social roles. The notion is not well understood outside the legal profession, and even inside the profession it is probably not understood well enough. Part of the problem is that the expression itself is ambiguous, denoting at least two very different types of circumstance. Moreover, problems arising out of conflicts of interest are most obvious in formal types of relationship, such as that which obtains between lawyer and client. These have few counterparts in ordinary day-to-day life.

Our purposes here will be twofold. In the first place, we shall endeavor to distinguish among the different kinds of conflicts of interest. It is important not only for lawyers but for others as well—doctors, journalists, social workers—to be sensitive to the possibility that they may be involved in a conflict of interest. For this reason our discussion in what follows will utilize examples, where possible, not only from law but from other areas as well. In the second place, we shall attempt with respect to each of these types of conflict to isolate what it is exactly that makes the circumstance ethically interesting. Why should the ethically competent attorney be wary of conflict of interest? It is not enough to say, as many discussions of conflict of interest seem to, that you or your client may be caused to suffer for such inattention. That may be so, but the question still must be faced as to whether such penalties ought to be paid.

The two situations denoted by the term "conflict of interest" have very different ethical characteristics. Sometimes the concern is that an attorney either has or may come to have conflicting obligations. In other cases the concern is that some fact has called into question the loyalty of the attorney. Henceforth we will use the term "conflict of obligation" to refer to the first type of situation and will reserve the term "conflict of interest" exclusively for the second type. A third concept of conflict of interest has occasionally commanded the attention of philosophers. It obtains whenever there are two interests such that the satisfaction of either precludes the satisfaction of the other: One person may want the air conditioner on and another may want it off; or Jones may want the air conditioner on but may not be willing to pay the resulting electric bill. Although it will be important at points to note conflicts falling under this concept—we can call them "interests that are in conflict"—this notion will not be a central topic of this chapter.

CONFLICTS OF OBLIGATION: ACTUAL AND POTENTIAL

Dexter, who used to box as a boy, has just started teaching his son and some of the youngsters from the neighborhood the basic elements of the sport. Working with heavily padded gloves, the boys have done well during several practice sessions and seem to be ready for their first matches. With Dexter serving as referee, the second bout begins with Dexter's son contending in the ring. Dexter tries to be fair as the two boys land punches on each other but nevertheless feels uncomfortable as he struggles to suppress any suggestion of favoritism toward his son. The match is a close one, and he wonders how the other boy will feel if he gives the bout to his son. He wonders how his son will feel if he gives the bout to the other boy. (Dexter's situation is reminiscent of one that befell a judge several hundred years ago. In the West of Ireland there is a memorial that tells the story. The judge had the misfortune to be on the bench when his son was brought before the court, accused, and found guilty of a capital offense. He resigned his position after sentencing his son to death.)

At the core of Dexter's uneasiness is an ethical dilemma that he has unwittingly brought upon himself. For Dexter is a father, and in at least one widespread view of that role, he has an obligation to be a partisan supporter of his young son. But Dexter is also the referee in a boxing match. As such his obligation is to be evenhanded and fair. Clearly there is nothing wrong with being a father, and clearly there is nothing wrong with being a referee. But there does seem to be something morally perilous about refereeing a match in which one's son is a contestant. With respect to one and the same youngster, Dexter must be both a partisan supporter and a disinterested judge: how can he meet either obligation without compromising his ability to fulfill the other? It is of little solace that there may be a right or a best answer to the dilemma: "If you have to decide between being a bad referee and a bad father, always choose . . ." Regardless of the answer, Dexter is in the unenviable position of having to decide what kind of creep he is going to be. The situation he has brought upon himself is one in which his obligations conflict with one another. Although the dilemma may be unresolvable once it has arisen, had he been sufficiently attentive to the ethical implications of the roles of father and referee, Dexter could have avoided the problem in the first place. For instance, he could have put off the boxing matches until he found someone else to referee them. But conflicts of obligation are not always that simple.

Flynn is driving along in her car with her two friends Chang and Ripley. Out of nowhere, a bus collides with her vehicle. Chang and Ripley are injured and require medical attention. While Flynn is not hurt, her car is damaged. A few weeks later the three meet with attorney Parker to discuss suing the bus company for damages. The evidence supports the bus driver's being at fault, and Parker agrees to take the case. Chang's medical bills total $14,000; Ripley's, $3,000. Flynn's car requires $1,500 worth of repairs. Taking into account other costs to his clients, Parker files suit against the bus company for $25,000. As Parker has anticipated, the bus company files a countersuit against Flynn, claiming that the accident was her fault. At trial each side has the chance to present its case, and the jury is asked to decide who is at fault and how much each has to pay to whom. Horrified, Parker listens as the jury finds Flynn and the bus company equally at fault and equally liable for $17,000 in medical bills.[1]

Why is Parker horrified? If Flynn, the driver of the car, were Parker's sole client, Parker would be obligated to discuss with her the option of filing an appeal. There is a chance that Flynn could escape the $8,500 judgment against her and perhaps even recover the cost of repairing the car. Filing an appeal might be a very good idea. But if Chang and Ripley were

[1]The facts here are adapted from *Jedwabney v. Philadelphia Transportation Company,* 390 PA 231, 135 A.2d 252 (1957).

Parker's only clients, suggesting an appeal would be absurd. They have essentially won their case. Merely to mention the word "appeal" to Flynn may be to betray Chang and Ripley. If Flynn decides to appeal, their award could be delayed for years. Conceivably, they might never receive payment. The authors of Canon 6 of the old A.B.A. Canons of Professional Ethics (superseded in 1970) had this situation in mind when they wrote that "a lawyer represents conflicting interests when, in behalf of one client, it is his duty to contend for that which duty to another client requires him to oppose." Parker has an obligation to Flynn to discuss with her the advisability of an appeal. And simultaneously he has an obligation to Chang and Ripley not to discuss with Flynn the advisability of an appeal. Parker is caught in a classic conflict of obligations.

But where exactly did Parker go wrong? We can appreciate, perhaps, that fathers should not referee boxing matches in which their sons are contenders. But what practical rule can attorneys adhere to that will serve to protect them against having to decide which client they are going to betray?

Without doubt, the most commonly given reply to our question is the injunction to be found in Matthew: "No man can serve two masters: for either he will hate the one, and love the other; or else he will hold to the one, and despise the other." While there may be wisdom in this New Testament language, it seems unlikely that Matthew's words can helpfully illuminate professional responsibility in law. In the first place, lawyers do not serve their clients as servants do their masters. For masters are owed obedience by those who serve them. Lawyers only rarely have obligations to obey their clients. For the most part, their service is autonomous. They are paid in order that they may do their work. In the second place, most practicing attorneys have no ethical problems in providing legal services for more than one client. If the Matthew rule were taken to be applicable to legal practice, it would entail the preposterous conclusion that no lawyer can have more than one client! While this would clearly reduce the incidence of conflicts of obligation in legal practice, it is hardly a suggestion that any attorney would take seriously. In this situation, Parker could not even decide to represent Chang and Ripley simultaneously. And indeed because Parker like every other attorney is an "officer of the court," he is as beholden to the judicial system as he is to his client. He is in the service of both. A strict application of the Matthew rule would thus preclude anyone from ever serving as anybody else's attorney.

A more promising approach would be for Parker to foresee at once that conflicting obligations are a possibility and to withdraw from the case. When Flynn, Ripley, and Chang sit down to tell their problem to Parker (who has not yet agreed to be their attorney), Parker must anticipate that, given the occurrence of certain events, he will be faced with an actual conflict of obligation if he agrees to represent all three clients. The bus company may file a countersuit against Flynn and the jury may find Flynn liable for the injuries sustained by the two passengers. If these things happen—and there is no way effectively to prevent their occurrence—Parker will be required to betray at least one of his clients. For that reason he may agree to represent Flynn or he may agree to represent Chang and Ripley; he may not agree to represent all three. The bare possibility that a conflict of obligation may arise would require the conscientious attorney, under this rule, to decline simultaneous representation of potentially conflicting interests. A responsible attorney must therefore be sensitive to the potential for conflict and be ready to step aside should a conflict of obligation be a possibility. On this account, the Matthew rule should be modified to prohibit an attorney from agreeing to serve more than one client when there is any reason to believe that meeting professional obligations to one of the clients might make it impossible to meet professional obligations to the other.

Like the original Matthew rule, this version will effectively prevent the occurrence of actual conflicts of obligation. But also like the Matthew rule, it may be a more draconian measure than is justified by the problem it seeks to prevent. For one thing, it will mean that the general public will have to support many more attorneys. Unless cases are dropped, additional lawyers will have to be employed whenever a potential conflict of obligation arises. While this may be financially beneficial for those in the legal profession, it may cause an erosion of public trust in lawyers, especially if less drastic measures can do the job.[2]

The presence of multiple attorneys may also promote more litigiousness than is necessary. Where

[2]See Thomas D. Morgan, "The Evolving Concept of Professional Responsibility," 90 *Harvard Law Review* (1977): 702, 727.

Chang and Ripley might be able to reach agreement with Flynn in an informal setting, it may be that such agreement will be difficult if both sides are represented by attorneys *before* an actual conflict has arisen. Geoffrey C. Hazard has helpfully illuminated this point.

> In respect to these broader terms in which conflict of interest is defined, the culture of law itself is a contributing determinant. The point can be made more clearly by considering cultures that sharply contrast in this regard. In this country, the ideals of due process, private property, and formal equality (that is, equality in legal status) lead to the definition of human relationships in legal terms. They also imply that adjudication is a normal and in some sense an ideal form of resolving disputed relationships. A derivative of this premise is that the role of partisan advocate and counselor is a normal, primary, and perhaps idealized one for a lawyer to play. By way of sharp contrast, in Japanese culture the ideals of concord and deference to traditional authority predominate. The definition of human relationships in legal terms is regarded as the exhibition of something like anti-social tendencies. A derivative of this premise is that in Japan it is uncommon to resort to legal assistance and more uncommon still for lawyers to assume the role of partisan rather than neutral expositor of the law. Within both countries, certainly this one, the degree of "legalism" in definition of relationships varies with specific context, as already suggested. But when an American lawyer is consulted, the client's orientation to the problem is usually adversarial, precisely because the lawyer's normal or expected role is that of partisan. Hence the fact that a client has consulted a lawyer can signify that the client contemplates a legally assertive course of action and itself is a step in the direction of defining a divergency of interest as a conflict of interest.[3]

If the potential for conflict of interest is well enough understood by the attorney and the prospective clients, it may be that agreement can be reached as to what the attorney's obligations will be should events occur that might precipitate an actual conflict of obligations. The obligations that Parker has to clients, he has because they have delegated responsibilities to him. If the clients explicitly forbear delegating to Parker responsibilities that may give rise to a conflict of obligations, then, since Parker cannot then find himself in an actual conflict, he will have no reason to decline representation of all three. Let us see how this might work.

The scene is once again Parker's initial interview with Flynn, Chang, and Ripley. The subject of the conversation is whether Parker will agree to represent any or all of the three in their proposed lawsuit against the bus company. The three potential clients have just completed recounting to Parker their story of the mishap and its consequences. Parker speaks:

"Based on what you all tell me, the three of you appear to have a solid case against the bus company. You are all in agreement that the accident was caused by the bus driver. If the rest of the evidence holds up, we would have a very good chance of prevailing at trial. But the bus company will not take this lying down. We can expect that they will file a countersuit against you, Ms. Flynn, and try to prove that the accident was your fault. From what you all tell me, it doesn't look as though they will succeed. But they might. No one can be certain which way the jury will go. If the jury finds you to be at fault, you will be held liable for the injuries your two friends have sustained. That will be a problem for you, and it may be a problem for your two friends. But it will also be a problem for me.

"As Ms. Flynn's attorney, I would ordinarily have the responsibility of advising her on whether she should file an appeal in the hope of getting a new trial and overturning the jury's judgment against her. The bus company will have won its lawsuit against you, Ms. Flynn, but there may be something we can do about it on appeal. If there is, while that will be a good thing for you, it may not be such a good thing for your two friends here. An appeal and a new trial will take a great deal of time, and during that period, Mr. Chang and Mr. Ripley, you will not have received any money to pay your medical bills. You will essentially have won your case, and yet, because of my responsibilities to Ms. Flynn, I will be doing work that will delay your payment and possibly subject you to the difficulties of an appeal. If we are 'successful' on appeal, there could be a second trial that would probably not net you one extra penny. Just as I would ordinarily have an obligation to advise and to represent Ms. Flynn in connection with her appeal, I would

---

[3]From Geoffrey C. Hazard, Jr., *Ethics in the Practice of Law* (New Haven, Conn.: Yale University Press, 1978). Copyright by Seven Springs Farm Center. Reprinted by permission of the author and publisher.

ordinarily have an obligation not to work to overturn any judgment in your favor. In short, I think that any responsible attorney would have some reservations about taking on all three of you as clients.

"There may be, however, something that we can do now that will prevent such a conflict from arising later on. For example, if you, Ms. Flynn, were to stipulate now in our agreement that I am to have no responsibility to advise you and no responsibility to represent you concerning any matter that may arise subsequent to the jury's verdict in this case, then I believe that that would take care of my reservations. I will advise you now that if the jury should return a judgment against you, it would be wise immediately to seek legal counsel on the question of appeal. I will be happy to suggest the names of several attorneys who would be able to help you to make your decision, should the need arise. On the other hand, if you two gentlemen were to stipulate now in our agreement that I am being retained, not merely to press the claims that you three have against the bus company, but equally to defend Ms. Flynn against any countersuit the company might file against her—at trial, on appeal, and if necessary at retrial—then it may be that we can reach agreement in that way. Perhaps we will want to discuss the responsibility for fees in the event it becomes necessary to file for an appeal. In any case, if we decide to go this second route, I would want to have it clearly stated in our agreement that the appeals process may delay and even jeopardize any payment to you that the courts may find owing.

"There is possibly a third option which the three of you may wish to consider. We could agree that in the event that the jury returns a judgment against Ms. Flynn, I will have neither the responsibility to advise her nor the authority to represent her on appeal and thereafter unless the two of you explicitly consent to my doing so in full understanding of what the consequences might be.

"I think that I can live quite comfortably with any of these three options. It will probably be less expensive and there will be less duplication of effort if the three of you proceed, for now, with one attorney. But you should consider carefully that your interests might diverge, now or later on, and that it may be better to bring in a second attorney or to accept that it may be costly to some of you if I work to meet all the responsibilities you have delegated to me. Why don't you talk over these arrangements among yourselves, and if one of them seems suitable, I will be happy to draw up the appropriate agreement. On the other hand, if you feel it is better to go with separate attorneys, I will be happy to recommend several who can do the work."

Here, attorney Parker is treating a potential conflict of obligation, not as a flashing red signal to stop, but rather as a problem that can be resolved to the advantage of his clients. When a potential conflict of obligation becomes apparent, it is clear that the first step ought to be disclosure. The lawyer-client relationship tends to be an unfamiliar one to many lay persons, and explaining the problem can serve to clarify the nature of an attorney's obligation to a client. The second step, on this analysis, would be to set out ways in which the dilemma can be prevented from arising. Is it possible for clients to specify and limit the attorney's responsibility and authority so that the conflict cannot arise? Can clients explicitly waive certain rights or disavow expectations in order to consent to multiparty representation that would otherwise be ethically questionable? Is it possible adequately to advise clients in advance of those circumstances under which independent counsel should be sought? At the very minimum—and this may not be enough—the attorney should tell clients precisely what he or she will do in the event that a conflict of obligations arises and should secure from each client a consent that is informed by adequate knowledge of the consequences. What is suggested here is not so much a rule as a set of ethical strategies. To be sure, there will be many occasions in which a conscientious attorney, committed to doing the best for clients, can do nothing better than decline simultaneous representation. But it is often possible for an ethically competent lawyer to fashion a framework for cooperation that will serve all of the clients well.[4]

Our discussion of conflict of obligation has focused thus far on problems arising in simultaneous representation of divergent interests. But similar problems arise out of successive representations. Although most of an attorney's obligations to a client

---

[4]One option that Parker does not discuss is that Chang and Ripley sue the bus company *and Flynn* for their injuries. Has a conflict of obligations prevented Parker from giving his best advice to two of his clients? Nor does Parker discuss with Flynn the possibility that Chang and Ripley may have caused the accident—and their own injuries—by interfering with Flynn's driving. Perhaps Ripley interfered, but not Chang.

end when the lawyer-client relationship is dissolved, there is one that does not: The obligation of confidentiality typically comes into play in conflicts involving the former client.

For several years Mr. Gould refers legal questions arising in the course of his business to Kimura, his attorney. As Gould's business grows, he eventually takes his legal matters to another firm. Several years afterwards, Mrs. Gould shows up in Kimura's office to talk with him about getting a divorce from her husband. Because of Kimura's earlier relationship with Mr. Gould, Kimura knows a fair amount about the businessman's assets. He may have information that could be very useful to Mrs. Gould if there is litigation regarding a property settlement. But at the same time, Kimura is under an obligation not to disclose the information to anyone unless Mr. Gould's permission is obtained. If Kimura agrees to serve as Mrs. Gould's attorney in the divorce proceedings against the former client, he will have the obligation to serve as her "zealous advocate," using all the means at his disposal to prevail in the courts. If there is something Kimura has learned from his former client that is crucial or even helpful to his current client, Kimura will be caught in a second type of conflict of obligation. He must advise and represent his current client to the best of his ability; yet, at the same time, he may have information essential to her welfare that he is not at liberty to utilize or divulge. Once the actual conflict of obligations becomes apparent to Kimura, it becomes patently clear that he must withdraw immediately as Mrs. Gould's attorney. He must abandon her. Indeed, he is not even permitted to explain in any detail the reasons for his withdrawal; to do so may be to violate the confidences he is obligated to preserve.

Conflicts of obligations arising out of successive representation are not manageable in the same way as those arising out of simultaneous representation. There is no longer a continuing relationship with one of the parties and not always an opportunity to hammer out agreements to the advantage of all. It is also frequently a nice question whether, without first exploring in detail the nuances of a new client's case, there is a potential conflict of obligation arising out of confidential communications from a prior client. Suppose Kimura had handled only one or two minor matters twelve years ago. Suppose most of what Kimura learned while serving as Mr. Gould's attorney has since become generally known. Since it may be difficult if not impossible to determine in advance whether one has confidential information from a prior client that could be helpful or even critical to a potential client whom one is interviewing for the first time, attorneys should probably err on the side of caution and decline representation when there is a possibility that zealous advocacy may be incompatible with the preservation of a former client's confidences.

One possible solution is to obtain the former client's consent. Waiving confidentiality, Mr. Gould can explicitly permit Kimura to represent his wife in the divorce action. A second solution might be to put the new client on notice that the attorney might withdraw at any moment without explanation. Perhaps there are some clients who would accept representation under such conditions. But the attorney may have an obligation to the court not to abandon clients in the midst of litigation. More to the point, the sudden decision to abandon a client can itself compromise the former client's confidences. Mr. Gould's wife could infer that the attorney knows something that would be useful to her that he cannot tell her. For this reason, unless there is consent from the former client, an attorney should disqualify himself or herself from representing any client where the matters under consideration are substantially related to matters considered in representing a former client.[5] Good judgment is called for in making this decision.

An attorney's good judgment is also a requirement where vicarious disqualification is a possibility. Suppose it had not been Kimura who represented Gould but Kimura's law partner. Must Kimura then decline representation of Mrs. Gould? Or suppose it had been Mr. Kimura's wife who represented Mr. Gould in his business transactions, or merely the attorney with whom Kimura shared office space. Kimura may be comfortable in the knowledge that he knows nothing whatever about Mr. Gould's financial status, past or present. From Kimura's perspective, we no longer have a potential conflict of obligations. From Mr. Gould's perspective, however, we may have a towering appearance of impropriety. It may look for all the world as if Kimura is relying on confidential information gained from an earlier slender

[5]This is essentially the standard applied in *T.C. Theater Corp.* v. *Warner Bros. Pictures*, 113 F. Supp. 265 (S.D.N.Y. 1953), and specified in the Model Rules of Professional Conduct.

or indirect relationship with Gould, information that is now being used to further the cause of one who has it in for Gould. Moreover, Gould may not be able to elaborate on his suspicions and Kimura may not be able to defend himself against the charges without disseminating the very information that is intended to be confidential. In terms of its effect on clients' willingness to trust lawyers, the appearance of betrayal is every bit as damaging as the real thing. Clients may refrain from sharing their confidences with their attorneys because they fear that the information may someday be used against them. This will mean that attorneys may be less able to give clients good advice. Hence, conflict of obligation in successive client representations, as an ethical problem for the practitioner, merges gradually into the profession's obligation to prevent flagrant appearances of impropriety among its members.

It is in this context that we are brought to the final point in our discussion of conflicts of obligation. For if the evidence that a court is permitted to examine supports the conclusion that an attorney may have relied on confidential information entrusted to him (or to his partner) by his present adversary; if it appears that there was an opportunity for him to be entrusted with such information and that the information could have been utilized on behalf of his present client against the former client, then a court may well be inclined to disqualify him as the client's attorney and to vacate any judgment he may have gained on his client's behalf. As one court put it: "An attorney must avoid not only the fact, but even the appearance, of representing conflicting interests."[6] If the system of adjudication is to work, if it is to succeed in generating judicial decisions that are likely to be just and that the community can accept as just, it must preserve appearances. The trial may have been defective because one of the parties had improper or inadequate representation. Indeed, in *Jedwabney* v. *Philadelphia Transportation Co.* (on which we loosely based our saga of Parker, Flynn, Chang, and Ripley), the attorney, who we assume *was* horrified, stood by as the Company won a new trial because the driver of the automobile was not adequately informed of his attorney's potentially conflicting obligations. The judge felt that the driver had not been "given the chance to make an informed choice." In his dissenting opinion in the case, Justice Musmanno laments that the two injured passengers who had won their verdict must once again "be subjected to the turmoil, the expense, the loss of time, the worry and the agony which accompany a trial—with the possibility of drowning in a river they have already crossed."[7] But the community has a competing interest in ensuring that judicial proceedings preserve the appearance of propriety. Clients may indeed be ill-served if attorneys neglect such conflicts. While this is not the whole reason for lawyer attention to the potential for conflict, it is certainly part of it.

CONFLICTS OF INTEREST: PERSONAL AND STRUCTURAL

In the preceding section we have seen how attorneys can get into ethical trouble if their obligation to one client is in potential or actual conflict with their obligation to another. A second type of conflict occurs when attorneys themselves have interests that may incline them away from fulfillment of their obligations to clients. Problems of this general type can arise wherever there are clear obligations associated with a social position. Consider the following:

1. The Anodyne Pharmaceutical Corporation is introducing a new drug for the treatment of hypertension. In its effort to promote sales as the drug enters the market, it offers expensive premiums to physicians who prescribe sufficient quantities before a certain date. Physicians who do this can choose a home stereo system, an all-expenses-paid vacation for two in Hawaii, or a self-propelled lawnmower. Dr. Brisby

[6] *Edelman* v. *Levy,* 346 N.Y.S. 2d 347 (1973).

[7] *Jedwabney* v. *Philadelphia Transportation Co.:* see note 1 above. It is a nice question, but one we will table, whether the Company ought to have had the standing to complain to the court and to win an appeal on the basis of the conflict of obligation on the part of the other side's attorney. The injured party—the driver of the car—never saw fit to protest that he had been unfairly treated. On the other hand, since the driver's attorney also represented the passengers, is it reasonable to expect that the court would hear of the driver's complaint through his attorney? How might a judge decide if a new trial is required because one of the parties was possibly not properly represented?

switches his patients over to the new drug and opts for the Hawaiian vacation.

2. For the past nine years, the four to six hundred students who take Professor Darnay's introductory-level political science course each semester have been required to read *An Introduction to Politics* written by Professor Darnay himself. The book costs $30, and Professor Darnay collects $4 in royalties from the publisher for every copy that is sold. Professor Darnay is the only professor who teaches this course, and student advisors regularly recommend it for prelaw undergraduates. Because new editions of the text are published regularly and are specifically assigned by the instructor, used books are seldom available for purchase.

3. Wiggins is the purchasing agent for a small municipality. He has responsibility for the final decision on all significant purchases made by the city government. For the past seven years, the city has purchased all of its automobiles from Ray's Motors. Ray, the owner and general manager of the company, is Wiggins's brother-in-law.

Now let us examine some similar cases in legal settings.

4. Big Jake, a reputed underworld leader, has a reputation for distributing extravagant gifts whenever things go well. After prevailing in a criminal case against him, Jake sends expensive presents to the prosecuting attorney on the other side, to the judge, and to all twelve of the jurors.

5. Mullens, who has been struck by an automobile and is recovering from injuries, contacts Taney, an attorney, about suing the driver of the car. Taney declines to take the case but recommends that Mullens see Hargitty, a specialist in personal injury cases. Mullens seems agreeable and remains in the office while Taney telephones Hargitty and schedules an initial interview. Taney and Hargitty have a standing agreement that whenever Taney refers a case to her, Hargitty will give him a small amount of work in connection with the case and will pay him one-third of whatever fee she obtains. Mullens is not aware of the arrangement.

6. Three years ago, in doing some estate planning, Scribner drafted a will for Whipple who was then seventy-eight years old. Now Whipple has died, and his Last Will and Testament is in probate. The will that Scribner earlier prepared for his client provides that one-third of the deceased's substantial estate go to his "good friend and faithful attorney, Scribner."

To begin, let us note that in the first three of the foregoing situations, we are not looking at conflicting obligations. Each actor can be said to have a personal interest in the outcome of the transaction but not an obligation to pursue that interest. Dr. Brisby clearly has no obligation to accept the Hawaiian vacation. While Professor Darnay, one assumes, is not completely disinterested as regards the $4,000 he collects annually from students he requires to purchase his book, he has no obligation to collect these funds. Wiggins, one supposes, is not displeased that some of the city's business has gone to a member of his family; still, it would not have been wrong for him to step aside and allow someone else to select the most competitive bid and issue the contract. There is certainly no obligation to take every opportunity to enrich oneself (and one's relatives), especially when one occupies a social position in virtue of which one is beholden to others, as the doctor is to his patients, as the teacher is to his students, and as the purchasing agent is to the citizens of his community.

Nor are we necessarily looking at a series of betrayals. Dr. Brisby's patients, let us suppose, will not suffer for having been switched to the new medication. Other conscientious professors use Darnay's *An Introduction to Politics*. And Wiggins's municipality is not being made to pay exorbitant prices for second-rate automobiles. We will suppose then that Dr. Brisby's patients, Professor Darnay's students, and the citizens of Wiggins's municipality are not the victims of deliberate efforts to shortchange them; indeed, they are not victims at all. Under different circumstances, other doctors, professors, or purchasing agents might reasonably have made the same choices without the extra incentives.

Let us suppose then that, despite their expectation that they might receive expensive gifts from the overjoyed Jake, the prosecutor, the judge, and the jurors do their very best not to let possible benefits for themselves affect either their effort or their judgment; even without Jake's reputation for largesse, the outcome might have been the same. Let us suppose that Taney has the highest regard for Hargitty's legal abilities and might well choose to go to her himself if the need arose. Finally, let us accept that Scribner did not twist Whipple's arm in order to get him to sign the will; it was Whipple's own idea to give a portion of the estate to Scribner, and, while Scribner did not object, other attorneys might well have found the bequest to Scribner to be unexceptional had they been drafting the will. Our concern here is not with the reasonableness or unreasonableness of the actions undertaken in behalf of the clients; it is rather with the acceptances of the gift and the referral fee and with the drafting of the will, enriching fiduciaries who are beholden to others.

It might be plausibly suggested that what is ethically perilous in these cases is the possibility that judgment might be affected despite the care taken to avoid influence. Subconsciously, the expectation that one has something to gain may play a role in one's deliberations. To the extent that this is so (*ex hypothesi;* one cannot know it is not so), one may not be doing the most responsible work that can be done under the circumstances. While we might suppose in setting up our examples that other attorneys, judges, etc., might have acted similarly even without a comparable personal interest in the outcome, it may not be possible for one who is subject to a conflicting personal interest to be equally confident about what a disinterested judgment would look like. Without the attorney's knowing about it, a personal interest in the matter may compromise the ability to exercise independent professional judgment on behalf of a client. Standing to benefit from specific advice or representation, the attorney also has an interest in underestimating the degree to which advantage to self may interfere with the fulfillment of obligations to the client. And so for many—perhaps for all—it may be ethically imprudent to trust one's own opinion that professional judgment will be unaffected by personal interest.

Still, an attorney might be confident—let us suppose, for the sake of discussion, reasonably so—that her independent judgment will not be compromised by a personal interest. Is there reason still for the responsible attorney to be concerned about conflict of interest? Does "reasonable" confidence that independent judgment will not be affected suffice to satisfy an attorney's doubts about the propriety of proceeding in the face of a conflicting personal interest?

In a professionalized legal system such as ours, people are not expected to understand their legal situation without professional counsel, nor are they expected to be able to secure that to which they are legally entitled unless they have access to professional services available only through licensed attorneys. Clients are thus sitting ducks for unscrupulous attorneys, and in general they know it. Legal advice may further the attorney's interests more than the client's, and legal action can benefit the attorney at the client's expense. For this reason loyalty to the client must be an overriding obligation of attorneys if the general public is to trust members of the legal profession. To the extent that lay persons believe that people generally pursue their own interests, attorneys must make a special effort to try to get across to clients that it will be the clients' interests that will be determinative of the lawyer's advice and representation and that the lawyer's personal interests will not compromise that loyalty to the clients. It is clearly part of the profession's responsibility that this be done. It is also in the profession's enlightened interest.

The duty of loyalty thus has two parts. There is a guarantee that the profession makes to a client on behalf of the attorney that he or she will exercise independent judgment on the client's behalf and will be a zealous advocate in representing the client's interests within the judicial system. That part is satisfied when the attorney is confident that significant personal interests will not interfere with independent judgment or zeal. But, additionally, there is a second guarantee: that the attorney will not give reason to believe that the loyalty has been compromised. A lawyer may be confident that potentially compromising influences are not having an effect, and we may suppose that such confidence is reasonable in the light of the attorney's experience. But one cannot be equally confident that others, believing attorneys to be as self-interested as anyone else, will be ready to accept the attorney's own assurances that personal interests played no role in professional judgment. In each of the six cases above, the existence of the conflicting personal interest calls into question the propriety of an action that would otherwise be unexceptional. If it becomes known that physicians participate in Anodyne's sales promotion plan, patients may be less willing to accept the advice of doctors. One cannot be sure whether a prescription is being written because the patient needs a new medication or because the physician needs a self-propelled lawnmower. Likewise, the students in Professor Darnay's class may underestimate the significance of his book on the grounds that it is being assigned, not because of some independent judgment as to its quality and appropriateness, but rather because Darnay needs the supplement to his income. His action may be construed as exploitative of his students. Thirdly, Wiggins's award of the contract to his brother-in-law can call into doubt the integrity of the governmental process. Suspicions will be aroused and confirmed that government offices do not serve the community so much as they serve the officeholders.

It is not difficult to appreciate how the fairness of Big Jake's trial is called into question by his distribution of expensive gifts. By way of comparison, suppose that the losing quarterback in an important professional football game were to receive from the owner of the winning team the sum of $100,000 in a brown paper bag. Suppose it were widely publicized that this transfer had taken place only a few hours after the conclusion of the game, a game in which the quarterback, normally a star player, had played badly. Consider how the bare fact that the money had changed hands can compromise the integrity of the game. Apart from whether or not the quarterback deliberately shaved points or threw the game; apart from whether or not the payments were made in satisfaction of some agreement made earlier; in the light of the payment, we have good reason to wonder whether what took place in the stadium was a genuine football game or an elaborate charade engineered to create the appearance of a fair test. Under the circumstances, the outcome of the game gives us scant reason to believe that the winners were the better football players. Likewise, if a trial is to serve as a social procedure for settling disputed questions, it is crucial that key participants in the transaction keep themselves above reproach. As with the role of quarterback, the positions of judge, prosecutor, and juror can create golden opportunities for self-enrichment at the expense of the apparent integrity of the process. The social positions themselves would lack point in the absence of a commitment not to benefit oneself in ways that *can be construed* as abusive of the privileges attaching to the roles. Thus, with only a few minor exceptions, the American Bar Association Code of Judicial Conduct (adopted in 1972) provides that "[n]either a judge nor a member of his family residing in his household should accept a gift, bequest, favor, or loan from anyone. . . ." Specifically barred is the acceptance of gifts from donors whose interests have come or are likely to come before the judge. Comparable constraints are applicable to the roles of juror and prosecutor.

Taney's referral of the Mullens case to Hargitty raises questions that are similar to those in the Dr. Brisby example. The existence of the referral fee calls into question the purpose of Taney's advice: Is it being given for the client's benefit or for the attorney's? Even if the attorney's recommendation is sound and the client is not being charged an unreasonable amount, few lay people, unschooled in the intricacy of the legal process, are likely to believe Taney when he says, with a straight face, that the kickback had no influence whatever on his professional judgment. To the extent that such referral fees are customary, the profession runs the risk that the general public will become aware of the practice and will look upon such recommendations with cynicism.[8]

Scribner's decision to draft the Whipple will, making himself a beneficiary, raises a different problem. Since Scribner *was* carrying out Whipple's instructions (and since Whipple is now dead), there is no occasion here for a client to lose trust. If eyebrows are raised at all, they will be those of the disinherited friends and relatives. Instead of decisively settling Whipple's intentions regarding the disposition of his estate, Scribner's document raises questions of undue influence and overreaching on the attorney's part, perhaps even questions of fraud arising out of the fiduciary relationship. Roman law would not permit the individual drawing a will to receive a legacy under it, and today the laws of some states provide that such a circumstance give rise either to a presumption or an inference of undue influence.[9] Not only is it the case that Scribner may not receive the portion of the estate that Whipple wanted him to have; his interest as a beneficiary of the will he was drafting can suffice to void the entire document. Since he is a beneficiary,

[8]Though there are differences in the way they approach the problem, the Canons of Professional Ethics (Canon 34, Division of Fees), the Code of Professional Responsibility (DR 2-107, Division of Fees Among Lawyers), and the Model Rules of Professional Conduct (Rule 1.5, Fees) each prohibit the financial arrangement contemplated by Taney and Hargitty. Nothing, however, would prohibit Taney from charging Mullens a reasonable fee for advising him to retain Hargitty.

[9]*State* v. *Horan,* 21 Wis. 2d 66, 123 N.W. 2d 488 (1963).

Scribner's own testimony regarding the validity of the will can be called into question. Clearly, if Scribner had wanted to do his best work for his client, he would have suggested, without recommending names, that Whipple retain some other attorney of his own choosing to draft a codicil providing for the bequest.[10] In part, this is a matter of prudence and competence. To do any less is to do less than one's best work for one's client. But in this case the expected outcome of the shoddy legal workmanship involves a substantial benefit for the attorney. The conflict of interest could hardly be more glaring.

The conflicts of interest that are of most concern to the legal profession are those in which the attorney reaps a substantial financial benefit quite apart from payment for work done on the case. But as all of us value things other than money, the possibilities for conflicts of interest are perhaps as far-ranging as human desire itself. Service to a client can suffer if an attorney is uncomfortable unless in control of the client or, alternatively, uncomfortable unless the client is involved in the making of all decisions; if the attorney is worried about being too aggressive or not aggressive enough; or if the attorney is insufficiently concerned or too much concerned about competency to handle a client's problem. Conflicts can arise as a consequence of assuming too many responsibilities. Which client's affairs can be put on a back burner? Which pressing problem am I going to neglect today?[11] Becoming a responsible attorney is in large measure a matter of coming to understand the personal tensions here and learning to manage or to avoid the problems. It is often difficult to adapt one's self to the constraints of a professional role.

Some conflicts of interest, however, are neither personal in the sense just discussed nor the product of some special financial interest. These cannot be averted merely by referring the case to another attorney. Such conflicts are systemic: rooted in the institutional context of the professional role. Attorneys are paid for their work, and, under the hourly fee arrangements governing much attorney income, there is an ineradicable conflict of interest every time a lawyer advises a client to get legal help with a problem and that he or she is available to do the job. The conflict comes to the fore also whenever a professional advises a client to purchase additional professional services. The lawyer has a clear financial interest in the advice. Some may think the problem could be ameliorated if attorneys were paid flat salaries in prepaid legal-services plans rather than on an hourly rate or a fee-for-service basis. But, instead of solving the problem, this arrangement merely changes its effect. The employee on a flat salary can be supposed to have an interest in working less for the same amount of money. Thus the incentive for a salaried attorney might be to say to prospective clients, not that they need professional services when they do not, but rather that they do not need professional services when in fact they do.

The problem is well understood in the medical context. The fee-for-service system has for years been criticized for encouraging unnecessary medical treatment. Conversely, health maintenance organizations (HMOs) which pay doctors on a salary basis have been criticized for not providing patients with needed medical services. The patient belonging to an HMO may spend less time in the hospital than a similar patient whose medical bills are paid for on a fee-for-service basis. But it is difficult to tell in practice whether the HMO patient is being deprived of needed care or whether the fee-for-service patient is paying for unneeded care. Conflicts of interest at this level require very careful specification of the concept of a need, medical or legal, and consideration of alternative incentive systems that can suffice to provide for those needs. The trick is to specify the details of a social structure that will assure the clients (or patients) that the services they receive are services they need, and the services they are denied are services they don't need. This is perhaps the most difficult question arising in the area of conflict of interest. At this writing, there is no favored answer. . . .

---

[10]This is the advice given by Henry Drinker, *Legal Ethics* (New York: Columbia University Press, 1953), p. 94.

[11]A useful source here is Andrew S. Watson, "A Psychological Taxonomy of Lawyer Conflicts," in his *The Lawyer in the Interviewing and Counselling Process* (Indianapolis: The Bobbs-Merrill Company, Inc., 1976), pp. 94–100.

88

LARRY MAY

Conflict of Interest

The classic clash between personal interests and professional principles occurs in cases of conflict of interest. The paradigm of a responsible professional, so it is often said, is that person who can scrupulously avoid conflicts of interest by keeping personal considerations completely out of his or her professional judgments.

Conflicts of interest are to be avoided, so the prevailing wisdom has it, because the professional's objective judgment is compromised, making it less likely that he or she can act in a principled way. When a professional has a conflict of interest, the professional's self is divided, with one part of the self pulled toward serving the interests of his or her client, and the other part of the self pulled toward personal gain (or some other interest) at the expense of serving the client's interests. *Black's Law Dictionary* defines such conflicts in terms of "a clash between public interest and the private pecuniary interest of the individual concerned."

. . . Michael Davis correctly states the major moral difficulty with conflicts of interest:

> If a lawyer does not at least warn his client of the conflict, he does more than weaken a guarantee worth preserving. He presents himself as having a judgment more reliable than in fact it is. He invites a trust the invitation itself betrays.[1]

As I shall argue in this section, Davis is largely correct, but for the wrong reasons. Davis goes wrong, as do most modern theorists, in believing that there is a type of professional judgment that is trustworthy and reliable in that it is completely uninfluenced by the material considerations of one's other interests.

Lawyers have perpetuated the view that professionals can and should be expected to serve absolutely the interests of their clients, a view stated well by Wolfram:

> Whatever may be the models that obtain in other legal cultures, the client-lawyer relationship in the United States is founded on the lawyer's *virtually total* loyalty to the client and the client's interests. . . . The entrenched lawyerly conception is that the client-lawyer relationship is the embodiment of centuries of established and stable tradition.[2] (emphasis added)

Other professionals have come to model themselves on this ideal of the Anglo-American legal profession.

The idea that professionals should serve "virtually total[ly]" the interests of their clients is at best unrealistic and at worst deceptive. It is unrealistic, as we will see, because it asks lawyers to blind themselves to their own interests in ways that are nearly impossible, and because it ignores the fact that there is often no objectively right way to conceive of someone's interests. It is deceptive because it creates false expectations of loyalty on the part of clients, expectations that when thwarted lead clients to a position where they lose control over their cases. The clients unknowingly render themselves vulnerable to possible abuses of trust that they would otherwise remain vigilantly on guard against. Lawyers betray the trust they have solicited when they act as if they were capable of rendering judgments in their clients' interests that are unaffected by their other interests.

Many factors intrude upon a professional's judgment, rendering the notion of a "virtually total loyalty" in serving the client's interest itself quite suspicious. Consider again the case of lawyers. Lawyers who are in private practice must be constantly concerned about paying the rent—indeed, many lawyers find themselves spending so much time getting, keeping, and billing clients that they come to regard the practice of law as a type of business. Yet rarely is this the picture of lawyers that lawyers themselves present to the public. In addition, the lawyers I have known are often highly ambitious individuals who see the pursuit of a particular client's case as a means of furthering their own careers. Furthermore, lawyers also have political agendas. As Wolfram and others have pointed out, "Even in pro bono representations, the ideological or altruistic motives that induce a lawyer to offer legal services" can often obscure the pursuit of the client's interests.[3] All of these factors make it unrealistic to think that lawyers can offer "virtually total loyalty" to

---

[1] [Michael Davis, "Conflict of Interest," *Business and Professional Ethics Journal* 1, no. 4 (summer 1982): 17–27], p. 21.

[2] [Charles Wolfram, *Modern Legal Ethics* (St. Paul, MN: West, 1986)], p. 146.

[3] Wolfram [*Modern Legal Ethics*], p. 313.

their client's interests, a loyalty lawyers nonetheless continue to claim to be the hallmark of their profession.

It is an infringement of client autonomy for professionals to deny clients the knowledge they need to decide whether to entrust themselves to a particular professional. It is deceptive of professionals to present themselves as capable of rendering objective judgments when they are aware of conflicts that will make it even more likely than normal that their "objective" judgments are compromised. This is why some conflicts of interest are morally problematic. But if a professional is quite open about the interests he or she has, or is likely to have, that are at odds with the client's interest, and secures from the client an understanding and consent to the lawyer's continued service under these circumstances, many conflicts of interest are no more troubling, from the moral point of view, than other cases of consensual client services.

It may be objected that in order for possible conflicts to be disclosed, my proposal calls for professionals to be able to identify what all of their interests are, a feat sometimes not feasible. On my view, professionals need to be, or to become, self-reflective concerning their interests. But this is no more troublesome for my view than it is for any other view of conflicts of interest. The traditional view, for instance, which calls for professionals to *avoid* all conflicts of interest surely must also call for professionals to be, or to become, aware of what their interests are that may conflict with the client's interests. My view is no worse off than the traditional view.

It may be further objected that I have misidentified the morally suspicious feature of conflicts of interest. Some might claim that the difficulty with all conflicts of interest is that they create temptation for wrongdoing. There are two things to be said about such a view. First, my consideration of the postmodern conception of the self leads me to think that at least some conflicts of interest are not occasions for wrongdoing at all but manifestations of the perfectly legitimate situation in which one has multiple and conflicting motivations. Second, the wrongdoing occurs, when it does, because of a presumed promise that all of the professional's other interests have been subordinated to the client's interests. But when professionals stop claiming that they can subordinate all of their other interests, the basis of the wrongdoing also begins to disappear. Disclosed conflicts that are consented to are not temptations for wrongdoing because the client has waived the right that would otherwise be the basis of a claim of wrongdoing due to the conflict of interest.

From the standpoint of deception and client autonomy, real estate brokers are better off than lawyers. Real estate brokers make it quite well known that they are working toward the consummation of real estate sales and that their income depends on securing higher rather than lower prices for these pieces of real estate. While they sometimes claim to represent the interests of the buyer, and in this sense perpetuate a deception, they do not claim to serve these interests absolutely. Those who are in the market for real estate are made much more aware of the conflicted nature of the brokers they encounter than is true of those who find themselves in need of legal counsel. In contrast, lawyers make it very difficult for a client to see the possible ways in which the client's interests will not necessarily be served. In this way, lawyers infringe client autonomy especially when they continue to assert so strongly that they are uniquely situated to devote themselves to the client's interests.

At this point it may be useful to consider a case of conflict of interest that I would find morally problematic. A scientist forms a corporation to support the research he is doing to find a cure for a certain disease. Many people who have this disease contribute money to the corporation. It is clear that the scientist's future research is now driven by a desire for personal monetary gain. But he contends that he has relieved himself of any problematic conflicts of interest by clearly disclosing to potential investors and to the university that is his primary employer that he has a strong personal monetary interest in the research he is conducting. Is there a morally problematic aspect to this case?

In my assessment, the people who have the disease in question and who contribute to the scientist's research corporation are not likely to be able to make informed decisions about what is best for themselves because their hopes for a cure for their own disease will cloud their judgments. In such cases it may not be possible for the scientist to rely on the consent given by those to whom he has disclosed a conflict of interest. For this reason, in similar kinds of cases, professionals should avoid such conflicts even when disclosure and consent are present. While these cases need to be addressed one by one, a general guideline could be that whenever an affected party is unlikely to be able to give fully informed consent, the professional should withdraw when conflicts of interest arise.[4]

Next, consider a different kind of case taken from engineering. A mechanical engineer is asked to give an informal opinion about a matter which the company he works for is planning to bring before the product standards committee of his profession at large. This engineer helps his work associates draft a letter of inquiry that is then submitted to his profession's product standards committee for review. As it turns out, this very engineer serves on the relevant product standards committee and is assigned the task of responding to the inquiry (which he had helped draft) in behalf of the professional committee. The engineer gives a ruling favorable to the drafters of the inquiry, who also happen to be his associates at the company for which he works. A competing company is placed in a disadvantageous position as a result of the ruling and eventually goes into bankruptcy. Needless to say, the ruling also works to the advantage of the engineer's own company. In 1982 the United States Supreme Court reviewed a similar case and held that the professional association had acted wrongly in allowing the engineer to review an inquiry he himself had helped to draft.[5]

Since it is true that professional engineers must staff such committees as the professional product standards committee discussed above, and since most engineers are employed by private organizations that will need to get rulings from such committees, conflicts of interest will almost inevitably manifest themselves in such contexts. In my view it was not initially wrong for the engineer in question to consult with his work associates and also to draft a response to the inquiry made by his work associates. Surely it is a mistake to think that professionals must never assume those roles that will possibly conflict with other roles they *may* play. In the case at issue, the engineer needed to inform the professional organization as well as the parties who would possibly be affected by the professional organization's ruling, and resign from the committee if any of those potentially affected objected to his remaining on the committee.

Deception and infringement of client autonomy are the key moral problems when personal interest conflicts with client interest. If the engineer in the case discussed above had informed all relevant parties that he had a special, work-related interest in the outcome of the product standards review he was preparing, and if these people had consented to let him remain on the committee, and if he had continued to notify others who might come to rely on the report, then the writing of this report would have posed no special moral problems. As it was, though, the people who relied on the report did not have sufficient knowledge of the writer's interests to be able to assess it properly; their autonomy was infringed through the lack of such disclosure. They were put into a vulnerable position which they would otherwise have wanted to guard against. In what follows, I attempt to set out a new model for understanding the fiduciary duties that have traditionally been seen as the basis for requiring professionals to avoid potential and actual conflicts of interest.

. . . I will propose a more moderate position that builds on some of the postmodern insights but mediates them in light of the discussion of communitarianism and critical theory that permeated the previous chapters of this book. A socially responsive professional will both be influenced by the socialization of his or her environment and take responsibility for a fair amount of this socialization. Most importantly, the socially responsive self will not merely withdraw into the self-indulgence that often characterizes postmodern conceptions of the self.

In law and other professional contexts, there is thought to be a fiduciary relationship between professional and client. *Black's Law Dictionary* defines *fiduciary* as follows:

> The term is derived from the Roman law, and means (as a noun) a person holding the character of a trustee, or a character analogous to that of a trustee, in respect to the trust and confidence involved in it and the scrupulous good faith and candor which it requires.[6]

A "fiduciary relation" establishes a situation in which various professionals "in equity and good conscience" are "bound to act in good faith and with due

---

[4]I am grateful to Carl Wellman for urging me to see that this refinement of my view was called for.

[5]See *American Society of Mechanical Engineers* v. *Hydrolevel Corporation* (72 L Ed 2d 330) 1982. For an extended discussion of this case see May, "Professional Actions and the Liabilities of Professional Associations: ASME vs. Hydrolevel Corp." Also see [Paula Wells, Hardy Jones, and Michael Davis, *Conflicts of Interest in Engineering* (Dubuque, IA: Kendall/Hart, 1986)], pp. 1–24.

[6]*Black's Law Dictionary,* p. 563.

regard to interests of one reposing the confidence."[7] When professionals are viewed as fiduciaries, they are thought to be bound to act as if their interests were those of their client and hence to sacrifice their own interests for the sake of their client's interests.

It is instructive to contrast this situation with that of the standard way that two parties are viewed if they are not in a fiduciary relationship. In his book *The Critical Legal Studies Movement,* Roberto Unger rightly points out that in law, nonfiduciary relations are ones in which neither party is thought to owe anything to the other: "the other party's interests can be treated as of no account as long as the rightholder remains within his zone of discretionary action."[8] The contrast between normal commercial relations and fiduciary relations is quite striking—surely there is a middle position that would more appropriately apply to conflict-of-interest cases. Like Unger, in this section I will strive for a view of fiduciary relations that takes account of the reality of professional life.

Unger proposes a fiduciary standard that "requires each party to give some force to the other party's interests, though less than to his own."[9] This proposal is a compromise between the overly minimalistic notion of simple contractual obligation, which some might apply to professional-client relationships, and the unrealistic selflessness of the legal model of fiduciary duty. Unger goes too far here. Surely it is not too much to require professionals to place the interests of their client at least on a par with their most strongly held personal interests. The special status afforded professionals calls for some serious attempt to serve the client's interest. In order to give proper care to the client, the client's interest must be given serious weight, and this means that it should be at least *equal* to the professional's most strongly held personal interests.

Those who have voluntarily placed themselves in positions of trust concerning the interests of others must give careful consideration to those interests. But it is simply a mistake to demand selfless service to the client's interest. Since "virtually total loyalty" is not a realistic possibility in professional life, the chief duty of professionals cannot be absolute service to their client's interests. The chief professional duty concerning conflicts of interest should be merely the duty of full disclosure, along with the duty to withdraw from serving the client if the client finds the disclosed conflict objectionable. It is too much to expect professionals to have a duty to be totally loyal or to place the interests of their client significantly above their own interests. As I have indicated, the perpetuation of the myth that professionals have these more strenuous duties is both unrealistic and deceptive.

It is important to note that many of the most serious harms that occur in conflict-of-interest cases result from one party's becoming less vigilant on the assumption that another party is serving absolutely the first party's interests. When the professional raises expectations of total loyalty and trustworthiness, he or she is indeed implicated in whatever harms result from the ensuing diminished vigilance of the client. This is also true of those expectations raised by the profession of which a given professional is a member. But as with other collective responsibilities, an individual can diminish or possibly extinguish his or her personal responsibility by taking steps to overcome the expectations raised by the profession at large. By explicitly stating the interests the professional has that are likely to conflict with the interests of the client, the professional at least partially distances himself or herself from the expectations of objectivity that the rest of the profession may raise. This heightens the vigilance of the client and makes him or her less likely to be harmed.

Professional responsibility is not merely a matter of conforming to the fiduciary duties one has, even if we understand these duties in the way in which I have suggested. Rather, it is important that elements of shame exist alongside the guilt that is associated with the direct violation of a professional duty. Even when a professional has done all he or she can do to avoid harm to a client, the professional should deeply regret whatever harms nonetheless occur, and when harms result from actions taken by the profession as a whole, shame is often not at all misplaced.[10] But the appropriateness of such shame should not lead us to think that professionals have a *duty* to serve absolutely the interests of their client, such that they should feel guilt whenever they let personal interest interfere with the pursuit of the client's interest. As I have argued, such

[7]Ibid., p. 564.

[8]Roberto Mangabeira Unger, *The Critical Legal Studies Movement* (Cambridge, MA: Harvard University Press, 1983), p. 83.

[9]Ibid., p. 83.

[10]See May, "Metaphysical Guilt and Moral Taint," in [Larry May and Stacey Hoffman, eds., *Collective Responsibility* (Savage, MO: Rowman & Littlefield, 1991)].

guilt is appropriate only in certain cases involving deception or infringement of client autonomy.

I have tried to provide a new basis for understanding what is morally problematic about some conflicts of interest in professional life. In arguing that the deceptiveness and infringement of client autonomy of certain conflicts of interest are their undoing, I have indicated a straightforward strategy for rendering many conflicts of interest morally unproblematic, namely, full and open disclosure of potential conflicts by the professional. This strategy is an example of . . . negotiated compromising. . . . In general, professionals have for too long mistakenly thought that they can and should avoid all conflicts of interest, as if it were possible for the professional thereby to provide objective judgments and absolutely loyal service for the client. I have provided a challenge to this assumption that has drawn on a postmodern perspective of social and personal conflicts. At least in this case, reliance on some postmodern ideas has not thrown us into a moral abyss[11] but rather has clarified the picture of a certain part of the moral landscape we call professional life.

89

Wheat v. United States

486 U.S. 153 (1988)

CHIEF JUSTICE REHNQUIST delivered the opinion of the Court.

The issue in this case is whether the District Court erred in declining petitioner's waiver of his right to conflict-free counsel and by refusing to permit petitioner's proposed substitution of attorneys.

I

Petitioner Mark Wheat, along with numerous codefendants, was charged with participating in a far-flung distribution conspiracy. Over a period of several years, many thousands of pounds of marijuana were transported from Mexico and other locations to southern California. Petitioner acted primarily as an intermediary in the distribution ring; he received and stored large shipments of marijuana at his home, then distributed the marijuana to customers in the region.

Also charged in the conspiracy were Juvenal Gomez-Barajas and Javier Bravo, who were represented in their criminal proceedings by attorney Eugene Iredale. Gomez-Barajas was tried first and was acquitted on drug charges overlapping with those against petitioner. To avoid a second trial on other charges, however, Gomez-Barajas offered to plead guilty to tax evasion and illegal importation of merchandise. At the commencement of petitioner's trial, the District Court had not accepted the plea; he was thus free to withdraw his guilty plea and proceed to trial.

Bravo, evidently a lesser player in the conspiracy, decided to forgo trial and plead guilty to one count of transporting approximately 2400 pounds of marijuana from Los Angeles to a residence controlled by Victor Vidal. At the conclusion of Bravo's guilty plea proceedings on August 22, 1985, Iredale notified the District Court that he had been contacted by petitioner and had been asked to try petitioner's case as well. In response, the Government registered substantial concern about the possibility of conflict in the representation. After entertaining some initial discussion of the substitution of counsel, the District Court instructed the parties to present more detailed arguments the following Monday, just one day before the scheduled start of petitioner's trial.

At the Monday hearing, the Government objected to petitioner's proposed substitution on the ground that Iredale's representation of Gomez-Barajas and Bravo created a serious conflict of interest. The Government's position was premised on two possible conflicts. First, the District Court had not yet accepted the plea and sentencing arrangement negotiated between Gomez-Barajas and the Government; in the event that arrangement were rejected by the court, Gomez-Barajas would be free to withdraw the plea and stand trial. He would then be faced with the prospect of representation by Iredale, who in the meantime would have acted as petitioner's attorney. Petitioner, through his participation in the drug distribution scheme, was familiar with the sources and size of Gomez-Barajas' income, and was thus likely to be called as a witness for the Government at any subsequent trial of Gomez-Barajas. This scenario

[11]See Edith Wyschogrod's *Saints and Postmodernism* [Chicago: University of Chicago, 1990] for another attempt at arguing that postmodernism can be conceived as a nonrelativistic standpoint. . . .

would pose a conflict of interest for Iredale, who would be prevented from cross-examining petitioner and thereby from effectively representing Gomez-Barajas.

Second, and of more immediate concern, Iredale's representation of Bravo would directly affect his ability to act as counsel for petitioner. The Government believed that a portion of the marijuana delivered by Bravo to Vidal's residence eventually was transferred to petitioner. In this regard, the Government contacted Iredale and asked that Bravo be made available as a witness to testify against petitioner, and agreed in exchange to modify its position at the time of Bravo's sentencing. In the likely event that Bravo were called to testify, Iredale's position in representing both men would become untenable, for ethical proscriptions would forbid him from cross-examining Bravo in any meaningful way. By failing to do so, he would also fail to provide petitioner with effective assistance of counsel. Thus, because of Iredale's prior representation of Gomez-Barajas and Bravo and the potential for serious conflict of interest, the Government urged the District Court to reject the substitution of attorneys.

In response, petitioner emphasized his right to have counsel of his own choosing and the willingness of Gomez-Barajas, Bravo, and petitioner to waive the right to conflict-free counsel. Petitioner argued that the circumstances posited by the Government that would create a conflict for Iredale were highly speculative and bore no connection to the true relationship between the co-conspirators. If called to testify, Bravo would simply say that he did not know petitioner and had no dealings with him; no attempt by Iredale to impeach Bravo would be necessary. Further, in the unlikely event that Gomez-Barajas went to trial on the charges of tax evasion and illegal importation, petitioner's lack of involvement in those alleged crimes made his appearance as a witness highly improbable. Finally, and most importantly, all three defendants agreed to allow Iredale to represent petitioner and to waive any future claims of conflict of interest. In petitioner's view, the Government was manufacturing implausible conflicts in an attempt to disqualify Iredale, who had already proved extremely effective in representing Gomez-Barajas and Bravo.

After hearing argument from each side, the District Court noted that it was unfortunate that petitioner had not suggested the substitution sooner, rather than two court days before the commencement of trial. The court then ruled:

> [B]ased upon the representation of the Government in [its] memorandum that the Court really has no choice at this point other than to find that an irreconcilable conflict of interest exists, I don't think it can be waived, and accordingly, Mr. Wheat's request to substitute Mr. Iredale in as attorney of record is denied.

Petitioner proceeded to trial with his original counsel and was convicted of conspiracy to possess more than 1000 pounds of marijuana with intent to distribute, in violation of 21 U.S.C. §846, and five counts of possessing marijuana with intent to distribute, in violation of §841(a)(1). . . .

II

The Sixth Amendment to the Constitution guarantees that "[i]n all criminal prosecutions, the accused shall enjoy the right . . . to have the Assistance of Counsel for his defence." . . .

The Sixth Amendment right to choose one's own counsel is circumscribed in several important respects. Regardless of his persuasive powers, an advocate who is not a member of the bar may not represent clients (other than himself) in court.[1] Similarly, a defendant may not insist on representation by an attorney he cannot afford or who for other reasons declines to represent the defendant. Nor may a defendant insist on the counsel of an attorney who has a previous or ongoing relationship with an opposing party, even when the opposing party is the Government. The question raised in this case is the extent to which a criminal defendant's right under the Sixth Amendment to his chosen attorney is qualified by the fact that the attorney has represented other defendants charged in the same criminal conspiracy.

In previous cases, we have recognized that multiple representation of criminal defendants engenders special dangers of which a court must be aware. . . .

Petitioner insists that the provision of waivers by all affected defendants cures any problems created by the

[1]Our holding in Faretta v. California, 422 U.S. 806 (1975), that a criminal defendant has a Sixth Amendment right to represent *himself* if he voluntarily elects to do so, does not encompass the right to choose any advocate if the defendant wishes to be represented by counsel.

multiple representation. But no such flat rule can be deduced from the Sixth Amendment presumption in favor of counsel of choice. Federal courts have an independent interest in ensuring that criminal trials are conducted within the ethical standards of the profession and that legal proceedings appear fair to all who observe them. Both the American Bar Association's Model Code of Professional Responsibility and its Model Rules of Professional Conduct, as well as the rules of the California Bar Association (which governed the attorneys in this case), impose limitations on multiple representation of clients. Not only the interest of a criminal defendant but the institutional interest in the rendition of just verdicts in criminal cases may be jeopardized by unregulated multiple representation.

For this reason, the Federal Rules of Criminal Procedure direct trial judges to investigate specialty cases involving joint representation. In pertinent part, Rule 44(c) provides:

> [T]he court shall promptly inquire with respect to such joint representation and shall personally advise each defendant of his right to the effective assistance of counsel, including separate representation. Unless it appears that there is good cause to believe no conflict of interest is likely to arise, the court shall take such measures as may be appropriate to protect each defendant's right to counsel.

Although Rule 44(c) does not specify what particular measures may be taken by a district court, one option suggested by the Notes of the Advisory Committee is an order by the court that the defendants be separately represented in subsequent proceedings in the case. . . .

To be sure, this need to investigate potential conflicts arises in part from the legitimate wish of district courts that their judgments remain intact on appeal. As the Court of Appeals accurately pointed out, trial courts confronted with multiple representations face the prospect of being "whip-sawed" by assertions of error no matter which way they rule. If a district court agrees to the multiple representation, and the advocacy of counsel is thereafter impaired as a result, the defendant may well claim that he did not receive effective assistance. On the other hand, a district court's refusal to accede to the multiple representation may result in a challenge such as petitioner's in this case. Nor does a waiver by the defendant necessarily solve the problem, for we note, without passing judgment on, the apparent willingness of Courts of Appeals to entertain ineffective assistance claims from defendants who have specifically waived the right to conflict-free counsel.

Thus, where a court justifiably finds an actual conflict of interest, there can be no doubt that it may decline a proffer of waiver, and insist that defendants be separately represented. . . .

Unfortunately for all concerned, a district court must pass on the issue of whether or not to allow a waiver of a conflict of interest by a criminal defendant not with the wisdom of hindsight after the trial has taken place, but in the murkier pretrial context when relationships between parties are seen through a glass, darkly. The likelihood and dimensions of nascent conflicts of interest are notoriously hard to predict, even for those thoroughly familiar with criminal trials. It is a rare attorney who will be fortunate enough to learn the entire truth from his own client, much less be fully apprised before trial of what each of the Government's witnesses will say on the stand. A few bits of unforeseen testimony or a single previously unknown or unnoticed document may significantly shift the relationship between multiple defendants. These imponderables are difficult enough for a lawyer to assess, and even more difficult to convey by way of explanation to a criminal defendant untutored in the niceties of legal ethics. Nor is it amiss to observe that the willingness of an attorney to obtain such waivers from his clients may bear an inverse relation to the care with which he conveys all the necessary information to them.

For these reasons we think the District Court must be allowed substantial latitude in refusing waivers of conflicts of interest not only in those rare cases where an actual conflict may be demonstrated before trial, but in the more common cases where a potential for conflict exists which may or may not burgeon into an actual conflict as the trial progresses. In the circumstances of this case, with the motion for substitution of counsel made so close to the time of trial, the District Court relied on instinct and judgment based on experience in making its decision. We do not think it can be said that the court exceeded the broad latitude which must be accorded it in making this decision. Petitioner of course rightly points out that the Government may seek to "manufacture" a conflict in order to prevent a defendant from having a particularly able defense counsel at his side; but trial courts are undoubtedly aware of this possibility, and must take it into consideration along with all of the other factors which inform this sort of a decision. Here the District Court was confronted not simply with an attorney who wished to represent two coequal defendants in a straightforward criminal prosecution; rather, Iredale proposed to defend three conspirators of varying stature in a complex drug distribution scheme. The Government intended to call Bravo as a witness for the prosecution at petitioner's trial.[2] The Government might readily have tied certain deliveries of marijuana by Bravo to petitioner, necessitating vigorous cross-examination of Bravo by petitioner's counsel. Iredale, because of his prior representation of Bravo, would have been unable ethically to provide that cross-examination.

Iredale had also represented Gomez-Barajas, one of the alleged kingpins of the distribution ring, and had succeeded in obtaining a verdict of acquittal for him. Gomez-Barajas had agreed with the Government to plead guilty to other charges, but the District Court had not yet accepted the plea arrangement. If the agreement were rejected, petitioner's probable testimony at the resulting trial of Gomez-Barajas would create an ethical dilemma for Iredale from which one or the other of his clients would likely suffer.

Viewing the situation as it did before trial, we hold that the District Court's refusal to permit the substitution of counsel in this case was within its discretion and did not violate petitioner's Sixth Amendment rights. Other district courts might have reached differing or opposite conclusions with equal justification, but that does not mean that one conclusion was "right" and the other "wrong." The District Court must recognize a presumption in favor of petitioner's counsel of choice, but that presumption may be overcome not only by a demonstration of actual conflict but by a showing of a serious potential for conflict. The evaluation of the facts and circumstances of each case under this standard must be left primarily to the informed judgment of the trial court.

The judgment of the Court of Appeals is accordingly affirmed.

JUSTICE MARSHALL, with whom JUSTICE BRENNAN joins, dissenting. . . .

The Court's resolution of the instant case flows from its deferential approach to the District Court's denial of petitioner's motion to add or substitute counsel; absent deference, a decision upholding the District Court's ruling would be inconceivable. Indeed, I believe that even under the Court's deferential standard, reversal is in order. . . .

At the time of petitioner's trial, Iredale's representation of Gomez-Barajas was effectively completed. As the Court notes, Iredale had obtained an acquittal for Gomez-Barajas on charges relating to a conspiracy to distribute marijuana. Iredale also had negotiated an agreement with the Government under which Gomez-Barajas would plead guilty to charges of tax evasion and illegal importation of merchandise, although the trial court had not yet accepted this plea arrangement. Gomez-Barajas was not scheduled to appear as a witness at petitioner's trial; thus, Iredale's conduct of that trial would not require him to question his former client. The only possible conflict this Court can divine from Iredale's representation of both petitioner and Gomez-Barajas rests on the premise that the trial court would reject the negotiated plea agreement and that Gomez-Barajas then would decide to go to trial. In this event, the Court tells us, "petitioner's probable testimony at the resulting trial of Gomez-Barajas would create an ethical dilemma for Iredale."

This argument rests on speculation of the most dubious kind. The Court offers no reason to think that the trial court would have rejected Gomez-Barajas's plea agreement; neither did the Government posit any such reason in its argument or brief before this Court. The most likely occurrence at the time petitioner moved to retain Iredale as his defense counsel was that the trial court would accept Gomez-Barajas's plea agreement, as the court in fact later did. Moreover, even if Gomez-Barajas had gone to trial, petitioner probably would not have testified. The record contains no indication that petitioner had any involvement in or information about crimes for which Gomez-Barajas might yet have stood trial. The only alleged connection between petitioner and Gomez-Barajas sprang from the conspiracy to distribute marijuana, and a jury already had acquitted Gomez-Barajas of that charge. It is therefore disingenuous to say that representation of both petitioner and Gomez-Barajas posed a serious potential for a conflict of interest.

Similarly, Iredale's prior representation of Bravo was not a cause for concern. The Court notes that the prosecution intended to call Bravo to the stand at petitioner's trial and asserts that Bravo's testimony could well have "necessitat[ed] vigorous cross-examination . . . by peti-

[2] Bravo was in fact called as a witness at petitioner's trial. His testimony was elicited to demonstrate the transportation of drugs that the prosecution hoped to link to petitioner.

tioner's counsel." The facts, however, belie the claim that Bravo's anticipated testimony created a serious potential for conflict. Contrary to the Court's inference, Bravo could not have testified about petitioner's involvement in the alleged marijuana distribution scheme. As all parties were aware at the time, Bravo did not know and could not identify petitioner; indeed, prior to the commencement of legal proceedings, the two men never had heard of each other. Bravo's eventual testimony at petitioner's trial related to a shipment of marijuana in which petitioner was not involved; the testimony contained not a single reference to petitioner. Petitioner's counsel did not cross-examine Bravo, and neither petitioner's counsel nor the prosecutor mentioned Bravo's testimony in closing argument. All of these developments were predictable when the District Court ruled on petitioner's request that Iredale serve as trial counsel; the contours of Bravo's testimony were clear at that time. Given the insignificance of this testimony to any matter that petitioner's counsel would dispute, the proposed joint representation of petitioner and Bravo did not threaten a conflict of interest.[3]

Moreover, even assuming that Bravo's testimony might have "necessitat[ed] vigorous cross-examination," the District Court could have insured against the possibility of any conflict of interest without wholly depriving petitioner of his constitutional right to the counsel of his choice. Petitioner's motion requested that Iredale either be substituted for petitioner's current counsel or be added to petitioner's defense team. Had the District Court allowed the addition of Iredale and then ordered that he take no part in the cross-examination of Bravo, any possibility of a conflict would have been removed. Especially in light of the availability of this precautionary measure, the notion that Iredale's prior representation of Bravo might well have caused a conflict of interest at petitioner's trial is nothing short of ludicrous. . . .

[3]The very insignificance of Bravo's testimony, combined with the timing of the prosecutor's decision to call Bravo as a witness, raises a serious concern that the prosecutor attempted to manufacture a conflict in this case. The prosecutor's decision to use Bravo as a witness was an 11th-hour development. Throughout the course of plea negotiations with Bravo, the prosecutor never had suggested that Bravo testify at petitioner's trial. At Bravo's guilty-plea proceedings, when Iredale notified the District Court of petitioner's substitution motion, the prosecutor conceded that he had made no plans to call Bravo as a witness. Only after the prosecutor learned of the substitution motion and decided to oppose it did he arrange for Bravo's testimony by agreeing to recommend to the trial court a reduction in Bravo's sentence. Especially in light of the scarce value of Bravo's testimony, this prosecutorial behavior very plausibly may be viewed as a maneuver to prevent Iredale from representing petitioner at trial. Iredale had proved to be a formidable adversary; he previously had gained an acquittal for the alleged kingpin of the marijuana distribution scheme. . . .

JUSTICE STEVENS, with whom JUSTICE BLACKMUN joins, dissenting. . . .

As Justice Marshall demonstrates, the Court exaggerates the significance of the potential conflict. Of greater importance, the Court gives inadequate weight to the informed and voluntary character of the clients' waiver of their right to conflict-free representation. Particularly, the Court virtually ignores the fact that additional counsel representing petitioner had provided him with sound advice concerning the wisdom of a waiver and would have remained available during the trial to assist in the defense. Thus, this is not a case in which the District Judge faced the question whether one counsel should be substituted for another; rather the question before him was whether petitioner should be permitted to have *additional* counsel of his choice. I agree with Justice Marshall that the answer to that question is perfectly clear.

Accordingly, although I agree with the Court's premise that district judges must be afforded wide latitude in passing on motions of this kind, in this case it is abundantly clear to me that the District Judge abused his discretion and deprived this petitioner of a constitutional right of such fundamental character that reversal is required.

90

MONROE H. FREEDMAN

Professional Responsibility of the Criminal Defense Lawyer: The Three Hardest Questions

In almost any area of legal counseling and advocacy, the lawyer may be faced with the dilemma of either betraying the confidential communications of his client or participating to some extent in the purposeful deception of the court. This problem is nowhere more acute than in the practice of criminal law, particularly in the representation of the indigent accused. The purpose of this article is to analyze and attempt to resolve three of the most difficult issues in this general area:

1. Is it proper to cross-examine for the purpose of discrediting the reliability or credibility of an adverse witness whom you know to be telling the truth?
2. Is it proper to put a witness on the stand when you know he will commit perjury?
3. Is it proper to give your client legal advice when you have reason to believe that the knowledge you give him will tempt him to commit perjury?

These questions present serious difficulties with respect to a lawyer's ethical responsibilities. Moreover, if one admits the possibility of an affirmative answer, it is difficult even to discuss them without appearing to some to be unethical.[1] It is not surprising, therefore, that reasonable, rational discussion of these issues has been uncommon and that the problems have for so long remained unresolved. In this regard it should be recognized that the Canons of Ethics, which were promulgated in 1908 "as a general guide,"[2] are both inadequate and self-contradictory.

I. THE ADVERSARY SYSTEM AND THE NECESSITY FOR CONFIDENTIALITY

At the outset, we should dispose of some common question-begging responses. The attorney is indeed an officer of the court, and he does participate in a search for truth. These two propositions, however, merely serve to state the problem in different words: As an officer of the court, participating in a search for truth, what is the attorney's special responsibility, and how does that responsibility affect his resolution of the questions posed above?

The attorney functions in an adversary system based upon the presupposition that the most effective means of determining truth is to present to a judge and jury a clash between proponents of conflicting views. It is essential to the effective functioning of this system that each adversary have, in the words of Canon 15, "entire devotion to the interest of the client, warm zeal in the maintenance and defense of his rights and the exertion of his utmost learning and ability." It is also essential to maintain the fullest uninhibited communication between the client and his attorney, so that the attorney can most effectively counsel his client and advocate the latter's cause. This policy is safeguarded by the requirement that the lawyer must, in the words of Canon 37, "preserve his client's confidences." Canon 15 does, of course, qualify these obligations by stating that "the office of attorney does not permit, much less does it demand of him for any client, violations of law or any manner of fraud or chicane." In addition, Canon 22 requires candor toward the court.

The problem presented by these salutary generalities of the Canons in the context of particular litigation is illustrated by the personal experience of Samuel Williston, which was related in his autobiography.[3] Because of his examination of a client's correspondence file, Williston learned of a fact extremely damaging to his client's case. When the judge announced his decision, it was apparent that a critical factor in the favorable judgment for Williston's client was the judge's ignorance of this fact. Williston remained silent and did not thereafter inform the judge of what he knew. He was convinced, and Charles Curtis[4] agrees with him, that it was his duty to remain silent.

In an opinion by the American Bar Association Committee on Professional Ethics and Grievances, an eminent panel headed by Henry Drinker held that a lawyer should remain silent when his client lies to the judge by saying that he has no prior record,

---

[1]The substance of this paper was recently presented to a Criminal Trial Institute attended by forty-five members of the District of Columbia Bar. As a consequence, several judges (none of whom had either heard the lecture or read it) complained to the Committee on Admissions and Grievances of the District Court for the District of Columbia, urging the author's disbarment or suspension. Only after four months of proceedings, including a hearing, two meetings, and a de novo review by eleven federal district court judges, did the Committee announce its decision to "proceed no further in the matter."

[2]AMERICAN BAR ASSOCIATION, CANONS OF PROFESSIONAL ETHICS, Preamble (1908).

[3]WILLISTON, LIFE AND LAW 271 (1940).

[4]CURTIS, IT'S YOUR LAW 17–21 (1954). See also Curtis, *The Ethics of Advocacy,* 4 STAN. L. REV. 3, 9–10 (1951); Drinker, *Some Remarks on Mr. Curtis' "The Ethics of Advocacy,"* 4 STAN. L. REV. 349, 350–51 (1952).

despite the attorney's knowledge to the contrary.[5] The majority of the panel distinguished the situation in which the attorney has learned of the client's prior record from a source other than the client himself. William B. Jones, a distinguished trial lawyer and now a judge in the United States District Court for the District of Columbia, wrote a separate opinion in which he asserted that in neither event should the lawyer expose his client's lie. If these two cases do not constitute "fraud or chicane" or lack of candor within the meaning of the Canons (and I agree with the authorities cited that they do not), it is clear that the meaning of the Canons is ambiguous.

The adversary system has further ramifications in a criminal case. The defendant is presumed to be innocent. The burden is on the prosecution to prove beyond a reasonable doubt that the defendant is guilty. The plea of not guilty does not necessarily mean "not guilty in fact," for the defendant may mean "not legally guilty." Even the accused who knows that he committed the crime is entitled to put the government to its proof. Indeed, the accused who knows that he is guilty has an absolute constitutional right to remain silent.[6] The moralist might quite reasonably understand this to mean that, under these circumstances, the defendant and his lawyer are privileged to "lie" to the court in pleading not guilty. In my judgment, the moralist is right. However, our adversary system and related notions of the proper administration of criminal justice sanction the lie.

Some derive solace from the sophistry of calling the lie a "legal fiction," but this is hardly an adequate answer to the moralist. Moreover, this answer has no particular appeal for the practicing attorney, who knows that the plea of not guilty commits him to the most effective advocacy of which he is capable. Criminal defense lawyers do not win their cases by arguing reasonable doubt. Effective trial advocacy requires that the attorney's every word, action, and attitude be consistent with the conclusion that his client is innocent. As every trial lawyer knows, the jury is certain that the defense attorney knows whether his client is guilty. The jury is therefore alert to, and will be enormously affected by, any indication by the attorney that he believes the defendant to be guilty. Thus, the plea of not guilty commits the advocate to a trial, including a closing argument, in which he must argue that "not guilty" means "not guilty in fact."[7]

There is, of course, a simple way to evade the dilemma raised by the not guilty plea. Some attorneys rationalize the problem by insisting that a lawyer never knows for sure whether his client is guilty. The client who insists upon his guilt may in fact be protecting his wife, or may know that he pulled the trigger and that the victim was killed, but not that his gun was loaded with blanks and that the fatal shot was fired from across the street. For anyone who finds this reasoning satisfactory, there is, of course, no need to think further about the issue.

It is also argued that a defense attorney can remain selectively ignorant. He can insist in his first interview with his client that, if his client is guilty, he simply does not want to know. It is inconceivable, however, that an attorney could give adequate counsel under such circumstances. How is the client to know, for example, precisely which relevant circumstances his lawyer does not want to be told? The lawyer might ask whether his client has a prior record. The client, assuming that this is the kind of knowledge that might present ethical problems for his lawyer, might respond that he has no record. The lawyer would then put the defendant on the stand and, on cross-examination, be appalled to learn that his client has two prior convictions for offenses identical to that for which he is being tried.

Of course, an attorney can guard against this specific problem by telling his client that he must know about the client's past record. However, a lawyer can never anticipate all of the innumerable and potentially critical factors that his client, once cautioned, may

[5]Opinion 287, Committee on Professional Ethics and Grievances of the American Bar Association (1953).

[6]Escobedo v. Illinois, 378 U.S. 478, 485, 491 (1964).

[7]"The failure to argue the case before the jury, while ordinarily only a trial tactic not subject to review, manifestly enters the field of incompetency when the reason assigned is the attorney's conscience. It is as improper as though the attorney had told the jury that his client had uttered a falsehood in making the statement. The right to an attorney embraces effective representation throughout all stages of the trial, and where the representation is of such low caliber as to amount to no representation, the guarantee of due process has been violated." Johns v. Smyth, 176 F. Supp. 949, 953 (E.D. Va. 1959); Schwartz, Cases on Professional Responsibility and the Administration of Criminal Justice 79 (1962).

decide not to reveal. In one instance, for example, the defendant assumed that his lawyer would prefer to be ignorant of the fact that the client had been having sexual relations with the chief defense witness. The client was innocent of the robbery with which he was charged, but was found guilty by the jury—probably because he was guilty of fornication, a far less serious offense for which he had not even been charged.

The problem is compounded by the practice of plea bargaining. It is considered improper for a defendant to plead guilty to a lesser offense unless he is in fact guilty. Nevertheless, it is common knowledge that plea bargaining frequently results in improper guilty pleas by innocent people. For example, a defendant falsely accused of robbery may plead guilty to simple assault, rather than risk a robbery conviction and a substantial prison term. If an attorney is to be scrupulous in bargaining pleas, however, he must know in advance that his client is guilty, since the guilty plea is improper if the defendant is innocent. Of course, if the attempt to bargain for a lesser offense should fail, the lawyer would know the truth and thereafter be unable to rationalize that he was uncertain of his client's guilt.

If one recognizes that professional responsibility requires that an advocate have full knowledge of every pertinent fact, it follows that he must seek the truth from his client, not shun it.[8] This means that he will have to dig and pry and cajole, and, even then, he will not be successful unless he can convince the client that full and confidential disclosure to his lawyer will never result in prejudice to the client by any word or action of the lawyer. This is, perhaps, particularly true in the case of the indigent defendant, who meets his lawyer for the first time in the cell block or the rotunda. He did not choose the lawyer, nor does he know him. The lawyer has been sent by the judge and is part of the system that is attempting to punish the defendant. It is no easy task to persuade this client that he can talk freely without fear of prejudice. However, the inclination to mislead one's lawyer is not restricted to the indigent or even to the criminal defendant. Randolph Paul has observed a similar phenomenon among a wealthier class in a far more congenial atmosphere:

> The tax adviser will sometimes have to dynamite the facts of his case out of the unwilling witnesses on his own side—witnesses who are nervous, witnesses who are confused about their own interest, witnesses who try to be too smart for their own good, and witnesses who subconsciously do not want to understand what has happened despite the fact that they must if they are to testify coherently.[9]

Paul goes on to explain that the truth can be obtained only by persuading the client that it would be a violation of a sacred obligation for the lawyer ever to reveal a client's confidence. Beyond any question, once a lawyer has persuaded his client of the obligation of confidentiality, he must respect that obligation scrupulously.

II. THE SPECIFIC QUESTIONS

The first of the difficult problems posed above will now be considered: Is it proper to cross-examine for the purpose of discrediting the reliability or the credibility of a witness whom you know to be telling the truth? Assume the following situation. Your client has been falsely accused of a robbery committed at 16th and P Streets at 11:00 p.m. He tells you at first that at no time on the evening of the crime was he within six blocks of that location. However, you are able to persuade him that he must tell you the truth and that doing so will in no way prejudice him. He then reveals to you that he was at 15th and P Streets at 10:55 that evening, but that he was walking east, away from the scene of the crime, and that, by 11:00 p.m., he was six blocks away. At the trial, there are two prosecution witnesses. The first mistakenly, but with some degree of persuasion, identifies your client as the criminal. At that point, the prosecution's case depends on this single witness, who might or might not be believed. Since your client has a prior record, you do not want to put him on the stand, but you feel that there is at least a chance for acquittal. The second prosecution witness is an elderly woman who is somewhat nervous and who wears glasses. She testifies truthfully and accurately that she saw your client at 15th and P Streets at 10:55 p.m. She has corroborated the erroneous testimony of the

[8] "[C]ounsel cannot properly perform their duties without knowing the truth." Opinion 23, Committee on Professional Ethics and Grievances of the American Bar Association (1930).

[9] Paul, The Responsibilities of the Tax Adviser, 63 HARV. L. REV. 377, 383 (1950).

first witness and made conviction virtually certain. However, if you destroy her reliability through cross-examination designed to show that she is easily confused and has poor eyesight, you may not only eliminate the corroboration, but also cast doubt in the jury's mind on the prosecution's entire case. On the other hand, if you should refuse to cross-examine her because she is telling the truth, your client may well feel betrayed, since you knew of the witness's veracity only because your client confided in you, under your assurance that his truthfulness would not prejudice him.

The client would be right. Viewed strictly, the attorney's failure to cross-examine would not be violative of the client's confidence because it would not constitute a disclosure. However, the same policy that supports the obligation of confidentiality precludes the attorney from prejudicing his client's interest in any other way because of knowledge gained in his professional capacity. When a lawyer fails to cross-examine only because his client, placing confidence in the lawyer, has been candid with him, the basis for such confidence and candor collapses. Our legal system cannot tolerate such a result.

> The purposes and necessities of the relation between a client and his attorney require, in many cases, on the part of the client, the fullest and freest disclosures to the attorney of the client's objects, motives and acts. . . . To permit the attorney to reveal to others what is so disclosed, would be not only a gross violation of a sacred trust upon his part, but it would utterly destroy and prevent the usefulness and benefits to be derived from professional assistance.[10]

The client's confidences must "upon all occasions be inviolable," to avoid the "greater mischiefs" that would probably result if a client could not feel free "to repose [confidence] in the attorney to whom he resorts for legal advice and assistance."[11] Destroy that confidence, and "a man would not venture to consult any skillful person, or would only dare to tell his counsellor half his case."[12]

Therefore, one must conclude that the attorney is obligated to attack, if he can, the reliability or credibility of an opposing witness whom he knows to be truthful. The contrary result would inevitably impair the "perfect freedom of consultation by client with attorney," which is "essential to the administration of justice."[13]

The second question is generally considered to be the hardest of all: Is it proper to put a witness on the stand when you know he will commit perjury? Assume, for example, that the witness in question is the accused himself, and that he has admitted to you, in response to your assurances of confidentiality, that he is guilty. However, he insists upon taking the stand to protest his innocence. There is a clear consensus among prosecutors and defense attorneys that the likelihood of conviction is increased enormously when the defendant does not take the stand. Consequently, the attorney who prevents his client from testifying only because the client has confided his guilt to him is violating that confidence by acting upon the information in a way that will seriously prejudice his client's interests.

Perhaps the most common method for avoiding the ethical problem just posed is for the lawyer to withdraw from the case, at least if there is sufficient time before trial for the client to retain another attorney.[14] The client will then go to the nearest law office, realizing that the obligation of confidentiality is not what it has been represented to be, and withhold incriminating information or the fact of his guilt from his new attorney. On ethical grounds, the practice of withdrawing from a case under such circumstances is indefensible, since the identical perjured testimony will ultimately be presented. More important, perhaps, is the practical consideration that the new attorney will be ignorant of the perjury and therefore will be in no position to attempt to discourage the client from presenting it. Only the original attorney, who knows the truth, has that opportunity, but he loses it in the very act of evading the ethical problem.

---

[10]2 MECHEM, AGENCY § 2297 (2d ed. 1914).

[11]Opinion 150, Committee on Professional Ethics and Grievances of the American Bar Association (1936), quoting THORNTON, ATTORNEYS AT LAW § 94 (1914). See also Opinion 23, *supra* note 8.

[12]Greenough v. Gaskell, 1 Myl. & K. 98, 103, 39 Eng. Rep. 618, 621 (Ch. 1833) (Lord Chancellor Brougham).

[13]Opinion 91, Committee on Professional Ethics and Grievances of the American Bar Association (1933).

[14]See Orkin, *Defense of One Known to Be Guilty,* 1 CRIM. L.Q. 170, 174 (1958). Unless the lawyer has told the client at the outset that he will withdraw if he learns that the client is guilty, "it is plain enough as a matter of good morals and professional ethics" that the lawyer should not withdraw on this ground. Opinion 90, Committee on Professional Ethics and Grievances of the American Bar Association (1932). As to the difficulties inherent in the lawyer's telling the client that he wants to remain ignorant of crucial facts, see note 8 *supra* and accompanying text.

The problem is all the more difficult when the client is indigent. He cannot retain other counsel, and in many jurisdictions, including the District of Columbia, it is impossible for appointed counsel to withdraw from a case except for extraordinary reasons. Thus, appointed counsel, unless he lies to the judge, can successfully withdraw only by revealing to the judge that the attorney has received knowledge of his client's guilt. Such a revelation in itself would seem to be a sufficiently serious violation of the obligation of confidentiality to merit severe condemnation. In fact, however, the situation is far worse, since it is entirely possible that the same judge who permits the attorney to withdraw will subsequently hear the case and sentence the defendant. When he does so, of course, he will have had personal knowledge of the defendant's guilt before the trial began.[15] Moreover, this will be knowledge of which the newly appointed counsel for the defendant will probably be ignorant.

The difficulty is further aggravated when the client informs the lawyer for the first time during trial that he intends to take the stand and commit perjury. The perjury in question may not necessarily be a protestation of innocence by a guilty man. Referring to the earlier hypothetical of the defendant wrongly accused of a robbery at 16th and P, the only perjury may be his denial of the truthful, but highly damaging, testimony of the corroborating witness who placed him one block away from the intersection five minutes prior to the crime. Of course, if he tells the truth and thus verifies the corroborating witness, the jury will be far more inclined to accept the inaccurate testimony of the principal witness, who specifically identified him as the criminal.[16]

[15]The judge may infer that the situation is worse than it is in fact. In the case related in note 23 *infra*, the attorney's actual difficulty was that he did not want to permit a plea of guilty by a client who was maintaining his innocence. However, as is commonly done, he told the judge only that he had to withdraw because of "an ethical problem." The judge reasonably inferred that the defendant had admitted his guilt and wanted to offer a perjured alibi.

[16]One lawyer, who considers it clearly unethical for the attorney to present the alibi in this hypothetical case, found no ethical difficulty himself in the following case. His client was prosecuted for robbery. The prosecution witness testified that the robbery had taken place at 10:15, and identified the defendant as the criminal. However, the defendant had a convincing alibi for 10:00 to 10:30. The attorney presented the alibi, and the client was acquitted. The alibi was truthful, but the attorney knew that the prosecution witness had been confused about the time, and that his client had in fact committed the crime at 10:45.

If a lawyer has discovered his client's intent to perjure himself, one possible solution to this problem is for the lawyer to approach the bench, explain his ethical difficulty to the judge, and ask to be relieved, thereby causing a mistrial. This request is certain to be denied, if only because it would empower the defendant to cause a series of mistrials in the same fashion. At this point, some feel that the lawyer has avoided the ethical problem and can put the defendant on the stand. However, one objection to this solution, apart from the violation of confidentiality, is that the lawyer's ethical problem has not been solved, but has only been transferred to the judge. Moreover, the client in such a case might well have grounds for appeal on the basis of deprivation of due process and denial of the right to counsel, since he will have been tried before, and sentenced by, a judge who has been informed of the client's guilt by his own attorney.

A solution even less satisfactory than informing the judge of the defendant's guilt would be to let the client take the stand without the attorney's participation and to omit reference to the client's testimony in closing argument. The latter solution, of course, would be as damaging as to fail entirely to argue the case to the jury, and failing to argue the case is "as improper as though the attorney had told the jury that his client had uttered a falsehood in making the statement."[17]

Therefore, the obligation of confidentiality, in the context of our adversary system, apparently allows the attorney no alternative to putting a perjurious witness on the stand without explicit or implicit disclosure of the attorney's knowledge to either the judge or the jury. Canon 37 does not proscribe this conclusion; the canon recognizes only two exceptions to the obligation of confidentiality. The first relates to the lawyer who is accused by his client and may disclose the truth to defend himself. The other exception relates to the "announced intention of a client to commit a crime." On the basis of the ethical and practical considerations discussed above, the Canon's exception to the obligation of confidentiality cannot logically be understood to include the crime of perjury committed during the specific case in which the lawyer is serving. Moreover, even when the intention

[17]See note 7 *supra.*

is to commit a crime in the future, Canon 37 does not require disclosure, but only permits it. Furthermore, Canon 15, which does proscribe "violation of law" by the attorney for his client, does not apply to the lawyer who unwillingly puts a perjurious client on the stand after having made every effort to dissuade him from committing perjury. Such an act by the attorney cannot properly be found to be subornation—corrupt inducement—of perjury. Canon 29 requires counsel to inform the prosecuting authorities of perjury committed in a case in which he has been involved, but this can only refer to perjury by opposing witnesses. For an attorney to disclose his client's perjury "would involve a direct violation of Canon 37."[18] Despite Canon 29, therefore, the attorney should not reveal his client's perjury "to the court or to the authorities."[19]

Of course, before the client testifies perjuriously, the lawyer has a duty to attempt to dissuade him on grounds of both law and morality. In addition, the client should be impressed with the fact that his untruthful alibi is tactically dangerous. There is always a strong possibility that the prosecutor will expose the perjury on cross-examination. However, for the reasons already given, the final decision must necessarily be the client's. The lawyer's best course thereafter would be to avoid any further professional relationship with a client whom he knew to have perjured himself.

The third question is whether it is proper to give your client legal advice when you have reason to believe that the knowledge you give him will tempt him to commit perjury. This may indeed be the most difficult problem of all, because giving such advice creates the appearance that the attorney is encouraging and condoning perjury.

If the lawyer is not certain what the facts are when he gives the advice, the problem is substantially minimized, if not eliminated. It is not the lawyer's function to prejudge his client as a perjurer. He cannot presume that the client will make unlawful use of his advice. Apart from this, there is a natural predisposition in most people to recollect facts, entirely honestly, in a way most favorable to their own interest. As Randolph Paul has observed, some witnesses are nervous, some are confused about their own interests, some try to be too smart for their own good, and some subconsciously do not want to understand what has happened to them.[20] Before he begins to remember essential facts, the client is entitled to know what his own interests are.

The above argument does not apply merely to factual questions such as whether a particular event occurred at 10:15 or at 10:45.[21] One of the most critical problems in a criminal case, as in many others, is intention. A German writer, considering the question of intention as a test of legal consequences, suggests the following situation.[22] A young man and a young woman decide to get married. Each has a thousand dollars. They decide to begin a business with these funds, and the young lady gives her money to the young man for this purpose. Was the intention to form a joint venture or a partnership? Did they intend that the young man be an agent or a trustee? Was the transaction a gift or a loan? If the couple should subsequently visit a tax attorney and discover that it is in their interest that the transaction be viewed as a gift, it is submitted that they could, with complete honesty, so remember it. On the other hand, should their engagement be broken and the young woman consult an attorney for the purpose of recovering her money, she could with equal honesty remember that her intention was to make a loan.

Assume that your client, on trial for his life in a first-degree murder case, has killed another man with a penknife but insists that the killing was in self-defense. You ask him, "Do you customarily carry the penknife in your pocket, do you carry it frequently or infrequently, or did you take it with you only on this occasion?" He replies, "Why do you ask me a question like that?" It is entirely appropriate to inform him that his carrying the knife only on this occasion, or infrequently, supports an inference of premeditation, while if he carried the knife constantly, or frequently, the inference of premeditation would be negated. Thus, your client's life may depend upon his recollection as to whether he carried the knife frequently or

[18]Opinion 287, Committee on Professional Ethics and Grievances of the American Bar Association (1953).

[19]*Ibid.*

[20]See Paul *supra* note 9.

[21]Even this kind of "objective fact" is subject to honest error. See note 16 *supra.*

[22]Wurzel, Das Juristische Denken 82 (1904), translated in Fuller, Basic Contract Law 67 (1964).

infrequently. Despite the possibility that the client or a third party might infer that the lawyer was prompting the client to lie, the lawyer must apprise the defendant of the significance of his answer. There is no conceivable ethical requirement that the lawyer trap his client into a hasty and ill-considered answer before telling him the significance of the question.

A similar problem is created if the client has given the lawyer incriminating information before being fully aware of its significance. For example, assume that a man consults a tax lawyer and says, "I am fifty years old. Nobody in my immediate family has lived past fifty. Therefore, I would like to put my affairs in order. Specifically, I understand that I can avoid substantial estate taxes by setting up a trust. Can I do it?" The lawyer informs the client that he can successfully avoid the estate taxes only if he lives at least three years after establishing the trust or, should he die within three years, if the trust is found not to have been created in contemplation of death. The client then might ask who decides whether the trust is in contemplation of death. After learning that the determination is made by the court, the client might inquire about the factors on which such a decision would be based.

At this point, the lawyer can do one of two things. He can refuse to answer the question, or he can inform the client that the court will consider the wording of the trust instrument and will hear evidence about any conversations which he may have or any letters he may write expressing motives other than avoidance of estate taxes. It is likely that virtually every tax attorney in the country would answer the client's question, and that no one would consider the answer unethical. However, the lawyer might well appear to have prompted his client to deceive the Internal Revenue Service and the courts, and this appearance would remain regardless of the lawyer's explicit disclaimer to the client of any intent so to prompt him. Nevertheless, it should not be unethical for the lawyer to give the advice.

In a criminal case, a lawyer may be representing a client who protests his innocence, and whom the lawyer believes to be innocent. Assume, for example, that the charge is assault with intent to kill, that the prosecution has erroneous but credible eyewitness testimony against the defendant, and that the defendant's truthful alibi witness is impeachable on the basis of several felony convictions. The prosecutor, perhaps having doubts about the case, offers to permit the defendant to plead guilty to simple assault. If the defendant should go to trial and be convicted, he might well be sent to jail for fifteen years; on a plea of simple assault, the maximum penalty would be one year, and sentence might well be suspended.

The common practice of conveying the prosecutor's offer to the defendant should not be considered unethical, even if the defense lawyer is convinced of his client's innocence. Yet the lawyer is clearly in the position of prompting his client to lie, since the defendant cannot make the plea without saying to the judge that he is pleading guilty because he is guilty. Furthermore, if the client does decide to plead guilty, it would be improper for the lawyer to inform the court that his client is innocent, thereby compelling the defendant to stand trial and take the substantial risk of fifteen years' imprisonment.[23]

Essentially no different from the problem discussed above, but apparently more difficult, is the so-called *Anatomy of a Murder* situation.[24] The lawyer, who has received from his client an incriminating story of murder in the first degree, says, "If the facts are as you have stated them so far, you have no defense, and you will probably be electrocuted. On the other hand, if you acted in a blind rage, there is a possibility of saving your life. Think it over, and we will talk about it tomorrow." As in the tax case, and as in the case of the plea of guilty to a lesser offense, the

[23]In a recent case, the defendant was accused of unauthorized use of an automobile, for which the maximum penalty is five years. He told his court-appointed attorney that he had borrowed the car from a man known to him only as "Junior," that he had not known the car was stolen, and that he had an alibi for the time of the theft. The defendant had three prior convictions for larceny, and the alibi was weak. The prosecutor offered to accept a guilty plea to two misdemeanors (taking property without right and petty larceny) carrying a combined maximum sentence of eighteen months. The defendant was willing to plead guilty to the lesser offenses, but the attorney felt that, because of his client's alibi, he could not permit him to do so. The lawyer therefore informed the judge that he had an ethical problem and asked to be relieved. The attorney who was appointed in his place permitted the client to plead guilty to the two lesser offenses, and the defendant was sentenced to nine months. The alternative would have been five or six months in jail while the defendant waited for his jury trial, and a very substantial risk of conviction and a much heavier sentence. Neither the client nor justice would have been well served by compelling the defendant to go to trial against his will under these circumstances.

[24]See TRAVER, ANATOMY OF A MURDER (1958).

lawyer has given his client a legal opinion that might induce the client to lie. This is information which the lawyer himself would have, without advice, were he in the client's position. It is submitted that the client is entitled to have this information about the law and to make his own decision as to whether to act upon it. To decide otherwise would not only penalize the less well-educated defendant, but would also prejudice the client because of his initial truthfulness in telling his story in confidence to the attorney.

III. CONCLUSION

The lawyer is an officer of the court, participating in a search for truth. Yet no lawyer would consider that he had acted unethically in pleading the statute of frauds or the statute of limitations as a bar to a just claim. Similarly, no lawyer would consider it unethical to prevent the introduction of evidence such as a murder weapon seized in violation of the fourth amendment or a truthful but involuntary confession, or to defend a guilty man on grounds of denial of a speedy trial.[25] Such actions are permissible because there are policy considerations that at times justify frustrating the search for truth and the prosecution of a just claim. Similarly, there are policies that justify an affirmative answer to the three questions that have been posed in this article. These policies include the maintenance of an adversary system, the presumption of innocence, the prosecution's burden to prove guilt beyond a reasonable doubt, the right to counsel, and the obligation of confidentiality between lawyer and client. . . .

[25]Cf. Kamisar, *Equal Justice in the Gatehouses and Mansions of American Criminal Procedure,* in CRIMINAL JUSTICE IN OUR TIME 77–78 (Howard ed. 1965):

> Yes, the presence of counsel in the police station may result in the suppression of truth, just as the presence of counsel at the trial may, when a client is advised not to take the stand, or when an objection is made to the admissibility of trustworthy, but illegally seized, "real" evidence.
>
> If the subject of police interrogation not only cannot be "coerced" into making a statement, but need not volunteer one, why shouldn't he be so advised? And why shouldn't court-appointed counsel, as well as retained counsel, so advise him?

91

MARTHA MINOW

Breaking the Law: Lawyers and Clients in Struggles for Social Change

Buckeroo Banzai, in his strange comic-book kind of movie, uttered this classic line: "Wherever you go, there you are." I have pondered this line for years now, and I have been looking for a chance to give a rejoinder. Is this my chance? How about: "Wherever you are, there you go"? No? Well, how about: "Wherever you stand, there you see"? This one I feel fairly confident about. Wherever we stand affects what we see and know; who we are affects what interests us, what we notice. . . .

This effect of where we stand on what we know and perceive poses a challenge to any of us interested in politics: how can we interest others in our causes? And even if others are interested, how can we convey the urgency we feel to others more remote from our issues? I think this problem extends also to relationships between attorneys and clients; how can attorneys understand the interests of clients, from the clients' point of view? The clients' case is the most important one to them, but one of many for the attorney; this alone indicates the distance between attorney and clients. To focus the problem of stance and interests further, I would like to explore here the issues posed by clients who are interested in pursuing social and political change: What can and what should lawyers serving such clients do for them? In particular, what can and what should lawyers do for clients who entertain breaking the law as one of their strategies for achieving social change?

Now, already, you may be formulating a response. But if so, I wonder with whom you have begun to identify—the lawyer? The clients? Whose problem is this, anyway? . . .

A distinctive feature of struggles for social change in the United States is the persistent efforts to work within the legal system, especially the courts. In other countries, including democratic ones, legislative reform and labor union activities represent the most critical avenues for internal, lawful change. Therefore the rules of politics—if they be rules—govern those struggles. In the United States, especially in the twentieth century, feminists, civil rights advocates, environmentalists, and others, have turned to the courts for protection, for efforts at persuasion, and for dramatic presentations to audiences beyond the courtroom. Some of the presentations intend to dramatize the failures of the legal system itself or to arouse public sympathy despite the courts' intransigence. Sometimes, the strategy produces change. The triumph of change announced by the judiciary in *Brown v. Board of Education* accentuates the dramatic story of the National Association for the Advancement of Colored Peoples's ("NAACP") efforts to build precedents, case-by-case, to surmount racial segregation.

Some might idealistically, others more cynically, describe this process as the alternative to violent revolution. John F. Kennedy wrote that "those who make peaceful revolution impossible make violent revolution inevitable." Thus, our legal system can be defended as a process of conducting orderly change. Yet, from the vantage point of those who seek social change, the legal system itself often seems unavailing. Consider the experience of Myra Bradwell who sought unsuccessfully to obtain admission to the Illinois bar. She challenged her exclusion in state court and then in the United States Supreme Court; she placed her confidence in the legal system to correct her exclusion. The Supreme Court, however, in 1873 refused to read the privileges and immunities guaranteed by the Constitution as assuring a woman's right to enter the professions. Bradwell tried to demonstrate the errors in the court's approach, but the federal system let her down.

Even ostensible successes often carry with them negative consequences. Margaret Sanger faced several prosecutions and served time in jail for violating a federal law, the Comstock Act, against advocating and dispensing information about birth control. She later shifted her strategy and worked alongside the medical profession for a reinterpretation of the onerous Comstock Act, under which she had faced prosecution. A federal court in 1936 ultimately accepted the argument she helped to frame in a test case: the Act itself was construed to permit doctors to prescribe contraceptives for the purpose of saving life or promoting the well-being of their patients. The decision was a victory, of sorts. Yet it put doctors—at that time, almost entirely male doctors—in charge of female contraception, and spawned a legacy of medical control over reproduction that we still struggle with today. The very effort to work within the law achieved an immediate successful legal result at the cost of considerable compromise, specifically loss of control by women. Moreover, Sanger's strategy appealed to racist and anti-immigrant attitudes in order to build public support for birth control. She argued that birth control would help limit the reproductive rates of racial minorities and immigrants; in so appealing, she strengthened the very prejudices against the people she wanted to assist. . . .

As these examples suggest, the very effort to make legal arguments may require accepting assumptions and terms of debate that advocates most deeply wish to challenge. One example of this problem arises particularly in arguments for equality on behalf of groups that have been excluded or degraded historically: women, people of color, gays and lesbians, and people with disabilities. To assert a claim of unequal treatment, the individual must declare that he or she is "like" those accorded the desired treatment. This argument buys into the belief that difference justifies inequality. If a woman, for example, is really different (from the implicit but unstated norm of a man) then she can be treated differently by the law. If we argue for insurance coverage for maternity needs by acknowledging the uniqueness of pregnancy, we may refuel justifications for other rules predicated on women's uniqueness, such as rules excluding women from some work because of potential dangers to reproduction. Should advocates for women's rights talk of women's special needs after divorce or instead push for equal—meaning identical—treatment for men and women in allocating property, alimony, child custody? Similar dilemmas arise in arguments for persons with disabilities who seek inclusion and accommodation. . . .

Because of these and other limitations with the legal system, it should not be surprising that people interested in social change throughout human history have periodically violated or bypassed the law. Well-known figures in American history have deliberately disobeyed particular laws in the service of conscience or principle. Some of these figures—those vindicated by history—now stand as heroes to be studied by school children. Besides Henry David Thoreau, Mahatma Gandhi, and Martin Luther King, Jr., less well-known and more varied individuals have engaged in deliberate acts of disobedience to law in an effort to change the laws or the larger society. . . .

Some have protested wars, the manufacturing of armaments, slavery, and racial segregation. Some have objected to particular taxes, employment practices, or economic oppression. This first, basic argument justifies disobedience in the face of particular rules that seem to implicate individuals in immoral actions or coercion to violate their own beliefs. Some who refuse conscription into the military may do so on the grounds that they wish no part in fighting a war; some refuse to pay taxes to a government engaged in a war because they seek to avoid complicity with the governmental policy. Adherence to competing, and compelling or even prior norms, such as religious beliefs, makes some conclude that disobeying the law is not only justifiable but at times obligatory.

A contrasting, second reason for disobedience is to disturb the premises of the legal system that itself excludes or degrades an entire class of people; suffragists who sought voting rights for women illustrated this motive repeatedly before convincing the nation to amend the Constitution. . . .

Still others have explored the real power of even seemingly powerless people to challenge centralized power by withholding consent and by engaging in dramatic challenges. This view perhaps manifests the belief that the government itself is not obviously legitimate, and that the people's consent to governmental authority, in a democracy, must be earned over and over again. The actual exercise of consent carries with it its opposite—the withdrawal or refusal of consent. And in the power to wield this opposite, some find a strength to challenge governmental and economic power they find unjust. . . .

Finally, for some, disobeying the law is essential to accomplishing the ends that they hold dear. Consider Harriet Tubman, one of the most courageous guides of fugitive slaves through the Underground Railroad. She engaged in resistance to law neither to arouse sympathy nor to publicize her cause, but to achieve her cause. For Tubman, secrecy, not publicity, was essential to the act of disobedience. Respect for justice and divine inspiration meant defiance and contempt for human law by those engaged in the underground railroad struggle. Similar arguments for hidden disobedience have been made by sanctuary movement participants on behalf of immigrants lacking legal entry to the United States, and by members of the Resistance to the Nazis during World War II.

A similar argument could be made, at this very moment, for some women who fear growing restrictions on abortion rights. Some have proposed that women master abortion techniques and perform them illegally. Others have proposed importation of the French pill RU 486, which is not available legally in the United States. An initial tactic is to press the pharmaceutical industry and the federal Food and Drug Administration to test and license the drug. Another is to seek to import the drug under an exception permitted for experimental purposes. Some, whom for obvious reasons I will not cite here, are exploring illegal importation of the drug. Obviously, the goal of each of these tactics is to enable women to terminate unwanted pregnancies—to achieve the end currently hindered by the law. . . .

Lawyers need lawbreakers; lawyers need clients. In this basic sense, there may be little conflict between lawyers and lawbreaking clients. The lawyers serve their profession and earn their livings by providing representation for people who run afoul of the law. This coincidence of interests should be no less present where the lawbreakers act out of conscience and a political motivation to seek social change than where lawbreakers act out of greed, uncontrolled passion, or other motives for breaking the law. . . .

So what factors may enter into an individual lawyer's decision about whether to represent someone who has violated the law for political reasons? I am concerned here not with those lawyers who identify with the political cause or who view their jobs as working for social change. I mean to focus on those more numerous other lawyers who may once or periodically in a career accept a client unlike the others, and those lawyers who may consider what a call to pro bono service should mean. The lawyers' fields of expertise, training, and other commitments will influence their judgments about whether to represent a politically-motivated lawbreaker. Some lawyers will be sympathetic to the client's cause and willingly provide representation. Some public interest law firms are organized to do just that. And perhaps clients should turn only to such lawyers. The client may not be particularly well-served by a lawyer who reluctantly takes on the case but shows no sympathy for the cause or for the means selected by the client.

Nonetheless, I would like to suggest that a lawyer presented with a client who has violated the law for political reasons at least think about the following argument before concluding that this is not a desirable case. The argument is not the standard view that everyone is entitled to a lawyer, nor the claim that the lawyer should not second-guess the client's goals because the adversary system depends upon the strong presentation of conflicting views by lawyers equipped for this task. Instead, I would argue that the lawyer should try to understand how the legal system itself needs people who are willing to break the law for political reasons. Such people provide one of the checks on the system's otherwise effective and often well-placed curbs on social change. Even if the lawyer does not agree with the client's ultimate purposes, or with the client's chosen methods, part of the lawyer's role should include presenting in terms that the legal system itself can understand the reasons for violations of its rules. The legitimacy of the system itself requires confrontation with disobedience defended by individuals who view compliance as immoral or by individuals seeking to persuade lawful officials to change. Moreover, the idea that governmental power can be supported through reasons itself requires grappling with the reasons why some would disobey the law.

This encounter with the reasons of those who disobey will not always yield acceptance by the government. When Martin Luther King, Jr., and members of the civil rights movement disobeyed a restraining order directing them not to march in Birmingham, Alabama, the state trial court responded with contempt sanctions. The Supreme Court ultimately affirmed, even though the same Court conceded the unconstitutionality of the underlying parade ordinance and restraining orders. King and the other contemnors did have excellent legal representation. Nonetheless, the Court ruled against them. This result is not actually what interests me here, although it has occasioned considerable important debate. Instead, I believe that the arguments on behalf of King and the others were crucial at least in assuring the preservation of those arguments inside the authoritative documents of the dissenting opinions and even minor paragraphs in the majority opinion. Present now in the law's official record, these arguments can give rise to study and to renewed questions about the demands of the law.

What were these arguments? They included both the argument that the ban against the march reflected illegitimate segregationist powers in that city, and the argument that the denial of the parade permit was itself illicit discrimination and waiting to challenge that denial in court would undermine the momentum of a political movement coordinated with the calendar of the inspirational religious holidays of Good Friday and Easter. Including these arguments within the formal official reports improved the legal system by introducing criticisms of its operations and by demonstrating its partiality in at least two senses. First, the arguments exposed the biases of all the legal officials, from the trial judge who granted the ex parte restraining order in the middle of the night, to the Supreme Court Justices worried three years later about urban riots. Second, the arguments highlighted the limited scope of the law as a moral authority in the lives of people oppressed by it and inspired by contrasting communal and religious norms of justice.

I suggest that these kind of arguments need to be made when people disobey the law for political reasons. The arguments remind those in power of their own biases and limited understandings, based on their positions. And the arguments remind those outside the system that other norms may at times warrant the courage to break the state's law. Although presenting these arguments may seem to collide with the usual lawyerly perspective, the challenge of these claims sharpens the lawyer's most critical skills and underscores the importance of lawyers to the system. Lawyers are important not as administrative flunkies but as advocates for the points of view that the judges—present and past—may not fully understand. So although this may seem counter-intuitive, and not the working assumption of most lawyers, it is in the lawyer's professional self-interest as well as job description to take on representation of politically motivated lawbreakers, and to relish doing so. Thus, whatever place the individual lawyer's judgment should play in decisions about what clients to accept, the lawyer's personal view should take a back seat to the system's own need for challenges couched in terms that its officials may understand. . . .

But what *should* a lawyer do if consulted before the client actually violates the law for political reasons? My own sense is that the lawyer should try to provide clear and complete legal advice detailing the possible and probable consequences of violations. The lawyer should also explore with the client the reasons for compliance with the governing law, and alternative avenues to breaking the law. But the lawyer should also remember that the client has the choice to make on both moral and tactical grounds. If the lawyer wants to make or help make that choice, then the lawyer should join the client as a comrade rather than serve in the role of legal adviser. . . .

Lawyers who are willing to represent political lawbreakers, and who find no obligation to breach the confidences of those clients, may nonetheless betray a contrast between their own perspectives and that of their clients in the course of representation. The grave risk is that lawyers will defend politically motivated lawbreakers in ways that recapitulate the very failure of the legal system that inspired the lawbreaking actions. In other words, there is a danger that the defense will pursue avenues that undermine the client's purposes or beliefs.

One such danger is that the defense will argue that there was no violation, that the individual actually complied with the law or reasonably was mistaken about it. From the lawyer's perspective, winning the case may seem more important than the particular argument used for the victory. Procedural arguments and claims about mistake can sometimes work effectively, and lawyers are often quite pleased to devise technical arguments that avoid the heat of the controversy while yielding victory for their clients. Of course, some clients may be similarly delighted with such results; they might well want to "get off" and avoid punishment through whatever argument the lawyers can muster. But for others, the point of the protest is to demonstrate the error or injustice of the law, to dramatize their cause, or otherwise express the collision between their views and the state's position. To devise excuses or claim there was no violation can make a mockery of such purposes. Arguments that sidestep the issue presented by the client's conduct, or that render ambiguous the client's motives or understanding, can jeopardize the seriousness of the client's actions and contradict the client's self-understandings.

A related danger is that the lawyers will use particular arguments that besmirch or degrade the client's commitments. The lawyer would not intend to harm the client, but would proceed by considering what legal arguments have the greatest chance of winning, and what techniques of persuasion similarly are most likely to work in a given tribunal. Yet, this calculus pursued by the lawyer may underplay or ignore other concerns of the client. For example, a lawyer may challenge a sodomy statute by arguing that gay sexuality deserves constitutional privacy protection even though it is distasteful or abnormal. The argument would emphasize that privacy protection is important precisely to shield individual choices from potential social disapproval. Such an argument may seem even more damaging to the client's self-concept and political purposes than would losing the case. Where victory itself is unlikely in court, the client may prefer tactics that articulate his or her genuine view. Some clients may feel this way regardless of the likelihood of success on the merits. The client may in this sense view the legal process as constitutive, at least in part, of the values at stake. Law in this sense is not merely an instrumental game but part of the language for imagining and creating a different kind of world.

Finally, the lawyer may conduct the defense in ways that serve the lawyer's own interests more than the interests of the clients. The lawyer could be interested in publicity, when the client is not. Or vice versa: the lawyer could seek to avoid publicity while the client would be delighted to have it. The lawyer could be interested in the ultimate cause rather than the immediate interests of the clients. Or the lawyer could be interested in the clients' immediate concerns more that the clients are. . . .

All of these steps require the lawyer to learn to take the perspective of the client. That may be just what is difficult for the lawyer to do. Yet that is also what lawyers, at their best, do. Lawyers make vivid and understandable the perspective of a client who may seem entirely wrong from the perspective of the prosecutor or the court. To do this, lawyers themselves have to come to understand at least some of what motivates and inspires the clients. This task is, if anything, more important where the clients have placed themselves against the prevailing order. . . .

CREDITS

JANE HARRIS AIKEN, "Sexual Character Evidence in Civil Actions: Refining the Propensity Rule," *Wisconsin Law Review,* 1997, No. 6. Copyright © 1997 by The Board of Regents of the University of Wisconsin System. Reprinted by permission of the Wisconsin Law Review.

EGBEKE AJA, "Crime and Punishment: An Indigenous African Experience," *The Journal of Value Inquiry,* Vol. 31, pp. 353–368, 1997. Used with kind permission of Kluwer Academic Publishers.

JONAS ALSÉN, "An Introduction to Chinese Property Law," *Maryland Journal of International Law and Trade,* Vol. 20, Spring 1996.

P. S. ATIYAH, *Promises, Morals and Law,* Oxford University Press, 1981. Copyright © 1981 P. S. Atiyah. Reprinted by permission of Oxford University Press.

JOHN AUSTIN, *The Province of Jurisprudence Determined* by John Austin, edited by Wilfrid E. Rumble. Copyright © 1995 Cambridge University Press. Reprinted with the permission of Cambridge University Press.

MICHAEL D. BAYLES, "Legally Enforceable Commitments," *Law and Philosophy,* Vol. 4, 1985. Used with kind permission of Kluwer Academic Publishers.

LYNN BERAT, "South African Contract Law," *Loyola of Los Angeles International and Comparative Law Review* (formerly known as *Loyola of Los Angeles International and Comparative Law Journal*), Vol. 14, 1992, pp. 507–527. Reprinted by permission of the author and publisher.

ROBERT BORK, *The Tempting of America, The Political Seduction of the Law,* The Free Press, 1990. Copyright © 1990 by Robert H. Bork. Reprinted with the permission of The Free Press, a Division of Simon & Schuster, Inc..

NICHOLAS CAPALDI, "Affirmative Action: Con" in Albert G. Mosley and Nicholas Capaldi, *Affirmative Action: Social Justice or Unfair Preference?* Rowman & Littlefield, 1996. Reprinted by permission of the publisher.

JULES L. COLEMAN, *In Harm's Way: Essays in Honor of Joel Feinberg,* Jules Coleman and Allen Buchanan, editors. Reprinted by permission of Cambridge University Press.

JEREMY COOPER, "Poverty and Constitutional Justice in India," *Mercer Law Review,* Vol. 44, 1993. Reprinted with permission from Mercer Law Review.

KIMBERLÉ CRENSHAW et al., editors, *Critical Race Theory: The Key Writings That Formed the Movement.* Copyright © 1995 The New Press. Reprinted by permission of The New Press.

JUDITH DECEW, "Constitutional Privacy, Judicial Interpretation and *Bowers vs. Hardwick,*" *Social Theory and Practice,* Vol. 15, Fall 1989, pp. 285–303. Reprinted by permission of the publisher.

PATRICK DEVLIN, *The Enforcement of Morals,* Oxford University Press, 1965. Copyright © 1965 Oxford University Press. Reprinted by permission of Oxford University Press.

RONALD M. DWORKIN, *Law's Empire,* Cambridge, Mass.: Harvard University Press, 1986. Copyright © 1986 by Ronald Dworkin by the President and Fellows of Harvard College. Reprinted by permission of the publisher; *Taking Rights Seriously,* Cambridge, Mass.: Harvard University Press, 1977. Copyright © 1977, 1978 by Ronald Dworkin. Reprinted by permission of the publisher; "Do We Have a Right to Pornography?" from *Oxford Journal of Legal Studies,* Vol. 1, pp. 177–212, 1981. Reprinted by permission of Oxford University Press.

RICHARD A. EPSTEIN, *Takings: Private Property and the Power of Eminent Domain,* Cambridge, Mass.: Harvard University Press, 1985. Copyright © 1985 by the President and Fellows of Harvard College. Reprinted by permission of the publisher; "A Theory of Strict Liability," *Journal of Legal Studies,* Vol. 2, January 1973. Copyright © 1973 by the University of Chicago. Reprinted with the permission of the publisher.

WILLIAM N. ESKRIDGE, JR., "Beyond Lesbian and Gay 'Families We Choose,'" from *Sex, Preference and Family: Essays on Law and Nature,* edited by David Estlund and Martha Nussbaum. Copyright © 1997 by Oxford University Press, Inc. Used by permission of Oxford University Press, Inc.

JOEL FEINBERG, *Doing and Deserving.* Copyright © 1970 Joel Feinberg. Reprinted by permission of the author.

JOHN FINNIS, *Natural Law Theory: Contemporary Essays,* ed. Robert P. George, Oxford: Clarendon Press, 1992. Reprinted by permission of Oxford University Press.

GEORGE P. FLETCHER, "Fairness and Utility in Tort Theory," *Harvard Law Review,* Vol. 85, No. 3, January 1972. Copyright © 1972 by The Harvard Law Review Association. Reprinted with permission from the publisher and the author.

DEBORAH L. FORMAN, "Unwed Fathers and Adoption," *Texas Law Review,* Vol. 72, No. 5, April 1994. Reprinted by permission of the publisher.

JEROME FRANK, *Law and the Modern Mind,* Tudor Publishing, 1936.

MONROE H. FREEDMAN, "Professional Responsibility of the Criminal Defense Lawyer," reprinted from *Michigan Law Review,* June 1966, Vol. 64, no. 8. Copyright © 1966 by The Michigan Law Review Association. Professor Freedman has expanded and updated his analysis in his book, *Understanding Lawyer's Ethics,* Matthew Bender, 1990.

CHARLES FRIED, *Contract as Promise,* Cambridge, Mass.: Harvard University Press. Copyright © 1981 by the President and Fellows of Harvard College. Reprinted by permission of the publisher; "The Lawyer as Friend: The Moral Foundations of the Lawyer–Client Relation," *The Yale Law Journal,* Vol. 85, pp. 1060–1089. Reprinted by permission of The Yale Law Journal Company and Fred B. Rothman & Company.

R. J. GERBER, "Is the Insanity Test Insane?" from *American Journal of Jurisprudence,* Vol. 20, 1975, pp. 112, 116–132. Reprinted by permission of the author.

CHERYL I. HARRIS, "Whiteness as Property." Copyright © 1995 *Critical Race Theory: The Key Writings That Formed the Movement* edited by Kimberlé Crenshaw, et al., reprinted by permission of The New Press.

H. L. A. HART, *The Concept of Law,* Second Edition, Oxford, Clarendon Press, 1997. Used by permission of Oxford University Press.

H. L. A. HART and A. M. HONORÉ, *Causation in the Law,* Second Edition, Oxford, Clarendon Press, 1985. Reprinted with permission from Oxford University Press.

A. M. HONORÉ, "Property, Title, and Redistribution" from *Equality and Freedom,* ed. by Carl Wellman, published by Archiv fur Rechts- und Sozialphilosophie, 1977.

DAN M. KAHAN, "What Do Alternative Sanctions Mean?" from *The University of Chicago Law Review,* No. 2, Spring 1996. Reprinted by permission of the publisher.

IMMANUEL KANT, *The Metaphysics of Morals,* ed. Mary Gregor. Cambridge University Press, 1996. Reprinted by permission of the publisher.

ANTHONY KENNY, *Freewill and Responsibility,* London: Routledge, 1978. Copyright © 1978 Routledge. Reprinted by permission of the publisher.

KENNETH KIPNIS, *Legal Ethics.* Copyright © 1986 Prentice-Hall, Inc.. Reprinted by permission of Prentice-Hall, Inc., Upper Saddle River, NJ.

JACQUELINE KRIKORIAN, "A Different Form of Apartheid?" from *Queen's Law Journal,* Vol. 21, Fall 1995. Reprinted by permission of the author and the publisher.

RAE LANGTON, "Whose Right? Ronald Dworkin, Women and Pornographers," *Philosophy and Public Affairs,* Vol. 19, Fall 1990. Copyright © Fall 1990 by Princeton University Press. Reprinted by permission of Princeton University Press.

CHARLES R. LAWRENCE III, "If He Hollers Let Him Go" from *Words That Wound,* Mari Matsuda, ed. Reprinted by permission of Charles R. Lawrence III.

ROBERT B. LEFLAR, "Personal Injury Systems in Japan," *University of Hawaii Law Review,* Vol. 15, 1993, pp. 742–756. Reprinted by permission of the publisher.

EDWARD H. LEVI, *An Introduction to Legal Reasoning,* The University of Chicago Press, 1949. Reprinted by permission of the author and the University of Chicago Press.

DAVID LUBAN, *Lawyers and Justice.* Copyright © 1989 by Princeton University Press. Reprinted by permission of Princeton University Press.

LARRY MAY, *Masculinity and Morality.* Copyright © 1998 Cornell University. Used by permission of the publisher, Cornell University Press; *The Socially Responsive Self: Social Theory and Professional Ethics,* University of Chicago Press, 1996. Originally published in *Professional Ethics and Social Responsibility,* Daniel E. Wueste, editor, Rowman & Littlefield, 1994. Reprinted by permission of Rowman & Littlefield Publishers.

MITCHELL MCINNES, "The Question of a Duty to Rescue in Canadian Tort Law," *The Dalhousie Law Journal,* vol. 13, no. 1, May 1990, pp. 85–122. Reprinted by permission of the author.

MARTHA MINOW, "Breaking the Law: Lawyers and Clients in Struggles for Social Change," 52 *University of Pittsburgh Law Review* 723, 1991. Reprinted by permission of the publisher.

MARTHA MINOW and MARY LYNDON SHANLEY, "Relational Rights and Responsibilities: Revisioning the Family in Liberal Political Theory," *Hypatia,* Vol. 11, No. 1, Winter 1996, pp. 9–29. Reprinted by permission of Indiana University Press.

MICHELE MOODY-ADAMS, "On Surrogacy: Morality, Markets, and Motherhood," *Public Affairs Quarterly,* April 1991. Reprinted by permission of the publisher.

ALBERT G. MOSLEY, "Affirmative Action: Pro" in Albert G. Mosley and Nicholas Capaldi, *Affirmative Action: Social Justice or Unfair Preference?* Rowman & Littlefield, 1996. Reprinted by permission of the publisher.

STEPHEN MUNZER and JAMES W. NICKEL, "Does the Constitution Mean What It Always Meant?" This article originally appeared in 77 *Columbia Law Review,* 1029 (1977). Reprinted by permission of the publisher and the authors.

ANSHU NANGIA, "The Tragedy of Bride Burning in India." Originally printed in 22 *Brooklyn Journal of International Law,* 637 (1997).

NELL JESSUP NEWTON, "Compensation, Reparations, and Restitution," *Georgia Law Review,* Vol. 28, 1994, pp. 453–467. Copyright © 1994 Nell Jessup Newton. Reprinted by permission of the author.

ROBERT NOZICK, *Anarchy, State and Utopia,* Basic Books, 1974. Copyright © 1974 by Basic Books, Inc. Reprinted by permission of Basic Books, a member of Perseus Books, L. L. C.

MARTHA NUSSBAUM, "Equity and Mercy," *Philosophy and Public Affairs,* Vol. 22, No. 2, 1993. Copyright © 1993 by Princeton University Press. Reprinted by permission of Princeton University Press.

RORY O'CONNELL, "Natural Law: Alive and Kicking?" from *Ratio Juris,* vol. 9, no. 3, 1996, pp. 258–82. Reprinted with permission from Blackwell Publishers Ltd.

R. P. PEERENBOOM, "What's Wrong with Chinese Rights? Toward a Theory of Rights with Chinese Characteristics," *Harvard Human Rights Journal,* Vol. 6, 1993, pp. 29–57. Copyright © 1993 by The President and Fellows of Harvard College. Reprinted by permission of the publisher.

LOIS PINEAU, "Date Rape: A Feminist Analysis," *Law and Philosophy,* Vol. 8, 1989, pp. 217–243. Used with kind permission of Kluwer Academic Publishers.

RICHARD A. POSNER, *The Problems of Jurisprudence,* Cambridge, Mass.: Harvard University Press, 1986. Copyright © 1986 by the President and Fellows of Harvard College. Reprinted by permission of the publisher; *Economic Analysis of Law,* Fifth Edition, Aspen Publishers, 1998. Reprinted by permission of the publisher.

DAN ROSEN and CHIKAKO USUI, "The Social Structure of Japanese Intellectual Property Law," *UCLA Pacific Basin Law Journal,* Vol. 13, Fall 1994, pp. 32–38, 69. Reprinted by permission of the authors.

FREDERICK SCHAUER, "Formalism." Reprinted by permission of The Yale Law Journal Company and Fred B.

Rothman & Company from *The Yale Law Journal,* Vol. 97, No. 4, March 1988, pp. 509–548.

MARY L. SHANLEY, "Fathers' Rights, Mothers' Wrongs: Reflections on Unwed Fathers' Rights and Sex Equality," *Hypatia,* Vol. 10, No. 1, Winter 1997, pp. 73–74, 83–103. Reprinted by permission of Indiana University Press.

A. JOHN SIMMONS, "Historical Rights and Fair Shares," *Law and Philosophy,* Vol. 14, 1995. Used with kind permission of Kluwer Academic Publishers.

PATRICIA SMITH, "Feminist Legal Critics: The Reluctant Radicals" in *Radical Philosophy of Law,* edited by David Caudill and Stephen Jay Gould, pp. 73–87 (Amherst, NY: Humanity Books). Copyright © 1995 Humanity Books. Reprinted by permission of the publisher.

CASS R. SUNSTEIN, *Legal Reasoning and Political Conflict,* Oxford University Press, 1996. Used by permission of Oxford University Press, Inc.

ROBERTO MANGABEIRA UNGER, *The Critical Legal Studies Movement,* Cambridge, Mass.: Harvard University Press, 1986. Copyright © 1986 by the President and Fellows of Harvard College. Reprinted with permission from the publisher.

JAMES WEINSTEIN, "First Amendment Challenges to Hate Crime Legislation," *Criminal Justice Ethics,* Volume 11, Number 2, Summer/Fall 1992, pp. 6–13, 15–20. Reprinted by permission of The Institute for Criminal Justice Ethics, 555 W. 57th Street, Suite 601, New York, NY 10019.

ALAN WERTHEIMER, "Unconscionability and Contracts," *Business Ethics Quarterly,* Vol. 2, No. 4, October 1992, pp. 479–496. Reprinted by permission of the publisher and author.

CHRISTINE M. WISEMAN, "Representing the Condemned: A Critique of Capital Punishment," *Marquette Law Review,* Vol. 79, No. 3, Spring 1996, pp. 731–744; 750–758. Reprinted by permission of the publisher.